W9-CKH-110

Life Care Planning

and

Case Management

Handbook

Second Edition

Life Care Planning
and
Case Management

Handbook
Second Edition

Edited by

Roger O. Weed

Ph.D., CRC, LPC, CLCP,
CCM, CDMS, FNRCA, FIALCP

Georgia State University
Atlanta, GA

CRC PRESS

Boca Raton   London   New York   Washington, D.C.

**W
84.7
L722
2004**

Library of Congress Cataloging-in-Publication Data

Life care planning and case management handbook / edited by Roger O. Weed.—2nd ed.
   p. cm.
   Includes bibliographical references and index.
   ISBN 0-8493-1511-5 (alk. paper)
     1. Life care planning—Handbooks, manuals, etc. I. Weed, Roger O.

RM930.7.L54 2004
362.1'6—dc22   2003065399
                                                                                    CIP

This book contains information obtained from authentic and highly regarded sources. Reprinted material is quoted with permission, and sources are indicated. A wide variety of references are listed. Reasonable efforts have been made to publish reliable data and information, but the author and the publisher cannot assume responsibility for the validity of all materials or for the consequences of their use.

Neither this book nor any part may be reproduced or transmitted in any form or by any means, electronic or mechanical, including photocopying, microfilming, and recording, or by any information storage or retrieval system, without prior permission in writing from the publisher.

All rights reserved. Authorization to photocopy items for internal or personal use, or the personal or internal use of specific clients, may be granted by CRC Press LLC, provided that $1.50 per page photocopied is paid directly to Copyright Clearance Center, 222 Rosewood Drive, Danvers, MA 01923 USA. The fee code for users of the Transactional Reporting Service is ISBN 0-8493-1511-5/04/$0.00+$1.50. The fee is subject to change without notice. For organizations that have been granted a photocopy license by the CCC, a separate system of payment has been arranged.

The consent of CRC Press LLC does not extend to copying for general distribution, for promotion, for creating new works, or for resale. Specific permission must be obtained in writing from CRC Press LLC for such copying.

Direct all inquiries to CRC Press LLC, 2000 N.W. Corporate Blvd., Boca Raton, Florida 33431.

Trademark Notice: Product or corporate names may be trademarks or registered trademarks, and are used only for identification and explanation, without intent to infringe.

Visit the CRC Press Web site at www.crcpress.com

© 2004 by CRC Press LLC

No claim to original U.S. Government works
International Standard Book Number 0-8493-1511-5
Library of Congress Card Number 2003065399
Printed in the United States of America 1 2 3 4 5 6 7 8 9 0
Printed on acid-free paper

FOREWORD

In 1999 the first edition of the *Life Care Planning and Case Management Handbook* was published. It brought together a number of important and valuable contributors within the practice of life care planning. As is the case within our unique area of practice, they stem from a variety of backgrounds, but they come together to contribute as a team to our advanced practice specialty. Now Dr. Roger O. Weed has wisely determined that it is time for an update to that important work, and after reviewing this new contribution, I could not agree more.

Dr. Weed and I first met in 1984. This was approximately 8 years after I had begun working on the development of the basic tenets, methodologies, and principles of life care planning and 3 years after the publication of *Damages in Tort Actions*. No one to that point in time had come to life care planning with greater enthusiasm or interest. Since that time no one has proven to share my vision for life care planning with greater dedication and effort. Dr. Weed has been a dedicated colleague, researcher, writer, lecturer, teacher, and a tremendous overall contributor to the advanced practice of life care planning. In recognition of his work he was invited to participate in *A Guide to Rehabilitation* (Deutsch & Sawyer, 1985–2003, AHAP Press, White Plains, NY). He has, without question, been a major moving force in the advancement of life care planning for the past two decades. He has done this by always remaining a team player who stays focused on what is good for life care planning and the practitioners as a whole. We have always shared a philosophy of openly contributing in our lectures and our texts all of the latest information and research we have available. Dr. Weed never holds anything back, and this latest text is a prime example of that philosophy.

The 2004 edition of the *Life Care Planning and Case Management Handbook* will prove to be a necessary desktop reference for every advanced practitioner of life care planning. In its opening chapters it defines the roles played by each of the key team members working with the life care planner. It provides life care planners with the insights critical to successful interaction with medical, health-related professionals and economic team members they are most likely to encounter as they work to build a successful and accurate life care plan.

The book then goes on to provide up-to-date information on the disabilities most frequently encountered by the life care planner. Most importantly, we are not just lecturing on current information, but we are providing critical resources for being able to bring ourselves up to date on a day-to-day basis. This is what makes a book a critical desktop reference.

v

053285179

This handbook then moves on to address issues typically left out of similar texts — issues made critical by *Daubert v. Merrell Dow* in the forensic setting, issues that should be critical even in the nonforensic setting. I refer to ethics, standards, research, and certification, all of which are thoroughly and professionally addressed within these pages.

It is easy to see that this text is the progression of a career, in which Dr. Weed has both written and edited many other books, chapters, and articles. He has been instrumental in not only helping to develop the advanced practice of life care planning but also helping to develop the market for the product we produce. Congratulations to Dr. Weed and all of the contributors on an excellent work. Congratulations to those fortunate enough to be working with a copy of this text on their desktop.

Paul M. Deutsch, Ph.D., C.R.C., C.C.M., C.L.C.P., F.I.A.L.C.P.,
Licensed Mental Health Counselor
Fellow — International Academy of Life Care Planning

INTRODUCTION

As reported in the first edition, life care planning has become a profession unto itself. It continues to grow and flourish with more training programs than ever in existence. As this goes to press, Kaplan College has launched an online distance learning program and has partnered with Medipro Seminars to offer the on-site portion to qualify for certification. Instructors observe that more physicians and allied health professionals are attending training. In addition, the *Journal of Life Care Planning* was introduced in 2002, as was the Foundation for Life Care Planning Research. Conceptually, the process, methods, and standards associated with future care build upon the foundation of appropriate and coordinated medical and ancillary care for people who have experienced significant medical adversity, and the process for identifying needs is described in the following pages.

Purpose

This book is intended to bring together the many concepts regarding developing life care plans into one publication, as well as offer current state-of-the-art thought, beliefs, and procedures. It is the editor's view that this highly specialized health care industry offers a valuable contribution to managed care and quality of life issues for persons with catastrophic disabilities. Having a solid foundation from which to practice will advance the entire industry. The intended audience for the book is anyone who has a role in planning for complex medical care. Families, clients, medical professionals, allied health care professionals, and representatives of the legal profession are included. It seems that life care planning is ideal for managed care, if the focus is on quality of care while maximizing the purchasing power of available resources.

Book Structure

The book is presented in four sections. The first chapter represents an overview of the history as well as the current practice of life care planning with a view toward the future. Section I, comprised of Chapters 2 through 11, spotlights various professions commonly associated with developing a life care plan. The professional roles are outlined, and suggestions for planning are offered for those unfamiliar with the various specialties. Each author was asked to provide an overview of his or her area of specialty as well as identify specific life care planning issues and topics. Obviously, not all contributors who possibly could be participants are included. For example, dietitian, recreational therapist, music therapist, and various medical specialties that are considered either too closely aligned to the others or not routinely part of the team are not included in the book.

Section II, comprised of Chapters 12 through 21, has been expanded and focuses on selected disabilities for which life care planning has been utilized. Certainly, current practice seems to encompass mostly injury-related disabilities, but the field is slowly expanding into disease and emotional disabilities if the required care is complicated or complex. Two examples are HIV and transplantation care plans. Chapters on mental illness and geriatrics have been added as a result of emerging needs in these areas. Also, the chapter on audiology, located in Section I, necessarily includes topics relating to a specific disability that overlap with the section on selected disabilities.

Section III, Forensic Considerations, is included in the book given that one of the first published uses of the life care plan was through the legal profession. And although future care planning is much broader in contemporary times, the legal roots are still obvious. This section represents a highly specialized civil litigation enterprise that has different "rules" with which most people outside of the legal profession are not familiar. The section includes basic concepts and perspectives from both plaintiff and defense attorneys. A unique contribution is the inclusion of the story of a father and a caregiver in a case where the life care plan was instrumental in settling litigation. Most people cannot fully appreciate what it must be like to have a family member involved in a traumatic injury and have to deal with major medical decisions as well as legal issues. Therefore, this chapter is included to offer some insight into these areas.

The fourth and final section is General Issues, and it covers important topics that are not easily aligned with other areas. Ethical issues transcend all categories and probably are the basis for the longevity of the life care planning industry. Ethical life care planners who adhere to a code of conduct will assure the future. Technology also transcends all categories and has immensely impacted the efficiency and professionalism of completing the life care plan. This industry has dramatically changed in the last 1 to 2 years and presents a major challenge for life care planners to keep abreast of new technology. Life care planning certification is the logical step in assuring minimum qualifications, although many persons who call themselves life care planners are not certified or educated in this particular area. Hopefully, voluntary use of qualified life care planners will encourage others to pursue this specialized training. Along with qualifications and ethics is the concept of basic research associated with the value of life care plans. A chapter that is a reprint of initial research on reliability is included. With the establishment of the Foundation for Life Care Planning Research, much more is expected to be published in the near future. A chapter on the Americans with Disabilities Act (ADA) as it relates to life care planning has been added to educate the readers about certain specialized ADA topics not previously covered. As in the first edition, the location of resources is a huge obstacle for beginning life care planners. Networking among life care planners clearly reveals the tremendous thirst for data that can be used for planning. Some sources are well known, while others are obscure. The sources listed represent a significant amount of work and sharing of knowledge. The final chapter is new and provides guidelines for equipment selection and replacement.

This edition of the book includes three appendices: the first is the Standards of Practice as published by the International Academy of Life Care Planners, the second is the Standards and Code of Professional Ethics published by the Commission on Health Care Certification (the board that issues the certified life care planner credential), and the third is a list of life care planning-related references. It is my hope that this publication will advance the profession another level and the information will assist all who read it by improving their knowledge and professional skills.

Roger O. Weed, Ph.D., C.R.C., C.C.M., C.D.M.S., C.L.C.P., L.P.C.
Fellow — International Academy of Life Care Planning

ACKNOWLEDGMENTS

There are a number of people who have contributed to helping this book become a reality. Certainly, first to be recognized are the contributors, who represent a major powerhouse of knowledgeable movers and shakers in the life care planning field from a wide range of specialties. One person, Dr. Paul Deutsch, acknowledged as the father of life care planning, has for many years maintained strong support for my work in this field, and I was honored to have him write the foreword to this edition. My department chair, Dr. JoAnna White, supported this venture by providing funding for Georgia State University doctoral student, Ann Landes, who spent many hours assisting with editing chapters.

I also think it is valuable to recognize others who have been instrumental in my career. Of course, my parents have primary credit for my existence as well as urging me to break the mold of local tradition by continuing my education. I was raised in a very small town where high school graduates commonly went to work in the timber industry. In fact, one of my peers could not understand why I would go to college when I could make almost as much money as a college graduate right out of high school. At the time, I did not have a good answer for him. However, he is now "between jobs" due to the massive turndown in the local economy, which is based almost entirely on wood products and logging.

Dr. Timothy Field, who in 1984 was a professor at the University of Georgia, agreed to be my Ph.D. major advisor after a few years of mentoring and advising me in my professional life. I can truly convey that Dr. Field has been a major positive factor in my professional life. He has opened many doors, been supportive beyond the call of duty, and shown me new horizons. I also acknowledge Debra Berens, who at the time of this edition has, for 14 years, been a major cheerleader, editor, organizer, co-author, and overall superb and talented colleague.

Last but certainly not least, my wife, Paula, has always encouraged me to do professionally whatever I wanted. This support resulted in many moves and job changes for her, and she has never wavered. All in all, I believe that many people have observed more capability in me than I saw in myself. Through good fortune, outstanding resources, and a lot of assistance, this text comes to fruition.

THE EDITOR

Roger Weed, Ph.D., L.P.C., C.L.C.P., C.R.C., C.D.M.S., C.C.M., F.N.R.C.A., F.I.A.L.C.P., professor and graduate rehabilitation counseling coordinator at Georgia State University, is a licensed professional counselor, certified life care planner, certified rehabilitation counselor, certified disability management specialist, certified case manager, fellow of the International Academy of Life Care Planners, and fellow of the National Rehabilitation Counseling Association. He has authored or co-authored approximately 100 books, articles, and book chapters. He has been honored with several awards for his work, including the 1997 and 1991 Outstanding Educator by the International Association of Rehabilitation Professionals, the 1993 National Professional Services Award from the American Rehabilitation Counseling Association, and the 2003 Research Excellence Award from the College of Education at Georgia State University. In addition, he is listed in several editions of *Who's Who in the World*.

Dr. Weed is the ethics chair for the International Academy of Life Care Planners and associate editor of the *Journal of Life Care Planning*. He is one of the five founders of the national training program leading to life care planning certification. He is also a past chair of the Georgia State Licensing Board for professional counselors, marriage and family therapists, and social workers, as well as a past president of the International Association of Rehabilitation Professionals (IARP) (previously known as the National Association of Rehabilitation Professionals in the Private Sector).

Dr. Weed maintains a nationwide private consulting practice specializing in catastrophic rehabilitation and rehabilitation professional training. In addition, he holds adjunct faculty status with the Center for Assistive Technology and Environmental Access at the Georgia Institute of Technology and courtesy faculty at the University of Florida.

CONTRIBUTORS

Paul Amsterdam
Rehab Equipment Consulting
South Orange, New Jersey

Raymond L. Arrona
Parent
Mesa, Arizona

Dan M. Bagwell
Rehabilitation Professional Consultants
San Antonio, Texas

Debra E. Berens
Rehabilitation Consultant
Atlanta, Georgia

Richard Paul Bonfiglio
Medical Director
HealthSouth
Harmarville Rehabilitation Hospital
Pittsburgh, Pennsylvania

Elizabeth Brown
Paul M. Deutsch & Associates
Oviedo, Florida

Melissa A. Brown
Department of Physical Medicine and
  Rehabilitation
University of Texas Southwestern Medical
  Center
Dallas, Texas

Paul M. Deutsch
Paul M. Deutsch & Associates
Oviedo, Florida

Everett G. Dillman
President
International Business Planners, Inc.
El Paso, Texas

Tyron C. Elliott, Esq.
The Elliott Law Firm
Manchester, Georgia

Randall W. Evans
Mentor
ABI Network
Chapel Hill, North Carolina

Vic S. Gladstone
American Speech-Language-Hearing
  Association
Rockville, Maryland

Lee D. Gunn IV, Esq.
Gunn Merlin Professional Association
Tampa, Florida

Tracy Raffles Gunn
Attorney
Fowler, White, Boggs, Banker, P.A.
Tampa, Florida

Phala A. Helm
Department of Physical Medicine and
  Rehabilitation
University of Texas Southwestern Medical
  Center
Dallas, Texas

Anna N. Herrington
Rehabilitation Counselor
Atlanta, Georgia

Carolyn W. Higdon
The University of Mississippi
Oxford, Mississippi

Larry Higdon
American Speech-Language-Hearing
  Association
Austin, Texas

Nicole M. Hilligoss
Promedica Research Center
Tucker, Georgia

Sherie L. Kendall
University of Kentucky
Lexington, Kentucky

Julie A. Kitchen
Paul M. Deutsch & Associates
Orlando, Florida

Peter Lubinskas
Commission on Health Care Certification
Wallingford, Connecticut

V. Robert May III
Commission on Disability Examiner
  Certification
Midlothian, Virginia

Ileana Seoane McCaigue
Occupational Therapist
Suwanee, Georgia

Patricia McCollom
LifeCare Economics, LTD.
Management Consulting & Rehabilitation
  Services, Inc.
International Academy of Life Care
  Planners
Ankeny, Iowa

Robert H. Meier, III
Director, Amputee Services of America
Manager, theARMteam
Thornton, Colorado

LaRhea A. Nichols
University of Texas
San Antonio, Texas

Art Peddle
HealthSouth Corporation
Norcross, Georgia

Susan Riddick-Grisham
Care Manager
Life Care Planner
Richmond, Virginia

David Ripley
Medical Director
Shepherd Center
Atlanta, Georgia

Anne Sluis Powers
Private Practice
Atlanta, Georgia

Amy M. Sutton
Scottish Rite Children's Hospital
Atlanta, Georgia

Randall L. Thomas
National Center for Life Care Planning
Madison, Mississippi

Lewis E. Vierling
Management Consulting & Rehabilitation
  Services, Inc.
Ankeny, Iowa

Mamie Walters
Caregiver and Certified Natural Health
  Professional
Smyrna, Georgia

Thomas M. Ward
Physiatrist
Little Rock, Arkansas

Roger O. Weed
Georgia State University
Atlanta, Georgia

Terry Winkler
Ozark Area Rehabilitation Services
Springfield, Missouri

ABOUT THE CONTRIBUTORS

Paul Amsterdam, ATS, is starting his 23rd year as a specialist in the field of rehabilitation medical equipment. He comes from a family of three generations in this industry, starting in 1929 with the founding of Amsterdam Bros., one of the country's first orthotic and surgical supply stores.

Mr. Amsterdam is a nationally certified assistive technology specialist. He has helped to create and participated in over 100 wheelchair clinics in rehabilitation hospitals, developmental centers, and schools for the disabled throughout the New York–New Jersey Metropolitan area. He has been a featured columnist for *Case Manager* magazine and other publications for the last 5 years.

Mr. Amsterdam is considered an expert in wheelchair mobility and adaptive seating. He makes full assessments of functional needs, designs custom positioning seating systems, and offers alternatives in decubitus prevention as well as manual and power mobility options. He provides complete evaluations for both adults and pediatrics with a wide range of physical disabilities.

Paul is currently director of marketing at Rehabco, one of the oldest rehab equipment companies in the country. He also runs his own consulting firm, Rehab Equipment Consulting, which works nationwide with case managers, insurance providers, and life care planners on medical equipment issues. Rehab Equipment Consulting helps create the medical equipment portion of a life care plan, saving time for the planner, and adding veracity and defensibility to that portion of the plan by having it reviewed by a certified specialist in the field. Mr. Amsterdam is also available for expert witness testimony.

He may be contacted at (973) 762-1657 or via e-mail at Braceman@msn.com.

Raymond L. Arrona began his career in 1967 as an independent contractor with Wear-Ever Aluminum, Inc., Alcoa Aluminum's first subsidiary, which marketed Wear-Ever Cookware and Cutco Cutlery. He quickly achieved one of the company's coveted positions as division manager and relocated from Arizona to Georgia in 1976 where he was President and CEO until 1997 of RASAR Management Services, Inc./dba Vector Marketing, which represents the Cutco Cutlery product. He also operated as Vector's southern zone division manager for the states of Georgia and South Carolina. In late 1997, he joined a start-up company, QuestCom, which develops websites for businesses. Since the publication of the first edition of this book, he has relocated with his daughter, Anita, to Mesa, Arizona, where he owns Pride of the Valley, an upscale shared direct mail card deck, an affiliate of Pride of the City.

Mr. Arrona experienced every father's nightmare when his daughter, Anita, was tragically injured in an accident caused by a drunk driver. "The impact of Anita's accident has been far reaching in all areas of my family's life, including the personal, financial, spiritual, educational, judicial, professional, and friendship levels. No emotion has been immune from the effects of that tragic day. It is my wish that by telling Anita's story, it will in some way help others through similar situations, or assist in allowing life care planners to gain insight into our family as we continue to deal with this life-changing event."

Dan M. Bagwell, B.S.N., R.N., C.L.C.P., C.C.M., C.D.M.S., is chief executive officer of Rehabilitation Professional Consultants, Inc., and president of Dan Bagwell & Associates, both of which are located in San Antonio, TX. Mr. Bagwell is a registered nurse, licensed in the state of Texas. He received a Bachelor of Science in Nursing in 1978 from the University of Mississippi School of Nursing. He is a certified life care planner, certified case manager, and certified disability management specialist. Mr. Bagwell provides adult and pediatric catastrophic case management and life care planning services for individuals in Texas and throughout the U.S. His clinical nursing experience spans 24 years, 19 of which have been dedicated primarily to medical case management. In addition to case management, his clinical experience has included critical care nursing and service as an officer in the U.S. Air Force Nurse Corps and Air Force Reserves. Mr. Bagwell completed the USAF Flight Nurse School in 1979 and performed duties as a medical crew director and flight nurse in Tactical Aeromedical Evacuation. He served as president and co-founder of Life Care Personal Living Centers, a residential care facility specializing in the care of individuals with severe neurological injuries. Mr. Bagwell has given presentations, lectures, and symposiums concerning life care planning at regional, national, and international conferences. He has authored and co-authored articles and other textbook chapters in life care planning. Mr. Bagwell serves as a courtesy instructor in the advanced life care planning curriculum with the University of Florida and Intelicus (now MediPro), where he teaches advanced life care planning in solid organ transplantation.

Debra E. Berens, M.S., C.R.C., C.C.M., C.L.C.P., is a certified rehabilitation counselor and certified life care planner in private practice in Atlanta, GA. She has a private consulting practice that specializes in assessment, research, and development of life care plans for adults and children with catastrophic injuries and disabilities. Ms. Berens also is a part-time instructor in the graduate rehabilitation counseling program at Georgia State University as well as adjunct faculty with the University of Florida/Intelicus (now MediPro) nationwide training program in Life Care Planning for Advanced Catastrophic Case Management. She is one of the initial developers of course content for an online professional certificate program in life care planning that began in July 2003. She completed a 5-year term as commissioner on the national Commission on Rehabilitation Counselor Certification (CRCC) in 2001 where she was a member of the Ethics Committee charged with revising the Professional Code of Ethics for Rehabilitation Counselors and also served as chair of the Standards and Credentials Committee. She is active in both state and national rehabilitation organizations and is a past president of the Professional Rehabilitation Specialists of Georgia (PRSG), the state chapter of the International Association of Rehabilitation Professionals (IARP). She has contributed over the years to writings and publications in the field of rehabilitation and life care planning and currently serves as associate editor of the *Journal of Life Care Planning*.

Richard Paul Bonfiglio, M.D., is the medical director of HealthSouth Harmarville Rehabilitation Hospital in Pittsburgh, PA. He is board certified by the American Board of Physical Medicine and Rehabilitation. Dr. Bonfiglio has previously served as the medical director of several nationally recognized rehabilitation facilities, including the Lake Erie Institute of Rehabilitation and the Bryn Mawr Rehabilitation Hospital. He has also maintained close academic ties, including having served as residency program director at the Schwab Rehabilitation Center.

Dr. Bonfiglio's clinical practice within the field of physical medicine and rehabilitation has included providing care to children and adults with traumatic brain injuries, spinal cord injuries, amputations, and acute and chronic pain problems. He is an internationally recognized speaker on rehabilitation topics.

Dr. Bonfiglio has been involved for years in the review and critical analysis of life care plans. His interests include the development of a strong medical foundation to enhance the accuracy and reliability of these plans. He is also an expert in life expectancy determinations for individuals following catastrophic illnesses and injuries. He has been on the faculty of the Rehabilitation Training Institute (now MediPro Seminars) for life care planning since its inception.

Dr. Bonfiglio has sustained a strong clinical practice within the field of physical medicine and rehabilitation, providing care to children with a variety of physical and cognitive impairments, and children and adults with traumatic brain injuries, spinal cord injuries, amputations, and acute and chronic pain problems.

Elizabeth "Beth" Brown has been working on the development of life care planning resources and foundational research for over 5 years with Paul M. Deutsch & Associates. She has single-handedly streamlined the manner in which research is accomplished, producing credible results and accurate information. She has trained other life care planners on her research techniques and serves as a guide in the industry on how to be creative, responsive, and persuasive in data collection. Beth is a guest speaker at conferences on life care planning and has contributed to both this text and *A Guide to Rehabilitation*.

Melissa A. Brown, M.S., C.R.C., is a faculty associate in the Department of Physical Medicine and Rehabilitation at the University of Texas Southwestern Medical Center at Dallas, as well as a vocational rehabilitation counselor. She serves as medical case manager for the Physical Medicine and Rehabilitation Department's clinical practice and is the consulting vocational rehabilitation counselor for the North Texas Burn Rehabilitation Model System.

Paul M. Deutsch, Ph.D., C.R.C., C.C.M., C.L.C.P., F.I.A.L.C.P., is a licensed mental health counselor with a Ph.D. in rehabilitation counseling and counseling psychology in his 31st year of practice. He specializes in working with catastrophic disabilities resulting from either birth or a traumatic onset. Dr. Deutsch is best known for having developed the basic tenets, methodologies, and processes of life care planning. He first published on life care planning as a fundamental tool of case management in his 1981 text (*Damages in Tort Actions*, Deutsch, Paul M. and Raffa, Fred). Dr. Deutsch has contributed 12 volumes and more than 50 peer-reviewed journal articles and chapter contributions, including "A Guide to Rehabilitation," Deutsch, Paul M. and Sawyer, Horace; "Innovations in Head Injury Rehabilitation," Deutsch, Paul M. and Fralish, Kathleen; and "Damages in Tort Actions," Deutsch, Paul M., and Raffa, Fred.

Recently, Dr. Deutsch led a team including Lori Allison, Roger Weed, Patricia McCollom, Debbie Berens, and Terri Winkler in the development of Kaplan College's life care planning curriculum.

Dr. Deutsch has taught as an adjunct professor at several universities and lectured widely through the U.S. and Europe. In the 1980s and early 1990s he worked extensively in the former Soviet Union with colleagues of Alexander Romanovich Luria. He has worked extensively in the areas of brain injury and spinal cord injury rehabilitation, among other areas. His experience includes co-ownership and directorship of a brain injury rehabilitation center in the 1980s and later ownership and management of a long-term residential and supported work program for severe brain injury patients.

He has remained active in research efforts and in the past few years has helped to spearhead the formation of the Foundation for Life Care Planning Research along with Dr. Roger Weed, Dr. Christine Reid, Patricia McCollom, M.S., R.N., and Susan Riddick, R.N. The primary work of this foundation is research on the reliability and validity of the life care planning process. Related areas of research may include life expectancy as it is influenced by effective life care planning, as well as case management and all appropriate related life care planning research. In a short time the foundation has forged multiple university relationships and developed successful fund-raising efforts. The results have allowed the foundation to begin funding several doctoral dissertation projects as well as other research efforts.

Dr. Deutsch is active in the profession's efforts to support and educate nurses and rehabilitation counselors involved in forensic consultation about Daubert-related issues. He has developed the core materials for the profession's amicus curiae brief that was filed in the Texas Seventh District Court of Appeals and is in the process of developing educational materials to be made available to all interested professionals.

Everett G. Dillman, Ph.D., an educator and business consultant, is president of International Business Planners, Inc. Dr. Dillman has been active in governmental, business, and financial circles in the Southwest for over 30 years. During this period he has served on the advisory board of the Lubbock Division of the Small Business Administration as well as on the board of directors of several profit and civic organizations. Dr. Dillman has served on the Board of Directors of the National Association of Forensic Economists and on the Steering Committee for Forensic Rehabilitation of the National Association of Rehabilitation Professionals in the Private Sector. He has published extensively in both the vocational and economic areas.

Tyron C. Elliott, J.D., is a practicing trial lawyer with over 30 years of experience. His practice focuses on the area of neurolaw, which deals with brain and spinal cord injuries. Mr. Elliott primarily represents persons who have received traumatic injuries. He is an adjunct professor at Emory University School of Medicine in Atlanta, where he lectures on legal-medical issues. He is also an advocate member of the American Board of Trial Advocates and has given lectures and programs throughout the U.S., Canada, and Mexico. Mr. Elliott is the executive editor of the *Neurolaw Letter* and has contributed several articles on brain injury and related litigation.

Randall W. Evans, Ph.D., A.B.P.P., is President of the MENTOR ABI Network. The MENTOR ABI Network provides community-based services for persons with ABI across the U.S. Dr. Evans is a Clinical Neuropsychologist and is Board Certified in Rehabilitation Psychology. He is also a Fellow of the National Academy of Neuropsychology. Dr. Evans was formerly a Research Fellow with the National Institutes of Health where his research focused on neuro-pharmacology and neuro-psychological test development. He obtained post-doctoral training in the Division of Neurosurgery at the University of California Medical School in San Diego and the Department of Psychiatry at the University of North Carolina Medical School in Chapel Hill.

Dr. Evans has published extensively on many topics relevant to brain injury rehabilitation. His works have appeared in the *New England Journal of Medicine*, *Archives of Physical Medicine and Rehabilitation*, *Developmental Neurology*, and a host of other peer review journals. Dr. Evans has published over 50 papers and book chapters.

Vic S. Gladstone, Ph.D., C.C.C. (Audiology), is associate director for audiology for the American Speech-Language-Hearing Association in Rockville, MD. He obtained his B.S. in speech pathology and audiology and his M.S. in audiology from Penn State University, and his Ph.D. in audiology from the University of Maryland. For 28 years Dr. Gladstone was a professor and director of audiology at Towson University in metropolitan Baltimore. While at Towson, he initiated the graduate audiology program and directed the audiology clinic. Dr. Gladstone has participated in numerous consultative activities, including providing direct clinical services to children and their families and in industrial environments.

Lee Gunn practices with Gunn Merlin Professional Association in Tampa, FL. He specializes in complex personal injury and insurance coverage and bad faith on behalf of plaintiffs. He is board certified as a trial attorney by both the Florida Bar and the National Board of Trial Advocacy, is a member of the American Board of Trial Advocates, is and AV rated. Prior to January 2000, Lee spent 18 years practicing as a defense attorney representing major insurers, hospitals, and product manufacturers.

Tracy Raffles Gunn is a shareholder with Fowler White Boggs Banker P.A. in Tampa, FL. Ms. Gunn specializes in appellate practice with an emphasis on tort and insurance issues. She is board certified in appellate practice and is AV rated by Martindale Hubbell. She serves on the Executive Council of the Appellate

Practice Section of the Florida Bar, chairs the Amicus Curiae Committee of the Florida Defense Lawyers Association, and is appointed by the Florida Supreme Court to serve on its Committee on Standard Jury Instructions in Civil Cases.

Phala A. Helm, M.D., is professor and a past chairperson of the Department of Physical Medicine and Rehabilitation at the University of Texas Southwestern Medical Center at Dallas and is internationally known for her work in burn rehabilitation. She is the director and principal investigator for the National Institute on Disability and Rehabilitation Research (NIDRR)-funded North Texas Burn Rehabilitation Model System, establishing state-of-the-art treatment standards and outcome measures for burn rehabilitation management.

Anna N. Herrington, M.S., is a graduate of the rehabilitation counselor training program and a counseling psychology doctoral student at Georgia State University in Atlanta, GA.

Carolyn Wiles (Watkins) Higdon, Ph.D., C.C.C.-S.L.P., owns and operates a private practice in assistive technology in Georgia. Her practice includes assistive technology for all ages, as well as educational consulting, forensics and life care planning, catastrophic health care of acquired brain injury and trach- and ventilator-dependent patients, and mediation and legal consulting. Dr. Higdon testifies as an expert witness in assistive technology for all ages, is a past chair of the Georgia Board of Examiners for Speech Pathology and Audiology, and is a past chair of Division 12 of American Speech-Language-Hearing Association (ASHA), the AAC Division. Dr. Higdon is a fellow of the ASHA, is active in multiple professional organizations, and has taught and consulted in Russia, Eastern Europe, Hong Kong, China, Costa Rica, and Thailand. Dr. Higdon is an ASHA consultant to the American Medical Association in the areas of augmentative and alternative communication and current procedural terminology (CPT) codes. Dr. Higdon is the chair of the Department of Communicative Disorders and the director of the Center for Speech and Hearing Research in the School of Applied Sciences at the University of Mississippi (Oxford, MS), and is an adjunct clinical associate professor at the University of Mississippi Medical Center in Jackson, MS.

Larry Higdon, M.S., C.C.C. (Audiology), is vice president for professional practices in audiology of the American Speech-Language-Hearing Association (ASHA) and is owner/audiologist of a private practice in Austin, TX. His practice includes both direct-service delivery and legislative consulting services, in which he is a lobbyist on behalf of various health and educational organizations, including the Texas Speech-Language-Hearing Association (TSHA). Prior to entering private practice full time, Larry served on the faculty of the University of Texas-Pan American, where he also served 1 year as interim program director, and at Southwest Texas State University. At each institution he was the director of clinical services, a product of his previous experience as a practitioner and administrator of hospital and community clinic programs. He has served as liaison to the Texas Education Agency, Department of Health, Department of Human Services, Medicaid, Texas Insurance Council, and the hearing aid dealers association.

Active in state and national professional organizations, he is a former president of TSHA and is the immediate past president of the Texas Speech and Hearing

Foundation. He is chair of the TSHA Publications Board and managing editor of the *Texas Journal of Audiology and Speech-Language Pathology (TEJAS)*. As an ASHA member he has served as chair of numerous committees and boards (Long Range Strategic Planning, Honors, Public Policy Advocacy, Clinical Fellowship Year) and has been very active in the standards programs of ASHA.

Mr. Higdon is a fellow of ASHA and has received the honors of TSHA and its highest leadership recognition award, the Jack L. Bangs Award.

Nicole M. Hilligoss, M.S., C.R.C., L.P.C., C.P.R.P., is a certified rehabilitation counselor, licensed professional counselor, and certified psychiatric rehabilitation practioner. She works as a clinician and research assistant at the Promedica Research Center in Tucker, GA. Her research interests include nonpharmacologic interventions in schizophrenia and vocational strategies in severe and persistent mental illness.

Sherie L. Kendall, Ph.D., received her doctorate from Indiana University School of Medicine in medical neurobiology, with a minor in anatomy. Eli Lilly Neuroscience Discovery Research Laboratories, Indianapolis, awarded her a women's health internship to study gender differences in models of brain ischemia for her dissertation. As an NIH fellow at the University of Kentucky, she is participating in advanced studies in therapeutic and translational research. Dr. Kendall's current research centers on gender-related differences in HIV-associated dementia and its relationship to recreational drug use. Dr. Kendall is a National Institutes of Drug Abuse Travel Award-winning international speaker in her area of research. She has presented the results of her research at scientific meetings in Europe, Canada, and across the U.S. Professionally Dr. Kendall is active in the Society for Neuroscience, the Symposia on Biology of Aging, and the American Association for the Advancement of Science. Dr. Kendall has dedicated her career to advancing women's health by translating basic scientific knowledge derived from experimental modeling of human pathology to the clinical research arena.

Julie A. Kitchen, C.C.M., C.D.M.S., C.L.C.P., is a certified life care planner with Paul M. Deutsch & Associates in Oviedo, FL. She has been involved in life care planning research and preparation for 20+ years. She is a current faculty member of Intelicus (now MediPro) in coordination with the University of Florida, teaching life care planning to others throughout the country. She has authored a number of book chapters, articles, and monographs in professional journals.

Peter Lubinskas serves as the director of the Commission on Health Care Certification (CHCC). Mr. Lubinskas is from Wallingford, CT, and received his Bachelor of Business Administration from the College of William and Mary. While enrolled in William and Mary and following his graduation in 1999, Mr. Lubinskas oversaw the Richmond, VA, operations of a home health care nursing firm, developing policies and procedures in accordance with Virginia Commonwealth guidelines, and served as the company liaison to all Departments of Social Services and the Department of Medical Assistance Services. He came to the CHCC from the Department of Medical Assistance Services where he served as the provider enrollment contract manager. Mr. Lubinskas was responsible for maintaining a comprehensive provider network of 47,000 medical and allied health care providers enrolled in the Virginia Medicaid Program. Additionally, he was responsible for the enrollment and certification of hospitals, practitioners, mental health service providers, and skilled nursing facilities within the Commonwealth. He implemented state and federal regulations governing the administration of health care professionals and facilities operating within the Commonwealth as well.

V. Robert May III received his doctorate in rehabilitation from Southern Illinois University–Carbondale and is currently the executive director of the National Association of Disability Evaluating Professionals (NADEP) and executive administrator of the Commission on Health Care Certification (CHCC). He taught functional capacity evaluation and impairment rating protocols at the University of Florida–Gainesville in the Department of Rehabilitation from the fall of 1992 through the fall semester of 1996. He currently serves as adjunct professor in the Department of Rehabilitation, Rehabilitation Institute, Southern Illinois University, where he oversees validation research studies of the NADEP functional capacity evaluation protocols and life care plan certification examination. Dr. May is on the faculty of the National Association of Disability Evaluating Professionals where he instructs physicians and therapists in impairment rating and functional capacity evaluation protocols in major training sites in Canada and the U.S. He maintains an outpatient industrial therapy center and a work capacity evaluation practice in two health clubs in Richmond, VA. His local therapy business May Physical Therapy Services, LLC offers physical/aquatic therapy services, strength and conditioning training, and work disability/functional capacity evaluations. In addition to the therapy and evaluation businesses he has consulted with the Coca-Cola Bottling Company, Overnite Transportation, Inc., and the Washington, D.C., Metropolitan Transit Authority regarding analyzing their jobs to ensure compliance with the Americans with Disabilities Act of 1990. Dr. May has lectured in China, Canada, and the U.S. on measuring work function, and has authored over 60 peer-reviewed journal articles and book chapters on industrial rehabilitation and federal/state legislation governing occupational medicine practices. His textbook, *NADEP Guide to Functional Capacity Evaluation with Impairment Rating Applications*, was recently published and is co-edited with Dr. Michael Martelli. He holds certification as a certified disability examiner, category II.

Ileana Seoane McCaigue, O.T.R./L., C.D.R.S., has been a practicing certified and licensed occupational therapist since 1977 when she graduated from the Medical College of Georgia in Augusta. She has worked in management and in direct care with patients of all ages and disabilities ranging from the neonatal intensive care unit to the nursing home. Her specialty interests and focus of treatment has been with adolescents and adults with acquired brain injuries, neurological disorders, or learning disabilities, especially in relation to adaptive driver rehabilitation. She is also a certified driver rehabilitation specialist and has been involved in driver rehabilitation since 1979. Ms. McCaigue has testified as an expert witness regarding issues related to transportation and home modification needs. She also assists in the development of life care plans in relation to these functional areas.

Patricia McCollom, R.N., M.S., C.R.R.N., C.D.M.S., C.C.M., C.L.C.P., is president and nurse consultant for LifeCare Economics, LTD., and Management Consulting

& Rehabilitation Services, Inc., and is CEO of the International Academy of Life Care Planners, Ankeny, IA. A graduate of the master's program in rehabilitation, Drake University, Ms. McCollom has extensive experience in care of individuals with head trauma, spinal cord injury, and other catastrophic injury. She is a past national president of the Association of Rehabilitation Nurses, former chair of the National Task Force on Case Management, and past chair of the Commission for Case Manager Certification (CCMC). She was elected by CCMC in 2003 to serve a 5-year position on the Foundation for Rehabilitation and Research. At the national level, she teaches case management practice and life care planning. She currently is vice president of the Board of Directors of the Foundation for Life Care Planning Research. The author of many articles on rehabilitation, case management, and life care planning, Ms. McCollom contributed the chapters on case management, burn rehabilitation, and cancer rehabilitation to the 2002 Mosby text *Rehabilitation Nursing*, 3rd edition and the section on life care planning to the 1997 *Advanced Rehabilitation Nursing Practice Core Curriculum*, published by the Association of Rehabilitation Nurses. She co-authored the section on amputations in the Mosby publication *Case Management Clinical Practice Guidelines* and the chapter on life care planning in the September 2001, F.A. Davis text: *The Nurse and the Law*. Ms. McCollom is a co-author of *The Expert's Role as an Educator Continues: Meeting the Demands Under Daubert* (2002). She is one of four principal developers of the certificate course in life care planning, initiated by Kaplan College in July 2003. Ms. McCollom is the editor of the *Journal of Life Care Planning*.

Robert H. Meier, III, M.D., is a physiatrist who has provided amputation rehabilitation during the past 34 years for some 3000+ persons with amputations. He previously directed amputee services at The Institute for Rehabilitation and Research in Houston, TX and the University of Colorado Health Sciences Center in Denver, CO. He received his M.D. degree and PM&R residency training from Temple University in Philadelphia. He has served on the faculties of Rehabilitation Medicine at Temple University, Baylor College of Medicine and the University of Colorado Health Sciences Center. He is now in private practice and is Director of the Amputee Services of America, a comprehensive outpatient rehabilitation program devoted solely to the rehabilitation of persons with one or more amputations, located in Thornton, CO. In addition, Dr. Meier serves as the Manager of theARMteam, a group of amputation rehabilitation specialists who consult nationally on the needs and most cost-effective services provided for complex amputee problems. Dr. Meier is the Director of Medical Rehabilitation Services for Kindred Hospital Denver and is on the active medical staff of the North Valley Rehabilitation Hospital. He also is the rehabilitation consultant for the Institute for Limb Preservation in Denver, CO, a multi-specialty medical group providing services for persons whose limbs are in jeopardy from cancer or trauma. He speaks nationally and internationally on various rehabilitation and amputation topics and has written many articles and book chapters. His most recent text, *Functional Restoration of Adults and Children with Upper Extremity Amputation*, was co-edited with Diane Atkins and published by Demos in 2004. Dr. Meier has been involved with Life Care Planning since 1976.

LaRhea Nichols, R.N., M.S.N., is an assistant professor and transplant administrator of the Organ Transplantation Programs at the University of Texas Health

Science Center at San Antonio (UTHSCSA). She has worked in the transplant field since 1979 and administrates a multiorgan transplant program specializing in heart, lung, kidney, pancreas, and liver transplants. She received her A.D.N., B.S.N., and M.S.N. degrees in nursing from the University of Nebraska Medical Center, College of Nursing. Prior to her appointment at UTHSCSA she worked in transplant units at the University of Iowa and Clarkson Hospital in Omaha, NE. She is a certified transplant coordinator, is a member of the North American Board of Transplant Coordinators, and currently maintains professional affiliations with the National Transplant Coordinator Organization. Mrs. Nichols is a frequent speaker and lecturer in the area of organ transplantation in addition to her educational responsibilities as assistant professor with UTHSCSA.

Art Peddle, L.P.T., graduated from Georgia State University with a B.S. degree in physical therapy and from David Lipscomb College with a B.A. degree in psychology. He has had very extensive experience in the field of physical therapy and in multiple disciplines specializing in the areas of industrial occupational medicine, orthopedic physical therapy, sports medicine physical therapy, and neurophysical therapy. He has worked in rehabilitation centers, hospitals, and private practice. His experience has included life care planning and consultation for a variety of physical therapy situations. He presently works with HealthSouth Corporation in Norcross, GA. He is a member of the APTA.

Susan Riddick-Grisham, R.N., C.C.M., C.L.C.P., maintains a private consulting practice specializing in care coordination for individuals with catastrophic injuries and life care planning. She has authored or co-authored several publications in the area of life care planning. A popular trainer, Ms. Riddick-Grisham has presented educational programs on case management, life care planning, and medical legal consultation.

David Ripley, M.D., M.S., C.R.C., F.A.A.P.M.&R., is the medical director of brain injury research and medical director of postacute services for the Shepherd Center in Atlanta, GA. He is board certified in physical medicine and rehabilitation and a fellow of the American Academy of Physical Medicine and Rehabilitation. Prior to entering medical school, Dr. Ripley received a master's degree in vocational rehabilitation counseling from Georgia State University and worked as a vocational rehabilitation counselor; he retains certification as a rehabilitation counselor (CRC). He serves on several committees and is on the Board of Directors of the Brain Injury Resource Foundation in Georgia. His clinical practice at the Shepherd Center involves providing inpatient and outpatient medical and rehabilitation care to individuals with neurological impairment, including brain injury and spinal cord injury, and providing medical oversight and direction of Shepherd Pathways, the rehabilitation day program for individuals with acquired brain injury.

Anne Sluis Powers, Ph.D., R.N., was an assistant professor of clinical medicine in the Department of Family Medicine and Psychiatry at University of Nevada School of Medicine in Reno. Dr. Powers is a licensed psychologist and registered nurse who has co-authored five books regarding life care planning. She provides services clinically to medical patients and those with catastrophic injuries and illnesses.

Amy M. Sutton, R.N., B.S.N., M.A., C.L.C.P., is a certified life care planner and Ph.D. student at Georgia State University studying counseling psychology. She received two bachelor's degrees in psychology and nursing from Purdue University and Indiana University and a master's degree in psychology from Ludwig Maximillian's University in Munich, Germany. Amy lived and worked as a home health nurse in Germany for 4 years. During her graduate studies in Germany, Amy conducted a 6-week internship/research project in South Africa on AIDS education in the public school system. As a registered nurse, Amy has worked in pediatric critical care, pediatric and adult home health, and inpatient pediatric rehabilitation. She is currently employed with Scottish Rite Children's Hospital in Atlanta in the pediatric rehabilitation unit, and she is working with Roger Weed and Debbie Berens in life care planning. Simultaneously, Amy is a full-time student at Georgia State University where she completed and published (lead author) a life care plan validation study.

Randall L. Thomas, Ph.D., C.R.C., N.C.C.C., is president of the National Center for Life Care Planning. He is a licensed psychologist, national board-certified counselor, and certified rehabilitation counselor. He is associated with TecSolutions, a software development company for care management and life care planning activities. He has provided expert testimony in the field of rehabilitation and life care planning in numerous states throughout the U.S. He has authored or co-authored numerous articles in the fields of rehabilitation and case management/life care planning software. He is active in the training and education of life care planning. He has served on the Mississippi Board of Psychological Examiners as a member and executive secretary and has also served as a member of the Mississippi Worker's Compensation Advisory Counsel. He is a member of numerous national organizations and has served as president of the Mississippi chapter of International Association of Rehabilitation Professionals.

Lewis Vierling, M.S., N.C.C., N.C.C.C., C.R.C., C.C.M., is vice president and vocational rehabilitation consultant, Management Consulting & Rehabilitation Services, Inc. (Mc/RS), in Ankeny, IA. A graduate of the master's program in counseling, Drake University, Mr. Vierling has 28 years of experience in providing counseling and vocational services. He consults as a case manager for postacute catastrophically injured individuals. Additionally, he was a member of a vocational rehabilitation advisory panel/project team, responsible for the development of a vocational rehabilitation program for a national managed care company. In 2002, Mr. Vierling was elected to serve a 4-year term on the national Commission for Case Manager Certification.

In June 1999, the U.S. Supreme Court cited the results of his vocational evaluation in a landmark Americans with Disabilities Act (ADA) decision, *Murphy v. United Parcel Services, Inc.* When the Equal Employment Opportunity Commission (EEOC) issued new instructions to address the definition of disability under ADA, Mr. Vierling's vocational research was cited from the Murphy decision providing examples of "Class of Jobs" relating to work as a major life activity. He has provided numerous vocational evaluations in ADA litigation, and because of his interest in the process, he is a member of the Supreme Court Historical Society.

Mr. Vierling writes an "ADA Update" column for *The Case Manager*, the official journal of the Case Management Society of America. *The Case Manager* refers to him as its "resident ADA expert." He is author of *Court Decisions Involving the Americans with Disabilities Act: A Resource Guide for Rehabilitation Professionals*, published in the fall of 2002 by Elliott & Fitzpatrick, Inc. He has also authored a series of ADA articles in *The Case Manager* discussing the implications of Supreme Court ADA decisions on the practice of case management. Mr. Vierling has written and presented nationally on ADA, catastrophic injury, and return-to-work and vocational rehabilitation issues.

Mr. Vierling was appointed by Governor Terry Branstad to the Iowa Commission on Persons with Disabilities and served from 1984 until 1994. In 1988, he was elected chairperson of the commission and also became a member of the President's Committee on Employment of People with Disabilities. The commission was actively involved in advocating for passage of the ADA legislation. As a result of those efforts, Mr. Vierling was invited by President George Bush to the signing of the ADA bill at the White House on July 26, 1990. In September 1992, he received a congratulatory letter from President Bush for efforts to promote full and harmonious compliance with the ADA legislation.

A national certified counselor (NCC), national certified career counselor (NCCC), certified rehabilitation counselor (CRC), and certified case manager (CCM), he is also a certified instructor for the Career Development Facilitator Curriculum (CDF), a national training program for paraprofessionals seeking certification.

Mamie Walters, C.N.H.P., pursued a career in music theory and composition until 1981 when she became co-owner and successfully operated a cutlery distributorship for 6 years. During this period she met Ray Arrona, who was with Vector Marketing Corporation. Her business acumen led to a national promotion as senior assistant to the executive vice president of sales and marketing for the southern zone with Vector. In March 1994, this position ended and Ms. Walters pursued her education full time. In January 1995, she began working as a private hire for Ray Arrona, natural and legal guardian of Anita Arrona for several years. Ms. Walters is a certified natural health professional and is currently enrolled and active in the doctor of naturopathy program. She is also a member of the American Naturopathic Practitioners Association and EarthSave International.

Thomas M. Ward, M.D., is a board-certified physiatrist in private practice in Little Rock, AR. He graduated from the University of Kansas Medical School in 1985. He served his internship at the University of California in Los Angeles and finished his residency in physical medicine and rehabilitation at the University of Minnesota. His practice is devoted entirely to the outpatient treatment of musculoskeletal and neuromuscular disorders including the late effects of brain injury, stroke, spinal cord injury, multiple sclerosis, pediatric cerebral palsy, and degenerative disc conditions of the axial spine.

Terry Winkler, M.D., C.L.C.P., is in private practice as a board-certified physiatrist in physical medicine and rehabilitation and as a sub-specialist in Spinal Cord Injury Medicine in Springfield, MO. He is a past medical director of Cox Hospital Rehabilitation Program and medical director of the Curative Rehabilitation Center, a freestanding outpatient rehab program. His practice focuses on spinal cord injury, acquired brain injury, amputations, and life care planning. Dr. Winkler serves on committees reviewing research grants concerning spinal cord injury, and peer reviews articles for publication in the Archives of Physical Medicine and Rehabilitation. Dr. Winkler has numerous publications regarding life care planning and has contributed to every major text in the field of life care planning, contributed to a college text on rehabilitation record systems, has written on the effects of aging with SCI, and will serve as the medical editor of the new *Guide to Rehabilitation* (Ahab Press). Dr. Winkler holds an academic appointment as clinical associate faculty at the University of Florida–Gainesville and MediPro Seminars where he teaches life care planning. At Southern Missouri State University in Springfield, MO he teaches differential diagnosis to the masters level physical therapy students. Dr. Winkler's undergraduate training was at Louisiana Tech University. He attended LSU Medical School and then completed residency training in rehabilitation medicine in Little Rock, AR. Past honors include The Americas Award, Alumnus of the Year LA Tech Univ., "Who's Who among Young Americans," and the Jean Claude Belot Award from Harvard University health sciences program. In addition to his active medical practice, Dr. Winkler is a certified life care planner, serves as a commissioner on the Commission for Health Care Certification, the Foundation of Life Care Planning, and the editorial board of the *Journal of Life Care Planning*.

CONTENTS

SECTION III: Forensic Considerations

SECTION IV: General Issues

1

LIFE CARE PLANNING: PAST, PRESENT, AND FUTURE

Roger O. Weed

INTRODUCTION

In the first edition of this text I wrote that life care planning has become a major buzzword in the field of professional rehabilitation. Many people who have little knowledge about published concepts in life care planning are using the term *life care plans* in order to generate business. I recall reading a deposition from a Ph.D.-level "life care planner" who, when asked by the opposing attorney about resources in life care planning, revealed that it was his opinion there were no written resources or training programs in life care planning. This discourse occurred in 1996, after there already existed a national certification in life care planning. It was repeated in 2003 by two "experts," one of who claimed there were no training programs but also claimed to be one of the founders of the life care planning industry.

Clearly, life care planning continues to be the standard by which other plans are to be measured with regard to the management of catastrophic impairments. The published methods, concepts, and procedures are an effective means to determine the road map of care as well as to identify reasonable needs and costs associated with any impairment. However, not everyone is demonstrating quality practice; many do not know of existing standards of practice; and many professionals are resisting standardization of the concept. Perhaps it is helpful to again review this profession as a foundation for this book.

The Past

The original issuance of life care plans appeared in a legal publication, *Damages in Tort Actions* (Deutsch & Raffa, 1981), which established the guidelines for determining damages in civil litigation cases. By 1985 the life care plan was introduced to the health care industry in *Guide to Rehabilitation* (Deutsch & Sawyer, 1985). One of the first nationwide rehabilitation professional training programs was organized by Dr. Paul Deutsch and offered on September 16–17, 1986, in Hilton Head, SC, where more than 100 rehabilitation professionals from

0-8493-1511-5/04/$0.00+$1.50
© 2004 by CRC Press LLC

throughout the U.S. assembled to begin the process of learning about life care plans. Initially the training comprised approximately 2 days to introduce rehabilitation professionals to the overall concepts and the format that was published in *Guide to Rehabilitation*. It also became evident that many people were practicing life care planning in a variety of ways, some of which appeared to be contrary to the intended goals and purposes of ethical rehabilitation practice. In addition, as previously mentioned, many people were using the term *life care planning* as it became more popular, but had little or no awareness of the appropriate uses or practices associated with this emerging industry.

In the fall of 1992 five rehabilitation professionals, Richard Bonfiglio, M.D., Paul Deutsch, Ph.D., Julie Kitchen, C.D.M.S., Susan Riddick, R.N., and Roger Weed, Ph.D., met to discuss the apparent problems associated with the life care planning industry. Concerned that fragmentation and poor standardization would result in the overall decline of the industry, they decided to develop a concentrated training program consisting of eight 2-day tracks representing the various aspects of life care planning.

Track I was a basic overview of life care planning process methods, standards, and formats. Track II was designed to include the vocational aspects of clients whose life care plans appropriately included work-related opinions. Track III addressed effective case management strategies within the complex medical environment. Track IV outlined the various forensic rehabilitation issues to which many rehabilitation professionals, willingly or unwillingly, are subjected. Track V focused specifically on spinal cord injury issues, and Track VI identified brain injury issues. Track VII was an overview of the long-term care issues for other physical and emotional disabilities as well as some disease processes. Track VIII was organized to focus more explicitly on business and ethical practices, including the use of technology in life care planning.

Following this process, a management company (Rehabilitation Training Institute) was contracted to set up training programs throughout the U.S. Before the first flyers were fully distributed, the first of the organized tracks (scheduled for November 1993) was filled. Two introductory courses were developed — one on the West Coast and the other on the East Coast. It appeared obvious that there were a number of rehabilitation professionals who were interested in pursuing continuing education related to life care planning, and several participants requested official recognition for their educational efforts. Dr. Horace Sawyer of the University of Florida was approached, and he agreed to pursue an official certificate of completion through the University of Florida's Continuing Education Department. A private–public partnership between the Rehabilitation Training Institute and the University of Florida was formed and named Intelicus. The five founders have donated the program content to Intelicus, and although some continue as faculty, they no longer have control over the content or management. Over the years these courses have been adjusted to focus on the roles and responsibilities that more specifically identify with life care planners based on participant comments and research. There are currently six modules with a provision for home study included. Intelicus was purchased by Medipro Seminars in 2003.

Although an initial description of life care planning was offered by Drs. Deutsch and Raffa in *Damages in Tort Action*, collaboration with leaders and organizations resulted in an agreed upon definition:

> A <u>Life Care Plan</u> is a dynamic document based upon published standards of practice, comprehensive assessment, data analysis and research, which provides an organized concise plan for current and future needs with associated costs, for individuals who have experienced catastrophic injury or have chronic health care needs. [Source: Combined definition of the University of Florida and Intelicus annual life care planning conference and the American Academy of Nurse Life Care Planners (now known as the International Academy of Life Care Planners) presented at the Forensic Section meeting, NARPPS annual conference, Colorado Springs, CO, and agreed upon April 3, 1998.]

Although the certificate from the University of Florida underscored the value of obtaining education specific to this specialized profession, it did not provide the assurance of ethical practice or the professional identity that was desired by people who had invested thousands of dollars and much of their time in the training process. Several certification boards were contacted, with three indicating an interest in leading the way to certification. Eventually the Commission on Disability Examiner Certification (now known as the Commission on Health Care Certification — CHCC) based in Richmond, VA, and directed by V. Robert May, Rh.D., assumed the responsibility, and the first certifications were offered in the spring of 1996. (For information regarding the requirements for certification, see Chapter 30.)

It should be noted that Intelicus is not the only route for obtaining the necessary education to qualify to sit for certification (also see The Present). Professionals or organizations seeking to support the life care planning credential can develop programs that meet the board's criteria.

Finally, life care plans have historically been subject to intense scrutiny in a variety of rehabilitation fields, including managed care, workers' compensation claims, civil litigation, mediation, reserve setting for insurance companies, and federal vaccine injury fund cases.

The Present

At present the life care planning industry continues to grow, change, and modify the scope of practice associated with catastrophic case management. The International Academy of Life Care Planners is well established and publishes basic standards of practice. The *Journal of Life Care Planning* has been launched. Kaplan College (online training leading to certification), Medipro Seminars, Capital Law School paralegal program, the Institute for Medical-Legal Education, International Association of Rehabilitation Professionals, and many other organizations have been preapproved for training related to obtaining or maintaining certification. The Foundation for Life Care Planning Research has been established and supports doctoral student dissertations and other qualified research efforts. Two national life care planning summits with endorsements from several organizations have been completed leading to transdisciplinary and transorganizational consensus on many topics and issues.

Although life care planning principles can be used in almost any aspect of care management, it is particularly useful in complex medical cases since the principles and methods that have been developed:

Provide for needed quality care

Reduce errors and omissions

Allow fewer clients to drop through the cracks

Reduce the failure to take into account various aspects that have an effect on the ultimate outcome of the client's medical care (Weed & Riddick, 1992; Weed, 1995a)

Complex case management has become a specialty in its own right, and indeed, there is the certified case manager designation that has emerged as another buzzword. Good case managers, professionals who are able to work consistently in a complex and often adversarial system, are very valuable professionals.

Since the first edition, certification continues to attract a variety of health care professionals and there are now certified life care planners in Canada and just about every state. The CLCP (certified life care planner) credential is about the only rehabilitation counselor- and case management-related certification that did not allow grandfathering; all CLCP were required to pass the exam.

Sometimes arguments are raised that life care planners should be people with nursing backgrounds only (Weed, 1989). In addition, one article proposed that only professionals with at least a doctorate should be considered qualified to develop life care plans (Weed, 1997). However, in the view of the organizers of the national life care planning training program, it is the expectation that various professionals are qualified to practice in areas of their knowledge, skills, and abilities. For example, a rehabilitation nurse who has recently graduated from nursing school is ill prepared to handle catastrophic cases. On the other hand, a master's-level vocational counselor who has spent several years working specifically in spinal cord injury rehabilitation may be extremely qualified to developed life care plans for that population. In addition, it is expected that life care planning members are part of a team, and it is further expected that team members will practice within their knowledge area. Historically it has been common for vocational counselors and rehabilitation nurses to work together to develop vocational and medical rehabilitation plans (Riddick & Weed, 1996).

In current practice, many organizations and hospitals have adopted life care planning procedures for discharge planning (Riddick & Weed, 1996; Weed & Riddick, 1992; Weed & Field, 2001). There are also allied health professionals (such as occupational therapists, physical therapists, speech/language pathologists, nurses, dietitians, counselors, psychologists, dentists, audiologists, etc.) who develop projected care based on the published formats used in life care planning. Although it is important that the various participants in the training have a rehabilitation education and relevant certification in their area of specialty before engaging in the life care planning process, this by itself is certainly not enough; additional education and experience are necessary (Weed, 1989, 1997). In order to identify some of the basic methodologies used in the industry and to underscore the relevance of the chapters included in this book, a review of the current standards is appropriate. Life care planning includes various topics that assure the effectiveness of the overall plan. Items included are explained in Table 1.1.

Once it is determined that a life care plan is appropriate, locating a qualified life care planner is necessary. Certainly individuals who have completed the certificate program through the University of Florida and others who have achieved the national board-certified life care planner designation should be qualified, and visiting the certification board's website (www.cdec1.com) will provide a list. There are other people who have had extensive experience who may supplant the need for a "designated" life care planner. Questions regarding the planner's qualifications, which include education, work experience, life care planning experience, research knowledge and experience, certifications in legitimate rehabilitation areas, and, in the area of civil litigation, forensic experience, would be relevant (Table 1.2). It may also be important to determine the consultant's awareness of life care planning with regard to his or her expertise or knowledge about the certified life care planning designation, courses completed on life care planning, references and publications relevant to life care planning, and knowledge of professionals who have been movers and shakers in the life care planning field. It is important to understand that the only certification that specifically has ethics for life care planners is the CLCP.

It is relevant to determine the consultant's commitment to the profession by inquiring as to which organizations he or she participates in. Many professionals pay dues to associations but do not participate in professional development, committees, or other profession-enhancing activities. It is also pertinent to determine if the professional has contributed time and effort by either volunteering to work with clients, speaking on relevant issues, holding office with professional organizations, or writing for publications. Receiving awards, honors, or peer recognition is also pertinent.

Other questions to ask may include the consultant's industry experience. If the practitioner is expected to work in personal injury litigation, then experience in this arena seems appropriate. Other specialty industries exist and the rules differ, such that it is often extremely important to ensure that the practitioner's experience covers these specialized fields (Weed, 1994, 1996).

Having an example life care plan may be appropriate to determine if the prospective professional establishes a medical foundation for his or her opinions and uses checklists and forms for other health professionals in the specific area of expertise. In general, it is expected that a physician be involved in the plan's medical opinions. Miscellaneous information may help determine if the consultant has a current vita that outlines his or her experiences, as well as any history of ethics or malpractice complaints.

Step-by-Step Procedures

Assuming that the rehabilitation professional is qualified to assess and project a lifetime care plan for a client and is knowledgeable in the topics to be covered, the next step is to begin the process of the life care plan (Table 1.3). First, of course, the referral must be made to the life care planner and basic information, including time frames, billing agreements, retainer information, and information

Table 1.1   Life Care Plan Checklist

Projected Evaluations: Have you planned for different types of nonphysician evaluations (for example, physical therapy, speech therapy, recreational therapy, occupational therapy, music therapy, dietary assessment, audiology, vision screening, swallow studies, etc.)?

Projected Therapeutic Modalities: What therapies will be needed (based on the evaluations above)? Will a case manager help control costs and reduce complications? Is a behavior management or rehab psychologist, pastoral counseling, or family education appropriate?

Diagnostic Testing/Educational Assessment: What testing is necessary and at what ages? Vocational evaluation? Neuropsychological? Educational levels? Educational consultant to maximize 94–142?

Wheelchair Needs: What types and configuration of wheelchairs will the client require? Power? Shower? Manual? Specialty? Ventilator? Reclining? Quad pegs? Recreational?

Wheelchair Accessories and Maintenance: Has each chair been listed separately for maintenance and accessories (bags, cushions, trays, etc.)? Have you considered the client's activity level?

Aids for Independent Functioning: What can this individual use to help himself or herself? Environmental controls? Adaptive aids? Omni-reachers?

Orthotics/Prosthetics: Will the client need braces? Have you planned for replacement and maintenance?

Home Furnishings and Accessories: Will the client need a specialty bed? Portable ramps? Hoyer or other lift?

Drug/Supply Needs: Have prescription and nonprescription drugs been listed, including size, quantity, and rate at which to be consumed? All supplies such as bladder and bowel program, skin care, etc.?

Home Care/Facility Care: Is it possible for the client to live at home? How about specialty programs such as yearly camps? What level of care will he or she require?

Future Medical Care — Routine: Is there a need for an annual evaluation? Which medical specialties? Orthopedics? Urology? Internist? Vision? Dental? Lab?

Transportation: Are hand controls sufficient or is a specialty van needed? Can local transportation companies be used?

Health and Strength Maintenance: What specialty recreation is needed? Blow darts? Adapted games? Row cycle? Annual dues for specialty magazines? (Specialty wheelchairs should be placed on wheelchair page.)

Architectural Renovations: Have you considered ramps, hallways, kitchen, fire protection, alternative heating/cooling, floor coverings, bath, attendant room, equipment storage, etc.?

Potential Complications: Have you included a list of potential complications likely to occur such as skin breakdown, infections, psychological trauma, contractures, etc.?

Future Medical Care/Surgical Intervention or Aggressive Treatment: Are there plans for aggressive treatment? Or additional surgeries such as plastic surgery?

Orthopedic Equipment Needs: Are walkers, standing tables, tilt tables, body support equipment needed?

Vocational/Educational Plan: What are the costs of vocational counseling, job coaching, tuition, fees, books, supplies, technology, etc.?

Reprinted with permission. Roger O. Weed, Ph.D.

Table 1.2   Checklist for Selecting a Life Care Planner

☑ Professional's **qualifications**?
- **Education**, including degrees and continuing education? If doctorate, was the university accredited? (Some have mail-order graduate degrees or diplomas from "universities" that are less than stellar.)
- **Work** experience?
- **Life care planning** experience?
- **Research** knowledge and experience?
- **Certifications or licenses**? Generally accepted rehabilitation certifications include **CLCP** (certified life care planner), **CRC** (certified rehabilitation counselor), **CDMS** (certified disability management specialist), **CVE** (certified vocational evaluator), **CRRN** (certified rehabilitation registered nurse), **CCM** (certified case manager), diplomate or fellow **ABVE** (American Board of Vocational Experts).
- **Forensic experience** (if appropriate)? Familiar with the rules pertaining to experts? Have they testified? Do they have a list of cases in which they testified at deposition or trial for the previous 4 years? Plaintiff/defense ratio?

☑ Prospective consultant's **awareness** of life care planning?
- Are they a board-**certified** life care planner?
- Have they achieved the **certificate** in life care planning offered through the University of Florida?
- Have they completed **courses** offered by a noted program on life care planning? (e.g., Rehabilitation Training Institute, Intelicus, University of Florida, NARPPS, et al.)
- Can they cite life care planning **references**?
- Do they subscribe to the *Journal of Life Care Planning*?
- Do they know some of the **professionals** associated with life care planning publications and training? (e.g., Terry Blackwell, Richard Bonfiglio, Paul Deutsch, Julie Kitchen, Robert Meier, Sue Riddick-Grisham, Horace Sawyer, Connie Sunday, Randall Thomas, Roger Weed, Terry Winkler, Jim Young)

☑ **Commitment** to the profession?
- Are they a member of the International Academy of Life Care Planners? What professional and disability-specific **organization**(s) do they belong to? (Are these legitimate or fringe organizations such as a for-profit owned by an individual or group with little recognition or substance?)
- Do they **participate** in professional development?
- Have they **contributed** their time and effort by volunteering services to clients in need, speaking, holding office with professional organizations, writing articles, chapters, or books?
- Have they received **awards, honors, peer recognition**?

☑ **Industry** experience?
- Workers' compensation or federal Office of Workers' Compensation Programs?
- Personal injury?
- Social Security?
- State rehabilitation?

(continued)

Table 1.2 (Continued)   Checklist for Selecting a Life Care Planner

- ■ Longshore workers?
- ■ Jones Act?
- ■ Federal Employees Liability Act (FELA)?
- ■ Long-term and short-term disability?
- ■ Specialize in a particular disability?
- ☑ **Medical foundation** for opinions established?
  - ■ Use established published **checklists** and **forms**?
  - ■ Routinely consult with a **physician** as part of the team?
  - ■ Include other **health professionals** as appropriate (e.g., OT, PT, SLT, RT, audiology, neuropsych, etc.)?
- ☑ **Other**
  - ■ What and how do they **bill** for their services? Do they charge different rates for interview, records review, deposition, or trial?
  - ■ Do they have a current curriculum **vita**?
  - ■ History of **ethics** complaints or **arrests**?

Reprinted with permission. Roger O. Weed, Ph.D.

release topics, must be discussed (Weed & Field, 2001). Second, it is important to obtain as complete a copy of the medical records as possible, including nurses' notes, physicians' orders, ambulance report, emergency records, consultant's reports, admission and discharge reports, and laboratory and radiographic reports.

It may also be useful to obtain additional information from the client or family in the form of depositions, interrogatories, or other records. Employment records, tax records, and school records are usually helpful if there are vocational issues to be included in the report. If the client is a young child with no educational or medical history, then it would be of value to survey in extensive detail the family history, including mother and father, aunts and uncles, and grandparents (Weed, 1996). In some situations, siblings may have school and other history that may be useful. Occasionally videotapes of the client prior to the injury or day-in-the-life videos may be compiled by the attorney and can be useful, particularly in civil litigation defense cases or insurance consulting where the client is not readily accessible to the consultant.

An initial interview should occur at the client's residence if possible (whether facility or home), and appropriate people should be invited to the interview, which may include parents, spouse, siblings, or caregivers. In general, initial interviews will last from 3 to 5 hours. When the professional attends the interview it is important to use interview forms or checklists that will help structure the interview and ensure that topics appropriate to be discussed are covered. There may be supplemental forms for pediatric cases, brain injury, assistive technology, activities of daily living, and others. It is useful to obtain a copy of the life care plan checklist to educate the client and family members as to the purpose of the life care plan. It is recommended that a camera or video recorder be used to record the living situation, medications, supplies, and equipment used for the client. For example, a home may need to be modified and photographs are useful for documentation.

Table 1.3 Step-by-Step Procedure for Life Care Planning

1. **Case Intake:** When you talked with the referral source, did you record the basic referral information? Time frames discussed? Financial/billing agreement? Retainer received (if appropriate)? Arrange for information release?

2. **Medical Records:** Did you request a **complete** copy of the medical records? Nurses' notes? Doctors' orders? Ambulance report? Emergency room records? Consultant's reports? Admission and discharge reports? Lab/x-ray/etc.?

3. **Supporting Documentation:** Are there depositions of the client, family, or treatment team that may be useful? Day-in-the-life videotapes? And if vocational issues are to be included in report, school records (including test scores), vocational and employment records, tax returns?

4. **Initial Interview Arrangements:** Is the interview to be held at the client's residence? Have you arranged for all appropriate people to attend the initial interview (spouse, parents, siblings)? Did you allow 3 to 5 hours for the initial interview? (Some consultants or defense experts may not be permitted direct access to the client or treating health care professionals.)

5. **Initial Interview Materials:** Do you have the initial interview form for each topic to be covered? Supplemental form for pediatric cases, CP, traumatic brain injury (TBI), spinal cord injury (SCI) as needed? Do you have a copy of the life care plan checklist? Example plan to show the client? Camera or video camcorder to record living situation, medications, supplies, equipment, and other documentation useful for developing a plan?

6. **Consulting with Therapeutic Team Members:** Have you consulted with and solicited treatment recommendations from appropriate therapeutic team members (if able to do so)?

7. **Preparing Preliminary Life Care Plan Opinions:** Do you have information that can be used to project future care costs? Frequency of service or treatment? Duration? Base cost? Source of information? Vendors?

8. **Filling in the Holes:** Do you need additional medical or other evaluations to complete the plan? Have you obtained the approval to retain services of additional sources from the referral source? Have you composed a letter outlining the right questions to assure you are soliciting the needed information?

9. **Researching Costs and Sources:** Have you contacted local sources for costs of treatment, medications, supplies, equipment? Or do you have catalogs or flyers? For children, are there services that might be covered, in part, through the school system?

10. **Finalizing the Life Care Plan:** Did you confirm your projections with the client and family (if appropriate)? Treatment team members? Can the economist project the costs based on the plan? Do you need to coordinate with a vocational expert?

11. **Last but Not Least:** Have you distributed the plan to all appropriate parties (client, if appropriate, referral source, attorney, economist, if there is one)?

Reprinted with permission. Roger O. Weed, Ph.D., Susan Grisham, R.N.

In general, it is useful to consult with the therapeutic team members if possible. As noted above, there may be personal injury litigation defense cases or insurance consulting where this is not possible. It is also reasonable to retain the services of a physician or other individuals as appropriate when treatment team members are not available to discuss the case or the caregivers are not specialized. Also, some treating physicians are not experts in the particular disability or are reluctant to provide recommendations, in which case it may be appropriate to arrange for specialty evaluations by other medical professionals.

There is a special note that should be made with regard to medical foundation for cases that have some or many medically based needs. There are people who are not physicians who claim that they need not have any more medical foundation than their own experience. There are others who assert they merely are administratively writing down the notes dictated to them by physicians and are not making independent judgments about the efficacy of recommendations. In this author's opinion, a qualified life care planner must be a collaborator, participant, and author of the life care plan. For a detailed review of this issue, see "The Life Care Planner: Secretary, Know-It-All, or General Contractor? One Person's Perspective" (Weed, 2002).

Once a preliminary life care plan opinion is arranged, it should include frequency of the service or treatment, cost, duration of the treatment, source of information, and perhaps vendors for the services or products listed.

It is not uncommon for basic evaluations to reveal various holes that may require additional medical or other evaluations to be appropriate. For example, a neuropsychologist may be required in brain injury cases. It is important that the consultant compose a list of questions that will assist the evaluator in addressing questions that are specific to the life care plan (Blackwell et al., 1994a,b; Weed & Field, 2001). For example, neuropsychologists may do an outstanding job in writing reports and listing the results of tests but may be less than adequate in identifying functional limitations that result from the disability, as well as revealing specific treatment options with costs so that a projection of its estimated value can be determined.

Once a life care plan has been completed, it is common for the planner to research the costs of treatment, medications, supplies, and equipment. There are occasions where catalogs will provide the necessary resource, particularly for products that are commonly available through mail order or for locations where the services or products are limited. In some states, depending on the jurisdiction (e.g., civil litigation, workers' compensation, long-term disability, etc.), there may be a need to identify collateral sources. A common collateral source is a "free" service often offered through the school systems for qualified students. There may also be special rules regarding the costs associated with products. One state, for example, requires that costs of products and service for workers' compensation insurance cases be only a certain percentage above Medicare/Medicaid reimbursement schedules.

Once the life care plan is approaching finalization, it may be appropriate to consult with the client and family (if appropriate) to determine that historical information is accurate and that the topics included in the life care plan are appropriate. Once the life care plan is complete, it is the responsibility of the life care planner to distribute the life care plan to appropriate resources. The life care planner should be mindful of the rules within the industry to avoid distribution of a plan to inappropriate sources. In the case of civil litigation, the attorney who retains the consultant's service determines the appropriate recipient(s).

The Future

The future of life care planning seems bright indeed. Since the life care plan first emerged in the rehabilitation literature in 1985, the concept has grown immensely to represent the most effective case management method within the industry, particularly with regard to complex medically challenging cases (Blackwell et al., 1997; Deutsch et al., 1989b; Kitchen et al., 1989; Weed & Sluis, 1990). As this book goes to press, many of the topics that were considered the future for life care planning just a few years ago have already become the present (Deutsch, 1994). Life care planning in the areas of reserve setting for insurance companies, managed care organizations, workers' compensation, personal injury, facility discharge planning, and government-funded vaccine injury programs has strongly endorsed the concept. In civil injury litigation, the Daubert ruling (1993) will continue to alter how some professionals develop life care plans by encouraging the practice of using consistent, researched, and critiqued methods of developing opinions (see chapters on forensics and perspectives by defense and plaintiff attorneys for more information).

It is predicted that areas of mental health (especially serious lifelong illness such as schizophrenia), geriatrics, mediation, facility-based life care planning, special needs trusts for children, divorces, and assisting families with financial and estate planning will increase. For example, in a divorce case where the settlement was based somewhat on the cost of a persistent vegetative state client living at home, the soon-to-be ex-wife was aware that the child's father planned to place the client in a facility because it was less expensive and therefore would reduce his obligation for child support. The care planner was initially asked to identify a reasonable care plan.

In addition, based on participants in recent training programs, experts from a variety of health care-related occupations (physicians, occupational therapists, physical therapists, and speech and language pathologists) will participate individually and as members of a team. Health maintenance organizations will use this methodology to assist with the projection of costs for their catastrophically impaired patient population. Managed care is a current phenomenon that has special application to life care planning. If the goal is to manage care, then using life care planning procedures is a viable option. The design is an excellent method to avoid errors and omissions. Unfortunately, the term *managed care* often really means *managed costs*. If health maintenance organizations truly wish to enhance care outcomes for their patients, then we will observe many case management professionals involved in training programs focused on life care planning. At least one nationwide case management firm has adopted the basic life care planning procedure to work with insurance companies for catastrophic injuries in an attempt to assist them with overall rehabilitation planning and projection of costs. Structured settlement companies use the life care plan to develop proposals for settlements and estate planning. Facility and hospital discharge planners will use the method for more effective patient and family education as well as for assurance of comprehensive care.

Additionally, life care planning research, already under way (Sutton et al., 2002 and reprinted in this text), will increase in number and sophistication with an eye toward underscoring reliability and validity criteria as well as enhancing the standards of practice.

CONCLUSION

Life care planning has emerged as an effective method for the prediction of future care needs and costs. The industry continues to grow and develop new horizons. It is of specific importance that a coordinated effort with standardized approaches be promoted in order that the industry as a whole progresses and becomes more effective. As more professionals, including allied health professionals, become involved in this process, the industry will mature and develop more effective outcome measurements. Some universities are developing doctoral programs to endorse or encompass life care planning procedures and methods. In fact, a 2003 unpublished study of accredited graduate rehabilitation counselor training programs revealed that two thirds offer training in life care planning (Isom et al., 2003). In civil litigation, defense attorneys have increasingly turned to rehabilitation professionals to consult on life care planning issues. It is incumbent on the rehabilitation professional to assure that services offered are consistent with the standards of the industry. Building on the work of others, rather than reinventing the wheel, will assist in achieving this goal.

REFERENCES

Blackwell, T., Kitchen, J., & Thomas, R. (1997). *Life Care Planning for the Spinal Cord Injured.* Athens, GA: E & F Vocational Services.

Blackwell, T., Sluis Powers, A., & Weed, R. (1994a). *Case Management for the Brain Injured* (foreword by James S. Brady). Athens, GA: E & F Vocational Services.

Blackwell, T., Weed, R., & Sluis Powers, A. (1994b). *Case Management for the Spinal Cord Injured.* Athens, GA: E & F Vocational Services.

Deutsch, P. (1994). Life care planning: into the future. *Journal of Private Sector Rehabilitation,* 9, 79–84.

Deutsch, P. & Raffa, F. (1981). *Damages in Tort Action,* Vols. 8 & 9. New York: Matthew Bender.

Deutsch, P. & Sawyer, H. (1985). *Guide to Rehabilitation.* New York: Ahab Press.

Deutsch, P., Weed, R., Kitchen, J., & Sluis, A. (1989a). *Life Care Plans for the Head Injured: A Step by Step Guide.* Athens, GA: Elliott & Fitzpatrick.

Deutsch, P., Weed, R., Kitchen, J., & Sluis, A. (1989b). *Life Care Plans for the Spinal Cord Injured: A Step by Step Guide.* Athens, GA: Elliott & Fitzpatrick.

Isom, R., Marini, I., & Reid, C. (2003). Life care planning: Rehabilitation education curricula and faculty needs. *Journal of Life Care Planning,* 2(3), 171–174.

Kitchen, J., Cody, L., & Deutsch, P. (1989). *Life Care Plans for the Brain Damaged Baby: A Step by Step Guide.* Orlando, FL: Paul M. Deutsch Press.

Riddick, S. & Weed, R. (1996). The life care planning process for managing catastrophically impaired patients. In *Case Studies in Nursing Case Management,* 61–91. Gaithersburg, MD: Aspen.

Sutton, A., Deutsch, P., Weed, R., & Berens, D. (2002). Reliability of life care plans: a comparison of original and updated plans. *Journal of Life Care Planning,* 1, 187–194.

Weed, R. (1989). Life care planning questions and answers. *Life Care Facts,* 1, 5–6.

Weed, R. (1994). Life care plans: expanding the horizons. *Journal of Private Sector Rehabilitation,* 9, 47–50.

Weed, R. (1995a). Life care plans as a managed care tool. *Medical Interface,* 8, 111–118.

Weed, R. (1995b). Objectivity in life care planning. *Inside Life Care Planning,* 1, 1–5.

Weed, R. (1996). Life care planning and earnings capacity analysis for brain injured clients involved in personal injury litigation utilizing the RAPEL method. *Journal of NeuroRehabilitation,* 7, 119–135.

Weed, R. (1997). Comments regarding life care planning for young children with brain injuries. *The Neurolaw Letter*, 6, 112.

Weed, R. (2002). The life care planner: secretary, know-it-all, or general contractor? One person's perspective. *Journal of Life Care Planning*, 1, 173–177.

Weed, R. & Field, T. (2001). *The Rehabilitation Consultant's Handbook*, 3rd ed. Athens, GA: Elliott & Fitzpatrick.

Weed, R. & Riddick, S. (1992). Life care plans as a case management tool. *The Individual Case Manager Journal*, 3, 26–35.

Weed, R. & Sluis, A. (1990). *Life Care Plans for the Amputee: A Step by Step Guide*. Boca Raton, FL: CRC Press.

I

THE ROLES OF LIFE CARE
PLAN TEAM MEMBERS

2

THE ROLE OF THE PHYSIATRIST IN LIFE CARE PLANNING

Richard Paul Bonfiglio

INTRODUCTION

An appropriate life care plan guides the provision of ongoing daily, medical, and rehabilitative care for an individual status post catastrophic injury or illness (Bonfiglio, 1999). However, for a life care plan to appropriately provide for the needs of most individuals, the plan must have a strong medical foundation. Medical care recommendations must be medically necessary and appropriate.

The individual's unique needs, desires, and aspirations should be considered. The long-term implications of care, including preventing secondary complications, enhancing functional outcome, reducing suffering, and improving quality of life, must be considered (Braddom, 1996).

Physicians specializing in physical medicine and rehabilitation (also known as physiatrists) are uniquely trained and qualified to aid in the development and foundation of forward-looking life care plans. Physical medicine and rehabilitation is the medical specialty that focuses on patient long-term functional outcome. Additionally, rehabilitation physicians understand the unique physiology of individuals with medical conditions like spinal cord injuries and traumatic brain injuries that cause severe impairments and many potential secondary medical conditions. The team approach that is essential to life care plan development and implementation is also the key to the rehabilitation approach to patient care.

There is significant legislative and judicial pressure to reduce compensation and limit awards for pain and suffering. Therefore, establishment of the actual losses and ongoing medical and rehabilitative needs becomes increasingly important for litigation (Cooper & Vernon, 1996; Romano, 1996). An individual having suffered a catastrophic injury or illness usually has extensive ongoing lifetime medical, rehabilitative, and daily living care needs. Physiatrists can help prognosticate regarding these ongoing needs and the impact that such care has on life expectancy.

Thus, a sound medical foundation for a life care plan provided by a physician specializing in physical medicine and rehabilitation can help address the patient's individual medical condition, premorbid medical issues, potential medical

0-8493-1511-5/04/$0.00+$1.50
© 2004 by CRC Press LLC

complications, patient and family preferences, and desired functional outcome, and by that significantly enhance the usefulness of the life care plan.

LIFE CARE PLANNING IMPLICATIONS

Ensuring the availability of appropriate ongoing medical, rehabilitative, and daily care needs has been significantly enhanced by the development of the science of life care planning. However, the foundation for many life care plans is limited by the plan developer's experience and the frequently marginal input from treating physicians. Especially in developing a plan for an individual with complex health care needs or a catastrophic injury, the life care planner and the treating physicians may have very little experience in dealing with a person with similar medical issues, especially for a patient with a spinal cord or traumatic brain injury.

Without adequate medical guidance, the life care plan may not provide for all of the unique needs of the individual, including ongoing medical subspecialist visits, diagnostic testing, and treatment options. Additionally, the recommended services, equipment, and supplies may not be adequate over the individual's lifetime to prevent secondary complications. The recommended services may not allow for recent or reasonably anticipated future developments in medical and rehabilitative care, including technological and service delivery advances. Conversely, the plan may include items that are not necessary to meet the specific needs of an individual patient.

For example, technological advancements and market forces have led to the development of a wide array of adaptive equipment. Environmental control systems allow individuals with virtually any consistent motor activity to control electronic devices and access and use computers, including the Internet. There are now numerous wheelchair options. Powered chairs can be navigated with a variety of inputs, and many power chairs have a self-reclining option. There are even power chairs that can climb stairs. Ceiling-anchored lift devices can ease daily care needs. Identifying the most appropriate adaptive equipment for a severely injured individual is aided with the input from a physician in physical medicine and rehabilitation.

CHOOSING THE RIGHT PHYSIATRIST

Physicians specializing in physical medicine and rehabilitation (physiatrists) are uniquely qualified to provide a strong foundation for life care planning, based on their training and experience in providing medical and rehabilitative services to individuals with various disabilities (DeLisa et al., 1993; Downey et al., 1994; Fletcjer, 1992; Sinaki et al., 1993). Physiatrists are, by their training, experienced in dealing with individuals who have catastrophic functional problems. Additionally, physiatrists are trained to anticipate the long-term needs of their patients.

Rehabilitation care is often essential to maximizing the abilities of individuals with significant disabilities. Rehabilitation physicians generally direct the provision of such services in rehabilitation settings. Relying on these physicians to help develop a long-term plan is a natural extension of their usual practice.

However, physiatrists are usually optimists. Obtaining realistic information and projections requires selecting a physiatrist expert appropriately. The following checklist can help with the selection of a physiatrist as an expert witness in a case for an individual with a catastrophic injury or complex health care needs and resultant significant disability:

- Completion of residency from a recognized leading program
- Board certification in physical medicine and rehabilitation
- Training or experience in applicable area of subspecialization (like traumatic brain injury or spinal cord injury)
- Previous publications and national presentations, especially on related topics
- Academic appointment
- Recognized by rehabilitation peers
- Experience with testimony
- Comfort with litigation process
- Reputation for objective, thorough assessment and ethical practice

In this author's opinion, physicians who combine clinical practice and experience with medicolegal work are usually more credible than those who exclusively provide medical opinions.

Initial contact with the physiatrist should help establish the physician's accessibility, availability, and ability to articulate regarding the key issues in establishing the extent of the individual's ongoing needs. Physicians appearing to avoid the attorney's or life care planner's contact generally make inadequate witnesses. Review of the physicians' past testimony, especially regarding comparable cases, may be useful in delineating the physicians' opinions regarding key areas.

ROLE OF THE PHYSIATRIST

Since the physiatrist may be called on to make projections regarding patient life expectancy which will serve as the medical basis for lifelong care needs, thoroughness in patient evaluations and medical record review is essential. Requesting a sample report is appropriate for judging the physician's examination and documentation adequacy. Physiatrists are usually team-oriented and are willing collaborators because of the nature of the profession. Physiatrists should be identified who consider the life care planner to be part of the patient's care team.

Hopefully, the involved physiatrist can be educated about the need for financial settlement to facilitate the provision of needed ongoing medical and rehabilitative services for the injured individual. In litigation-related cases, the physiatrist must educate the jury about all aspects of the involved individual's disabling condition and its implications. Disability not only often results in physical or cognitive limitations, but also may have emotional and psychological implications. The additional energy requirements and time of performing tasks with a disability often take a toll on the patient.

An individual's disability can also affect the person's family. New family dynamics may add to the person's emotional pressure.

Rehabilitation physicians can also play a key role in a team evaluation of an individual with a catastrophic injury or complex health care needs. Evaluations that include measurement of the patient's functional abilities by various team members, including physical, occupational, and speech therapists; psychologists; vocational counselors; and rehabilitation nurses, are becoming more common. These evaluations serve as a stronger foundation for life care planning development. Physicians in complementary areas of specialization, including neurologists, psychiatrists, neurosurgeons, orthopedists, and urologists, may also be involved. The physiatrist can play a key role in coordinating these evaluations and developing a holistic approach to the resulting clinical impressions and recommendations.

COMMON PATIENT SCENARIOS

Individuals' Status Post Spinal Cord Injury

Rehabilitation evaluation for a person after a spinal cord injury is particularly important because of the alteration in physiology that accompanies such an injury (Blackwell et al., 2001). Virtually every organ system is affected. As an example, blood pressure maintenance is significantly impacted by higher-level spinal cord injuries, secondary to the loss of central connections for the autonomic nervous system. During the early period after spinal cord injury, especially during spinal shock, hypotension is common. During the early rehabilitation process, orthostatic hypotension can interfere with progress. Orthostatic measures like support stockings and an abdominal binder are important treatment measures. Even during the long course, accommodations may be needed, especially with position changes.

After the initial period of spinal shock, the impaired autonomic control can lead to autonomic dysreflexia or hyperreflexia for individuals with higher-level spinal cord injuries, especially above thoracic level 6. Sensations that in an individual with an intact spinal cord would lead to noxious stimulation can trigger this response. Common triggers are bladder overdistention, excessive skin pressure, constipation, and sunburn. Initial treatment should include elimination of the precipitating factor and changing position, especially elevating the individual's head. Medication management may also be needed, especially when the condition recurs frequently. If this condition is left untreated, life-threatening blood pressure elevations and cardiac arrhythmias can occur (Blackwell et al., 2001).

Management of the individual with a spinal cord injury's neurogenic bladder is also essential. Periodic urological evaluations should be included in all life care plans for the spinal cord injured. Additionally, periodic urologic diagnostic testing is needed. At a minimum, this should include regular bladder and renal ultrasound testing, urinalyses, urine cultures, and cystometrograms. Additional tests that may be needed include intravenous pyelograms and laboratory testing, including electrolytes, BUN, and creatinine.

There are many other alterations in physiology after a spinal cord injury, resulting in conditions like spasticity and impaired thermal regulation. Additionally, there are many possible secondary complications like osteoporosis, contractures, heterotopic ossification, pressure ulcers, urinary tract stones, and a perforated abdominal viscus. Evaluation of the likelihood or presence of these conditions in an individual case can be done by a physiatrist (see Chapter 18 for more details).

Traumatic Brain Injury

Traumatic brain injuries can range from mild to those leading to persistent vegetative state. Although extensive medical and daily care is required for anyone in a persistent vegetative state, the provision of services still should be specific to the individual's needs and can be influenced by many factors, including the family support system, available community resources, and architectural considerations.

Individuals with severe traumatic brain injuries usually require ongoing medical, rehabilitative, and daily care services (Rosenthal et al., 1990). A physiatrist can help to delineate the needed care. This medical foundation can aid the life care planner in establishing the medically most appropriate plan. Maximizing the individual's functional improvement is important. Anticipating potential future complications is also needed (more information is available in Chapter 13).

Even for an individual diagnosed as having a mild traumatic brain injury, the functional implications may be very significant. Neuropsychological testing to determine the extent of these functional effects is important. A physiatrist can help to translate these functional limitations to life care planning effects.

Chronic Pain

Many individuals develop chronic pain because of trauma or illness. Establishing the etiology and relating it to a specific event can be difficult. Additionally, defining the extent of pain and its functional implications can be problematic. Because of the experience of physiatrists in looking at functional implications of disease and disability, they can be helpful in establishing such links. Chronic pain is also a frequent sequela of spinal cord and brain injuries (for additional information, see Chapter 17).

Amputation

A physiatrist can help determine the appropriate prosthetic device for an individual after an amputation. Recognizing the functional implications of an amputation and appropriate adaptive equipment is also within the experience of physiatrists. Many amputees experience vascular and chronic pain, and physiatrists are appropriate resources for this care as well (also see Chapter 12).

LIFE EXPECTANCY DETERMINATIONS

Provision of adequate funding for lifetime medical, rehabilitative, and daily care needs is dependent on an accurate prediction of life expectancy. Unfortunately, there is no medical literature for individuals with catastrophic injuries that projects life expectancy *based on the level of care* that is typically outlined in a life care plan. Additionally, the medical literature addressing life expectancy for those with catastrophic injuries or illnesses leading to brain or spinal cord injury has many other flaws. The literature does not generally reflect current health care provision or technological advances. Additionally, such population studies do not address the unique situation of any particular patient. Therefore, an estimate provided by an experienced physiatrist can better predict life expectancy. However, such determinations require a thorough review of available medical records, especially to identify the already existing medical conditions and secondary complications that have occurred. The physiatrist can help determine which complications can be prevented or treated with the services outlined in the life care plan and which are likely to occur despite the recommended ongoing medical and rehabilitative care. The physiatrist can provide an opinion of the effect of the patient's underlying condition and secondary complications on life expectancy.

TESTIMONY

In litigation-related cases, physiatrists can provide the medical foundation for plaintiff life care plans (Cooper & Vernon, 1996; Council on Ethical and Judicial Affairs, 1997; Culver, 1990; Romano, 1996). Recognizing the unique needs of patients with disabilities is a regular part of the practice of physical medicine and rehabilitation.

Physiatrists can equally well evaluate plaintiff-generated life care plans for medical accuracy and necessity. Determining whether recommended medical services are medically necessary and appropriate is important to the defense.

Physiatrists can also provide testimony regarding the medical basis for life expectancy determinations.

Example Case

Each entry in the life care plan requires certain data. Each recommendation must include the medical specialty, start date, stop date, frequency of service, and duration. A base or procedure cost is added that will allow an economist to estimate the total value of the services or procedures. To provide an example, in the table that follows are a few entries associated with the care of a 73-year-old woman with C5–C6 tetraplegia, which is within the domain of the physiatrist.

Recommendation[a]	Dates	Frequency	Expected Cost
Outpatient spinal cord injury reevaluation to include MD, RN, OT, PT, RT, dietary	2004 to life expectancy	1 time per year	$850–1200 each
IVP or renal ultrasound, CBC, UA, and others as needed	2004 to life expectancy	1 time per year	Included in yearly evaluation
Physiatrist	2004 to life expectancy	4 times per year	$156 per visit
Urologist	2004 to life expectancy	2 times per year	$120–150 per visit
KUB	2004 to life expectancy	1 time per year	$65.77 each
Orthopedist	2004 to life expectancy	1 time per year	$100–125 per visit

[a] Partial plan only. Illustration of physician-related minimum needed data.

SUMMARY AND CONCLUSIONS

The appropriate physician expert in physical medicine and rehabilitation can provide opinions regarding:

- Nature and extent of individual patient's disability and residual abilities
- Patient's disease and disability past and future natural history
- Potential future medical complications
- Medical basis of vocational potential
- Delineation of individual's functional limitations, including physical, cognitive, emotional, and fatigue aspects
- Medical basis of needed equipment, supplies, home modifications, transportation needs, nursing, therapy, and other care services
- Life expectancy

The use of a physiatrist to bolster medical foundation for a life care plan for all venues, and in litigation, can facilitate the jury's deliberations regarding adequacy of awards. Such decisions are particularly important when the individual requires regular ongoing lifetime care.

Additionally, the physiatrist can help with implementing life care plans by determining the timing and extent of provision of specific medical services. Maximizing functional gains should be a focus of the rehabilitative and life care planning process effort. For a summary of questions that a life care planner might ask, see medical-related topics in the Life Care Plan Checklist, in Chapter 1.

REFERENCES

Blackwell, T., Krause, J., Winkler, T., & Stiens, S. (2001). *Spinal Cord Injury Desk Reference: Guidelines for Life Care Planning and Case Management*. New York: Demos.

Bonfiglio, R.P. (1999). The role of the physiatrist. In R. Weed, Ed., *Life Care Planning and Case Management Handbook*. Boca Raton, FL: CRC Press, pp. 15–21.

Braddom, R.L. (1996). *Physical Medicine & Rehabilitation*. Philadelphia: W.B. Saunders.

Cooper, J., & Vernon, S. (1996). *Disability and the Law*. London: Jessica Kingsley Publishers.

Council on Ethical and Judicial Affairs. (1997). *American Medical Association: Code of Medical Ethics*. Chicago: American Medical Association.

Culver, C.M. (1990). *Ethics at the Bedside*. Hanover, NH: University Press of New England.

DeLisa, J.A. et al. (1993). *Rehabilitation Medicine Principles and Practice*, 2nd ed. Philadelphia: J.B. Lippincott.

Downey, J.A. et al. (1994). *The Physiologic Basis of Rehabilitation Medicine*, 2nd ed. Stoneham, MA: Butterworth-Heinemann.

Fletcjer, C.F. et al. (1992). *Rehabilitation Medicine: Contemporary Clinical Perspectives*. Philadelphia: Lea & Febiger.

Romano, J.L. (1996). *Legal Rights of the Catastrophically Ill and Injured*. Norristown, PA: Rosenstein & Romano.

Rosenthal, M. et al. (1990). *Rehabilitation of the Adult and Child with Traumatic Brain Injury*, 2nd ed. Philadelphia: F.A. Davis.

Sinaki, M. et al. (1993). *Basic Clinical Rehabilitation Medicine*, 2nd ed. St. Louis, MO: Mosby.

3

THE ROLE OF THE NURSE CASE MANAGER IN LIFE CARE PLANNING

Susan Riddick-Grisham

INTRODUCTION

The components of the nursing process, a framework for providing care, include assessment, nursing diagnosis, outcome identification, planning, implementation, and evaluation to ensure a systematic approach for delivering care. These core competencies when applied to the practice of case management involve a collaborative process that assesses, plans, implements, coordinates, monitors, and evaluates the options and services required to meet an individual's health needs, using communications and available resources to promote quality, cost-effective outcomes (CMSA, 1995). Because of their clinical assessment skills, multidisciplinary communication background, and experience to anticipate and coordinate needed treatment, nurses have remained an invaluable resource to the field of case management. Case management for the individuals with catastrophic injury or chronic illness involves a diagnosis with complex medical and psychosocial issues. Life care planning was developed to serve as a tool to facilitate the practice of complex health care and catastrophic injury case management by providing a consistent methodology for analyzing the complex needs dictated by the onset of the disability (Weed & Riddick, 1992). Today effective case management and life care planning both rely on the principles of the nursing process to create an integrated continuum with measurable outcomes.

INTEGRATION OF CARE MANAGEMENT, FINANCIAL MANAGEMENT, AND INFORMATION SHARING

Following World War II, insurance companies hired nurses and social workers to manage the physical, emotional, and social needs of severely disabled veterans (Blancett & Flarey, 1996). Case management grew as it was widely used in the management of individuals with mental illness. Employers and insurance companies, faced with escalating claims costs, court awards, and rising health care costs,

0-8493-1511-5/04/$0.00+$1.50
© 2004 by CRC Press LLC

used case management services to assess a claim and set goals and timetables to project costs, all to ensure effective use of their dollars spent.

Today case management continues to play a pivotal role in the evolving health care system by decreasing fragmentation and duplication of services, increasing communication and collaboration among all members of the care team, and improving patient adherence to treatment. These actions improve achievement of measurable and durable outcomes, using health care dollars efficiently.

Drs. Paul Deutsch and Horace Sawyer (1985), in *A Guide to Rehabilitation*, first introduced the concept of life care planning to the rehabilitation professional in 1985. Life care planning was developed as a tool to facilitate case management of catastrophically injured or chronically ill individuals. Life care planning was a direct result of the realization that what was needed was a consistent methodology for analyzing all of the needs dictated by the onset of catastrophic disability through to end of life expectancy. Life care planning offered a methodology that considered the disability, the patient and family, and the process of age and disability combining over time to create phase changes in needs, and further considered the most current research on the disability process. The process also considers the treatment team's recommendations based on needs-driven considerations.

The life care planning process is a means by which the nurse case manager can develop a consistent, well-organized approach to the management of complex cases. The scope of life care planning has extended to areas such as managed care, insurance reserve setting, discharge planning, elder care, and others. A comprehensive and thorough life care plan (LCP) is designed to allow for an integrated continuum of care addressing the integration of care management, information/communication, and finance mechanisms (see Figure 3.1).

Care and treatment of the catastrophically injured or chronically ill patient often involves multiple treatment providers in a number of treatment settings, all with their own treatment protocols and outcomes. The nurse case manager is frequently the member of the care team who manages the patient across all settings from acute hospitalization to discharge home and return to the community and employment. The life care plan itself can provide that basis for shared communication and expectations among all care providers, along with the patient and family. The nurse case manager, serving as the implementer of the plan, can act as the liaison of the information, dispensing it to the appropriate individuals at the appropriate times, so as to ensure efficient decision making, appropriate financial expenditures, and planned and measurable outcomes.

THE ROLE OF THE NURSE CASE MANAGER

Case management in its broadest terms reflects the phases of the nursing process; it is process in action (Blancett & Flarey, 1996). Lydia E. Hall (1963), a rehabilitation nurse, first theorized about the nursing practice in her Core, Care, and Cure Model. In 1973 the American Nursing Association (ANA) legitimized the nursing process. In 1991 and later in 1998 the ANA defined the nursing process to include assessment, diagnosis, outcome identification, planning, implementation, and evaluation.

The nursing process is a framework for providing nursing care to patients, families, and communities. It provides an orderly and systematic approach to

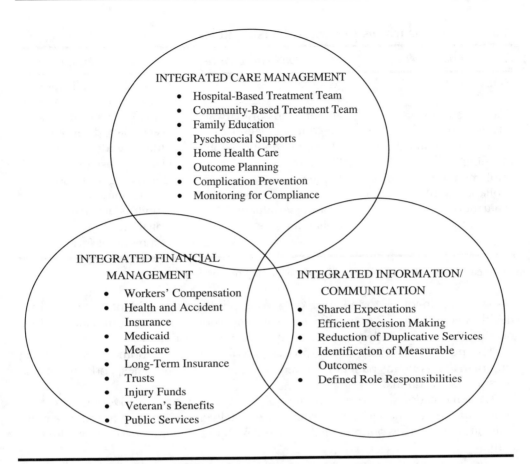

INTEGRATED CARE MANAGEMENT

- Hospital-Based Treatment Team
- Community-Based Treatment Team
- Family Education
- Pyschosocial Supports
- Home Health Care
- Outcome Planning
- Complication Prevention
- Monitoring for Compliance

INTEGRATED FINANCIAL MANAGEMENT

- Workers' Compensation
- Health and Accident Insurance
- Medicaid
- Medicare
- Long-Term Insurance
- Trusts
- Injury Funds
- Veteran's Benefits
- Public Services

INTEGRATED INFORMATION/ COMMUNICATION

- Shared Expectations
- Efficient Decision Making
- Reduction of Duplicative Services
- Identification of Measurable Outcomes
- Defined Role Responsibilities

Figure 3.1   Integrated continuum.

defining a plan for patient-centered care that is appropriate to use throughout a lifetime in all settings. Throughout the nursing process the nurse collects and analyzes data to identify health care needs and determine priorities of care goals. The types of data collected can include objective or obvious data, subjective data, variable or changing data, or constant data. The major tasks of the assessment include collection, validation, and organization of data.

The nurse then plans and implements an individualized plan of care with measurable outcomes. This is followed by an evaluation of the patient's response to the plan, determining whether the patient goals have been achieved. If the patient's needs change or goals are not achieved, the nurse modifies the original plan of care. This ongoing continuum of care essentially provides a framework for guiding clinical practice.

Every step of nursing process is essential to, and is closely interrelated with, the other steps. During the diagnosis and assessment phase, the nurse collects data about the patient from a variety of sources, including the patient, family, significant others, health care personnel, medical records, and literature. This information is used for problem identification so that planning and implementation are appropriate to the patient's needs.

Table 3.1 Comparisons of Various Nursing Roles

Nursing Process	Case Management Process	Life Care Planning Process
Assessment	Assessment	Data collection includes assessment
Diagnosis (nursing diagnosis)	Understands primary and secondary diagnoses	Understands primary and secondary diagnoses
Outcome identification	Outcome identification	Outcome identification
Planning	Planning/research	Planning/research
Implementation (involves collaboration)	Implementation	Consulting and possible implementation[a]
Evaluation	Monitors/evaluates	Monitors/evaluates
	Collaborates	Collaborates
		Testimony (if forensic)

[a] Life care plans that are used in legal cases may not be implemented.

This step involves formulating diagnostic statements that identify the patient's health-related problems. Once an assessment is made, the nurse formulates various nursing diagnoses as they pertain to the nursing care model.

The next step of the nursing process involves the development of a nursing care plan that contains patient-centered goals, expected outcomes, and appropriate nursing interventions.

Implementation is the action step of the nursing process. During this step, problem-oriented individualized client care is delivered according to the care plan. This often involves working collaboratively with other members of the health care team.

The last step of the process is evaluation/monitoring. The success of implemented interventions, achievement of expected outcomes, resolution of nursing diagnoses, and accuracy and completeness of assessment data are evaluated. This step provides for the revision of the nursing care plan as necessary.

The entire process is sequential and interrelated. Each step depends on the previous one. The sequence is logical, orderly, and systematic. The plan is established based on patient needs, and nursing care is provided according to the plan.

These core competencies can be applied to the practice of case management that involves a collaborative process that assesses, plans, implements, coordinates, monitors, and evaluates the options and services required to meet an individual's health needs, using communications and available resources to promote quality, cost-effective outcomes (CMSA, 1995). Case management for the individual with a catastrophic injury or chronic illness involves a diagnosis with complex medical and psychosocial issues. Life care planning was developed to serve as a tool to facilitate the practice by providing a consistent methodology for analyzing the complex needs dictated by the onset of the disability. Case management and life care planning both rely on the principles of the nursing process to create an integrated continuum (see Figure 3.1).

Although a nursing education gives the basic skills used in the life care plan process, a high level of expertise is required to address the complex issues involved in life care planning. Within the life care planning field there are a number of roles that can be filled by a nurse case manager. Those could include but may not be limited to:

Life Care Plan Expert — Develops life care plan. Is prepared to provide expert testimony if the case is in litigation.

Life Care Plan Consulting Expert — Develops life care plans in nonlitigious situations or offers consulting services addressing life care plan critique and analysis to lawyers or insurance companies. Is not expected to provide expert testimony.

LCP Research Assistant — Assists a life care planner in performing medical records analysis or research. Is not expected to provide expert testimony.

Life Care Plan Implementer/Case Manager — Implements the life care plan utilizing traditional case management.

Legal Nurse Consultant — Assist with discovery, conducts research, reviews medical records, identifies standards of care, prepares reports and summaries on the extent of injury or illness, and locates expert witnesses. See Table 3.2 for a medical-legal checklist.

LIFE CARE PLAN SURVEY RESEARCH

In the Life Care Plan Survey 2001, it was noted that 56% of the respondents were registered nurses (Neulicht et al., 2002). Nurses who enter into the practice of life care planning must have an understanding of the medical and rehabilitation issues involved with varying complex medical conditions that they will be asked to address. Another key component of life care planning involves that ability to develop a consistent, valid, and reliable approach to data collection. There are various software programs available to assist in this process.

For those who decide to function in the capacity of a life care plan expert, there is the expectation that one will be required to testify in deposition or trial. These situations are often stressful and time-consuming. In light of recent challenges presented by the Daubert rulings (see Chapters 24 and 25), the future of life care planning as a forensic tool is dependent upon life care plan research focused on identifying quantifiable outcomes and establishing the reliability and validity of the process of life care planning. Nurses who act as life care plan experts will be expected to understand basic research methodology. See Table 3.3 for desirable traits for the nurse life care planner.

PROVIDING LIFE CARE PLAN SUPPORT SERVICES

The nurse case manager may choose a role that is more supportive in nature. Nurses are often hired by the life care plan experts to provide support services, which could include medical record reviews, research, and some of the traditional case management services (Table 3.4).

There are times when the scope of the nurse case manager's role occurs only after the completion of the life care plan, when the financing mechanisms are in place. This often involves the implementation of the care plan utilizing funds that have been set aside in a trust. The life care plan serves as a road map for the

Table 3.2 Medical-Legal Consultation Checklist

☑ **Medical Records Analysis**
Organize and tab; define in layman's terms; describe number of operative procedures and invasive procedures; use of pain medication; special consultations; number of days in ICU or other special placements; complications experienced; physician names and specialties; discharge disposition

☑ **Medical Research**
Relevant articles and books; MEDLINE; software; networking; define content, highlight, organize, and educate attorney

☑ **Experts**
Location of appropriate experts; coordination of referral to expert; securing services of appropriate experts, including liability, causation, and damage experts

☑ **Deposition: Review and Summarization**
Development of deposition questions and attendance at deposition. Review and summarize deposition to highlight damage and treatment issues

☑ **Case Management**
Assessment of medical condition; coordination of medical care and physician referral; coordination of information with attorney, client/family, physician to physician

☑ **Attendance at Medical Exam**
Documentation of physician/client interview and assessment

☑ **Demonstrative Evidence**
Overheads; charts; graphs; photos; videotape; medical illustration and medical equipment; arrange for day-in-the-life and script; help develop settlement brochures

☑ **Life Care Plan/Life Care Plan Review**
Development of a life care plan that identifies appropriate and reasonable care for individuals who have sustained catastrophic injury or chronic illness; review of existing life care plan for overlap and duplication of services; check costs for regional accuracy; assess planner's potential for bias; check math calculations; review for effective rehabilitation and potential to avoid complications; assure all appropriate topics are included in plan

☑ **Vocational Issues**
Identify vocational experts and coordinate evaluation; discuss issues related to placeability, earnings capacity, rehabilitation plan, vocational handicaps, work life expectancy, and related issues

nurse case manager and family to allow for proactive decision making focused on maintaining outcomes and prevention of costly complications.

PROVIDING LEGAL SUPPORT SERVICES

Nurse case managers with life care planning experience are often hired by law firms to act as consultants to assist them in a number of different areas, including medical records review, medical research, identification of experts, and case management. Table 3.5 summarizes topics associated with a comprehensive

Table 3.3 Desirable Traits for the Nurse Life Care Planner

- Know inpatient medical-surgical or acute rehabilitation services
- Have emergency medical experience
- Possess verbal and analytical reasoning skills
- Have the ability to communicate with variety of cultural, educational, and experiential backgrounds
- Possess problem-solving, negotiation, and conflict resolution skills
- Be computer literate for research and communication
- Have knowledge of professional resources and access
- Have the ability to critically analyze literature
- Understand the scope and limitations of medical and allied health fields
- Have pharmacology knowledge
- Know normal laboratory values
- Know drug actions/interactions
- Know pathophysiology of different disabilities
- Have basic abnormal psychology knowledge
- Know the effects of trauma on coping and psychological functioning
- Deal effectively with stress
- Pay attention to details
- Be well organized
- Document the work in the file
- Maintain meticulous files
- See the big picture
- Have self-confidence
- Be objective and professional
- Stay within area of expertise

Table 3.4 Support Functions as Performed by the LCP Research Assistant

- Conduct patient assessment
- Synthesize medical information
- Research medical treatment options
- Research medical literature
- Obtain vendor quotes
- Locate treatment providers and procure services
- Communicate with patient/family/treatment providers/attorneys
- Identify community resources
- Identify collateral source information

medical records analysis, which can be an enormous help to lawyers who have limited medical knowledge.

In addition to the above, the attorney may ask a nurse case manager to review a life care plan to evaluate methodological appropriateness of medical conclusions. The forensic chapter includes suggestions for accomplishing this goal.

Many nurse case managers who perform these support services choose to obtain legal nurse consulting certification, which is offered by the American Association of Legal Nurse Consultants (see resources below).

Table 3.5 Checklist for a Comprehensive Medical Records Analysis

- ☑ **Primary/Secondary Diagnoses:** Have you thoroughly reviewed the records to identify primary and other diagnoses?
- ☑ **Hospitalization Days:** List all hospitals and treatment programs. Summarize the dates and days in each. Include the number of days in specialized care such as ICU or rehabilitation.
- ☑ **Operative Procedures:** What operations were performed, on what date, and by whom, and what was the surgeon's specialty area (orthopedics, neurosurgery, plastic, ophthalmology, etc.)? What kind of anesthesia was used (local or general)? How long was the operation? Were there any complications?
- ☑ **Medications:** What medications were administered? Why were they administered (infections, pain, bowel or bladder program, blood loss, anxiety, etc.)? Include the name, dosage, route of administration (oral, IV, IM, sublingual, catheter). Note any abnormal reactions and long-term effects.
- ☑ **Treatment Team:** Identify all treating physicians by name, specialty, address, and telephone.
- ☑ **Consultations:** Have you identified all consultations during treatment (e.g., endocrinology, infectious disease, pulmonology, radiology, urology, cosmetic, etc.)?
- ☑ **Invasive Procedures:** Note Foley catheters, intravenous, G-tube feeds, etc. Include length of required treatment and how much.
- ☑ **Posthospitalization Treatment:** What postacute programs or treatment programs were included? Day treatment? Home care? Include dates, purpose, and outcomes.
- ☑ **Complications:** List complications and dates, for example, septic shock, chronic infections such as urinary and respiratory, contractures, skin breakdown, adverse reactions to medications, psychological, etc. Include future risk factors such as bone nonunion, traumatic arthritis, etc.
- ☑ **Report Writing:** Have you explained the medical records so that your reader can understand them (e.g., decubitus = skin breakdown; debride = clean the wound; etc.)?
- ☑ **Recommendations:** Should additional evaluations or treatment be offered? What effect does the incident have on the client's ultimate functioning or work?

For the nurse case manager who is interested in providing expert services, additional training and professional development are recommended. It is important to understand what attorneys are looking for when hiring a qualified life care planner. It is essential to outline the exact nature of the service that will be provided. This is especially true for nurse life care planners. Life care planning often involves the process of developing opinions regarding vocational planning and loss of earnings capacity. For most nurses this is outside the scope of their expertise. It is recommended that the nurse case manager clearly communicate what he or she is prepared to address in the life care plan report. This can be accomplished by development of a clear, concisely worded referral letter.

It is also important that anyone who serves as an expert develop a basic understanding of the litigation process and the role of the expert witness. In life care planning it is especially important to understand the need for the medical evidentiary foundation for each item of the life care plan.

Nurses are bound to practice within the definition of the Nurse Practice Act for the individual state in which they practice. Additionally, the nurse case manager/life care planner is held to the Practice Standards and Code of Ethics for each organization joined or certification obtained. Each of these organizations provides opportunities for continued education and growth.

RELATED CERTIFICATIONS AND ORGANIZATIONS

There are several organizations that offer credentials for case management and related certifications. Some are listed below.

- CCM — Certified Case Manager, offered by the Commission for Case Management Certification; (847) 818-0292 or www.ccmcertification.org
- CMCN — Certified Managed Care Nurse, offered by the Board of Managed Care Nursing; (804) 527-1905
- CMC — Case Manager, Certified, offered by the American Institute of Outcomes Case Management; (562) 945-9990 or www.aiocm.org
- RN-NCM — Registered Nurse–Nurse Case Manager, offered by American Nurses Credentialing Center; (800) 284-2378
- CMC — Care Manager Certified, offered by the National Academy of Certified Care Managers; (800) 962-2260
- A-CCC — Continuity of Care Certification, Advanced, offered by the National Association for Certification of Care; (877) 661-0066
- CSWCA — Certified Social Work Case Manager, offered by the National Association of Social Workers Credentialing Center, Specialty Certifications; (800) 638-8799, ext. 409
- COHN/CM — Certified Occupational Health Nurse, offered by the American Board for Occupational Health Nurses; (630) 789-5799

Legal Nurse Certification

- LNCC — Legal Nurse Consultant Certified, offered by the American Association of Legal Nurse Consultants; (877) 402-2562

Life Care Plan Certification

- CLCP — Certified Life Care Planner, offered by the Commission for Health Care Certification; (804) 378-7273 or www.cdec1.com
- AANLCP — Certified Nurse Life Care Planner, offered by the American Association of Nurse Life Care Planners; (888) 575-4047 or www.aanlcp.org

Life Care Plan Organizations

- IALCP — International Academy of Life Care Planners; (800) 531-5146 or www.IALCP.com
- AANLCP — American Association of Nurse Life Care Planners; (888) 575-4047 or www.aanlcp.org

Case Management Organizations

CMSA — Case Management Association of America; (501) 225-2229
NACCM — The National Academy of Certified Care Managers; (800) 962-2260
ARN — Association of Rehabilitation Nurses; (800) 229-7530
IARP — International Association of Rehabilitation Professionals; (800) 240-9059

CONCLUSION

The nurse case manager can play a pivotal role in the ongoing management of the catastrophically injured or chronically ill patient. Because their clinical assessment skills, multidisciplinary communication background, and experience to anticipate and coordinate needed treatment, nurses have remained an invaluable resource to the field. Life care planning was developed to serve as a tool to facilitate the practice by providing a consistent methodology for analyzing the complex needs dictated by the onset of disability. Case management and life care planning both rely on the principles of the nursing process to create an integrated continuum.

Within the specialized field practice referred to as life care planning there are many roles that can be served by the nurse case manager. By combining the basic skills of the nursing process with an understanding of life care planning, along with extensive knowledge of the clinical aspects of the presenting disability, an experienced nurse is an excellent professional to provide life care planning services.

REFERENCES

Blancett, S. & Flarey, D. (1996). Case studies in nurse case management. *Health Care Delivery in a World of Managed Care*, 1, 1–5.
Case Management Society of America (CMSA). (1995). *Standards of Practice.*
Countiss, R. (2002). Amicus curiae brief. *Journal of Life Care Planning*, 1, 8–31.
Deutsch, P. & Sawyer, H. (1985). *Guide to Rehabilitation*. White Plains, NY: Ahab Press.
Hall, L.E. (1963). Center for nursing. *Nursing Outlook*, 11, 805.
Kendall, S.L. & Deutsch, P.M. (2002). Research methodology for life care planners. *Journal of Life Care Planning*, 1, 157–168.
Neulicht, A., Riddick-Grisham, S., Hinton, L., Costantini, P., Thomas, R., & Goodrich, B. (2002). Life Care Plan Survey 2001. *Journal of Life Care Planning*, 1, 97–148.
Reimas, C.L., Cohen, E.L., & Redman, R. (2001). Nurse case management role attributes: fifteen years of evidence-based literature. *Lippincotts' Case Management*, 6, 230–242.
Riddick, S. & Weed, R. (1996). The life care planning process for managing catastrophically impaired patients. In S. Bancett & D. Flarey, Eds., *Case Studies in Nursing Case Management*, 61–91. Gaithersburg, MD: Aspen.
Weed, R. & Riddick, S. (1992). Life care plans as a case management tool. *Individual Case Manager*, 3, 26–35.

4

THE ROLE OF THE VOCATIONAL COUNSELOR IN LIFE CARE PLANNING

Debra E. Berens and Roger O. Weed

INTRODUCTION

The *Dictionary of Occupational Titles* (*DOT*), 4th edition (U.S. DOL, 1991a, p. 52) defines vocational rehabilitation counselor as one who "counsels handicapped individuals to provide vocational rehabilitation services." Such services generally include interviewing and evaluating clients, conferring with medical and professional personnel and analyzing records to determine type and degree of disability, developing and assisting clients throughout the rehabilitation plan (or program), and aiding clients in outlining and obtaining appropriate medical and social services. The *DOT* further states that vocational counselors may specialize in a type of disability (e.g., spinal cord injury, traumatic brain injury, amputation, burn, visual impairment, hearing impairment, chronic pain, etc.). The role of the vocational rehabilitation counselor in life care planning expands this definition and is specific to persons who are catastrophically impaired and have limited access to the labor market. This role has become more defined since the early 1980s, when life care planning was first introduced into the literature (Deutsch & Raffa, 1981). In today's climate, vocational counselors serve as an instrumental member of the rehabilitation team to coordinate assessments in an effort to measure a person's aptitude, achievement levels, and transferable work skills. These assessments help determine one's potential for future work activity, such as full- or part-time employment, sheltered or supported employment, or, in cases where work activity is not a realistic goal, to achieve their highest level of productivity or independent living. The essential premise underlying vocational rehabilitation is that involvement in work or some productive, meaningful activity is the goal of one's rehabilitation program (Weed & Field, 1994, 2001; Marme & Skord, 1993). And if return to work or productive activity is appropriate, then the needs and steps to achieve that goal must be included in the life care plan.

Vocational rehabilitation counselors who work within the life care planning arena generally are rehabilitation professionals who have a minimum of a master's

0-8493-1511-5/04/$0.00+$1.50
© 2004 by CRC Press LLC

degree in rehabilitation counseling, hold one or more national certifications in the field of rehabilitation, and have extensive training and experience in the areas of evaluation and assessment, catastrophic case management, transferable work skills, earnings capacity analysis, and job placement (Weed & Field, 1994, 2001). Vocational counselors can be credentialed in a number of areas, most notably CRC (certified rehabilitation counselor), CDMS (certified disability management specialist), CCM (certified case manager), CVE (certified vocational evaluator), ABVE (American Board of Vocational Experts), and CLCP (certified life care planner). Credentials can also be obtained from other organizations that, on the surface, appear to be based more on profit making than on advancing the role and function of the rehabilitation professional. While some of these credentials may be valuable, the authors strongly encourage those professionals interested in pursuing further credentials to thoroughly research the history of the organization and scrutinize the validity of the offer.

VOCATIONAL REHABILITATION COUNSELOR AS TEAM MEMBER

Vocational rehabilitation counselors with advanced degrees and appropriate credentials are properly trained, qualified, and fully prepared to complete life care plans. They can be found working in a variety of fields, including workers' compensation, personal injury, health or disability insurance/managed care, federal Office of Workers' Compensation Programs, and state vocational rehabilitation agencies. Additionally, many facilities (for example, specialty centers of excellence such as Shepherd Center in Atlanta, GA) employ rehabilitation counselors to assist in the evaluation and, when appropriate, transition of a client into other services for return to work assistance or to achieve his or her highest productivity.

Vocational rehabilitation counselors must be knowledgeable and stay within the accepted standards and guidelines of the particular jurisdiction for which they are preparing the life care plan. For instance, in the workers' compensation arena, the vocational counselor must work within the established definitions of disability and return to work hierarchy (see Weed & Field, 1994, 2001, Chapter 3). This also includes the "odd lot" doctrine that has been defined by case law as "any work that the client may be able to perform which would be of limited quantity, dependability or quality, and for which there is no reasonably stable market for their labor activities" (*Clark v. Aqua Air Industries*, 1983; *Gil Crease v. J.A. Jones Construction Company*, 1982). In comparison, vocational rehabilitation counselors within the disability insurance arena, such as long-term disability/short-term disability (LTD/STD), will be expected to provide information on the status of the client's "any/own occupation," as well as the client's vocational potential and the cost of future vocational/educational needs. Similarly, vocational rehabilitation counselors within the personal injury arena will need to determine if the client has vocational potential and to what degree. They will also need to provide information on the cost of the client's expected future vocational/educational needs in an effort to identify vocational damages associated with the injury or disability.

Regardless of the specific jurisdiction, vocational rehabilitation counselors in life care planning must be able to determine first if a client can work and, if so, what work he or she can perform. This determination would include providing information on not only the types of vocational activity a client can be expected to perform, but also the cost, frequency, and duration or replacement of any training or assistance (such as job coach, vocational counseling, rehabilitation technology, modified or custom-designed workstation, supported employment, tuition/books, or other specialized education programs) that may be required to reach the goal (Weed & Riddick, 1992). Depending on the type of disability, the vocational rehabilitation counselor will work with a variety of medical and allied health professionals in determining one's vocational potential and providing information for the life care plan.

Professionals such as physicians and medical specialists, physical therapists, occupational therapists, speech/language pathologists, recreation therapists, nurses, psychologists, neuropsychologists, audiologists, counselors or other mental health professionals, and, in the case of school-age clients, school personnel all work with the vocational rehabilitation counselor to provide information for the life care plan. Generally, team members whose primary responsibilities are for cognitive and psychosocial remediation interact more with vocational counselors than do other team members, and interactions are more effective when focused on adaptive work behaviors such as ability to relate with co-workers and supervisors (Sbordone & Long, 1996). In some cases, the nurse case manager for a client with catastrophic injuries will be the primary person for the life care plan, and the vocational rehabilitation counselor must work in conjunction with the nurse to gather and disseminate vocationally relevant information (also see Chapter 3). It is common for the vocational rehabilitation counselor to rely on the client's primary physician (if available to the expert based on legal protocol), typically a physiatrist, also known as a specialist in physical medicine and rehabilitation (PM&R), in determining a client's functional level and potential to perform vocational activity. In appropriate cases, the vocational counselor may request a functional capacity evaluation (FCE), which may also be known as a physical capacity evaluation or functional capacity assessment, to objectively delineate a client's physical functioning. The FCE can provide objective, hard data regarding the client's ability to perform various physical demands (lifting, standing, walking, sitting, pushing/pulling, etc.), which are usually performed in a facility that specializes in occupational health information. The FCE provides a snapshot view of a client's abilities on one particular day (evaluation may be conducted over 2 days), and given the outcome of the testing, the client's work capacity from a physical standpoint is determined. Additional factors that the vocational counselor must take into consideration in assessing a client's physical capacities are the client's ability to perform work activity over time (endurance), his/her subjective complaints, test validity/reliability (often associated with the examiner as well as the tests), and secondary gain issues (Matheson et al., 2002). In summary, the FCE is just one of many pieces of information used by the vocational counselor in assessing a client's vocational potential.

It is the responsibility of the vocational rehabilitation counselor to maintain a vocational focus on issues related to the life care plan. Most important, the counselor needs to work with the team to establish a medical or psychological foundation to support a client's work potential. A case in which the authors consulted illustrates the need to establish a medical foundation. The case involved a 50-year-old iron-metal construction worker who fell 70 to 90 feet from scaffolding and received multiple orthopedic injuries. The nurse case manager assigned to the case referred the client for a vocational evaluation to determine his work potential. Results from the vocational evaluation coupled with the client's reported high motivation to return to work seemed to suggest that he had the capacity to return to work in some area related to his previous work experience. The vocational rehabilitation counselor then proceeded to conduct a labor market survey to identify actual jobs in his area. Although on the surface it appeared that the case was progressing appropriately (at least from the case manager's perspective), it was learned through contacts with the client's treating physician that it was his opinion the client was permanently and totally disabled from work. Indeed, the client applied for and was approved for Social Security Disability Insurance (SSDI) benefits, which further confirmed he was permanently and totally disabled. The physician furthermore indicated that his recommendations with regard to the client's vocational potential had not been solicited by the case manager. In fact, the physician was unaware that a vocational rehabilitation plan had been developed to return the client to work, and he obviously did not support the plan. This is a clear example of the importance of interacting with a client's medical care providers (when able) to establish a foundation to support the vocational plan.

Vocational Assessment/Evaluation

The terms *vocational assessment* and *vocational evaluation* have been used over the years in rehabilitation literature to generally describe the process of gathering data and determining a person's potential for work activity. Botterbusch (1987) defines vocational assessment as "more limited in scope" than vocational evaluation and cites the Vocational Evaluation and Work Adjustment Association (1983) definition of vocational evaluation, which "incorporates medical, psychological, social, vocational, educational, cultural, and economic data" (p. 191). In Siefker (1992), it is noted that the two phrases "do not describe a significantly different process and can be considered synonymous" (p. 1). For purposes of this chapter, the phrases will be used interchangeably to describe the comprehensive evaluation of a client's biographical and social history, education and work history, medical and other pertinent records (employment/personnel records, school records, parent's school records in pediatric cases, etc.), psychological/neuropsychological records, and actual vocational test results in determining vocational potential.

In compiling data for the life care plan, it is within the role of the vocational counselor to recommend and obtain a formal vocational assessment/evaluation, particularly in the case of a client who:

- Is of working age (generally age 16 to 60)
- Has no or an unclear vocational goal
- Has no work history or a series of short, sporadic jobs
- Has not been determined permanently and totally disabled (i.e., is thought to have some vocational potential)

For clients who are catastrophically injured, it is important for the vocational evaluation to be as specific as possible and to take into account the client's personality traits, interests, aptitudes, and physical capabilities so as to adequately identify appropriate vocational options (Weed & Field, 1994, 2001). In their book *Counseling the Able Disabled*, Deneen and Hessellund (1986) describe some of the most common reasons for vocational testing. Below is a modified version of the list that is felt to be most relevant to life care planning:

1. Provide information about a person's interests, mental and physical abilities, and temperament with respect to work.
2. Support, clarify, and document impressions gained during interviews.
3. Discover job interests and potential vocational objectives.
4. Objectively and accurately describe the client's likes, dislikes, needs, and abilities rather than rely solely on verbal interview information.
5. Observe and evaluate the client's physical stamina, endurance, agility, and ability as related to work performance.
6. Evaluate the degree to which a particular impairment is a physical disability or handicap.

Vocational assessments can vary depending on the particular jurisdiction in which the case is involved. For example, vocational evaluations performed for workers' compensation typically do not include personality testing in determining suitable employment. These evaluations generally focus on interests, aptitudes, and physical capacities as well as the client's demonstrated work history. It is the authors' opinion that vocational evaluations that do not address personality factors or testing should be closely scrutinized as to why such assessment tools are not included. Is it an oversight on the part of the evaluator? Is the evaluator not qualified to administer personality tests? Is the evaluator relying upon government data associated with the job history as published in the *DOT* and the *Transitional Classification of Jobs* (Field & Field, 2004)? Or is there a deliberate attempt not to define personality traits, which may have a positive or negative effect on the client's vocational potential? Even in workers' compensation cases, at least one court ruled on appeal that a client's vocational interests were relevant and necessary (Weed & Field, 1994, 2001).

When referring for a vocational evaluation, the vocational rehabilitation counselor must review the evaluator's credentials and specify which areas to assess. (Also see the section on referring for neuropsychological testing later in this chapter.) The vocational counselor should be concerned not only with the expertise and experience of the evaluator, but also with the technical or scientific aspects of a particular assessment tool and the way in which the test results will be used (Kapes & Mastie, 1988; Siefker, 1992). In developing a life care plan, the vocational rehabilitation counselor must be able to translate results from the vocational evaluation into requirements for the life care plan (Weed & Field, 1994, 2001). Such requirements may include cost for training, transportation, tuition, specialized or adaptive equipment, and maintenance and replacement schedules of needed equipment (Siefker, 1992). For example, the authors were involved in identifying the costs associated with completing a master's degree and pursuing a Ph.D. for a triple amputee who was a teacher at the time of his electrical injury. Not only were costs included in the life care plan for education requirements, but also costs of transportation, prosthetic devices, maintenance and replacement, clothing

Table 4.1   Selected Issues Related to Vocational Assessment

Speeded, timed, and untimed tests	Speeded and timed tests may be biased against physically impaired clients. Untimed tests may not reveal how competitive a client may be.
Individual vs. group tests	Usually the group test is offered for economic reasons and is more general. Individually administered tests allow for examiner comment regarding effort and behavioral observation.
Short "screening" vs. in-depth testing	Vocational evaluators often use short tests for achievement, intelligence, aptitude, and interest screening. Tests such as the Wide Range Achievement Test-Revised (WRAT-R), Self-Directed Search, General Aptitude Test Battery (GATB), Slosson Intelligence Test, and others are not as precise as more detailed tests (e.g., Wechsler). Many evaluators are not qualified to administer more precise tests.
Tests vs. on-the-job evaluation	In order of general priority for best assessment: ■ On the job with an employer ■ On the job based on general standard by professional evaluator ■ Work sample ■ Individually administered test ■ Group test
Leaving out personality factors	It is common in workers' compensation to leave out interest and personality factors when developing an opinion. Basic information with regard to interests, work values, and personality as it relates to work is recommended.

Reprinted with permission. Roger O. Weed, Ph.D.

allowance (due to increased wear and tear on garments as result of prosthetic use), and computer and other assistive technology needed to assist the client in attaining his vocational goal of education administrator. This case example also demonstrates that a client's ability to achieve a vocational goal is closely related to other life care plan issues such as ability to perform activities of daily living (ADLs), accessible housing and transportation, psychological adjustment to disability, home/attendant care, wheelchair or mobility needs, and others. This case also provides an example of the inclusive approach the vocational rehabilitation counselor must use in conducting a comprehensive assessment of the client and interrelating realistic occupational goals with all other aspects of the client's care.

In addition to having a comprehensive evaluation performed, the vocational rehabilitation counselor must be sensitive to how the specific tests are administered. For example, group vs. individual; time, speeded, or untimed; paper and pencil vs. computer administered vs. work sample; short vs. long form; normed vs. nonnormed; and objective vs. subjective, to name a few (see Table 4.1). In general, group tests are not as specific as individual tests (Anastasi, 1982; Siefker, 1992), and speeded or timed tests are usually biased against catastrophically impaired persons. In clients who are motorically or cognitively impaired, tests that are timed may reveal a lower score than is intellectually indicated given that the score is based on speed rather than ability. Additionally, situational or job-specific tests that evaluate a person's ability for work activity in an actual work environment are more favorable and yield more accurate results than a work sample assessment in which job tasks are simulated. Some authors suggest that a client's vocational potential can be most effectively determined when the workplace is used as the primary site of all rehabilitation activity. They further indicate that no other location can be compared to the workplace for face validity and actual job activities (Sbordone & Long, 1996).

Much has been written on the various vocational assessment tools given to persons with a disability (see *A Guide to Vocational Assessment*, 2000; *A Counselor's Guide to Career Assessment Instruments*, 1988; *Vocational Assessment & Evaluation Systems: A Comparison*, 1987; and *Vocational Evaluation in the Private Sector*, 1992). The following list is provided to give an overview of some of the more common or well-known tools used in the vocational assessment/evaluation of persons who are catastrophically impaired. The reader is referred to the publications referenced above for a description of each test and information regarding its usefulness for specific populations of persons with a disability.

Intelligence:
- Wechsler Intelligence Scales (preschool, child, and adult versions; the standard of the industry)
- Stanford–Binet Scales (child and adult)
- Slosson Intelligence Test (brief and very general)
- Raven Progressive Matrices (reasoning)

Personality:
- Minnesota Multiphasic Personality Inventory-III (MMPI-III) (also in Spanish)
- 16 Personality Factors (16 PF)
- Myers-Briggs Type Indicator (MBTI)
- Personality Assessment Inventory (PAI)
- Rorschach Inkblot Test

Interest:
- Strong–Campbell Interest Inventory
- Career Assessment Inventory (CAI)
- Self-Directed Search (SDS)
- Kuder Occupational Interest Inventory

Aptitude:
- General Aptitude Test Battery (GATB)
- Apticom
- Armed Services Vocational Aptitude Battery (ASVAB)
- Differential Aptitude Tests (DAT)
- McCarron Dial System
- Crawford Small Parts Dexterity
- Hester Evaluation System
- Purdue Pegboard

Achievement:
- Wide Range Achievement Test (WRAT as revised)
- Woodcock–Johnson Psychoeducational Battery
- Peabody Individual Achievement Test
- Basic Occupational Literacy Test (BOLT)

Work Sample:
- VALPAR (www.valparint.com)
- Jewish Employment and Vocational Service (JEVS) (www.jevs.org)

Assessment of Physical Functioning:
- Vineland Social Maturity Scale
- PULSES (*p*hysical condition, *u*pper limb, *l*ower limb, *s*ensory, *e*xcretory, *s*upport factors)
- Barthel Inventory of Self-Care Skills

In conjunction with objective test results, the vocational rehabilitation counselor should consider the client's behavior during the interview and test session. Behavioral observations are an integral part of the vocational assessment process and should always be interpreted with the actual test results and client's history, assuming the test was one that lends itself to such observation (Siefker, 1992). The qualified vocational evaluator is attuned to behavioral issues that may affect test results (e.g., pain behaviors, visual/hearing difficulties, need for medication or rest breaks, fatigue, cultural issues and language barriers, and environmental issues, such as: Is the room too hot or cold? Is it early or late in the day?). Likewise, the client's behavior may reveal areas of concern or discrepancy that may warrant further investigation (e.g., Was the client late for the testing session? What are the nonverbal behaviors? Is his or her appearance and grooming appropriate?). Behavior is a valid indication of how one will respond in certain situations, whether it is in a work environment or social/community setting.

In addition to behavioral observations, information about a client's abilities and skills obtained through educational and work experience may be more valid than test results (Weed & Field, 1994, 2001; Siefker, 1992). For this reason, a transferable skills analysis is an essential component of the vocational evaluation and for determining a client's vocational potential. Simply described, a transferable skills analysis gives a profile of the worker traits required of a specific occupation. It is used primarily for clients with a documented work history and takes into consideration one's work experience and residual functional capacities to determine appropriate vocational options. The *DOT* and *Transitional Classification of Jobs* (*COJ*) are necessary to compile a transferable skills analysis, and some experts utilize various computer programs to assist with managing large amounts of data (Gibson, 2003; McCroskey, 2001; Truthan, 1997). Also, the Occupational Information Network (O*Net) has been designed to replace the *DOT* eventually; however, the O*Net does not yet offer a way to conduct a transferability analysis that can be used with reliability in formulating opinions for Social Security disability determinations and personal injury cases, and the *DOT* continues to be the vocational resource of choice at the present time. See the vocational resources section later in this chapter for a description of these and other relevant vocational publications.

Neuropsychological Evaluations in Return to Work Prediction

Neuropsychological evaluations are performed on clients following a brain injury or neurological disease and are essential in identifying the relationships that exist between one's brain and behavior or, more specifically, between one's actions and abilities and his or her higher-level cognitive processes (Evans, 1999; Gabel et al., 1986). It is within the role of the vocational rehabilitation counselor to refer a client for a neuropsychological evaluation in cases where there is documented or suspected brain injury/impairment. According to Gabel et al. (1986), referral to a neuropsychologist is appropriate to assess problems of a more long-standing nature and includes areas such as visual, auditory, or tactile processing difficulties; constructional apraxia (copying designs or free drawing); abstract reasoning or concept formation; receptive or expressive language deficits; attention/concentration deficits; and short- or long-term memory problems. Neuropsychological testing is valuable not only to assess a client's current behavioral and learning problems (i.e., to establish a functional baseline), but also to establish prognosis, monitor and document changes over time, and assist in the planning of the rehabilitation program (Evans, 1999).

Historically, the focus of neuropsychological testing has been on the determination of brain damage and its location. Presently, there is a growing interest within neuropsychology to focus on the client's capacity to function in everyday life. The prediction of work behavior is the second most frequent reason for referral to neuropsychological evaluations. However, such evaluations are somewhat limited by a lack of norms based on specific job types and specific client population, and more work is needed in this area (Sbordone & Long, 1996).

Neuropsychologists and vocational rehabilitation counselors generally share the goal of facilitating the client's transition to an active and productive life. Vocationally speaking, neuropsychological evaluations should assist the vocational counselor in identifying the client's vocational capabilities and behaviors and in planning for his successful entrance into an appropriate work environment or, at minimum, to achieve his highest level of functioning/productivity (Sbordone & Long, 1996). For this reason, neuropsychological evaluations are helpful for both adult and children or pediatric clients and, as with vocational evaluations, must be as specific as possible.

For purposes of life care planning, results from neuropsychological evaluations must relate specifically to the client's function and ability and also provide recommendations for future care needs. Problems in thinking and reasoning, information processing speed, attention/concentration, and long- or short-term memory are vocational barriers that need to be accurately assessed (Sbordone & Long, 1996). Additionally, psychosocial and interpersonal relationship skills need to be assessed such that there is an obvious need for strong communication and collaboration between vocational rehabilitation counselors and neuropsychologists in the interest of maximizing return to work and identifying life care planning recommendations.

Table 4.2 Neuropsychologist Questions

In addition to the standard evaluation report, add the following as appropriate.

1. Please describe, in layman terms, the damage to the brain.
2. Please describe the effects of the accident on the client's ability to function.
3. Please provide an opinion on the following topics:
   a. Intelligence level? (include pre- vs. postincident if able)
   b. Personality style with regard to the workplace and home?
   c. Stamina level?
   d. Functional limitations and assets?
   e. Ability for education/training?
   f. Vocational implications — style of learning?
   g. Level of insight into present functioning?
   h. Ability to compensate for deficits?
   i. Ability to initiate action?
   j. Memory impairments (short-term, long-term, auditory, visual, etc.)?
   k. Ability to identify and correct errors?
   l. Recommendations for compensation strategies?
   m. Need for companion or attendant care?
4. What is the proposed treatment plan?
   a. Counseling? (individual and family)
   b. Cognitive therapy?
   c. Reevaluations?
   d. Referral to others (e.g., physicians)?
   e. Other?
5. How much and how long? (Include the cost per session or hour and reevaluations.)

© 1992, Roger O. Weed, Ph.D., C.R.C., C.D.M.S., F.N.R.C.A. (partially adapted by R. Frazier, Ph.D.), reprinted with permission.

Neuropsychological testing helps determine how much assistance is needed in the home, on the job, at school, and within the community. When referring for a neuropsychological evaluation, it is prudent for the vocational rehabilitation counselor to know to whom he or she is making the referral and the credentials of the neuropsychologist. Experience has shown that the most qualified neuropsychologist not only has a Ph.D. in clinical psychology and is board certified as a neuropsychologist, but also has experience in evaluating persons across all levels of severity of brain injury and has demonstrated a commonsense approach to evaluation and test interpretation.

Once a referral is made to a neuropsychologist, it is recommended that the vocational counselor provide specific questions to the neuropsychologist, which, when answered, would provide information needed specifically for the life care plan. The effects of brain trauma can be found in any or all aspects of one's life, including interpersonal, vocational, educational, recreational, and activities of daily living. It is the role of the neuropsychologist to evaluate the long-term or lifelong effects of brain injury on the client's ability to function (Evans, 1999; Weed, 1994). Suggested questions specifically pertinent for the life care planning process are listed in Table 4.2. Rehabilitation counselors should ask neuropsychologists to answer the questions as part of their evaluation for life care planning.

As stated previously, neuropsychological evaluations are useful in both adult and pediatric cases. The interested reader is referred to the book *Neuropsychological Assessment* (Lezak, 1995) for detailed information on neuropsychological evaluations. According to Lezak (1976), the basic neuropsychological battery contains both individually administered tests and paper-and-pencil tests that are self-administered. The individually administered tests can take up to 3 hours, and the paper-and-pencil tests can take from 3 to 6 hours, depending on the extent of the client's impairment(s). The paper-and-pencil tests should not be timed; however, the individually administered tests are timed. Especially in the case of pediatric clients, neuropsychological evaluations are often given over two sittings in order to avoid fatigue factors. Again, the vocational rehabilitation counselor is cautioned to be sure the neuropsychologist provides a comprehensive evaluation that is sensitive to the client's particular needs and provides information that is relevant for life care planning. Similar to vocational evaluations, neuropsychological evaluations are not done with a single test but instead are a compilation of data based on test results and interpretation and behavioral observations. It is recommended, and good practice, for the vocational counselor to establish a mechanism to meet or speak directly with the neuropsychologist to discuss test results and solicit his or her input for life care planning.

For purposes of this chapter, a brief overview of some of the more common evaluation tools for each age group is given. For additional information, refer to Chapter 6.

Pediatric: Neuropsychological Evaluations

Pediatric cases present many unique challenges for the life care planner (Weed, 2000). One challenge is that there is little, if any, history on which to rely, and practitioners are hesitant to make future care predictions. For this reason, neuropsychological evaluations are particularly helpful with children to help qualify and quantify the impact of a child's brain injury on his or her functioning and behavior (Weed, 1996). Although there are many assessment tools to evaluate pediatric clients, the Halstead–Reitan and Luria–Nebraska batteries are the most frequently used in the neuropsychological assessment of children (Gabel et al., 1986).

According to Gabel et al. (1986), perhaps the greatest usefulness of the Halstead–Reitan batteries is the establishment of objective baseline data that can clarify a child's strengths and weaknesses and be helpful in outlining educational strategies and programs to enhance his or her capabilities. In comparison, the Luria–Nebraska Children's Neuropsychological Test Battery can be administered to children ages 8 to 12 years and focuses on functional systems involved in brain–behavior relationships. A third common assessment battery for children is the Kaufman Assessment Battery for Children (K-ABC) (1983 and revisions), which is individually administered to children ages 2 to 12 years old and measures intelligence and achievement. Last, a useful tool to assess infants who have experienced brain trauma from age 2 months to 30 months is the Bayley Scales of Infant Development (1969 and revisions). The scales are considered to be the best measure of infant development and provide valuable data regarding early mental and motor development and developmental delay. Other scales of infant developmental attainment are the Cattelle Scales of Infant Development and the Vineland Adaptive Behavior Scales (1984 and revisions).

Adult: Neuropsychological Evaluations

Whereas there are numerous neuropsychological assessment tools from which to choose when evaluating children for life care planning, there are significantly more tests for adult assessments. Below is a brief list of some of the more common neuropsychological tools for adults and areas they evaluate. For more information and descriptions on the listed tests, refer to Lees-Haley's *Last Minute Guide to Psychological and Neuropsychological Testing* (1993).

- Wechsler Adult Intelligence Scale, 3rd edition (WAIS-III) (intelligence)
- Wisconsin Card Sorting Test (executive or higher-order functions)
- Boston Naming Test (language)
- Rey Auditory Verbal Learning (memory)
- Wechsler Memory Scale–Revised (WMS-III) (memory)
- Stroop Color Test (mental control)
- Serial 7s or Serial 3s (attention)
- Benton Visual Retention Test (visual memory)
- Gates–MacGinitie Reading Tests (reading academic skills)
- Hooper Visual Organization Test (visual perception)
- Woodcock–Johnson (academic and cognitive assessment)
- Haptic Intelligence Test (intelligence); used for clients with visual impairment
- Leiter Intelligence Test (intelligence); used for clients with hearing impairment
- Hisky–Nebraska Aptitude Test (aptitude); used for clients with hearing impairment

In summary, neuropsychological evaluations for clients with brain impairment are usually essential in the field of life care planning to assess both the near- and long-term effects of brain damage on one's functioning and developmental levels. Information obtained through neuropsychological testing can be crucial in developing the appropriate future care planning of a client with a traumatic brain injury. Inasmuch as neuropsychological evaluations are vital to life care planning, test results for young children are very variable. Generally, IQ test results are not considered of substantial value until the child reaches school age. Additionally, it is generally more preferable to rely on school children's standardized achievement test scores than on actual grades as a true measure of their achievement. In referring a client for neuropsychological testing, the vocational counselor should ensure that the evaluator reviews all available medical and academic records and that the evaluation includes developmental assessments in addition to the standardized test batteries. It is common to include in the life care plan provisions for neuropsychological reevaluations at specific life stages in the client's development or at specific time intervals throughout one's life expectancy in order to assess and monitor the client's functioning abilities. This also applies to the assessment of aging on brain injury or neurological impairment (Weed, 1998).

Wage Loss and Earnings Capacity Analysis

In addition to contributing information relevant to a client's vocational and educational outlook with regard to life care planning, the vocational counselor also may be asked to assess the client's loss of earnings capacity. According to one source, future medical care and loss of earnings capacity are directly related to the education and experience of most vocational counselors. The vocational counselor can offer valuable input in three critical areas: lost capacity to earn an income, loss of opportunity to be employed (loss of access to the labor market), and cost of future medical care (Weed & Field, 1994, 2001). The first and second areas will be described in this chapter. The third area, establishing the cost of future medical care, is referenced throughout this book and will not be covered specifically in this section. Also, refer to Table 4.3 for a summary of the necessary details associated with vocational aspects appropriate for the life care plan.

Table 4.3   Life Care Planning Questions Regarding Vocational Needs

- First determine if vocational aspects have been considered or are already under way (e.g., already initiated by insurance company or attorney).
- What interview information have you obtained from the client (e.g., work skills, leisure activities, education, work, functional ability)?
- Have you obtained copies of relevant medical records?
- Have you obtained work-related information (such as tax returns, job evaluations, school and test records, training history, and treating physician comments)?
- Does the client need testing before determining vocational potential (e.g., vocational evaluation; psychological, neuropsychological, or physical capacities testing)? Also, is the evaluation a quality and valid appraisal?
- If there is work potential, is there a need for justifying a plan by performing a labor market survey? (If LMS, what method is used? e.g., direct contact with employers vs. statistics or publications.)
- What is the client's expected income, including benefits? (If personal injury litigation, then pre- vs. postinjury capacity.)
- If there is an apparent market for the client's labor, is there a need for a job analysis? (And if an analysis was completed, was it done according to the Americans with Disabilities Act guidelines?)
- What are the estimated costs of the vocational plan?
  - Counseling, career guidance? (When does it start/stop, frequency and cost? e.g., 30 hours over 6 months at $65/hour.)
  - Job placement, job coaching, or supported employment costs?
  - Tuition or training, books, supplies? (Include dates for expected costs, e.g., technical training for 2 years at $400/year for 1997–1999.)
  - Rehabilitation or assistive technology; accommodations or aides; costs for work, education, or training (e.g., computer, printer, workstation, tools, tape recorder, attendant care, transportation — include costs and replacement schedules)?
- What effect, if any, does the injury have on work life expectancy (e.g., delayed entry into workforce, less than full-time, earlier retirement, expected increased turnover, or time off for medical follow-up or treatment)?

Reprinted with permission. Roger O. Weed, Ph.D.

Table 4.4   Establishing a Foundation for Earnings Capacity

Client Age	Factors to Consider
0–1 year of age	Review of family history (i.e., parents, older siblings, aunts/uncles, and grandparents) to include education and work records as a way to establish family patterns.
2–5 years of age	Same as above plus day care records/observations, church school observations, preschool records, pediatrician records, family videotapes, baby books if well maintained by parents, developmental records, neuropsychological evaluations, or other relevant records.
6–18 years of age	Review of family history, school records (including standardized test scores, academic grades, honors, disciplinary records, and extracurricular activities), pediatrician records, neuropsychological testing, vocational testing, or other relevant records.
18+ years of age	Review of employment/personnel records, school records, tax records, military records, community/civic involvement, neuropsychological testing, vocational testing, or other relevant information.

Reprinted with permission. Roger O. Weed, Ph.D.

With regard to lost earnings capacity, it is first necessary to establish the client's wages at the time of injury. This can be fairly simple for a client who was working at the time of injury in a job that is considered representative of his or her earnings potential. In pediatric cases or for young clients who may have been working but had not yet established a clear vocational identity, the process can be more challenging. The issue of identifying earnings capacity can be divided into four client populations (Weed, 1996):

1. Clients injured at birth or in the neonatal period
2. Clients injured before they reach school age (and have no academic grades or standardized test scores)
3. Clients injured before establishing a career identity
4. Clients injured after having an established work history representative of their vocational potential

Clearly, there are differences in the way the vocational counselor considers information based on the age of the client at the time of injury. Table 4.4 outlines some considerations to make in establishing a foundation for earnings capacity in all four age groups.

The listed factors can be a good predictor or give a reasonable approximation of what the client could have done prior to the injury (preinjury earnings or capacity). Obviously, the more history and documentation there is, the better and more accurate a foundation can be established with regard to earnings capacity.

The vocational counselor must determine the level of the client's functioning both before the injury (preinjury) and after the injury (postinjury) as it relates to the types of jobs the client could hold now or in the future. In general, wage loss refers to the amount of money (wages) lost by the client as a result of the injury and is based on his or her actual past work history. Earnings capacity, on the other hand, refers to the loss of future earnings related to what would be considered a reasonable estimation of the client's work potential (capacity) (Weed & Field, 1994, 2001).

In some cases, it may be possible to determine that a client is permanently and totally disabled from the workforce based on his or her work history and type of injury. Such an example includes the case of a 58-year-old career truck driver who was involved in a motor vehicle accident and has tetraplegia resulting from a spinal cord injury at C4 level. Although it may be arguable that the client could possibly be employed as a dispatcher or in some other related job in the trucking industry, it is not likely given his advanced age and the fact that he would require extensive job modification and rehabilitation technology, as well as an employer willing to make the modifications and employ the client. In such cases, the actual earnings of the client would be the basis on which to project wage loss (Blackwell et al., 1992).

In other cases, it may be more appropriate to identify a client's pre- vs. postinjury earnings capacity in categories of jobs rather than specific job titles. For example, in cases where the client is a child or young adult with no clearly established work history, the vocational expert can identify categories of jobs that are representative of types of workers (such as skilled or unskilled) and can then identify certain jobs that fall under those categories (such as lawyer or laborer) to determine the client's earnings capacity. Another alternative is to estimate the client's pre- vs. postinjury education capacity. For example, if the client is expected to have the educational capacity of a high school graduate, average earnings representative of a high school graduate can be used. Similarly, average earnings of individuals with a 4-year degree, master's degree, and doctorate or professional-level degree can be determined based on education level.

To determine wage loss or loss of earnings capacity, the vocational expert essentially evaluates the client's preinjury and postinjury employability (defined in Weed & Field, 1994, 2001, as possessing the skills, abilities, and traits necessary to perform a job) and compares the two. Once the counselor has evaluated the difference in pre- and postinjury earnings capacity, the economist then calculates the total amount of lost earnings capacity over the client's work life expectancy (Siefker, 1992). See Chapter 11 on the role of the economist in life care planning for further information.

There are many factors and approaches to consider when determining future wage loss and earnings capacity analysis. Of the many approaches, the RAPEL method considers most of the factors (Weed & Field, 1994, 2001). The RAPEL method, developed by Weed (1994), offers a comprehensive approach to determining earnings capacity analysis, particularly in forensic cases. (See Chapter 24 for additional information.) The approach incorporates a *rehabilitation* plan (or life care plan for the client who is more catastrophically impaired), information with regard to the client's *access* to the labor market (employability), information with regard to the client's *placeability* (defined as the likelihood that the client could successfully be placed in a job), *earnings* capacity, and *labor* force participation or work life expectancy. Generally, if there is a reduction in the client's life expectancy as a result of his or her injury, there also will be a reduction in the work life expectancy. The experienced vocational counselor would express this reduction in a percentage of loss or number of years lost in the labor market. For more information on the topic of wage loss/earnings capacity analysis, refer to Dillman (1987) and Chapter 11 in this text.

LABOR MARKET SURVEY AND JOB ANALYSIS

The labor market survey is designed to reveal current information about a specific job market (Weed & Field, 1994, 2001). Questions include:

1. Do jobs of a particular nature exist in the economy?
2. If these jobs exist, are they available locally?
3. If available locally, are these jobs open to my client?
4. What do these jobs pay (including benefits)?

Part of the opinion regarding an adult client's earnings capacity may be related to the current labor market. Obviously, a pediatric case would not include a specific employer-by-employer analysis; however, data that are collected by the government with regard to the future outlook of an occupation may be included. See Table 4.5 for common topics included in the labor market survey (summarized from Weed & Field, 1994, 2001).

It should be noted that the way in which the consultant asks questions could skew the results toward a desired direction. In an example case, a plaintiff's expert revealed that a client who had chronic pain was unemployable and used as partial justification the results of a labor market survey. She reported that the survey revealed that the client would not be an acceptable candidate for sedentary jobs that were directly in line with her work history. Following the deposition, the defense expert contacted the same employers and distinctly different information was provided. It was hypothesized that the consultant asked questions in a way that solicited support for her conclusions. Ethics, on the part of some consultants, can also be suspect. In another case, contact with the employers listed in another consultant's notes revealed that no employer on the list recalled being contacted with regard to a labor market survey, therefore raising the question of whether a survey had actually been performed.

Once a prospective job is located, it may be appropriate to conduct a job analysis (Weed & Field, 1994, 2001; Weed et al., 1991; Blackwell et al., 1992). The analysis is designed to determine if job traits match the worker's traits and therefore represent a reasonable probability of employment. There are specific guidelines that consultants must follow in order to make sure that they are conducting the analysis according to published standards. Indeed, one successful malpractice lawsuit resulted when a nurse completed a "job analysis" that consisted of less than one page (*Drury v. Corvel*, as cited by Oakes, 1994). The topics covered in the analysis did not follow published standards. In fact, it appeared as if the nurse was unaware that the government and others have published on this topic.

It is important that the life care planner, who may not be a vocational expert, be aware that when he works with the vocational aspects of the plan, the vocational expert must provide a proper foundation for her opinion. For more information, the reader is encouraged to review these topics in the *Rehabilitation Consultant's Handbook* (Weed & Field, 1994, 2001) or the *Revised Handbook for Analyzing Jobs* (U.S. DOL, 1991c).

Table 4.5   Labor Market Survey Checklist

Introduction (include the following identifying information for report)
   Name
   Age
   Date of injury
   Type of injury and medical limitations
   Work experience
   Education
   Other historical information
   Vocational test results
Method(s) Used (What method(s) was (were) used to obtain the information? Suggest
   starting with residual employability profile by VDARE for worker traits.)
   Personal Contacts (as appropriate) with:
      Personal network
      Yellow pages
      City directory or *Haynes Directory*
      Chamber of Commerce
      Professional and trade associations
      Job service
      Vocational rehabilitation
      Other
   Publications
      Wage rates for selected occupations (state)
      Occupational supply and demand (state Department of Industry and Trade or
         Labor)
      State career information systems (or similar)
      Manufacturing directory (SIC codes)
      Bureau of Labor Statistics; e.g., area wage survey (federal)
      Census Bureau (federal)
      Job service microfiche/posted jobs (state)
      Classified ads or job flyers
      Identified discrete jobs related to client's experience
      Labor Market Access Analysis (LMA; 1991 computer program)
      Other
   Results
      Employers contacted — approximately 10
      Job(s) available
      Wages and benefits (holidays, vacation, sick, medical, dental, personal leave, etc.)
      Training/education needed
      Willingness to work with disabled
      Accessibility/architectural barriers
      Other
   Conclusions (the professional's opinion)
      Placeability
      Expected income
      Other related comments

Reprinted with permission. Roger O. Weed, Ph.D.

VOCATIONAL RESOURCES

The vocational counselor has many resources available to assist in assessing a client's vocational potential and making appropriate recommendations for the life care plan. Below are listed a few of the more valuable reference materials used by the vocational counselor:

- *Dictionary of Occupational Titles (DOT)*, 4th edition (1991). Contains definitions of 12,741 job titles and descriptions of jobs found in the national economy. Data compiled by the U.S. Department of Labor. Now available in revised format on CD-ROM (Field & Field, 1995). This publication is expected to be eliminated when the O*Net (see below) is activated on the World Wide Web.
- *Transitional Classification of Jobs (COJ)* (2004). Contains worker trait profiles of the 72 U.S. Department of Labor worker traits for each of the 12,741 *DOT* job titles. The worker traits are assigned a code and rated. Also includes information on the O*Net database.
- *Occupational Outlook Handbook (OOH)* (2003). Clusters jobs by occupation and gives information with regard to employment potential, labor market trends, salary, requirements, and training needed to enter the occupation. Updated versions available online at http://www.bls.gov/oco/.
- *The Enhanced Guide for Occupational Exploration (GOE)* (1991). Provides descriptions of all jobs organized within related job clusters and includes information pertaining to academic and physical requirements, work environment, salary and outlook, typical duties, skills and abilities required, and where to obtain additional information.
- *The Revised Handbook for Analyzing Jobs (RHAJ)* (1991). Gives descriptions on how to examine individual jobs to determine suitability for a client.
- *Job Analysis and the ADA: A Step-by-Step Guide* (1992). This is another option for a comprehensive guide for determining the suitability of a job for clients with disabilities.
- O*NET, the Occupational Information Network. A comprehensive database of worker attributes and job characteristics. Contains over 900 occupational units (OUs). As the replacement for the *Dictionary of Occupational Titles*, O*NET will be the nation's primary source of occupational information. However, it is not useable in its present form for transferability of skill analysis (manual or computerized). Available online at http://online.onet-center.org/.

The above-listed resources use data compiled by the federal government, with many published by the government. In addition to the ones listed, there are other state, regional, and local publications specific to occupations found in certain geographic areas. For various approaches to transferable skills analysis, see Weed (2002) and the associated special-issue journal on this subject.

For additional print and computer resources available to the vocational rehabilitation counselor, the following may be useful:

- SkillTRAN (Truthan, 1997). A telephonic system of ordering job search and transferable skills information. Also other resources for purchase; (800) 827-2182 or www.skilltran.com.
- Vertek, Inc. (Gibson, 2003). Developed the OASYS computerized job-matching program; (800) 220-4409 or www.Vertekinc.com.
- McCroskey Vocational Quotient System (MVQS) (McCroskey, 2001). Job–person matching, transferable skills analysis, values, needs, vocational interest and personality reinforcer (VIPR) type indicator, and earning capacity estimation system; (612) 569-0680 or http://www.vocationology.com.
- Passport to Data on CD-ROM (includes the *DOT, COJ, OOH*, and *RHAJ*) (Field & Field, 1995). Also extensive print resources. Available through Elliott & Fitzpatrick, (800) 843-4977 or www.elliottfitzpatrick.com.
- Job Accommodation Network (JAN), Office of Disability Employment Policy, U.S. Department of Labor (1984). Offers free consulting service that provides information about job accommodations, the Americans with Disabilities Act (ADA), and the employability of people with disabilities; (800) 526-7234 or http://www.jan.wvu.edu/.

For other websites, see Weed & Field (1994, 2001).

CONCLUSION

This chapter is designed to outline some of the vocational factors that a life care planner may encounter if a client is expected to work. If the life care planner does not have the expertise to develop opinions in this specialized area, it may be reasonable to obtain services of a vocational expert and ensure that the vocational expert includes the relevant areas, as described in this chapter, and has sufficient expertise to develop reasonable opinions. Some of the topics included in this chapter are designed to assist the nonvocational expert with an overview so that appropriate questions can be asked in order to enhance the ultimate life care plan, reduce overlap or duplication in services, and facilitate the client's return to employment and achievement of his or her highest level of functioning.

REFERENCES

Anastasi, A. (1982). *Psychological Testing*, 5th ed. New York: Macmillan.

Blackwell, T., Conrad, D., & Weed, R. (1992). *Job Analysis and the ADA: A Step-by-Step Guide*. Athens, GA: E & F Vocational Services.

Botterbusch, K.F. (1987). *Vocational Assessment and Evaluation Systems: A Comparison*. Menomonie, WI: University of Wisconsin Materials Development Center.

Clark v. Aqua Air Industries, 435 So. 2d 492 (1983).

Crease, G. v. J.A. Jones Construction Company, 425 So. 2d 274 (LA App. 1982).

Deneen, L. & Hessellund, T. (1986). *Counseling the Able Disabled*. San Francisco: Rehab Publications.

Deutsch, P. & Raffa, F. (1981). *Damages in Tort Actions*, Vol. 8. New York: Matthew Bender.

Dillman, E. (1987). The necessary economic and vocational interface in personal injury cases. *Journal of Private Sector Rehabilitation*, 2, 121–142.

Evans, R. (1999). The role of the neuropsychologist in life care planning. In R. Weed, Ed., *Life Care Planning and Case Management Handbook*, Boca Raton, FL: CRC Press, 65–75.

Field, J.E. & Field, T.F. (1995). *Passport to Data*. Athens, GA: Elliott & Fitzpatrick (computer program).

Field, J.E. & Field, T.F. (2004). *Transitional Classification of Jobs*. Athens, GA: Elliott & Fitzpatrick.

Gabel, S., Oster, G., & Butnik, S. (1986). *Understanding Psychological Testing in Children*. New York: Plenum Publishing.

Gibson, G. (2003). *Oasys*. Bellevue, WA: Vertek, Inc. (computer program).

Kapes, J. & Mastie, M., Eds. (1988). *A Counselor's Guide to Career Assessment Instruments*, 2nd ed. Alexandria, VA: National Career Development Association.

Lees-Haley, P. (1993). *The Last Minute Guide to Psychological and Neuropsychological Testing: A Quick Reference for Attorneys and Claims Professionals*. Athens, GA: Elliott & Fitzpatrick.

Lezak, M.D. (1995). *Neuropsychological Assessment*, 3rd ed. New York: Oxford University Press.

Marme, M. & Skord, K. (1993). Counseling strategies to enhance the vocational rehabilitation of persons after traumatic brain injury. *Journal of Applied Rehabilitation Counseling*, 24, 19–25.

Matheson, L., Rogers, L., Kaskutas, V., & Dakos, M. (2002). Reliability and reactivity of three new functional assessment measures. *Work*, 18, 41–50.

McCroskey, B. (2001). *The McCroskey Vocational Quotient System 2001*, version 1.1. Brooklyn Park, MN: Vocationology, Inc. (computer program).

Oakes, M. (1994). *Drury v. Corvel*. Retrieved June 20, 2003, from http://www.oakes.org/webdoc14.htm.

Power, P. (2000). *A Guide to Vocational Assessment*, 3rd ed. Austin, TX: Pro-Ed.

Sbordone, R.J. & Long, C.J., Eds. (1996). *Ecological Validity of Neuropsychological Testing*. Delray Beach, FL: St. Lucie Press.

Siefker, J.M., Ed. (1992). *Vocational Evaluation in Private Sector Rehabilitation*. Menomonie, WI: University of Wisconsin Materials Development Center.

Truthan, J. (1997). *SkillTRAN, LLC*. Spokane, WA: SkillTRAN, LLC (computer program).

U.S. Department of Labor (U.S. DOL). (1984). *Job Accommodation Network*. Washington, DC (computer program).

U.S. Department of Labor (U.S. DOL). (1991a). *Dictionary of Occupational Titles*. Washington, DC.

U.S. Department of Labor (U.S. DOL). (1991b). *Enhanced Guide for Occupational Exploration*. Washington, DC.

U.S. Department of Labor (U.S. DOL). (1991c). *Revised Handbook for Analyzing Jobs*. Washington, DC.

U.S. Department of Labor (U.S. DOL). (2002–2003). *Occupational Outlook Handbook*. Washington, DC. Available at http://www.bls.gov/oco/.

Weed, R. (1994). Evaluating the earnings capacity of clients with mild to moderate acquired brain injury. In C. Simkins, Ed., *Guide to Understanding, Evaluating and Presenting Cases Involving Traumatic Brain Injury for Plaintiff Lawyers, Defense Lawyers and Insurance Representatives*. Washington, DC: National Head Injury Foundation.

Weed, R. (1996). Life care planning and earnings capacity analysis for brain injured clients involved in personal injury litigation utilizing the RAPEL method. *Journal of Neurorehabilitation*, 7, 119–135.

Weed, R. (1998). Aging with a brain injury: the effects on life care plans and vocational opinions. *The Rehabilitation Professional*, 6, 30–34.

Weed, R. (2000). The worth of a child: earnings capacity and rehabilitation planning for pediatric personal injury litigation cases. *The Rehabilitation Professional*, 8, 29–43.

Weed, R. (2002). The assessment of transferable work skills in forensic settings. *Journal of Forensic Vocational Analysis*, 5, 1–4 (special issue editorial).

Weed, R. & Field, T. (1994). *Rehabilitation Consultant's Handbook*, 2nd ed. Athens, GA: Elliott & Fitzpatrick.

Weed, R. & Field, T. (2001). *Rehabilitation Consultant's Handbook*, 3rd ed. Athens, GA: Elliott & Fitzpatrick.

Weed, R. & Riddick, S. (1992). Life care plans as a case management tool. *The Individual Case Manager Journal*, 3, 26–35.

Weed, R., Taylor, C., & Blackwell, T. (1991). Job analysis for the private sector. *NARPPS Journal and News*, 6, 153–158.

5

THE ROLE OF THE PSYCHOLOGIST IN LIFE CARE PLANNING

Anne Sluis Powers and Randall L. Thomas

INTRODUCTION

As a member of the interdisciplinary rehabilitation team, the psychologist can play numerous roles. This chapter will consider the roles of inpatient and outpatient psychological services, as well as the ways a psychologist can work with individuals with disabilities, their support systems, and the rehabilitation team (also see Chapter 6, which discusses the role of the neuropsychologist). Several different topics will be considered: (1) choosing a psychologist, (2) psychological issues common to rehabilitation, (3) the psychologist's role in assessment and diagnosis, (4) psychological testing, (5) types of psychological treatment, (6) ethical standards for the psychologist, (7) specialty guidelines for the forensic psychologist, and (8) the interface between the psychologist and life care planner.

CHOOSING A PSYCHOLOGIST

The following is an overview of the psychological training and preparation of the licensed psychologist. Though psychologists may vary in theoretical orientation, their academic requirements are consistent with the requirements of the American Psychological Association. Rehabilitation professionals should be well informed of the psychologist's credentials when selecting one and, in order to make the most appropriate referrals, should be aware of their theoretical orientation.

- A licensed psychologist almost always has a doctoral degree from an accredited university program or professional school that has been approved by the American Psychological Association (or deemed equivalent, in some select cases). Psychologists are required to complete a 1900-hour predoctoral internship in an approved program, followed by a minimum of a 1-year full-time equivalent postdoctoral internship supervised by a licensed psychologist.

0-8493-1511-5/04/$0.00+$1.50
© 2004 by CRC Press LLC

■ The candidate petitions the state board of psychological examiners for the right to take the written examination in professional psychology, which must be passed within state-legislated parameters. Then the candidate takes an oral examination based on legal and ethical issues for the state in which she or he intends to practice. Successful passage of both examinations allows licensure within that state. It is only then that the person may use the title *psychologist*. Use of the title without proper licensure constitutes a violation of legal statutes and ethical principles.

■ Psychologists practice within the scope of their training and experience, and this may vary widely. It will be important for those engaged in life care planning to ascertain whether a psychologist has specific personal and professional experience in working with rehabilitation clients and their families. It may be helpful to choose a psychologist who has subspecialized in health, medical, or rehabilitation psychology or who has additional training as a registered nurse or rehabilitation counselor.

The following is a brief description of widely accepted theoretical orientations used by practicing psychologists (Altmaier, 1991).

■ **Psychoanalytic psychologists** generally follow the theory and principles established by Sigmund Freud, including examination of early childhood and familial relationships, along with conflicts presumed to originate in early developmental stages.

■ **Psychodynamic psychologists** incorporate the theories of those following Freud (Alfred Adler, Harry Stack Sullivan, Karen Horney, Erik Erikson, and others). These psychologists also focus on aspects of relationships presumed to originate in infancy and childhood.

■ **Developmental psychologists** examine how individuals seem to be developing relative to their age-related peers, which may be useful following catastrophic events occurring before adulthood.

■ **Behavioral psychologists** analyze environmental and personal factors that can be identified and altered in the interest of improving the incidence and frequency of desirable behaviors and decreasing the amount of problematic behaviors in an individual.

■ **Cognitive-behavioral psychologists** incorporate behavioral principles and also consider the roles of thoughts and feelings in acquiring and maintaining certain behaviors. Both behavioral and cognitive-behavioral psychologists can help develop systematic behavior change programs.

■ **Health psychologists** tend to adhere to the systems approach: no part of a system operates exclusive of others. Therefore, they adhere to the biopsychosocial model. In the rehabilitation process health psychologists work with a multidisciplinary team of health professionals (e.g., physicians, nurses, physical therapists, occupational therapists, case managers) to determine the treatment plan and its implementation.

■ **Rehabilitation psychologists** practice within the broad field of psychology. Rehabilitation psychology is the application of psychological knowledge and understanding on behalf of individuals with disabilities and society through such activities as research, clinical practice, teaching, public education, development of social policy, and advocacy. Rehabilitation psychologists participate in a broad range of activities, including clinical care, program development, service provision, research, education, administration, and public policy. The American Board of Professional Psychology (ABPP) recognizes rehabilitation psychology as a specialty area of practice within psychology.

- ■ **Industrial psychologists** analyze work environments to enhance productivity through the human element. Considerations include management style; environmental factors such as work site layout, music, and color; employee assistance programs; policy development; attention to group dynamics; and other factors.

It will be important to choose a psychologist who is able to work well with an interdisciplinary team and who understands the roles of the various rehabilitation professionals. The psychologist should be properly licensed to eliminate concerns of credibility, and his or her orientation, when appropriate, should be relevant to the client's situation from a biopsychosocial-spiritual perspective, addressing the client's needs holistically.

PSYCHOLOGICAL ISSUES COMMON TO REHABILITATION

The Family

Emotional Issues

Initially following catastrophic injury or the diagnosis of a life-threatening illness, the issue facing the client and family is that of survival. Will the person live or die? For family members, the initial reaction is usually one of panic. As this response subsides, feelings of disorientation and loss of control are common. It may be very difficult to concentrate, and family members may become confused by what they perceive to be different types of information coming from different sources. Feelings of disequilibrium continue for quite some time in many families, with members feeling in control one day and quite out of control the next. Behaviors that can signal these reactions include anger over both significant and seemingly trivial issues, concrete or very literal thinking, efforts to participate in the loved one's care in ways that are inappropriate, and neglect of other significant areas of one's life.

Functional Issues

Once it seems apparent that the client will survive the initial crisis, the focus will shift toward issues of functional abilities and quality of life. Will the client be able to talk, eat, walk, and care for themselves, return to normal family roles and responsibilities, return to school, or earn a living? Different levels of anxiety are associated with the different stages of stabilization and rehabilitation. Family members need a forum for discussing some of these concerns that is private and separate from the client, in addition to being involved in family therapy with their loved one. They may need assistance with relaxation strategies, help with prioritizing decisions, or to find as much information as necessary to make good judgments.

Denial

Denial is a defense mechanism that is initially protective, keeping families from feeling overwhelmed by the enormity of a catastrophic event. However, denial of facts prevents the family from dealing with real issues and consequences that must eventually be addressed. The rehabilitation team treads a fine line, wanting to support optimism and hopefulness, while presenting data about deficits and limitations that may endure. Encourage family members to focus on one day at a time without letting expectations for the future affect the client's immediate needs. Gently asking family members "How does he/she seem to you?" or asking them to describe how their loved one did things prior to the illness or injury may allow an assessment of the family's degree of denial or acceptance.

Letting go of denial may lead to expressions, directly or indirectly, of anger. Anger may be expressed toward the client, others perceived as responsible for the injury or illness, medical care providers, the legal system, family members, God, or others. Dealing with anger and frustration effectively may require the assistance of a mental health professional, who will suggest appropriate problem-solving strategies and may assist with various stress management techniques.

Other psychological concerns commonly seen in family members include:

- Fatigue
- Depression
- Sleep disturbance
- Criticisms from other family members and friends regarding care provided for the client
- Feelings of hopelessness, helplessness, and guilt
- Constriction of social activities and opportunities for social support
- Changes in the quality of the relationship with the injured or ill person

At this point, it is important for the rehabilitation team to remember how *family* may be defined. Certainly where issues of consent are concerned, legal statutes apply. We must not forget that the client's self-defined "family" may include those with whom no formal, legal ties exist. These relationships may, in fact, be closer than those within the biological family, including relationships with a significant other, close friends, stepfamily members, and so on. Some close relationships may have been defined within legal documents such as durable powers of attorney or living wills; the client's wishes should be respected and followed within the scope of the law. Extended family members should be supported with mental health services every bit as much as members of the client's biological family.

It is important to note that psychological issues may surface and then reemerge over and over: developing a relationship with a caring provider that can endure over time, as the need arises, may be essential to a family's adjustment.

The Client

Rehabilitation clients can face tremendous challenges: physically, cognitively, emotionally, behaviorally, financially, and socially. Following traumatic brain injury, disordered and inappropriate features may emerge as a result of altered brain functioning (DeBoskey & Morin, 1985). For those with other kinds of injuries, it is important to remember that subtle brain injuries may have also occurred. Subtle or obvious problems may become apparent with regard to attention, concentration, memory, problem solving, insight, judgment, affective issues, pain management, and coping.

Problematic behaviors can include periods of the following:

- Agitation
- Irritability
- Outbursts of anger
- Inappropriate statements
- Inappropriate sexual behavior
- Egocentrism
- Concrete thinking
- Impulsivity
- Emotional lability
- Denial of deficits
- Suspicion or paranoia
- Anxiety
- Depression
- Apathy
- Obsessiveness
- Inertia
- Social immaturity
- Dependency
- Eating disorders

The Behavioral Psychology Approach

When a psychologist with a behavioral orientation is asked to consult regarding these problematic areas, several things will occur. The psychologist will be interested in input from all members of the rehabilitation team in order to determine when problems occur and possible patterns in the problematic behavior (Bellak et al., 1990). The client may be observed during therapies and quiet times for several days while the psychologist notes patterns of behavior. These behaviors will be charted on a 24-hour log and used as baseline data.

In general, behavioral interventions will be specifically described and the team will be asked to chart information about client responses. It is common for behavioral problems to increase for a short period of time when the behavioral program is instituted. The psychologist will look for decreases in the frequency, intensity, and duration of problem behaviors over time. Do not become concerned if the behavioral program does not instantly solve behavioral issues: modifications are commonly required and consistency in application is essential.

The following describes how a behavioral psychologist might work to assist the client in resolving problems.

- The psychologist may be able to **identify patterns of events** that precede the problem behavior. For example, a client may become agitated when a specific family member visits. Perhaps that family member is doing something that contributes to the problem. In other cases, clients become agitated when the stimulation level in the environment becomes excessive, when they become tired, or when they are uncomfortable.
- The psychologist will also try to **identify the impact or effect** of the client's behavior. For example, if an inappropriate behavior is followed by an event that the client perceives as reinforcing (e.g., getting to stop doing a painful physical therapy exercise when he yells, or being given a milkshake as a distraction), the probability is that the inappropriate behavior will continue or even worsen with time. The psychologist will recommend different ways of responding to inappropriate behaviors that will lessen the likelihood of recurrence. It will be of utmost importance for the entire team to follow the behavioral plan consistently.
- Rehabilitation team members are in a unique position of being able to **model** ways of interacting with clients. Family members may be at a loss as how to respond to angry outbursts or episodes of poor social judgment. The team can show family members how to simplify language when speaking to someone who cannot think abstractly, how to distract a client who is focusing inappropriately, and how to ignore certain behaviors in order to eliminate the reinforcing power of attention.
- As a client's level of awareness and insight improves, it will be important to **involve the client** in the setting of behavioral goals. Explaining treatment rationales and getting the client to take responsibility for her own behavioral problem will increase her investment in the process and, ultimately, in the success of the program. Clients can keep track of progress on charts, in memory logs, or other creative ways that measure successes over time.

The Process of Adjustment to Disability

As insight improves, adjustment concerns become central. Individuals follow very similar patterns of adjustment to disability. Cohn (1961) has described a five-stage process of adjustment. The first stage is **shock**, wherein denial or minimization is common. In the second stage, **expectancy for recovery**, the client may admit to current deficits but continues to expect a quick and complete recovery. As the extent of the disability becomes apparent, **mourning** occurs. Depression, suicidal ideation, suicidal attempts, and disengagement from or active resistance to the therapy process are common during this stage and should be identified. During the fourth stage, **defense**, the adjustment process begins. The person reaches a critical point where either denial or moves toward independence tend to occur. The final stage, **adjustment**, occurs when the client has a realistic appraisal of the disability and begins to focus on moving forward with life.

Posttraumatic Stress Disorder

When traumatic injuries have occurred, posttraumatic stress disorder (PTSD) can result. According to the American Psychological Association (1994) in the *Diagnostic and Statistical Manual of Mental Disorders*, 4th edition, text revision (DSM-IV, TR, 2000) criteria, PTSD follows from exposure to "an extreme traumatic stressor … that involves actual or threatened death or serious injury" (p. 424) to the self or someone else, or finding out about such an event experienced by a loved one. The person's response must involve "intense fear, helplessness, or horror; a persistent avoidance of stimuli associated with the trauma; a numbing of general responsiveness; and persistent symptoms of increased arousal" (DSM-IV, TR, p. 424). The symptoms must be present for over 1 month and cause clinically significant distress or impairment in daily functioning (DSM-IV, TR, 1994). The epidemiology of posttraumatic stress disorder varies, with 50 to 80% of those experiencing a devastating disaster going on to develop symptoms of the disorder (Kaplan & Sadock, 1991). The likelihood of developing PTSD correlates positively with the severity of the stressor.

Therapeutic Strategies

Early intervention programs are now being used to encourage clients to talk about their traumatic experiences in a supportive context. Behavior therapy, cognitive therapy, hypnosis, and some experimental approaches have been used (Hammond, 1990). Group therapy can be particularly effective when members of the group have shared similar precipitating events. Family therapy is often useful because of the high incidence of marital disruption caused by PTSD symptoms. Medication therapy may be indicated in clients who are seriously affected and are not responding optimally to other therapeutic interventions. Hospitalization may be required during periods of severe symptoms or when there is a risk of suicidal or violent behavior.

It is important to note that clients adjust to disability in highly individual ways. The stages of adjustment within the individual can vary as well. Often, personal stressors will arise that can lead to a revisiting of adjustment issues (e.g., changes in a personal relationship may lead to further examination of the impact of the disability). It may be quite helpful for the client to have a relationship with a psychologist who can be available, repeatedly if needed, for periods of brief therapy.

THE PSYCHOLOGIST'S ROLE IN ASSESSMENT AND DIAGNOSIS

Psychologists are asked frequently to contribute to the initial assessment of a rehabilitation client. Generally, psychologists enter the picture in the rehabilitation facility, rather than during the acute hospitalization. In complex cases, however, it may be helpful to have psychological input during the transitional phase between acute hospitalization and rehabilitation placement.

The psychologist may address the following factors:

- Medical diagnosis
- Preexisting conditions (medical conditions, mental health issues)
- Premorbid health beliefs and behaviors (religious beliefs about health care, degree of compliance with medical treatment in the past, health-related practices, quality of prior relationships with health care providers, use of alternative medicine, degree of faith in Western medicine, etc.)
- Educational background
- Employment history (job titles and stability of employment)
- Medications, including side effects and interactions
- Functional limitations
- Physical rehabilitation potential, from a team perspective
- Premorbid personality characteristics
- Marital status and stability of primary relationship
- Role within family prior to injury or illness (e.g., wage-earner status, parenting responsibilities, household management tasks, financial obligations, relationship with extended family)
- Financial resources
- Extent of social support network
- Substance use and abuse history
- Abuse history (physical, emotional, sexual)
- Legal history
- Coping resources and compensatory strategies
- Community resources
- Adjustment, including stage of adaptation to disability
- Affective status (depression, anxiety, anger, etc.)
- Suicidal potential and lethality
- Insight
- Judgment
- Potential for posttraumatic stress disorder
- Compliance with treatment
- Initiative and motivation
- Passivity vs. proactivity
- Beliefs about outcomes
- Role of spirituality, past and present

Following a psychological evaluation, the team should be able to "see" who the client was prior to the injury or onset of illness, how the event has impacted the client and his or her support system in the present, and what changes can be anticipated in the future.

PSYCHOLOGICAL TESTING

A number of psychological instruments can provide valuable information when planning care for a rehabilitation client. This section will identify some psychological tests that may be given, along with descriptions of the types of data they will generate.

Behavioral Assessment of Pain Questionnaire® (BAP)

This 390-item questionnaire investigates issues related to the management of chronic pain (Lewandowski & Tearnan, 1993). Answers reveal the client's perception of pain and its severity, health care use patterns, degree of physical activity and activity avoidance behaviors, spousal influences on pain and wellness, physician influences on pain and wellness, perceived quality of the physician–patient relationship, nonproductive pain beliefs, coping strategies used, mood, and use of medications. Treatment recommendations are generated for managing the physician–patient relationship, reducing pain behaviors, examining pain beliefs, and addressing use of drugs and other substances. A posttreatment questionnaire is available for outcome evaluation.

Beck Anxiety Inventory® (BAI)

Twenty-one physical and emotional symptoms are listed in this questionnaire. The client rates whether symptoms experienced within the past week are absent or are mild, moderate, or severe in intensity. Scores indicate whether symptoms of anxiety are within normal range or range from mild to severe. The physical symptoms within the inventory must be evaluated with medical diagnoses in mind: many may be manifestations of disease processes rather than symptoms of anxiety, though the severity of symptoms may be affected by anxiety as well.

Beck Depression Inventory® (BDI)

The inventory contains 21 sets of statements related to depressing thoughts, feelings, and behaviors. The client circles the statement that most accurately describes symptoms during the past week. Scores indicate whether symptoms of depression are within normal range or range from mild to severe. Suicidal ideation, intent, and plan are assessed by one set of statements within the inventory.

Beck Suicide Inventory® (BSI)

This inventory contains 21 sets of statements related to suicidal ideation, intent, and plan. The client circles the statement that most accurately describes symptoms experienced during the past week. Scores indicate the degree of suicide ideation. It is important to use clinical data, in addition to a suicide inventory, when assessing suicidal thinking or lethality.

Coping Resources Inventory for Stress® (CRIS)

CRIS measures perceived coping resourcefulness based on transactional models of stress (Curlette et al., 1992). According to these models, stress is the outcome of a perceived imbalance between demands and coping resources. CRIS scales measure self-disclosure, self-directedness, confidence, acceptance, social support, financial freedom, physical health, physical fitness, stress monitoring, tension control, structuring abilities, problem solving, cognitive restructuring, functional beliefs, and social ease. An overall Coping Resources Effectiveness Score is computed, along with primary and composite scales, wellness-inhibiting items, and validity keys.

Geriatric Depression Scale® (GDS)

This scale asks 30 yes/no questions about thoughts, feelings, and activities related to depression in older adults. Scores range from normal to severe.

Millon Behavioral Health Inventory® (MBHI)

This 150-item true/false questionnaire is designed to assess psychological characteristics of patients receiving general medical care or evaluation. It contains 20 scales that provide data regarding coping factors related to the physical health care of adult medical patients. It can help identify possible psychological or psychosomatic complications, and may help predict responses to illness or medical treatment. The inventory takes about 20 minutes to complete and assumes an eighth-grade reading level. The MBHI report generates hypotheses that must be used as one facet of a total patient evaluation.

Millon Clinical Multiaxial Inventory-III ® (MCMI-III)

This self-report instrument contains 175 true/false items designed to assess personality disorders and clinical syndromes described in the *Diagnostic and Statistical Manual* (DSM-IV, TR). It can assist the clinician in developing individualized treatment plans and help identify potential barriers or obstacles to treatment. The MCMI-III assumes an eighth-grade reading level.

Minnesota Multiphasic Personality Inventory-A® (MMPI-A)

This inventory is an empirically based test of psychopathology, derived specifically for adolescents (Archer, 1992). It is used primarily to aid in problem identification, diagnosis, and treatment planning in a variety of settings, including hospitals, clinics, school counseling programs, private practice, and correctional facilities. There are 478 true/false items. Administration time takes up to an hour and assumes a sixth-grade reading level. Family problems, eating disorders, and chemical dependency issues are addressed.

Minnesota Multiphasic Personality Inventory-2® (MMPI-2)

This inventory is the restandardized version of the original MMPI, an empirically based test of adult psychopathology. It is used to measure objectively psychopathology across a broad range of client settings where social or personal adjustment problems are acknowledged or suspected. The MMPI-2 can aid in identifying appropriate treatment strategies and potential difficulties with treatment. The inventory contains 567 true/false test items and assumes a reading level of sixth grade (Greene, 1991).

The MMPI-2 is an extremely sophisticated psychological assessment instrument, and it is beyond the scope of this chapter to present the test in detail. However, the test yields several validity indexes that measure a client's degree of psychological sophistication and any attempts to fake psychological health or to present a more deviant picture. Ten basic clinical scales measure symptomatic and characterological symptoms, and numerous subscales assess subtle and obvious aspects of psychological functioning. The consistency of responses and attentiveness while taking the test are also assessed.

Personality Assessment Inventory® (PAI)

The PAI is a 344-item inventory that provides a broad-based assessment of mental disorders. The PAI includes 4 validity scales, 11 clinical scales, 5 treatment scales, and 2 interpersonal scales. Clinical scales are clustered in neurotic, psychotic, personality disorders, and behavioral disorders.

State-Trait Anxiety Inventory® (STAI)

Charles Spielberger developed this inventory to measure the anxiety level of individuals. It consists of two 20-item self-report scales designed to assess anxiety proneness and the current level of anxiety. The test is appropriate for those with a seventh-grade education or higher and requires approximately 15 minutes to administer.

Wechsler Adult Intelligence Scale-Revised® (WAIS-III)

This test is based upon a definition of intelligence as "the aggregate or global capacity of the individual to act purposefully, to think rationally, and to deal effectively with his environment" (Wechsler, 1944). The subtests evaluate verbal intelligence and performance intelligence. The test is of value for determining intellectual functioning for occupational, educational, and neuropsychological purposes.

Wechsler Intelligence Scale for Children-4th Edition® (WISC-IV)

Wechsler (1944) applied the same definition of intelligence as noted above under WAIS-III to the development of a measure of intellectual functioning in children aged 6 years 0 months to 16 years 11 months. Twelve subtests classify verbal intelligence and performance intelligence. The WISC-IV is often administered as part of a neuropsychological test battery.

Wide Range Achievement Test-3rd Edition® (WRAT-3)

This is a norm-referenced test designed to measure current arithmetic, word recognition, and spelling skills. Results provide grade equivalents, standard scores, and percentile rankings for an individual. The spelling and arithmetic subtests can be administered individually or in groups. The reading subtest is individually administered. Jastak and Wilkinson (1984) report greater test–retest reliability on the reading and spelling subtests than on the arithmetic subtest.

Woodcock–Johnson® III Test (Achievement and Cognitive Abilities)

The Woodcock–Johnson Test (2001) is widely used by educators and psychologists. It is individually administered and measures achievement in the areas of reading, mathematics, written language, knowledge, and cognitive abilities in the areas of cognitive factors, oral language, and differential aptitudes. The test is divided into two major parts: achievement and cognitive abilities.

Academic achievement is measured in the following areas: mathematics, written language, knowledge, skills, and reading.

Cognitive factors measured include: comprehension–knowledge, long-term retrieval, visual–spatial thinking, auditory processing, fluid reasoning, processing speed, short-term memory.

TYPES OF PSYCHOLOGICAL TREATMENT

Different psychotherapeutic approaches have been used with success with those who have had a catastrophic injury or illness. Often an appropriate mixture of therapeutic approaches is needed to provide the client with the maximum benefit. When completing a life care plan, it will be important to include therapeutic modalities that will address the patient's changing needs over time, and to allow some flexibility so that the patient may enter and exit therapy as life experiences occur.

- **Individual therapy** allows the person to explore issues of a personal nature in a protected and private manner. The individual will need time and privacy to explore the feelings of loss related to the disability or illness. Having a confidential relationship with one therapist over time will facilitate disclosure and allow the therapist and client to develop individualized approaches to treatment issues. The therapist can help the client deal with personal feelings about relationships, manage the fluctuating emotions that emerge, develop plans for behavioral change, troubleshoot potential problem areas, and work on reintegration goals. In many instances, individual therapy can offer the client that opportunity to practice new skills and to bounce ideas off of a caring, neutral party in ways that are potentially less threatening than doing so with a relative or friend.

  Individual therapy should be requested approximately three times per week during the rehabilitation facility phase. Once the individual is stabilized and participating in outpatient therapies, weekly visits for the first 3 to 6 months are appropriate. Check with the psychologist regarding issues specific to the individual that may require more intensive monitoring (e.g., suicidality).

- **Biofeedback** (Basmajian, 1989) is a helpful modality for many clients as well, particularly those dealing with psychophysiological problems such as hypertension, muscle tension disorders, pain problems, and stress disorders. Biofeedback techniques help the client learn more about his or her individual responses to stressors and ways that he or she can learn to intervene directly, often without using medications or other medical interventions. Physical and occupational therapists have found biofeedback to be a helpful adjunct in neuromuscular reeducation programs.

When adding biofeedback therapy to the life care plan, request approximately 12 hour-long weekly sessions initially, in order to learn and apply the technique. Follow-up visits can be scheduled every 2 weeks for 2 months, then once a month for 2 months. Check with your biofeedback referral source for recommendations.

■ **Hypnotherapy** is a somewhat controversial therapeutic technique that can be helpful for some clients. When practiced by a competent therapist, hypnotic techniques can help a client change behaviors he is already willing to change (Hammond, 1990). For example, a person who wishes to quit smoking may find hypnotic suggestions regarding smoking cessation to be very powerful in encouraging abstinence. Hypnosis may also be a helpful stress management technique for some. Hypnotherapy is not useful, however, for helping clients accurately retrieve "suppressed memories."

■ **Family therapy** is an extremely important therapeutic modality. A catastrophic injury or illness has profound effects on family functioning, and these effects need to be dealt with by involving the entire family. Changes in role behavior, role expectations, marital relationships, communication pathways, financial status, and family goals will require sensitive support and negotiation (Lezak, 1988). When completing a life care plan, family therapy should be considered when major life transitions are encountered (e.g., child leaving home, death in the family, major illness diagnosed) by any family member. Family therapy sessions can provide a good forum for discussing quality of life issues, the development of living wills and advanced directives, and renegotiating family rules.

■ **Group therapy** is helpful for many rehabilitation clients. Good cases can be made for including the client in group therapy designed specifically for one type of injury (e.g., spinal cord injuries only) and for more heterogeneous groups. An important consideration when selecting a group will be the members' functional communication level rather than functional physical level. Having a mixture of participants who are operating at different stages of adaptation to their disabilities can be helpful in providing newer members with hope and inspiration. A skilled group leader will acknowledge the various stages of adaptation while sensitively encouraging the group to progress to a focus on abilities rather than disabilities, to hope rather than despair.

When completing a life care plan, include a group therapy modality on a regular basis (some groups meet weekly, others less often) for the first 6 months at least, if the client shows willingness to participate. Many groups become "leaderless" after this period of time, transitioning from professionally led to a self-help format.

■ **Pain management** is an important subspecialty area that requires mention. Following catastrophic injury, pain problems are often related to the tissue damage that has occurred. Pain management strategies usually include the use of medications and, hopefully, relaxation techniques (Hanson & Gerber, 1990). As time passes, however, the client will need to reduce his or her reliance on potentially addictive pain medications and to increase independence in managing pain. A pain management specialist can help the client learn relaxation techniques, cognitive strategies, reactivation steps, and ways of dealing with the psychological components of pain.

If pain continues to be a focus of treatment after physical stabilization has occurred, consider a referral to a pain specialist. Pain is no longer merely a symptom: it has become a problem and needs to be addressed in an intensive manner.

THE INTERFACE BETWEEN LIFE CARE PLANNER AND PSYCHOLOGIST

Most life care planners are familiar with the role of the psychologist. The interface between the life care planner and the psychologist can be productive as the life care planner requests long-term care recommendations. However, there are a number of areas that the psychologist and the life care planner should be aware of to reduce the possibility of miscommunication.

Initially, the life care planner should determine if the psychologist involved is a treating psychologist or has been retained by one of the attorneys as an expert witness for specific purposes of providing expert testimony or providing an independent medical evaluation. In nearly all cases, the psychologist will be either a treating psychologist or a retained expert.

Psychologists often treat individuals with catastrophic injuries, and those clients may become involved in litigation. Therefore, the psychologist may be familiar with the litigation process and should be familiar with requests for records, discovery depositions, and occasionally testifying as a treating psychologist. The psychologist's office can be expected to have policies and procedures describing how to respond to requests for records and related activities concerning the litigation process.

However, the treating psychologist may not be familiar with the role of life care planners, and an explanation of the process, along with specific questions, will be helpful. The psychologist may be concerned as to your role and why all of these questions are being asked. Perhaps reference to this chapter would be helpful. Some cases may be involved in litigation and extra care should be exercised to assure no rules or boundaries are crossed.

Psychologists are generally oriented toward patient care, and the type of information life care planners solicit is familiar to the psychologist. For example:

- What is the client's diagnosis?
- What is the client's current treatment program?
- What is the client's projected course of treatment?
- What is the client's projected prognosis?

Typically psychologists are comfortable projecting the number of sessions per week or per year and treatment time frame. In addition, they can provide cost for psychological services as a part of the life care planning process.

The life care planner communicating with the treating psychologist or retained expert psychologist should inquire regarding specific services. The following is an outline that can aid communication between the life care planner and the psychologist:

1. Projected evaluations (include duration and frequency; consider the effects of aging).
2. Psychotherapy/counseling (consider group, family, and individual sessions). Remember that counseling and psychotherapy are similar and somewhat dependent on the setting. Options may include:
    ■ Biofeedback
    ■ Counseling regarding sexual dysfunction (e.g., associated with spinal cord or brain injury)
    ■ Individual counseling regarding behavioral management
    ■ Family counseling for family members' adjustment
    ■ Group counseling
    ■ Family consultation (disability education, behavior management)
3. Psychologist/neuropsychological testing, to include intellectual assessment, academic assessment, interest assessment, personality assessment, neuropsychological functioning. Provide approximate ages at which the assessments should occur.
4. Psychological services related to pain management.
5. Personal care attendant for issues related to mental capacity/incapacity.
6. Recommendations related to restrictive/least restrictive environment.
7. Computer hardware/software related to socialization/independence.
8. Case management related to psychological care.
9. Psychiatric hospitalization — inpatient or partial hospitalization.
10. Chemical dependency treatment.
11. Opinions and recommendations relating to vocational outlook (personality, trauma, intelligence, etc.).
12. For litigation-related injury cases, an opinion regarding the person's pre- vs. postinjury functioning.
13. Referral to other professionals such as psychiatrist for medication.

Psychologists can provide valuable information to the life care planner as the life care report is being developed. However, both life care planner and psychologist should clearly be aware of their roles, boundaries, and limitations.

Once the psychologist has provided the list of recommendations, it is suggested the life care planner type up the recommendations and return them to the psychologist for review and signature. This provides the psychologist the opportunity to look for any areas of miscommunication or areas of omission. The written document also provides documentation of the participation of the professionals involved in the planning process.

In addition, the life care planner may request the psychologist to sign the document listing the recommendations. Having a signed form in the file reduces the potential for a challenge of the life care planner's testimony being based on hearsay since the recommendations were only provided orally and not in a written

Table 5.1 Psychologist-Related Checklist

☑ Did the psychologist provide a diagnosis?

☑ Does the report contain information about the person's able to function in everyday life (e.g., in a job, in her own behalf, under stress, etc.)?

☑ Is the client competent, or should he have a guardian for contracts, finances, and judgment? Or a personal care attendant?

☑ What is the difference in the person's functioning ability pre- vs. postincident (if an injury)?

☑ Should the client be referred to another professional for treatment or evaluation (e.g., psychiatrist for medication, biofeedback for pain, etc.)?

☑ What effects does the person's psychological functioning have on his or her vocational potential?

☑ What is the specific treatment plan? (Include frequency, duration, and expected costs. Example, individual treatment for 1 time/week for 6 months at $100/week and then group treatment for 36 months, 48 weeks/year at $40/session.)

☑ Are there recommendations that are family related (such as therapy, consultation, or education for parents and siblings)?

☑ Did the psychologist offer an opinion with regard to global assessment of functioning (GAF)?

form. The courts typically allow life care planners significant leeway regarding hearsay. Life care planners solicit oral recommendations from health care members in the normal course of their business (see reference to federal rules 702 and 703 in the Chapter 24). However, due to the potential for an error in communication, and the extent to which that error may affect the admissibility of testimony in forensic cases (and the rare occasion where the psychologist may change his opinion), the life care planner is well advised to at least request the psychologist to review and sign the list of recommendations. For a summary checklist (that might also be useful to provide to the psychologist), see Table 5.1. (For additional questions, see Chapter 6 regarding the neuropsychologist's role.)

ETHICAL/PRACTICE STANDARDS FOR PSYCHOLOGIST

The primary national association for psychologists is the American Psychological Association (APA) (http://www.apa.org). Based in Washington, D.C., the APA is a scientific and professional organization that represents psychology in the U.S. With more than 155,000 members, APA is the largest association of psychologists worldwide. The 2002 APA Ethics Code was published in the December 2002 issue of the *American Psychologist*. Electronic copies of the ethics code are available at http://www.apa.org/ethics/.

Some licensed psychologists have chosen to not join the APA. However, most state licensing laws for psychologists incorporate the APA Ethics Code into the licensing law. Therefore, even though a psychologist may not be a member of the APA, he or she is very likely held to the ethical code of the APA based on the specific stature of the state in which he or she is licensed.

Psychologists are licensed to practice at the state level, not the national level. Each state has a unique license law that describes the practice of psychology in that particular state.

SPECIALTY GUIDELINES FOR FORENSIC PSYCHOLOGIST

The "Specialty Guidelines for Forensic Psychologist" (1991) represent a joint statement of the American Psychology–Law Society and Division 41 of the APA. In addition, the guidelines have also been endorsed by a majority vote of the American Academy of Forensic Psychology. The guidelines do not represent an official statement of the APA. They provide assistance to psychologists and others who are interested about the process psychologists will follow when they are involved in a litigation event or retained as an expert witness.

A copy of the "Specialty Guidelines for Forensic Psychologists" may be obtained from http://www.unl.edu/ap-ls/foren.pdf.

THE INDIVIDUALS WITH DISABILITIES EDUCATION ACT

Since 1975, the federal government has played an important role in ensuring that children with disabilities receive the best possible education through the Individuals with Disabilities Education Act (IDEA). President Bush's sweeping reforms in the No Child Left Behind Act made fundamental improvements in elementary and secondary education to enhance the education of children with disabilities by supporting accountability for results, expanded parental choice, a focus on what works, and increased local flexibility. A psychologist, often the most important professional in this specialty area, who evaluates for purposes of IDEA is responsible for education-related recommendations only. However, outside consultation can influence what is perceived as education. The life care planner who is developing a pediatric plan should endeavor to contact the school psychologist as a part of the information gathering process. In many injury cases, school testing may also provide the foundation for preinjury functioning.

Case Example

The patient is a 28-year-old female that is 30 months postinjury. She had significant physical injuries, including injury to her brain, in a motor vehicle accident. She has deficits in organizational skills. She tires easily. Neuropsychological testing reveals significant impairment in the ability to maintain attention and concentration. Problem-solving ability is impaired. She is clinically depressed. Memory impairments are present. Short-term and long-term memory are impaired. Auditory and visual memory are also impaired. In addition, she has impaired receptive language and chronic pain.

The life care planner held a phone conference with the patient's treating psychologist, Dr. Mary Smith. Following the phone conference, Dr. Smith's recommendations were typed and sent to her for review and signature. A sample summary with request for confirmation is below:

List of Items and Services

Recommendations/information from Dr. Mary Smith, psychologist, on April 23, 2003, regarding Ms. Susan Jones:

1. **Diagnosis**
   Acquired brain injury, PTSD, impaired mobility, impaired memory, and chronic pain.
2. **Psychological Evaluation**
   Annual psychological evaluations for 4 years, then PRN.
   Neuropsychological exam, one per year for next 3 years, then PRN.
3. **Counseling and Psychological Services**
   Counseling two times a week for 1 hour each session for next 3 years, then one session per week for 4 years. She should continue to receive counseling and psychological services because of her ongoing medical and psychological problems. She will need counseling regarding her self-concept and relationship issues.
   She will need pain management services and cognitive retraining services. If pain continues, additional psychological services of 20 sessions (1 hour per session) per year are recommended until pain levels abate.
4. **Counseling for Family**
   Support services and counseling for family for next 2 years. Approximately 50 counseling hours per year.
5. **Implications for Current and Future Adjustment to Disability**
   She will need assistance with day-to-day problem solving and planning. I am unable to provide a specific number of hours per day for attendant care, but she may need an attendant 24 hours per day due to cognitive deficits, safety issues, and poor judgment.
6. **Case Management Services**
   She will need a case manager 4 hours per month to coordinate services.
7. **Specialized Services**
   She will need a vocational assessment to determine if she can return to work (which is unlikely) and to assist with avocational activities.

CONCLUSION

This chapter has reviewed the ways in which a trained, experienced rehabilitation psychologist can participate as a member of the rehabilitation team. In rehabilitation, much attention is given to the preservation and restoration of functioning. Psychological issues can color the work of rehabilitation in subtle and obvious ways and should be carefully considered when planning for the client's care.

It is also important to remember that the relationship a psychologist establishes with a client can continue for many years following the catastrophic injury or diagnosis of illness. As a life care planning professional, you can ensure that your client receives the emotional and behavioral support needed to achieve his or her goals of functional independence.

REFERENCES

Altmaier, E.M. (1991). Research and practice roles for counseling psychologists in health care settings. *The Counseling Psychologist*, 19, 342–364.

American Psychiatric Association. (2000). *Diagnostic and Statistical Manual of Mental Disorders*, 4th ed., text revision. Washington, DC: American Psychiatric Association.

Archer, R.P. (1992). *MMPI-A: Assessing Adolescent Psychopathology*. Hillsdale, NJ: Lawrence Erlbaum Associates.

Basmajian, J.V., Ed. (1989). *Biofeedback: Principles and Practice for Clinicians*. Baltimore: Williams & Wilkins.

Bellack, A.S., Hersen, M., & Kazdin, A.E., Eds. (1990). *International Handbook of Behavior Modification and Therapy*, 2nd ed. New York: Plenum Press.

Cohn, N. (1961). Understanding the process of adjustment to disability. *Journal of Rehabilitation*, 27, 16–22.

Curlette, W.L., Aycock, D.W., Matheny, K.B., Pugh, J.L., & Taylor, H.F. (1992). *Coping Resources Inventory for Stress Manual*. Atlanta, GA: Health Prisms.

DeBoskey, D.S. & Morin, K. (1985). *A "How to Handle" Manual for Families of the Brain Injured*. Tampa, FL: Tampa General Rehabilitation Center.

Greene, R.L. (1991). *The MMPI-2/MMPI: An Interpretive Manual*. Boston: Allyn and Bacon.

Hammond, D.C., Ed. (1990). *Handbook of Hypnotic Suggestions and Metaphors*. New York: W.W. Norton.

Hanson, R.W. & Gerber, K.E. (1990). *Coping with Chronic Pain: A Guide to Patient Self-Management*. New York: Guilford Press.

Jastak, S. & Wilkinson, G. (1984). *Wide Range Achievement Test-Revised Administration Manual*. Wilmington, DE: Jastak Associates.

Kaplan, H.I. & Sadock, B.J. (1991). *Synopsis of Psychiatry: Behavioral Sciences, Clinical Psychiatry*, 6th ed. Baltimore: Williams & Wilkins.

Lees-Haley, P.R. (1993). *The Last-Minute Guide to Psychological and Neuropsychological Testing: A Quick Reference for Attorneys and Claims Professionals*. Athens, GA: Elliott & Fitzpatrick.

Lewandowski, M.J. & Tearnan, B.H. (1993). *Behavioral Assessment of Pain Questionnaire*. Reno, NV: Pendrake.

Lezak, M.D. (1988). Brain damage is a family affair. *Journal of Clinical and Experimental Psychology*, 10, 111–123.

Specialty guidelines for forensic psychologists. (1991). *Law and Human Behavior*, 15, 655–665.

Wechsler, D. (1944). *The Measurement of Adult Intelligence*, 3rd ed. Baltimore: Williams & Wilkins.

Woodcock, R.W., McKrew, K.S., & Mather, N. (2001). *Woodcock-Johnson III Tests of Cognitive Abilities*. Itasca, IL: Riverside Publishing.

6

THE ROLE OF THE NEUROPSYCHOLOGIST IN LIFE CARE PLANNING

Randall W. Evans

INTRODUCTION

Modern-day clinical neuropsychology is roughly 60 years old, although the use of neuropsychological data has undergone considerable change within the last 10 years or so. It could be safely argued that the primary use of neuropsychological test data until very recently was to assist in neurological diagnosis and localization of cognitive and mental functions to various brain regions. The pioneer works of Ward Halstead, Ralph Reitan, and Alexander Luria exemplified the early localization studies. Their work has since been built upon by such notable neuropsychologists and behavioral neurologists as Edith Kaplan, Arthur Benton, Frank Benson, Henry Hecaen, Antonio Damasio, Martin Alpert, and Nelson Butters, to name but a few. The contributions of these and others have established the field of clinical neuropsychology as a very respected clinical addition to related fields such as neurology, neuropsychiatry, gerontology, physiatry, neuropharmacology, and psychopathology.

THE FOCUS OF NEUROPSYCHOLOGY

Until recently, most practicing neuropsychologists focused their efforts on determining and assisting neurological or neuropathological diagnoses, particularly as such diagnoses were applied to localization of brain dysfunction and extent of that dysfunction. Additionally, neuropsychologists are often asked to assist in the determination of whether brain dysfunction is thought to exist at all. The following populations are often the subjects of neuropsychological inquiry:

- Persons who have experienced neurological insults, for example, traumatic brain injury, stroke, anoxic events
- Persons undergoing dementia evaluations

0-8493-1511-5/04/$0.00+$1.50
© 2004 by CRC Press LLC

- Persons suspected of developmental disabilities including autism, attention deficit disorder, learning disabilities, and other related disabilities
- Persons with neuropsychiatric disorders — Tourette's syndrome, Korsakoff's syndrome, conversion disorders, and other related syndromes
- Persons undergoing neuropharmacological interventions

Besides assessing persons in these categories, some neuropsychologists, notably those employed in university-based medical centers, are involved in the uses of neuropsychological data in the broad study of brain and behavior relationships. Additionally, *research* neuropsychologists continually work to refine test construction and test development, in many respects in response to emerging neuroimaging developments. In these areas neuropsychological test data are used to cross-validate and complement new imaging techniques.

During the last decade, neuropsychologists have turned their attention increasingly toward the use of neuropsychological data to predict short- and long-term outcomes in various patient populations. Initially, the interest in outcomes tended to focus on specific cognitive functions, for example, the relationship of current performance on memory tests to long-term memory functioning.

However, most of these studies did not focus on performance of neuropsychological test data as outcome predictors, failing to show how such performance related to more functional outcomes, such as a person's ability to return to work or to live independently. This lack of attention to what the industry refers to as ecological validity severely limits practical use of this rather sophisticated data.

CONTRIBUTIONS TO THE LIFE CARE PLAN

With regard to the life care planning process, the contributions of the neuropsychologist are at least twofold (Blackwell et al., 1994). At a minimum, a neuropsychologist with significant experience with a given population or diagnostic group can contribute his or her experiential database to the short- and long-term prognostic issues as reflected in the patient's neuropsychological test profile. This is somewhat analogous to the expert witness scenario. Additionally, the neuropsychologist can relate neuropsychological test performance to what is known in the literature as to how such performance relates to short- and long-term outcome, keeping in mind the importance of addressing the ecological validity of the projected outcome (Evans, 1996). With these two issues in mind, this chapter will review:

- Commonly used neuropsychological inquiry approaches/test batteries.
- Neuropsychological assessment literature as it relates to outcome prediction.
- Common applications of neuropsychological data as they relate to the life care planning process.
- A case example of neuropsychological data utilization in a life care plan.
- A summary commentary regarding future contributions of the neuropsychologist to the life care planning process. As an example, this chapter will occasionally focus on the traumatic brain injury (TBI) population.

NEUROPSYCHOLOGICAL BATTERIES IN CURRENT USE

This section will describe some of the more commonly used neuropsychological test batteries and the theoretical underpinnings underlying those approaches. However, a brief discussion of the overall assumptions of neuropsychological assessment is in order.

Background Information

Ever since the French neurologist Broca discovered the anterior language center of the brain in 1865, medical practitioners have waged an aggressive campaign to articulate the relationships between distinct brain regions and human behavior. That campaign, well over a hundred years old, continues now with the support of sophisticated neuroimaging techniques as complementary tools. Modern-day neuropsychology is concerned with the diagnosis and treatment of persons with, or suspected of having, various forms of brain dysfunction or brain damage. The tools of the neuropsychologist are well-normed test procedures, observation of patient function, detailed history taking, and an extensive working knowledge of those practitioners from Professor Broca and beyond. The neuropsychological exam is a dynamic process that must be flexible to the condition of the patient and to the very reason for the examination itself. There is a growing awareness in the field that whatever test strategy is used must address the day-to-day needs of the examinee. No longer is it appropriate to report neuropsychological performance in statistical terms. The performance of the patient on test procedures must be tied to the direct relevance of his or her ability to survive and prosper in today's world. Therefore, the neuropsychologist can have a healthy and meaningful contribution to the life care planning process.

Halstead–Reitan Neuropsychological Test Battery (HRB)

The most commonly used neuropsychological test battery is the Halstead–Reitan Battery (HRB), although most practitioners use supplementary measures based on patient status, diagnosis, data utilization need, and the referral question. Table 6.1 illustrates the tests used in the HRB together with the primary functions measured by each test.

These measures are basic to the HRB approach and it is almost always the case that the neuropsychologist will supplement this battery with additional tests relative to the issues raised above. Additionally, tests of emotional and personality functioning are usually included in a comprehensive evaluation. The test results are then analyzed from several perspectives. According to the HRB approach, four levels of inference are used:

- **Level of performance**. This is a comparative analysis based on well-established norms whereby the person's actual performance is compared to a cutoff level, which reflects the probability of statistical variance. In the HRB approach, for example, a score below a statistical level determines the *probability* of brain dysfunction.

Table 6.1 Halstead–Reitan Neuropsychological Test Battery

Test Name	Primary Function(s) Measured
Halstead Category Test	Concept formation, reasoning, learning, judgment, mental flexibility
Tactual Performance Test	Psychomotor coordination, tactile and kinesthetic
Abilities, incidental memory (spatial)	
Seashore Rhythm Test	Auditory perception, sustained attention and concentration
Speech Sounds Perception Test	Sustained attention and concentration, language processing, auditory–verbal perception
Trail Making Test	Visual scanning, visual sequencing, speed of information processing
Wechsler Adult Intelligence Scale	Verbal and performance intelligence
Sensory Perceptual Examination	Auditory, visual, and tactile discrimination
Aphasia Screening Test	Various aspects of language ability and usage, basic arithmetic abilities, praxis skills
Finger Oscillation and Dynamometer	Simple motor speed and grip strength

- **Pattern of performance**. This analytical approach attempts to take into account not only levels of performance but also that certain pathological conditions (i.e., a severe learning disability) usually show a *pattern* of deficit on the neuropsychological exam. This level-of-inference approach often takes years of experience by the examiner to refine as well as considerable experience with specific populations or specific diagnostic groups.
- **Pathognomonic signs**. This is a yes–no type of approach where the mere *presence* or *absence* of certain performance indicators suggests brain damage or brain dysfunction. For example, a clear sign of aphasia or neglect often constitutes a pathognomonic sign strongly suggestive of brain dysfunction.
- **Right–left comparisons**. Certain tests measure performance of either the left or right side of the body (i.e., motor skills, perceptual skills), and therefore the examiner will look for *discrepancies* between the two sides. In this type of analysis, performance that is influenced by factors peripheral to the central nervous system must be taken into account.

These analytical approaches articulated by Halstead and Reitan decades ago are still quite pertinent today and can also be readily applied to other neuropsychological methods and batteries. There are several noteworthy advantages to the HRB approach, the most prominent of which is the extensive norms and research that accompany it. However, its prognostic utility is divided between good and poor. It is good from the perspective of predicting future psychometric performance. It is limited, however, in that it has not been adequately correlated to the neuropsychological performance of everyday life (i.e., ability to work, cook, manage money, and prioritize). Only in cases of very poor performance on the

HRB can reliable inferences be made about ecologically valid performance issues. Finally, the HRB is limited in circumstances where frequent and repeated testing is necessary, as in pharmaceutical studies, because of limited alternate form availability.

Other Approaches

More than 30 years ago, A.R. Luria and Anne-Lise Christensen began publishing clinical and research observations that eventually led to the development of the *Luria–Nebraska Neuropsychological Battery*. This battery, while intending to measure many of the same motor, perceptual, and cognitive functions elicited by the HRB approach, has less of a following than the HRB. The Luria approach inherently places a premium on the importance of behavioral observations of the examinee in interpreting performance relevance, thereby limiting its use with psychometrists or those with limited patient experience. Additionally, most neuropsychologists would argue that an examiner using the Luria battery (vs. the HRB) must have a very firm grounding in neuropsychological theory as well as a considerable background in the history of the patient, further limiting its use to a smaller examiner base. The reader is referred to the works of Golden et al. (1980) and Purisch (1999) for additional information on the Luria approach to neuropsychological assessment. It should be noted that the Luria approach has never been routinely applied to issues of long-term outcome or ecological validity, except in cases of significant injury or significant impairment.

One of the more popular, flexible approaches to neuropsychological inquiry is the *Iowa–Benton Approach (IBA)*, which is tied to the exhaustive work of Arthur Benton and his colleagues (2000). The IBA is considered a hypothesis-generating approach. The IBA provides the examiners with a wide range of tools that can be customized to the functioning level of the patient and to the needs of the referral question(s). There is, however, a *core battery* to support this approach, which gives a broad sampling of the patient's performance and which can be referred to normative data sets. Benton believed that any approach to neuropsychological assessment should be viewed "in the same way as we view the physical or neurological examination, i.e., as a logical, sequential decision making process rather than the administration of a fixed battery of tests." For a more extensive review of neuropsychological test batteries, see Lezak (1995).

Modern-day neuropsychologists use a combination of proven assessment techniques (e.g., the HRB) and a compilation of newly devised and newly standardized approaches that are much more patient and referral question focused than previous strategies. For example, test batteries and specific tests have been established for patients with specific diagnoses or impairment, including:

- Neurotoxic exposure
- HIV-positive exposure
- Acquired neurological injury
- Learning disabilities
- Developmental disabilities
- Neuropsychiatric disorders
- Dementia and other amnesic disorders

The current movement away from presence vs. absence of damage/dysfunction, with less focus on localization issues, will in this author's opinion result in neuropsychological approaches that are more user friendly to the referring party, as well as more tightly focused on the clinical needs of the person under examination. In many respects, tailored evaluations, which are reinforced by valid norms, move in the desired direction toward ecologically valid interpretations of complex test findings. Again, refer to the expansive review of available neuropsychological test procedures presented by Lezak (1995).

NEUROPSYCHOLOGICAL INQUIRY AND OUTCOME PREDICTION

As mentioned above, until recently, most neuropsychological examinations focused on the identification of cognitive assets and deficits in persons who are suspected of cerebral dysfunction, compromise, or injury. Localization of lesions or dysfunction is becoming less important, except in rare circumstances, in these evaluations with the progress of neuroimaging procedures (e.g., magnetic resonance imaging [MRI], positron emission tomography [PET], and single proton emission computerized tomography [SPECT]. On the positive side, however, neuroimaging procedures used in combination with neuropsychological procedures will likely lead to exciting advances toward the understanding of brain and behavior relationships.

Essential to the life care planning process is the accuracy of predicting client need and the resources necessary to meet those projected needs (Evans, 1996). While some studies have addressed the predictive power of neuropsychological performance to patient outcome, most studies in the literature address the correlation between *current test performance* and *future test performance*, ignoring the social, vocational, or independent living competencies of the person examined as they relate to test performance. Therefore, much of the neuropsychological test literature is of minimal or no value to the life care planner, who inherently seeks information that has more global functional inferences.

Listed in Table 6.2 are references to important studies that address the relationship of neuropsychological test performance to outcomes that may be of interest to the life care planner. This list is not intended to be exhaustive; rather, it is a starting point for further research.

Table 6.2 Neuropsychological Literature Relating to Global Outcome Measures: Traumatically Brain Injured Patients

Authors/Date	Outcomes Measured	Population Studied
Wehman et al., 1995	Return to work	Severe TBI
Giacino & Zasler, 1995	Coma recovery	Severe TBI
Goldstein & Levin, 1995	Cognition and behavior	TBI > age 50
Dikmen & Machamer, 1995	Neuropsychological and psychosocial levels	TBI patients (literature review)
Cifu et al., 1997	Return to work	TBI patients (mixed)
Vogenthaler et al., 1989	Return to work, independent living	TBI patients

These studies certainly can provide a benchmark for outcome prediction based on neuropsychological test performance. However, the notable shortcomings of such studies are twofold. First, neuropsychological data alone tell only part of the story — the cognitive and emotional one. Neuropsychological data often fall short when addressing the client's overall adaptation to loss or injury; they usually do not address environmental management issues (i.e., ergonomic considerations) to compensate for cognitive losses and changes. Second, these studies do not offer long-term follow-up on the reliability and validity of predicted outcomes. The predictability/reliability issue is particularly important in cases of mild to moderate injury in which the issue of permanent loss or permanent inability to compensate is less certain (Levin et al., 1982; Rizzo & Tranel, 1996). As the measured deficit becomes more severe, the reliability of predicted outcome usually increases. Several literature reviews have been published regarding short- and long-term outcomes following traumatic brain injury. Refer to the references at the end of this chapter.

Global Measures Influencing Outcome Following TBI

There are certain accepted truths in the TBI literature relating to short- and long-term outcome following traumatic brain injury. These usually relate to mechanisms surrounding the injury and to certain injury factors. Laaksonen (1994) summarized these issues:

Mechanisms	Factors
1. Lesion or injury	Localization
	Size
	Speed of development
2. Individual factors of patient	General state of health, age
	Degree of brain function dominance
	Intellectual capacity
	Motivation, interests, etc.
3. Factors regarding therapy	Time of treatment after onset
	Therapeutic methods
	Therapy expertise
	Duration/access to treatment

Many of these global influences can be gathered directly by the neuropsychologist (particularly the individual patient factors). The neuropsychological literature is filled with hundreds of studies addressing the influence of mechanism and patient factors, such as patient long-term functioning. The life care planner and the neuropsychologist should have ready access to this literature and should be prepared to reference this literature as part of the life care plan.

APPLICATIONS TO THE LIFE CARE PLANNING PROCESS

Thus far, most of the discussion in this chapter as to the role of the neuropsychologist in the life care planning process has focused on the relevance to neuropsychological test performance as related to short- and long-term outcome. While this is a very important contribution to the neuropsychologist's repertoire, experienced neuropsychologists also have considerable background in other areas of *clinical* neuropsychology, such as psychodiagnosis, counseling, crisis intervention, and family and patient education. These areas must also be addressed in the life care planning process. In what may best be described as a consultative role in these areas outside of formal neuropsychological evaluations, the neuropsychologist can contribute to a life care plan with the following issues:

- Identification of client risk for developing various psychological conditions requiring intermittent or ongoing treatment
- Identification of client need for periodic psychological or neuropsychological evaluations
- Identification of compensatory mechanisms and resources that may reduce or alleviate handicap caused by the injury
- Integration of allied health (occupational therapy, physical therapy, speech and language therapy, social work, vocational services) records and evaluations into a cohesive working plan to maximize the cognitive and emotional performance of the client
- Expert witness testimony, particularly in relating neuropsychological data to long-term functioning
- Integration of existing neuropsychological literature as supportive/related material to the neuropsychological performance estimates made in the life care plan
- Participation in rehabilitation assessments and rehabilitation team conferences that integrate team findings into the life care plan

In these areas, the neuropsychologist is used as an "on demand" consultant. His or her ability to assist the life care planner must be at a level where he or she can articulate existing rehabilitation and evaluative data into a cohesive and pragmatic story that takes into account current and anticipated databases and industry-accepted practices. This integration, when articulated in the context of relevant neuropsychological research and applied literature, will result in a well thought out, well-designed *empirically driven* contribution to the life care plan.

Beyond the Neuropsychological Evaluation

In the case of traumatic brain injury, it is the opinion of this author that the neuropsychologist must go well beyond the contributions of the neuropsychological evaluation to have the optimum impact in the life care planning process. Most neuropsychological evaluations are at risk to fall short of meeting the ultimate requirement of the life care plan: to make reliable predictions of functional outcome and the resources necessary and available to maintain the predicted functioning level. Neuropsychological evaluations, by definition, usually focus on describing the individual's functioning at the time of inquiry, with estimates as to how such functioning may change over time (Christensen & Uzzell, 1994). While certain test performance levels may be statistically unlikely to change over the lifetime of the person, one's ability to adapt and compensate can change. The neuropsychologist ideally should be able to describe what conditions and circumstances need to exist for such changes to occur. In a similar vein the neuropsychologist, with input from other rehabilitation professionals, can project cognitive, emotional, and behavioral circumstances that can reduce the risk for exacerbation of existing handicaps or regression of the same.

Case Study Illustration

A patient, M.C., was referred to this author by his life care planner. At the time of referral, M.C. was approximately 9 months status after a severe brain injury sustained in an automobile accident. Until the injury, M.C. was a high-functioning, 52-year old sales executive, with a supportive wife and two adolescent children. There were no significant preinjury medical problems, nor was there any history of familial neurological dysfunction or disease. M.C. had a college education and had recently been promoted in his job, secondary to exemplary performance. After the injury, M.C. received immediate medical intervention (within 20 minutes) by Emergency Medical Services (EMS) and was transported to a nearby neurotrauma center. His initial Rancho Los Amigos Score (RLAS) Level was III, indicative of a severe injury; additionally, his initial Glasgow Coma Score (GCS) was 5, again indicative of severe injury. His initial hospital course was uncomplicated and approximately 1-week postinjury his RLAS score had progressed to IV and his GCS was 10. These early signs of improvement suggested a potentially good recovery. However, approximately 10 days postinjury M.C. suffered an episode of status epilepticus (a severe seizure, despite taking Dilantin prophylactically), and it was suspected that the patient suffered anoxic injury to the brain as well. Following this episode, the patient regressed to a RLAS III, a state that lasted for 5 days. Two months postinjury the patient had stabilized at an RLAS V, at which time he started an extensive course of inpatient rehabilitation.

Following a 3-month inpatient stay, which was complemented by an additional 4 months of outpatient treatment, the patient's life care planner was brought in to begin to assemble the life care plan (LCP). This author was asked to address the following referral questions:

- Determine the patient's current neuropsychological status and the likelihood for change within the next year.
- Determine a course of neuropsychological treatment, both short- and long-term.
- Determine the likelihood of whether the patient will be capable of competitive employment following his course of treatment.
- Determine what supports, if any, are likely to maintain or improve the patient's neuropsychological abilities once discharged to home.
- Determine the cognitive issues that will facilitate or limit the patient's ability to live independently (i.e., without the support of paid assistance).
- Provide relevant literature that supports the conclusions above.

These six questions could not have been better stated. That is, the life care planner insisted that the neuropsychologist integrate current test performance to issues that had ecological validity, such as the ability to return to work, the ability to live independently, durability of outcome, and the supports necessary to maintain outcome. With these referral questions well understood, the neuropsychologist proceeded with a flexible neuropsychological test battery (in this case the IBA) with certain additions that had literature relevant to the referral questions. The neuropsychological evaluation concluded with the following critical points:

■ The patient's memory deficits were very severe and unlikely to change significantly, based upon the depth and chronicity of the memory impairment. Similarly, severe problems with initiation and persistence were likely to be lifelong. M.C.'s attention span was very short, and he constantly needed redirection to all evaluation and treatment procedures.

■ The patient's cognitive deficits were considered consistent not only with severe TBI, but also with cerebral anoxia.

■ Treatment interventions would yield the highest probability of success if performed in very familiar surroundings (i.e., M.C.'s home) given the patient's inability to generalize.

■ It was highly unlikely that the patient would ever be capable of competitive employment, although participation in a supported employment situation may prove some success.

■ M.C., though in fairly good shape physically and medically, would likely require constant cueing from family members to complete his activities of daily living. Nonetheless, the patient should never be left alone for any extended period of time (greater than 15 minutes), secondary to chronic inability to assess potential hazards in his environment.

■ A follow-up neuropsychological evaluation was recommended at the 18-month anniversary of his injury in order to determine his neurometric status and to make additional recommendations for compensatory strategies.

The actual neuropsychological report contained dozens of test scores, percentiles, and other pertinent data. The summary statement, however, reflected the above-noted conclusions that were relevant to the LCP. The actual test data, combined with the extensive experience of the examiner, combined with detailed reference to the neuropsychological literature, supported the above-noted conclusions. Such integration is imperative for the outcome of a useful LCP. (Editor's note: Also see Chapter 13 for the checklist of questions for the neuropsychologist.)

CONCLUSION

Modern-day practices in neuropsychology can contribute significant value-added services to the life care planner in cases of neurological injury or disease. Traumatic brain injury was used as an example throughout this text. As is often the case, the experience base of both parties will have direct correlation to the reliability and validity of conclusions and recommendations made with the LCP. A critical element, however, of those contributions made by the neuropsychologist needs to be determined at the time of the initial evaluation. It is very important that the life care planner clearly articulate that he or she desires that the neuropsychological data not only be integrated with data from other examinations, but also be relevant to the global functioning issues addressed in the plan. If this expectation of data usage is not clarified, such issues are at risk of not being addressed, significantly lessening the contributions of the examination procedures. Supporting the conclusions with references to relevant research also strengthens the contributions of the neuropsychologist. Finally, it is incumbent that the neuropsychologist clarify what factors in the person's environment (home, work, school, etc.) either support or serve as detriments to the patient's neuropsychological abilities. The neuropsychologist must recognize that the patient's world lies outside the examiner's office and that the patient is constantly faced with a dynamic set of conditions that must be managed within the context of disrupted cognitive, emotional, and behavioral conditions.

REFERENCES

Benton, A. (2000). *Exploring the History of Neuropsychology: Selected Papers*. Oxford: Oxford University Press.

Blackwell, T.L., Powers, A.S., & Weed, R.O. (1994). *Life Care Planning for Traumatic Brain Injury*. Athens, GA: Elliot & Fitzpatrick.

Christensen, A.L. & Uzzell, B.P. (1994). *Brain Injury and Neuropsychological Rehabilitation*. Hillsdale, NJ: Erlbaum Associates.

Cifu, D.X., Keyser-Marcus, L., Lopez, E., Weyman, P., Kreutzer, J., Englander, J., & High, W. (1997). Acute predictors of successful return to work 1 year after traumatic brain injury: a multicenter analysis. *Archives of Physical Medicine and Rehabilitation*, 78, 125–131.

Dikmen, S. & Machamer, J.E. (1995). Neurobehavioural outcomes and their determinants. *Journal of Head Trauma Rehabilitation*, 10, 74–86.

Evans, R.W. (1996). Commentary and an illustration on the use of outcome data in life care planning for persons with acquired neurological injuries. *NeuroRehabilitation*, 7, 157–162.

Giacino, J.T. & Zasler, N.D. (1995). Outcome after severe traumatic brain injury: coma, the vegetative state, and the minimally responsive state. *Journal of Head Trauma Rehabilitation*, 10, 40–56.

Golden, C.J., Hammeke, T.A., & Purisch, A.D. (1980). *The Luria-Nebraska Neuropsychological Test Battery Manual (Revised)*. Los Angeles: Western Psychological Services.

Goldstein, F.C. & Levin, H.S. (1995). Neurobehavioral outcome of traumatic brain injury in older adults: initial findings. *Journal of Head Trauma Rehabilitation*, 10, 57–73.

Laaksonen, R. (1994). Cognitive training methods in rehabilitation of memory. In A.L. Christensen & B.P. Uzzell, Eds., *Brain Injury and Neuropsychological Rehabilitation*. Hillsdale, NJ: Erlbaum Associates.

Levin, H.S., Benton, A.L., & Grossman, R.H. (1982). *Neurobehavioral Consequences of Closed Head Injury*. New York: Oxford University Press.

Lezak, M.D. (1995). *Neuropsychological Assessment*, 3rd ed. New York: Oxford University Press.

Purisch, A.D. (1999). Forensic use of the Luria-Nebraska Neuropsychological Battery. In C.J. Golden, Ed., T*he Luria-Nebraska Neuropsychological Battery: Twentieth Anniversary Handbook*, 165–185, Los Angeles: Western Psychological Services

Rizzo, M. & Tranel, D., Eds. (1996). *Head Injury and Postconcussive Syndrome*. New York: Livingstone Press.

Vogenthaler, D.R., Smith, K.R., & Goldfader, P. (1989). Head injury: a multivariate study, predicting long term productivity and independent living outcome. *Brain Injury*, 3, 369–385.

Wehman, P.H., West, M., Kregel, J., Sherron, P., & Kreutzer, J. (1995). Return to work for persons with traumatic brain injury: a data-based approach to program development. *Journal of Head Trauma Rehabilitation*, 10, 27–39.

7

THE ROLE OF THE OCCUPATIONAL THERAPIST IN LIFE CARE PLANNING

Ileana Seoane McCaigue

INTRODUCTION

The principal role of the occupational therapist in the life of an individual with a disability is to serve as an impartial facilitator, focusing on the potential functional abilities that he or she may be capable of performing with modifications as needed. When participating in the life care planning process, as whenever an evaluation is conducted, the occupational therapist assesses the person as a whole entity, with occupational performance areas ranging from activities of daily living to work activities and play or leisure skills.

Occupational therapy comes from the word *occupation*, or "purposeful activity" (Hinojosa et al., 1993). Occupational therapists use purposeful activities, therapeutic tasks, and exercises to achieve functional outcomes established for each person with a disability. Occupational therapy by definition as adopted and approved by the Representative Assembly of the American Occupational Therapy Association, Inc., is "the therapeutic use of self-care, work and play activities to increase independent function, enhance development, and prevent disability; may include adaptation of task or environment to achieve maximum independence and to enhance quality of life" (American Occupational Therapy Association, April 1986).

QUALIFICATIONS OF AN OCCUPATIONAL THERAPIST

An occupational therapist (OT) or occupational therapy assistant (OTA) graduates from a university or college accredited by the Accreditation Council for Occupational Therapy Education of the American Occupational Therapy Association, Inc. An entry-level OT must achieve a Bachelor of Science or basic Master of Science degree to be eligible to take a national certification examination. On passing this exam OTs are entitled to use the credentials OTR after their name to delineate themselves as registered occupational therapists by the National Board for the

0-8493-1511-5/04/$0.00+$1.50
© 2004 by CRC Press LLC

Table 7.1 Examples of Specializations within Occupational Therapy

Area of Specialty	Initials
Certified hand therapist	CHT
Certified driver rehabilitation specialist	CDRS
Board certified in pediatrics	BCP
Board certified in neurorehabilitation	BCN
Certified work capacity evaluator	CWCE

Accreditation of Occupational Therapy, Inc. (NBCOT, Inc.), formerly known as the American Occupational Therapy Certification Board, Inc. (AOTCB, Inc.), until April 1996 (Low, 1997). Occupational therapy assistants, upon graduating from a 2-year program with an Associate of Science degree, also take a national examination to become certified as COTAs.

Under certain state regulations, some occupational therapists and occupational therapy assistants are required to apply for licensure in order to practice. Once licensure requirements are met, the OTR or COTA then may apply an "L" to his or her credentials — OTR/L or COTA/L — to designate his or her qualifications to practice in the state of his or her choice and abide by the guidelines set therein. State licensure requires renewal by the respective qualifying state licensure board and varies as to the frequency per state, but is usually either annually or biannually. Licensure renewal generally requires a specified number of contact hours or continuing education credits to be met within the licensure period. National recertification by the NBCOT, Inc., is currently elective, with the certification period effective for 5 years.

Additional specialty certifications are also available for occupational therapists with expertise in certain areas of practice (Table 7.1). Occupational therapists can qualify to sit for a certification examination in the clinical or practice areas of hand rehabilitation and merit the additional credentials of CHT (certified hand therapist). In the area of driver rehabilitation, the credentials of CDRS can be added, designating that therapist as a certified driver rehabilitation specialist upon passing this specialty examination. The practice areas of pediatrics and neurorehabilitation are two other clinical designations that can be achieved, applying the credentials of BCP (board certified in pediatrics) and BCN (board certified in neurorehabilitation) to identify the occupational therapist as a specialist in these areas. Certifications are also available, not necessarily via a certifying organization, but by programs offering extensive training courses. These include the area of work capacity evaluation by which an individual can earn the credentials of CWCE (certified work capacity evaluator). Some occupational therapists may choose to seek the assistive technology practitioner or (as of 2002) rehabilitation engineering technologist certifications from the Rehabilitation Engineering and Assistive Technology Society of North America (also referred to as RESNA). Additional specialty certifications, though too numerous to list, are available in almost every branch of occupational therapy practice from pediatrics to geriatrics.

Besides the basic Bachelor or Master of Science degrees, an OT can continue his or her education within the field of occupational therapy and pursue an advanced master's degree or doctorate in selected universities throughout the U.S. Other countries have schools of occupational therapy; however, they are not accredited by the American Occupational Therapy Association. Upon entry into this country foreign therapists must pass a national registration examination qualifying them to have at least the same entry-level skills that graduates from the accredited schools in America have acquired. They must then apply for certification and licensure, as would any new therapist. Supervision is then provided by the hiring facility for a designated period of time until they achieve status as a resident or return to their native country.

OCCUPATIONAL THERAPY AREAS OF OVERLAP WITH OTHER PROFESSIONS

Since occupational therapists practice in a multitude of settings ranging from the hospital environment and nursing homes to community-based settings such as clients' homes, schools, and work sites, the settings often determine what role the occupational therapist plays within the treatment team. For example, when treating the client or patient who has difficulties with transfers from multiple surfaces in the home, the occupational therapist may be designated as the primary therapist to work on bathroom and car transfers. The physical therapist may be the primary therapist focusing on bed mobility and bed transfers. Though both disciplines are capable of performing these techniques given their training, these roles are delineated many times to avoid duplication of services or fees for service. Another example is that though the physical therapist is primarily responsible for ambulation and the client's status for mobility within her environment, the occupational therapist must also be aware of her status and how to ambulate her safely. This is necessary so that the occupational therapist can encourage the client to perform activities of daily living (ADLs), which will require mobility and transfers to and from varying surface heights, to achieve independence in her basic and higher-level self-care skills.

The schematic diagram in Figure 7.1 depicts 10 professional fields or areas of practice with which the profession of occupational therapy interacts or overlaps. The primary professions that are most directly involved with the occupational therapist's treatment from a life care planning perspective are the life care planner, physician, psychologist, speech/language pathologist, and physical therapist. Depending on the setting, nursing may also be involved with the OT in acute care with the rehabilitation counselor or the case manager for the overall care of that client. The occupational therapist must follow the guidelines for care based on the presenting problems, potential for return to prior level of functional abilities, availability of resources for the continuum of care outside the respective facility, and the client's own desire or motivation to progress with his or her rehabilitation. In the educational setting, the focus of care is on the development or habilitation of skills that are educationally driven, such as the self-care tasks of taking off and putting on a jacket, snapping fasteners, pulling pants up or down, handling a spoon or fork for feeding, drinking from a cup, toileting, and manipulating tools for drawing, coloring, painting, cutting, and writing while being able to sit to attend with appropriate behavior. Prevocational tasks are also emphasized since many children with multiple handicaps are often not able to continue in the

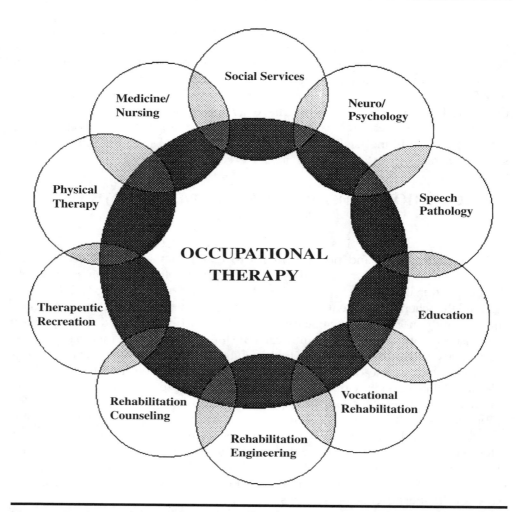

Figure 7.1 Schematic depiction of the interrelationship of occupational therapy among 10 professions with which services are coordinated, depending on the providers' settings.

higher levels of education and are placed out of high school in job settings suitable to their capabilities. The fields of overlap in these settings are with educators, school social workers, psychologists, speech/language pathologists, school nurses, physical therapists, and vocational specialists.

Some areas of common overlap covering the gamut of professionals with whom occupational therapists interact as part of a global plan of care for mutual clients are as follows:

■ **Medicine/Nursing:** Review of medications and disease processes, determining medical stability in relation to rehabilitation potentials, case management, posttraumatic or postsurgical wound management, hand rehabilitation needs for possible surgical intervention, splinting or immobilization needs, range of motion maintenance, visual skills assessment, and developmental assessments.

- **Neuropsychology:** Individual and group dynamics, cognitive assessment and retraining, perceptual evaluation, functional needs assessment, developmental assessments, psychosocial skills, community reentry skills, and predriving skills assessment of potential to drive safely.
- **Physical Therapy:** Ambulation, functional mobility and positioning needs, transfers assessment and training, developmental assessments and treatment, accessibility needs, wound management, physical agent modalities and hand rehabilitation, prosthetics, physical capacities assessment for determining return to work potential and therapy needs to achieve goals.
- **Speech Pathology:** Dysphasia evaluation with resultant swallowing and feeding needs for treatment, augmentative communication needs assessment, visual and auditory perceptual skills assessment and treatment, cognitive assessment and retraining, and oral motor evaluation and treatment.
- **Vocational Rehabilitation:** Evaluation and assessment of prevocational skills, determining potential to return to previous work capacity or other appropriate job possibilities, job site assessment and modifications needed, work-related or transferable skills retraining needs, and potential placements.
- **Rehabilitation Counseling:** Case management, determination of work or job skills status, accessibility issues, activities of daily living and driving status, and life care planning.
- **Social Services:** Psychosocial factors affecting rehabilitation potential and abilities, medication and case management, funding sources, family and community resources, and risk management issues.
- **Therapeutic Recreation:** Assessment and therapeutic intervention for play/leisure skills specific to the client's interests, accessibility issues for community activities, and assistive technology to adapt activities deemed as appropriate in relation to the clients' capabilities and leisure interests.
- **Rehabilitation Engineering:** Assistive technology design, fabrication, and implementation of low- and high-tech equipment and devices; accessibility issues and needs for home or environmental modifications; and technology, positioning, and mobility equipment needs to enable transport to job sites.
- **Education:** School performance needs and capabilities, developmental assessments and remedial tasks, school-related self-care skills, accessibility needs to maneuver in classroom and general school environment, prevocational training and modifications needed for job sites, assistive technology for low- and high-tech needs in the classroom, predriving skills and possible driving potential to determine vocational placement, cognitive training in compensatory strategies, and handwriting training.

In every case or setting the occupational therapist must consider the innate desires of the adult or child with whom he or she is working. This should be considered the main focus of the treatment plan: to engage that individual in his or her program and enable him or her to achieve the goals outlined by the client and by the team of professionals involved with his or her care.

COMMON TERMS USED IN THE FIELD OF OCCUPATIONAL THERAPY

The uniform terminology established for occupational therapy practitioners was revised for the third edition published in 1994, to replace the previous document adopted in 1989 (see Low, 1997). The Uniform Terminology Grid was originally developed by Dr. Winnie Dunn in 1988 (Table 7.2) (see Dunn et al., 1994). It was later revised and translated into the pictorial representation of the most current 1994 uniform terminology definitions, which included the addition of performance contexts (not shown). Due to the extensive number of terms used in the evaluation, assessment, and treatment process, only those items that relate to the terms within the performance areas, performance components, and performance contexts are listed within this publication.

THE OCCUPATIONAL THERAPY FRAMEWORK FOR EVALUATION AND TREATMENT

There are three critical aspects of performance in which occupational therapists are trained and instructed to evaluate when assessing the needs of each person with a presenting disability. These are skills or behaviors represented in the (1) **performance areas** of activities of daily living, work and productive activities, and play or leisure activities; (2) **performance components** of sensorimotor components, cognitive integration/cognitive components, and psychosocial skills/psychological components; and the (3) **performance contexts** of the temporal aspects and the environment (Dunn & McGourty, 1989). Once these interrelated aspects are utilized to complete an evaluation of the person with a disability, the occupational therapist can assess the gestalt or global needs of the individual. A framework is then developed for intervention, and the therapist then gives a prognosis for that person's ability to achieve the functional outcomes established based on these factors (Dunn & McGourty, 1989).

Performance Areas

Performance areas are those activities of primary concern for the occupational therapist that cover the broad category of daily living skills that are considered typical for each person. Terms used within this domain are as follows:

Activities of daily living — Self-maintenance tasks.
- **Grooming:** Obtaining and using supplies; removing body hair (use of razors, tweezers, lotions, etc.); applying and removing cosmetics; washing, drying, combing, styling, and brushing hair; caring for nails (hands and feet), skin, ears, and eyes; and applying deodorant.
- **Oral hygiene:** Obtaining and using supplies; cleaning mouth; brushing and flossing teeth; or removing, cleaning, and reinserting dental orthotics and prosthetics.
- **Bathing/showering:** Obtaining and using supplies; soaping, rinsing, and drying body parts; maintaining bathing position; and transferring to and from bathing positions.

- **Toilet hygiene:** Obtaining and using supplies; clothing management; maintaining toileting position; transferring to and from toileting position; cleaning body; and caring for menstrual and continence needs (including catheters, colostomies, and suppository management).
- **Personal device care:** Cleaning and maintaining personal care items, such as hearing aids, contact lenses, glasses, orthotics, prosthetics, adaptive equipment, and contraceptive and sexual devices.
- **Dressing:** Selecting clothing and accessories appropriate to time of day, weather, and occasion; obtaining clothing from storage area; dressing and undressing in a sequential fashion; fastening and adjusting clothing and shoes; and applying and removing personal devices, prostheses, or orthoses.
- **Feeding and eating:** Setting up food; selecting and using appropriate utensils and tableware; bringing food or drink to mouth; cleaning face, hands, and clothing; sucking, masticating, coughing, and swallowing; and management of alternative methods of nourishment.
- **Medication routine:** Obtaining medication, opening and closing containers, following prescribed schedules, taking correct quantities, reporting problems and adverse effects, and administering correct quantities by using prescribed methods.
- **Health maintenance:** Developing and maintaining routines for illness prevention and wellness promotion, such as physical fitness, nutrition, and decreasing health risk behaviors.
- **Socialization:** Accessing opportunities and interacting with other people in appropriate contextual and cultural ways to meet emotional and physical needs.
- **Functional communication:** Using equipment or systems to send and receive information, such as writing equipment, telephones, typewriters, computers, communication boards, call lights, emergency systems, Braille writers, telecommunication devices for the deaf, and augmentative communication systems.
- **Functional mobility:** Moving from one position or place to another, such as in-bed mobility, wheelchair mobility, and transfers (wheelchair, bed, car, tub, toilet tub/shower, chair, floor). Performing functional ambulation and transporting objects.
- **Community mobility:** Moving self in the community and using public or private transportation, such as driving or accessing buses, taxicabs, or other public transportation systems.
- **Emergency response:** Recognizing sudden, unexpected hazardous situations and initiating action to reduce the threat to health and safety.
- **Sexual expression:** Engaging in desired sexual and intimate activities.

Work and productive activities — Purposeful activities for self-development, social contribution, and livelihood.

- **Home management:** Obtaining and maintaining personal and household possessions and environment. This includes clothing care, cleaning, meal preparation and cleanup, shopping, money management, household maintenance, and safety procedures.

Table 7.2   Uniform Terminology Grid: Occupational Therapy

PERFORMANCE COMPONENTS	Grooming	Oral Hygiene	Bathing	Toilet Hygiene	Dressing	Feeding & Eating	Medication Routine	Socialization	Functional Communication	Functional Mobility	Sexual Expression	Home Management	Care of Others	Educational Activities	Vocational Activities	Activities	Play or Leisure Exploitation	Play or Leisure Performance
A. SENSORY/MOTOR COMPONENT																		
1. Sensory integration																		
a. Sensory awareness																		
b. Sensory processing																		
(1) Tactile																		
(2) Proprioceptive																		
(3) Vestibular																		
(4) Visual																		
(5) Auditory																		
(6) Gustatory																		
(7) Olfactory																		
c. Perceptual skills																		
(1) Stereognosis																		
(2) Kinesthesia																		
(3) Body scheme																		
(4) Right–left discrimination																		
(5) Form constancy																		
(6) Position in space																		
(7) Visual closure																		
(8) Figure ground																		
(9) Depth perception																		
(10) Topographical orientation																		
2. Neuromuscular																		
a. Reflex																		
b. Range of motion																		
c. Muscle tone																		
d. Strength																		
e. Endurance																		
f. Postural control																		
g. Soft tissue integrity																		
3. Motor																		
a. Activity tolerance																		
b. Gross motor coordination																		
c. Crossing the midline																		
d. Laterality																		
e. Bilateral integration																		
f. Praxis																		
g. Fine motor coordination/dexterity																		
h. Visual–motor integration																		
i. Oral–motor control																		

Table 7.2 (Continued) Uniform Terminology Grid: Occupational Therapy

PERFORMANCE COMPONENTS	Grooming	Oral Hygiene	Bathing	Toilet Hygiene	Dressing	Feeding & Eating	Medication Routine	Socialization	Functional Communication	Functional Mobility	Sexual Expression	Home Management	Care of Others	Educational Activities	Vocational Activities	Activities	Play or Leisure Exploitation	Play or Leisure Performance
B. COGNITIVE INTEGRATION AND COMPONENTS 1. Level of arousal																		
2. Orientation																		
3. Recognition																		
4. Attention span																		
5. Memory a. Short-term																		
b. Long-term																		
c. Remote																		
d. Recent																		
6. Sequencing																		
7. Categorization																		
8. Conceptual formation																		
9. Intellectual operations in space																		
10. Problem solving																		
11. Generalization of learning																		
12. Integration of learning																		
13. Synthesis of learning																		
C. PSYCHOLOGICAL SKILLS AND PSYCHOLOGICAL COMPONENTS 1. Psychological a. Roles																		
b. Values																		
c. Interests																		
d. Initiation of activity																		
e. Termination of activity																		
f. Self-concept																		
2. Social a. Social conduct																		
b. Conversation																		
c. Self-expression																		
3. Self-management a. Coping skills																		
b. Time management																		
c. Self-control																		

Column group headers: *Performance Areas* — *Activities of Daily Living* (Grooming, Oral Hygiene, Bathing, Toilet Hygiene, Dressing, Feeding & Eating, Medication Routine, Socialization, Functional Communication, Functional Mobility, Sexual Expression); *Work Activities* (Home Management, Care of Others, Educational Activities, Vocational Activities); *Play or Leisure* (Activities, Play or Leisure Exploitation, Play or Leisure Performance).

©1988, Winnie Dunn. Reprinted with permission for this publication by Winnie Dunn, Ph.D., O.T.R., F.A.O.T.A., the originator of the Uniform Terminology Grid in 1988. The American Occupational Therapy Association's Terminology Task Force, led by Dr. Dunn and comprised of five members, modified the grid to include the performance contexts in 1994 to replace the previous 1989 document.

- **Care of others:** Providing for children, spouse, parents, pets, or others, such as giving physical care, nurturing, communicating, and using age-appropriate activities.
- **Educational activities:** Participating in a learning environment through school, community, or work-sponsored activities, such as exploring educational interests, attending to instruction, managing assignments, and contributing to group experiences.
- **Vocational activities:** Participating in work-related activities. This includes vocational exploration, job acquisition, work or job performance, retirement planning, and volunteer participation.

Play or leisure activities — Intrinsically motivating activities for amusement, relaxation, spontaneous enjoyment, or self-expression.

- **Play or leisure exploration:** Identifying interests, skills, opportunities, and appropriate play or leisure activities.
- **Play or leisure performance:** Planning and participating in play or leisure activities. Maintaining a balance of play or leisure activities with work and productive activities and activities of daily living. Obtaining, using, and maintaining equipment and supplies.

Performance Components

Performance components are the fundamental human abilities that are required for successful engagement in performance areas. Terms within this framework area are as follows:

Sensorimotor components — The ability to receive input, process information, and produce output.

- *Sensory information:*
  Sensory awareness — Receiving and differentiating sensory stimuli.
  Sensory processing — Interpreting sensory stimuli.
  1. **Tactile:** Interpreting light touch, pressure, temperature, pain, and vibration through skin contact/receptors.
  2. **Proprioceptive:** Interpreting stimuli originating in muscles, joints, and other internal tissues that give information about the position of one body part in relation to another.
  3. **Vestibular:** Interpreting stimuli from the inner ear receptors regarding head position and movement.
  4. **Visual:** Interpreting stimuli through the eyes, including peripheral vision and acuity, and awareness of color and pattern.
  5. **Auditory:** Interpreting and localizing sounds, and discriminating background sounds.
  6. **Gustatory:** Interpreting tastes.
  7. **Olfactory:** Interpreting odors.
  Perceptual processing — Organizing sensory input into meaningful patterns.
  1. **Stereognosis:** Identifying objects through proprioception, cognition, and the sense of touch.

2. **Kinesthesia:** Identifying the excursion and direction of joint movement.
3. **Pain response:** Interpreting noxious stimuli.
4. **Body scheme:** Acquiring an internal awareness of the body and the relationships of body parts to each other.
5. **Right–left discrimination:** Differentiating one side from the other.
6. **Form constancy:** Recognizing forms and objects as the same in various environments, positions, and sizes.
7. **Position in space:** Determining the spatial relationship of figures and objects to self or other forms and objects.
8. **Visual closure:** Identifying forms or objects from incomplete presentations.
9. **Figure ground:** Differentiating between foreground and background forms and objects.
10. **Depth perception:** Determining the relative distance between objects, figures, or landmarks and the observer, and changes in planes of surfaces.
11. **Spatial relationships:** Determining the position of objects relative to each other.
12. **Topographical orientation:** Determining the location of objects and settings and the route to the location.

- *Neuromusculoskeletal information:*

  Reflex — Eliciting an involuntary muscle response by sensory input.

  Range of motion — Moving body parts through an arc.

  Muscle tone — Demonstrating a degree of tension or resistance in a muscle at rest and in response to stretch.

  Strength — Demonstrating a degree of muscle power when movement is resisted, as with objects or gravity.

  Endurance — Sustaining cardiac, pulmonary, and musculoskeletal exertion over time.

  Postural control — Using righting and equilibrium adjustments to maintain balance during functional movements.

  Soft tissue integrity — Maintaining anatomical and physiological condition of interstitial tissue and skin.

- *Motor information:*

  Gross coordination — Using large muscle groups for controlled, goal-directed movements.

  Crossing the midline — Moving limbs and eyes across the midsagittal plane of the body.

  Laterality — Using a preferred unilateral body part for activities requiring a high level of skill.

  Bilateral integration — Coordinating both body sides during activity.

  Motor control — Using the body in functional and versatile movement patterns.

  Praxis — Conceiving and planning a new motor act in response to an environmental demand.

Fine coordination/dexterity — Using small muscle groups for controlled movements, particularly in object manipulation.

Visual–motor integration — Coordinating the interaction of information from the eyes with body movement during activity.

Oral–motor control — Coordinating oropharyngeal musculature for controlled movements.

Cognitive integration and cognitive components — The ability to use higher brain functions.

- **Level of arousal:** Demonstrating alertness and responsiveness to environmental stimuli.
- **Orientation:** Identifying person, place, time, and situation.
- **Recognition:** Identifying familiar faces, objects, and other previously presented materials.
- **Attention span:** Focusing on a task over time.
- **Initiation of activity:** Starting a physical or mental activity.
- **Termination of activity:** Stopping an activity at an appropriate time.
- **Memory:** Recalling information after brief or long periods of time.
- **Sequencing:** Placing information, concepts, and actions in order.
- **Categorization:** Identifying similarities of and differences among pieces of environmental information.
- **Concept formation:** Organizing a variety of information to form thoughts and ideas.
- **Spatial operations:** Mentally manipulating the position of objects in various relationships.
- **Problem solving:** Recognizing a problem, defining a problem, identifying alternative plans, selecting a plan, organizing steps in a plan, implementing a plan, and evaluating the outcome.
- **Learning:** Acquiring new concepts and behaviors.
- **Generalization:** Applying previously learned concepts and behaviors to a variety of new situations.

Psychosocial skills and psychological components — The ability to interact in society and to process emotions.

- *Psychological information:*
  Values — Identifying ideas or beliefs that are important to self and others.
  Interests — Identifying mental or physical activities that create pleasure and maintain attention.
  Self-concept — Developing the value of the physical, emotional, and sexual self.
- *Social information:*
  Role performance — Identifying, maintaining, and balancing functions one assumes or acquires in society (e.g., worker, student, parent, friend, religious participant).
  Social conduct — Interacting by using manners, personal space, eye contact, gestures, active listening, and self-expression appropriate to one's environment.

      Interpersonal skills — Using verbal and nonverbal communication to interact in a variety of settings.

      Self-expression — Using a variety of styles and skills to express thoughts, feelings, and needs.

■ *Self-management information:*

      Coping skills — Identifying and managing stress and related factors.

      Time management — Planning and participating in a balance of self-care, work, leisure, and rest activities to promote satisfaction and health.

      Self-control — Modifying one's own behavior in response to environmental needs, demands, constraints, personal aspirations, and feedback from others.

Performance Contexts

Situations or factors that influence an individual's engagement in desired and required performance areas. These are taken into consideration when determining the function and dysfunction in relation to performance areas and performance components, as well as in planning treatment intervention. Terminology used within this category is as follows:

Temporal aspects
- **Chronological:** Individual's age.
- **Developmental:** Stage or phase of maturation.
- **Life cycle:** Place in important life phases, such as career cycle, parenting cycle, or educational process.
- **Disability status:** Place in continuum of disability, such as acuteness of injury, chronicity of disability, or terminal nature of illness.

Environment
- **Physical:** Nonhuman aspects of contexts that include the accessibility to and performance within environments having natural terrain, plants, animals, buildings, furniture, objects, tools, or devices.
- **Social:** Availability and expectations of significant individuals, such as spouse, friends, and caregivers; also includes larger social groups that are influential in establishing norms, role expectations, and social routines.
- **Cultural:** Customs, beliefs, activity patterns, behavior standards, and expectations accepted by the society of which the individual is a member. Includes political aspects, such as laws that affect access to resources and affirm personal rights; also includes opportunities for education, employment, and economic support.

Reprint permission granted for "Uniform Terminology, Third Edition" by the American Occupational Therapy Association, Inc., the original publisher and copyright holder. Portions of this document were reprinted for clarification of the terms listed on the previous grid as well as to explain the framework for practice.

SPECIFIC ISSUES WITH SPECIFIC POPULATIONS

Pediatrics (Birth to 21 Years of Age)

Access to Services

To obtain occupational therapy services for children, several avenues of funding are possible. Services can be funded by either private pay, private health insurance, hospital grants, private foundation or corporate grant monies, federal Medicaid or via federal public laws affecting accessibility, education, and assistive technology needs. Since most families with special needs children are financially unable to bear the long-term costs of therapy and equipment needs privately, supplemental funding is a necessity. The following are some of the sources or options available to access occupational therapy services:

> **Private Health Insurance:** With the advent of managed care and the establishment of health maintenance and preferred provider organizations, the insurance carriers often dictate the amount of services that they will cover via an internal case manager or insurance representative. Usually intervals of therapy services are funded on a short-term basis with a designated number of visits, requiring justification and rationalization by the external facility case manager and the therapist where services are being provided. If the guardian or parent has the standard health insurance option, therapy service coverage varies per each individual plan. It may be covered by the previously standard 80 to 90% reimbursement rate for fees for service or hourly rates with a standard deductible, or it may have to be appealed in order to be added to the plan as an addendum via the appeals process. However, in any of these scenarios, the fees are usually based on charges that are considered to be reasonable or usual and customary by the insurance carrier at sometimes discounted reimbursement rates for the service provider. Due to the lifetime cap usually placed on such policies, additional supplemental funding is often sought to meet the remainder of therapy needs over a longer period of the child's life.
>
> **Hospital Grants or Private Foundation and Corporate Funds:** Many major hospitals have funds set aside either via fund-raising drives that involve community efforts or via donations made by physicians, private individuals, employees, or major companies. In order to qualify for these funds or for those through any private organization that offers assistance for charitable causes, the child's parent(s) or guardian(s) must complete a hospital application form from the Social Services Department or the human resources division of an organization. They may then be referred to funds from United Way, the Kiwanis Club, the Lions Club, the Shriners, or other monies that have been set aside for specific patient populations in need of resources for medical assistance, which includes occupational therapy services since they are generally considered medically necessary to accomplish functional outcomes. (Please refer to the section Other Public and Private Sources of Funding for a reference on how to obtain information regarding these grants and organization assistance programs.)

Medicaid: As part of the assistance offered by the federal government to individuals requiring medical assistance via Title XIX or Medicaid, each state has mandatory services it must provide, as well as optional services it can provide on a discretionary basis to its beneficiaries. Occupational therapy is listed as an optional service (Dunn & McGourty, 1989) that may be provided by each state and that is funded at the same level of reimbursement as the mandatory services if offered (e.g., at 50 to 80% of the cost of the fee-for-service or procedure). Often the insurance carriers of the Medicaid funding will use the Medicare guidelines for reimbursement as a model. Therefore, as with Medicare and private insurance justifications, the occupational therapist or case manager for the service provider must seek prior approval for the services proposed to be provided based on an assessment of the child. The therapist or case manager must familiarize himself with the Medicaid terminology in order to receive adequate and continued reimbursement for the child's ongoing treatment. The occupational therapist or case manager must also be knowledgeable regarding the appeals process and verbiage that will help to justify the services and equipment being denied.

One of the more difficult areas of occupational therapy to receive funding via Medicaid is in the recommendation of adaptive equipment or assistive technology needs of a child. Since assistive technology is not listed as a separate service under Medicaid regulations, the funding of technology has been identified through eight primary sources, one of which is occupational therapy services (Angelo & Lane, 1997).

In justifying any services or equipment, the occupational therapist must keep in mind that the functional limitations must be directly associated with the child's disability, that the services and equipment are warranted due to functional outcomes or goals that she will assist the child in achieving, and that this will ultimately improve the child's abilities, independence, and overall quality of life.

There are several waiver programs available through Medicaid. For those children with disabilities whose parents' income level exceeds the poverty range required for standard Medicaid eligibility, there is the Medicaid-Deeming Waiver Program (formerly known as Katie Beckett Program), which provides financial assistance for skilled medical and rehabilitation services. For additional information on the federal programs available for funding via Medicaid or other government assistance, individuals can contact the state Department of Family and Children's Services (DFACS) or the local state Medicaid office for specific waiver program information.

Public Laws Affecting Education and Funding: Table 7.3 gives a comparison of requirements of disability statutes affecting public schools for the Americans with Disabilities Act (ADA, Title II), Section 504 of the Rehabilitation Act of 1973, and Individuals with Disabilities Education Act (IDEA), which took the place of Public Law 94-142 (The Education for All Handicapped Children Act) (Angelo & Lane, 1997). Specifics of these public laws will not be detailed; however, they impact those services that will improve accessibility for children to services, facilities, etc. (e.g., IDEA regarding

Table 7.3 A Comparison of Requirements of Disability Statutes Affecting Public Schools

		AMERICANS WITH DISABILITIES ACT (Title II)	SECTION 504 OF THE REHABILITATION ACT OF 1973	INDIVIDUALS WITH DISABILITIES EDUCATION ACT
Who Must Comply?	Scope of Coverage	All Programs and Activities of State and Local Governments.	All Programs and Activities of Recipients of Federal Financial Assistance.	State and Local Education Agencies Funded Under the Individuals with Disabilities Education Act.
Who is Protected?	Definition of Disability	Non-categorical—Covers Persons with a Physical or Mental Impairment that Substantially Limits a Major Life Activity, Persons Who Have a Record of an Impairment that Substantially Limits a Major Life Activity, and Persons Who are Regarded as Having Such an Impairment.*	Non-categorical—Covers Persons with a Physical or Mental Impairment that Substantially Limits a Major Life Activity, Persons Who Have a Record of an Impairment that Substantially Limits a Major Life Activity, and Persons Who are Regarded as Having Such an Impairment.*	Categorical—Covers Specified Disabilities Only.
Oversight	Complaints	U.S. Department of Education, Office for Civil Rights.	U.S. Department of Education, Office for Civil Rights.	State Education Agency.
Planning for Compliance	Administrative Requirements	Requires Self-Evaluation. Requires Transition Plan if Structural Modifications are Needed if 50 or More Employees.	Requires Self-Evaluation. Requires Transition Plan if Structural Modifications are Needed.	Requires Triennial State Plan Submitted to Office of Special Education Programs.
	Designation of Responsible Employee	Requires ADA Coordinator if 50 or More Employees.	Requires Section 504 Coordinator if 15 or More Employees.	Not Required.
	Grievance Procedures	Required if 50 or More Employees.	Required if 15 or More Employees.	Not Required.
	Public Notice	Requires On-Going Notice of Nondiscrimination on the Basis of Disability.	Requires On-Going Notice of Nondiscrimination on the Basis of Disability.	Requires Notice to Parents of Child Find Activities.
Employment	Reasonable Accommodation	Required for Qualified Applicants or Employees with Disabilities, Unless Entity can Demonstrate Undue Hardship.	Required for Qualified Applicants or Employees with Disabilities, Unless Entity can Demonstrate Undue Hardship.	Not Required.
	Written Job Description	Advisable—Not Specifically Required.	Advisable—Not Specifically Required.	Not Required.
Facilities	Program Accessibility	Requires Services, Programs, and Activities in Existing Facilities to be Readily Accessible When Viewed in Their Entirety.	Requires Services, Programs, and Activities in Existing Facilities to be Readily Accessible When Viewed in Their Entirety.	Not Required.
	Facilities Accessibility	Requires Compliance with ADAAG or UFAS in New Construction or Alterations Begun On or After 1/26/92.	Requires Compliance with ANSI (R1971) in New Construction or Alterations Begun On or After 6/3/77; Compliance with UFAS On or After 1/18/91.	Not Required.
	Maintenance of Accessible Features	Required.	Not Required.	Not Required.
Communication Requirements	Auxiliary Aids and Services	Required for Persons with Visual, Hearing, and Speech Disabilities if Necessary to Provide Effective Communication.	No Requirement Specified. Obligation Exists to Provide Effective Communication.	Required Only if Written into the Student's Individualized Education Program.

*A student who is covered under the 2nd or 3rd prongs of the definition of individuals with disabilities, and who does not also have a physical or mental impairment that substantially limits a major life activity, is not entitled either to special education and/or related services or to regular education with related services. It is also important to note that protection under Title II and Section 504 is specifically afforded to qualified individuals with disabilities. Not every person with a disability is qualified.

"Not Required" means that there is no requirement in the statute or regulations relating to this specific issue.

"No Requirement Specified" means that the requirement is not specifically mentioned in the statute or regulations, but that other provisions of the regulations indicate an obligation exists.

"Advisable—Not Specifically Required" means that although the statute and regulations do not specifically require a certain action, such actions will assist school districts in complying with other provisions of the ADA and Section 504.

page 1 of 2

General Nondiscrimination Requirements for Public Schools	AMERICANS WITH DISABILITIES ACT (Title II)	SECTION 504 OF THE REHABILITATION ACT OF 1973	INDIVIDUALS WITH DISABILITIES EDUCATION ACT
Child Find	Requires Location and Identification of All Qualified Children with Disabilities Who are Not Receiving a Free Appropriate Public Education (K-12).*	Requires Location and Identification of All Qualified Children with Disabilities in Jurisdiction Who are Not Receiving a Free Appropriate Public Education (K-12).	Requires Location and Identification of All Children with Disabilities in Jurisdiction Birth to Twenty-One.
Parental Notice	Required.*	Required.	Required.
Free Appropriate Public Education (FAPE)	Required.*	Required.	Required.
Education Plan	Requires that the Student's Program be Described with Sufficient Specificity to Demonstrate that the Student's Needs have been Assessed on an Individual Basis (An Individualized Education Program Document is Not Specifically Required).*	Requires that the Student's Program be Described with Sufficient Specificity to Demonstrate that the Student's Needs have been Assessed on an Individual Basis (An Individualized Education Program Document is Not Specifically Required).	An Individualized Education Program Document (IEP) is Required.
Procedural Safeguards	Required. (Compliance with Requirements in IDEA will be Considered Compliance Under the ADA).*	Required. (Compliance with Requirements in IDEA will be Considered Compliance Under Section 504).	Required.
Evaluation Procedures	Required.*	Required.	Similar and Additional Requirements to those in Section 504 and Title II.
Placement Team	Requires Group, Including Individuals Knowledgeable About the Child, Meaning of Evaluation Data, and Placement Options.*	Requires Group, Including Individuals Knowledgeable About the Child, Meaning of Evaluation Data, and Placement Options.	Requires Group, Including Individuals Knowledgeable About the Child, Meaning of Evaluation data, and Placement Options.
Educational Setting	Requires Most Integrated Setting Appropriate.*	Requires Most Integrated Setting Appropriate.	Requires Least Restrictive Environment.
Non Academic Programs	Requires Equal Opportunity to Participate.*	Requires Equal Opportunity to Participate.	Requires Equal Opportunity to Participate.
Pre-School (ages 3-5 years)	Requires Equal Opportunity to Participate.*	Requires Equal Opportunity to Participate.	Requires a Free Appropriate Public Education.
Adult Education Programs	Requires Equal Opportunity to Participate.*	Requires Equal Opportunity to Participate.	Not Required.
Reasonable Modification	Requires Reasonable Modification of Policies, Practices, and Procedures of All Public Entities.	No Requirement Specified. General Obligation Exists to Make Reasonable Modification of Recipients' Policies, Practices, and Procedures.	Not Required.
Confidentiality	No Requirement for Students, but School Districts Must Maintain Employees' Medical Files Separate from Employees' Personnel Files to Ensure Against Unwarranted Disclosure of the Employees' Disability.	No Requirement for Students, but School Districts Must Maintain Employees' Medical Files Separate from Employees' Personnel Files to Ensure Against Unwarranted Disclosure of the Employees' Disability.	Requires Protection of Special Education Student Records and Conformance with Family Educational Rights and Privacy Act (FERPA).

*These Requirements are described in Subpart D of the U.S. Department of Education's Section 504 Regulation.
The U.S. Department of Justice interprets the general non-discrimination provisions in Title II to cover discriminatory conduct that is specifically prohibited under Subpart D of the Section 504 Regulation.

Funded by the National Institute on Disability and Rehabilitation Research of the U.S. Department of Education
Adaptive Environments Center, ADA National Access for Public Schools Project   Schools Hotline 1-800-893-1225

(617) 695-1225 V/TDD   (617) 482-8099 Fax

January 1996

Page 2 of 2

Reprinted with permission from the Adaptive Environments Center, 374 Congress Street Suite 301, Boston, MA 02210 identification of free and appropriate public education for children with disabilities).

Section 504 and the ADA require that those students with disabilities who do not qualify for special education services have access to all activities and programs offered within their schools in grades K through 12. For those students who qualify for special education services, the IDEA mandates that these children receive "free and appropriate public education" (Angelo & Lane, 1997) through the establishment of an Individualized Education Plan (IEP) as part of due process within the public school system for children up to age 21. Since occupational therapy is listed as a related service under the IDEA, a child must first qualify for special education in order to receive occupational therapy funded by the provisions of the IDEA. The states' educational agencies set the specific guidelines for what qualifies children for special education services of varying categories (e.g., orthopedically impaired vs. other health impaired, speech impaired, specific learning disability, autistic or intellectually disabled — mildly, moderately, severely, or profoundly). Therefore, reference should be made to the *Special Education Handbook*, which each state should have printed for information on qualification guidelines to have a child receive special education, and possible related therapy and services.

Special education funds are limited to students who are eligible for special education and related services determined by an IEP. For students who are not eligible for special education services, and in the event that occupational therapy services are required as an issue of access to education, determination of the extent of school responsibility is made under the provision of Section 504 through a 504 plan. However, it is important to note that unlike the provisions for implementation of the IDEA, there is no federal funding of services provided as a result of Section 504 procedures.

Other Public and Private Sources of Funding: In addition to the previously referenced sources of coverage for occupational therapy services and assistive technology, the Department of Human Resources within individual states may have reference materials regarding private and public sources of funding for persons with disabilities. The state of Georgia, for instance, based on the Technology-Related Assistance for Individuals with Disabilities Act of 1988 or Tech Act (Public Law 103-213, as amended in 1994), funded a project in 1991 via a federal grant through RESNA (Rehabilitation Engineering and Assistive Technology Society of North America) and NIDRR (National Institute on Disability and Rehabilitation Research) (Angelo & Lane, 1997). This project became known as Tools for Life, Georgia's Assistive Technology Program, a service of the Department of Labor, rehabilitation services. The manual produced by this program describes not only funding for therapy services and assistive technology, but also funding information in general over a wide area of coverage needs. Listed are 28 public and 60 private sources of funding for persons with disabilities of all ages. To obtain a copy of the manual, entitled *Dollars and Sense: A Guide to Solving the Funding Puzzle and Getting Assistive Technology in Georgia* (Weeks et al., 1997), contact:

Georgia Department of Labor, Office of Vocational Rehabilitation
"Tools for Life" Program
2 Peachtree St., 35th Floor
Atlanta, GA 30303
(800) 497-8665 or (404) 657-3084
TDD: (404) 657-3085
Fax: 404-657-3086

Common Measures of Evaluation

Children are evaluated to determine if occupational therapy is needed to meet developmental milestones or functional goals being hindered by their disability. These assessments can be performed from clinical observations and testing materials that have been normed with standardized information for the child's specific age and gender. Table 7.4 is a partial list of evaluation and screening tools that have been used by occupational therapists in a variety of pediatric settings for assessing the treatment needs of children of varying ages.

Long-Term Considerations

When an occupational therapist evaluates a child for a life care plan, his or her professional assessment should consider not only the immediate needs within the settings in which the child currently participates, but also those needs that the child may have later in life. This is determined from knowledge of the child's diagnosis and clinical predictors of cognition, longevity or expected life span, and presenting capabilities, which are determined as potentially realistic, given the presenting limitations. For example, a 15-year-old child has had an acquired brain injury of the left hemisphere since the age of 7 years due to blunt trauma from a beating. He has the presenting problems of right-sided hemiplegia or paralysis with functional use of his right hand to assist the now dominant left hand and is functionally ambulatory with an ankle-foot orthosis (AFO). He exhibits distractibility with limited sustained attention, problems with visual convergence or merging visual focus on near objects, and a cognitive level of a mildly intellectually impaired person. His abilities include performing his basic self-care skills independently with minimal assistance for setup of the activities (e.g., assistance to organize clothes in drawers for easy access and selection by color, item type, etc.). He is able to perform simple job tasks in a structured setting, can compute simple problems and math skills with use of a calculator, and can make simple change. He has the potential to live in a supported living setting given these skills. Considerations should be made as to whether he has the potential to be a safe and independent driver within familiar, local routes vs. extended distances, and whether, in consultation with a vocational counselor, he will be able to support himself via independent employment or supported employment options. Given that he probably has a normal life span expectancy, these are concerns that the occupational therapist needs to evaluate and assess with input from the parents, physician, rehabilitation team, educators, and school vocational placement counselors, among others, in order to fully assess his lifetime maximum functional potential.

Table 7.4   Partial Listing of Occupational Therapy Pediatric Screen Tools

- Activities of Daily Living Skills Inventory
- Battelle Developmental Inventory
- Bayley Scales of Infant Development-2nd Edition
- Beery Developmental Test of Visual–Motor Integration (VMI)-Revised
- BRIGANCE Diagnostic Inventory of Early Development
- Bruininks–Oseretsky Test of Motor Skills
- Carolina Curriculum for Infants and Toddlers with Special Needs
- Clinical Observations-Ayres'
- De Gangi–Berk Test of Sensory Integration
- Denver Developmental Screening Test
- Detroit Tests of Learning Aptitude
- Developmental Programming of Infants and Young Children
- Developmental Test of Visual Perception, 2nd Edition
- Erhardt Hand Development Prehension Test
- Evaluation Tool of Children's Handwriting (ETCH)
- Fiorentino Reflex Testing
- First STEP Screening for Evaluating Preschoolers
- Functional muscle strength testing
- Grip and pinch strength measurements
- Hawaii Early Learning Profile (HELP)
- Hooper Visual Organization Test
- Jebsen Hand Function Test for Children
- Milano Comparetti Reflex Testing
- Miller Assessment of Preschoolers (MAP)
- Motor-Free Visual Perception Test-Revised
- Movement Assessment of Infants
- Neonatal Behavioral Assessment Scale (Brazelton)
- Peabody Developmental Motor Scales
- Pediatric Evaluation of Disability Inventory (PEDI)
- Purdue Pegboard
- Quality of Movement Checklist
- Range of Motion Measurements
- Sensory Integration and Praxis Tests (SIPT)
- Symbol Digit Modalities Test
- Test of Auditory Perceptual Skills (TAPS)-Revised
- Test of Sensory Function in Infants
- Test of Visual Motor Integration
- Test of Visual Motor Skills (TVMS)-Revised
- Test of Visual Perceptual Skills (TVPS)-Upper and Lower Levels-Revised
- Visual Skills Appraisal
- Wide Range Achievement Test-3 (WRAT-3)
- Wilbarger Sensorimotor History

Adults (21 Years and Older)

Transportation — Driving vs. Dependence

The ability to transport oneself independently is an issue of great consideration in an individual's access to gainful employment and community resources; therefore, much emphasis is placed on assessing a person's ability to drive with the limitations imposed by a disability. An occupational therapist who has received specialized education and training within the area of driving rehabilitation should be able to ascertain whether a person with a disability can independently and *safely* operate a car or van via extensive predriving clinical and road performance testing.

An occupational therapist can be certified to perform driving assessments and training via two channels. A CDI (certified driving instructor) certificate, the same test taken by commercial driving school instructors, can be acquired after passing a test given by the state Department of Motor Vehicles after establishing the facility as a driving school. In order to become certified as a certified driver rehabilitation specialist (CDRS), the occupational therapist must pass a certification examination administered by an independent testing agency contracted by the Association for Driver Rehabilitation Specialists (ADED, 2003). This certification examination encompasses a wide knowledge base of varying disabilities from orthopedic or spinal cord considerations to more abstract and less obvious problems of persons with mild to moderate acquired brain injuries and other neurological disorders. Before a determination of the potential to drive can be made, many factors must be assessed. These include, but are not limited to, the following:

- **Medical History/Medications:** An accurate medical history with a definitive diagnosis and list of current medications is imperative to review before assessing further predriving skills. Seizure status, medical precautions with regard to the diagnosis or presenting problems, psychiatric complications, and the stability of the medication routines are all critical factors that need to be addressed to accurately determine potential for driving.
- **Visual/Ocular Motor Skills:** Acuity at near and far distances, peripheral fields, tracking, convergence, quick localization, saccades, stereopsis or depth perception, desensitization to color, etc.
- **Visual Perceptual Skills:** Color perception, figure ground discrimination, spatial relations, form constancy, visual closure, visual memory, etc.
- **Physical/Motor Skills:** Range of motion and strength in all available extremities; sensation for light touch, joint proprioception and kinesthetic awareness, temperature discrimination and any paresthesias or abnormal sensations; eye–hand and eye–foot reaction times bilaterally; gross and fine motor coordination, muscle tone, and the limitations imposed by weakness or spasticity; static and dynamic sitting balance; transfer skills; activity tolerance and endurance with effects of fatigue assessed; functional reach patterns; etc.
- **Cognitive/Perceptual Skills:** Anticipatory perception is critical to being able to formulate and execute defensive maneuvers, along with the judgment and perception of time distance in order to carry out the actions needed to avoid a collision. Processing speed is an integral factor in all of the above skills, as is the ability to compensate for reduced processing via other cognitive strategies (e.g., automatically allowing extra space to provide more time for reaction planning). Problem-solving or reasoning skills based on situational cues, such as determining potential vs. actual road hazards and judgment of safety conditions, are critical skills needed to safely drive. This should be tested through controlled static and dynamic

methods prior to exposing the person with a disability to a potentially risky road situation.

Once the history and skill areas have been evaluated, the information should be reviewed to determine if the person has met criteria considered to be indicators of safe, functional performance. Criteria are usually established by the facility or evaluator providing the service and vary according to the norms chosen on selected tests or by the preference of the evaluator to road test all individuals with disabilities vs. borderline to good candidates for safe performance. Prior to road testing, adaptive equipment or assistive technology may be prescribed by the occupational therapist with the vehicle equipment to be used matching the recommended setup as closely as possible. Based on the predriving assessment, the type of vehicle to be used and the specific equipment needs are determined. Table 7.5 is a tool developed to assist the occupational therapist and case manager in determining whether a car or van is most likely to be needed to meet the client and his or her family's needs.

Should the person with the disability pass the road test, then a final assessment and determination is made of the adaptive equipment and driving restrictions that will be needed for safe and independent operation of the selected vehicle. The greatest cost is calculated to be for vehicular modifications, especially if the person has a disability that requires driving a van with high-tech needs (e.g., a person with a triple amputation or high-level quadriplegia). Table 7.6 and Table 7.7 outline the possible adaptive equipment needs in a car for a client as a driver or for a van with the person with the disability driving or riding as a passenger. In Table 7.6 some possible presenting problems and diagnoses are listed along the left-hand column. The headers list the major types of assistive technology that are currently available for car modification. Since the equipment is much more extensive for van modifications, Table 7.7 lists some of the possible presenting problems more typical for van drivers in the heading across the top of the pages, while the current available basic technologies for vans are itemized vertically. In both tables equipment needs can be determined basically by matching the presenting problems with the types of equipment checked across the tables for those specific problems. Where there is a possible vs. probable need, the final decision on this equipment choice must be made with the clinical and road assessments completed to get an accurate picture of the client's needs. In preparing a life care plan where there may be projected or hypothetical needs in the future life span of the individual with a disability, the occupational therapist would want to give the life care planner a complete equipment list, including possible or optional items. In other words, if a client driving from a wheelchair has a *possible need* for a headrest with a touch pad for primary controls, this should be part of the itemized and projected costs for this client. This is especially applicable if he or she is a child at the time the life care plan is being developed and has been assessed as having potential to be a driver in the future.

Liability or Responsibility

A point of great concern is when a person with a disability has a history of multiple accidents prior to the driving assessment or when the person does not

Table 7.5 Van vs. Automobile Selection

**OCCUPATIONAL THERAPY
ADAPTIVE DRIVER REHABILITATION
VEHICLE SELECTION ASSESSMENT**

Patient: _____ Age: _____ Sex: M F   Status: S M W D

Diagnosis: _____ Onset: _____

Referred By: _____ Phone: (___) _____ Referral Date: __/__/__

Date of Evaluation: __/__/__ Evaluator: _____, ___OTR/L ___CDRS

Licensure Status: ___Current ___Temporary Permit ___Expired ___Pending Other: _____

Driving Status: ___Pending Evaluation ___Cleared to Drive ___Unsafe/Inappropriate to Drive

___Status Uncertain Other: _____

QUESTIONNAIRE	YES	NO
1. Is the client wheelchair dependent for long distance/endurance mobility (traveling distances for work, school campus, shopping, etc.)?		
2. Is the client unable to independently transfer into or out of a car without fatigue or shortness of breath?		
3. If wheelchair dependent and able to transfer self into a car, is the client unable to maneuver self and wheelchair to fold and store the wheelchair behind the front seat?	(x2)	(x2)
4. Does the client live alone or is responsible for independent mobility/transportation needs?		
5. Do more than two passengers need to ride with the client for outings or other activities of daily living (shopping, laundromat, restaurant dining, etc.)?		
6. Is the client's illness or disability of a progressive nature where a wheelchair would be possibly needed during the next eight to ten years?	(x2)	(x2)
7. If ill, would the client possibly need to be transferred via wheelchair to a nearby physician and/or hospital? (Where the family member/friend would not be able to perform a stand/pivot or sliding board transfer with the client?)	(x2)	(x2)
8. Will the client's height, weight, size and/or disability make it physically straining over a short and/or long term to assist with transfers, possibly causing a resultant secondary injury to another individual?		
9. Will the client need to efficiently and expediently enter or exit his/her vehicle often during the course of his/her daily routines (work, school, etc.)?		
10. Is the client comfortable driving a vehicle larger than a standard car?		
RESPONSE TOTALS: If the number in this column is GREATER, then a VAN would be the vehicle of preference .... →		
If the number in THIS column is GREATER, then an AUTOMOBILE would be the vehicle of preference .... →		

ISM: 1/97

Table 7.6 Adaptive Car Equipment — Client as Driver

Legend: X = Probable Need   P = Possible Need   *If unable to adjust seating with 6-way power seat.

Diagnosis/Problems	Door Handle Opener	Power Steering	Adaptive Side/Pana Mirrors	Left Sided Hand Controls	Right Sided Hand Controls	Adaptive Steering Device	Parking Brake Extension	Left Foot Gas Pedal	Floor Pedal Extensions	Turn Signal Adaptor	Gear Shift Extension	Car Topper	Seat Harness	*Seat Cushion
1. Hemianopsia, reduced peripheral vision and/or neck arom			X											
2. Paraplegia/ paraparesis and greater left U.E. strength		X		X		X (Left)	X					P	P	P
3. Paraparesis and greater right U.E. strength		X			X	X (Left)	X				X	P	P	P
4. Right hemiplegia/ paresis		X	P			X (Right)		X						P
5. Left hemiplegia/ paresis		X	P			X (Left)				X				P
6. Dwarfish (short stature/limbs)	P	X	P			P	X		X					
7. Arthritis and reduced joint arm (JRA, etc.)	X	X	P			P	P		P					P
8. Right L.E. amputee								X						P
9. Left L.E. amputee							X							P
10. Bilater L.E. amputee, left U.E. greater strength		X		X		X (Right)	X						P	
11. Bilater L.E. amputee, right U.E. greater strength		X			X	X (Left)	X				X		P	
12. Right U.E. amputee		X				X (Left)				P	X			
13. Left U.E. amputee		X			X	X (Right)				X				
14. Triple amputee; both L.E. and right U.E. w/prosthesis and able to transfer; unable to store wheelchair		X	P	X		X (Right)	X			P	X	P		P
15. Triple amputee: both L.E. and left U.E. w/prosthesis and able to transfer; unable to store wheelchair		X	P		X	X (Left)	X			X				
16. Upper extremity weakness — able to transfer, but not store wheelchair	P	X				P						X		

ISM: 1/97

Table 7.7 Adaptive Van Equipment

Legend: X = Probable Need   P = Possible Need   O = Option/Choice   * = Bilateral U.E. Amputee   ** = R or L U.E. Amputee

Adaptive Equipment/Assistive Technology	Wheelchair Transfer to Driver's Seat	Client to Drive from Wheelchair	Wheelchair Driver with U.E. Weakness	W/C Driver with Limited U.E. Arom	Decreased Trunk/Neck Control	Transport Family in Rear of Van	Client Riding as a Passenger in W/C in Van
1. Electric door openers:	X	X	X	X	X	X	
A. Key activated toggle	X	P	P			X	
B. Magnetic keyless	O	O	O	O	O		
C. Electronic remote control	O	O	O	O	O		
2. Wheelchair lifts and controls:							
A. Fully automatic	X	X	X	X	X	X	O
B. Semi-automatic							X
C. Folding platform						X	O
D. Rotary platform	O	O	O	O	O	O	O
3. Door entry: full size van	O	O	O	O	O	O	X
A. Raised Roof and door	P	X	P	P	X	O	P
B. Lowered Floor in center	P	X	X	X	X	O	P
C. Lowered floor driver's side		X	X	X	X	O	
D. Entry/courtesy lighting	X	X	X	X	X	X	X
4. Door entry: Mini Van Chrysler/Ford lowered floor (size/space permitting)							
A. Fully auto. ramp and doors	X	X	X	X	X	X	
B. Manual system for opening							X
5. Driver position:							
A. Removable driver's seat	X	X	X	X	X	P	
B. Auto. wheelchair tiedown	X	X	X	X	X	X	O
C. 3 Point shoulder/lap belt	X	X	X	X	X	X	
D. Power seat base	X					X	
E. Power mirrors	X	X	X	X	X	X	
F. Head rest w/tough pad for primary controls	P	P	X	X	X	O	

Table 7.7 (Continued)   Adaptive Van Equipment

Legend: X = Probable Need   P = Possible Need   O = Option/Choice   * = Bilateral U.E. Amputee   ** = R or L U.E. Amputee

Adaptive Equipment/Assistive Technology	Wheelchair Transfer to Driver's Seat	Client to Drive from Wheelchair	Wheelchair Driver with U.E. Weakness	W/C Driver with Limited U.E. Arom	Decreased Trunk/Neck Control	Transport Family in Rear of Van	Client Riding as a Passenger in W/C in Van
6. Steering system:							
A. Standard power steering	P	P				P	
B. Low or reduced effort			X	X		X	
C. Zero effort steering controls			P	P	X	O	
D. Tilt wheel on column	X	X	X	X	X	X	
E. Horizontal steering	P	P	P	P	P	P	
F. Steering column extension	P	P	P	X	X	O	
G. Standard wheel size	X	P	P		P	O	
H. REDUCED WHEEL SIZE		P	P	X	P	O	
I. Joystick (4-way) control	P	P	P (if severe)	P (if severe)	P	P	
7. Steering devices:							
A. Spinner knob	X	X	X	X	X	X	
B. Tri-pin or v-grip	P	P	P	P	P	O	
C. Palmar clip		P	P	P		O	
D. Amputee ring**		P	P	P		O	
E. Steering disc (floor)*							
8. Brake and acceleration system:							
A. Standard power brakes	X	P			P	P	
B. Reduced effort brakes		P	P	P		P	
C. Mechanical hand controls	X	P	P	P	P	P	P
D. Electronic gas/brake (EGB)		P	P	P		P	
E. Parking brake extension	X	P				P	
F. Power parking brake	O	P	X	P	X	O	

9. Accessory controls:							
A. Standard primary and secondary controls	P						X
B. Electronic/touch pad for secondary controls		P	P	P	P	P	
C. Modified primary controls: (turn signals, horn and dimmer switch, wipers, cruise control set)	P		P	P	P	O	
D. Modified secondary controls: (windows and locks, headlights, windshield washers, heat/AC, cruise control On)	P		P	X (if severe)	X (if severe)	O	
10. Miscellaneous:							
A. Passenger wheelchair tiedown system	P		P	P	P	P	X
B. Unoccupied wheelchair transport lock	X						
C. Sliding board transfers	X						
D. Chest restraint	P		P	P	P		P
E. Emergency communications device (cellular phone or CB radio)	X		X	X	X	X	X
F. Dual (back-up) battery system	X		X	X	X	X	
G. Rear heat/AC systems	X		X	X	X	X	X

ISM: 1/97

demonstrate the ability to compensate for the limitations imposed by his or her disability and is considered to be unsafe to operate a motorized vehicle independently. This could occur during the predriving evaluation process, on completion of the road test, or after the person has been cleared to drive because of seizures or other changes in his or her physiological or emotional status. For liability purposes and as a matter of professional responsibility, any service provider who has concerns regarding a disabled individual's abilities to drive should make the treating team aware of his or her concerns and should document this concern. Efforts should then be made to inform the person with the disability and his or her family of these concerns. Whether the physician, occupational therapist, case manager, or other health and rehabilitative care professional reports the person with the disability is a decision that is usually made according to the provider's facility procedures or to the degree of risk that the reporting person agrees to assume regarding this person's and the public's safety.

An occupational therapist performing a driving evaluation should routinely assess past driving history and performance as part of the intake information. The person being evaluated should be aware that the state Department of Motor Vehicles could be contacted to verify any prior record of accidents or restrictions as part of the driving assessment. If this person is found to be unsafe to begin or continue to drive independently or is recommended to drive under restricted conditions (e.g., low-volume traffic areas on familiar routes during daytime and good weather conditions), the occupational therapist usually sends a copy of the report to the state Department of Motor Vehicles (DMV), depending on the philosophy of the provider's facility and the regulations for that particular state regarding disabilities and driving status. There are states that require mandatory reporting of a person who sustains a disabling injury or illness by a physician or other medical personnel. However, other states do not require a person with a disability to be reported, and the assumption is made that anyone can report anyone who feels a citizen is unsafe to drive (e.g., because of either alcoholic or drug intake, a disability affecting physical abilities, or a psychiatric condition).

When an occupational therapist, case manager, psychologist, physician, or other service provider makes a report to recommend that a person with a disability be restricted from driving in some manner, then the individual's case is referred to the Medical Advisory Board of that state's Department of Motor Vehicles (DMV) or Public Safety. The Medical Advisory Board notifies the person with the disability of a licensure suspension pending review and is then charged with the task of obtaining additional medical information to make the determination whether to reinstate licensure with or without recommended restrictions. Though the reporting person's information is regarded as confidential and can be requested to be anonymous, the person who was reported can have the DMV subpoenaed to provide the name of the person filing the charges through an attorney or the proper legal procedures. Therefore, it is in the best interest of the occupational therapist or service provider making the report to notify the person with the disability of his or her intent to report him or her to the DMV. He or she should also know that this referral is based on the information obtained from clinical data or road testing during the driving evaluation, or from the family and other service providers of incidents that have occurred since the person was cleared to drive and that warrant concern regarding the individual's or the public's safety.

To find out whether the state in which a client resides and in which he or she plans to drive has mandatory reporting requirements, contact the state's Department of Motor Vehicles or Department of Public Safety. To locate an occupational therapist or driver educator who has been certified to assess a client's potential to begin or return to safe and independent driving, contact:

The Association for Driver Rehabilitation Specialists
711 S. Vienna St.
Ruston, LA 71270
(800) 290-2344
http://www.driver-ed.org/

HOME HEALTH CARE

With the evolution of managed care and more controlled use of services by Medicare and private insurance carriers in the continuum of care, home health occupational therapy and rehabilitation services in general are being ordered more often by physicians with internal case managers' input for provision of treatment after the acute care phase of a disability or injury. Home health services are often implemented when the patient or person after an injury or disability will require a greater period of time to prepare for outpatient rehabilitation than is warranted in the specific policy of the insurance carrier or if there are no further pressing medical problems that would require continued hospitalization under Medicare guidelines. The home health recipient must be determined to be homebound, unable to transport himself or herself by either driving, transferring independently into the passenger side of a vehicle, or independently calling and arranging for a taxi or transportation service of some type. The reasons that determine the person to be homebound must be of a medical or functional nature (e.g., wheelchair dependence with poor transfer and balance skills, oxygen dependency, poor endurance, bed mobility dependence, generalized weakness, visual or other sensory impairments, etc.) that would impede independent mobility.

For occupational therapy and other rehabilitation services to be covered by Medicare, services must be considered medically necessary. A reasonable length of time and frequency of treatment sessions must be determined based on the number of limiting factors and presenting problems (e.g., bathroom doorways are too narrow for a wheelchair and there are no financial or community resources to widen door entries; sponge bathing is not feasible on a permanent basis since there is a good prognosis for return to independent ambulation with a walker or other aid).

Some of the areas that occupational therapists typically evaluate in assessing the total needs of a home health patient include, but are not limited to, the following:

■ **Orientation/Cognition:** Awareness of person, place, date, and event or situation; short- and long-term memory; judgment regarding personal safety; affect; presence or absence of mental confusion; following visual vs. verbal directions; ability to recall and repeat immediate information and retention over a period of time, along with the ability to communicate functionally to indicate needs.

■ **Psychosocial Status:** Emotional state during evaluation; ability to express feelings appropriately; social outlets or family and community resources; presence or absence of social isolation; insight into disability; degree of motivation or inner drive toward recovery and achievement of functional independence. Resources for community services following discharge may be recommended to assist with problems of chronic depression, emotional lability, etc. (e.g., adult day care, etc.).

■ **Physical Status:** Vital signs at the time of assessment and treatment sessions, such as blood pressure and pulse (especially with any secondary problem of hypertension, when regular nursing visits are not mandated by orders, or when any history of cardiovascular or cardiac conditions exists); range of motion or functional joint mobility for upper extremities specifically, and overall for the lower extremities as they affect self-care tasks; upper extremity strength, including hand grip and pinch measures; muscle tone, specifically for the presence or absence of spasticity and synergy patterns of arm use; active movements and overall coordination for gross and fine motor skills; hand dominance and sensation or sensory deficits, including any paresthesias, ocular motor and visual skills; sitting and standing balance and activity work tolerance and endurance.

■ **Perceptual Testing:** Motor-free visual perceptual skills; left–right discrimination abilities; body image or concept and self-esteem; the presence or absence of unilateral neglect; other skills areas that could hinder self-care tasks.

■ **Functional Abilities:** Activities of daily living skills for basic self-care (dressing, feeding, bathing, hair care, oral hygiene, shaving/makeup, transfers, bed mobility, general ambulation status), as well as for higher self-care tasks such as homemaking (cooking, washing dishes, cleaning, laundry, bed making), reading, telling time, making change and money management, telephone skills, and potential to return to prior level of independent mobility or transportation before illness or injury.

■ **Orthotics/Prosthetics:** Any splints, slings, anterior foot orthoses, or other ambulation aid, prosthetic limb, or other appliance that was recommended and provided prior to return home; those positioning and facilitative appliances or supplies that should be recommended based on the initial home health visit for greater functional abilities and the prevention of deformity over a long period of time.

■ **Assistive Devices and Adaptive Equipment Needs:** Any items that were provided or recommended and for which arrangements were made for delivery prior to discharge from the hospital (safety belt, bedside commode, hospital bed, wheelchair, rolling walker, hemi-walker, quad cane, reacher, dressing stick, long-handled shoehorn, bath sponge, etc.); those items that will be needed to enable full or prior functional independence in the home (handheld shower spray, tub transfer bench, leg lift and transfer loop, nonskid bath and floor mats, etc.).

■ **Architectural Barriers:** If wheelchair or walker dependent, especially on a long-term basis, measurement of inside doorways into the bathroom and access to other areas of the home is critical with recommendations for feasible or reasonable modifications; access to resources to make modifications, especially for ramp ways or railings that may be needed to overcome exterior and interior steps; assessment of the exterior walkways for even surfaces, especially if broken concrete or asphalt, gravel, grass, or dirt and significant surface irregularities are present.

Another key factor is determining the *prognosis* for achieving maximum functional potential in order to attain the outcomes or goals mutually developed by the therapist and the patient. Generally these goals are determined as close as possible to the functional levels exhibited prior to the injury or illness. However, it appears that the most important or key determinant of coverage is the ability to show continual and steady progress in order to further justify the utilization of skilled occupational therapy services or those services that cannot be carried out by a home health aide or other paraprofessional. Without the need for skilled intervention by a professional to carry out the activities directed to meet functional goals and the evidence of graded and steady progress, Medicare will scrutinize the therapy charges and often deny coverage. The billing facility can appeal these rulings through the established appeals process. If the appeal is denied, then a hearing can be requested and scheduled for an independent review of the Medicare carrier's decision to deny coverage. Chances for repeal of denials vary, but often have been favorable when terminology and wording have been simplified into less "rehab verbiage" and more functional, understandable language in order to clarify the procedures, intent of treatment, and functional outcomes.

Aging and Geriatric Long-Term Care

If after receiving home health occupational therapy and other nursing or rehabilitative services in the home, the person with a disability is unable to live independently or reach a level of function appropriate for outpatient care, then supported living options need to be explored. There is funding assistance available through Medicaid known as the Medicaid Independent Care Waiver Program that offers financial resources for skilled nursing and rehabilitation services, as well as personal attendant care, with the goal of maintaining a person with a disability in the community rather than in a nursing home. Should an individual not be able to obtain placement in this program, then the alternatives would be to look at placement in a state-funded or private nursing home or a personal care home, or to acquire attendant care in the patient's home at the expense of the family or other private resources. There are also retirement communities that offer several levels of care, from monitoring or supervisory visits to skilled inpatient nursing services; however, these are usually very expensive and are paid for from private resources. At this level of independence, occupational therapy is usually available by private payment. However, if the person develops a medical condition that requires admission into the skilled nursing unit of that community or into a hospital that would make him or her eligible for Medicare coverage under Part A, he or she could then be eligible to receive occupational therapy and other skilled services under Medicare Part B. These services could be provided either in the skilled nursing facility or in the home, as long as the services were deemed medically necessary and continued progress was shown toward achieving functional outcomes.

OCCUPATIONAL THERAPY IN LIFE CARE PLANNING

The Role of the Occupational Therapist as a Team Member

Unless the occupational therapist is the author of the life care plan, the role of the occupational therapist is to assist the life care planner in determining the activities of daily living, the work and play or leisure needs of a person with a disability throughout life expectancy. The areas of need would be assessed based on the framework for evaluation and treatment within the profession of occupational therapy outlined previously. This would include any assessment or intervention services, and assistive technology or adaptive equipment that would be needed to maintain the quality of life, as well the level of maximum functional independence. Once the global needs of the individual are determined, the occupational therapist could then assist in the cost determination for those services and equipment identified. Consideration must also be given to the duration expectancy of each item of equipment recommended (e.g., replacement of a tub transfer bench every 6 to 8 years, depending on weight and other factors). This information would then be used to determine the overall cost of the life care plan for the individual with the disability with the occupational therapy component as one piece in the total life puzzle for that person.

Case Example: Evaluation and Identification of Concerns Requiring Occupational Therapy

Mr. A. is a 6-foot-1-inch-tall, 50-year-old, married, black male weighing 220 pounds who sustained an on-the-job injury when he fell off a warehouse loading dock, causing primary trauma to his cervical or neck area. He experienced severe neck pain, plus headaches and muscle spasms of his neck, shoulders, and back. He ultimately underwent two cervical fusions after unsuccessful discectomies within a period of 18 to 20 months after his original injury. Mr. A. reported no history of hypertension or arthritis until after this work injury occurred. Radiologic studies verified the evidence of degenerative joint changes, especially in his cervical and shoulder regions (C3–T1 vertebral discs). He also complained of paresthesias in both his upper extremities with tingling, numbness, and cold sensations, greater toward his hands. Mr. A. lives with his wife and two children, both dependent minors. His wife works full-time during the day. Since he has been considered as having a catastrophic injury and unable to return to gainful employment due to the continued spasms, need for a permanent cervical collar, and other sensorimotor and functional limitations, he spends the day alone at home. He received 6 months of physical therapy on an outpatient basis; however, no home health services or occupational therapy was reportedly received by the client during his rehabilitation period.

An occupational therapy consult was recommended in order to provide information to complete a life care plan by an independent rehabilitation counselor. The occupational therapist was requested to assess Mr. A.'s activities of daily living skills, home environment safety issues, and status regarding safe and independent driving since he was driving to appointments with questionable safety, as reported by his case manager. A home visit was scheduled in order to assess Mr. A.'s needs with the following information obtained:

- **Medications:** At the time of the interview, Mr. A. was taking six different types of medication for pain and spasms, edema, hypertension, and arthritis. He was unable to recall the names, frequency, or dosages for five of six prescriptions, and his blood pressure during the initial visit was 172/132, suggesting he was not taking them as scheduled. Side effects he reported as a result of these medications included dizziness, sleepiness, fatigue, and generalized weakness. He also reported a tendency to drop items if held in his hands for longer than a few seconds at or above shoulder level.

- **Orientation/Cognition/Perception:** Mr. A. reported difficulty with sustained and focused attention, tending to shift focus rather quickly, and consequently, he had problems with short-term memory and retention of information. He was oriented to the date and day by use of compensatory aids such as a calendar, and was cognizant of the occupational therapist's profession and purpose for the home visit. No problems were noted with ocular pursuits, left–right discrimination, or general visual perceptual abilities. Processing speed was, however, noted to be delayed for visual information, especially when compensatory trunk or torso motions were needed to compensate for an inability to rotate his neck due to the cervical collar. Mentation was found to be functional for general money management skills and telling time; however, Mr. A. had difficulty following verbal and visual directions for more than two steps in a sequence, and reported difficulty with reading and phone use due to fatigue and spasms in his arms from elevating reading materials or the telephone for greater than 30 seconds at a time. Judgment regarding safety was assessed as questionable due to his continuing to drive long distances when unable to fully scan visually and rotate his trunk.

- **Physical Status:** On evaluation of active range of motion, muscle tone, and upper extremity strength, Mr. A. was found to have limitations in his scapular and shoulder areas. This was estimated to be partially due to the need to keep the cervical collar in position at all times to prevent continuous and uncontrolled spasms posteriorly or toward the back of his neck into hyperextension. Shoulder motions, though limited, were found to be within functional limits, except for external rotation of his upper arms bilaterally, preventing him from reaching the back of his neck and top of his head without significant stress to his neck and back areas. No limitations were found for elbow, forearm, and hand motions; however, hand grip and pinch strength were very poor for a man of his large stature and above-average height (e.g., 18 pounds left hand grip with 9 pounds of lateral pinch, and 14 pounds for the dominant right hand grip with 6.5 pounds for lateral pinch).

- Muscle tone at rest was palpated and found to be normal when no active movement was initiated; however, with any degree of assisted or independent motion, severe tremors and fasciculations of the upper arm and forearm muscles were noted in each limb. Muscle tone was normal for the lower extremities, as were range of motion and strength, except for the quadriceps and hamstrings muscle groups, with difficulty standing from a stooping or semi-squatting position observed.

■ Bilateral gross and fine motor coordination was observed to be slow and rather labored for rapid and alternating motions of the forearms, wrists, and fingers. Isolated finger movements were very slow, requiring visual compensation to complete. Ocular motor skills were found to be within normal limits for range of motion and speed of visual skills; however, Mr. A.'s hand skills moved at a much slower rate than did his eyes, making eye–hand skills delayed. This translated to his writing skills, being very crowded and illegible with irregular flow, hastening rather quickly when a tremor was building in his forearm musculature. With printing and number writing, his legibility improved due to the ability to make shorter, more controlled strokes, allowing small rest breaks for the hand-to-forearm motions.

■ Sensation was found to be impaired for stereognosis or discrimination of objects by touch only and joint awareness or position sense for the wrists and hands, but intact for sharp/dull discrimination, light touch, and hot/cold perception for the rest of the upper and lower extremities.

■ **Activities of Daily Living/Functional Status:** The following areas of self-care were assessed:

Dressing Skills — Independently performed using Taylor sitting for socks, shoes, and shoe fasteners.

Feeding Skills — Independent for hand-to-mouth motions; however, required assistance to cut meat, unless very tender; to open containers if not easily removable; and to use mug, unless lightweight and plastic with a handle to secure grip for drinking and avoid dropping or spillage.

Hair Care — Independent with compensatory positioning using trunk flexion to reach top of head with lateral trunk flexion to comb sides.

Oral Hygiene — Independent with electric toothbrush with minimal loosening of collar to allow rinsing.

Shaving — Independent with modified positioning. By leaning against the bathroom wall to block hyperextension, Mr. A. could release the front half of the collar enough to shave by his sense of feel. Since there are sensory deficits in his wrists and hands, this seemed rather risky, especially without use of the wall mirror that was on the wall perpendicular to the head-supporting wall.

Toilet Transfers — Due to his height, Mr. A. experienced neck, shoulder, and back pains when coming to a stand from a standard-height toilet without adaptation, though able to perform independently.

Tub Transfers and Bathing — Able to perform without assistance; however, Mr. A. uses poor judgment in his hand placements for supporting himself when stepping into and out of tub. He places one hand/arm on the sink counter that stands at the near end of shoulder reach, while the other holds onto a towel bar to step. Once one foot is into the tub, the edge of the tub tile is grasped, though no grab bar or true edge is available. For bathing Mr. A. uses a soft collar, which he states he loosens briefly to wash the neck and reports he is able to shower independently by supporting himself in standing with the tile wall while flexing or leaning his trunk laterally to reach leg and foot lifted up. This is another area of questionable judgment and safety to consider in making equipment recommendations.

Chair and Car Transfers — Again Mr. A. is able to perform these independently, but with strain to his neck, shoulder, and back areas from low surfaces.

Mobility — In bed Mr. A. uses a tubular cervical pillow in the supine or faceup position with the front half of the hard collar removed. He replaces the collar front to turn himself or to stand from this lying position. Ambulation is independent without assistive devices inside the home or on even, familiar surfaces; however, on uneven or outdoor grounds and surfaces, he prefers to use a straight cane to assist with balance. Stairs and steps are performed independently with the use of railings or for only one to two steps; however, if there are a number of steps and he is unfamiliar with their size and placement, he requires contact guard or supervision and cueing to maneuver them safely due to his inability to look down to see them accurately. Driving to familiar locations, though one requires highway driving of greater than 30 miles' distance, is performed in his four-door sedan with automatic transmission, bucket seats, one driver's sideview mirror, and the standard rearview mirror. This, again, is another area of concern for judgment regarding safety since Mr. A. is unable to turn or rotate his trunk to either side more than 40 to 50° to compensate for his inability to move his head and neck to scan side to side before making decisions for intersection entries and exits.

Homemaking Skills — Areas of concern in this higher-level skill area for daily tasks were cooking with the use of knives for food preparation and the sensory deficits; stovetop cooking with an inability to see accurately to look into pots, skillets, etc.; and oven cooking in an overhead oven due to Mr. A.'s difficulty with elevating his arms more than just briefly to place a hot item into or remove from the cavity of the oven to place on a counter or table with questionable vision. The cleaning, bed making, and a majority of the laundry tasks were performed by either his daughters or his wife, though Mr. A. did use a stool to sit to transfer clothing from the washer to the dryer. He attempted to carry a basket of clothes to and from the laundry to the rooms; however, he was unable to sustain the hold due to tingling and numbness in his arms and hands with sustained holding.

Money Management and Bill Paying — This has always been done by Mrs. A.; therefore, it was not an area of concern for writing skills needed. Because Mr. A.'s signature is illegible most of the time and extensive writing is not feasible with standard pens or pencils, this is an area of concern for written expression of other sorts.

Assistive Technology for Assistive Devices or Adaptive Equipment — No equipment or devices were available in the home or provided from previous rehabilitation services as per report by Mr. A., verified by his wife and case manager.

■ **Architectural Barriers:** From the driveway to the front porch, a series of two short steps of only 5 inches in height for one and 4 inches for the other exist, with a railing along each side of the steps. At the front door another step measuring 6 inches high was evident. Because of his familiarity with his entryways, Mr. A. has had no observable or reportable problems with maneuvering these steps. There are no steps at the back and side entrances into the home, and the interior doorways and furniture setup are adequate since he is not dependent on a walker or wheelchair to ambulate (though he does use a straight cane outside on uneven surfaces to assist with equilibrium or balance and righting reactions).

■ **Avocational/Leisure Status:** Mr. A. enjoys playing cards and reading, though he is unable to do these activities due to his inability to hold his arms elevated for long periods of time; attending or watching spectator sports such as baseball, basketball, and football games; attending church services and activities; and participating in a support group via his psychologist's office for persons with orthopedic disabilities.

Projection of Occupational Therapy Needs

It was determined that Mr. A. would require a period of home health occupational therapy services for education and training on self-care, leisure, and safety issues. Equipment needs for provision of home-based services are as follows (costs presume one time only unless otherwise noted):

1. A slantboard to reduce reading and writing strain by supporting the upper body, preferably on an elevated surface to have Mr. A.'s hand level with his eyes. In addition, the use of lightweight clamps to hold reading materials and a ledge at the base of the slantboard are recommended. *Estimated cost*: $175.

2. A gooseneck extension for a phone holder or the provision of a speaker telephone. The gooseneck may be the preferred choice to enable private conversations as desired without having to hold the mouthpiece by hand. *Estimated cost*: $85.

3. Enlarged or built-up handles for writing, cooking, and other utensils or hand tools to reduce the grip strength needed for sustained holding and greater control. In addition, a right-angle rocker cutting knife with a serrated edge and an adapted cutting board are recommended, along with the use of prism lenses to look downward for chopping or other food preparation tasks and stovetop cooking as well. *Estimated costs*: $30 for five rolls of foam tubing to be added to handles — replace every 2 to 3 years; $35 for a rocker knife — replace every 15 years; $55 for an adapted cutting board — replace every 15 years; $70 for a prism lens.

4. Use of dycem with the daily in-home tasks to secure items on counters, food trays, tables, or other surfaces. *Estimated cost*: $45 for a 16-inch by 2-yard roll every 10 years.

5. A reacher for use in the kitchen, bath, or cabinets and closets to obtain items out of reach, especially in overhead positions. *Estimated cost*: $75 — replace every 20 years.

6. A portable, folding cart on locking casters for carrying items throughout the home to enable ease of performance with laundry and meal preparation tasks especially. *Estimated cost*: $55 — replace every 20 years.

7. Nonskid material on bath mats and throw rugs (preferably eliminated), as well as a surface coating on the steps outside the home to avoid slipping and potential falls, especially when wet. *Estimated cost*: $85.

8. A wall grab bar to improve safety for standing transfers into and out of the tub area, as well as a shower seat with a back for washing in a safer seated position; long-handled bath sponge to wash the legs and back; and handheld shower spray to enable safe rinsing. *Estimated costs*: $35 for the wall grab bar; $75 for the shower seat; $20 each for the long-handled bath sponges — replace every 2 years; $55 for the handheld shower — replace every 15 years.

9. A portable elevated cushion for seating that would offer lumbar and cervical supports that could be used in the home and car. *Estimated cost*: $85 — replace every 15 years.

10. Adaptive convex mirrors placed on bilateral sideview mirrors, a panoramic rearview mirror or Panamirror, and possible use of side/fender or windshield frame mirrors to aid with visual compensation for scanning, reaction/response time for unexpected obstacles in peripheral fields, and decision making regarding intersection crossings due to poor head/neck and limited trunk motions. (In addition, using four-way stops or traffic lights at intersections, driving on low-volume local routes in daytime and good weather, and driving during daily schedules when low medication side effects are expected once routine is stabilized are also recommended.) *Allowance for the above*: $225 — may replace when the automobile is replaced.

Outpatient occupational therapy was recommended to assess Mr. A.'s predriving and road performance capabilities. This will help to determine his potential to drive safely and independently using compensatory strategies and adaptive equipment for vehicular modifications as needed. In addition, physical therapy (or conditioning in a community fitness program) and an exercise physiologist were also recommended in order to strengthen his leg musculature to assist with squatting and stooping motions, which would be needed to compensate for limited upper body abilities (service costs not calculated).

Frequency and Focus of Treatment

Home-based occupational therapy was projected to be needed at a frequency of three times a week for 4 weeks, reducing to two times a week for 6 to 8 additional weeks to cover all areas outlined for activities of daily living retraining, work simplification, energy conservation education and training, upper extremity strengthening, education on compensatory positioning with the use of assistive devices and adaptive equipment, and home program instruction. Outpatient occupational therapy would be needed for approximately six sessions lasting from 3 to 5 hours for the initial evaluation and 1 to 2 hours for the remainder of the visits for further road testing and training with anticipated equipment needs. These are anticipated to be such items as bilateral adaptive sideview convex and possible fender mirrors with a panoramic rearview mirror, and a steering knob at the seven o'clock wheel position, along with an adaptive seat cushion and head/neck support to improve positioning and comfort. *Estimated costs*: For therapy, $85 to $100 per session per visit for home health; for driving services, $125 per hour for 15 hours; for devices, $385.

Discontinuation of Occupational Therapy Services

Once Mr. A. was found to be safe and reliable for following a medication schedule and for the use of assistive technology and compensatory strategies in the home, he could be discharged from home health occupational therapy services. Prior to discharge, however, client and family education would be needed to suggest that he continue to be monitored regarding his medication routine and the effects this could have on his driving safety. If Mr. A. follows the recommended driving protocols established via a structured adaptive driving program to drive at intervals between certain medications to prevent significant side effects impeding his skills, as well as driving within given restrictions of low-volume, daylight, good weather times on familiar local short-distance routes, then discharge from outpatient occupational therapy services can be recommended. However, annual screenings by occupational therapy for overall activities of daily living, including driving status and compliance, should be continued for a period of 3 to 5 years to ensure the client's, his family's, and the public's safety. Should any significant changes in medication, physiological, or psychological status occur, then the wife should have the ability to contact the physician to order occupational therapy follow-up regarding the client's judgment for safety, especially with regard to his driving skills.

Cost Estimates

Because fees for service or charges vary among facilities, and the use of an appropriate facility will be primarily based on the location relative to the client's home, costs cannot be accurately estimated without performing a market survey of the facilities and services available within the immediate surrounding areas. Once a suitable home health agency and outpatient facility have been identified that provide the recommended occupational therapy services outlined previously, the hourly or program fees charged by each of these services can be multiplied by the number of hours projected via the assessment performed to predict a more accurate total cost for occupational therapy services needed.

CONCLUSION

Occupational therapy is a health and rehabilitative profession that can serve a vital role in the development of a life care plan for an individual with a disability caused by illness or injury. Through the occupational therapist's expertise in activity analyses, clinical and behavioral observations, and formal and informal testing methods, an accurate assessment of a person's functional abilities with regard to activities of daily living and work and play or leisure skills can be obtained. As a team member assessing the global needs of a child, adult, student, client, or patient, depending on the setting, the occupational therapist brings to the life care plan a unique perspective into the realm of purposeful activities. Occupational therapy generally focuses on the client's functional independence and adaptive activity performance using assistive technology or task modifications, as needed, to achieve the desired outcomes. Occupational therapy can serve as the link to productive living — the link that enables the person with a disability to live a safe and independent life to his or her fullest potential with the quality he or she deserves.

ACKNOWLEDGMENTS

Special thanks and much appreciation are extended to Ryan and Lorena McCaigue for supporting their mother and her efforts in writing this chapter, and to Vivian and Phillip Gammell for their emotional support, technical expertise, and assistance in compiling the text. To Chris Bosonetto-Doane, M.S., O.T.R./L., Elizabeth Garrett, Ph.D., David Goudelock, M.A., C.R.C., C.D.M.S., C.C.M., C.L.C.P., Vicki Sadler, M.Ed., C.R.C., C.D.M.S., C.C.M., C.L.C.P., Michael J. Weeks, and Ray Wight, much gratitude is expressed for offering objective feedback to help the reader acquire a clearer understanding of the intent of this chapter, as well as professional support and encouragement to its author.

REFERENCES

ADED. (2003). Fact Sheets. Retrieved June 26, 2003, from http://www.driver-ed.org/i4a/pages/index.cfm?pageid=102

American Occupational Therapy Association. (April 1986). Dictionary definition of *occupational therapy*. Adapted and approved by the Representative Assembly, April 1986, to fulfill Resolution 596-83. (Available from AOTA, 4720 Montgomery Lane, P.O. Box 31220, Bethesda, MD 20824-1220.)

Angelo, J. & Lane, S., Eds. (1997). *Assistive Technology for Rehabilitation Therapists*, 211–240. Philadelphia: F.A. Davis.

Dunn, W., Foto, M., Hinojosa, J., Schell, B.A., Thomson, L.A., & Hertfelder, S. (1994). Uniform terminology, third edition: application to practice. *The American Journal of Occupational Therapy*, 48, 1055–1059.

Dunn, W. & McGourty, L. (1989). Application of uniform terminology to practice. *The American Journal of Occupational Therapy*, 43, 817–831.

Hinojosa, J., Sabari, J., & Pedretti, L. (1993). Position paper: purposeful activity. *The American Journal of Occupational Therapy*, 47, 1081–1082.

Low, J.F. (1997). NBCOT and state regulatory agencies: allies or adversaries? *The American Journal of Occupational Therapy*, 51, 74–75.

Weeks, M.J., Kniskern, J., & Phillips, C.P. (Winter 1997). *Dollars and Sense: A Guide to Solving the Funding Puzzle and Getting Assistive Technology in Georgia*. Atlanta, GA: "Tools for Life" Program Publication.

8

THE ROLE OF THE PHYSICAL
THERAPIST IN LIFE CARE
PLANNING

Art Peddle

INTRODUCTION

Physical therapists serve as facilitators of health. They treat patients with a broad range of potential participation from other professionals, family, and friends. An open mind-set to any given patient and situation is crucial to the enhancement and facilitation of health. The treatment of signs and symptoms, pain, irritation, lesions, catastrophic injury, and dysfunction are given viable solutions from the unique perspective of balanced deliverance of effective physical therapy skills. This creates a synergistic application of physical therapy with the patient's willingness to be responsible toward maximizing his or her health and function. Cooperation with all professionals, financial supporters, family members, and friends contributes to the overall facilitation of health. Insight to innovative and new techniques as applied to a specific patient's needs is an opportunity to promote physical therapy skills with the positive participation by the patient. It is vitally important that the well-being of each patient be considered in long-term and short-term care.

THE LIFE CARE PLANNING PROCESS

In dealing with life care issues, there are fundamental questions and paradigms of thinking to be asked of the physical therapist and others involved in the care of the patient or client, such as:

- What was the level of health, function, and lifestyle before the injury, disease, lesion, or dysfunction?
- What level of health, function, lifestyle can be achieved given the present status of the patient and his or her physiological, social, psychological, financial, and spiritual environment?

0-8493-1511-5/04/$0.00+$1.50
© 2004 by CRC Press LLC

- What are the ideal, hopeful goals and plans, balanced with the real goals and plans?
- What are the integrated thoughts on parameters and boundaries of the patient's thinking in relationship to the process of healing and health?

The physical therapist and all persons involved in life care planning should integrate their plans with the following concepts being interwoven in their health care delivery process:

- "Seek first to understand, before you are understood." (Covey, 1989, p. 239)
- "Walk a mile in my shoes." (Song performed by Joe South)
- "Do unto others as you would have them do unto you." (Matthew 22:39 (paraphrased), KJV)
- "Understand the patient's languages of love" — care and receiving. (Chapman, 1995)

As we examine life care goals and priorities for the patient, we are building a foundation of true principles to develop our skilled delivery of physical therapy. Therefore, we return the patient, as much as possible, to full health and function with basic human dignity, rights, and privileges. If full health and function are not attainable, then at the very least we should create a plan, delivery, and environment of highest quality and dignity of life, minimizing suffering and creating a door of hope for tomorrow. This also allows us to participate in one of the greater values of life, the opportunity to fellowship and relate to a person's unique experience of life, a form of shared enlightenment.

Again, the attitude for delivery is based on how we would want to be treated in any given situation. This attitude counteracts selfish goals and stirs physical therapists to strive for the best scenario and outcome, for the goal is quality of life. This way of life care planning requires commitment to the process. It includes active responsibility and participation of both the physical therapist and the patient.

THE EVALUATION

The physical therapist has the unique capability of providing a large spectrum of evaluative techniques as well as evaluative protocol. The evaluation process is a multilevel course of action. Full detailed evaluation processes can occur on various levels or may be specific parameters, as well as being appropriate to special situations.

In the general areas of medical studies and patient situations, a physical therapist is presented with a variety of evaluative techniques. These include the areas of orthopedics, neurology, soft tissue dysfunction, wound care, sports medicine, hand therapy, industrial medicine, and catastrophic injury to specific or multiple areas. The physical therapist can also specify evaluative techniques by age groups, including pediatric, youth, adult, and geriatric populations. Besides the areas of physical dysfunction and areas of given diagnostic diseases, lesions, or injury, a comparative evaluation and preparation for return to life evaluations can be delivered. Evaluations that involve return to life skills, including activities of daily living (ADL), function, work-related skills, ergonomic analysis, sports-related skills, and overall total life skills can be offered with the appropriate parameters in order to be specific or holistic in nature.

The evaluation process involves consideration of the adaptability of the patient and the circumstances in which the patient is placed. Evaluations can involve specific areas of spine, extremities, and body systems, as well as specific areas of dysfunction and injury. General areas of consideration and evaluation involve the following.

Intake Interview

1. Review the existing medical history and subjective information.
2. Interview the patient. This involves a general subjective overview, including verbal contributions from the patient, type of injury, surgical history, disease process, and dysfunction. Other areas involved in subjective information include present job situation, activity level before and after injury, previous types of physical therapy received, and medical care received.
3. Consider psychosocial questions and interview as they relate to the present dysfunction. Other professionals may have covered psychosocial issues, but it is always appropriate to establish a baseline of understanding of other involved issues in the patient's dysfunction.
4. As appropriate, communicate with family and friends about observed subjective and objective information.

General Evaluation Input

The subjective information and input obtained from the client is established as the baseline for other evaluation considerations. Pain evaluations using standardized questionnaires as well as various tests have benefits for cross-correlation and reliability of subjective information. These essential baseline data of pain characteristics assist in leading the therapist toward establishing present dysfunction and potential for further dysfunction and other complicating factors.

General characteristic complaints of pain are to be established, such as:

1. The location, duration, and frequency of the pain.
2. The specific qualities of the pain — constant, intermittent, diffused, localized, sharp, numb, burning, dull, tingling, radiating, quick, or sustained.
3. Examples of specific pain (e.g., night pain, pain upon arising in the morning, pain with activity, pain throughout the day).
4. Clarify the pain intensity by using a scale — 0 being no pain and 10 being acute pain.
5. Examples of activities that increase pain and activities that decrease pain (e.g., sitting, standing, walking, lying, bending, massage, ice, heat).
6. Is the pain getting better, worse, or remaining the same?
7. What is the maximum length of time the patient can perform any particular function, such as sitting, standing, walking, and driving?

Pain questionnaires should also reveal relationships between how much function the patient can perform and at what level the pain occurs, such as how much can the patient lift and carry? What provides relief? What positions and body ergonomics or equipment assist in decreasing pain and promoting function? Pain drawings and various standard pain scales are other informative tools to be utilized for comparative information, with coordination of other data.

Past medical history and personal information also are important to understanding the direction of evaluation, treatment, and plans for function and health care. The new standards and parameters established under the Health Insurance Portability and Accountability Act (HIPAA) have to be considered in all aspects of care and planning.

Referral questions such as return to work, work duty load, time load, consistency testing, and impairment ratings are also directional in evaluative and care process.

Objective Evaluation

Objective evaluation will analyze basic functional activities, such as the patient's gait; sitting, standing, and rolling activities; and appropriate supportive devices.

Observation of the basic structure of the anatomy, weight-bearing capabilities, and appropriate body landmarks is an essential part of this examination. One should note appropriate posture, compared to the correct anatomical position, and specific noted deviations. Considerations for historical body habits, adaptive shortening, and contractures are important data. Also note the self-limiting or compensated functions and adaptations the patient has made. These can occur voluntarily and or involuntarily.

Other observations should include:

1. Basic soft tissue evaluation
2. Appropriate understanding of joint position
3. Intervertebral movement
4. Normal joint movement
5. Range of motion (ROM), including cardinal and diagonal planes
6. Gait analysis
7. Flexibility
8. Manual muscle testing
9. Strength testing with technologies and instruments
10. Functional test
11. Sensory tests
12. Special tests

Special tests can target specific examination of any given extremity or body part. These tests rule out various complications and evaluate appropriate function and dysfunction.

Other appropriate evaluations include:

■ A **neurological exam** would include basic reflexes as well as appropriate strength measuring, with manual muscle testing and sensory examination. It should be noted that during the evaluation any cross-correlation with a basic generalized assessment can be made with more specific evaluations, including functional aspects of a work capacity assessment (WCA), functional capacity assessment (FCA), and isokinetic, neurological, and balance testing and sensation tests.

- **Joint mobility evaluations** include the normal ROM, correct anatomical position, appropriate accessory movements, and physiological movements.
- **Soft tissue evaluations** include palpation of tissue, noting restrictions, trigger points, pliability, and plastic and elastic responsiveness. The evaluation of soft tissue and tender points should include restrictive qualities and tenderness nature and the response of the tissue (Jones et al., 1995). The evaluation of articular structures should include pain, irritation, and inflammation status as well as movement patterns being evaluated. The functioning of soft tissue and joint structures as a synergistic pattern should be noted. Functioning activities such as sit to supine and return, rolling to supine, side lying and return, and overhead reach are part of the evaluation. The evaluation of functional positions and assuming positions, including the quality of movement as well as any centralization or peripheralization of pain, signs, and symptoms should be considered in this process.
- Other palpation skills include evaluating muscle play, restriction, guarding, reflex contractions, soft tissue restrictions, trigger point, and referred pain. **Intervertebral movement evaluation** is based on a numerical scale set between 0 and 6, with 0 being anklylosed and 6 being unstable; 3/6 is normal. The intervertebral movement can also be classified as hypomobile, hypermobile, and painful. The general evaluation can be broad or specific.

Work Capacity Assessment (WCA) and Functional Capacity Assessment (FCA)

The terms *work capacity assessment* and *functional capacity assessment* are sometimes used synonymously (Blankenship, 1989; Polinsky, 1983). They can also be more definitive, with WCA being an evaluation used for baseline of work capacities. The FCA would involve a more direct study of basic, functional activities of daily living, with the potential of also evaluating work-related activities. The WCA/FCA can be done at the beginning, middle, or end of any treatment evaluation process, or as part of a total perspective of life care planning depending on what is needed. There can also be varying degrees of specific details in the WCA, since the parameters are determined by the physical therapist's understanding of the goals of the evaluation process. The WCA/FCA can occur during the initial stages of the life care planning process or can be extended throughout the span of the life care plan. Follow-up assessments are to upgrade and adjust the goals and plans for the patient, as well as to update the baseline data for reevaluation. All physical therapy evaluations are done in coordination with other professionals and their evaluations. Integrating the results of other health professional's assessments into the physical therapy plan allows for a more holistic approach in achieving the goals for the individual patient.

There are a number of evaluative techniques in the areas of WCA and FCA that are effective and appropriate for any given situation in the life care planning process. According to Blankenship (1989, p. 122), "the WCA or the FCA is an evaluation of physical capabilities and limitations as they relate to work, recreation, and ADL. It describes the optimum and maximal capabilities in terms of strength, endurance, related joint problems, fine and gross motor coordination, limiting factors and methods of functional and task performance." Therefore, in order to make a more accurate assessment, the WCA/FCA should involve measurements of different activities.

Nonmaterial Handling and Positional Tolerance

General areas tested in basic functioning include:

1. Lifting, which includes level lift, floor to table, and carrying
2. Pushing to maximum tolerance
3. Pulling to maximum tolerance
4. Standing, sitting, and kneeling tolerance
5. Bending, stooping, and squatting
6. Walking, climbing, and balance
7. Coordination activities, including the upper and lower extremities with gait analysis and gait function
8. Pivots, forward reach, overhead reach, etc.

The evaluation often requires an assessment of time and repetitive parameters specifically defined as not required, occasional (up to one third of the time), frequent (one third up to two thirds of the time), and constant (over two thirds).

Material Handling, Lifting Tests, Strength Tests

These tests can take on specific work or functional aspects. Various lifting tests have been developed to improve consistency, reliability, validity, and standardization of data to be applied to evaluation and supportive conclusions, results, and directions of rehabilitation.

Isometric lift test, strength test with one repetition, repetitive loads, dynamic and static, grip test, and other integrated techniques utilizing new technologies, programs, and standardized techniques and database are part of the evaluative tools available. These tests are also cross-correlated often to arrive at reliability, validity, and consistency of effort parameters. Many tests, e.g., EPIC (Employment Potential Improvement Corporation, developed by Matheson, available at http://www.epicrehab.com), have criteria and standards for application, databasing, and analysis.

Activities of Daily Living

Establishment of proper body ergonomics and posture during functional ADL, as well as work-related activities, is important not only in establishing and facilitating present health, but also in preventing further dysfunction and injury. It is important that ergonomics be applied in the evaluation process as a tool to determine the patient's capabilities (physically and mentally) in comprehending the issues of proper body mechanics. In the evaluative functional capacity/work capacity arena, proper ergonomics and posture will need modifications based on equipment handling capabilities and the use of adaptive equipment.

Functional aspects of ADL, such as personal grooming, hygiene, and dressing, are issues that are often considered in the FCA (also see Chapter 7 on the occupational therapist's role). Areas of nutrition and speech can also be evaluated by a qualified physical therapist with appropriate training. Some aspects of the FCA, as well as other aspects of WCA, are often overlapped in the expertise area with the occupational therapist, speech therapist, recreational therapist, ergonomic specialist, and appropriate physician specialist. In any evaluative process, standard body mechanics are to be evaluated by the therapist during the lifting task portion, as well as basic functional activities task, in order to ensure the most advantageous body mechanics for handling basic ADL functions and work functions.

Evaluation for sports and other specific recreational skills needs to be considered in the evaluative process. There is a correlation between functional skills, work skills, and sports or recreation skills. Collating these concepts provides for efficiency of movement, as well as promoting correct body function and health, within the parameters of the given dynamics of the patient's physical challenges.

Evaluation of body mechanics is crucial to determine potential for "wear and tear" on the patient. Appropriate alternatives, suggestions, and varying procedures and skills for handling any given dysfunction should be understood. Full comprehension of these procedures and skills will enhance the development of proper use of strength, as well as minimize irritation and pain. Also, with proper evaluation of the patient's present knowledge and skill, the need for further training or education can be developed. The role of the physical therapist from the basic evaluative process or WCA/FCA can essentially be refined or specified for any catastrophic impairment.

When performing the evaluative process and listing objective findings, substantial data are important to assist the delivery of health care to the patient. Gathering of data and information in the objective format also plays an important role in defending the patient's present situation and in presenting the plan for future services. Skilled assessment is vital in giving direction for the best possible outcome for the patient's return to health, as well as providing long-term care. It is appropriate to develop parameters allowing for changes in the patient's function and health and in the patient's environmental situation and basic home lifestyle. Adaptability and changes in preparing the patient for return to work or work activities are crucial in understanding the format for performing the evaluative FCA or WCA.

Isokinetic Testing

Isokinetic testing provides a technologically advanced approach to human performance testing, rehabilitation, and exercise. The test allows all major joints of the body, including the upper extremities, lower extremities, and trunk, to be evaluated and compared. Bilateral testing, as well as comparative testing, can differentiate between muscle groups in the isokinetic test. Isokinetic exercise is performed at a constant speed throughout the range of motion. As the muscle applies force, it is resisted by appropriate proportional opposing force. Therefore, the speed of movement is kept constant. The isokinetic evaluation process or exercise provides an excellent means of qualifying many aspects of movement and function, including muscle torque, work, fatigue, ROM, and peak torque levels. As the sophistication of technology improves, more accurate and appropriate measuring devices will allow for basic data and parameters in which to assess body function. The isokinetic test can also be used in a cross-correlation with functional measurements being taken, as well as manual muscle testing and basic lifting capabilities. This cross-correlation can help define the patient's present level of activity and assist in determining symptom magnification and inappropriate illness behavior parameters.

Neurological Evaluation

As in the general evaluation given earlier, the neurological examination can be an expanded appraisal involving specific parameters. It involves specific emphasis on neurological and neuromuscular mechanisms of the body, including muscle test and evaluations, sensory tests, functional and neuromuscular developmental sequencing and evaluations, and specific injury evaluations to the central nervous system or peripheral nervous system. Associated dysfunction as in gait, transfers, dressing, grooming, hygiene, sports, and work can also be neurologically evaluated.

Cardiovascular Fitness Evaluation/Cardiovascular Profile

Cardiovascular fitness evaluations incorporate a range of specifically applied stress testing under the supervision of the physician and appropriate professionals, including a physical therapist. The cardiovascular appraisal is often involved in the FCA/WCA, which establishes a minimal level of conditioning protocol that could include treadmill, bicycle ergometer, or step-climbing evaluations. All these tests have basic guideline parameters. Often a cardiovascular clearance evaluation is needed before other evaluations, WCA, and FCA can be performed. The pertinent physician or professional may give appropriate parameters under which the cardiovascular system may be stressed or tested.

Neuromuscular, Balance, and Coordination Evaluations

The neuromuscular skeletal function is evaluated in specific areas or systems and holistic body systems and functions. This evaluation can involve the study of the balance system of the body in relationship to gait and functional activities. Proper consideration for a proprioceptive feedback system in static and dynamic functional activities is measured. This evaluation can involve specific job activities, sports activities, and ADL, with coordination, balance, and skill being integrated into foundation data. The criteria involve general standardized tests, as well as specific tests designed by the physical therapist to the given situation based on age, developmental sequencing, and specific goals of the functional or life care demands.

Gait Evaluation

Gait evaluation involves specific and/or general evaluation of the patient's ambulatory status in a variety of environment situations. Consideration for adaptive equipment, tools, and prosthetics is part of this evaluative process.

Return to work and physical demand categories as published by the Department of Labor, in combination with consistency of performance, positional tolerances, and lifting tests and other evaluative procedures, create a viable tool to have a "systematic process of measuring and developing an individual's ability to perform meaningful tasks on a safe and dependable basis" (Hanoun Medical, 2002).

Evaluation Recommendations

The role of the physical therapist as a facilitator in health care is to treat, train, condition, and assist in the direct structure and setting of goals for the patient. Basic communication to the patient, family, professionals, and financial parties serves as a primary directive of achieving the life care planning process. It should be understood from the physical therapist's point of view that his or her establishment of feedback into the life care planning process is crucial in developing a long-term solution for the patient's care. Proper structured treatment, evaluation, follow-up physical therapy, and training involves clear communications among the professionals involved so that all forms of facilitation to functioning are utilized.

THE LIFELONG PHYSICAL THERAPY PLAN

An attitude of openness and understanding should be the goal while preparing the patient for the highest level of independence. This same directive should be applied when providing options for those who will need long-term or lifelong physical therapy. Examples of this attitude and structure are as follows: A patient who is in need of a wheelchair and is dependent upon the wheelchair for most of his or her life will develop other dysfunctions. Typically there is greater wear and tear on the upper extremities, cervical, neck, thoracic, and spine, due to having to handle a greater load of total body function in the upper extremities and upper trunk and neck areas. It is important to understand that lower extremities that are not functioning do not provide support and therefore cannot be used in functional skills. This greater demand of activity and function is placed on the remaining working cardiovascular, neuromuscular, and skeletal systems. Patients or clients are susceptible to greater breakdown of all involved systems and structures. Effective planning involves addressing the immediate dysfunction in preparing the patient to develop a higher level of independence and future preparation. It should also be understood that the patient would in all probability have an increased ratio of wear and tear factors and greater susceptibility to further lesions and insult in his or her remaining systems and structures.

The dysfunctional areas of the body and mind will still need suitable care and support. These would include areas of strength, ROM, hygiene, wound care, tissue function, and basic vascular and neurological functional considerations. Sometimes injured areas become hypersensitive, even though not functional. Phantom and referred pain can occur in the dysfunctional area.

As in any treatment or evaluation process, the therapist should be open-minded and aware of any new studies or opportunities to increase the function and promote the facilitation of health in the injured area. This especially applies for adaptive equipment. The progressive use of equipment, awareness of advanced technology, and foresight to predict need are essential. For example, a lower-level tetraplegic patient would commonly require a primary power wheelchair for basic ambulating. However, there are occasions in which an additional manual wheelchair would provide the patient with a variety of sitting postures, backup to the power chair, and an opportunity for the wheelchair to be used as a piece of exercise equipment. The manual wheelchair provides an excellent source of exercise potential and opportunity for the patient to develop some control and direction in ambulating.

Thoughtful modifications and supplements to the patient and the given situation, with appropriate equipment, should be considered for both short-term and long-term care. This allows the physical therapist and the life care planning team to develop a full perspective in returning the patient to the highest level of independence and an appropriate, dignified lifestyle. Motivating, encouraging, and challenging the patient to use equipment and supportive devices is part of the evaluative, training, and treatment process.

Financial considerations include original equipment, maintenance, modifications, and replacement equipment. All these factors are to be considered over the patient's life span. As the patient changes and various challenges are presented, considerations for equipment should be appropriate to the life care plan and goals. Financial support for equipment and the evaluative process should be based on the highest goals and principles presented.

Physical Therapy Treatment

In the life care planning process, an evaluation establishes the baseline for treatment throughout the process. In many situations, specific treatment by the physical therapist is required and involves not only therapy, but also ongoing evaluation. Physical therapy treatment may involve eight basic categories:

1. Education
2. Conditioning
3. Physical medicine treatment
4. Function-specific and ADL-specific treatment
5. Occupational and industrial physical therapy
6. Sports physical therapy
7. Total life relationship skills and integration treatment
8. Boundaries and communication skills

Education involves an emphasis on ergonomic principles applied to posture and body mechanics, and essential principles for carrying out assisted or independent programs of conditioning, strengthening, ROM, and functional care. Education in ADL, functional, sports, and work-related skills is delivered to all parties involved. It is important that these skills are developed in the patient's real-world setting and that there is ample opportunity to implement them in an appropriate manner — with supervision, leading toward independence as a baseline goal. The appropriate support of professionals and family members in the real-world setting will require adaptive thinking.

Establishment of specific patient potential in any given area needs to be determined and understood by the patient and team members. An understanding of the patient's situational lifestyle, critical work demands, task analysis, functional activities, and recreational plans is important. The patient's understanding of educational information presented and the development of a functional delivery by the patient in handling basic nonmaterial ergonomics and essential material ergonomics should be considered. Material handling and nonmaterial handling ergonomics are not just a matter of work-related issues, but also of functional ADL and the total environment.

Integration into the whole aspect of the patient's life care with the life care planning team on an as-needed and program-developmental basis will be required. This will probably require the physical therapist to coordinate with the patient/client, other professionals, and family members to follow through with essential concepts of physical therapy education.

Conditioning involves aerobics, cardiovascular, and physiological conditioning. It should be noted that in conditioning, appropriate adaptations to the patient's/client's needs will be made and evaluated, as well as developed into a working solution by the physical therapist. Strengthening, which will incorporate specific muscle dynamics, will be used to increase strength levels for performing functional activities, work activities, sports activities, and ADL. Specific areas of strengthening can involve techniques in cardinal and diagonal planes, which can involve singular movements or multidirectional movements. The physical therapist has at his or her disposal the use of many strengthening techniques, including isometrics, isotonics, isokinetics, plyometrics, and proprioceptive neuromuscular facilitation (PNF). Strengthening could involve rotational, multidirectional facets to prepare the patient for a variety of lifestyle situations. Mobility, stretching, and flexibility categories are used synonymously to describe appropriate mobility exercises to ensure basic principles of full functional ROM in both physiological and accessory patterns. Using balanced concepts of strengthening without strain or further injury is of vital importance in designing a program specific to the individual patient and situation.

The integration of all conditioning factors with functional skills, ADL skills, work skills, and sports skills should be considered and integrated into life care planning. Specific neuromuscular, balance, and coordination activities allow the integration of the central nervous system and the peripheral nervous system to handle ADL, functional, work, and sports activities. Ballistics and dynamics are stresses to be applied to prepare the patient to handle a variety of velocity forces and changes that occur in any lifestyle situation. This can involve specificity of training at various speeds and various levels of physical performance.

Physical medicine treatment includes the use of appropriate medications, modalities, manual therapy, and specific exercises. Physical therapy medicine is used for basic signs and symptoms, which may include pain management, wound care, and improving function. Physical medicine includes the areas of specialized program development or treatment, which could include relaxation techniques, weight control, and appropriate uses of supportive devices, equipment, and braces.

Function-specific and ADL-specific treatment are specific treatment programs the physical therapist can use to encourage increased functional capabilities, such as in gait, transfers, personal hygiene and grooming, speech, and general ADL.

Occupational and industrial physical therapy involves the process of creating a situation in which a patient/client may progress from a beginning level of handling any job task to the actual performance of the job. The job-specific program can involve a program starting in the clinic and being transferred to the on-site job location. *Work hardening*, *work conditioning*, and *work start* are synonymous terms to describe this process.

Sports physical therapy involves the direct relationship of physical therapy in establishing appropriate conditioning and training, structure, and protocol. This skilled development of parameters and goals creates an atmosphere that develops independent training techniques, as well as independence to continue higher levels of sport or sports-specific performance.

Total life relationship skills and integration treatment involves the physical therapist working with the patient, family, and total environmental in developing a workable plan structured for assisting the patient in facilitating his or her full health at the highest level possible. This total life care integration involves a coordination of all previous physical therapy treatments and evaluations with the potential for upgrading, changing, and adapting any given treatment plan and program.

Boundaries and communication skills involve personal and relationship effort and education, utilizing appropriate psychological consultation and study. The skills and techniques gained will enhance the positive effectiveness of a caring serving professional.

EXIT PROGRAM AND CARE RESOLUTION

Preparing the exit program involves a combination of compiling all previous evaluations, treatment, data, and observation processes in communication with the associated team members to arrive at a conclusion of the involvement process in the patient/client. During the exit program, appropriate recommendations and postdischarge plans are made from the physical therapist's point of view with preferred sequencing, as well as postdischarge plans for status to returning to full lifestyle situations. Options and variations of any program, as well as reentry into a program, are open for consideration, as is proper application of newly found situations.

Follow-up care resolution is a broad category involved in interpreting the appropriateness and efficacy of the evaluative and treatment process from the patient's perspective. It also involves the physical therapist's perspective in the areas of physical ergonomic integration into basic life, concepts of preventative physical medicine, appropriate concerns for future update and recheck, and any issue of compliance. This involves a process of communication between the patient and all team members in restoring the patient to the highest level of function and a dignified lifestyle.

SYMPTOM MAGNIFICATION

Symptom magnification or inappropriate illness behavior is an issue that is present in the life care process and involves many complications and issues. Physical therapists, as well as other professionals, have attempted to arrive at appropriate systems tests and evaluative procedures for giving suitable feedback and baseline data to establish appropriate behavior in any given situation. General considerations for inappropriate illness behavior and symptom magnification are behaviors that are out of proportion to the impairment. It should be understood that symptom magnification is a behavior that is improper but does not implicate a reason or motive for that behavior. Furthermore, it should also be understood that there could be a psychosocial basis for some behaviors that do not necessarily originate from a physiological or organic basis.

In determining symptom magnification or inappropriate illness behavior it should be understood that there are often degrees and levels at which it is expressed. Some of these levels are extreme and can impede the appropriate fair process of assisting a person to achieve a healthy lifestyle. In addition, there are forms of symptom magnification that exist on a low level that are intrinsic to basic lifestyle teachings. Therefore, appropriate considerations for establishing objective information, as well as objective treatment, require skill and fitting consultation from the team of life care planners and associated professionals.

If the physical therapist is involved in the identification of the type of symptom magnifier, which could be classified in the areas of an experimenter, a refugee, a game player, and a psychogenic type of magnification, consultation with the appropriate professional should be performed and used (Blankenship, 1989). Appropriate test questionnaires and scales administered by the physical therapist, or previously by associated professionals, can be considered as part of the evaluative process. It should also be noted that in understanding, evaluating, and commenting on appropriate and inappropriate illness behavior, one should have an open mind and be alert to cross-correlation factors in the evaluative and treatment processes.

An example of this would be a patient being asked to perform a cardinal plane ROM by lifting his arm over his head, but the patient states or demonstrates that he cannot lift his arm above 70° of shoulder flexion. Then when asked to take off his shirt, he is able to demonstrate taking his shirt off over his head, thus demonstrating his ability to flex his shoulders above 100° or more of shoulder flexion. Cross-correlation of specific evaluative techniques and functional techniques assists in determining the reliability and validity of the patient's status. In communicating this information, the physical therapist should use the expression "the data presents itself." Another way to express performance is to use the phrase "the patient demonstrated (this or that)." Therefore, the therapist avoids conjecture and judgment when communicating.

PHYSICAL THERAPY CHARGES

Basic rates in physical therapy for services rendered are wide and varied. Each profession and professional has his or her requirements and specific insights into delivery of any evaluation and treatment process. The following numbers are given as a broad perspective and are estimates for considering lifelong life care planning issues and are subject to change with all basic life situational economics, as well as specific professional demands.

- Basic physical therapy treatment and conditioning range from $65 to $200 per hour.
- General evaluative techniques, depending on the extensiveness of the techniques, range from $60 to $1000.
- These techniques could involve a beginning basic physical therapy evaluation of $65 (average charge) to more specific exams running $200.
- WCAs and FCAs range from a modified WCA/FCA costing $200 to a more extensive WCA/FCA costing $1000.

Again, there is such a wide variety in pricing that it is best to be specific to the physical therapist involved in the analysis, evaluation, and treatment processes to determine the best life care planning situation. As in other life care planning areas, considerations for "how I would like to be treated" and what is fair should be a basis for appropriate structuring for financial reimbursement.

ESTABLISHING A KNOWLEDGE BASE

The physical therapist should establish an appropriate information system in order to accomplish the following:

1. Provide a means of examining the specific case issues as a professional.
2. Establish appropriate correlations between injury and patient types.
3. Establish appropriate protocol for returning the patient to his or her lifestyle and life situation.
4. Establish appropriate modifications for further patient assistance and study.

CASE STUDY

The client, a 23-year-old female, suffered a burst fracture of the first vertebrae in her lumbar spine (L1) resulting in a conus medullaris (spinal cord) injury following an exercise-related injury. She is ambulatory (although impairment is obvious) but uses a cane when outside of the home for stability and safety. She participated in a functional capacity evaluation, which was completed over a 2-day period due to the client's fatigue and reduced endurance.

Results of the evaluation are as follows:

- Unable to complete Kasch Step Test due to fatigue in lower extremities.
- Unsteady balance while stepping when fatigued.
- After 15 minutes of continuous walking, client was visibly fatigued with decreased control of lower extremities and trunk during ambulation.
- Difficulty with crouching (consistently lost balance).
- No difficulty sitting for 30 to 40 minutes at one time.
- No difficulty crawling.
- Difficulty with higher-level coordination/balance activities.
- Validity of the isometric strength testing reflects decreased strength/balance.
- Dynamic progressive lifting test discontinued after client lifted 24 pounds due to rating of very heavy load.
- Functioning in sedentary–light physical demand category due to lack of endurance.
- Significant postural, lower extremity strength, balance, and endurance deficits.
- Highly motivated client with "enormous potential to improve."
- Recommend 6-week rehabilitation therapy program to address deficits, night splinting to prevent further deformity of toes, vocational counseling.

Results of the muscle skeletal evaluation are as follows:

■ Significant increase in thoracic kyphosis (outward curvature of the spine at the top of the back) with scoliosis (sideways deviation of the spine)
■ Left shoulder $3/4$ inch lower than right shoulder; right iliac crest $1/4$ inch higher than left
■ Posture in forward head, rounded shoulder stance
■ Decreased muscle mass in gastroc and lower leg area with increased toe flexion

Projected Evaluations			
Recommendation (by whom)	*Year Initiated*	*Frequency/Duration*	*Expected Cost*
Physical therapy evaluations (PT)	2002 to life	1–2 times/year for 1–2 more years, then follow-up with physiatrist and biannual PT evaluation as part of spinal cord injury review	$181–341/year through 2000 at $90.40–$170.60 for 30- to 60-minute consult; additional PT costs part of biannual review (not included in this sample)
Projected Therapeutic Modalities			
Recommendation (by whom)	*Year Initiated*	*Frequency/Duration*	*Expected Cost*
Rehabilitation therapy to address posture, strength, balance, and endurance deficits (includes physical therapy and occupational therapy) (PT)	2002	3 times/week for 6 weeks	$2,837.50 total at $155–175 average for first visit and $155–160 average for subsequent visits (cost will vary depending on length of visit and specific treatment)
Health and strength maintenance via supervised exercise program by PT at a model spinal cord injury center's fitness center	2003	Expect 3 times/week to life	$340/year

CONCLUSION

The role of the physical therapist is vital in life care planning in many cases. There exists the opportunity to facilitate good health, to minimize suffering and pain, and to restore patients or clients to the highest functional level of life. The experienced physical therapist is capable of being an effective leader and director of life care planning. The physical therapist, as a responsible leader, accepts the challenges of encouraging responsibility in the patient and team members. When participating in the life care planning process, if the physical therapist seeks to apply the principles of "seek first to understand before you are understood" (Covey, 1989, p. 239) and "do unto others as you would have them do unto you" (Matthew 22:39 (paraphrased), KJV), the outcome will be an integration of the spiritual and physical worlds. This philosophy offers an appropriate balance of structure, goals, and priorities to enhance the life care planning paradigm.

ACKNOWLEDGMENTS

The author wishes to acknowledge all the educators, mentors, associates, and work professionals, as well as friends and family, who have contributed in the past to my profession as a physical therapist. Some of the material in this chapter was based on readings from Polinsky Rehabilitation, Keith Blankenship's *Industrial Rehabilitation*, *The Five Love Languages* by Chapman, *Strain-Counterstrain* by Jones et al. Other conceptual contributors are Health South's Rehabilitation, Gordon Cummings, Stanley Paris, and John Barnes. This chapter seeks to introduce the general population of professionals who are involved in life care planning, with a general overview of insights to physical therapists and their role in the life care planning process. It encompasses information I have read and received from a variety of sources, integrating those ideas and resources with my experience and opportunities in providing life care planning in the past and present. There are many excellent sources of further specific details, evaluations, and treatments available to those concerned. It is of vital importance that we apply our skills, training, and knowledge with appropriate understanding balanced with growth.

REFERENCES

Barnes, J. (1989). *Myofascial Release Treatment*. Available from Myofascial Release Treatment Center, Rt. 30-252, Suite 1, 10S Leopard Rd., Paoli, PA 19301.

Blankenship, K. (1989). *Industrial Rehabilitation*. Athens, GA: American Therapeutic.

Chapman, G. (1995). *The Five Love Languages*. Chicago: Northfield Publishing.

Covey, S. (1989). *The Seven Habits of Highly Effective People*. New York: Simon & Schuster.

Hanoun Medical (2002). [Brochure]. 12 Ashwarren Rd. Downsview, Greenwood, CO 80111.

Jones, L., Kusunose, R., and Goering, E. (1995). *Strain-Counterstrain*. Jones Strain-Counter-Strain, Inc., 1501 Tyrell Lane, Boise, ID 83706.

Polinsky Medical Rehabilitation Institute. (1983). *Functional Capacity Assessment*. Available from Polinsky Medical Rehabilitation Institute, 530 East 2nd St., Duluth, MN 55805.

9

THE ROLE OF THE SPEECH-LANGUAGE PATHOLOGIST AND ASSISTIVE TECHNOLOGY IN LIFE CARE PLANNING

Carolyn W. Higdon

INTRODUCTION

Individuals with communication disorders present complex, confusing, and often frustrating challenges to the life care planner. Communication is defined as the transmission or exchange of thoughts and information from one individual to another, whatever the means (e.g., speech, manual sign, gestures, or other graphic symbols). Communication may be linguistic or nonlinguistic. Communication itself is an abstract concept, with disorders in communication, defined by brain-monitoring technology, sophisticated differential diagnoses, and an ability to understand normal and abnormal human speech and language. The best-qualified person to evaluate and make recommendations in this specific area is the speech-language pathologist (SLP). The area of study is accurately referred to as communication sciences and disorders, which includes speech-language pathology and audiology. Speech-language pathology includes cognitive communication, speech, language, and swallowing.

As we begin the second century of neuroscience, we have embarrassingly little information about how speech and language develops in the normal human brain, and understanding of how these processes can be disrupted is also extremely primitive. To a large extent, this predicament results from severe technological limitations in the study of human anatomy and physiology that have prevailed until recently. Either techniques have been too invasive for use with human subjects or, for those less invasive techniques (conventional electroencephalography), the information generated is difficult to interpret, particularly with regard to normal function.

Brain imaging refers to a group of radiological techniques that differentiate abnormal from normal brain structures. Newer imaging techniques permit

0-8493-1511-5/04/$0.00+$1.50
© 2004 by CRC Press LLC

examining live brain tissue integrity without cranial penetration, now allowing SLPs to gather very sophisticated information about the brain and communication. Brain imaging is divided into static and dynamic techniques. Static techniques identify the anatomical structures of the brain and include computed tomography (CT) and magnetic resonance imaging (MRI). Dynamic techniques examine brain functional anatomy or physiology and include regional cerebral blood flow, single-photon emission computed tomography (SPECT), and positron emission tomography (PET).

In addition to imaging techniques, several other diagnostic techniques may be chosen to gather cognitive and language function information from the brain. The electroencephalogram (EEG) is a graphic representation of the potential differences between two separated points on the scalp surface that represent brain transmitted electrical potentials or the electrical activity generated by brain cells. Electrical potentials are called brain waves. Brain electrical activity mapping represents a topographic mapping of the temporally recorded EEG activity of the electrical potentials from the brain. Brain electrical activity mapping provides greater clinical insight into brain physiology than an EEG (Bhatnagar & Andy, 2003).

Electromyography (EMG) is the visual record of muscular electrical activity during spontaneous and voluntary movements. Electromyography is used to determine the nerve or muscle pathology when clinical evidence is either absent, equivocal, or needs confirmation. An examination of the quality, speed, and magnitude of electrical impulses in muscles can help detect nerve or muscle damage. It can also differentiate among muscle disease (myopathy), atrophy of spinal motor neurons (neuropathy), interruption of nerve supply (denervation), and neuromuscular (myoneural) problems.

Evoked potentials refer to normal electrical activities of the central nervous system that occur in response to specific and controlled sensory stimulation. Whether the sensory stimulus is *visual*, *somatosensory*, or *auditory*, evoked brain responses are recorded using electrodes referred to the spinal cord, brainstem, and scalp. Visual evoked potentials are used to evaluate electrical conduction along the optic nerve, optic tract, lateral geniculate, optic radiations, and visual cortex. Somatosensory evoked responses are elicited by simulation of contralateral peripheral nerves. Clinical conditions in which somatosensory evoked potentials are of diagnostic value include multiple sclerosis, brain injuries, brain death, posterior column spinal cord lesions, and lesions of the peripheral nerves. Evoked response audiometry is the electrophysiological assessment of auditory functions. It measures changes in neural activity that occur in the auditory acoustic stimuli. Evoked response audiometry is used for assessing the functioning of the auditory neural pathway to predict hearing thresholds in patient populations that are difficult to test. In evoked response audiometry, the most commonly measured responses are the *auditory brainstem responses (brainstem auditory evoked response).*

Dichotic listening is a noninvasive neuropsychological tool that involves auditory stimuli and is commonly used for assessing cerebral dominance. It involves presenting simultaneous but partially different auditory stimuli to both ears. The attention factors are minimized by requiring subjects to simultaneously attend to both ears and report the stimuli they perceive. When the linguistic material presented in both ears is largely similar and spoken in the same voice, attending to the stimuli from both ears poses processing difficulties. The neurolinguistic implications of these findings are that right ear performance can serve as an index for determining degrees of language lateralization. Strong support for the stronger contralateral auditory projections in dichotic listening came when the dichotic testing results were supported by the observation of the left language lateralization by hemispheric infusion of sodium amobarbital.

The lumbar puncture (spinal tap) is used for diagnosing various infections and hemorrhages of the central nervous system that are not observable from the CT scan. Chemical analysis of the obtained cerebrospinal fluid helps in the differential diagnosis of multiple sclerosis, neurosyphilis, Guillain–Barre syndrome, carcinomatous meningitis, and neuropathies. Lumbar puncture is contraindicated in cases of increased intracranial pressure because of the possibility of a brainstem herniation (Bhatnagar & Andy, 2003). These are a few commonly used radiological diagnostic techniques that directly apply to the management of neurological patients who are commonly seen by practicing speech-language pathologists, primarily in medical settings.

Improvements in computers during the last two decades have significantly enhanced our ability to study aspects of human anatomy and physiology otherwise inaccessible (e.g., deep structures of living brains), and to consider sophisticated experimental questions (e.g., the temporal course of neural function and the nature of individual differences). Thus, in many ways these techniques have placed us on the threshold of the first century of human neuroscience.

Neuroscience is significant in the process of life care planning because it allows life care planners the critical, and now more measurable, information to make projections about disability related to the communication disorders, as well as provides thoughtful input into the long-term medical, educational, clinical, rehabilitative, psychosocial, recreational, vocational, and technology needs of the individuals. Access to neuroscientific information also mandates that the life care planner carefully identify the speech-language pathologist in the life care planning process, to ensure that the SLP demonstrates the knowledge and skills necessary to provide irrefutable information that will stand up under scrutiny of other team members in the life care planning process, as well as from other medical, legal, and funding sources.

This chapter will discuss the role of the speech-language pathologist and the advanced areas of training and preparation needed to demonstrate the level of knowledge and skills in communication sciences and disorders necessary in life care planning. Qualifications and credentials of a speech-language pathologist are reviewed (ASHA, 1989), along with the assessment process and funding and economic considerations that impact the area of speech-language pathology (ASHA, 1991). Neurolitigation considerations for the speech-language pathologist expert are discussed in the second half of the chapter. The whole concept of taking a role in the life care planning process is a new consideration for the speech-language pathologist, who will provide an integral part in the development of the life care plan for individuals with communication or swallowing deficits. The credibility and complexity of communication disorders is just beginning to be recognized, as well as the impact that deficits in communication disorders have on multiple parts of the life care plan. If the life care planner recognizes that an individual has a communication deficit, the SLP may furnish information in the areas of cognitive communication, vocational, educational, aids to independent living, psychosocial, speech, language, swallowing, medical complications, and future medical planning.

THE ROLE OF SPEECH-LANGUAGE PATHOLOGIST IN LIFE CARE PLANNING

The purpose of a life care plan is to identify the comprehensive and individualized needs of a person as they relate to a disability or chronic illness with relevant associated cost considerations. These needs are the operational components of a life care planning process. They should never be compromised or manipulated. The costs assigned to these needs are determined by the geographical consumer rate for the identified services and equipment. The costs can be developed through understanding the range of available funding streams, creative and innovative ways of negotiating, available resources, and the cost projection analyses that accompany such planning.

The speech-language pathologist must be well grounded in the theory of normal development in all ages, in any previous learning or developmental problems affecting the individual, and in the current status of the individual, and must be able to predict future functioning of the individual. Many times speech-language pathologists will practice in the treatment of either the pediatric or the adult population. This frequently precludes the speech-language pathologist from being able to look backward or beyond to make accurate recommendations about future functioning needs.

It is always useful for the speech-language pathologist, who is consulting in the life care planning process, to be able to be actively engaged in the clinical treatment of individuals and their families. This enhances the SLP's credibility, because the speech-language pathologist should have realistic estimates of current needs and prognostic predictions. However, it is also imperative that the consulting speech-language pathologist have a fluid understanding of the current literature and research that directly or indirectly impacts the area of communication sciences and disorders. This includes knowledge of the most current assessment procedures, state-of-the-art assistive technology, trends in pharmacology and medical care, and possible needs in the areas of residential and geriatric care (ASHA, 1993).

QUALIFICATIONS AND CREDENTIALS OF A SPEECH-LANGUAGE PATHOLOGIST FOR LIFE CARE PLANNING PURPOSES

The generally accepted national standard for practice in speech-language pathology (communication sciences and disorders) is the American Speech-Language-Hearing Association (ASHA) certificate of clinical competence in speech-language pathology (CCC-SLP). The ASHA CCC-SLP requires a master's degree in speech-language pathology, completion of a 1-year clinical fellowship, and successful passage of the national examination. For states with licensure, the legal right to practice will vary with the individual licensing acts. Most licensure laws were modeled after the ASHA CCC standard (ASHA, 1996). Licensure, unlike certification, is mandatory for those states that regulate the practice of audiology and speech-language pathology. In many states, licensure requirements parallel those

Table 9.1 State Licensure for SLPS and Audiologists

Alabama	Kentucky	Ohio
Alaska	Louisiana	Oklahoma
Arizona	Maine	Oregon
Arkansas	Massachusetts	Pennsylvania
California	Michigan[a]	Rhode Island
Colorado[b]	Minnesota	South Carolina
Connecticut	Mississippi	Dakota+
Delaware	Missouri	Tennessee
District of Columbia[a]	Montana	Texas
Florida	Nebraska	Utah
Georgia	Nevada	Vermont[a]
Hawaii	New Hampshire	Virginia
Idaho[a]	New Jersey	Washington
Illinois	New Mexico	West Virginia
Indiana	New York	Wisconsin
Iowa	North Carolina	
Kansas	North Dakota	

[a] Does *not* regulate the professions of audiology and speech-language pathology.

[b] Regulates only audiology.

of ASHA certification. Further, ASHA certification will satisfy many of the requirements of state licensure when you apply for reciprocity. Table 9.1 shows the states with licensure of speech-language pathologists and audiologists.

These individuals may hold additional credentials through their state education agency. Often, the state education agency requirements do not equate to the national standard, requiring only a bachelor's degree and education certification in a state to practice. Speech-language pathologists with specific interests may hold additional certifications determined by societies and organizations interested in developing credentials to define expertise in a particular area, such as the Rehabilitation Engineering and Assistive Technology Society of North America (also known as RESNA) or the special interest divisions of ASHA. The special interest divisions within ASHA are listed in Table 9.2.

Codes of ethics for all organizations in which an individual holds membership must be acknowledged and followed. Ethics is defined as "the study of standards of conduct and moral judgment ... and the system or code of morals of a particular profession" (ASHA, 2003). When applied to a field or professional area, such as augmentative communication, or a profession, such as audiology or speech-language pathology, the ethical conduct of practitioners is embodied both in a code (or canons) of ethics and in standards of practice. Each speech-language pathologist or audiologist must comply with the code of ethics for his or her discipline. The code of ethics for a discipline is typically developed by the professional association serving it. The ASHA Code of Ethics sets forth the fundamental principles and rules considered essential to the preservation of the highest standards of integrity and ethical conduct to which members of the profession of speech-language pathology and audiology are bound. All profes-

Table 9.2 ASHA Special Interest Divisions

Division	
1	Language learning and education
2	Neurophysiology and neurogenic speech and language disorders
3	Voice and voice disorders
4	Fluency and fluency disorders
5	Speech science and orofacial disorders
6	Hearing and hearing disorders: research and diagnostics
7	Aural rehabilitation and its instrumentation
8	Hearing conservation and occupational audiology
9	Hearing and hearing disorders
10	Issues in higher education
11	Administration and supervision
12	Augmentative and alternative communication
13	Swallowing and swallowing disorders (dysphagia)
14	Communication disorders and sciences in culturally and linguistically diverse populations
15	Gerontology
16	School-based issues

sional activity must be consistent with the code of ethics. The Principle of Ethics II, Rule B, especially important in the area of assistive technology, states "individuals shall engage in only those aspects of the profession that are within their competence, considering their level of education and training. ..." (ASHA, 2003a).

When funding is available, third-party intermediaries in most instances require the ASHA CCC and licensure. The national certification standards are generally tied to the ASHA CCC for both funding by third-party intermediaries and for service delivery. On the other hand, other certifications in existence, such as the education agency certification, traditionally do not equate to the CCC. If you are not familiar with an individual and his credentials, it is wise to contact ASHA and the state licensing board to determine his credentials. It is also important to note that licensing laws usually relate to direct patient assessment and treatment in the state where the service is provided, but do not address review of records or expert testimony. The national certification is a generic certification whereby the individual has met the minimum entry-level requirements across a broad spectrum of knowledge areas in communication sciences and disorders. When funding is available, third-party intermediaries use as a guideline the requirements for service delivery established by Medicare and Medicaid (i.e., ASHA CCC-SLP) and, where applicable, a current state license.

Speech-language pathologists who have the expertise to provide information in their area must also understand and participate in transdisciplinary integrated assessment and treatment models, have knowledge of funding streams and creative funding, be knowledgeable about state and federal policy, laws, and changes in these laws and policies, and be knowledgeable of collaborative sources and how to build them. They must also be able to provide clear, concise, understandable documentation that is written in a defensible but understandable format with functional milestones and goals available. For a complete communication assessment and many of the services related to delivery of care for individuals exhibiting communication and swallowing difficulties described in this chapter, it is advisable that the consulting speech-language pathologist hold a doctoral-level degree with emphasis in the areas of assistive technology. (See Appendix 9.1 for an outline of relevant information.)

Speech-Language Pathologist's Training and Preparation

The competent SLP has received preparation in the following areas, as they relate to human communication, swallowing, and development across the life span:

- Theories and processes of normal development and aging, including motor, cognitive, social-emotional, and communication
- Physiology of speech production and swallowing, including respiration, phonation, articulation, resonance, and the vocal/aerodigestive tract
- Embryological, genetic factors in development, including the development of craniofacial structures and the nervous system
- Anatomic structures, neuroanatomy, and neurophysiology supporting speech, language, hearing, swallowing, and respiration
- Organic etiologies of disorders of communication and swallowing
- Psychological and psychosocial influences on communication and swallowing
- Neurolinguistic, linguistic, cultural, and social influences on communication
- Theories of speech perception and production, language development, and cognition
- Ethics related to diagnosis, treatment, and professional conduct
- Basic computer theory and systems applications, including frequently used software and input and output devices, as they relate to evaluation and treatment of language and communication, augmentative and alternative communication (AAC), and swallowing
- Interpersonal communication, human learning, counseling theories and practices, and family systems and systems theory

The speech-language pathologist who is consulting on a life care plan should demonstrate an advanced knowledge and understanding of health care and educational facility practices; the common diseases and conditions affecting human communication, swallowing, and development across the life span; and medical, educational, surgical, and behavioral treatment as they relate to communication disorders, including knowledge of:

- Medical terminology
- Physicians' orders, confidentiality, legal issues in medical practices, and information and data systems management
- Elements of the physical examination and vital sign monitors
- Medical and laboratory tests and their purposes
- Medical record documentation practices

- Pharmacologic factors affecting communication and cognitive processes, development, and behavior
- Assistive technology, augmentative and alternative communication approaches, and the range of bioengineering adaptations used in medical settings
- Concepts of quality control and risk management
- Concepts in medical setting environmental safety (such as universal precautions, procedures, and infection control principles; radiation exposure precautions; and the Safe Medical Devices Act)
- Team processes
- Performance improvement processes
- Theories, concepts, and practices in outcomes measures
- Theories and concepts related to the impact of psychosocial and spiritual needs and the individual's cultural values on health care services
- Voice and laryngeal health and disorders
- Respiratory functions, tracheostomy tubes, and respiratory support requirements
- Neuroanatomy, neuropathology, and the neurophysiological support of swallowing, speech, language and related cognitive abilities, and the effects of diseases and disorders of the nervous system
- Concepts in human nutrition and hydration needs and their disorders
- Methods and interpretations in neuroimaging and other forms of anatomic imaging
- Esophageal, oropharyngeal, laryngeal, and neurologic tumors
- Concepts in neuropsychology and psychiatric and psychosocial disorders
- Common medical conditions
- Educational terminology
- Federal mandates related to education
- Broad understanding of curricula and literacy
- Educational philosophy of state education agencies
- Medical and surgical management of communication and swallowing

The speech-language pathologist should be able to demonstrate advanced skills and abilities in diagnostics, treatment, and service delivery. The SLP should be able to review medical records and conduct succinct clinical case histories and interviews, to gather relevant information related to communication and swallowing, and to select and administer appropriate diagnostic tools and procedures and treatment for communication and swallowing disorders that are functionally relevant, family-centered, culturally sensitive, and theoretically grounded.

The SLP should be able to:

- Obtain a representative sample and describe articulation and voice production in meaningful, accurate, and reliable terminology that addresses intelligibility and the audio-perceptual judgments of quality, tension, pitch, loudness, variability, steadiness, oral and nasal resonance, and severity of the disorder
- Interpret a range of acoustic and physiologic measures of voice production
- Demonstrate skills in instrumental assessments (acoustic, aerodynamic, electroglottographic, electromyographic, manometric, and ultrasonic measures)

- Apply techniques that ensure validity of signal processing, analysis routines, and elimination of task or signal artifacts
- Use one or more techniques for imaging the larynx, vocal tract, and nasopharynx, (flexible/rigid endoscopy, ultrasonography, or stroboscopy)
- Select and implement training and treatment procedures appropriate for speech prostheses and orthotics (tracheoesophageal puncture prosthesis, electrolarynges, speaking trachs and one-way valves, palatal lifts, voice amplifiers, voice output communication aids, obturators, and palatal augmentation prostheses)
- Conduct an oropharyngeal swallow examination accurately identifying abnormal structures and functions; identify symptoms, medical conditions, and medications pertinent to dysphagia; interpret and document examination findings; use instrumental techniques for screening and diagnosis of oropharyngeal dysphagia and for biofeedback in dysphagia management
- Conduct reliable and accurate modified barium swallow procedures following a standard protocol that includes identification of structural abnormalities; swallowing motility disorders; presence, time, and etiology of aspiration; and appropriate treatment techniques (posture, maneuvers, bolus modification)
- Determine patient management decisions regarding oral/nonoral intake, diet, risk precautions, candidacy for intervention, and treatment strategies
- Select and appropriately apply aided and unaided communication, including both linguistic and nonlinguistic modes and methods
- Locate and access assistive technology, services, and funding sources
- Work effectively with interpreters and translators and use assistive listening devices when needed for patient care
- Communicate findings and treatment plans in a manner that is fitting and consistent with health care facility procedures
- Counsel and educate patients and families and work within family systems to elicit participation in the treatment plan and work as a member of a health educational care team

The speech-language pathologist will need to consider all of the following categories, regardless of the age of the individual, in the development of information for the life care plan: an oral and pharyngeal swallowing (dysphagia) assessment to include modified barium swallows, videostroboscopy evaluation, prostodontic intervention, and palatal prostheses; cognitive communication information; auditory processing information to include central auditory processing, augmentative communication assessment information, assistive technology assessment information, voice and vocal information including videostroboscopy, and Botox assessment information; oral peripheral motor information; hearing acuity information; assistive listening device; and cochlear implant information.

The critical information obtained from a thorough communication sciences and disorders assessment must be considered within all the parameters of the life care plan itself. In other words, any and all areas that are impacted by deficits in communication and swallowing must be addressed with recommendations, if deemed appropriate by the evaluating speech-language pathologist. These parameters include projected evaluation, projected therapeutic modalities, diagnostic testing and educational assessment, mobility (including accessories and maintenance of mobility technology), aids for independent functioning, orthotics and prosthetics, home furnishing and accessories, pharmacology needs, home/facility care, future medical care, transportation, health and strength maintenance, architectural renovations, potential complications, orthopedic equipment needs, vocational/educational planning, assistive technology in the areas of sensory deficits, cognitive challenges, and communication disorders (including hearing and processing difficulties needing assistive listening devices). (See Appendix 9.2 for an outline of the above.)

TERMINOLOGY IN THE FIELD OF COMMUNICATION SCIENCES AND DISORDERS

The importance of terminology relative to our communication with other professionals and the general public, as well as the very special needs of international and transdisciplinary communication and development, has become increasingly apparent. In addition to improved consistency in the use of terms, there is the need to carefully examine what meanings the developing jargon may have to other individuals who rely primarily on a dictionary and common sense. Although many people in the field may know what is meant by a given term, others may not share the same meaning. Some terms used by many people in one country may not easily translate into other languages. Even more apparent, with the diversity of people in the world today, care must be exercised to consider multiple interpretations of a term, sometimes affected by the perspective of one's culture.

Because of the transdisciplinary nature of the medical-legal-clinical world, there are also problems of various disciplines using other jargon to describe essentially the same phenomenon, act, or characteristic. These problems reflect the need for an emerging field like life care planning to develop an internally consistent and logical terminology that will facilitate the international and transdisciplinary development of the field. It is important to actively educate individuals on the life care planning team concerning specific terminology that defines and describes areas of assessment and treatment within the field of communication sciences and disorders.

The Speech-Language Pathologist's Review of Records and Intake

The speech-language pathologist must perform his or her own case intake, consisting of talking with the referral source, determining the time frames needed to complete testing, arranging the financial and billing agreements, and arranging for a release of all pertinent information. Additional testing needed may be identified at this time or during the initial interview arrangements.

The speech-language pathologist will then review a copy of the medical records to include:

■ Nursing notes
■ Doctor's orders
■ Other services' reports
■ Educational information

- ■ Vocational information
- ■ Day-in-the-life videos
- ■ Other relevant documentation, depending on the etiology and diagnosis

A thorough assessment battery is then administered, gathering information from the spouse, family, or other relatives, including the clients themselves. This step may also include the opportunity for the speech-language pathologist to consult and interview other team members whose information may have a bearing on final recommendations of the speech-language pathologist. At this time, if additional medical, clinical, vocational, or educational information or evaluations are needed, requests for these additional information-gathering steps should be submitted to the referral source. A letter may be composed outlining the correct questions with supporting data to ensure that the speech-language pathologist has the opportunity to solicit the needed information.

At the completion of the assessment, the speech-language pathologist must be able to provide a written report, documenting the test results, observations, and conclusions with clear recommendations. These recommendations must be detailed to include a projection of future care costs, frequency of service or treatment, duration, base cost, source of information, and recognized vendors or manufacturers, current prices, collaborative sources, and categories of information. It is recommended that the consulting speech-language pathologist be knowledgeable about the local sources and costs of these recommendations, either through direct contact with suppliers or through catalog and desktop/computerized research. Recommendations from the speech-language pathologist should be discussed with the client and family, treatment team members, and other life care team members if they directly impact the final recommendations and the cost analysis of the plan by the economist. Any coordination and agreement needed between team members including the economist should occur at this time. A draft of the communication sciences and disorders assessment and recommendations report should be written and distributed to the life care planner for review relative of the accuracy and completeness of the information. The speech-language pathologist must be able to explain, from a life care planning perspective, the reasons and rationales that are relative to their recommendations. These must be lifelong recommendations and objectives, developed in an integrated format. Once the document is correct and complete, a final draft should be compiled and distributed to the life care planner and the referral source. It should be determined, by these two parties, whether the written documentation should be sent to other internal life care planning team members, including the family and client and to external individuals.

ASSESSMENT PROCESS

There are four methods of gathering and interpreting quantitative and qualitative information about the client that should be used in the communication sciences and disorders assessment process by the speech-language pathologist. These four measures are a collection of the initial database, interview procedures, clinical assessment, and formal assessment procedures (Dunn & Dunn, 1991). Often more than one method is used to gather information about the same aspect of a client's skills and abilities, the context, the activity, or the use of technology or equipment. Information collected should include the reason and need for referral, medical diagnosis, and educational and vocational background information. This information is collected during the referral and intake phase, and its purpose is to provide preliminary data for planning the assessment. The interview takes place during the identification phase as a means of gathering information regarding the consumer and his or her needs. It is important that the consumer, family members, rehabilitation or education professionals, and other care providers be interviewed.

Formal assessment procedures are administered in a prescribed way and have set methods of scoring and interpretation. Therefore, they can be duplicated and analyzed. They may or may not be standardized. Clinical assessment techniques involve skilled observation of the consumer and are used throughout the assessment process. These techniques may be structured so that a series of steps is followed to determine specific skills, or it may be intentionally left unstructured to see what takes place. Observation can be done during a simulated task in a clinic setting or in a context familiar to the consumer such as a classroom or workplace. Differential diagnosis is an ongoing and essential component of the assessment process and one that requires an advanced level of understanding and perspective about the trauma or injury.

PEDIATRIC AND ADOLESCENT ASSESSMENTS

Evaluating children (pediatric and adolescent) presents complex and challenging issues, complicated by the catastrophic nature of the disease, disability, or trauma and frequently challenged by the almost insurmountable task of planning a child's life. For these reasons, it is critical to make accurate and thorough projections and careful analysis of the disability; educate team members and caregivers about the pediatric disabilities and develop a differential diagnostic therapeutic approach to service delivery to the child. The list of pediatric and adolescent considerations in the communication sciences and disorders assessment is lengthy, detailed, and can be complex. It is important to disclose that the list is not all-inclusive, because changes occur as research and science enhance the process.

There are areas that warrant consideration when performing a communication evaluation for a pediatric or adolescent individual that are not considered, or at least not in the same detail, when evaluating an adult. Chronological age and pretrauma development are used as the normal benchmarks against which to measure the disability issues. Routine medical needs must be addressed to the pediatric specialists who would provide the information that impacts a child's communication development. These include pediatric physiatry, otolaryngology, pediatric neurology, developmental medicine, audiology, dental/orthodontic, prosthodontist, and pediatric neuro-ophthalmology and ophthalmology. It should be noted here that there is a trend in the medical specialty fields to identify specialists who work solely with adolescents. Additional cognitive and educational information is gathered from the following sources:

- Educational consultants to private and public educational programs
- Personal caregivers and attendants
- Pediatric neuropsychological assessment

- Occupational and physical therapy
- Vision and hearing specialists
- Evaluators of driving
- Programs for the development of social and pragmatic skills
- Prevocational and vocational training programs

FEDERAL MANDATES AND POLICIES

The SLP, as an outcome of the assessment results, frequently provides assistive technology (AT) or augmentative and alternative communication (AAC) recommendations. Assistive technology is defined as any technology used to enable individuals to perform tasks that are difficult or impossible due to disabilities (Lloyd et al., 1997). AAC itself is defined as the supplement or replacement of natural speech or writing using aided or unaided symbols, and the field is referred to as the clinical/educational practice to improve the communication skills of individuals with little or no functional speech (Lloyd et al., 1997). It is important to be knowledgeable about the laws and policies that support the use of AT or AAC. The list of federal mandates that relate to the use of assistive technology, the development of assistive technology services (evaluation and therapy), and the integration of assistive technology devices and services into medicine, education, independent living, and vocational arenas is lengthy. A partial list of mandates, listed in Table 9.3, continues to change (and improve) and is not considered to be inclusive. It is included to give readers an idea of the growing list of political directives that acknowledge the consumer's need for assistive technology devices and services.

Industrial advancements and competition have driven the recent development of assistive technology devices, but the development of services and service delivery in the U.S. has been influenced significantly by federal legislation. Over the last 40 years, the federal government has enacted a series of bills and initiatives

Table 9.3 Federal Mandates

Section 504 of the Rehabilitation Act of 1973
Rehabilitation Act of 1973, reauthorization and amendments of 1993 and 1998
Individuals with Disabilities Education Act (IDEA), PL 101-476
Technology-Related Assistance for Individuals with Disabilities Act of 1988, PL 100-407
Technology-Related Assistance for Individuals with Disabilities Act Amendments, PL 103-218
Americans with Disabilities Act (ADA) of 1990, PL 101-336
Goals 2000: Educate America Act, PL 103-85
Improving America's Schools Act, PL 103-382
Telecommunications Act of 1996, PL 104-104
Telecommunications for the Disabled Act of 1982
Telecommunications Accessibility Enhancement Act of 1988
Rehabilitation Act, Section 508
Decoder Circuitry Act

requiring federal agencies, states, and private industry to support the employment of people with disabilities. Milestones over the 40 years include the following most recent legislation.

The Rehabilitation Act of 1973 mandates reasonable accommodation in federally funded employment and higher education for assistive technology and services. This act has established several important principles upon which subsequent legislation has been based. These include *reasonable accommodations* in employment and in secondary education. The act mandates that employers and institutions of higher education receiving federal funds seek to accommodate the needs of employers and students who have disabilities. It specifically prohibited discrimination in employment or admission to academic programs solely on the basis of a handicapping condition. Sections 503 (educational institutions) and 504 (employers receiving federal funds) of this act describe both reasonable accommodations and *least restrictive environment* (LRE), a term relating to the degree of modification in a job or academic program that is acceptable. Many of the efforts to achieve accommodations in the least restrictive environment involved the use of assistive technologies.

The Education for All Handicapped Children Act (EHA) of 1975 extends reasonable accommodations for students from ages 5 to 21, providing a free, appropriate public education (FAPE). This act initiated procedures to ensure that each public school system identifies and provides all children with disabilities with an education. States were also mandated to establish procedures for enforcement. Assistive technology plays a more significant role in gaining access to educational programs. The act created the Individual Education Plan (IEP) to be made for all students with disabilities. This act, also known as PL 94-142, established the right of all children to a free and appropriate education, regardless of handicapping condition. When PL 94-142 passed, children with disabilities who were not in school programs or those who were but who were not receiving services began Individual Education Plans (IEPs) with measurable goals, assistive technology, and services. Lack of local services or lack of funding was not a reason to deny services. The impact of this law has been far reaching. Devices ranging from sensory aids (visual and auditory) to augmentative communication devices to specialized computers have been utilized to provide access to educational programs for children with disabilities. Several additional acts leading up to PL 94-142 gave the foundation for the passage of this act.

The passage of the Elementary and Secondary Education Act (PL 89-10) in 1965 to improve quality of education for individuals and the passage of Elementary and Secondary Education Amendments for Children with Handicaps (PL 89-313) established the foundation for future legislation dealing with children with handicaps. The zero reject principle is the principle developed out of EHA, stating that all children, regardless of the severity of their disability, have a right to special education services. These services are provided by the local education agency (LEA) in the least restrictive environment. The Handicapped Infants and Toddlers Act of 1986 extended the preceding act to children ages 5 and under, expanding emphasis on educationally related assistive technology.

The 1986 amendment to the Rehabilitation Act of 1973 required all states to include provision for assistive technology services in the rehabilitation plans of the state vocational rehab agencies. Section 508 mandates equal access to elec-

Table 9.4 Tech Act Priorities

To promote public awareness of assistive technology at the national level

To provide training and education about assistive technology on a national basis for stakeholders, including other national social service and business organizations, members of the insurance and health care industry, and public office holders/policy makers

To develop positions on a full range of national assistive technology- and disability-related issues and to share these positions with other organizations or policy makers, as needed, to ensure that the views of the states and territories and their consumers with regard to assistive technology service delivery are adequately represented

To provide a forum for exchanging information and promoting the system change accomplishments and activities of the Tech Act projects

To identify the need and opportunities for the development of nationally conducted activities to increase access to assistive technology

To develop and promote a national agenda

tronic office equipment for all federal employees. Technology-Related Assistance for Individuals with Disabilities Act (Tech Act) of 1988 mandates consumer-driven assistive technology services and system changes in the states. This act created the development of the Tech Act programs throughout the country. The act was reauthorized in 1994. This legislation authorized funds for states to establish and implement a consumer-responsive, statewide program of technology-related assistance for individuals with disabilities, including identification of barriers to administering this assistance. Table 9.4 lists the priorities for the continuation of Tech Act activities.

The Americans with Disabilities Act (ADA) (PL 101-336) of 1990 prohibits discrimination based on disability in employment, transportation, and telecommunications. The ADA furthers the goal of full participation of people with disabilities by giving civil rights protection to individuals with disabilities that are like those provided to individuals on the basis of race, sex, national origin, and religion. It guarantees equal opportunity for individuals with disabilities in employment, public accommodations, transportation, state and local government services, and telecommunications. President Bush signed the ADA into law on July 26, 1990. Copies of the full Americans with Disabilities Act of 1990 may be obtained at no cost from the U.S. Subcommittee on Disability Policy, 113 Hart, Senate Office Building, Washington, DC 20510. The ADA Private Transportation Hotline is (202) 224-6265.

The Individuals with Disabilities Education Act (IDEA) of 1991 (Public Law 105-17 and the reauthorization of PL 94-142) mandates that all local educational agencies provide assistive technology devices and services to benefit students with disabilities. The IDEA mandate includes that local educational agencies be responsible for providing assistive technology devices and services if these are required as part of the child's educational or related services or as a supplementary aid or service. Assistive technology devices are identified in the IDEA as "any item, piece of equipment or product system, whether acquired commercially off the shelf, modified, or customized, that is used to increase, maintain, or improve the functional capabilities of children with disabilities" (Section 300.5).

The definition of an assistive technology device, as provided in the IDEA, is very broad and gives IEP teams the flexibility that they need to make decisions about appropriate assistive technology devices for individual students. Assistive technology includes a range of low and high technology, hardware and software, and technology solutions that are generally considered instructional technology tools if they have been identified as educationally necessary and documented in the student's IEP. The need for assistive technology is determined by the student's IEP committee as *educationally* necessary. Assistive technology service is any service that directly assists a child with a disability in the selection, acquisition, and use of an assistive technology device. The term includes (1) the evaluation of the needs of a child with a disability, including a functional evaluation of the child in the child's customary environment; (2) purchasing, leasing, or otherwise providing for the acquisition of assistive technology devices by children with disabilities; (3) selecting, designing, fitting, customizing, adapting, applying, retaining, repairing, or replacing assistive technology devices; (4) coordinating and using other therapies, interventions, or services with assistive technology devices, such as those associated with existing education and rehabilitation plans and programs; (5) training and technical assistance for a child with a disability or, if appropriate, that child's family; and (6) training or technical assistance for professionals (including individuals or rehabilitation services), employers, or other individuals who provide services to employ or are otherwise substantially involved in the major life functions of children with disabilities (Section 300.6). The rules and regulations for special education in each state may also address the provision of assistive devices and services in various sections of the state's educational policy and regulations, including the definition of assistive devices, the definition of service, within what parts of the IEP assistive technology may be included (related services, supplemental aids and services, etc.), whether assistive technology is needed to provide the student a FAPE, whether an assistive technology assessment is needed, if assistive technology is needed for the student to participate in local or state testing, and whether the technology is needed in a nonschool setting.

The reauthorization of the Rehabilitation Act of 1973 (1992) mandates rehabilitation technology to be a primary benefit to be included in the rehabilitation plan for the state rehabilitation agencies. The rehab plan was required to include how assistive technology will be used in the rehabilitation process of each individual client. In 1992, Congress passed the reauthorization of the Rehabilitation Act of 1973. This legislation (PL 102-569) makes the rehabilitation act consistent with the principles of self-determination of the ADA, and it is more consumer responsive than the original version. Rehabilitation technology is defined in this law to include rehabilitation engineering and assistive technology devices and services. Under this legislation each state must specify how assistive technology devices and services or work site assessments are to be provided. The individualized written rehabilitation plan (IWRP, but now referred to as the Individual Work Plan, or IWP) must include the provisions of rehabilitation technology services to assist in the implementation of intermediate and long-term objectives, and rehabilitation technology is exempt from what are termed comparable benefits funding considerations. The latter concept means that vocational rehabilitation monies are considered to be the first source of funding for purchase of assistive technology regardless of whether the individual has other funding sources. Also included within the mandate of this legislation was the continuation of rehabilitation engineering research centers, which focus on one or more core areas of research and development.

The Ticket to Work and Work Incentive Improvement Act of 1999 provides consumer choices for the provision of vocational rehabilitation and job training and other support services. The Ticket to Work and Work Incentive Improvement Act of 1999 has a number of incentives that can be offered to benefit recipients to help them reintegrate into the workplace. Agencies that provide employment training and job placement to people with disabilities will receive a fixed portion of that person's prospective Social Security case benefit when the individual goes back to work and in the first few years during the individual's employment.

The New Freedom Initiative (February 2001) increases funding for research and development of assistive technology resources nationwide. Although not legislation, this initiative also promotes full access to the community for people with disabilities through expanded transportation options, educational opportunities, and greater integration into the workforce. Readers should refer to Appendix 9.4 for funding terminology information.

Speech-language pathologists (and audiologists) must address the unique privacy concerns, both ethical and regulatory, that confront individuals who rely on assistive technology and the speech-language pathologists and other practitioners who provide them with services (Blackstone et al., 2002). The Health Insurance Portability and Accountability Act of 1996 (HIPAA) was created by Congress to provide guidelines for the protection of health care information and to establish standard formats for the electronic transmission of clinical data such as claims, referrals, explanation of benefits (EOB), remittance advices (RAs), and others. Although there are nine separate elements to the HIPAA legislation, the Department of Health and Human Services (DHHS) has thus far promulgated three in the form of final regulatory rules, the privacy rule and the transaction and code set rules, and the security of health care data as they are generated and stored by providers and others who have access to this protected information.

The privacy rule of HIPAA is intended as a federal floor to protect the privacy of individually identifiable health information contained in a patient's medical record. The protected information includes a patient's name, address, Social Security number, financial data, or any other identifying information in addition to the medical record itself. The rule creates substantial new compliance issues for covered entities, which include virtually all health care providers, health plans, health information clearinghouses, and those business associates who engage directly or through contractual arrangements with any of the above. It also covers paper files containing this protected information that is not yet in electronic form. In short, it covers all information, including both hard and soft files. The compliance date for the privacy rule was April 14, 2003. Substantial civil and criminal penalties, up to and including jail time, can be assessed for noncompliance.

The final HIPAA privacy rule covers all individually identifiable health care information in any form, electronic or nonelectronic, that is held or transmitted by a covered entity such as a health care provider, a third-party payer, or any of

Table 9.5 HIPAA Helpful Websites

http://eduserv.hscer.washington.edu/bioethics/topics/consent.html
http://humansubjects.stanford.edu/manual/chapters/ch8_1_informed.html
http://www.professional.asha.org/resources/legislative/hipaa.cfm

their business associates who come into contact with these data. Under HIPAA, there are legal penalties for covered entities that receive or use unauthorized information intentionally. SLPs, by transmitting personal health information (PHI) in electronic form, are regulated by HIPAA. The following points about HIPAA and assistive technology should be followed to remain compliant.

SLPs should consider assistive devices that facilitate the security of PHI by providing essential design features, vocabulary, and training that emphasize the rights to privacy and informed consent of individuals who rely on assistive devices, strategies, and techniques. The SLP is responsible for making sure the PHI is not openly accessible. New devices offer both text and audio-data logging. These logs potentially put the user at risk if they are available to others. All AAC users should receive a copy of the provider's Notice of Privacy Practices. The Notice of Privacy Practices explains how the provider will use the individual's PHI and outlines the provider's confidentiality program. SLPs should educate themselves on HIPAA regulations, should conduct a gap analysis of their practice policies and procedures, and should undertake a compliance implementation program. The privacy and safety of individuals using communication boards and AAC devices should be considered when including personal information (name, address, phone number, religion, political affiliation, etc.). Remember that not all assistive technology users understand the privacy issues either. Eavesdropping, communication partners speaking loudly to interpret the message, and people reading what is on the screen are all potential violations of privacy. Assistive technology users need training to learn to protect their privacy and need help selecting vocabulary such as "Please do not read my display." Assistive technology users also need training to coordinate their speech output to conform to public expectations of conversations, help to lower the volume of their device, password protection and encryption of the message buffer and data logging system in the assistive technology device to protect the user's content, and privacy/confidentiality training for their communication partners. Table 9.5 has HIPAA helpful websites.

SPEECH-TO-SPEECH RELAY SYSTEM

Individuals with speech disabilities who live in the U.S. (including Puerto Rico and the Virgin Islands) have available the free telephone service called Speech to Speech (STS) 24 hours a day. This service provides communication assistants (CAs) for people with difficulty being understood by the public on the telephone. The Federal Communications Commission (FCC) in Washington, D.C., regulates relay service. STS is provided through an extensive telecommunications relay service and is available during limited hours in Sweden and Australia. STS is provided through the TTY relay in each state. Unlike TTY, STS enables people with speech disabilities to communicate by voice through a CA, as many people with speech difficulties have difficulty typing. People with speech disabilities can dial toll-free to reach a patient, trained CA who is familiar with many speech patterns and has excellent language recognition skills. This CA makes telephone calls for them and repeats their words exactly in a three-way calling environment. Every month users make about 6000 calls nationally (2003). STS is the only way for many people to telephone others not accustomed to their speech. STS's website is http://www.stsnews.com/. The STS listserv is stslistserv@stsnews.com. One can also access STS by dialing 711 and asking for Speech to Speech.

MANUFACTURERS' ROLES

Manufacturers' roles in assistive technology are often disputed and discussed. The responsibility of the manufacturer/vendor/representative varies depending on the expertise of the assistive technology team and the expertise of the SLP. The Communication Aids Manufacturers Association (CAMA) is an association of suppliers of augmentative communication devices and systems. Devices are designed into a prototype device to convert it to a version that can be fabricated in small quantities and tested with potential users. Testing of this production prototype is commonly referred to as *alpha testing* and is normally conducted as an in-house function by the manufacturers. Once the device appears to be functioning properly, several additional replicas are fabricated. During this development stage, the manufacturer is able to determine potential problems that may develop during the manufacturing phase and the prototypes can be evaluated more extensively by several individuals, usually clinicians and consumers simultaneously (*beta testing*). This accomplishes the identification of potential problems in the product, evaluation of product documentation to ensure that it is clear and useful, and evaluation of the product with a variety of individuals with disabilities to identify the target population as accurately as possible. Manufacturing then occurs, by which a working prototype of the AAC device is converted into a device that is then produced. For a complete listing of the CAMA members and additional vendors, please refer to Appendix 9.5. Additional information and resources specific to each CAMA company are listed at the CAMA website (www.aacproducts.com). Appendix 9.6, Selected AAC Websites, also has a wealth of AAC and AT resources.

FUNDING AND ECONOMIC ISSUES

There are a variety of financing and funding options for services and technology needs that a qualified speech-language pathologist could recommend for support in the life care planning process. It is the consulting speech-language pathologist's responsibility to understand where and how to access this information on collateral funding sources. These include public programs such as maternal and child health, education, vocational rehabilitation, developmental disability programs, Department of Veterans Affairs programs, and Older Americans Act programs. There are alternative funding sources such as loans, libraries, foundations, and charitable organizations, as well as understanding options under the U.S. tax code, and the issues of civil rights, universal access, and telecommunications (Appendix 9.3).

Information on current initiatives and emerging promising best practices related to the funding and acquisition of technology and services is also available and should be considered in the development of the life care plan for the areas of speech-language pathology and assistive technology. Knowledge of policy and funding information adds credibility and strength to this portion of the life care planning process. Frequently, recommended technology and services in the areas of communication sciences and disorders/speech-language pathology are costly and require a lengthier and more complex plan of treatment than some other areas of the plan. If the consultant in this area can show his or her ability to understand and develop funding options and plans, the success of this portion of the plan is strengthened. The speech-language pathologist who is involved in the life care planning process must have a current and accurate analysis of the marketplace with regard to the cost of services and technology or other goods needed in his or her portion of recommendations in the life care process. This also directly relates to potential policy changes in health care and education that may directly affect specific recommendations in the areas of communication sciences and disorders and current funding terminology (Appendix 9.4).

MEDICAL CODING

Medical coding is useful to life care planners and SLPs for documentation and billing purposes. *Current Procedural Terminology*, 4th edition (*CPT*) is a systematic listing and coding of procedures and services performed by physicians, based upon the procedure being consistent with contemporary medical practice and being performed by many physicians in clinical practice in multiple locations. Each procedure is identified with a five-digit code. Prior to 2001, SLPs used the CPT code 92597 for AAC evaluations for use and fitting of a voice prosthetic or AAC device to supplement oral speech and the CPT code 92598 for modification of a voice prosthetic or AAC device or supplemental oral speech. CPT codes 92506 (speech and language evaluation) and 92507 (treatment of speech and language disorders) were also used. In January 2001, the Centers for Medicare and Medicaid Services (CMS) assigned temporary *HCPCS Level II G codes* to services related to AAC devices that were being reviewed prior to inclusion in the *CPT* manual. Once CPT codes for these services are assigned, the G codes are deleted. The HCPCS Level II G codes are listed in Table 9.6.

In January 2003, five CPT codes specifically for AAC services replaced the G codes. These codes and definitions are listed in Table 9.7. These codes are used specifically for all AAC services (evaluation, reevaluation, and therapy). Readers should be cautioned in two regards. First, readers should refer to the *AMA CPT Code Manual* (2003) and the ASHA website (http://www.professional.asha.org) for clarification of the AAC codes or for further information on any of the speech, language, and hearing codes. Medical codes are always subject to updating and changes, so clinicians should stay current with medical coding terminology. Second, readers need to remember that there are Level II HCPCS national codes for speech-generating and non-speech-generating devices, called K codes (Table 9.8). The device codes (K codes) are specifically for devices, accessories, and software. The CPT codes are for evaluation and treatment services. Readers will also find a wealth of resources in Appendix 9.7 (Toll-Free Phone Numbers

Table 9.6   Temporary HCPCS Level II G Codes for AAC Services

G0197   Evaluation of patient for prescription of speech-generating devices describes the services to evaluate a patient to specify the speech-generating device recommended to meet the patient's needs and capacity for use

G0198   Patient adaptation and training for use of speech-generating devices describes the services delivered to the patient to adapt the device to the patient and train him or her in its use

G0199   Reevaluation of patient using speech-generating devices describes the services to reevaluate a patient who has previously been evaluated for a speech-generating device and either is currently using a device or did not have a device recommended

Table 9.7   CPT Codes and Definitions for AAC Services

CPT 92605	Evaluation for prescription of non-speech-generating augmentative and alternative communication device
CPT 92606	Therapeutic service(s) for the use of non-speech-generating device, including programming and modification
CPT 92607 (replaces G0197)	Evaluation for prescription for speech-generating augmentative and alternative communication device; face-to-face with the patient; evaluation, first hour [For evaluation for prescription for a non-speech-generating device, use 92605]
CPT 92608	Each additional 30 minutes (list separately in addition to code for primary procedure) [Use 92608 in conjunction with 92607]
CPT 92609 (replaces G0195)	Therapeutic services for the use of speech-generating device, including programming and modification

and Hotlines), Appendix 9.8 (Internet Resources), and Appendix 9.9 (Periodicals and Newsletters).

NEUROLITIGATION

Following the development of the complete plan by the life care planner, it is possible that the plan will become part of neurolitigation. Success in neurolitigation frequently depends on the quality and quantity of expert evidence, which directly relates to the presentation of the life care plan, especially during medical malpractice cases and traumatic brain injury and spinal cord injury cases. Courts may admit the life care plan into evidence and rely on those plans as the predicate for compensatory damage awards when a well-qualified rehabilitation specialist prepares those plans. Included should be a list of treatment interventions that are reasonable and necessary and that show the real need for the individual to incur the expenses noted in the plan, and accurate, reasonable, and conservative costs for future care. Speech-language pathologists participating in the life care planning

Table 9.8 K Codes

K0541	Speech-generating device, digitized speech, using prerecorded messages, less than or equal to 8 minutes recording time
K0542	Speech-generating device, digitized speech, using prerecorded messages, greater than 8 minutes recording time
K0543	Speech-generating device, synthesized speech, requiring message formulation by spelling and access by physical contact with the device
K0544	Speech-generating device, synthesized speech, permitting multiple methods of message formulation and multiple methods of device access
K0545	Speech-generating software program, for personal computer or personal digital assistant
K0546	Accessory for speech-generating device, mounting system
K0547	Accessory for speech-generating device, not otherwise classified

Note: The fee schedule amounts for each code are dependent on the current Medicare Fee Schedule. A speech-generating device (SGD) is the Medicare terminology for a AAC device.

process need to appreciate these requirements and understand their possible role in neurolitigation. It is possible that the consulting speech-language pathologist will have to give testimony in a deposition concerning his or her area within the life care plan, or may be considered as an expert witness if the case goes to trial. The speech-language pathologist will be responsible for answering questions and explaining his or her portions of the life care plan.

Regardless of particular knowledge, skills, experience, training, or education, the expert who is able to clearly articulate his opinions and conclusions, who understands the dynamics of the litigation process, and who comports with commonsense techniques for presenting testimony is the expert the attorney wishes to use to advance his or her client's cause. Obviously, the expert must be both professional and knowledgeable in demeanor and appearance, must be familiar with the various types of rehabilitation programs and therapeutic services available, must possess an in-depth knowledge of the current literature, and understand and be able to explain intervention strategies employed at all levels of treatment. Being able to explain the complexities involved in extremely specialized fields of expertise, without appearing to condescend to lay jurors, is particularly important.

The following is a list of general considerations that speech-language pathologists who function as experts for the purpose of explaining their part of the life care planning process should espouse:

1. Tell the truth. Then you will not have to remember what you said.
2. Phrase your answers with care. Be conscious of what they will look like in black and white.
3. Answer only the question asked; do not volunteer information.
4. Do not answer a question that you do not understand. It is not up to you to educate the examiner, and if he misuses words common in your profession, do not explain distinctions or ask questions as to what he means; it is up to him to formulate an intelligible question.

5. Do not guess, speculate, or assume anything. You only know what you have seen or heard; there is a difference between what you know and whether you have information concerning a particular subject.

6. Do not be positive about a subject unless you are; it is no crime to fail to remember or to be vague if that is the truth.

7. Do not adopt the examiner's phraseology or conclusions. If the question contains a false assumption ("Isn't it true that all communication tests are conducted in this manner?"), or terms that are not precisely correct ("So you *frequently* performed this treatment for this patient?"), point out the language you do not wish to accept and stick to the facts. Beware of questions that start with "Isn't it fair to say" or that attempt to paraphrase or summarize your previous testimony on a particular point.

8. Do not explain the manner in which you reached your answer, because such invariably involves other facts concerning which you have not been asked.

9. Do not testify concerning a document that is an exhibit until you have read it over thoroughly. Do not discuss documents that are not exhibits unless specifically asked about them, and then do not be positive about their content unless you are certain of your answer. Make no assumptions about documents.

10. Never get upset, explain, or argue with the examiner. You are liable to say things that are not correct, and in any event, it is not your duty to help him in this task.

11. If an objection to a question is made by counsel who retains you, listen very carefully, as it may provide information as to some underlying snare.

12. Avoid small talk, levity, ethnic or derogatory slurs of any kind, and even the mildest obscenity. Better to come across as formal than as a non-serious or offensive person.

13. If at any time during the deposition you realize you previously said something that was a mistake or incorrect, correct the error as soon as possible. Do not waive your right to read and sign a deposition. Should a realization of an error arrive after the deposition has been completed, you should make such correction on the errata sheet that will be supplied to you at the time you are asked to sign off on the deposition as transcribed.

Presentation of testimony by selected members of the rehabilitation team in litigation can be of immense benefit to counsel, the court, and lay jurors in furthering the understanding and costs associated with present and future needs and care and treatment, and in providing a framework on which an insurer or jury can justify a substantial settlement or award. One's abilities to be effective in this regard are aided by a clear understanding of one's role as an expert witness and the ability to interact with others and clearly articulate one's specialized knowledge in the areas at issue, placed in the context of a full understanding of the dynamics of the litigation process and an awareness of the techniques of proper presentation.

HOT TOPICS IN SPEECH-LANGUAGE PATHOLOGY

The following is a list of hot topics in the field of speech-language pathology/communication disorders. These topics will continue to develop over the next several years, affecting recommendations in life care plans. Life care planners are encouraged to monitor these topics and to be assured that they are always on the cutting edge of this information as they develop strong well-written and well-researched life care plans.

Development of specific treatment guidelines in neurological treatment of communication disorders (e.g., cognitive communication, aphasia, apraxia, dysarthria, and dementia)

Development of research in gastroesophageal reflux disease (GERD)

Efficacy and evidence-based studies to determine what treatments are effective

Development of a stronger presence with funding streams and sources

Improving treatment outcomes with all areas of treatment

Development of instrumentation to improve diagnostic and treatment measures (fiberendoscopy, e-stimulation, cervical auscultation, deep pharyngeal stimulation)

Increased inclusion as a member of medical surgical teams for management of head and neck issues (e.g., laryngectomees, palatal surgeries, vocal cord surgeries) and brain surgeries (e.g., removal of tumors, control postcerebral vascular accidents, seizure controls)

Increased research and treatment of progressive neurological diseases such as Parkinson's, dementia, Alzheimer's, and multiple sclerosis

Increased research participation with neurotroaphic cortical electrode implantation

Increased research with speech-language treatment postcochlear implants

Research with pharmacological therapeutic interventions to improve communication in patient with communication disorders

CASE STUDY

Disability

The client, Merrie Chrismoss, reportedly experienced asphyxia at birth and has cerebral palsy, which mildly impairs her ability to control her extremities, and possible mild brain dysfunction, which may impair her ability to learn. At the time of the interview, she was 2 years and 9 months of age. She did not demonstrate a functional ability to speak, but was alert and responsive to the environment.

A complete series of tests was administered, including cognitive and oral–motor (results will not be included in this brief example) evaluations appropriate for her age, and the child clearly appeared capable of participation in speech and language therapy. The rehabilitation plan below was part of a comprehensive life care plan; however, only the appropriate topics for the speech-language therapist are included.

Partial Rehabilitation Plan

Recommendation	Dates	Frequency	Expected Cost
Medical Needs			
Swallow study with videofluoroscopy	2004–2024	Yearly to October 2007, then at ages 16 and 22	$400
Otolaryngologist	2004–2008	Yearly to October 2008, then optional depending on complications	$200 (estimate)
Nutrition consult	2004–2024	Yearly to age 6, then at ages 14 and 22	$50 each
Drooling medication	2004 to life expectancy	Daily	$100/year (estimate)
Optional pulmonology	Only if complications	Unknown	Unknown
Home and Accessories			
Environmental control unit	2004 to life expectancy	Replace every 5 years	$640 + $50/year maintenance and updates
Assistive Technology Supplies/Equipment			
Augmentative and alternative communications (AAC)	2004 to life expectancy	*Evaluation:* 1 time/year through school and then every 5 years; specialty evaluation begins in 2007 *Devices:* Replace every 5 years from 2007 to life	$0 for school $1800 evaluation $2000 now $6000–7000 in 2007 and every 5 years thereafter
Wheelchair mount and latching system for AAC	2004 to life expectancy	When power wheelchair is replaced	$1200
Power pack for AAC	2004 to life expectancy	When wheelchair is replaced	$595 for power chair $400 for manual
Summer AAC camp in lieu of summer therapy	2005–2027	Yearly	$2000 plus $1000 (estimate) for transportation
Speech and language therapy	2004–2024	Weekly	$0, provided by school system; also see education

(continued)

Partial Rehabilitation Plan (Continued)

Recommendation	Dates	Frequency	Expected Cost
Assistive Technology Supplies/Equipment (continued)			
MyoTrac 2 Biofeedback portable unit	2004–2024	As part of therapy and swallowing program	$1600 every 5 years (with 1-year warranty); pack of 10 sensors $65 (replace one every 3 months)
Education Related			
Adapted education program	2008–2024	Public school schedule	No additional cost
Work/study station in home (school to provide equipment and software for education program)	2008–2014	Update 2014, 2024	$1000 (2008) $2000 (2014) $8000 (2024)
Computer, printer, oversize monitor, initial operating software and setup	2004 to life expectancy	Replace every 5 years	$2700 + $50/year switches
Specialized software	2004 to life expectancy	Yearly	$2000 in 2004, then $500/year
Multiphone for AAC	2012	1 time only	$300
Technical support/engineer	2008–2024	2008, 2014, 2024	$1200 (2008), then $300 in 2014 and $300 in 2024
Nonamplified auditory trainer	2004–2024	Replace every 5 years	$1500

CONCLUSION

The opportunity to participate in the life care planning process should not be taken lightly. It is one of the most rewarding parts of the profession of speech-language pathology for this author. It requires professionals who are respected among their peers for their hard work, diligent study, research, data collection and use, expert testimony, and even their ability to explain their results and information in written form. Standards must be placed on what the industry expects from its consultants when the consultants provide strong, useful assessments and recommendations. It is time for life care planners to set a level of accountability, responsibility, and recognition for the consultants that they use to develop the communication and swallowing areas of the life care plan, and it is time for speech-language pathologists to empower themselves for this process.

REFERENCES

American Medical Association. (2003). Current Procedural Terminology CPT 2004. Chicago, IL: Author.

American Speech-Language-Hearing Association. (1989). Competencies for speech-language pathologists providing services in augmentative communication. *ASHA*, 31, 61–64, 107–110.

American Speech-Language-Hearing Association. (1991). Augmentative and alternative communication. *ASHA*, 33 (Suppl. 5), 8–12.

American Speech-Language-Hearing Association. (1993). Preferred practice patterns for the professions of speech-language pathology and audiology. *ASHA*, 35 (Suppl. 11), 25–26, 27–28, 49–50, 51–52, 61–62, 87–88.

American Speech-Language-Hearing Association. (1996). Scope of practice in speech-language pathology. *ASHA*, 36 (Suppl. 16), 12–15.

American Speech-Language-Hearing Association. (2003a). Code of ethics. *ASHA*, 36 (Suppl. 13), 1–2.

American Speech-Language Hearing Association. (2003b). Speech-to-Speech Relay. Retrieved April 8, 2003, from http://www.asha.org/takeaction/Speech-to-Speech-Relay.cfm.

Bhatnagar, S. & Andy, O. (2003). *Neuroscience for the Study of Communicative Disorders*, 2nd ed. Baltimore: Williams & Wilkins.

Blackstone, S., Higgenbotham, J., & Williams, A. (2002). Privacy in the information age. *The ASHA Leader*, 7, 12–13.

Dunn, L. & Dunn, L. (1991). *Peabody Picture Vocabulary Test*, rev. ed. Circle Pines, MN: American Guidance Service.

Lloyd, L., Fuller, D., & Arvidson, H. (1997). *Augmentative and Alternative Communication: A Handbook of Principles and Practices*. Boston: Allyn & Bacon.

Venkatagiri, H. (1996). The quality of digitized and synthesized speech: what clinicians should know. *American Journal of Speech-Language Pathology, A Journal of Clinical Practice*, 5, 24–28.

Appendix 9.1 Communication Sciences and Disorders/SLP Assessment Process

1. **WHO** is a qualified speech-language pathologist for life care planning purposes?
   A. Training, licensure, certification, and practice settings
   B. Ability to network
   C. Integrated transdisciplinary model
   D. Knowledge of funding streams and creative funding
   E. Knowledge of state and federal policy, laws, and procedures
   F. Knowledge of the development of collaborative sources
2. **WHAT** will a qualified speech-language pathologist need?
   A. Review of all pertinent medical, vocational, educational, pharmacological, and sociological information
   B. Differences between a staff speech-language pathology evaluation and the type of data needed to support a life care plan and to support the medical-legal challenges
   C. Time needed to complete a communication sciences and disorders assessment
   D. Understanding of related professional information and how it impacts and affects the speech-language information and plans
   E. An ability to understand future trends and their application to the life care plan
3. **COMPONENTS** of a communication disorders assessment
   A. Oral and pharyngeal swallowing (dysphagia) assessment to include modified barium swallows, videostroboscopy evaluations, prostodontic intervention, and palatal prostheses
   B. Cognitive communication information
   C. Audiological information to include central auditory processing information
   D. Augmentative communication assessment information
   E. Assistive technology assessment information
   F. Voice (to include videostroboscopy, Botox assessment information, etc.)
   G. Oral peripheral motor information
   H. Hearing acuity information
   I. Assistive listening device or cochlear implant information
4. **WRITTEN** documentation prepared in a defensible but understandable plan with functional milestones and goals
   A. Ability to determine lifelong goals and functional outcomes
   B. Ability to understand how to develop services and technology needs over time
   C. Ability to explain how decisions within other areas of the life care plan will impact assessment, treatment, and technology needs within the communication sciences and disorders part of the plan
   D. Ability to explain present data in terms of future impact

Appendix 9.2   Communication Sciences and Disorders: Checklist for Life Care Planning

____ 1. Does the funding source understand the purpose and usefulness of a complete evaluation from a speech-language pathologist?

____ 2. Check qualifications, credentials, and areas of expertise of the speech-language pathologist you have selected to provide the information.

____ 3. Does the speech-language pathologist understand the concepts of the life care planning process and how the information provided by him or her will be used?

____ 4. Is the speech-language pathologist aware of the professional content areas within communication sciences and disorders that must be included/considered in the report to the life care planner?

    A. Expressive language

    B. Receptive language

    C. Cognitive communication

    D. Oral and pharyngeal dysphagia

    E. Augmentative communication

    F. Assistive technology

    G. Hearing and auditory processing as it relates to communication

    H. Voice and voicing aspects

    I. Fluency and rate

____ 5. Can the speech-language pathologist provide the results in a timely manner that meets deadlines?

____ 6. Has the speech-language pathologist been provided access to all available and necessary records, including medical, educational, vocational, and specialized testing?

____ 7. Are the client and family available for a thorough test battery? Are there access restrictions?

____ 8. Once information is gathered, is the speech-language pathologist able to provide thorough written documentation with clear recommendations?

____ 9. Have the questions in the following areas been considered during the communication sciences and disorders assessment?

Evaluations/Assessments

____ Have all the necessary assessments in the areas of communication sciences and disorders (language, speech, swallowing, augmentative communication, assistive technology, hearing, central auditory processing, videostroboscopy, modified barium swallow studies) been considered?

____ When will reassessments be scheduled?

____ At what ages or levels of functioning will these reassessments (or additional assessments) be considered?

Therapy

____ How will necessary therapies be identified?

____ How will collaborative sources be used?

Appendix 9.2 (Continued)   Communication Sciences and Disorders: Checklist for Life Care Planning

Assistive Technology

____ How will technology recommendations for augmentative communication be integrated with other assistive technology recommendations or other assistive technology that is already present?

____ Consider the use of low and high technology to include wheelchairs, environmental controls, vision equipment, hearing aids, computers, adaptive aids, assistive listening systems.

____ Have maintenance schedules, maintenance contracts, extended warranties, and replacement schedules been considered?

____ What is the range of assistive technology that is needed?

____ Have the following been considered: computers, means of access, size of screens, assisted listening, low technology communication needs, high technology communication needs, memory aids, swallowing program equipment, necessary software, ancillary battery power, systems to integrate augmentative communication with computers for complete system development, adapted phones, variety of synthetic and digitized voices, amount of memory needed in computerized systems, positional items for mounting and portability?

Home Furnishing/Accessories

____ How will assistive technology within the existing home and environment be included?

____ Have probable vs. potential environmental changes been considered?

Drug Supplies and Needs

____ Is there a need for medications for saliva control?

____ Have all pharmacological interventions been recommended for motor control (ataxia, tremors, etc.), for memory enhancement, for seizure control?

____ Have potential side effects of drugs or pharmacological intervention plans been considered in relationship to all areas of communication, swallowing, or auditory processing? These drug recommendations directly impact treatment recommendations and must be aggressively considered in the plan.

Future Medical Care

____ What annual evaluations will be needed?

____ What specialties will need to repeat the evaluations for specific treatment needs and recommendations?

Potential Complications

____ What complications could potentially occur as a result of poor treatment or no treatment in the areas where recommendations have been made?

____ What complications in speech, language, swallowing, communication, cognitive communication, oral–motor, hearing, and processing could occur with this etiology during the life span?

Appendix 9.2 (Continued) Communication Sciences and Disorders: Checklist for Life Care Planning

Vocational Planning

_____ How will communication, hearing, and language/speech recommendations as well as augmentative communication and assistive technology recommendations integrate with vocational plans and needs at this time and in the future?

Educational Planning

_____ How will communication, hearing, and language/speech recommendations as well as augmentative communication and assistive technology recommendations integrate with educational plans and needs at this time and in the future?

_____ What systems and equipment are available within educational programs (primary, secondary, and postsecondary)?

_____ Is the software appropriate for cognitive needs and projections in the future?

_____ Have specialized camps, summer training programs, specialized preschools, and specialized short-term programs for upgrading and improvement as well as further training needs in the future been considered?

_____ 10. Is the speech-language pathologist able to explain from a life care planning perspective the reasons and rationales relative to the recommendations?

_____ 11. Does the speech-language pathologist understand how to develop lifelong recommendations and objectives? An integrated plan?

_____ 12. Is the speech-language pathologist able to give detailed specifications in the written documentation that allows the life care planner the ability to develop life care plan specifics (i.e., vendors, dates, current prices, specific individuals, collaborative sources, categories of information)?

_____ 13. Once the draft of the life care plan is complete, is the speech-language pathologist furnished a draft for careful review relative to the accuracy and completeness of the information?

_____ 14. Is the speech-language pathologist aware that the data collection and analysis (evaluation) information may be presented to an insurance carrier, in testimony through deposition, or at a trial?

Appendix 9.3   Funding and Financing

Public Programs

Medicaid and Medicare

Required and optional services
Intermediate care facilities for persons who are mentally retarded (ICFs/MR)
Early and Periodic Screening, Diagnosis and Treatment (EPSDT)
Section 2176 Home- and Community-Based (HCB) Waivers
Community-Supported Living Arrangements

Maternal and Child Health

Maternal and Child Health Block Grant
Children with Special Health Care Needs
Special Projects of Regional and National Significance (SPRANS)

Education

Individuals with Disabilities Education Act (IDEA) state grants (Part B)
IDEA: Programs for Infants and Toddlers with Disabilities and Their Families (Part H)
State-operated programs (89-313)
Vocational education
Head Start

Vocational Rehabilitation

State grants
Supported employment
Independent living (Parts A, B, and C)

Social Security Benefits

Title II: Social Security Disability Insurance (SSDI)
Title XVI: Supplemental Security Income (SSI)
Work Incentive Programs
Developmental disability programs
Department of Veterans Affairs programs
Older Americans Act programs

Alternative Financing

Revolving loan fund
Lending library
Discount program
Low-interest loans
Private foundations
Service clubs
Special state appropriations
State bond issues
Employee accommodations program
Equipment loan program
Corporate-sponsored loans

Appendix 9.3 (Continued)   Funding and Financing

Charitable organizations

Funding Options through Private Insurance

Health insurance
Workers' compensation
Casualty insurance
Disability insurance

Funding Options through the U.S. Tax Code

Medical care expense deduction
Business deductions
Employee business deductions
ADA credit for small business
Credit for architectural and transportation barrier removal
Targeted jobs tax credit
Charitable contributions deduction

Appendix 9.4   Funding Glossary

Access: Generally refers to an individual's ability to obtain public or private health insurance coverage. Also used to indicate an individual's ability to easily obtain health services. That ability may be affected by restrictions on enrollees' distance from health care, waiting time to receive services, or individual's capability to communicate with providers, as well as to comprehend and carry out treatment instructions. Access may also be impacted by restrictions imposed on the physicians' choice of treatment options and various cost-containment strategies.

Accountable health plans (AHPs): Under leading health reform proposals, vertically integrated organizations of providers and insurers that offer a standard benefit package approved at the national level by Congress and a federal board or commission. Accountable health plans would be certified by the states and would be required to publish reports on their prices, patient satisfaction, and health outcomes. These health plans would fully integrate the financial, managerial, clinical, and preventive aspects of health care. Accountable health plans are also referred to as certified health plans, alliance health plans, accountable health partnerships, and qualified health plans under current reform bills.

Actual acquisition cost: The pharmacist's net payment made to purchase a drug product, after taking into account such items as purchasing allowances, discounts, rebates, and the like.

Actual charge: The amount a physician or other provider actually bills a patient for a particular medical service, procedure, or supply in a specific instance. The actual charge may differ from the usual, customary, prevailing, or reasonable charge.

Acute care: Medical care for health problems or illnesses that are short-term or intense in nature.

Administrative costs: The costs assumed by a managed care plan for administrative services such as claims processing, billing, and overhead costs.

Appendix 9.4 (Continued)   Funding Glossary

Adverse selection: Among applicants for a given group or individual program, the tendency for those with an impaired health status, or who are prone to higher than average utilization of benefits, to be enrolled in disproportionate numbers and lower deductible plans. See *community rating*.

Aged: For purposes of Medicare enrollment, persons 65 years of age or over are considered to be aged. Medicaid eligibility is determined on the basis of financial need for people who meet Supplemental Security Income eligibility criteria (aged, blind, or disabled individuals) and Aid to Families with Dependent Children criteria (adults and children). Eligibility determinations are made for an entire economic unit or case (sometimes a family) based on whether one member of a case meets the criteria. For example, an aged case could consist of a 66-year-old male and his 63-year-old wife. In contrast, a disabled enrollee could be over 65 years of age.

Agency for Health Care Policy and Research (AHCPR): The agency of the Public Heath Service responsible for enhancing the quality, appropriateness, and effectiveness of heath care services.

Allied health professionals: Nonphysician health workers, including, but not limited to, nurses, pharmacists, respiratory therapists, phlebotomists, pulmonary therapists, occupational therapists, recreational physical therapists, lab technicians, social workers, and dental hygienists.

All payer system: A reimbursement set up where all insurers reimburse providers using the same accounting system.

Alternative delivery system: A phrase that describes nontraditional health insurance programs that finance and provide health care to members. These include health maintenance organizations (HMOs) and preferred provider organizations (PPOs).

Ambulatory care: Health care services provided on an outpatient basis. No overnight stay in the hospital is required. The services of ambulatory care centers, hospital outpatient departments, physicians' offices, and home health care services fall under this heading.

Ambulatory surgery: Any minor surgical procedures that can be performed at any type of medical facility on an outpatient basis — not requiring an overnight stay.

Claim: The formal demand by the insured to collect reimbursement for a loss covered under an insurance policy.

Claims clearinghouse system: System that allows electronic claims submission through a single source.

Claims review: The method by which an enrollee's health care service claims are reviewed before reimbursement is made. The purpose of this monitoring system is to validate the medical appropriateness of the provided services and to be sure the cost of the service is not excessive.

Clearinghouse capability: Company capable of submitting electronic and paper claims to several third-party payers.

Clinical indicator: A tool used to monitor and evaluate care to assure desirable outcomes and to explain or prevent undesirable outcomes.

Clinical practice guidelines: Guidelines that specify the appropriate course(s) of treatment for specified health conditions.

Closed-panel HMO: Employment system in which physicians staffing an HMO are employed solely by the HMO.

Appendix 9.4 (Continued)   Funding Glossary

Coinsurance: A cost-sharing requirement under a health insurance policy that provides that the insured will assume a portion or percentage of the costs of covered services. After the deductible is paid, this provision forces the subscriber to pay for a certain percentage of any remaining medical bills — usually 20%.

Community rating: A method health insurers use to determine the premium costs for a group it is planning to insure. Under this system, the insurer bases the premiums on the average health care costs of the community, not the age, sex, occupation, or health of individual subscribers.

Competitive medical plan (CMP): An organization defined by the federal Medicare program that provides enrolled members with physician, hospital, and laboratory services on a capitation basis. These services are provided primarily by physicians who are under contract, employed by, or partners in the CMP. A CMP has fewer restrictions imposed than a federally qualified health maintenance organization, but may be a state-licensed HMO.

Comprehensive major medical coverage: A form of health insurance that combines the coverage of basic medical expense contracts and specialized medical care contracts into one comprehensive plan. These plans have both a deductible and coinsurance.

Consolidated Omnibus Reconciliation Act (COBRA): Federal law enacted in 1985. It permits an employee who has been terminated or has a reduction in work hours to continue his or her health insurance coverage for a period of up to 18 months. This law also covers the employee's dependents.

Continuous quality improvement (CQI): A quality model that incorporates statistical tools to analyze processes and improvement in quality care.

Contract: An agreement by which the insurer agrees to provide insurance benefits, to protect against losses, and to provide a written statement outlining the insurance provisions. The insured agrees to pay the insurer a set fee, called a premium, and other considerations.

Contributory: A general term that describes any employee insurance plan where the employee pays part of the premium.

Co-payment: Co-payments are a type of cost-sharing under Medicaid whereby insured or covered persons pay a specified flat amount per unit of service or unit of time, and the insurer pays the rest of the cost.

Cost-per-case limits: Reimbursement limits imposed by the government on each Medicare admission to hospitals.

Cost-sharing: The general set of financing arrangements whereby the consumer must pay out of pocket to receive care, either at the time of initiating care or during the provision of health care services, or both. Cost-sharing can also occur when an insured pays a portion of the monthly premium for health care insurance.

Cost shifting: A practice by health insurers to increase premiums for one group of business to offset costs from another line of business, like Medicare and Medicaid recipients.

Exclusivity clause: A part of a contract that prohibits physicians from contracting with more than one health maintenance organization or preferred provider organization.

Expenditures: Under Medicaid, expenditures refers to an amount paid out by a state agency for the covered medical expenses of eligible participants.

Experience rating: A system where an insurance company evaluates the risk of an individual or group by looking at the applicant's health history.

Appendix 9.4 (Continued)   Funding Glossary

Extended care: Long-term care, ranging from routine assistance for daily activities to sophisticated medical and nursing care for those needing it. The care, covered under certain insurance policies, can be provided in homes, day care centers, or other facilities.

Family planning services: Family planning services are any medically approved means, including diagnosis, treatment, drugs, supplies and devices, and related counseling that are furnished or prescribed by or under the supervision of a physician for individuals of childbearing age for purposes of enabling such individuals freely to determine the number or spacing of their children.

Federally qualified HMOs: HMOs that meet certain federally stipulated provisions aimed at protecting consumers, e.g., providing a broad range of basic health services, assuring financial solvency, and monitoring the quality of care. HMOs must apply to the federal government for qualification. The process is administered by the Office of Prepaid Health Care of the Health Care Financing Administration (HCFA), Department of Health and Human Services (DHHS).

Fee-for-service: The traditional way of billing for health care services. Under this system, there is a separate charge for each patient visit and the service provided.

First-dollar coverage: Health policies that pay all medical expenses up to a predetermined limit, without a deductible charge.

Fiscal agent: A fiscal agent is a contractor that processes or pays vendor claims on behalf of the Medicaid agency.

Fiscal intermediary: The agent (Blue Cross or an insurance company, for example) that has contracted with providers of service to process claims for reimbursement under health care coverage. In addition to handling financial matters, it may perform other functions such as providing consultative services or serving as a center for communicating with providers and making audits of providers' records.

Fiscal year: Any 12-month period for which annual accounts are kept. The federal government's fiscal year extends from October 1 to the following September 30.

Fixed fee: An established fee schedule for pharmacy services allowed by certain government and private third-party programs in lieu of cost-of-doing business markups.

Formulary: A list of selected pharmaceuticals and their appropriate dosages felt to be the most useful and cost-effective for patient care. Organizations often develop a formulary under the aegis of a pharmacy and therapeutics (P&T) committee. In HMOs, physicians are often required to prescribe from the formulary.

Freedom of choice: Legislation restricting or eliminating the right of insurers to narrow the subscribers' selection of providers in return for a price discount.

Freestanding hospital: Any hospital that is not affiliated with a multihospital system.

Gatekeeper: A component of an independent practice association HMO that requires a subscriber to see a primary physician and get the physician's approval before seeing a specialist about a medical condition.

Generic substitution: Substituting a generic version of a branded off-patent pharmaceutical for the branded product when the latter is prescribed. Some HMOs and Medicaid programs mandate generic substitution. Mandatory generic substitution within the Medicare program is currently being debated in Congress.

Appendix 9.4 (Continued)   Funding Glossary

Global budget: A budget that would determine the total amount of money that a geographic area could spend each year for health care. Under a global budget, providers and hospitals receive predetermined payments. As an enforcement mechanism for staying within budget, providers and hospitals will not receive additional funding if their costs exceed their budgeted payments.

Infant mortality rate: Deaths in the first year of life per 1000 births. The U.S. rate in 1990 was 9.1, 19th among developed countries. According to the U.S. General Accounting Office, 50% of these deaths are due to lifestyle factors, 20% due to environmental factors, 20% due to biological factors, and 10% due to inadequate health care.

Inpatient hospital services: Inpatient hospital services are items and services furnished to an inpatient of a hospital by the hospital, including bed and board, nursing and related services, diagnostic and therapeutic services, and medical or surgical services.

Intensive care: Skilled nursing services prescribed by a physician, delivered with the guidance of a registered nurse. Scope of care is provided to individuals with serious medical conditions that persist for long periods of time.

Intermediate care facility: An intermediate care facility is an institution furnishing health-related care and services to individuals who do not require the degree of care provided by hospitals or skilled nursing facilities as defined under Title XIX (Medicaid) of the Social Security Act.

Job-lock: The inability of an individual to change employers for fear of losing health coverage, particularly if the employee or a dependent has a preexisting condition.

Laboratory and radiological services: Professional and technical laboratory and radiological services ordered by a licensed practitioner, provided in an office or similar facility (other than a hospital outpatient department or clinic) or by a qualified lab.

Legend drug: A drug product that cannot be dispensed legally without a prescription.

Long-term care: Continuous health care delivered by a hospital or other health care institution to a patient for 30 days or more.

Magnetic resonance imaging: State-of-the-art machine used as a diagnostic tool, using magnetic waves to produce comprehensive pictures of the anatomy.

Managed care: A term coined originally to refer to the prepaid health care sector, e.g., HMOs and CMPs, where care is provided under a fixed budget and costs are managed. Increasingly, the term is being used by many analysts to include PPOs and even forms of indemnity insurance coverage that incorporate preadmission certification and other utilization controls.

Maximum allowable cost, or reasonable cost range: A maximum cost is fixed for which the pharmacist can be reimbursed for selected products, as identified in a formulary.

Medicaid: A government program that covers medical expenses for the poor and certain other classes of uninsured people, established by Title XIX of the Social Security Act. Each state administers its own program. Medicaid is funded by both the state and federal governments.

Medicaid buy-in: A provision in certain health reform proposals whereby the uninsured would be allowed to purchase Medicaid coverage by paying premiums on a sliding scale based on income.

Medicaid Management Information System: Federally developed guidelines for computer system design to achieve national standardization of Medicaid claims processing, payment, review, and reporting for all health care claims.

Appendix 9.4 (Continued)   Funding Glossary

Medically needy: Under Medicaid, medically needy cases are aged, blind, or disabled individuals or families and children who are otherwise eligible for Medicaid and whose income resources are above the limits for eligibility as categorically needy but are within limits set under the Medicaid state plan.

Medical savings accounts (MSAs): An account into which individuals can contribute a limited amount to cover medical costs or to buy insurance. Contributions to the accounts are sometimes tax deductible. MSAs are often cited as an incentive to limit health spending. Also called medical IRAs.

Practice variation: An assessment of the patterns of a practitioner's practice to determine if the practitioner provides care that is significantly different from others with similar practices. If there is a significant difference, the practitioner's practice is analyzed to determine the reasons for the variation and whether that practitioner's practice patterns should be modified.

Preferred provider organization (PPO): Type of health insurance program where a limited group of physicians and hospitals provide a broad range of medical care for a predetermined fee. Patients using the group providers usually have their health care expenses covered in full. Those covered under the PPO who do not use the preferred providers for care usually have to pay for a portion of their medical expenses.

Prepaid group practice plans: Organized medical groups of essentially full-time physicians in appropriate specialties, as well as other professional and subprofessional personnel, who, for regular compensation, undertake to provide comprehensive care to an enrolled population for premium payments that are made in advance by the consumer or their employers.

Prescribed drugs: Prescribed drugs are drugs dispensed by a licensed pharmacist on the prescription of a practitioner licensed by law to administer such drugs, and drugs dispensed by a licensed practitioner to his own patients. This item does not include a practitioner's drug charges that are not separable from his other charges, or drugs covered by a hospital's bill.

Preventative care programs: Often called wellness programs, these programs use exercise and health education and promotion as vehicles to keep people healthy and good insurance risks.

Primary care: General medical care that typically deals with common injuries and illness.

Prior authorization: The approval a provider must obtain from an insurer or other entity before performing certain procedures using certain medical products or admitting a patient electively, in order for the service to be covered under the plan.

Prospective financing: Financing for health care services based on prices or budgets determined prior to the delivery of service. Payments can be per unit of service, per member, or per time period. In all its forms prospective financing differs from cost-based reimbursement, under which a provider is paid for costs incurred.

Prospective Payment Assessment Commission (ProPAC): A 15-member commission, appointed by the director of the Office of Technology Assessment, that makes recommendations to the secretary of Health and Human Services on various aspects of the diagnosis-related group system of Medicare reimbursement.

Providers: Physicians, hospitals, and other health care organizations that treat individuals for illness and injuries.

Appendix 9.4 (Continued)   Funding Glossary

Rate setting: A form of financing under which hospitals or nursing homes are paid prices that are prospectively determined, generally by a state agency. Prospectively determined prices may be paid by all payers for all covered services, as in all payer systems, or by only some payers. The unit of payment can be service, patient, or time period. See *prospective financing*.

Rational drug therapy: Prescribing the right drug for the right patient, at the right time, in the right amounts, and with due consideration for relative costs.

Reasonable charge: In processing claims for supplementary medical insurance benefits, carriers use HCFA guidelines to establish the reasonable charge for services rendered. The reasonable charge is the lowest of the actual charge billed by the physician or supplier, the charge the physician or supplier customarily bills his patients for the same services, and the prevailing charge that most physicians or suppliers in that locality bill for the same service. Increases in the physicians' prevailing charge levels are recognized only to the extent justified by an index reflecting changes in the costs of practice and in general earnings.

State plan: The Medicaid State Plan is a comprehensive written commitment by a Medicaid agency to administer or supervise the administration of a Medicaid program in accordance with federal requirements.

Stop loss: That point at which a third party has reinsurance to protect against the overly large single claim or the excessively high aggregate claim during a given period of time. Large employers, who are self-insured, may also purchase reinsurance for stop-loss purposes.

Supplemental Security Income (SSI): SSI is a program of income support for low-income aged, blind, and disabled persons established by Title XVI of the Social Security Act.

Therapeutic substitution: A practice entailing a pharmacist's dispensing a drug felt to be therapeutically equivalent to the drug prescribed by a physician without obtaining permission from the prescribing physician. Generally, the P&T committee of an HMO will formally approve therapeutic substitutions that it feels are permissible, and only those so designated can be made by the pharmacist dispensing for the HMO.

Third-party administrator: Individual or company that contracts with employers who want to self-insure the health of their employees. They develop and coordinate self-insurance programs, process and pay the claims, and may help locate stop-loss insurance for the employer. They also can analyze the effectiveness of the program and trace the patterns of those using the benefits.

Third-party liability: Under Medicaid, third-party liability exists if there is any entity (i.e., other government programs or insurance) that is or may be liable to pay all or part of the medical cost or injury, disease, or disability of an applicant or recipient of Medicaid.

Total quality management (TQM): See *continuous quality improvement*.

Universal access: The availability of affordable public or private insurance coverage for every U.S. citizen or legal resident. There is no guarantee, however, that all individuals will actually choose to, or have the funds to, purchase coverage. See *universal coverage*.

Universal coverage: The guaranteed provision of at least basic health care services to every U.S. citizen or legal resident. See *universal access*.

Usual, customary, and reasonable charges: Method of reimbursement used under Medicaid by which state Medicaid programs set reimbursements rates using the Medicare method or a fee schedule, whichever is lower.

Appendix 9.4 (Continued)   Funding Glossary

Utilization review: A tool used by providers, health care organizations, and insurance companies to influence the use of health care resources with the objective of containing costs.

Vendor: A medical vendor is an institution, agency, organization, or individual practitioner that provides health or medical services.

Vendor payments: In welfare programs, direct payments are made by the state to such providers as physicians, pharmacists, and health care institutions rather than to the welfare recipient himself.

Waiver: A rider or clause in a health insurance contract excluding an insurer's liability for some sort of preexisting illness or injury. Also refers to a plan amendment, such as a HCFA waiver or plan modification.

Waivers (Section 1115 or 1915(b)): Section 1115 of the Social Security Act grants the secretary of Health and Human Services broad authority to waive certain laws relating to Medicaid for the purpose of conducting pilot, experimental, or demonstration projects. Section 1115 demonstration waivers allow states to change provisions of their Medicaid programs, including eligibility requirements, the scope of services available, the freedom to choose a provider, a provider's choice to participate in a plan, the method of reimbursing providers, and the statewide application of the program. Projects typically run 3 to 5 years. States cannot change the federal Medicaid assistance percentage through a waiver.

Appendix 9.5   Vendor List

Ablenet, Inc.
1081 Tenth Ave. SE
Minneapolis, MN 55414-1312
Telephone: (800) 322-0956
E-mail: customerservice@ablenetinc.com
Website: http://www.ablenetinc.com

Adamlab
55 East Long Lake Rd.
Mailstop PMB-337
Troy, Michigan 48098
Telephone: (248) 594-6997

Adaptivation
2225 W 50th St., Suite 100
Sioux Falls, SD 57105-6525
Telephone: (800) 723-2783
E-mail: info@adaptivation.com
Website: http://www.adaptivation.com

Appendix 9.5 (Continued)   Vendor List

Applied Human Factors, Inc.
P.O. Box 228
Helotes, TX 78023
Telephone: (888) 243-0098
E-mail: sales@ahf-net.com
Website: http://www.ahf-net.com

Assistive Technology, Inc.
7 Wells Ave.
Newton, MA 02459
Telephone: (800) 793-9227
E-mail: customercare@assistivetech.com
Website: http://www.assistivetech.com

CAMA Administrative Office
P.O. Box 1039
Evanston, IL 60204-1039
Telephone: (800) 441-2262
E-mail: cama@northshore.net
Website: http://www.aacproducts.org

Dyanavox Systems, L.L.C.
2100 Wharton, Suite 400
Pittsburgh, PA 15203-1942
Telephone: (800) 344-1778
E-mail: sales@dynavoxsys.com
Website: http://www.dynavoxsys.com

Enabling Devices/Toys for Special Children
385 Warburton Ave.
Hastings on Hudson, NY 10706
Telephone: (800) 832-8697
E-mail: customer_support@enablingdevices.com
Website: http://www.enabingdevices.com

Enkidu Research, Inc.
247 Pine Hill Rd.
Spencerport, NY 14559
Telephone: (800) 297-9570
E-mail: info@enkidu.net
Website: http://www.enkidu.net

Hearit, L.L.C.
8346 North Mammoth Dr.
Tucson, AZ 85743-1046
Telephone: (800) 298-7184
E-mail: hearitllc@hearitllc.com
Website: http://www.hearitllc.com

Appendix 9.5 (Continued)   Vendor List

Madentec, LTD.
9935-29A Ave.
Edmonton, Alberta T6N 1A9
Canada
Telephone: (877) 623-3682
E-mail: sales@madentec.com
Website: http://www.madentec.com

Mayer-Johnson, Inc.
P.O. Box 1579
Solana Beach, CA 92075-7579
Telephone: (800) 588-4548
E-mail: mayerj@mayer-johnson.com
Website: http://www.mayer-johnson.com

Poppin and Company
Communication Materials
P.O. Box 176
Unity, ME 04988
Telephone: (207) 437-2746
E-mail: poppin@uninets.com
Website: http://www.poppinandcompany.com

Prentke Romich Company
1022 Heyl Rd.
Wooster, OH 44691-9744
Telephone: (800) 262-1984
E-mail: info@prentrom.com
Website: http://www.prentrom.com

Tash, Inc.
3512 Mayland Court
Richmond, VA 23233
Telephone: (800) 463-5685
E-mail: tashinc@aol.com
Website: http://www.tashinc.com

Toby Churchill, LTD.
20 Panton St.
Cambridge, CB2 1HP
United Kingdom
Telephone: 011-44-1223-576117
E-mail: sales@toby-churchill.com
Website: http://www.toby-churchill.com

Appendix 9.5 (Continued)   Vendor List

Turning Point Therapy & Technology Inc.
P.O. Box 310751
New Braunfels, TX 78131-0751
Telephone: (877) 608-9812
E-mail: support@turningpointtechnology.com
Website: http://www.turningpointtechnology.com

Words+, Inc.
1220 West Ave. J
Lancaster, CA 93534-2902
Telephone: (800) 869-8521
E-mail: support@words-plus.com
Website: http://www.words-plus.com

Zygo Industries, Inc.
P.O. Box 1008
Portland, OR 97207-1008
Telephone: (800) 234-6006
E-mail: ZYGO@zygo-usa.com

Appendix 9.6   Selected AAC Websites

Communication Aid Manufacturers

1. Communication Aid Manufacturers Association (CAMA)
   http://www.aacproducts.org
   CAMA is an organization of the major manufacturers of augmentative and
   alternative communication (AAC) software and hardware products. CAMA
   conducts workshops throughout the U.S. every year. CAMA will also send packets
   of catalogs upon request.

2. AbleNet
   http://www.ablenetinc.com
   AbleNet produces a variety of communication aids, switches, and other adaptive
   devices. It will loan a package of equipment with an accompanying training script
   for in-service training. The website offers links for the products catalog, AAC
   news, frequently asked questions, and other AAC-related websites.

3. Adaptivation
   http://www.adaptivation.com
   Adaptivation distributes assistive technology to persons with disabilities.
   Adaptivation products include the Chipper, Voice Pal, and many other related
   devices and the accessories that go with them. The website includes links for its
   product catalog, domestic and foreign dealers, upcoming workshops, and other
   AAC-related websites.

Appendix 9.6 (Continued)   Selected AAC Websites

4. Adaptive Switch Laboratories, Inc.

    http://www.asl-inc.com

    Adaptive Switch Laboratories, Inc., is a company that makes and sells a variety of switches and mounting kits. Its products are compatible with a variety of wheelchairs. Product catalogs and price lists can be found on its website. The ASL website also includes information about educational seminars and leasing programs.

5. AMDi

    http://www.amdi.net

    AMDi designs electronic devices for governmental, industrial, and commercial customers. Some of its products include the Tech/Speak, Tech/Talk, and Tech/Four. Its website provides the product catalog and price list.

6. Assistive Technology, Inc.

    http://www.assistivetech.com

    Assistive Technology, Inc., is the manufacturer of the Gemini AAC device and universally accessible Macintosh computer, suited to a range of input methods. Assistive Technology also produces LINK, a talking keyboard. The website includes links to its products catalog and upcoming tradeshows and conferences.

7. Aurora Systems, Inc.

    http://www.aurora-systems.com

    Aurora Systems, Inc., is a company that provides computer software for people with learning disabilities, augmentative communication needs, and speech disabilities. The Aurora Systems, Inc., website contains purchasing information and a support system center for its products.

8. Communication Devices Inc.

    http://www.comdevices.com

    Communication Devices, Inc., is the manufacturer of the Holly.com line of augmentative communication devices. This website also has links to other AAC websites.

9. Consultants for Communication Technology

    http://www.ConCommTech.com

    Consultants for Communication Technology products include the KeyWi and KeyWi2 lines of software, which enable a laptop computer to become a complete communication device without the need for an external synthesizer. Other products include an environmental control system. The website includes links for the company's product catalog, downloads of a demo of its software, and the opportunity to hear the synthesized voices that are included with the KeyWi software.

10. Crestwood Communication Aids, Inc.

    http://www.communicationaids.com

    Crestwood Communication Aids, Inc., has a variety of light-tech products that are easy to use and affordably priced. Its website includes links to its catalog.

11. DynaVox Systems

    http://www.dynavoxsys.com

    Products by DynaVox Systems include the DynaMyte 3100, the DynaVox 3100, and the Dynavox line of software by both Macintosh- and IBM-compatible computers. The DynaVox Systems website includes links for tech tips, upcoming trade shows, and finding a DynaVox representative in your area.

Appendix 9.6 (Continued)   Selected AAC Websites

12. Electronic Speech Enhancement, Inc.

    http://www.speachenhancer.com

    The entrepreneurs at Electronic Speech Enhancement, Inc., developed a technology called speech enhancement to combat the challenge of making speech clearer, not just louder. The ESE website includes links for its products and its ordering process.

13. Enabling Devices

    http://www.enablingdevices.com

    Enabling Devices, a division of Toys for Special Education, Inc., is dedicated to providing affordable learning and assistive devices for the physically challenged. The website for enabling devices includes links to its products catalog and an online shopping option. This website also includes links to many other related websites.

14. Enkidu

    http://www.enkidu.net

    Enkidu distributes AAC devices that feature dynamic display and synthesized speech. These devices come in handheld, palmtop, and tablet sizes. The Enkidu website has links to contact the company and frequently asked questions and answers.

15. The Great Talking Box Company

    http://www.greattalkingbox.com

    The Great Talking Box Company distributes affordable communication devices such as EasyTalk, DifiCom 2000, and e-talk, along with accessories. The Great Talking Box Company website has other useful information such as trade show and sales information.

16. Gus Communications, Inc.

    http://www.gusnic.com

    Some of the products offered by Gus Communication, Inc., include a software package that is compatible with any Windows-based personal computer. The Gus Communications, Inc., website includes links for its products, ordering, and demos of its products that can be downloaded onto any IBM-compatible computer.

17. IntelliTools

    http://www.intellitools.com

    IntelliTools develops and markets computer products for special education. The company's mission is to help children with educational challenges (physical and cognitive) and optimize their social and academic participation and success. Products by IntelliTools include Creativity Tools, Curriculum Resources, and SwitchIt! Software. Along with information about its products, the IntelliTools website also includes links for tutorials and training, technical support, product demos, and links to other AAC-related websites.

18. LC Technologies, Inc.

    http://www.eyegaze.com

    LC Technologies, Inc., is a company that manufactures the Eyegaze Communication System, a system that "empowers people to communicate with the world by only the movement of their eyes." Its website includes product brochures and prices. In addition, it also provides papers and presentations by individuals who have used or worked with Eyegaze Communication Systems.

Appendix 9.6 (Continued)   Selected AAC Websites

19. Luminaud, Inc.

    http://www.luminaud.com

    Luminaud, Inc., is a manufacturer and supplier of a wide range of electronic speech equipment and tracheostomy products. Some of its products include Minivox, Chattervox, and other voice amplification products. Its website includes its products catalog and price lists and links to other AAC-related websites.

20. Madentec

    http://www.madentec.com

    Madentec is a company that distributes products such as the computer enhancer Tracker 2000, a head-pointer access system. In addition, it sells a variety of electronic aids for environmental control. The Madentec website also includes frequently asked questions and links that provide games to play using Tracker 2000.

21. Mayer-Johnson, Inc.

    http://www.mayer-johnson.com

    Mayer-Johnson, Inc., offers products for special needs and education. Products by Mayer-Johnson, Inc., include Picture Communication Symbols, BoardMaker software Picture Communication Symbols*, and many other AAC-related devices and materials. Its website includes links to other AAC websites and the product catalog, as well as upcoming conferences and tech support for the Mayer-Johnson line of products. *Picture Communication Symbols (PCS) are copyrighted © 1981–2000, Mayer-Johnson, Inc. All rights reserved.

22. Prentke Romich Company

    http://www.prentrom.com

    The Prentke Romich Company (PRC) produces a number of devices that take advantage of Minspeak semantic compaction. This vocabulary system features over 4000 vocabulary words available on a single overlay. Prentke Romich Company has a variety of training options, including video conferencing and web-based modules. The PRC website offers links to its product catalog, product representatives, training seminars, and conferences, as well as a link to other AAC-related websites.

23. RJ Cooper & Associates

    http://www.rjcooper.com

    RJ Cooper & Associates makes products for persons with special needs, including special software and hardware adaptations. RJ Cooper & Associates also sells a variety of switches and related devices, including the Big Baby Switch especially designed for babies. Its website includes a single switch arcade game that can be downloaded to a computer as well as links to its TechWeek vacation, lectures, and workshops.

24. Saltillo Corporation

    Saltillo Corporation is a company that distributes communication products for nonspeaking individuals. Its products are designed to be easy to use by the communicator and his or her support staff. The Saltillo Corporation website contains details and purchasing information about ChatBox and its accessories, among other AAC devices. The website also contains helpful technical support, distributor locations, and its rental policies.

Appendix 9.6 (Continued)   Selected AAC Websites

25. Slater Software Inc.

    http://www.slatersoftware.com

    Slater Software, Inc., is the producer of the Picture It, Pixreader, and Pixwriter software packages that teach literacy skills to children with special needs. Its website includes descriptions of products along with Adaptive Plays and Interactive Books. It also includes a link to the products catalog.

26. Synergy

    http://www.speakwithus.com

    Synergy is a company that makes AAC/computer systems and a wide range of software and adaptive inputs. Synergy offers an AAC/functional computer system for both Macintosh- and IBM-compatible computers. Its website includes links for funding assistance, frequently asked questions, and upcoming workshops and lectures.

27. Tash, Inc.

    http://www.tashinc.com

    Tash, Inc., is the manufacturer of a variety of switches, adaptive devices, and mounting devices. Its website offers online shopping and the option of requesting a catalog.

28. Words+, Inc.

    http://www.words-plus.com

    Words+, Inc., is a company dedicated to improving the quality of life for people with disabilities. Its products include computer software, the Freedom 2000, and the Message Mate line of products. The Words+, Inc., website includes links for its products catalog, upcoming workshops, and links to other AAC-related websites.

29. ZYGO Industries, Inc.

    http://www.zygo-usa.com

    ZYGO Industries, Inc., is the manufacturer of the Macaw family of digitized AAC systems. ZYGO Industries, Inc., also manufactures a variety of other assistive technology devices. It has a CD-ROM and videotape that contains samples of its products. Its website includes links to its product catalog and a link to information about funding for assistive technology.

AAC Associations

30. American Speech-Language-Hearing Association (ASHA)

    http://professiona.asha.org/resources/divs/div_12.cfm

    Home page for Special Interest Division 12 (AAC). Available once you register at the ASHA website: http://www.asha.org/speech/disabilities/disabilities.cfm

    This page is user-friendly and available to the public. It is a good reference for those beginning to learn about AAC. This page provides general information about AAC, including information about putting together an AAC team and selecting a device.

31. International Society for Augmentative and Alternative Communication (ISAAC)

    http://www.isaac-online.org

    ISAAC is an international organization devoted to advancing augmentative and alternative communication (AAC). The mission of ISAAC is to improve communication and the quality of life for people with severe communication impairments. ISAAC does this by facilitating information exchange and focusing attention on work in the field. The ISAAC website provides links to AAC resources, publications, events, and conferences.

Appendix 9.6 (Continued)   Selected AAC Websites

32. U.S. Society for Augmentative and Alternative Communication (USSAAC)

    http://www.ussaac.org

    USSAAC is a national chapter of ISAAC devoted to advancing augmentative and alternative communication (AAC) in the U.S. The mission is to improve communication and the quality of life for people with severe communication impairments by facilitating information exchange through its conferences and a quarterly newsletter titled *Speak UP!*

Education Sites

33. The AAC-RERC (Augmentative and Alternative Communication — Rehabilitation Engineering Research Center on Communication Enhancement)

    http://www.aac-rerc.org

    The AAC-RERC is dedicated to assisting individuals who use AAC by advancing and promoting AAC technologies and supporting individuals that use, manufacture, and recommend them. The AAC-RERC is funded by the National Institute on Disability and Rehabilitation Research (NIDRR, Grant H133E980026). The website includes current information on Medicare funding policies, research on improving AAC technologies for young children, and links to vendor websites and university AAC sites.

34. AAC at Penn State

    http://aac.hhdev.psu.edu/Research.htm

    The website describes current research in AAC, including some on improving AAC technology for young children. It also describes research programs directed toward improving clinical practice and enhancing outcomes for individuals who use AAC. Penn State is also a partner in the AAC-RERC (Augmentative and Alternative Communication — Rehabilitation Engineering Research Center on Communication Enhancement; see 34 above).

35. AACworld at Purdue

    http://www.soe.purdue.edu/aac

    In addition to information about augmentative and alternative communication (AAC) and assistive technology (AT) courses at Purdue, this website provides several types of resource material for researchers and practitioners, including abstracts of master's and doctoral theses, recent AAC research at Purdue, and links to other sites of potential value, including the Assessment Research Center (which includes information about the electronic alternate assessment procedures developed at Purdue as Indiana's response to PL 105-17) and universities with which Purdue is currently collaborating, such as the Centre for Augmentative and Alternative Communication (CAAC) at the University of Pretoria, South Africa, and the University of Cologne, Germany.

36. California State University–Northridge

    http://www.csun.edu/cod/conf2001/proceedings/index.html

    The proceedings of CSUN's 2001 conference, "Technology and Persons with Disabilities," includes research on assistive technology and its use with children and adults. An index of the conference proceedings can be accessed at http://www.csun.edu/cod/conf2001/proceedings/alphaproceedings.html.

Appendix 9.6 (Continued)   Selected AAC Websites

37. Closing the Gap

    http://www.closingthegap.com

    This website includes product information on new hardware and software and current issues involving AT and AAC. It also has links to newsletter articles and how to subscribe to the bimonthly newsletter.

38. Communication Aids for Language and Learning (CALL) Centre, University of Edinburgh

    http://callcentre.education.ed.ac.uk

    The CALL Centre is a Scottish National Resource and Research Centre located within the University of Edinburgh's Department of Equity Studies and Special Education, in the Faculty of Education.

39. Trace Research and Development Center

    http://www.trace.wisc.edu

    This website provides information on all types of assistive technology, including AAC. The comprehensive nature of the site provides students with the broad perspective they will need to work effectively with clients who require technology beyond a communication device. The front page is organized into four headings: New and Highlighted Items, Designing a More Useable World, Cooperative Electronic Library (Co-Net), and Publications and Media Catalog. The last two sections relate to AAC most directly. Co-Net includes information on products, people, and services, publications and media, and also includes text documents. For the most up-to-date product information, the website directs the user to the ABLEDATA website (see 43 below).

40. The University of Nebraska–Lincoln AAC website

    http://www.aac.unl.edu

    The University of Nebraska–Lincoln (UNL) AAC website contains academic and clinical training information, as well as vendor information for people working with AAC. It also provides a variety of links to AAC and other speech-language pathology sites.

Other AAC Resources

41. AAC Intervention.com

    http://www.aacintervention.com

    AAC Intervention.com is a website that sells products to aid in making overlays for early intervention with AAC. It also provides helpful information on how to begin using AAC with a nonspeaking child. This website has some unique features such as local and national presentation/conference dates and tips of the month.

42. ABLEDATA

    http://www.abledata.com

    ABLEDATA is a federally funded project whose primary mission is to provide information on assistive technology and rehabilitation equipment available from domestic and international sources to consumers, organizations, professionals, and caregivers within the U.S. Its website includes links for resource centers, product information, and other AAC-related websites.

Appendix 9.6 (Continued)   Selected AAC Websites

43. Augmentative Communication, Inc.

    http://www.augcominc.com

    Augmentative Communication, Inc., publishes *Alternatively Speaking* (*AS*) and *Augmentative Communication News* (*CAN*), newsletters that together provide the latest information on hot topics in the field, discussion of vital issues for AAC stakeholders, and news from the AAC community. The Augmentative Communication, Inc., website also provides links for presentations, articles in the publications, and other AAC-related websites.

44. Communication Independence for the Neurologically Impaired (CINI)

    http://www.cini.org

    Founded by speech-language pathologists, people with ALS, and family members, CINI is the only not-for-profit organization solely devoted to improving the quality of life for persons with ALS/MND (Lou Gehrig's disease). The organization disseminates information about the communication technology that can help them. The website includes pages on frequently asked questions, related resources and links, a glossary, publications, and names of manufacturers.

Additional Resources

Additional resources can be obtained by:

- Checking references and appendices in the four original texts cited and the other publications cited (e.g., the Lloyd et al. text has extensive appendices on developers, manufacturers, vendors, and associations as of 1997)
- Checking websites with the typical cautions used when one browser websites
- Subscribing to the ASHA SID 12 newsletter in particular and specific volumes, including *Augmentative and Alternative Communication Newsletter*, June 2001, Vol. 10, No. 2, pp. 32–33 (an issue devoted to a bibliography of AAC books, chapters, and journals
- Subscribing to ISAAC's official journal — *Augmentative and Alternative Communication*

The above information is reprinted with permission from the American Speech-Language-Hearing Association and Special Interest Division 12, Augmentative and Alternative Communication.

Additional Links to Other AAC-Related Sites

AAC-RERC

http://aac-rerc.com

AAC-RERC is the Rehabilitation Engineering Research Center on Communication Enhancement. This is one of a network of RERCs funded by the National Institute on Disability and Rehabilitation Research (NIDRR) of the U.S. Department of Education.

ABLEDATA

http://www.abledata.com

ABLEDATA is a federally funded project whose primary mission is to provide information on assistive technology and rehabilitation equipment available from domestic and international sources to consumers, organizations, professionals, and caregivers within the U.S.

Appendix 9.6 (Continued)   Selected AAC Websites

ACOLUG

http://www.temple.edu/inst_disabilities/acolug

ACOLUG is a listserv created to exchange ideas, information, and experiences on augmentative communication by people from all over the world. By using e-mail, people who use augmentative communication and their friends and families discuss issues related to augmentative communication, such as equipment, funding, learning techniques, and supports. Anyone can join and there is no cost.

Apraxia-Kids

http://www.apraxia-kids.org/

The Apraxia-Kids Internet Resources provides comprehensive information regarding Childhood Apraxia of Speech. The site, which is appropriate for both families and professionals, includes expert articles on diagnosis, treatment, AAC, related disabilities, an e-mail discussion list, a monthly online newsletter, message boards, and resource listings. Additionally, there is a research section with the latest news on apraxia research.

ASHA

http://www.asha.org

ASHA is the American Speech-Language-Hearing Association. ASHA is the professional organization of speech-language pathologists (SLPs) and audiologists. SLPs are the primary service providers for people who rely on AAC and are generally the best resource on an AAC team for addressing language issues. ASHA has a special interest division, SID-12, that addresses AAC.

ATIA

http://www.atia.org

ATIA is the Assistive Technology Industry Association. ATIA organizes an annual conference on assistive technology.

Augmentative Communication, Inc.

http://www.augcominc.com

Augmentative Communication News and *Alternatively Speaking* provide the latest information on hot topics in the field, discussion of vital issues for AAC stakeholders, and news from the AAC community.

CAMA

http://www.aacproducts.org

The Communication Aid Manufacturers Association (CAMA) is a not-for-profit organization of the world's leading manufacturers of augmentative and alternative communication (AAC) software and hardware products. CAMA conducts more than 30 1-day workshops throughout the U.S. each year.

C.H.E.R.A.B.

http://www.apraxia.cc

The Communication Help, Education, Research, Apraxia Base Foundation websites are for anyone who cares for a child that has delayed speech, a speech disorder, is a late talker, etc., as well as for those who care for a child that has received a diagnosis of apraxia.

Appendix 9.6 (Continued)   Selected AAC Websites

Childhood Apraxia of Speech Association of North America (CASANA)

http://www.apraxia.org

The Childhood Apraxia of Speech Association is a not-for-profit organization whose mission is to strengthen the support systems in the lives of children with apraxia so that each child is afforded his or her best opportunity to develop speech.

Consortium for Assistive Technology Outcomes Research (CATOR)

http://www.atoutcomes.org

CATOR conducts research dedicated to improving measurement science for assistive technology (AT), reducing barriers to the use of AT outcome measures, and understanding the processes for AT adoption and abandonment.

CSUN

http://www.csun.edu/cod/

California State University–Northridge

(CSUN) Center on Disabilities organizes the annual Conference on Technology and Persons with Disabilities. CSUN also offers the Assistive Technology Applications Certificate Program.

CTG

http://closingthegap.com

Closing the Gap organized an annual conference on computer technology for people with disabilities and publishes a newsletter.

ISAAC

http://www.isaac-online.org

ISAAC is the International Society for Augmentative and Alternative Communication. Membership is open to anyone interested in AAC. ISAAC activities include a biennial conference and sponsorship of *AAC Journal*. Many ISAAC national chapters address more local interests.

PEC

http://www.toolcity.net/~coonster/shout/

The Pittsburgh Employment Conference for Augmented Communicators is the largest gathering in the world of people who rely on AAC. Topics of interest to employment-age individuals are addressed at the annual conference.

RESNA

http://www.resna.org

RESNA (Rehabilitation and Assistive Technology Society of North America) is an interdisciplinary association of people with a common interest in technology and disability. Its purpose is to improve the potential of people with disabilities to achieve their goals through the use of technology. It serves that purpose by promoting research, development, education, advocacy, and the provision of technology and by supporting the people engaged in these activities. RESNA was founded in 1979 as a not-for-profit organization. There are currently over 1600 individual and 150 organizational members.

Appendix 9.6 (Continued)   Selected AAC Websites

USSAAC

http://www.ussaac.org
USSAAC (U.S. Society for Augmentative and Alternative Communication) is the U.S. chapter of ISAAC.

WheelchairNet

http://www.wheelchairnet.org
WheelchairNet is a community for people who have a common interest in (or in some cases a passion for) wheelchair technology and its improvement and successful application. WheelchairNet is a virtual community — a community that exists only in cyberspace. Cyberspace is just a way of referring to the Internet. It's a community organized along the lines of a real town. This virtual town is inhabited, visited, and managed by people who have an interest in wheelchairs and how wheelchairs can best serve the needs of people who use them. WheelchairNet is operated by the RERC on Wheeled Mobility at the University of Pittsburgh.

Appendix 9.7   Toll-Free Phone Numbers and Hotlines

AMC Cancer Information Line
(800) 525-3777

American Association on Mental Retardation
(800) 424-3688

American Council of the Blind
(800) 424-8666

American Diabetes Association, Inc.
(800) 232-3472

American Foundation for the Blind
(800) 232-5463

American Liver Foundation
(800) 223-0179

American Paralysis Association
(800) 225-0292

American Parkinson Disease Association
(800) 223-2732

American Speech-Language-Hearing Association
(800) 638-8255

American Spinal Cord Injury
(800) 962-9629

Appendix 9.7 (Continued)   Toll-Free Phone Numbers and Hotlines

American Trauma Society
(800) 556-7890

Arthritis Foundation
(800) 283-7800

Association for Retarded Citizens of the U.S. (ARC)
(800) 433-5255

AT&T National Special Needs Center
(800) 833-3232

Beginnings
(800) 541-4327

Better Hearing Institute Hearing Helpline
(800) EAR-WELL

Blind Children's Center
(800) 222-3566

The Candlelighters Childhood Cancer Foundation
(800) 366-2223

Captioned Films for the Deaf
(800) 237-6213

Center for Special Education Technology
c/o Council for Exceptional Children
(800) 873-8255

Consumer Product Safety Commission
(800) 638-2772

Cornelia deLange Syndrome Foundation
(800) 535-3323

Dial a Hearing Screening Test
(800) 222-3277

Disabilities AT&T, National Special Needs Center
(800) 233-1222
(800) 833-3232

Dyslexia Society, Orton
(800) 222-3123

Easter Seal Society
(800) 221-6827

Appendix 9.7 (Continued) Toll-Free Phone Numbers and Hotlines

Educators Publishing Service, Inc.
Specific Language Disabilities
(Dyslexia) (800) 225-5750

Epilepsy Foundation of America
(800) 332-1000

ERIC Clearinghouse on Adult Career and Vocational Education
(800) 848-4815

Family Support Network
(800) 852-0042

Federal Hill-Burton Free Care Program
(800) 638-0742

Federal Internal Revenue Service
(800) 829-1040

Financial Aid for Education Available from the Federal Government
(800) 333-INFO

Georgia Assistive Technology Project
(Atlanta) (800) 497-8665
(Warm Springs) (800) 578-8665

Georgia Relay Center
(800) 255-0135 (Voice to TT)
(800) 255-0056 (TT to Voice)

Guide Dog Foundation for the Blind
(800) 548-4337

Handicapped Media, Inc.
(800) 321-8708

Handicapped Travel Divisions, National Tour Assoc.
(800) 682-8886

Head Injury Foundation, National
(800) 444-6443

Health Resource Center
(800) 544-3284

Hearing Helpline
(800) 327-9355

Hearing Information Center, Senior Hearing Aids
(800) 622-3277

Appendix 9.7 (Continued) Toll-Free Phone Numbers and Hotlines

Higher Education and Adult Training of People with Handicaps (HEATH Resource Center)
(800) 54-HEATH

Huntington's Disease Society of America
(800) 345-4372

IBM National Center for Person with Disabilities
(800) 426-4832

International Shriners Headquarters
(800) 237-5055

Job Accommodations Network (JAN)
(800) 526-7234

Job Opportunities for the Blind (JOB)
(800) 638-7518

John Tracy Clinic on Deafness
(800) 522-4582

Juvenile Diabetes Foundation Hotline
(800) 223-1138

Kidney Foundation, National
(800) 622-9010

Kidney Fund, National
(800) 638-8299

The Lighthouse National Center for Vision and Aging
(800) 334-5497

Lupus Foundation of America
(800) 558-0121

Medicare, Hotline (800) 672-3071

Medigap, U.S. Dept. of Health and Human Services
(800) 638-6833

Modern Talking Picture Service, Inc.
(800) 237-6213

Muscular Dystrophy Association
(800) 358-7240

Muscular Sclerosis, GA Regional Office
(800) 822-3379

Appendix 9.7 (Continued)   Toll-Free Phone Numbers and Hotlines

National AIDS Hotline
(800) 342-AIDS

National Alliance for the Mentally Ill (NAMI)
(800) 950-NAMI

National Association for Parents of the Visually Impaired
(800) 562-6265

National Association for Rehabilitation Facilities
(800) 368-3513

National Association for Sickle Cell Disease, Inc.
(800) 421-8453

National Cancer Institute Information
Service (800) 4-CANCER

National Center for Sight
(800) 221-3004

National Committee for Citizens in Education
(800) NETWORK

National Council on Aging
(800) 424-9046

National Cystic Fibrosis Foundation
(800) 344-4823

National Down Syndrome Congress
(800) 232-6372

National Down Syndrome Society
(800) 221-4602

National Eye Care Project Helpline
(800) 222-EYES

National Headache Foundation
(800) 843-2256

National Head Injury Foundation (NHIF)
(800) 444-6443

National Health Information Center (NHIC)
(800) 336-4797

National Hearing Aid Society Hearing Aid Hotline
(800) 521-5247

Appendix 9.7 (Continued) Toll-Free Phone Numbers and Hotlines

National Information Center for Children and Youth with Disabilities (NICHCY)
(800) 999-5599

National Information Clearinghouse for Infants with Disabilities and Life-Threatening Conditions
(800) 922-9234, ext. 201

National Information System Vietnam Vets/Children
(800) 922-9234

National Insurance Consumer Hotline
(800) 942-4242

National Library Service for Blind & Physically Handicapped
(800) 424-8567

National Multiple Sclerosis Society
(800) 624-8236

National Organization for Rare Disorders (NORD)
(800) 447-6673

National Organization on Disability
(800) 248-ABLE

National Parkinson Foundation
(800) 327-4545

National Rehabilitation Information Center (NARIC)
(800) 346-2742

National Retinitis Pigmentosa Foundation
(800) 638-2300

National Reye's Syndrome Foundation
(800) 233-7393

National Sexually Transmitted Diseases Hotline
(800) 227-8922

National Spinal Cord Injury Association
(800) 962-9629

National Stroke Association
(800) 367-1990

National Tuberous Sclerous Association
(800) CAL-NTSA

North American Riding for the Handicapped Assoc., Inc.
(800) 369-7433

Appendix 9.7 (Continued)   Toll-Free Phone Numbers and Hotlines

Occupational Hearing Service
(800) 222-EARS

Orton Dyslexia Society
(800) 222-3123

Parkinson's Disease Foundation, Inc.
(800) 457-6676

Parkinson's Education Program
(800) 344-7872

Practitioner's Reporting System
(800) 638-6725

The Rural Disability Information Service
(800) 732-0323

State Library for the Blind and Physically Handicapped
(800) 662-7726

Tele-Consumer Hotline
(800) 323-1124

TRIPOD GRAPEVINE, Service for Hearing Impaired
(800) 352-8888

United Cerebral Palsy Association
(800) 872-5827

Veterans Administration Office
(800) 831-6515

INFORMATION ON 1-800 NUMBERS
(800) 555-1212

Appendix 9.8   Internet Resources

About elder law
http://www.naela.com/naela/hotlinks.htm#ElderlawResources

Adaptive Solutions
Assistive Technology Tracker
www.adaptive-sol.com

Alexander Graham Bell Association for the Deaf
http://www.agbell.org

Appendix 9.8 (Continued)   Internet Resources

Alliance for Technology Access
http://www.ataccess.org

ALS Association
http://www.alsa.org

American Association on Mental Retardation
http://www.aamr.org

American Foundation for the Blind, Technology Center
http://www.afb.org

American Medical Association
http://www.ama-assn.org

American Physical Therapy Association
http://www.apta.org

American Speech-Language-Hearing Association
www.asha.org

Americans with Disabilities Act Document Center
http://janweb.icdi.wvu.edu

Assistive Technology, Inc.
http://www.assistivetech.com/info-faq-funding.htm

Assistive Technology Tracker
www.adaptive-sol.com

Audible, Inc.
www.audible.com

Augmentative Communication
http://www.augcomm.com/products.html

Augmentative Communication On-Line User Group (ACOLUG)
www.temple.edu/inst_disabilities/acolug

Blissymbolics Communication International
http://home.istar.ca/~bci/

Brain Actuated Technologies, Inc.
www.brainfingers.com

California Relay Service
1-800-735-2929

California State University–Northridge, Center on Disabilities
http://www.csun.edu/cod/

Appendix 9.8 (Continued)   Internet Resources

CALL Center, University of Edinburgh
http://callcenter.education.ed.ac.uk

Center for International Rehabilitation Research Information and Exchange (CIRRIE)
http://cirrie.buffalo.edu

Centers for Disease Control and Prevention
http://www.cdc.gov

Centers for Disease Control *Morbidity and Mortality Weekly Report*
http://www.cdc.gov/epo/mmwr/mmwr.html

Clinical Research Abstract
http://www.med.upenn.edu/cra

Communication Aids Manufacturers Association
www.aacproducts.com

Communication Aids Manufacturers Association (CAMA)
www.aacproducts.org

Communication Independence for the Neurologically Impaired (CINI)
http://www.cini.org

Council for Exceptional Children
http://www.cec.sped.org

Council for Licensure Enforcement and Regulation (CLEAR)
http://www.clearhq.org

Cyberlink Interface
www.brainfingers.com

Department of Veterans Affairs
http://www.va.gov

Design to Learn
www.designtolearn.com

Division of Vocational Rehabilitation
State of New Mexico Department of Education
http://www.state.nm.us/dvr/vragencies.htm

Doug Dodgen and Associates
AAC Feature Match Software
http://www.dougdodgen.com

Dragon Dictate Systems
www.dragonsys.com

Appendix 9.8 (Continued)   Internet Resources

Eisenhower National Clearinghouse for Math and Science Education
http://www.enc.org

Equal Access to Software and Information (EASI)
http://www.rit.edu/~easi/

Eye/Muscle Operated Switch (EMOS)
www.mctos.com

Food and Drug Administration
http://www.fda.gov

GMR Labs
http://www.aimnet.com/~roark/

Guillan-Barre Syndrome Disability Resources
http://www.adsnet.com/steinhi/html/gbs/gbsabel.html

Harris Communications
15159 Technology Dr.
Edan Prairie, MN 55344-2277

Health Care Financing Administration
www.hcfa.gov

Health Care Financing Administration (HFAC)
http://www.hcfa.gove/medicaid/medicaid.htm

Health care law
http://www.arentfox.com/telemedicine.html

HMS School for Children with Cerebral Palsy
Philadelphia, PA
www.hmsschool.org

Human Factors and Ergonomics Society (HFES)
HFES is one of the major professional organizations for practitioners and researchers
in ergonomics and human factors.
http://hfes.org

Institute of Medicine
http://www.nas.edu/iom

International Society for Augmentative and Alternative Communication (ISAAC)
http://www.isaac-online.org

Internet Disability Resources, Mary Barros-Baily and Dawn Boyd, AHAB Press, Inc., 2
Gannett Dr., Suite 200, White Plains, NY 10604-3404.
E-mail: AHAB4@aol.com

Appendix 9.8 (Continued)   Internet Resources

ISAAC
www.isaac-online.org

Keyboard Alternatives and Vision Solutions
www.keyalt.com

Krown Manufacturing, Inc.
www.krowntty.com

Kurzweil Applied Intelligence
www.kurz-ai.com

LifeSpan Access Profile
Don Johnston Company
http://www.donjohnston.com

List of disability sites
http://www.nde.state.ne.us/ATP/listsites.html

Madentec
www.madentec.com

Muscular Dystrophy Association (MDA)
http://www.mdusa.org

Nathaniel H. Kornreich Technology Center
www.kornreich.org

National Easter Seal Society
http://www.easter-seals.org

National Federation of the Blind (NFB)
http://www.ngb.org

National Information Center for Children and Youth with Disabilities (NICHY)
http://www.nichy.org

National Information Center for Children and Youth with Handicaps (NICHCY)
http://www.nichcy.org

National Institutes of Health
http://www.nih.gov

National Organization for Competency Assurance (NOCA)
http://www.noca.org

National Organization on Disability
http://www.nod.org

National Spinal Cord Injury Association
http://www.spinalcord.org

Appendix 9.8 (Continued)   Internet Resources

National Technical Institute for the Deaf
http://www.rit.edu/~418www/

Net Connection to CD & S
http://ww.mankato.msus.edu/dept/comdis/kuster2/welcome.html

Oklahoma Able Tech home page
http://www.okstate.edu/wellness/at-home.htm

PennTech-Central Instructional Support Center
http://www.cisc.k12.pa.us/

Pittsburgh Employment Conference (PEC)
SHOUT@agi.net
Prentke Romich Company (PRC)
www.prentrom.com

Quality Indicators for Assistive Technology Services
http://www.quiat.org

Rehabilitation Engineering and Assistive Technology Society of North America (RESNA)
RESNA is an interdisciplinary association of people with a common interest in
technology and disability. This association promotes research, development,
education, advocacy, and the provision of technology.
www.resna.org

Rehabilitation Engineering and Assistive Technology Society of North America (RESNA)
http://www.resna.org

RESNA Credentialing Examination in Assistive Technology
http://www.resna.org/certify/index.html

Social Security Disability Administration Disability Information
http://www.ssa.gov

Special Interest Division 12
www.professional.asha.org/sidivisions/sid_12.htm

Speech to Speech
http://www.stsnews.com

Technical Assistance Project
http://www.resna.org/taproject/at/statecontacts.html

Texas Commission for the Blind — blindness-related links
http://link.tsl.state.tx.us/www
www.ITCB.dir/blind/shtml

The Arc (of the U.S.)
http://www.thearc.org

Appendix 9.8 (Continued) Internet Resources

Trace Center — University of Wisconsin–Madison
gopher://trac.wisc.edu:70/1/netmenus/fintech

Trace Research and Development Center
http://trace.wisc.edu

Training and Technical Assistance Center for Professionals Serving Students with Disabilities
http://tac.elps.vt.edu/htmldocs/augcom.html

Turning Point Technologies
(877) 608-9812

United Cerebral Palsy, Funding for Assistive Technology
http://www.ucpa.org

United Way of America home page
http://www.unitedway.org

University of Nebraska–Lincoln
AAC Vendors Information
http://aac.unl.edu/

University of Washington Speech and Hearing Sciences Department
UW AugComm
http://depts.washinton.edu/augcomm
This site has been established as part of the UW Tele-Collaboration Project to provide information and resources for professionals and community members with an interest in AAC.

Upshaw Institute for the Blind
Technology Information and Resources Services
http://www.upshawinst.org

U.S. Government site for Medicare information
http://www.medicare.gov

USSAAC (U.S. Chapter of ISAAC)
USAAC@aol.com

Wisconsin Assistive Technology Initiative
http://aac-rerc.com
http://wati.org

World Health Organization
http://www.who.ch/

Appendix 9.8 (Continued)   Internet Resources

Wynd Communications
http://www.wyndtell.com

YAACK (Augmentative Communication Connecting Young Kids)
http://www.mrtc.org/~duffy/yack/index.html

Appendix 9.9   Online Assistive Technology Resources

Ability Hub

AbilityHub.com's purpose is to help users find information on adaptive equipment and alternative methods available for accessing computers. Ability Hub's founder is Dan Gilman, a certified ATP (assistive technology practitioner) with RESNA.

ABLEDATA

A national database of information on more than 17,000 products that are currently available for people with disabilities.

Access Board

An independent federal agency. Contains information on Section 508 of the Rehabilitation Act, as amended requiring that electronic and information technology developed, procured, maintained, or used by the federal government be accessible to people with disabilities. In 1998, the board established an Electronic and Information Technology Access Advisory Committee (EITAAC) to help the board develop standards under Section 508.

Accessible Website Design Resources

Connects to a Government Services Administration (GSA) site with links to several organizations with "how-to's" on designing websites for accessibility for people with disabilities, including a link to "Top Ten Mistakes in Web Design."

Alliance for Technology Access

Provides location information for the Alliance for Technology Access regional centers. The Alliance assists individuals with disabilities access technology, mainly through computer resources.

Apple's Disability Solutions

Information on computer access solutions for individuals with disabilities.

Assistive Technology Funding and Systems Change Project (ATFSCP)

Assistive technology funding and systems change information.

Appendix 9.9 (Continued)   Online Assistive Technology Resources

AT Quick Reference Series

This TechConnections resource provides quick reference guides for work-related accommodations, such as Voice Input Systems, accessible calculators, mouse alternatives, one-handed keyboards, and other assistive technologies.

AZtech, Inc.

Information on transforming inventions into products for individuals with disabilities.

Breaking New Ground Resource Center

Provides information and resources on assistive technology for agricultural workers and agricultural work sites. In 1990, the Outreach Center of Breaking New Ground became a part of the USDA AgrAbility program.

Center for Information Technology Accommodation (CITA)

Legislation and policies on information systems accessibility, including the Assistive Technology Act of 1998.

Closing the Gap

Closing the Gap's role is to provide information on microcomputer materials and practices that can help enrich the lives of persons with special needs.

Consortium for Citizens with Disabilities (CCD)

CCD is a working coalition of more than 100 national consumer, advocacy, provider, and professional organizations working together with and on behalf of the 54 million children and adults with disabilities and their families living in the U.S. The CCD has several task forces on various disability issues, such as employment and training, developmental disabilities, health, Social Security, long-term services and supports, telecommunications and technology, rights, etc.

Cornucopia of Disability Information (CODI)

A wealth of information relating to disabilities, including topics such as aging, statistics, computing, centers for independent living, and universal design. This site is based at the State University of New York–Buffalo.

CPB/WGBH National Center for Accessible Media

"Making Educational Software Accessible: Design Guidelines, Including Math and Science Solutions." These guidelines represent an ambitious initiative to capture access challenges and solutions and present them in a format specifically designed to educate and assist educational software developers. The detailed guidelines and solutions specific to math and science are unique to this document. This work is the result of a 3-year project funded by the National Science Foundation's Program for Persons with Disabilities. The CPB/WGBH National Center for Accessible Media developed this document with input from a distinguished board of advisors with expertise in accessible design, assistive technology, and the education of students with disabilities.

Appendix 9.9 (Continued)   Online Assistive Technology Resources

DISABILITY Resources on the Internet

This site was created and is maintained by Jim Lubin, a person with quadriplegia.

Do-It Internet Resources

Resources are listed in many categories, including general resources, education, technology, legal, social, and political issues.

EPVA Assistive Technology

The Eastern Paralyzed Veterans Association (EPVA) launched a website for assistive technology in 2002. Available at this site are product reviews on wheelchairs and cushions and a tech guide on driving aids, transfer devices, and exercise equipment.

Equal Access to Software and Information (EASI)

EASI is part of the Teaching, Learning, and Technology Group, an affiliate of the American Association of Higher Education. EASI's mission is to promote the same access to information and resources for people with disabilities as everyone else.

Federal Communications Commission (FCC)

Contains the Telecommunications Act of 1996 and links to FCC's Disabilities Issues Task Force that contain press releases and reports that affect telecommunications and technology issues for people with disabilities.

IBM Special Needs Solutions

Information on IBM computer access solutions for persons with disabilities.

International Center for Disability Resources on the Internet

The center will collect and present best practices in areas related to disability and accessibility issues. The center will collect disability-related Internet resources, including resources that may be helpful to the disability community.

Job Accommodation Network (JAN)

A service of the U.S. Department of Labor's President's Committee on Employment of People with Disabilities, JAN provides information about job accommodation and the employability of people with functional limitations. Publishes quarterly reports on the number of cases handled by information and ADA-related concerns, among many other outcome data statistics.

Learning Disabilities OnLine

Interactive guide to learning disabilities for parents, teachers, and children.

National Clearing House of Rehabilitation Training Materials (NCHRTM)

Download AT-related documents from this site. Sample titles include Assistive Technology: Practical Intervention Strategies; ADA: Train the Trainer Program; and Reasonable Accommodations in the Workplace.

Appendix 9.9 (Continued)   Online Assistive Technology Resources

National Rehabilitation Information Center (NARIC)

NARIC is a library and information center on disability and rehabilitation. More than 50,000 National Institute on Disability and Rehabilitation Research (NIDRR)-funded, other federal agency, and private disability-related publications are held and abstracted by NARIC in its REHABDATA database, searchable online.

National Institute on Disability and Rehabilitation Research (NIDRR)

NIDRR, part of the U.S. Department of Education, manages and funds more than 300 projects on disability and rehabilitation research, including 56 state and U.S. territory assistive technology projects and several Rehabilitation Engineering Research Centers.

On a Roll — Talk Radio

Talk Radio focusing on life and disability news, updated daily. While at the site, check out the RealAudio archives of this award-winning radio talk show.

One-Hand Typing

Information on free downloads, how-to manuals, therapists, and more.

TeamRehab Report

A monthly magazine for professionals in rehabilitation technology and services.

Trace Research & Development Center

The Trace Center conducts research aimed at improving technology that can benefit individuals with disabilities by making it more accessible in four main areas: communication, control, computer access, and next-generation communication information and transaction systems.

West Virginia Rehabilitation Research and Training Center (WVRRTC)

Information resources on vocational rehabilitation, including links to the Job Accommodation Network and Project Enable.

WheelchairNet

WheelchairNet is a continuously developing resource for a broad community of people who are interested in wheelchairs: consumers, clinicians, manufacturers, researchers, funders. It contains resources for lifestyle, wheelchair technology and research developments, discussions, products, industry product standards, funding, services, etc.

World Wide Web Consortium (W3C)

The W3C, an international industry consortium, was founded in October 1994 to lead the World Wide Web to its full potential by developing common protocols that promote its evolution and ensure its operability. The W3C also includes the World Accessibility Initiative, which provides guidelines on website accessibility.

Appendix 9.10 International Sites

AAATE

http://www.fernuni-hagden.de/FTB/AAATE.html

ARATA

http://www.iinet.net.au/~sharano/arata

International Center for Disability Resources on the Internet

The center will collect and present best practices in areas related to disability and accessibility issues. The center will collect disability-related Internet resources, including resources that may be helpful to the disability community.

Untangling the Web: Where Do I Go for Disability Information?

Lists websites in many categories, including general information resources, disability legislation, employment resources, and more.

Yuri Rubinsky Insight Foundation: webABLE!

Contains an accessibility database that provides links to an extensive list of Internet resources related to disability and accessibility. Resources include mailing lists, websites, and newsgroups.

Appendix 9.11   Periodicals and Newsletters

ABLEDATA, 8455 Colesville Rd., Suite 935, Silver Springs, MD 20910; Telephone: (800) 227-0216, (301) 588-9284; Fax: 301-587-1967.

Alternatively Speaking, Augmentative Communication, Inc., 1 Surf Way, Suite 237, Monterey, CA 93940; Telephone: (408) 649-3050; Fax: 408-646-5428; newsletter.

Augmentative Communication News, Augmentative Communication, Inc., 1 Surf Way, Suite 237, Monterey, CA 93940; newsletter.

The Bumpy Gazette, Repro-Tronics, Inc., 75 Carver Ave., Westwood, NJ 07675; Telephone: (800) 948-8453; Website: http://www.repro-tronics.com/.

Closing the Gap Resource Directory, P.O. Box 68, Henderson, MN 56044; Telephone: (612) 248-3294.

Conn SENSE Bulletin, Special Education Center, Technology Lab, The University of Connecticut, U-64, Room 227, 249 Glenbrook Rd., Storrs, CT 06269-2064; Telephone: (203) 486-0172.

The ISAAC Bulletin, 49 The Donway West, Suite 308, Toronto, ON M3C 3M9, Canada; Telephone: +1-416-385-0351; Fax: +1-416-385-0352; E-mail: secretariat@isaac-online.org; Website: www.isaac-online.org.

REACH/Rehabilitation Engineering Associates, Telephone: (800) 485-5040; newsletter.

SpeakUp!, c/o Beatrice Bruno, P.O. Box 21418, Sarasota, FL 34276; Telephone: (941) 312-0992; Fax: 941-312-0992; E-mail: usaac@comcast.com; Website: www.usaac.com.

Spotlight on AAC, Prentke Romich Company, Inc., 1022 Heyl Rd., Wooster, OH 44691; Telephone: (800) 262-1984, ext. 440.

Technology Resource Directory, Susan Mack, Exceptional Parent, 1170 Commonwealth Ave., 3rd Floor, Boston, MA 02134-9942.

Voices, Hear Our Voices, Newsletter Department, 1660 L St. NW, Suite 700, Washington, DC 20036; Telephone: (205) 930-9025.

WorkTech, Seaside Education Associates, Inc., P.O. Box 6341, Lincoln Center, MA 01773; newsletter.

10

THE ROLE OF THE AUDIOLOGIST IN LIFE CARE PLANNING

Carolyn W. Higdon, Larry Higdon, and Vic S. Gladstone

Audiology, an autonomous profession that encompasses both health care and educational professional areas of practice, is involved with the study of hearing and balance and their related disorders. The audiologist is the independent hearing health care professional who provides comprehensive diagnostic and habilitative/rehabilitative services for all areas of auditory, vestibular, and related disorders. These services are provided to individuals across the entire age span from birth to adulthood, which is in concert with the goals of a life care plan; to individuals from diverse language, ethnic, cultural, and socioeconomic backgrounds; and to individuals who have multiple disabilities (ASHA, Spring 1996). Within life care planning, the audiologist should be involved in pediatric and adult rehabilitation efforts when clients experience decreased hearing sensitivity, auditory processing problems, auditory neuropathy (auditory dys-synchrony), or balance problems. Clients may experience auditory deficits, due to genetic or natural aging factors, ear disease, brain injury, auditory processing dysfunction, environmental noise exposure, or reactions to medications that are ototoxic or vestibulotoxic.

Life care planners seeking information on current audiology preferred practices, technical papers, position statements, reimbursement codes, standards, and certification and licensure will find the American Speech-Language-Hearing Association (ASHA) webportal (professional.asha.org or asha.org) the most comprehensive site for peer-reviewed documentation of practice issues and currency of reimbursement codes. The ASHA Code of Ethics (ASHA, 2003), revised January 1, 2003; scope of practice (ASHA, Spring 1996); preferred practice patterns for the profession of audiology (ASHA, 1997); Joint Audiology Committee Clinical Practice (1999) statements and algorithms; and current reimbursement code funding are documents (ASHA, 2004) of significant interest to life care planners seeking best practices information and quality hearing health care for their clients. The information is also available on the ASHA webportal.

0-8493-1511-5/04/$0.00+$1.50
© 2004 by CRC Press LLC

Services provided by audiologists include the ability to:

■ Test and diagnose hearing and balance disorders
■ Select, fit, and dispense hearing aids and assistive devices
■ Provide audiologic/aural (re)habilitation services
■ Educate consumers and professionals on prevention of hearing loss
■ Participate in hearing conservation programs to help prevent workplace-related and recreational hearing loss
■ Consult for federal, state, and local agencies in reducing community noise
■ Conduct research

Audiology services are available in the following work settings:

1. Colleges and universities
2. Public and private schools
3. Hospitals
4. Community-based hearing and speech centers
5. State and local health departments
6. Private practices
7. Rehabilitation centers
8. Nursing care facilities
9. Industry
10. State and federal governmental agencies
11. Military

Audiology can be categorized by either the setting in which one practices or the population one serves. Bess and Humes (1995) identified the following specialty areas in which audiologists generally practice. The *pediatric audiologist* concentrates on the audiologic management of children of all ages. The pediatric audiologist is often employed in a children's hospital or a health care facility primarily serving children. The *medical audiologist* works with patients of all ages and is more concerned with establishing the site and cause of a hearing or balance problem. Medical audiologists are typically employed in hospitals as part of either a hearing and speech department or a department of otolaryngology (i.e., ear, nose, and throat). Some audiologists who work in a medical environment perform intraoperative monitoring, which involves monitoring central and peripheral nerve function during surgical procedures. The *rehabilitative/dispensing audiologist* focuses on the management of children or adults with hearing impairment. Rehabilitative audiologists are often in private practice and may specialize in the direct dispensing of hearing aids in addition to offering other audiologic rehabilitation services. Rehabilitative audiologists are also employed by a variety of health care facilities (e.g., hospitals and nursing homes). *The industrial audiologist* provides consultative hearing conservation services to companies whose workers are exposed to high noise levels. The industrial audiologist may be in private practice or work on a part-time basis. The *forensic audiologist* serves as an expert witness in legal issues related to hearing and balance. The forensic audiologist may serve as an expert witness for the plaintiff or defense in compensation cases

Figure 10.1 Audiology specialties. (From Bess, F. & Humes, L. (1995). *Audiology: The Fundamentals,* **2nd ed., p. 7. Baltimore: Williams & Williams. Reprinted by permission.)**

and may also serve as a consultant in community or environmental noise issues. Finally, the *educational audiologist* serves children in the schools and is employed or contracted by the educational system. Many audiologists, not just those in academic environments, engage in basic and applied research that is not only essential to understanding human auditory function but also necessary in order to develop testing materials and procedures and improved amplification systems.

BASIC AUDIOLOGIC PROCEDURES

When referring a patient to an audiologist for a basic audiologic assessment, one may expect certain basic procedures to be conducted to quantify and qualify hearing loss on the basis of responses to acoustic stimuli and to screen for other associated communication disorders. These include a pure tone hearing test (ASHA, 1978), speech audiometry (ASHA, 1988), and acoustic immittance (ASHA, 1991b) procedures accomplished in accordance with American National Standards Institute standards (ANSI, 1981, 1986, 1987, 1991, 1992, 1996) and under Centers for Disease Control (CDC) standard health care precautions guidelines (CDC, 1988; U.S. Department of Labor, 1998). Of course, the basic audiologic procedures may be modified depending on the age or level of cooperation of the patient.

Clinical Process for a Basic Audiologic Assessment

The clinical process for a basic audiologic evaluation includes (ASHA, 1999):

- A case history
- Otoscopic evaluation
- External ear canal examination and cerumen management, if necessary
- Assessment, which includes:
  — Air conduction and bone conduction threshold measures with appropriate masking (pure tone testing)
  — Speech recognition thresholds or speech awareness thresholds with appropriate masking
  — Word recognition (speech discrimination) measures with appropriate masking
  — Acoustic immittance testing (tympanometry, static compliance, and acoustic reflex measures)
  — Other procedures, which include, but are not limited to, otoacoustic emissions screening, speech and language screening, communication inventories, and screening for auditory processing disorders and other related auditory disorders.

External Ear Canal Examination and Cerumen Management

The external ear canal examination is performed to remove debris from the ear canal to allow the audiologist to perform the assessment or to perform rehabilitative or hearing aid procedures. The need for cerumen (ear wax) management is required when there is an accumulation of debris that would preclude the audiologist from obtaining valid and reliable assessment results and, in many cases, improve auditory sensitivity. Established procedures include (ASHA, 1991a; Ballachandra & Peers, 1992; Roeser & Crandell, 1991):

- Mechanical removal
- Irrigation
- Suction

It should be noted that in some states cerumen management is not within the scope of practice of audiologists. Reimbursement for the service varies by state and region and also from third-party payers.

Pure Tone Testing

An audiologist using a calibrated electronic device called an audiometer measures hearing. An audiogram is a graphic representation of hearing. It relates intensity (loudness) as a function of frequency (pitch). Frequency, measured in hertz (Hz), is plotted along the abscissa, and intensity, measured in decibels (dB), is plotted along the ordinate. For a simplistic explanation of the various sounds and definitions of hearing loss, see Figure 10.2.

A person wears earphones and the audiologist presents tones at varying frequencies and intensities for each ear. When the individual hears the tone, he

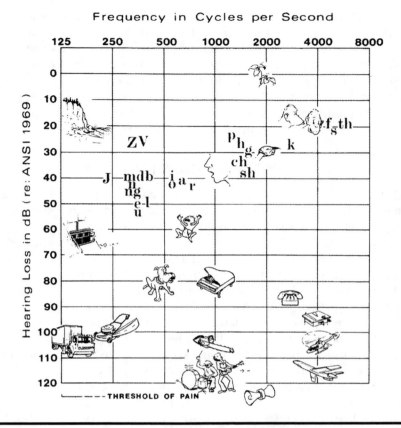

Figure 10.2   Frequency spectrum of familiar sounds plotted on standard audiogram. (From Northern, J. & Downs, M. (1991). *Hearing in Children*, 4th ed., p. 17. Baltimore: Williams & Williams. Reprinted by permission).

or she responds by raising his or her hand. When the tone is heard at the lowest intensity level two out of three times, the audiologist records this intensity level for each frequency on the audiogram. This level is called threshold. Thresholds for the left ear are plotted with a blue *X* and thresholds for the right ear are plotted with a red *0*. Normal hearing is considered to be between −10 and +15 dB HL. Hearing level (HL) is the number of decibels relative to normal hearing, which is 0 dBHL on the audiogram. The example audiogram indicates normal hearing in the left ear and a hearing loss in the right ear.

The area enclosed by the two wavy lines is called the speech banana. This area represents the frequencies and intensities of spoken English and assists the audiologist in explaining how a hearing loss may affect a person's ability to understand speech. In the example audiogram, the person will not be able to hear speech sounds above 1000 Hz in the right ear because his thresholds are out of the speech banana. Were this person to have this degree of hearing loss in both ears, he may be expected to have difficulty understanding high-frequency speech sounds such as *s*, *f*, *th*, *p*, *t*, *k*, *sh*, and *ch*, for example. In addition, he may be expected to have considerable difficulty understanding conversational speech in the presence of background noise, such as in a cafeteria.

Audiograms (Figure 10.3) are very important because they can indicate whether a person has a hearing loss and also the type and degree of loss he or she has. There are three principal types of hearing loss directly associated with the peripheral auditory mechanism: conductive (a problem in the outer or middle ear), sensorineural (a problem in the inner ear or the eighth cranial nerve, which carries the auditory signals to the brain), and mixed conductive and sensorineural loss. Other nonperipheral auditory deficits may include auditory processing disorders and an auditory neuropathy (auditory dys-synchrony).

SPEECH AUDIOMETRY

A second part of the basic testing includes speech audiometry where the audiologist evaluates how well a person can hear and understand speech. Speech audiometry consists of speech threshold and word recognition (understanding) or speech discrimination testing. Speech threshold testing determines how soft a speech sound a person can recognize, whereas word recognition testing tells the audiologist what percentage of conversational speech is correctly understood at a particular intensity level. One method of obtaining a word recognition/speech discrimination score is called the articulation gain function (Figure 10.4) (or performance intensity/phonetic balance function). This method assures that the patient's maximum score possible will be identified (ASHA, 1988).

Most people understand conversational speech maximally at approximately 40 dB above their speech threshold. The evaluator starts by presenting the speech level at 40 dB above the patient's speech threshold and reading a list of 50 single-syllable words with the person instructed to repeat back each word.

The percentage correct score at 40 dB above a person's threshold is then plotted. If 100% correct is not achieved, the test is repeated using a similar list of words at 50 dB above the person's threshold, and that score is plotted. This procedure is repeated until the person's best score is obtained. The score in the example graph indicates that the person will understand speech 90% of the time as long as it is 60 dB above threshold.

Acoustic Immittance

Acoustic immittance, sometimes referred to as acoustic impedance, measures the mobility of the middle ear system. The middle ear is basically a vibratory system consisting of the eardrum and the three middle ear bones: the malleus, incus, and stapes. The middle ear is responsible for taking acoustic energy (sound) and transferring it via mechanical energy from the outer ear to the fluids in the inner ear. The functioning of the middle ear affects the way people hear. Tympanometry is a measure of the mobility of the middle ear (compliance) as a function of middle ear pressure, measured in dekapascals (daPa). The results are displayed on a graph called a tympanogram (Figure 10.5), and interpretation of these results can help indicate the site of the lesion or what is causing a hearing loss (ASHA, 1991b).

An electroacoustic immittance meter is used to measure the middle ear function. A plug is inserted into the ear canal, and the instrument takes the measurements and graphs the information.

AUDIOGRAM

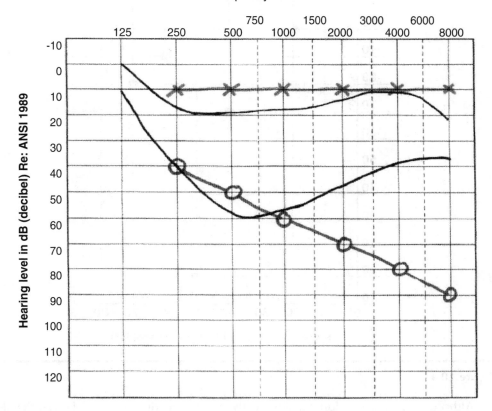

Figure 10.3

There are five basic types of tympanograms:

Type A	Middle ear pressure is between +100 and 150 daPa Compliance is normal	
Type A$_s$	Middle ear pressure is normal Compliance is reduced	Otosclerosis
Type A$_d$	Middle ear pressure is normal Compliance is increased	Disarticulation
Type B	Middle ear pressure cannot be measured due to fluid Compliance is reduced	Middle ear effusion
Type C	Middle ear pressure is reduced	Eustachian tube dysfunction

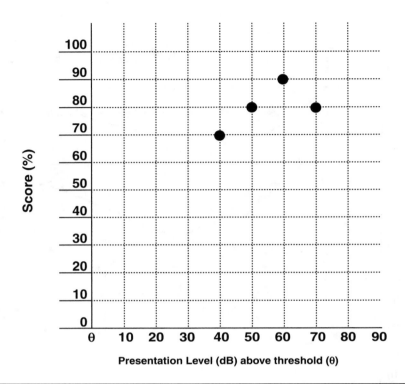

Figure 10.4

Although these procedures are typically conducted during an audiologic evaluation, they may be modified to meet the special needs of children and other difficult-to-test patients. For patients that cannot or will not tolerate earphones, test signals (tones and speech) can be presented through loudspeakers strategically placed within the sound-attenuated test booth. The patient will either look toward the sound or be taught to place a peg in a board, ring on a peg, block in a box, etc., in response to the sound. At that moment, the patient's positive response behavior will be reinforced. Successive trials will enable the audiologist to establish threshold or an acceptable estimate of hearing level.

PEDIATRIC AUDIOLOGIC ASSESSMENT

Pediatric audiologic assessment is usually conducted on infants and young children (under 5 years of age) (ASHA, 1993) and other individuals whose developmental levels preclude the use of standard adult audiologic assessment procedures. The assessment typically requires an audiologist skilled in pediatric assessment and will involve multiple office visits. The clinical process is essentially the same as that for a basic audiologic assessment prior to attempting to obtain test results. The assessment may include one or more assessment tools (acoustic immittance measures, audiologic (re)habilitation and education needs assessment,

TYMPANOGRAMS

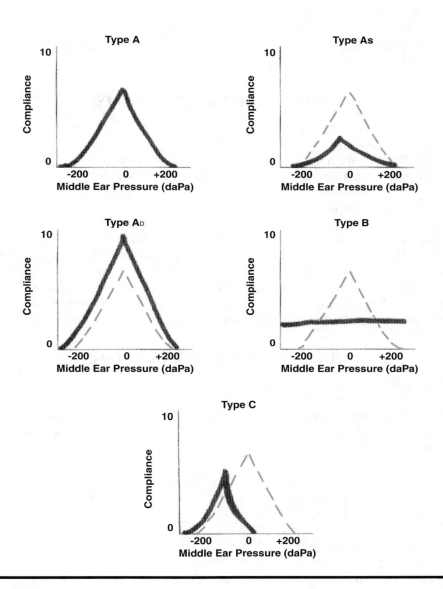

Figure 10.5

otoacoustic emissions (OAE), electrophysiologic assessment, and other developmentally appropriate behavioral procedures). Behavioral testing measures include:

- Visual Reinforcement Audiometry (VRA)
- Conditioned Play Audiometry
- Tangible Reinforcement Operant Conditioning Audiometry (TROCA)
- Visual Reinforcement Operant Conditioning Audiometry (VROCA)
- Behavioral Observation Audiometry (BOA)

COMPREHENSIVE (ADVANCED) AUDIOLOGIC ASSESSMENT

The comprehensive audiologic assessment includes the measures utilized in a basic audiologic assessment, but further encompasses specific procedures or batteries of specific procedures that are viewed as separate entities for purposes of service delivery.

OTOACOUSTIC EMISSIONS (OAES)

OAEs are acoustic signals generated by the inner ear of healthy ears in normal-hearing individuals. The acoustic signals are by-products of the activity of the outer hair cells in the cochlea. The clinical significance is that they are evidence of a vital sensory process arising in the cochlea, and OAEs only occur in a normal cochlea with normal hearing. OAEs are a powerful diagnostic tool that assist audiologists in ruling out unusual auditory disorders, where there are unexplained differences in hearing between two ears, when a sudden hearing loss occurs, in medical-legal cases, and in cases of questionable validity of hearing test results.

The OAE evaluation is relatively quick (approximately 5 minutes per ear) and is noninvasive. A soft rubber tip is inserted in the ear canal and a series of comfortably loud tones or clicks are presented. No response is necessary from the patient; he or she only needs to sit quietly while the test is being conducted. OAEs can be completed at any age from shortly after birth to above 90.

AUDITORY EVOKED RESPONSE (AER)

An AER assessment describes the clinical status of the auditory neural pathway and associated sensory elements, and assists in differential diagnosis and in estimating threshold sensitivity. The assessment may also be conducted with patients who are difficult to test by conventional behavioral methods for the purposes of site of lesion identification or in resolution of conflicting data (ASHA, 1999).

Patients are prepared for the assessment by placement of recording electrodes on the head, and they wear earphones for introduction of stimuli. The AER procedures may include:

- Electrocochleography (EcohG)
- Auditory brainstem response (ABR)
- Auditory middle latency response (AMLR)
- Auditory late (long latency) response (ALR)
- P300 response
- Mismatched negativity (MMN) response

NEUROPHYSIOLOGIC INTRAOPERATIVE MONITORING

Neurophysiologic intraoperative monitoring involves continuous direct or indirect electrophysiologic measurement and interpretation of myogenic and neural responses to intraoperative events or modality-specific, controlled stimulation in the course of surgery on or in the vicinity of those structures. The important aspect of intraoperative monitoring is the online moment-to-moment correlation between the changes in neurophysiologic responses and intraoperative events.

The principal objectives of neurophysiologic intraoperative monitoring are (1) to avoid intraoperative injury to neural structures, (2) to facilitate specific stages of the surgical procedure, (3) to reduce the risk of permanent postoperative neurological injury, and (4) to assist the surgeon in identifying specific neural structures (ASHA, 1992).

BALANCE (VESTIBULAR) SYSTEM ASSESSMENT

Clinical indications for a vestibular or balance system assessment are when a patient presents with nystagmus, complaints of vertigo, balance dysfunction, or gait abnormalities; or when peripheral or central vestibulopathy is suspected (ASHA, 1997). A balance system assessment is prompted by medical referral or by the results of an audiologic assessment. A balance system assessment is conducted to:

- Detect pathology within the vestibular or balance system
- Determine probable site of lesion
- Monitor change in balance function
- Determine the contribution of the visual, vestibular, and proprioceptive systems to functional balance
- Determine coordinated motor control recovery from induced sway
- Counsel regarding the effects of balance system dysfunction

The clinical process may include but is not limited to the following tests:

- Electronystagmography (ENG) — Surface electrodes are placed around the eyes to measure the vestibule-ocular reflex (VOR). The corneo-retinal potential is recorded and subsequent measurements of coordinated eye movement and nystagmus can be made. Subtests may include gaze nystagmus, oculomotor tests, such as saccades, smooth pursuit, and optokinetics, objective and subjective head shake, torsion swing, Dix–Hallpike maneuver, static positional tests, bithermal caloric irrigations, ice caloric irrigations, and failure of fixations suppressions (FFS).
- Computerized rotary chair — Surface electrodes are placed around the eyes to measure phase, gain, and symmetry of VOR. The patient is seated in a darkened room in a computer-driven chair, which rotates around the Earth's vertical axis.
- Computerized dynamic posturography (CDP) — During the Sensory Organization Test (SOT), six conditions are presented that alter visual and somatosensory input. The Motor Control Test (MCT) evaluates automatic motor responses to several computer-induced platform movements. CDP is advantageous for patients with balance disorders, neurologically or orthopedically compromised patients, and patients for whom standard VOR tests are nonsignificant or incomplete. It also serves as a quantitative method for evaluating the efficacy of vestibular rehabilitation.

- Individuals with a positive Dix–Hallpike maneuver may be candidates for a canalith repositioning maneuver, such as the Semont procedure or the Epley procedure.

COCHLEOTOXIC DRUG THERAPY (AUDIOLOGIC MANAGEMENT)

Permanent hearing loss or balance disorders caused by ototoxic drugs can have serious vocational, educational, and social consequences. These effects may be minimized or even prevented if the ototoxic process is detected early in treatment. Any drug with the potential to cause toxic reactions to structures of the inner ear, including the cochlea, vestibule, semicircular canals, and otoliths, is considered ototoxic (Govaerts et al., 1990). Drug-induced damage affecting the auditory and vestibular systems can be called, respectively, cochleotoxicity and vestibulotoxicity. Over 200 drugs have been labeled ototoxic (see list in Govaerts et al., 1990; Lien et al., 1983; Rybak, 1986). Different ototoxic drugs can cause either permanent or temporary structural damage of varying degree and reversibility (Bendush, 1982; Brummett, 1980). The actual frequency of cochleotoxicity associated with specific drugs is unclear because of inconsistencies in reported data (Powell et al., 1983; Kopelman et al., 1988; Pasic & Dobie, 1991).

Although the role and responsibility for designing and implementing an auditory monitoring program for cochleotoxicity rests with the audiologist, the implementation and continuation of such a program requires a collaborative effort between the audiologist, physician, and other medical center personnel. The relationship between cochleotoxicity and drug administration parameters such as dosage, duration of treatment, and serum concentration is highly variable (Barza & Lauermann, 1978; Fausti et al., 1992, 1993; Schentag, 1980). An attending physician, therefore, cannot rely solely on dosage or serum concentration to predict the risk of ototoxicity. The prospective assessment of hearing function remains the only reliable method for detecting the presence of cochleotoxicity prior to symptomatic hearing loss. Evidence suggests that high-frequency audiometry is the method of choice for the earliest detection of ototoxic hearing loss (Fausti et al., 1990; Frank & Dreisbach, 1991; Frank, 1990; Laukli & Mair, 1985; Valente et al., 1992).

The basic cochleotoxicity monitoring program requires (ASHA, 1994):

- Specific criteria for identification of toxicity
- Timely identification of at-risk patients
- Pretreatment counseling regarding potential cochleotoxic effects
- Valid baseline measures (pretreatment or early in treatment)
- Monitoring evaluations at sufficient intervals to document progression of hearing loss or fluctuation in sensitivity
- Follow-up evaluations to determine posttreatment effects

If ototoxic hearing loss results in a communication deficit, the audiologist will recommend audiologic rehabilitation (including amplification if necessary), assistive listening devices, speech-reading, etc. Audiologic rehabilitation management should begin as soon as possible after the hearing loss is identified.

AUDIOLOGIC (AURAL) REHABILITATION ASSESSMENT

Audiologic rehabilitation assessment evaluates and describes the receptive and expressive communication skills of individuals with a hearing loss or related hearing disorders. Individuals of all ages are assessed on the basis of results from the audiologic assessment, hearing aid or assistive system/device assessment, fitting, or orientation; sensory aid assessment; and communication needs or preferences.

The assessment includes an evaluation of the impact of the loss of hearing on the individual and his or her family/caregiver. The assessment may result in the development of a culturally appropriate audiologic rehabilitation management plan, including, when appropriate (ASHA, 1997):

- Fitting and dispensing recommendations, and educating the consumer and family/caregivers in the use of and adjustment to sensory aids, hearing assistive devices, alerting systems, and captioning devices
- Counseling relating to psychosocial aspects of hearing loss and processes to enhance communication competence
- Skills training and consultation concerning environmental modifications to facilitate development of receptive and expressive communication
- Evaluation and modification of the audiologic management plan

AUDIOLOGIC (AURAL) REHABILITATION MANAGEMENT

Audiologic rehabilitation is provided to persons of all ages who have any degree or type of hearing loss on the basis of the results of the audiologic rehabilitation assessment. Audiologic rehabilitation facilitates receptive and expressive communication of individuals with a hearing loss or related hearing disorders, and results in achievement of improved, altered, augmented, or compensated communication processes. Performance in both clinical and natural environments is considered. The family/caregiver plays an integral part of the rehabilitation process.

Short- and long-term functional communication goals and specific objectives are determined from assessment and direct the framework for treatment. They are reviewed periodically to determine continued relevance and appropriateness (ASHA, 1995b, 1997, 2002).

When it comes to dealing with hearing loss, some think that simply obtaining hearing aids or other listening devices is the rehabilitation. Audiologic rehabilitation, however, is a much broader concept. It focuses on reducing difficulties related to hearing loss and listening. The overall goal is to maximize communication success in everyday environments and situations.

Audiologic rehabilitation services may include:

- Learning how to listen
- Learning how hearing loss affects speech
- Learning skills in speech-reading (lip-reading, facial expression, gestures, body language)
- Building confidence in handling communication situations
- Learning what to do when you do not get the message

- Learning how to use your hearing aids or cochlear implant
- Learning about different kinds of technology to improve communication
- Learning how to advocate for yourself
- Learning what your rights are under various laws
- Promoting family and caregiver understanding and support of your needs
- Learning how you can make it easier for your family to communicate with you

Audiologists and speech-language pathologists often collaborate in delivering aural rehabilitation services. Depending on the patient's particular need, one or the other professional may take a lead.

For example, the audiologist:

- Would be responsible for fitting and dispensing hearing aids, sensory aids, and assistive listening devices, and training you how to use them
- Can provide counseling about your hearing loss and processes to enhance communication
- Can provide skills training concerning environmental modifications to facilitate development of receptive and expressive communication
- Can conduct aural rehabilitation assessment and design a management plan

The speech-language pathologist:

- Would be responsible for evaluating receptive and expressive communication skills and providing services to develop or improve receptive and expressive communication
- Can provide treatment focusing on comprehension of language in oral, signed, or written modes
- Can provide treatment dealing with speech and voice production
- Can provide treatment such as auditory training and speech-reading
- Can provide training in communication strategies

Retrieved from http://www.asha.org/hearing/rehab/gen_aur_rehab.cfm.

AUDIOLOGIC (RE)HABILITATION FOR CHILDREN

Specific services for children depend on individual needs as dictated by the current age of the child, the age of onset of the hearing loss, the age at which the hearing loss was discovered, the severity of the hearing loss, the type of hearing loss, the extent of hearing loss, and the age at which amplification was introduced. The audiologic rehabilitation plan is also influenced by the communication mode the child is using. Examples of communication modes are speaking/listening/looking, cued speech, manually coded English, total communication, auditory-oral, auditory-verbal, and American Sign Language.

The most debilitating consequence of onset of hearing loss in childhood is its disruption to learning speech and language. The combination of early detection of hearing loss and early use of amplification has been shown to have a dramatically positive effect on the language acquisition abilities of a child with hearing loss. In fact, infants identified with a hearing loss by 6 months can be expected to attain language development on a par with hearing peers.

Audiologic habilitation/rehabilitation services for children typically involve:

- **Training in auditory perception.** This includes activities to increase awareness of sound, identify sounds, tell the difference between sounds (sound discrimination), and attach meaning to sounds. Ultimately, this training increases the child's ability to distinguish one word from another using any remaining hearing. Auditory perception also includes developing skills in hearing with hearing aids and assistive listening devices and how to handle easy and difficult listening situations.
- **Using visual cues.** This goes beyond distinguishing sounds and words on the lips. It involves using all kinds of visual cues that give meaning to a message such as the speaker's facial expression, body language, and the context and environment in which the communication is taking place.
- **Improving speech.** This involves skill development in production of speech sounds (by themselves, in words, and in conversation), voice quality, speaking rate, breath control, loudness, and speech rhythms.
- **Developing language.** This involves developing language understanding (reception) and language usage (expression) according to developmental expectations. It is a complex process involving concepts, vocabulary, world knowledge, use in different social situations, narrative skills, expression through writing, understanding rules of grammar, etc.
- **Managing communication.** This involves the child's understanding the hearing loss, developing assertiveness skills to use in different listening situations, handling communication breakdowns, and modifying situations to make communication easier.
- **Managing hearing aids and assistive listening devices.** Because children are fitted with hearing aids at young ages, early care and adjustment are done by family members or caregivers. It is important for children to participate in hearing aid care and management as much as possible. As they grow and develop, the goal is for their own adjustment, cleaning, and troubleshooting of the hearing aid and, ultimately, taking over responsibility for making appointments with service providers.

Services for children occur in the contexts of early intervention (ages birth to 3) and school services (ages 3 to 21) through the Individuals with Disabilities Education Act (IDEA). In early intervention, an Individualized Family Service Plan (IFSP) is developed and may include audiology services, speech-language pathology services, the services of teachers of the deaf and hard-of-hearing, and the services of other professionals as needed. When the child turns 3, an Individualized Education Program (IEP) is developed. The services provided are designed to maximize the child's success in the general education environment. Again, the IEP may specify audiology services, speech-language pathology services, and the services of teachers of the deaf and hard-of-hearing. Each professional has a role to play in the child's educational achievement and success.

ASSISTIVE LISTENING DEVICES (ALDS)

An ALD is any type of device that can help a person function better in day-to-day communication situations. An ALD can be used with or without hearing aids to overcome the negative effects of distance, background noise, and poor room acoustics. So even though a patient has a hearing aid, assistive listening devices can offer greater ease of hearing (and therefore reduced stress and fatigue) in many day-to-day communication situations. (Retrieved from http://www.asha.org/hearing/rehab/assist_tech.cfm.)

Examples of ALDs include:

1. **Personal frequency-modulated (FM) systems** are like a miniature radio station operating on special frequencies assigned by the Federal Communications Commission. The personal FM system consists of a transmitter microphone used by the speaker and a receiver used by you, the listener. The receiver transmits the sound to your hearing aid either through direct audio input or through a looped cord worn around your neck.

    FM systems/auditory trainers have been standard equipment for children with hearing loss in educational settings for many years. Audiologists are the uniquely qualified professionals to select, evaluate, fit, and dispense FM systems. Before selecting an FM system for personal use it is necessary to assess auditory capacity and the current level of auditory and communication function and to identify other factors related to device use. The issue of potential damage to the auditory mechanism should be considered when fitting any assistive listening device. This is of special concern when considering the fitting of a self-contained FM system to a person with near normal hearing, mild hearing loss, or fluctuating hearing loss (ASHA, 2002). All amplification equipment is subject to failure; therefore, daily monitoring is required (Bess, 1988). Periodic comprehensive monitoring of the FM system by the audiologist includes electroacoustic analysis, probe microphone measurements, and other in-depth troubleshooting measures. In addition, the periodic assessments of hearing and of performance with the FM device are necessary to monitor stability of hearing, appropriate device settings, function, and degree of benefit. The evaluations should be performed at least annually for adults and children 5 years of age and older. For children under 5 years of age and for individuals with fluctuating or conductive hearing loss, the follow-up evaluations should be much more frequent.

    If a self-contained FM system is going to be used, decisions must be made relative to the gain, frequency response, input/output functions, and saturation sound pressure level requirements for the individual listener. During the preselection process, assessments may include, but are not limited to, audiological assessment, observation of auditory performance in representative settings, consultation with the user or others knowledgeable about the user's performance, questionnaires and scales, hands-on demonstration, and a trial period. Other factors to be considered in the preselection process include (ASHA, 2002):

- The person's ability to wear, adjust, and manage the device
- Support available in the educational setting (e.g., in-service to teachers, classmates)
- Acceptance of the device
- Appropriate situations and settings for use
- Time schedule for use
- Compatibility with personal hearing aids and other audio sources as well as options for coupling
- Individual device characteristics and accessories
- External source interference (e.g., pagers, radio stations, computers, etc.)
- Cost and accessibility
- Legislative mandates

Personal FM systems are useful in a variety of situations such as listening to a travel guide, in a classroom lecture, in a restaurant, in a sales meeting, listening to a book review, in nursing homes, in senior centers, etc.

FM systems are also used in theaters, places of worship, museums, public meeting places, corporate conference rooms, convention centers, and other large areas for gathering. In this situation, the microphone/transmitter is built into the overall sound system. Patients are provided with an FM receiver that can connect to their hearing aid or to a headset.

2. **Infrared systems** are often used in the home with TV sets. They, like the FM system, are also used in large-area settings like theaters.

   Sound is transmitted using infrared light waves. The TV is set at a volume comfortable for family members. The infrared system transmitter transmits the TV signal to the receiver, which can be adjusted to a desired volume. Thus, TV watching as a family becomes pleasurable for all. It is not blaring for family members with normal hearing.

3. **Induction loop systems** are most common in large-group areas. They can also be purchased for individual use.

   An induction loop wire is permanently installed (perhaps under a carpet) and connects to a microphone used by a speaker. (In the case of individual systems, a wire loop is laid on the floor around the listener and the speaker.) The person talking into the microphone creates a current in the wire that makes an electromagnetic field in the room. When the patient switches his or her hearing aid to the T (telecoil/telephone) setting, the hearing aid telecoil picks up the electromagnetic signal and the patient can adjust its volume through the hearing aid.

4. **One-to-one communicators** are sometimes used in a restaurant, a nursing home situation, or riding in a car, when the patient wants to be able to easily hear one person. Or perhaps she is delivering a lecture or running a meeting and a person in the audience has a question. The person with the question is given a microphone to speak into. The sound is amplified and delivered directly into the speaker's hearing aid (or headset if she does not have a hearing aid), and the speaker can adjust the volume to her comfort level. When using the one-to-one communicator, the speaker does not have to shout, private conversations can remain private, and, when in a car, her eyes can remain on the road.

5. There are many other assistive listening devices such as telephone amplifying devices for cordless, cell, digital, and wired phones; amplified answering machines; amplified telephones with different frequency responses; paging systems; computers; wake-up alarms; etc.

6. There are also **alerting devices** that signal when a sound occurs. For example, there are doorbell, knock-at-the door, or phone alerting devices; fire alarm/smoke alarm devices; baby-cry devices or room-to-room sound alerting systems; vibrating clock alarms; vibrating paging systems; vibrating watch alarms; etc. Many use strobe light or conventional light to alert; others use vibrating systems to alert.

HEARING AID SELECTION AND FITTING

Myth: Hearing aids restore hearing to normal just as an eyeglass prescription can restore vision to 20/20.

Fact: Hearing aids do not restore hearing to normal. Just as eyeglasses do not cure vision problems, hearing aids do not cure hearing loss. Like eyeglasses, hearing aids provide benefit and improvement. They can improve hearing and listening abilities, and they can substantially improve quality of life.

Any individual who subjectively reports and audiometrically demonstrates hearing loss of a degree that interferes with communication should be considered for fitting with amplification. The clinical process is initially the same as that for a basic audiologic assessment. The complete audiologic assessment and needs assessment is necessary to initiate a treatment plan that may include amplification. Pre-hearing aid selection in conjunction with determination of the treatment plan is necessary prior to initiating the selection regimen.

The patient must be counseled to include an explanation of the potential benefits and limitations associated with personal amplification. The fitting of a personal amplification system and verification of its appropriateness for the communication needs of the patient, family, and caregiver are necessary requisites. There must be validation of the benefit to and satisfaction of the patient, family, and caregiver. In many cases it is necessary to demonstrate a support system is in place to assist in maximizing the use and maintenance of the personal amplification system. The clinical decision-making process is based on professional judgment and individual patient characteristics that may significantly influence the nature and course of the selection and fitting process. The process may vary by audiologist and may vary based on the patient needs, cooperation, comprehension, and process setting. The procedures listed below require the completion of an audiologic assessment within the prior 6 months. (Most audiologists will require their own assessment at the time of the hearing aid selection process.)

The audiologic clinical process may include, but is not necessarily limited to, the following (ASHA, 1998, 1999) (the components are not designed to be all-inclusive):

■ Recent history of auditory function
■ Appropriate physical examination (e.g., otoscopy)

- Cerumen (ear wax) management
- Sprathreshold loudness measurements
- Ear impressions
- Hearing aid selection procedure
- Hearing aid performance verification in 2 cc coupler and in the real ear for quality control
- Individual or group orientation to amplification
- Unaided/aided communication inventory
- Individual or group hearing aid follow-up
- Qualitative assessment of amplification
- Measurement of satisfaction and benefit
- Unaided and aided speech recognition measures

Hearing aids differ in design, size, the amount of amplification, ease of handling, volume control, and availability of special features. But they do have similar components, which include:

- A microphone to pick up sound
- Amplifier circuitry to make the sound louder
- A receiver (miniature loudspeaker) to deliver the amplified sound into the ear
- Batteries to power the electronic parts

Some hearing aids also have ear molds (earpieces) to direct the flow of sound into the ear and enhance sound quality.

STYLES OF HEARING AIDS

In-the-canal and *completely-in-the-canal* aids are contained in a tiny case that fits partly or completely into the ear canal. They are the smallest aids available and offer cosmetic and some listening advantages.

All parts of *in-the-ear* aids are contained in a shell that fills in the outer part of the ear. These aids are larger than canal aids and, for some people, may be easier to handle than smaller aids.

All parts of *behind-the-ear* aids are contained in a small plastic case that rests behind the ear; the case is connected to an ear mold by a piece of clear tubing. This style is often chosen for young children for safety and growth reasons.

The majority of hearing aids sold today are canal hearing aids and in-the-ear hearing aids.

There are also special hearing aids built to handle very specific types of hearing losses. For example, a *bone-conduction hearing aid* uses a headband and a bone vibrator for individuals who have no ear canal or outer ear. There are hearing aids that route sounds coming to one ear over to the other ear for use by individuals who have no hearing in one ear. In special cases, hearing aids can be built into glasses for individuals who need that type of fitting. There are hearing aids available that can accommodate virtually any kind of hearing loss.

TYPES OF HEARING AIDS

Hearing aids are distinguished by their technology or circuitry. In the early days, hearing aid technology involved vacuum tubes and large, heavy batteries. Today, there are microchips, computerization, and digitized sound processing used in hearing aid design.

- *Conventional analog hearing aids* are designed with a particular frequency response based on your audiogram. The audiologist tells the manufacturer what settings to install. Although there are some adjustments, the aid essentially amplifies all sounds (speech and noise) in the same way. This technology is the least expensive, and it can be appropriate for many different types of hearing loss.
- *Analog programmable hearing aids* have a microchip that allows the aid to have settings programmed for different listening environments such as quiet conversation in your home, noisy situations like a restaurant, or large areas like a theater. The audiologist uses a computer to program the hearing aid for different listening situations depending on the individual hearing loss profile, speech understanding, and range of tolerance for louder sounds.
- Some aids can store several programs. As the listening environment changes, a wearer can change the hearing aid settings by pushing a button on the hearing aid or by using a remote control to switch channels. The aid can be reprogrammed by the audiologist if hearing or hearing needs change. These aids are more expensive than conventional analog hearing aids, but generally have a longer life span and may provide better hearing in different listening situations.
- *Digital programmable hearing aids* have all the features of analog programmable aids but use digitized sound processing to convert sound waves into digital signals. A computer chip in the aid analyzes the signals of your environment to determine if the sound is noise or speech and then makes modifications to provide a clear, amplified distortion-free signal. Digital hearing aids are usually self-adjusting. The digital processing allows for more flexibility in programming the aid so that the sound it transmits matches a specific pattern of hearing loss. This digital technology is the most expensive, but it allows for improvement in programmability, greater precision in fitting, management of loudness discomfort, control of acoustic feedback (whistling sounds), and nose reduction.

SPECIAL FEATURES FOR HEARING AIDS

Many hearing aids have optional features that can be built in to assist in different communication situations. Some options are:

- *Directional microphone.* Some hearing aids have a switch to activate a directional microphone that responds to sound coming from a specific direction, as occurs in a face-to-face conversation. A patient can switch from the normal nondirectional (omnidirectional) setting, which picks up sound almost equally from any direction, to focus on a sound coming from in front. When the directional microphone is activated, sound coming from behind is reduced.

- *Telephone switch.* Some hearing aids are made with an induction coil inside. You can switch from the normal microphone "on" setting to a "T" setting to hear better on the telephone. (All wired telephones produced today must be hearing aid compatible.) In the T setting, environment sounds are eliminated, and the patient only picks up sound from the telephone. Furthermore, he can talk without his hearing aid "whistling" because the microphone of the hearing aid is turned off.
- The T setting can also be used in theaters, auditoriums, houses of worship, etc., that have induction loop or FM installations. The sound of the talker, who can be a distance away, is amplified significantly more than any background noises. Some hearing aids have a combination M (microphone)/T (telephone) switch so that while listening with an induction loop, the wearers can still hear nearby conversation.
- *Direct audio input.* Some hearing aids have a direct-audio-input capability that allows them to plug in a remote microphone or an FM assistive listening system, connect directly to a TV, or connect with other devices such as a computer, CD player, tape player, radio, etc. (Retrieved from http://www.asha.org/hearing/rehab/hearing_aids.cfm.)

Federal and state regulations may require a medical evaluation and clearance from a licensed physician prior to hearing aid purchase.

Advances in digital signal processing in recent years have opened the way for digital hearing aids to become the standard of current audiologic practice. The current emphasis for research and development is on specific features such as directional technology and digital noise reduction to maximize speech understanding and sound quality. The introduction of digital noise reduction (DNR) has provided greater ease of listening for many hearing-impaired individuals based on subjective measures. The challenge remains to develop algorithms that separate speech from noise. Notable technological developments are also being made in the field of implantable hearing devices. Apart from the more commonly employed cochlear implant technology, there has also been growth in the use of middle ear implants and, more recently, bone-anchored hearing aids suitable for single-sided hearing loss.

AUDITORY NEUROPATHY

Dr. Charles I. Berlin (1999) suggests that auditory neuropathy (AN) is better named auditory dys-synchrony because it is a disorder of the timing of the auditory nerve. Auditory neuropathy is a confusing diagnosis that has sparked conflict among audiology professionals.

Dr. Linda Hood (1998) indicates that AN is a term presently used to describe a condition, found in some patients ranging in age from infants to adults, in which the patient displays auditory neural function at the level of the VIIIth (vestibulo-cochlear) nerve. These characteristics are observed on clinical audiologic tests as normal otoacoustic emissions in the presence of an absent or severely abnormal auditory brainstem response. These patients are distinguished from patients with space-occupying lesions, such as VIIIth nerve tumors, or multiple sclerosis, in that radiological evaluation yields normal results and even the most peripheral responses from the VIIIth nerve are absent. Patients with AN require a different management approach to their auditory and communication problems from approaches used with patients with usual peripheral hearing losses. The characteristics of AN most likely reflect more than a single etiology, and thus the disorder(s) may more accurately be described as auditory neuropathies.

AUDITORY PROCESSING DISORDERS ASSESSMENT (AS PERFORMED BY AN AUDIOLOGIST)

Auditory processing disorders (APDs) is the current terminology for what was referred to in earlier literature as central auditory processing disorders (CAPDs). With current research and improved diagnostic tools we now know that not all auditory processing disorders can be related to a central origin. An APD assessment helps to define the functional status of the central auditory nervous system (CANS) and central auditory processes.

The assessment is indicated for individuals of all ages who have symptoms or complaints of hearing difficulty with documented normal peripheral auditory function; have a central nervous system (CNS) disorder potentially affecting the central auditory system; or have learning problems possibly related to the auditory difficulties. The APD assessment is to be conducted with other audiologic, speech, and language tests, as well as neuropsychological tests, to evaluate the overall communication behavior, including spoken language processing and production, and educational achievement of the individual (ASHA, 1999).

ASHA (1996) in the *American Journal of Audiology* defined (central) auditory processing disorders as a problem in one or more of six areas:

1. Sound localization and lateralization (knowing where in space a sound source is located)
2. Auditory discrimination (usually with reference to speech, but the ability to tell that one sound is different from another)
3. Auditory pattern recognition (musical rhythms are one example of an auditory pattern)
4. Temporal aspects of audition (auditory processing relies on making fine discriminations of timing changes in auditory input, especially differences in timing by the way input comes through one ear as opposed to the other)
5. Auditory performance decrements with competing acoustic signals (listening in noise)
6. Auditory performance decrements with degraded acoustic signals (listening to sounds that are muffled, missing information, or for some reason not clear — the best example is trying to listen to speech taking place on the other side of a wall; the wall filters or blocks out certain parts of the speech signal, but a typical listener can often understand the conversation)

The interpretation of results is derived for multiple tests; there is no single test to determine the presence of an auditory processing disorder. The APD battery of tests may involve a series of appointments over a period of time. The test results will be measured against age-appropriate norms and knowledge of the CANS in normal and disordered states. The procedures in an APD battery should be viewed as separate entities for purposes of service delivery and reimbursement.

The clinical process is as follows:

- Appropriate communication, medical, and educational history is taken.
- Assessment is typically part of an intradisciplinary (audiology and speech-language pathology) approach.
- Patient is prepared for behavioral and electrophysiologic assessment of the CANS.
- Types of central auditory behavioral tests include:
  — Tests of temporal processes
  — Tests of dichotic listening
  — Low redundancy monaural speech tests
  — Tests of binaural interaction

Central auditory electrophysiologic tests include:

- Auditory brainstem response (ABR)
- Middle latency evoked response (MLR)
- N1 and P2 (late potentials) responses (P300)
- Mismatched negativity (MMN)
- Middle ear reflex
- Crossed suppression of otoacoustic emissions

AUDITORY PROCESSING DISORDERS MANAGEMENT (AS PERFORMED BY AN AUDIOLOGIST)

The comprehensive rehabilitation of and management of APDs may include interventions directed to acoustic signal enhancement, improvement of language and cognitive capacities, skills development, use of compensatory strategies, employment of listening strategies, and improvement of the listening environment (ASHA, 1990, 1996). Management (treatment) is conducted to improve auditory processing, listening, spoken language processing, and the overall communication process. Improvements in auditory processing and listening can benefit learning and daily living activities.

APD management is recommended when there is a likelihood of improving communication behavior in any age group. Any individual who is documented to have an APD after completion of the APD test battery, and who is impaired or compromised on the basis of the results, is a candidate for management (treatment). Generalization of skills and strategies is enhanced by extending practice to the natural environment through collaboration among key professionals (ASHA, 1999).

The clinical process may be, but is not limited to, the following (ASHA, 1999):

■ A treatment plan is formulated based on the patient's complaints, symptoms, history, central auditory test results, and functional performance deficits.
■ Treatment may be conducted in an intradisciplinary (audiology and speech-language pathology) and interdisciplinary manner.
■ The treatment plan should incorporate several major approaches:
— Auditory training and stimulation
— Communication and educational strategies
— Metalinguistic and metacognitive skills and strategies
— Assistive listening devices
— Acoustic enhancement and environmental modifications of the listening environment

Tinnitus Management

Tinnitus, more commonly spoken of as ringing in the ear or head noise, has been experienced by almost everyone at one time or another. It is defined as the perception of sound in the head when no external sound is present. In addition to ringing, head noises have been described as hissing, roaring, pulsing, whooshing, chirping, whistling, and clicking. Ringing and head noises can occur in one ear or both ears and can be perceived to be occurring inside or outside the ear. Tinnitus can accompany hearing loss. It can exist independent of a hearing loss.

Tinnitus cannot be measured objectively. Rather, the audiologist relies on information provided in describing the tinnitus. The audiologist will ask questions like:

■ Which ear is involved? Right? Left? Both?
■ Is the ringing constant? Do you notice it more at certain times of the day?
■ Can you describe the sound or the ringing?
■ Does the sound have a pitch to it? High pitch? Low pitch?
■ How loud does it seem? Does it seem loud or soft?
■ Does the sound change or fluctuate?
■ Do you notice conditions that make the tinnitus worse, e.g., when drinking caffeinated beverages, when taking particular medicines, or after exposure to noise?
■ Does the tinnitus affect your sleep? Your work? Your ability to concentrate?
■ How annoying is it? Extremely so? Not terribly bothersome?

Knowing the cause of tinnitus is a relief, instead of having to live with the uncertainty of the condition. When tinnitus is demystified, stress level (which can make tinnitus worse) is frequently reduced, and there is a feeling of greater control.

The most effective treatment for tinnitus is to eliminate the underlying cause. Because tinnitus can be a symptom of a treatable medical condition, medical or surgical treatment can take place to correct the tinnitus.

Unfortunately, in many cases the cause of tinnitus cannot be identified, or medical or surgical treatment is not the appropriate course of action. In these cases, the tinnitus itself may need to be treated.

Drug therapy, vitamin therapy, biofeedback, hypnosis, electrical stimulation, relaxation therapy, counseling, habituation therapies, and tinnitus maskers are among many forms of management available. Audiologists and otolaryngologists routinely collaborate in identifying the cause and providing treatment. A treatment that is useful and successful for one person may not be appropriate for another.

Tinnitus maskers look like hearing aids and produce sounds that mask, or cover up, the tinnitus. The masking sound acts as a distractor and is usually more tolerable than the tinnitus. It is an external noise and some people find it preferable to the sound in their heads. The characteristics of the tinnitus (pitch, loudness, location, etc.) that you described for the audiologist determine what kind of masking noise might bring relief. If you have a hearing loss as well as tinnitus, the masker and the hearing aid may operate together as one instrument. Like all other treatments for tinnitus, maskers are useful for some, but not all, people.

The scope of practice of audiologists is described below and should demonstrate the breadth and depth of knowledge and skill audiologists possess.

American Speech-Language-Hearing Association[1] (ASHA) Audiology Scope of Practice

The practice of audiology includes (ASHA, 1996):

1. Activities that identify, assess, diagnose, manage, and interpret test results related to disorders of human hearing, balance, and other neural systems
2. Otoscopic examination and external ear canal management for removal of cerumen in order to evaluate hearing or balance, make ear impressions, fit hearing protection or prosthetic devices, and monitor the continuous use of hearing aids
3. Conducting an interpretation of behavioral, electroacoustic, or electrophysiologic methods used to assess hearing, balance, and neural system function
4. Evaluation and management of children and adults with central auditory processing disorders
5. Supervision and conducting of newborn hearing screening programs
6. Measurement and interpretation of sensory and motor evoked potentials, electromyography, and other electrodiagnostic tests for purposes of neurophysiologic intraoperative monitoring and cranial nerve assessment
7. Provision of hearing care by selecting, evaluating, fitting, facilitating adjustment to, and dispensing prosthetic devices for hearing loss, including hearing aids, sensory aids, hearing assistive devices, alerting and telecommunication systems, and captioning devices
8. Assessment of candidacy of persons with hearing loss for cochlear implants and provision of fitting, programming, and audiological rehabilitation to optimize device use

---

[1] See resources section for address and phone number.

9. Provision of audiological rehabilitation, including speech reading, communication management, language development, auditory skill development, and counseling for psychosocial adjustment to hearing loss for persons with hearing loss and their families and caregivers

10. Consultation with educators as members of interdisciplinary teams about communication management, educational implications of hearing loss, educational programming, classroom acoustics, and large-area amplification systems for children with hearing loss

11. Prevention of hearing loss and conservation of hearing function by designing, implementing, and coordinating occupational, school, and community hearing conservation and identification programs

12. Consultation and provision of rehabilitation to persons with balance disorders using habituation, exercise therapy, and balance retraining

13. Designing and conducting basic and applied audiologic research to increase the knowledge base, to develop new methods and programs, and to determine the efficacy of assessment and treatment paradigms; dissemination of research findings to other professionals and to the public

14. Education and administration in audiology graduate and professional education programs

15. Measurement of functional outcomes, consumer satisfaction, effectiveness, efficiency, and cost–benefit of practices and programs to maintain and improve the quality of audiological services

16. Administration and supervision of professional and technical personnel who provide support functions to the practice of audiology

17. Screening of speech-language, use of sign language (e.g., American Sign Language and cued speech), and other factors affecting communication function for the purposes of an audiologic evaluation or initial identification of individuals with other communication disorders

18. Consultation about accessibility for persons with hearing loss in public and private buildings, programs, and services

19. Assessment and nonmedical management of tinnitus using biofeedback, masking, hearing aids, education, and counseling

20. Consultation to individuals, public and private agencies, and governmental bodies, or as an expert witness regarding legal interpretations of audiology findings, effects of hearing loss and balance system disorders, and relevant noise-related considerations

21. Case management and service as a liaison for the consumer, family, and agencies in order to monitor audiologic status and management and to make recommendations about educational and vocational programming

22. Consultation with industry on the development of products and instrumentation related to the measurement and management of auditory or balance function

23. Participation in the development of professional and technical standards

Credentials Held by Audiologists

As health professionals concerned with the welfare of the patients they serve, audiologists must possess certain credentials to practice audiology. These credentials signify a specific level of education and competence that serve to protect consumers. Certification and licensure are the two most common credentials possessed by audiologists. Table 10.1 delineates the characteristics of certification and licensure.

In order to be certified by the American Speech-Language-Hearing Association and licensed/registered/certified by a particular state regulatory board or agency to practice audiology, one must possess either a master's or doctoral degree earned from an accredited college or university audiology graduate program. A doctoral degree in audiology will be required for new graduates effective 2007. College and university graduate audiology programs seek accreditation from the Council on Academic Accreditation of the American Speech-Language-Hearing Association. This ensures that graduates of these programs are eligible for the certificate of clinical competence (CCC) issued by the Council for Clinical Certification of ASHA. The U.S. Department of Education and the Council on Recognition of Postsecondary Accreditation have approved ASHA as a credentialing agency. The standard on which the certificate of clinical competence in audiology (CCC-A) is based has served as the foundation for most states' licensing laws. ASHA's national certification standards have undergone costly scientific tests of validity (ASHA, 2004b). ASHA-certified audiologists possess specific knowledge and competencies and must pass a national examination as well as maintain currency through continuing education.

Additionally, most states require audiologists to be licensed, registered, or certified in order to practice audiology in that particular state. Each state's licensing or regulatory board has specific educational and competency requirements, which are assessed through examination. Renewal of state credentials usually requires maintenance of currency through continuing education.

Referral Considerations

Referrals to audiologists can be made directly by contacting the office, center, hospital, or facility in which the audiologist is employed. The American Speech-Language-Hearing Association, (301) 897-5700, or the American Academy of Audiology, (703) 790-8466, or a state speech-language-hearing association can provide the names of audiologists practicing in specific geographic areas. ASHA maintains a referral source (PROSERV) on its consumer website at www.asha.org.

It is important and helpful to be aware of the types of test procedures and terminology used by audiologists. This will assist the case manager in making appropriate referrals and in conversing knowledgeably with the audiologist. The following is a listing of some of the test procedures and terminology used by audiologists:

Table 10.1   Characteristics of Certification and Licensure

Purpose:	grants recognition to <u>practitioners</u> who have met certain qualifications	protects the <u>public's</u> life, health safety or economic well being
Function:	restricts the use of the designated title to individuals who choose to meet the qualifications	restricts scope of practice so that it is illegal for unlicensed individuals to provide the services
Qualifications:	formal education, experience, personal characteristics, and completion of examination	may piggy-back on qualifications required for certification
Establishment of Regulations:	developed and approved by members of the association	developed by regulatory body and approved according to the state's Administrative Procedure Act
Provider:	usually a private association	state agency
Status:	voluntary	mandatory
Penalties for Violation:	• rescind membership • rescind certification	• admonishment • license revocation • monetary fine • restrictions on practice • incarceration • license suspension
Continuing Education:	certifying entity may sponsor continuing education opportunities for members; <u>may</u> be required for recertification	may be required for licensees to renew

ASHA State Policy Division
10/10/95-aew

Types of Hearing Loss

Conductive: Abnormalities of the outer or middle ear

Sensorineural: Abnormalities of the inner ear

Mixed: Combination of conductive and sensorineural

Central: Abnormalities of the central auditory nervous system

Assessment Procedures

Behavioral Observation Audiometry (BOA): Controlled observation of responses (i.e., changes in behavior such as quieting, arousal from sleep, eye shift, eye widening, eyebrow raising, body movement, and head turn) to acoustic stimuli

Visual Reinforcement Audiometry (VRA): Reinforcement with lighted toys when the child turns toward the sound source

Conditioned Play Audiometry (CPA): Conditioning the child to respond to the stimulus through game playing

Conventional Audiometry: Hand-raising or button-pushing response to stimulus

Auditory Evoked Potentials (AEPs): Measurement of changes in electrical activity of the auditory nervous system in response to acoustic stimuli

Otoacoustic Emissions (OAEs): Measurement of sound generated by motion of the outer hair cells

(Central) Auditory Processing Evaluation (APDs): Assessment of the central auditory system to process complex auditory stimuli

Mode of Presentation

Soundfield: Testing via loudspeakers; does not allow a unilateral or asymmetrical hearing loss to be ruled out

Air Conduction: Testing via earphones; allows each ear to be evaluated in isolation

Bone Conduction: Testing via a bone vibrator; directly stimulates better cochlea function

Test Battery

Frequency-Specific Information: Absolute vs. minimum response

Speech Awareness Threshold (SAT): Lowest intensity level at which there is awareness of speech

Speech Reception Threshold (SRT): Lowest intensity level at which a spondee word can be repeated 50% of the time

Word Recognition Ability: Percentage of monosyllabic words repeated correctly when presented at a comfortable listening level

Acoustic Immittance: Previously explained

Tympanometry: Measurement of the mobility of the tympanic membrane/middle ear system as a function of varying degrees of air pressure in the external ear canal

    a. *Static Compliance:* Mobility of the tympanic membrane/middle ear system

    b. *Equivalent Volume:* Ear canal volume

Acoustic Reflex Measurements: Observation of the contraction of the muscles of the middle ear in response to loud sounds

Outcomes of Audiology Services

Outcomes of audiology services may be measured to determine treatment effectiveness, efficiency, cost–benefit analysis, and consumer satisfaction. Specific outcome data may assist consumers to make decisions about audiology service delivery. The following listing describes the types of outcomes that consumers may expect to receive from an audiologist:

1. Interpretation of otoscopic examination for appropriate management or referral
2. Identification of populations and individuals with or at risk for hearing loss or related auditory disorders:
   a. With normal hearing or no related auditory disorders
   b. With communication disorders associated with hearing loss
   c. With or at risk of balance disorders, and tinnitus
3. Professional interpretation of the results of audiological findings
4. Referrals to other professions, agencies, or consumer organizations
5. Counseling for personal adjustment and discussion of the effects of hearing loss and the potential benefits to be gained from audiological rehabilitation and sensory aids, including hearing and tactile aids, hearing assistive devices, cochlear implants, captioning devices, and signal/warning devices
6. Counseling regarding the effects of balance system dysfunction
7. Selection, monitoring, dispensing, and maintenance of hearing aids and large-area amplification systems
8. Development of culturally appropriate, audiologic, rehabilitative management plans, including, when appropriate:
   a. Fitting and dispensing recommendations, and educating the consumer and family/caregivers in the use of and adjustment to sensory aids, hearing assistive devices, alerting systems, and captioning devices
   b. Counseling relating to psychosocial aspects of hearing loss and processes to enhance communication competence
   c. Skills training and consultation concerning environmental modifications to facilitate development of receptive and expressive communication
   d. Evaluation and modification of the audiologic management plan
9. Preparation of a report summarizing findings, interpretation, recommendations, and audiologic management plan
10. Consultation in development of an Individualized Education Program (IEP) for school-age children or an Individualized Family Service Plan (IFSP) for children from birth to 36 months old
11. Provision of in-service programs for personnel and advising school districts in planning educational programs and accessibility for students with hearing loss
12. Planning, development, implementation, and evaluation of hearing conservation programs

Impact of Hearing Loss on Communication

Case managers and other individuals should be aware of the impact hearing loss can have on communication. Generally speaking, a conductive (outer or middle ear) hearing loss, which cannot be medically remediated, can be adequately benefited through amplification. It must be cautioned that young children commonly experience conductive hearing loss due to ear and upper respiratory infections. Although these episodes are usually self-limiting or respond to medical intervention when necessary, some children persist with conductive hearing loss, which may affect their speech and language development. These children should be referred to an audiologist as well as a speech-language pathologist.

An individual with a sensorineural (inner ear) hearing loss, however, can be expected to experience some degree of difficulty *understanding* speech, particularly when the listening environment is less than ideal. This means that when a person with a sensorineural hearing loss is greater than 3 to 4 feet from the source of the sound or when there is noise in the background (there almost always is *some* noise in the background), that person will likely misunderstand some of what is being said. This is because the pattern of hearing with a sensorineural hearing loss is typically worse in the high frequencies or pitches and better in the low frequencies or pitches. In order to understand speech clearly, we must hear all the pitches equally well. The vowels are generally low in pitch (and loud) compared to consonants, which are high in pitch (and soft).

A properly fitted hearing aid can be extremely beneficial. However, it is important for all to recognize that even with appropriate amplification, individuals with sensorineural hearing loss might still have difficulty understanding what is being said, particularly with noise in the background.

How to Communicate with Hard-of-Hearing People

The following suggestions are examples of effective strategies for communicating with individuals with hearing impairment:

1. *Positioning:*
   a. Be sure the light, whether natural or artificial, falls on your face. Do not stand with the sun to your back or in front of a window.
   b. If you are aware that the hard-of-hearing person has a better ear, stand or sit on that side.
   c. Avoid background noise to the extent possible.
2. *Method:*
   a. Get the person's attention before you start talking. You may need to touch the person to attract attention.
   b. Speak to the hard-of-hearing person from an ideal distance of 3 to 6 feet in face-to-face visual contact.
   c. Speak as clearly as possible in a natural way.

    d. Speak more slowly to the hard-of-hearing person. Pausing between sentences will assist the listener.

    e. Do not shout. Shouting often results in distortion of speech and it displays a negative visual signal to the listener. Do not drop your voice at the end of the sentence.

    f. If the person does not understand what you said, rephrase it.

    g. When changing the subject, indicate the new topic with a word or two or a phrase.

3. *Physical:*

    a. Do not obscure your mouth with your hands. Do not chew or smoke while talking.

    b. Facial expressions and lip movements are important clues to the hard-of-hearing person. Feelings are more often expressed by nonverbal communication than through words.

4. *Attitude:*

    a. Do not become impatient.

    b. Stay positive and relaxed.

    c. Never talk about a hard-of-hearing person in his or her presence. Talk *to* them, not *about* them.

    d. Ask what you can do to facilitate communication.

First Aid for Hearing Aids

The following are some suggestions for troubleshooting minor hearing aid difficulties:

For These Symptoms	Read Paragraphs
Hearing aid dead	1–5, 9
Working, but weak	1–9, 12
Works intermittently	3–5, 9
Whistles	6, 8, 10, 11
Sounds noisy, raspy, shrill	3–5, 8, 10, 11
Sounds hollow or mushy	1, 2, 7

Causes, Tests, and Remedies[2]

1. Cause: Dead or rundown battery. Test: Substitute new battery. Remedy: Replace worn-out battery.

2. Cause: Battery reversed in holder so that positive end is where negative end should be. Test: Examine. Remedy: Insert battery correctly.

---

[2] Adapted from Sonotone Corporation, Longwood, FL.

3. Cause: Poor contacts at cord receptacle of battery holder due to dirty pins or springs. Test: With hearing aid turned on, wiggle plugs in receptacles and withdraw and reinsert each plug and the battery. Remedy: Rub accessible contacts briskly with lead pencil eraser, then wipe with clean cloth moistened with dry-cleaning liquid. Inaccessible contacts usually can be cleaned with a broom straw dipped in cleaning fluid.

4. Cause: Internal break or near-break inside receiver cord. Test: While listening, flex all parts of cords by running fingers along entire length and wiggle cords at terminals. Intermittent or raspy sounds indicate broken wires. Remedy: Replace cords with new ones. Worn ones cannot be repaired satisfactorily.

5. Cause: Plugs not fully or firmly inserted in receptacles. Test: While listening, withdraw and firmly reinsert each plug in turn. Remedy: Insert correctly.

6. Cause: Ear tip not properly seated in ear. Test: With the fingers, press the receiver firmly into the ear and twist back and forth slightly to make sure that the ear tip is properly positioned. Remedy: Position correctly.

7. Cause: Ear tip plugged with wax or with drop of water from cleaning. Test: Examine ear tip visually and blow through it to determine whether passage is open. Remedy: Disconnect ear tip from receiver, then wash ear tip in lukewarm water and soap, using pipe cleaner or long-bristle brush to reach down into the canal. Rinse with clear water and dry. A dry pipe cleaner may be used to dry out the canal; blowing through the canal will remove surplus water.

8. Cause: Insufficient pressure of bone receiver on mastoid. Test: While listening, press the bone receiver more tightly against the head with the fingers. Remedy: Bend the receiver headband to provide greater pressure. Your audiologist who is more skilled in maintaining conformation with the head preferably does this.

9. Cause: Battery leakage (resulting in poor battery connections). Test: Examine battery and battery holder for evidence of leakage or corrosion. Remedy: Discard the battery and wipe the holder terminals carefully with cloth dampened (not wet) in warm water.

10. Cause: Receiver close to wall or other sound-reflecting surfaces. Test: Examine. Remedy: Avoid sitting with the fitted side of the head near a wall or other surfaces. Such surfaces tend to reflect the sound from the receiver so that it is more readily picked up by the microphone, thus causing whistling.

11. Cause: Microphone worn too close to receiver. Test: Try moving instrument to provide wider separation between it and the receiver. Remedy: Avoid wearing microphone and receiver on same side of body or close together.

12. Cause: Plastic tubing not firmly seated at hearing aid or ear tip ends, or tubing so sharply bent as to block the passage of sound through it. Test: Examine and check for tightness at ends. Remedy: Push tubing ends firmly onto nubs. See that there is no kink or sharp bend. Replace the tubing if necessary.

Behaviors of Children at Risk for Auditory Disorders[3]

Certain characteristic behaviors by children should alert parents and teachers to be concerned about their hearing. Some of the signs are:

1. Often misunderstands what is said
2. Constantly requests that information be repeated
3. Has difficulty following oral instructions
4. Gives inconsistent responses to auditory stimuli
5. Turns up the volume of the television, radio, or stereo
6. Gives slow or delayed response to verbal stimuli
7. Has poor auditory attention
8. Has poor auditory memory (span and sequence)
9. Is easily distracted
10. Has difficulty listening in the presence of background noise
11. Has poor receptive and expressive language
12. Has difficulty with phonics and speech sound discrimination
13. Learns poorly through the auditory channel
14. Has reading, spelling, and other learning problems
15. Exhibits behavior problems
16. Says "huh" or "what" frequently

Indicators Associated with Hearing Loss[4]

Some common indicators associated with hearing loss include:

1. Family history of hearing loss
2. *In utero* infection (e.g., cytomegalovirus, rubella, syphilis, toxoplasmosis)
3. Craniofacial anomalies, including those with morphological abnormalities of the pinna and ear canal
4. Birth weight less than 1500 grams (3.3 pounds)
5. Hyperbilirubinemia at a serum level requiring exchange transfusion
6. Ototoxic medications, including, but not limited to, chemotherapeutic agents, or aminoglycocides used in multiple courses or in combination with loop diuretics
7. Bacterial meningitis and other infections associated with sensorineural hearing loss
8. Severe depression at birth with Apgar scores of 0 to 4 at 1 minute or 0 to 6 at 5 minutes
9. Prolonged mechanical ventilation 5 days or longer (e.g., persistent pulmonary hypertension)
10. Stigmata or other findings associated with a syndrome known to include a sensorineural or conductive hearing loss
11. Parent/caregiver concern regarding hearing, speech, language, or developmental delay

---

[3] Adapted from the Fisher's Auditory Problems Checklist.
[4] Adapted from the Draft Joint Committee on Infant Hearing 1993 position statement.

12. Head trauma associated with loss of consciousness or skull fracture
13. Recurrent or persistent otitis media with effusion for at least 3 months
14. Neurofibromatosis type II and neurodegenerative disorders
15. Anatomic deformities and other disorders, which affect eustachian tube, function

Costs Related to Amplification

The cost of hearing aids varies from approximately $500 to $2500 per instrument depending upon type and options. A single behind-the-ear instrument may be as little as $500, while a digital instrument will typically cost $2100 to $2500. Middle ear implantable instruments may run $25,000, plus $5000 per year for technical support. Many patients with disabilities may need manufacturer support to ensure they are capable of operating the volume control and other instrument options. Digital hearing aids often have an external control much like a television remote control. Care must be given to ensure appropriate fitting and follow-up services. Pitfalls that must be avoided are indiscriminate fitting of patients with amplification not appropriate for their loss and insufficient follow-up and audiologic/aural rehabilitation.

- A hearing aid should be effective for 3 to 5 years before *replacement* is necessary. It is wise to purchase replacement and repair warranties.
- A standard factory *warranty* will be 1 to 2 years.
- *Battery costs* may vary depending on the severity of the hearing loss and the power required of the hearing aid. A package of six batteries will cost $4 to $5. The average life expectancy for a battery is approximately 10 days to 2 weeks when the instrument is worn during waking hours. If an instrument is out of warranty, the cost of repair is approximately $150 to include a 1-year warranty.

Children under 21 are entitled to mandatory hearing services, including hearing aids, under Medicaid. Hearing aid coverage for adults is optional and varies from state to state. A list of state Medicaid office contacts can be found on the following link: http://cms.hhs.gov/medicaid/tollfree.asp.

Although Medicare does not pay for hearing devices in fee-for-service plans, hearing aids may be covered by Medicare+Choice plans, such as health maintenance organizations. The Centers for Medicare and Medicaid Services (CMS) clarified in 2001 that Medicare carriers should pay for diagnostic audiologic tests regardless of a hearing aid recommendation.

Funding Issues Related to Audiological Services

Obviously, people with the financial resources to pay privately for these devices and services will be able to obtain what they need. However, most rely upon alternative funding and specific issues are revealed below:

- Medicaid: States must cover hearing aids for children through the Early and Periodic Screening, Diagnosis, and Treatment Program. Coverage for adults is optional and rarely included in a state plan.
- Medicare: Medicare does not cover hearing aids or tests related to hearing aids. Social health maintenance organizations (SHMOs) are part of a demonstration project that includes some long-term care. All SHMOs cover hearing aids. As risk HMOs enter the Medicare market, many are providing partial coverage of hearing aids. For example, the Medicare HMO might cover $500 of a hearing aid. Some states and regional third-party payers allow balance billing — check in your state and with your dispensing audiologist.
- Private Health Plans: Most do not cover hearing aids unless there is a labor union contract such as the United Automobile Workers (UAW), which covers the costs related to one hearing aid every 3 years. The benefit is not limited to automobile workers but is found in many contracts negotiated by the UAW. Another example of a union contract is the California Public Employees Retirement System, which offers a hearing benefit to retirees enrolled in Medicare managed care plans. Some private plans such as Blue Cross and Blue Shield may cover a hearing aid if the need is related to an accident or illness.

Special Issue: Cochlear Implants

As referenced above, the audiologist may evaluate clients for the cochlear implant — telephone (303) 790-9010. This device is implanted in nearly 10,000 children and adults who are profoundly hearing impaired or deaf due to genetic factors, ototoxic drugs, meningitis, rubella, and head trauma. A criterion for candidacy primarily requires that the auditory nerve must not be destroyed. General guidelines include:

- Be at least 1 year of age (with anticipation of even younger in near future)
- Have severe to profound bilateral sensorineural deafness
- Demonstrate no significant benefit from traditional amplification
- Strong family support
- No medical contraindications to surgery
- For children, a supportive school system
- For adults, appropriate expectations
- Have the ability to pay for the device and services — the total cost of an implant in 1995 was more than $40,000, not including replacements (see example care below)

With regard to children, there appears to be a controversy regarding the device. Although promoters report that children can more effectively learn language with the implant, they are neither a normal-hearing person nor deaf. The child may not fit in the deaf subculture and may experience ridicule from others that can adversely affect social development. On the other hand, individuals who became deaf before learning language commonly do not read higher than the third- or fourth-grade level. This barrier, of course, can significantly affect their vocational outlook.

COCHLEAR IMPLANT CENTERS

There are various cochlear implant centers around the country. Teams of professionals work together with adults and children from start to finish. Team members include an audiologist, otologist/surgeon, medical specialists as needed, psychologist, counselors, and speech-language pathologists. They work with potential candidates and their families to determine candidacy for an implant, perform the surgery, and provide follow-up care both through the center and through local agencies or school districts near the cochlear implant recipient.

The Clinical Process

Once a person is referred to the cochlear implant center, extensive testing is done to determine if the person is a suitable candidate. This evaluation usually includes extensive audiologic testing, psychological testing, examination and tests performed by the surgeon, x-rays, magnetic resonance images, physical examination, and counseling to assure suitability and motivation to participate in the process. It is important that the candidate understands what the implant will and will not do and the commitment required for care and follow-up services.

Once the decision is made to go ahead, the surgery is done. Sometimes it involves an overnight stay in the hospital, and sometimes it is done on an outpatient basis.

About 4 to 6 weeks after surgery, the person returns to the center to be fitted with the microphone and speech processor and to activate and program (called *mapping*) the implant. The initial fitting process is done over several days and may include additional visits over several months. The reason is that as each electrode in the cochlea is activated, it must be adjusted and programmed into the speech processor. As the person develops skill in using the implant, further adjustments and reprogramming are required. Once the optimum program is obtained, then fewer visits are required. Usually there are annual visits to the center for check-ups.

Both children and adults are involved in extensive rehabilitation services from an audiologist, speech-language pathologist, teachers, and counselors as they learn to listen, improve speech, use speech-reading, and handle communication. They are taught how to use the implant and how to respond to the sounds they are receiving. If one has heard before, sounds through the cochlear implant may seem unnatural at first. If a person has never heard, they must be taught what the sounds are.

COCHLEAR IMPLANT MECHANISM

Cochlear implants have external (outside) parts and internal (surgically implanted) parts.

The *external parts* include a microphone, a speech processor, and a transmitter. The *microphone* looks like a behind-the-ear hearing aid. It picks up sounds — just like a hearing aid microphone does — and sends them to the speech processor.

The *speech processor* may be housed, with the microphone, behind the ear, or it may be a small box worn in a chest pocket. The speech processor is a computer that analyzes and digitizes the sound signals and sends them to a transmitter worn on the head just behind the ear.

The *transmitter* sends the coded signals to an implanted receiver just under the skin.

The *internal (implanted) parts* include a receiver and electrodes. The *receiver* is just under the skin behind the ear. The receiver takes the coded electrical signals from the transmitter and delivers them to the array of electrodes that have been surgically inserted into the cochlea. The *electrodes* stimulate the fibers of the auditory nerve and sound sensations are perceived. (Retrieved from http://www.asha.org/hearing/rehab/cochlear_implant.cfm.)

EXAMPLE CASE

Below is an example *portion* of a plan for a 6-year-old child, profoundly hearing impaired due to meningitis at the age of 1, who met the criteria for evaluation. His parents were very bright based on educational achievements and testing. Both were employed by the school system. The child and an older sibling were both judged to be intellectually gifted.

Recommendation	Dates	Frequency	Expected Cost
Speech-language therapy and assistive technology prescriptions	1996–2014 (25 years old)	3 times/week average during school year and 2 times/week for 10 weeks during summer; then 1 time/week at ages 20–25	$0 provided by school system under IDEA for school year; if private pay, during summers and ages 22–25 expected cost $100/hour
Education	1996–2007	School year	$0 provided under IDEA
TTY text telephone unit; recommend Superprint 4425 (includes printer, auto answer, ring flasher, etc.)	1999 (10 years old) to life	Every 10 years	$387–$500 (includes 1-year warranty)

TTY unit uses regular phone line; however, units are unable to distinguish between incoming TTY calls or voice calls. A separate phone line dedicated for the TTY unit may be appropriate. Cost for additional phone line installation is estimated between $100 and $110 plus monthly charge of approximately $35. Does not include long-distance charges that are usually higher due to length of time to transmit written words rather than spoken words. Cost cannot be projected. Internet access cost is $23.95/month.

| Portable TTY with printer | 1999 (10 years old) | Every 5 years (estimate) | $500 (includes 1-year warranty) |

(continued)

Recommendation	Dates	Frequency	Expected Cost
TTY refill paper 3/pack of 2¼-inch thermal paper	1999 (10 years old)	Every 3 months or as needed depending on use	$3 and $4/package $12 and $16/year (estimate)
TTY batteries (6)		Yearly or more depending on use	$19.50 at $6.50 for 2/package
Sonic Alert or Silent Call Alerting System, including receiver, transmitters, and rechargeable battery	1996	Sonic Alert: 1 time only Silent Call: every 10 years or more (estimate)	Sonic Alert: $259.80 with 1-year warranty Silent Call: $539.80 with vibrating unit and 2-year warranty
Door knock signaler with light	1996	Every 10 years	$29.95 and $34.95 each
Portable smoke detector with strobe	1996	Every 10 years	$175
Allowance for batteries, light bulbs, etc.	1996	Batteries: monthly Bulbs: yearly depending on use	$50/year (estimate)
OPTIONAL Baby-cry alerter (assumes marriage and child)	Estimate 2019 (30 years old)	1 time only (assumes marriage and family)	Sonic Alert: $39.95 (may also be used as smoke detector)
OPTIONAL Silent Call Sleep Alert charger unit	1996	Every 10 years or more (estimate)	$106.95
OPTIONAL Cochlear implant (1)	1996	One replacement over life	$40,744 (includes all costs for first year)
Follow-up for cochlear implant	1997 or 1 year after implant performed	1/year	$300/visit for 3 hours at $100/hour
Hearing/ audiologic rehab therapy	1996 to age 22	4–5 hours/week average through high school, then 1–2 hours/week to age 22	$100/hour
Speech therapy	1996 to age 22	4–5 hours/week average through high school, then 1–2 hours/week to age 22	$100/hour

(continued)

Recommendation	Dates	Frequency	Expected Cost
Service contract for external speech processor and headset (internal device has 99-year warranty)	1996 to life	Every 2 years	$595 for 2 years (after 3-year manufacturer's warranty expires)
Programming, map adjustment and tuning, general maintenance	1996 to life	1 time/week for first 2 months, then 1 time every other week for 2 months, then 1 time/month for 3 months, then every 3 months to age 16 (2005), then every 6 months thereafter	1996: $0, included in cost of implant 1997–2005: $400/year 2006+: $200/year at $100/hour
Replacement cords and batteries	1996 to life	Every 3 months for 2 cords at $10 each 1 time/year for 2-pack batteries at $10/year	$90/year
Replacement headset	1999 (after 3-year warranty) to life	Project 3–4 upgrades over lifetime	$500 (estimate) every 3 years
Upgrade external processor	2001 (estimate)	1 time only	$5500 (estimate) each upgrade

Note 1: No provision for technology advances.
Note 2: Economist to determine present value.

Interpreter	1996 to lifetime	6 hours/day, 5 days/week during school (August–June) to 2007, then expect 2–4 hours/week average to lifetime	$0 provided through school system through age 18, then expect 2–4 hours/week average at $15/hour for medical, dental, contracts, legal, and other non-education-related activities

RESOURCES SPECIFICALLY FOR ALDS

Harc Mercantile
Kalamazoo, MI
(800) 438-4272 (V)
(800) 413-5245 (TTY)
www.harcmercantile.com

Harris Communications
Eden Prairie, MN
(800) 825-6758 (V)
(800) 825-9187 (TTY)
www.harriscomm.com

Hear-More, Inc.
Farmingdale, NY
(800) 881-4327 (V/TTY)
www.hearmore.com

Hitec
Burr Ridge, IL
(800) 288-8303
www.hitec.com

MVM Technical Corporation
1 Union Square West, Room 210
New York, NY 10003

Potomac Technology
Rockville, MD
(800) 433-2838
www.potomactech.com

Soundbytes
New York, NY
(800) 667-1777
www.soundbytes.com

United TTY Sales
Olney, MD
(866) 889-4872
www.UnitedTTY.com

Weitbrecht Communications
Santa Monica, CA
(800) 233-9130 (V/TTY)
www.weitbrecht.com

Some Other Distributors of Assistive Listening Devices

Audio Enhancement
www.audioenhancement.com

Centrum Sound
members.aol.com/centrumweb

Hear You Are, Inc.
Stanhope, NJ
(201) 347-7662 (V)
(201) 347-7662 (F)
hearyouare@aol.com

Heidico
Reno, NV
(702) 324-7104 (V/TTY/F)

Hello Direct
www.hello-direct.com

Radio Shack
www.radioshack.com

Sound Associates
www.soundassociates.com

Sound Remedy
New York, NY
(212) 242-1036 (V/F)

There are also many centers across the country where individuals can examine the types of assistive listening devices available in order to determine which products to purchase. To locate an assistive device demonstration center in your area, call the American Speech-Language-Hearing Association's Action Center at (800) 638-8255, e-mail actioncenter@asha.org, or call Self Help for Hard of Hearing People, Inc. (SHHH) at (301) 657-2248 (voice) or (301) 657-2249 (TTY).

Selected Resources for Information, Services, and Products

Information

Alexander Graham Bell Association for the Deaf
3417 Volta Place, NW
Washington, DC 20007
(202) 337-5220 (V/TTY)

American Academy of Audiology
11730 Plaza America Dr., Suite 300
Reston, VA 20190
(703) 790-8466

American Association for the Deaf-Blind
814 Thayer Ave., Room 302
Silver Spring, MD 20910
(301) 588-6545 (V/TTY)

American Association for Deaf Children
10th and Tahlequah Streets
Sulfur, OK 73086
(800) 942-ASDC

American Athletic Association for the Deaf
3607 Washington Blvd., #4
Ogden, UT 84403
(801) 393-5710 (V)
(801) 393-7916 (TTY)

American Speech-Language-Hearing Association
10801 Rockville Pike
Rockville, MD 20852
(301) 897-5700
(202) 651-5051 (V)
(202) 651-5052 (TTY)

Helen Keller National Center for Deaf-Blind Youths and Adults
111 Middle Neck Rd.
Sands Point, NY 11050
(516) 944-8900 (V)
(516) 944-8637 (TTY)

National Association for the Deaf
814 Thayer Ave., Room 302
Silver Spring, MD 20910
(301) 587-1788 (V)
(301) 587-1789 (TTY)

National Information Center on Deafness
Gallaudet University
800 Florida Ave. NE
Washington, DC 20002

Products/Services

Canines

Paws with a Cause
1235100th St. SE
Byron Center, MI 49315
(800) 253-PAWS

Cochlear Implant

Cochlear Corporation
Suite 200
61 Inverness Dr. East
Englewood, CO 80112
(800) 523-5798

Interpreters

Registry of Interpreters for the Deaf
9719 Colesville Rd., Suite 310
Silver Spring, MD 20910
(301) 608-0050 (V/TTY)

General Products

HARC Mercantile, LTD.
1111 West Centre Ave.
P.O. Box 3055
Kalamazoo, MI 49003
(800) 445-9968 (V)
(800) 413-5245 (TTY)

General Products

LS&S Group
P.O. Box 6783
Northbrook, IL 60065
(800) 317-8533
E-mail: lssgrp@aol.com

General Products

NFSS Communications
8120 Fenton St.
Silver Spring, MD 20910
(888) 589-6671 (V)
(888) 589-6670 (TTY)
E-mail: sales@nfss.com

General Products

Potomac Technology
One Church St., Suite 402
Rockville, MD 20850
(301) 762-4005 (V)
(301) 762-0851 (TTY)

Tactile Aids

Audiological Engineering Corporation
35 Medford St.
Somerville, MA 02143
(800) 283-4601 (V)
(800) 955-7204 (TTY)

CONCLUSION

In many life care plans audiological services can be a critical component. In personal injury litigation common sequelae from head trauma can destroy or reduce hearing, disrupt balance, and produce serious ringing in the ears (tinnitus). In medical illness, malpractice, or mistakes the audiologist is commonly an important member for diagnosis and treatment of hearing dysfunction. Of particular interest is the role the audiologist can play with regard to children. Hearing deficits can seriously hamper educational achievement that can lead to poor social adjustment and a poor vocational outlook. Indeed, many deaf children are initially diagnosed mentally retarded and do not receive services during critical developmental periods. This chapter assists the life care planner with information related to the roles and responsibilities of the audiologist and provides resources for information, services, and products.

REFERENCES

American National Standards Institute. (1981). *Reference Equivalent Threshold Force Levels for Audiometric Bone Vibrators*. New York: Acoustical Society of America.

American National Standards Institute. (1986). *Artificial Head Bone for the Calibration of Audiometer Bone Vibrators*. New York: Acoustical Society of America.

American National Standards Institute. (1987). *Specifications for Instruments to Measure Aural Acoustic Impedance and Admittance* (ANSI S3.39-1987). New York: Acoustical Society of America.

American National Standards Institute. (1991). *Maximum Permissible Ambient Noise Levels for Audiometric Test Rooms* (ANSI S3.1-1991). New York: Acoustical Society of America.

American National Standards Institute. (1992). *Method for Manual Pure-Tone Audiometry* (ANSI S3.211978) (R1992). New York: Acoustical Society of America.

American National Standards Institute. (1996). *Specifications for Audiometers* (ANSI S3.1996). New York: Acoustical Society of America.

American Speech-Language-Hearing Association. (1978). Manual pure-tone threshold audiometry. *ASHA*, 20, 297–301.

American Speech-Language-Hearing Association. (1984). Competencies for aural rehabilitation. *ASHA*, 26, 37–41.

American Speech-Language-Hearing Association. (1988). Guidelines for determining threshold level for speech. *ASHA*, 30, 85–89.

American Speech-Language-Hearing Association. (1990). Audiological assessment of central auditory processing: an annotated bibliography. *ASHA*, 32 (Suppl. 1), 13–30.

American Speech-Language-Hearing Association. (1991a). External auditory canal examination and cerumen management. *ASHA*, 34 (Suppl. 7), 22–24.

American Speech-Language-Hearing Association. (1991b). Acoustic immittance: a bibliography. *ASHA*, 33 (Suppl. 4), 1–44.

American Speech-Language-Hearing Association. (1992). Neurophysiologic intraoperative monitoring. *ASHA*, 34 (Suppl. 7), 34–36.

American Speech-Language-Hearing Association. (1994). Guidelines for the audiologic management of individuals receiving cochleotoxic drug therapy. *ASHA*, 36 (Suppl. 12), 11–19.

American Speech-Language-Hearing Association, (1995b). Acoustics in educational settings: position statement and guidelines. *ASHA*, 37 (Suppl. 14), 15–19.

American Speech-Language-Hearing Association. (1996). Central auditory processing: current status of research and implications for clinical practice. *American Journal of Audiology*, 5, 41–54.

American Speech-Language-Hearing Association (Spring 1996). Scope of practice in audiology. *ASHA*, 38 (Suppl. 16), 12–15.

American Speech-Language-Hearing Association. (1997). *Preferred Practice Patterns for the Professions of Speech-Language Pathology and Audiology.* Rockville, MD: author.

American Speech-Language-Hearing Association. (1998). Position statement and hearing aid fitting guidelines for adults. *ASHA*, 40 (Suppl. 18).

American Speech-Language-Hearing Association. (1999). Guidelines: competencies in auditory evoked potential measurement and clinical applications. *ASHA*, 41 (Suppl. 19), 23–28.

American Speech-Language-Hearing Association. (2003). Code of ethics. Retrieved 6/15/03 from http://www.asha.org/about/ethnics/.

American Speech-Language-Hearing Association. (2004a). Reference list of position statements, guidelines, definitions, and relevant papers. Retrieved 1/15/04 from http://asha.org/members/deskref_journals.

American Speech-Language-Hearing Association. (2004b). Guidelines for fitting and monitoring FM systems. Retrieved 1/15/04 from http://asha.org/hearing/gen_audiology.cfm.

Ballachandra, B.B. & Peers, C.J. (1992). Cerumen management: instruments and procedures. *ASHA*, 32, 43–46.

Barza, M. & Lauermann, M. (1978). Why monitor serum levels of gentamicin? *Clinical Pharmacokinetics*, 3, 202–215.

Bendush, C.L. (1982). Ototoxicity: clinical considerations and comparative information. In A. Whelton & H.C. Neu, Eds., *The Aminoglycosides: Microbiology, Clinical Use and Toxicology.* New York: Marcel Dekker.

Berlin, C.I. (1999). Managing patients with auditory neuropathy/auditory dys-synchrony. Retrieved April 10, 2003, from http://www.medschool.lsumc.edu/otor/dys.html.

Bess, F.H. (Ed.). (1988). *Hearing Impairment in Children.* Parkton, MD: York Press.

Bess, F.H. & Humes, L.E. (1995). *Audiology: The Fundamentals.* Baltimore: Williams & Wilkins.

Brummett, R.E. (1980). Drug-induced ototoxicity. *Drugs*, 19, 412–428.

Centers for Disease Control. (1988). *Universal Precautions for the Prevention of Transmission of HIV, HBV, and Other Bloodborne Pathogens in Health Care Settings*, 37, 24.

Fausti, S.A., Frey, R.H., Henry, J.A., Knutsen, J.M., & Olson, D.J. (1990). Reliability and validity of high frequency (8–20kHz) thresholds obtained on a computer based audiometer as compared to a documented laboratory system. *Journal of the American Academy of Audiology*, 1, 162–170.

Fausti, S.A., Henry, J.A., Schaffer, H.I., Olson, D.J., Frey, R.H., & Bagby, B.C. (1993) High frequency monitoring for early detection of cisplatin ototoxicity. *Archives of Otolaryngology-Head and Neck Surgery*, 119, 661–668.

Fausti, S.A., Henry, J.A., Schaffer, H.I., Olson, D.J., Frey, R.H., & McDonald, W.J. (1992). High frequency audiometric monitoring for early detection of aminoglycoside ototoxicity. *Journal of Infectious Diseases*, 165, 1026–1032.

Fisher, L.I. (no date). *Fisher Auditory Problems Checklist.* Cedar Rapids, IA: Grant Wood Area Education Agency.

Frank, R. & Dreisbach, L.E. (1991). Repeatability of high frequency thresholds. *Ear and Hearing*, 12, 294–295.

Frank, T. (1990). High frequency hearing thresholds in young adults using a commercially available audiometer. *Ear and Hearing*, 11, 450–454.

Govaerts, P.J., Claes, J., Van De Heyning, P.H., Jorens, P.G., Marquet, J., & De Broe, M.E. (1990). Aminoglycoside-induced ototoxicity. *Toxicology Letters,* 52, 227–251.

Hood, L.J. (1998). Auditory neuropathy: what is it and what can we do about it? *The Hearing Journal,* 51, 10–18.

Joint Audiology Committee on Clinical Practice. (1999). *Clinical Practice Statements and Algorithms.* Rockville, MD: American Speech-Language-Hearing Association.

Joint Committee on Infant Hearing. (1993). Position statement. *ASHA,* 6, 38–41.

Kopelman, J., Budnick, A.S., Sessions, R.B., Kramer, M.B., & Wong, G.Y. (1988). Ototoxicity of high dose cisplatin by bolus administration in patients with advanced cancers and normal hearing. *Laryngoscope,* 98, 858–864.

Laukli, E. & Mair, L.W.S. (1985). High frequency audiometry: normative studies and preliminary experiences. *Scandinavian Audiology,* 14, 151–158.

Lien, E.J., Lipsett, L.R., & Lien, L.L. (1983). Structure side effect sorting of drugs. VI. Ototoxicities. *Journal of Clinical and Hospital Pharmacy,* 8, 15–33.

Pasic, T.R. & Dobie, R.A. (1991). Cis-platinum ototoxicity in children. *Laryngoscope,* 101, 985–991.

Powell, S.H., Thompson, W.L., & Luthe, M.A. (1983). Once daily vs. continuous aminoglycoside dosing: efficacy and toxicity in animal and clinical studies of gentamicin, netilmicin, and tobromycin. *Journal of Infectious Diseases,* 147, 918–932.

Roeser, R. & Crandell, C. (1991). The audiologist's responsibility in cerumen management. *ASHA,* 33, 51–53.

Rybak, L.P. (1986). Drug ototoxicity. *Annual Review of Pharmacology and Toxicology,* 26, 79–99.

Schentag, J.J. (1980). Aminoglycosides. In W.E. Evans, J.J. Schentag, & W.J. Jusko, Eds., *Applied Pharmacokinetics: Principles of Therapeutic Drug Monitoring.* San Francisco: Applied Therapeutics.

U.S. Department of Labor. *Occupational Exposure to Bloodborne Pathogens: Request for Information.* Occupational Safety and Health Administration, Docket H370A, September 9, 1998.

Valente, M.L., Gulledge-Potts, M. Valente, M., French-St. George, J., & Goebel, J. (1992). High frequency thresholds: sound suite versus hospital room. *Journal of the American Academy of Audiology,* 3, 287–294.

11

THE ROLE OF THE ECONOMIST IN LIFE CARE PLANNING

Everett G. Dillman

INTRODUCTION

An economist is frequently called upon to compute the present value of the future medical and care costs set forth in a life care plan prepared by a specialist. Although the economist generally will have little or no input in the development of the plan, he or she does have an interest in how the plan is structured and what it contains. This chapter examines the content of life care plans from the point of view of an economist and identifies some areas of potential concern.

The structure of the life care plan, including what elements are covered, will differ to some extent from author to author. Experience has shown, however, that there are a number of consistent patterns that emerge, some of which will cause difficulty for economic analysis (Dillman, 1987, 1988). The areas of concern from an economic point of view include (1) cost categories, (2) items that should be included, (3) timing of the items, (4) the use of actual or annual averages, and (5) the emphasis placed on trivial items. Each of these elements is discussed in more detail.

CATEGORIES OF COSTS

In making the economic evaluation the economist must consider the fact that the costs of the various items included in the plan will not remain static over time but can be expected to increase with inflation. The historical rates of increase will differ depending upon the particular item, as the prices of some things tend to increase faster than others. For instance, the inflation of doctors' fees and hospital costs has historically been much greater than the inflation for such items as bandages, hospital beds, and other commodities.

In considering future inflation, the economist generally looks at the past inflation of the type of good being evaluated. Although it may be possible to develop data series for many individualized items, the economic analysis will generally place the items into the broad classifications of medical services, non-medical services, medical commodities, and nonmedical commodities.

0-8493-1511-5/04/$0.00+$1.50
© 2004 by CRC Press LLC

Two of the categories, medical services and medical commodities, are subsets of the Consumer Price Index (CPI) and are defined by the Bureau of Labor Statistics (http://www.bls.gov/cpi/home.htm, 2003). These definitions as well as those for the other two categories follow.

Medical Services

This category involves professional and hospital services. Included are payments for physicians, dentists, and other professionals such as optometrists, ophthalmologists, opticians, psychologists, and therapists. Chiropractors and nurse practitioners are also included. The category of hospital services includes nursing home care. Hospital services for inpatients, such as pharmacy, laboratory tests, radiology, short-stay units, ambulatory surgery, physical therapy, and emergency room fees billed by the hospital, also fall into this category.

Medical Commodities

The medical commodities classification includes:

1. Prescription drugs and medical supplies. This includes all drugs and medical supplies dispensed by prescriptions. Also included are all prescription-dispensed over-the-counter drugs, i.e., those drugs that are obtained over the counter but are prescribed by the doctor and dispensed by the pharmacist.
2. Internal and respiratory over-the-counter drugs. This includes all nonprescription medication taken by swallowing or inhaling, as well as suppositories or enemas.
3. Topicals and dressings. Includes all nonprescription medicines and dressings used externally.
4. Medical equipment for general use. Includes nonprescription medical equipment not worn or not used for supporting the body. Included in this group are nonprescription male and female contraceptives. Whirlpools and vaporizers are also included.
5. Supportive and convalescent medical equipment. This category includes all supportive and convalescent medical equipment and auxiliaries to such equipment. Also included are prostheses, crutches, wheelchairs, and associated accessories.
6. Hearing aids. Includes all types of hearing aids and the cost of testing and fitting of the hearing aid.

Nonmedical Services

The nonmedical services category is concerned with all personal services that are not included in medical services. Examples would include services such as lawn care and auto repair. Some services that are medical related will fall into this group, such as wheelchair repair and maintenance of a van wheelchair lift. Nonprofessional attendant care (when not provided through a health care provider) can be classified as a nonmedical service.

Since the long-term inflation rate of nonmedical services is less than that for medical services, when there is a doubt as to the correct classification, the conservative approach would be to place the service item in the nonmedical services category.

Nonmedical Commodities

The nonmedical commodities category includes all the commodity (i.e., nonservices) items that do not fall under medical commodities. Such items might be specialty foods, housing and alterations to housing, automobiles, games, bedding, and computers.

The historical inflation rates of each of these categories are given by the appropriate subseries of the Consumer Price Index or, in the case of the nonmedical services, the average increase in hourly wages in the private nonagricultural economy. These are shown in Table 11.1 to Table 11.6.

WHAT SHOULD BE INCLUDED

The life care plan should include all medical and care items (both services and commodities) that will be, or should be, incurred because of the incident in question. Which specific items to include is usually not a question for the economist. The economist needs to make sure that only marginal costs are considered. In addition, the value of the items or services should be evaluated even if provided at no cost by family members, significant others, or some other collateral source. Each of these concepts will be briefly discussed.

Marginal Costs

A marginal cost can be defined as an additional or extra cost that is incurred because, and only because of, the injury in question. For instance, the entire cost of a new car (every 3 years or so) would generally *not* be considered a marginal cost. The individual would normally need transportation even if not injured. What would be appropriate, however, is the additional cost required by the nature of the limitations. A van rather than a regular car might be necessary to transport a client in a wheelchair. If so, the additional cost of a van instead of a regular car would be appropriate. Any special modifications such as a lift or special controls would also qualify as a marginal cost. To obtain the marginal cost, one would subtract the cost of a normal item (for instance, a compact car) from the cost of the recommended item.

Items such as television sets, radios, and books are often set forth in life care plans. In some cases, the inclusion of such items may be justified because of the specifics of the case, but often the items are duplications of what the individual would normally have purchased without the injury and therefore are not a marginal cost and should not be a part of the plan. (Editor's note: Marginal costs may be included in the rare case where no compensation for lost earning capacity is included.)

Table 11.1   Consumer Price Index for Medical Components: All Urban Consumers

Year	All Items CPI 1982–1984 = 100.0	Medical Care 1982–1984 = 100.0
1935	13.7	10.2
1936	13.9	10.2
1937	14.4	10.3
1938	14.1	10.3
1939	13.9	10.3
1940	14.0	10.4
1941	14.7	10.4
1942	16.3	10.7
1943	17.3	11.2
1944	17.6	11.6
1945	18.0	11.9
1946	19.5	12.5
1947	22.3	13.5
1948	24.1	14.4
1949	23.8	14.8
1950	24.1	15.1
1951	26.0	15.9
1952	26.5	16.7
1953	26.7	17.3
1954	26.9	17.8
1955	26.8	18.2
1956	27.2	18.9
1957	28.1	19.7
1958	28.9	20.6
1959	29.1	21.5
1960	29.6	22.3
1961	29.9	22.9
1962	30.2	23.5
1963	30.8	24.1
1964	31.0	24.6
1965	31.5	25.2
1966	32.4	26.3
1967	33.4	28.2
1968	34.8	29.9
1969	36.7	31.9
1970	38.8	34.0
1971	40.5	36.1
1972	41.8	37.3
1973	44.4	38.8
1974	49.3	42.4
1975	53.8	47.5
1976	56.9	52.0
1977	60.6	57.0
1978	65.2	61.8
1979	72.6	67.5

(continued)

Table 11.1 (Continued)   Consumer Price Index for Medical Components: All Urban Consumers

Year	All Items CPI 1982–1984 = 100.0	Medical Care 1982–1984 = 100.0
1980	82.4	74.9
1981	90.9	82.9
1982	96.5	92.5
1983	99.6	100.6
1984	103.9	106.8
1985	107.6	113.5
1986	109.6	122.0
1987	113.6	130.1
1988	118.3	138.6
1989	124.0	149.3
1990	130.7	162.8
1991	136.2	177.0
1992	140.3	190.1
1993	144.5	201.4
1994	148.2	211.0
1995	152.4	220.5
1996	156.9	228.2
1997	160.5	234.6
1998	163.0	242.1
1999	166.6	250.6
2000	172.2	260.8
2001	177.1	272.8

Source: U.S. Department of Labor. Bureau of Labor Statistics.

Value of the Items

Care must be taken to include the type and extent of all additional commodities and services necessitated by the injury, even if these have been, or are expected to be, provided without direct out-of-pocket cost to the client. For example, an injured party may require 24-hour, 7-days-a-week attendant care, which has been provided in the past by family members. Even if the family members are able and willing to continue to provide the services, from an economic point of view the value of the services should be estimated and included as a part of the life care plan. In economics, this is called the opportunity cost.

The concept of marginal cost may also come into play when assigning a value to some of the services provided. That is, some of the services provided by the family member would have been provided even without the injury and consequently should not be double counted. For instance, if the injured party is a young child who requires constant care, only the additional care necessitated by the injury should be considered. The normal and customary care a mother and other family members would provide the child should not be considered an additional cost necessitated by the injury.

Table 11.2   Consumer Price Index for Medical Commodities: All Urban Consumers

Year	Medical Commodities 1982–1984 = 100.0	Prescription Drugs 1982–1984 = 100.0	Nonprescription Drugs and Medical Supplies December 1986 = 100.0	Internal and Respiratory Over-the-Counter Drugs 1984–1986 = 100.0	Nonprescription Medical Equipment and Supplies 1982–1984 = 100.0
1935	31.7	30.6			
1936	31.6	30.6			
1937	31.8	30.8			
1938	32.0	31.0			
1939	31.9	31.0			
1940	31.8	31.0			
1941	32.0	31.4			
1942	32.8	32.2			
1943	33.0	32.5			
1944	33.3	33.1			
1945	33.6	33.5			
1946	34.2	34.6			
1947	36.7	38.1			
1948	38.6	41.2			
1949	39.2	42.2			
1950	39.7	43.4			
1951	40.8	45.5			
1952	41.2	46.0			
1953	41.5	46.0			
1954	42.0	46.9			
1955	42.5	47.6			
1956	43.4	49.0			
1957	44.6	50.7			
1958	46.1	53.0			
1959	46.8	54.2			
1960	46.9	54.0			
1961	46.3	52.2			
1962	45.6	50.1			
1963	45.2	48.9			
1964	45.1	48.3		38.8	
1965	45.0	47.8		39.0	
1966	45.1	47.7		39.4	
1967	44.9	46.8		39.8	
1968	45.0	46.0		40.8	
1969	45.4	46.6		41.2	

(continued)

Table 11.2 (Continued) Consumer Price Index for Medical Commodities: All Urban Consumers

Year	Medical Commodities 1982–1984 = 100.0	Prescription Drugs 1982–1984 = 100.0	Nonprescription Drugs and Medical Supplies December 1986 = 100.0	Internal and Respiratory Over-the-Counter Drugs 1984–1986 = 100.0	Nonprescription Medical Equipment and Supplies 1982–1984 = 100.0
1970	46.5	47.4		42.3	
1971	47.3	47.4		43.9	
1972	47.4	47.2		44.3	
1973	47.5	47.1		44.8	
1974	49.2	48.2		46.8	
1975	53.3	51.2		51.8	
1976	56.5	53.9		55.3	
1977	60.2	57.2		59.1	
1978	64.4	61.6		63.3	69.1
1979	69.0	66.4		68.0	73.3
1980	75.4	72.5		74.9	79.2
1981	83.7	80.8		84.2	86.5
1982	92.3	90.2		93.3	94.5
1983	100.2	100.1		100.3	100.4
1984	107.5	109.7		106.5	105.1
1985	115.2	120.1		112.2	109.6
1986	122.8	130.4		117.7	115.0
1987	131.0	140.8	103.1	123.9	119.6
1988	139.9	152.0	108.1	130.8	123.9
1989	150.8	165.2	114.6	138.8	131.1
1990	163.4	181.7	120.6	145.9	138.0
1991	176.8	199.7	126.3	152.4	145.0
1992	188.1	214.7	131.2	158.2	150.9
1993	195.0	223.0	135.2	163.5	155.9
1994	200.7	230.6	138.1	165.9	160.0
1995	204.5	235.0	140.5	167.0	166.3
1996	210.4	242.9	143.1	170.2	169.1
1997	215.3	249.3	145.4	173.1	171.5
1998	221.8	258.6	147.7	175.4	174.9
1999	230.7	273.4	148.5	175.9	176.7
2000	238.1	285.4	149.5	176.9	178.1
2001	247.6	300.9	150.6	178.9	178.2

Source: U.S. Department of Labor. Bureau of Labor Statistics.

Table 11.3 Consumer Price Index for Medical Services: All Urban Consumers

Year	Medical Care Services 1982–1984 = 100.0	Professional Medical Services 1982–1984 = 100.0	Physician's Services 1982–1984 = 100.0	Dental Services 1984–1986 = 100.0	Eye Care 1982–1984 = 100.0	Professional Services December 1986 = 100.0
1935	8.3		11.1	13.4		
1936	8.3		11.2	13.4		
1937	8.4		11.2	13.7		
1938	8.4		11.2	13.8		
1939	8.5		11.2	13.8		
1940	8.5		11.2	13.8		
1941	8.5		11.3	13.8		
1942	8.8		11.5	14.2		
1943	9.2		12.3	14.8		
1944	9.6		12.8	15.6		
1945	9.9		13.1	16.3		
1946	10.4		13.7	17.2		
1947	11.3		14.6	18.7		
1948	12.1		15.2	19.7		
1949	12.5		15.5	20.5		
1950	12.8		15.7	21.0		
1951	13.4		16.3	21.8		
1952	14.3		17.0	22.3		
1953	14.8		17.4	23.0		
1954	15.3		18.0	23.7		
1955	15.7		18.6	24.0		
1956	16.3		19.1	24.4		
1957	17.0		20.0	25.0		
1958	17.9		20.6	25.8		
1959	18.7		21.3	26.4		
1960	19.5		21.9	27.0		
1961	20.2		22.4	27.1		
1962	20.9		23.1	27.8		
1963	21.5		23.6	28.6		
1964	22.0		24.2	29.4		
1965	22.7		25.1	30.3		
1966	23.9		26.5	31.3		
1967	26.0	30.9	28.4	32.8		
1968	27.9	32.5	34.5	39.2		
1969	30.2	34.7	36.9	41.7		
1970	32.3	37.0	38.0	43.4		
1971	34.7	39.4	39.3	44.8		
1972	35.9	40.8	42.9	48.2		
1973	37.5	42.2	48.1	53.2		
1974	41.4	45.8	53.5	56.5		
1975	46.6	50.8	58.5	60.8		
1976	51.3	55.5	63.4	65.1		
1977	56.4	60.0	69.2	70.5		

(continued)

Table 11.3 (Continued)   Consumer Price Index for Medical Services: All Urban Consumers

Year	Medical Care Services 1982–1984 = 100.0	Professional Medical Services 1982–1984 = 100.0	Physician's Services 1982–1984 = 100.0	Dental Services 1984–1986 = 100.0	Eye Care 1982–1984 = 100.0	Professional Services December 1986 = 100.0
1978	61.2	64.5	30.0	34.6		
1979	67.2	70.1	32.1	37.1		
1980	74.8	77.9	76.5	78.9		
1981	82.8	85.9	84.9	86.5		
1982	92.6	93.2	92.9	93.1		
1983	100.7	99.8	100.1	99.4		
1984	106.7	107.0	107.0	107.5		
1985	113.2	113.5	113.5	114.2		
1986	121.9	120.8	121.5	120.6		
1987	130.0	128.8	130.4	128.8	103.5	102.4
1988	138.3	137.5	139.8	137.5	108.7	108.3
1989	148.9	146.4	150.1	146.1	112.4	114.2
1990	162.7	156.1	160.8	155.8	117.3	120.2
1991	177.1	165.7	170.5	167.4	121.9	126.6
1992	190.5	175.8	181.2	178.7	127.0	131.7
1993	202.9	184.7	191.3	188.1	130.4	135.9
1994	213.4	192.5	199.8	197.1	133.0	141.3
1995	224.2	201.0	208.8	206.8	137.0	143.9
1996	232.4	208.3	216.4	216.5	139.3	146.6
1997	239.1	215.4	222.9	226.6	141.5	151.8
1998	246.8	222.2	229.5	236.2	144.1	155.4
1999	255.1	229.2	236.0	247.2	145.5	158.7
2000	266.0	237.7	244.7	258.5	149.7	161.9
2001	278.8	246.5	253.6	269.0	154.5	167.3

Source: U.S. Department of Labor. Bureau of Labor Statistics.

In some life care plans an attendant or aide is priced at the going rate, as if one were to directly hire and become the employer. In other plans, the service is considered to be provided by a home care provider. If the direct-hire approach is to be recommended, consideration must be given to the following:

1. The hourly wage must be at least the federal minimum wage.
2. The employer (i.e., the client) will be responsible for the withholding and payment of all Social Security taxes. Arrangements must be made for the filing of all reports in a timely fashion.
3. Provision must be made for vacations, sickness, or other unavailability of the employee.
4. The client will be responsible for hiring and training. The turnover of such employees can be expected to be very high.

Table 11.4   Consumer Price Index for Hospital Services: All Urban Consumers

Year	Hospital and Related Services 1982–1984 = 100.0	Hospital Services December 1996 = 100.0	Inpatient Hospital Services December 1996 = 100.0	Outpatient Services December 1986 = 100.0
1978	55.1			
1979	61.0			
1980	69.2			
1981	79.1			
1982	90.3			
1983	100.5			
1984	109.2			
1985	116.1			
1986	123.1			
1987	131.6			103.3
1988	143.9			112.5
1989	160.5			124.7
1990	178.0			138.7
1991	196.1			153.4
1992	214.0			168.7
1993	231.9			184.3
1994	245.6			195.0
1995	257.8			204.6
1996	269.5			215.1
1997	278.4	101.7	101.3	224.9
1998	287.5	105.0	104.0	233.2
1999	299.5	109.3	107.9	246.0
2000	317.3	115.9	113.8	263.8
2001	338.3	123.6	121.0	281.1

Source: U.S. Department of Labor. Bureau of Labor Statistics.

The administrative tasks necessary when an employee is used may prove too burdensome for the client, who is, after all, injured or at least in need of assistance. Although family members may assume the responsibility for these administrative matters, it is not incumbent upon them to do so. In most cases, the preferred treatment would be to assume that attendant costs would be provided by a home care agency. (Editors' note: For a detailed explanation of costs associated with private hire, see Thomas, R. & Kitchen, J., 1996, Private hire: the real costs, *Inside Life Care Planning*, 1, 1, 3–5.)

DELIVERY PERIOD AND AMOUNT

In computing the present value of the life care plan the economist must know the timing of each cost element as well as the length of time the element will be needed. There are two separate considerations concerning the delivery period: *when* the element will be needed (including replacements) and for *how long* it will be needed.

Table 11.5   Historical Hourly Earnings for Nonagricultural Wage and Salary Employees, 1947–2001

Year	Hourly Wages	Year	Hourly Wages
1947	1.13	1975	4.53
1948	1.23	1976	4.86
1949	1.28	1977	5.25
1950	1.34	1978	5.69
1951	1.45	1979	6.16
1952	1.52	1980	6.66
1953	1.61	1981	7.25
1954	1.65	1982	7.68
1955	1.71	1983	8.02
1956	1.80	1984	8.32
1957	1.89	1985	8.57
1958	1.95	1986	8.76
1959	2.02	1987	8.98
1960	2.09	1988	9.28
1961	2.14	1989	9.66
1962	2.22	1990	10.02
1963	2.28	1991	10.34
1964	2.36	1992	10.59
1965	2.46	1993	10.83
1966	2.56	1994	11.12
1967	2.68	1995	11.43
1968	2.85	1996	11.82
1969	3.04	1997	12.28
1970	3.23	1998	12.78
1971	3.45	1999	13.24
1972	3.70	2000	13.75
1973	3.94	2001	14.33
1974	4.24		

Source: Economic Report of the President, February 2002.

Table 11.6   Average Annual Increases for Medical and Care Costs

Cost Category	Data Series	Average Annual Rate of Increase (1947–2001)
Medical services	Medical care services CPI	6.12%
Medical commodities	Medical care commodities CPI	3.61%
Nonmedical services	Average hourly earnings	4.82%
Nonmedical commodities	All items (CPI)	3.91%

Source: Table 11.1 to Table 11.5.

The life care planner should attempt to be as specific as possible as to exactly when a procedure or item will be required. Estimates such as "when needed" or "as required" are often seen in life care plans but cannot be evaluated by the economist.

Statements such as "two operations will be required over his lifetime" are less precise than the economist would prefer but can be used and evaluated. In such a case, the economist may make the estimate by assuming that the procedures will occur at equal time intervals over the life expectancy. As an alternative, the economist may total the costs for all like procedures and divide by the number of years of life expectancy to give an annual amortized cost. This would represent the average annual cost for the procedures. If the delivery times are given as a range (e.g., every 3 to 5 years), the economist may space the delivery at the mean (e.g., 4 years) or, again, compute an annual average. Using an average per year is slightly less accurate than using given amounts in specific years, however. The problem is that in many cases, the exact timing is not known.

Statements such as "an operation will be needed within the next 10 years" are very imprecise but still may be evaluated. The most conservative evaluation would place the timing at the beginning of the period if the inflation rate is expected to exceed the discount rate, or at the end of the period if the interest rate is expected to exceed inflation. A compromise evaluation may be made by timing the procedure at the midpoint of the stated duration or by averaging the cost over this period and using an annual average.

The duration of the delivery period is also a very important consideration. The life care plan should note when the element is to start (usually identified by age) and when it is to end. Statements such as "these costs will continue until he reaches adulthood" provide little information.

Many of the elements identified in the life care plan will be delivered over the life expectancy of the injured party. The question may arise as to what is the life expectancy of the client given the medical condition. Changes to the life expectancies set forth in the typical mortality table are not an economic determination but rather a medical one. The economist should be made aware of any modifications to a normal life expectancy made by a specialist. It should be emphasized that the client's life expectancy should be based on the assumption of the provision of first-class care as set forth in the life care plan. For this reason, data from studies of the mortality rates of patients with like conditions but who did not have the advantages of first-class care should not be used, uncritically, as evidence of a changed life expectancy for the client.

ACTUAL OR AVERAGE ANNUAL

The costs of the various items may be stated in terms of a specific value in 1 or more years or may be stated in terms of an average cost per year. For instance, assume a medical item costs $12,000 and will have to be replaced every 4 years. The life care planner may opt to average the expenditures as $3000 per year. The present value of items listed in these two ways will differ slightly because of the math involved. If the initial costs and the replacement periods are known exactly, then analyzing the data based on a specific amount in a given year will be slightly more accurate than using the average per year. The problem in most cases, however, is that both the initial costs and the length of the replacement periods are estimates, averages, or ranges. When this is the case, little accuracy will be lost by allocating the costs on an average basis.

ECONOMY OF EFFORT

A comprehensive life care plan will contain a large number of items, some of which cost little and some of which cost a great deal. Experience has shown that most of the costs are concentrated in just a relatively few items, usually those elements associated with care, such as the costs of doctors, hospitals, nurses, LPNs, or attendants. The total value of the commodity items generally represents only a small proportion of the total costs.

Many life care plans set forth trivial commodity items in minute detail. Some go as far as to estimate the number of additional boxes of facial tissue that will be used annually. On the other hand, the same plan may set forth two or more care options that differ by many thousands (or even hundreds of thousands) of dollars per year. In many cases, the care options will be assigned a cost, but detailed discussion as to the relative benefits of each option will not be given. The reader of the plan will have little or no idea of the relative advantages or disadvantages of the various care options.

The life care plan would be strengthened if the major research, development, and discussion were concentrated on needs that make the greatest impact on total costs. That is, the important items should be emphasized. In many cases, even if the marginal costs of the trivial items (such as facial tissue) were eliminated from the analysis, there would be little difference in the final total cost of the life care plan.

TOTAL LIFETIME VALUES

The only important total cost, over the life expectancy, that needs to be considered in a life care plan is the total present value. This is the number the jury will be asked to consider to provide for the lifetime medical and care needs of the client. Present value considers the rates of price inflation as well as the earning power of money (i.e., interest).

When a life care planner gives a total lifetime value of the recommended items by adding all of the items over life expectancy, the results may be confusing and even misleading. If such a total is intended to represent present value, the implicit assumption is that inflation and interest will cancel out. Unless the economist uses the total offset discounting method, the present value calculation will always differ from the lifetime total. These differences will invariably cause confusion.

CONCLUSIONS

When an economist is called upon to compute the present value of the future medical and care costs set forth in a life care plan prepared by a specialist, he or she must rely on the accuracy of data, including the need, the dollar values, the timing, and the duration. Since the life care plan is the foundation for the economic analysis, the economist has an interest in how the plan is presented.

This chapter has looked at life care plans from the economist's point of view and has made a number of recommendations.

REFERENCES

Dillman, E. (1987). The necessary economic and vocational interface in personal injury cases. *Journal of Private Sector Rehabilitation*, 2, 121–142.
Dillman, E. (1988). *Economic Damages and Discounting Methods*. Athens, GA: Elliott & Fitzpatrick.

II

SELECTED DISABILITIES: TOPICS AND ISSUES

12

LIFE CARE PLANNING FOR THE AMPUTEE

Robert H. Meier, III and Roger O. Weed

INTRODUCTION

The physiatrist has been trained in the team approach to provide rehabilitative care to persons with simple and complex disabilities. The physiatrist should serve as an ally with the life care planner in determining the ideal outcome of rehabilitative care. In addition, if the physiatrist has been the care provider throughout the active rehabilitation treatment phase, he or she also will have insights into the psychosocial issues of the person with the disability that will enhance the life care plan. The physiatrist can also medically case manage the variety of health professionals and treatments that are necessary, especially in cases of catastrophic disability. The physiatrist is an excellent resource to provide rehabilitative care and determine equipment costs.

For the person with an amputation, the physiatrist should have the ability to provide meaningful information for the life care plan, especially in the following areas (Meier & Atkins, 2004):

1. Point of maximum medical improvement
2. Life expectancy
3. Expected functional outcomes
4. Prosthetic service
5. Frequency of prosthetic replacement
6. Adaptive equipment needs
7. Architectural modifications for function
8. Attendant care hours and level of service
9. Psychosocial needs
10. Vocational and avocational expectations and modifications
11. Future medical needs
12. Future surgical needs

If the local physiatrist is unable to provide useful life care planning information, there is a network of specialized physiatrists who have years of experience in

0-8493-1511-5/04/$0.00+$1.50
© 2004 by CRC Press LLC

working with the rehabilitation of specific areas of disability. These physiatric specialists can be located through the life care planner network. They should have extensive experience in providing health care for a person with an amputation. The physiatrist can be of great service to the life care planner in indicating the appropriate level of functional outcome to be achieved and the future needs for the amputee.

PHASES OF AMPUTATION REHABILITATION

The loss of a body part(s) is an emotionally traumatic experience. Yet most persons who sustain an amputation can look forward to a fulfilling life of meaningful function using contemporary prosthetic designs. The key to successful prosthetic rehabilitation is having an understanding of the desired functional outcome and the rehabilitative process necessary for achieving that outcome. In addition, the physiatrist should provide a time framework for the achievement of the ideal outcome. The physiatrist can also outline the most cost efficient array of rehabilitative services to achieve the desired rehabilitation goals.

To understand the rehabilitative process for a person with an amputation, it is best to consider the following phases of amputation rehabilitation. These phases, while somewhat artificial, do interweave and flow from one to the next. By knowing the phase of the amputation rehabilitative process, the case manager/life care planner can identify the issues to be considered in each phase and assist the amputee toward the next phase. The hallmarks of each phase can be used to determine if the amputee is successfully moving through the phases or is delayed in a phase. Being delayed in a phase of rehabilitative care can detract from the best functional or psychosocial outcome and can also add to the costs of health care.

The phases for amputation rehabilitation staging and the setting in which they are usually accomplished in today's health systems are:

OUTPATIENT (usually, although trauma related is commonly inpatient)
    1. Preoperative
INPATIENT
    2. Surgical
    3. Acute postsurgical (some inpatient and some outpatient)
OUTPATIENT
    4. Preprosthetic
    5. Prosthetic prescription and fabrication
    6. Prosthetic training
    7. Community reentry
    8. Vocational/avocational
    9. Follow-up

Hallmarks of each phase have been assigned to measure the progress of the person with an amputation from one phase to the next (Table 12.1). There is usually some overlap from one phase to the next, and the person may move more quickly through one phase than another (Meier, 1994). The focus throughout all these phases is on the needs and desires of the amputee. The person's ability

Table 12.1   Medical and Rehabilitation Progression of Amputation

Phase	Hallmarks
1. Preoperative	Assess body condition and patient education; discuss surgical level, postoperative rehabilitation, and prosthetic plans
2. Amputation surgery	Length, myoplastic closure, soft tissue coverage, nerve reconstruction handling, and rigid dressing
3. Acute postoperative	Wound healing, pain control, proximal body motion, and emotional support
4. Preprosthetic	Shaping and shrinking amputation stump, increasing muscle strength, and restoring patient locus of control
5. Prosthetic fabrication	Team consensus on prosthetic prescription and experienced prosthetic fabrication
6. Prosthetic training	Increase wearing of prosthesis, mobility, and activities of daily living (ADL) skills
7. Community reintegration	Resume roles in family and community activities; regain emotional equilibrium and healthy coping strategies; pursue recreational activities
8. Vocational rehabilitation	Assess and plan vocational activities for future; may need further education, training, or job modification
9. Follow-up	Provide lifelong prosthetic, functional, medical, and emotional support; provide regular assessment of functional level and prosthetic problem solving

to adapt to an altered body image and, in some cases, an altered lifestyle is essential for achieving the idealized outcome. Paying attention to and providing service for their psychosocial well-being is paramount to successful rehabilitative outcomes.

Preoperative

On a few occasions, the patient is delayed in the decision for an amputation. This is an ideal time for the rehabilitation team to assess and begin a treatment plan focusing on function of the remaining extremities. This is also an appropriate time to practice preventive care to maintain full range of motion and strength in the proximal limb muscles of the side to be amputated and also in the intact limb. An aerobic conditioning program should be provided during this phase since this type of exercise will hasten the postoperative functional recovery, especially in the use of a leg or arm prosthesis.

Amputation Surgery and Reconstruction Phase

Amputation surgery should proceed as a reconstructive surgery that will provide a residual limb with the best function, regardless of whether a prosthesis is likely to be prescribed. A reconstructive philosophy of amputation is best accomplished by a surgeon who has performed a number of amputations and understands contemporary prosthetic options and ideal functional outcomes.

Acute Postoperative Phase

This is a time for wound healing and pain control. Usually there is wound care necessary until the sutures are removed. The rehabilitation focus is on the remaining limbs and instructing the amputee in preventive exercise for the amputated limb and the intact limbs. Psychosocial support is essential during this period of loss for the individual.

Preprosthetic Phase

This period is usually accomplished on an outpatient basis. Once the sutures are removed, attention is paid to shaping and shrinking the residual limb in preparation for prosthetic casting. This is a good time to educate the amputee and the family regarding the prosthetic options available, and to develop and review the rehabilitation plan, if it has not previously been accomplished. At this time careful therapeutic attention should be paid to aerobic conditioning and strength training. Emotional stresses should be anticipated that surround change in body image, function, family roles, and income. Empowering the amputees to view themselves as healthy individuals and to regain the locus of control in their lives is an important component of this phase.

Prosthetic Fabrication

At this phase, the team, including the amputee, should decide on a prosthetic prescription that best meets the person's needs and desires (Meier, 1995). More and more, the prosthetic prescription is also dependent on what a third-party payer will sponsor. It is preferable that a prosthetist who is frequently experienced in fitting the specific level of amputation be used to fabricate the prosthesis. The time framework from prosthetic casting until final fitting of the prosthesis should be presented to the amputee and the rehabilitation team for planning purposes.

As a general rule, the lower-limb amputee should be fitted within 8 weeks of amputation and the arm amputee fitted within 4 to 6 weeks of amputation surgery. If the upper-limb amputee is delayed in fitting, his or her chances of using a prosthesis for bimanual activities decreases significantly. Such amputees become accustomed to performing activities in a one-handed manner and therefore do not find the prosthesis to be of much assistance in performing daily activities.

Prosthetic Training

This phase is most often accomplished in an outpatient therapy setting with therapists who have trained many amputees with similar levels of amputation and similar types of prosthetic components. It is important that the therapist has worked with the types of prosthetic components included in the prosthesis. Today's prosthetic technology is changing so quickly that it is important the treating therapist keep abreast of the latest componentry and understand the biomechanics of each component. This phase should continue until the expected level of functional outcome has been achieved. The length of treatment time will vary depending on the level of amputation, the amputee's health, level of function

Table 12.2   Functional Expectations for the Below-Knee Amputee

1. Wears the prosthesis during all waking hours
2. Walks on level and uneven surfaces
3. Climbs stairs step over step
4. Drives a car (if desired)
5. Can fall safely and arise from the floor
6. Can run (if cardiovascular status permits)
7. Can hop without the prosthesis
8. Participates in avocational interests
9. Has returned to same or modified work
10. Does not use any gait aid
11. Performs aerobic conditioning exercise (if cardiovascular system permits)
12. Knows how to inspect skin of the amputated and nonamputated legs and foot
13. Knows how to change stump socks to accommodate for soft tissue changes
14. Knows how to buy a correctly fitting shoe for the remaining foot
15. Independent in activities of daily living (ADL)
16. Understands the necessity of follow-up

prior to the amputation, associated injuries, and medical problems. The rehabilitation team should proceed with gradual prosthetic wearing and functional training with the goal of achieving the idealized functional outcomes listed in Table 12.2, Table 12.3, and Table 12.4. The rehabilitation treatment plan should focus on the level of function necessary for community reintegration and on vocational and avocational outcomes.

Community Reintegration

Persons with amputations should begin to resume their roles in their family and community as quickly as possible following the amputation. Prosthetic training can assist with community reintegration by providing meaningful function. A psychologist or social worker should assist amputees in developing productive social interactions with their family, friends, peers, and other persons in their community.

Vocational Rehabilitation

The physiatrist should be closely involved during this phase of amputee rehabilitation. The physiatrist is most knowledgeable in the expected level of prosthetic use in a variety of vocational settings. The physiatrist is also best suited to place the work restrictions in relationship to the level of amputation and functional outcome. Working as a team, the case manager, the physiatrist, and the vocational rehabilitation specialist can provide an excellent support system for the amputee and enhance his or her successful return to the workplace.

While vocational rehabilitation should begin shortly following the amputation, return to the workplace may require a functional capacity evaluation, work site evaluation, and perhaps work site modification. Generally, it is ill advised to

Table 12.3 Functional Expectations for the Above-Knee Amputee

(Greater energy expenditure than for below-knee prosthetic use)

1. Wears the prosthesis during all waking hours
2. Walks on level and uneven surfaces
3. Climbs stairs step over step (some may do one step at a time)
4. Drives a car (if desired)
5. Can fall safely and arise from the floor
6. Can hop without the prosthesis
7. Participates in avocational interests
8. Has returned to same or modified work
9. Does not use any gait aid (some may need a cane)
10. Performs aerobic conditioning exercise (if cardiovascular system permits)
11. Knows how to inspect skin of the amputated and nonamputated legs and foot
12. Knows how to buy a correctly fitting shoe for the remaining foot
13. Independent in activities of daily living (ADL)
14. Understands the necessity of follow-up
15. A few can run with high-level training

Table 12.4 Functional Expectations for the Above- or Below-Elbow Amputee

1. Independent in donning and doffing the prosthesis
2. Independent in activities of daily living (ADL)
3. Can write legibly with remaining hand
4. Has successfully switched dominance (if necessary)
5. Drives (if desired)
6. Has returned to work (same or modified job)
7. Can tie laces with one hand or with the remaining hand and the prosthesis
8. Uses a button hook easily
9. Has prepared a meal in the kitchen
10. Has been shown adaptive equipment for the kitchen and ADL
11. Has performed carpentry and automotive maintenance (if desired)
12. Wears prosthesis during all waking hours
13. Uses the prosthesis for bimanual activities
14. Understands the necessity of follow-up

provide a vocational prognosis until the person has achieved maximum functional outcome with or without the prosthesis.

Vocationally, it appears that people with traumatic amputation who have received rehabilitation from a center of excellence have better vocational outcomes than people with disabilities in general (Weed, 2001; Weed & Atkins, 2004). Educational achievement seems to correlate well with work following amputation. In one study, 70.8% of people with amputation who had some college or a college degree were able to work postinjury (Weed et al., 1997). In a second study, also based on a sample from a center of excellence, 58.4% of upper-extremity amputees were able to work postinjury. The amount of time the person wore the prosthesis and the amount of education were positively correlated with work (Atkins, as cited in Weed & Atkins, 2004). As the person aged, the employment rates declined by about 45% per each decade.

Also, in 2001, a study conducted in the Netherlands with a sample of 652 lower-limb amputees revealed that 64% of the population was working at the time of the study, 31% had work experience but were not working, and 5% had no work experience. Consistent with studies in the U.S., people who worked found employment in less physically demanding jobs. Of those who quit working within 2 years of the amputation, 78% reported that amputee-related factors played a role in their decision. They also commonly reported problems with obtaining workplace modifications (Schoppen et al., 2001).

The life care planner who prepares the future expected care for a person with an amputation obviously should consult a vocational expert for recommendations if there is a reasonable expectation for employment. In most cases, job modifications and educational support will be appropriate. For sample suggestions for assistive technology, see Weed and Field (2001) and Weed and Atkins (2004).

Follow-Up

In order to ensure the most appropriate level of prosthetic function, prevent prosthetic problems, and address emotional adjustment to amputation, a regular and periodic program of rehabilitation follow-up should be provided for the amputee. Once the ideal level of function has been achieved and the amputee is wearing a definitive prosthesis, the person should be seen in regular follow-up on an annual or every-other-year basis. This schedule permits measurement of the functional outcomes of amputation rehabilitation. It also serves to enhance the education of the amputee regarding preventive care and further prosthetic needs.

Restoration of meaningful function, body compensation, and emotional adaptation to an amputation take a significant time from the amputation until the patient is well stabilized. This process of amputation and its rehabilitation will generally take the majority of 12 to 18 months in most patients. Certainly prosthetic fitting and training take less than the 12 to 18 months, but the true return to a full life cannot be hurried and the achievement of maximum medical improvement falls within this 12- to 18-month framework.

DEMOGRAPHICS OF LIMB AMPUTATION

Amputation of the leg is more common than amputation of the arm and occurs in a 3:1 ratio. The leg amputee is usually a person in the sixth or seventh decade of life who sustains the amputation because of occlusive arterial vascular disease. Often this person also has associated diabetes mellitus. In addition to the vascular disease in the legs, there is often accompanying arterial disease in the coronary and cerebral arteries. With associated diabetes, the complications can include peripheral neuropathy, renal disease, and diminished eyesight. All of these comorbid factors can diminish the functional outcomes expected from prosthetic rehabilitation.

The arm amputee is usually a young man who has sustained a work-related injury. The amputation most frequently involves the right arm and most often results in a below-elbow (transradial) amputation of the dominant arm. The arm amputee, unlike the leg amputee, can function independently with the use of one arm. Full-time functional prosthetic use in the arm amputee is less likely to occur than in the leg amputee.

PHANTOM AND RESIDUAL LIMB PAIN

This phenomenon occurs in most patients immediately following the amputation surgery and usually subsides during the first 4 to 6 weeks after the amputation. In only a few amputees does phantom limb pain become so problematic that it interferes with the quality of life. Phantom pain should not be treated with narcotics other than during the acute postoperative period. A variety of medications can be used to alleviate this pain. Popular are tricyclic antidepressants such as amitriptyline or trazadone, gabapentin (Neurontin), and carbamazepine (Davis, 1993). In addition, early in the 21st century there are a number of other medications that are being used in the treatment of phantom pain. These include baclofen, tizanadine, Topamax, Marinol, Lidocaine patches, Zostrix, and Mexitil. These medications affect the way the body processes pain messages in the peripheral and central nervous systems. Other physical modalities have been utilized but have met with varied success depending on the individual amputee. If the phantom pain interferes greatly with the quality of life or prosthetic function, an amputee pain specialist should be consulted. Often, pain in the amputee is related to the level of anxiety, depression, and altered sleep that is present. Posttraumatic stress disorder is often present and may contribute to the level of perceived pain. Problematic pain in the amputee must be approached using emotional counseling and not just medications or modalities.

Pain in the residual limb should be differentiated from phantom pain. Often, residual limb pain is caused by a poorly fitting prosthesis and can be alleviated with socket modifications. Residual limb pain may also be caused by the development of a neuroma from a peripheral nerve that was severed at the time of the amputation. There are a variety of conservative and surgical methods to attempt to decrease the pain from a neuroma (Sherman et al., 1980).

LEVELS OF LIMB AMPUTATION

In general, the longer the length of the residual limb, the better the prosthetic function that can be expected. In the leg, amputation below the knee (transtibial) provides for lower energy expenditure than the use of an above-knee (transfemoral) prosthesis. Salvaging the leg at a below-knee level is now the goal of leg amputation surgery in the U.S. (Moore & Malone, 1989). Disarticulation levels for the arm and leg have certain relative contraindications and should be carefully considered on an individual basis. Full-thickness skin and soft tissue coverage are also helpful in achieving ideal prosthetic functional outcomes. However, with the new gel liner interfaces, scarred skin and poor soft tissue coverage can be dealt with in a more satisfactory manner than in the past.

PROSTHETIC PRESCRIPTION

There has been an explosion of available prosthetic components in the past 10 years, and it is hard to keep up with the constant barrage of new options for the amputee. Most of the new components have added to the expense of the prosthesis with little or no demonstration that they have enhanced the functional outcome. Many of the new components are lighter weight and therefore more comfortable to wear. New prosthetic foot designs have added the ability to run and jump, and these desired functions were not previously possible with the older component designs (Esquenazi & Torres, 1991). The use of electric components for the arm amputee has not been universally applied in the U.S. This technology remains less frequently prescribed than the conventional body-powered designs. The prices of prostheses, especially those using the new socket designs and components, have risen dramatically. A high-tech above-knee prosthesis frequently will cost between $17,000 and $76,000 (highest cost, for example, is the C leg — a computerized knee system available through Otto Bock), while an above-elbow myoelectric arm can cost $60,000 to $120,000. With costs at these levels, it is imperative that the amputee be treated in a comprehensive interdisciplinary center of amputation rehabilitative excellence.

The usual components required for a prosthetic leg include the socket, a foot/ankle complex, and a means of suspension. Of course, for the above-knee prosthesis, a knee component is also prescribed. An estimate of ability to use a prosthesis, designated as K functional levels, has been established as justification for various prosthetic technology sophistication choices. See Table 12.5 for an outline of criteria.

For the arm amputee, there is a socket that fits onto the residual limb, and for the below-elbow amputee, a wrist joint, a terminal device, and a suspension

Table 12.5 Functional Ability Estimates for Lower-Extremity Prosthesis

K Level	Description
0	Does not have the ability or potential to ambulate or transfer safely with or without assistance and a prosthesis does not enhance the quality of life or mobility
1	Has the ability or potential to use a prosthesis for transfers or ambulation on level surfaces at fixed pace; typical of the limited and household ambulator
2	Has the ability or potential for ambulation with the ability to navigate environmental barriers such as curbs stairs or uneven surfaces; typical of the limited community ambulator
3	Has the ability or potential for ambulation with variable pace; typical of the community ambulator who has the ability to navigate most environmental barriers and may have vocational therapeutic or exercise activity that demands prosthetic utilization beyond simple locomotion
4	Has the ability or potential for prosthetic ambulation that requires high-impact stress or energy levels typical of the prosthetic demands of the child, active adult, or athlete; add on option/accessory for wheelchair

Table 12.6 Advantages and Disadvantages of Various Upper-Limb Prostheses

Type	Pros	Cons
Cosmetic (passive)	Most lightweight	High cost if custom made
	Best cosmesis	Least functional
	Least harnessing	Low-cost gloves stain easily
Body powered	Moderate cost	Most body movement to operate
	Moderately lightweight	Most harnessing
	Most durable	Least satisfactory appearance
	Highest sensory feedback	
Externally powered (myoelectric and switch control)	Moderate or no harnessing	Heaviest
	Least body movement to operate	Most expensive
	Moderate cosmesis	Most maintenance
	More function-proximal levels	Limited sensory feedback
Hybrid (cable elbow/ electric TD)	All cable excursion to elbow	Electric TD weights forearm (harder to lift)
	Increased TD pinch	Good for elbow disarticulation (or long above elbow)
Hybrid (electric elbow/ cable TD)	All cable excursion to TD	Least cosmesis
	Low effort to position TD	Lower pinch force for TD
	Low-maintenance TD	

TD = terminal device.

Source: Esquenazi et al., 1989.

system are required elements of the prescription. Terminal devices can be a hook or a hand (Sears, 1991). The hand can be passive or it can move. For the above-elbow amputee, an elbow joint is prescribed. In considering the arm prosthetic prescription, the team needs to consider the three basic prosthetic designs available. They are a passive prosthesis that provides mainly cosmetic restoration, one that is cable controlled by body power, or one that has electric moving parts. A comparison of these types of arm prostheses is presented in Table 12.6 (Esquenazi et al., 1989).

Partial Hand

This level of amputation can be handled in several ways. Many partial-hand amputees choose to not wear any prosthetic restoration. However, if cosmesis is desired, a cosmetic glove can be fabricated. This is usually made from a mold taken of the residual hand. A custom-made silicone glove that is hand-colored can provide excellent cosmesis and is reasonably durable. However, if it is worn at work, a protective glove should be worn. Another manner to prosthetically handle this level is to make an opposition bar that can provide improved prehension between the prosthetic bar and the residual moving parts of the hand. If the thumb has been amputated, an excellent prosthetic thumb can be fabricated. The functional and cosmetic results from this prosthesis often decrease the need for surgical reconstruction of the amputated thumb.

Wrist Disarticulation/Below Elbow (Transradial)

The below-elbow prosthesis is usually composed of a double-walled plastic laminate socket that fits intimately over the residual limb. A locking, quick-change wrist unit is commonly prescribed through which the terminal device is attached to the forearm shell. This wrist unit permits ease of change of various terminal devices and locks the terminal device in a position of function when handling heavier objects. For most men who will return to heavy-duty work, a body-powered prosthesis will be useful. For the businessman or white-collar worker, a myoelectric or a passive cosmetic prosthesis may be preferable (Meier & Atkins, 2004; Meier, 1996).

Elbow Disarticulation/Above Elbow (Transhumeral)

The prosthetic options at this level of restoration are body-powered or electric control. The electric prosthesis is many times the expense of the body-powered arm. For a very short above-elbow level of amputation, an electric prosthesis may be the only functional restoration that is reasonable.

Shoulder Disarticulation

This level can be fitted with a lighter-weight endoskeletal design with a passive elbow joint and a moving terminal device. At this proximal level of amputation, an electric prosthesis will permit more functional motion of the component parts. However, it is heavier to wear and much more costly.

Partial/Hindfoot

Often this level of amputation can be fitted with a full-length insole with toe filler that fits inside the shoe. This insole can usually be interchanged between various shoes. The bottom of the shoe may need to be modified to provide a more normal gait pattern.

Below Knee (Transtibial)

The prosthesis that is currently used for this level of amputation was popularized in the mid-1950s. It is called a patellar tendon-bearing (PTB) design. It was originally designed to place superincumbent body weight on the remaining anatomic landmarks that were pressure tolerant. It relieves pressure from the pressure-intolerant areas of the residual stump. For this level, the prosthetic prescription includes the design of the prosthetic socket, a foot/ankle complex, and a means of suspending the prosthesis on the residual leg. A current popular suspension design is called the triple S system or the silicone suction suspension. A silicone sleeve is worn against the skin and a knurled pin extends from the distal end. This pin locks inside a coupling in the distal end of the prosthetic socket. The silicone sleeve provides additional padding to the inside of the socket against the skin. Other types of gel liners are in vogue today and have made prosthetic leg wearing more comfortable. These liners reduce the number of skin problems seen with prosthetic wear and function.

Knee Disarticulation/Above Knee (Transfemoral)

The contemporary socket design for the above-knee amputee has changed in the 1980s and 1990s (Leonard & Meier, 1993). There are a number of designs available, but the one in greatest use is a narrow mediolateral, ischial containment design. New socket designs also include thermoplastic inner liners that have improved the comfort of prosthetic wearing. Gel liners are also available for this level of amputation. A variety of knee units are also available that provide differing degrees of knee stability and cosmesis with gait.

The new C knee has become available and is a computerized knee mechanism that permits programmed stability at the knee. At the time of this writing, the knee had not been in use for very long in the U.S., and controlled studies as to its efficacy in prescription were under way. It does add significantly to the cost of an above-knee prosthesis, so it should be carefully matched to the correct amputee (for information, see http://www.ottobockus.com/products/op_lower_cleg.asp).

Hip Disarticulation

This is a difficult level to fit comfortably and to have the amputee walk successfully with the prosthesis. This level of amputation should be handled by a prosthetist who makes 10 or more of this type of prosthesis a year. More important, for best success, this amputee should have his or her rehabilitation in a center that has trained a number of amputees to wear this type of prosthesis with good results.

Prosthetic Complications

A well-fitted prosthesis is in intimate contact with the skin of the residual limb. There are shearing forces applied to the skin in arm and leg prostheses. In the leg amputee, there are also direct pressures applied from the prosthesis to the skin of the residual leg. These forces can create skin pressure problems. These issues are usually addressed with prosthetic socket modifications or the use of gel–skin interfaces. A differing socket design may also be necessary to change the forces applied to the skin. In addition, use of a prosthesis will usually cause an occasional superficial skin infection that can usually be treated in a brief time with topical or oral antibiotics.

Prosthetic Costs

Because of the high cost of prosthetics, a team of experienced amputee rehabilitation specialists should develop a prescription. To have the prosthetist develop the prescription in a vacuum is almost a conflict of interest and should be avoided.

When assembling the prosthetic costs of the life care plan, it is essential that the life care planner understand what estimate the prosthetist is providing. There are at least three ways of pricing a prosthesis. There is a usual and customary cost. This cost would be the full, nondiscounted, non-Medicare allowable cost that usually will have significant markup built into the numbers provided from the prosthetic laboratory. Almost never is this price paid to the prosthetist for the final prosthetic device. The more appropriate number to use for prosthetic costs is the Medicare allowable one. This is the most usual price that will be paid for a prosthesis. Some managed care and insurance providers will discount from the Medicare allowable fee schedule or will provide an add-on amount that will be a specific percentage above the Medicare allowable reimbursement schedule.

Also, if the life care planner is obtaining price quotations from a variety of prosthetic facilities, it is imperative that the same L codes be utilized when pricing the prosthesis. The L code is the Medicare system of providing specific numbers for specific prosthetic components. If specific L codes are not used in obtaining the variety of quotes, it will be like comparing apples and oranges. However, it may be of benefit to obtain a variety of prosthetic price quotes and provide a range in the life care plan using a high estimate, a low estimate, and the median price. Prosthetic pricing does vary from laboratory to laboratory for the exact same prosthesis. Prosthetic price quotes also can vary dramatically from one region of the U.S. to another.

Prosthetic Replacement

Within the first 2 years following the amputation, several socket changes are usually necessary to accommodate the rapid soft tissue changes that occur. These changes improve the prosthetic fit and comfort of wearing. Usually, after this time, a prosthesis should last the amputee from 3 to 5 years before a replacement prosthesis is prescribed. Certainly, the level of activity in using the prosthesis will affect the frequency with which these replacements are needed. Modifications to the prosthesis are usually needed once every 6 months on average. An estimate for routine prosthetic maintenance should be obtained from a prosthetic facility, but on average, it is estimated that 10% of the original cost of the prosthesis be provided once the warranty of the prosthesis has expired.

Complete replacement of a leg prosthesis is generally felt to be essential for the active prosthetic wearer every 3 to 5 years. This provides a mean of 4 years between new prosthetic fabrication.

For the conventional, body-powered arm prosthetic user, the same replacement schedule is provided as for the leg. For the electric arm prosthesis, the replacement schedule increases to every 7 years.

LIFE CARE PLANNING WITH THE PHYSIATRIST

There are three differing scenarios for physiatric involvement with life care planning. The best scenario is when the physiatrist to be involved with the life care plan has been the treating physiatrist throughout the individual's rehabilitation process. In this scenario, the physiatrist has become quite involved with developing and facilitating the amputee's rehabilitation treatment goals and plan. Having worked with the amputee through the phases of amputation rehabilitation, this physiatrist can give the most useful prognostic information for the life care plan. The physiatrist will have a clear picture of the amputee's psychosocial support system and his or her needs and desires, as well as the amputee's preamputation lifestyle and how likely it will be to achieve the desired quality of life postamputation.

Another scenario can occur when the physiatrist who has been asked to participate in the life care plan has never been involved with the amputee's rehabilitation program. This physiatrist should evaluate the individual to provide meaningful information for a life care plan. Often, this requires a visit from the amputee to the physiatrist, or the physiatrist will visit the amputee for a thorough assessment. This may be accomplished over a 1- to several-day period of time, depending on the complexity of the case. Almost always, this evaluation will be performed during an outpatient visit. The evaluation usually includes the physiatric assessment and visits with an occupational therapist, a physical therapist, a psychologist, and a prosthetist. Other rehabilitation professionals and consultants may be included in this evaluation depending on other areas of disability or comorbid factors that are present. The product of this evaluation should be a report that provides all the information that a life care planner will find useful in developing the final plan. For this reason, it is essential that the life care planner pose all of the important questions he wishes the physician to address before the evaluation process begins.

The evaluation process by the physiatrist should include the elements that are clearly delineated during the evaluation and the physiatrist's opinions that are to be included in the life care document. These items should include:

1. History
2. Past medical history
3. Review of systems, including thorough assessment of pain
4. Medications
5. Psychosocial history
6. Activity status — before the amputation and at the time of the evaluation
7. Vocational history
8. Avocational history
9. Prosthetic history
10. Adaptive equipment used
11. A typical 24-hour period in the life of the amputee at the time of the assessment
12. Achievement of maximum medical improvement
13. Future needs:
    Prosthetic
    Emotional
    Rehabilitative
    Medical
    Surgical
    Equipment
    Architectural modifications
    Attendant care
    Vocational options
    Follow-up plan
    Health maintenance and preventive care
14. Specifically stated goals obtained from the amputee for his or her future

A third manner for physiatric involvement in life care planning is the "curbside consultation." In this instance, the physiatrist does not have the advantage of evaluating the amputee but instead reviews the case records and provides input into the life care plan based on the physiatrist's experience with similar patients. This manner of physiatric involvement can be very useful to the life care planner in helping to assure that important life care planning issues for a person with an amputation are not overlooked.

High-Voltage Electrical Burn Amputees

This category of amputee often has significant comorbid issues that should be considered in the life care plan. These issues have to do with the nature of a high-voltage electrical injury. Often there are multiple amputations because of the extensive nature of the electrical damage to the bones and soft tissues. In addition, there are often large skin areas that are grafted. Also, there is often unusually shaped anatomy of the residual limb(s). For all these reasons, staged and prolonged reconstructive plastic and orthopedic surgery may be indicated and may delay or interrupt prosthetic fitting and functional use of one or more of the prostheses.

Often this type of burn involves the arms and can result in bilateral arm amputations. On occasion, the arms are lost bilaterally above the elbows or at both shoulders. These types of amputees require treatment in a center of excellence that works with a number of this type of complicated amputee if the best prosthetic devices and prosthetic training are to be achieved. Sending the amputee from home to a center of excellence will have transportation costs involved in the plan.

Another complication to be considered for the life care plan is the development of cataract formation. If cataracts are to form secondary to the electrical injury, they will occur within 2 years of the initial injury. Also, there are often peripheral nerve injuries secondary to the electrical burn, and if these are incomplete injuries, they may not show their extent of recovery for 3 to 4 years. Occasionally a brain injury is also experienced from electrical current, and the expert should be alert for signs and symptoms that may indicate a need for a neuropsychological evaluation.

Potential Complications

Potential complications are dependent on the reason for the amputation (trauma, electrocution, diabetes, cancer, cardiovascular disease, etc.), fit of prosthesis (if one is used), work demands, living environment, quality of medical treatment, and other factors. However, common considerations include (Weed, 2001; Weed & Sluis, 1990):

1. Some of the most common complications are psychological in nature. In many cases, psychological counseling will be provided while the client is an inpatient and may be continued following discharge from acute care. In one case, a client who experienced a traumatic hemipelvectomy (including loss of sexual, bowel, and bladder functioning) experienced significant

depression, was hospitalized for suicidal ideation, and had undergone a significant amount of psychological counseling following discharge. In this case, the family unit fell apart and a number of family counseling issues were raised.

2. In the event of amputations where the client wears a prosthesis, one would expect the probability of occasional skin breakdown. In one case, a client suffered amputations as a result of an electrical injury. In this situation, the skin loses its integrity due to the burn. The client may require surgical intervention in order to repair skin breakdown.

3. Bone spurs occasionally become a problem and may require surgery.

4. Phantom pain or sensations are very common, at least during acute recovery, and may need some sort of treatment.

5. Other complications include osteoarthritis, which may be experienced in the knees and lower back, as well as back pain that may be experienced due to an abnormal gait. Fit of the prosthesis is of paramount importance to avoid these kinds of complications. In addition to proper fit, specific gait training to educate the client as to proper body mechanics will be important.

6. Another often overlooked complication has to do with weight gain. Weight gain affects the fit of the prosthesis, requiring either adjustment or a complete refabrication of the socket.

7. Complicated recoveries from other injuries may be a result of the inability of the client to manage self-care during periods of injury or illness. For example, an individual who is a triple amputee (bilateral below knee and dominant arm at the shoulder) may be unable to take care of himself for even bowel and bladder care or other survival needs should he injure his other arm.

8. Knee problems when not wearing the prosthesis are often a complication for bilateral below-knee amputees. It is sometimes much easier to avoid the time it takes to put on a prosthesis by simple walking on one's knees in order to get around the house, such as going to the bathroom at night or trying to get out of the house in case of an emergency. After years of using this method to move around, it is not uncommon for clients to experience knee problems.

9. While working in hot environments or having to exert considerable effort to walk or engage in physical activity with a prosthesis, sweating can become an irritating problem. Prostheses tend to feel heavy and awkward and will require an approximate 10% increase in energy for a single below-knee amputation and much more energy expenditure with multiple amputations (Friedmann, 1981). It does not take an educated observer to understand that a bilateral above-knee amputee will expend considerable energy simply getting from one place to another. In fact, many amputees may prefer to use a wheelchair to do things quicker. In addition, an upper-extremity amputee, such as a shoulder disarticulation, requires the addition of a mechanical arm or a Utah arm, which also requires considerable effort. This may result in excessive sweating and irritation as well. In addition, working in a hot environment, such as outdoors in the summertime in the south or in a boiler room indoors, may become intolerable.

10. Neuromas are also fairly frequent and can be quite irritating if the prosthesis impacts the area where the neuroma resides. Often surgery is the treatment of choice.

EXAMPLE CASE

This North Carolina client was 14 years old at the time of the traumatic amputation of both legs. She has a right above-knee amputation (AKA) and Syme's amputation of her left foot.

The sample only includes relevant physician recommendations and prosthetic entries.

CONCLUSION

The physiatrist should play a valuable role in assisting in the development of the life care plan for the person who has sustained an amputation. Emphasis should be placed on the amputee achieving the ideal level of function with an appropriate rehabilitation program. Just providing a prosthesis is not the same as providing an integrated rehabilitation program that includes a prosthesis. The emphasis should be placed on the amputee's needs and desires. Measuring the functional outcome, the success of community reintegration, and the individual's emotional adaptation to the changes in their life is important in developing an accurate life care plan. The physiatrist should serve as an invaluable collaborator with the life care planner in order to develop the most accurate and comprehensive life care plan.

Routine Future Medical Care — Physician Only

Recommendation (by whom)	Year Initiated/Suspended	Frequency	Expected Cost
Multidisciplinary amputee team clinic evaluation at an amputee center of excellence (RM)	2002 (during summer) through 2006 (age 18)	1-time comprehensive evaluation, then 1 time/year evaluation (during summers) through 2006	2002: $452 (includes doctor, clinic fees, bilateral lower-extremity x-rays, amputee coordinator, PT, OT, prosthetist, nursing, other allied health specialists as needed, etc.) 2003: $452 2004: $452 2005: $452 2006: $452 Also includes airfare at $614 each trip for 2 passengers (client + 1 caregiver) + 2 nights' lodging at $118–158 total

Note 1: It is expected the client will participate in a comprehensive evaluation beginning the summer of 2002 and one time each summer until she completes high school (2006). Travel costs assume that the client plus one parent/caregiver will travel together.

Note 2: See also outpatient prostheses and gait training following prostheses fitting.

Recommendation (by whom)	Year Initiated/Suspended	Frequency	Expected Cost
Physiatrist/physical medicine and rehabilitation (PM&R) with experience in bilateral lower-extremity amputations (RM)	2002 (following evaluation by amputee center of excellence) to life expectancy	1 time every 6 months (average) through 2006, then 1 time/year to life expectancy (assumes client's amputations are stable by 2006)	2002–2006: $900 total at $100 (average estimate) per evaluation Then 2007±: $100/year (average estimate) plus
X-rays of bilateral stumps (RM)	2002 through 2006 (age 18)	1 time/year, each leg, through 2006	2002–2006: Included in evaluation

Recommendation (by whom)	Year Initiated/Suspended	Frequency/Duration	Expected Cost
Orthopedist to monitor for orthopedic problems as client ages, i.e., back problems, pain related to altered gait, etc. (RM)	Beginning 2032 (age 45) to life expectancy	2032 and every 3 years (average) to life expectancy	Initial in 2032: $150 (average estimate) 1 time only + $79 for travel Follow-up visits beginning 2035: $100 (average estimate) + $79/travel every 3 years (average) to life expectancy
X-rays of lumbar spine with pelvis (RM)	Beginning 2032 (age 45) to life expectancy	2032 and every 3 years (average) to life expectancy	Lumbar spine with pelvis: $120 every 3 years to life expectancy (to be done at time of orthopedic visit)

Note 1: The client is expected to experience increased degenerative problems as a result of her injuries and will require follow-up beginning approximately 30 years postinjury related to sequelae associated with long-term bilateral lower-extremity prosthetic use as well as long-term manual wheelchair use.

Note 2: Need for x-rays (other than those outlined above) or other diagnostic or orthopedic studies is dependent on orthopedist evaluation and cannot be predicted at this time. See Potential Complications for related orthopedic complications.

Projected Evaluations — Nonphysician (Allied Health Evaluations)

Recommendation (by whom)	Year Initiated/Suspended	Frequency/Duration	Expected Cost
Physical therapy evaluation (RM)	2002–2006	Included in comprehensive amputee center of excellence evaluation; see also outpatient gait training/prosthesis training at time of each new prostheses	2002–2006: Included in cost of evaluation

Note: The physiatrist states physical therapy evaluations are not recommended (unless complications) and assumes the client receives an annual comprehensive evaluation through the summer of 2006, as well as qualified prostheses/gait training at time of each new prostheses.

Projected Evaluations — Nonphysician (Allied Health Evaluations) (Continued)

Recommendation (by whom)	Year Initiated/Suspended	Frequency/Duration	Expected Cost
Recreation therapy evaluation (RW)	2002 through high school	1 time/year through school system	$0; no cost for school-related activities if provided by school system under IDEA*

*IDEA refers to the federal Individuals with Disabilities Education Act, which provides services through the school system to students with disabilities.

Recommendation (by whom)	Year Initiated/Suspended	Frequency/Duration	Expected Cost
Wheelchair seating and positioning evaluation (RW)	2002	Every 2–3 years (average) through 2006 (age 18), then every 5 years (average) to life expectancy Consistent with wheelchair replacement	Included in cost of wheelchair Note: If the client changes wheelchair vendors, seating evaluation fees may incur
Adapted driving evaluation (RW)	2004 (16 years old)	1-time-only evaluation	$300 (estimate)

Note: The client is expected to be able to drive when she reaches driving age; however, a formal driving evaluation is recommended to assess her abilities and safety behind the wheel and to ensure her vehicle is appropriately modified according to her needs. See also Transportation.

OPTIONAL

Recommendation (by whom)	Year Initiated/Suspended	Frequency/Duration	Expected Cost
Occupational therapy home accessibility evaluation to also include ADL training and home management skills (RW)	2002	1 time only	$150–200 (estimate) for in-home evaluation by OT or other qualified specialist with report and recommendations Note: Equipment vendor to also accompany therapist to home to determine home needs at $0

Note: The client's current home is not fully accessible for her and does not appear to be reasonably modifiable. An in-home accessibility evaluation is recommended to enhance her safety and functional independence in her current home or to evaluate any potential new home to ensure appropriate modifications are made according to her needs.

Projected Therapeutic Modalities

Recommendation	Initiated/Suspended	Frequency/Duration	Expected Cost
Outpatient prostheses and gait training upon receipt of prosthetic devices at an amputee center of excellence (RM)	2002 to life expectancy	2002: 6–8 weeks following receipt of initial prostheses	Initial evaluation: $260 Training for 5 times/week for 6–8 weeks: $2700–7200 at $90–180/1-hour session. *Note:* The client likely will participate in more training during the 6- to 8-week period as she gets used to her legs; however, frequency cannot be determined and no additional cost included Also includes airfare at $614 each trip for 2 passengers (client + one caregiver), as well as 6–8 weeks of lodging at $2478–4424 total for 2 at $59–79/night
		2006 to life expectancy: 4 sessions at time of each new prosthesis	2006+: $400–480 (estimate) for 4 sessions at $100–120/session (estimate) at time of prostheses replacement Includes transportation to Charlotte at $154/trip + 1 overnight stay at $85–95 (estimate) (for client + caregiver) at time of each prostheses training

Projected Therapeutic Modalities (Continued)

Recommendation	Initiated/Suspended	Frequency/Duration	Expected Cost
Note 1: Initial 6 to 8 weeks of prostheses/gait training is expected to be provided by the amputee specialists, as well as any subsequent training needed at time of the yearly comprehensive evaluations through the client's age 18. Training after the client's age 18 is expected to be provided in Charlotte by qualified and trained therapists experienced in amputee rehabilitation.			
Note 2: It is expected that the client also will receive minimal prosthetic training by the prosthetist at the time of fittings, adjustments, and prostheses replacement. Cost included in cost of prostheses.			
Prosthetist follow-up (RM)	2002 to life expectancy	Once receive temporary prostheses, expect on average every 2 weeks for 3 months, then 1 time/month (minimum) until time of definitive prostheses; once in definitive prostheses, expect on average every 6 months (minimum) and as needed to life expectancy	Cost for initial evaluation and measuring expected to be included in cost of prostheses Cost for adjustments and follow-up every 6 months to life included in yearly maintenance
Recreation therapy for recreation and leisure activities (RW)	2002 through high school (2006)	As needed and determined by school system	$0; provided by school system under IDEA

Mobility Needs, Accessories, and Maintenance

Recommendation (by whom)	Year Purchased	Replacement	Expected Cost
Quickie LXI folding lightweight transportable manual wheelchair (RM) Motorized scooter for mobility assistance (RM)	2002 (current need) to life expectancy	Option 1, Left BK Every 2–3 years (average) through 2006 (age 18, expected end of skeletal growth), then every 5 years (average) as adult	Option 1, Left BK Prosthesis $3500–4000 with cushion and seat belt every 2–3 years (average) through 2006, then every 5 years (average) to life expectancy

	Option 2, Left Syme's		Option 2, Left Syme's Amputee
	Every 2–3 years (average) through 2006, then every 3–4 years (average) as adult		$3500–4000 with cushion and seat belt every 2–3 years (average) through 2006, then every 3–4 years (average) as adult to life expectancy
	Every 5–7 years (average) to life expectancy		2047: $3000–3100 (average) every 5–7 years to life expectancy
	2047 (beginning age 60) to life expectancy		

Note 1: A manual wheelchair is recommended throughout the client's lifetime to provide her with a means of mobility during times when her prostheses are in for repairs/maintenance or for other complications such as skin breakdown, fatigue, or other times when she is unable to use the prostheses.

Note 2: If the client remains a left leg Syme's amputee and does not have the left leg revised to a below-knee (BK) amputation (see Option 1), she is expected to rely more on the wheelchair for mobility assistance and ambulate using the prostheses for short distances only. For purposes of future care planning, both options are shown above with regard to wheelchair replacement schedules, presuming the chair will be used more if she remains a Syme's amputee and less if her leg is revised to a BK amputation.

Note 3: A motorized scooter is recommended beginning at age 60 due to expected degenerative changes in the client's shoulders and back and an increased need for motorized mobility assistance. After age 60, a manual wheelchair is expected to be used as backup mobility assistance.

Shower wheelchair for bathing (RM)	2002 (assumes wheelchair accessible home with roll-in shower, see pg. 12)	Every 5 years (average) to life expectancy	$350 (average) every 5 years (average) to life expectancy
Sports wheelchair to participate in wheelchair athletics, i.e., basketball, etc. (RM, RW)	2002	Every 5 years (average) to 2017 (age 30)	Sports chair: $2200 (estimate)

Note: The client reportedly was involved in basketball and other sports activities prior to the injury and continues to express an interest in participating in wheelchair athletics as a recreational outlet.

Mobility Needs, Accessories, and Maintenance

Recommendation (by whom)	Year Purchased	Replacement	Expected Cost
Jay Combi wheelchair cushion (HK)	2002 to life expectancy	1 time every 2 years (average) to life expectancy	$450 every 2 years (average) to life expectancy
Manual wheelchair maintenance (RW)	2003 to life expectancy	1 time/year after 1-year warranty expires (does not apply to years new chair is purchased + 1-year warranty after each purchase)	Option 1, Left BK $100/year (average) to 2006, then $100 every other year to life expectancy (includes tires, casters, labor, and preventative maintenance) Option 2, Left Syme's $100/year (average) to life expectancy
Shower chair maintenance (RW)	2003 to life expectancy	1 time/year after 1-year warranty expires	$20–40/year (average) to life expectancy
Motor scooter maintenance (RW)	2048	1 time/year after 1-year warranty expires	$320/year (includes 2 gel batteries); does not include tire replacement, which is unknown and depends on use

Orthotics/Prosthetics

Recommendation (by whom)	Year Purchased	Replacement	Expected Cost
Right Leg: Right above-knee (AK) prosthesis with C leg and Genesis 2 multiaxial foot (RM)	2002 2002 (presumes left leg amputation revised to below knee)	Right Leg: AK temporary/preparatory prosthesis for 6–12 months, then AK definitive prosthesis estimated in 2003	Right Leg: AK temporary prosthesis: $17,551 for 6–12 months Then 2003: AK definitive prosthesis with C leg: $43,351

Left Leg:
Option 1 – Preferred
Left below-knee (BK) prosthesis with Genesis 2 multiaxial foot (RM)

AK socket: 1 time/year (average) to 2005 (age 18), then replace at time of AK prosthesis replacement; if Option 1, left BK, replace AK every 3 years (average) to 2047 (age 60), then every 5 years (average) to life expectancy; if Option 2, Syme's, replace every 5–6 years (average) to 2047, then every 7–8 years (average) to life expectancy

AK socket: $11,204 1 time/year (average) to 2005, then at time of AK prosthesis replacement
Note: See replacement column for AK replacement schedule if Option 1 or Option 2

Left Leg:
Option 1 – Preferred
BK temporary prosthesis for 3–6 months, then definitive prosthesis in 2002–03 and every 3 years (average) to 2047 (age 60), then every 5 years (average) to life expectancy
BK socket: 1 time/year (average) through 2006 (age 18), then replace at time of prosthesis replacement

Left Leg:
Option 1 – Preferred
BK temporary prosthesis: $7828 for 3–6 months
Then
BK definitive prosthesis at $14,555
BK Sockets: $6884 (includes 2 gel locking liners) 1 time/year (average) through 2006, then at time of BK prosthesis replacement

Option 2
Left flex Syme's prosthesis (RM)

Syme's prosthesis: Every 3 years (average) to 2047 (age 60), then every 5 years (average) to life expectancy

Initial Syme's prosthesis for 3–6 months at $8220 (temporary prosthesis generally not appropriate for this level), then replacement Syme's (reusing flex foot): $5,369 for 2 years (average,) then replace entire prosthesis at $8220 and every 3 years (average) to 2047, then every 5 years (average) to life expectancy

2002 (presumes left leg remains a Syme's ankle disarticulation amputation)

Orthotics/Prosthetics (Continued)

Recommendation (by whom)	Year Purchased	Replacement	Expected Cost

Note 1: The physiatrist recommends, for best outcomes for the client, her left leg amputation probably should be revised to a below-knee amputation. For purposes of future care planning, both options — Option 1, left BK amputation (preferred), and Option 2, continuing the left Syme's amputation — are included.

Note 2: To provide a realistic reference point, expected costs for prostheses included in the plan are based on reasonable negotiated rates for catastrophic workers' compensation cases with similar kinds of prosthetic needs.

Note 3: There are a variety of other prostheses that are available and have more specifically designed legs and feet that can be used for specific athletic activities; however, the client's skin grafts on lower extremities probably will not tolerate significant athletic activities, and sport prostheses are not recommended at this time. Sport prostheses could be an option in the future depending on outcomes from skin grafts, left BK amputation, integrity of skin on stumps, and specific activity or sport; however, cost for sport prostheses is not included in plan totals. As a more likely alternative, see sports wheelchairs. Additionally, the client may choose to use swimming prostheses in the future; however, individuals with bilateral amputations at the client's level commonly choose to swim without prostheses and no cost for swimming prostheses is included in plan totals.

Note 4: After her prostheses are replaced the first time, it is expected she will use the old prostheses as backup to her primary ones and recycle each prosthesis at the time of replacement into a backup prosthesis.

Note 5: During periods of rapid growth or significant weight gain or loss, the client may need her prosthetic sockets replaced more frequently. However, frequency and occurrence cannot be predicted and no cost for additional sockets is included in plan totals. See also Potential Complications.

| Stump shrinkers to reduce swelling and preserve size and shape of stump when not wearing prostheses (DZ) | 2002 | Four shrinkers for each leg for the first year (minimum), then unknown depending on condition of stumps | Right AK shrinker: $280 for minimum of 1 year at $70/each, then unknown
Option 1 — Preferred
Left BK shrinker: $200 for minimum of 1 year at $50/each, then unknown
Option 2
Left Syme's shrinker: $200 for minimum of 1 year at $50/each, then unknown |

Gel liners (RM)	2003	Every 6–12 months (average) through 2006 (age 18), then 1 time/year (average) depending on wear and tear and care and treatment	AK: $2338 for 2 liners every 6–12 months (average) through 2006, then 1 time/year (average) to life expectancy Option 1 — Preferred Left BK: $2922 for 2 liners (includes 1 liner with locking pins) at time of socket and prosthetic replacement and $2338 every 6–12 months (average) through 2006 on years (average) through 2006 when socket or prosthesis not replaced, then 1 time/year (average) to life expectancy Option 2 Left Syme's: $2338 for 2 liners every 6–12 months (average) through 2006, then 1 time/year (average) to life expectancy

Note: Given the extent of the client's injuries and the integrity of her skin, gel liners are expected to be needed throughout her lifetime to protect and preserve her skin and provide reduction in sheer forces when using the prostheses.

Prostheses maintenance to include general maintenance and repairs (does not include gel liners) (RM, DZ)	2003 to life expectancy	Yearly maintenance (does not include years in which new prostheses are purchased; see prostheses replacement schedules)	5% cost of *each* prosthesis per year (Note: Does not apply to years in which prostheses are replaced; however, does apply to years in which only sockets are replaced)

Supply Needs

Supply needs and costs change from time to time and are representative of the client's current need.

Recommendation (by whom)	Purpose	Cost per Unit	Cost per Year
Allowance for miscellaneous supplies such as wound dressings, sterile gauze pads, 4 × 4s, Kerlix rolls, wood application sticks, ointments, saline solution, Eucerine lotion, Vitamin E or other lubricating skin lotions or creams, etc. (RM, RW)	Stump skin care and wound care	Yearly allowance	2002: $150–200 (estimate) during time of active wound healing 2003 to life expectancy: $50/year (average estimate) *Note:* If complications or chronic nonhealing wounds, expected cost of yearly supplies to be more in the $150 (average) range depending on extent of wounds; however, increased cost of supplies not included in plan totals

Transportation

Recommendation (by whom)	Year Purchased	Replacement	Expected Cost
Vehicle hand controls (RM, RW)	2003 (age 16)	Every 5–7 years (average) at time of vehicle replacement	Basic hand controls: $650 (estimate)

Note 1: Although the client is expected to be able to drive when she reaches driving age, a formal driving evaluation is recommended to evaluate her driving potential and need for vehicle modifications. If adapted driver training is required to learn to use the vehicle modifications, cost is $500 for estimated five sessions at $100/session.

Note 2: Hand controls are recommended as backup on days when client is unable to use leg prostheses for driving.

Recommendation (by whom)	Year Initiated	Frequency	Expected Cost
Vehicle with automatic transmission and power package, including power brakes, power steering, and power windows (RM, RW)	2003 (age 16) to life expectancy	Every 5–7 years (average) at time of vehicle replacement	$0–1500 depending on make and model of vehicle
Cellular telephone to be used by client for emergency communication (RW)	2002 to life expectancy	Every 5–7 years (estimate)	$0; no cost included as this is considered a common item used by general population
Braun Scooter Lift Jr. with spring assist (RM)	2048 (age 60) to life expectancy	Every 5–7 years (average)	Beginning 2047: $935 (approximate) and every 5–7 years to life expectancy
Maintenance		1 time/year after warranty expires	$100/year (average)
Installation		Every 5–7 years (average)	$110 each installation

Note 1: The scooter lift may be reinstalled into a new vehicle if it has been well maintained and presents no safety issues.

Note 2: The scooter lift assumes the client will have a vehicle of the size and type to support the lift and effectively transport the scooter. As an alternative to scooter lift on vehicle, the client may need an accessible wheelchair van with lift for scooter, especially on days when she is unable to wear her prostheses and unable to independently put her scooter in the car. However, cost for accessible van is not included in plan totals.

Future Medical Care, Surgical Intervention, Aggressive Treatment

Recommendation (by whom)	Year Initiated	Frequency	Expected Cost
Full-thickness skin graft over left knee (RM)	2002	1 time only, if successful	$30,000–35,000 (approximate); includes surgeon, anesthesia, OR, hospital stay, etc.

Note 1: Skin graft to left knee is indicated for both Option 1, left BK amputation, and Option 2, left Syme's amputation.

Note 2: The client's plastic surgeon states she expects the client will require multiple debridements and skin grafts to her right and left legs; however, she is unable to project the number of surgeries or the age or time of expected surgeries, and costs are not included in future care plan. It is presumed that the client will receive quality care by the amputee center of excellence and will have optimal outcomes such that the potential need for debridements and skin grafts will be reduced.

Future Medical Care, Surgical Intervention, Aggressive Treatment (Continued)

Recommendation (by whom)	Year Initiated	Frequency	Expected Cost
Right AK stump and left stump revision due to bony overgrowth (RM)		Expect 1 time for each leg prior to 2006 (age 18)	Bilateral stump revisions: $27,715–32,910 (includes surgeon, OR time, anesthesia, 2-day hospitalization, and other associated charges related to hospital stay)
Option 1 — Preferred Left leg revised to below-knee (BK) amputation (RM) Option 2 Full-thickness skin graft over left Syme's stump to enhance weight bearing (RM)		1-time-only BK amputation 1 time only, if successful	Option 1 — Preferred $18,000 (approximate); includes surgeon, anesthesia, OR, hospital stay, etc. Option 2 $30,000–35,000 (approximate); includes surgeon, anesthesia, OR, hospital stay, etc.

Note: The client is expected to have an approximate 2-month recovery and rehabilitation if Option 1, left BK amputation.

Potential Complications

Note: Potential complications are included for information only. No frequency or duration of complications is available. No costs are included in the plan.

■ Chronic skin breakdown/wounds on stumps and at site of anticipated prostheses that require additional skin grafts, skin flaps, or other surgery to close. The client's plastic surgeon states that she expects the client to have recurrent skin breakdown at amputation sites on both legs.

■ Hypertrophic scarring that may require surgery to correct.

■ Increased phantom pain or phantom sensations that require medication or other treatment (neuromuscular stimulation, etc.) to treat.

- Orthopedic or neurologic problems, including poor posture due to altered gait, back problems and back pain related to abnormal gait, osteoarthritis in left knee or knee contractures, neuromas, and heterotopic ossification or bony overgrowth or bone spurs on stumps that are more significant than expected and that require additional surgery to correct. The records document heterotopic ossification already in the client's right leg/stump that may require surgery to remove. If surgery, expect approximate 4-day inpatient hospitalization.

- Significant weight gain or loss that affects prostheses fit and requires more adjustments than expected, including more frequent replacement of sockets and prostheses than expected.

- Vascular compromise or other vascular issues that require treatment, including medication.

- Increased risk for falls and reinjury due to impaired mobility skills and increased fatigue associated with bilateral lower-extremity prosthetic use. The client also may need orthopedic equipment such as a cane for stability as she ages or crutches if able to wear only one prosthesis.

- Poor psychological adjustment to disability and functional limitations.

- Failure to maintain prostheses or perform proper skin care, which results in increased maintenance, replacements, or increased stump skin problems. Stability of prostheses also may affect client's functional abilities.

- Excessive sweating that affects fit of prostheses and durability of liners.

- Need for prescribed medication related to amputations. As an example, the client was prescribed Neurontin, 600 mg, 3 times/day for phantom pain/sensations; Zoloft, 50 mg, 1 time/day for depression; and APAP/Codeine, 300 mg, as needed for pain upon discharge from the hospital in October 2001.

REFERENCES

Davis, R. (1993). Phantom sensation, phantom pain and stump pain. *Archives of Physical Medicine Rehabilitation*, 74, 79–84.

Esquenazi, A., Leonard, J.A., & Meier, R.H. (1989). Prosthetics. *Archives of Physical Medicine Rehabilitation*, 70 (Suppl.), 207.

Esquenazi, A. & Torres, M.M. (1991). In L.W. Friedmann, Ed., *Physical Medicine and Rehabilitation Clinics of North America*. Philadelphia: W.B. Saunders. pp. 299–309.

Friedmann, L. (1981). Amputation. In W. Stolov & M. Clowers, Eds., *Handbook of Severe Disability*. Washington, DC: U.S. Department of Education, Rehabilitation Services Administration.

Leonard, J.A. and Meier, R.H. (1993). Upper and lower extremity prosthetics. In J.A. DeLisa, Ed., *Rehabilitation Medicine: Principles and Practices*. Philadelphia: J.B. Lippincott. pp. 669–696.

Meier, R.H. (1994). Upper limb amputee rehabilitation. In A. Esquenazi, Ed., *Prosthetics: State of the Art Reviews*. Philadelphia: Hanley & Belfus.

Meier, R.H. (1995). Rehabilitation of the person with an amputation. In R.B. Rutherford, Ed., *Vascular Surgery*. Philadelphia: W.B. Saunders. pp. 2227–2248.

Meier, R.H. (1996). Upper limb prosthetics: design, prescription and application. In C.A. Peimer, Ed., *Surgery of the Hand and Upper Extremity*. New York: McGraw-Hill. pp. 2453–2468.

Meier, R. & Atkins, D. (2004). *Functional Restoration of Adults and Children with Upper Extremity Amputation*. New York: Demos Publishing.

Moore, W.S. & Malone, J.M., Eds. (1989). *Lower Extremity Amputation*. Philadelphia: W.B. Saunders.

Schoppen, T., Boonstra, A., Groothoff, J., Vries, J., Goeken, L., & Eisma, W. (2001). Employment status, job characteristics, and work-related health experience of people with a lower limb amputation in the Netherlands. *Archives of Physical Medicine Rehabilitation*, 82, 239–245.

Sears, H.H. (1991). Approaches to prescription of body-powered and myoelectric prosthetics. In L.W. Friedmann, Ed., *Prosthetics: Physical Medicine and Rehabilitation Clinics of North America*. Philadelphia: W.B. Saunders. pp. 361–371.

Sherman, R.A., Sherman, C.J., & Gail, N.A. (1980). Survey of current phantom limb treatment in the United States. *Pain*, 8, 85–99.

Weed, R. (2001). Contemporary life care planning for persons with amputation. *Orthotics and Prosthetics Business News*, 10, 20–22, 24, 26, 28, 30.

Weed, R. & Atkins, D. (2004). Return to work issues for persons with upper extremity amputation. In D. Atkins and R. Meier, Eds., *Functional Restoration of Adults and Children with Upper Extremity Amputation*. New York: Demos Publishing.

Weed, R. & Field, T. (2001). *The Rehabilitation Consultant's Handbook*, 3rd ed. Athens, GA: E & F Vocational Services.

Weed, R., Kirkscey, M., Mullins, G., Dunlap, K., & Taylor, C. (1997). Return to work rates in case of amputation. *Journal of Rehabilitation Outcomes Measurement*, 1, 35–39.

Weed, R. & Sluis, A. (1990). *Life Care Plans for the Amputee: A Step by Step Guide*. Boca Raton, FL: CRC Press.

13

LIFE CARE PLANNING FOR ACQUIRED BRAIN INJURY

David Ripley and Roger O. Weed

INTRODUCTION

Acquired brain injury (ABI) is one of the leading causes of neurological impairment in the U.S. and accounts for over 1 million visits to the emergency room each year (Centers for Disease Control, 1999; Kraus et al., 1984). ABI is the leading cause of neurological impairment for individuals between the ages of 16 and 30 years of age. Acquired brain injury technically includes brain damage as a result of cerebrovascular disease (or stroke), but for the purposes of this chapter, the focus will predominately be on brain injury of traumatic etiology.

Creating an appropriate life care plan for an individual with acquired brain injury can be a formidable challenge. The brain, as the neurological control center for the body, affects almost every aspect of physiological functioning. Damage to the brain therefore can affect almost every function (Kaufman et al., 1993; Kraus, 1991; Macciocchi et al., 1993; Piek, 1995; Rosenthal, 1990). Practitioners in the field of brain injury rehabilitation must be prepared to deal with problems in essentially every organ system in the body, as well as a variety of cognitive and behavioral problems (Uomoto & Brockway, 1992; Wood, 1987).

Because the majority of people who sustain a brain injury are young at the time of their injury, in the time of their lives when career goals are being set and established, it is difficult in many circumstances to estimate lifetime earning capacity and needs (Corthell, 1993; Dikmen et al., 1994; Goodall et al., 1994; Horn & Zasler, 1996; Ip et al., 1995; Stapleton et al., 1989; Wehman et al., 1988; Zasler, 1997). Additionally, as acute trauma management and medical and rehabilitation care improves, the survival of patients with these injuries continues to increase (High et al., 1996; Kreutzer et al., 2001). The result is that many more people survive with increasingly complex medical and rehabilitation problems. Due to the variability in recovery following traumatic brain injury, life care planners are often forced to develop, in a sense, multiple care plans to accommodate the different potential outcomes that may occur in a single individual.

0-8493-1511-5/04/$0.00+$1.50
© 2004 by CRC Press LLC

DEFINITIONS

Due to a variety of descriptions used by medical professionals throughout the years, and the problems this caused with communication, the American Congress of Rehabilitation Medicine (ACRM) in 1993 proposed a uniform nomenclature for brain injury. The following definitions are part of the ACRM's recommendations (American Congress of Rehabilitation Medicine Head Injury Interdisciplinary Special Interest Group, 1993):

> *Acquired brain injury* — Damage to the brain that occurs after the brain has developed; may be due to trauma, surgery, intracranial bleeding, ischemia, or tumor.
>
> *Traumatic brain injury* — Damage to the brain caused by trauma. One form of acquired brain injury.
>
> *Coma* — Specific diagnostic term indicating lack of arousability, including loss of sleep–wake cycles on EEG, and lack of meaningful interaction/response to the environment.
>
> *Vegetative state* — Patients who have no meaningful response to the environment after their eyes are open.
>
> *Persistent vegetative state* — A vegetative state that persists longer than 3 months, or 1 year if due to trauma.
>
> *Locked-in syndrome* — A condition in which patients are awake, capable of communication, aware of their environment, but unable to move or speak.
>
> *Minimally responsive* — Patients who are no longer comatose or vegetative but remain severely disabled (used for patients who are demonstrating inconsistent responses to stimuli yet have some meaningful interaction with the environment).

EPIDEMIOLOGY

It is estimated that approximately 3 million traumatic brain injuries occur in the U.S. each year. In 1996, there were an estimated 600,000 hospitalizations for a primary diagnosis of TBI. The U.S. Centers for Disease Control and Prevention (CDC, 1999) have determined that the annual combined total incidence for TBI is estimated to be 102 cases per 100,000 people. It is useful to break down the incidence of TBI based on injury severity. Various methods of rating injury severity are used and will be discussed later in the chapter. However, the incidence when breaking down by injury severity is 14 per 100,000 for severe TBI, 15 per 100,000 for moderate TBI, and 131 per 100,000 for mild TBI.

There are several risk factors associated with a higher risk for TBI. Males are more than twice as likely than females to sustain a TBI. Additionally, patients with brain injury tend to be from lower socioeconomic groups, have a history of substance use or abuse, and have a history of engaging in risky behaviors. Additionally, brain injured patients are likely to live in an urban area. Alcohol is frequently involved in accidents resulting in brain injury and is considered to be the most common preventable cause of TBI. Education about safety, such as wearing seat belts and bicycle helmets, and not driving while intoxicated seems to have contributed to a slight decline in the incidence of hospitalization following TBI in recent years.

Brain injury generally follows a *bimodal* distribution with respect to age. The largest peak is in late adolescence and early adulthood, when individuals are more likely to engage in high-risk activities. The later peak begins for individuals older than age 65, when falls become more common. Because the largest peak occurrence is in the period of time from late adolescence to early adulthood, life care planning for this group is particularly challenging, as lifelong concerns must be taken into consideration, including aging and aging issues, education, vocational rehabilitation, and community reintegration. Age may also be correlated with outcomes, as older individuals (over age 65) tend to have a slower recovery following brain injury.

COSTS

The costs associated with treating traumatic brain injury are estimated to be $48.3 billion annually. Costs associated with hospitalization are estimated to be $31.7 billion. Fatal brain injuries cost the U.S. $16.6 billion each year (CDC, 1999; Cope & O'Lear, 1993).

Review of model systems data (Traumatic Brain Injury Model Systems, 1993) reveals that the average cost for inpatient treatment of a case of severe TBI was approximately $120,000. This estimate was based on the cost for acute hospital care and acute inpatient rehabilitation and does not include rehabilitation efforts after the patient has left the hospital; it also does not include physicians' fees.

ETIOLOGY

ABI of nontraumatic etiology may include cerebrovascular accidents (stroke), bleeding within the brain, infections, tumors, or surgery. A cerebrovascular accident (CVA), commonly called a stroke or a brain attack, occurs as a result of *thromboembolic* phenomenon, usually as a result of vascular disease. A *thrombus* is a clot of fibrin, platelets, and blood cells that can form on the inner lining of blood vessels. This thrombus may *embolize*, or travel from the location where it was formed to another area, where it can become lodged, blocking blood flow. Nontraumatic ABIs may also occur as a result of lack of oxygen getting to the brain due to problems with the lungs, heart, or bleeding. Some ABIs are due to hemorrhage within the brain due to vascular disease or aneurysms that have ruptured. Another significant cause of ABI is due to tumors, both benign and malignant. Additionally, damage to the brain may occur as sequelae from intracranial surgery.

Traumatic brain injuries can occur as a result of trauma from a number of causes. The most frequent cause is from motor vehicle accidents, accounting for almost two thirds of all injuries. The second most frequent cause is falls. Falls are the most common cause of TBI in the elderly and very young. Assaults are the third most common cause overall, and in urban areas, assaults may actually be a greater cause than falls. Other less common causes of TBI include sports and recreational injuries, work-related injuries, and miscellaneous injuries, such as being struck by falling objects. At least half of all traumatic brain injuries involve alcohol consumption in one way or another, and alcohol represents the single most preventable cause of TBI in the U.S. (Corrigan, 1995).

ANATOMY OF THE BRAIN

Coverings

The brain is protected by a number of layers of differing tissue. A layer of skin is the outermost covering, followed by a layer of connective tissue and muscle. The bony calvarium, or skull, provides the greatest protection of the brain. Fractures of the skull are present in a number of brain injuries and are generally associated with a more severe injury. Under the skull are three distinct layers that provide the direct cover of the brain. The outermost, thickest layer is called the *dura mater* and is attached to the inner layer of the skull in many places. Underneath this layer is the *arachnoid mater*, which derives its name from its similarity in appearance to a spider web. The arachnoid mater follows the surface of the brain closely, but does not follow the surface down deep into the crevices, or *sulci*, on the surface of the brain. The innermost layer of covering is called the *pia mater*, and this layer does follow the brain into the sulci.

Cerebral Cortex

The outer surface of the brain is called the cerebral cortex. There are many convolutions of the surface of the brain, which serve to increase the surface area of the outside of the brain. The bulges are referred to as *gyri*, and the involutions are referred to as *sulci*, as mentioned above. The origination of neural messages to the rest of the body, for the most part, occurs on the surface of the brain. In most cases, seizure activity also originates at the level of the cortex.

The cortex of the brain is divided into lobes (see Figure 13.1) that represent areas of specific functioning. The *frontal lobe* is responsible for higher cognitive processes, such as planning, organization, and problem solving. It is also the part of the brain responsible for control of impulsive and instinctual behavior (Grafman et al., 1996). Lastly, the origination of motor activity occurs in the most posterior portion of the frontal lobe.

The *parietal lobe* is predominately concerned with the registration of sensory information, particularly the ability to sense when something has touched the skin. Other types of sensory information are processed in this area, and the parietal lobe gives us the ability to orient objects in space, follow a map, and appreciate music. Mathematical ability is also predominately located in the parietal lobe. Individuals with damage to the parietal lobe will often exhibit *neglect*, or lack of awareness of part of their own body.

The *temporal lobes* are located on the side of the brain. These lobes are critical in the registration of auditory information and are critical in the understanding and formulation of language. The inner portion of the temporal lobes also contains structures that are responsible for memory formation, as well as the origination of emotions. Individuals with seizures most frequently have damage to their temporal lobe.

The *occipital lobe* is located on the most posterior aspect of the brain. Visual information is registered and processed here. Individuals with damage to this area will have *cortical blindness*, which is an inability to see because of failure of the brain to recognize the neural signals sent from the eyes.

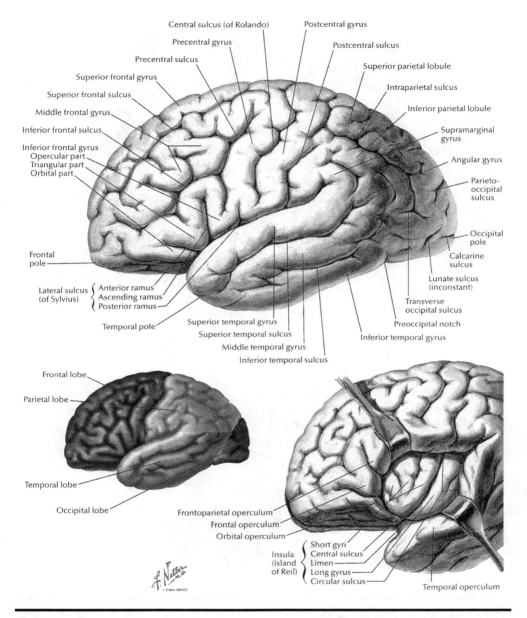

Figure 13.1 Cerebrum, lateral views. (From Netter, F.H., *Atlas of Human Anatomy*, 2nd ed., Icon Learning Systems, 1997. With permission.)

Midbrain

The midbrain (Figure 13.2) contains a number of structures whose predominate activities are to receive signals transmitted from other parts of the brain or from elsewhere in the body, and to modify the signal before transmitting it on to where it ultimately will act. Structures within the midbrain help to control movement, interpret sensory information, and also help with such activities as controlling our

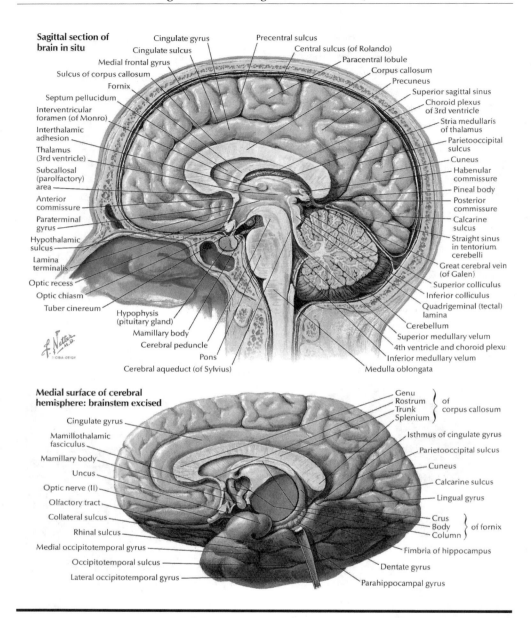

Figure 13.2 Cerebrum, medial views. (From Netter, F.H., *Atlas of Human Anatomy*, 2nd ed., Icon Learning Systems, 1997. With permission.)

level of consciousness. Patients who are comatose or who are in a persistent vegetative state have impaired functioning in the midbrain.

Brainstem

The brainstem (Figure 13.2) is the most inferior portion of the brain and is not always considered a part of the brain at all. However, this part of the brain is critical for basic life-sustaining functions, as it is responsible for regulating breathing and heart rates. Most of the cranial nerves exit here, so the brainstem is intimately involved in the transmission and reception of sensory and motor information of the head, such as tongue movement, facial movement, and sensation. Because all sensory and motor information to and from the body and brain must travel through the brainstem, even a very small area of damage to the brainstem can have devastating effects on the patient.

Cerebellum

The cerebellum is an area of the brain that facilitates coordinated motor movements. There are extensive neural pathways between the cerebellum and other areas of the brain concerned with motor movement. Individuals with damage to the cerebellum exhibit *ataxia*, or lack of control of smooth, coordinated movements. Interestingly, patients with ataxia often have no problems with strength and often have the muscle strength to carry out any activity you ask. However, they lack an ability to control their limbs' movements, such that it is often difficult or impossible for them to perform basic activities like picking up a glass or walking.

BRAIN INJURY CLASSIFICATION

Brain injuries can be classified by a number of methods (Marshall et al., 1992; Teasdale et al., 1992). Acquired brain injuries are generally classified as traumatic, anoxic/hypoxic, vascular, or other. Anoxic or hypoxic brain injuries occur when areas of the brain do not receive enough oxygen. This is frequently the cause of secondary injury after a traumatic injury, but may also occur independently of trauma. The most frequent cause of hypoxic brain injury is secondary to myocardial infarction or heart failure. During resuscitative efforts for a heart attack, the brain may be deprived of oxygen for several minutes. Vascular brain injuries, commonly called strokes, most commonly occur as a result of thromboembolic phenomena. However, other types of vascular brain injuries include aneurysms, arteriovenous malformation, and spontaneous intracranial hemorrhages. Finally, damage to the brain may occur as a result of viral or bacterial infections, metabolic derangements, or tumors.

Traumatic brain injuries, the broadest category of acquired brain injury, may be further subdivided a number of ways. One of the most basic methods of subcategorization is to divide them between *open* or *closed*. Open injuries are those injuries in which there is disruption of the scalp and skull, creating the possibility that the brain may be contaminated by material from the outside environment. Penetrating brain injuries are a type of open injury, in which a foreign body (such as a bullet) passes through the skull and outer coverings of the brain into the brain tissue itself. Closed head injuries are those in which the skull remains intact and the brain is not exposed to the outside environment, although significant damage may occur from the impact of the brain against the inner part of the skull, or from shearing of axons secondary to rotational forces.

Medical professionals caring for survivors of brain injury will also classify the injuries based on severity. The most common, widely utilized method of classification is the *Glasgow Coma Scale*, a method that classifies injuries based on clinical presentation (see Table 13.1). A medical professional will rate the patient's response in three separate areas: eye opening, motor response, and verbal

Table 13.1 The Glasgow Coma Scale

Patient's Response		Score
Eye opening		
	Spontaneously	4
	To voice	3
	To painful stimulus	2
	No eye opening	1
Motor		
	Follows commands	6
	Localizes to pain	5
	Withdraws from pain	4
	Flexor response	3
	Extensor response	2
	No motor response	1
Verbal		
	Oriented	5
	Converses but disoriented	4
	Inappropriate words	3
	Incomprehensible verbal utterances	2
	Not vocalizing	1
Total		
	(Sum of score from each of three areas)	(3–15)
	Injury classification:	
	Severe	3–8
	Moderate	9–12
	Mild	13–15

Note: A score with a T (e.g., 8T) means the patient was intubated for airway purposes and may be unable to fully respond.

response. The scale gives scores for each of the areas, which are summed to give a total score that can be used to rank the severity of the injury. Individuals who score 3 to 8 are said to have a severe injury, from 9 to 12 a moderate injury, and from 13 to 15 a mild injury. This information may be useful to predict the outcome and likelihood of long-term impairments (Clifton et al., 1993; Teasdale et al., 1998; Zafonte et al., 1996).

Other methods of rating injury severity are available but not as widely utilized. One alternative method of injury classification uses duration of *posttraumatic amnesia* as the best method of predicting outcomes following traumatic brain injury (Zafonte et al., 1997). Other methods of classification have tried to use radiographic findings, such as location and size of lesions on computed tomography (CT) or magnetic resonance imaging (MRI) (Teasdale et al., 1992). However, the correlation between radiographic findings and clinical presentation is often poor.

Another broad categorization of brain injury is to divide between *diffuse* and *focal* brain injuries. Diffuse injuries are generally due to shearing injury to the axons and generally occur deep within the brain, but across a broad area. Focal injuries occur with trauma to one specific region of the brain. These two types of injury may occur concomitantly. In general, focal injuries result in shorter periods of unconsciousness than diffuse injuries. Individuals with diffuse axonal injury (DAI) may have prolonged periods of unconsciousness from several days to weeks. In general, individuals with DAI have a prolonged recovery period compared to those with focal injuries (Berker, 1996; Bontke & Boake, 1991).

INITIAL TREATMENT

When a patient presents to the emergency room following TBI, the initial activities focus on life preservation. Often, concomitant injuries preclude addressing the brain injuries until later in the course of treatment. However, for those patients with severe injuries, the initial protocols involve rating the patient's level of arousal using the Glasgow Coma Scale, and some form of neuroradiographic imaging. At this time, CT scan remains the preferred type of image, due to the relatively faster speed with which images can be obtained and the fact that the types of damage that require emergency surgical intervention show much more readily on CT than MRI. However, there is some discussion about whether newer MRI techniques are more sensitive to intracranial injury (Horn & Zasler, 1996; Levin, 1992; Marshall et al., 1992; Piek, 1995; Rappaport et al., 1992).

Once the patient is stabilized, a more detailed assessment of the injury will occur, and further treatment may be recommended. For severe injuries, assessment by a neurosurgeon will usually occur. If there is evidence of specific, severe types of bleeding or increased pressure inside the head, surgery will be performed to evacuate the blood or alleviate the pressure. Sometimes an intracranial pressure monitor will be placed to accurately measure the pressure inside the brain.

Patients frequently require assistance with basic life functions. They may be placed on a mechanical ventilator to help them breathe. For prolonged management, sometimes a tracheotomy is performed to facilitate prolonged ventilator support. Additionally, for patients that are unconscious for prolonged periods of time, a feeding tube may be surgically introduced. Many patients with severe injury will also sustain injuries to other parts of their body as well. Surgical attention is often necessary during the early hospitalization to address fractures, damaged internal organs, internal bleeding, and other medical concerns.

INITIAL REHABILITATION CARE

While patients are still in the hospital, physical and occupational therapy referrals should occur to maintain joint range of motion and strength and to begin working on activities of self-care. The more severely injured patients should be referred to a rehabilitation facility following their acute hospitalization to begin the work of trying to be restored to their highest level of functioning. An assessment by a physiatrist, a medical doctor with training in physical medicine and rehabilitation (PM&R), is important during this phase, to facilitate the coordination of services and medical treatment to promote the best outcome following TBI (Almli & Finger, 1992; Berker, 1996; Bontke et al., 1993; Rosenthal, 1990; Semlyen et al., 1998).

Patients will often require further medical and rehabilitation care after medical concerns are stabilized (Cope, 1995). Several different levels of rehabilitation care are possible, and the best appropriate level of care depends on the acuity of the concomitant medical issues as well as the level of functioning of the patient (Evans, 1992; Hall & Cope, 1995; Mazmanian et al., 1993; Schmidt, 1997). Patients who cannot participate or tolerate several hours of therapy each day are most appropriately sent to a subacute rehabilitation program until they can tolerate a more aggressive therapy program. The most common level of rehabilitation care *is acute inpatient rehabilitation*, where patients receive 3 or more hours of therapy a day from several different therapy disciplines (i.e., physical therapy, occupational therapy, speech therapy), as well as ongoing medical attention (Malec & Basford, 1996). Once patients are medically stable and safe to be managed at home, therapy efforts transition to an outpatient setting. *Rehabilitation day programs* are therapy programs designed for individuals who still need therapy from several different disciplines in a team format, but no longer need as close medical attention as individuals in the acute inpatient setting. Some individuals will not need the interdisciplinary model of therapy, but only require therapy from one or two disciplines; then single-service outpatient therapy is indicated.

MEDICAL COMPLICATIONS

An adept life care planner who works with patients with brain injury must be aware of the potential medical complications that arise following brain injury and their impact on recovery, long-term function, and reintegration in the community. As the brain is the control center for all neurological processes in the body, damage to the brain can result in complications to almost every organ system. It is beyond the scope of this chapter to discuss all complications, although there are several common complications that we will describe (Bigler, 1989; Bloomfield, 1989; Bontke et al., 1993; Cifu et al., 1996a; Corrigan & Mysiw, 1988; Jore et al., 1993; Katz & Alexander, 1994; Kaufman et al., 1993; Kraus, 1984, 1991; Piek, 1995; Russell-Jones & Shorvon, 1989; Uomoto & Brockway, 1992).

Cranial Complications

Damage to the cranial nerves frequently occurs following TBI. As a result, patients may have difficulty with basic sensory functions, such as vision, hearing, smell, and taste. Facial paresis is frequently seen, with resultant difficulty in oromotor functions, as in speaking, chewing, and swallowing. The vestibular apparatus in the inner ear may be damaged, with resultant dizziness and balance disorders. This by itself may lead to problems with standing, walking, and transfers. It is very common for the olfactory nerve, the cranial nerve that controls sense of smell, to be damaged due to its structure, sometimes resulting in problems with eating and appetite. Fractures of the temporal bone, a part of the skull, can result in disruption of the cranial nerve associated with hearing, resulting in hearing impairment.

Many patients will have significant difficulty with vision problems following brain injury. Problems may range from inability to see objects in certain parts of the field of vision (sometimes referred to as a field cut) to blurry or double vision. This may be due to damage to the visual pathways within the brain, to damage to the nerves that control eye movements, or to damage to the eye itself. An evaluation by a neuro-ophthalmologist, a physician with training in neurological disorders that affect vision, is sometimes very helpful.

Endocrine Disorders

Endocrinology is the study of hormones and their function. Many hormones are regulated or secreted by the pituitary gland, a structure at the base of the brain. The pituitary can frequently be damaged during injury to the brain due to its location and structure. Common endocrine disorders following brain injury include syndrome of inappropriate diuretic hormone (SIADH), growth hormone deficiency, and irregularities of gonadal steroid production. Endocrinopathies are much more evident in women, because menstrual irregularities, as a result of altered pituitary–gonadal axis functioning, may persist for a year or longer after brain injury. This may also be a source of problems with infertility following injury.

Pulmonary Complications

Patients with severe traumatic brain injury frequently have respiratory failure as sequelae of the initial trauma. As a result, patients often require mechanical ventilation with a breathing machine (ventilator). Sometimes physicians must perform a tracheotomy, or a surgically created hole, to allow the patient to breath and to help prevent complications from prolonged ventilator management. Patients who are immobile for prolonged periods of time are at a higher risk for developing pneumonia. A pulmonary embolus, or a blood clot that lodges in the blood vessels of the lungs, is also a potential complication of prolonged immobility.

Cardiovascular Complications

Direct effects of brain damage on the heart are infrequent. However, immobility may lead to secondary complications over time. The most common is the formation of deep vein thromboses (DVTs) or blood clots in the veins. These clots can be potentially life threatening, as they can break free and lodge in the lung vessels causing a pulmonary embolus, as noted above. DVTs may also result in postphlebitic syndrome, or a painful condition of inflammation of the veins. Another complication that may lead to cardiovascular damage is called central storming, in which abnormally high levels of stimulant hormones, like adrenaline, can be released into the bloodstream, resulting in fevers, high heart rates, and high blood pressure. This phenomenon can result in heart damage to people who are susceptible.

Neurological Complications

Typical neurological problems include weakness, sensory deficits, and the above-mentioned cranial nerve problems. Individuals who have had a brain injury are at increased risk for developing seizures. Presence of a penetrating brain injury, skull fracture, or significant amounts of subarachnoid blood increases the risk for seizures. The upper motor neuron syndrome is possibly the most frequently seen neurological complication after all forms of brain injury, with its constellation of symptoms of weakness, spasticity, and increased reflexes. Spasticity is a velocity-dependent increase in motor tone that is seen frequently following damage to motor nerves in the central nervous system. This is such a profound problem after brain injury that it will be discussed in detail later in the chapter. Additionally, cognitive and behavioral problems are frequent neurological complications and will also be discussed in more detail later.

Gastrointestinal Complications

Patients frequently exhibit dysphagia, or impairment in the ability to swallow, as a result of weakness of the pharyngeal muscles. Often, patients require the placement of a feeding tube to prevent aspiration of food and to allow for feeding while the pharyngeal muscles remain weak. Additional gastrointestinal problems may include incontinence secondary to neurological impairment of the muscles controlling bowel function or alternatively from cognitive impairment. Constipation is frequently seen due to the same alteration in neurological functioning of the bladder, or often due to medications.

Genitourinary Complications

Neurological control of the bladder may be impaired, resulting in incontinence. However, most cases of incontinence following brain injury are a result of disinhibition instead of true neurological impairment. Patients with neurological impairment of bladder function may retain urine, which can lead to other problems, including frequent infections of the urinary tract, infection of the kidneys, and renal and bladder stones. Sexual dysfunction may also be an issue, although again, these problems are predominately behavioral as opposed to physiological impairment of sexual functioning. Frequently, sexual inhibition may occur as a result of altered body image due to impairments such as weakness, spasticity, or changes in physical appearance due to the injury, although more frequently, patients become sexually disinhibited due to damage to the areas of the brain responsible for control of impulsive behavior (Kreuter et al., 1998). Sexual functioning is an area that is frequently overlooked by medical professionals. In women, infertility may occur secondary to the endocrine changes mentioned earlier.

Musculoskeletal Complications

Musculoskeletal complications are very common following brain injury. Damage to the motor nerves in the brain may result in the upper motor neuron syndrome, which consists of the constellation of symptoms of spasticity, weakness, and hyperreflexia. Areas of weakness can vary depending on where the damage is located in the brain. Due to the brain's structural organization, damage on one side of the brain results in weakness on the opposite side of the body. Additionally, the weak side is frequently associated with spasticity. If unchecked, spasticity and immobility may ultimately result in *contractures*, which is tightening of the soft tissues and shortening of tendons around a joint resulting in a reduction in the patient's mobility. As a result of associated trauma, brain injured patients also frequently have associated fractures, peripheral nerve injuries, or soft tissue damage that can also make rehabilitation difficult. An interesting musculoskeletal problem that sometimes occurs following traumatic brain injury is *heterotopic ossification*, a condition in which bone is formed inappropriately in soft tissue

Table 13.2 Potential Cognitive Problems after TBI

Apathy	Impulsivity	Irritability	Aggression
Depression	Lability	Silliness	Denial
Forgetfulness	Memory problems	Bizarre ideation	Slovenliness
Anxiety	Sexual problems	Substance abuse	Spatial neglect
Anasognosia	Attention deficit	Fatigue	Social problems

areas. This problem, if left untreated, can result in ankylosis, or fusion of a joint, such that moving it is impossible. Extremity pain may also be a problem, due to inherent damage to the extremity or from neurological damage to the sensory pathways.

Cognitive Problems

Damage to the brain can result in any number of changes in mental function, including changes in personality. The specific changes, of course, depend on the specific structures damaged. Very commonly, brain injured patients experience problems with memory, attention, and arousal, as well as difficulties with language and communication (Seel et al., 1997). Even patients who experience a relatively good recovery will often have subtle cognitive deficits that make returning to work or living independently difficult. A list of potential cognitive problems after TBI can be found in Table 13.2 (Groswasser & Stern, 1998).

RECOVERY FROM TBI

Recovery from brain injury is a highly variable process. Severely injured patients recover *in general* along a set of stages, classified as the Rancho Los Amigos Scale of Cognitive Functioning (see Table 13.3). Patients do not always progress through each stage in a stepwise fashion; some patients may skip one or more stages. This scale has its greatest usefulness in communicating with other team members about the condition of the patient, although at times it is helpful for family members, particularly when patients are in an agitated state. Some families find it somewhat comforting to know that the agitated state is part of a normal recovery process following TBI.

Most sources indicate that full neurological recovery of the brain following a severe injury takes approximately 1 year. Although this is a good estimate for most patients, there are certainly exceptions, and some patients have demonstrated significant recovery even after 1 year. Researchers are learning more about the process of neuroplasticity and factors affecting better outcomes (Ginsberg et al., 1997; Pike & Hamm, 1997).

LONG-TERM IMPAIRMENTS

Impairments following brain injury may include almost any complication imaginable. However, there are certain impairments that occur with such regularity after TBI that they warrant special mention. These impairments are the main issues

Table 13.3   Rancho Los Amigos Scale of Cognitive Functioning—Revised

Stage	Name	Description
Level I	Unresponsive: total assistance	Complete absence of change in behavior when presented any stimulus.
Level II	Generalized response: total assistance	Generalized reflex response to painful stimuli; may increase or decrease activity in response to repeated auditory stimuli; responds to external stimuli with generalized physiological changes; gross body movement; responses may be significantly delayed.
Level III	Localized response: total assistance	Withdraws from painful stimuli; may turn away or toward auditory stimuli; may track object that passes across visual field or blink to visual threat. Responds inconsistently to simple commands; may respond to some people and not others.
Level IV	Agitated/aggressive: maximal assistance	Alert, in heightened state of activity. Purposeful attempts to remove tubes and restraints; may exhibit aggressive or flight behavior. Emotionally labile, unable to cooperate with rehabilitation efforts. Verbalizations are incoherent and inappropriate to activity or environment.
Level V	Confused-inappropriate: maximal assistance	Alert, not agitated, disoriented. Frequent brief periods of nonpurposeful sustained attention. Severely impaired memory. Unable to learn new information. May demonstrate inappropriate use of external objects. Able to converse on a social and automatic level for brief periods of time.
Level VI	Confused-appropriate: moderate assistance	Inconsistently oriented to person, time, and place. Able to attend to highly familiar tasks in nondistracting environment for prolonged periods of time. Able to use memory aid with assistance. Begins to show carryover for relearned familiar tasks. Verbal conversations are appropriate in familiar and structured situations.
Level VII	Automatic-appropriate: minimal assistance	Consistently oriented to person and place within highly familiar environments. Able to attend to highly familiar tasks in nondistracting environment for at least 30 minutes with minimal assistance to complete tasks. Minimal supervision for new learning. Shallow recall of personal activities. Superficial awareness of his/her condition but unaware of specific impairments and the limits they place on the ability to safely, accurately, and completely carry out household, work, and leisure ADLs.

(continued)

Table 13.3 (Continued)   Rancho Los Amigos Scale of Cognitive Functioning—Revised

Stage	Name	Description
Level VIII	Purposeful-appropriate: standby assistance	Consistently oriented to person, place, and time. Able to attend to and complete familiar tasks for 1 hour in distracting environment. Able to recall and integrate past and recent events. May be able to use memory aids with supervision; aware of impairments on a superficial level but needs assistance to undertake appropriate corrective action. May demonstrate low frustration tolerance, irritability, and become argumentative. May be able to recognize socially inappropriate behavior and take corrective action with assistance.
Level IX	Purposeful-appropriate: standby assistance on request	Able to independently shift back and forth between tasks and complete them accurately for at least 2 consecutive hours. Uses memory devices appropriately when reminded; may be able to initiate and carry out steps in familiar household, work, and leisure tasks with assistance when requested. Aware of and acknowledges impairments and disabilities when they interfere with task completion and takes appropriate corrective action with supervision when requested. May continue to have low frustration tolerance, irritability, and depression, but able to monitor social interaction more appropriately with only standby assistance. May be able to think about consequences of actions or decisions when requested.
Level X	Purposeful-appropriate: modified independent	Able to handle multiple tasks simultaneously in all environments but may require periodic breaks. Able to independently procure, create, and maintain own assistive memory devices. Independently initiates and carries out self-care, household, community, work, and leisure tasks, but may require more time or compensatory strategies to complete them. Able to independently think about the consequences of decisions or actions but may require more than the usual amount of time or compensatory strategies to select the appropriate decision or action. Social interactions are fairly consistently appropriate.

that cause long-term problems after brain injury. Any life care plan for a patient who is traumatically severely injured should be sure to address these particular issues.

Weakness — Damage to the motor cortex or motor pathways may lead to weakness. Severe enough damage will result in paralysis. Weakness is usually the biggest factor affecting a person's ability to perform activities of self-care, such as dressing, grooming, and feeding. It may also impair an individual's ability to walk and move about and, in extreme cases, may lead to the necessity of assistance with transfers.

Spasticity — Spasticity, as mentioned earlier in the chapter, often remains a huge obstacle to independence after a brain injury. Spasticity is often associated with weakness and further complicates the patient's ability to move and perform activities of self-care. Furthermore, severe spasticity places the patient at risk for a number of other complications, such as contractures and skin breakdown. Much of the medical treatment following traumatic brain injury centers around the prevention and treatment of spasticity. A number of medical interventions in the treatment of spasticity have become available in recent years. Aside from oral medications and therapeutic interventions such as splinting, casting, bracing, and range-of-motion exercises, patients are frequently treated with a variety of injections for spasticity. These may include nerve blocks using ethanol or phenol or, more commonly now, botulinum toxin injections. A newer treatment device, the intrathecal pump, may be surgically implanted to provide a higher concentration of medicine for spasticity directly at the level of the spinal cord, where it is most effective. The advantage to this technique is that it allows greater control over the administration of medicine, while avoiding many of the side effects associated with oral administration of medication. This treatment is not for everyone, however, and should be discussed with the patient's doctor. Finally, various surgical techniques may be used, usually as last-resort efforts, for treatment of spasticity. These include various tendon-lengthening procedures, rhizotomy, or cordotomy.

Behavioral problems — Although other issues may be more of a focus of medical treatment, it is often behavioral issues that prevent successful community reintegration and return to gainful employment. Patients may have low frustration tolerance, impaired judgment, and, in many cases, emotional lability or frank aggression that hinder successful rehabilitation outcomes. Behavioral problems are usually addressed on a number of levels, including psychological counseling, behavior modification plans, medications, and, in worst cases, inpatient neurobehavioral treatment programs.

Cognitive — Several studies have examined the frequency of patients' complaints following traumatic brain injury. The most common complaint in all studies is problems with memory. Areas of the brain associated with memory formation are particularly susceptible to damage following trauma, due to their proximity to bony protuberances inside the skull. Additionally, these structures are particularly susceptible to anoxic damage as well, which can occur secondarily following trauma. Deficits in attention, motivation, and sensory input can also secondarily result in memory problems.

Aging — As noted below in the vocational category, aging with a brain injury can result in a faster than average decline physically as well as cognitively. Reduced physical skills and judgment can also result in additional injury as time passes. Indeed, once a person has experienced a brain injury, he or she is much more likely to have a second injury than people without a brain injury. Also, for some mild to moderately brain injured clients, social isolation and awareness of deficits eventually erode the hope and optimism that occur while progress is being made, and behavior and emotional problems may rise several years after the original insult. These problems are not as much related to aging as to the passage of time and the slow realization that they will never achieve their preinjury levels and may be unable to enjoy normal social and love relationships (Trudel & Purdum, 1998).

COMMUNITY REINTEGRATION

Successful return to the community remains a significant challenge given all of the potential barriers a patient may face due to the impairments sustained as a result of the injury (Smith-Knapp et al., 1996; Wall et al., 1998). With changes in personality, and behavioral problems, interpersonal relationships often become difficult. Many patients require ongoing supervision for safety reasons, which interferes with social activities. Driving a motor vehicle is a significant concern, and a formal driving evaluation should be performed by a therapist trained to look for the specific problems that may interfere with safe driving.

An additional issue frequently seen is return to recreational activities. A high percentage of brain injury patients engaged in high-risk activities prior to their injury (Chesnut et al., 1993). In fact, it is often engagement in high-risk activities that led to the brain injury in the first place. It is extremely important that individuals protect themselves against a second injury, particularly while the brain is healing. The *second impact syndrome*, in which a person healing from one injury is exposed to a second injury, may result in exponentially worse or even fatal outcomes, even with a relatively minor second injury. It is therefore extremely important that the patient be restricted from engaging in activities that may place him at risk for another injury. A therapeutic recreation specialist may be helpful in identifying and developing appropriate leisure interests after brain injury as well as helping develop techniques to pursue those interests when physical and cognitive impairments make them difficult. In addition, substance abuse may adversely affect recovery and ultimate outcome, further complicating the vocational and life care planning needs (Corrigan, 1995).

VOCATIONAL REHABILITATION

Return to gainful employment after brain injury remains a significant challenge (Cifu et al., 1997; Dikmen et al., 1994; Goodall et al., 1994; Ip et al., 1995; Stapleton et al., 1989; Wehman et al., 1988, 1993; Zasler, 1997). Most studies indicate that

Table 13.4 Neuropsychologist Questions

In addition to the standard evaluation report, add the following as appropriate:
1. Please describe, in layman terms, the damage to the brain.
2. Please describe the effects of the accident on the client's ability to function.
3. Please provide an opinion to the following topics:
   a. Intelligence level? (include pre- vs. postincident if able)
   b. Personality style with regard to the workplace and home?
   c. Stamina level?
   d. Functional limitations and assets?
   e. Ability for education/training?
   f. Vocational implications — style of learning?
   g. Level of insight into present functioning?
   h. Ability to compensate for deficits?
   i. Ability to initiate action?
   j. Memory impairments? (short-term, long-term, auditory, visual, etc.)
   k. Ability to identify and correct errors?
   l. Recommendations for compensation strategies?
   m. Need for companion or attendant care?
4. What is the proposed treatment plan?
   a. Counseling? (individual and family)
   b. Cognitive therapy?
   c. Reevaluations?
   d. Referral to others? (e.g., physicians)
   e. Other?
5. How much and how long? (include cost per session or hour and reevaluations)

© Roger O. Weed, with acknowledgment to Robert Frasier.

following a severe brain injury, approximately 10 to 20% of individuals return to work within a 1- to 2-year period following their injury. Even with milder brain injuries, work-related issues often become the major problem due to significant problems with interpersonal relationships and behavioral changes (Baker, 1990; Chwalisz, 1992; DePompei & Williams, 1994). Most traumatic brain injuries occur in individuals between the ages of 16 and 30, a time in most people's lives when education is being completed and career goals established. For those who have completed their education, the cognitive problems often prohibit the use of previously gained knowledge. Additionally, memory problems may make further education or training impossible, in the worst cases.

It is strongly recommended that individuals undergo a neuropsychological evaluation to determine their capacity for education and work (Macciochi et al., 1998; Weed, 1996, 1998). A proper, thorough neuropsychological evaluation will give information about how the patient learns and processes information, and will help the vocational rehabilitation counselor in establishing appropriate return to work goals (also see Table 13.4 for checklist of questions to the neuropsychologist). Many clients, in fact, are unable to return to competitive employment due to their impairments, or need significant support and assistance to do so. Many patients have no difficulty obtaining employment, but have a great deal of trouble maintaining employment. Research regarding employment suggests that the most difficult to place long term are people with mental illness and brain injury.

In order to adequately assess the vocational and life planning needs of a person with a brain injury, it is recommended that, as clinical judgment dictates, other allied health professionals be considered. The occupational therapist may be an appropriate referral for an assessment for seating and positioning, adaptive aids, and other vocationally related issues. For some clients, activities of daily living training, including household safety, would be included. The speech and language pathologist will be instrumental in determining augmentative communications and assistive technology for clients with more severe injuries, as well as in providing an assessment of receptive and expressive speech and language. They also often offer cognitive remediation strategies. A physical therapist is often the most appropriate referral to determine the client's true physical capabilities by compiling a functional capacity assessment (or physical capacity assessment) that is more detailed than most physicians can report. For the young adult or pediatric case, an educational consultant can be very important to maximize the client's educational potential. Under the Individuals with Disabilities Education Act (IDEA), the public school system is responsible for providing specialized services to children with disabilities. However, many of these clients are unserved for a variety of reasons. One reason is that the client has not been adequately assessed in order to identify deficits that would meet the criteria for specialized education. Another reason is that the client may meet the definition, but the school's funding is inadequate and the school will fail to provide appropriate support. Educational consultants who are familiar with the rules often can negotiate the appropriate education protocol.

Several methods of vocational assistance have been developed, including sheltered workshops and supported employment. The supported employment model involves a job coach who spends time with the patient at the work site and assists with training the patient for the job, accommodations of the work space if necessary, and helping with problems that may occur if needed. Much of the support involves educating the employer about the nature of brain injury (McMahon & Shaw, 1991; Wehman et al., 1993).

In addition, the effects of aging with a brain injury may affect work life expectancy (Weed, 1998). Data reveal that many clients with a brain injury cognitively or physically deteriorate at a faster rate and appear years older than their chronological age; it is not uncommon for clients to depart from work (i.e., retire early) at an age younger than that of most able-bodied workers. Reduced physical skills from the initial injury means the person has less of a reserve than the average person, so as she ages, she may reach the threshold of dependence at an earlier age. There also may be an increased risk of Alzheimer's disease at an earlier age, leading to loss of independence earlier than the average person (Chandra et al., 1989; Gedye et al., 1989; Cifu et al., 1996b; Rosenthal, 1990; Thompson et al., 1997). For example, it may be appropriate to phase work out and phase a day program or volunteer activities in by the time the client is in her 50s. The decline in work life can also be a result of moving from full-time to part-time work as well as earlier retirement.

CASE STUDY

The 32-year-old client was riding a motorcycle that was hit by a car. At the time of the interview, 3 years postinjury, he stated that he did not remember the incident or anything a couple of weeks prior to the incident. Following the incident, his first consistent memory is approximately 2 to 3 months later. He was treated for 2 months in an acute care hospital and then for 5 months in a brain injury rehabilitation hospital. The client was diagnosed with severe traumatic brain injury with physical and cognitive deficits, including ventriculoperitoneal shunt and orthopedic injuries requiring extensive care.

Neuropsychological testing results concluded that the client had sustained a very severe traumatic brain injury. Testing revealed reduced intellectual capacity of one standard deviation, perhaps slightly more, below preinjury levels. His primary deficit is in visual/motor problem solving. He is able to sight read beyond a high school level. He has significant deficits in mathematical calculations, with overall performance at a level much lower than expected given his preinjury educational level. No anomia was noted, and he is able to mildly retrieve words without perseveration or intrusive errors. He has significant difficulty with fine motor coordination, with reduced range in the left upper extremity. He has significantly improved executive function from prior testing, which is the most promising part of the overall evaluation, although he continues to exhibit occasions of temper outbursts. He has moderately to severely impaired short-term memory, especially with verbal short-term memory given the absence of consolidation of information. He has a positive affect, although he has times of unhappiness/frustration, and is basically functioning in a more adaptive manner.

He has a young daughter and must be supervised when with her. The wife is supportive and has quit work to be his caregiver. He must have someone available for assistance with judgment, safety, food preparation, and financial commitments. Work is not a reasonable goal, although volunteer activities part-time would be therapeutic.

CONCLUSION

Thousands of our citizens experience a brain injury each year. The more knowledgeable one is about this specialized industry, the better equipped one is to obtain effective treatment while controlling costs and complications. Life care plans can effectively help ask the right questions and guide the individual, family, and funding source through the complex maze of rehabilitation and long-term care. Effective vocational rehabilitation can help integrate the person back into the community, perhaps as an employed, productive individual. In order to accomplish these monumental tasks, numerous professionals and family members must work together in a collaborative fashion to achieve common goals.

LIFE CARE PLAN

Note: For purposes of this plan, the following initials are placed in parentheses according to their respective recommendations:

JP = Jeffrey Preston, M.D., physiatrist
MC = Michael Cathy, M.D., psychiatrist
RH = Robert Hampton, M.D., ophthalmologist
IR = Ian Raston, M.D., hand surgeon
WW = William White, M.D., internist
AP = Amy Passy, P.T., physical therapist
JH = John Hurry, Psy.D., neuropsychologist
RW = Roger Weed, Ph.D., certified life care planner

Routine Future Medical Care — Physician Only

Recommendation (by whom)	Initiated/Duration	Purpose	Expected Cost
Physiatrist (JP)	4 times/year to life expectancy	Monitor overall rehabilitation program and prevent/reduce complications, etc.	$276–320/year at $69–80/visit (see Note 1 below)
X-rays: left hip, knee, or shoulder (JP)	3 times/year to life expectancy	Monitor development of expected degenerative joint disease	Range: $609–1365/year at $203–455 each, 3 times/year to life
Head CT scan (JP)	1 time/year to life expectancy	Assess integrity of shunt	CT scan: $2173–2296/year to life
Head MRI (JP)	Every 5 years to life	Monitor structural changes to brain	MRI: $3016–4370 every 5 years to life
EEG (JP)	1 time/year to life expectancy	Assess brain wave activity due to high risk for seizures	EEG: $854/year to life

Note 1: Cost for physiatrist does not include one-time new patient evaluation at $100 to $150 required by one physiatrist.

Note 2: Costs for x-rays, CT scan, MRI, and EEG include both diagnostic study and physician interpretation fee. Cost range for MRI depends on whether the study is done with or without contrast. If done with contrast, an additional fee for the contrast dye will incur.

Routine Future Medical Care — Physician Only (Continued)

Recommendation (by whom)	Initiated/Duration	Purpose	Expected Cost
Neurologist (JP)	2 times/year to life expectancy	Monitor neurological status	$148–460/year at $74–115/visit
Orthopedic surgeon (JP)	2 times/year to life expectancy	Monitor orthopedic status and development of expected degenerative joint disease	New patient: $180, 1 time only Follow-up: $120–160/year to life at $60–80/visit
Note: See also expected future left knee and hip replacement surgery recommended by Dr. Preston.			
Neuro-ophthalmologist (RH)	2 times/year to life expectancy	Monitor visual impairments	$160/year at $80/visit
Note: Economist to deduct cost of routine ophthalmology follow-up since it is recommended for the general population.			
Psychiatrist (MC)	4–6 times/year for 2–3 years, then 2–3 times/year to life expectancy	Medication management	$288–432/year for 2–3 years, then $144–216/year to life at $72/visit
Hand surgeon (IR)	1 time/year to life expectancy	Monitor left-hand problems related to neurological disorder	$60/year to life expectancy
Internist (WW)	4 times/year to life expectancy	General medical care and treatment	$424/year at $106/visit

Note: The internist reports the client is expected to require more frequent visits and at a higher level per visit than typically expected of the general population. Visits included in the plan are over and above recommendations for the general population.

Note: The client also may need evaluation and follow-up by specialists, including neurosurgeon, urologist, and others as needed depending on complications and at the discretion of his treating physicians. See also Potential Complications.

Projected Evaluations — Nonphysician

(Include all allied health evaluations)

Recommendation (by whom)	Dates	Frequency/Duration	Expected Cost
Physical therapy evaluation to assess gait changes (JP)	2001 to life expectancy	1 time/year to life expectancy	$200–250/year to life expectancy

Note 1: According to the records, the client was discharged from physical therapy in April 2001 and transitioned to a home exercise program. The therapist recommended physical therapy reevaluation in 3 to 4 months to determine maintenance of his function and carryover of skills.

Note 2: See also Health and Strength Maintenance for ongoing fitness program.

Occupational therapy evaluation to evaluate for and monitor adaptive equipment needs (JP)	2001 to life expectancy	1 time/year to life expectancy	$300–350/year to life expectancy

Note: According to the physiatrist, speech therapy does not appear to be indicated for the client and no recommendations are made for yearly speech evaluations or therapy to monitor his status and provide recommendations depending on needs.

Home accessibility evaluation by qualified occupational therapist (RW)	2001	1 time only	$90 for in-home occupational therapy evaluation with recommendations

Note: Although the client's home generally appears appropriate for him at this time, a home accessibility evaluation is reasonable and appropriate to evaluate the home and make recommendations for additional modifications to ensure the client maintains his highest level of independence and function in his home, especially given an expected further decline in physical functioning as he ages.

Projected Therapeutic Modalities

Recommendation (by whom)	Year Initiated	Frequency/Duration	Expected Cost
Physical therapy to develop, monitor, and supervise fitness program and home exercise program (JP)	2001	4 times/year to life expectancy	$988/year to life for four 1-hour sessions/year at $247/session

Note: See also Health and Strength Maintenance for ongoing fitness program.

Recommendation (by whom)	Year Initiated	Frequency/Duration	Expected Cost
Neuropsychologist consultation for coping strategies, adjustment issues, cognitive remediation, and behavior management strategies (JH)	2001	4–6 times/year to life expectancy	$392–840/year to life at $98–140 (depends on length of visit)

Note 1: It is likely the client also will need counseling episodically throughout his lifetime, especially during transitional times in his life (i.e., mid-30s, middle age, elderly, etc.), as well as during life-changing events that may occur (i.e., birth of second child, expected in January 2004, etc.). Frequency and duration of counseling are unknown, and no additional cost is included in plan totals.

Note 2: The client's wife/family also may need counseling as needed throughout their life expectancy depending on circumstances. The neuropsychologist states he is available to the client and wife as needed, typically for telephonic intervention related to various issues/questions that arise, at no additional cost to the client. The physiatrist also states the client's family/wife may need counseling intervention at some time in the future.

Recommendation (by whom)	Year Initiated	Frequency/Duration	Expected Cost
Case manager experienced in working with clients with a brain injury to problem solve, coordinate care, client advocate, etc. (RW)	2001	2 hours/month (average) to life expectancy	$1800–2136/year (average) to life expectancy at $75–89/hour (does not include mileage to appointments and to meet with client)

Financial planner/consultant (JH)	2001 to life expectancy	2 hours/month (average)	$1920–2400/year (average) to life expectancy at $80–100/hour (estimate)

Note: The client requires assistance and oversight with legal and business contracts, budgeting, financial planning, major decision making, and other money management decisions. Although his wife currently performs these activities, it is recommended a financial consultant, independent from the family, be utilized.

Diagnostic Testing/Educational Assessment

Recommendation (by whom)	Year Initiated	Frequency/Duration	Expected Cost
Neuropsychology evaluations (JH)	2020–2025 (50–55 years of age), then repeat 5 years later	2 times over course of lifetime	$1200–1600 total at $600–800/evaluation

Wheeled Mobility Needs, Accessories, and Maintenance

Recommendation (by whom)	Year Purchased	Replacement Schedule	Expected Cost
Power scooter (JP)	2001 to life expectancy	Scooter: Every 5 years (average)	Scooter: $2700–2900 every 5 years average
Scooter maintenance (RW)	2002	Batteries: 1 time/year (average) to life expectancy	Batteries (2): $180/year at $89.95 each
		1 time/year after warranty expires	Maintenance: $100/year (average estimate)

Note 1: The physiatrist recommends a power scooter for prolonged mobility assistance and extended outings in the community. See also scooter lift for vehicle below.

Note 2: The client states (and records confirm) that he previously used a manual wheelchair for mobility assistance and no longer requires the chair. For purposes of future care planning, it is presumed the wheelchair is available in the home for his use in the future, if needed, and no cost for replacement is included in plan totals.

Home Furnishings/Aids for Independent Function

Recommendation (by whom)	Year Purchased	Replacement Schedule	Expected Cost
Shower/tub bench with back (JP)	2001 (already has)	Every 5 years (average) to life expectancy	$48.95–59.95 every 5 years (average) to life expectancy
Elevated toilet seat (JP)	1997 (already has)	N/A; see Note below	N/A; see Note below

Note: The client states he no longer uses this item; however, for purposes of future care planning, it is presumed the elevated toilet seat is available in the home for his future use, if needed, and no cost for replacement is included in plan totals.

Recommendation (by whom)	Year Purchased	Replacement Schedule	Expected Cost
Allowance for daily planner/scheduler, memory book and other compensatory tools, handheld shower, cordless phone, etc. (JH, RW)	2001 (already has some items)	1 time/year allowance to life expectancy	$50/year (average) to life expectancy

Orthotics/Prosthetics

Recommendation (by whom)	Year Purchased	Replacement Schedule	Expected Cost
Custom left ankle, foot orthosis (AFO) (JP)	2015 or 2020 (age 45 or 50)	Every 2–3 years (average) to life expectancy	$600–1000 every 2–3 years (average) to life (includes measuring, molding, casting, fittings, and adjustments)

Note 1: The physiatrist states the client also may benefit from custom insoles or orthopedic footwear due to his altered gait; however, no information is available regarding specific type or kind of orthopedic supply and no additional cost is included in plan totals. See Potential Complications.

Note 2: The orthotist suggests replacement every 1 to 2 years (average) depending on wear and tear, maintenance, and need or changes in the client's mobility and musculoskeletal structure.

Orthopedic Equipment Needs

Recommendation (by whom)	Year Purchased	Replacement Schedule	Expected Cost
Cane with offset handle (JP, WW)	2001 (already has)	Every 10 years (average) to life expectancy	$20–25 every 10 years (average) to life expectancy
Standard folding walker (JP, WW)	2000 (already has)	Every 10 years (average) to life expectancy	$70–85 every 10 years (average) to life expectancy

Note 1: The client currently uses a cane with offset handle for mobility assistance primarily in the community. The physiatrist recommends both a cane and walker be available to him throughout his life expectancy. If a rolling walker is needed, cost is $200 to $270 each.

Note 2: The physiatrist also recommends a power scooter for long-distance outings in the community (see scooter, below).

Drug Needs

Drug needs and costs are representative of the client's current need and may change from time to time.

Recommendation (by whom)	Purpose	Cost per Month	Cost per Year
Clonazepam (Klonopin), 0.5 mg, 2 times/day (MC)	Seizure prevention	$21.12–43.59 for 60 tablets/month	$257–530/year to life expectancy
Oxybutynin (Ditropan), 5 mg, 3 times/day (WW)	Bladder control and management	$17.11–25.79 for 90 tablets/month	$208–314/year to life expectancy
Zanaflex, 4 mg, $\frac{1}{2}$ tablet in A.M., $\frac{1}{2}$ tablet at noon, 1 tablet at bedtime ($1\frac{1}{2}$ tablets/day) (WW)	Reduce spasticity/ataxia	$34.27–42.59 for 30 tablets/month	$730–907/year to life expectancy
Baclofen, 20 mg, 3 times/day (WW)	Reduce spasticity/ataxia	$25.92–47.69 for 90 tablets/month	$315–580/year to life expectancy
Propranolol LA (Inderal), 60 mg, 2 times/day (WW)	Reduce spasticity/ataxia	$47–61.79 for 60 tablets/month	$572–752/year to life expectancy

Note: According to the physiatrist, the client is expected to require these or similar medications throughout his life expectancy. The internist also states medications are expected to be needed throughout his lifetime.

Supply Needs

Supply needs and costs are representative of the client's current need and may change from time to time.

Recommendation (by whom)	Purpose	Replacement Schedule	Cost per Year
Prism glasses (RH)	Reduce double vision	Expect replacement every 1–2 years (average)	$283 for frames and lenses every 1–2 years (average) to life expectancy

Note 1: According to the ophthalmologist, the client's vision impairment as related to the brain injury is expected to remain the same over his lifetime. He states there will probably be no new problems with his vision assuming no additional or further ocular trauma occurs. See also Potential Complications.

Note 2: The client states he does not use other supplies related to injuries received in the incident.

Home/Facility Care

Recommendation (by whom)	Year Initiated/Suspended	Hours/Shifts/Days of Attendance or Care	Expected Cost
Competent companion for assistance, safety, and supervision in the home (JP, JH)	2001	10–12 hours/day, 7 days/week, 365 days/year to life expectancy	$35,953–65,700/year to life expectancy at $9.85–15/hour
Child care assistance (JP, JH)	2001	As needed	Defer to economist for loss of child care services

Note 1: The client's wife currently performs the function of a live-in caregiver.

Note 2: Of the nine home health agencies contacted in the client's local area, only one agency offered a live-in caregiver and the service currently was not available due to staffing shortages and difficulty hiring and retaining live-ins. When and if available, live-in at the one agency is $139.20/day.

Note 3: The neuropsychologist states the client does not require overnight *awake* care and should be able to summon emergency assistance if needed.

Note 4: Both the neuropsychologist and physiatrist state the client is expected to have difficulty with child-raising activities with his 2-year-old daughter and his expected second child in January 2004 and requires child care assistance. Economic value of time that a father normally spends in child-rearing and child-raising activities and that which is lost due to the client's injury are deferred to the economist.

Note 5: The cost of in-home care may be reduced through negotiation with the home health agency for long-term contract, private hire, or if family or friends assume some of the care.

Yard care and interior/exterior home maintenance and repairs (per interview)	2001	N/A	Defer to economist as part of loss of household services

Note: The client's home is in obvious need of repair due to damage caused by maneuvering the wheelchair in the home, i.e., damage to doorways, flooring, walls, etc. The client states he is unable to do the repairs and is unable to paint or do other interior/exterior home maintenance tasks since the injury.

Transportation

Recommendation (by whom)	Year Purchased	Replacement	Expected Cost
Cellular telephone for emergency communication (RW)	2000 (already has)	Every 5 years (estimate)	N/A (had preinjury)
Scooter lift for vehicle (RW)	2001 or when scooter purchased; see scooter	Every 5–7 years (average) to life expectancy or at time of vehicle replacement	$2500 every 5–7 years (average) for hoist arm scooter lift

Note: Although the client received satisfactory scores in the behind-the-wheel adapted driving evaluation in July 2001, the neuropsychologist opines that driving is not recommended due to judgment impairments and slow processing that impairs his ability to act quickly or in emergencies.

Health and Strength Maintenance (Leisure Time Activities)

Recommendation (by whom)	Year of Purchase or Attendance	Replacement or Attendance Schedule	Expected Cost
Fitness program: Option 1 Gym membership (JP) Option 2 Home exercise equipment to include treadmill, parallel bars, and multistation exercise machine	2001 to life expectancy	N/A; already has equipment; plan for 2-time replacements (estimate) over his lifetime	N/A; no additional cost over general population 2011: $3000 (estimate) 2021: $3000 (estimate)

Note 1: The physiatrist recommends a physical conditioning/exercise program under the supervision of a physical therapist to monitor and oversee/supervise fitness program. See also physical therapy for recommended four times/year physical therapist supervision.

Note 2: The physical therapist suggests a recumbent stationary bicycle also may be useful for the client.

Recommendation (by whom)	Year of Purchase or Attendance	Replacement or Attendance Schedule	Expected Cost
Membership to National Brain Injury Association and local support groups/networking (RW)	2001 to life expectancy	Yearly membership	$35/year to life expectancy

Vocational/Educational Plan

Recommendation (by whom)	Year Initiated/Suspended	Purpose	Expected Cost
Computer with monitor, printer, Internet access, software package, and other features (RW)	1-time-only replacement estimated in 2002 (approximately 4 years after purchase of current computer in 1998)	Increase independence for educational and recreational activity	$2000 (average) for 1-time-only replacement in approximately 2002

Note 1: Dr. Preston states in his deposition that a personal computer is medically indicated for the client to include possible access for environmental control unit (ECU) or adaptive devices integration in the future.

Note 2: A one-time-only replacement cost for computer and related equipment/supplies is included in plan. Replacement after that is presumed to be consistent with use of a personal computer by the general population.

Note: The client has no competitive vocational potential. Volunteer activity is a best option for him to increase his sense of productivity, self-worth, and provide a sense of purpose. If professional services are required in the future to develop or cultivate an alternate volunteer program for the client, expect 20 to 40 hours for vocational counseling and related services, including vocational evaluation, labor market research, job site analysis, etc., at $75 to $89/hour. However, costs for these services are not included in the plan.

Architectural Considerations

(List considerations for home accessibility and modifications.)

The client currently lives with his wife and 2-year-old daughter in a ranch-style house that has been modified to accommodate him and generally appears appropriate for his current needs. A ramp has been constructed to the back door, which is the entrance the client uses to enter and exit the home, and grab bars have been installed in the bathroom. The front entrance has steps leading to the front door, although no handrail is available and the client demonstrates he generally is able to ascend and descend the stairs with difficulty in a modified fashion and with altered gait.

The client requires a one-story home with accessibility features and minimal, if any, stairs. If stairs, he requires handrails. See also home accessibility evaluation for one-time-only evaluation to assure the home is accessible both now and for the future as he ages and experiences an expected reduction in his physical capabilities.

Future Medical Care, Surgical Intervention, Aggressive Treatment

Recommendation (by whom)	Year Initiated	Frequency	Expected Cost*
Eye muscle surgery (RH)	2002–2003 (age 32–33)	1 time only, if successful	$5000 (approximate)
Left total knee replacement (JP)	2020 (age 50)	Initial knee replacement in 2020, then every 10–12 years (average) knee revision to life expectancy	Replacement in approximately 2020: $30,948
Left knee revision (JP)	Approximately 2030–2032 and every 10–12 years (average) thereafter to life expectancy		1st revision: $35,608
			2nd revision: $34,378
Left total hip replacement (JP)	2020 (age 50)	Initial hip replacement in 2020, then every 10–12 years (average) hip revision to life expectancy	Replacement in approximately 2020: $31,568
Left hip revision (JP)	Approximately 2030–2032 and every 10–12 years (average) thereafter to life expectancy		1st revision: $39,811
			2nd revision: $37,479

* Expected cost for knee and hip replacement/revision includes surgeon fee and average hospital charges and does not include surgeon assistant fee, if applicable, anesthesiologist fee, or subacute or rehab unit stay. One case of a client similar in age to this client with diagnosis of degenerative joint disease required total knee replacement at a cost of $40,733, inclusive.

Note 1: The physiatrist states he expects the client to require joint replacement in both left hip and left knee due to altered gait and increased wear and tear on his lower-extremity joints as well as expected degenerative joint disease. He states the severity of the degenerative joint disease depends on maintenance of the client's weight and overall health and fitness.

Note 2: According to one orthopedic surgeon who performs knee and hip replacement surgeries, knee and hip prostheses last on average 10 to 12 years (based on geriatric population); however, the client may require more frequent revision due to his young age at time of projected initial replacement and expected increased activity level (more so than geriatric activity level). See also Potential Complications.

Note 3: For purposes of future care planning and based on the physiatrist's recommendation for initial hip and knee joint replacement at approximately age 50, presume two hip and knee revisions over the client's lifetime at approximately age 60 to 62 and age 72 to 74.

Note 4: The orthopedic surgeon states joint revision surgeries are more difficult than the initial replacement surgery and each subsequent revision is more difficult than the previous one. Recovery also tends to take longer. However, no additional cost for extended recovery is included in plan totals for revision surgeries.

Note 5: Pain medication is expected to be needed following each joint revision surgery as well as probable anti-inflammatory medication. Exact kind, dose, and duration of medication are unknown and no additional cost for medications is included in plan totals.

Note 6: Orthopedic visits following joint replacement/revision generally include one post-op visit (at no cost) plus three other visits at 3, 6, and 12 months postreplacement/postrevision at $60 to $80/visit. Routine follow-up also includes AP and lateral x-rays of hip at $174.25/x-ray and knee at $261.25/x-ray at each post-op visit. Additional medical needs following joint replacement/revision likely include postoperative physical therapy and probable long-term need for cane or walker for mobility assistance. Aqua therapy also may be indicated following joint replacement/revision.

Ventriculoperitoneal (VP) shunt revision (JP)	Approximately 2011 (15 years after initial shunt placement)	1 time only, assuming no complications	Neurosurgeon evaluation: $286 Revision surgery: $28,927

Note 1: The client was released from the care of his neurosurgeon in February 1998 to be followed by the physiatrist and return as needed if there were complications with his shunt or changes in his neurologic status. The physiatrist states it is probable the client will require at least one shunt revision over his lifetime due to expected complications.

Note 2: Expected cost for VP shunt revision includes surgeon fee and hospital charges only and does not include diagnostic studies that may be needed such as abdominal x-rays or head CT scan, or anesthesiology charges. See head CT scan, which may be used for diagnostic purposes at time of shunt revision.

Potential Complications

Note: Potential complications are included for information only. No frequency or duration of complications is available. No costs are included in the plan.

■ Neurologic problems, including increased risk for seizures, shunt complications, increased spasticity that is expected to get worse over time, etc., which require aggressive treatment (including Botox injections), diagnostic tests, and prescription medication.

■ Psychological difficulties, including poor adjustment to disability, anger, aggression, irritability, depression, poor social behavior, increased social isolation, increased risk for suicide if not getting adequate care, etc., which could require medication and psychotherapy or hospitalization to treat. The psychiatrist states the client is at higher risk for affective symptoms. Additionally, the neuropsychologist states an anger management program may be an option in the future.

■ Increased risk for early onset of dementia due to the effect of traumatic brain injury and the aging process, as well as more prone to earlier onset of memory problems and overall decline in cognitive abilities associated with aging.

■ Increased risk for falls and additional injuries (i.e., bone fractures, secondary brain injury, etc.) due to spasticity, impulsivity, poor balance, and reduced physical abilities. The physiatrist states there is a very high probability of the client experiencing falls with resultant fractures. The neuropsychologist states a second brain injury would be devastating and the client would not recover to the extent he has recovered from the primary brain injury.

■ Musculoskeletal and mobility problems due to altered gait. May require custom orthopedic footwear and insoles. May also experience additional hand problems, depending on his neurological status, that require surgical correction. May require more frequent hip or knee revisions than normally expected or have longer than expected recovery following joint revisions.

■ Urology problems if Ditropan medication becomes ineffective and urology services are needed, including evaluation, diagnostic studies, other medications, surgery, etc.

■ Visual problems, including additional or further ocular trauma or need for other aggressive treatment/surgery to correct or improve his double vision caused by left trochlear nerve palsy and partial oculomotor palsy.

■ More extensive or expensive medical care and equipment than expected.

■ Adverse reaction to long-term use of medication(s).

REFERENCES

Almli, C.R. & Finger, S. (1992). Brain injury and recovery of function: theories and mechanisms of functional reorganization. *Journal of Head Trauma Rehabilitation*, 7, 70–77.

American Congress of Rehabilitation Medicine Head Injury Interdisciplinary Special Interest Group. (1993). Definition of mild traumatic brain injury. *Journal of Head Trauma Rehabilitation*, 8, 86–87.

Baker, J.E. (1990). Family adaptation when one member has a head injury. *Journal of Neuroscience Nursing*, 22, 232–237.

Berker, E. (1996). Diagnosis, physiology, pathology and rehabilitation of traumatic brain injuries. *International Journal of Neuroscience*, 85, 95–220.

Bigler, E.D. (1989). Behavioural and cognitive changes in traumatic brain injury: a spouse's perspective. *Brain Injury*, 3, 73–78.

Bloomfield, E.L. (1989). Extracerebral complications of head injury. *Critical Care Clinics*, 5, 881–892.

Bontke, C.F. & Boake, C. (1991). Traumatic brain injury rehabilitation. *Neurosurgery Clinics of North America*, 2, 473–482.

Bontke, C.F., Lehmkuhl L.D., Englander, J., Mann, N., Ragnarsson, K.T., Zasler, N.D., Graves, D.E., Thoi, L.L., & Jung, C. (1993). Medical complications and associated injuries of persons treated in the traumatic brain injury model systems programs. *Journal of Head Trauma Rehabilitation*, 8, 34–46.

Centers for Disease Control, National Center for Injury Prevention and Control. (1999). *Traumatic Brain Injury in the United States: A Report to Congress.* Atlanta, GA: Author.

Chandra, V., Kokmen, E., Schoenberg, B.S., & Beard, C.M. (1989). Head trauma with loss of consciousness as a risk factor for Alzheimer's disease. *Neurology*, 39, 1576–1578.

Chesnut, R.M., Marshall, L.F., Klauber, M.R., Blunt, B.A., Baldwin, N., Eisenberg, H.M., Jane, J.A., Marmarou, A., & Foulkes, M.A. (1993). The role of secondary brain injury in determining outcome from severe head injury. *Journal of Trauma*, 34, 216–222.

Chwalisz, K. (1992). Perceived stress and caregiver burden after brain injury: a theoretical integration. *Rehabilitation Psychology*, 37, 189–203.

Cifu, D.X., Kaelin, D.L., & Wall, B.E. (1996a). Deep venous thrombosis: incidence on admission to a brain injury rehabilitation program. *Archives of Physical Medicine and Rehabilitation*, 77, 1182–1185.

Cifu, D.X., Keyser-Marcus, L., Lopez, E., Wehman, P., Kreutzer, J.S., Englander, J., & High, W. (1997). Acute predictors of successful return to work 1 year after traumatic brain injury: a multicenter analysis. *Archives of Physical Medicine and Rehabilitation*, 78, 125–131.

Cifu, D.X., Kreutzer, J.S., Marwitz, J.H., Rosenthal, M., Englander, J., & High, W. (1996b). Functional outcomes of older adults with traumatic brain injury: a prospective, multicenter analysis. *Archives of Physical Medicine and Rehabilitation*, 77, 883–888.

Clifton, G.L., Kreutzer, J.S., Choi, S.C., Devany, C.W., Eisenberg, H.M., Foulkes, M.A., Jane, J.A., Marmarou, A., & Marshall, L.F. (1993). Relationship between Glasgow Outcome Scale and neuropsychological measures after brain injury. *Neurosurgery*, 33, 34–38.

Cope, D.N. (1995). The effectiveness of traumatic brain injury rehabilitation: a review. *Brain Injury*, 9, 649–670.

Cope, D.N. & O'Lear, J. (1993). A clinical and economic perspective on head injury rehabilitation. *Journal of Head Trauma Rehabilitation*, 8, 1–14.

Corrigan, J.D. (1995). Substance abuse as a mediating factor in outcome from traumatic brain injury. *Archives of Physical Medicine and Rehabilitation*, 76, 302–309.

Corrigan, J.D. & Mysiw, W.J. (1988). Agitation following traumatic head injury: equivocal evidence for a discrete stage of cognitive recovery. *Archives of Physical Medicine and Rehabilitation*, 69, 487–492.

Corthell, D.W. (1993). *Employment Outcomes for Persons with Acquired Brain Injury.* Washington, DC: Research and Training Center WU-SMW, National Institute on Disability and Rehabilitation and Research.

DePompei, R. & Williams J. (1994). Working with families after TBI: a family-centered approach. *Topics in Language Disorders*, 15, 68–81.

Dikmen, S.S., Temkin, N.R., Machamer, J.E., Holubkov, A.L., Fraser, R.T., & Winn, H.R. (1994). Employment following traumatic head injuries. *Archives of Neurology*, 51, 177–186.

Evans, R.W. & Ruff, R.M. (1992). Outcome and value: a perspective on rehabilitation outcomes achieved in acquired brain injury. *Journal of Head Trauma Rehabilitation*, 7, 24–36.

Gedye, A., Beattie, B.L., Tuokko, H., Horton, A., & Korsarek, E. (1989). Severe head injury hastens age of onset of Alzheimer's disease. *Journal of the American Geriatrics Society*, 37, 970–973.

Ginsberg, M.D., Zhao, W., Back, T., Belayev, L., Stagliano, N., Dietrich, W.D., & Prado, R. (1997). Three-dimensional autoradiographic image-processing strategies for the study of brain injury and plasticity. *Advances in Neurology*, 73, 239–250.

Goodall, P., Lawyer, H.L., & Wehman, P. (1994). Vocational rehabilitation and traumatic brain injury: a legislative and public policy perspective. *Journal of Head Trauma Rehabilitation*, 9, 61–81.

Grafman, J., Schwab, K., Warden, D., Pridgen, A., Brown, H.R., & Salazar, A.M. (1996). Frontal lobe injuries, violence, and aggression: a report of the Vietnam Head Injury Study. *Neurology*, 46, 1231–1238.

Groswasser, Z. & Stern, M.J. (1998). A psychodynamic model of behavior after acute central nervous system damage. *Journal of Head Trauma Rehabilitation*, 13, 69–79.

Hall, K.M. & Cope, D.N. (1995). The benefit of rehabilitation in traumatic brain injury: a literature review. *Journal of Head Trauma Rehabilitation*, 10, 1–13.

High, W.M., Hall, K.M., Rosenthal, M., Mann, N., Zafonte, R., Cifu, D.X., Boake, C., Bartha, M., Ivanhoe, C., Yablon, S., Newton, C.N., Sherer, M., Silver, B., & Lehmkuhl, L.D. (1996). Factors affecting hospital length of stay and charges following traumatic brain injury. *Journal of Head Trauma Rehabilitation*, 11, 85–96.

Horn, L.J. & Zasler, N.D. (1996). *Medical Rehabilitation of Traumatic Brain Injury*. Philadelphia: Hanley & Belfus.

Ip, R.Y., Dornan, J., & Schentag, C. (1995). Traumatic brain injury: factors predicting return to work or school. *Brain Injury*, 9, 517–532.

Jorge, R.E., Robinson, R.G., Starkstein, S.E., & Arndt, S.V. (1993). Depression and anxiety following traumatic brain injury. *Journal of Neuropsychiatry and Clinical Neuroscience*, 5, 369–374.

Katz, D.I. & Alexander, M.P. (1994). Traumatic brain injury. Predicting course of recovery and outcome for patients admitted to rehabilitation. *Archives of Neurology*, 51, 661–670.

Kaufman, H.H., Timberlake, G., Voelker, J., & Pait, T.G. (1993). Medical complications of head injury. *Medical Clinics in North America*, 77, 43–60.

Kraus, J.F. (1991). Epidemiologic features of injuries to the central nervous system. In D.W. Anderson, Ed., *Neuroepidemiology: A Tribute to Bruce Schoenberg*, 333–357. Boca Raton, FL: CRC Press.

Kraus, J.F., Black, M.A., Hessol, N., Ley, P., Rokaw, W., Sullivan, C., Bowers, S., Knowlton, S., & Marshall, L. (1984). The incidence of acute brain injury and serious impairment in a defined population. *American Journal of Epidemiology*, 119, 186–201.

Kreuter, M., Dahllof, A.G., Gudjonsson, G., Sullivan, M., & Siosteen, A. (1998). Sexual adjustment and its predictors after traumatic brain injury. *Brain Injury*, 12, 349–368.

Kreutzer, J., Kowlakowski, S., Ripley, D., Cifu, D., Rosenthal, M., Bushnik, T., Zafonte, R., Englander, J., & High, W. (2001). Charges and lengths of stay for acute and inpatient rehabilitation treatment of traumatic brain injury 1990–1996. *Brain Injury*, 15, 763–774.

Levin, H.S. (1992). Head injury and its rehabilitation. *Current Opinion in Neurology and Neurosurgery*, 5, 673–676.

Macciocchi, S.N., Littlefield, L.M., & Diamond, P.T. (1998). Neuropsychological assessment and functional capacity. *Neurorehabilitation*, 11, 67–74.

Macciocchi, S.N., Reid, D.B., & Barth, J.T. (1993). Disability following head injury. *Current Opinion in Neurology*, 6, 773–777.

Malec, J.F. & Basford, J.S. (1996). Postacute brain injury rehabilitation. *Archives of Physical Medicine and Rehabilitation*, 77, 198–207.

Marshall, L.F., Marshall, S.B., Klauber, M.R., Van Berkum, C.M., Eisenberg, H., Jane, J.A., Luerssen, T.G., Marmarou, A., & Foulkes, M.A. (1992). The diagnosis of head injury requires a classification based on computed axial tomography. *Journal of Neurotrauma*, 1, S287–S292.

Mazmanian, P.E., Kreutzer, J.S., Devany, C.W., & Martin, K.O. (1993). A survey of accredited and other rehabilitation facilities: education, training and cognitive rehabilitation in brain-injury programmes. *Brain Injury*, 7, 319–331.

McMahon, B. & Shaw, L. (1991). *Work Worth Doing*. Orlando, FL: PMD Press.

Piek, J. (1995). Medical complications in severe head injury. *New Horizons*, 3, 534–538.

Pike, B.R. & Hamm, R.J. (1997). Activating the posttraumatic cholinergic system for the treatment of cognitive impairment following traumatic brain injury. *Pharmacology, Biochemistry and Behavior*, 57, 785–791.

Rappaport, M., Dougherty, A.M., & Kelting, D.L. (1992). Evaluation of coma and vegetative states. *Archives of Physical Medicine and Rehabilitation*, 73, 628–634.

Rosenthal, M. (1990). Rehabilitation of the adult and child with traumatic brain injury, 2nd ed. Philadelphia: Davis.

Russell-Jones, D.L. & Shorvon, S.D. (1989). The frequency and consequences of head injury in epileptic seizures. *Journal of Neurology, Neurosurgery and Psychiatry*, 52, 659–662.

Schmidt, N.D. (1997). Outcome-oriented rehabilitation: a response to managed care. *Journal of Head Trauma Rehabilitation*, 12, 44–50.

Seel, R.T.,Kreutzer, J.S., & Sander, A.M. (1997). Concordance of patients' and family members' ratings of neurobehavioral functioning after traumatic brain injury. *Archives of Physical Medicine and Rehabilitation*, 78, 1254–1259.

Semlyen, J.K., Summers, S.J., & Barnes, M.P. (1998). Traumatic brain injury: efficacy of multi-disciplinary rehabilitation. *Archives of Physical Medicine and Rehabilitation*, 79, 678–683.

Smith-Knapp, K., Corrigan, J.D., & Arnett, J.A. (1996). Predicting functional independence from neuropsychological tests following traumatic brain injury. *Brain Injury*, 10, 651–661.

Stapleton, M., Parente, R., & Bennett, P. (1989). Job coaching traumatically brain injured individuals: lessons learned. *Cognitive Rehabilitation*, 7, 18–21.

Teasdale, G.M., Pettigrew, L.E., Wilson, J.T., Murray, G., & Jennett, B. (1998). Analyzing outcome of treatment of severe head injury: a review and update on advancing the use of the Glasgow Outcome Scale. *Journal of Neurotrauma*, 15, 587–597.

Teasdale, G., Teasdale, E., & Hadley, D. (1992). Computed tomographic and magnetic resonance imaging classification of head injury. *Journal of Neurotrauma*, 1, S249–S257.

Thompson, J.D., Schellenberg, G.D., & Larson, E.B. (1997). Head injury and risk of Alzheimer's disease by apolipoprotein E genotype. *American Journal of Epidemiology*, 146, 373–384.

Traumatic Brain Injury Model Systems. (1996). *Traumatic Brain Injury Facts and Figures*, Vol. 1. Detroit: Traumatic Brain Injury Model Systems National Data Center.

Trudel, T. & Purdum, C. (1998). Aging with a brain injury, long term issues. *The Rehabilitation Professional*, 6, 37–41.

Uomoto, J.M. & Brockway, J.A. (1992). Anger management training for brain injured patients and their family members. *Archives of Physical Medicine and Rehabilitation*, 73, 674–679.

Wall, J.R., Rosenthal, M., & Niemczura, J.G. (1998). Community-based training after acquired brain injury: preliminary findings. *Brain Injury*, 12, 215–224.

Weed, R. (1996). Life care planning and earnings capacity analysis for brain injured clients involved in personal injury litigation utilizing the RAPEL method. *Journal of Neurorehabilitation*, 7, 119–135.

Weed, R. (1998). Aging with a brain injury: the effects on life care plans and vocational opinions. *The Rehabilitation Professional*, 6, 30–34.

Wehman, P., Kregel, J., Sherron, P., Nguyen, S., Kreutzer, J., Fry, R., & Zasler, N. (1993). Critical factors associated with the successful supported employment placement of patients with severe traumatic brain injury. *Brain Injury*, 7, 31–44.

Wehman, P., Kreutzer, J., Wood, W., & Morton, M.V. (1988). Supported work model for persons with traumatic brain injury: toward job placement and retention. Special issue: traumatic brain injury. *Rehabilitation Counseling Bulletin*, 31, 298–312.

Wood, R.L. (1987). *Brain Injury Rehabilitation: A Neurobehavioural Approach*. London: Croom Helm.

Zafonte, R.D., Hammond, F.M., Mann, N.R., Wood, D.L., Black, K.L., & Millis, S.R. (1996). Relationship between Glasgow Coma Scale and functional outcome. *American Journal of Physical Medicine and Rehabilitation*, 75, 364–369.

Zafonte, R.D., Mann, N.R., Millis, S.R., Black, K.L., Wood, D.L., & Hammond, F. (1997). Posttraumatic amnesia: its relation to functional outcome. *Archives of Physical Medicine and Rehabilitation*, 78, 1103–1106.

Zasler, N.D. (1997). The role of medical rehabilitation in vocational reentry. *Journal of Head Trauma Rehabilitation*, 12, 42–56.

14

LIFE CARE PLANNING FOR THE BURN PATIENT

Melissa A. Brown, Phala A. Helm, and Roger O. Weed

INTRODUCTION

The development of the life care plan for the burn patient is best begun imme-diately following the injury to ensure provision of adequate medical, emotional, social, and financial support for the patient and family. There is an enormous investment of health care manpower, time, money, and facilities in the acute treatment of burn patients and in restoring them to health (Herndon & Blakeney, 2002; Feck et al., 1978). The treatment process is long, arduous, demanding, complex, and expensive (Fisher & Helm, 1984; Helm & Fisher, 1988). The rehabilitation process begins as soon after initial hospital admission as possible. The end point of rehabilitation is not easily defined, but can continue for up to 2 years after discharge (Helm & Cromes, 1995).

A basic knowledge of the incidence, classification, and pathophysiology of burn injury is essential to the medical case manager. In the U.S., 1.5 to 2.0 million persons per year sustain burn injuries, 6000 to 12,000 of which result in death. Approximately 55,000 to 100,000 injuries require hospitalization, and of those, 50% will develop either temporary or permanent disability (Fisher & Helm, 1984; Committee on Trauma Research, 1985; Rice & MacKenzie, 1989). Those at greatest risk for burn injuries are young children (2 to 4 years) and young adult males (17 to 25 years). The upper extremity is the most commonly involved body part in burn injury, followed by the neck and head. Injury to these areas obviously affects function and appearance and can result in disability (Demling & LaLonde, 1989).

The causes of burns include scalds in 30% (or 40% if flash burns are included), contact burns in 15%, fires in 33%, chemical in 6%, electrical in 5%, and radiation in 1% (Pruitt et al., 2002).

0-8493-1511-5/04/$0.00+$1.50
© 2004 by CRC Press LLC

CLASSIFICATION OF BURNS

Burn injuries are usually classified by the extent of body surface area (BSA) of skin involved and the depth of the burn. Traditionally, burn depth was classified as first, second, and third degree. Today burn depth has been reclassified as superficial (first degree), partial (second degree), full (third degree), and deep full thickness (fourth degree). The depth of burn injury refers to the skin layers that have been destroyed.

- *Superficial* (first degree) burns involve only the superficial epidermis and usually require 3 to 7 days for healing with no scarring.
- *Superficial partial-thickness* (second degree) burns involve the epidermis and the dermis excluding hair follicles, sweat glands, and sebaceous glands and should heal in less than 21 days with minimal scarring.
- *Deep partial-thickness* (also second degree) burns involve the epidermis and most of the dermis, requiring more than 21 days for healing, and may develop severe hypertrophic scarring.
- *Full-thickness* (third degree) burns result in total destruction of the skin, both epidermis and dermis, and may involve additional tissue. Full-thickness burns of any significant size require skin grafting.
- *Deep full-thickness* (fourth degree) burns involve muscle or bone and are usually a result of prolonged contact with heat or an electrical injury and may require flap coverage or amputation (Fisher & Helm, 1984).

Burn injuries are also classified in terms of the percentage of total body surface area (TBSA) involved. The percentage of partial- and full-thickness burns should be indicated separately. The American Burn Association (ABA) classifies burn injuries as mild, moderate, and major. Moderate and major burns require hospitalization.

- Minor burns are defined as those less than 15% TBSA partial thickness (10% for children and elderly) and less than 2% full thickness unless the eyes, ears, face, or perineum are involved.
- Moderate burns include 15 to 25% TBSA (10 to 20% for children under 10 and adults over 40) regardless of depth and 2 to 10% full-thickness burns unless the eyes, ears, face, or perineum are involved.
- Major burns include greater than 25% partial-thickness burns (20% for children and adults over 40); greater than 10% full-thickness burns; all burns involving the face, eyes, ears, feet, and perineum; all burns that are electrical or involve inhalation injury; all burns with ancillary injury (fracture, tissue trauma, etc.); and all burns involving a person with factors that suggest poor risk secondary to age or illness (Hartford, 2002; Cromes & Helm, 1993).

THE SKIN: CONSEQUENCES OF BURNS

Skin is the largest organ system in the human body and the tissue most affected by burn injury. The purpose of skin is to keep body fluids inside, regulate body temperature by controlling perspiration, prevent infection, and decrease the effect of radiation from the sun. The skin is composed of two layers: the epidermis (or outer layer) and the dermis (or inner layer). The epidermis contains cells that produce skin color and form the outer protective layer of skin. The dermis lies below the epidermis and is composed of connective tissue, capillaries, collagen, and elastic fibers. It provides structural and nutritional support to the epidermis and the skin appendages (i.e., hair follicles, sweat glands, and sebaceous glands) and contributes to the skin elasticity. Full-thickness burns that involve both the epidermis and dermis will result in hair loss and sweat gland and sebaceous gland loss. Beneath the dermis is a layer of fat and connective tissue. Muscle, bone, and tendons lie below this layer. Sensory nerve endings are distributed throughout the skin and subcutaneous layer. Therefore, depending on the depth, a burn injury may result in a permanent altered ability to sense pain, touch, and temperature (Fisher & Helm, 1984).

REHABILITATION

Rehabilitation of the burn patient begins during acute hospitalization and may last for several months postdischarge (Hartford, 2002; Choctaw et al., 1987). Upon discharge it is likely that some wounds are not completely healed. Wound care is one focus of the outpatient rehabilitation program, along with positioning, splinting, range of motion (ROM), exercise, and conditioning. After discharge the rehabilitation process increasingly focuses on independence in daily activities, increased physical conditioning, and psychological adaptation to burn sequelae (Buschbacher, 1996; Cromes & Helm, 1993).

A prolonged rehabilitation course is inherent to a burn injury. A large burn may require a year or more of rehab intervention. A rule of thumb for serious injuries is 1 year of rehabilitation followed by another year to regain function (which may not be back to what it was preincident). Treatment should be initiated in a timely manner before burn scar maturation; otherwise, complications can occur, resulting in more prolonged treatment and increased cost of care. The burn scar takes 6 to 18 months to mature, and it is during this time that the scar can be successfully mobilized to prevent contractures, deformities, and hypertrophic banding. After the scar matures, correction of most deformities and cosmetic abnormalities requires expensive surgical procedures with rehabilitation follow-up afterward to maintain functional gains (Cromes & Helm, 1993).

Outpatient Services

In order to provide appropriate outpatient rehabilitation services, it may be necessary to temporarily relocate the patient and perhaps a family member near a recognized burn center (Hartford, 2002). A comprehensive outpatient burn rehabilitation program may entail 6 hours per day for 5 days per week, with a gradual decrease in frequency of treatment to three times per week (TIW), and then two times per week (BIW). Initially the patient may require 24-hour attendant care from a family member or health care provider for assistance with activities of daily living. A severe burn may require several weeks or even months of assistive care. If spouses or family members are providing attendant care or transportation, reimbursement for their time and services should be considered.

Physician follow-up visits are needed approximately every 1 to 2 weeks in the initial outpatient stage, with frequency decreasing to once or twice per month as long as the patient is on physical therapy or occupational therapy treatment, and for the first few weeks after treatment is stopped. To make sure the patient is maintaining function after therapy has stopped, physician follow-up should continue but gradually decrease to once every 3 months, biannual, and annual visits, unless unforeseen complications arise.

Psychological Evaluation

Psychological intervention begins in the acute hospitalization phase and may continue on a weekly basis for several months postdischarge, depending in part on the preinjury emotional stability of the individual. Because of pain, disrupted sleep, rigors of treatment, slowness of progress, interruption of lifestyle patterns, concern about physical and cosmetic outcomes, and not being able to work, as well as a host of other possibilities, the patient may display emotional difficulties (Watkins et al., 1989; Cromes & Helm, 1993). Disfigurement can affect self-concept, body image, comfort in interpersonal situations, and acceptance in the workplace (Sheffield et al., 1988). Psychological services should be available to spouses, caregivers, and families. Individual and family counseling interventions may be more pertinent after discharge. Severe burns are more likely to result in long-term quality of life problems with both physical and psychosocial aspects (Cobb et al., 1990).

One burn center, through research, has developed an outline of seven adaptive stages and suggested interventions (Watkins et al., 1989). The stages can be summarized as follows. (Note: Although the following stages are common, many people may skip stages or fail to progress, leading to long-term sequelae.)

1. Survival anxiety. Questions such as "How bad is it?" or "Will I live?" are predominant. Observable behavior includes agitation, restlessness, poor concentration, and poor cooperation initially. The intervention is orientation and explanation of the person's situation.
2. The problem of pain. Comments such as "I hurt" or "The medicine is wearing off too fast" become common. Observable behavior includes

reports of pain, increased demands, and typically poor cooperation with treatment. The intervention is adequate amounts of medication.

3. The search for meaning. Questions such as "Why did this happen?" or "Why me?" or "What did I do to deserve this?" emerge. The person's behavior may be recounting the events, anger at self or others, guilt, or they "can't figure it out." The intervention is to assist the person in finding his or her own answer or validation.

4. Investment in recuperation. At some point it can be expected that the person will begin to understand that he needs to be a part of the rehabilitation process and may ask questions about progress or inquire about what more he can do. The behavior changes to an interest in procedures, decreasing requests for assistance, and increased participation in treatment. The intervention is to offer more education about his situation.

5. Acceptance of losses. Many people will go through this stage several times based on treatment and progress. They may observe that they have forever been changed. For people with serious burns, disfigurement, and functional loss, one can expect concerns about "never being the same." Their behavior may be sad mood, tearfulness, decreased appetite, and temporary sleep disturbance. The intervention is to legitimize their view and assist with a realistic concept of permanent losses. It is important to assure clients that life after a burn can be pleasurable and valued despite losses.

6. Investment in rehabilitation. The client further invests herself in the process. She wants to know what functionally can be done her way and requests assistance and information. Her behavior can be expected to show a renewed interest in continuing treatment and interest in rehabilitative programs. The intervention is commending her on her efforts and gains.

7. Reintegration of identity. The expected last stage leads the person to reflect on who he is after recovery and how the burn has changed his life. His behavior can be described as a return to preburn functioning as much as possible (and in many cases, full functional return). His identity as a burn victim is complete and may result in a continuing interest in burn care, peer counseling to other burn patients, or retraining into another job. At this point the intervention is termination of psychological services.

Vocational Rehabilitation

Vocational rehabilitation issues should be addressed early in the outpatient phase of the rehabilitation process. Frequent communication with employers should be encouraged to maintain a positive work relationship and to allay fears of loss of employment. Acquisition of a detailed job description or a job analysis (based on established standards) can be used to focus therapy plans and concentrate on job-related skills. When job modifications and returning to a former job are unrealistic, vocational evaluation and training can be initiated in the latter stages of medical rehabilitation and reconstructive procedures. Burn patients are frequently able to return to work before scars are mature. Options for part-time employment or light duty should be explored with the employer to help alleviate financial stress and the establishment of dependency patterns. However, a large portion of burn victims are unable to return to the same job as preincident. A study of patients at the University of Washington revealed that only 37% of survivors 2 years postinjury had returned to their same job, with the same employer and without accommodation. Almost one half had taken disability, or not returned to work, or had some degree of job disruption (Brych et al., 2001).

To facilitate or maximize the potential for the return to work of an individual that is permanently impaired requires the involvement of a competent rehabilitation counselor (a board-certified rehabilitation counselor (CRC) is preferred) who has the training, expertise, and knowledge to conduct an assessment of the person's physical, cognitive, and emotional functioning levels. A vocational evaluation by a certified vocational evaluator may be justified. A psychological assessment and functional capacity evaluation may also be needed. The effect of a burn on the person's ability to work is very individual. The range can be no real loss of functioning to missing body parts and prostheses to deal with. In fact, in life care planning a common scenario is an electrical burn that may result in multiple amputations, mild brain impairment, and vision loss. From a vocational point of view, one study, which included amputations from electrical burns, and patients who received treatment from a center of excellence, seemed to have a better return to work rate than people with disabilities in general (Weed et al., 1997). Since being productive is one of the most valued personal traits, assisting clients with returning to work is an extremely important outcome.

COMPLICATIONS

Burn complications can be extensive and involve every part of the body. In addition, vocational, psychological, and family functioning can be significantly altered. The following burn sequelae (Table 14.1) have been arranged according to body systems with suggestions for rehabilitation intervention, frequency and duration of treatment, and surgical options. Although these lists are not all-inclusive, the most significant and common burn injury-related complications and treatment options have been listed.

CASE STUDY

The client (age 60 at the time of the injury) was working as lineman. He stated he was in a bucket hooking up a transformer and apparently hit with a 24,000-volt shock. The current reportedly entered his body through his left ear and exited through his rib cage, side of left hand, and top of left foot.

The client's areas of greatest injuries/burns reportedly include entire the left side of his face, including mouth (substantially restricting his mouth opening), the ear, left side of neck, chest, trunk, and back. He also reportedly received burn injuries to bilateral upper extremities, left leg, thigh, and hip area from electrical injury. Additional problems as a result of the electrical injury reportedly include memory impairment.

Table 14.1   Complications Associated with Burn Injury

Problem	When/Where Occurred	Results in	Dx Tests	Rehab Intervention	Duration of Treatment	Surgical Options
Musculoskeletal						
Heterotopic ossification	Usually occurs in large joints such as elbows, knees, and hips	Severely limited ROM and loss of function	X-ray, bone scan	PT/OT to provide ROM within functional limits, splinting, continuous passive motion (CPM) unit	6 months from dx	If HO does not absorb on its own, surgical intervention is indicated, followed by therapy for wound care and ROM and/or CPM 5 times/week to TIW for 6–12 weeks to obtain max results
Joint ankylosis	Usually occurs in small joints of fingers and toes; may occur in other joints	Frozen or locked joint often leaving digit in an awkward position	X-ray	No rehab intervention		Consider surgical pinning of joint or digit in a more functional position
Osteomyelitis	Usually occurs from a very deep burn with exposed bone, resulting in a long-term chronic open wound; may occur months after date of injury	Chronic open wound.	X-ray, bone scan	Requires extended wound care and possible hospitalization for IV antibiotics	Can occur intermittently for years	Surgical debridement of dead tissue; amputation may be required
Scoliosis	Usually occurs in children with unilateral (asymmetric) hip, trunk, and shoulder burns	Spinal curvature; if child hits a growth spurt, structural spinal deformity can occur with wedging of vertebrae	X-ray to R/O structural deformity	Functional scoliosis will respond to therapy using paraffin, sustained stretch, and ROM of trunk	Monitor semiannually until age 18	May require surgery for early release of hip or axillary contracture and/or z-plasty, or skin grafting down sides of trunk to release tight skin

Table 14.1 (Continued) Complications Associated with Burn Injury

Problem	When/Where Occurred	Results in	Dx Tests	Rehab Intervention	Duration of Treatment	Surgical Options
Reflex sympathetic dystrophy (RSD), shoulder/hand syndrome	Usually begins in acute phase of burn before wound closure; questionable etiology but seems to be related to immobility for long periods of time; occurs in both partial- and full-thickness burns, primarily in the hands	Hypersensitive hand with painful swollen joints, tapered, shiny fingers, and moist skin; if not treated immediately and aggressively, can result in permanent contracture deformities	X-ray, clinical exam	Stellate block immediately followed by vigorous physical therapy modalities of paraffin and sustained stretch, ultrasound, ROM and exercise, and desensitization; splinting may be indicated to prevent contracture; a 1-week trial of steroids may reduce pain and swelling	Early dx and tx are the keys to successful intervention; treatment time varies	None; sympathectomy rare
Kyphotic deformity	Occurs in children and thin adults with anterior chest and shoulder burns	Decreased respiratory function, spinal deformity	X-ray	Physical therapy for paraffin and sustained stretch, ROM, exercise and serial casting of the trunk, clavicular strap for shoulders	Until scar matures at 6–12 months postburn if no surgery	Axillary contracture releases and/or release of skin of anterior chest with skin grafting for adequate chest expansion
Joint subluxation	Can occur before wound healing is complete or as a result of tight scar tissue; usually occurs in small joints such as finger MPs, thumb, and toes	Permanent ankylosis or deformity	X-ray	Anticipate and treat early with splinting or casting to prevent	Until scar matures at 6–12 months postinjury	Surgical release of scar tissue will sometimes correct
Boutonniere finger deformity	Occurs in deep burns to the dorsal aspect of the fingers and hand, resulting in exposed or burned extensor tendons	Permanent deformities severely compromising hand function	Clinical exam, x-ray	Prevention is the key; requires specific treatment protocol for positioning, hand therapy, wound care, and finger casting	6 weeks or until tendon is covered	None
Swan neck deformity	Contracture of intrinsic muscles of the hands and/or volar plate rupture	Permanent finger deformity severely compromising hand function	X-ray, clinical exam	Stretching of intrinsic muscles, splinting of hand	Until ROM plateaus	None; if problematic, reconstructive procedures for better positioning of finger

Condition	Cause/Occurrence	Clinical Presentation	Diagnosis	Treatment	Duration	Surgical Procedure
Mallet finger deformity	Usually occurs in full-thickness burns of dorsal fingers and involves the insertion of the extensor tendon	Inability to extend the DIP joint of the finger	Clinical exam	Splint 24 hours/day for reattachment of ruptured extensor tendon	24 hours/day for 6 weeks	None; if no reattachment, pin in extension required
Muscle contracture	Develops from protective posturing to decrease pain, may occur without skin involvement	Loss of ROM	Clinical exam	Physical therapy for stretching program and serial casting	3–4 months	Surgical release is rarely required
Joint capsule contracture	Secondary to skin contracture, primarily in shoulder and fingers	Loss of ROM; may result in permanent deformity	Clinical exam	PT/OT for stretching program, ultrasound	3- to 4-month trial	Surgical release
Exposed bone	Occurs in deep full-thickness burns	Prolonged open wound	R/O osteomyelitis	Intense wound care protocol, including burr hole stimulation to promote growth of granulation tissue	Daily wound care until wound bed is ready for grafting	Skin graft or flap procedure
Exposed tendons	Occurs in deep full-thickness burns	Prolonged wound care and permanent deformities if not treated appropriately; may result in tendon rupture	Clinical exam	Intense wound care program to stimulate granulation tissue and prepare wound for surgery; splinting, casting, and orthotics may be needed for positioning and protection of tendon	Daily wound care and 24-hour splinting until tendon is covered	Surgical procedures for tissue flap and/or skin graft
Septic arthritis	May occur in joints associated with open wounds and/or joints without open wounds	Warm, painful, swollen joints and possible joint fusion	X-ray	ROM within pain limitation; oral or IV antibiotics	Condition can last for several weeks	May require surgical incision and drainage
Postischemic hand syndrome	Can occur from prolonged application of pneumatic tourniquet during grafting procedure	Numb, stiff, swollen hand	Clinical exam	OT program of massage, Coban wraps, and compression gloves to reduce swelling	5 times/week to TIW until problem resolves	None
Residual joint pain	Occurs primarily in hands and knees after wound healing and into the rehab program, perhaps from microtrauma to joints secondary to exercise program	Results in aching joints in absence of redness, warmth, or swelling and with negative x-rays	Clinical exam, x-ray	Usually controlled with over-the-counter analgesics or anti-inflammatory medications	Condition can persist for years	None

Table 14.1 (Continued) Complications Associated with Burn Injury

Problem	When/Where Occurred	Results in	Dx Tests	Rehab Intervention	Duration of Treatment	Surgical Options
Limb amputation	Occurs with full-thickness and deep full-thickness burns, and electrical injuries	Loss of extremity		Prior to prosthetic fitting, ROM, strengthening, and stump conditioning to prepare the limb for prosthesis; prosthetic fitting, gait training, and activities of daily living	TIW for 6–8 weeks; mobility aids such as wheelchair or crutches may be needed; a replacement schedule for the prosthesis should be considered	Surgical modification of the stump may be required to improve skin integrity and padding for the prosthesis
Shortened extremity	Occurs in the growing child when scar tissue crosses a joint and inhibits bone growth	Permanent shortened extremity	Clinical exam, extremity measurements	Child should be followed semiannually for extremity measurements and spinal screening	Follow until adult or bone maturity: 18 for girls, 24 for boys	Surgical release of scar tissue may be necessary to prevent permanent deformity

Neurological

Problem	When/Where Occurred	Results in	Dx Tests	Rehab Intervention	Duration of Treatment	Surgical Options
Generalized peripheral neuropathy	Occurs during the first 3–6 weeks postinjury	Sensory loss and distal weakness of upper and lower extremities Although improvement is generally seen, some weakness can be permanent.	EMG, NVC, muscle test	Therapy program consisting of muscle reeducation, strengthening, and electrical stimulation; weekly muscle test to monitor progress; assistive devices for ADLs; splints and AFOs for positioning to prevent contracture	Generally plateaus within 3–6 months	None
Mononeuropathy	Occurs anytime during the initial hospitalization; commonly affected nerves include the median, ulnar, peroneal, radial, and brachial plexus	Residual weakness and sensory loss extending down from the level of lesion	EMG, NVC, muscle test	Therapy program consists of muscle reeducation, strengthening, electrical stimulation, ROM, and specialized splinting; weekly muscle test to monitor return of function	Duration of treatment and recovery rate varies depending on the level of lesion; the more proximal the level of the lesion, the longer the intervention; 3 months to 2 years	None

Neuroma	A hypersensitive nerve ending or nerve bundle that occurs when an injured nerve tries to repair itself, generally after a surgical procedure	Localized hypersensitive, painful area	Clinical exam	Therapy program of desensitization techniques such as tapping, vibration, and massage; steroid injection	TIW from 6–8 weeks	A persistent neuroma may require surgical removal

Skin

Open wounds	Occurs with partial- and full-thickness burns	Painful wounds (prolonged wound healing usually results in worse scarring)	Clinical exam	Hydrotherapy, debridement, and wound care by an experienced rehab professional at a burn center	Wound care should be done by a professional 3–5 times/week and by a trained family member or caregiver on the other days; partial-thickness burns without complications heal in approximately 21 days; full-thickness burns, depending on the size, can take months to heal	Full- and/or split-thickness skin grafts for deep partial- and full-thickness burns will decrease pain and healing time
Chronic open wounds	Occurs with infection as MRSA, scratching, fragile skin, pressure, shearing, or blistering	Prolonged wound care, cellulitis, multiple hospitalizations	Wound culture to R/O MRSA	Oral and/or IV antibiotics may be indicated; hydrotherapy, debridement, and wound care	Wounds can heal and then reopen for years, especially when MRSA is the cause; treatment is required intermittently for several weeks depending on wound size	Surgical excision of the wound and debridement; skin grafting
Blistering	Generally occurs in early stages of wound healing from shearing of new skin	Open wounds on previously healed skin	Clinical exam	Requires a specific wound care protocol; may require oral antibiotics	The blistering stage generally lasts from 2–6 weeks	Occasionally skin grafting

Table 14.1 (Continued)   Complications Associated with Burn Injury

Problem	When/Where Occurred	Results in	Dx Tests	Rehab Intervention	Duration of Treatment	Surgical Options
Depigmentation/ hyperpigmentation	Noticed in newly healed skin	Uneven skin tones		May want to try camouflage makeup to improve cosmesis; vendors of camouflage makeup are often difficult to identify and locate; the makeup is expensive and uncomfortable for some patients	Skin tones can continue to change and improve for 6 months to 2 years, but will never totally return to normal	Pigmentation procedures
Hypertrophic scars	Generally occur in nongrafted areas of deep partial- and/or full-thickness burns with prolonged wound healing; usually occur more often in children and individuals with darker pigmented skin or very fair skin; if a burn wound loses its redness in 3 months, hypertrophic scarring usually does not occur; chances for hypertrophic scarring decrease if full-thickness or deep partial-thickness burns are grafted early	Red and/or purple, thick, lumpy, firm scar tissue that is warm to touch, hypersensitive, and may be painful	Clinical exam	Compression garments are worn for scar flattening, to decrease itching, and control pain; intermediate compression garments, such as isotoner gloves and elastic net, should be worn 23 hours/day for 2–4 weeks posthealing; these should be followed with custom-made compression garments that should be worn for 23 hours/day; two sets of garments should be ordered each time and will need to be replaced every 2–3 months Silicone sheets can be worn over scars for at least 12 hours/day for 4 weeks to facilitate flattening and scar maturation; may cause maceration of skin Clear plastic face masks and neck collars for optional methods of pressure	Compression garments are worn for 6–24 months or until scars are mature; mature scars are pliable, softer, flatter, cool to the touch, and lighter in color Worn 23 hours/day for 6–24 months; may require periodic revisions May require multiple or alternating splints to be worn for several months; splints will be revised periodically as scar tissue band softens and stretches Indefinite	After the scars mature, surgical reconstructive procedures, such as scar excision or tissue expanders, may be an option; this is often a time-consuming process, as reconstructive procedures are often done in stages requiring wound care and therapy between surgeries to obtain maximum benefit

Painful scars	Usually occur over the lateral chest wall and medial arm	Sensitive, painful scars; can interfere with sleep	Scar palpation	Splints for scar banding; worn over compression garments to apply additional pressure; web spacers or otoform may be worn under garments for additional pressure Camouflage makeup Treat with silicone gel sheets underneath compression garments; ice massage, vibrator, ultrasound scar massage, or desensitization can offer some relief, as well as steroid injections	Can last for up to 2 years	In severe painful cases, can be surgically removed
Skin contracture	Can occur anywhere in the burned area, causing bands of scar tissue that limit motion	Decreased ROM and function	Clinical exam, ROM measurements	Aggressive therapy protocol, including paraffin and sustained stretch, scar massage, portable vibrator to break up scar tissue, fluidotherapy, ROM, and exercise program Serial splinting and casting to prevent further loss of ROM and hopefully gain ROM Different joints require specific splinting protocols that may involve alternating splints and/or multiple splint changes	Therapy is recommended 3–5 times/week for several months; frequent cast changes and splint revisions can be expected; often the role of therapy is to keep the contracture from worsening until a surgical release can be performed	Surgical contracture releases are often done in stages in order to obtain maximum range; wound care and therapy are required between surgical procedures
Microstomia (small mouth)	Occurs with facial and lip burns	Decreased mouth opening resulting in compromised dental hygiene and poor nutritional status	Clinical exam, mouth opening measurements	Therapy protocol, including scar massage, mouth exercises with cones and appliances, or mouth stretchers; plastic face mask and cervical collars may also be indicated	Therapy 3–5 times/week until problem resolves	In severe cases surgical releases may be indicated

Table 14.1 (Continued)   Complications Associated with Burn Injury

Problem	When/Where Occurred	Results in	Dx Tests	Rehab Intervention	Duration of Treatment	Surgical Options
Ectropion (contraction of scar tissue of the eyelid or eversion of the eyelid caused by contraction of facial skin)	Occurs with deep facial burns and or burns to the eye area; usually becomes obvious during acute hospitalization	Inability to close the eyes, thereby causing corneal damage due to drying	Clinical exam, ophthalmology consult	Therapy, including scar massage and stretching	Daily therapy until problem resolves	Surgical intervention for release and skin grafting is usually indicated
Skin infection	Occurs when healed burned skin develops pustules from clogged pores and/or ingrown hair follicles; infection secondary to MRSA	Skin irritations characterized by weeping pustules and open wounds; requires prolonged wound care	R/O MRSA	Antibiotics and wound care; severe cases may require hospitalization and IV antibiotics If MRSA is diagnosed, Bactroban ointment and extended wound care may be indicated	May occur intermittently for years	Wound excision and grafting in severe cases of MRSA
Fingernail burns	Occurs with deep hand burns	Deformed nails with ragged sharp edges that catch on clothing, etc.	Clinical exam	Therapist can trim and grind nails; scar tissue massage over fingers to decrease pull at base of nail	Continue therapy until problem resolves	May require surgical removal and/or modification; reconstructive procedures to graft from toenails has been successful
Hair follicle loss	Most disfiguring with full-thickness burns to the scalp and forehead involving the eyebrows	Permanent hair loss and poor cosmesis	Clinical exam	Wigs or hairpieces, as well as hats and glasses, can be used to improve appearance	Items will be needed indefinitely without reconstructive procedures	Reconstructive procedures using tissue expanders have been successful with scalp burns; however, it often requires multiple procedures over several years depending on the size of the burn; eyebrows may be reconstructed with hair transplants or tattooing
Ingrown hairs	Usually occurs on men's faces and necks with thick scarring	Local infection	Clinical exam	Treat local infection with wound care and antibiotics	May occur intermittently for years	Surgical intervention to remove ingrown hairs may be required when large areas are involved

Loss of sebaceous glands	Occurs in full-thickness burns or with hypertrophic scarring	Dry, cracked skin and/or itching.	Clinical exam	Requires lubrication of skin 2–3 times/day	Permanent	None
Loss of skin innervation	Occurs in full-thickness burns and in areas of thick hypertrophic scars	Easily traumatized skin	Test for sensory loss	Patient education; protective clothing such as gloves and knee pads; fleece-lined shoes and custom insoles can help decrease traumatization; may require occupational modifications or vocational change	Permanent	None
Decubitus ulcer	Generally associated with long-term ICU hospitalization; most commonly occurs over bony prominences such as heels and sacrum	Prolonged rehab process; adherent scar tissue over the defect	Clinical exam	Prevention is the key; Roho mattresses are preferred over constant airflow beds due to the poor positioning associated with airflow beds; requires an extensive wound care protocol, including hydrotherapy, debridement, packing, and bandaging	Can take several months to heal	May require surgical flap procedure
Marjolin's ulcer (squamous cell carcinoma)	Develops from chronic open wounds (wounds that close and reopen over a prolonged period of time); rare — occurs in 0.1 of 0.01% of burns	Malignancy	Wound biopsy	Awareness of complication		Requires surgical procedure and wound closure
Allergic reactions	Healed skin becomes irritated due to lubricants, pressure garments, soaps, detergents, etc.; it is difficult to identify the irritating agent	Weeping wounds, burning, and itching; prolongs healing time and can interfere with return to work	Clinical exam	Discontinue use of topical agents, lotions, garments, and soaps for 2–4 days; begin substituting with alternative products, adding one at a time; may need short course of topical or oral steroids	Once the irritating product is discontinued, the problem resolves in 1–2 weeks	None
Itching	Can occur in any burned area after burn is healed	Open wounds from scratching	Clinical exam	Skin lubrications and antihistamine	Possibly years	None

Table 14.1 (Continued) Complications Associated with Burn Injury

Problem	When/Where Occurred	Results in	Dx Tests	Rehab Intervention	Duration of Treatment	Surgical Options
Psychological, Social, Vocational						
Psychosocial problems	Psychosocial and/or emotional difficulties manifest at any time during the burn recovery and rehab process and are often related to the etiology of the burn; spouses and caregivers may also experience emotional distress	Poor body image and decreased self-esteem; sexuality problems; increased dependency or sick role; anxiety related to loss of control; depression; fear of dying; anxiety over the future; posttraumatic stress disorder; discomfort in interpersonal situations and lack of acceptance in the workplace and/or fear of workplace Anxiety and distress related to fear of losing a loved one or material possessions; anxiety regarding ability to provide care for patient; concern for the future and economic issues	Psychiatric consult on all inpatients, rehab psychological evaluation for outpatients	Psychotropic medication if indicated; individual therapy sessions; support group participation; training in relaxation techniques; give patient appropriate options regarding treatment schedule, etc. Participation in individual therapy sessions and spousal support group; adequate family training	Psychological intervention may be prolonged or periodic in nature	Long-term emotional problems in burn patients appear to be the exception; some reports suggest that more severe burns are more likely to result in long-term quality of life problems with both physical and psychological aspects; others indicate that emotional problems may be more frequent in persons with more than 30% TBSA burns or if visible areas, such as the face and hands, are involved

Vocational problems	Vocational concerns usually begin to surface as the physical rehab process comes to an end, particularly if the burn was work related; both physical and psychological factors can impair function in the workplace, i.e., intolerance for heat and cold extremes, skin sensitivity to exposure to the sun or chemical agents, fatigability and reduced stamina, poor concentration, fear of workplace, decreased functional ROM and strength, and psychological adaptation	Delayed return to work	Functional capacity evaluation, comprehensive medical evaluation identifying functional limitations, vocational evaluation	Initiate formal vocational rehabilitation program as soon as patient is medically stable; encourage open and frequent communication with employer; obtain a comprehensive job description or complete job site evaluation; consider physical modification of job site and/or job tasks; participation in a formal work hardening program; identify a modified work schedule, or light duty, and encourage progressive return to full-time and regular duties	Approximately 90% of persons admitted to burn centers return to their preburn functional levels within 1 year; size, depth, and location (hands) are factors that influence time to return to work; surgical reconstructive procedures may also delay return to work	If return to one's preburn job is not feasible, consideration must be given to modifying that job, changing to a new job that might require retraining, or accepting permanent disability; decreased earning potential is a concern, as are difficulties in qualifying for Social Security Disability Insurance (SSDI)
Return to school problems	Can occur in any school child who receives a burn injury, but is usually a bigger problem when the child has had a lengthy absence from school; children may be concerned about appearance, discomfort due to compression garments and splints, and acceptance of peers	Posttraumatic stress disorder, anxiety, depression	Psychological evaluation	Prepare teachers and students for the burned child's return by having a therapist, social worker, or nurse give a special presentation of the "A Back to School" program allowing students and teachers to see garments and splints and ask questions about burn injuries; individual therapy sessions		
Sleep disturbances	Generally occurs after hospital discharge; can be secondary to pain and discomfort from burn wounds and/or splints; may also result from fear related to injury or anxiety relative to the future	Nightmares or night terrors, decreased energy and coping skills, or depression due to inadequate rest and sleep	Psychological evaluation may be indicated	Psychological intervention and desensitization and relaxation techniques; sleep medication	Usually improves with time and improved physical health; may require sleep medication up to 1-year postinjury	

Table 14.1 (Continued) Complications Associated with Burn Injury

Problem	When/Where Occurred	Results in	Dx Tests	Rehab Intervention	Duration of Treatment	Surgical Options
			Other			
Visual impairment	May occur with facial burns or electrical injuries	Burned or damaged corneas; may result in permanent partial loss of vision or blindness or cataracts in electrical injuries	Ophthalmology exam and follow-up	After wound healing or in conjunction with wound healing and burn rehab program, patient will need to participate in a rehab program for blind/visually impaired for ADL, mobility training, etc.	Several months depending on degree of visual loss	Corneal transplant
Hearing loss	Probably secondary to antibiotics	Hearing loss that may be permanent	ENT consult and audiological evaluation	In severe cases, training in sign language and lip reading may be indicated; hearing aids	Several months depending on degree of hearing loss	Cochlea implants offer limited improvement
Amputation of body parts	Deep full-thickness burns to ears, noses, fingers, and/or toes can result in amputations	Deformity and disfigurement, impaired body image, and emotional difficulties		Although it is very expensive, excellent prostheses are available from one who specializes in cosmetic prostheses Psychiatric/psychological intervention may be indicated	Replacement schedule for prostheses is 5–7 years Psychological support may be indicated periodically or continuously for several months	Reconstructive plastic surgery
Speech impairment	Occurs with prolonged intubation with endotracheal tube and when severe inhalation injuries are associated with burn injury	Hoarseness and decreased volume	ENT consultation	Speech therapy	Generally resolves or improves over extended time	None

Deconditioning	1–1.5% loss of strength per day of bed rest; loss of strength and muscle mass plateaus after 2 weeks of continuous bed rest, but can result in an overall strength loss of 25–40%	Decreased strength, endurance	Depending on individual's age and medical hx, a stress test to evaluate cardiac status is indicated	Formal conditioning program under the supervision of a therapist' activities utilizing treadmill and life cycle or similar equipment, and weight training are indicated in a progressive program	Formal conditioning program can last 10–12 weeks, after which the individual can be placed on a home program using home exercise equipment or through a health club; this should be a lifetime commitment	None
Poor dental hygiene	Occurs with prolonged intubation and ICU stays	Tooth decay, chipping of teeth	Dental exam	Cooperate with dentist to improve dental hygiene		None

Abbreviation Key

ADL	Activities of daily living	MP	Metacarpophalangeal joint
AFO	Ankle-foot orthosis	MRSA	Methicillin-resistant Staph Aureus
BIW	2 times/week	NVC	Nerve velocity conduction
DIP	Distal interphalangeal	OT	Occupational therapy
dx	Diagnosis	PT	Physical therapy
EMG	Electromyography	R/O	Rule out
ENT	Ear, nose, and throat	ROM	Range of motion
HO	Heterotopic ossification	TBSA	Total body surface area
hx	History	TIW	3 times/week
ICU	Intensive care unit	tx	Treatment

The life care plan, based on medical records, interview, physiatrist burn physician, orthopedist, plastic surgeon, gastroenterologist, and neuropsychologist recommendations, included the following.

RESOURCES

In addition to the references associated with this chapter, information regarding burn rehabilitation is available from the American Burn Association and its professional journal. They can be located at http://www.ameriburn.org.

Another resource for burn survivors is the Phoenix Society located on the Internet at http://www.phoenix-society.org.

Probably best known for free burn care for children is the Shriners. The Shriners have four primary locations:

51 Blossom St.	3229 Burnet Ave.
Boston, MA 02114	Cincinnati, OH 45229
(617) 722-3000	(513) 872-6000
815 Market St.	2425 Stockton Blvd.
Galveston, TX 77550	Sacramento, CA 95817
(409) 770-6600	(916) 453-2000

CONCLUSION

It is unrealistic to think that the total rehabilitation of the burn patient is dependent on the actual therapy treatment experience. Carryover and consistent follow-through by the patient for splinting regimens and home exercise programs must be stressed for maximum recovery. Giving patients control of appropriate options (type of medication, dressing change schedule, treatment schedule, etc.) can facilitate the process of their becoming more responsible and independent in their care. Nonetheless, the rehab process for a burn patient can totally overwhelm the patient's life, as well as the life of the patient's family. Therefore, the identification and attention to psychological problems is necessary throughout the rehabilitation process to address the impact of emotional difficulties on compliance and successful community reentry (Helm & Cromes, 1995). Overall, burn rehabilitation is complex, expensive, and involves considerable time and effort on the part of the client. This chapter outlines many of the concerns and goals regarding treatment. Compliance and effective treatment can maximize the ultimate outcome and reduce complications.

LIFE CARE PLAN

Note: For purposes of this plan, the following initials are placed in parentheses according to their respective recommendations:

RW   = Robert Weldon, M.D., reconstructive surgeon
RD   = Reggie Doppler, Ph.D., neuropsychologist
EE   = Eve Erickson, orthopedic surgeon
DT   = Denny Truffle, M.D., physiatrist
RV   = Renee Vector, M.D., gastroenterologist
ROW = Roger Weed, Ph.D., certified life care planner

Routine Future Medical Care — Physician Only

Recommendation (by whom)	Year Initiated and Frequency	Purpose	Expected Cost
Plastic/reconstructive surgeon (RW)	1 time/year to life expectancy	Monitor hypertrophic burn scar and existing skin coverage	$52–66/year
Note: The surgeon suggests more frequent follow-up if the client undergoes surgical intervention for scar revision/repair. See surgical interventions.			
Orthopedic surgeon (EE)	Every 2 years over next 10 years (2010)	Monitor orthopedic problems/complications	$220 total for 5 visits at $44/visit
Physiatrist (DT)	2 times/year to life expectancy	Overall rehabilitation follow-up regarding therapy and equipment needs	$120/year to life expectancy at $60/visit

Note: The physiatrist recommends regular follow-up every 6 months indefinitely.

Projected Evaluations — Nonphysician

(Include all allied health evaluations)

Recommendation (by whom)	Year Initiated	Frequency/Duration	Expected Cost
None recommended unless additional surgery			See next section and Potential Complications page

Projected Therapeutic Modalities

Recommendation (by whom)	Year Initiated	Frequency/Duration	Expected Cost
Physical therapy to develop/implement home exercise program (DT)	2000	1–3 sessions initially, then 3 times/week for 1–2 weeks (average) every 2–3 years to life for monitoring and compliance	Initial sessions at $310 total, then $240–480 every 2–3 years to life expectancy at $80/visit
Case management (ROW)	Unknown	See Note below	See Note below
Counseling (individual/family) for adjustment, support, coping, education, etc. (RD)	2000	2000: 1 time 2001–life: 4 times/year to life expectancy	2000: $80 2001+: $320/year to life at $80/visit*

Note 1: The physiatrist states the client may need special accommodations for lifting due to scars and contractures around his upper extremities. However, no information is available on specific accommodations and no cost included in plan totals. See also Health and Strength Maintenance.

Note 2: The client likely will need increased therapy if he has surgery to release contractures in his upper extremities. See future surgical interventions.

Note: Currently, the client does not exhibit case management needs and no cost is included for services. If complications and/or scar revision/reconstruction surgery occur in the future, case management services will need to be implemented at an estimated 4 hours/month for 6 months surrounding the time of surgery. Cost for case management services is $75 to $85/hour.

*Cost for follow-up sessions is with a master's-level counselor as recommended by the neuropsychologist.

Diagnostic Testing/Educational Assessment

Recommendation (by whom)	Year Initiated	Frequency/Duration	Expected Cost

None indicated at this time. The neuropsychologist states that, assuming no changes have occurred since initial evaluation, the client likely has stabilized in his functioning during the past year and the need for neuropsychological reexamination is limited. He states reevaluation may be indicated if changes are noted and that quarterly follow-up as listed in the previous section is warranted to monitor his adjustment. If needed, cost for neuropsychological reevaluation for established patient is $440.

Mobility Needs

Recommendation (by whom)	Year Purchased	Replacement Schedule	Expected Cost
Wheeled mobility system (EE, DT)	Anticipate 2006 (age 70)	1 time only	$3000 (average) depending on model and type

Note 1: Although the client currently uses a cane for mobility assistance, the orthopedic surgeon states that it is expected the client will need a wheelchair as he ages and his function/mobility decreases. The physiatrist states that the client would not have sufficient function in his left arm to maneuver a manual chair and will require a power scooter.

See also orthopedic equipment.

Mobility System Accessories and Maintenance

Recommendation (by whom)	Year Purchased	Replacement Schedule	Expected Cost
Scooter maintenance (ROW)	2007 (or 1 year after purchase of wheelchair)	1 time/year to life expectancy after 1-year warranty expires	$200/year (includes 2 gel batteries, tires, and maintenance)

Aids for Independent Function

Recommendation (by whom)	Year Purchased	Replacement Schedule	Expected Cost
Cordless telephone (ROW)	2000	Every 5 years (average)	$50 (average)
Shower chair/bench (EE)	1998 (already has)	N/A; do not expect replacement	N/A

Note: The client reportedly has a shower chair/bench and raised toilet seat.

Recommendation (by whom)	Year Purchased	Replacement Schedule	Expected Cost
Bedside commode (EE)	2000	1-time-only purchase	$100–150

Home Furnishings and Accessories

Recommendation (by whom)	Year Purchased	Replacement Schedule	Expected Cost
Chair with lift capability (ROW)	2000	N/A; 1-time-only purchase	$155–325 (lift cushion placed in any chair) to $850 (average) (recliner chair with power lift)

Note: Based on the client interview and observation, due to poor lower-extremity and left arm strength, assistance is needed for him to get from a sitting to a standing position.

Portable ramp at time of wheeled mobility system (can be used with either manual wheelchair or power scooter) (ROW)	2006 (age 70) or when use mobility system	N/A; 1-time-only purchase	$196–340 (depends on 3- or 5-foot ramp)

Drug/Supply Needs

Drug/supply needs and costs change from time to time and are representative of the client's current need.

Recommendation (by whom)	Purpose	Cost per Unit	Cost per Year
Allowance for miscellaneous items such as cocoa butter cream, sunscreen, Benadryl 1% lotion, etc. (RW, DT)	Skin emollient, sunburn protection, itch relief	As needed	$50/year (average)

Home/Facility Care

Recommendation (by whom)	Initiated/Suspended	Hours/Shifts/Days	Expected Cost
Competent companion (RD); currently performed by the family	2000 to life expectancy	Equivalent to live-in (10–12 hours/day with unpaid overnight)	1. In-home assistance: Up to $135–177/day equivalent to competent companion live-in if through home health agency 2. Loss of household services: Defer to economist to calculate loss of household services

Note 1: The neuropsychologist states the client is dependent on his wife/family and the likelihood of his resuming a fully independent lifestyle is unlikely. He also reports the client's capacity for independent function is greatly reduced. In addition, the wife reportedly left the workforce following the injury to care for the client.

Note 2: The client and his wife state he is unable to carry laundry and perform most housekeeping tasks and reportedly relies on his wife for laundry, shopping, driving to medical appointments, housecleaning, meal preparation, etc. This information as well as the neuropsychological test results, which indicate impairment in the areas of problem solving, attention/concentration, memory, etc., further support that the client requires a competent companion (which currently is provided by his wife) to help with executive functions, memory, and other household tasks. If the client's wife is no longer available to provide these services, then he would have need for all services associated with basic household management to be purchased through an agency. Cost equivalent for his wife's services if purchased through a private-duty home health agency would be $135 to $177/day or $13.50 to $14.75/hour for 10 to 12 hours equivalent to live-in. One agency offered CNA services at $11.50/hour up to 24 hours or $10/hour for 24-hour assistance; however, the CNA did not perform housecleaning and other services outside direct client care, and costs from this agency are not included in plan totals.

Note 3: Of the six private-duty home health agencies contacted in the client's area, none provide live-in services. Cost for 10 to 12 hours/day of companion/homemaker (equivalent to live-in) ranges $135 to $177/day. Cost of in-home care may be less if negotiated with home health agency, through private hire, or if family members provide some or all of the care.

Note 4: No provision is included for increased homemaking services following any surgery and/or as client ages due to expected reduced function.

Transportation

Recommendation (by whom)	Year Purchased	Replacement Schedule	Expected Cost
Mileage to appointments in Columbia, SC (ROW)	2000 to life expectancy	4 times/year to life	$104/year for 80 miles round-trip (approximately) at $0.325/mile

Note: Mileage includes counseling and physician appointments and presumes the client will schedule some appointments on the same day to avoid additional trips.

Braun Lift Jr. (ROW)	2006 (age 70)	N/A: 1-time-only purchase	Lift: $1045 (includes installation) plus maintenance at $100/year (average) after 1-year warranty

Note 1: Beginning it 2006 when it is expected the client will begin to use a scooter for outings and community mobility, he will require a Braun Lift to transport the wheelchair/scooter when in the community. Lift can be reinstalled into new vehicle if appropriate.

Note 2: The client states he does not drive other than occasional trips to visit his family approximately 5 miles from his home. It is presumed his wife or competent companion is available to drive the vehicle to take him to appointments, etc. See in-home care for equivalent agency costs for companion.

Health and Strength Maintenance (Leisure Time Activities)

Recommendation (by whom)	Year of Purchase or Attendance	Replacement or Attendance Schedule	Expected Cost
Daily exercise to include stretching and walking (DT)	2000 to life expectancy	Daily	N/A
Home exercise program to include weights/dumbbells for strengthening (DT)	2000 to life expectancy	1-time-only purchase	$7.90 for 1 pair of dumbbells up to $50 for set of 1- to 5-pound dumbbells

Vocational/Educational Plan

Recommendation (by whom)	Year Initiated/Suspended	Purpose	Expected Cost
Not applicable			

Architectural Considerations

(List considerations for home accessibility and/or modifications.)

The client currently lives in a small ranch home where he and his wife have resided for the past 30 years. The home is not barrier-free or accessible to the extent that it will need to be when he begins to use a scooter. If the client relies on a scooter for mobility inside the home in the future (anticipated at age 70), he will require a one-level, barrier-free, fully accessible home with features including wider doorways and hallways, smooth floor coverings, ramps, grab bars in bathroom, etc. Expect cost for accessibility features to be 10 to 20% over cost of average home in local area.

Economist to deduct cost of average home in local area.

Orthopedic Equipment Needs

Recommendation (by whom)	Year Purchased	Replacement Schedule	Expected Cost
Straight cane for mobility (interview)	1998 (already has)	N/A; expect no replacement	N/A
Walker (EE)	2003 (age 67)	1-time-only purchase	$57–70 depending on type/model

Note 1: Although it is anticipated that the client will use a scooter at approximately age 70 for mobility when out in the community, he will continue to need a cane and/or walker for backup to wheelchair and for household ambulation.

Future Medical Care, Surgical Intervention, Aggressive Treatment

Recommendation	Year Initiated	Frequency	Expected Cost
Scar revision, local and distant tissue transfers, skin grafting (RW)	2000	Unknown; depends on nature of hypertrophic burn scar and existing skin covrage	Unknown; see Note 1 below

Note 1: The surgeon states it is likely the client will require scar revision/repair at some time over the course of his lifetime; however, he reports he is unable to calculate the cost as the kind and extent of surgery depend on the client's skin integrity and scar/contracture formation. Requests have been made of the plastic surgeon to estimate approximate cost of surgery; however, at the time of plan development, the surgeon responded that the costs cannot be calculated. Further attempts are being made to identify costs.

Note 2: At the time of reconstructive surgery, he will also require physical/occupational therapy following each surgery at $960 to $3200 total (previously estimated by physiatrist at three to five times/week for 4 to 8 weeks); in-home skilled nursing for wound care/dressing changes; pain and antibiotic medication; and other services that may be required that cannot accurately be predicted. See also next entry.

| Pressure garments following scar revision surgery (RW) | Compression to reduce/prevent hypertrophic scar formation in arms, trunk, and neck | Generally replaced every 3 months up to 12 months of use following each surgical procedure | Face mask: $64–88 each
Neck strap: $44 each
Vest with sleeves: $120–147 each
(Note: The client requires 2 of each) |

Note 1: According to the surgeon, the client will require pressure garments throughout his lifetime following scar revision surgery. Garments generally are worn for up to 12 months following each surgical procedure and require replacement every 3 months (average) depending on wear and tear.

Note 2: Expect two of each pressure garment replaced every 3 months for up to 12 months.

Note 3: Cost does not include additional charges for fittings and accessories such as zippers and linings, silicon sheeting for skin, adhesive tape, or gel.

Potential Complications

Note: Potential complications are included for information only. No frequency or duration of complications is available. No costs are included in the plan.

Reduced/compromised skin integrity requiring more extensive and/or frequent scar revision/repair or skin grafting than expected and more frequent follow-up by reconstructive surgeon, including increased need for pressure garments, medications (pain and/or antibiotic medication), physical therapy, in-home nursing and/or attendant care, etc.

Increased contractures and/or poor outcome from any future revision surgery. If contractures worsen, could further reduce his independent function and require increased in-home care needs and/or increased need for adaptive equipment. The surgeon states the client experiences a proliferative healing process/hypertrophic burn scar formation that makes him prone to future difficulties.

Orthopedic complications (i.e., development of heterotopic ossifications, bone spurs, arthritis, etc.) that require surgery, aggressive therapy, medication, splints, etc., to treat.

Altered protective sensation in skin that could result in further damage or injury.

Increased risk of infections if skin breakdown and/or wounds do not heal properly.

Psychological maladjustment to disability (i.e., depression, ineffective coping, social isolation/withdrawal, etc.) that requires more frequent follow-up, medication, and/or hospitalization to treat.

REFERENCES

Buschbacher, R.M. (1996). Deconditioning, conditioning, and the benefits of exercise. In R.L. Braddom, Ed., *Physical Medicine & Rehabilitation*, 687–708. Philadelphia: W.B. Saunders.

Brych, S., Engrav, L., Rivara, F., Ptacek, J., Lezotte, D. Esselman, P., Kowalske, K., & Gibran, N. (2001). Time off work and return to work rates after burns: systematic review of the literature and a large two-center series. *Journal of Burn Care & Rehabilitation*, 22, 401–405.

Choctaw, W.F., Eisner, M.E., & Wachtel, T.L. (1987). Courses, prevention, prehospital case, evaluation, emergency treatment, and prognosis. In B.M. Achover, Ed., *Management of the Burn Patient*, 4–5. Los Altos, CA: Appleton & Lange.

Cobb, N., Maxwell, G., & Silverstein, P. (1990). Patient perception of quality of life after burn injury: results of an eleven-year survey. *Journal of Burn Care & Rehabilitation*, 10, 251–257.

Committee on Trauma Research. (1985). *Injury in America: A Continuing Public Problem.* Washington, DC: National Academic Press.

Cromes, G.H., Jr. & Helm, P.A. (1993). Burns, in M. Eisenberg, R. Glueckauf, & H. Zaretsky, Eds., *Medical Aspects of Disability*, 92–104. New York: Springer Publishing Company.

Demling, R.H. & LaLonde, I.C. (1989). *Burn Trauma.* New York: Thieme Medical Publishers.

Feck, G., Baptiste, M.S., & Tate, C.L., Jr. (1978). *An Epidemiological Study of Burn Injuries & Strategies for Prevention.* Washington, DC: U.S. Department of Health, Education, and Welfare, Public Health Services.

Fisher, S.V. & Helm, P.A. (1984). *Comprehensive Rehabilitation of Burns.* Baltimore: Williams & Wilkins.

Hartford, C.E. (2002). Care of outpatient burns. In D. Herndon, Ed., *Total Burn Care*, 2nd ed., 40–49. New York: W.B. Saunders.

Helm, P.A. & Cromes, G.F., Jr. (1995). Burn injury rehabilitation. In The National Rehabilitation Hospital Research Center, Ed., *The State-of-the-Science in Medical Rehabilitation*, IV1–IV22. Falls Church, VA: Birch & Davis Associates.

Helm, P.A. & Fisher, S.V. (1988). Rehabilitation of the patient with burns. In J.A. DeLisa, Ed., *Rehabilitation Medicine Principles & Practice*, 821–839. Philadelphia: J.B. Lippincott.

Herndon, D. & Blakeney, P. (2002). Teamwork for total burn care: achievements, directions and hopes. In D. Herndon, Ed., *Total Burn Care*, 2nd ed., 11–15. New York: W.B. Saunders.

Pruitt, B., Goodwin, C., & Mason, A. (2002). Epidemiological, demographic and outcome characteristics of burn injury. In D. Herndon, Ed., *Total Burn Care*, 2nd ed., 14–30. New York: W.B. Saunders.

Rice, D.P. & MacKenzie, E.J. (1989). *Cost of Injury in the United States: A Report to Congress.* Atlanta, GA: Centers for Disease Control.

Sheffield, C.G., Irons, G.B., Muehal, P., Jr., Malie, J.F., Ilstrup, D.M., & Stonnington, H.H. (1988). Physical & psychological outcome after burn. *Journal of Burn Care & Rehabilitation*, 9, 172–177.

Watkins, P., Cook, L., May, R., & Ehleben, C. (1989). Psychological stages of adaptation following burn injury: AS method for facilitating psychological recovery of burn victims. *Burn Care Commentary*, 5, 1–23 (Humana Burn Center, Augusta, GA).

Weed, R., Kirkscey, M., Mullins, G., Dunlap, K., & Taylor, C. (1997). Return to work rates in case of amputation. *Journal of Rehabilitation Outcomes Measurement*, 1, 35–39.

15

LIFE CARE PLANNING FOR THE HIV/AIDS PATIENT

Sherie L. Kendall

INTRODUCTION

Just over 20 years ago the first case of what would be called acquired immuno-deficiency syndrome (AIDS) was described (CDC, 1981). The U.S. Centers for Disease Control, now known as the Centers for Disease Control and Prevention (CDC), began reporting an unusually high incidence of the uncommon *Pneumocystis carinii* pneumonia (PCP) and a rare cancer, Kaposi's sarcoma, among young gay men in San Francisco, New York, and other cities. Therefore, AIDS was initially considered almost exclusively a male, homosexual disease. Then the number of new cases began increasing rapidly among persons with hemophilia A and other recipients of blood transfusions. Another distinct population of victims emerged from the intravenous drug users' community. Prognosis at that time was imminent death, the cause and prevention of which were unknown.

Because AIDS was appearing in diverse populations, an infectious agent was suspected as the cause (Prusiner, 2002). The mode of transmission seemed to be through sexual contact or blood product exposure. By 1983–1984 the pathogen responsible for the progressed disease state of AIDS was identified as human immunodeficiency virus (HIV). Within a year a blood test was developed for diagnosing HIV infection, thus safeguarding the blood supply, allowing the extent of the epidemic and individual infection to be defined and forecast, and eventually the evaluation and monitoring of therapeutic interventions (Montagnier, 2002). Present therapies have extended the life span for the treated HIV patient; however, neither an absolute cure nor a preventative vaccine is currently available. Since new infections continue to exceed the number of HIV-related deaths, the population living with HIV infection is burgeoning. UNAIDS estimated that in 2002 HIV was acquired by 5 million people, while HIV-related mortality accounted for 3.1 million deaths. Now in the third decade since identification, HIV/AIDS has become a true infectious disease pandemic with an estimated 42 million people in the world infected at the end of 2002 (UNAIDS, 2002).

0-8493-1511-5/04/$0.00+$1.50
© 2004 by CRC Press LLC

Epidemiology of HIV/AIDS in the U.S.

Human immunodeficiency virus type 1 (HIV-1) has been clearly identified as the primary cause of AIDS, which results from the destruction of CD4+ T lymphocytes of the immune system. Another strain of the human retrovirus found in western Africa, HIV-2, also causes AIDS. Additionally, there are clades, or subtypes, of HIV-1 that are different from those commonly found in the U.S. and Europe (Kitchen, 1995). The major clades are lettered A through G, with clade A having four subtypes (Sande et al., 2001). While clade B is currently the most prevalent in the developed world, international travel facilitates communication of the different varieties of HIV to all world regions. Genetic variants have arisen not because HIV replicates with a higher rate of mutation than is common, but because HIV generates 10 billion virions/day. At this rate, every possible mutation in the HIV genome can be produced every day. The genetic versatility of HIV permits the virus to become drug resistant and avoid antibody detection by vaccines and disease screening tests (Johnson, 1998).

As early as 1983, the U.S. Department of Health and Human Services (DHHS) declared the HIV epidemic to be the nation's foremost health priority (National Institute of Mental Health, 2000). National vital statistics data are discerning measures of HIV-related mortality and how HIV-related deaths have changed over the course of the HIV epidemic. Currently, HIV is the fifth leading cause of death for Americans between the ages of 25 and 44. This represents a decline in AIDS-related deaths by 70% from the mortality peak in 1995 when HIV was the leading cause of death in this age group (National Center for Health Statistics, 2002; CDC, 2002b). The decline in mortality coincides with the emergence of new HIV therapies in the past decade. Unfortunately, the rate of new infection has not been similarly reduced. Approximately 40,000 people in the U.S. acquire HIV annually (CDC, 2001a). By the end of 2002, the CDC estimated that an alarming 950,000 people in the U.S. were infected with HIV and perhaps 25% of them were unaware of their infection (Fleming et al., 2002; Sande & Volberding, 1999). These numbers represent a substantial health care burden, loss of work time and resources, and significant case management responsibilities for this population.

An estimated 362,827 persons in the U.S. were living with AIDS at the close of 2001. Of those reported AIDS cases, infection exposure categories ranked (1) men who have sex with men, (2) injecting drug use, and (3) heterosexual contact. For women, heterosexual contact was the number one exposure risk for HIV infection, followed by injecting drug use. Pediatric HIV infection is almost entirely due to mother-to-child transmission either before or during birth, or after birth by breast-feeding. The gender distribution of these AIDS cases is 70% men and 30% women. The fastest-growing newly infected HIV population is young to middle-aged women, and heterosexual sex is the fastest-growing method of transmission (CDC, 2002b). Clearly the face of HIV/AIDS is changing from the initial perception that it was a male, homosexual disease to an infection spread by heterosexual contact in the mainstream of society.

Natural History

Transmission of HIV occurs through exchange of body fluids, particularly blood, breast milk, and genital secretions. Risk of transmission is present in sexual encounters, infected needle sticks, blood product and tissue reception, birth and breast-feeding. Because a vaccine against HIV is not anticipated in the near future, prevention of new infection cases is limited to behavior modification of high-risk behaviors such as injection drug use and unprotected sexual intercourse and minimizing other risk factors such as genital ulcers, multiple sex partners, and history of sexually transmitted diseases. Postexposure prophylaxis is moderately effective in reducing the rate of transmission and generally recommended after a significant intravenous exposure or sexual exposure and to reduce mother-to-child transmission for the fetus of an infected woman who becomes pregnant.

After HIV has been transmitted to a person, there ensues an incubation period of 2 to 3 weeks. The subsequent acute retroviral syndrome lasts 1 to 3 weeks; however, only 50 to 90% of patients are symptomatic in this stage. The range and severity of symptoms in primary HIV infection vary considerably, with an acute mononucleosis-like illness developing in about 40% of patients. Generally, it is characterized by fever, lethargy/malaise, pharyngitis (sore throat), rash on the body, mucocutaneous ulcerations, adenopathy (swollen lymph nodes), myalgias, and weight loss. Gastrointestinal disorders include nausea/vomiting, diarrhea, hepatosplenomegaly, and oropharyngeal candidiasis. Neurologic symptoms may appear as headache, meningoencephalitis, peripheral neuropathy, facial palsy, brachial neuritis, Guillain-Barré syndrome, and cognitive/affective impairment (Bartlett, 2001).

With recovery from the acute HIV syndrome, an antiviral immune response occurs (seroconversion) and a state of chronic HIV infection is entered that may be clinically asymptomatic, or minimally symptomatic before the development of overt immunodeficiency. This clinical latency period is marked by viral replication within lymphoid tissues and declining numbers of CD4+ lymphocyte cells in the immune system. In an untreated patient, the asymptomatic stage usually continues for 7 to 10 (average of 8) years. However, for reasons that are only beginning to be understood, the disease progresses differently in some people such that slow, intermediate, and rapid progressors to the symptomatic and AIDS stages have been seen clinically, as well as long-term nonprogressors. The onset of symptomatic HIV infection may present with persistent fever, headache, fatigue, unintentional weight loss of more than 10% (wasting), chronic diarrhea, idiopathic thrombocytopenic purpura, and adenopathy. In addition to these direct effects of viral infection, tumors such as Kaposi's sarcoma and some rather virulent opportunistic infections (OIs) can appear at this time even though the immune system is only moderately suppressed, e.g., bacterial pneumonia and tuberculosis. Chronic skin conditions such as seborrheic dermatitis, oral or vaginal candida, herpes zoster, herpes simplex, and oral hairy leukoplakia may be seen (Powderly, 2001). The immune system is progressively impaired as CD4+ cell counts continue to decline, allowing the clinical expression of an AIDS indicator condition.

The average time from the diagnosis of an AIDS-defining condition to death is 16 months. In the untreated patient of HIV infection, survival from time of HIV infection is about 10 years. For the HIV-positive patient receiving current antiretroviral (ARV) therapy and prophylaxes against OIs, survival and quality of life are appreciably better than those of the untreated HIV patient recounted in this natural history of HIV infection. However, the ARV treatments introduced in the last decade have not been used therapeutically long enough to define the extended survival they provide (Bartlett, 2001; Masci, 2001).

Classification

The classification, surveillance, and reporting of HIV/AIDS are based on the case definitions for adults and children over the age of 18 months that have been developed by the CDC. The CDC has developed special criteria for infants less than 18 months of age that take into account mother-to-child transmission. The AIDS surveillance case definition was revised in 1985, 1987, and 1993 to incorporate additional illnesses that were found to be associated with HIV infection. The current case definition of AIDS recognizes the following AIDS indicator conditions (Bartlett, 2001; CDC, 1992; Masci, 2001; Powderly, 2001).

AIDS Indicator Conditions

*Candidiasis of esophagus, trachea, bronchi, or lungs

*Cervical cancer, invasive

*Coccidioidomycosis, extrapulmonary

Cryptococcosis, extrapulmonary

Cryptosporidiosis with diarrhea for >1 month

Cytomegalovirus (CMV) infection of any organ except liver, spleen, or lymph nodes; eye

Herpes simplex with mucocutaneous ulcer for >1 month, or esophageal or pulmonary involvement

*Histoplasmosis, extrapulmonary

HIV-associated dementia: disabling cognitive or other dysfunction interfering with occupation or activities of daily living

*HIV-associated wasting: involuntary weight loss of >10% of baseline plus chronic diarrhea (two or more loose stools per day for ≥30 days) or chronic weakness and documented enigmatic fever for ≥30 days

*Isoporosis with diarrhea for >1 month

Kaposi's sarcoma in patient under 60 years (or *over 60 years)

Lymphoma

Mycobacterium avium complex (MAC) or *M. kansasii*

**Mycobacterium tuberculosis*

Nocardiosis

Pneumocystis carinii pneumonia

*Pneumonia, recurrent bacterial (two or more episodes in 12 months)

Progressive multifocal leukoencephalopathy

**Salmonella* septicemia (nontyphoid), recurrent

Toxoplasmosis of internal organ

*Laboratory evidence of HIV infection is required

The 1993 revision (CDC, 1992) also added immunologic parameters of CD4+ lymphocyte counts less than 200 cells/mm$_3$ or a CD4+ percentage of total lymphocytes of less than 14% as diagnostic of AIDS for HIV-infected adults and adolescents. By 1993 and 1994 this immunologic criteria, rather than AIDS-defining conditions, resulted in almost half of the AIDS cases reported (Sande & Volberding,

1999). An expansion of the case definition for HIV/AIDS stages the progression of HIV according to the patient's clinical condition (categories A, B, and C) and CD4+ cell count (classes 1, 2, and 3). Because class 3 is an AIDS indicator condition, HIV-positive patients staged as A3 and B3 as well as C1, C2, and C3 are defined as having progressed to AIDS (Bartlett, 2001).

Clinical Conditions Categories

A. Asymptomatic, or persistent generalized lymphadenopathy or acute HIV infection
B. Symptomatic (not A or C)
C. AIDS indicator condition present

CD4 Count Classification

1. Greater than or equal to 500 cells/mm^3, greater than 29%
2. 200 to 499 cells/mm^3, 14 to 28%
3. Less than 200 cells/mm^3, less than 14%

Laboratory Criteria

The most recent revision (CDC, 1999) incorporated "the reporting criteria for HIV infection and AIDS into a single case definition." The definition of HIV infection implemented in 1993 was revised to include HIV screening tests as laboratory evidence of HIV with regard to AIDS-defining conditions for adults, adolescents, or children aged greater than or equal to 18 months. A reportable case of HIV infection must meet at least one of the following criteria:

■ Positive result on a screening test for HIV antibody, e.g., repeatedly reactive enzyme immunoassay, followed by a positive result on a confirmatory (sensitive and more specific) test for HIV antibody, e.g., Western blot or immunofluorescence antibody test
■ Positive result or report of a detectable quantity on any of the following HIV virologic (nonantibody) tests:
    — HIV nucleic acid (DNA or RNA) detection, e.g., DNA polymerase chain reaction (PCR) or plasma HIV-1 RNA
    — HIV p24 antigen test, including neutralization assay
    — HIV isolation (viral culture)

Clinical or Other Criteria

If the above laboratory criteria are not met, then one of the following must be met:

■ Diagnosis of HIV infection, based on the laboratory criteria above, that is documented in a medical record by a physician
■ Conditions that meet criteria included in the case definition for AIDS (CDC, 1992)

CLINICAL MANAGEMENT OF HIV INFECTION

HIV Lab Studies/Blood Analysis

HIV testing and diagnosis should always be carried out under the CDC Guidelines for Counseling, Testing and Referral (CDC, 2001b). The patient's best interest requires early diagnosis to preserve the broadest possible range of treatment options in managing the disease. Once antibody testing establishes diagnosis, two other tests for markers of HIV infection are important in managing the illness. Viral load tests of the amount of virus in the bloodstream indicate the expected rate of disease progression. The higher the viral load, the faster the disease is expected to progress. White blood cell tests for counts of CD4+ lymphocyte cells or percent of CD4+ cells in the total lymphocyte cell population indicate how far the disease has progressed in suppressing the immune system. These tests are used to determine when to initiate therapy, relative success of therapy, and when to change therapy. Both viral load tests and CD4+ cell counts are recommended upon diagnosis of HIV seropositive status to establish a baseline, at initiation of ARV therapy, 4 weeks later, and then every 3 to 4 months thereafter. Resistance testing is used to determine the optimal therapy choice either prior to initiation of therapy or when current therapy fails.

HIV Antibody Testing

Screening for HIV infection is by the detection of antibody specific to the virus in the blood by reactive enzyme-linked immunosorbent assay (ELISA). A second positive ELISA followed by a positive Western blot detection of several HIV antibodies confirms diagnosis. The patient is termed *HIV seropositive* because the blood analysis or serology is positive for HIV.

If acute HIV infection is suspected, a negative ELISA may be followed by a Western blot and plasma HIV RNA test. Acute HIV infection, which precedes seroconversion, is defined by detection of HIV RNA in the plasma on the same day as a negative Western blot for antibodies (Princeton, 2003). Seroconversion should be verified 3 to 4 months later by an ELISA. Sensitivity and specificity of these tests are greater than 98%; however, indeterminate results can be obtained. Patients with high-risk exposure should be retested in 2 to 3 months. Patients with indeterminate serology and a low-risk behavior history are almost never positive and retesting is optional.

The ELISA and Western blot test processes are time- and labor-intensive. Some other serologic tests have been developed to speed the return of results or provide the privacy of home testing. To improve consumer acceptance of testing, both a urine sample and a saliva sample test have been developed, but the Food and Drug Administration (FDA) has approved neither of these two tests.

Viral Load Testing

Viral load tests are used for evaluating and monitoring the effectiveness of ARV therapy. Lower levels of virus in the blood are associated with reduced risk for progression to AIDS status, infection, and death. Successful ARV therapy will diminish or stabilize viral load. An increasing viral load while on ARVs is indicative of therapeutic failure and possibly the emergence of viral resistance. Current viral load tests can detect as few as 50 copies of virus. The most desirable range of viremia is undetectable. An undetectable viral load is prognostic of the best clinical outcome, but it does not mean that HIV has been eradicated. Viremia is a measure of HIV in the blood only. Other reservoirs of virus reside in lymph tissues, bone marrow, the brain, and genital secretions. The DHHS recognizes two quantitative determinations of viral load: one is reverse transcriptase-PCR (RT-PCR) for viral RNA and the other is the branched-chain DNA assay (bDNA). These two assays give different numbers for the same patient sample because the bDNA detects more viral subtypes than the RT-PCR. Therefore, it is inappropriate to compare results from the different tests.

CD4+ Cell Testing

Counts of CD4+ lymphocytes are an indicator of immune system health. The level of CD4+ cells correlate well with the risk of opportunistic infections and tumors. The normal CD4+ cell count is $1000/mm^3$, but even a count of $500/mm^3$ is considered high for the HIV-positive patient. In the high cell count range there is no immediate danger. In the medium range of 300 to $500/mm^3$ serious symptoms are uncommon, but there is an increased risk for shingles, thrush, skin infections, and bacterial pulmonary infections. Many researchers consider this the optimal time to initiate ARV therapy, especially if viral activity is significant. In the low range of less than $300/mm^3$, the risk of infection is greatest and preventative treatment, or prophylaxis, for some major infections is usually initiated. A CD4+ cell count of less than $200/mm^3$ is an AIDS-defining condition.

Resistance Testing

When HIV can replicate in the presence of an ARV drug it has the opportunity to mutate to avoid the drug's activity. If a drug is unable to completely suppress HIV replication, viral resistance can emerge. Incomplete suppression can occur in a number of ways. The drugs prescribed may not be completely effective against the patient's strain of HIV, or the patient may have difficulty adhering to the treatment regimen and miss doses of the drugs. Resistance testing can help in the selection process for an effective therapeutic treatment strategy. Two kinds of resistance testing are available: phenotypic and genotypic. In phenotypic testing, a sample of the patient's HIV is exposed to various drugs, and the relative effectiveness of the drugs against that strain of HIV is measured. In genotypic testing the genetic structure of the patient's HIV is determined and compared to the structure of ARV targets. Mutations in the patient's HIV structure that are known to thwart ARV targets are identified. A rational choice for the new ARV regimen can be based on the results of this resistance testing.

Antiretroviral Therapy

The progress medical science is making toward eradicating HIV is encouraging. While it must be understood that antiretroviral agents (ARVs) cannot be considered a cure, they do represent viable, potent therapies for this infectious disease. A positive HIV test is not good news, but with these drugs, it is no longer a death sentence. Many HIV-positive people are living 15 years or longer with appropriate case management.

The first ARV, a nucleoside reverse transcriptase inhibitor, was released in 1986. Therapeutic research during the 1990s developed two new classes of ARVs, protease inhibitors and nonnucleoside reverse transcriptase inhibitors. Studies of treatment with combinations of three to four of these drugs were found to slow progression of HIV infection to AIDS status and improve survival. The multidrug therapies are termed *highly active antiretroviral therapy* (HAART). The goal of anti-HIV therapy is to suppress viremia in order to preserve or restore immune function and to prevent the emergence of drug resistance by patient adherence to treatment regimen.

Since many ARVs were expedited through the development process, investigation of their long-term adverse effects, toxicities, and drug interactions must be continued. Some toxicities have become well recognized such as abnormal fat redistribution and metabolic disorders, e.g., glucose intolerance, hyperlipidemia, lactic acidosis, and hepatic steatosis (Princeton, 2003). Patient adherence is difficult to maintain since the treatment regimens are complex and laden with minor, but troubling, side effects. Complete patient compliance with therapy is vitally important because viral resistance to the drugs emerges as adherence diminishes (Masci, 2001).

The U.S. DHHS (2002) has developed guidelines for initiation of anti-HIV treatment based on a combination of clinical symptomology, viral load, and CD4+ count. These guidelines are tiered in three levels:

1. When the patient is asymptomatic, CD4+ cell count is above $350/mm^3$, and viral load is below 30,000 (bDNA) or below 55,000 (RT-PCR), the recommendation is variable. Some would treat and some would delay initiating treatment and observe.
2. When the patient is asymptomatic, CD4+ cell count is less than $350/mm^3$, and viral load is above 30,000 (bDNA) or above 55,000 (RT-PCR), the recommendation is to offer treatment. However, the recommendation's strength is based on the patient's interest in initiating therapy and the prognosis of disease-free survival.
3. When the patient is symptomatic (sick — AIDS, OI, fever), the recommendation is to treat regardless of CD4+ cell count and viral load.

HAART is the cornerstone of anti-HIV therapy. The use of only two ARVs or any monotherapy is generally not recommended because these therapies may not completely suppress HIV replication, thus allowing viral resistance to emerge. The hallmark of successful therapy is a 5- to 7.5-fold drop in viral load within 4 weeks and a 10-fold decrement within 8 weeks. The long-term goal of HAART is to maintain viral load below the limits of detection, i.e., undetectable. The durability of the initial treatment regimen is predicated upon the efficacy of the drugs against the virus, their tolerability by the patient, and ultimately by the patient's adherence to the regimen.

There are several reasons to change the components of a drug therapy. One is when the primary goals of HAART are not met by the first therapy regimen selected. Since HIV can become resistant to all drugs, future treatment options could be limited by the initial and secondary drug choices. The standard of care of the HIV patient changes with the accumulation of knowledge and the development of new drugs. Therefore, it is sometimes prudent to delay making therapeutic changes in anticipation of future drug development. Other major reasons to consider changing drug regimens include:

- Viral load increase by threefold above the lowest measurement obtained or viral rebound to detectable levels after being undetectable
- CD4+ counts continue to fall even with decreases in viral load
- Clinical symptoms of HIV/AIDS develop or worsen
- Significant drug intolerance or toxicity
- Less than 95% patient adherence
- Pregnancy

At the present time, there are at least 16 antiretroviral medications approved either individually or in co-formulation for HIV therapeutic intervention. These drugs are classified in three categories: nucleoside/nucleotide reverse transcriptase inhibitors (NRTIs), nonnucleoside reverse transcriptase inhibitors (NNRTIs), and protease inhibitors (PIs). They include the following:

Drug Brand Name (Class)	Generic Names
Combivir® (NRTI)	lamivudine and zidovudine
Epivir® (NRTI)	lamivudine, 3TC
Hivid® (NRTI)	zalcitabine, ddC
Retrovir® (NRTI)	zidovudine, ZDV, azidothymidine, AZT
Trizivir™ (NRTI)	abacavir sulfate with lamivudine and zidovudine
Videx® and Videx® EC (NRTI)	didanosine, ddI
Viread™ (NRTI)	tenofovir disoproxil fumarate
Zerit® (NRTI)	staduvine, d4T
Ziagen® (NRTI)	abacavir sulfate
Rescriptor ® (NNRTI)	delavirdine mesylate
Sustiva™ (NNRTI)	efavirenz
Viramune® (NNRTI)	nevirapine
Agenerase® (PI)	amprenavir
Crixivan® (PI)	indinavir sulfate
Fortovase® (PI)	saquinavir
Invirase® (PI)	saquinavir mesylate
Kaletra® (PI)	lopinavir and ritonivir
Norvir® (PI)	ritonavir
Viracept® (PI)	nelfinavir mesylate

Recommended HAART incorporates one choice from column A and one from column B:

Column A	Column B
Crixivan	AZT plus ddI
Kaletra	AZT plus 3TC or Combivir
Norvir plus Fortovase	d4T plus ddI
Sustiva	d4T plus 3TC
Viracept	Trizivir

Alternative HAART recommendations incorporate one choice from column A and one from column B:

Column A	Column B
Agenerase	AZT plus ddC
Fortovase	ddI plus 3TC
Norvir	
Rescriptor	
Viracept plus Fortovase	
Viramune	
Ziagen	

The medical follow-up of individuals on any pharmacological therapy must be maintained, as well as diligent case management, to closely monitor the patient's condition and changing needs. Case management/medical issues associated with the use of these drugs include routine follow-up with general chemistry and hematologic evaluations on a schedule established by the physician as well as monitoring of viral load and CD4+ counts.

Drug Profiles

Nucleoside/Nucleotide Reverse Transcriptase Inhibitors (NRTIs)

This class of drugs provided the first efficacious antiretroviral treatment. They are analogs of the nucleosides or nucleotides used to build the DNA of the virus. When the reverse transcriptase enzyme uses an analog in the replication process, an incomplete virus is produced that is nonfunctional. Adverse reactions common to this class of drugs include lactic acidosis with or without hepatomegaly, and steatosis. Viral resistance to these drugs usually evolves from point mutations in the virus specific for the particular drug so that cross-resistance between drugs is usually incomplete.

Abacavir

The limiting adverse effect to this drug is a hypersensitivity reaction, which can be fatal. The reaction usually occurs within the first 6 weeks of drug administration, but resolves after discontinuation of the drug. Abacavir is one of three drugs comprising Trizivir™. There are no food restrictions.

Didanosine

Using this medication can cause painful chronic peripheral neuropathies that produce a mild, reversible, stocking-and-glove pattern of discomfort in about 10% of individual users. Pancreatitis may occur in 1 to 2% and may be severe, even fatal. Toxicities can include headache, insomnia, rash, and gastrointestinal disturbances. Should be taken 30 minutes before or 2 hours after a meal.

Lamivudine

Resistance to this drug can develop rapidly if monotherapy is used or if viral replication is not completely suppressed. The drug is generally well tolerated, but side effects can include nausea, diarrhea, anemia, low white blood cell count, and pancreatitis (especially in children). Renal failure would require the dosage to be decreased. Lamivudine is one of three drugs comprising Trizivir™. It has also been approved for use with Zidovudine and marketed as Combivir®. There are no food restrictions.

Stavudine

A dose-related peripheral neuropathy occurs in 19 to 24% of individuals with advanced disease and in 14% of those with less advanced HIV disease. Other adverse effects may include headache, gastrointestinal disturbances, anemia, neutropenia, pancreatitis, and elevated hepatic transaminases. Renal failure would require the dosage to be decreased. The drug may be taken without regard to food.

Tenofovir

This is the only nucleotide analog currently approved for clinical use. The nucleotide analog does not require intracellular phosphorylation for activation, as do the nucleoside analogs. It may have broader activity than the other drugs of this class. Adverse effects can include elevations in creatine kinase, hepatic transaminases, and triglycerides, neutropenia, fatigue, headache, and worsening of peripheral neuropathies. Should be taken with food.

Zalcitabine

The major adverse effect is peripheral neuropathy presenting as a burning sensation. Other side effects include rash, stomatitis, fever, ototoxicity, anemia, leukopenia, and thrombocytopenia. Pancreatitis is rare, but can be fatal. Renal failure would require the dosage to be decreased. Do not take with didanosine. There are no food restrictions. Do not take with antacids.

Zidovudine

Therapy-limiting effects may include anemia and leukopenia. Other side effects are headache, fatigue, rash, nausea, gastrointestinal disturbances, and seizures. A reversible myopathy may appear with prolonged use. This drug has been shown to decrease mother-to-child transmission. Zidovudine is one of three drugs comprising Trizivir™. It has also been approved for use with Lamivudine and marketed as Combivir®. The drug may be taken without regard to food.

Nonnucleoside Reverse Transcriptase Inhibitors (NNRTIs)

This class of drugs differs structurally from the NRTIs. Rather than substituting a dysfunctional component in the DNA-building process, they actually bind to the reverse transcriptase, thus inactivating the enzyme of synthesis. Viral resistance to this class of drugs evolves rapidly if any single drug is used as a monotherapy. Broad cross-resistance between agents in this class is common.

Delavirdine

Rash, headache, fatigue, and gastrointestinal disturbances are the common adverse effects. Other side effects include insomnia, myalgia, elevations in uric acid, transient elevations in liver functions, anemia, neutropenia, and thrombocytopenia. Do not take with didanosine. The drug should be taken an hour apart from antacids.

Efavirenz

Rash commonly occurs early in treatment and then resolves within the month. Cholesterol may increase by 10 to 20% in some patients. Because this drug penetrates the blood–brain barrier, some central nervous system (CNS) disturbances may occur, including dizziness, changes in sleep and dreams, abnormal thinking, and difficulty concentrating. These symptoms typically resolve within a month. Delusions, abnormal behavior, depression, and elevated liver enzymes may also occur. Taking the drug at bedtime minimizes the drug effects on activities of daily living. Avoid taking the drug with high-fat meals.

Nevirapine

Rash occurs in 7 to 15% of patients and is more common in women, but can usually be tolerated with antihistamine use. Other common adverse effects are headache and depression — less commonly fatigue, nausea, diarrhea, fever, myalgia, elevated liver function, and mean corpuscular volume. This drug is not compatible with oral hormone contraceptives. There are no food restrictions.

Protease Inhibitors (PIs)

This class of drugs inhibits HIV protease, the enzyme that cleaves viral polyproteins to functional HIV proteins. When protease is inhibited, infectious HIV virions are not produced. Toxicities generally appearing in this class of drugs are metabolic effects on lipids and glucose and body composition changes. Complete cross-resistance of the virus to PIs does not evolve initially. However, cross-resistance may broaden over time as mutations in the virus accumulate so that sequential use of PIs may not be possible.

Amprenavir

The most common side effects are rash, paresthesias, and gastrointestinal disturbances. Because this drug is a sulfonamide, it must not be taken by those with hypersensitivity reactions to sulfa. This drug is not compatible with oral hormone contraceptives. Vitamin E supplements should not be taken. Amprenavir interacts with several other drugs, elevating serum levels of some drugs and itself being reduced in serum by others. A thorough reference should be consulted before prescribing. Should be taken an hour apart from antacids and didanosine. Avoid taking the drug with high-fat meals.

Indinavir

Adverse effects that are noteworthy include nephrolithiasis, which occurs infrequently and requires a temporary interruption of treatment for 1 to 3 days. Adequate hydration is critical. Other side effects include rash, nausea, thrombocytopenia, headache, diarrhea, insomnia, stomatitis, asymptomatic hyperbilirubemia, and elevated hepatic transaminases. Indinavir interacts with several other drugs, elevating serum levels of some drugs and its own serum level being reduced by others. A thorough reference should be consulted before prescribing. The drug dose should be taken with water either 1 hour before or 2 hours after a meal.

Lopinavir

Lopinavir is co-formulated with ritonavir to elevate its plasma concentration to therapeutic levels and marketed as Kaletra®. Adverse effects may include elevated triglycerides, cholesterol, hepatic enzymes, and glucose. Other side effects may be asthenia, headache, rash, diarrhea, nausea, and vomiting. Lopinavir inhibits the P450 CYP3A metabolic path and like other PIs has many drug interactions. A thorough reference should be consulted before prescribing. The drug dose should be taken with food.

Nelfinavir

Side effects are generally mild and are primarily diarrhea, but can include nausea, rash, depression, asthenia, and mild fatigue. Nelfinavir inhibits the P450 CYP3A metabolic path and like other PIs has many drug interactions. A thorough reference should be consulted before prescribing. The drug dose should be taken with food and can be dissolved in water.

Ritonavir

The most common side effects are gastrointestinal: nausea, diarrhea, vomiting, anorexia, abdominal pain, and taste perversion. Other adverse effects may include paresthesias, elevated cholesterol, and elevated hepatic enzymes. Ritonavir binds to several cytochrome P450 isoforms, and interacts with several drugs. It will reduce levels of oral contraceptives and theophylline, among others. A thorough reference should be consulted before prescribing. Refrigeration is recommended. The drug should be taken with food.

Saquinavir

Adverse effects are generally mild and include diarrhea, nausea, and abdominal discomfort. Other side effects may include jaundice, elevated liver function, headache, confusion, seizures, rash, asthenia, and paresthesias. Saquinavir is metabolized by CYP3A4, and interactions with other drugs that affect that metabolic path are common. A thorough reference should be consulted before prescribing. The drug dose should be taken within 2 hours of a full meal.

Investigational Drugs

Although HAART may durably suppress HIV replication without the emergence of viral resistance, the HIV variants hosted by a particular patient may still develop reduced susceptibility to current drugs through incomplete adherence to treatment regimen. Sometimes declines in immune function develop in the presence of viral suppression. The possibility also exists that the current HAART drugs will prove too toxic to be used indefinitely. Furthermore, HIV is known to be sequestered in memory cells of the immune system and harbored in other privileged sites in the body that are inaccessible to ARV therapeutics so that HIV cannot be eradicated from the body. New therapeutics will be required to facilitate salvage therapy. Ongoing basic and clinical research is aimed at addressing the need for superior drug efficacy, improved patient adherence, reduced toxicity, better tolerance, and more treatment options (Feinberg, 2002).

The antiretroviral agents currently approved for therapeutic intervention act to inhibit either the reverse transcriptase or the protease enzyme of viral synthesis. New classes of drugs under current development are aimed at different viral targets, including the virion's entry to the cell (fusion inhibitors) and its activation after synthesis (integrase inhibitors) (Ritchie, 2001). Twelve anti-HIV drugs representing all these drug classes are presently in clinical trials (Cohen, 2002). Early-access programs are available for qualifying patients to participate in studies of investigational drugs through the pharmaceutical company. Usually the primary care physician must initiate the recommendation of the patient to the program.

Newly Approved Drugs

As this chapter goes to press, the U.S. Food and Drug Administration has approved two new HIV therapeutic drugs.

The first of the fusion inhibitor (FI) class of medications received accelerated approval on March 13, 2003. Fuzeon® (FI)/enfuvirtide is remarkable because it is effective against HIV infection resistant to other currently available drugs, thus adding a new component to HIV therapy. The drug is given by subcutaneous injection. Adverse reactions may include allergic reaction, especially at the injection site, and increased risk for pneumonia. Roche Pharmaceuticals of Nutley, NJ, will distribute the drug under a license from Trimeris, Inc., of Durham, NC.

A seventh protease inhibitor was approved on June 20, 2003. Reyataz® (PI)/ata-zanavir is noteworthy for being given in a single pill, once per day, with food. As with all drugs in this class, a significant safety concern is hyperlipidemia. Bristol-Myers Squibb Company of Princeton, NJ, produces it.

Opportunistic Infections and Malignancies

By weakening the immune system, HIV permits the opportunity for infectious disease and malignancy to attack any organ system. HIV is also known to alter the natural progression of several common infections such as syphilis and hepatitis B and C. Most HIV/AIDS-related mortality is caused by these comorbid conditions. The incidence of opportunistic infection varies between different transmission exposure populations such as men who have sex with men or intravenous drug users. Prevalence of certain OIs varies with geographical region such as histo-plasmosis, which is endemic to the Ohio and Mississippi River Valleys. However, the CD4+ cell count is a reliable marker for incidence of specific OIs. When the CD4+ cell count falls to between 250 and 500/mm^3, HIV-positive individuals usually experience minor OIs such as oropharyngeal candidiasis (thrush) and the development of active tuberculosis disease. Cryptosporidiosis and tumors of Kaposi's sarcoma or lymphoma may emerge with CD4+ cell counts between 150 and 200/mm^3. When the CD4+ cell count range is between 75 and 125/mm^3, more severe opportunistic infections such as *Pneumocystis carinii* pneumonia, *Mycobacterium avium* complex, herpes simplex virus, toxoplasmosis, cryptococ-cosis, and esophageal candidiasis may appear. Cytomegalovirus retinitis occurs with CD4+ counts of less than 50/mm^3. Prolonged survival has been shown with MAC and PCP prophylaxis as well as with HAART (Sande & Volberding, 1999). The U.S. Public Health Service and the Infectious Diseases Society of America developed guidelines for preventing OIs among persons infected with HIV in 1995 and updated them in 1997, 1999, and 2002. The major changes in the most recent update primarily address the discontinuance of prophylaxis upon recon-stitution of the immune system. Overall, HAART is still recognized as the most effective approach to OI prevention. The guidelines address 19 OIs (CDC, 2002a). The more frequently reported HIV/AIDS-related malignancies and OIs and their preventions and standard treatments are described here.

Vaccinations

Vaccination with influenza vaccine and pneumococcal vaccine is recommended for all HIV-infected adults. Hepatitis vaccination for HBV is the standard of care. Vaccination for HAV is recommended for those who have HCV or chronic liver disease or are sexually active and are seronegative for HAV. Diphtheria/tetanus vaccine should be boosted every 10 years. Other vaccines that should be administered in those not previously vaccinated include measles, mumps, and rubella, as well as inactivated polio. All live virus vaccines are contraindicated (Bartlett, 2002; Princeton, 2003; Sande & Volberding, 1999).

Opportunistic Infection, Suppressive Therapy, and Treatment

Pulmonary disease is a major source of morbidity and mortality in HIV-infected individuals. The number one life-threatening OI for HIV-infected patients is *Pneumocystis carinii* pneumonia, which is suppressible with the prophylactic use of trimethoprim-sulfamethoxazole (TMP/SMX) (Bactrim or Septa), Dapsone, aerosolized pentamidine (NebuPent), or Atovaquone (Mepron). Bactrim has the advantage of also being prophylactic against *Toxoplasma gondii* and some other bacterial infections. Patients who are at risk of PCP are those with CD4+ counts of <200; those with oropharyngeal candidiasis; those with persistent fever of more than 2 weeks; and those who have had prior PCP. Treatment medications include TMP/SMX, Dapsone, pentamidine, Clindamycin/Primaquine, and Atovaquone (Mepron). *Recurrent bacterial pneumonia* is an AIDS indicator condition. Pneumococcal vaccination with Pneumovax is the standard of care. Empiric treatment should not be commenced until the infecting bacteria are characterized. Although penicillin-resistant strains are appearing, effective treatment can be made with second- and third-generation cephalosporins or TMP/SMX.

Mycobacterium tuberculosis (TB) is a frequent but treatable cause of morbidity and mortality in the HIV-positive population. Most HIV-associated TB disease is the result of activation of dormant TB infection and can emerge even in the presence of CD4+ counts in excess of 300. Biannual TB skin testing by purified protein derivative (PPD) is recommended. HIV infection alters the natural history of TB so that those who are HIV positive are far more likely to contract TB. Latent TB may be suppressed by isoniazid (INH) therapy given for 12 months. Although many strains of TB are becoming antibiotic resistant, TB can be treated and cured with a multidrug regimen usually commencing with four drugs, then reducing the number of drugs over the course of treatment. Some of the more common drugs of treatment include INH, rifampin (Rifadin), rifabutin (Mycobutin), ethambutol (Myambutol), and pyrazinamide (PZA).

Another frequently occurring, serious OI is *Mycobacterium avium* complex. MAC is a term for two related bacteria: *Mycobaterium avium* and *Mycobaterium intracellulare* (MAI). When CD4+ counts drop below 50, MAC can become disseminated, seriously eroding quality of life and reducing survival. MAC bacteremia is associated with fever/sweats, progressive anemia, painful joints, gastrointestinal cramping, nausea/vomiting, diarrhea, and wasting. Prophylaxis should be considered, after excluding TB, when the CD4+ count falls below 100. Azithromycin (Zithromax) is the preferred prophylactic, but two other drugs are also approved — clarithromycin (Biaxin) and rifabutin (Mycobutin) — for all HIV-infected patients with CD4+ counts of less than 100.

Fungal infections seen in HIV/AIDS patients include candidiasis, cryptococcosis, histoplasmosis, coccidioidomycosis, and aspergillosis. *Candidiasis* is the most commonly seen OI in HIV/AIDS patients and is seen at all stages of immunosuppression. Vaginal candidiasis (yeast), followed by oropharyngeal (thrush) and esophageal candidiasis, is the usual order of presentation of this infection. Candidiasis is routinely being treated topically with ketoconazole (Nizoral), clotrimizole (Nystatin, Gyne-Lotrimin), or miconazole (Monistat 3) when possible, reserving the systemic drugs such as fluconazole (Diflucan), amphotericin, and itraconazole (Sporanox) for more severe fungal infections. *Cryptococcus neoformans* is the most frequently occurring life-threatening fungal infection, usually affecting those with CD4+ counts below 50. Cryptococcosis most often presents as disseminated disease. Cryptococcal meningitis is the most common manifestation, but pneumonia is also seen. This infection should be treated aggressively with amphotericin, followed by suppressive therapy with fluconazole. *Histoplasmosa capulatum* is endemic to the midwestern U.S. and found in bird droppings. It causes acute pulmonary disease. The preferred therapy for disseminated histoplasmosis is amphotericin. *Coccidioides immitis* is endemic to the southwestern U.S. and Mexico. Most patients with this infection have CD4+ counts under 250. The clinical presentation of coccidioidomycosis is acute pulmonary infection. Disseminated disease should be treated with amphotericin, followed by suppressive therapy with ketoconazole or fluconazole for life. *Aspergillosis* is seen infrequently and usually only in advanced AIDS. The lungs are most commonly involved, and secondarily the brain. The treatment of choice is amphotericin.

Cytomegalovirus infection is a common HIV-related pathogen causing retinitis, colitis, and encephalopathy. Most people are infected with dormant CMV, but active disease emerges in 20 to 40% of HIV/AIDS patients, particularly in those with CD4+ counts of less than 50. *CMV ritinitis* accounts for the 75 to 85% of CMV disease and is the leading cause of blindness in AIDS patients. Symptoms include blurry vision, light flashes, and floaters. A therapy specific for CMV retinitis is surgical implantation of a ganciclovir pellet (Vitrasert) in the affected eye together with oral Ganciclovir. The implant is effective for several months, but will not protect the other eye from CMV (Princeton, 2003). *CMV colitis* presents with abdominal pain, diarrhea, anorexia, weight loss, and fever. *CMV encephalopathy* is usually seen as radiculopathy. This occurs as a spinal cord syndrome with lower-extremity weakness, spasticity, areflexia, urinary retention, and hypoesthesia. Subacute encephalitis caused by CMV also occurs in AIDS patients. Personality changes, difficulty concentrating, headaches, and sleepiness frequently are present. The best prophylaxis is effective ARV therapy to restore the immune system. Initial acute therapy is with IV Ganciclovir. Maintenance therapy throughout the life of the patient is critical for CMV retinitis because the virus is only suppressed by Ganciclovir and not eliminated. Oral Ganciclovir is nearly as effective as I.V. Ganciclovir was at delaying reactivation of CMV retinitis . Toxicity and viral resistance may limit Ganciclovir therapy. Foscarnet and Cidofovir may provide alternate therapies (Sande & Volberding, 1999).

Herpes viruses cause a number of symptoms in immunocompetent people and are responsible for substantial morbidity in immunosuppressed HIV/AIDS patients where their symptoms are more severe and of longer duration. This family of viruses includes CMV, described above, as well as herpes simplex viruses I and II and herpes zoster. *Herpes simples virus I* produces cold sores or fever blisters primarily around the mouth, but they can also occur on the genitalia. Other symptoms include fever, fatigue, swollen glands, and muscle pain. *Herpes simples virus II* produces painful ulcers on the genitals or anus. Symptoms preceding an outbreak are similar to influenza. *Herpes zoster* (shingles) causes a painful rash along a particular dermatome, which is a reactivation of previous chicken pox infection. Suppression and treatment are accomplished with acyclovir (Zovirax), famciclovir (Famvir), or valacyclovir (Valtrex).

Toxoplasma gondii is associated with cerebral toxoplasmosis in the majority of patients. It is the second most common opportunistic infection of the eye. It may also cause pneumonia. *T. gondii* is one of the most common tissue parasites found in humans and is hosted by the domestic cat as well as many other mammals and bird species. Humans can become infected by coincidental exposure to cat feces or by eating raw or undercooked meat. In an immunocompetent individual, the parasite is usually dormant, causing no signs or symptoms; however, in the patient with depressed cellular immunity, the parasite may become activated and cause full-blown disease. Among individuals with AIDS, 3 to 40% develop toxoplasmic encephalitis (Smith, 1994). Persons with *T. gondii* are at risk for developing toxoplasmosis and should begin suppressive therapy when their CD4+ count falls below 100. The most common regimens are TMP/SMX (Bactrim or Septa), pyrimethamine in combination with sulfadiazine, and Dapsone plus pyrimethamine (Daraprim). Patients with toxoplasmosis encephalitis must be on chronic suppressive therapy for life.

Cryptosporidium parvum is a serious parasitic OI. Cryptosporidiosis causes profuse, watery diarrhea with crampy abdominal pain, fatigue, anorexia, and nausea/vomiting. CD4+ cell counts under 200 facilitate this illness. The infection is easily transmitted by contact with feces. Hand washing is the best protection against contamination. Cryptosporidiosis is not cured, only suppressed, and is more likely to reappear as the immune system is progressively impaired. Symptoms may be reduced by paromomycin, spiramycin, or erythromycin and other anti-diarrheal agents.

Malignancies

Kaposi's sarcoma, non-Hodgkin's lymphomas (NHLs), and invasive cervical cancer are malignancies indicative of AIDS in HIV-infected individuals (Krown, 1996). Squamous carcinoma conjunctiva is known as an AIDS-associated cancer. Other neoplasms that are likely AIDS associated include Hodgkin's disease, plasmacytoma, leiomyosarcoma (pediatric), and seminoma (Sande and Volberding, 1999). Both males and females with prolonged immunodeficiency exhibit a high frequency of noninvasive intraepithelial lesions (warts) of the anogenital squamous epithelium that may be precursors to invasive cancer. The sexually transmitted human papillomaviruses (HPVs) are suspected of causing these lesions and neoplasms. AIDS-associated malignancies may increase in frequency as their long latency periods are exceeded by prolonged survival provided by HAART.

LIFE CARE PLANNING CONSIDERATIONS FOR THE HIV/AIDS PATIENT

The approval in 1996 of several antiretroviral drugs and tests for quantifying viral load transformed the care of HIV patients. Case management strategies in the past primarily addressed cost-effective treatment of the primary disease for a relatively short time horizon. The new primary disease treatment protocols have significantly slowed the progression of HIV infection and prolonged survival in many patients. The extension of life span has broadened case management guidelines for the HIV-infected patient in scope, direction, and responsibilities. One new facet of case management is the psychosocial adaptations of living long-term with HIV/AIDS. This not only includes the psychological health of HIV-positive persons and their families, caregivers, and health-related professionals, but also the immense financial and job market accommodations that are required.

Life care planning for the individual living with AIDS or symptomatic HIV can cover a wide array of needs. To be as inclusive as possible in outlining the potential areas of needs, a checklist may prove helpful. The following checklist is for planning purposes. In the interest of space, not every possible concern has been detailed. However, this checklist will guide the interested party in the systematic thought process needed to comprehensively consider the need areas (Kitchen, 1995).

Life Care Planning: Needs Checklist for the HIV/AIDS Patient

Physical impairment/considerations:
Hemiplegia
Loss of balance
Loss of strength
Paralysis
Coordination
Fatigue
Weakness
Clumsiness
Ataxia
Reduced functional capacity
Pain
Visual acuity
Physical stamina and endurance
Loss of bowel control
Arthralgia
Arthritis
Fibromyalgia

Cognitive impairment/neuropsychological considerations:
Depression
Dementia
Intellectual impairment
Inattention
Forgetfulness
Reduced concentration
Expressive/receptive speech
Aphasia
Dysarthria

Adjustment disorder
Apathy
Disorientation
Social isolation
Delirium
Manic disorder
Psychotic disorder
Anxiety disorder
Adjustment disorder
Respiratory considerations:
Bacterial infection
Lymphoma
Fungi
Mycobacteria
Pneumocystis
Kaposi's sarcoma
Viral infections
Tuberculosis
Gastrointestinal considerations:
Abdominal pain
Painful elimination
Hepatomegaly
Cholecystitis
Colitis
Enteritis
Megacolon/colon perforations
Pancreatitis
Intestinal obstruction
Mucosal biopsy
Neurological considerations:
Meningitis
Focal CNS lesions
Encephalitis
Headache
Myelopathy
Cranial nerve palsies
Seizures
Peripheral neuropathy
Demyelinating neuropathy
General health considerations:
Diarrhea
Painful elimination
Apathy
Anorexia
Dysphagia
Poor intake (painful mouth/throat)
Medication reaction/interaction
Adverse drug reactions

Chronic pain
Esophageal disease
Fever
Malnutrition
Weight loss
Malabsorption
Wasting syndrome
Candida (oral/esophageal/vaginal)
Sleep disorder

Hematologic considerations:

Anemia
Leukemia
Bone marrow disorders
Leukopenia
Thrombocytopenia

Cardiovascular considerations:

Pericarditis
Pulmonary hypertension
Myocardial involvement
Vascular abnormalities
Arrhythmias
Venous thrombosis and pulmonary embolism

Endrocinologic considerations:

Hypothalamic-pituitary
Adrenal
Glucocorticoid hormones (Cortisol)
Mineralocorticoid hormone deficiency (renal sodium wasting, hypotension, hypokalemia, metabolic acidosis)
Thyroid
Gonad
Pancreas
Mineral homeostasis
Lipid metabolism
Wasting syndrome

Renal considerations:

Fluid imbalance
Electrolyte imbalance
Acid–base disturbance
Acute tubular necrosis
Metabolic acidosis
HIV-associated nephropathy
Hemolytic uremic syndrome
Dialysis

Dermatologic considerations:

Infections
Shingles
Herpes virus infection
Hairy leukoplakia

Neoplastic disease
Seborrheic dermatitis
Hypersensitivity rashes

Oral considerations:
Candidiasis
Gingivitis
Periodontitis
Herpes simplex
Herpes zoster
Bacterial lesions
Cytomegalovirus ulcers
Hairy leukoplakia
Warts

Neoplastic disease:
Kaposi's sarcoma
Lymphoma
Carcinoma
Recurrent aphthous ulcers

Life Care Planning: Recommendations Checklist

Allied health evaluations:
Physical therapy
Occupational therapy
Speech therapy
Respiratory therapy
Recreational therapy
Psychology
Neuropsychology
Vocational/educational
Financial planning
Seating/mobility
Adaptive driving

Medical (evaluations and follow-up):
Physiatry
General medicine
Dental
Podiatry
Oncology
Dermatology
Neurology
Rheumatology
Anesthesiology (pain control)
Nutritional
Gynecological/obstetrics
Psychiatry
Gastroenterology

Urological
Plastic/reconstruction
Pulmonary
Cardiology
Ophthalmology
Diagnostics, such as TB testing, MRI, CT scans, pap smear, etc. (see list below)
Routine preventative immunizations (i.e., pneumonia vaccine, hepatitis B)

Laboratory testing (Bartlett, 2001):
HIV serology
CBC
CD4 count
Quantitative plasma HIV RNA
Chemistry profile, including renal function and liver function tests
Toxoplasma serology (immunoglobulin G, or IgG)
Chest x-ray
PPD
STD screen; syphilis and chlamydia urine screen (women)
Baseline fasting lipid profile and glucose in all candidates for HAART therapy
Hepatitis screen: HAV and HBV (to determine candidates for vaccine); HCV (in all injection drug users); and active hepatitis screen by determination of transaminase levels
Pap smear (if none in the past year)

Optional tests:
- CMV serology
- HAV antibody
- Varicella antibody
- G6PD (sometimes done at baseline in those with high risk — African Americans and men of Mediterranean heritage)

Sequential tests:
- HIV RNA plasma levels: baseline confirmatory test at 2 to 4 weeks, then every 3 months if stable, or more frequently with initiation of antiretroviral therapy or change in therapy
- CD4 count: baseline and then every 3 to 6 months +/– confirmatory test if outlier results
- PPD: annual in high-risk patients with persistently negative results
- RPR: annual syphilis test in sexually active patients
- Pap smear: baseline and 6 months, then annually if negative
- CBC: baseline and every 3 to 6 months (as a component of CD4 count)

Therapeutic drug monitoring:
- AZT-CBC every 3 months or more frequently
- ddC, ddI , d4T — peripheral neuropathy
- Nevirapine — liver function tests, especially during first 6 weeks

- Protease inhibitors +/– NNRTI — fasting lipid profile at baseline and in 3 to 6 months; subsequent frequency depends on risks and test results
- Fasting levels necessary for triglycerides that are used to determine LDL; should be done after 8- to 12-hour fast

Therapeutic modalities:
Physical therapy
Occupational therapy
Speech therapy
Respiratory therapy
Recreational therapy
Therapy/counseling (group, individual)
Career guidance/counseling
Staff training
Family counseling
Family education
Patient education
Driver's education (with adaptations)
Legal/financial counseling
Spiritual support/counseling
Caregiver support
Case management
Leisure pursuits

Equipment considerations:
Mobility equipment (wheelchairs/scooters, etc., manual/power)
Equipment repairs/maintenance
Emergency call equipment (Wander guard/cell phone, Call Alert, other safety systems)
Home furnishings (to conserve physical energy)
Lift recliner
Accessible setting
Mobile stools
Reachers
Environmental control devices/maintenance and repair
Ramping
Stair-glide
Elevator
Hospital bed/mattress
Special-size linens/blankets
Washer/dryer (for excess laundry requirements)
Feeding pumps (parenteral/enteral feeding)
Scale
Handheld shower
Shower bench
Handrails

Medical equipment:
Suction machine
Apnea monitor

Oxygen concentrator

Liquid oxygen

Ventilator

Humidifier

Miscellaneous supplies (medical):

Catheters

Feeding bags

Suction catheters

Syringes

Diapers

Bed pads

Gloves

Creams/powders

Gauze/tapes

Masks

Thermometers

Blood pressure monitors

Garbage bags

Wipes

Paper towels

Antibacterial soaps

Architectural renovations/medical retrofitting:

Barrier-free design

Grab bars in bathroom

Temperature guards

Call system

Orthotics:

As prescribed

Orthopedic equipment:

(For strength maintenance and mobility)

Walkers

Parallel bars

Canes

Crutches

Bath seat

Aids for independent function:

Built-up plates/utensils

One-handed equipment

Voice-activated computer/software

Adaptive clothing

Infection control devices:

Sharps/needle/contaminant storage and destruction

Decontaminant cleaners

Medications:

Antiretrovirals

Protease inhibitors

Palliative care

Pain treatment

        Oral

        IV

        Feeding supplements

        Dietary supplements

        Vitamin therapy

Attendant/nursing care:

        Respite care

        Caregiver support

        Hospice care

        Home health aide

        Driver

        Nursing care

        Home maintenance (interior/exterior)

Surgical/aggressive intervention:

        Ports for total parenteral nutrition (TPN) access

        Plastic surgical repairs

        Pain control devices (implanted)

        Surgical treatment of complications

        Tumor removal

Complications:

        Hospital care

        Clinic care

        Secondary infections

        Falls

        Accidents

        Medical complications (myriad)

        Financial

Costs of Care

There is one certainty when considering the costs of care for the HIV/AIDS patient: there is no way to predict with certainty the costs of care. The medical management of the HIV/AIDS patient cannot be projected very far into the future because the course of the disease and its complications vary widely between patients. New treatment therapeutics and regimens, which are continuously being brought to the clinic, can change the treatment plan repeatedly. Although one can become knowledgeable about the most frequently encountered complications and the range of care and associated costs, it is not possible to state within a reasonable degree of rehabilitation probability the frequency of occurrence, the severity of occurrence, the duration of a complication, or its best treatment strategy at some future time. Therefore, a practical way to predict a treatment course, project its costs, and feel comfortable that adequate services and funding have been identified does not exist. This effectively limits the amount of information for quantifying the costs of complications that can be provided in a life care plan.

More extensive primary disease therapies used over lengthier periods of time and the concomitant extension in life expectancy for the HIV patient that has occurred over the past decade have increased costs of care significantly compared to life care plans prepared 10 years ago. In addition to the costs for treating the primary HIV infection, common complications in HIV disease management must be considered in projecting the costs of care. The most common complication of HIV disease is the occurrence of opportunistic infections, which can substantially influence the total sphere of costs. Improved prophylaxes and treatment protocols for more opportunistic infections result in the prescription of more drugs over the course of the disease, which also raises the costs of care.

Opportunistic infection management can be a major expenditure, especially when one factors in the ongoing prophylactic treatment after the initial acute infection has subsided or when the patient's condition indicates prophylaxis be commenced. For example, the routine use of Diflucan for persons with CD4+ counts of less than 100 would cost almost $100,000 for each major infection prevented. Another example to consider is the medication for CMV infections. Oral Ganciclovir as a prophylaxis of CMV disease reduced the rate of CMV disease by nearly 50%; however, oral Ganciclovir costs approximately up to $20,000 per year. At higher CD4+ counts, health care costs are principally due to primary disease therapy and not opportunistic infection management. The primary treatment therapy remains the most expensive cost consideration, however; costs for prophylaxis and treating complications increase as the CD4+ counts decrease. Table 15.1 presents the costs of agents recommended for prophylaxis or treatment of the more frequently encountered opportunistic infections among adults with HIV.

The medical management of the HIV/AIDS patient is not limited to primary disease treatment and control of opportunistic infections. Other health care resources such as consultations with specialists, tests, particular procedures, and health care facility usage are regularly employed to monitor and manage the course of the disease and its complications. Table 15.2 presents some health care resource costs. The costs are presented in 2003 dollars as econometrically updated from the originally reported 1995 dollars (Gable et al., 1996). The 1995 dollar costs were revised to represent 2003 dollar costs based on the cumulative increase in the medical care component of the U.S. Department of Labor's Consumer Price Index, 1995 (annual) vs. June 2003.

These tables do not present home care costs such as attendants or nursing services that the patient may periodically require. The cost of attendant or skilled nursing care will vary by the severity and duration of the specific episode of the complication. In early disease stages the patient may only need outpatient treatment, while in later stages the patient may require intermittent hospitalization or home-based attendant care with visiting skilled nursing. Eventually disease progression may necessitate skilled nursing care and perhaps home-based hospice care.

When computing the potential cost of attendant care services, it is important to factor volunteer or nonpaid hours into the total costs of care. It is common for the patient's family, significant other, spouse, or other volunteers to provide health care services when sufficient funding to acquire paid help is lacking. Particularly in determining costs of care in the life care planning (forensic) arena, these volunteer hours must be accounted for in the total cost of care. In other words, the services that a spouse, friend, or volunteer provide have a value. The proper method to assess the value of such services is to determine what it would cost to replace these services in the labor market. This is typically done by

Table 15.1   Wholesale Acquisition Costs of Agents Recommended for Preventing Opportunistic Infections among Adults Infected with HIV

Pathogen	Drug/Vaccine	Dose	Estimated Annual Cost/Patient US$
Pneumocystis carinii	Trimethoprim-sulfamethoxazole	160/800 mg daily	135
	Dapsone	100 mg daily	72
	Aerosolized pentamidine	300 mg every A.M.	1185
	Atovaquone	1500 mg daily	11,627
Mycobacterium avium complex	Clarithromycin	500 mg twice daily	2843
	Azithromycin	1200 mg weekly	3862
	Rifabutin	300 mg daily	3352
Cytomegalovirus	Ganciclovir (oral)	1000 mg 3 times/day	17,794
	Ganciclovir implant (lasts 6–9 months)		5000
	Ganciclovir (IV)	5 mg/kg of body weight daily	13,093
	Foscamet (IV)	90–120 mg/kg of body weight daily	27,770–37,027
	Cidofovir (IV)	375 mg every other week	20,904
	Fomivirsen (intravitreal)	1 vial every 4 weeks	12,000
	Valganciclovir	900 mg daily	21,582
Mycobacterium TB	Isoniazid	300 mg daily	23/9 months of therapy
	Rifampin	600 mg daily	294/2 months
	Pyrazinamide	1500 mg daily	194/2 months
Fungi	Flucconazole	200 mg daily	4603
	Itraconazole capsule	200 mg daily	5340
	Itraconazole solution	200 mg daily	5673
	Ketoconazole	200 mg daily	1230
Herpes simplex virus	Acyclovir	400 mg 2 times/day	1384
	Famciclovir	500 mg 2 times/day	5311
	Valacyclovir	500 mg 2 times/day	2538
Toxoplasma gondii	Pyrimethamine	50 mg weekly	49
	Leucovorin	25 mg weekly	888
	Sulfadiazine	500 mg 4 times/day	1490
Streptococcus pneumoniae	23-valent pneumococcal vaccine	One 0.5-ml dose intramuscularly	13
Influenza virus	Inactivated trivalent influenza vaccine	One 0.5-ml dose intramuscularly	3

(continued)

Table 15.1 (Continued)Wholesale Acquisition Costs of Agents Recommended for Preventing Opportunistic Infections among Adults Infected with HIV

Pathogen	Drug/Vaccine	Dose	Estimated Annual Cost/Patient US$
Hepatitis A virus	Hepatitis A vaccine	Two 1.0-ml doses intramuscularly	124
Hepatitis B virus	Recombinant hepatitis B vaccine	Three 10- to 20-μg doses intramuscularly	70
Bacterial infections	Granulocyte-colony-stimulating factor (IV)	300 μg 3 times/week	29,406
Varicella-zoster virus	Varicella-zoster immune globulin	Five 6.25-ml vials	562

Reprinted with permission from Medical Economics Company, Inc., a division of Thomson Medical Economics. "Wholesale Acquisition Costs of Agents Recommended for Preventing Opportunistic Infections among Adults Infected with Human Immunodeficiency Virus," as printed in *Drug Topics Red Book*, 2000, Montvale, NJ; as noted in *CDC-MMWR Recommendations and Reports*, June 14, 2002/51(RR08), 1–46; *Guidelines for Preventing Opportunistic Infections among HIV-Infected Persons — 2002; Recommendations of the U.S. Public Health Service and the Infectious Diseases Society of America.*

contracting through a home health agency to provide the level of care required based on the home health regulations in a specific state.

This discussion of costs also leads to a consideration of the availability of funding for the proper treatment of early intervention and prophylaxis for OIs. As is typical in the general population, funded health care has been proven to reduce overall costs of health care since preventative steps can be taken that reduce actual costs per incidence of medical need. That is true in the HIV/AIDS population as well. If funding is not available for primary disease medications or for preventative treatment of OIs, costs can escalate due to complications and opportunistic infections, resulting in more hospital stays and a foreshortened life expectancy.

Other considerations in providing care for the HIV patient include social services, palliative treatment, i.e., pain management, psychological support, and home health requirements. Home health requirements can include services provided and arranged through an agency (home health agency), private home health hires, friends, family services, community or church volunteers, and local service programs. A central aspect of home health care is providing a stable environment in which adherence to the treatment regimen can be maintained to avoid the possibility of viral resistance even if directly observed therapy becomes necessary.

The economic impact on the individual through loss of work productivity, quality of life, self-esteem, and will to live merit consideration in assessing the costs of living with HIV infection. Services must be provided to empower the HIV/AIDS individual in all spheres of life.

Table 15.2   Cost of HIV+/AIDS: Health Care Resource Use Costs (2003 dollars econometrically updated from 1995 dollars)

Resource Use	Unit of Treatment	Cost per Unit ($)
Amikacin levels	Tests	201
Barium swallow	Procedure	312
Blood chemistries	Test	47
Blood culture	Test	235
Blood gas	Test	79
Bone marrow biopsy	Procedure, physician, laboratory tests	1158
Bone marrow	Test	287
Bone marrow and culture (MAC)	Test	634
Brain biopsy	Procedure, hospital (3 days), laboratory tests, physician	15,576
Bronchoscope	Procedure	2181
Catheter placement	Procedure	3116
CD4+ cell count	Test	211
Chest radiograph	Test	156
Colonoscopy (biopsy)	Procedure	720
Complete blood count test	Test	3
Consultation (oncologist)	Visit	232
Cryptococcal antigen titer	Test	89
CT scan/CAT	Procedure	935
CT scan (noncontrast)	Procedure	467
CT chest, abdomen, head	Procedure, contrast material	2804
Dermatologic biopsy	Procedure	391
Detached retina	Treatment, hospitalization	4673
Dilantin level	Test	70
Electroencephalogram	Test	779
Endoscopy (biopsy)	Procedure	779
Emergency room visit	Visit	391
Foscarnet administration induction	Treatment	9615
Foscarnet administration maintenance	Treatment	1561
Foscarnet induction monitoring	Test/cycle	760
Foscarnet maintenance monitoring	Test/cycle	913
Ganciclovir administration induction	Treatment	6255
Ganciclovir administration maintenance	Treatment	1444
Ganciclovir induction monitoring	Test/cycle	140
Ganciclovir maintenance	Test/cycle	278
Home (drug) administration	Visit	156
Home care	Visit	350
Hospital physician visit	Visit	195
Hospitalization	Day	1544
Intensive care unit	Day	3087

(continued)

Table 15.2 (Continued) Cost of HIV+/AIDS: Health Care Resource Use Costs (2003 dollars econometrically updated from 1995 dollars)

Resource Use	Unit of Treatment	Cost per Unit ($)
Induced sputum	Procedure	547
Indwelling catheter	Procedure	3087
Infected catheter	Treatment and replacement	3739
Intralesional injections	Procedure	156
Lipase and triglycerides	Test	55
Lumbar puncture	Procedure, laboratory tests	733
Lumbar puncture	Associated tests	342
Lymphoma biopsy	Procedure, hospital (1 day), physician, laboratory tests	3894
Magnesium test	Test	31
Magnetic resonance imaging	Procedure	1869
Office visit (physician)	Visit	79
Ophthalmology examination	Test	312
Ophthalmology examination (follow-up)	Test	235
PPD skin test	Test	15
Pulmonary function test	Test	71
Radiation therapy, 2 to 3 weeks		17,133
Serum amylase	Test	24
Specialized test battery	Tests	1558
Sputum smear and culture sensitivities	Test	326
Toxoplasmosis titer	Test	55
TPN	TPN material and home infusion charges (9 days)	577
TPN laboratory work	Test	125
Transfusion	Each	779
Wasting syndrome diagnostic workup	Clinical tests	3116

Note: CT = computerized tomography.

Reprinted with permission: Costs of HIV+/AIDS at CD4+ counts disease stages based on treatment protocols, *Journal of Acquired Immune Deficiency Syndromes and Human Retrovirology,* 12:413–420, 1996, Lippincott-Raven Publishers, Philadelphia.

Viatical Settlements

There is available to individuals facing a life-threatening illness a unique financial resource, viatical settlements, which allow individuals to sell their life insurance policy for cash. This process is called viaticating and is quite simple. It requires no invasive process, just a single application form, which the patient (client) completes. These settlements provide valuable financial resources to help patients restore control over their lives and facilitate options they might not otherwise have, such as noninsured or experimental medical treatments, keeping their home, and even meeting day-to-day living expenses.

Viatical settlement is not a new concept. The term comes from the Latin *viaticum*, meaning "provision for a journey." Viatica were the supplies that Roman soldiers were given in preparation for their journeys into battle (presumably journeys from which they might not return). In essence, a viaticum was the provision a soldier needed for the closing phase of his life. The analogy is that a person wishing to viaticate is preparing for the closing phase of his or her life.

Initially, the viatical settlement industry was comprised of an informal network of small insurance settlement companies serving primarily the AIDS community. The process was expanded to include persons with other life-threatening illnesses such as cancer or Alzheimer's disease who could benefit from the financial resources made available to individuals through the viatical settlement process for the cost of hospitalization, treatment, home care, or other expenses, including day-to-day living expenses. Now the selling of an insurance policy does not require justification. Any person can sell any policy and use the proceeds as desired, even to take a vacation.

Viatical settlements are available in all 50 states. There are no restrictions on how the funds may be used, which restores some control to the patient for making decisions he or she feels are necessary. All types of insurance policies, including term, whole life, universal life, or group (employer paid) policies, may be viaticated. Policy values of just $10,000 to well over $1 million have been sold for viatication. The viatication process usually takes 3 to 6 weeks to complete. Many insurance settlement providers are active in the field today. Some will offer to buy the policy directly; others will seek offers to purchase from several funding sources. The Medical Escrow Society (800-334-3211, www.lifeassets.net) is one example of such a service provider.

The value of the insurance policy (the amount paid to the policy owner) is determined by several factors, including prevailing interest rates, premium obligations, and projected life expectancy. The National Association of Insurance Commissioners (NAIC) has established pricing guidelines. Viators (patients) generally receive between 50 and 80% of the face value of the insurance policy. Generally, the longer the life expectancy, the less the viatical settlement company is likely to pay for that individual's policy because the company must assume responsibility for maintaining the policy for a longer period of time. The proceeds from a viatical settlement may, however, impact certain means-based entitlement programs such as Medicaid. Furthermore, under current law, the proceeds from a viatical settlement are taxable as income for federal tax purposes. However, several states have adopted or are considering specific regulations or provisions, which may include:

1. State and city tax-free treatment of viatical settlement proceeds to encourage the use of these settlements.
2. Prevention of the brokering of life insurance policies to individual investors who are looking for speculative returns without due regard for the policy owner's welfare.

3. Requiring viatical companies to maintain a minimum level of capital or surety bond to fund the purchase of life insurance policies as part of the viatical settlement process to help ensure that companies can fund settlements and to prevent the involvement of viatical settlement companies that may put people at financial risk.

4. Requiring licenses and other strictly enforced reporting mechanisms for viatical settlement companies and limiting licenses to companies with well-established operations. (For more information, contact the Viatical Association of America, 800-390-1390.)

Case Management: A Critical Component

Case management of individuals with HIV/AIDS is vitally important — not only in managing the case from a direct economic standpoint, but also from managing the case from an early intervention/prevention standpoint. It is imperative that case managers keep themselves informed on the scope of knowledge available on HIV/AIDS, on new treatment modalities and their uses, on resistance issues, and on side effects. In addition, the case manager must be able to communicate effectively with physicians and to address nutritional issues, adherence of patients to therapy, financial issues, and psychological issues such as loss of identify and self-esteem.

Because the field is changing rapidly, the effective case manager will subscribe to professional journals that are devoted to the subject, e.g., the *Journal of Acquired Immune Deficiency Syndromes and Human Retrovirology*, Lippincott-Raven Publishers, Philadelphia, and learn to browse the Internet efficiently. Suggested websites include National Health HOTLINES, government agencies, and professional organizations; private-sector AIDS services, information, and advocacy groups; AIDS lobby/watchdog groups; and other AIDS-related information sources. Information from the Centers for Disease Control and Prevention (CDC) is also available on the Internet.

When case managing an HIV/AIDS client, the health professional should encourage patients to become self-advocates. This will empower the person with HIV/AIDS to become involved with the treatment of the disease, rather than being a victim of the disease. Delays in treatment are not only costly, but also life threatening. Some suggested activities for both the case management professional and the patient are:

1. Join the local AIDS organization, the county AIDS consortium, and the state board.
2. Attend conferences on AIDS, arming oneself with information to share.
3. Call local health departments or HIV/AIDS organizations for information.
4. Seek out pharmacists who have taken the time to become familiar with the new treatment modalities.
5. Become involved in local support groups.

There are a multitude of state and federal programs that can be of assistance if one is willing to invest the time and energy to become involved and informed. Additional information can be found by contacting entities listed in the Resources section. These include AIDS hotline numbers (national and state level), government health agencies and professional societies, private-sector services and advocacy groups, AIDS lobby/advocacy/watchdog groups, other AIDS-related information sources, patient assistance programs made available through pharmaceutical companies, and pharmaceutical information.

CONCLUSION

The AIDS epidemic continues to present unrelenting challenges to the medical profession. While medical science has made progress in reducing the frequency and duration of complications, improving quality of life of those affected and extending survival, an absolute cure or preventative vaccination remains elusive. The progression of this disease is unpredictable, which presents significant obstacles to the life care planner, since, unlike most diseases, complications and the course of the illness cannot be accurately anticipated. The life care plan will rely heavily on the recommendations of the individual's physician and relevant research. The life care planner who chooses to specialize in the HIV/AIDS arena must be aware of the myriad of complications and remain contemporaneous with evolving HIV/AIDS medical research. Accordingly, he or she must also be committed to regularly updating the plan based on the client's ever-changing circumstances and emerging information.

ACKNOWLEDGMENTS

The author thanks Julie A. Kitchen, C.C.M., C.L.C.P., of Paul M. Deutsch & Associates for significant contributions to the text. Her professional expertise and perspective were invaluable for the Life Care Planning Considerations for the HIV/AIDS Patient, Viatical Settlements, and Case Management: A Critical Component sections.

As past medical virologist-epidemiologist for the Centers for Disease Control, and state epidemiologist serving in both Arizona and Kentucky, Glyn G. Caldwell, M.D., brought his considerable experience and discernment to bear on the medical management aspects of the text. His overview of the structure of the chapter and attention to veracity of the information detail are greatly appreciated.

Ardis Hoven, M.D., is medical director of the Bluegrass Care Clinic at the University of Kentucky, which is supported by the Ryan White Title III CARE Act Early Intervention Services. Her specialization in HIV medicine made her mentorship in producing the text particularly valuable.

As program director of the Ryan White Title III-funded Bluegrass Care Clinic and specialist in HIV medicine, Alice Thornton, M.D., generously gave her time and direction in practical application of clinical concepts.

Sherie Kendall, Ph.D., is supported by the Department of Internal Medicine, Division of Infectious Diseases, at the University of Kentucky and grants from the National Heart, Lung and Blood Institute (K30 HL04 163) and the National Institute on Aging (T32 AG00242-09).

RESOURCES

http://www.hopkins-aids.edu/links/links_hot.html

Government Agencies/Professional Societies

AIDS Clinical Trials Information Service (ACTIS): (800) TRIALS-A (800-874-2572), (800) 243-7012 (TTY); P.O. Box 6421, Rockville, MD 20859-6421

AIDS Treatment Information Service/CDC (ATIS): 800-H*I*V-0440 (800-448-0440)

American Medical Association (AMA): 535 Deerborn St., Chicago, IL 60610; (312) 645-5000

American Public Health Association (APHA): 1015 Fifteenth St., Washington, DC 20005; (202) 789-5600

American Red Cross: 1750 K St. NW, Suite 700, Washington, DC 20006; (202) 973-6025

American Red Cross AIDS Education Office: 1730 D St. NW, Washington, DC 20006; (202) 737-8300

American Social Health Association (ASHA): P.O. Box 13827, Research Triangle Park, NC 27709; (800) 227-8922; see also HOTLINES, above

The Americans with Disabilities Act Information and Assistance Hotline: 800-949-4232 (V/TTY)

Business & Labor Information Service (CDC NAC): (800) 458-5231, (800) 243-7012 (deaf/TDD); links business organizations and labor groups with resources for developing HIV/AIDS in the workplace programs

CDC Hotline: Also listed below

Centers for Disease Control and Prevention (CDC): 1600 Clifton Rd. NE, 26 Executive Park, Atlanta, GA 30333; (404) 639-3311

The Centers for Disease Control Hotline: (800) 343-AIDS (800-342-2437)

The Centers for Disease Control and Prevention (CDC) National AIDS Information Clearinghouse Materials Catalogue and Business Responds to AIDS Resource Services: P.O. Box 6003, Rockville, MD 20849-6003; (800) 458-5231, (301) 763-5111 in Maryland, 9 A.M. to 7 P.M. Monday through Friday; additional numbers: (800) 243-7012 (TDD/deaf access), (301) 217-0023 (international)

Department of Health and Human Services (see also listing for U.S. Public Health Service, below): Office of the Secretary, 200 Independence Ave. NW, Room 615-F, Washington, DC 20201; (202) 245-6296

Experimental Treatment Infoline (see also New York listings): (800) 633-7444 (New York State only), (212) 239-5523 in other states; provides up-to-date information on experimental treatments via Touch-Tone

Food and Drug Administration (FDA): 5600 Fishers Lane, Rockville, MD 20857; (301) 443-2410

FDA Center for Drug Research: Office of the Director, 5600 Fishers Lane, Room 13B-45, Rockville, MD 20857; (301) 443-2894

Health Resources and Services Administration (HRSA): HRSA AIDS Program Office, 5600 Fishers Lane, Parklawn Bldg., Rockville, MD 20857 — (301) 443-4588; Substance Abuse and Mental Health Services Administration

(SAMHSA), SAMHSA Office on AIDS, 5600 Fishers Lane, Room 12C-10, Rockville, MD 20857 — (301) 443-5305; U.S. PHS Public Affairs Office, H. H. Humphrey Bldg., Room 725-H, Rockville, MD 20857 — (202) 245-6867

Hemophilia and AIDS/HIV Network for the Dissemination of Information (HANDI): 110 Greene St., Suite 303, New York, NY 10012; (212) 431-8541, (800) 42-HANDI

Intergovernmental Health Policy Project (IHPP) at George Washington University AIDS Policy Center: 2021 K St. NW, Suite 800, Washington, DC 20006; (202) 872-1445

National Adoption Information Clearinghouse: (301) 231-6512

National AIDS Hotline: (800) 342-2437 (24 hours a day, daily); (800) 243-7889 (TTY/TDD); (800) 342-AIDS (English hotline); (800) 344-SIDA (Spanish hotline); (301) 217-0023 (international line)

National Clearinghouse for Alcohol and Drug Information — Center for Substance Abuse Prevention (CSAP): (800) 729-6686

National Indian AIDS Hotline: (800) 283-24370

National Hemophilia Foundation (NHF): (212) 219-8180

National Herpes Hotline: (919) 361-8488, 9 A.M. to 7 P.M., EST, weekdays

National Institutes of Health (NIH) Office of the Director, Bldg. 1, Room 344, 6003 Executive Blvd., Bethesda, MD 20892; (301) 496-4000 (main information number); for information on AIDS clinical trials at the NIH Clinical Center, (800) AIDS-NIH (800-243-7644), Monday through Friday, 12 to 3 P.M. (EST)

National Library of Medicine (NLM): The National Library of Medicine provides numerous AIDS informational resources, including three online AIDS databases: AIDSLINE, AIDSDRUGS, and AIDSTRIALS. To obtain a free information packet, call (800) 638-8480. National Institutes of Allergy and Infectious Diseases (NIAID), Office of Communications, Bldg. 31, Room 7A-32, Bethesda, MD 20892; (301) 496-5717. National Cancer Institute (NCI), Bldg. 31, Room 11A-48, 6003 Executive Blvd., Bethesda, MD 20892; (301) 496-4000.

National Minority AIDS Council (NMAC): 1931 Thirteenth St. NW, Washington, DC 20009; (202) 483-6622, (202) 544-1076; Fax: 202-483-1135, 202-544-0378

National Native American AIDS Prevention Center (NNAAPC): 3515 Grand Ave., Suite 100, Oakland, CA 94610; (510) 444-2051

National Pediatric & Family HIV Resource Center: 30 Bergen St., ADMC #4, Newark, NJ 07103; (973) 972-0410, (800) 362-0071; Fax: 973-972-0399; Website: www.pedhivaids.org

National Sexually Transmitted Diseases HOTLINE/CDC: (800) 227-8922, 8 A.M. to 11 P.M., EST, weekdays

Rural AIDS Network (RAN): 1915 Rosina, Santa Fe, NM 87501; (505) 986-8337

Substance Abuse and Mental Health Services Administration (SAMHSA) — Drug Abuse Information and Treatment Referrals Hotline: (800) 662-HELP

Teen AIDS Hotline: (800) 283-2473 (AIDS info and grief counseling), 8:30 A.M. to 1 P.M., 2 to 5 P.M., Monday through Friday

U.S. Agency for International Development (USAID) HIV/AIDS Division/AIDS Control and Prevention Project (AIDSCAP): Room 1200, SA-18, Washington, DC 20523-1817; (703) 875-4494

U.S. Conference of Mayors: 1620 I St. NW, 4th Floor, Washington, DC 20006; (202) 293-7330

U.S. Public Health Service (PHS): 200 Independence Ave. SW, Washington, DC 20201; (202) 472-4248

Visual AIDS (U.S. government. effort to increase AIDS awareness through image, video, etc.): 131 West 21st St., 3rd Floor, New York, NY 10011; (212) 206-6758

Private-Sector Services and Advocacy Groups

ACT UP: Local chapter contacts (within ARIC's *PWA Resource Guide*)

AIDS Action Council (AIDS legislative watchdog group): 1875 Connecticut Ave. NW, Washington, DC 20009; (202) 986-1300, ext. 47; Fax: 202-986-1345. Contacts: Winnie Stachelberg, Derek Hodel.

AIDS Project Los Angeles (APLA): 6721 Romaine St., Los Angeles, CA 90038; (213) 962-1600. Contacts: Stephan Korsia, Stephen Bennett (CEO). Available publications: *I Heard It through the Grapevine* newsletter (see entry in AIDS newsletters).

AIDS Research Information Center, Inc. (ARIC, Inc.): 20 South Ellwood Ave., Suite #2, Baltimore, MD 21224-2241; Tel./Fax: (410) 342-ARIC (410-342-2742). Contact: Lee Hardy. Available publications: *ARIC's AIDS Medical Glossary*, a 500-page medical reference in layman's language (donation requested); *The DIRT* (on AIDS) newsletter (see entry in AIDS newsletters).

AIDS Treatment Data NETWORK: 611 Broadway, Suite 613, New York, NY 10012; (212) 260-8868; Fax: 212-260-8869 (national), 800-734-7104. Contacts: Ken Fornataro, Joel Beard. Available publications: *Treatment Review* newsletter (see entry in AIDS newsletters); Simple Facts Information Sheets, information on drugs and diseases in AIDS in plain language; *AIDS/HIV Experimental Treatment Directory*, a directory of trials for New York, New Jersey, Connecticut, Philadelphia, and Washington, D.C. (Note: These and other materials are available in Spanish.)

American Foundation for AIDS Research (AmFAR): 733 Third Ave., 12th Floor, New York, NY 10017; (212) 682-7440, (800) 764-9346; Fax: 212-682-9812. Contact: Donald Moschberger. Available publications: *AIDS/HIV Treatment Directory*, currently available treatments for AIDS and the trials in which they are being used. Updated quarterly. Subscription rates are $55 for individuals ($77 outside the U.S.) and $125 for physicians and institutions ($150 outside the U.S.). For information, (800) 764-9346. TxLINK, a searchable database version of the *AIDS/HIV Treatment Directory*, available on IBM-compatible diskette. Prices and ordering information are the same as for the *Directory*, (800) 764-9346. *AIDS/HIV Clinical Trial Handbook*, answers the most frequently asked questions about participating in clinical trials in easy-to-understand, nontechnical language. Available in English and Spanish, (800) 764-9346. *AIDS Targeted Information* (*ATIN*), a publication sponsored by AmFAR. *ATIN* is published monthly and provides abstracts of (and critical commentary on) the latest scientific and medical literature. *ATIN* highlights significant scientific reports and is a fairly good digest of the AIDS publication maze. Published by Williams & Wilkins, 428 East Preston St., Baltimore, MD 21202. Subscriptions are $225/year, (212) 682-7440.

American Lung Association (of South Alleghenies) (TB and AIDS info): 634 Main St., P.O. Box 67, Johnstown, PA 15907; (814) 536-7345; Fax: 814-539-5919. Contact: Philip J. Cynar.

Carl Vogel Foundation: 2025 I St. NW, Suite 917, Washington, DC 20006; (202) 289-4898. Contact: Ron Mealy, executive director.

Center for Natural and Traditional Medicine: P.O. Box 21735, Washington, DC 20009; (202) 387-3645, (202) 234-9632; Fax: 202-332-2132 (dedicated). Contact: Kaiya Montaocean, co-director.

Community Research Initiative on AIDS (CRIA): 275 7th Ave., 20th Floor New York, NY 10001; (212) 924-3934; Fax: 212-924-3936. Contact: Bette Smith.

Direct Action for Treatment Access (DATA) (alternative/holistic AIDS treatment advocacy) and Consumer Coalition for Health Choices: P.O. Box 60391, Palo Alto, CA 94306-0391; (415) 321-6670, 9 A.M. to 9 P.M.; Fax: 415-323-3864 (W), 415-323-6051; CompuServe account: 71702,760 (71702.760@compuserve.com). Contact: Steven Wm. Fowlkes.

Direct AIDS Alternative Information Resources (DAAIR) (alternative/holistic treatments information): 31 E. 30th St., Suite 2, New York, NY 10016; (212) 689-8140. Contact: Fred Bingham.

Drug Reform Coordination Network (DRCNet): 4455 Connecticut Ave. NW, Suite B-500, Washington, DC 20008-2302; (202) 362-0030; Fax: 202-362-0032

Gay Men's Health Crisis (GMHC) (see also New York listings): 129 W. 20th St., New York, NY 10011; (212) 807-6664; Fax: 212-337-3565; GMHC AIDS Information HOTLINE: (212) 807-6655, Monday through Friday, 10 A.M. to 9 P.M., Saturday, 12 to 3 P.M. Available publications: *Treatment Issues* newsletter (see entry in AIDS newsletters).

Human Rights Campaign Fund (Gay/lesbian rights and AIDS issues lobby group): 1012 14th St. NW, Suite 607, Washington, DC 20005; (202) 628-4160; Fax: 202-347-5323. Contact: Tim McFeeley.

Mobilization Against AIDS (MAA): (415) 863-4676; Fax: 415-863-4740. Contact: Ben Carlson.

National AIDS Network: 729 Eighth St. SE, Suite 300, Washington, DC 20003.

National AIDS Treatment Advocacy Project: 72 Orange St., #3C, Brooklyn, NY 11201; (718) 624-8541; Fax: 718-624-8399. Contact: Jules Levin.

National Association of People with AIDS: 1413 K St. NW, 7th Floor, Washington, DC 20005; (202) 898-0414, (800) 673-8538; Fax: 202-898-0435; NAPWA-Link computer BBS: (703) 998-3144 (8-N-1)

National Council of Churches/AIDS Task Force: 475 Riverside Dr., Room 572 New York, NY 10115; (212) 870-2421

National Council of Churches/Minority Task Force on AIDS: Same address as above, but Room 456; (212) 749-1214

National Gay/Lesbian Health Foundation: 1638 R St. NW, Suite 2, Washington, DC 20007; (202) 797-3708. Contact: Bill Scott.

National Gay and Lesbian Task Force (NGLTF) (Gay/lesbian rights and AIDS lobby group): 1734 14th St. NW, Washington, DC 20009-4309; (202) 332-6483

National Women's Health Network: 1325 G St. NW (Lower Level), Washington, DC 20005; (202) 347-1140

Parents and Friends of Lesbians and Gays (P-FLAG): P.O. Box 27605, Washington, DC 20038-4605; (202) 638-4200. Book offer: *Family AIDS Support Notebook*, basic information for the families of people with HIV/AIDS.

The People with AIDS Coalition Hotline (see also New York listings): (212) 532-0568, (800) 828-3280

Pharmaceutical Research and Manufacturer's Association (drug information): 1100 Fifteenth St. NW, Washington, DC 20005; (202) 835-3400. Contacts: Gerald Mossinghoff, John Petricciani, M.D. Available publications: *AIDS Medicines in Development*, annual report on new AIDS drugs and vaccines in development. Free.

Project Inform: 205 13th St., Suite 2001, San Francisco, CA 94103-2461; (415) 558-9051, (800) 822-7422. Contact: Martin Delaney. Available Publications: *PI Perspective* newsletter, wise words (by and for women with HIV) and other treatment information.

PWA Health Group: 31 W. 26 St., New York, NY 10010; (212) 532-0289. Available publications: *Notes from the Underground* newsletter (see entry in AIDS newsletters).

The Sheridan Group: (202) 462-7288; Fax: 202-483-1964. Contact: Tom Sheridan.

Test Positive Aware Network: 1340 West Irving Park Rd., P.O. Box 259, Chicago, IL 60613. Contact: John Krotz, director. Available publications: *Positively Aware* newsletter (see entry in AIDS newsletters).

Treatment Action Group (offshoot of ACTUP Treatment and Data Committee, now independent): 147 Second Ave., #601, New York, NY 10003; (212) 260-0300

Treatment Action Network (Project Inform's treatment activist organization; same address as Project Inform, above): (415) 558-8669, (415) 626-7231; Fax: 415-558-0684. Contacts: Anne Donnelly, Tom Wonsiewicz, David Lewis.

Women Alive: (800) 554-4876. This is a new national hotline staffed by HIV-positive women volunteers. This hotline is geared toward HIV-positive women who would like peer support or treatment information. Open Monday, Wednesday, and Friday, 11 A.M. to 6 P.M. (Pacific time), 2 to 9 P.M. (Eastern time).

Women and AIDS Resource Network (WARN): P.O. Box 020525, Brooklyn, NY 11202; (718) 596-6007

Women Organized to Respond to Life Threatening Diseases (WORLD): P.O. Box 11535, Oakland, CA 94611; (510) 658-6930. Available publications: *WORLD/MUNDO* newsletter (see entry in AIDS newsletters).

Women's AIDS Resource Movement (WARM) (a part of Tampa AIDS Network): P.O. Box 8333, Tampa, FL 33674; (813) 237-6455

Palliation

Alliance for Cannabis Therapeutics (ACT) and Marijuana/AIDS Research Service (MARS) (advocacy for the use of marijuana): P.O. Box 21210, Kalorama Station, Washington, DC 20009; (202) 483-8595; Fax: 202-797-9543

American Chronic Pain Foundation (info on coping with chronic pain): P.O. Box 850, Rocklin, CA 95677

International Pain Foundation (info on pain research/treatment): 909 NE 43rd St., Suite 306, Seattle, WA 98105

Roxane Pain Institute Association Doleur France-Amerique (France–USA Pain Society): Michel Dubois, MD, president of the Cancer/AIDS Pain HOTLINE (24 hours/day): (800) 335-9100

Family and Population Planning

Planned Parenthood Federation of America (PPFA) (HIV info and safe sex education): 810 Seventh Ave., New York, NY 10019; (212) 541-7800

The Population Institute (info on how overpopulation helps spread disease worldwide): 110 Maryland Ave. NE, Washington, DC 20002

State AIDS Info Hotlines

Alabama: (800) 228-0469

Alaska: (800) 478-AIDS; (907) 276-4880 (nationwide)

Arizona: (602) 420-9396

Arkansas: (800) 364-2437 (instate); (501) 661-2408 (elsewhere)

California: (800) 367-2437 (Northern California); (415) 863-2437 (nationwide); (415) 864-6606 (TTY/TDD); (800) 922-2437 (Southern California); (800) 553-2437 (Southern California TTY/TDD); 213-876-2437 (Los Angeles)

California Department of Health Office of AIDS: (800) 367-AIDS (within Northern California); (800) 922-AIDS (within Southern California); P.O. Box 942732, Sacramento, CA 94234-7320

Colorado: (800) 252-AIDS; (303) 782-5186 (Denver only)

Connecticut: (800) 342-AIDS

Delaware: (800) 422-0429

District of Columbia: (202) 332-AIDS; (800) 322-7432 (metro D.C. and Virginia)

Florida: (800) 352-AIDS; (800) 243-7101 (in Haitian Creole); (800) 545-SIDA (in Spanish)

Georgia: (800) 551-2728; (404) 876-9944 (nationwide); (404) 876-9944 (Atlanta)

Hawaii: (808) 321-1555; (808) 922-1313 (nationwide)

Idaho: (800) 677-AIDS

Illinois: (800) 243-AIDS; (800) 782-0423 (TTY/TDD)

Indiana: (800) 848-AIDS; (800) 972-1846 (TTY/TDD)

Iowa: (800) 445-AIDS

Kansas: (800) 232-0040

Kentucky: (800) 654-AIDS

Louisiana: (800) 992-4379 (instate); (504) 944-2437 (elsewhere); (504) 944-2492 (TDD)

   New Orleans: (800) 992-4379

Maine: (800) 851-AIDS (instate); (800) 775-1267 (elsewhere)

Maryland: (800) 638-6252; (410) 945-AIDS (Baltimore); (800) 322-7432 (metro D.C. and Virginia); (301) 949-0945 (Hispanic AIDS Hotline); (410) 333-2437 (Baltimore area only TTY)

Massachusetts: (800) 235-2331; (617) 536-7733 (nationwide); (617) 437-1672 (TTY/TDD)

Michigan: (800) 872-AIDS; (800) 826-SIDA (Spanish); (800) 332-0849 (TTY/TDD); (800) 750-TEEN (teen line)

Minnesota: (800) 248-AIDS; (612) 870-0700 (nationwide)

Mississippi: (800) 826-2961

Missouri: (800) 533-AIDS

Montana: (800) 233-6668; (800) 675-2437 (Eastern Montana AIDS Hotline); (800) 663-9002 (Western Montana AIDS Hotline)

Nebraska: (800) 782-AIDS

Nevada: (800) 842-AIDS

New Hampshire: (800) 752-AIDS

New Jersey: (800) 624-2377; (201) 926-8008 (TTY/TDD)

New Mexico: (800) 545-AIDS

New York: (718) 638-2074; (800) 872-2777 (counseling, Monday through Friday, 2 to 8 P.M., Saturday and Sunday, 10 A.M. to 6 P.M.); (800) 541-2437 (taped information, 24 hours; counselors, Monday through Friday, 8 A.M. to 8 P.M., Saturday and Sunday, 10 A.M. to 6 P.M.); (800) 633-7444 (treatment information); (800) 233-7432 (Spanish)

GMHC AIDS Hotline: (212) 807-6655 (Monday through Friday, 10 A.M. to 9 P.M., Saturday, 12 to 3 P.M.); (212) 645-7470 (GMHC TDD)

Long Island AIDS Hotline: (516) 385-AIDS (Monday through Friday, 9 A.M. to 9 P.M., tape after hours); (800) 233-SIDA (Albany)

Long Island People with AIDS Hotline: (516) 225-5700

Mothers of PWAs (outside of New York): (800) 828-3280 (available Monday, Wednesday, and Friday, 2 to 6 P.M.)

NY State Gay/Lesbian Task Force AIDS Information HOTLINE: (800) 221-7044 (funded by Gay/Lesbian Task Force, New York: 212-807-6016)

People with AIDS Coalition Hotline: (212) 647-1420 (staffed by HIV-positive people)

North Carolina: (800) 342-AIDS

North Dakota: (800) 472-2180; (701) 224-2376 (nationwide)

Ohio: (800) 332-AIDS; (800) 332-3889 (TTY/TDD)

Oklahoma: (800) 535-AIDS

Oregon: (503) 223-AIDS; (800) 777-2437 (within area codes 503, 206, and 208)

Southern Oregon HIV/AIDS Resources: http://id.mind.net/community/pride/resource.htm

Pennsylvania: (800) 662-6080; (215) 545-2212 (Critical Path AIDS Project Hotline); (215) 463- 7160 (publications orders)

Puerto Rico: (800) 981-5721 (Linea de Infor SIDA y Enfermedades de Transmision Sexual); (809) 765-1010 (nationwide)
Rhode Island: (800) 726-3010; (800) 442-7432 (Spanish)
South Carolina: (800) 322-AIDS
South Dakota: (800) 592-1861
Tennessee: (800) 525-AIDS
Texas: (800) 299-AIDS
Utah: (800) 366-AIDS; (800) 487-2100 (nationwide)
Vermont: (800) 882-AIDS
Virgin Islands: (809) 773-AIDS
Virginia: (800) 533-4148; (800) 322-7432 (Hispanic line)
Washington: (800) 272-AIDS
West Virginia: (800) 642-8244
Wisconsin: (414) 273-AIDS; (800) 334-2437
Wyoming: (800) 327-3577

Note: Physicians and other health care professionals are encouraged to consult other sources and confirm the information contained in the Johns Hopkins website listed below because no single reference or service can take the place of medical training, education, and experience. Consumers are cautioned that this site is not intended to provide medical advice about any specific medical condition they may have or treatment they may need, and they are encouraged to call or see their physician or other health care provider promptly with any health-related questions they may have.

Copyright © 1997–2003. The Johns Hopkins University on behalf of its Division of Infectious Diseases and AIDS Service. All rights reserved. Reprinted with permission: HIV/AIDS Hotlines: United States. Johns Hopkins AIDS Service-Related Links. http://www.hopkins-aids.edu/links/links_hot.html.

REFERENCES

Bartlett J.G. (2001). *The Johns Hopkins Hospital 2002 Guide to Medical Care of Patients with HIV Infection*, 10th ed. Philadelphia: Lippincott Williams & Wilkins.

Bartlett J.G. (2002). *The 2002 Abbreviated Guide to Medical Management of HIV Infection.* Baltimore: Johns Hopkins University, Division of Infectious Diseases.

Centers for Disease Control (CDC). (1981). Pneumoncystis pneumonia — Los Angeles. *MMWR*, 30, 250–252.

Centers for Disease Control and Prevention (CDC). (1992). Revised classification system for HIV infection and expanded surveillance case definition for AIDS among adolescents and adults. *MMWR*, 41 (RR17).

Centers for Disease Control and Prevention (CDC). (1999). Guidelines for national human immunodeficiency virus case surveillance, including monitoring for human immunodeficiency virus infection and acquired immunodeficiency syndrome. *MMWR*, 48 (RR13), 1–31.

Centers for Disease Control and Prevention (CDC). (2001a). HIV and AIDS — United States, 1981–2001. *MMWR*, 50, 430–434.

Centers for Disease Control and Prevention (CDC). (2001b). Revised guidelines for counseling, testing, and referral. *MMWR*, 50 (RR19), 1–58.

Centers for Disease Control and Prevention (CDC). (2002a). Guidelines for preventing opportunistic infections among HIV-infected persons — 2002. *MMWR*, 51 (RR08), 1–46.

Centers for Disease Control and Prevention (CDC). (2002b). U.S. HIV and AIDS cases report through December 2001. *HIV/AIDS Surveillance Report*, 13, 1–44.

Cohen, J. (2002) Confronting the limits of success. *Science*, 296, 2320–2324.

Feinberg, M. (2002) The interface between pathogenesis and treatment of HIV Infection. In E. Emini, Ed., *The Human Immunodeficiency Virus: Biology, Immunology, and Therapy*, chap. 10. Princeton, NJ: Princeton University Press.

Fleming, P.L. et al. (2002). HIV Prevalence in the United States, 2000. 9th Conference on Retroviruses and Opportunistic Infections, Seattle, WA, February 24–28, 2002. Abstract 11.

Gable, C., Tierce, J., Simison, D., Ward, D., & Motte, K. (1996). Costs of HIV+/AIDS at CD4+ counts disease stages based on treatment protocols. *Journal of Acquired Immune Deficiency Syndromes and Human Retrovirology*, 12, 413–420.

Johnson, R. (1998). *Viral Infections of the Nervous System*, 292. Philadelphia: Lippincott-Raven.

Kitchen, J. (1995). Acquired immune deficiency syndrome. In P. Deutsch & H. Sawyer, Eds., *A Guide to Rehabilitation*, Vol. 2, 31.1–31.99. White Plains, NY: Ahab Press.

Krown, S. (1996). AIDS-associated malignancies. In *Cancer Chemotherapy and Biological Response Modifiers*, Annual 16, chap. 19, 441–461. New York: Elsevier Science.

Masci, J.R. (2001). *Outpatient Management of HIV Infection*, 3rd ed. Boca Raton: CRC Press.

Montagnier, L. (2002). A history of HIV discovery. *Science*, 298, 1727–1728.

National Center for Health Statistics. (2002). Deaths: final data for 2000. *National Vital Statistics Reports*, 50 (15).

National Institute of Mental Health. (2000). Human immunodeficiency virus (HIV)/acquired immunodeficiency syndrome (AIDS) research. Fact Sheet, September.

Powderly, J.G., Ed. (2001). *Manual of HIV Therapeutics*, 2nd ed., 33–47. Philadelphia: Lippincott Williams & Wilkins.

Princeton, D.C. (2003). *Manual of HIV AIDS Therapy*. Laguna Hills, CA: Current Clinical Strategies.

Prusiner, S. (2002). Discovering the cause of AIDS. *Science*, 298, 1726–1727.

Ritchie, D. (2001). Antiretroviral agents. In W. Powderly, Ed., *Manual of HIV Therapeutics*, 2nd ed., 33–47. Philadelphia: Lippincott Williams & Wilkins.

Sande, M. Gilbert, D., & Moellering, R., Jr., Eds. (2001). *The Sanford Guide to HIV/AIDS Therapy*, 10th ed., 11. Hyde Park, VT: Antimicrobial Therapy.

Sande, M. & Volberding, P. (1999). *The Medical Management of AIDS*, 6th ed. Philadelphia: W.B. Saunders.

Smith, G. (1994). Treatment of infections in the patient with acquired immunodeficiency syndrome. *Archives of Internal Medicine*, 154, 949–973.

UNAIDS. (2002). *AIDS Epidemic Update*, December.

U.S. Department of Health and Human Services (DHHS). (February 4, 2002). Guidelines for the Use of Antiretroviral Agents in HIV-Infected Adults and Adolescents. http://aidsinfo.nih.gov/guidelines/adults/AAMay23.pdf.

16

LIFE CARE PLANNING FOR
DEPRESSIVE DISORDERS,
OBSESSIVE-COMPULSIVE
DISORDER, AND
SCHIZOPHRENIA

Nicole M. Hilligoss

The impact of mental illness on the cost of health care and productivity has been largely underestimated. Mental illness affects about one in five adults or about 22.1% of Americans age 18 and older (Reiger et al., 1993). In 1998, these prevalence rates translated into about 44.3 million people in the U.S. (National Institute of Mental Health (NIMH), 2001). Of the 10 leading causes of disability in the U.S., 4 of these disabilities are mental disorders: major depression, bipolar disorder, obsessive-compulsive disorder, and schizophrenia (Murray & Lopez, 1996). Psychiatric illness programs have not traditionally used life care planners. However, life care planning for mental illness can be considered an untapped market since the disease is lifelong and requires reasonably predictable care (Hilligoss, 2003). The prediction of expected care can be summarized in a life care plan (Weed, 1999; Weed & Field, 2001). In order to provide an accurate life care plan, it is important to consider the complexity of mental illness, including symptoms, treatment, and impact on functioning. The following sections will provide an overview of major depressive disorder, bipolar disorder, obsessive-compulsive disorder, and schizophrenia. At the end of the chapter, implications for life care planning will be considered, including a checklist to help create the life care plan and an example of a life care plan for individuals with schizophrenia.

MAJOR DEPRESSIVE DISORDER

The leading cause of disability worldwide in individuals aged 5 years and older (measured in the number of years lived with a disabling condition or illness) is major depression (Murray & Lopez, 1996). In any given year, about 9.5% of the

0-8493-1511-5/04/$0.00+$1.50
© 2004 by CRC Press LLC

adult U.S. population (Reiger et al., 1993) or about 18.8 million individuals (NIMH, 2001) have a depressive disorder. The term *depressive disorders* includes major depressive disorder (MDD), dysthymic disorder, and bipolar disorder (also see Bipolar Disorder section). MDD and dysthymia share similar clinical features; however, they differ in duration and severity. Dysthymia is characterized by mild depressive symptoms with a duration of at least 2 years (American Psychiatric Association (APA), 2000a). MDD is associated with greater impairment and severity of symptoms; therefore, it will be the focus of the rest of the section.

Epidemiology and Course of Illness

The Epidemiologic Catchement Area Study (ECA) sponsored by the National Institutes of Health estimated, in adults, the 1-month prevalence of MDD at 2.2% and a lifetime prevalence of 5.8% (Robins & Reiger, 1991). However, other studies have found significantly higher lifetime prevalence estimates, with a 26% rate in women and a 12% rate in men (APA, 2000a). A major depressive episode often occurs after an individual experiences a severe psychosocial stressor such as divorce or death of a loved one. MDD can occur at any age, but the average age of onset is in the late twenties. The disorder may develop suddenly or take days or weeks to become clinically diagnostic. The duration of MDD is varied, and untreated episodes typically last 6 months or longer (APA, 2000a). Some individuals will later develop bipolar disorder after experiencing a hypomanic or manic episode. It is estimated that 50 to 85% of individuals with MDD will have another episode (Mueller et al., 1999). Typically, functioning returns to baseline after an episode resolves, but 20 to 35% of individuals will have some residual functional impairment (APA, 2000a). There appears to be a genetic component in the development of MDD, with higher prevalence rates among first-degree relatives (APA, 2000a).

Symptoms

MDD is characterized by one or more major depressive episodes, with an absence of any hypomanic, manic, or mixed episodes. The fundamental feature of a major depressive episode is a persistent depressed mood that lasts at least 2 weeks or loss of interest or pleasure in almost all activities. Other symptoms of a major depressive episode include changes in sleep, appetite, weight, or psychomotor activity; lack of energy; feeling guilty or worthless; decreased ability to focus, think, or make decisions; and thoughts of death or suicidal thoughts, plans, or attempts (APA, 2000b). At least four of these symptoms must be present and last for at least 2 weeks in order to meet the criteria of a major depressive episode. MDD can range from mild to severe, with a corresponding range in loss of functioning. Individuals with MDD can have psychotic features where delusions (false, irrational beliefs) and hallucinations are present. Catatonic features may also be present, where there is a severe change in motor movements and behavior (i.e., an individual may remain motionless, engage in bizarre postures, or stop speaking) (APA, 2000b).

Treatment

The American Psychiatric Association has established treatment guidelines for MDD (APA, 2000a) and has conceptualized treatment into three phases: (1) the acute phase, during which the goal is to induce remission; (2) the continuation phase, during which the goal is to preserve remission; and (3) the maintenance phase, during which the goal is to prevent future episodes. Both pharmacotherapy and psychotherapeutic interventions are used to meet these goals. Treatment recommendations will vary based on the severity and characteristics of the depressive episodes and response to treatment.

Pharmacotherapy

Antidepressants

Antidepressant medications are utilized during all phases of treatment. Commonly prescribed antidepressants include tricyclics, monoamine oxidase inhibitors (MAOIs), and selective serotonin reuptake inhibitors (SSRIs). Tricyclic agents include amitriptyline, clomipramine, doxepin, and imipramine. Studies estimate that about 50 to 75% of individuals respond to tricyclics, compared with a placebo response rate of 25 to 33% (Depression Guidelines Panel, 1993; Klein et al., 1980; Klerman & Cole, 1967; Potter et al., 1998). Common side effects of tricyclics include cardiac or autonomic (i.e., orthostatic hypotension, dizziness), anticholinergic (i.e., dry mouth, urinary retention, blurred vision), and neurobehavioral (i.e., memory impairment, psychomotor stimulation, tremors) (Pies, 1998). MAOIs include phenelzine and tranylcypromine. MAOIs have similar efficacy in treating MDD as tricyclics (APA, 2000a). Individuals taking MAOIs must avoid certain foods and beverages such as aged cheese or meats, fava beans, and red wine because a serious, life-threatening interaction (hypertensive crisis) may occur (Pies, 1998). Common side effects of MAOIs include orthostatic hypotension, weight gain, sexual impairment side effects, and neurological effects such as headache and insomnia (APA, 2000a). SSRIs include fluoxetine, fluvoxamine, paroxetine, and citalopram. SSRIs are generally as effective as other classes of antidepressants and may be more helpful than tricyclics (APA, 2000a). Common side effects of SSRIs include sedation, insomnia/agitation, gastrointestinal distress, sexual side effects, and weight gain (Pies, 1998).

Adjunctive Medications

If an individual does not have an adequate response to antidepressant medications, other agents may be added in hopes of greater efficacy. Lithium has demonstrated efficacy in up to 50% of individuals that do not respond to antidepressant therapy alone (Price et al., 1986). Individuals with psychotic symptoms are often prescribed antipsychotic agents. Additionally, one antipsychotic agent, olanazpine, has shown efficacy when combined with fluoxetine in treatment-resistant depression (Shelton et al., 2001). Lastly, electroconvulsive therapy (ECT) may be considered in moderate to severe depression and in depression with psychotic features. ECT has shown superior efficacy over antidepressant therapy (Janicak et al., 1985).

Psychotherapeutic Interventions

Cognitive behavior therapy has the most evidence of any psychotherapy approaches in treating MDD successfully (APA, 2000a). The goals of cognitive therapy are to identify and change irrational beliefs and distorted attitudes, thereby reducing depressive symptoms. Additionally, other theoretical orientations that may be used in MDD include behavior therapy, interpersonal therapy, and psychodynamic therapy. Individuals with MDD often have marital and family issues, so therapy with the spouse or family may be helpful. Group therapy may also be beneficial in individuals with MDD.

Vocational Impact of MDD

Individuals that are depressed may have decreased motivation, poor initiative, lack of drive, and low energy (Fischler & Booth, 1999). These symptoms can make it difficult to learn new skills. Individuals with MDD may have irritability that negatively effects relationships with co-workers. They may be overly sensitive to criticism and have difficulty coping with others. The symptoms of MDD can make it difficult for an individual to stay on task or complete a project. Stress tolerance is decreased in MDD; therefore, a high-stress, fast-paced work environment may be inappropriate.

Reasonable Accommodations

Accommodations for an individual with MDD will depend on the severity of symptoms. It is important to offer flexibility in scheduling to allow for appointments for medication management or therapy. A quiet workstation away from distractions may improve attention and focus. A predictable routine can help minimize stress and maintain stamina. Hourly goals can help with maintaining work pace. Working in a team may decrease feelings of loneliness. Lastly, new information or new job skills may require extra instruction and additional time to learn. Providing written instructions can help improve accuracy and aid in retention.

Costs of MDD

Major depressive disorder is a costly illness in terms of both direct costs (i.e., hospitalizations, doctor's visits, medications) and indirect costs (i.e., missed work, reduced productivity, quality of life). The annual cost of MDD is estimated at $43 billion, and missed work accounts for $17 billion (American College of Occupational and Environmental Medicine (ACOEM), 2002). MDD has been shown to be equivalent to coronary heart disease in terms of reduced productivity, and it is estimated that people with MDD function at an even lower rate than people with hypertension, diabetes, or arthritis (ACOEM, 2002). In terms of cost of treatment, SSRIs may be cost-effective over tricyclic agents, even though the SSRIs have higher up-front acquisition costs (Frank et al., 2001). Factors that contribute to the cost-effectiveness of SSRIs include higher rates of compliance and reduced rates of physician visits, laboratory monitoring, and hospitalizations (Conner et al.,

1999). The SSRIs show comparable costs across the various agents (Crown et al., 2001).

BIPOLAR DISORDER

Clinical classifications on bipolar disorder first appeared around the turn of the century, when Emil Kraepelin divided psychotic disorders into two major categories: manic-depressive insanity and dementia praecox (Wyatt, 2001). These terms are the predecessors of bipolar disorder and schizophrenia, respectively. According to the *Diagnostic and Statistical Manual of Mental Disorders, IV, text revision* (DSM-IV-TR) (APA, 2000b), there are two classifications of bipolar disorder: bipolar I and bipolar II. Individuals with bipolar I have experienced at least one episode of mania, while individuals with bipolar II have not. Instead, they experience a milder form of mania termed *hypomania*. Both of these mood states will be further explained in the Symptoms section. Bipolar I is typically more severe and disabling than bipolar II. Unless otherwise stated in the text, in the following sections the term *bipolar disorder* refers to bipolar I.

Epidemiology and Course of Illness

The Epidemiologic Catchement Area Study estimated the prevalence of bipolar I and bipolar II disorder in the adult population at 0.8 and 0.5%, respectively (Robins & Reiger, 1991). Approximately 2.3 million American adults have a bipolar disorder (NIMH, 2001). The ECA study reports the mean age of onset at 21 years old (Robins & Reiger, 1991). Disturbingly, it is estimated that almost 70% of individuals with bipolar disorder who seek help are misdiagnosed, commonly with unipolar depression (Hirschfeld et al., 2003). There are generally an equal number of men and women affected with bipolar disorder, although their course of illness may be different. Women tend to have more depressive than manic episodes, while in men manic episodes typically equal or exceed depressive episodes (APA, 2000b). Rapid cycling is also more common in women than men (APA, 2000b). Current research indicates that bipolar disorder is likely a result of genetic predisposition combined with environmental influences, including stressful events (Rush, 2003).

Bipolar disorder can have a devastating impact on quality of life. When left untreated, an individual may experience 10 or more episodes of mania and depression over his or her lifetime (Goodwin & Jamison, 1990). As many as 60% of individuals with bipolar disorder experience chronic interpersonal and occupational impairments (APA, 2002). The divorce rates among these individuals are two to three times higher than those of the general population (Manning et al., 1997). The ECA study found that individuals with bipolar disorder were the most likely of all of the mentally ill groups to have a history of previous suicide attempts. In fact, 25 to 60% of all individuals with bipolar disorder will attempt suicide at least once in their lifetime, and 18.9% succeed (Robins & Reiger, 1991).

The course of illness in most individuals is chronic, often with alternating periods of depression and mania. Symptoms typically reduce for a period of time between these episodes; however, 20 to 30% of individuals continue to have residual mood symptoms (APA, 2000b). About 10 to 15% of individuals with bipolar disorder have rapid cycling, which is defined as four or more episodes of mania, mixed mania, hypomania, or depression, occurring in a 12-month period (Bowden, 1996).

Symptoms

Symptoms associated with bipolar disorder include mania, hypomania, depressive, and mixed states. Psychotic features may occur with all of these states except hypomania. Psychotic features are defined as a break with reality characterized by delusions and hallucinations. The DSM-IV-TR (APA, 2000b) criteria for each of these mood states are detailed below.

Mania

The characteristics of mania include:

- Mood disturbance for at least 1 week: abnormal and persistently elevated, expansive, or irritable mood
- Pressured speech: talkative, with pressure to keep talking, difficult to interrupt
- Distractibility: difficulty maintaining attention, distracted by irrelevant information or stimuli
- Flight of ideas: racing thoughts, frequently changing subjects
- Inflated self-esteem or grandiosity: an exaggerated sense of self-importance or of one's status, accomplishments, wealth, talents, or beauty
- Decreased need for sleep: sleeps very little or not at all, may deny need for sleep
- Impulsivity: difficulty controlling impulses and may engage excessively in pleasurable activities without regard for potential consequences (i.e., gambling, sexual activity with strangers, or lavish spending of money)
- Increase in goal-directed activity or psychomotor agitation

Hypomania

Hypomania and mania share the same characteristics. However, in hypomania the symptoms are not severe enough to cause significant vocational or social impairment or to warrant hospitalization. Additionally, psychotic features are never present during a hypomanic episode (APA, 2000b).

Depressive Episode

To meet the criteria for a depressive episode, each symptom must be present nearly every day (i.e., not occurring occasionally). The criteria for a depressive episode are as follows:

- Depressed mood occurring most of the day for at least 2 weeks
- Significantly reduced interest or pleasure in all or almost all activities occurring most of the day

- Significant weight loss or weight gain or change in appetite
- Insomnia or hypersomnia
- Psychomotor agitation or retardation that is observable by others
- Feelings of worthlessness or excessive/inappropriate guilt, which may take on a delusional quality
- Fatigue or lack of energy
- Decreased ability to think or focus or make decisions
- Recurrent thoughts of death and/or suicidal ideation, plan or attempt

Mixed Episode

A mixed episode occurs when the criteria for both a manic and depressive episode are met at the same time nearly every day for at least 1 week (APA, 2000b). A mixed episode causes severe impairment and may lead to hospitalization. During a mixed state, it is common to have agitation, difficulty sleeping, significant changes in appetite, psychosis, and suicidal thoughts.

Treatment

The APA *Practice Guidelines for the Treatment of Patients with Bipolar Disorder* provide the following treatment guidelines and goals (APA, 2002):

- Perform a thorough diagnostic evaluation.
- Evaluate the safety of the patient and others and determine a treatment setting.
- Establish and maintain a therapeutic alliance.
- Monitor the patient's psychiatric status.
- Provide psychoeducation about bipolar disorder.
- Enhance treatment compliance.
- Promote regular patterns of activity and sleep.
- Anticipate stressors.
- Identify new episodes early.
- Minimize functional impairments.

To achieve these goals, a combination of pharmacologic and psychotherapeutic interventions is required.

Pharmacotherapy

Medications are used to treat acute manic symptoms, alleviate depression, and prevent future episodes. Common categories of drugs that are used to treat bipolar disorder include mood stabilizers, antidepressants, and adjunctive agents. Currently, there are only three agents that are approved by the Food and Drug Administration (FDA) for the treatment of bipolar disorder: lithium, valproate, and olanzapine (K. Littrell, personal communication, June 1, 2003). Psychiatrists often prescribe off-label for bipolar disorder, which means prescribing medications that are on the market and may be effective, but have not been FDA-approved for a particular illness.

Lithium

Lithium has been the mainstay of bipolar pharmacologic treatment. It was first found to have antimanic properties in 1949 (Cade, 1999), but was not widely prescribed for bipolar disorder in the U.S. until the mid-1960s (Jefferson et al., 1987). Lithium demonstrates efficacy in the treatment of acute mania, depressive episodes, and prevention of recurrent episodes (Goodwin & Jamison, 1990). Side effects are reported in up to 75% of individuals that take lithium (Jefferson et al., 1987; Goodwin & Jamison, 1990). Side effects of lithium include excessive thirst, excessive urination, memory problems, tremor, weight gain, and drowsiness/tiredness (Lenox & Husseini, 1998). Rates of noncompliance range from 18 to 53%, and the side effect most often reported as the reason for discontinuing lithium is memory problems (Goodwin & Jamison, 1990). Toxic effects and overdose can occur and are more common with high serum levels. Monitoring of serum plasma levels is an important aspect of lithium treatment. Initially, close serum monitoring is required to find the optimal therapeutic dose and to avoid toxicity. It is recommended that renal and thyroid function be tested regularly because lithium use may disrupt these processes (APA, 2002).

Valproate

Valproate, an anticonvulsant, is another agent commonly used in the treatment of bipolar disorder. Valproate has demonstrated efficacy in the treatment of acute mania and some evidence of effectiveness in acute bipolar depression and maintenance (APA, 2002). Common side effects of valproate include sedation, gastrointestinal distress, tremor, increased appetite, and weight gain. There may be life-threatening adverse reactions, but such events are rare. Dosing is established through blood serum monitoring. Toxicity and overdose are not common with routine dosing. It is recommended that liver function and hematologic measures be assessed on a regular basis (APA, 2002).

Olanzapine

Olanzapine is an atypical antipsychotic indicated for use in schizophrenia and, more recently, bipolar disorder. Olanzapine has demonstrated efficacy in acute mania and some evidence of effectiveness in depressive symptoms, maintenance, and rapid cycling (Tohen et al., 1999; Sanger et al., 2001, 2003). Common side effects of olanzapine include somnolence, agitation, insomnia, dry mouth, constipation, and weight gain. Unlike lithium and valproate, olanzapine does not require serum monitoring.

Adjunctive Medications

Other medications that are used in bipolar disorder include antipsychotics, benzodiazepines/tranquilizers, antidepressants, and anticonvulsants. Antipsychotics are typically used to treat acute mania and psychotic symptoms. Benzodiazepines or tranquilizers are also used to treat acute mania because of their sedative effects. Antidepressants are used for bipolar depression; however, caution and close monitoring are required because these agents may induce mania (APA, 2002). Some research indicates that other anticonvulsants such as lamotrigine and gabapentin may be effective in treating bipolar disorder (Fogelson & Sternback, 1997; Wang et al., 2002). More research is needed to better quantify the beneficial effects of adjunctive medications.

Psychotherapeutic Interventions

The APA practice guidelines for the treatment of bipolar disorder (2002) recommend the use of psychoeducation and psychotherapeutic interventions. The primary goals of these treatments are to decrease distress, improve functioning, and reduce the risk and severity of future episodes. While psychotherapeutic interventions alone are typically not effective in the treatment of acute mania, they do demonstrate efficacy with bipolar depression (Zaretsky et al., 1999). Treating bipolar depression without antidepressants can be especially beneficial in individuals who have antidepressant side effects, antidepressant-induced mania, or rapid cycling. In addition to individual therapy, individuals with bipolar disorder may also benefit from family therapy, group therapy, and support groups.

Vocational Impact of Bipolar Disorder

Bipolar disorder can result in significant difficulties in the workplace. Hirschfeld and colleagues (2003) found that employment rates of individuals with bipolar disorder dropped from 49% in 1992 to 40% in 2000. During a manic phase, symptoms such as grandiosity, distractibility, poor judgment, and excessive or inappropriate motivation can result in severe consequences on the job. A person experiencing manic symptoms has reduced interpersonal functioning, poor time management, difficulty maintaining attention, and may be distracting to co-workers. The individual may be unpredictable, unreliable, and irrational. At the most extreme, the individual experiencing mania can be dangerous to himself or herself and to others in the workplace. An individual experiencing a depressive episode may have lack of motivation, lack of energy, social withdrawal, and decreased ability to attend and focus (Fischler & Booth, 1999).

Reasonable Accommodations

Functional limitations and reasonable accommodations will vary according to the individual based on differences in episode, symptom severity, and effective coping strategies. Accommodations could include job sharing or job restructuring, putting all workplace communications in writing, and allowing time off for appointments and hospitalization, if needed. Increasing the structure of the workday and developing hourly goals can also be helpful. It is important to provide regular feedback in both job performance and interactions with others. Providing a quiet workstation with minimal distractions can improve attention and focus. Educating a supervisor or co-worker about the early signs of mania could also be helpful in providing appropriate interventions early in the episode, thereby reducing functional impairment.

Costs of Bipolar Disorder

Bipolar disorder is a costly illness, in terms of both economics and impact on quality of life. The most costly intervention for bipolar disorder is hospitalization. Begley and colleagues (1998) report that the average cost per person with a single manic episode is $11,720. This estimate rose to $624,785 for individuals with chronic episodes. It is estimated that 64% of individuals with bipolar disorder are noncompliant, meaning they do not take their medications as prescribed (Li et al., 2002). Direct health care costs rise in individuals who delay or do not take mood stabilizers during their first year of treatment (Li et al., 2002). Medication noncompliance can lead to relapse and rehospitalization — a costly cycle. While newer medications may be more expensive, there is some evidence that shows that new medications help reduce overall costs, due to improved efficacy (Namjoshi et al., 2002).

OBSESSIVE-COMPULSIVE DISORDER

Worry, doubts, and superstitious behavior are often a part of everyday experiences. Many people spend some time worrying, especially when psychosocial stressors are high. When worries become excessive or irrational or when certain actions are perceived as necessary to counteract these thoughts, then obsessive-compulsive disorder (OCD) is suspected. Important clinical features of OCD are that the thoughts and actions must be time-consuming (greater than 1 hour per day), cause marked distress, and significantly impair everyday activities (APA, 2000b).

Epidemiology and Course of Illness

OCD was once considered to be a rare disease by mental health professionals. People with OCD often did not seek treatment. OCD came to be recognized as a more common illness when the National Institute of Mental Health found that more than 2% of the population has OCD, which makes it more common than bipolar disorder and schizophrenia (U.S. Department of Health and Human Services (U.S. DHHS), 1996). People with OCD come from all ethnic backgrounds, and men and women are affected in equal numbers. Generally, the onset of OCD is any age between preschool and adulthood. Most people develop OCD by the age of 40 years (March et al., 1997). Up to 50% of individuals with OCD report that their symptoms began during childhood (March et al., 1997). OCD often goes unrecognized even after an individual seeks treatment. It is estimated that the average person with OCD sees three to four different doctors and spends 9 years seeking treatment before the correct diagnosis is made (March et al., 1997). OCD appears to have a genetic component and is linked to tic disorders (U.S. DHHS, 1996). The symptoms are most likely due to a reduction in the levels of serotonin in the brain or other neurotransmitter dysfunction (U.S. DHHS, 1996; March et al., 1997). OCD symptoms are often chronic, although there may be periods of time when the symptoms are less severe.

Symptoms

Most people with OCD have both obsessions and compulsions. Obsessions are thoughts, images, or impulses that are persistent and perceived by the individual as unwanted, intrusive, and beyond control (APA, 2000b). However, the individual with obsessions is able to recognize that these thoughts are a product of his or her own mind. The obsessive thoughts are perceived as disturbing and result in high levels of distress and anxiety. Individuals experiencing obsessions often cope by ignoring or suppressing the thoughts or attempting to neutralize them through another thought or behavior, which is a compulsion. Therefore, compulsions are repetitive actions or thoughts that an individual performs in order to make obsessions go away. Compulsive behaviors in OCD are not pleasurable, but used to reduce or prevent anxious feelings or worries (APA, 2000b). Common obsessions include the following (APA, 2000b):

- Fear of contamination (i.e., by touching a doorknob or shaking hands)
- Repeated doubts (i.e., wondering if the stove was left on or if a check was signed)
- A need to have things in a certain order or organized a certain way, often symmetrically (i.e., lining up shoes a certain way, positioning canned goods according to size, type)
- Aggressive or horrifying images (i.e., slapping someone, shouting obscenities at work)
- Sexual imagery (i.e., pornographic images)

Common compulsions include the following (APA, 2000b):

- Repetitive behaviors (i.e., hand washing, ordering, checking, touching, hoarding)
- Repetitive mental acts (i.e., praying, counting, repeating words or phrases)

Treatment

Treatment of OCD includes both medications and psychotherapeutic interventions. Most people require the use of both modalities, as only 20% experience symptom remission with medications alone (March et al., 1997). The Expert Consensus Guidelines for the Treatment of Obsessive-Compulsive Disorder (March et al., 1997) divide treatment into two phases: acute and maintenance. The respective treatment goals during the acute and maintenance phases are to end the current OCD episode and prevent future episodes. Most treatment occurs on an outpatient basis, as hospitalization is rarely necessary for the treatment of OCD.

Pharmacotherapy

Antidepressants

Serotonin reuptake inhibitors (SRIs) are the mainstay of pharmacologic treatment of OCD. SRIs include clomipramine (a tricyclic antidepressant) and SSRIs such as fluoxetine, fluvoxamine, paroxetine, sertraline, and citalopram. Antidepressants that do not have serotonergic properties are typically not effective in the treatment of OCD (Pies, 1998). If OCD symptoms do not diminish after an SRI is initiated, it is recommended that the dosage be increased to the maximum dose for at least 4 to 6 weeks. If the response is still inadequate, the ineffective SRI should be discontinued and another SRI initiated (March et al., 1997).

Adjunctive Medications

If symptoms do not respond to conventional treatment, then another strategy is the use of adjunctive medications. Commonly used adjunctive medications include clomipramine, benzodiazepines (i.e., clonazepam, alprazolam, lorazepam), antipsychotics (i.e., haloperidol, pimozide, risperidone), and buspirone (an antianxiety agent) (March et al., 1997). Adjunctive medications are not used alone, but added on to the existing medication regime. It is important to monitor for increased medication side effects or interactions when using multiple agents. Sedation is a common side effect of these medications, so it may be necessary to take them at bedtime.

Psychotherapeutic Interventions

Cognitive behavior therapy (CBT) is recommended for all individuals with OCD (March et al., 1997). CBT techniques utilized in the treatment of OCD include exposure and response or ritual prevention. Exposure consists of having the individual come into contact with a feared stimulus (i.e., dirty objects, shaking hands, etc.). The goal of this technique is to reduce anxiety with each exposure session. Response or ritual prevention is another key element to this process. This technique is defined as preventing the individual from any actions that are used to reduce anxiety when exposed to the feared stimulus (March et al., 1997), for example, not permitting the individual to wash his or her hands after touching something perceived as contaminated. Other CBT techniques used in OCD include thought stopping, distraction, and contingency management.

Individuals with OCD may also benefit from psychoeducation about the illness and ways to manage symptoms. Also, support groups can be helpful because they provide an outlet for individuals to share experiences and receive peer support.

Vocational Impact of OCD

OCD can have a devastating impact on vocational functioning. Commonly, individuals with OCD will work at a slow pace as a result of coping with obsessions and compulsions. An individual may feel compelled to check and recheck his or her work or a need to do certain rituals while working that make ordinary tasks take an extended period of time to complete. Individuals with OCD have a lower tolerance for stress. Everyday occurrences such as shaking someone's hand or counting money might induce obsessive thoughts and compulsive behaviors. Also, a stressful work environment can contribute to the severity and frequency of OCD symptoms. Distractibility can occur because the individual with OCD is often preoccupied with symptoms, detracting from the ability to concentrate and focus (Fischler & Booth, 1999).

Reasonable Accommodations

An individual with OCD will work better in an environment that offers predictability and routine. This can help keep stress levels to a minimum and reduce the need to make decisions throughout the day, which may be prove difficult, especially when symptoms are moderate to severe. It may be helpful to allow some flexibility in the setup of the workspace. Providing hourly goals may help establish pace of work. A workstation that is not in close proximity to co-workers may decrease anxiety and distractibility. Lastly, flexible scheduling should be offered to accommodate medication management and CBT appointments.

Costs of OCD

Although hospitalization is generally not required in the management of OCD, it remains a costly illness from both an economic and quality of life perspective. In 1990, the total costs of OCD were estimated to be $8.4 billion, which was 5.7% of the estimated costs of all mental illnesses combined for that year ($147.8 billion) (Dupont et al., 1995). More research is needed to better quantify the costs of OCD. In regards to quality of life, individuals with OCD have dysfunction in all areas. OCD has a negative impact on an individual's interpersonal relationships, and significant others may become part of the destructive symptom cycle by enabling rituals. In these cases, it is especially important to include significant others in the treatment plan, including the use of marriage and family therapy.

SCHIZOPHRENIA

In 1896, Emil Kraeplin provided the first descriptions of the disease known today as schizophrenia (Wyatt, 2001). After decades of studying the mentally ill, Kraepelin began to categorize individuals by their course of symptoms. He used the term *dementia praecox* to describe individuals whose psychotic symptoms began early in life and continued on a deteriorating course (Wyatt, 2001). In 1911, Eugene Bleuler coined the term *schizophrenia* for the illness that Kraepelin called dementia praecox, because he thought it was a more fitting description of the illness. The word schizophrenia means a splitting (schizo) of the mind (phrenia), and not a split personality, which is a common public misperception about the illness (Wyatt, 2001).

Early treatments for schizophrenia such as hypoglycemic coma, seizure therapy, and frontal lobotomies were typically unsuccessful and even harmful for the patient. Schizophrenia treatment was revolutionized in the early 1950s with the introduction of the first antipsychotic agent, chlorpromazine (Thorazine), allowing many patients to be treated in the communities instead of in hospitals (Siegfreid et al., 2001). In the early 1990s, pharmacotherapy entered another more promising phase with the introduction of the first atypical antipsychotic agent, clozapine. The atypical agents offer increased efficacy and reduced serious side effects when compared with the older, conventional agents.

Epidemiology and Course of Illness

The ECA study found the annual prevalence rate for schizophrenia to be about 1.3% of the population (Robins & Reiger, 1991), translating into about 2.2 million people in the U.S. The incidence rate is similar across diverse geographical, cultural, and socioeconomic categories. The onset of schizophrenia can be gradual or sudden, but many individuals display signs that something is wrong (i.e., decreased sociality, withdrawal, unusual behavior) before actual psychotic symptoms are apparent (U.S. DHHS, 1999). The age of onset is typically adolescence to early adulthood, with men typically having an earlier onset than women. It is unusual to develop schizophrenia after the age of 40 (McEvoy et al., 1999). Earlier onset is associated with poorer outcomes, which may be attributed to the loss of age-appropriate milestones in the areas of education, interpersonal relationships, and employment (U.S. DHHS, 1999). The course of schizophrenia is often chronic and disabling. Individuals may have periods of acute psychosis alternating with periods of symptom remission or a constant level of residual symptoms that can greatly impair functioning. Schizophrenia subtypes (based on symptoms) include paranoid, disorganized, catatonic, undifferentiated, and residual (APA, 2000b).

Schizophrenia is primarily a problem of brain functionality rather than brain structure. While the role of dopamine imbalance has been well documented, other neurotransmitters appear to be involved in schizophrenia as well, including serotonin, acetylcholine, norepinephrine, glutamate, and GABA. While the causes of schizophrenia are unknown, scientists believe it is a combination of genetic predisposition and environmental factors that most likely occur *in utero* during the development of the brain (U.S. DHHS, 1999).

Symptoms

The two main categories of symptoms in schizophrenia are positive symptoms and negative symptoms. The term *positive* refers to occurrences that are added to one's ordinary experience, while the term *negative* refers to aspects of life that are taken away from one's ordinary experience.

Positive Symptoms

Positive symptoms include hallucinations, delusions, disorganized speech, and disorganized or catatonic behavior. Hallucinations can occur in all sensory modalities, but the most common are auditory. Auditory hallucinations are usually in the form of voices. A voice may provide a running commentary on a person's actions or thoughts; there may be two or more voices talking to each other or a single voice that commands a person to do things such as pray out loud or hide in the basement.

Delusions are false beliefs and may take on a bizarre quality such as believing one is from another planet or that one has two heads. Common categories of delusions include the following:

- Paranoid (believing one is being tracked by the CIA, is the victim of a communist plot, etc.)

- Grandiose (believing one is the president, a rock star, a religious prophet, etc.)
- Referential (believing that a song on the radio or popular novel is about oneself, etc.)
- Thought broadcasting (believing that one's thoughts are broadcasting out loud so that others can hear them)
- Somatic (believing one's teeth are soft or loose, that one's body is shrinking, etc.)

Negative Symptoms

Negative symptoms include flat affect (facial expressions of emotion are absent), alogia or poverty of speech (fluency and amount of speech are markedly reduced), avolition or lack of motivation or drive (decreased ability to initiate and continue goal-directed behaviors, little interest in any activity), anhedonia (loss of ability to feel pleasure, emptiness), anergia (lack of energy), and asociality (social isolation and withdrawal).

Associated Symptoms or Features

Other symptoms often found in schizophrenia include cognitive dysfunction (i.e., impaired memory, executive functioning, concentration, abstract thinking, etc.), inappropriate affect, dysphoric or depressed mood, anxiety, odd psychomotor activities (i.e., rocking, pacing), odd mannerisms or behaviors, and sleep disturbances. Common comorbid conditions include substance abuse, anxiety disorders, personality disorders, and other medical conditions/illnesses. It is important to note that treatment noncompliance is very common and further complicates the clinical picture of schizophrenia. It has been reported that 75% of individuals with schizophrenia stop taking their medication within 2 years of leaving a hospital or treatment program, which greatly increases the risk of relapse and rehospitalization (Weiden et al., 1994).

Treatment Phases of Schizophrenia

There is no cure for schizophrenia. Treatment involves a broad range of interventions, both pharmacotherapy and psychosocial, designed to reduce the frequency and severity of symptoms and to improve functioning. The American Psychiatric Association has established treatment guidelines for schizophrenia (APA, 1997) and has conceptualized the treatment of schizophrenia into three phases: (1) acute phase, (2) stabilization phase, and (3) stable phase.

The acute phase is characterized by florid psychosis where an individual has severe delusions, hallucinations, negative symptoms, and disorganized thinking. Individuals in this stage are often unable to care for themselves and may be violent, homicidal, or suicidal. The goals of treatment during the acute phase are to reduce the acute symptoms and improve functioning. Clients should receive care in the least restricted environment that will preserve safety and allow for effective treatment. Treatment should include the implementation of antipsychotic medication, as well as nonpharmacologic treatments aimed at reducing stress and overstimulation and establishing a therapeutic relationship between the client and treatment team. Psychoeducation about schizophrenia should be provided at this phase to both clients and their families.

The stabilization phase typically lasts 6 months or more after the onset of the acute episode. Although the severity of the psychotic symptoms is reduced, symptoms are still present and can fluctuate in intensity. Functioning is improved, but some impairment remains. Treatment goals during the stabilization phase include minimizing stress, minimizing the likelihood of relapse, improving community functioning, and continued reduction of symptoms. During this phase, it is important to provide clients with psychoeducation regarding the importance of medication in reducing relapse. Pharmacologic interventions include the continued use of antipsychotics and other agents to reduce symptoms and relapse. The APA expressly discourages the reduction in dose or discontinuation of effective medications for at least 6 months after the resolution of the acute phase (APA, 1997). Psychotherapeutic interventions include psychoeducation, social skills training, group therapy, and prevocational training.

The stable phase is characterized by relatively stable symptoms that are less severe than those experienced during the acute phase. Residual symptoms may be more nonpsychotic in nature, such as circumstantial thoughts or speech, overvalued ideas rather than delusions, and mild to moderate negative symptoms. Treatment goals during the stable phase include optimizing functioning and quality of life, minimizing the risk of relapse, and monitoring for medication side effects. Pharmacologic interventions include maintenance therapy of effective medications (antipsychotics and others) while minimizing medication side effects. Nonpharmacologic interventions include independent living skills training, social skills training, cognitive rehabilitation, and vocational rehabilitation (APA, 1997).

Treatment Refractory Schizophrenia

A substantial portion of individuals with schizophrenia are considered treatment refractory or resistant. The criteria for treatment refractory schizophrenia are as follows: (1) persistent, moderately severe, positive symptoms; (2) at least a moderately severe illness overall; (3) poor social/occupational functioning during the last 5 years; and (4) drug refractory, i.e., lack of improvement on at least two conventional antipsychotics (Kane et al., 1988). Treatment refractory individuals are often highly symptomatic, with higher rates of service use and rehospitalization. The reported prevalence rates of refractory schizophrenia range from 20 to 40% to 60% or greater when the definition of *refractory* is broadened to include social, vocation, and cognitive dysfunction (Hegarty et al., 1994; Prein & Cole, 1968; Essock et al., 1996). Adjunctive medications or higher antipsychotic dosing are often used in refractory individuals.

Pharmacotherapy

Antipsychotics

The expert consensus guidelines (McEvoy et al., 1999) recommend that atypical antipsychotics be employed as first-line therapies over conventional antipsychotics unless a client is having good results with minimal side effects on a conventional agent or if the client does not take oral medications regularly (noncompliant); then a depot formulation (long-acting shot) should be used. At this time, depot formulations are only available as conventional antipsychotics. Conventional antipsychotics are associated with troublesome and serious side effects such as tardive dyskinesia (abnormal, involuntary movements commonly of the mouth, face, or extremities) and extrapyramidal symptoms (restlessness, tremors, muscle contractions, and rigidity). Many atypical agents have shown equal efficacy in positive symptoms as conventional agents and superior efficacy in the treatment of negative symptoms and cognitive symptoms (McEvoy et al., 1999). The atypical agents are not without side effects. Common side effects associated with the use of atypicals include drowsiness/sedation, dry mouth, constipation, dizziness, orthostatic hypotension, nausea, extrapyramidal symptoms (but reduced in comparison with conventional symptoms), and weight gain.

Adjunctive Medications

Polypharmacy is becoming increasingly common in psychiatry, including the use of more than one antipsychotic agent (Stahl, 1999). The rationale for the use of multiple agents is the desire to target different neurotransmitter receptor sites thought to be part of the disease process in schizophrenia. However, there is little controlled research on the efficacy of combination therapy. Clark and colleagues (2002) examined New Hampshire Medicaid pharmaceutical claims from 1995 to 1999 and found the following information about changes in prescription practices in the treatment of schizophrenia and schizoaffective disorder: (1) prescriptions of multiple antipsychotics increased from 5.7 to 24.3%; (2) prescriptions for antidepressants increased from 18.5 to 35.6%; (3) prescriptions for antianxiety medications increased from 19.9 to 33.5%; and (4) prescriptions for mood stabilizers increased from 17.7 to 30.0%.

Anticonvulsants/Mood Stabilizers

Commonly prescribed anticonvulsants/mood stabilizers include valproate, carbamazepine, and lithium. These agents have shown some evidence of augmenting antipsychotic response, improving mood, and reducing agitation, aggression, and irritability (APA, 1997; Fein, 1998). Dosing is generally the same as the dosing that would be used in seizure or mood disorders (APA, 1997). Anticonvulsants are generally well-tolerated agents. Carbamazepine may interact with other drugs, including reducing the serum levels of antipsychotics and benzodiazepines (antianxiety medications). Common side effects of anticonvulsants include neurological symptoms (i.e., double vision, blurred vision, fatigue) and gastrointestinal distress (i.e., nausea, indigestion, vomiting, and diarrhea) (Keck & McElroy, 1998).

Antidepressants

It has been noted for many years that a large portion of people with schizophrenia exhibit depression-like symptomatology. Estimates of the prevalence of depression in this population range from 7 to 65% (Bartles & Drake, 1988; DeLisis, 1990).

The expert consensus guidelines (McEvoy et al., 1999) recommend utilizing an SSRI (i.e., fluoxetine, paroxetine, sertraline, etc.) as first-line treatment. SSRIs may increase the serum concentrations of certain antipsychotics. Common side effects of SSRI treatment include gastrointestinal distress, insomnia, and sexual dysfunction (Tollefson & Rosenbaum, 1998).

Benzodiazapines/Anxiolytics

Benzodiazepines (i.e., lorazepam, diazepam, clonazepam, etc.) are often implemented during acute psychosis and may augment antipsychotic response and decrease agitation and anxiety (APA, 1997). Additionally, patients with certain motor disturbances, such as akathisia, may show improvement with the use of benzodiazepines (Siegfreid et al., 2001). Generally, benzodiazepines have few drug interactions. Common side effects of benzodiazepines include sedation and drowsiness (Ballenger, 1998).

Anticholinergics

Anticholinergic medications (i.e., benzotropine mesylate, trihexyphenidyl hydrochloride, amantadine, etc.) are used to prevent and treat extrapyramidal side effects. It is commonly necessary to use anticholinergics in individuals that are prescribed conventional agents. The use of these agents should be reconsidered whenever a change in the antipsychotic dosage is made, as lower dosages may have reduced side effects (APA, 1997). Anticholinergics generally do not interact with other drugs. Side effects of anticholinergics include dry mouth, dry eyes, urinary retention, constipation, and memory disturbances (Stanilla & Simpson, 1998).

Vocational Impact of Schizophrenia

Employment is a critical aspect of reintegration into the community. In recent years, the importance of employment among individuals with schizophrenia has received renewed interest, and more supported employment programs are available. However, most people with severe and persistent mental illness remained unemployed, at a rate as high as 85 to 100% (Anthony et al., 1990; National Organization on Disability, 1998). There are many factors that contribute to such low rates of employment, including residual positive and negative symptoms, interpersonal skills deficits, cognitive impairments, relapse, lack of appropriate vocational programs, and stigma. However, the benefits of paid employment are far reaching, including an association with total symptom improvement, lower rates of hospitalization, and decreased rates of emotional discomfort (Bell et al., 1996).

Functional Limitations and Reasonable Accommodations

Functional limitations will vary according to the individual based on differences in symptoms (both severity and domain) and effective coping strategies. Positive symptoms can make it difficult for clients to concentrate, handle stress, and interact with others. Negative symptoms can result in lack of motivation and energy, difficulty with initiating and completing a work task, and impaired social skills. Cognitive symptoms have a negative impact on concentration, attention, memory, and ability to problem solve or learn new information. Additionally, cognitive symptoms can cause difficulties in a client's ability to prioritize, filter out irrelevant information, and function socially.

Reasonable accommodations for clients with schizophrenia will vary according to individual needs and may change over time. Typically accommodations are not costly, as they are not usually structural. Common categories of accommodations (Manusco, 1990; Pratt et al., 1999) include the following:

- Human assistance (i.e., job coach, additional training, co-worker mentoring)
- Changes to the physical environment (i.e., room dividers to decrease distractions or enclosed office space)
- Changes in workplace policy (i.e., job sharing, job restructuring, schedule flexibility to accommodate medical/therapy/rehabilitation appointments)
- Changes in workplace communication (i.e., putting all work requests in writing, scheduling daily planning sessions to develop hourly goals)

Vocational Programs

Vocational program models include clubhouse programs, transitional employment, agency-sponsored or consumer-operated businesses, and supported employment. A review of 17 studies of various employment programs found supported employment to have the best outcomes, with 58% of individuals in supported employment obtaining jobs, compared with a rate of 21% of individuals in traditional programs (Bond et al., 1997). The basic tenent of supported employment is any client can hold a job in the competitive workforce if provided the proper supports. Important features of supported employment include integration with treatment, client choice, ongoing, time-unlimited supports on or off site, and integrated settings.

Costs of Schizophrenia

It is estimated that schizophrenia costs the U.S. about $32.5 billion dollars per year (NIMH, 2003a). When measured in disability adjusted life years (DALYs), the impairment of active psychosis is equal to tetraplegia (quadriplegia) (NIMH, 2003b). The largest portion of the cost of schizophrenia is generated from hospitalizations for initial episodes and relapses (Thieda et al., 2003). Half of the relapses are a result of medication noncompliance, and the other half are due to lack of treatment efficacy (Weiden & Olfson, 1995). Decreasing hospitalization rates and utilizing outpatient programs instead of inpatient treatment could reduce the economic burden of schizophrenia. One study found that intensive outpatient treatment resulted in a savings in hospital costs of about $8000 per client (Dickstein et al., 1988). This program resulted in annual savings of $272,767, based on reductions in hospitalization rates.

Treating individuals with schizophrenia with the atypical antipsychotics instead of conventional antipsychotics can also help reduce overall costs, despite that the initial costs of the atypical agents are significantly higher than the conventional drugs (Davies et al., 1998; Finley et al., 1998; Palmer et al., 1998; Hamilton et al., 1999). A review of 22 studies found that in most cases, the atypical antipsychotics were at least cost-neutral and may be cost-effective when compared with conventional agents (Hudson et al., 2003). It can be difficult to measure the cost-effectiveness of antipsychotic agents, especially when outcomes are expanded to include not just reduction in hospitalization, but also improvements in quality of life. More controlled research is needed to better quantify the cost benefits of atypical antipsychotics vs. conventional agents.

CASE STUDY

John is a 40-year-old single man who was diagnosed with schizophrenia at the age of 17. He has been hospitalized five times and attempted suicide at the age of 20. His primary symptoms include auditory hallucinations and delusions. The voices he hears often instruct him to do things such as "Don't go outside!" or "Don't eat that food, it's poisoned!" His delusions are mostly of a paranoid nature. He believes that he is monitored by the CIA through a chip implanted in his ear. When he walks down the street he feels like others are staring at him. Sometimes he thinks that people are speaking in code about him at the supermarket. John also has a lack of motivation and drive. On a bad day, he stays on the couch for hours, barely moving. He sometimes has difficulty keeping up his hygiene. John often has trouble with his concentration and memory. To overcome this, he carries a small notebook with him everywhere he goes to remind him of things he needs to do such as appointments, grocery shopping, and laundry.

John takes many medications on a daily basis and requires the use of a medication organization box to keep track of them. Despite this, sometimes he still forgets his medication. John occasionally has delusions about his medications, believing that they are poisoned or hurting his body in some way. He sees his psychiatrist once a month for medication management. He also attends individual and group therapy once a week. John has received social skills training, psycho-education, and vocational counseling in the past. He lives independently with a roommate. Previously, he lived in a group home.

Although he had his first break at 17, John did complete high school. He has not had any other formal education. His work history is sporadic, with long periods of unemployment. He has worked as a grocery bagger, stocker, fast food worker, pizza deliverer, and landscaper. He has morning sedation from his medications and is often late if he has to be at work before 11:00 A.M. His chronic lateness resulted in several job terminations. John is currently unemployed but wants to work. He wants to try vocational counseling again because he is having a hard time finding a job on his own.

John receives Social Security Disability Insurance (SSDI) payments and has Medicare. His parents also contribute substantially to his living costs. John's parents want funds set up for when they are deceased, so that John will continue to receive appropriate treatment. They want to hire a life care planner to help them create these plans. Table 16.1 provides a sample life care plan for schizophrenia based on the format published in Deutsch and Sawyer (1993).

Table 16.1 Example Life Care Plan for John for Estate Planning

Routine Medical Care

Description	Purpose	Frequency/Duration	Costs per Visit	Costs per Year
Psychiatry	Medication management	Minimum of 1 time/month to life (may be 1 time/week during acute phase)	$100	$1200
Dentist/teeth cleaning	Many psychotropic medications cause dry mouth, which may lead to dental problems	2 times/year to life	$70	$140
Primary care physician/general medical care	Monitoring of overall health; increased prevalence of comorbid conditions such as obesity, insulin resistance, diabetes, STDs	1 time/year, average	$100	$1200

Psychotherapeutic Interventions

Therapy	Age/Year Initiated	Age/Year Discontinued	Treatment Frequency	Base Cost per Session
Individual	2003	Lifetime	1 time/week for 6 months (stabilization phase), then 1–2 times/month average	$100/session
Group	2003	Expect lifetime	1 time/week up to 6 months (stabilization), then 1–2 times/month average	$40/session
Psychoeducation	2003	Expect 6 months, then unknown	2 times/month for 6 months; follow-up sessions as needed	$30/session

Table 16.1 (Continued) Example Life Care Plan for John for Estate Planning

Psychotherapeutic Interventions (continued)

Therapy	Age/Year Initiated	Age/Year Discontinued	Treatment Frequency	Base Cost per Session
Social skills training, group format	2003	Expect 6 months, then unknown	1 time/week during the stabilization phase, then less frequent depending on symptoms, level of social dysfunction, ability to learn new skills	$30/session
Case management	Age of onset/stabilization phase	Expect 6 months, then unknown	1 time/week during stabilization phase, then less frequent	$65/session

Diagnostic Testing

Diagnostic Recommendation	Age/Year Initiated	Age/Year Discontinued	Frequency	Base Cost per Year
MRI (brain)	2003	2003	Expect 1 time only	$1500
Psychological evaluation/testing	2003	2003	Expect 1 time only	$300–600

Medication/Supply Needs

Medication/Supply	Age/Year Initiated	Age/Year Discontinued	Cost per Month
Antipsychotic	2003	Lifetime	Atypical = $200–500/month Conventional = $60–100/month
Anticonvulsant/mood stabilizer	2003	May be lifetime	$50–200/month Lab costs = $100–150/lab
Antidepressant	2003	Minimum 9 months, then reevaluate	$100–250/month, then unknown

			Length of Treatment	Costs per Day
Benzodiazepine Anticholinergic	2003	In conjunction with conventional antipsychotic, possibly with atypical antipsychotic	6 months, then re-evaluate Unknown, dependent on symptoms	$90/month $20–150/month
Medication organizer	Age of onset		Lifetime	Nominal (>$5); replace as needed

Acute and Facility Care

Facility Description	Description/Purpose	Length of Treatment	Costs per Day
Hospitalization	Inpatient treatment; indicated if individual is a threat to himself or others; initiate medications and provide stabilization	Expect 2–4 weeks for stabilization in 2003; additional hospitalizations may be indicated in future	$700+/day
Option 1 Residential treatment	Supervised housing + day treatment; indicated if individual is unable to complete activities of daily living (including taking medications as prescribed) without high level of assistance	Same as above	$200+/day
Option 2 Partial hospitalization/day treatment	Day treatment; does not include housing; indicated if individual needs increased daily structure	Same as above	$150+/day
Option 3 Group home	Living quarters and meals; no treatment is provided	Same as above	$35+/day

Table 16.1 (Continued) Example Life Care Plan for John for Estate Planning

Vocational/Education Plan

Recommendation	Age/Year Initiated	Age/Year Discontinued	Frequency	Costs per Session
Vocational counseling	2003	2004	1–2 times/week average, 48 weeks	$60–70/session
Vocational testing	2003	2003	1 time only	$750
Supported employment — may include job coaching, telephone contact, workplace visits, meetings with employer	2004	2004	2 sessions or more per week, for 48 weeks, then less frequent as indicated	$40–70/session

Potential Complications

- Poor compliance due to side effects of medications or other factors leading to relapses and hospitalizations
- Adverse reactions to medications (e.g., drowsiness, dry mouth, constipation, dizziness, orthostatic hypotension, sedation, nausea, and weight gain)
- Job placement difficulties that require more than one occasion of support
- Loss of family support (e.g., death of one or both parents) resulting in relapse, requiring more psychological support than planned
- Movement disorders (such as tardive dyskinesia (TD) or extrapyramidal symptoms (EPS)), which can be permanent and debilitating
- Dental complications from long-term use of medications

CONCLUSION

It is important to understand the complexity of mental illness when creating a life care plan. Factors to consider include the expected course of illness, chronicity of symptoms, and response to treatment. The most costly treatment modality is hospitalization. Individuals with a chronic, disabling course of illness may require multiple hospitalizations or longer-term stays. Treatment noncompliance is a major issue to consider, given that it is a widespread phenomenon and is associated with poorer outcomes and higher costs.

Despite the differences among various mental illnesses in symptoms, treatment, and degree of disability, there are common areas to consider when creating a life care plan for this population. The checklist provided in Table 16.2 can help the life care planner cover the various areas required to create a plan for individuals with mental illness. Given the high costs of mental illness in both direct costs and quality of life issues, life care planning is definitely a needed, but untapped resource.

Table 16.2 Life Care Plan Checklist for Mental Illness

- Psychotherapeutic Interventions: What types of therapy will be needed? Are there family or marriage issues that need to be addressed? How complex is the treatment plan? Will a case manager be needed to coordinate care? Are support groups available? Is substance abuse present? If so, what treatments will be needed?

- Diagnostic Testing: Often times other illnesses need to be ruled out before a diagnosis of mental illness is made, especially in cases where symptoms might overlap with brain abnormalities (i.e., tumors). What tests are needed to rule out other illnesses? Will a psychological battery be needed? What level of education has the individual completed? Is separate educational testing needed as well?

- Medication/Supply Needs: Medication regimens can consist of multiple medications at various dosages. Some require blood serum monitoring, which will add to the overall cost. What medications are indicated (including daily dosages and how supplied)? Are they available in generic?

- Routine Medical Care: How often will the individual need to see a psychiatrist? In what kind of treatment setting will medication management take place? Will there be regular monitoring by other staff such as nurses? Comorbid conditions are common in people with mental illness. Will annual health checks be preformed by medical personal, including laboratory assessments?

- Acute and Facility Care: Is the illness at an acute stage where inpatient treatment is required? What is the expected course of illness? Are multiple hospitalizations likely? What impact do symptoms have on functioning? Is family present in individual's life? Is the individual capable of independent living? If not, what level of support is required?

- Vocational/Education Plan: What is the individual's work history? What vocational services are offered in his or her geographical area? Has vocational potential been assessed? What are the costs of supported employment?

REFERENCES

American College of Occupational and Environmental Medicine. (2002). ACOEM Evidence-Based Statement, A Screening Program for Depression. Author. Accessed on May 12, 2003, at http://www.acoem.org/guidelines/article.asp?ID=54.

American Psychiatric Association. (1997). *Practice Guidelines for the Treatment of Schizophrenia.* Washington, DC: Author.

American Psychiatric Association. (2000a). *Practice Guidelines for the Treatment of Patients with Major Depressive Disorder.* Washington, DC: Author.

American Psychiatric Association. (2000b). *Diagnostic and Statistical Manual of Mental Disorders*, 4th ed., text revision. Washington, DC: Author.

American Psychiatric Association. (2002). *Practice Guidelines for the Treatment of Patients with Bipolar Disorder.* Washington, DC: Author.

Anthony, W.A., Cohen, M., & Farkas, A. (1990). *Psychiatric Rehabilitation.* Boston: Center for Psychiatric Rehabilitation.

Ballenger, J.C. (1998). Benzodiazepines. In A.F. Schatzberg & C.B. Nemeroff, Eds., *Textbook of Psychopharmacology*, 2nd ed., chap. 14. Washington, DC: American Psychiatric Press.

Bartles, S.J. & Drake, R.E. (1988). Depressive symptoms in schizophrenia: comprehensive differential diagnosis. *Comprehensive Psychiatry*, 29, 467–483.

Begley, C.E., Annegers, J.F., Swann, A.C., Lewis, C., Coan, S., Schnapp, W.B., & Bryant-Comstock, L. (1998). The lifetime cost of bipolar disorder in the U.S.: an estimate for new cases in 1998. *Pharmacoeconomics*, 19, 483–495.

Bell, M.D., Lysaker, P.H., & Milstein, R.M. (1996). Clinical benefits of paid work activity in schizophrenia. *Schizophrenia Bulletin*, 22, 51–67.

Bond, G.R., Drake, R.E., Mueser, K.T., & Becker, D.R. (1997). An update on supported employment for people with severe mental illness. *Psychiatric Services*, 48, 335–346.

Bowden, C.L. (1996). Rapid cycling among bipolar patients. *Primary Psychiatry*, 3, 40.

Cade, J.F. (1999). Lithium salts in the treatment of psychotic excitement. *Australian and New England Journal of Psychiatry*, 33, 615–618.

Clark, R.E., Bartels, S.J., Mellman, T.A., & Peacock, W.J. (2002). Recent trends in antipsychotic combination therapy of schizophrenia and schizoaffective disorder: implications for state mental health policy. *Schizophrenia Bulletin*, 28, 75–84.

Conner, T.M., Crismon, M.L., & Still, D.J. (1999). A critical review of selected pharmacoeconomic analyses of antidepressant therapy. *Annals of Pharmacotherapy*, 33, 364–372.

Crown, W.H., Treglia, M., Meneades, L., & White, A. (2001). Long-term costs of treatment for depression: impact of drug selection and guideline adherence. *Value Health*, 4, 295–307.

Davies, A., Langley, P.C., Keks, N.A., Catts, S.V., Lambert, T., & Schweitzer, I. (1998). Risperidone versus haloperidol. II. Cost-effectiveness, *Clinical Therapeutics*, 20, 196–213.

DeLisis, L.E. (1990). *Depression in Schizophrenia.* Washington, DC: American Psychiatric Press.

Depression Guidelines Panel. (1993). *Clinical Practice Guideline Number 5: Depression in Primary Care, Treatment of Major Depression*, HHS Publication 93-0551. Rockville, MD: Agency for Health Care Policy and Research.

Deutsch, P. & Sawyer, H. (1993). *Guide to Rehabilitation.* New York: Mathew Bender.

Dickstein, D., Hanig, D., & Grosskopf, B. (1988). Reducing treatment costs in a community support program. *Hospital and Community Psychiatry*, 39, 1033–1035.

DuPont, R.L., Rice, D.P., Shiraki, S., & Rowland, C.R. (1995). Economic costs of obsessive-compulsive disorder. *Medicine Interface*, 8, 102–109.

Essock, S.M., Hargreaves, W.A., Covell, N.H., & Goethe, J. (1996). Clozapine's effectiveness for patients in state hospitals: results from a randomized trial. *Psychopharmacology Bulletin*, 32, 683–697.

Fein, S. (1998). Treatment of drug-refractory schizophrenia. *Psychiatry Annals*, 28, 215.

Finley, P.R., Sommer, B.R., Corbitt, J.L., Brunson, G.H., & Lum, B.L. (1998). Risperidone: clinical outcome predictors and cost-effectiveness in a naturalistic setting. *Psychopharmacology Bulletin*, 34, 75–81.

Fischler, G. & Booth, N. (1999). *Vocational Impact of Psychiatric Disorders*. Gaithersburg, MD: Aspen Publishers.

Fogelson, D.L. & Sternback, H. (1997). Lamotrigine treatment of refractory bipolar disorder. *Journal of Clinical Psychiatry*, 58, 271–273.

Frank, L., Revicki, D.A., Sorensen, S.V., & Shih, Y.C. (2001). The economics of selective serotonin reuptake inhibitors in depression: a critical review. *CNS Drugs*, 15, 59–83.

Goodwin, F.K. & Jamison, K.R. (1990). *Manic-Depressive Illness*. New York: Oxford University Press.

Hamilton, S.H., Revicki, D.A., Edgell, E.T., Genduso, L.A., & Tollefson, G. (1999). Clinical and economic outcomes of olanzapine compared with haloperidol for schizophrenia: results from a randomized clinical trial. *Pharmacoeconomics*, 15, 469–480.

Hegarty, J.D., Baldessarini, R.J., Tohen, M., Waternaux, C., & Oepen, G. (1994). One hundred years of schizophrenia: a meta-analysis of the outcome literature. *American Journal of Psychiatry*, 151, 1409–1416.

Hilligoss, N. (2003). Life care planning for people with severe and persistent mental illness: an overlooked practice setting? *Journal of Life Care Planning*, 2, 56–72.

Hirschfeld, R.M., Lewis, L., & Vornik, L.A. (2003). Perceptions and impact of bipolar disorder: how far have we really come? Results of the National Depressive and Manic-Depressive Association 2000 survey of individuals with bipolar disorder. *Journal of Clinical Psychiatry*, 64, 161–174.

Hudson, T.J., Sullivan, G., Feng, W., Owen, R.R., & Thrush, C.R. (2003). Economic evaluations of novel antipsychotic medications: a literature review. *Schizophrenia Research*, 60, 199–218.

Janicak, P.G., Davis, J.M., Ericksen, S., Change, S., & Gallagher, P. (1985). Efficacy of ECT: a meta-analysis. *American Journal of Psychiatry*, 142, 297–302.

Jefferson, J.W., Greist, J.H., Archerman, D.L., & Carroll, J.A. (1987). *Lithium Encyclopedia for Clinical Practice*, 2nd ed. Washington, DC: American Psychiatric Press.

Kane, J.M., Honigfeld, G., Singer, J., & Meltzer, H. (1988). Clozapine for the treatment-resistant schizophrenic. *Archives of General Psychiatry*, 45, 789–796.

Keck, P.E. & McElroy, S.L. (1998). Antiepileptic drugs. In A.F. Schatzberg & C.B. Nemeroff, Eds., *Textbook of Psychopharmacology*, 2nd ed., chap. 21. Washington, DC: American Psychiatric Press.

Klein, D.F., Gittleman, R., Quitkin, F., & Rifkin, A. (1980). *Diagnosis and Drug Treatment of Psychiatric Disorders: Adults and Children*, 2nd ed. Baltimore: Williams & Wilkins.

Klerman, G.L. & Cole, J.O. (1967). Clinical pharmacology of imipramine and related antidepressant compound. *International Journal of Psychiatry*, 3, 267–304.

Lenox, R.H. & Husseini, K.M. (1998). Lithium. In A.F. Schatzberg & C.B. Nemeroff, Eds., *Textbook of Psychopharmacology*, 2nd ed., chap. 10. Washington, DC: American Psychiatric Press.

Li, J., McCombs, J.S., & Stimmel, G.L. (2002). Cost of treating bipolar disorder in the California Medicaid (Medi-Cal) program. *Journal of Affective Disorders*, 71, 131–139.

Manning, J.S., Haykal, R.F., Connor, P.D., & Akiskal, H.S. (1997). On the nature of depressive and anxious states in a family practice setting: the high prevalence of bipolar II and related disorders in a cohort followed longitudinally. *Comprehensive Psychiatry*, 38, 102–108.

Manusco, L.L. (1990). Reasonable accommodations for workers with psychiatric disabilities. *Psychosocial Rehabilitation Journal*, 14, 3.

March, J.S., Frances, A., Carpenter, D., & Kahn, D.A. (1997). The expert consensus guidelines for the treatment of obsessive-compulsive disorder. *Journal of Clinical Psychiatry*, 58 (Suppl. 4).

McEvoy, J.P., Scheifler, P.L., & Frances, A., Eds. (1999). The expert consensus guideline series: treatment of schizophrenia. *Journal of Clinical Psychiatry*, 60 (Suppl. 11).

Mueller, T.I., Leon, A.C., Keller, K.B., Solomon, D.A., Endicott, J., Coryell, W., Warshaw, M., & Maser, J.D. (1999). Recurrence after recovery from major depressive disorder during 15 years of observational follow-up. *American Journal of Psychiatry*, 156, 1000–1006.

Murray, C.J.L. & Lopez, A.D., Eds. (1996). Summary: The Global Burden of Disease: A Comprehensive Assessment of Mortality and Disability from Diseases, Injuries, and Risk Factors in 1990 and Projected to 2020. Harvard School of Public Health on behalf of the World Health Organization and the World Bank. Cambridge, MA: Harvard University Press. Accessed on May 1, 2003, at http://www.who.int/msa/mnh/ems/dalys/into.htm.

Namjoshi, M.A., Rajamannar, G., Jacobs, T., Sanger, T.M., Risser, R., Tohen, M.F., Breier, A., & Keck, P.E. (2002). Economic, clinical and quality-of-life outcomes associated with olanzapine treatment in mania. Results from a randomized controlled trial. *Journal of Affective Disorders*, 69, 109–118.

National Institute of Mental Health. (2001). The Numbers Count: Mental Disorders in America, NIMH Publication 01-4584. Accessed on May 1, 2003, at http://www.nimh.nih.gov/publicat/numbers.cfm.

National Institute of Mental Health. (2003a). Mental Illness in America. Accessed on May 1, 2003, at http://www.applesforhealth.com/illamerica.html.

National Institute of Mental Health. (2003b). The Impact of Mental Illness on Society. Accessed on May 1, 2003, at http://www.nimh.nih.gov/publicat/burden.cfm.

National Organization on Disability. (1998). Annual Report. Accessed on May 3, 2003, at http://www.nod.org/annualreport.html.

Palmer, C.S., Brunner, E., Ruiz-Flores, L.G., Paez-Agraz, F., & Revicki, D.A. (1998). A cost-effectiveness clinical decision analysis model for schizophrenia. *American Journal of Managed Care*, 4, 345.

Pies, R.W. (1998). *Handbook of Essential Psychopharmacology*. Washington, DC: American Psychiatric Press.

Potter, W.Z., Manji, H.K., & Rudorfer, M.V. (1998). Tricyclics and tetracyclics. In A.F. Schatzberg & C.B. Nemeroff, Eds., *Textbook of Psychopharmacology*, 2nd ed., chap. 10. Washington, DC: American Psychiatric Press.

Pratt, C.W., Gill, K.J., Barrett, N.M., & Roberts, M.M. (1999). *Psychiatric Rehabilitation*. San Diego: Academic Press.

Prein, R.F. & Cole, J.O. (1968). High-dose chlorpromazine in chronic schizophrenia. *Archives of General Psychiatry*, 18, 482–495.

Price, L.H., Charney, D.S., & Heninger, G.R. (1986). Variability of response to lithium augmentation in refractory depression. *American Journal of Psychiatry*, 143, 1387–1392.

Reiger, D.A., Narrow, W.E., Rae, D.S., Mandersheid, R.W., Locke, B.Z., & Goodwin, F.K. (1993). The de facto mental and addictive disorders service system. Epidemiologic Catchment Area prospective 1-year prevalence rates of disorders and services. *Archives of General Psychiatry*, 50, 85–94.

Robins, L.N. & Reiger, D.A. (1991). *Psychiatric Disorders in America: The Epidemiologic Catchment Study*. New York: The Free Press.

Rush, A.J. (2003). Toward an understanding of bipolar disorder and its origin. *Journal of Clinical Psychiatry*, 64 (Suppl. 6), 4–8.

Sanger, T.M., Grundy, S.L., Gibson, P.J., Namjoshi, M.A., Greaney, M.G., & Tohen, M.F. (2001). Long-term olanzapine therapy in the treatment of bipolar I disorder: an open-label continuation study. *Journal of Clinical Psychiatry*, 62, 273–281.

Sanger, T.M., Tohen, M., Vieta, E., Dunner, D.L., Bowden, C.L., Calabrese, J.R., Feldman, P.D., Jacobs, T.G., & Breier, A. (2003). Olanzapine in the acute treatment of bipolar I disorder with a history of rapid cycling. *Journal of Affective Disorders,* 73, 155–161.

Shelton, R.C., Tollefson, G.D., Stahl, S., Gannon, K.S., Jacobs, T.G., Buras, W.R., Bymaster, F.P., Zhang, W., Spencer, K.A., Feldman, P.D., & Meltzer, H.Y. (2001). A novel augmentation strategy for treating resistant major depression. *American Journal of Psychiatry*, 158, 131–134.

Siegfreid S.L., Fleischhacker, W., & Lieberman, J.A. (2001). Pharmacological treatment of schizophrenia. In J.A. Lieberman & R.M. Murray, Eds., *Comprehensive Care of Schizophrenia*, chap. 4. London: Martin Duntz.

Stahl, S.M. (1999). Antipsychotic polypharmacy, part 1: therapeutic option or dirty little secret? *Journal of Clinical Psychiatry*, 60, 425–426.

Stanilla, J.K. & Simpson, G.M. (1998). Treatment of extrapyramidal side effects. In A.F. Schatzberg & C.B. Nemeroff, Eds., *Textbook of Psychopharmacology*, 2nd ed., chap. 19. Washington, DC: American Psychiatric Press.

Thieda, P., Beard, S., Richter, A., & Kane, J. (2003). An economic review of compliance with medication therapy in the treatment of schizophrenia. *Psychiatric Services*, 54, 508–516.

Tohen, M., Sanger, T.M., McElroy, S.L., Tollefson, G.D., Chengappa, K.N., Daniel, D.G., Petty, F., Centorrino, F., Wang, R., Grundy, S.L., Greaney, M.G., Jacobs, T.G., David, S.R., & Toma, V. (1999). Olanzapine versus placebo in the treatment of acute mania. *American Journal of Psychiatry*, 156, 702–709.

Tollefson, G.D. & Rosenbaum, J.F. (1998). Selective serotonin reuptake inhibitors. In A.F. Schatzberg & C.B. Nemeroff, Eds., *Textbook of Psychopharmacology*, 2nd ed., chap. 11. Washington, DC: American Psychiatric Press.

U.S. Department of Health and Human Services (U.S. DHHS). (1996). *Obsessive-Compulsive Disorder*, revised, Publication 99-3755. Bethesda, MD: Author, National Institutes of Health, National Institutes of Mental Health (reprinted in 1999).

U.S. Department of Health and Human Services (U.S. DHHS). (1999). *Mental Health: A Report of the Surgeon General*. Rockville, MD: Author, Substance Abuse and Mental Health Services Administration, Center for Mental Health Services, National Institutes of Health, National Institutes of Mental Health.

Wang, P.W., Santosa, C., Schumacher, M., Winsberg, M.E., Strong, C., & Ketter, T.A. (2002). Gabapentin augmentation therapy in bipolar depression. *Bipolar Disorder*, 4, 296–301.

Weiden, P., Rapkin, B., & Mott, T. (1994). Rating of medication influences (ROMI) scale in schizophrenia. *Schizophrenia Bulletin*, 20, 297–310.

Weiden, P.J. & Olfson, O. (1995). Cost of relapse in schizophrenia. *Schizophrenia Bulletin*, 21, 419–429.

Wyatt, R.J. (2001). Diagnosing schizophrenia. In J.A. Lieberman & R.M. Murray, Eds., *Comprehensive Care of Schizophrenia*, chap. 1. London: Martin Duntz.

Weed, R., Ed. (1999). *Life Care Planning and Case Management Handbook*. Boca Raton, FL: CRC Press.

Weed, R. & Field, T. (2001). *The Rehabilitation Consultant's Handbook*, 3rd ed. Athens, GA: E&F Vocational Services.

Zaretsky, A.E., Segal, S.V., & Gemar, M. (1999). Cognitive therapy for bipolar depression: a pilot study. *Canadian Journal of Psychiatry*, 44, 491–494.

17

LIFE CARE PLANNING ISSUES FOR
PEOPLE WITH CHRONIC PAIN

Thomas M. Ward and Roger O. Weed

INTRODUCTION

Significant pain can be experienced as a result of a multitude of medical problems. The most common is associated with low back pain, an affliction experienced by 80% of the population sometime during their lifetime (Moreo, 2003; Cailliet & Helberg, 1981). Objective definitions of pain have eluded researchers (Weed, 1987). No pain literature available to these writers has been able to satisfactorily define pain objectively. Pain appears to be a subjective experience measured by self-report (Sternbach, 1968, 1974; Shealy, 1976; Fordyce, 1976; Melzak, 1973; Merskey, 1964, 1972; Skinner, 1974; Loeser, 1980; Bresler, 1979; Ramsey, 1979; Engel et al., 1970; IASP, 1979). Research indicates that the pain threshold is similar from person to person and culture to culture, but pain tolerance can vary dramatically (Shealy, 1976). Sternbach (1968) has simply stated that "pain is a hurt we feel" (p. l).

Sternbach (1974) has also identified more than 100 words that people use to describe their pain, revealing how difficult it is to objectively quantify. Pain seems clearly not merely a neurophysiological event, but a combination of variables complicated by evidence that pain is not simply what a patient says it is (Fordyce, 1976). Most patients can describe how intense their pain is, but attempts to describe the quality has led to the development of the McGill-Melzack Pain Questionnaire in an effort to standardize treatment approaches (Meissner, 1982).

For purposes of this chapter, chronic pain can be described as daily pain that has lasted anywhere from 6 months to 1 year after the original pain incident. Although there is controversy regarding definitions, most physicians agree that *acute pain* is from the date of onset to 1 month, *subacute pain* is defined as daily pain lasting from 1 to 6 months, and *chronic pain* can thereafter be defined as lasting 6 months or longer (National Institute of Disability and Rehabilitation, 1993).

Chronic pain and the subsequent costs to society, however, do not necessarily include all individuals who have had pain of some type or another for longer than a year. In general, the diagnosis of chronic pain becomes broader as it includes the psychological stress and disruption to the everyday quality of life of

0-8493-1511-5/04/$0.00+$1.50
© 2004 by CRC Press LLC

individuals who suffer from it. There are an estimated 30 to 40 million adults (representing 15 to 20% of the population) in this country who suffer from chronic pain (Moreo, 2003; Brownlee & Schaf, 1997). Each year millions of people seek relief at hospitals or pain clinics. The overall cost in lost workdays, medical treatment, and additional psychological counseling can be enormous. If directly related to back pain, the cost is estimated at $25 billion (Moreo, 2003). Counting back pain, migraine and headache pain, osteoarthritis, rheumatoid arthritis, fibromyalgia, failed surgical fusion lumbar or cervical spine, reflex sympathetic dystrophy, causalgia, diabetic neuropathy, and cancer pain, estimates exceed over $40 billion annually. Of the workforce, complaints of pain and related complications of pain result in one quarter of all the sick days taken, or to put it another way, over 50 million lost workdays per year are due to pain (Brownlee & Schaf, 1997; Beecher, 1959; Davis, 1975).

The history of pain management actually probably dates back to the first known practicing doctors. It has been said that 80% of patient problems prompting a visit to a physician are the direct result of some form of pain — acute, subacute, or chronic. However, most recently, with the advent of chronic pain management programs, more comprehensive multidisciplinary team management for chronic pain and the associated disability/psychological stress/depression and subsequent functional loss have sprung up. Now there are pain management centers in nearly every major metropolitan area in the U.S. Pain management has become a subspecialty recognized by the American Medical Association, and numerous societies offer continuing medical education, seminars, legislative lobbying assistance, and national boards of directors to oversee the problems associated with the disease state now classified as chronic pain. Beginning in 1911, workers' compensation laws were enacted to require employers to assume the cost of occupational disability without regard to fault (Weed & Field, 2001). These laws have dramatically altered the recovery of the individual injured in the workforce since that time. However, additional aspects involving litigation have become more prevalent in the last 20 to 30 years. Because of litigation, an adversarial role between the workplace and the injured worker often develops.

Also of interest are the recent efforts to reduce health care costs by any and all means. Thus, again, injured workers suffering chronic pain ailments are often given little, if any, direct assistance, and anecdotally it appears that legal assistance through litigation has become necessary to allow the patient to pursue more comprehensive treatment of his chronic pain condition. It can be said that if a patient truly has significant chronic pain, it will disrupt every aspect of his or her life. This includes vocational as well as avocational pursuits, sleep, and routine daily activities such as dressing, bathing, hygiene, and self-care. Exercise, relationships, sexual relationships, and financial stresses will all ensue. In this way, a comprehensive approach to the treatment of the chronic pain patient embodies all the aforementioned areas, as it focuses attention on restoring the patient to a level of independence to the extent that it is possible. The long-range goal is to achieve a degree of independence of the patient from the health provider. Recent studies seem to indicate that those individuals suffering from chronic pain who are not seeing physicians or receiving constant medical attention may do better overall than those individuals who do seek chronic pain management for years at a time (Ernonoff, 1997).

DIAGNOSTIC EFFORTS IN WORKUP

The first thing necessary for any patient suffering from pain of 6 months' duration or longer is to review what medical attention he or she has been receiving from the standpoint of diagnostic evaluations, medical consultations, laboratory and x-ray, and surgical intervention. Before any comprehensive management addressing the other areas mentioned above can be initiated, it should be ascertained that the patient does not have a remedial or correctable cause for his or her chronic pain. The scope of diagnostic evaluations of the patient with chronic pain is quite numerous. Magnetic resonance imaging (MRI) of the affected area, computed tomography (CT) scanning, plain-film x-rays, myelograms, electromyographic muscle examinations and nerve conduction velocity, and invasive procedures such as laparoscopic surgical evaluation, epidural steroid injections and differential blocks, and diskograms are all helpful in the diagnosis of axial skeletal-related cervical, thoracic, or lumbar spine pain resulting from disk injuries or fractures.

Occasionally multiple specialty consultations are required to achieve such thorough evaluations in our present era of medical specialties. Inclusive of this would be a psychologist for determination via psychological testing, such as with the Minnesota Multiphasic Personality Inventory or other assistive testing, to determine a patient's psychological status as it pertains to his or her pain complaints. Benefits of having several specialists evaluate the patient will be that significant overlap of observations, including questionable symptom magnification with litigious patients with secondary gain in mind, will be noted from a variety of clinicians' vantage points. Despite being a suspicious point of view to include in an evaluation of the patient with pain, it is nonetheless necessary, as certainly questions will arise later regarding the authenticity of the patient's symptoms. Occasionally it will be difficult to show from the objective testing standpoint that pain has an organic cause that is immediately observable with the aforementioned testing (Beecher, 1959). In these instances, chronic pain management specialists can add a further backdrop from which to define and further assess the patient's pain complaints. There are a number of sensory feedback loops to the central nervous system, including the sympathetic nervous system, bones, joints, ligaments, muscles, and, ultimately, the dermatomes of the peripheral nervous system. Despite the insurance company's desire to be shown where the pain is coming from, many times pain resulting from trauma does not reveal the presence of a herniated disk, fracture, or ruptured ligaments. In these instances, additional documentation or proof as to the nature of the patient's pain complaints will be required.

APPROACHES TO MANAGEMENT OF PAIN

Following a complete evaluation of the workup requiring the aforementioned tests, consultation with the psychologist or psychiatrist and subsequent psychological testing batteries, differential nerve blocks, MRI scans, etc., the patient may be placed in a variety of settings for continued pain management and treatment (Aronoff & Wilson, 1978; Bowsher, 1989; Bresler, 1979; Davis, 1975; Ericson, 1996; Walsh & Dumit, 1988).

Of recent prevalence is the anesthesiologist-based pain management clinic. The majority of these clinics function in an outpatient surgical setting or in the confines of a local hospital. The anesthesiologist in this case has been trained through specialty residency training for the performance of injections of anesthetic agents and narcotics into different regions, thereby blocking the local neuroanatomy and allowing for the cessation of the pain symptom complex. Depending upon the nature of the pain and its subsequent causes, the patient may require surgical intervention. The most common surgeons involved in spine ailments, including cervical and lumbar spine pain, are the neurosurgeon and the orthopedic surgeon. Specialists in these areas in most major metropolitan regions are familiar with causes and treatment of pain and will offer surgical remedies for their relief.

Another resource for treatment for pain would be the less aggressive, more conservative outpatient rehabilitation or physiatrist office. In this setting the comprehensive nature of the pain is addressed from a number of areas, including medications, sleep restoration, diet and exercise, orthotics, therapy, electrical stimulation devices, and other neurological diagnostic workups. The decision as to which resource to employ is often selected by the patient.

The majority of patients in the physician author's outpatient clinic have typically been injured for over a year and have already been evaluated by either a neurosurgeon or orthopedic surgeon. Many of them have already undergone surgical intervention and have subsequently been referred to an anesthesiologist where additional aggressive management is pursued through injection therapy with narcotics or local anesthetics (Spengler et al., n.d.). At that juncture, the anesthesiologist also employs a number of medications and usually initiates a psychological evaluation including biofeedback and stress management. Depending upon the benefits of those measures, an additional referral is made to other physicians such as physiatrists, where exercise programs, further medication adjustments, orthotics, diet, sleep restoration, stress management, and family counseling are usually initiated. Outpatient physical therapy may be employed on a number of different occasions throughout the chronological time frame from the original injury, surgical intervention, anesthesiological intervention, and, ultimately, for rehabilitation and restorative functional gains.

If an individual has already undergone several surgeries and a number of injections, then a physician may be reluctant to send her back for more surgery. It should be remembered that each patient needs to have a thorough evaluation of her present condition to determine the etiology of her pain. If a patient's pain has not been evaluated for 2 or more years, despite a thorough documentation of the presence of a nonoperative lesion from the past, then it is quite possible that further evaluation and diagnostic x-ray information may need to be obtained.

LIFE CARE PLANNING AND CHRONIC PAIN

Individual types of pain are especially variable and are almost beyond the scope of this short chapter. A listing of types of injuries that can result in chronic pain requiring lifetime medical care would include the following:

- Spinal cord injury — cervical, thoracic, lumbar with paraplegia, or tetraplegia (also known as quadriplegia)
- Lumbar, cervical, or thoracic spine injury
- Herniated disk

- Spinal cord infarctions
- Spinal cord fractures or axial spine fractures
- Neuropathy
- Causalgia
- Chronic regional pain syndrome (reflex sympathetic dystrophy)
- Multiple orthopedic fractures and subsequent claudication injuries
- Cancer of any organ or any tissue type
- Traumatic brain injury
- Abdominal problems
- Genital/urinary problems
- Pulmonary problems
- Osteoarthritis
- Rheumatoid arthritis
- Systemic lupus erythematosus
- Fibromyalgia
- Trigeminal neuralgia
- Motor vehicle accidents
- Failed spinal surgeries
- Orthopedic joint replacement surgery, including hip and knee surgeries
- Vascular injuries, including angina
- Peripheral vascular injuries
- Peripheral vascular ischemia with crush injuries
- Headaches, including migraine, cluster, and tension headaches
- Brachial plexus injuries
- Pelvic inflammatory disease
- Environmental toxins and exposures

The medical needs and future care for these conditions run the gamut and require a coordinated effort of services that are individually determined. Some of the considerations include the following.

Psychological Considerations

In the comprehensive management of chronic pain, psychological testing and treatment for depression, anxiety, and stress are all components required for maximum improvement. All chronic pain patients should have psychological counseling and psychological testing somewhere in the course of their pain diagnosis or management. The family will also require assistance in coping with the patient's pain problems, as it is very disruptive to the normal activities of family life following an injury or illness that causes chronic pain. Depending upon when the life care planner becomes involved in the case, an evaluation by a psychologist is commonly recommended, as well as subsequent further recommendations of biofeedback and stress management on a weekly basis for at least 1 year to improve the patient's ability to initiate and maintain a program that will benefit him for the lifetime of his complaint.

There are numerous additional resources from which the chronic pain patient can draw. Self-help groups and certain newsletters are available for individual diseases that the patient can access through the Internet. Local chapters, usually located by Internet searches, of the larger disease diagnoses that cause chronic pain may be available. These include rheumatoid arthritis foundation groups, fibromyalgia groups, spinal cord injury and recovery groups, brain injury recovery groups, multiple sclerosis groups, local diabetes foundations, and others.

It should be noted that self-treatment through alcohol or illicit drug use is a common feature of our society, which probably increases with the advent of chronic pain. Recently, additional guidelines have been released by the American Academy of Pain Medicine (http://www.painmed.org), the World Institute of Pain (http://www.iapsar.org/WIP/WIP-base.htm), and the American Academy of Pain Management (http://www.aapainmanage.org). All entities now recognize the therapeutic use of chronic narcotic analgesia for chronic pain. However, medical societies in local as well as state medical boards are concerned about the use of chronic narcotic analgesia for chronic pain. This view seems to reflect our fears of addiction and the subsequent costs and problems that addiction has caused in our society. As this may be a national resource book for life care planning, it is likely that the reader may find in his or her locality a remaining bias toward the avoidance of use of chronic narcotic analgesia for the treatment of chronic pain. Multidisciplinary pain programs that employ psychologists, social workers, anesthesiologists, orthopedic surgeons, neurosurgeons, neuropsychologists, physiatrists, and allied health professionals are often quite familiar with the local political flavor of the area and will be one of the better resources in determining what a patient's needs are in general, as well as giving him or her an understanding of what the trends throughout the nation are at that time.

Additional Considerations for Chronic Pain Management

As mentioned above, a multidisciplinary team is the best resource for thorough and comprehensive management of chronic pain. Typically the needs of the patient will require five or six comprehensive measures to maximize the outcome of the patient's ability to manage his own condition after a period of 6 months to a year. Most outpatient treatment of a chronic pain patient will result in a very brief 1- to 2-month period of intense evaluation and management followed by a middle period of 3 to 6 months of continued weekly monitoring or monthly monitoring and establishing of a management program that will fit the patient's needs. Biofeedback, stress management, counseling, psychological testing, and family counseling will be included. Additional areas for maximizing the patient's independence will include diet, weight loss, and exercise. Normally, most patients with chronic pain have a hard time functioning in the upright position and the normal gravity environment. For that reason, exercise programs, especially ones employing a pool, are very popular and quite prevalent and seem to best suit the needs of the chronic pain exercise program prescription.

The physician author of this chapter prescribes a six-step comprehensive program in the treatment of chronic pain patients. Note that this occurs in the rehabilitation setting, since the majority of the patients seen in this setting have already undergone anesthesia and surgery. A comprehensive, conservative chronic pain management program would consist of the following areas:

1. *Exercise.* A program including a pool for both strength conditioning and checking the effects of the central nervous system related to exercise with serotonin and norepinephrine release. Additional cardiovascular and pulmonary conditioning for weight-loss assistance is also a key element of this.

2. *Diet.* A thorough review is usually achieved with a dietary journal kept by the patient for 2 weeks. After the journal is reviewed, recommendations are made with specific restrictions of foods that are clearly harmful to the patient's diet. For additional help with diet, reading materials and instructions are added for food selection, and a basic understanding of carbohydrates, fats, and protein is taught. Subsequently, the patient's weight is taken on a weekly basis for his next several visits and further assistance and encouragement are given.

3. *Sleep restoration.* Patients cannot handle the daily stress of chronic pain without adequate sleep. Sleep achieves a degree of relaxation and resets the thermostat of the central nervous system. The sleep-deprived patient will have more difficulty responding to minute-to-minute changes in his or her day and thereby will be much less adaptable to his or her chronic pain condition than those who are sleeping through the night. Pharmacological agents for this are often needed to restore the patient to a restful night's sleep. Additional concerns would be for patients who have sleep apnea or other obstructive forms of sleep disturbance. Sleep centers are usually run and directed by a pulmonologist or neurologist and are available in most metropolitan areas. This physician author has used these clinics as an assistive consultation in helping the patient to return to a more restful night's sleep.

4. *Pharmacological agents.* Here again, the recitation of all medications that are prescribed and used in current pain management would be beyond the scope of this short chapter. Mainly they would fall into five categories:

   4.1. Antidepressants, consisting of Prozac, serotonin, and, in general, tricyclic antidepressants and anxiolytics.

   4.2. Medications for the resolution of nerve pain, which consist of Tegretol, Dilantin, Phenobarbital, Neurontin, and Depakote.

   4.3. Muscle relaxants, consisting of Soma, Skelaxin, Robaxin, Flexeril, Baclofen, Parafonforte, and occasionally Valium or anxiolytics that would fit into this category as well.

   4.4. Nonsteroidal antiinflammatory drugs (NSAIDs) or other nonnarcotic analgesics that also assist with the reduction in inflammatory joint changes. These would consist of ibuprofen (Advil, Motrin, and others), Releve, Relafen, Oravail, etc.

   4.5. Narcotic analgesia. This would depend on efforts of resolving the pain from all other measures. Examples include methadone, Percodan, morphine, Duragesec patches, etc.

   4.6 Side effects. All of the above commonly have side effects that affect patient compliance and comfort. For example, NSAIDs can cause gastrointestinal upset, ulcers, and liver and kidney damage. Opioids often result in physical dependence and cause dizziness, fatigue, concentration impairments, drowsiness, nausea, impaired vision, and constipation. Also, some of the newer medications can reach $100,000 per year in cost.

5. *Physical therapy and outpatient modalities.* Usually patients who have chronic pain also have a sedentary lifestyle as a consequence of trying to avoid pain. A brief burst of physical therapy for 2 to 4 weeks following the intake of a new patient may prove useful. This is usually aimed at providing the modality that may have already been used in other efforts of physical therapy. The difference with the use of physical therapy at this time is to try other physical therapy prescriptions and also to allow patients the use of transcutaneous electric nerve stimulation (TENS) or percutaneous electrical stimulation (PES) units, or other locally available stimulation units to attempt to decrease their pain. Further sessions of physical therapy throughout the course of the patient's lifetime may also be necessary depending upon brief or prolonged periods of inactivity, which will result in a loss of strength and function. In general, the nature of the comprehensive, conservative measures implemented for chronic pain management attempts to keep the patient from losing significant degrees of function for prolonged periods of time by instituting an exercise program. Nonetheless, a once-per-year physical therapy evaluation may be necessary to forestall more remedial forms of functional loss.

   For back pain and other selected central nervous system-generated pain, injections into the spinal canal area can provide relief, but often must be repeated regularly and can cause numerous side effects (e.g., nausea, vomiting, headache, transient weight gain, and infections).

6. *Orthotics and other adaptive equipment.* These products can usually be procured at the local orthotist or prosthetist or durable medical equipment supplier. There are a number of self-care adaptive aids, such as long-handled reachers, button hooks, and assistive devices for eating, grooming, and daily household tasks. In addition, under this heading would fall the grouping of spinal orthoses such as cervical pillows or orthopedic braces for sleeping and comfort in sitting, driving, walking, and moving about. From this standpoint, electric mobility devices, power chairs, assistive bathing devices, and personalized aids could all be considered for prescription. Throughout it should be mentioned that the patient's condition is not presumed to be static. Occasional retesting and obtaining x-rays and, in some cases, other surgical, neurosurgical, or orthopedic surgery interventions may be required.

In addition to the above, various surgical options may be available for structurally identifiable reasons and well-selected patients. Intrathecal morphine pumps, spinal cord stimulators, and repeat surgery are examples. However, there are high failure rates and costs are substantial (Moreo, 2003). Spinal fusions can total $18,000 to $25,000. Implanted pumps can cost $15,000 to $32,000 for the surgery, an average of $300 per month for medication and other follow-up charges, and $10,000 to $21,000 for pump replacement. Spinal cord stimulation initially can be expected to reach $15,000 to $20,000 or more, and then another $2500 per year for follow-up.

Determining Patient's Functioning Level

The patient's needs, at the time of intake as a chronic pain patient and throughout life, can be ascertained most effectively through an outside source of local physical therapy where functional capacity evaluations are performed. A functional capacity evaluation (FCE) (also referred to as a physical capacity assessment) is usually an 8-hour assessment that is typically performed over a 2-day period. During this assessment the patient's autonomic functions are evaluated, including heart rate, respiratory rate, and skin temperature. Other measurements, such as a visual analog scale of pain, may also be performed.

The majority of the testing includes performance of a variety of tasks that are observed and are also repeated in a number of different fashions to ascertain the patient's reliability from one task to the next. Typically, insurance companies and other health care providers will request these, as will the workplace at the time of a patient's disability. They are useful for disability determination, but are typically not adequate for disability rating. Disability ratings come under a different evaluation. Many times the consultants who have been working with the patient throughout the months are not capable or are not interested in performing disability evaluations. Determining individuals who are willing and capable to perform these assessments can be the source of difficulty in bringing the patient's legal problems to a close. The reader should be aware that the validity of the FCE results has been challenged, particularly in litigation settings, and the value of the results may be only as good as the equipment used and the evaluator's expertise (King et al., 1998).

Life Care Planning and Chronic Pain and Future Concerns

In making preparations in the life care plan for the needs of a patient with chronic pain, it becomes necessary to take into consideration all of the measures listed above. To this end, identifying someone who will follow the patient and participate in a comprehensive chronic pain management multidisciplinary team approach is preferred. If, however, that is not possible, then the needs from a chronic pain future life care plan would include all of the steps mentioned in the evaluation and treatment of a chronic pain patient at the initial intake. It should be noted that from a chronic pain standpoint, efforts are directed at making the individual with chronic pain self-reliant and avoiding constant medical intervention. Although this is the desired outcome, it is very time-consuming to achieve this goal, and as with any long-term disease problem, it becomes necessary for routine reevaluations and upgrades in the individual program. Cost estimates for chronic pain include medication and equipment repair and replacement, and 1- to 2-year reevaluations with x-rays, blood work, and consultations of the individual specialists will be necessary. It may also be necessary to include physical therapy and psychological counseling reevaluations. As the patient with chronic pain ages, additional evaluations and treatments with upgrades in equipment and possible surgical interventions may also be required. It once again becomes necessary to include in an exhaustive fashion a comprehensive listing of the patient's problems and some future prognosis as to the deterioration of these diagnostic considerations.

CASE STUDY

The following life care plan was prepared for a patient who fell on stairs at her home, resulting in a back injury. After attempts at conservative treatment, back surgery was accomplished on two occasions with poor results. The client was referred to a specialist for a dorsal column stimulator, which failed to provide long-term relief. Following the surgery, she was referred to a pain clinic and the attending psychiatrist diagnosed her with dissociate identity disorder. Her history included intestinal bypass for obesity. She had also been hospitalized on occasion for psychiatric reasons. At the time of the plan she remained essentially nonfunctional and did not drive, work, or clean her home. Her bed was relocated to the living room to avoid stairs or excessive movement. Her husband was supportive and actively assisted in her rehabilitation efforts.

CONCLUSION

Chronic pain has the ability as a diagnostic entity to cause as much disruption in patient care as do the functional, psychological, and social losses involved in the original injury. It should be noted that as a specialty chronic pain is developing and should be available in its broadest sense from the multidisciplinary approach nearly everywhere in the U.S. A carefully arranged initial intake with subsequent development of the six categories outlined should place the life care planner in the position to expertly assess and recommend the appropriate level of care for patients with chronic pain. However, as with all diseases, individuals with chronic pain will suffer variable outcomes based upon their individual application of the programs outlined for them. The responsibility of the patient in chronic pain is not unlike that of a diabetic, who, although having undergone a comprehensive study and treatment program, nonetheless is left on a daily basis to provide the right type of treatment for his or her own condition. It is incumbent upon the patient to adopt new lifestyle measures, restrict activities, and habituate certain aspects such as biofeedback and relaxation, and not just do the easy thing, which is to take a pill or apply a TENS unit. Patient compliance in this regard is key, and assistance through psychological counseling and frequent monitoring is often the best hope for achieving some degree of success in modifying a patient's former lifestyle to include measures necessary for a chronic pain management program. The goal of chronic pain planning, therefore, is not to reduce the pain to the level it was before the injury, but to modify the pain such that the patient can enjoy an enhanced quality of life and maintain a reasonable degree of function. It is also pertinent to note that a comprehensive treatment plan that uses all six outlined areas mentioned above will offer the best chance of success, rather than a patient selectively using two or three modalities. The goal is to reduce the patient's perceived level of pain to where certain activities that were prohibitive or restrictive are now possible. Clearly this does not necessarily mean that the patient will be able to perform all activities. It is along these lines that the compromise between where the patient was and where the patient is now needs to be identified. In this context, the patient can be encouraged to achieve some degree of compromise with the condition of chronic pain and a future activity level that is beyond where he or she has been functioning. In light of these issues, the life care plan can be a valuable adjunct to assist the chronic pain patient.

REFERENCES

Aronoff, G. and Wilson, R. (1978). How to teach your patients to control chronic pain. *Behavioral Medicine*, July, 29–35.

Beecher, H. (1959). *Measurement of Subjective Responses*. New York: Oxford University Press.

Bowsher, D. (1989) Assessment of the chronic pain sufferer. *Journal of Surgical Rounds for Orthopedics*, 2, 70–73.

Bresler, D. (1979). *Free Yourself from Pain*. New York: Simon & Schuster.

Brownlee, S. & Schaf, J. (March 17, 1997). Quality of life. *U.S. News and World Report*, 54–62.

Cailliet, R. & Helberg, L. (1981). Organic musculoskeletal back disorders. In W. Stolov and M. Clowers, Eds., *Handbook of Severe Disability*. Washington, DC: U.S. Department of Education, Rehabilitation Services Administration.

Davis, R. (1975). *Clinic Orthopedics and Related Research*, 112, 76–80.

Ernonoff, W. (1997). *Current Review of Pain*, 1, 320–324.

Engel, G., MacBryde, C., & Blacklow, R. (1970). *Signs and Symptoms*, 5th ed. Philadelphia: J.P. Lippincott.

Ericson, J.C. (1996). Pain. In D. Green, Ed., *Medical Management of Long Term Disability*, 2nd ed., 303–312. Boston: Butterworth-Heinmann.

Fordyce, W.E. (1976). *Behavioral Methods for Chronic Pain and Illness*. St. Louis: C.V. Mosby.

IASP. (1979). International association for studies on pain, subcommittee on taxonomy. *Pain*, 6, 249–252.

King, P., Tuckwell, N., & Barrett, T. (1998). A critical review of functional capacity evaluations. *Physical Therapy*, 79, 852–866.

Meissner, J. (1982). McGill-Melzack Pain Questionnaire. *ASHP Signal*, 24–37.

Melzak, R. (1973). *The Puzzle of Pain*. New York: Basic Books.

Merskey, H. (1964). An Investigation of Pain in Psychological Illness. Unpublished doctoral dissertation. Oxford, England.

Merskey, H. (1972). Personality traits of psychiatric patients with pain. *Journal of Psychosomatic Research*, 16, 163–166.

Moreo, K. (2003). *Managing Low Back Pain*. Miramar, FL: author.

National Institute of Disability and Rehabilitation Research. (1993). Chronic back pain. *Rehab Brief*, 15.

Ramsey, R. (1979). The understanding and teaching of reaction to pain. *Bibliotheca Psychiatrica*, 159, 114–140.

Shealy, C. (1976). *The Pain Game*. Los Angeles: Celestial Arts.

Skinner, B.F. (1938). *Behavior of Organisms*. New York: Appleton-Century-Crofts.

Spengler, D., Loeser, J., & Murphy, T. (n.d.). Orthopedic Aspects of Chronic Pain Syndrome. Unpublished manuscript.

Sternbach, R.A. (1968). *Pain: A Psychophysiological Analysis*. New York: Academic Press.

Sternbach, R.A. (1974). *Pain Patients: Traits and Treatment*. New York: Academic Press.

Walsh, M.E. & Dumit, D. (1988). The treatment of the patient with chronic pain. In J.L. Delisa, Ed., *Rehabilitation Principles and Practice*, 707–725. Philadelphia: J.B. Lippincott.

Weed, R. (1987). Pain basics. *Journal of Private Sector Rehabilitation*, 2, 65–71.

Weed, R. & Field, T. (2001). *The Rehabilitation Consultant's Handbook*, 3rd ed. Athens, GA: E&F Vocational Services.

LIFE CARE PLAN
Roberta Melvins

TABLE OF CONTENTS

Roger O. Weed, Ph.D., C.R.C., C.D.M.S.,
C.L.C.P., F.N.R.C.A.
P.O. Box 2133
Duluth, Georgia 30096

LIFE CARE PLAN
Projected Therapeutic Modalities

Client Name: Roberta Melvins
Date of Birth: 4/11/59
Date of Injury: 7/7/2000
Date Prepared: 8/27/2001

Therapy	Age/Year at Which Initiated	Age/Year at Which Suspended	Treatment Frequency	Base Cost per Year	Growth Trends	Recommended by:
Pain support group; individual, couples, and crisis therapy; medication supervision	43/2002	Life expectancy	Group at $50/week Individual at $125, 1 to 2 times/week for 2½ years, then 25 sessions/year (average) to 2007	$2400 (group) $6000–12,000 (individual) to 6/1994, then $3125 to 12/31/2007	To be determined by economist	Dr. Hertz
Occupational therapy; included as part of inpatient pain program	43/2002	3–4 months	2 times per week, 1 hour per session as part of pain program	See pain program		Dr. Hertz
Physical therapy	43/2002	3–4 months	2 times per week, 1 hour per session following pain program	$1920–3200 at $80–100/hour	To be determined by economist	Dr. Hertz

Format reproduced with permission of Dr. Paul M. Deutsch. Adapted from the *Guide to Rehabilitation*. LCare_2_DOC

Roger O. Weed, Ph.D., C.R.C., C.D.M.S.,
C.L.C.P., F.N.R.C.A.
P.O. Box 2133
Duluth, Georgia 30096

LIFE CARE PLAN

Diagnostic Testing/Educational Assessment

Client Name: <u>Roberta Melvins</u>
Date of Birth: <u>4/11/59</u>
Date of Injury: <u>7/7/2000</u>
Date Prepared: <u>8/27/2001</u>

Diagnostic Recommendation	Age/Year at Which Initiated	Age/Year at Which Suspended	Per Year Frequency	Base Cost per Year	Growth Trends	Recommended by:
Psychological testing, IQ and psychological status testing	43/2002	43/2002	1 time only	$500–600	To be determined by economist	Dr. Hertz

Format reproduced with permission of Dr. Paul M. Deutsch. Adapted from the *Guide to Rehabilitation*. LCare_3_DOC

LIFE CARE PLAN
Wheelchair Needs

Roger O. Weed, Ph.D., C.R.C., C.D.M.S.,
C.L.C.P., F.N.R.C.A.
P.O. Box 2133
Duluth, Georgia 30096

Client Name: Roberta Melvins
Date of Birth: 4/11/59
Date of Injury: 7/7/2000
Date Prepared: 8/27/2001

Wheelchair Type	Age/Year at Which Purchased	Replacement Schedule	Purpose of Equipment	Base Cost	Growth Trends	Catalog or Supplier Reference
Three-wheel power chair, rear-wheel drive (e.g., Pride)	43/2002	Every 5 years	Mobility, independence, and avoid complications	$3000–3500 Maintenance: expect $150/year after 1-year warranty	To be determined by economist	Adaptive Equipment Specialists

Format reproduced with permission of Dr. Paul M. Deutsch. Adapted from the *Guide to Rehabilitation.* LCare_4_DOC

LIFE CARE PLAN
Wheelchair Accessories and Maintenance

Roger O. Weed, Ph.D., C.R.C., C.D.M.S.,
C.L.C.P., F.N.R.C.A.
P.O. Box 2133
Duluth, Georgia 30096

Client Name: Roberta Melvins
Date of Birth: 4/11/59
Date of Injury: 7/7/2000
Date Prepared: 8/27/2001

Wheelchair Accessory/Maintenance	Age/Year at Which Purchased	Replacement Schedule	Purpose	Base Cost	Growth Trends	Catalog or Supplier Reference
Maintenance, carry bags, wheelchair batteries, and charger		Yearly	Maintenance and supplies	$100	To be determined by economist	Sammons-Preston

Format reproduced with permission of Dr. Paul M. Deutsch. Adapted from the *Guide to Rehabilitation*. LCare_5_DOC

Roger O. Weed, Ph.D., C.R.C., C.D.M.S.,
C.L.C.P., F.N.R.C.A.
P.O. Box 2133
Duluth, Georgia 30096

LIFE CARE PLAN
Aids for Independent Function

Client Name: Roberta Melvins
Date of Birth: 4/11/59
Date of Injury: 7/7/2000
Date Prepared: 8/27/2001

Equipment	Age/Year at Which Purchased	Replacement Schedule	Equipment Purpose	Base Cost	Growth Trends	Catalog or Supplier Reference
Reachers or other aids	43/2002	Yearly	Aides for independent functioning	$50 average	To be determined by economist	Sammons-Preston or other supplier

Format reproduced with permission of Dr. Paul M. Deutsch. Adapted from the *Guide to Rehabilitation*. LCare_6_DOC

LIFE CARE PLAN

Orthotics/Prosthetics

Roger O. Weed, Ph.D., C.R.C., C.D.M.S.,
C.L.C.P., F.N.R.C.A.
P.O. Box 2133
Duluth, Georgia 30096

Client Name: <u>Roberta Melvins</u>
Date of Birth: <u>4/11/59</u>
Date of Injury: <u>7/7/2000</u>
Date Prepared: <u>8/27/2001</u>

Equipment Description	Age/Year at Which Purchased	Replacement Schedule	Equipment Purpose	Base Cost	Growth Trends	Supplier
Right leg ankle/ foot orthosis	1/2002	Every 3 years	Support body weight, avoid falls, reduce complications	$406.64	To be determined by economist	Butte Limb & Brace
Straps	9/1999	Every 8–12 months	Attach ankle-foot orthosis (AFO) to leg	$10		

Format reproduced with permission of Dr. Paul M. Deutsch. Adapted from the *Guide to Rehabilitation*. LCare_7_DOC

Roger O. Weed, Ph.D., C.R.C., C.D.M.S.,
C.L.C.P., F.N.R.C.A.
P.O. Box 2133
Duluth, Georgia 30096

LIFE CARE PLAN
Drug/Supply Needs

Client Name: Roberta Melvins
Date of Birth: 4/11/59
Date of Injury: 7/7/2000
Date Prepared: 8/27/2001

Supply Description	Drug (Prescription)	Purpose	Per Unit Cost	Per Year Cost	Growth Trends	Recommended by:
	Methadone, 10 mg, 3 times/day Ativan, 2 mg, 3 times/day	Pain control Antianxiety	$9.76/30 $12.62/90	$356 $153	To be determined by economist Total = $509	Dr. Hertz

Note: Medications listed are representative of current and future needs. Specific prescriptions may change.

Format reproduced with permission of Dr. Paul M. Deutsch. Adapted from the *Guide to Rehabilitation*. LCare_9_DOC

Roger O. Weed, Ph.D., C.R.C., C.D.M.S.,
C.L.C.P., F.N.R.C.A.
P.O. Box 2133
Duluth, Georgia 30096

LIFE CARE PLAN
Home/Facility Care

Client Name: Roberta Melvins
Date of Birth: 4/11/59
Date of Injury: 7/7/2000
Date Prepared: 8/27/2001

Facility Recommendation	Home Care/Service Recommendations	Age/Year at Which Initiated	Age/Year at Which Suspended	Hours/Shifts/Days of Attendance or Care	Base Cost per Year	Growth Trends
Pain management program		43/January 1, 2002	3½ weeks		$7000–8000	To be determined by economist
	Companion, psychological support, aide, and house maintenance	2001	Life expectancy	Husband performs these functions; expect 2 days/week at $36/day if hired	$0 if continued marriage or $3744 if hired	To be determined by economist

Format reproduced with permission of Dr. Paul M. Deutsch. Adapted from the *Guide to Rehabilitation*. LCare_10_DOC

LIFE CARE PLAN
Future Medical Care — Routine

Roger O. Weed, Ph.D., C.R.C., C.D.M.S.,
C.L.C.P., F.N.R.C.A.
P.O. Box 2133
Duluth, Georgia 30096

Client Name: Roberta Melvins
Date of Birth: 4/11/59
Date of Injury: 7/7/2000
Date Prepared: 8/27/2001

Routine Medical Care Description	Frequency of Visits	Purpose	Cost per Visit	Cost per Year	Growth Trends	Recommended by:
Psychiatrist follow-up	As needed	Review of medications	See projected therapeutic modalities	N/A		Dr. Hertz
Neurological/ orthopedic follow-up (not including x-ray, lab, or other diagnostic costs, e.g., MRI = $1000–1200)	1 time/year to life expectancy	Prescribe braces, follow-up to back surgery, and prevent complications	$100 (average)	$100	To be determined by economist	Dr. Hertz

Format reproduced with permission of Dr. Paul M. Deutsch. Adapted from the *Guide to Rehabilitation*. LCare_11_DOC

Roger O. Weed, Ph.D., C.R.C., C.D.M.S.,
C.L.C.P., F.N.R.C.A.
P.O. Box 2133
Duluth, Georgia 30096

LIFE CARE PLAN
Transportation

Client Name: Roberta Melvins
Date of Birth: 4/11/59
Date of Injury: 7/7/2000
Date Prepared: 8/27/2001

Equipment Description	Age/Year at Which Purchased	Replacement Schedule	Equipment Purpose	Base Cost	Growth Trends	Catalog or Supplier Reference
Option 1 Handicap-accessible van with lift and hand controls	43/2002	Every 5–7 years (trade-in value to be determined by economist)	Mobility and independence	$42,000–45,000	To be determined by economist (reduce by cost of client vehicle estimate value of $12,000, then by cost of average vehicle at trade-in)	Handicapped Services, Inc.
Option 2 Car with trunk lift and hand controls	43/2002	Every 5–7 years	Mobility and independence	$1200–1750 ($400–550 hand controls; $1000–1200 trunk lift; car must be equipped with power steering and brakes)	To be determined by economist	Adaptive Equipment Specialists

Format reproduced with permission of Dr. Paul M. Deutsch. Adapted from the *Guide to Rehabilitation*. LCare_12_DOC

Roger O. Weed, Ph.D., C.R.C., C.D.M.S.,
C.L.C.P., F.N.R.C.A.
P.O. Box 2133
Duluth, Georgia 30096

LIFE CARE PLAN
Health and Strength Maintenance

Client Name: Roberta Melvins
Date of Birth: 4/11/59
Date of Injury: 7/7/2000
Date Prepared: 8/27/2001

Equipment Description	Special Camps or Programs	Age/Year of Purchase or Attendance	Replacement or Attendance Schedule	Base Cost	Growth Trends	Catalog or Supplier Reference
Universal gym with physical conditioning components/ stationary bike/weights		2002	1 time only	$500–1500	To be determined by economist	Sports Town

Format reproduced with permission of Dr. Paul M. Deutsch. Adapted from the *Guide to Rehabilitation*. LCare_13_DOC

Roger O. Weed, Ph.D., C.R.C., C.D.M.S., C.L.C.P.,
F.N.R.C.A.
P.O. Box 2133
Duluth, Georgia 30096

LIFE CARE PLAN
Architectural Renovations

Client Name: Roberta Melvins
Date of Birth: 4/11/59
Date of Injury: 7/7/2000
Date Prepared: 8/27/2001

Accessibility Needs		Accessibility Needs		Costs
Ramping	X	Bathroom	X	Cost estimated at 10–15% over average home
Light/environmental controls	X	Sink	X	
Floor coverings (if wheelchair is used inside)	X	Cabinets	X	
Hallways	X	Roll-in shower		
Doorways	X	Temperature control guards		
Covered parking	X	Heater		
Kitchen		Fixtures		
Sinks/fixtures		Door handles		
Cabinets		Additional electrical outlets		
Appliances		Central air/heat		
Windows		Therapy/equipment storage	?	
Electric safety doors		Attendant bathroom		
Fire alarm	X	Single-story home; no steps	X	

Format reproduced with permission of Dr. Paul M. Deutsch. Adapted from the *Guide to Rehabilitation.* LCare_14_DOC

Roger O. Weed, Ph.D., C.R.C., C.D.M.S., C.L.C.P., F.N.R.C.A.
P.O. Box 2133
Duluth, Georgia 30096

LIFE CARE PLAN
Potential Complications

Client Name: Roberta Melvins
Date of Birth: 4/11/59
Date of Injury: 7/7/2000
Date Prepared: 8/27/2001

Complications	Estimated Costs	Growth Trend
Rehospitalized for psychological/psychiatric care and crises management; electroconvulsive therapy costs approximately $1000 each treatment	No duration or frequency available; costs not included in plan	
Failed back with additional surgery required		
Falls and reinjury		
Adverse reactions to medications		

Format reproduced with permission of Dr. Paul M. Deutsch. Adapted from the *Guide to Rehabilitation*. LCare_15_DOC

Roger O. Weed, Ph.D., C.R.C., C.D.M.S.,
C.L.C.P., F.N.R.C.A.
P.O. Box 2133
Duluth, Georgia 30096

LIFE CARE PLAN
Vocational/Educational Plan

Client Name: Roberta Melvins
Date of Birth: 4/11/59
Date of Injury: 7/7/2000
Date Prepared: 8/27/2001

Recommendation	Age/Year at Which Initiated	Age/Year at Which Suspended	Purpose	Base Cost	Growth Trends	Recommended by:
Client appears unemployable; final determination based on progress in treatment						

Format reproduced with permission of Dr. Paul M. Deutsch. Adapted from the *Guide to Rehabilitation*. LCare_16_DOC

Roger O. Weed, Ph.D., C.R.C., C.D.M.S.,
C.L.C.P., F.N.R.C.A.
P.O. Box 2133
Duluth, Georgia 30096

Client Name: Roberta Melvins
Date of Birth: 4/11/59
Date of Injury: 7/7/2000
Date Prepared: 8/27/2001

LIFE CARE PLAN

Future Medical Care
Surgical Intervention or
Aggressive Treatment Plan

Recommendation (Description)	Age/Year Initiated	Frequency of Procedure	Per Procedure Cost	Per Year Cost	Growth Trends	Recommended by:
Based on history, client likely to be rehospitalized for psychological reactions to disability	Unknown	Unknown	Unknown	Unknown	Unknown	Dr. Hertz

Format reproduced with permission of Dr. Paul M. Deutsch. Adapted from the *Guide to Rehabilitation*. LCare_17_DOC

18

LIFE CARE PLANNING FOR
SPINAL CORD INJURY

Terry Winkler and Roger O. Weed

INTRODUCTION

Spinal cord injury (SCI) historically has been described by physicians as one of the most catastrophic conditions in medicine (Kennedy, 1986). In ancient Egyptian times, it was considered a condition not to be treated since patients died and the demise reflected on the physician's ability if attempts to cure them failed. Clinical features were first described in great detail by Hippocrates around 400 B.C. Paraplegia and neurogenic bowel and bladder were observed. However, since complications were poorly understood and modern medications were unavailable, an early death was the common result. It was not until this century that significant strides were made based on medical research begun particularly in England in 1944 at the Stoke Mandeville Hospital. In the U.S. the first federally funded research program was established in Arizona in 1970. Since its early beginnings, the research center has been moved to the University of Alabama with contributing support by 16 spinal cord rehabilitation programs throughout the U.S. Research data are now available regarding a plethora of issues, and life expectancy as well as quality of life have significantly improved. Fortunately, there have been many positive changes in health care and in society for spinal cord injured patients. Technology is rapidly changing and continues to provide positive changes in life expectancy and quality of life for the spinal cord injured. However, there are a number of physicians and health care providers who continue to hold a somewhat pessimistic view of spinal cord injury. Indeed, as late as 1947, Dr. William Asher described the paralyzed patient as follows:

> Picture the pathetic patient lying long abed, the urine leaking from his distended bladder, the lime draining from his bones, the blood clotting in his veins, the flesh rotting from his seat, the scybala stacking up in his colon, and the spirit draining from his soul. (Asher, 1947, p. 967)

One goal of this chapter is to provide the background information that life care planners need to prevent the above portrait from developing in a spinal cord

0-8493-1511-5/04/$0.00+$1.50
© 2004 by CRC Press LLC

injured person's life. The rehabilitation professional should become involved with the spinal cord injury patient immediately after the acute hospital care (Winkler, 1997). The life care planner must have a thorough working knowledge of the physiological effects, the most common side effects, and proper medical interventions of spinal cord injury. He or she must work with other health professionals to provide counseling for the patient and the family, and offer suggestions for environmental modifications, equipment, and services for the patient that offer greater mobility and independence. This chapter is intended to provide a foundation of basic medical knowledge of spinal cord injury, vocational information, functional abilities of people with spinal cord injury, and future medical and nonmedical needs, and to serve as an introduction to life care planning and spinal cord injury (Blackwell et al., 2001). It is imperative that the life care planner go beyond this chapter to the references cited to develop a deeper understanding of the issues that have an impact on life care planning in spinal cord injury.

PREVALENCE OF SPINAL CORD INJURY

The most current discussion of epidemiological factors of spinal cord injury can be found in Bette Go et al. (1995). The model systems data provide good information on general trends in spinal cord injury. It should, however, be pointed out that the model systems data perhaps are skewed toward individuals who have a higher level of lesion and an adequate funding source. Individuals who have lower-level or incomplete spinal cord injuries or who do not have adequate funding for extended hospital stays tend to be treated locally rather than referred to the model systems. Krause and colleagues (1975) found an incidence of spinal cord injury of 32 cases per million per year who survived or reached a hospital, with an additional 21 cases per million per year dying prior to reaching the hospital. Griffin and colleagues (1985) describe an incidence that approached 55 per million, with 35 cases per million surviving to reach the hospital.

The incidence of spinal cord injury has been reported as low as 29 cases per million to a high of 60 cases per million in various studies. There appears to be some variability from state to state regarding the exact rate of spinal cord injury. However, overall the annual rate of hospitalized individuals with spinal cord injury is between 30 and 40 cases per million. This would correspond with between 7000 and 10,000 new cases of spinal cord injury per year in the U.S. The prevalence of individuals with spinal cord injury at any one given time in the U.S. is between 180,000 and 230,000 persons (Go et al., 1995).

CAUSES OF SPINAL CORD INJURY

Gibson (1992) has described the four leading causes of spinal cord injury as motor vehicle accidents, falls, violence, and sports injuries (Table 18.1).

Automobile accidents remain the number one cause of traumatic spinal cord injury, but a decline has been reported (Go et al., 1995). The peak incidence occurred between 1978 and 1980 at 47% and has recently dropped to as low as 38%, reported in 1990. This reduction in motor vehicle accidents and spinal cord injury may be attributed in part to the improved safety features of some automo-

Table 18.1 Causes of Spinal Cord Injury

Injury Source	Percent of Total Injuries
Motor vehicle accidents	45%
Falls	20%
Violence	15%
Sports	15%
Other	5%

biles. Another interesting trend is the reduction of sports-related spinal cord injuries that has occurred over the last 15 years. Spinal cord injuries as a result of falls have increased by 5% in the same period of time, and spinal cord injury as a result of violence has almost doubled from 1978 to 1990. In some areas, violence is the number two cause of spinal cord injury. Louisiana ranks it as the number two cause, resulting in 32% of its reported cases of spinal cord injury (Lawrence et al., 1992).

Go et al. (1995) pointed out that the etiology of spinal cord injury differs substantially by age, gender, and race. The most common age of injury is 19 years, with a range of 16 to 30. Males account for 80% of all spinal cord injuries. The mean age at the time of spinal cord injury from 1973 through 1992 has increased by 4.9 years, with the mean age of 28.5 years increasing to a mean age of 33.4 years. This trend has important implications. Since older persons with spinal cord injury tend to have more preexisting major medical conditions and are more likely to have tetraplegia (previously known as quadriplegia), they therefore develop a higher rate of secondary complications and more frequent hospitalizations than their counterparts (Go et al., 1995; Roth et al., 1992).

As perhaps expected, there are seasonal variations, with the lowest number of spinal cord injuries occurring during the winter months, particularly February. The highest number of spinal cord injuries occurs during the summer months, with July having the highest incidence. Half of all spinal cord injuries occur on a weekend day, with 20% occurring on Saturday, which is nearly double the rate of spinal cord injury occurring during weekdays.

Of all spinal cord injured people, 55% have tetraplegia, with the remainder having paraplegia. Tetraplegia is defined as paralysis or partial paralysis in four extremities, with paraplegia being paralysis or partial paralysis in two extremities. Between 50 and 55% of all spinal cord injuries have some sparing of sensation, motor function, or both sensation and motor function and can be classified as incomplete.

FUNCTIONS OF THE SPINAL CORD

Spinal cord injury is a traumatic insult to the spinal cord that can result in alterations of normal motor, sensory, and autonomic function (Blackwell et al., 2001; Staas et al., 1993). The discussion will be confined to traumatic spinal cord injury; however, the principles will apply to spinal cord injury of all etiologies.

The spinal cord has three basic functions:

1. It serves as a conduit to bring sensory messages from the body and internal organs to the brain, where the brain can monitor activities of all structures and act as a central processing unit to interpret messages from the body.
2. In a similar fashion, it carries messages from the brain to the effector organs or structures in the body. In this regard, the spinal cord can be viewed as a series of cables or connections between the brain and the body.
3. It provides protective and coordination function whereby reflex mechanisms protect the body (e.g., withdrawal reflexes) and other centers facilitate or coordinate some bodily functions, such as urination, which is controlled by the micturition center in the sacral cord.

This is, of course, a simplification of the spinal cord. The spinal cord is a tremendously complex structure with literally hundreds, if not thousands, of functions being performed. Many of the body's autonomic functions are coordinated and regulated at least in part in the spinal cord, and we have learned that the modulation and control of pain is in part based in the spinal cord. There is a very complicated group of interneurons and proprioneurons in the spinal cord whose roles are to facilitate or inhibit the activity of other neurons in the spinal cord. There is virtually no bodily function occurring below the level of the foramen magnum that is not influenced in some way by the integrity of the spinal cord. Therefore, the number of complications and problems that occur as a direct result of spinal cord injury are enormous, with implications for almost every body system (Schoenen, 1991).

THE SPINAL COLUMN: BASIC ANATOMY

The spinal column consists of 33 vertebrae, intervertebral disks, and ligaments (Blackwell et al., 2001). The vertebrae provide a weight-bearing structure, the spinal column that houses and protects the spinal cord. In addition, the vertebral column allows a great deal of flexibility in the cervical and lumbar spines. There is a relatively high degree of rigidity in the thoracic spine, easily identified by the rib cage, which provides support and protection for the internal organs.

The vertebrae are divided into five segments:

- Seven cervical vertebrae (neck): These support the head and provide a great deal of mobility. There are eight spinal nerves, C1 through C8. This is accomplished by the first cervical vertebra having a spinal nerve exiting above and below it, with each vertebral body from that level down having a spinal nerve exiting below the vertebra.
- Twelve thoracic vertebrae support the ribs.
- Five lumbar vertebrae (lower back) allow flexion and extension, some rotation and side bending.
- Five sacral vertebrae provide a base of support and attachment for the pelvis.
- Four coccygeal vertebrae are fused together and form the tailbone.

Each vertebral body is separated by an intervertebral disk that is made of cartilage and acts as a shock absorber and cushion for the spinal column. The intervertebral disks make up one fourth of the total height of the spinal column and allow a great deal of flexibility between vertebral bodies. The vertebral disks have the ability to herniate and can cause injury to the spinal cord or nerve root in cases of severe herniation.

Numerous ligaments are responsible for maintaining the integrity of the spinal column and its alignment. Two of the most important are the anterior longitudinal ligaments on the front of the vertebral bodies and the posterior longitudinal ligaments on the back of the vertebral bodies. If either of these ligaments is torn, the column is said to be unstable and this greatly increases the likelihood of spinal cord injury or damage.

The central nervous system is made up of the brain and the spinal cord. It is completely encased in a very strong protective membrane, the dura mater, and is bathed in cerebrospinal fluid. The spinal cord begins at the base of the skull, the foramen magnum, and extends to the L1 or L2 vertebral level, ending in the shape of a cone called the conus medullaris. From the conus medullaris down, nerve roots continue down through the spinal canal to exit at their proper levels. These nerve roots are referred to as the cauda equina.

It is important to note that there is a disparity between the bony level and the neurological level. For example, the nervous segments that are adjacent to the L1 vertebral body in the spinal canal are S2, S3, and S4. Therefore, an injury to the L1 vertebral body would result in damage to S2, S3, and S4 nerves. This is a very important concept in life care planning. When developing a life care plan (LCP), it is extremely important that the life care plan be developed for the neurological level of injury, not the bony level of injury.

SPINAL CORD DAMAGE

Spinal cord damage can occur in several ways, some of which include (Blackwell et al., 2001):

1. Overstretching or tearing of the nervous tissue of the spinal cord.
2. Direct pressure on the spinal cord from bony fragments, bulging disks, or hematoma.
3. Swelling and edema can produce increased pressure and decreased blood flow in the area of the spinal cord injury, leading to further damage.

The initial spinal cord injury usually does not result in a complete disruption of the cord, and it is generally felt that high-dose steroids, such as methylprednisolone, given within 4 hours of the spinal cord injury may have some beneficial effect, although there are conflicting reports in this regard. Intense research in spinal cord injury treatment and intervention may hold the most promise of providing some relief from the effects of injury. However, to date there is no cure for spinal cord injury and none foreseeable in the near future.

It is possible to determine the mechanism of injury in spinal cord injury by reviewing x-rays and computed tomography (CT) scans. Axial compression alone, such as from a diving accident, will result in a burst-type fracture. Rotation combined with flexion is the most damaging type of force on a spinal column, and it will result in disruption of the posterior ligamentous structure (Staas et al., 1993). Central cord syndromes are the result of a hyperextension injury. Injury to the thoracic spine requires much greater forces due to the protective effect of the rib cage and the stability of the spine. These are usually only involved in very high speed vehicular-type traumas or accidents that involve very high forces. They also can occur when the occupant is ejected from the vehicle (Zigler & Field, 1992).

Distraction forces placed at a vertebral body can result in a Chance fracture. This type of injury is observed in motor vehicle accidents where only a lap belt is worn. This can be prevented with the use of a shoulder harness belt in addition to the lap belt. A similar injury occurs in automobiles that are provided with passive restraints in which the shoulders are restrained but the hips are not. A collision can result in the person's hips moving forward, causing a hyper flexion of the neck and resultant spinal cord injury at a higher level. Another recent reported phenomenon is high tetraplegia to children and smaller adults as a result of air bag deployment.

The stability of the spinal column is determined by the intactness of the anterior and posterior longitudinal ligaments as well as the vertebral body and will dictate whether surgery is needed. Surgical decompression even a number of years after the spinal cord injury can result in improvement. This issue is of the utmost importance in cervical spinal cord injury where, for example, a late decompression can result in a person with C5 motor function having an improvement in C6 motor function, which would make a tremendous difference in his functional outcome. In general, for the lower-level spinal cord injury, decompression is not as crucial. Acute spinal cord injury surgical management may include traction, halos, bracing, Harrington or similar rods, and fusion.

SPINAL CORD INJURY CLASSIFICATIONS

It is important to establish a worldwide standard for the nomenclature and classification of spinal cord injury. Without this, it is impossible to perform meaningful spinal cord injury research from center to center or country to country. Likewise, it is impossible to view spinal cord injury in terms of life care planning and to critique and review and make recommendations in life care planning without a standardized classification system.

In response to this need, the American Spinal Injury Association (ASIA) and the International Medical Society of Paraplegia developed a worldwide nomenclature system (American Spinal Injury Association/International Medical Society of Paraplegia, 2000). This system of classification gives key sensory levels to identify dermatomes of injury and key muscle levels to identify the levels of muscle functions. Spinal cord injuries may be *complete* or *incomplete* with partial sparing. The ASIA classification system includes a level for the sensory impairment and a level for the motor impairment, as well as a letter designation for the degree of completeness (also see Blackwell et al., 2001).

The scale, once known as the modified Frankel classification system and now as the ASIA Impairment Scale (also see Figure 18.1), is used to describe completeness, with five classes being recognized:

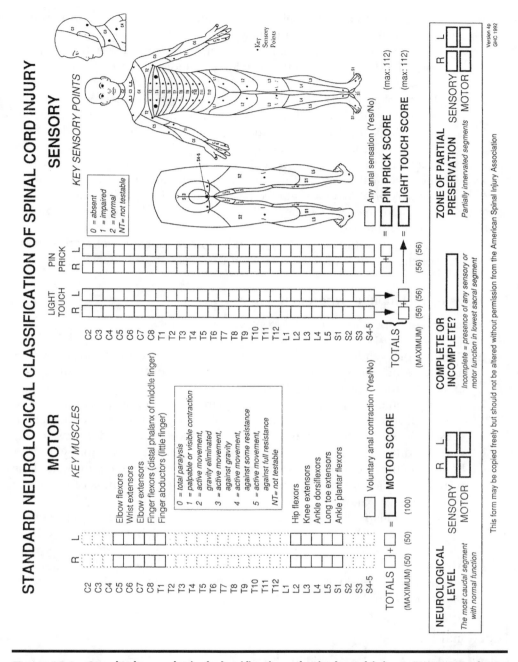

Figure 18.1 Standard neurological classification of spinal cord injury. (From American Spinal Injury Association, 2000 & 2002.)

Class A: Complete spinal cord injury: No motor or sensory function is preserved in the sacral segments S4–S5.

Class B: Incomplete spinal cord injury: Sensation but not motor function preserved below the level of injury; includes the sacral segments S4–S5.

Class C: Incomplete spinal cord injury: Motor function is preserved below the neurological level, and more than half of the key muscles below the neurological level have a muscle grade of less than 3 (Grades 0 to 2). No functional motor strength.

Class D: Incomplete spinal cord injury. Motor function is preserved below the neurological level, and at least half of the key muscles below the neurological level are graded at 3 or more. The person may be able to use the motor function, for example, for a brief transfer, or ambulate short distances.

Class E: Complete return of all motor and sensory function below the level of the lesion, but may have abnormal reflexes.

Examples of Incomplete Syndromes

The following are specific types of incomplete syndromes:

1. Central cord syndrome. Central cord syndrome is said to be present when the individual has paralysis greater in the upper extremity than the lower extremities, and sacral sensory sparing.
2. Brown–Sequard syndrome. Brown–Sequard syndrome is a hemisection of the spinal cord and is characterized by ipsilateral paralysis with contralateral sensory loss from two segments below the level of the lesion down.
3. Cauda equina syndrome. Cauda equina syndrome is an injury to the lumbosacral nerve roots within the neural canal below the conus medullaris resulting in a loss of bowel and bladder control and weakness of the lower extremities or paralysis.
4. Conus medullaris syndrome. An injury to the spinal cord at the level of the conus and the lumbosacral nerve roots, which results in areflexic bladder and bowels and lower-limb paralysis.
5. Anterior cord syndrome. A lesion that produces variable loss of motor function and sensitivity to pinprick and temperature while preserving proprioception.

Functional Effects

Spinal cord injury is considered to be a permanent condition, with very few people experiencing significant long-term recovery from the disability. Individuals with complete spinal cord injury have very little improvement in general; only 2% will improve to a ASIA Class D. Of those who present with a ASIA Class B, 20% will improve to a ASIA Class D or E. For ASIA Class C, 50% will improve to a ASIA Class D or E. The length of time since spinal cord injury is also a factor in prognosis. Individuals who have had no improvement within the first 6 months to 1 year are considered to have permanent injury with no likelihood for significant functional improvement.

Upper motor neuron (UMN) lesions in general refer to a lesion in the spinal cord that occurs at the T11 or T12 level or higher. Tetraplegics have a UMN lesion. UMN lesions are characterized by increased spasticity with intact reflex bladder and bowel functioning and sexual functioning, in general.

Lower motor neuron (LMN) injuries occur at T12 or below, usually seen in paraplegics, especially cauda equina syndromes. In general, LMN lesions have impairment of the reflex arcs that control bowel and bladder functioning and sexual functioning. These individuals will have flaccid bowel and bladder functioning, which results in much greater difficulty controlling bowel and bladder incontinence. In general, erectile function in the male is impaired.

Individuals with intact reflex voiding mechanisms of the bladder and the bowel may experience less complications, infections, and incontinent episodes.

POTENTIAL COMPLICATIONS OF SPINAL CORD INJURY

Numerous physiological changes occur in almost every system of the body as a result of spinal cord injury (Blackwell et al., 2001). In addition, there are a host of complications that occur as a result of spinal cord injury. A comprehensive discussion of these factors and issues is beyond the scope of this chapter. However, an introduction to the topic is useful and necessary to understand the implications for life care planning. At the conclusion of this chapter, several references for more in-depth discussion of these issues are offered.

Cardiovascular

Normal physiological control of the arteriovenous system and the heart are lost in spinal cord injury from the injured vertebral level down. The portion of the spinal cord that controls the heart directly ranges from T1 to T7. Injuries at this level or above result in altered cardiovascular physiology, not only of the vasculature, but of the heart proper.

Hypotension

Loss of blood pressure (BP) control is a very common problem in spinal cord injury. Higher-level spinal cord injuries result in orthostatic hypotension in which the individual experiences a drop in blood pressure and an elevating heart rate in response to attempting to sit up. These episodes tend to improve with time; however, a select group of individuals may continue to have this throughout the remainder of their lives and require very aggressive management in order to tolerate a sitting posture. Orthostatic hypotension is most commonly seen in individuals with a spinal cord injury at T6 or above. It can be quite severe and result in a patient having a fainting episode or loss of consciousness. Numerous techniques to assist in the management of this are available, including compression hose, abdominal binders, reclining chairs, and elevating leg rests. Physical therapists address this complication by progressive elevation with a tilt table. Medications useful in the management of orthostatic hypotension include ephedrine, tyramine, florinef, and ergotamine. Newer medications such as Proamatine (mido-drine), an alpha-adrenergic vasoactive agent, are more effective. The orthostasis will interfere with the number of hours a person can be in a wheelchair and with his or her ability to be out in the community for vocational or social activities.

Arrhythmias

High-level spinal cord injuries can result in bradyarrhythmias that can lead to cardiac arrest and standstill during tracheal suction. Patients at risk for this may require atropine or possibly placement of a pacemaker. A highly skilled caregiver who is capable of responding to such emergencies should be available.

Deep Vein Thrombus (DVT)

DVT has been recognized as a significant cause of morbidity and mortality in spinal cord injury. The incidence of DVT ranges from 47 to 100%, increasing the initial cost of hospitalization by 35%, and the annual direct cost of hospital care alone is estimated by DeVivo to be $178 million; these figures do not take into account the economic cost of lives lost to DVT (Consortium for Spinal Cord Injury, 1997b). One recent tragic loss occurred when a Kansas City Chief football player died after developing a DVT secondary to SCI. In SCI without prophylaxis DVT is likely to occur in well over 80% of cases (Waring & Karunas, 1991). The use of heparin has been demonstrated to be effective in reducing the incidence of DVT. Spasticity and its effects on the development of DVT have been studied. There are varying reports in the literature; however, overall, it is felt that increased spasticity may result in a decreased incidence of DVT in the acute sitting (Bors et al., 1954). Chin (personal communication, 1997) has studied DVT and the use of Lovonox (a low-molecular-weight heparin) in the prevention of DVT and has documented that Lovonox is extremely effective in reducing the acute incidence of DVT. The Consortium for Spinal Cord Injury (1997b) publication *Prevention of Thromboembolism* recommends low-molecular-weight heparin to prevent DVT in SCI.

Of those individuals who develop DVT, approximately one third can develop pulmonary embolus. Pulmonary embolus can be a life-threatening condition and result in death in a number of individuals. Venous Doppler studies and venograms are necessary to follow the DVT as are serial laboratory studies, such as Protimes. Once a DVT has developed, an individual will be treated for 6 months to 1 year, depending on clinical response. A small number of spinal cord injured people will develop a chronic DVT and require lifelong management with anticoagulation therapy. Some individuals with DVT and other comorbidities or injuries may require the placement of a vena cava filter to protect them from risk of pulmonary embolus. Of those individuals who do not develop DVT during the acute hospital stay, there is approximately 14 to 20% risk of developing a DVT at some point during their lifetime. The period of greatest risk for development of deep vein thrombosis seems to occur within the first 3 months of injury (Staas et al., 1993). If the person is 1 year out from the development of DVT and experiences increased swelling and temperature when anti-coagulation is stopped, this likely represents a permanent condition and will require lifelong anticoagulation treatment. Individuals who have experienced a DVT are twice as likely to develop a blood clot again in the same extremity at some point later in their life (Wyngaarden et al., 1988).

Autonomic Dysreflexia (AD)

AD is a life-threatening complication. The incidence of AD is 48 to 98% of people with tetraplegia and high paraplegia (Esmail et al., 2002) and most commonly occurs in individuals who have a spinal cord injury at T6 or above. The Consortium for Spinal Cord Injury has a comprehensive discussion of this condition and its treatment in *Acute Management of Autonomic Dysreflexia* ("Adults with SCI Presenting to Health-Care Facilities," 1997, as cited in Esmail et al., 2002), which defines a systolic blood pressure at or over 150 as a hypertensive urgency. It is important to remember that higher-level SCI uniformly leads to low blood pressure, and a BP reading ordinarily felt to be within normal limits would be elevated for a tetraplegic. AD is characterized by one or more of the following:

- Flushing or redness of the skin that develops above the level of the spinal cord injury
- General malaise
- Severe headache
- Elevated blood pressure
- Increased heart rate
- Occasionally, slowed heart rate

While AD commonly occurs at T6 or above, with the right type of stimulus (such as giving birth) it can occur at lower levels of spinal cord injury. This condition is extremely uncomfortable and can be life threatening. The patient may feel as if she is dying, and the sequela can cause an extreme and diffuse malaise. Individuals that have frequent and recurring autonomic dysreflexia or who tend to have alarmingly high blood pressures (i.e., diastolic pressure over 120 mmHg or systolic pressure over 200 mmHg) require ongoing use of medications such as Dibenzyline and Procardia. In addition, they will require a fail-proof emergency response system to ensure that they obtain required urgent care. The danger lies in the elevated blood pressure that can result in stroke and death. The life care plan should be designed in such a fashion as to make every effort to prevent the episodes by providing adequate supplies for frequent catheterization and bowel programs. Additionally, personal care attendants should be trained to properly assist in preventing the autonomic dysreflexia, or recognizing and treating it.

In incomplete spinal cord injuries, AD is generally not a significant problem. AD occurs as a result of some noxious stimulus, the most common being distended bowel or bladder. Other causes may be occult fractures, decubitus ulcers, infections, and abdominal lesions (ulcers or cholelithiasis). Improper positioning in the chair, as well as tight clothing or wrinkles in the clothing, has been reported to cause episodes of AD. In individuals who are experiencing increasing autonomic dysreflexia, a complete and thorough medical workup is indicated to determine the etiology of the AD.

AD is treated by identifying and relieving the noxious stimulus. In the case of bowel and bladder, the complication can be reduced or eliminated by emptying the bowel or bladder. In refractory cases of AD, medications such as Dibenzyline may be required. In acute episodes of AD, calcium channel blockers such as Procardia are indicated to gain control of the blood pressure while the underlying etiology is determined. Recent reports reveal that Captopril given sublingually may be a safer alternative (Esmail et al., 2002). Some centers are using Nitroglycerin paste on the chest wall as an alternative to Procardia.

The spinal cord injured patient is also at higher risk for developing peripheral vascular disease, both arterial and venous disease (Lee, 1991). There is also evidence that individuals with spinal cord injuries experience a greater rate of *coronary artery disease* and *myocardial infarction*. When all other risk factors are controlled for, such as sex, age, family history, and lifestyle, the individual with a spinal cord injury is twice as likely to develop coronary artery disease as the able-bodied counterpart (Yehutil, 1989; Kesseler, 1986; Duckworth, 1983; Dorey, 1990; Bauman et al., 1994). Schmitt et al. (1995) have pointed out that the leading cause of death for persons with neurologically incomplete paraplegia is ischemic heart disease.

Pulmonary

Individuals with spinal cord injuries below T12 have virtually no impairment of their pulmonary system. As the spinal cord injury levels rise from T12 to T5, there is a progressive loss of abdominal motor function and chest wall function that impairs expiration and cough. As the level rises further from T5 to T1, intercostal function is impaired and inspiratory and expiratory function are impaired. Jackson and Groomes (1991) have reported that approximately 70% of new spinal cord injured persons experience respiratory complications, with one third developing pneumonia.

The most critical level for pulmonary function is C3, C4, and C5, the neural segments that supply the phrenic nerve and the diaphragm. With injuries at this level and above, the individual is at high risk for relying upon a ventilator for pulmonary function. Spinal cord injury at levels C3 and above will result in total dependency on ventilators (Blackwell et al., 2001). These individuals require a whole host of support to maintain them, including high-level attendant care and frequent physician follow-up visits. In a select group of these individuals, phrenic pacers (although expensive) may be indicated and will result in a more physiological breathing mechanism. It can be expected that individuals with phrenic pacers will experience fewer respiratory complications, have an improved quality of life, and have improved longevity. Benefits include improved speech and smell, ease of transfers and mobility, reduced respiratory infections, reduced secretions, and possibly closing the trach site (Gittler et al., 2002). In high levels of spinal cord injury, careful monitoring of the pulmonary status is absolutely essential and problems must be reported immediately to the treating physicians. Individuals with vital capacities below 10 to 5 ml/kg are at greatest risk for respiratory failure and may require some assisted ventilation to prevent complications. Devices and techniques such as abdominal or quad coughs, abdominal binders, mechanical insufflation–exsufflation, high-frequency chest wall oscillation, incentive spirometry, and abdominal weights may be required (McKinley et al., 2002). Medications that may be required are antibiotics, updraft agents, theophylline, mucolytic drugs, and beta-agonist inhalers. Oxandrin, an oral anabolic steroid, has been shown to improve pulmonary function (Spungen et al., 1999). Four-Amino Pyrididine, a supplement in final Food and Drug Administration (FDA) clinical trials, may also improve vital capacity. This drug will be offered by Elan when cleared by the FDA.

Upper respiratory tract infections and pneumonias can be expected to occur at a higher frequency and require aggressive preventive care in order to limit morbidity and mortality. Tetraplegics should receive annual influenza vaccinations and a pneumococcal vaccination. The winter months are likely to be the most troublesome and may require daily respiratory therapy treatments, in order to prevent complications.

Individuals with high-level spinal cord injury will require a host of equipment, including ventilators, respiratory monitors, suctioning equipment, and pulse oxymetry. Additional emergency equipment will include a backup ventilator, a home generator system in the event of prolonged power failure, and an Ambu bag.

Additional factors that can complicate respiratory status in spinal cord injury are a progressing scoliosis, increasing spasticity, and syringomyelia. High spinal cord injury in females who become pregnant may also experience a worsening pulmonary status and require additional support during pregnancy.

Sleep Disturbances

Braun and colleagues (1982) have reported an increased incidence of sleep apnea in spinal cord injured patients. Consideration of monitoring of their condition is required in patients with symptoms of sleep apnea, particularly in patients who are overweight.

Gastrointestinal (GI)

Individuals with spinal cord injury experience a number of physiological changes in the function of their GI tract. There is a slowing of transient time through the GI system, and gastric acid secretion may increase (Consortium for Spinal Cord Injury, 1998).

Peptic Ulcer Disease

There is an increased risk and rate of development of peptic ulcer disease connected with a spinal cord injury. Almost all acute spinal cord injured people will have gastritis or peptic ulcer disease (Epstein, 1981; Kewalramani, 1979). GI bleeding is a very common early complication in spinal cord injury. The risk for GI bleeds and ulceration is higher in individuals with spinal cord injury at T6 and above. Prophylactic use of H2 blockers is common and medically appropriate. The GI bleeds frequently result in anemia after spinal cord injury (Gore et al., 1991).

Cholelithiasis

Individuals with spinal cord injury have an increased risk and rate of development of gallstones. Reports have suggested an increased rate from 3 to 11 times more likely to develop gallstones than the able-bodied population. It is generally believed that this may be related to a relative stasis in the gastrointestinal tract, an overproduction of bile by the gallbladder, or decreased gallbladder motility (Apstein & Dalecki-Chipperfield, 1987; Stone et al., 1990).

Individuals with UMN lesions may have an unaltered defecation reflex and respond to digital stimulation of the rectum with a reflex defecation. Individuals who do not have an intact anorectal reflex (LMN lesions) for defecation have a much more difficult time controlling bowel incontinence.

Dietary factors are used to assist in controlling bowel incontinence by maintaining a proper consistency of the stool. In addition, rectal suppositories such as Dulcolax, Enemeez (formally known as Therevac, Mini Enemas), and Magic Bullet may be necessary. Oral medications such as Metamucil, Colace, or Peri-Colace also may assist in bowel management. Miralax is an entirely new agent that appears to be very effective for SCI constipation.

Individuals with spinal cord injuries experience a high rate of hemorrhoids and rectal fissures that will require the assistance of gastroenterologists and colorectal surgeons. Spinal cord injured patients who have intractable diarrhea and difficulty controlling their incontinence may be candidates for a colostomy. Bowel incontinence poses serious social, recreational, and vocational limitations for the spinal cord injured patient. Individuals with high-level spinal cord injuries are dependent on others for assistance and management of their bowel incontinence. In addition, individuals with low-level spinal cord injury or paraplegias will require the assistance of an attendant during times of illness for management of their bowel program, and a personal care attendant will be required during times of illness that result in GI upset or diarrhea. Management of the neurogenic bowel can be quite time-consuming and require from 30 minutes to 3 hours or more for each event.

Metabolic Changes

Metabolic changes are numerous after spinal cord injury and can result in altered nutritional requirements, hypercholesterolemia, and dyslipidemia. Nutritional counseling and changes in the diet may be required to assist the patient with learning how to manage these complications. Exercise has been demonstrated to be beneficial in assisting and restoring a desirable HDL-to-LDL ratio.

Diabetes Mellitus

Diabetes mellitus (adult onset) is clearly related to spinal cord injury. Several studies have well established the glucose intolerance of individuals with spinal cord injury. There may be a relative insulin resistance present. Other factors may also include the decreased ability of the spinal cord injury patient to exercise and maintain fitness and the tendency to gain weight due to decreased activity (Duckworth, 1983; Bauman & Spungen, 1984; Formal, 1992).

Anemia

Anemia after spinal cord injury develops early. It was originally generally believed to represent only an acute incidence of blood loss and acute gastrointestinal problems. There are, however, individuals who continue to have ongoing difficulty with anemia that is clearly related to their injury. The exact etiology of the anemia remains elusive, although there are reports that there is decreased erythropoietin produced at the kidneys. It is clear that persistent anemia is likely a multifactorial problem (Hirsch et al., 1990). Treatment requires multivitamins, vitamin C, iron supplements, and occasionally Epogen.

Urinary Complications

Spinal cord injury results in a neurogenic bladder (urinary incontinence) in most people. The management program required depends on the level of spinal cord injury and the patient's unique bladder function or dysfunction. Upper motor neuron lesions may be managed with an external catheter if an intact reflex voiding mechanism is present. This technique is by far the most desirable if it is functional for the patient. It should be recognized that as a patient ages or changes occur with the spinal cord injury, the external condom catheter may not continue to be an effective method of urinary control.

Most patients with spinal cord injury will require intermittent catheterization (IC) performed four to six times daily. Spinal cord injured males with low-level lesions are the best suited for intermittent catheterization. Intermittent catheterization becomes increasingly more difficult in females, obese individuals, and individuals with high-level lesions. Indwelling Foley or suprapubic catheters may be required to manage the neurogenic bladder for these patients.

Detrusor-sphincter dyssynergia is common in SCI and leads to poor bladder emptying, urinary reflux, and, if unrecognized or not treated, renal failure. It is screened for with renal ultrasounds diagnosed with urodynamic studies. Treatment includes anticholenergic medications, sphincterotomy, and frequent intermittent catheterization (Wyndaele, 2002). Pudendal nerve blocks with Botox or Phenol are also effective (Tsai et al., 2002).

Individuals with spinal cord injury experience an increased rate of urinary tract infections and urosepsis and will require urinalysis, urine culture and sensitivities, and intermittent antibiotics. The cost of antibiotics in a population utilizing sterile IC is 43% of the cost of those using nonsterile IC, and using hydrophilic catheters reduces the risk for strictures (Wyndaele, 2002). Some individuals may require lifelong use of prophylactic antibiotics to reduce the incidence of urinary tract infections. Bladder and renal calculi are a common complication of spinal cord injury that should be screened annually and will require a urologist to manage. Bladder cancer is much more common in SCI, especially in those who use an indwelling Foley catheter. For SCI the risk of bladder cancer is 25 times higher, and the risk of mortality is 70 times higher than age- and gender-matched population in general. Looking at the SCI population, an indwelling Foley increases the risk of bladder cancer fivefold over other methods of bladder management (Groah et al., 2002). Urinary incontinence may lead to skin breakdown in the perineal area and result in decubitus ulcers that require expensive surgery. High-level spinal cord injury will mandate the assistance of a personal care attendant.

The individual with spinal cord injury will likely require catheters, leg drainage bags, night drainage bags, gloves, tape, Betadine, and other supplies. Follow-up evaluations will require renal ultrasounds, intravenous pyelograms (IVPs), urinalysis, urine cultures and sensitivities, urology visits, and urodynamic studies.

Goals of neurogenic bladder management include maintaining continence, preserving renal function, and reducing morbidity. A change in management of the system during the patient's lifetime may be required (Cardenas, 1992).

Musculoskeletal

A host of physiological changes occur after spinal cord injury, including body composition, lipid metabolism, energy expenditure, nutritional parameters, glucose and calcium metabolism, thermoregulation, and soft tissue changes (Yarkony, 1996). All of these affect the musculoskeletal system.

Approximately 40% of the spinal cord injured will have multiple fractures below the level of the injury. In addition, due to the extensive osteoporosis from the level of the lesion down, it can be anticipated that many spinal cord injured individuals will experience at least one long bone fracture during their lifetime. Long bone fractures below the level of the lesion are slow to heal or may not heal at all, resulting in a nonunion. Such fractures have to be evaluated carefully; they may require future surgical interventions or prolonged care and treatment. These fractures can be a source of ongoing pain and can produce autonomic dysreflexia symptoms in a patient. Fractures below the level of the spinal cord injury can result in the development of a nonunion or heterotopic ossification, both of which would require extended periods of treatment.

Fractures above the level of the lesion or in the upper extremities can interfere with rehabilitation care and make the patient more dependent on personal care services until the fracture and the resulting sequela have resolved.

Heterotopic ossification (HO) is a common complication of spinal cord injury by which the body begins making ectopic bone in an area where bone should not exist. Typically, this bone is formed in the soft tissues around a joint, most commonly in the hips, knees, shoulders, elbows, and ankles. The condition rarely occurs in small joints of the hands or feet. It is reported to occur in as many as 20 to 30% of spinal cord injured patients and can result in limited range of motion (ROM) of a joint. HO can lead to complications such as repeated skin breakdown, or it interferes with positioning and activities of daily living (ADL). Triple-phase bone scan is the earliest and most sensitive test to diagnose HO. Additional useful tests includes serum alkaline phosphatase and x-rays.

HO must be treated by a physical therapist with range of motion to prevent ankylosing of a joint. Medications that are useful include Indocin and Didronel and may require from 6 months to 1 year of treatment. When active HO is present, frequent follow-ups with a physiatrist, serial bone scans and x-rays, and serum phosphorus levels are required.

After HO has matured and has no longer been active for at least 1 year, and if the HO is causing interference with ADL, positioning, or skin breakdown, it can be surgically removed. Refractory HO that is not responsive to medication may benefit from radiation treatment, although there are conflicting reports in the literature regarding the efficacy of radiation treatment.

Once spinal cord injured patients have experienced HO, they have approximately a 50% chance of reactivating the disease sometime during their lifetime. Factors that will result in reactivation of the HO include fractures, infection, kidney stones, decubitus ulcers, and surgeries. Reactivated HO is treated the same as the original episode of HO, requiring Indocin, Didronel, physical therapy, and possibly radiation treatment. It also requires physician follow-up, bone scans, x-rays, and frequent laboratory evaluation.

Poikiothermia

Poikiothermia is related to a decreased ability to maintain body temperature. In an able-bodied person, body heat is generated through shivering and vasoconstriction and body heat is reduced through sweating and vasodilatation. These mechanisms are impaired in the patient with a spinal cord injury. The higher the level of injury, the more significant the poikilothermia. This loss of ability to regulate body temperature can be life threatening in individuals with spinal cord injury and require adequate safeguards to assist in maintaining body temperature. This includes central heating and air systems in their homes as well as good, functioning air-conditioning systems in their vehicles. Cellular telephones are required so that in the event the vehicle breaks down, the person can summon help. Spinal cord injured people are at risk for skin injury from exposure to extreme heat or cold and may, in fact, suffer life-threatening complications if exposed to the extremes of either temperature for longer than a brief period of time.

Osteoporosis

Osteoporosis is a common complication of spinal cord injury because as much as 50% of the bone mineralization may be lost within the first few months of the injury. This puts the patient at greater risk of fractures below the level of the lesion. In addition, it has been reported that fractures below the level of the lesion are much slower to heal or may not heal at all. Bone mineralization loss continues with aging, raising the risk of skeletal complications with the length of time from spinal cord injury onset.

Overuse Sydromes

Overuse sydromes and chronic pain of the upper extremities, shoulders, elbows, and wrists are common sequelae of spinal cord injury and can result in a decreased functional status of the patient. Up to 75% of patients may experience the development of peripheral nerve entrapment such as carpal tunnel syndrome and ulnar nerve entrapments at the wrists and elbow. Davidoff et al. (1991) have reported the incidents to be as high as 86%. Decreased shoulder functioning and increasing pain have been reported with aging. Rotator cuff impairment and tendonitis of the shoulders are common problems associated with spinal cord injury. At least one study reports upper-extremity complications occur earlier in females (Pentland & Twomey, 1991). Upper-extremity pains are commonly reported to exist in 75% of the spinal cord injured (Sie et al., 1992). Females seem to have greater difficulty with upper-extremity and shoulder pain than males. Musculoskeletal repetitive trauma injuries occur commonly in long-term SCI, but can be prevented with appropriate lifestyle or equipment modifications. Also, living independently without assistance increases the opportunity for repetitive use injuries (Groah et al., 2002).

Spasticity

Spasticity, an involuntary rhythmic contraction of a muscle, can result in increased disability by interfering with transfers, activities of daily living, and positioning in the chair, as well as interrupting sleep and causing pain. However, there also are some beneficial effects of spasticity such as assisting with weight shifts, improving circulation, helping to reduce skin breakdown, and at times use for functional purposes, such as a transfer.

Increasing spasticity can result from sitting on a foreign object, skin breakdown, infections, kidney stones, ingrown toenails, bony fractures, or other painful stimuli. Syringomyelia, a cyst in the spinal canal that can raise the level of injury if not treated, is a diagnosis that must be excluded when no other source of the increasing spasticity can be found.

Spasticity is treated by providing full range of motion to all involved joints at least twice a day with prolonged terminal stretch by the therapist. Standing in a standing frame or tilt table can help reduce spasticity. Avoiding extreme temperature changes, whirlpool treatments, and preventing bladder infections, constipation, and skin breakdown will also help.

Medications that are commonly useful in the treatment of spasticity include Baclofen, Dantrium, and Valium. Xanaflex is a newer antispasticity medication that is an alpha-blocker and can be helpful in cases not responding to other oral agents. In severe cases, the patient may require an intrathecal Baclofen (ITB) pump. Sudden withdrawal from ITB has been reported to have resulted in at least six deaths, and life-threatening syndromes in many others, which is felt to be an underrepresentation of the actual adverse events (Coffey et al., 2002). The authors report that noncompliance, human error, and mechanical malfunction occur, leading to these problems, and that any patient with ITB infusion is theoretically at risk. Such reports emphasize the duty of life care planners to develop plans that assure high-quality timely follow-up care and access to health care providers.

Surgery such as a rhizotomy may be considered. The patient may require motor point blocks or nerve blocks using phenol, alcohol, or Botox. Spasticity has been reported to increase with aging in spinal cord injury (Menter, 1995).

The results of increased tone and decreased range of motion are well-known complications of spinal cord injury. They can require surgical intervention, treatment with physical therapists, range of motion, standing frames, whirlpool treatments, peripheral nerve or motor point blocks, and splinting.

Decubitus Ulcers

Decubitus ulcers are a common and perhaps most costly complication of spinal cord injury. It is reported that most spinal cord injured patients will experience at least one decubitus ulcer. In the SCI population the annual incidence of decubitus ulcers is 23 to 30% (Byrne & Salzberg, 1996). Ulcers may be classified according to their level of involvement:

- *Grade I* is redness and induration of the skin.
- *Grade II* is superficial breakdown of the dermis.
- *Grade III* extends through the entire subcutaneous tissue but not into the muscle.
- *Grade IV* involves deep ulceration that extends into muscle tissue and to underlying bone.
- *Grade V* results in widespread extension of the ulcer into adjacent body joints or cavities.

The best management for decubitus ulcer is prevention; however, this is not always possible. Given the very best level of care, individuals can still develop decubitus ulcers. It particularly becomes a problem as the individual with spinal cord injury ages. Adequate seating systems and positioning in the chair with proper cushions are crucial in maintaining skin integrity and reducing the incidence of decubitus ulcers. In addition, adequate personal care attendants for hygiene and assistance in transferring and positioning are also necessary. Nutritional support is beneficial at reducing the risk of decubitus ulcers and at helping decubitus ulcers to heal.

Once decubitus ulcers have developed, a variety of treatments may be appropriate, including antibiotic ointments, debridement preparations, whirlpool treatments, and surgery. Recent wound care advancements include Regranex gel, Oxandran, electrical stimulation, and vacuum system to promote wound healing (McKinley et al., 2002). A scar is left in the area of a decubitus ulcer after healing and predisposes this area to further breakdown in the future. This complication can be a very expensive and time-consuming event. One model spinal cord injury treatment center reported that the cost of treatment for decubitus, where hospitalization was required (Stage III or IV), was $14,000 to $23,000 for U.S. hospitals, and a few of the more complicated cases at a model spinal cord injury center have topped $100,000 (Arthur Simon, M.D., personal communication, November 1999).

Infections are common complications that may be a direct result of skin breakdown, be it from virulent organisms transmitted to the patient by others via poor sterilization procedures or from community-acquired bacteria. Review of past medical records to determine the number of infections and the types of infections that the patient has suffered will serve as a useful guide for making projections about the future rates and types of infections the person is most likely to experience. In addition, the severity of the infections should be assessed to determine the level of care that will likely be required. For example, a patient who has had numerous infections with highly resistant organisms requiring hospitalizations and IV antibiotics is likely to continue to require that level of care.

Sexual Functioning

Spinal cord injury has a significant impact on sexual functioning in males and females. Sipski and Alexander (1992) reported that in males with UMN injuries, reflex erections are present in 70 to 90%. Ejaculation occurs in only 4% of these patients. In males with LMN lesions, approximately 20% achieve an erection, with 20% of these achieving ejaculation. Females with spinal cord injury have reported higher levels of reflex lubrication and psychogenic lubrication, with 50 to 75% reporting orgasm.

Male fertility is impaired in spinal cord injury. Techniques such as vibratory stimulation and electroejaculation may be used to harvest sperm for artificial insemination. Success rates vary from center to center but may approach 50%. In general, it is felt that the earlier the sperm is harvested after spinal cord injury, the greater the likelihood of successful pregnancy. Recent studies suggest the viability of sperm does not decline over time as previously thought (Brackett et al., 1998).

Spinal cord injured males may require assistive techniques for erectile dysfunctions such as prostaglandin penile injections, vacuum tumescence pumps, or penile implants. In general, penile implants are discouraged in the spinal cord injury population since they can lead to erosion and skin breakdown in the perineum. A newer treatment for erectile dysfunction is MUSE, an intraurethal suppository. Viagra and Lavita have proven useful to treat erectile dysfunction in SCI. Caverjet penile injections are required for some men with SCI.

Stiens reports that vibratory ejaculation and electrical stimulation result in semen retrieval in 67 to 97% of men with SCI. Assisted reproduction technologies available in order of complexity include intravaginal insemination, intrauterine insemination, *in vitro* fertilization, gamete intrafallopian transfer, and intracytoplasmic sperm injection, with costs ranging from $1000 to $14,000 (Blackwell et al., 2001).

In spinal cord injured females, half will not miss a menstrual cycle. Of those who have a delayed menses, all will begin normal menstruation within a 3- to 6-month period. The spinal cord injured female has no change in her fertility. Birth control becomes a major problem since the female is at high risk for development of deep vein thrombosis and birth control pills are known to increase the risk of DVT. It is generally recommended that birth control pills not be utilized. The Norplant implant is not recommended if there has been a preexisting history of DVT. Condom usage may be the method of choice for prevention of pregnancy in the spinal cord injured female.

Women with spinal cord injuries who become pregnant have a higher incidence of premature and low-birth-weight infants (Sipski & Alexander, 1992). In addition, females during the last trimester of pregnancy may experience more difficulty with urinary tract infections, decubitus ulcers, edema, autonomic dysreflexia, transfers, and self-care. Due to these complications, admission to the hospital during the 32nd week of pregnancy may be required. Breast-feeding in the tetraplegic female may be difficult due to positioning or due to its triggering autonomic dysreflexia. SCI mothers may require assistance with child rearing. The SCI mom will require a power wheelchair to assist her mobility with the infant and diaper bag. This need will continue until childbearing years are over or until the family growth is complete and the youngest child is old enough to follow parents' request. It has been reported that having a disability increases a woman's likelihood of physical, mental, or sexual abuse, with as many as 40% having experienced abuse (Ridington, 1989; Nosek et al., 1998; Harness-DiGloria, 1999).

Individuals with spinal cord injury should have access to counseling regarding their sexuality and relationships with others. Counseling can provide sex education to assist the couple in resuming sexual activity and to teach alternate techniques for giving and receiving sexual pleasure with the presence of a spinal cord injury.

FACTORS TO CONSIDER IN LIFE CARE PLANNING

A thorough and comprehensive review of the medical records from the acute care hospital stay and the initial rehabilitation stay should be performed to obtain the most accurate information available regarding the complications the patient has experienced that can have an impact on future medical needs. In addition, a thorough review of the most recent records from physical therapy and occupational therapy will provide valuable clues to the person's current functional status and equipment needs and will occasionally reveal complications. When reviewing the medical records, there are key items that should be searched for, since they can and do alter the future medical needs of the patient. In addition to the complications noted above, the list below is intended to be a partial list of important topics and issues to glean from records that can have an effect on life care plan entries.

Neurological Level

Knowing the neurological level of the patient is crucial as a starting point to determine future medical needs. Therefore, careful review of the records should be performed to determine the exact neurological level and completeness of the spinal cord injury. If this cannot be determined from the records, then the life care planner must obtain an accurate neurological level from a knowledgeable physician. In addition, knowing and describing accurately the neurological level of the patient serves as a baseline in the event that there is a change in the person's neurological status so that the change can easily be recognized by the caregivers.

Comorbidities

Comorbidities and other medical complications and problems of the patients are extremely important and can impact the life care plan. Complications such as coronary artery disease, peripheral vascular disease, preexisting renal disease, chronic obstructive lung disease, or diabetes mellitus have a significant interplay with the effects of spinal cord injury. Preexisting conditions can become much worse when combined with spinal cord injury and dictate that a higher level of care be provided. Some conditions, although not related to the traumatic spinal cord injury, are seriously complicated by the traumatic spinal cord injury and therefore mandate that the life care plan provide a higher level of care as a result of the spinal cord injury. For example, the insulin-dependent diabetic who becomes tetraplegic requires an increased level of attendant care to monitor blood sugar and give insulin injections, even though diabetes is not directly related to the spinal cord injury.

Preexisting disabilities combined with spinal cord injury can have a synergistic effect and require higher levels of care than would be required by the presence of either disability alone. For example, the blind individual who becomes paraplegic will require a much higher level of attendant care than the average paraplegic.

Functional Independent Measures (FIMs)

FIM scores are used to communicate the level of independence of the patient in many areas. The scale ranges from Level 7, fully independent, to Level 1, which requires total assistance. The rehabilitation record will reflect FIM scores in several areas, including dressing, bathing, grooming, transfers, medications, bowel and bladder, and mobility. If the FIM score is 5 or less in any category, then attendant care is needed to assist the patient in that area. While FIM scores are not the only way to determine what personal care services are needed by the individual, they are an excellent way to establish a baseline and provide objective documentation of the need. FIM scores considered along with level of SCI, and many other factors, will help determine need for personal assistance services (PAS). (Also see the discussion below.)

Equipment

Review of the records can also determine in part what equipment needs the patient has and what equipment needs have been met at that point. It is not necessary to recommend the exact same type and style of equipment that was recommended by the hospital, but it is important to review what has been provided to the patient and when it was provided prior to making any future recommendations. The equipment provided to or recommended for the individual may be a function of resources available rather than what was indicated or needed.

Various types of durable medical equipment will be required, although the amount and style depend on the level of injury and the competence of the patient. A life care plan should address wheelchair needs, home and ramp modifications, environmental control systems, equipment maintenance, security systems, transportation needs, cellular phones, and other appropriate equipment.

Position and posture are important variables affecting SCI performance. Problem solving and seating recommendations require a good working knowledge of physical impairment, wheelchair adaptation, seating systems, and the person's needs. Due to the complexity of the issue, an analytical working method is required (Bolin et al., 2000).

Equipment should be provided to allow the individual to maintain an active exercise program. Persons with higher-level spinal cord injuries, who are unable to voluntarily move the muscles, may be appropriate for functional electrical stimulation units to perform this activity for them. Functional electrical stimulation (FES) equipment has been around for as long as 20 years and has undergone significant refinement in recent years. Gittler (2002) provides a brief discussion of indications and costs of several options. Phrenic pacers improve pulmonary function with the basic hardware cost of $50,000. Vocare will improve bowel and bladder emptying, with a hardware cost of $40,000. The Freehand system, the Handmaster, and the Tetron Glove provide grasp, or key grip and release function for C5–C6 tetraplegics, costing $50,000. Although the Freehand system is no longer manufactured, a number of units are available for implantation. Each of these FES systems will require surgical or nonsurgical placement, training in its use, and ongoing maintenance/replacement cost. A variety of FES devices have been shown useful in maintaining cardiovascular health and improving lipid profiles in spinal cord injury (Wheeler et al., 2002).

Psychological and Social Adjustment

The rehabilitation and acute care record should provide information on family support and the patient's psychological adjustment to the disability. Patients who cope poorly or fail to complete initial rehabilitation are at much higher risk for experiencing complications and problems and will require a more intensive level of service in the life care plan. In addition, identifying social activities that were important to the patient prior to the spinal cord injury and establishing alternative ways to participate in these activities for the newly injured person are important goals of a life care plan.

FUTURE NEEDS

Functional Outcomes

The functional status of the patient is crucial in projecting future equipment needs and, specifically, personal assistance services needs. Careful consideration to the needs of a patient must be given and every attempt made to accurately represent the number of personal care hours that are required. PAS needs can represent the single most expensive part of the plan for higher-level injuries. For example, ventilator-dependent tetraplegics require 24-hour care. If PAS are purchased through an agency, at least licensed practical nurse (LPN)-level care will be provided. In many cases, there are no LPNs trained in ventilator care, in which case an RN will be required (check with the agency within each state with regard to its policies on this topic). At the other extreme, a lower-level paraplegic may be self-sufficient with a few hours of homemaker services. Underrepresentation of PAS needs will result in the patient not having adequate services to maintain him throughout his lifetime and will likely lead to a higher rate of complications and hospitalization and, in extreme cases, reduced life expectancy. Overestimating the PAS needs will result in an inaccurate, unjustifiable, and more expensive plan that is unfair to all parties involved.

There are a number of tables that can be used to provide a starting point on what a person's functional level is anticipated to be, given his or her neurological level of spinal cord injury. Comprehensive tables available include those published in Blackwell et al. (1994), Staas et al. (1993), and Braddom (1995). A more complete discussion of these issues can be found in Blackwell et al. (2001) and Harrell and Krause (2002).

The above references and tables are intended to serve only as guides in making projections about the types of support an individual will need. There are patients who will function with less care and others who will require much greater care, given their unique sets of circumstances; thus, each person must be evaluated individually. Failure of a patient to meet the projected level of independence does not necessarily mean the patient is not trying, is poorly motivated, or is malingering. The tables referred to above are general starting points. However, there are specific areas in each of these tables that these authors have serious disagreements with, and we do not, by noting them here, suggest that we wholeheartedly agree with the recommendations in these publications.

It is well recognized that the most expensive component of present and future care is the area of support services or personal assistance services. PAS includes attendant care, homemaker services, driver services, and home/lawn maintenance. Several studies have attempted to identify the average charges or expense for these services (Berkowitz et al., 1992, 1998; Devivo et al., 1995). These studies have attempted to identify cost of PAS as an average in cohorts, with questionable success. The studies do not in anyway represent the actual needs for PAS. Data from these studies are not intended to apply to a specific individual. In addition to limitations of the studies, the authors warn that the data should not be used to project the future needs of an individual. The LCP is a needs-based assessment and must be written to reflect the actual need of the person with SCI. Harrell and Krause (2002) specifically state, "it would be irresponsible, and a breach of our professional duties and responsibilities as life care planners, not to endeavor to articulate this need." Many factors affect the number of hours of PAS required as well as the level of training required. Some include the level of SCI, age at onset of SCI, sex, comorbidities, SCI complications, duration of SCI, effects of aging with SCI, obesity, cognitive ability, compliance, and level of psychological adjustment. Guidelines for hours of PAS have been published by the Consortium for Spinal Cord Injury (1999), *Outcomes Following Traumatic Spinal Cord Injury*. This has been adapted by Blackwell et al. (2001) and is presented with permission in Table 18.2. The guidelines are not intended to be prescriptive, but are a guide to understand PAS needs in SCI. In addition, it should be recognized that projections are based on the average SCI case (i.e., young, healthy, and male).

Relying on family members to provide PAS is inadequate and leads to adverse effects on the family. Burnout, fatigue, exhaustion, stress, loss of intimacy, and social isolation are some of the more common problems (Blackwell et al., 2001). Families serving as caregivers do so at considerable cost to themselves, increasing their risk for health problems. Caregivers who find that role stressful have a mortality risk 63% higher than noncaregivers over a 4-year period (Schulz & Beach, 1999). Private hire of PAS has hidden costs and problems described in the article by Thomas, Kitchen's discussion of "Private Hire: The Real Cost," which is summarized in Chapter 30. Harrell reports that the reality of self-managed care can be burdensome. "It is often difficult to find appropriate caregivers … the identification and screening of appropriate assistant candidates is difficult even for professionals" (Harrell, 2002).

In cases where a high level of PAS is required, recommending nursing home placement absent compelling reasons is considered at the very least inadequate and likely unethical. Harrell and Krause's (2002) comments earlier about the life care planners' obligation to develop a needs-driven report speaks to this issue. Nursing home placement typically results in a reduced quality of life for people

Table 18.2 Hours per Day of Assistance by Level of Injury and FIM™ Instrument

Level of Injury	Assistance Required	FIM™ [a]	NSCISC Median [b]	NSCISC Interquartile Range [c]
C1–C3	24-hour attendant care, to include homemaking	24 hours/day	24 hours/day	12–24 hours/day
C4	24-hour care, to include homemaking	24 hours/day	24 hours/day	16–24 hours/day
C5	Personal care[d]: 10 hours/day Homemaking[e]: 6 hours/day	16 hours/day	23 hours/day	10–24 hours/day
C6	Personal care: 6 hours/day Homemaking: 4 hours/day	10 hours/day	17 hours/day	8–24 hours/day
C7–C8	Personal care: 6 hours/day Homemaking: 2 hours/day	8 hours/day	12 hours/day	2–24 hours/day
T1–T9	Homemaking: 3 hours/day	2 hours/day	3 hours/day	0–15 hours/day
T10–L1	Homemaking: 2 hours/day	2 hours/day	2 hours/day	0–8 hours/day
L2–S5	Homemaking: 0–1 hours/day	0–1 hours/day	0 hours/day	0–2 hours/day

[a] Expected FIM™ instrument outcomes based on expert clinical consensus.
[b] Median FIM estimates, as compiled by NSCISC.
[c] Interquartile range for NSCISC FIM data.
[d] Personal care includes hands-on delivery of all aspects of self-care and mobility, as well as safety interventions.
[e] Homemaking activities include meal planning and preparation and home management.

Adapted from *Outcomes Following Traumatic Spinal Cord Injury: Clinical Practice Guidelines for Health-Care Professionals* by the Consortium for Spinal Cord Medicine, 13–20, by Paralyzed Veterans of America, 1999. Adapted with permission.

with SCI (Harrell, 2002; Duggan et al., 2002). Duggan et al. (2002) indicate that in today's managed care environment, a focus on cost containment has resulted in the SCI population being discharged earlier and more likely facing nursing home placement. The national SCI model system database reveals a significant increase in discharges to nursing homes from 3% in 1977 to 6% by 1993, and such discharges may be in excess of 8% today. The authors state, "the typical skilled nursing home facility may not be equipped to provide the necessary level and intensity of SCI care demanded" (2002). The study identified numerous problems in nursing home care, such as:

- Failure of staff to answer call buzzers
- Insufficient attention to personal privacy
- Absence of routine self-care activities, or self-care that was provided haphazardly or irregularly

- Failure to give bowel and bladder care timely with bowel and bladder routines virtually disappearing
- Functional gains made in rehab lost
- Verbal and physical abuse by staff
- Increased rates of complications experienced by the cohort
- Repeat hospitalizations, and an overall pattern of instability
- Lack of economic power as the reason for nursing home placement

The Supreme Court on June 22, 1999, decided *Olmstead v. L.C.* (527 U.S. 581, 1999), ruling that institutionalization of a person with a disability when a physician deems community treatment equally beneficial "is properly regarded as discrimination based on disability." President George W. Bush in his New Freedom Initiative committed to signing an order supporting the most integrated community-based settings for individuals with disabilities (Bush, 2001). In addition, the Department of Health and Human Services prepared a report for the Congress that indicates 90% of nursing homes do not have enough workers to properly care for patients (Pear, 2002). The report to Congress still has not been released to the public at the time of this writing. However, the preliminary implications by Kathryn Allen, Director, Health Care — Medicaid and Private Health Insurance Issues, are available from the U.S. General Accounting Office in publication GA0-01-1167T, titled *Implications of Supreme Court's Olmstead Decision Are Still Unfolding*. Nursing homes have been implemented as reservoirs of multiple antibiotic-resistant bacteria (Wiener et al., 1999). *JAMA* (September 1998, Volume 280, Number 12), in its medical news and perspectives section, discusses unacceptable nursing home deaths and reports that two thirds of deaths where autopsy was done revealed that the causes were treatable. In addition, 3113 nursing home residents died avoidable deaths from malnutrition, dehydration, urinary tract infection, bowel obstruction, or bedsores in 971 nursing homes in 1993 alone. Clearly recommending nursing home placement absent compelling reasons in this physician author's opinion is unacceptable life care planning practice.

Psychological and Vocational Rehabilitation Issues

Adjustment to disability and community reintegration are crucial factors that have an effect on quality of life and longevity. Clinical depression is five times more common in the SCI population than the general population (Kemp et al., 1999). Sufficient attention must be provided in this area in the life care plan to ensure that an adequate adjustment to disability is achieved by the patient, and that he can reassume a functional role in his community.

Vocational goals should be assessed when appropriate and require the expertise of a vocational counselor who is knowledgeable in spinal cord injury. Rehabilitation engineering or assistive technology may be very useful to the spinal cord injured patient's successful return to productivity (Weed & Field, 1994). Recreational activities have an important impact not only on the patient but on her family as well. Attempts should be made to assess the person's important preinjury recreational activities and to reintegrate her into these activities to the extent possible and appropriate given her injury level. For example, an outdoor enthusiast who hunted frequently may be accommodated with an all-terrain vehicle and appropriate hunting-assisted devices. Some activities may have specific benefits. For example, a tetraplegic may exercise the pulmonary system with blow darts.

As previously noted, sexual adjustment and marital relationship issues must be considered in the life care plan. Berkowitz et al. (1992) reports that the rate of divorce in SCI is twice as high as in the general population. Females with SCI reported a lack of meaningful relationship, and sexuality counseling is frustrating (Pentland et al., 2002). Appropriate counseling should be provided to both the individual with the spinal cord injury and the spouse or significant other. This may require consideration for family adjustment, which is frequently an issue after spinal cord injury. All members of the family, including the children, have suffered losses and may need to have available some level of support and counseling to assist with their readjustment.

The life care plan must ensure that the patient's highest functional level is achieved and maintained throughout his or her lifetime. The support services that are provided have the major impact in this area. Patients should have adequate access to individuals who can assist in improving and maintaining their strength, endurance, and range of motion. They should be given the opportunity to learn advanced wheelchair skills and improved community mobility.

Medical Follow-Up

The spinal cord injured patient will require physician evaluations and treatment. The required physician specialties and evaluations will depend on the patient's level of injury and unique situation. In general, every spinal cord injured person should have a physiatrist if one is available in the local community. Additional physicians and specialties based on individual needs that often are periodically required include urology, internal medicine, neurosurgery, orthopedist, pulmonary medicine, podiatry, and plastic surgery. Laboratory evaluations will include complete blood counts (CBCs), sequential multiple analysis (SMAs), urinalyses (UAs), urine cultures and sensitivities, renal ultrasounds, intravenous pyelograms (IVPs), electrocardiograms (EKGs), x-rays, and magnetic resonance imaging (MRI).

In most cases, periodic physical therapy and occupational therapy evaluations will be required. Additional support services may include respiratory therapy, particularly with a higher-level injury. Biannual, annual, or semiannual spinal cord injury evaluations (depending on individual needs) by a team of experts should be provided in order to reassess the patient's functional status, evaluate medication needs, train new caregivers, introduce new equipment and technology to the patient, reduce the likelihood of complications, and improve the level of overall care provided to the patient. These evaluations can be provided in a specialty spinal cord treatment center or by a local team that is particularly knowledgeable and expert in providing these services. A systematic assessment by an interdisciplinary team knowledgeable in SCI is essential (Whiteneck & Menter, 1993).

Transportation

Transportation to medical appointments, work, recreation, or shopping can be a significant issue for patients with spinal cord injuries. Initially, lower-level paraplegics may do well with an automobile and hand controls. A Braun car topper may be adequate for wheelchair storage, or a patient may be able to store the wheelchair behind the driver's seat. Tetraplegics or aging paraplegics may require an accessible van with a wheelchair lift. In general, parking should be covered since protection from the elements is important. Some vans are designed to fit into a standard garage. However, most have a raised roof that may prevent the use of standard carports or garages.

Supplies/Medications

As the life care planner probably expects, supplies can be a major part of the life care plan. Catheters and bladder management-related materials, chux, bowel program supplies, skin care products, dilatation sticks, latex gloves, sanitation supplies, etc., will be required. A strategy to assess this need is to obtain a list of suppliers and request a printout of the products obtained over the past 6 months. This list will usually provide a complete picture, including amount, size, usage, and cost. Often lists of medications from the pharmacist will reveal forgotten complications that should be considered in the life care plan. The plan should include provisions for changes for additional supplies in the future.

Vocational Considerations

Many individuals with a spinal cord injury will be able to enter the labor market (Devivo et al., 1995; Krause & Anson, 1996; Krause, 1996). The number one factor for successful employment is amount of education. As one may expect, the higher the education level, the more likely the spinal cord injured is able to find employment (Krause & Anson, 1996; Krause, 1996). Other influences include level of injury, with paraplegics more likely to be employed than tetraplegics. Race also seems to play a role, with Caucasians finding employment more often than minorities. With regard to race, it is interesting to note that current research reports that minority women are more likely to be employed than minority men, but Caucasian men are more likely to be employed than Caucasian women (Krause & Anson, 1996). With regard to age, spinal cord injured people in the age group of 41 to 50 were more likely to be employed than cohorts who were younger or older. One study reports that people working at the time of their injury had a better chance of finding employment than people who were not working (Devivo et al., 1995). Of interest, only 74% of the participants in one study were working at the time of their injury (Krause & Anson, 1996). Their employment rate was 25% at the time of the study. However, even if they were not currently working, 42% of Caucasians and 23% of minorities reported working at some point since their injury. It is also noted that it may take several years to adequately recover from injury and obtain employment skills. The employment rate continued to rise for more than 8 years postinjury. Krause (1996) also notes that clients who are socially active have a better chance of employment.

Earning capacity is another related issue. Even though the client may be employed, he may not be working full-time. In addition, clients' ability to choose jobs, ascend up the promotion ladder, and otherwise maximize their earning potential is likely compromised. They may also retire earlier or miss workdays due to medical treatment for complications or periodic evaluations. The comprehensive life care plan will reduce the potential for complications and provide vocational support that enhances the potential for suitable employment.

The life care plan should address the costs for assisting clients with preparing for employment if this work is a reasonable option. Potential costs could include:

- Tuition and fees
- Books and supplies
- Computer technology designed to reduce physical effort (such as IBM voice type, Dragon Dictate, Kurzweil, Voice Master, smaller keyboards, keyboard panel, head points, etc.)
- Workstations (such as AbleOffice, produced by the Center for Assistive Technology and Environmental Access, Georgia Institute of Technology, Atlanta, GA)
- Vocational evaluation, vocational counseling, job placement assistance, job coaching, and related costs

Many life care planners are not vocational experts and may easily overlook or fail to include support for this important quality of life issue. It is suggested that the life care planner include a vocational expert as a part of the team.

AGING WITH SPINAL CORD INJURY

Numerous changes occur as an individual ages, and people with spinal cord injury are no exception. In fact, there is evidence that the spinal cord injured tend to age faster or experience some of the changes commonly associated with aging earlier. The LCP should anticipate the change in functional status of the person due to SCI, and reflect changing equipment and PAS needs. A model of aging with SCI is useful in projecting functional decline (Menter, 1993). See Figure 18.2.

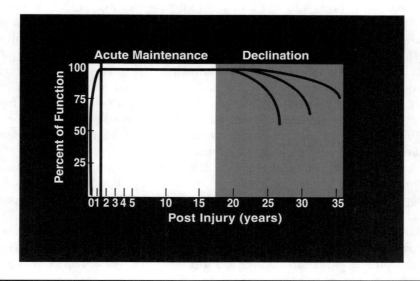

Figure 18.2 Model of aging and physical disability in SCI by Menter, 1993. Reprinted with permission.

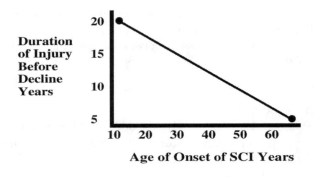

Figure 18.3   Decline after SCI relationship to age of onset of SCI. Reprinted with permission.

Essentially the graph has three components in terms of level of independence achieved, rate of decline, and length of maintenance phase. First is the level of functional recovery achieved with rehab after onset of SCI. Second is a maintenance phase of variable length in time from a few months to 20 years or more. The last identified phase is the declining phase due to aging, SCI complications, and comorbidities. The slope of this curve, or the rate of decline, is variable from person to person. Many individualized factors affect each component or phase of Menter's model of aging with SCI. Thompson and Kemp have described the effect of one variable, the age of the person at onset of SCI. When the person is older at onset of SCI, the maintenance phase is shorter in a linear inverse relationship; see Figure 18.3.

This phenomenon is a function of both the absolute age of the individual and the number of years the individual has had the disability. As a result, the patient has changing needs throughout the course of his lifetime. The life care plan should reflect this change in needs by incorporating appropriate services and equipment to meet the anticipated need as the individual ages. For example, it can be anticipated that an individual who has had a spinal cord injury for 20 to 25 years and has been using a manual wheelchair will have more difficulty with upper-extremity pain and complications and may consider switching to a power wheelchair. Similarly, the patient may have more difficulty with transfers and self-care needs and require a higher level of attendant care.

Secondary conditions of SCI are common. As life expectancy has increased for people with SCI, so has morbidity from secondary conditions. In a survey of 117 people with SCI with a mean proportion of 35 disabled life years, respondents reported having experienced, in the year prior to interview, a mean of 6.5 of 17 secondary conditions. The most prevalent were spasms, 87%; UTIs, 73%; skin breakdown, 66%; fatigue, 64%; chronic pain, 49%; bowel problems, 47%; autonomic dysreflexia, 46%; anxiety, 43%; and depression, 42%. Difficulty with independence with regard to activities of daily living and with access to medical care was significantly associated with reports of more secondary conditions (Meyers et al., 2000). Seekins and Ravesloot (2000) conducted a similar survey on 73 rural

SCI survivors in Montana who averaged 11 years since onset of SCI, reporting an average of 16 secondary conditions. This "suggests that many people with disabilities living in rural communities are faring far more poorly than might be expected" (Seekins & Ravesloot, 2000). Surveys of secondary conditions in veterans show a similar prevalence, confirming that serious but preventable secondary conditions are common and take an important toll on people living with SCI (Prysak et al., 2000).

Women aging with SCI have concerns unique and distinctive from males. Pentland has completed a review and describes the concerns felt to be essential for women with SCI to plan and prepare for their later years. Women are more likely to face the aging process alone. They report heavier menstrual flow with age, and wheelchair transfers cause "flooding" by creating surges in menstrual flow. Many in their early 40s report menopause symptoms. Frequency of UTIs and incontinence episodes increases as does bowel care needs. Worsening upper-limb pain interferes with ADL and sleep. Most experience fatigue and reduced stamina, making napping necessary. Those with partners report they are increasingly relying on them for PAS, which is perceived as both a threat and loss to both parties. Many report more "down" days, increased anxiety, marked absent-mindedness, and tearfulness. The age-related changes exacerbate the need for continual adjustment. The women indicated that well-trained attendants who are knowledgeable about SCI can play a significant role in averting medical problems (Pentland et al., 2002). Women in general required more PAS than men (Berkowitz et al., 1992).

For research regarding aging and spinal cord injury, excellent sources include Menter (1995), Stover (1995), Whiteneck et al. (1991), and Yarkony et al. (1988). Menter has described general physiological changes that occur with aging, such as:

- Loss of muscle mass
- Decreased strength
- Decreased range of motion
- Increasing osteoarthritis
- Increasing problems with urinary and bowel management

These aging-related risks combined together can lead to increased pain and decreased functional status. When these effects occur in the spinal cord injured, they are additive and accelerate the decline of the person's functional status. Menter's (1993) model of aging predicts a functional decline that will begin between 15 and 20 years postinjury for the average spinal cord injured patient. Some of the specific problems associated with aging include:

1. Pain has been reported to occur in over 90% of individuals with a spinal cord injury (Melzack, 1978). There are several types of pain that can increase with time. One type is musculoskeletal pain from overuse of the upper extremities, osteoarthritic changes, and other causes. Another type is a central pain from the spinal cord injury that is usually described as a burning dysesthetic-type pain that has been reported to increase with aging. A neurological pain can develop due to poor posture, arthritic changes at the spinal column, or peripheral nerve entrapments that will

further deteriorate the patient's functional status. Woozly and Young (1995) have reported that pain is frequently a major lifelong management issue in patients with traumatic myelopathy. Potential sources of the pain include bones, ligaments, spinal meninges, cauda equina, and the spinal cord itself (Schmitt et al., 1995). Local pain at the level of the spinal cord injury may be addressed with surgical procedures even after having been present for a number of years (Bohlman et al., 1994). In one report the cervical and shoulder pain in a cape-like distribution common in tetraplegia is felt to be related to an associated orthostatic hypotension (Cariga et al., 2002). Persistent pain is a prevalent problem of community-residing people with SCI and likely to affect activity levels (Widerstrom-Noga et al., 2002). Pain control techniques such as physical therapy, transcutaneous electrical nerve stimulation (TENS) unit, electrical stimulation, and whirlpool therapy should be considered. In some cases, the individual may require an inpatient pain management program.

2. Spasticity has been reported to increase with time and can become quite problematic and difficult to control. As an individual ages, he or she may no longer tolerate the medications to treat the spasticity and require the placement of an intrathecal Baclofen pump. Spasticity may require additional physical therapy, whirlpool treatments, or electrical stimulation to control.

3. Because as a person ages he has a decline in strength and increasing weakness, it is not surprising that fatigue has been reported as one of the most common problems affecting lifestyle and quality of life and is a difficult problem to treat. Contrary to popular belief, wheelchair propulsion and other functional activities such as transfers do not significantly increase upper-extremity strength (Kotajarvi et al., 2002). Fatigue can best be addressed by providing more assistive equipment, reducing the level of activity, or providing additional personal care services.

4. There is mounting evidence that there are physiological and hormonal changes in the spinal cord injured population that contribute to aging at a faster rate than the able-bodied population. Tsitouras and colleagues (1995) have documented abnormally low levels of serum testosterone, growth hormone, and insulin-like growth factors in individuals with spinal cord injuries that predispose the individual to age-related changes. Over time there is little doubt that other changes will be discovered that correlate with Menter's theory that the spinal cord injured person ages at a faster rate.

Spinal Cord Injury and Life Expectancy

A common question asked of the physician is related to the effects of the injury on life expectancy. Although treatment for complications has improved dramatically over time, available statistics continue to reflect a reduced life expectancy. However, life expectancy is clearly improving as care improves and complications are effectively managed. Morbidity and mortality associated with SCI are due not to the neurological deficits per se but to its complications. Survival rates greatly improved with systematic prevention and treatment of SCI complications. SCI survival in Israel was found to be only slightly lower for the hospitalized population

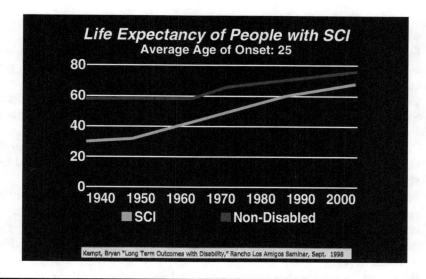

Figure 18.4   Life expectancy of people with SCI. Reprinted with permission.

in Israel. Surviving 5 years or longer predicts a long life expectancy (Catz et al., 2002). Figure 18.4 illustrates the trend of improving longevity.

In general, research demonstrates that the higher the injury, the more the loss. For example, a 40-year-old male tetraplegic who is ventilator dependent will statistically die sooner than a similar tetraplegic who is not on a ventilator, and a 40-year-old male paraplegic will statistically have a longer life expectancy than both tetraplegic patients noted above. Two discussions of life expectancy in SCI are provided in recent publications (DeVivo, 2002; Krause, 2002). DeVivo (2002) indicates that tables can only provide rough estimates of life expectancy, as categories are broad data with considerable variability within each category. Also, factors such as gender, race, time since injury, the trend toward longer life expectancy, and preexisting medical conditions should be considered. Krause (2002) argues that standard approaches to estimating life expectancy are inadequate, do not consider important social variables, and result in the most conservative estimates. In addition, Krause (2002) reports that individuals with Medicaid or Medicare as the primary sponsor of care have a 1.47 to 2.31 greater likelihood of mortality. Individuals having adequate access to care and PAS are going to have a lower rate of mortality and concludes that income is a major factor to be considered in life expectancy.

General Considerations

It is difficult to rely on statistics for specific clients since many elements can affect longevity. There are several factors to consider, such as:

- Diagnosis: The type and level of injury has the most obvious impact.
- Intelligence: The ability to comprehend, comply, and participate in the management of their injury directly affects quality of care. A patient with severe mental retardation or with a brain injury and a spinal cord injury

is less able to assist in his own care or recognize complications than someone who does not have a cognitive impairment.

■ Education: This probably is related to intelligence and refers to understanding the educational value of learning about their situation to prevent complications or to accommodate the disability.

■ Quality of care: Poor quality of care can lead to unobserved complications that can be life threatening. Good medical follow-up can intervene in complications before they become expensive or life threatening.

■ Compliance: Lack of compliance in medicine is a well-known problem. For example, a poor weight shift schedule can lead to serious and expensive skin breakdown care.

■ Personality and psychological state: Also related to compliance is the person's ability to train and get along with caregivers. Good and assertive communicators are better able to convey their needs than shy, ineffective patients. Also, clients with poor psychological adjustment may be harmful to themselves.

■ Family support: Another well-known and researched attribute is the client's family support system. Overall, the better the support, the better the recovery and adjustment.

■ Home vs. institution: The client's place of residence can have an effect by subjecting the patient to virulent diseases if she is in a nursing home. Also, staff who work for the facility are often less responsive to patients than staff whose paychecks come directly from the client. In addition, staff who work for a facility may have several patients to manage, whereas clients at home usually are the attendant's only responsibility.

Risk Factors

As with the general population, there are risk factors that the physician must consider when opining about the patient's life expectancy:

■ Age: As noted above, aging leaves patients with reduced ability to rebound from illness and complications.

■ Sex: Males generally are expected to have a shorter life span.

■ History of complications: Some patients have a history of problems that can be serious with regard to life expectancy. Upper respiratory infections, skin breakdown, and serious spasticity are just a few examples.

■ Diseases: As noted previously, patients with diabetes pose greater problems than patients without this disease. Preexisting cancer, diabetes, cardiovascular disease, or other diseases may be a factor.

■ Smoking: Smoking is a well-known life-reducing activity. Tetraplegics with already impaired respiration may be at even more risk.

■ Substance abuse: Alcoholism or drug addiction can significantly affect the patient's basic physical well-being, as well as detrimentally affect his or her judgment. For example, one patient who became a paraplegic from an automobile accident after drinking was rendered a tetraplegic when he had another motor vehicle accident after drinking.

■ Good or bad genetics: Family history has been linked to longevity.

In summary, to project the patient's life expectancy, the life care planner should consult a physician with regard to this topic in order to consider the individual's unique factors. A strong caution must be given on attempting to apply generalized statistics to a specific person with a spinal cord injury. Deutsch and Sawyer (1996) have an excellent discussion on the problems of "mindless use of data." The available information must be reviewed and interpreted by a physician experienced and knowledgeable in the field of spinal cord injury. Currently available data, in all likelihood, underrepresent true life expectancy of spinal cord injured individuals.

For patients who appear to have higher risk factors for shortened life expectancy, the life care planner should make fair and reasonable attempts to provide a level of care in the plan to reduce the risk to the extent possible.

CASE STUDY

This 46-year-old Missouri client was injured in a motor vehicle accident resulting in mild brain injury and C4–C5 spinal cord injury. The client demonstrates no functional capabilities with three of his extremities, although he has enough motion in his right upper extremity to control his wheelchair. He wears a tracheostomy (trach) as a result of his inability to cough appropriately, and suctioning of his secretions reportedly is required several times per day. Additionally, he speaks with the aid of a Passy Muir speaking valve that is attached to his trach. The client has experienced several complications, and the future medical care requirements are more detailed than most. The life care plan follows.

CONCLUSION

Spinal cord injury represents a complex array of medical challenges to the life care planner. Fortunately, enough research exists to effectively plan for the patient's needs with regard to care, products, supplies, and equipment. A detailed analysis of the patient's situation, review of medical records, and knowledge of the available literature, as well as the participation of a qualified physician, will assist the life care planner with a quality and effective road map of care that will enhance the patient's life.

LIFE CARE PLAN

Note: For purposes of this plan, the following initials are placed in parentheses according to their respective recommendations:

RE = Reedi Eates, M.D., gastroenterologist
RW = Roger Weed, Ph.D., certified life care planner
TW = Terry Winkler, M.D., consulting physiatrist

Routine Future Medical Care — Physician Only

Recommendation (by whom)	Year Initiated and Frequency	Purpose	Expected Cost
Physiatrist (TW)	3 times/year to life expectancy	Assess medical status to address/prevent complications	$300–600/year at $100–200/visit (depends on length of visit and complexity of exam)
Urologist (TW)	2 times/year to life expectancy	Monitor neurogenic bladder and urological functioning	$200–400/year at $100–200/visit
Renal ultrasound or renogram (TW)	Every other year to life expectancy		Ultrasound: $235–280
Cystoscopy/urodynamics (TW)	1 time/year to life expectancy		Cystoscopy: $325–400
Pulmonologist (TW)	3–6 times/year to life	Monitor respiratory status and tracheostomy	Initial: $100–400 (includes x-ray and pulmonary function tests)
Chest x-ray	1–2 times/year (average) to life expectancy		Follow-up: $65–170/visit $65–100 each (depending on single view, etc.)
Complete pulmonary function test (TW)	1–2 times/year (average) to life expectancy		$65–300 each (depending on specific tests needed)

Note 1: Costs do not include cultures of trachea secretions to survey for pathogens or other diagnostic tests that cannot accurately be determined at this time.

Note 2: The client continues to require a tracheostomy (trach). Presume trach and related supplies will be needed to life expectancy. See also related medical equipment and related supplies.

Provider	Frequency	Purpose	Cost
Orthopedist (TW)	1 time/year to life expectancy	Monitor heterotopic ossification formation and reduce or prevent complications	$100–200/year depending on length and complexity of visit

Note: Cost does not include x-rays or other diagnostic tests that cannot accurately be determined at this time.

Provider	Frequency	Purpose	Cost
Podiatrist (TW)	3 times/year (average)	Toenail care and cutting	Initial: $45–130 (depending on length of visit) Follow-up: $44–46/visit
Plastic surgeon (TW)	2–4 times/year (average) to life expectancy	Monitor skin care and prevent/manage skin breakdown	$164–328/year to life expectancy at $82/visit (2001)
Internist/general practitioner (TW)	2–4 times/year over and above general population	General medical care and treatment of acute complications	$120–320/year at $60–80 for Level III visit (2001)
Annual influenza vaccination (TW)	1 time/year		$20/year (2001)
Pneumococcal pneumonia vaccine (TW)	1 time only	1 time only	$25, 1 time only (2001)

Note 1: The frequency of routine future medical care assumes the client's complications are well controlled. It is expected that the client will experience complications; however, the frequency, type, and severity are difficult to predict. Also see Potential Complications.

Note 2: The client may also need evaluation and/or follow-up by other specialists, including gastroenterologist, pulmonologist, and others as needed depending on complications and at the discretion of his primary physician.

Projected Evaluations — Nonphysician

(Include all allied health evaluations)

Recommendation (by whom)	Year Initiated	Frequency/Duration	Expected Cost
Physical therapy evaluation (TW)	2002	1 time/year to life expectancy	$150–352 for initial 30- to 60-minute evaluation, then $150–180/year thereafter to life expectancy
Occupational therapy evaluation (TW)	2002	1 time/year to life expectancy	$150–352 for initial 30- to 60-minute evaluation, then $150–180/year thereafter to life expectancy
Nutritional/dietary evaluation (TW)	2002	1 time/year to life expectancy	$60–70/year for 1-hour consultation
Psychological evaluation (RW)	2002	1 time only	$125–175 (depending on specific tests administered)

Note: One of the psychologists contacted stated that he sees the client for a 1-hour initial visit at $125 to obtain a thorough case history and then will recommend psychological testing, if appropriate, based on the initial evaluation. If indicated, cost for testing is $300 to $400 at $100/hour for 3 to 4 hours of testing (approximately).

Recommendation (by whom)	Year Initiated	Frequency/Duration	Expected Cost
Therapeutic recreation evaluation with report and recommendations (RW)	2002	1 time only	$176–352 for 30- to 60-minute evaluation
Home accessibility evaluation (see also Architectural Considerations)	2002 (or when move to new home)	1 time only	$100 for 1-hour in-home OT evaluation (2001)

Note: An occupational therapist with experience and expertise in home accessibility and assistive technology is recommended to evaluate the client's home as well as make recommendations for assistive technology devices for in-home use.

Projected Therapeutic Modalities

Recommendation (by whom)	Year Initiated	Frequency/Duration	Expected Cost
Physical therapy (in addition to daily range of motion by caregivers) (TW)	2002	3 times/year to evaluate in-home program and make recommendations	$270–333/year at $90–111/visit
Counseling (individual and/or couple) for adjustment to disability, coping strategies, problem solving, etc. (RW)	Unknown*	Unknown*	Unknown*

*Note: The client's need for and frequency of counseling will be dependent upon outcome of psychological evaluation.

Sexual evaluation/counseling (TW)	2002	1-time evaluation	$0; included in urological evaluation

Note 1: Dr. Winkler suggests options that may be appropriate for the client include a trial dose of Viagra, an Erectaide device, and/or Prostaglandin injections; however, occurrence and frequency depend on outcome of urological evaluation. See also Potential Complications.

Note 2: Sexual counseling also may be a component of the comprehensive rehabilitation day program at the spinal cord injury rehabilitating center.

Case manager to problem solve, coordinate care, client advocate, hire caregivers, oversee case, etc. (RW)	2002 (immediate need)	4 hours/week (average) for 1 year, then 4 hours/month (average) to life expectancy	$15,600–16,432 for first year, then $3600–3792/year (average), thereafter at $75–79/hour

Diagnostic Testing/Educational Assessment

Recommendation (by whom)	Year Initiated	Frequency/Duration	Expected Cost
Optional Neuropsychological evaluation (RW)	2002	1 time only	$900 with report and recommendations

Wheelchair Needs

Recommendation (by whom)	Year Purchased	Replacement Schedule	Expected Cost
Invacare Action Arrow power wheelchair with joystick controls, recline system, elevated leg rests, arm rests, head rest, etc. (TW)	4/8/98 (already has)	Every 4–5 years depending on use	$16,074 retail (negotiated cost at $13,341)
Reclining manual wheelchair for backup mobility (TW)	2002 (immediate need)	Every 10 years (estimate) depending on amount of use	$3000 (average)
Shower wheelchair for bathing and hygiene (assumes accessible bathroom) (TW)	2002 (immediate need)	Every 4–5 years depending on wear and tear	$1500 (average)
Tilt table for stand-up capability (TW)	2002–2020 (age 65)	Every 10 years (estimate) depending on amount of use to 2020	$1184–3799 for manual table or electric/manual combination table (2001)

Wheelchair Accessories and Maintenance

Recommendation (by whom)	Year Purchased	Replacement Schedule	Expected Cost
Roho wheelchair cushion (TW)	2000 (already has)	Every 2 years (average)	$399
2 cushion covers		1 time/year	$50/year
Note: It is recommended the client have two cushion covers — one to be used as backup when the primary cover is being laundered or otherwise unable to be used.			
2 gel batteries for wheelchair (TW)	1998	1 time/year	$350 for pair

Note: According to the client's wheelchair vendor, a battery charger comes with the purchase of a wheelchair and, if properly used and maintained, should not need replacement sooner than the wheelchair. Replacement cost, if needed, is $450.

Recommendation (by whom)	Year Purchased	Replacement	Expected Cost
Power wheelchair maintenance (TW)	2002	1 time/year and as needed after 1-year warranty	Expect 10% cost of chair/year
Manual wheelchair maintenance (TW)	2003 (or 1 year after purchase of manual backup wheelchair)	1 time/year and as needed after 1-year warranty	Expect 10% cost of chair/year
Shower wheelchair maintenance (TW) (assumes accessible bathroom)	2003 (or 1 year after purchase of shower wheelchair)	1 time/year and as needed after 1-year warranty	$100/year (average)
Allowance for wheelchair carry bag, laptop tray, beverage holder, ECU holder, etc. (TW)	2002	1 time/year	$50/year (average)

Orthotics/Prosthetics

Recommendation (by whom)	Year Purchased	Replacement	Expected Cost
Bilateral resting hand splints (TW)	2002	1–2 times/year (average)	$33–60 standard (Sammons Catalog)
Bilateral resting ankle splints (TW)	2002	Every 2 years (average)	$40–65 standard (Sammons Catalog)

Assistive Technology/Aids for Independent Function

Recommendation (by whom)	Year Purchased	Replacement Schedule	Expected Cost
Mobile Arm Support Feeder with elevating forearm mechanism that attaches to wheelchair to assist with right-hand feeding (TW, RW) Training by occupational therapist in proper use (TW, RW)	2002 (upon completion of intensive and comprehensive rehabilitation program) to life expectancy	Every 5 years (average)	$325 (includes instruction manual and reclining wheelchair feeder bracket); if Winsford Feeder is needed, cost = $2960 (2001) $0; it is presumed training can be provided by the OT during the rehabilitation program and monitored by the OT during annual evaluations

Assistive Technology/Aids for Independent Function (Continued)

Recommendation (by whom)	Year Purchased	Replacement Schedule	Expected Cost
Allowance for assistive technology devices/aids for independent function such as mouth sticks, page turner, tabletop docking station, swivel docking station, pillow splints, handheld shower, etc. (RW)	2002	1 time/year to life expectancy	$100/year (average)
Computer system, printer, and Internet access (RW)	2002	Life expectancy	No cost over general population
Rehabilitation technology evaluation to develop in-home workstation (RW)	2002	1 time only to determine modifications and develop accessible work area for home use	$4000 (estimate) for evaluation and custom-designed area

Home Furnishings and Accessories

Recommendation (by whom)	Year Purchased	Replacement Schedule	Expected Cost
Invacare Hospital Bed (semielectric)	1998 (already has)	Frame: 1-time-only purchase (see Note 2)	$2030 (actual retail cost of current bed)
Excel 8000 air flotation mattress	1999 (already has)	Every 10 years (estimate) depending on wear and tear	$1798 (actual retail cost of current mattress)
Maintenance (to include mattress covers, etc.)	2002	1 time/year or as needed after warranty and depending on wear and tear	$100/year (estimate)

Note 1: If skin breakdown continues to be a problem, the client will require a high-technology skin pressure relief bed system (such as Clinitron or similar). Cost is up to $100/day or $36,500/year.

Note 2: An option to allow the client and his wife to sleep in the same bed is a queen-size adjustable bed by Invacare. Cost is $2100.

Recommendation	Year Purchased	Replacement Schedule	Expected Cost
Overbed table (TW)	2002	Every 15 years (estimate)	$100–200
Power Patient Lift System with split sling (TW)	2002 (immediate need)	Lift: 1 time only Sling: Every other year	Lift: $2604–3703 Sling: $165–198

Note 1: Dr. Winkler recommends a more advanced lift system that will be easier for the caregivers to use and will transfer the client in a safer way. The new lift also does not require the client to sit on the sling all day, which could potentially reduce the complications he has with skin breakdown.

Note 2: It is recommended the client have two lift slings — one to be used as backup when the primary sling is being laundered or otherwise unable to be used.

Recommendation	Year Purchased	Replacement Schedule	Expected Cost
Portable ramps (TW)	2002	1 time only	$300–330
Allowance for accessories such as lift maintenance, batteries for speaker telephone, urinals, transfer board, etc. (RW)	2002	1 time/year	$100/year (average)

Medical Equipment

Recommendation (by whom)	Year Purchased	Replacement Schedule	Expected Cost
Vacumax Suction Machine	1999 (already has)	Every 5 years	$800
Suction machine canister	N/A	1 time/month (average)	$109.20/year at $9.10 each
Humidifier	1999 (already has)	Every 5 years	$30–50

Note: If the client requires a more advanced humidifier or air purifier system, cost could be up to $445.

Medical Equipment (Continued)

Recommendation (by whom)	Year Purchased	Replacement Schedule	Expected Cost
Nebulizer with compressor	1999 (already has)	Every 5 years	$165
Air compressor for tracheostomy	1999 (already has)	Every 5 years	$800
Oxygen concentrator	1999 (already has)	Every 5 years	$3500
Pulse oximeter (TW)	2002 (current need)	Every 5 years	Handheld: $1850 Handheld with printer: $2000 Standard: $3000

Note 1: The client states the oxygen equipment is used on an as needed basis and more during winter months and/or times of complications.

Note 2: Dr. Winkler reports that based on a telephone conversation with the client and review of available records, it is presumed the client will require the trach and supplies as well as supplemental oxygen and equipment to life expectancy. For purposes of future care planning, the cost of the trach and related supplies/equipment is included to life.

Drug Needs

Medications will change over time and are representative of the client's current needs.

Recommendation (by whom)	Purpose	Cost per Unit	Cost per Year
Cytotec, 200 mcg, 1 time/day	Prevent ulcers	$128.49/120 tablets	$390.82/year
Albuterol solution, 2.5 mg/3 ml, 2 times/week average	Aid in breathing	$22.49/month (approximately)	$76.90/year (average) at 2 times/week (average)
Dulcolax (Bisacodyl), 10 mg, every other day (TW)	Bowel program	$5.41/30 tablets	$32.91/year
Baclofen, 10 mg, 4 times/day (TW)	Decrease spasticity	$23.49/90 tablets	$381.06/year

Recommendation (by whom)	Purpose	Cost per Unit	Cost per Year
Robitussin, cf. syrup, 5 ml, every 4 hours as needed	Expectorant and cough medication	$7.69/bottle	$184.56/year at 2 bottles/month (average estimate)
Ultram, 50 mg, 2 times/day (per client interview, 12/13/01)	Pain relief	$47.70–71.79 for 60 tablets	$580.35–873.45/year (2001)
Tylenol, 500 mg, 2 times/day (TW)	Pain relief	$12.78/120 tablets	$77.75/year
Vitamin C, 500 mg/day	Vitamin supplement	$1.49/60 tablets	$9.06/year
Zinc sulfate, 220 mg, 2 times/day	Mineral supplement	$14.49/60 tablets	$176.30/year
Allowance for additional as needed medications, i.e., Propulsid, Therevac mini-enemas, Bean-O, autonomic dysreflexia medication, etc.	Gastrointestinal difficulties, bowel management, abdominal gas, episodes of autonomic dysreflexia	N/A	$50/year (estimate)

Note 1: Antibiotics also are prescribed on a regular basis for infections. See Future Medical Care, for expected yearly cost of antibiotic treatment.

Supply Needs

Supplies will change over time and are representative of the client's current needs.

Recommendation (by whom)	Purpose	Cost per Unit	Cost per Year
#16 Foley catheter insertion tray, changed monthly (includes catheter and drainage bag)	Bladder management	$16.43/kit	$230.02/year (see Note below)

Note: According to Dr. Winkler, the client's Foley catheter may need to be changed more frequently during times of urinary tract infections or other complications. Expect approximately 14 catheter changes/year (average).

| Colorectal tube, approximately 1/month (RE) | Relief of distended abdomen | N/A | $0; client no longer uses; see Potential Complications |

Supply Needs (Continued)

Recommendation (by whom)	Purpose	Cost per Unit	Cost per Year
Adult diapers, 1/day (average)	Bowel incontinence	$77.44/case of 72	$392.58/year
Chux bed underpads, 4/day	Incontinence	$56/case of 150	$545.07/year
Power-free gloves, 3/day	Hygiene	$8.50/box of 100	$93.08/year
Tracheostomy collar, 1/month	Respiration	$3	$36/year
Disposable nebulizer, as needed	Respiration/airway clearance	$3	$72/year (approximately) at approximately 2/month
Oxygen cannulas, approximately 10/week	Respiration	$8/week	$416/year
Oxygen mask		$3 each	$36/year at 1/month (average) depending on use
Oxygen adapter for portable oxygen		$1.50 each	$18/year at 1/month depending on use
Trach supplies, including trach tube holders and trach drain bags	Aid in breathing	Expect 1/month depending on frequency of use	$44.80/year $16.25/year
Suction supplies, including cannisters, tubing, 14 Fr catheters, etc., as needed Aerosol tubing (100 feet)	Pulmonary care and aid in suctioning	Estimate 4 times/year depending on use	$76/year at $19 each
Passy–Muir speaking valve	Aid in speaking with tracheostomy	Expect 2 times/year (estimate)	$240/year at $120 each
Blood pressure cuff (purchased in 1998)	Monitor blood pressure	$85 (average) up to $120 (average) for digital every 10–15 years (estimate)	$5.67–12/year

Stethoscope (purchased in 1998)	Monitor heart rate	$15 every 15 years (estimate) or $50 for kit (includes blood pressure cuff and stethoscope)	$1/year or $3.33–5/year for both (Note: If kit purchased, eliminate separate cost for blood pressure cuff above)
Porta-Cath	IV access for antibiotics	N/A	$0; do not expect catheter replacement unless complication
Allowance for sterile gauze pads, kerlex tape, 4 × 4 sponges, Q-tips, ½-inch Dakin strips, foam heel protectors, TED hose for swelling, syringes, contact precaution gowns, rubbing alcohol, hydrogen peroxide, antiseptic wipes, various skin creams, donut ring, etc.	Wound and skin care	N/A	Expect $200/year (average)

Health and Strength Maintenance (Leisure Time Activities)

Recommendation (by whom)	Year of Purchase or Attendance	Replacement or Attendance Schedule	Expected Cost
Daily range of motion to extremities See also Assistive Technology/Aids for Independent Function	2002 to life expectancy	7 days/week, 365 days/year	$0; provided by in-home caregiver
In-home care (TW)	2002 to life expectancy	24 hours/day care, 365 days/year Minimum LPN level of care at 3 shifts/day; see also Note 6 below	LPN: $24–31/hour weekdays, $24–$32/hour weekends Note: One agency ($31 and 32/hour) bills holidays at 1½ time

Health and Strength Maintenance (Leisure Time Activities) (Continued)

Recommendation (by whom)	Year of Purchase or Attendance	Replacement or Attendance Schedule	Expected Cost
Skilled nurse visit, i.e., RN (TW)	2002 to life expectancy	2–6 hours/month (average)	RN: $28–37/hour or $90 (2001) to 105/visit (1999)

Note 1: According to Dr. Winkler, the client requires 24 hours/day care, including nighttime awake care for suctioning, positioning/turning, and emergencies. The agencies based on needs specify minimum LPN level.

Note 2: The client's caregiver must also provide transportation to medical appointments and errands, housekeeping, laundry, meal preparation, bathing, personal care, range-of-motion exercises, and respite to family members who currently provide most of the care.

Note 3: Dr. Winkler reports that the client's home health needs will increase during times of illness, infections, or other complications and states the client will require 24 hours/day care by an RN during those times. According to Dr. Winkler, estimate 7 days/year for 24-hour RN care for increased level of in-home skilled care due to expected complications. Cost of RN care at $28 to $37/hour for 24-hour RN care for increased days/year. Economist to deduct cost of LPN care for 7 days/year while RN care is provided.

Note 4: Economist to deduct the cost of 6 to 12 weeks of in-home nursing care on a one-time-only occurrence for the time in which the client is expected to be in the intensive rehabilitation program. Economist also to deduct expected 4 to 9 hospitalization days/year; see Future Medical Care entries below.

Recommendation (by whom)	Year of Purchase or Attendance	Replacement or Attendance Schedule	Expected Cost
Interior/exterior home maintenance (wife will do homemaker tasks) (TW)	2002 to life expectancy	Expect 2 hours/week (average)	$1040/year at $10/hour (average)

Transportation

Recommendation (by whom)	Year Purchased	Replacement Schedule	Expected Cost
Wheelchair-accessible van with automatic lift, raised roof, wheelchair tie-downs, etc. (TW)	2002 (immediate need)	Every 7–10 years or 70,000–80,000 miles	$42,000 (estimate) and $256/year mileage to appointments. Note to economist: Deduct cost of trade-in vehicle; deduct cost of average vehicle
Van accessibility maintenance (RW)	2003	1 time/year or as needed depending on wear and tear	$50/year average
Cellular telephone for emergency communication (RW)	2002	Every 5–7 years (estimate)	No additional cost over general population

Architectural Considerations

List considerations for home accessibility and/or modifications.

He requires a single-level, barrier-free home with widened hallways and doorways, smooth floor coverings, accessible bathroom to include roll-in shower and grab bars in wet areas, wheelchair ramps to front and back entrance/exit, equipment/storage room, and other accessibility features. His home also requires a backup generator in the event of a power failure. Although his oxygen and respiratory equipment are not used on a daily basis, an alternate or backup power source is recommended in the event of power failure when the equipment is in use. Estimated cost for standard generator is $2000, including installation (will not power home air-conditioning).

Current home is not modifiable. If a new home is constructed, expect cost to be 10 to 20% above cost of average home in the local area. Moving expenses to move the client's belongings from his current residence to a new residence are estimated at $5000. Economist is to deduct the value of an average home in the client's local area.

Future Medical Care, Surgical Intervention, Aggressive Treatment

Recommendation (by whom)	Year Initiated	Frequency	Expected Cost
Note 1: According to Dr. Winkler, the client is expected to have on average 4 to 9 days/year of hospitalization for urinary tract infections, upper respiratory infections, skin breakdown, and other complications related to his spinal cord injury at an average of $1200/day.			
Note 2: At the time of Dr. Winkler's examination, the client reportedly had a Grade II decubitus ulcer on his right ischial tuberosity that required immediate attention, and chronic osteomyelitis in his left ischial tuberosity. Information received subsequent to Dr. Winkler's evaluation reveals that the client has seen the plastic surgeon regarding his pressure sores and underwent aggressive wound care.			
Antibiotic treatment for complications related to urinary tract infections, indwelling Foley catheter, upper respiratory infections, etc. (TW)	2002	Oral antibiotics <u>Oral antibiotics</u> 1–2 courses/year (average) (estimate 3 tablets/day, 10 days average/course) <u>IV antibiotics</u> 1- to 2-week course (average) every 2–3 years (average) to life expectancy	<u>Oral antibiotics</u> $129–590/year to life at $129–295/course (2001) (range includes Ceftin to Levaquin antibiotcs) <u>IV antibiotics</u> $1567–3134 every 2–3 years at every 2–3 years for medications (2001) plus $223.89/day for RN to administer IV antibiotics 2 times/day (average) at $90/visit for 1–2 weeks (average) every 2–3 years (average) to life (2001)

Note 1: According to Dr. Winkler, the client is expected to require oral antibiotic treatment on a yearly basis and IV antibiotics on an intermittent basis for various complications related to the spinal cord injury throughout his life expectancy.

Note 2: The client states that he was prescribed oral Ceftin and Levaquin for his most recent infections and informs that he generally is no longer prescribed Cipro or Augmentin antibiotics. According to the infusion company, his last IV antibiotics were Vancomycin and Ceftazidime, administered in July 2000, and cost is based on his history of infusion therapy.

Comprehensive rehabilitation day program, including physiatry, nursing, respiratory therapy, PT, OT, seating and positioning, education/training, vocational services, community reintegration, etc. (TW)	2002 (immediate need)	6- to 12-week program (actual length of program will be determined following evaluation by rehabilitation team)	$21,120–42,240 at $704/day for 5 days/week program Airfare to treatment center: $268 (2001) round-trip (for client plus 1 attendant; see Note below) Accessible ground transportation to/from Atlanta airport: $180–190 at $90–95/trip for 20 miles one way (approximately) Lodging is included in per diem

Note 1: Economist is to deduct therapeutic evaluations, i.e., PT, OT, and dietary, for the year in which the client participates in the intensive rehabilitation program.

Note 2: Additional physicians and specialty services may be added to the day program (i.e., urology, psychology, sexual counseling, plastic surgery, etc.) depending on the client's needs and outcome of initial team evaluation. Type and amount of services, if any, cannot accurately be determined and no additional cost is included in plan.

Note 3: Assumes the client's wife will accompany him to the evaluation and will be his attendant.

Potential Complications

Note: Potential complications are included for information only. No frequency or duration of complications is available. No costs are included in the plan.

Skin breakdown/decubitus ulcers that could require surgery to correct. The client has a history of skin breakdown and hospitalizations for wound care with surgical intervention. Recent statistics regarding pressure sore treatment at a specialty spinal cord treatment center include $62,000 for 6-week hospitalization up to $92,000, including physician and operating room charges (source: Arthur Simon, M.D., plastic surgeon, 10/20/99).

Increased risk for respiratory complications, including pneumonia, embolus, lung collapse, upper and lower respiratory infections, etc., due to spinal cord injury and tracheostomy use, which could require extensive diagnostic studies, aggressive pulmonary treatment, and/or hospitalization. The client has a history of hospitalizations for pneumonia and has other respiratory problems.

Cardiovascular problems, including heart disease, high cholesterol levels, inflammation of veins with clots, deep venous thrombosis, electrolyte imbalance, heart irregularities, and feet/leg circulation problems.

Urological problems, including urinary tract infections, bladder/kidney stones or blockage, higher incidence of bladder cancer related to indwelling catheter, kidney failure, autonomic dysreflexia, etc. Additionally, the client may be a candidate for medications and/or devices for his erectile dysfunction.

Musculoskeletal problems, including poor posture, myosistis ossification, osteoporosis, pain especially in upper extremities, fractures, spinal column instability, contractures, heterotopic ossification, traumatic arthritis, etc., which could require x-rays, bone scans, and/or other diagnostic studies and aggressive treatment, including surgery. The client discloses daily pain in his upper extremities as well as a burning pain sensation in the back of his knees and calves.

Gastrointestinal problems related to chronic abdominal distention (i.e., ileus), constipation/impaction, digestive problems, bowel accidents/incontinence, etc., which require evaluation/follow-up by gastroenterologist, including abdominal x-rays and/or other diagnostic tests.

Neurological problems, including spasticity, syringomyelia, spinal cord cysts, etc. The client reports daily spasms that occur during transfers and at night, which wake him up. One option for treatment could be an intrathecal Baclofen pump implant. If needed, estimated average charges include one-time Baclofen trial therapy at $1320. If successful candidate, initial Baclofen pump implant at $18,060; physician follow-up and pump maintenance/refill (six times/year average) at $3660/year; and pump replacement every 4 years average at $14,700/replacement (source: Medtronic, 1996 data).

Cellulitis and/or ingrown toenails.

Metabolic problems, i.e., weight gain, increased risk for diabetes, poor diet/nutrition, loss of appetite, etc.

Psychological adjustment to disability, including increased fatigue, depression, social withdrawal, etc.

Adverse reaction to medications and/or problems with Porta-Cath that require replacement of device.

REFERENCES

American Spinal Injury Association/International Medical Society of Paraplegia. (2000). *International Standards for Neurological and Functional Classification of Spinal Cord Injury*, rev. ed. Chicago: American Spinal Injury Association.

Apstein, M. & Dalecki-Chipperfield, K. (1987). Spinal cord injury is a risk factor for gallstone disease. *Gastroenterology*, 92, 666–668.

Asher, R. (1947). On dangers of going to bed. *British Medical Journal*, 13, 967–968.

Bauman, W.A., Razam, M., Spungen, A.M., & Machac, J. (1994). Cardiac stress testing with thallium-201 imaging reveals silent ischemia in individuals with paraplegia. *Archives of Physical Medicine and Rehabilitation*, 75, 946–950.

Bauman, W.A. & Spungen, A.M. (1994). Disorders of carbohydrate and lipid metabolism in veterans with paraplegia or quadriplegia: a model for premature aging. *Metabolism*, 43, 749–756.

Berkowitz, M., Harvey, C., Greene, C.G., & Wilson, S.E. (1992). *The Economic Consequences of Traumatic Spinal Cord Injury*. New York: Demos Publications.

Berkowitz, M., O'Leary, P., Kruse, D.L., & Harvey, C. (1998). *Spinal Cord Injury: An Analysis of Medical and Social Cost*. New York: Demos Medical Publishing, Inc.

Blackwell, T., Krause, J., Winkler, T., & Stiens, S. (2001). *Spinal Cord Injury Desk Reference: Guidelines for Life Care Planning and Case Management*. New York: Demos.

Blackwell, T., Weed, R., & Powers, A. (1994). *Life Care Planning for Spinal Cord Injury*. Athens, GA: Elliott and Fitzpatrick.

Bohlman, H.H., Kirkpatrick, J.S., Delamarter, R.B., et al. (1994). Anterior decompression for late pain and paralysis following fractures of the thoracic lumbar spine. *Clinical Orthopedics*, 300, 24–29.

Bolin, I., Bodin, P., & Kreuter, M. (2000). Sitting position — posture and performance in C5-C6 tetraplegia. *Spinal Cord*, 38, 425–434.

Bors, E., Conrad, C.A., & Massell, T.B. (1954). Venous occlusion of the lower extremities in paraplegic patients. *Surgery, Gynecology and Obstetrics*, 99, 451–454.

Brackett, N.L., Ferrell, S.M., Aballa, T.C., Amador, M.J., & Lynne, C.M. (1998). Semen quality in spinal cord injury men: does it progressively decline postinjury? *Archives of Physical Medicine and Rehabilitation*, 79, 625–628.

Braddom, L.R., Ed. (1995). *Physical Medicine and Rehabilitation*. Philadelphia: W.B. Saunders.

Braun, S.R., Giovannoni, R., Levin, A.B., et al. (1982). Oxygen saturation during sleep in patients with SCI. *American Journal of Physical Medicine*, 61, 302–309.

Byrne, D.W. & Salzberg, C.A. (1996). Major risk factors for pressure ulcers in the spinal cord disabled: a literature review. *Spinal Cord*, 34, 255–263.

Bush, G.W., President, Initiative, February 2001. Available at www.whitehouse.gov/news/freedominitiative/freedominitiative.html.

Cardenas, D.D. (1992). Neurogenic bladder evaluation and management. *Physical Medicine and Rehabilitation Clinics of North America, Traumatic Spinal Cord Injury*, 3, 4.

Cariga, P., Ahmed, S., Mathias, C.J., & Gardner, B.P. (2002). The prevalence and association of neck (coat-hanger) pain and orthostatic (postural) hypotension in human spinal cord injury. *Spinal Cord*, 40, 77–82.

Catz, A., Thaleisnik, M., Fishel, B., et al. (2002). Spinal cord injury in Israel. *Spinal Cord*, 40, 595–598.

Coffey, R.J., Edgar, T.S., Francisco, G.E., Graziani, V., et al. (2002). Abrupt withdrawal from intrathecal Baclofen: recognition and management of a potentially life-threatening syndrome. *Archives of Physical Medicine and Rehabilitation*, 83, 735–741.

Consortium for Spinal Cord Injury. (1997a). *Clinical Practice Guidelines: Acute Management of Autonomic Dysreflexia. Patients with Spinal Cord Injury Presenting to Health-Care Facilities*. Washington, DC: Paralyzed Veterans of America.

Consortium for Spinal Cord Injury. (1997b). *Clinical Practice Guidelines: Prevention of Thromboembolism in Spinal Cord Injury*. Washington, DC: Paralyzed Veterans of America.

Consortium for Spinal Cord Injury. (1998). *Clinical Practice Guidelines: Neurogenic Bowel Management in Adults with Spinal Cord Injury.* Washington, DC: Paralyzed Veterans of America.

Consortium for Spinal Cord Injury. (1999). *Outcomes Following Traumatic Spinal Cord Injury: Clinical Practice Guidelines for Health-Care Professionals.* Washington, DC: Paralyzed Veterans of America.

Davidoff, G., Werner, R., & Waring, W. (1991). Compressive mononeuropathies and chronic paraplegia. *Paraplegia, 29,* 17–24.

Deutsch, P. & Sawyer, H. (1996). *Guide to Rehabilitation.* White Plains, NY: Ahab Press.

Devivo, M. (1989). Causes of death in spinal cord injury. *Archives of Internal Medicine,* 149, 1761–1766.

Devivo, M., Whiteneck, G., & Charles, E. (1995). The economic impact of spinal cord injury. In S. Stover, J. DeLisa, & G. Whiteneck, Eds., *Spinal Cord Injury Clinical Outcomes from the Model Systems,* 234–288. Gaithersburg, MD: Aspen.

DeVivo, M.J. (2002). Estimating life expectancy for use in determining lifetime cost of care. *Topics in Spinal Cord Injury Rehabilitation: Life Care Planning,* 7, 49–58.

Drory, L.N. (1990). Coronary artery disease. *Archives of Physical Medicine and Rehabilitation,* 71, 389–392.

Duckworth, W.C. (1983). Glucose intolerance in spinal injury. *Archives of Physical Medicine and Rehabilitation,* 64, 107–110.

Duckworth, W.C., Jallepalli, P., & Solomon, S.S. (1983). Glucose intolerance in spinal cord injury. *Archives of Physical Medicine and Rehabilitation,* 64, 107–110.

Epstein, N. (1981). GI bleeds in spinal cord injury. *Journal of Neurosurgery,* 54, 16.

Esmail, Z., Shalansky, K.F., Sunderji, R., et al. (2002). Evaluation of captopril for the management of hypertension in autonomic dysreflexia: a pilot study. *Archives of Physical Medicine and Rehabilitation,* 83, 604–608.

Formal, C. (1992). Metabolic and neurological changes after spinal cord injury. *Physical Medicine and Rehabilitation Clinics of North America, Traumatic Spinal Cord Injury,* 3, 1002.

Gibson, C.J. (1992). Overview of spinal cord injury. *Physical Medicine and Rehabilitation Clinics of North America,* 3, 699–709.

Gittler, M.S., McKinley, W.O., Stiens, S.A., Groah, S.L., & Kirshblum, S.C. (2002). Spinal cord injury medicine. 3 rehabilitation outcomes. *Archives of Physical Medicine and Rehabilitation,* 83 (Suppl. 1), S65–S71.

Go, B., Devivo, M., & Richards, J. (1995). The epidemiology of spinal cord injury. In S.L. Stover, J.A. DeLisa, & G.G. Whiteneck, Eds., *Spinal Cord Injury Clinical Outcomes from the Model Systems,* 21–51. Gaithersburg, MD: Aspen.

Gore, R., Mintzer, R., & Calenoff, L. (1991). Gastrointestinal complications of spinal cord injury, *Spine,* 6, 538–544.

Griffin, M.R., Opitz, J.L., Kurland, L.T., et al. (1985). Traumatic spinal cord injury in Omstead County, Minnesota, 1935 through 1981. *American Journal of Epidemiology,* 121.

Groah, S.L., Stiens, S.A., Gittler, M.S., et al. (2002). Spinal cord injury medicine 5. Preserving wellness and independence of the ageing patient with spinal cord injury: A primary care approach for the rehabilitative medicine specialist. *Archives of Physical Medicine and Rehabilitation,* 83(S1), S82–S89.

Groah, S.L., Weitzenkamp, D.A., Lammertse, D.P., et al. (2002). Excess risk of bladder cancer in spinal cord injury: evidence for an association between indwelling catheter use and bladder cancer. *Archives of Physical Medicine and Rehabilitation,* 83, 346–351.

Harness-DiGloria, D. (1999). Breaking the silence. *Paraplegic News,* 53, 18–20.

Harrell, W.T. & Krause, J.S. (2002). Personal assistance services in patients with SCI: modeling an appropriate level of care in a life care plan. *Topics in Spinal Cord Injury Rehabilitation: Life Care Planning,* 7, 38–48.

Hirsch, G.N., Menard, M.R., & Anton, H.A. (1990). Anemia after spinal cord injury. *Archives of Physical Medicine and Rehabilitation,* 71, 3–7.

Jackson, A.B. & Groomes, T.E. (1991). Incidents of respiratory complications following spinal cord injury. *Journal of American Paraplegia Society*, 14, 87.

Kemp, B., Krause, J.S., & Adkins, R. (1999). Depression among African-Americans, Latinos, and Caucasians with spinal cord injury: an exploratory study. *Rehab Psychology*, 44, 235–247.

Kennedy, E. (1986). Spinal cord injury: facts and figures. Birmingham, AL: University of Alabama.

Kesseler, B.I. (1986). Coronary artery disease in spinal cord injury. *The American Journal of Cardiology*.

Kewalramani, L.S. (1979). Neurogenic ulcers in spinal cord injury. *Journal of Trauma*, 19, 259–265.

Kotajarvi, B.R., Basford, J.R., & An, K. (2002). Upper-extremity torque production in men with paraplegia who use wheelchairs. *Archives of Physical Medicine and Rehabilitation*, 83, 441–446.

Krause, J. (1996). Employment after spinal cord injury: transition and life adjustment. *Rehabilitation Counseling Bulletin*, 38, 244–255.

Krause, J. & Anson, C. (1996). Employment after spinal cord injury: relation to selected participant characteristics. *Archives of Physical Medicine and Rehabilitation*, 77, 737–743

Krause, J.F., Frantice, P.T., Riggins, R.S., et al. (1975). Incidence of spinal cord lesion. *Journal of Chronic Disease*, 28, 471.

Krause, J.S. (2002). Accuracy of life expectancy estimates in life care plans: consideration of nonbiographical and noninjury factors. *Topics in Spinal Cord Injury Rehabilitation: Life Care Planning*, 7, 49–58.

Lanis, I. & Lammertse, D. (1992). The respiratory system and spinal cord injury. *Physical Medicine and Rehabilitation Clinics of North America*, 34, 725–740.

Lawrence, D.W., Bayakly, A.R., & Mathison, J.B. (1992). Traumatic Spinal Cord Injury in Louisiana: 1990. Annual Report. New Orleans, LA: Louisiana Office of Public Health.

Lee, B. (1991). *Management of Peripheral Vascular Disease in the Spinal Cord Injured Patient: The Spinal Cord Injured Patient Comprehensive Management*. Philadelphia: W.B. Saunders.

McKinley, W.O., Gittler, M.S., Kirshblum, S.C., Stiens, S.A., & Groah, S.L. (2002). Spinal cord injury medicine. 2. Medical complications after spinal cord injury: identification and management. *Archives of Physical Medicine and Rehabilitation*, 83 (Suppl. 1), S58–S64.

Medical News and Perspectives. 1998. *Journal of American Medical Association*, 280, 1038–1039.

Melzack, R. (1978). Pain and spinal cord injury. *Pain*, 4, 195–210.

Menter, R.R. (1993). Issues of aging with spinal cord injury. In E. Whiteneck, S. Charlifue, K. Gerhart, D. Lammertze, S. Manley, R. Menter, & K. Seedroff, Eds., *Aging with Spinal Cord Injury*, 1–8. New York: Demos Publications.

Menter, R. (1995). The effects of age at injury and on aging and the aging process. In S.L. Stover et al., Eds., *Spinal Cord Injury Clinical Outcomes from the Model Systems*. Gaithersburg, MD: Aspen.

Meyers, A.R., Mitra, M., Walker, D.K., Wilber, N., & Allen, D. (2000). Predictors of secondary conditions in a sample of independently living adults with high-level spinal cord injury. 6, 1–8.

Nosek, M.A., Howland, C.A., & Young, M.E. (1998). Abuse of women with disabilities: policy implications. *Journal of Disability Policy Study*, 8, 158–175.

Pear, R. 9 out of 10 Nursing Homes Lack Adequate Staff, Study Finds. *New York Times*, February 18, 2002.

Pentland, W.E. & Twoney, L.T. (1991). The weight bearing extremity in women with long term paraplegia. *Paraplegia*, 29, 521.

Pentland, W., Walker, J., Minnnes, P., et al. (2002). Women with spinal cord injury and the impact of ageing. *Spinal Cord*, 40, 374–387.

Prysak, G.M., Andresen, E.M., & Meyers, A.R. (2000). Prevalence of secondary conditions in veterans with spinal cord injury and their interference with life activities. *Topics in Spinal Cord Rehabilitation: Secondary Conditions*, 6, 34–42.

Ridington, J. (1989). Beating the "Odds": Violence and Women with Disabilities. Vancouver: Disabled Women's Network (position paper 2).

Roth, E.J., Lovell, N.L., Heinemann, A.W., et al. (1992). The older adult with a spinal cord injury. *Paraplegia*, 30, 520–526.

Schmitt, J., Midha, M., & McKenzie, N. (1995). *Diagnosis and Management of Disorders of the Spinal Cord.* Philadelphia: W.B. Saunders.

Schoenen, J. (1991). Clinical anatomy of the spinal cord: disorders of the Spinal Cord, *Neurological Clinics*, 9.

Schulz, R. & Beach, S.R. (1999). Care giving as a risk factor for mortality: the caregiver health effects study. *Journal of American Medical Association*, 282, 2215–2219.

Seekins, T. & Ravesloot, C. (2000). Secondary conditions experienced by adults with injury-related disabilities in Montana. *Topics in Spinal Cord Rehabilitation: Secondary Conditions*, 6, 43–53.

Sie, I.H., Waters, R.L., Adkins, R.H., and Gellerman, H. (1992). Upper extremity pain in the postrehabilitation spinal cord injured patient. *Archives of Physical Medicine and Rehabilitation*, 73, 44–48.

Sipski, M.L. & Alexander, C.J. (1992). Sexual function and dysfunction after spinal cord injury. *Physical Medicine and Rehabilitation Clinics of North America*, 34, 811–828.

Spungen, A.M., Grim, D.R., Straken, M., Pizzolato, P.M., & Bauman, W.A. (1999). Treatment with an anabolic agent is associated with improvement in respiratory function in persons with tetraplegia: a pilot study. *Mount Sinai Journal of Medicine*, 66, 201–205.

Staas, W., Jr., Christopher, S., Formal, A.M., & Gershkof, G. (1993). *Rehabilitation Medicines, Principles and Practice*, 2nd ed. Philadelphia: J.B. Lippincott.

Stone, J.M., Nino-Murciam, Wolfe, V.A, & Perkash, I. (1990). Chronic GI problems in spinal cord injury. *American Journal of Gastroenterology*, 85, 1114–1119.

Stover, S. (1995). *Spinal Cord Injury, Clinical Outcomes of Model Systems.* Gaithersburg, MD: Aspen.

Tsai, S., Lew, H.L., Date, E., & Bih, L. (2002). Treatment of detrusor-sphincter dyssynergia by pudendal nerve block in patients with spinal cord injury. *Archives of Physical Medicine and Rehabilitation*, 83, 714–717.

Tsitouras, P.D., Zhong, Y.G., Spungen, A.M., & Bauman, W.A. (1995). Hormone levels in patients with spinal cord injury. *Hormone and Metabolic Research*, 27, 287–292.

Waring, W.P. & Karunas, R.S. (1991). Acute spinal cord injuries and the incidence of clinically occurring thromboembolic disease. *Paraplegia*, 29, 8–16.

Weed, R. & Field, T. (2001). *The Rehabilitation Consultant's Handbook*, rev. ed. Athens, GA: Elliott & Fitzpatrick.

Wheeler, G.D., Andrews, B., Lederer, R., et al. (2002). Functional electrical stimulation-assisted rowing: increasing cardiovascular fitness through functional electric stimulation rowing training in persons with spinal cord injury. *Archives of Physical Medicine and Rehabilitation*, 83, 1093–1099.

Whiteneck, G. & Menter, R.R. (1993). Where do we go from here? In G. Whiteneck et al., *Aging with Spinal Cord Injury*, 361–369. New York: Demos Publications.

Whiteneck, G., Menter, R., Charlifue, S., et al. (1991). Impairment, disability, handicap, and medical expenses of persons aging with spinal cord injury. *Paraplegia*, 29, 613–619.

Widerstrom-Noga, E.G., Ducan, R., Felipe-Cuervo, E., & Turk, D.C. (2002). Assessment of the impact of pain and impairments associated with spinal cord injuries. *Archives of Physical Medicine and Rehabilitation*, 83, 395–404.

Wiener, J., Quinn, J.P., Bradford, P.A., et al. (1999). Multiple antibiotic-resistant Klebsiella and Eschericha coli in nursing homes. *Journal of American Medical Association*, 281, 517–523.

Winkler, T. (1997). Spinal cord injury and life care planning. In P. Deutsch & H. Sawyer, Eds., *A Guide to Rehabilitation*, 16.1–16.139. White Plains, NY: Ahab Press.

Woozly, R.M. & Young, R.R. (1995). *Diagnosis and Management of Disorders of the Spinal Cord.* Philadelphia: W.B. Saunders.

Wyndaele, J.J. (2002). Complications of intermittent catheterization: their prevention and treatment. *Spinal Cord*, 40, 536–541.

Wyngaarden, J.B. & Smith, L.H. (1988). *Cecil's Textbook of Medicine*, 18th ed., 384–387. Philadelphia: W.B. Saunders.

Yarkony, G.N. (1996). Rehabilitation of patients with spinal cord injury. In Randall L. Braddom, Ed., *Physical Medicine and Rehabilitation*. Philadelphia: W.B. Saunders.

Yarkony, G.N., Roth, E.J., Heinemann, A.W., et al. (1988). Spinal cord injury in rehabilitation outcome: the impact of aging. *Journal of Clinical Epidemiology*, 41, 173–177.

Yehutil, Y. (1989). Prevalence of heart disease in spinal cord injury. *Paraplegia*, 27, 58–62.

Zigler, J. & Field, B. (1992). Surgical procedures for spinal cord injury. *Physical Medicine and Rehabilitation Clinics of North America*, 3.4, 711–723.

19

LIFE CARE PLANNING FOR ORGAN TRANSPLANTATION

Dan M. Bagwell, LaRhea A. Nichols, and Roger O. Weed

INTRODUCTION

The transplantation of organs from one human being to another suffering from end-stage organ disease indeed represents a gift of life. Since the first successful kidney transplant was performed in 1954, organ transplantation has emerged from a dream to become a well-established science. This was due in large part to a handful of brilliant medical scientists who failed to give up on the prospect that transplantation of organs could become a reality. In the five decades that have followed, many thousands of individuals have received a new opportunity for life, through the selfless act of organ donation and the tireless dedication of health care workers and other concerned individuals and organizations devoted to saving lives through transplantation.

Until 1984, the allocation of organs for transplantation in the U.S. was largely unregulated and primarily coordinated by local organ banks scattered throughout the country. In 1984, Congress passed the National Organ Transplant Act (PL 98-507) from which the Task Force on Organ Transplantation was formed. Through this task force, initial transplantation guidelines were developed to include the creation of qualified organ procurement organizations (OPOs) and the formation of the Organ Procurement and Transplantation Network (OPTN) as authorized by PL 98-507. The OPTN is a partnership between the public and private sectors that serves as a system-wide link for all professionals involved in the system of donation and organ transplantation nationwide. The primary goals of the OPTN are to ensure the effectiveness, efficiency, and equity of organ sharing through a national system of organ allocation and to increase the supply of donated organs available for transplantation. Through a contract with the Health Resources and Services Administration of the U.S. Department of Health and Human Services, the OPTN is operated by the United Network for Organ Sharing (UNOS). UNOS has maintained this distinction for more than 16 years with four successive contract renewals. UNOS performs many valuable functions, but it is best known as the "holder of the list": the nation's list of patients awaiting cadaveric organ transplantation.

541

0-8493-1511-5/04/$0.00+$1.50
© 2004 by CRC Press LLC

As of July 1, 2001, there were 882 UNOS-certified programs within 260 transplant centers offering kidney, pancreas, pancreas islet cell, liver, intestine, heart, lung, and heart–lung transplantation (UNOS, 2002). UNOS certification is provided for transplantation programs that meet its strict standards for patient and graft survival rates, transplant volumes, surgeon and physician training, and nursing, laboratory, and hospital criteria. These standards are monitored through the OPTN to ensure that certified programs maintain compliance with certification criteria. All pretransplant and posttransplant patients are registered with UNOS along with their health status. Laboratory results, rejection incidence, infections, and other data are reported to UNOS at periodic intervals throughout the life of the patient. UNOS maintains an elaborate informational database (www.unos.org) providing statistical information, such as waiting lists by organ type, graft and patient survival by individual transplant center, and volume and types of organs transplanted.

As of August 2002, more than 80,000 persons were awaiting organ transplantation in the U.S. (UNOS, 2002). More than half of these individuals are diagnosed with end-stage renal disease (ESRD) and are awaiting kidney transplantation. It is estimated that by the year 2010, more than 95,000 people with ESRD will be awaiting kidney transplantation alone (USRDS, 2002). The prevalence of end-stage renal disease in the U.S. population is 1321 per million (USRDS, 2002). Primary etiologies of kidney failure are diabetes, hypertension, and glomerulonephritis. The prevalence of liver failure in the U.S. is 25 per million. Hepatitis C and alcoholic cirrhosis account for most liver failures requiring liver transplantation. Chronic obstructive lung disease and pulmonary fibrosis represent the most common etiologies for those 3600 persons awaiting lung transplantation. For the estimated 3400 individuals awaiting heart transplantation, there is an equal distribution of primary disease caused by coronary artery disease and cardiomyopathy.

LIFE CARE PLANNING IN TRANSPLANTATION

As with any chronic disease process or disabling injury, life care planning for individuals diagnosed with end-stage organ disease requires a thorough understanding of the disease process. Furthermore, until a suitable organ can be transplanted, life-sustaining medical treatment and care must be implemented. The client/patient's candidacy for organ transplantation must be determined with placement on the waiting list, in order to make a reasoned projection that transplantation will occur within the average wait time for a suitable organ. Depending on the specific organ involved and the extent of the disease, time can be an extremely important factor of patient survival. While persons with end-stage renal disease can be kept alive usually for many years on renal dialysis, those with liver failure and advanced heart and lung disease do not have the same opportunity. As such, some of these individuals will die awaiting transplantation. To address the issue of deaths while awaiting transplantation, the OPTN seeks to allocate organs to those who need them the most. In the case of liver failure, organs are allocated using a mortality risk score corresponding to the degree of medical urgency. Once candidacy is determined, comprehensive evaluations and ongoing follow-up are required until transplantation.

THE TRANSPLANT CANDIDACY PROCESS

Patients in need of transplantation are referred to transplantation centers through many different means. Generally, referrals are made through physicians specializing in end-organ disease such as nephrologists, gastroenterologists, cardiologists, or pulmonologists. Patients may also be referred by claims representatives of health insurance companies, with programs identified through a contractural relationship as their "centers of excellence" or "transplant institutes." Individuals may also refer themselves to transplant programs, which can be accomplished through the Internet (UNOS.com).

Prior to scheduling an initial evaluation, medical records are forwarded to the transplant center for review by a physician and a transplantation nursing coordinator. Patients are assigned to a pretransplantation nurse coordinator at the time of referral to begin the process of determining candidacy through a program's transplantation evaluation protocols. The pretransplant nurse coordinator is an invaluable resource to the life care planner, for he or she can assist in the analysis of program-specific medical evaluations and diagnostic protocols in preparation for transplantation.

Indications for transplantation (UNOS, 2002):
- End-stage organ failure not amenable to medical therapy
- Psychological stability and family support to sustain the patient through the transplant and complex postoperative regimen
- Age parameters: neonate to early 70s (varies greatly from center to center)

Contraindications for transplantation:
- Morbid obesity (greater than 35% body mass index)
- Metastatic cancer
- Uncontrolled systemic infection
- Pregnancy
- Psychological instability that will make compliance difficult
- Ongoing elicit substance abuse (past substance abuse requires a period of at least 6 months abstinence)
- Positive for human immunodeficiency virus (HIV) (may be considered in a few select centers)
- Cardiac ejection fraction less than 20% (unless patient is a heart transplant candidate)

Etiology of disease is important to review as certain underlying disease processes may recur and threaten the transplanted organ. Membranoproliferative glomerulonephritis and focal segmental glomerulosclerosis have fairly high recurrence rates (25 to 50%) within a few months to a year or more after kidney transplantation (Matthew, 1988; Verani & Dan, 1982). Hepatitis C is not cured by liver transplantation and recurs after transplantation, with 40 to 90% of patients exhibiting complications during the first postoperative year (Charlton & Seaberg, 1998). Graft hepatitis may lead to fibrosis and cirrhosis in up to 30% of patients.

Following the initial interview and evaluation, patient candidates will undergo rigorous medical testing to ensure the best possible outcomes during and following the transplant procedure. Typical diagnostics routinely performed during the pretransplantation evaluation period for all transplant candidates include the following:

Routine Laboratory: Blood type, white blood cell count (WBC), chemistry profile, serology studies (hepatitis A, B, and C; HIV; and rapid plasmin reagin (RPR)), histocompatibility leukocyte antigen (HLA) typing, 24-hour creatinine clearance (except for kidney transplant patients), and viral titers; cytomegalovirus (CMV), varicella, Epstein-Barr virus (EBV)

Other Basic Diagnostics: Skin testing for tuberculosis, chest x-ray (posterior–anterior (PA) and lateral), and electrocardiogram

Cardiac Evaluation (based on symptomatology or per protocol): echocardiogram, cardiac stress test, and possibly cardiac catheterization

Dental Consultation (to rule out infectious agents)

Standard Cancer Screening: Pap smear (women over age 18 or younger if sexually active), mammogram (women over age 40 or younger with positive family history), prostate-specific antigen (PSA) levels (men over age 40), and colonoscopy for men and women over age 50

Social Services Consultation with Possible Psychiatric Consultation

Additional Organ-Specific Diagnostics:

- *Kidney:* Voiding cystourethrogram (optional) for diabetics or those with a history of urinary tract infections
- *Liver:* Abdominal computed tomography (CT) scan or magnetic resonance imaging (MRI) to rule out hepatocellular carcinoma, evaluate the portal vein, and measure the size of the liver
- *Heart:* Cardiac catheterization for all patients to determine filling pressures and pulmonary resistance
- *Lung:* Ventilation perfusion scan of each lung to determine the specific lung to be removed during transplantation; pulmonary function tests to establish pretransplant baselines; CT scan of the chest to rule out lung cancer

Additional diagnostics may be required for further evaluation or interim treatment of a health problem prior to transplantation, if the typical diagnostics performed yield abnormal findings. Cardiac abnormalities found during echocardiography or cardiac stress testing may require cardiac catheterization for definitive results and treatment plans. This is not an infrequent occurrence, as persons with end-stage organ failure often have multiple organ system problems.

Completion of the initial evaluation period may take a few days to months. Following the evaluation period, the patient's data are collected and presented to a committee, review board, or perhaps individual physician for review and determination of transplant candidacy. Once approved, the prospective transplant recipient is notified and his data is forwarded for placement on the national waiting list for a cadaveric organ, or a living donation transplant is performed.

Living donation has increased dramatically from 2425 in 1991 to 5463 in 2000 (OPTN, 2001). The options for living donation are presented to most kidney and liver pretransplant patients and may be offered for lung transplant candidates at select programs. The primary mission for programs offering living donation is to "do no harm" to the potential donor while helping the recipient. This requires a thorough assessment of the living donor to ensure that he or she is in optimal health. The donor evaluation will generally include the following:

Laboratory: Blood type, WBC, chemistry profile, serology studies (hepatitis A, B, and C; HIV; and RPR), HLA typing with donor–recipient cross-match for kidney donation, and viral titers; CMV, varicella, EBV, urinalysis with urine culture, 24-hour creatinine clearance (two times), and, optimally, a glofil study to assess creatinine clearance for potential kidney donors.

Other Basic Diagnostics: Skin testing for tuberculosis, chest x-ray (PA and lateral) and electrocardiogram, CT scan or arteriogram to evaluate renal arteries/veins, anatomy of kidneys, and CT or MRI scan of the liver for potential living liver donors; a liver biopsy is often requested by the transplant physician for prospective liver donors.

Cardiology Evaluation: Based on the age of the donor, this may include echocardiogram and a cardiac stress test.

Social Services and Psychiatric Consultation

Following the donor evaluation, the results are often reviewed by a neutral third party that is not associated with the prospective transplant recipient. If the donor meets the requirements and is cleared for donation, then surgery is scheduled and performed.

Living donation remains a better choice for most patients, as shorter waiting times decrease morbidity and mortality. When the donor of a living related kidney and the recipient share histocompatibility antigens, significant improvements in long-term graft survival are seen.

The Waiting Period

Renal patients awaiting transplantation are followed at close intervals by their nephrologists through their respective dialysis units and nephrology offices. While awaiting transplantation, pre-kidney transplant patients will have blood specimens forwarded to the histocompatability laboratories (HLA) at periodic intervals (at least monthly) for cross-matching with prospective cadaveric kidney donors and for monitoring of antibodies associated with rejection. This represents an ongoing cost born by the recipient candidate until transplantation is accomplished. Likewise, the cost of donor evaluations and eventual organ procurement are assumed by the organ recipient. Patients on hemodialysis will continue to dialyze three times weekly for a period of 3 to 4 hours with each dialysis. Mean waiting times in 2001 for blood type O were 1248 days, and 1501 days for blood type B (OPTN, 2001). Waiting times may be extremely long for patients who are sensitized, or patients with a significant degree of preformed antibody such that the risk of immediate rejection is considerably higher. Unfortunately, these antibodies are formed when an individual is exposed to other human antigens such as pregnancy, prior blood transfusions, and prior transplantation. Newer protocols have been established to enhance the opportunities for these sensitized patients through the use of gamma-globulin infusion and plasmapheresis such that problematic antibodies are removed from the blood. This process has demonstrated some limited success in recent application, but general clinical utilization is still quite early.

Waiting periods for individuals with end-stage liver failure are variable and are determined on the basis of medical acuity of the prospective recipients. UNOS has assigned a new methodology for rating liver transplant patients on the waiting list, referred to as MELD, or the Model for End-stage Liver Disease. MELD is a "continuous disease severity scale that is highly predictive of the risk of dying from liver disease for patients waiting on the transplant list" (UNOS, 2002). This model incorporates the patient's bilirubin, international normalized ratio (INR), and creatinine in an equation that results in a patient score of up to 40 points. Liver organ candidates with higher scores are moved forward on the waiting list, thereby increasing their opportunity to receive an organ and hopefully reducing the number of deaths due to liver failure while awaiting transplantation. Of significance, the laboratory values must be repeated at regular intervals and entered into the national waiting list for the patient to maintain his place on the list. When the patient has 25 points or greater, he must have laboratory studies drawn every 7 days, and the results must be entered into the UNOS database within 48 hours of laboratory draws. Liver organ recipient candidates with lower scores will have laboratory draws with frequencies ranging from every 30 days to as long as 12 months. Liver candidates may be followed medically by their own gastroenterologist in conjunction with a transplant center, or they may be followed solely by the transplant center.

Lung failure patients are listed with UNOS as either status 1 or 7. Status 1 refers to an active status, while status 7 designates an on-hold status. Currently, there are no specific criteria in existence for those patients who are hospitalized or requiring mechanical ventilation. All prospective lung recipients are considered equally. Individuals suffering from end-stage lung disease are among the most acutely ill patients awaiting transplantation. Prior to transplantation, exacerbations of chronic obstructive lung disease may require frequent hospitalizations. Extended intubation and ventilation requirements are poor prognostic indicators for transplantation.

Heart transplant candidates are ranked through a status criteria system with designations as 1A, 1B, 2, or 7. To qualify as a status 1A, the recipient candidate must require mechanical circulatory support, mechanical circulatory support with objective medical evidence of significant device-related complications, mechanical ventilation, *or* continuous infusion of high-dose intravenous inotropic agents, *or* have an estimated life expectancy without a heart transplant of less than 7 days. To qualify for status 1B, heart transplant recipient candidates must have a left and/or right ventricular assist device in place and require intravenous inotropic medication. Those classified as status 2 do not meet the criteria for status 1A or 1B. Status 7 is applied to those patients deemed unsuitable for transplantation and are maintained in an on-hold status. The wait time for most adult heart transplant candidates is in excess of 1 year. As with patients awaiting lung transplantation, heart transplant candidates are also acutely ill and frequently require hospitalizations prior to transplant. It is not uncommon for these patients to require mechanical bridges to transplant, such as aortic balloon pump therapy or ventricular assist devices.

Individuals awaiting heart and lung transplants may have to relocate to live near their transplant centers, as the donor organs have a relatively short ischemic time and should be transplanted within 4 hours of organ procurement. If these organ recipient candidates reside at distances 2 or more hours from their transplant facility and do not have 24-hour coverage capability for emergency flight arrangements, then relocation to an area within the vicinity of the transplant center is necessary. At least one caretaker will need to be with the patient at all times to care for him, drive him to appointments, and be present at the time of transplant.

Finally, average waiting times for access to suitable organs vary from region to region, due to the length of the waiting lists and the volume of organs procured by each organ bank. The life care planner should research information available through UNOS or the OPO linked with the transplant program where a specific client/patient is registered. Each organ procurement organization computes its data on average waiting times for each organ type. Median waiting times (in days) by organ type for candidate information obtained from the OPTN waiting list through September 2000 were as follows:

- Heart: 206 (1999)
- Lung: 704 (1998)*
- Heart–lung: 889 (1997)*
- Liver: 517 (1998)*
- Kidney: 1099 (1997)*
- Pancreas: 179 (1999)
- Kidney–pancreas: 442 (1999)
- Intestine: 285 (1999)

*Pre-1999 median waiting times used where cohort sizes were less than 10 transplants.

Source: Milliman USA Research Report (2002).

ORGAN PROCUREMENT

Organs may be procured locally or regionally. The cost associated with cadaveric organ acquisition and procurement varies by the organ procurement organization with established standard acquisition costs (SAC). SAC fees are approved through the Medicare intermediaries of each state. These fees include charges from the donor hospital for testing of a donor after he or she has been declared brain dead. Typical charges include screening for infectious diseases, basic laboratory work, chest x-rays, hospital costs for use of the operating room and associated expenses for organ removal, surgical fees for organ removal, transportation of teams to outside hospitals by land (ambulance) or chartered air service, and the OPO's procurement coordinators and supplies. These SAC fees can be obtained by contacting the OPO in the region where the patient is listed for transplantation. For example, in South Texas, the OPO SAC fees *excluding* surgical fees and transportation charges are:

- Kidney: $19,100
- Liver: $20,800
- Split liver: $16,675
- Heart: $23,100
- Single lung: $12,900
- Bilateral lung: $33,400
- Pancreas: $17,925
- Small bowel: $15,300

Source: Texas Organ Sharing Alliance (2002).

TRANSPLANTATION

When a suitable donor becomes available, matching recipient candidates on the waiting list are notified and asked to come to the hospital. Upon arrival, consent forms are signed, blood work is drawn (CBC, chemistry profiles, HIV, hepatitis screens, CMV status, and HLA cross-matches for patients needing kidney transplants), a chest x-ray and EKG are performed, and a loading dose of immunosuppression is given prior to transplantation. In some instances, patients will be admitted and undergo the above described workups only to have the transplant cancelled, due to problems with the donor organ.

Table 19.1 provides an outline by organ type of average time spent in the operating room (OR), postoperative intensive care unit (ICU), and the general transplant ward, and the average length of stay. This outline was developed though an analysis of data from multiple large-volume transplant centers and only includes adult transplant recipient patients. Pediatric transplantation average lengths of stay are generally longer than those of adults, including time spent in the ICU.

The diseased organ for transplanted patients involving the liver, lung, and heart will be removed (or in the case of single-lung transplantation, one diseased lung removed) and the new organ transplanted in its place. In the instance of kidney transplantation, the native kidneys remain in place unless they are removed for reasons of infection or intractable hypertension. The newly transplanted kidney

Table 19.1   Average OR Time, Postoperative ICU Days, and General Transplant Ward Days, and Average Length of Stay by Organ Type

Transplant Type	Time in OR	Postoperative ICU Days	General Transplant Room Days	Average Length of Stay
Kidney	3 hours	1 day	6 days	7 days
Liver	3–6 hours	2 days	7 days	9 days
Lung (single)	3–5 hours	3 days	7 days	10 days
Lung (double)	$3^1/_2$–6 hours	3–4 days	7–10 days	14 days
Heart	$2^1/_2$–3 hours	2 days	5 days	7 days

is placed retroperitoneal in the lower abdomen adjacent to the bladder through an incision of the same location as an appendectomy. This position allows for fewer urological complications from ureter attachments and offers easier post-transplantation biopsy. In children, kidneys are placed intra-abdominally.

Immediately upon arrival to the ICU, extensive and specific postoperative monitoring is begun to include laboratory work, hemodynamic monitoring, fluid assessment, and administration of immunosuppressive medications, generally cyclosporin or Prograf. Daily drug levels will be drawn to monitor cyclosporine or Prograf levels in the blood. Patients receiving liver, lung, or heart transplants will remain on mechanical ventilation for at least a few hours. For many lung transplants, mechanical ventilation is required for as long as 3 days.

ORGAN-SPECIFIC POSTOPERATIVE MANAGEMENT

Following kidney transplant, postoperative care focuses upon monitoring urine output, replacing fluids, and maintaining normal electrolyte values. Foley catheters will be maintained for 3 to 5 days postoperatively. Transplanted kidneys may begin to function immediately, producing copious amounts of urine. Acute tubular necrosis may be seen, resulting from ischemia of the kidney tubules. Acute tubular necrosis necessitates an increased length of stay, along with dialysis for resolution and preservation of the patient's health.

Surgical complications from kidney transplantation are categorized into vascular, urologic, or lymphatic. Overall, surgical complications occur in less than 5% of kidney transplanted patients. Vascular complications include renal artery or vein thrombosis. The more common urologic complications seen postoperatively include ureteral obstruction, urinary leakage at the graft, and the occurrence of lymphoceles. All of these complications can potentially involve a return to surgery for repair, although obstructions caused by hematoma may resolve without intervention or perhaps with percutaneous drainage (Ginns et al., 1999). Renal artery thrombosis represents a very serious complication that may threaten graft survival. Ultrasonography of the new kidney is performed within the first 48 hours of transplantation to assess the status of the renal artery and vein and check for signs of ureteral obstruction.

Liver transplant patients begin their immediate postoperative period in much the same fashion as kidney transplants, although the focus of postoperative monitoring centers on the function of the new liver. Considerable blood loss and fluid shifts may have occurred in the operating room, often a result of the patient's pretransplant medical condition. Signs and symptoms of hemorrhage will be carefully monitored, and coagulapathies may be corrected with fresh frozen plasma. In addition to the standard Foley, nasogastric tubes, and venous access lines seen with all transplanted patients, liver transplant patients will arrive with at least two Jackson–Pratt drains placed for drainage. Hemodynamically, the patients may have difficulty with hypertension and electrolyte imbalance. Typical vascular complications include hepatic artery and portal vein thrombosis and occur in approximately 10% of liver transplantation cases. These may require a return to surgery for repair.

Two to three days of mechanical ventilation can be expected following lung transplantation. When sufficient tidal volume is reached along with an adequate spontaneous ventilatory rate and an alert mental status, the lung transplant recipient can be extubated. Chest tubes placed during surgery are generally removed postoperatively between days 6 and 8. Complications following lung transplantation include the reimplantation response; a combination of ischemia, reperfusion, and injury; and lymphatic discontinuity that may contribute to pulmonary edema (Ginns et al., 1999). Ventilatory management is much the same as usual postoperative management, except for those who are transplanted for chronic obstructive lung disease (COLD). These patients, who will continue with one hyperinflated lung in their chest, may be positioned with their native lung down to decrease mechanical pressure from the hyperinflated lung. Minimizing fluid intake is critical for these individuals, so as to reduce risk of pulmonary edema while maintaining hemodynamic stability.

Heart transplant recipients generally recover more quickly than patients undergoing open-heart surgeries. The hemodynamic monitoring and support of the transplant patient is similar to open-heart care. Bradycardia and junctional rhythms are not unusual in the transplant patient, and most patients will have pacing wires placed during the transplant procedure. Patients will also require small amounts of inotropic support for the first 2 to 3 days postoperatively. After a relatively short stay in the ICU for postoperative monitoring, the heart transplant patient can be moved to a general transplant ward for the remaining recovery period, typically 4 to 5 days. At the end of the first postoperative week, the patient will undergo an initial endomyocardial biopsy to monitor for rejection. The biopsy is performed in the cardiac catheter suite. The right internal jugular vein is catheterized, and bioptomes are advanced into the right ventricle for biopsy.

Throughout the entire hospitalization for patients receiving transplanted organs, transplant coordinators, social workers, and discharge coordinators are planning for and organizing a smooth transition to the home or alternative setting at the time of discharge. The average length of stay for transplant recipients has continued to shorten, as improvements in the entire transplantation process have been seen. Managed care influences have also contributed to shorter hospitalization stays. As a result, many transplant centers begin formal postoperative teaching classes prior to transplantation.

COMPLICATIONS OF ORGAN TRANSPLANTATION

Organ rejection and postoperative infection represent major complications following organ transplantation. Many other potential complications are also seen, and these are primarily the result of direct and indirect side effects of many of the necessary medications required for immunosuppression. Medical management of these individuals requires somewhat of a balancing act for transplant physicians, who strive to maintain viability of a transplanted organ through immunosuppressive therapy, while also attempting to reduce other potentially serious side effects these agents produce.

Rejection continues to represent one of the most common causes of graft failure. With an intact immune system, the body's natural response to a newly transplanted organ is rejection. Specific lymphocytes within the immune system

Table 19.2   Signs and Symptoms of Rejection by Organ Type and Commonly Employed Diagnostics in the Detection of Rejection

Transplant Type	Signs and Symptoms of Rejection	Common Diagnostics
Kidney	Flank tenderness; diminished urine output; weight gain; edema; increased serum creatinine	Chemistry profile, specifically serum creatinine; immunosuppressive levels; kidney biopsy
Liver	Increased bilirubin and GGT ; tenderness at operative site; usually asymptomatic of pain or discomfort	Bilirubin levels; GGT; immunosuppressant levels; liver biopsy
Lung	Increasing shortness of breath; infiltrates on chest x-ray; decreased FEV1; FEF 25–75 (PFTs)	Chest x-ray; exercise oximetry; pulmonary function tests; diagnostic bronchoscopy with bronchial lavage
Heart	Fatigue; peripheral edema; S3 gallop; pericardial friction rub; decreased ECG voltage	Rejection can only be monitored by endomyocardial biopsy

recognize the genetic blueprint of anything that is not native to the recipient. As a result of advances in HLA typing and cross-matching, hyperacute rejection today is almost extinct, although chronic rejection remains a serious unsolved complication. Organs donated and received between identical twins are the only transplants that will not require comprehensive immunosuppression. A wide spectrum of improved immunosuppressive agents that have contributed significantly to a drastic reduction in the incidence of acute cellular rejection for most transplanted organs is now available.

The diagnosis and treatment of rejection varies by organ type. Table 19.2 identifies common signs and symptoms of rejection by organ transplant type and the most common diagnostics utilized to identify early rejection.

IMMUNOSUPPRESSION

Advances in organ transplantation have been largely due to improvements in and the general availability of immunosuppressants. Fifty years ago, total body irradiation was the only form of immunosuppression available following transplantation. High-dose irradiation was required to prevent rejection, and most patients died from secondary marrow aplasia or overwhelming infection. Azathioprine was introduced in the early 1960s, representing a major advance in kidney transplantation. With prolonged graft survival demonstrated, a dramatic increase in the number of kidney transplant units was seen throughout the world. Steroids were soon added in combination with azathioprine to treat rejection and subsequently for prevention of rejection. This regimen was typically followed during the 1960s and 1970s, until cyclosporin became readily available in the early 1980s. With the introduction of cyclosporin, another dramatic breakthrough in allograft survival was seen. Graft and host survival was improved not only in kidney transplantation, but in liver and heart transplants as well. Many new immunosuppressant agents are currently under investigation that are promising for yet further dramatic improvements in transplantation outcomes. The production of monoclonal antibodies that recognize different cell surface markers on lymphocytes expands the opportunity for increased specificity of immunosuppression.

Transplant recipients will require immunosuppressive therapy throughout their life or the life of the graft. Most will receive at least dual-agent therapy, although protocols vary to include triple and quadruple therapy, along with a variety of other medications. Immunosuppressants represent a significant proportion of the long-term outpatient expenses incurred by transplanted individuals beyond the first 12 months following transplantation. The cost of standard immunosuppression alone typically ranges from $8000 to $13,000 per year (2002 dollars) (UNOS, 2002).

Managing immunosuppressant therapy can be a clinical challenge. Careful consideration is given to other necessary medications a patient may require for conditions other than end-stage organ disease. For example, there is increased metabolism of cyclosporine when administered with other medications such as phenytoin and Phenobarbital, thus decreasing its antirejection qualities. Conversely, drugs such as erythromycin and certain antifungal agents impair cyclosporin metabolism; therefore dosing must be adjusted accordingly.

Maintenance immunosuppressive agents commonly employed in today's transplant programs are listed in Table 19.3 and are identified by category, function, common side effects, and standard dosing.

Beyond maintenance immunosuppression, monoclonal or polyclonal antibodies add a new dimension to immunosuppression therapy and are utilized for induction therapy, as well as treatment of moderate to severe rejection (Table 19.4). These drugs are generally initiated in the hospital setting following transplantation, where patient response can be monitored. If well tolerated, they may be continued after discharge in the outpatient setting, although usually administered over a relatively short course (7 to 14 days). Should long-term monoclonal or polyclonal antibodies be required, a substantial increase in the cost of immunosuppression is seen with a single dose; average wholesale costs range from approximately $350 to as much as $1595 (*Drug Topics Red Book*, 2002).

INFECTION

Infection is a major cause of morbidity and mortality for transplanted patients. It has been estimated that more than 60% of transplanted patients encounter some type of infection within the first posttransplant year (Rubin, 1999). Clearly, the risk of infection is exceptionally high with an immunocompromised host.

Within the first month following transplantation, bacterial infections are most common and are generally related to the surgery and invasive procedures such as intravenous lines, drain tubes, and indwelling catheters. Prophylactic antibiotic coverage begins intraoperatively at most transplant centers. Beyond the first postoperative month, the effects of sustained immunosuppression predispose the patient to viral infections, such as CMV, EBV, and hepatitis B and C. Postoperative CMV infection is common and represents a serious problem and concern in organ transplant patients. The host patient can be infected with this virus when CMV mismatched organs are transplanted such that a CMV-positive donor organ is transplanted into a CMV-negative recipient. CMV has been cited as a risk factor for acute rejection (McLaughlin et al., 2002) and chronic rejection (Weinberg et al., 2001). Most centers will preferentially treat with an intravenous antiviral agent for up to 30 days, then convert to an oral agent for long-term treatment or prophylaxis (Rubin, 2000). In combination with antivirals, CMV hyperimmune globulin may also be administered at periodic intervals. Opportunistic infections are also seen beyond 6 months postoperatively.

Prevention of bacterial, viral, and fungal infections is critical for graft and host survival. Therefore, prophylactic treatment, primarily within the first year of transplantation, is standard practice. Thereafter, antibiotics and other antimicrobials are frequently prescribed with the onset of fever or other symptoms of potential infection.

Bactrim is a mainstay for most transplant program protocols for prevention of pneumocystic pneumonia. For those sensitive to sulfa preparations, pentamidine inhalation treatments are administered in an outpatient setting on a monthly basis. CMV prophylaxis (ganciclovir/valganciclovir) is usually administered for the first year following transplantation, as is acyclovir for herpes zoster prophylaxis. *Candida* prophylaxis (fluconazole, itraconazole) is also generally prescribed for the first year after transplantation.

OTHER COMPLICATIONS

In approximately 75% of renal transplant recipients, hypertension is a problem following transplantation. Blood pressure monitoring is an integral part of follow-up. Patients are taught to monitor their own blood pressure and are sent home with blood pressure monitoring equipment. Commonly prescribed antihypertensives utilized by transplant centers include nifedipine, Norvasc, atenolol, clonidine, and hydrochlorothiazide.

Hyperlipidemia is commonly seen in many transplanted patients, with rates of occurrence ranging from 29 to 62% posttransplantation (Backman & Morales, 2000). Cardiovascular disease remains the leading cause of late mortality in renal transplant patients. A cholesterol-lowering agent, such as Pravachol, Lipitor, or Lopid, is usually included in the medication regime. There is also a high incidence of gastrointestinal ulcers, and many transplanted patients require long-term use of H2 receptor antagonists such as Pepcid, Zantac, Prilosec, Prevacid, Nexium, or Protonix.

The onset of diabetes mellitus following transplantation has been reported in 10 to 15% of patients and has been linked to the combination of Prograf and steroids (Weir & Fink, 1999). Many patients require short-term insulin use, although a small percentage will remain insulin dependent. The highest incidence of insulin dependency following transplantation is in the African American and Hispanic population groups.

Transplanted patients also have a significantly heightened risk for malignancies. A 21-fold increased incidence of skin cancer has been reported in the transplanted population relative to the general population at large, along with a 28- to 49-fold increased incidence of lymphoproliferative disease (Penn, 2001).

Table 19.3   Maintenance Immunosuppression

Immunosuppressant	Category	Function	Common Side Effects	Maintenance Dosage
Prograf (Tacrolimus, FK 506)	Calcineurin inhibitor	Inhibits T cell function by impairing release of interleukin-2 (IL-2); binds to immunophilin FKBP (acute or cellular rejection prevention)	Hypertension Tremor Nephrotoxicity Diarrhea Hyperkalemia Insomnia Hyperglycemia	0.1– 0.3 mg/kg/day; generally given orally; may be given intravenously
Neoral (cyclosporine)	Calcineurin inhibitor	Inhibits T lymphocyte response by binding cyclophilin; also impairs IL-2 (acute or cellular rejection prevention)	Hypertension Tremor Nephrotoxicity Hirsutism Gingival hyperplasia Hypokalemia	5–15 mg/kg/day given in two divided doses
CellCept (Mycophenolate mofetil — MMF)	Selective antimetabolite	Blocks synthesis of guanosine, thus blocking T and B cell proliferation (acute and possibly humoral rejection prevention)	Diarrhea Nausea Abdominal discomfort Leukocytosis	1–3 g daily divided every 12 hours

Drug	Type	Mechanism	Side Effects	Dosage
Imuran (Azathioprine)	Antimetabolite	Inhibits T and B lymphocyteproliferation by inhibiting DNA and RNA synthesis	Leukopenia Thrombocytopenia Alopecia Anorexia Toxic hepatitis	1–3 mg/kg/day in a single daily dose
Rapamune (Sirolimus)	Macrolide antibiotic	Impairs capacity of cytokines to trigger T cells to enter cell division; inhibits B cell proliferation (possibly cellular and humoral rejection prevention)	Anemia Thrombocytopenia Leukopenia Hypertension Hypercholesterolemia	2–5 mg/day
Prednisone (Methylprednisolone, Solu-Medrol)	Corticosteroid	Inhibits lymphocyte proliferation; nonspecific anti-inflammatory agent	Increased appetite Cushingoid syndrome Hypertension Hyperglycemia Insomnia Mood swings GI upset Acne Osteoporosis Cataracts	5–10 mg/day for the treatment of acute rejection; may be given in doses up to 1–2 mg/kg IV

Table 19.4 Monoclonal and Polyclonal Antibodies (Immunosuppressive Induction and Rescue Agents)

Agent	Category	Function	Common Side Effects	Dosage
OKT3 (Muromonab-CD3)	Monoclonal antibody	Alteration of T cells by binding of CD3 T cell (treatment of acute rejection when conservative therapy fails)	Fever Body aches/chills Pulmonary edema Nausea/vomiting Diarrhea Tremors Aseptic meningitis	5 mg/day for 7–14 days according to center protocol
Simulect (Basiliximab)	Monoclonal antibody	Binds receptors of interleukin-2 (IL-2) complex; inhibits IL-2-mediated T lymphocytes	May predispose patients to infection or PTLD	Day of transplant: 20 mg IV Postoperative day 4: 20 mg IV
Zenapax (Daclizumab)	Monoclonal antibody	Binds receptors of IL-2 complex; inhibits IL-2-mediated T lymphocytes	Nausea/vomiting May predispose patients to infection or PTLD	1 mg/kg given every 14 days for a total of 5 doses
Thymoglobulin	Polyclonal immunoglobulin	Antibody may adhere to cell receptors, which reduces the amount of circulating T lymphocytes	Fever/chills Thrombocytopenia Leukopenia Myalgia Headaches	

LONG-TERM FOLLOW-UP

After discharge from the acute care setting, patients immediately begin their transplant clinic follow-up. With each clinic visit, laboratory studies are obtained to include CBC, chemistry profile, and immunosuppressant levels. Some transplant centers routinely biopsy transplanted kidneys annually or as indicated to monitor for rejection, while other centers biopsy within the first 12 months and only when there are demonstrable signs of rejection thereafter. Biopsies may be performed in an outpatient surgery setting under the guidance of ultrasound or through inpatient admission.

Heart transplant patients will undergo endomyocardial biopsy and follow-up chest x-rays. Heart biopsies begin at 7 to 10 days postoperatively. This is followed by weekly biopsies for 2 to 3 weeks, then monthly for 2 to 3 months, progressing to 60-day intervals, quarterly intervals, semiannual intervals, and, ultimately, biopsies on an annual basis.

Outpatient clinical follow-up with lung transplant patients will include laboratory monitoring, chest x-rays, and pulmonary function tests. Postoperative clinic visit intervals for these patients are generally scheduled weekly for 4 weeks, followed by 2-week intervals for approximately 8 weeks, monthly for 3 to 4 months, 60-day intervals for at least 4 months, and then quarterly. Patients are discharged with a handheld spirometer to encourage daily monitoring of pulmonary function.

Most transplant patients will average 20 to 35 outpatient transplant clinic visits during their first postoperative year. Assuming relative medical stability, clinic visits may be reduced and typically range from 5 to 15 per year thereafter. Hospital readmission is most common for infection or rejection, with the highest incidence of readmission for transplant complications following lung and kidney transplantation.

VOCATIONAL ISSUES

The risk of contracting infection, including communicable diseases, following transplantation represents a serious concern. These individuals will remain immunocompromised with the requirement for immunosuppression therapy. The risk of infection is usually greatest during the first postoperative year, until maintenance therapy is ultimately achieved. Work limitations are dependent to some degree on the type of transplantation, but it is usually recommended that patients avoid heavy manual labor or occupations where the risk of even minor injury is significant. The transplant may necessitate vocational retraining or assistance with work modification. During the first 3 to 6 months following transplantation, medical follow-up is frequent and intensive. Employers should be made aware of the importance of this medical follow-up and the impact this will have on return to work opportunities. In general, as with most people with disabilities, the individual should be evaluated for his or her skills, abilities, functional limitations, and other factors, and a medical professional should be involved in outlining vocational considerations (Weed & Field, 1994). In many cases, if not most, a graduated return to work schedule should be arranged (Lane & Weed, 1999).

Most people suffering from end-stage organ disease are unable to maintain gainful employment prior to transplantation. Adults who qualify for benefits through the Social Security Administration or other disability benefit programs are usually declared totally disabled and thus leave the workforce. Those who qualify for benefits solely on a disability basis may face a financial dilemma following successful transplantation, with an eventual loss of the benefits which they have relied upon for many years. This is particularly true for individuals with end-stage renal disease, who often remain on dialysis for many years before receiving their transplant. Within 2 to 3 years following successful transplantation, many of the transplant recipients who are below age eligibility for Social Security no longer qualify for disability benefits, to include Medicare, and must return to the workforce. While the transplanted patient usually feels liberated from certain death and can enjoy a greatly improved state of health, the prospects of failure in the attempt to return to work can be a frightening experience for one who has not been actively employed for many years. The vocational rehabilitation counselor should be consulted early in the planning stages of transplantation, for he or she will serve an important role for those planning to return to the workforce.

GRAFT AND PATIENT SURVIVAL

Both graft and patient survival continues to improve in all transplant organ categories, despite the necessity of transplantation from donors with less than optimal HLA compatibilities due to a growing waiting list of individuals needing organs and a plateau in the number of donors. This has been particularly true for kidney transplantation, where the results of living donor kidney transplants continue to be superior to those achieved with cadaver donors. An unexpectedly high rate of success has been seen even when transplants are performed between genetically unrelated spouses, in-laws, friends, and strangers, thus leading to an increase in the acceptance of these unconventional donors (Cecka & Terasaki, 2002). Longer-term graft and patient survival continues to be greatest for kidney transplants, while lung and combined liver and intestinal transplants have the shortest patient survival. Kidney transplanted patients also have the advantage of return to dialysis if the graft fails, and many have an opportunity for subsequent transplantation(s).

The annual report of the U.S. Organ Procurement and Transplantation Network provides extensive and timely reports concerning graft and patient survival rates, as well as other valuable information concerning the transplantation and organ donation process in the U.S. These reports are available to the general public and include specific data by transplant center, region, state, and nation. Table 19.5 provides current statistical information concerning graft and patient survival by organ type at 3 months, 1 year, 3 years, 5 years, and 10 years following transplantation in the U.S.

ESTIMATED COSTS FOR TRANSPLANTATION

Hospitalization costs for organ transplantation can vary substantially, and this variation is usually complication dependent (postoperative), with varying lengths of stay. Standard deviations reported by reliable databases are generally in excess of $100,000. The sections above in this chapter have included pertinent information needed by the life care planner to develop a comprehensive life care plan for individuals suffering from the most common forms of end-stage organ diseases and awaiting organ transplantation. As with other diagnostic groups, life care planning in transplantation must be individualized for each person, with consideration given to specific parameters applicable for the individual. Specific factors that should be considered in developing the life care plan include patient age, gender, blood type, transplant status, and transplant center, as these factors can affect recipient candidacy and specific waiting times for transplantation. Likewise, preoperative and postoperative protocols can vary from one center to the next, although most OPTN-certified transplant centers are similar. Center- and organ-specific immunosuppressant protocols do tend to vary, which over time can have a significant impact on cost.

Table 19.6 provides an estimate of average billed charges per transplant in the U.S. as of July 1, 2002, for the first year following transplantation.

CASE STUDY

Abbreviated Life Care Plan

James R. Doe is a 55-year-old, nondiabetic, married, Caucasian male diagnosed with end-stage renal disease secondary to drug-induced interstitial nephritis. He has required renal replacement therapy for just over 2 years, having attempted peritoneal dialysis initially, but now requiring hemodialysis due to loss of adequate peritoneal membrane over time from scarring secondary to recurring peritonitis. Mr. Doe has completed his initial evaluation for transplantation and has been advised that he is a good candidate for kidney transplantation. He is followed through the renal transplantation program of a high-volume transplantation center in Dallas, TX. In the absence of an available living related donor, he has been placed on the waiting list for a cadaveric organ. Based on his current status and placement on the waiting list, transplantation is anticipated within 2 years. This is confirmed by his transplant physician, pretransplantation coordinator, and the local organ procurement organization. Residual patient life expectancy is estimated at 15 years, assuming successful transplantation.

Mr. Doe is a high school graduate with 30 years experience as a cabinetmaker. He has been self-employed for 20 years and continues to work on a limited part-time basis. He admits to frequent periods of depression associated with his decline in health and requirement for dialysis. His wife of 32 years is somewhat apprehensive about his decision to proceed with transplantation, as she fears that her husband may die from the procedure. She is currently undergoing counseling through the transplantation center, to better understand the benefits and risks associated with kidney transplantation. Mr. and Mrs. Doe do not have children. Mr. Doe has a history of severe degenerative joint disease involving his bilateral knees and, to a lesser extent, his bilateral hips. Arthroplasty of the knees has been discussed but is currently on hold while Mr. Doe awaits kidney transplantation. He is otherwise in good health, with only mild hypertension that is well controlled on medication.

Upon completion of a comprehensive client and family interview and evaluation, review of the medical records, and consultation with key transplantation team members, a life care cost analysis was developed for Mr. Doe as follows.

Table 19.5 Graft and Patient Survival at 3 Months, 1 Year, 3 Years, 5 Years, and 10 Years (%)

Organ and Survival Type		Follow-Up Period				
		3 Months	1 Year	3 Years	5 Years	10 Years
Kidney: cadaveric donor	Graft survival	93.7%	89.2%	77.7%	61.3%	35.8%
	Patient survival	97.6%	95.0%	89.2%	81.3%	62.2%
Kidney: living donor	Graft survival	96.9%	94.7%	87.4%	76.0%	55.8%
	Patient survival	99.0%	97.8%	95.2%	90.5%	81.6%
Pancreas	Graft survival	88.5%	80.0%	52.9%	40.7%	16.2%
	Patient survival	97.8%	95.5%	86.5%	84.1%	65.2%
Kidney–pancreas	Kidney graft survival	94.8%	91.8%	83.3%	71.5%	41.5%
	Pancreas graft survival	87.7%	83.8%	77.2%	67.5%	45.5%
	Patient survival	96.9%	94.6%	89.6%	83.1%	65.2%
Liver: cadaveric donor	Graft survival	85.7%	80.3%	70.7%	64.0%	43.7%
	Patient survival	91.4%	87.0%	80.9%	75.1%	58.9%
Liver: living donor	Graft survival	79.8%	71.9%	78.5%	64.3%	53.3%
	Patient survival	88.3%	81.5%	85.0%	81.3%	65.6%
Intestine	Graft survival	77.7%	54.9%	56.6%	30.8%	—[a]
	Patient survival	90.9%	77.5%	57.9%	53.3%	—[a]
Heart	Graft survival	88.8%	84.4%	76.8%	67.7%	46.1%
	Patient survival	89.5%	85.1%	77.6%	69.6%	49.1%
Lung	Graft survival	85.6%	75.4%	55.7%	40.3%	16.8%
	Patient survival	86.5%	76.4%	57.2%	42.6%	19.3%

Heart–lung	Graft survival	69.2%	56.2%	45.7%	48.5%	26.5%
	Patient survival	71.3%	58.5%	45.1%	50.9%	27.1%
Kidney–liver	Kidney graft survival	84.6%	79.7%	60.1%	54.4%	40.6%
	Liver graft survival	85.9%	79.1%	61.8%	58.6%	47.4%
	Patient survival	92.6%	85.6%	71.3%	65.3%	59.2%
Kidney–heart	Heart graft survival	85.8%	76.8%	79.4%	71.6%	50.4%
	Kidney graft survival	85.5%	80.5%	82.3%	71.2%	36.0%
	Patient survival	82.4%	73.5%	85.2%	78.6%	51.3%
Liver–intestine	Intestine graft survival	62.6%	45.3%	46.4%	32.0%	—[a]
	Liver graft survival	63.8%	46.6%	44.9%	35.7%	—[a]
	Patient survival	69.4%	49.5%	48.3%	39.9%	—[a]

Notes: Multiorgan transplants are excluded except where specified.

Living donor transplants excluded unless explicitly listed. Heterotopic heart and liver transplants excluded.

Survival is calculated for transplants during 1998–1999 for 3 months and 1 year; 1996–1997 for 3 years; 1994–1995 for 5 years; and 1989–1990 for 10 years.

Graft survival follows individual transplants until graft failure. Patient survival follows patients from first transplant of this type until death. Counts for graft and patient survival are different because a patient may have more than one transplant for a type of organ.

[a] Suppressed due to small number (0 to 9).

Source: 2001 Annual Report of the U.S. Organ and Transplantation Network (OPTN) and Scientific Registry of Transplant Recipients (SRTR).

Table 19.6 Estimated U.S. Average Billed Charges per Transplant as of July 1, 2002 (First Year Following Transplant)

Transplant	Evaluation	Procurement	Hospital	Physician	Follow-Up[a]	Immuno-suppressants	Total
Heart	$16,800	$57,000	$210,400	$29,300	$68,100	$10,200	$391,800
Lung	$17,400	$58,200	$170,400	$27,100	$57,100	$12,800	$343,000
Heart–lung	$17,100	$115,200	$253,800	$37,400	$68,100	$12,800	$504,400
Liver	$17,200	$54,100	$131,800	$42,700	$58,400	$9400	$313,600
Kidney	$9500	$45,700	$32,800	$13,500	$31,200	$10,600	$143,300
Pancreas	$9500	$43,900	$40,200	$15,200	$31,200	$8900	$148,900
Kidney–pancreas	$9500	$89,600	$39,400	$15,200	$31,200	$10,600	$195,500
Cornea	$0	$0	$7900	$6300	$0	$0	$14,200
Bone marrow, autologous	$15,100	$33,000	$122,500	$16,000	$57,200	$0	$243,800
Bone marrow, allogenic related	$15,100	$33,000	$188,500	$9800	$106,700	$9000	$362,100
Bone marrow, allogenic unrelated	$15,100	$33,000	$257,500	$9800	$122,900	$9000	$447,300
Intestine	$31,000	$69,600	$593,500	$55,100	$58,400	$6900	$814,500

[a] Excludes retransplantation.

Source: Milliman USA Research Report: 2002 Organ and Tissue Transplant Costs and Discussion. Reprinted with permission.

LIFE CARE COST ANALYSIS
For
James R. Doe

Date of Report: 6/20/02
Date of Birth: 04/07/47
Current Age: 55.2 years
Normal (Average) Residual Life Expectancy: 23.8 years
Projected Residual Life Expectancy: 15 years

Diagnoses: End-stage renal disease secondary to biopsy-proven interstitial nephritis; degenerative joint disease, knees and hips; mild hypertension, well controlled; depressive features

Pretransplantation Expenditures

Service/Item	Begin at Age	Duration, Years	Frequency per Year	Average Unit Cost	Annual Cost	Lifetime Cost
Hemodialysis[a]	55	2	1	$114,245.00	$114,245.00	$228,490.00
Counseling (individual)	55	2	24	$162.04	$3888.89	$7777.78
Counseling (family/spouse)	55	2	15	$201.76	$3026.43	$6052.87
Case management	55	2	9	$425.00	$3825.00	$7650.00
Vocational evaluation	55	1	1	$1085.00	$1085.00	$1085.00
Vocational counselor	55	1	12	$450.00	$5400.00	$5400.00
Vocational counselor	56	1	6	$450.00	$2700.00	$2700.00
Vascular access surgery	55	2	1/2	$21,508.63	$10,754.31	$21,508.63
Antidepressant	55	2	365	$3.84	$1400.87	$2801.74
Ongoing transplant follow-up						
HLA typing/other labs	55	2	12	$470.00	$5640.00	$11,280.00
Clinic follow-up	55	2	6	$225.00	$1350.00	$2700.00

[a] Includes inpatient, outpatient, primary care physician/supplier, dialysis unit nursing, and other ancillary services.

Renal Transplantation and First Postoperative Year

Service/Item	Begin at Age	Duration, Years	Frequency per Year	Average Unit Cost	Annual Cost	Lifetime Cost
Transplantation hospitalization (75th percentile)	57	1	1	$100,435.00	$100,435.00	$100,435.00
Surgeons (operative)	57	1	1	$10,715.35	$10,715.35	$10,715.35
Other physician	57	1	1	$4250.00	$4,250.00	$4250.00
Donor organ	57	1	1	$30,139.72	$30,139.72	$30,139.72
Diagnostics						
CBC	57	1	20	$43.91	$878.14	$878.14
Metabolic profile	57	1	20	$70.04	$1400.84	$1400.84
Lipid panel	57	1	6	$131.72	$790.32	$790.32
Urinalysis	57	1	20	$28.23	$564.52	$564.52
Coagulation studies	57	1	4	$73.18	$292.71	$292.71
Antirejection levels	57	1	20	$91.00	$1820.00	$1820.00
Cultures	57	1	9	$78.41	$705.65	$705.65
Creatinine clearance	57	1	20	$67.95	$1359.02	$1359.02
Renal ultrasound	57	1	1	$554.06	$554.06	$554.06
Renal biopsy (inpatient)	57	1	1.5	$24,247.36	$36,371.04	$36,371.04
Medication						
Antirejection agents	57	1	365	$21.76	$7942.40	$7942.40
CellCept	57	1	365	$21.28	$7767.20	$7767.20
Steroid	57	1	365	$0.15	$54.75	$54.75
Bactrim	57	1	274	$1.25	$342.50	$342.50
Acyclovir	57	1	365	$3.08	$1124.20	$1124.20
Diuretic	57	1	365	$0.49	$178.85	$178.85
Calcium channel blocker	57	1	365	$2.90	$1058.50	$1058.50

Service/Item	Begin at Age	Duration, Years	Frequency per Year	Average Unit Cost	Annual Cost	Lifetime Cost
Medication (continued)						
Lipitor or Pravachol	57	1	365	$3.02	$1100.84	$1100.84
Antibiotics (other)	57	1	2	$130.44	$260.89	$260.89
Candida prophylaxis	57	1	365	$2.94	$1073.10	$1073.10
CMV prophylaxis	57	1	365	$4.28	$1562.20	$1562.20
Flu Vax	57	1	1	$47.50	$47.50	$47.50
PneumoVax	57	1	1	$100.31	$100.31	$100.31
Surgeon follow-up	57	1	6	$150.54	$903.23	$903.23
Nephrology/transplant management	57	1	13	$128.58	$1671.59	$1671.59
Hospital readmission	57	1	1.5	$20,003.64	$30,005.45	$30,005.45
Case management	57	1	9	$600.00	$5400.00	$5400.00
Counseling (individual)	57	1	10	$162.04	$1620.37	$1620.37
Counseling (family)	57	1	10	$201.76	$2017.62	$2017.62

Posttransplantation: Subsequent Years

Service/Item	Begin at Age	Duration, Years	Frequency per Year	Average Unit Cost	Annual Cost	Lifetime Cost
Transplant physician (nephrology)	58	12	7	$128.58	$900.09	$10,801.07
Surgical follow-up	58	12	1	$177.72	$177.72	$2,132.62
Diagnostics						
CBC	58	12	5	$43.91	$219.53	$2634.41
Metabolic profile	58	12	5	$70.04	$350.21	$4202.51
Lipid panel	58	12	1.5	$131.72	$197.58	$2370.97
Urinalysis	58	12	5	$28.23	$141.13	$1693.55
Antirejection levels	58	12	6	$91.00	$546.00	$6552.00
Cultures	58	12	1.5	$78.41	$117.61	$1411.29
Creatinine clearance	58	12	1	$67.95	$67.95	$815.41

Posttransplantation: Subsequent Years (Continued)

Service/Item	Begin at Age	Duration, Years	Frequency per Year	Average Unit Cost	Annual Cost	Lifetime Cost
Renal ultrasound	58	12	1.5	$554.06	$831.09	$9973.12
Renal biopsy (inpatient)	58	12	1	$24,247.36	$24,247.36	$290,968.31
Medication						
Antibiotics	58	12	3.5	$86.96	$304.37	$3652.41
Antirejection agents	58	12	365	$21.76	$7942.40	$95,308.80
CellCept	58	12	365	$21.28	$7767.20	$93,206.40
Diuretic	58	12	365	$0.49	$178.85	$2146.20
Calcium channel blocker	58	12	365	$2.90	$1058.50	$12,702.00
Lipitor or Pravachol	58	12	365	$3.02	$1100.84	$13,210.08
Steroid	58	12	365	$0.15	$54.75	$657.00
Hospital readmission	58	12	1	$20,003.64	$20,003.64	$240,043.63
Dialysis graft closure	58	1	1	$11,201.00	$11,201.00	$11,201.00
Counseling (individual)	58	1	10	$162.04	$1620.37	$1620.37
Counseling (family)	58	1	10	$201.76	$2017.62	$2017.62
Case management	58	12	3.5	$425.00	$1487.50	$17,850.00

Potential Care Needs

Service/Item	Begin at Age	Duration, Years	Frequency per Year	Average Unit Cost	Annual Cost	Lifetime Cost
Hemodialysis	60	2	1	$114,245.00	$114,245.00	$228,490.00
Graft failure retransplant (1st-year costs)	62	1	1	$268,487.87	$268,487.87	$268,487.87

Transplantation Centers

Retrieved July 29, 2003, from http://www.transweb.org/reference/sites/centers.htm.

Brigham and Women's Hospital's Transplant Programs: Heart, Kidney, Lung
British Columbia Transplant Society
Children's Hospital of Los Angeles
Cleveland Clinic Foundation Transplant Center
Emory University Division of Transplantation
Fairview University Children's Hospital
Henry Ford Health System transplant program
Howard University Transplant Center
Jackson Memorial Hospital
Johns Hopkins Comprehensive Transplant Center
Lied Transplant Center
London Health Sciences Center Multi-Organ Transplant Program (Canada)
Loyola University Medical Center Transplant Programs
Medical College of Georgia
Medical College of Virginia Hospitals of the VCU Health System
The Methodist Hospital Multi-Organ Transplant Center
Midwest Eye-Banks and Transplantation Center
National Institute of Transplantation
New York Presbyterian Hospital–Cornell Medical Center Organ Preservation
    Unit
New York University Medical Center Division of Transplant Surgery
Northwestern University Division of Organ Transplantation
Ochsner Multi-Organ Transplant Center
Oregon Health Sciences Center transplant program
Porter Transplant Service
St. John Health System Transplant Specialty Center
Stanford University Medical Center transplant program
State University of New York at Stony Brook transplant program
Texas Heart Institute
Texas Transplant Institute
Thomas E. Starzl Tranplantation Institute
Transplantation Program at Albany Medical Center
Tulane Multi-Organ Transplant Center
University Hospitals of Cleveland Transplant Program
University of Arizona Medical Center transplant program
University of California at Davis Transplant Center
University of California at Los Angeles' Transplant Program
University of California at San Diego's Heart Transplant Program
University of Florida South Health Sciences Center transplant surgery
University of Iowa Hospitals and Clinics
University of Kentucky Transplant Center
University of Maryland Transplant Services
University of Michigan Transplant Center–Michigan Transplant

University of Minnesota Transplant Surgery
University of Nebraska transplant program (Lied Transplant Center)
University of Oklahoma Health Sciences Center Transplant Program
University of Pennsylvania Health System transplant services
University of Southern California Liver Transplant Program
University of Tennessee (Memphis) Transplant Program
University of Texas Division of Immunology & Transplantation
University of Texas Health Science Center at San Antonio (organ transplantation
    program)
University of Toronto Multi-Organ Transplant Program (Canada)
University of Virginia Heart Center

Resources

Selected Organizations

United Network of Organ Sharing (UNOS)
P.O. Box 2484
Richmond, VA 23218
(804) 782-4800
http://www.unos.org

Coalition on Donation
700 N. 4th St.
Richmond, VA 23219
(804) 782-4920
http://www.shareyourlife.org

Transplant Speakers International, Inc.
P.O. Box 6395
Freehold, NJ 07728
(877) 609-4615
http://www.transplant-speakers.org

National Foundation for Transplants
1102 Brookfield, Suite 200
Memphis, TN 38119
(800) 489-3863 or (901) 684-1697
http://www.transplants.org

Minority Organ and Tissue Transplant Education Program
2041 Georgia Ave. NW
Ambulatory Care Center, Suite 3100
Washington, DC 20060
(202) 865-4888 or (800) 393-2839
http://www.nationalmottep.org

National Donor Family Council
c/o National Kidney Foundation
30 East 33rd St.
New York, NY 10016
(800) 622-9010
http://www.kidney.org/recips/donor/index.cfm

REFERENCES

Backman, L. & Morales, J.M. (2000). Is nonnephrotoxic immunosuppression a possibility? *Transplantation*, 69, 27–30.

Cecka, J. & Terasaki, P. (2002). *Clinical Transplants 2001*. Los Angeles: UCLA Immunogenetics Center.

Charlton, M. & Seaberg, E. (1998). Predictors of patient and graft survival following liver transplantation for hepatitis C. *Hepatology*, 28, 823–830.

Drug Topics Red Book. (2002). New York: Thompson Medical Economics.

Ginns, L., Cosimi, A.B., & Morris, P. (1999). *Transplantation*. Malden, MA: Blackwell Science.

Hauboldt, R. & Ortner, N. (July 2002). Organ and Tissue Transplant Costs and Discussion. Milwaukee, WI: Milliman USA Research Report.

Lane, G. & Weed, R. (1999). Transplantation issues in life care planning. In R. Weed, Ed., *Life Care Planning and Case Management Handbook*. Winter Park, FL: CRC Press.

Matthew, T.H. (1988). Recurrence of disease following renal transplantation. *American Journal of Kidney Disease*, 12, 85–96.

McLaughlin, K., Wu, D., et al. (2002). Cytomegalovirus seromismatching increases the risk of acute renal allograft rejection. *Transplantation*, 74, 813–816.

National Center for Health Statistics . (2002). *United States Life Tables*, Vol. 50, No. 6, Table 5, Life Table for White Males; United States 1999 . Author.

OPTN. (2001). Annual Report of the Organ Procurement and Transplantation Network and the U.S. Scientific Registry of Transplant Recipients (SRTR): Transplant Data 2001. Rockville, MD, and Richmond, VA: HHS/HRSA/OSP/DOT and UNOS. Available at http://www.optn.org/data/annualReport.asp port.asp.

Penn, I. (2001). Neoplasia following transplantation. In D. Norman & L. Turka, Eds., *Primer on Transplantation*. Mt. Laurel, NJ: American Society of Transplantation.

Physicians Fee Reference . (2002). Atlanta, GA: Wasserman Publications.

Rubin, R. (1999). Infection in the organ transplant recipient. In L.C. Ginns, A.B. Cosimi, and P.J. Morris, Eds., *Transplantation*, 747–769. Malden, MA: Blackwell Science.

Rubin, R. (2000). Prevention and treatment of cytomegalovirus in heart transplant patients. *The Journal of Heart and Lung Transplantation*, 19, 731–735.

Texas Organ Sharing Alliance (TOSA). (2002). Online, available at www.txorgansharing.org.

UNOS. (2002). United Network for Organ Sharing, Data. Online, available at www.UNOS.org.

USRDS. (2002). United States Renal Data System. Annual Data Report. Available at www.usrds.org.

Verani, R. & Dan, M. (1982). Membranous glomerulonephritis in renal transplant: a case report and review of the literature. *American Journal of Nephrology*, 2, 316–320.

Weed, R. & Field, T. (2001). *The Rehabilitation Consultant's Handbook*, rev. ed. Athens, GA: Elliott & Fitzpatrick.

Weinberg, A., Zhang, L., & Hayward A.R. (2000). Alloreactive cytotoxic CD4+ responses elicited by cytomegalovirus-infected endothelial cells: role of MHC class I antigens. *Viral Immunology*, 13, 37–47.

Weir, M.R. & Fink, J.C. (1999). Risk for posttransplant diabetes mellitus with current immunosuppressive medication. *American Journal of Kidney Diseases*, 34, 1–13.

20

LIFE CARE PLANNING FOR THE
VISUALLY IMPAIRED

Terry Winkler and Roger O. Weed

INTRODUCTION

Visual impairment can have a devastating effect on an individual, personally, emotionally, socially, and vocationally. Younger and Sardegna (1994) have pointed out that an individual's personality, past experiences with blindness, education, social and financial factors, mobility, occupation, cultural background, general physical condition, psychological readiness, and family support system will affect how he or she is able to deal with vision loss. The consequences of vision loss or impairment are all-encompassing, impacting every area of an individual's life. This demands that the rehabilitation professional develop a carefully thought out life care plan that meets the needs of the individual over a lifetime through all of the various areas affected. In addition, vision impairment encompasses a continuum of problems from low vision to total blindness. The level of preserved vision will affect the recommendations of the life care plan. Technology is rapidly changing and continues to provide interventions that have a tremendously positive effect on a visually impaired person's life and vocation.

The goal of this chapter is to provide background information that the life care planner will need to initiate a life care plan for visually impaired individuals. In addition, and perhaps more important, the chapter provides references to assist in locating resources for the visually impaired. The life care planner must have a thorough working knowledge of visual impairment, its effect and impact, and expertise regarding the types of equipment and technological advances for the visually impaired.

Definitions

Visual impairment may be divided into two main categories: low vision and blindness. Low vision is much more common than total blindness. From an educational standpoint, blindness is defined as visual acuity in both eyes of less than 20/200 or visual field of less than 20°, despite the best correction with glasses (Panek, 2002; Deutsch & Sawyer, 2003). In education, low vision is defined as

0-8493-1511-5/04/$0.00+$1.50
© 2004 by CRC Press LLC

visual acuity better than 20/200 but worse than 20/70 with correction (PL101-476, The Individuals with Disabilities Education Act). Additional important terminology distinctions are *severe visual impairment* and *legally blind*. *Severe visual impairment* is defined by Nelson and Dimitrova (1993) as the self or proxy reported inability to read ordinary newspaper print even with the best correction of glasses or contact lenses. In other words, severe visual impairment is not based on test of visual acuity. Rather, it measures perceived visual problems. *Legally blind* is used to indicate entitlement to certain government and private agency services. Low vision is defined by the American Academy of Ophthalmology (2003) to exist if ordinary eyeglasses, contact lenses, or lens implants do not give clear vision. People with low vision still have useful vision; however, this vision can be improved with visual aid devices. In addition, vision impairment is defined as having 20/40 or worse vision in the better eye even with eyeglasses. In most states, 20/40 is the point at which people can no longer obtain unrestricted driver's licenses (NIH, 2003).

Epidemiology

A variety of estimates are available at various sources regarding the numbers of individuals with low vision or blindness. Definitions of blindness and low vision vary with different authors or sponsoring organizations. This results in some variability of the numbers that are reported. The Prevention of Blindness Database estimates that in 1990 38 million people worldwide met the definition of blind (Tielsch et al., 1990) and more than 1 million in the U.S. (NIH, 2003). This was more than double the population reported in 1972 of 10 to 15 million. Thylefors et al. (1995) reported that 4.6% of the U.S. population met the definition for blindness and 14.4% met the definition of low vision. Nelson and Dimitrova (1993) reported a total number of U.S. citizens with blindness among civilian noninstitutionalized population of 4.3 million. They went on to say that they believed this number represented approximately half of all the individuals with visual impairments in the U.S. Nelson and Dimitrova's (1993) discussion of severe visual impairment revealed that the five states with the highest number of individuals meeting the definition were California, New York, Texas, Pennsylvania, and Florida. Florida had the highest rate of severe visual impairment at 22.6 persons per 1000. It was estimated that approximately 1,000,000 to 1,250,000 were of working age between 18 and 64. For persons aged 40 or older, Iowa, South Dakota, and North Dakota had the highest prevalence (NIH, 2003). In the national picture in 1990, more than 17 of every 1000 persons in the civilian noninstitutionalized population of the U.S. were severely visually impaired. Slightly over half a million met the definition of blindness in both eyes, with approximately 100,000 children meeting the definition of severely visually impaired. The National Information Center for Children and Youth with Disabilities estimates that for individuals under the age of 18, 12.2 per 1000 have visual impairments and 0.06 per 1000 have severe visual impairments, i.e., either legally or totally blind (Teplin, 1995). Some studies indicate that visual problems are strongly linked to race. For example, Tielsch et al. (1990) and the NIH (2003) reported that legal blindness is more common among black Americans than whites, and Hispanics have a higher prevalence of vision impairment than other races (NIH, 2003).

Etiology

A variety of conditions can lead to visual impairment. The most common causes of visual impairment vary with the age of the individual. Deutsch and Sawyer (2003) pointed out that the leading causes for children under the age of 5 include retrolental fibroplasia, neoplasm, infections, and injuries. The same is true for individuals ages 5 to 19. Over age 20, cataracts become the most common cause. During the 1970s, glaucoma was the second leading cause of blindness. However, 1992 data indicate that the most common causes of blindness in the U.S. are cataracts, trauma, amblyopia, and macular degeneration, respectively. This likely reflects a greater awareness, early detection, and treatment of glaucoma.

Low vision may occur from a variety of causes, which include birth defects, inherited diseases, injuries, diabetes, dacryoma, and cataracts. The most common cause is macular degeneration, which is a disease of the retina and causes damage to the central vision. Peripheral vision, however, is not affected. There are different types of low vision according to the American Academy of Ophthalmology (2003). Reduced central or reading vision is the most common; however, decreased peripheral vision may occur, or a loss of color vision, or the ability to adjust to light, contrast, or glare. The different types of low vision may require different kinds of assistance.

Traumatic etiology of eye injuries occurs in a variety of ways. They may be the result of chemical or ultraviolet burns, direct penetrating wounds, abrasions, lacerations, or violent shaking-type injuries, which can damage the retina. Burns to the eye, lacerations, and corneal abrasions can result in significant visual impairment. However, later scar tissue development can also be a complicating factor that leads to deteriorating vision. Detached retina can lead to blurred or altered vision, flashes of light, or total blindness in an eye.

Some medical conditions that are undiagnosed or not treated properly can lead to severe visual impairment. These include eye infections, glaucoma, cataracts, hydrocephalus, and vascular disease. The central causes of visual impairment would include stroke, traumatic brain injury, hydrocephalus, and tumors. A significant limitation to vision can occur from ocular motor injuries.

Functional Outcomes

The degree of visual loss may vary significantly with the more severe visual impairments leading to the most profound types of functional deficits. The age of onset and level of development before loss of sight occurs are critical factors in a person's ability to acquire skills and concepts. Vision may actually fluctuate or be temporarily influenced by factors such as fatigue, light glare, or inappropriate lighting. An understanding of the types of visual impairment is important, but generalizations about a person's visual functioning cannot be made solely on the basis of a diagnosis. Assessment of functional and vocational implications must be conducted on an individual basis, which in turn affects the nature of the final life care plan (Bristow, 1996; LaPlant et al., 1992).

The types of interventions that are required vary, depending on the nature of the visual impairment. For example, if peripheral vision is damaged, the person has tunnel vision and requires different interventions than an individual with macular degeneration, which would result in the loss of central vision with relative sparing of the peripheral vision. Or an individual may have night blindness where he has very little vision in dimly lit areas such as in retinitis pigmentosa, or he may have photosensitivity where his vision is severely impaired in the bright sunlight.

Special issues occur in very young children with visual impairment (Dodson-Burk & Hill, 1989; Matthews, 1996; Teplin, 1995). In fact, the child's development depends upon the severity of the visual impairment, type of visual loss, and age at onset of the vision deficit. The National Information Center for Children and Youth with Disabilities reports that a young child with visual impairment has little reason to explore interesting objects in the environment and misses opportunities to have experiences to learn. This lack of exploring will continue until learning becomes motivating or until intervention begins. Children with visual impairment may be unable to imitate social behavior and understand nonverbal cues because they are unable to see peers or parents. This creates obstacles to a growing child's independence. It is imperative that children with visual impairment be assessed early and receive appropriate interventions. They will require ongoing assessment as they grow and develop. An interdisciplinary approach will be beneficial in teaching self-care and daily living skills, as well as approaching educational and vocational issues. Deutsch and Sawyer (2003) have pointed out that even relatively minor impairment can result in vocational handicaps that limit the range of job alternatives available to an individual and reduce earning capacity. An example is color blindness, which can reduce the range of job opportunities that would otherwise be available. The degree to which total blindness results in permanent impairment and loss of earning capacity varies with the individual and depends on many personal and vocational factors. An infant or young child who has sustained the loss of an eye will require multiple careful follow-up appointments with the placement and replacement of an ocular prosthesis and conformer to promote development of the orbit. Failure to do this will result in some deformity of the forehead and face and will not allow placement of a cosmetic prosthesis.

Psychological Impact

Few conditions are as feared as blindness. As stated in the introduction, an individual's reaction is affected by personality, past experience, education, social and financial factors, mobility, occupation, cultural background, general physical condition, psychological readiness, and family support. Common psychological reactions include anxiety, depression, anger, and, perhaps the most limiting of all, fear. The individual may experience the five emotional stages of loss as defined by Dr. Elizabeth Kübler-Ross (1975): denial, anger, bargaining, depression, and finally acceptance. While not all individuals will experience each of the stages, and the length of time per stage may vary a great deal, some part or all of these reactions may occur.

Deutsch and Sawyer (2003) described a variety of sensory distortions that can occur early on, including a loss of position sense such as a sensation of floating. This disorientation is often exacerbated by the psychological problems that accompany visual impairments. In addition, an individual who has a sudden onset of total visual impairment may have more acute or severe psychological reactions than an individual who has had a slow onset of blindness and has had time to adjust along the way. Varying degrees of independence will be lost, with some individuals experiencing a high degree of dependence on others. This cannot be viewed as a lack of motivation on an individual's part. It should be recognized, as previously stated, that there are multiple factors involved that dictate the ultimate functional outcome from visual impairment. Most will experience a great deal of social isolation, frequently having difficulty in establishing relationships. Some individuals have a substantial difficulty in communicating with sighted people after the onset of their visual impairments. If the visual impairment occurs at a very young age, certain concepts such as visual spatial arrangements can be extremely difficult to grasp.

Psychological counseling will be crucial for individuals with visual impairment to assist in dealing with the impact of the disability. In addition, a variety of specialized training and equipment can be utilized to help improve the person's independence, which will have a positive psychological effect.

Aids to Independent Function and/or Durable Medical Equipment for the Visually Impaired

This need can be divided into two broad general categories: high-technology and low-technology devices. Devices exist to help individuals with low vision and individuals with total blindness. A low-vision device is an apparatus that improves vision. The American Academy of Ophthalmology (2003) cautions that no one device restores normal vision in all circumstances, so that different devices may be required for different purposes. Bristow (1996) reports that a rehabilitation professional should consider three types of aids for the visually impaired: tactile, auditory, and visual aids. Low-vision devices can be divided into optical and nonoptical devices. Optical devices use a lens or combination of lenses to produce magnification. There are five categories: magnifying spectacles, hand magnifiers, stand magnifiers, telescopes, and closed-circuit television. Nonoptical low-vision devices include large-print books, check-writing guides, large playing cards, large telephone dials, high-contrast watch faces, talking clocks and calculators, and machines that can scan print and read out loud.

Lighting is extremely important to individuals with low vision (Panek, 2002). As you age, your need for light to perform a task increases. On average, a 60-year-old person will need twice as much illumination as he or she needed when 20. A visually impaired person may require complete renovation or modification of the entire lighting system in his home or office in order to best accommodate his disability. In some cases, having light sources that can be portable or moved close to the work area, such as high-intensity lights on adjustable arms, are beneficial. Hat brims or visors can be useful in blocking annoying overhead light, and absorptive lenses, which can help control glare, should be considered.

Gail Pickering, an assisted technology specialist, has published an excellent chapter regarding assisted technology for the visually impaired in the 1996 edition of *A Guide to Rehabilitation* by Deutsch and Sawyer.* This article provides a comprehensive discussion of low-technology and high-technology devices and concludes with an exhaustive list of resources for obtaining the devices and information about their cost and use. Also see the resources list at the end of this chapter and the related chapter on assistive devices in Weed and Field (2001).

Examples of low-technology devices that should be included in a life care plan include check-writing guides, watches that can indicate time by voice, tactile clues or feeling, Braille, tape recorders, labels, timers, cooking cups, measuring cups, cooking devices, rulers, large-dial telephones, etc. High-Marks is a liquid paste that hardens to make colored fluorescent raised lettering for writing notes or labeling items that can be easily seen or appreciated tactilely. Label makers can make labels that are large print, Braille, or talking labels that will allow a person to organize her closets and wardrobes, among other uses. Pill splitters and liquid medication guides and measuring spoons are available. Individuals with diabetes and visual impairment will benefit from insulin-measuring devices that are accessible or perhaps a computerized insulin pump. Numerous kitchen devices are available, such as liquid-level indicators, elbow-length oven mitts to prevent burns, and vegetable- and meat-slicing guides. There are self-threading needles, magnetic padlocks (that do not require a combination or a key to open but use a magnetic sensor), typewriters, and letter-writing templates.

High-technology devices include portable money handling, accounting, and identification machines, portable Braille note takers, refreshable Braille displays that can integrate with TDD devices, and optical character reader devices such as the Optacon™. This device will scan printed material and convert it to a tactile display. Similar devices can be obtained that will convert the printed material to a computer file or voice synthesizer. Descriptive video services are available that will allow a visually impaired person to receive narrative descriptions of the visual portions of a television program. In order to receive this service, the person must have stereo VCR, DVD, or TV and a second audio program channel to receive the descriptive video service. These devices should be considered in every life care plan for a visually impaired person. Computers can be modified or adapted, such as utilizing a screen reader, a speech synthesizer to allow a visually impaired or blind person to access computer programs. Screen readers are available from Microsoft that will read the graphical portion of a computer program. Electromagnetic ovens can be used to heat food without flames or heating elements to reduce the risk of burns. Kurzweil™ readers, a computerized camera that scans print media and converts it to voice-synthesized output, are available.

Closed-circuit TV will allow the visually impaired person to modify printed text to an enlarged image or to an image that has enhanced contrast so that it may be easier read. Software programs are available that will scan books on disk for individual words or combinations of words.

Mobility devices are the most common aid, and the simplest is a cane. The proper length is important. The individual should flex the shoulder until the upper limb is parallel with the floor. The distance from the hand to the floor is the proper length for the cane. The cane should be lightweight, flexible, and easily collapsible, and the end of the cane is painted red to indicate to others that the individual has a visual impairment. High-technology mobility devices include a laser cane; examples are the Pathsounder™, the SonicGuide™, and the Mowat Sensor™. These devices operate either by sonar or by light beams. Walkmate™ is an electronic mobility device that vibrates to indicate when an obstacle is in the path. Some individuals will benefit from the Night Vision Aid, which will provide improved vision by amplifying available light. Aids are available that will help to orient an individual or familiarize a person with the environment that he or she is in (Galvin & Caves, 1996). Examples would be three-dimensional maps or tactile aids, verbal recordings, and sight descriptions of travel routes. A contemporary high-technology device for mobility is a Global Positioning Systems (GPS) device, which can literally help a person locate his or her position on the Earth accurate to within a few feet. These devices are now available with verbal directions and are available in models that can be installed in cars or be handheld. If the individual has turned the wrong way, the device will alert him to this fact. Digitized compasses are available also. Some areas or cities have transmitters in public areas such as telephones, restrooms, street signs, ATM machines, elevators, etc., which transmit information about the location.

Guide dog services are extremely beneficial for some visually impaired individuals. Most organizations provide a guide dog at no out-of-pocket cost to the person who qualifies. These organizations often have long waiting lists and fairly stringent criteria as to who may qualify to receive the animal. Although there may be no direct cost, there clearly are numerous expenses associated with a guide dog, including the cost of transportation to obtain the guide dog, training on how to use the animal, and lost wages if the individual is employed. The training varies from a couple of weeks to 6 to 8 weeks in length. Once the guide dog has been obtained, there are costs associated with maintaining the animal's health, tick and flea control, food, grooming, veterinarian care, and kennel stays. In addition, there may be some increased costs to maintaining the home. Appropriate modifications such as a fenced-in yard to allow the guide dog the opportunity to be out of the home during times when not working is essential. Periodic replacement of the guide dog's harness will also be required.

The individual with visual impairment may choose not to own a private vehicle and utilize public transportation or taxicab services for community mobility. Such costs must be included in the life care plan. If a private vehicle is maintained or the person lives in a town that has limited public transportation, then the cost of hiring a driver should be determined.

There are times and situations where the visually impaired individual's community mobility is best assisted by using a sighted companion as a guide. Some individuals do not adapt well to canine guides or the use of assistive mobility devices. There may be emotional or cognitive factors that demand a companion assist the visually impaired person with her community mobility. Indeed, in many cases, dependent on the activity level of the person, career choice, environment, etc., all of the mobility aids mentioned will be required or used.

PERSONAL CARE AND HOMEMAKER SERVICES

There are numerous activities that are required to maintain a home or to live with a measure of independence in the community. The life care planner must carefully evaluate the individual's unique situation and functional abilities and keep foremost in mind the safety of the person for whom the plan is being developed. In addition, it is important to recognize that marked changes in the person's functional status can occur with what would be otherwise relatively minor illnesses for sighted people. The life care plan should have adequate funding for personal care services and homemaker services to cover this eventuality. The visually impaired individual will benefit from some assistance in areas such as personal banking; identifying and marking bills for payments; labeling clothing; food shopping and storage; marking settings on the furnace, washing machine, microwave, and stove; some housecleaning; maintaining the home, lawn, and yard; and many other tasks.

When attending school, college, or seminars, note takers and readers may be required and should be considered in the life care plan (Hazekamp & Huebner, 1989). In most school settings, these services may be provided by the school system with funding from the Individuals with Disabilities Education Act (IDEA). There are also funding sources available through state, federal, and nonprofit resources if the person qualifies (Mendelson, 1987). Such funding can vary with jurisdiction and congressional funding.

Mobility training, available in many metropolitan areas, is essential for the visually impaired and requires a time-intensive initial training period and then updates on an annual or as needed basis. Mobility instructors will be required when there are any changes in the individual's life such as a new home or home modifications, a new job or change in one's present job, a move to a new city, or orientation to new stores and businesses that develop in the community. Changes in public transportation systems or bus routes may also require an additional training period. This is separate from orientation training that is required on an ongoing basis. For example, a visually impaired person will have times when strangers are required to be in the home, such as for home repairs, servicing for utilities, deliveries, etc. Having a trusted sighted companion present in the home during these times provides an extra measure of safety for the visually impaired person and his or her personal belongings.

Formal Rehabilitation

For the newly blind or severely visually impaired, a formal rehabilitation program should be undertaken. Topics that should be addressed at a minimum include communication with the sighted world, training in personal management and household tasks, accessing printed material, meal preparation and consumption, in-home and community mobility, and other activities of daily living. Mobility training should be refreshed at least on an annual or as needed basis and is somewhat dependent on changes in the person's life. Additional areas to be addressed would include Braille instructions, typing lessons, vocational training, and psychological counseling or adjustment.

CASE STUDY

The following excerpts of a life care plan are for a 49-year-old woman injured in a motor vehicle accident. She experienced a mild brain injury as well as blindness from a blood clot on her brain. The following is for illustration purposes only and does not constitute the complete life care plan.

Recommendation	Dates	Frequency	Expected Cost
Aids for Independent Function			
Arctic Business Vision software	2003–2033	Replace every 5 years	$1895
Arctic transport synthesizer	2003–2033	Replace every 5 years	$1295
Braille & Speak portable note taker	2003–2033	Replace every 3 years	$1794
Braille printer	2003–2033	Replace every 3 years	$3995
Duxbury Braille Translator	2003–2033	Replace every 5 years	$495
DUXWP Translator	2003–2033	Replace every 3 years	$295
Optic scanner	2003–2033	Replace every 5 years	$1500
Personal computer with voice control (JAWS and software only)	2003–2033	Update every 2 years	$1000, then $300 per 2 years
Refreshable Braille display	2003–2033	Replace every 5 years	$14,495
Talking money identifier	2003–2033	Replace every 5 years	$685
Maintenance for above equipment	2004–2027	Yearly with deduction for warranty	$500/year average
Mobility training	2003–2004	1 time only	$45,000
Seeing Eye dog	2003–2033	Every 12 years	$0 for dog $1500 year for food, grooming, veterinarian, flea and tick treatments
Allowance for aids such as canes, talking clock, watch, kitchen timer, blood pressure cuff, travel alarm, scale, yardstick, writing guide, garment labeler, talking books, etc.	2003–2033	Yearly	$300/year
Home Care			
Housekeeper	2003–2033	Weekly	$2080/year
Handyman	2003–2033	Weekly	$2080/year
Lawn maintenance	2003–2033	Seasonally (32 weeks)	$700/year
Personal assistance for shopping, etc.	2003–2033	10 hours/week	$6240
Home security	2003–2033	1 time only	$1500 + $25/month maintenance and monitoring

(continued)

Recommendation	Dates	Frequency	Expected Cost
Future Medical Care — Routine			
Physiatrist	2003–2033	3 times/year	$204/year
Neurologist	2003–2033	1 time/year	$54/year
Ophthalmologist	2003–2033	2 times/year	$224/year
Lab tests, including UA , Tegretol, and blood	2003–2033	2 times/year	$156–578/year
Transportation			
Taxi	2003–2033	As needed	$600/month average; economist to deduct average cost of car expense

CONCLUSION

Visual impairments can be caused by disease, injury to the eye or brain, or the natural process of aging. Although total blindness is relatively rare, low vision or vision disturbance (such as neglect or field cuts) can adversely affect the person's ability to live independently or work. This chapter is designed to suggest life care planner topics and services that need to be considered when developing a comprehensive plan. Since the causes of visual impairment are varied and specific functional limitations and medical care are individual, the life care planner should either have education or training in this specialized area or associate with someone who does. Fortunately, many resources and adaptive aids (see below) have been developed for enhancing the person's quality of life as well as productive functioning.

SELECTED RESOURCES

General Information

American Academy of Ophthalmology
P.O. Box 7424
San Francisco, CA 94120-7424
(415) 561-8500, ext. 223
http://www.eyenet.org

American Foundation for the Blind
11 Penn Plaza, Suite 300
New York, NY 10001
(800) 232-5463 (hotline)
(212) 502-7600
(212) 502-7662 (TDD)
http://www.afb.org/

Center for Assistive Technology and Environmental Access
Georgia Institute of Technology
490 10th St.
Atlanta, GA 30318
(404) 894-4960 (V/TTY)
Fax: 404-894-9320
http://www.catea.org

Glaucoma Research Foundation
200 Pine St., Suite 200
San Francisco, CA 94104
(800) 826-6693
(415) 986-3162
Fax: 415-986-3763
http://www.glaucoma.org

Lighthouse, International, Information and Resource Service (I&R)
111 East 59th St.
New York, NY 10022-1202
(212) 821-9200
(800) 829-0500
(212) 821-9703 (TTY)
Fax: 212-821-9707
http://www.lighthouse.org

National Association for Visually Handicapped
22 W. 21st St.
New York, NY 10010
(212) 889-3141
Fax: 212-727-2931
http://www.navh.org

National Eye Institute
Building 31, Room 6A32
31 Center Dr., MSC 2510
Bethesda, MD 20892-2510
(301) 496-5248
Fax: 301-402-1065
www.nei.nih.gov

VISIONS/Services for the Blind and Visually Impaired
Nancy D. Miller, Executive Director
500 Greenwich St., 3rd Floor
New York, NY 10013-1354
(888) 245-8333
(212) 625-1616
Fax: 212-219-4078
http://www.visionsvcb.org

Recorded Reading Materials

American Printing House for the Blind
1839 Frankfort Ave.
P.O. Box 6085
Louisville, KY 40206-0085
(800) 223-1839
(502) 895-2405
Fax: 502-899-2274
http://www.aph.org

Associated Services for the Blind
919 Walnut St.
Philadelphia, PA 19107
(215) 627-0600
Fax: 215-922-0692
http://www.libertynet.net/tildaasbinfo

Books On Tape, Inc.
P.O. Box 7900
Newport Beach, CA 92658-7900
800-626-3333

Braille Circulating Library
2700 Stuart Ave.
Richmond, VA 23220-3305
(804) 359-3743
Fax: 804-359-4777
BrailleCl@aol.com

Jewish Braille Institute of America, Inc.
110 East 30th St.
New York, NY 10016
(800) 433-1531
(212) 889-2525
Fax: 212-689-3692
http://www.jewishbraille.org

Library of Congress
National Library Service for the Blind and Physically Handicapped
1291 Taylor St. NW
Washington, DC 20542
(800) 424-8567
(202) 707-5100
(202) 707-0744 (TDD)
Fax: 202-707-0712
http://lcweb.loc.gov/nls

Recording for the Blind & Dyslexic
The Anne T. Macdonald Center
20 Roszel Rd.
Princeton, NJ 08540
(800) 221-4792
(609) 452-0606
Fax: 609-520-7990
http://www.rfbd.org

Xavier Society for the Blind
154 East 23rd St.
New York, NY 10010-4595
(800) 637-9193
(212) 473-7800

Large-Print Reading Materials

American Bible Society
1865 Broadway
New York, NY 10023
(212) 408-1200
http://www.americanbible.org

American Printing House for the Blind
1839 Frankfort Ave.
P.O. Box 6085
Louisville, KY 40206-0085
(800) 223-1839
(502) 895-2405
Fax: 502-899-2274
http://www.aph.org

Blindskills, Inc.
P.O. Box 5181
Salem, OR 97304-0181
(503) 581-4224
(800) 860-4224
Fax: 503-581-0178
http://www.blindskills.com

Doubleday Large Print Home Library
Membership Services Center
6550 East 30th St.
P.O. Box 6325
Indianapolis, IN 46206
(317) 541-8920

John Milton Society for the Blind
475 Riverside Dr., Room 455
New York, NY 10115
(212) 870-3336
Fax: 212-870-3229
http://www.jmsblind.org

National Association for Visually Handicapped
22 West 21st St.
New York, NY 10010
(212) 889-3141
Fax: 212-727-2931
http://www.navh.org

New York Times/Large Type Weekly
229 W. 43rd St.
New York, NY 10036
(800) 631-2580 (large-type weekly subscriptions)
(212) 556-1734 (office)
Fax: (212) 556-1748

TIME Large Edition
TIME Inc.
Time & Life Building
Rockefeller Center
New York, NY 10020-1393
(800) 552-3773
http://www.time.com

Ulverscroft Large Print (USA), Inc.
P.O. Box 1230
West Seneca, NY 14224-1230
(800) 955-9659
(716) 674-4270
Fax: 716-674-4195
http://www.ulverscroft.co.uk

Optical Reading and Illumination Devices

Bossert Specialties
3620 East Thomas Rd., Suite D-124
Phoenix, AZ 85018
(602) 956-6637
(800) 776-5885
Fax: 602-956-1008
http://bossertspecialties.com

Eschenbach Optik of America, Inc.
904 Ethan Allen Highway
Ridgefield, CT 06877
(203) 438-7471
(800) 396-3886
http://www.eschenbach.com

National Association for Visually Handicapped
22 W. 21st St.
New York, NY 10010
(212) 889-3141
Fax: 212-727-2931
http://www.navh.org

Membership Organizations

American Council of the Blind
1155 15th St. NW, Suite 1004
Washington, DC 20005
(800) 424-8666 (weekday afternoons, 2 to 5 P.M. Eastern Standard Time)
(800) 424-8666 (5 P.M. to midnight, recording only)
(202) 467-5081
Fax: (202) 467-5085
http://www.acb.org

Blinded Veterans Association
477 H St. NW
Washington, DC 20001-2694
(800) 669-7079 (message)
(202) 371-8880
Fax: 202-371-8258
www.bva.org

National Federation of the Blind
1800 Johnson St.
Baltimore, MD 21230
(410) 659-9314
Fax: 410-685-5653
http://www.nfb.org

Consumer Organizations

American Foundation for the Blind
National Technology Center
11 Penn Plaza, Suite 300
New York, NY 10001
(800) 232-5463
(212) 502-7773 (CTIB)
www.afb.org

Association for Macular Diseases, Inc.
210 East 64th St.
New York, NY 10021
(212) 605-3719

The Foundation Fighting Blindness
Executive Plaza I, Suite 800
11350 McCormick Rd.
Hunt Valley, MD 21031-1014
(888) 665-9010
(800) 683-5555
(800) 683-5551 (TDD)
(410) 785-9687 (TDD)
(410) 785-1414
Fax: 410-771-9470
http://www.blindness.org

Glaucoma Support Network
Glaucoma Research Foundation
200 Pine St., Suite 200
San Francisco, CA 94104
(800) 826-6693
(415) 986-3162
http://www.glaucoma.org

The Institute for Families of Blind Children
Mail Stop #111
P.O. Box 54700
Los Angeles, CA 90054-0700
(323) 669-4649
Fax: 323-665-7869

Lighthouse International
111 E. 59th St.
New York, NY 10022-1202
(212) 821-9200
(800) 829-0500
(212) 821-9703 (TTY)
Fax: 212-821-9707
http://www.lighthouse.org

Macular Degeneration Foundation, Inc.
P.O. Box 9752
San Jose, CA 95157-9752
(408) 260-1335
Fax: 408-260-1336
http://www.eyesight.org

National Association for Parents of Children with Visual Impairments, Inc.
P.O. Box 317
Watertown, MA 02471
(800) 562-6265
(617) 972-7441
Fax: 617-972-7444
http://www.spedex.com/napvi

National Association for Visually Handicapped
22 West 21st St.
New York, NY 10010
(212) 889-3141
Fax: 212-727-2931
http://www.navh.org

National Organization for Albinism and Hypopigmentation (NOAH)
P.O. Box 959
East Hampstead, NH 03826-0959
(800) 473-2310
Fax/voice: 603-887-2310
http://www.albinism.org

Adaptive Equipment Catalogs

National Federation for the Blind
Product Center
1800 Johnson Street
Baltimore, MD 21230
410-659-9314
www.nfb.org

LSS Group
P.O. Box 673
Northbrook, IL 60065
800-468-4789
www.LSSgroup.com

Maxi-Aids
P.O. Box 3209
Farmingdale, NY 11735
800-522-6294
www.maxiaids.com

Dog Guide Resources

Eye Dog Foundation for the Blind
512 North Larchmont Blvd.
Los Angeles, CA 90004
213-626-3370

Fidelco Guide Dog Foundation
P.O. Box 142
Bloomfield, CT 06002
203-243-5200

Leader Dogs for the Blind
1039 Rochester Rd.
Rochester, MN 48063
313-651-9011

Pilot Dogs, Inc.
625 West Town St.
Columbus, OH 43215
614-221-6367

Seeing Eye, Inc.
P.O. Box 375
Morristown, NJ 07960
973-539-4425

Southeast Guide Dogs, Inc.
4210 77th St. E
Palmetto, FL 33561
813-729-5665

REFERENCES

American Academy of Ophthalmology. (2003). Low Vision Facts, Questions and Answers. Available at http://www.eyenet.org/.

Bristow, D.C. (1996). Assistive technology. In P. Deutsch and H. Sawyer, Eds., *A Guide to Rehabilitation*. White Plains, NY: Ahab Press.

Deutsch, P.M. & Sawyer, H.W. (2003). *A Guide to Rehabilitation*. White Plains, NY: Ahab Press.

Dodson-Burk, B. & Hill, E.W. (1989). *An Orientation and Mobility Primer for Families and Young Children*. New York: American Foundation of the Blind.

Galvin, J.C. & Caves, K.M. (1996). Computer assisted devices and environmental controls. In R. Braddom, Ed., *Physical Medicine and Rehabilitation*. Philadelphia: W.B. Saunders.

Hazekamp, J. & Huebner, K.M. (1989). *Program Planning and Evaluation for Blind and Visually Impaired Students: National Guidelines for Educational Excellence*. New York: American Foundation for the Blind.

Kuebler-Ross, E. (1975). *Death: The Final Stage of Growth*. Englewood Cliffs, NJ: Prentice Hall.

LaPlante, M.P., Hendershot, G.E., & Moss, A.J. (1992). Assisted Technology Devices and Home Accessibility Features: Prevalence, Payment, Needs and Trends. Advanced data from the Vital Health Statistics, 217. Hyattsville, MD: National Center for Health Statistics.

Matthews, D.J. (1996). Examination of the pediatric patient. In R. Braddom, Ed., *Physical Medicine and Rehabilitation*. Philadelphia: W.B. Saunders.

Mendelson, S. (1987). *Financing Adaptive Technology: A Guide to Sources and Strategies for Blind and Visually Impaired Users*. New York: Smiling Interface.

Nelson, K.A. & Dimitrova, E. (1993). Severe visual impairment in the United States and each state. *Journal of Visual Impairment and Blindness*, 87, 80–85.

NIH. (2003). *Vision Problems in the U.S.: Prevalence of Adult Vision Impairment and Age-Related Eye Disease in America*. Bethesda, MD: National Eye Institute, National Institutes of Health.

Panek, W. (2002). Visual disabilities. In M. Brodwin, F. Tellez, & S. Brodwin, Eds., *Medical, Psychological and Vocational Aspects of Disability*. Athens, GA: Elliott & Fitzpatrick.

Teplin, S.W. (1995). Visual impairment in infants and young children. *Infant Young Children*, 8, 18–51.

Thylefors, V., Negrel, A., Pararajasegaram, R., & Dedzieky, K.Y. (1995). Available data on blindness update, 1994. *Ophthalmic Epidemiology*, 2, 5–39.

Tielsch, J.M., Sommer, A., & Witt, K. (1990). Blindness and visual impairment in an American urban population. *Archives of Ophthalmology*, 108, 236–241.

Younger, V. & Sardegna, J. (1994). *A Guide to Independence for the Visually Impaired and Their Families*. New York: Demos Publications.

Weed, R. & Field, T. (2001). *The Rehabilitation Consultant's Handbook*, rev. ed. Athens, GA: Elliott & Fitzpatrick.

21

APPLICATION OF LIFE CARE PLANNING PRINCIPLES IN ELDER CARE MANAGEMENT

Patricia McCollom

The continuation of living is compounded by the onset of chronic illnesses and disabling conditions as people age, resulting in increased use of health care resources (Fowler & Machisko, 1997). It is expected that by the year 2030, the number of persons age 65 and older will be 66 million and will make up 22% of the population (U.S. Department of Health and Human Services, 2000). Additionally, the population 85 years of age and older is projected to grow to 8.5 million in the year 2030 (Administration of Aging, 1999). As this age shift occurs, physiological aging is delayed, as compared to a century ago. With advances in medical treatment, persons are living longer and healthier into the sixth, seventh, and eighth decades, with greater periods of time in what is considered old age.

Increased age brings increased likelihood of functional loss and disability. As a result, costs for care and services increase. One study has reported that approximately 20% of community-dwelling older adults have some difficulty with activities of daily living, and this percentage doubles for persons who are more than 85 years old (Cohen & Van Nostrand, 1995). The effects of age-related changes on functional activities are summarized in Table 21.1.

Review of Table 21.1 demonstrates that the aging process itself results in expected physiological change. Coupled with lifestyle, nutrition habits, physical environment, and work history, expected physiological change varies. For those with chronic conditions, prescribed medications add an additional variable that impacts long-term health needs. For example, individuals with elevated blood pressure may be prescribed medication that increases susceptibility to falls, as a result of orthostatic hypotension. Facing long-term health needs, elders requiring care management can benefit from development of a life care plan. The life care plan becomes a distinct written resource for the individual and family, listing community resources, payer sources, contacts, and eligibility variables. Using this tool in elder care management benefits the individual, the family, and the case/care manager, as services are provided over a continuum of care.

0-8493-1511-5/04/$0.00+$1.50
© 2004 by CRC Press LLC

Table 21.1 Age-Related Changes on Functional Activities

Body System	Expected Change	Disease/Illness	Functional Consequences
Senses			
Vision	Degenerative change to pupils, iris, sclera, retina Decreased elasticity, opacity, and flattening of lens	Macular degeneration; cataracts	Need for increased lighting; sensitivity to glare; diminished adaptation to light/dark; poor eye coordination; decreased peripheral vision; decreased visual acuity; decreased depth perception
Hearing	Thickening of ear drum Decreased sensory receptors Auditory nerve degeneration	Deafness; chronic vestibular effects	Diminished ability to participate in conversation; safety problems
Smell/taste	Decreased sensitivity of neuroreceptors	Health impairments related to poor nutrition	Decreased appetite; safety problems
Touch	Decreased sensitivity of neuroreceptors	Impaired skin integrity related to pressure, pain, burns	Decreased response to tactile stimuli; safety problems
Musculoskeletal	Decreased muscle mass Loss of elasticity Decreased bone density Deterioration of articular cartilage Altered motor neuron conduction	Arthritis; muscle atrophy; bone fractures; chronic pain	Immobility; decreased strength and endurance; postural changes; impaired balance and coordination; decreased speed of movement and reaction time; body flexibility
Neurological	Decreased short-term memory Decreased processing of information Slowed reflexes Increased response time Sleep pattern changes	Decreased cerebral blood flow; stroke; dementia; depression	Decrease in adapting to new information; decreased ability to problem solve and integrate new information; difficulty in remembering or memorization; need for rest periods
Cardiopulmonary	Decreased pumping force of heart Blood pressure changes Weakening of respiratory muscles Decreased elasticity of cardiac valves Reduced chest wall function and vital capacity	Orthostatic hypotension; hypertension; cardiac failure; myocardial infarction; pulmonary infection	Reduced ability to exercise, work; need to pace energy; increase in fatigability; decreased endurance; shortness of breath

(continued)

Table 21.1 (Continued)   Age-Related Changes on Functional Activities

Body System	Expected Change	Disease/Illness	Functional Consequences
Integumentary	Decreased skin vascularity and thickness Diminished sweat glands Decreased thermo-regulatory control Nails thicken and become brittle Increased corns, callouses, nevi	Frequent bruising, skin tears; delayed healing time; infection of skin and nails; skin cancer	Poor body temperature control; susceptible to tissue damage
Gastrointestinal (GI)	Changes in teeth, gingivae Decreased saliva, gastric juices Decrease bowel motility Decreased blood flow to liver, pancreas, bowel	Nutrition deficits; dysphagia; constipation; elevated liver enzymes; weakening of wall of GI system; hiatal hernia; gastroesophageal reflux disease (GERD)	Decreased ability to maintain intake; swallowing problems; alternations in medication metabolism; change in protein metabolism
Endocrine	Reduced insulin secretion Decreased glucose tolerance Changes in hormone, enzyme production	Diabetes; hypoglycemia	Decreased endurance; monitoring of blood sugar necessary; specific nutritional intake required; prescription medication necessary
Genitourinary	Decreased renal blood flow Decreased muscle tone Decreased glomerular filtration, resulting in changes in acid–base balance	Electrolyte imbalance; recurrent urinary tract infection; urinary retention	Frequency of urination; stress incontinence; severe systemic effects with nausea, vomiting, or diarrhea

In many cases, a life care plan is developed for litigation. In geriatric care, however, it most likely is compiled for long-term care planning or family education. A life care plan in elder care management is distinguished from life care planning for litigation support in three ways:

- The life care plan is an outcome of elder care/case management services.
- The life care plan is developed in collaboration with the individual and family without regard to personal injury legal parameters.
- The life care plan identifies community resources and health care options from which the individual and family may choose.

BENEFITS FOR LIFE CARE PLANNING IN ELDER CARE

Benefits for life care planning in elder care may be specified in five areas. First, a life care plan for elder care management *enhances individual and family education*. Information in the plan includes physician appointments, procedures, medications, needed diagnostic or monitoring tests, home health care services, and chosen options for ongoing services. The document clearly and concisely lists needed information that can be readily accessed.

> *Case Example:* Robert R., age 81, was diagnosed with lung cancer, with metastasis to the lumbar spine. His primary caretaker was an 85-year-old brother. His physician prescribed over 17 medications to address Mr. R.'s health care needs. In the elder care management process, a life care plan was developed that included all medications, the reason for prescription dosage, time for administration, and side effects to note. The pharmacist's name, address, and telephone number were included for reference. Over the remaining 7 months of Mr. R.'s life, he and his brother used the life care plan medication list several times daily, as a support tool, to answer questions and confirm accuracy of administration.

Second, a life care plan in elder care management *facilitates integration of services*. Multiple options may exist for a given program to meet a specific need. When developing the plan in collaboration with the family, options are identified and choices regarding services are made. Services are therefore not duplicated.

> *Case Example:* In the life care plan of Mr. R., noted previously, supplemental nutrition services were needed, since he did not have the strength or endurance to prepare meals. Working with the family, a cooking and food shopping plan was developed with neighbors, to assure food met his tastes and appetite. Use of a community program was declined, due to institutional-style meals, with little fresh fruit or vegetables included.

Third, use of a life care plan in elder care management results in *decreased stress* for the individual and family. The plan delineates not only care and services, but associates costs, identifying the payer source. Prepared in a concise, clear form, the structure of the plan allows the individual and family to locate specific information related to needs, and to review the rationale for treatment and services.

> *Case Example:* Mr. R.'s extended family lived in a distant state. The life care plan's costs section assisted the family in supporting Mr. R.'s brother in decision making regarding home care assistance. Further, a plan was developed that included homemaker services and increased services, as his condition worsened.

Fourth, the life care plan in elder care management *provides a continuing resource to the family* through delineation of needs, rationale and outcomes for programs and services, and evaluation of services.

> *Case Example:* With implementation of the life care plan for Mr. R., the recommendation was for homemaker services once weekly. Listed within the plan was the expected outcome for this recommendation: laundry and household cleaning completed. Evaluation of this service by the care manager demonstrated lack of achievement of the outcome at 4 weeks. Services were increased to three times weekly, which demonstrated outcome achievement.

Finally, *access to community resources* is facilitated through life care planning in elder care management. The life care planner must locate and identify community resources consistent with the individual's needs and present the resources as options to consider.

> *Case Example:* When homemaker services were recommended to assist Mr. R. to remain in his home, such services were not covered by Medicare. Community options were identified and selection for services was made based upon comprehensive review of available options, rather than referral by hospital social service only.

The development of a life care plan in elder care management is based upon individual rights, choice, individual/family values, comprehensive assessment, appropriate resource use and planning, and implementing, monitoring, and evaluating recommended services. The plan is developed with the individual's informed consent or that of a guardian/conservator. By addressing an individual's rights, values, and preferences, the life care plan is removed from a litigation model to a model recognizing individual autonomy. Individual preferences, community resources, and financial abilities determine the plan.

ASSESSMENT

A life care plan used in elder care management is driven by clinical data about the individual, which provides a rationale for resource use. A systematic assessment of the individual's functional skills, cognitive status, limitations, needs, strengths, abilities, and resources (personal and community) is required.

An assessment of functional skills is critical to life care plan development. During assessment interview, consider questions about lifestyle, such as how does the individual spend the day and what activities take place outside the home (McCollom, 2000). Further questioning should define how the elder shops and carries out financial and household management. Review of functional evaluation completed by care providers may assist in clearly assessing the individual's functional status.

Environmental assessment must be integrated with functional assessment, to provide safety-related recommendations in the life care plan. External risk factors may include social isolation, lack of a support system, or geographic location. Internal risk factors for consideration in a life care plan include cognitive status, medications, depression, comorbid illnesses, and mobility.

Life care planning in elder care involves more nonmedical issues. As a result, the life care planner must be able to assess the individual's risk factors, potential problems, barriers, and options. Lifestyle and cultural implications must be considered. A life care planner's values may conflict with the individual's preferences or beliefs. Funding community resources or geographic barriers or family/cultural variables may make autonomy difficult.

Ultimately, the outcomes of an individually driven life care plan include improvements in patient and family satisfaction, education, and understanding of care options. Individual participation also increases involvement in care and service evaluation, which allows the individual some level of control over a difficult circumstance. Furthermore, self-reliance and self-determination are promoted. Table 21.2 provides an assessment tool for use in life care planning in elder care management.

Table 21.2   Elder Care Management Life Care Plan Assessment Tool

1.   Records review
2.   Contacts
3.   Guardian/conservator
4.   Health status
     History
     Review of systems
     Medications
        Pharmacist
        Program medications
     Nutritional status/eating habits
        Cultural specifications
        Illness impact
        Protein needs
     Height, weight
5.   Functional skills
     Self-care
     Cognition
     Communication
     Behavior
     Mobility
     Elimination
     Safety
     Household management
     Community involvement
     Evaluations completed

Table 21.2 (Continued)   Elder Care Management Life Care Plan Assessment Tool

6. Psychosocial status
    Family/friends
    Patient/family values
    Community support
    Mood, affect
    Coping mechanisms
    Stressors
    Substance use/abuse
    Sleep patterns
7. Environment
    Architectural barriers
    Health hazards
    Modification needs
    Transportation
    Community resources used
8. Financial status
    Income
    Assets
    Monthly costs
    Insurance
    Power of attorney
    Living will
9. Risk factors
    External
    Internal

PLAN IMPLEMENTATION AND MONITORING

Implementation of the life care plan reflects action based upon information analysis and synthesis. The plan identifies formal and informal supports and family involvement in the plan. Assignment is made to family, providers, or other resources for evaluation of ongoing needs and the efficacy of provider services.

MAXIMIZING RESOURCES

Life care planning in elder care management typically involves budgeting from limited financial resources and the creative use of community resources. Care and service options may include community or service/church groups; volunteers; private, personal pay; or alternative family resources.

Support services needed may include health screening through parish nurse programs or recreation programs. Respite care may be located through church or diagnosis-specific organizations.

Long-term-care insurance policies may provide alternative services support, such as adult day care, which may be incorporated into the life care plan.

SAMPLE LIFE CARE PLAN

Life Care Planning in Elder Care Management (Edited Version)

Patient:	Robert R.
Address:	6112 Edge Wood Dr. Salem, SC 02711
Date of Birth:	November 22, 1919
Telephone:	(972) 555-1212
Medical Diagnosis:	1. Lung cancer, with metastasis to the lumbar spine
	2. History of cardiac insufficiency and congestive heart failure
	3. Ateriosclerotic heart disease, status post stent placement
Physician:	T.O. Smith, M.D., Oncologist
Telephone:	(972) 555-1111
Hospital:	Adventist Care System 717 Hollyhock St. Salem, SC 02711
Telephone:	(972) 555-2222
Primary Care Giver:	Kurt R. (brother) 6114 Edge Wood Dr. Salem, SC 02711
Telephone:	(972) 555-1213

History: Robert R. is an 81-year-old male, retired, who resides alone in a three-bedroom condominium. The residence is on the second level of the building, with no elevator. He was diagnosed in December 2001 with cancer of the lung, with metastasis to the lumbar spine. He has a history of cardiac insufficiency and ateriosclerotic heart disease, with stent placement in December 2000. In July 2001, he began experiencing lower-back pain and increasing shortness of breath with exertion. Initial medical testing did not reveal the cause for symptoms, and he was treated with physical therapy for muscle strain. Increasing symptoms caused need for further evaluation. Magnetic resonance imaging (MRI) of the spine demonstrated carcinoma invading L4–L5. An MRI of the chest and abdomen demonstrated two lung tumors. Bronchoscopy confirmed squamous cell tumor of the lung. Chemotherapy was initiated.

Status at Time of Life Care Plan Development: Mr. R. was in a weakened condition, with poor nutritional status. He was isolated socially and unable to participate in household management. His 85-year-old brother was the primary caretaker. The brother was recovering from chemotherapy for treatment of non-Hodgkin's lymphoma. The brother's role was medication administration, transportation to physician appointments, and grocery buying. Elder care management was instituted on a private-pay basis by extended family, living in a distant state, to monitor health status and to promote quality of life.

MEDICAL CARE

Care/Need	Rationale	Outcome	Cost	Comments
Monitoring by cancer specialist as scheduled by the doctor; weekly appointments are scheduled during chemotherapy	The doctor must check blood to monitor the effects of chemotherapy	Complications will be avoided and energy levels will be monitored	Paid by Medicare and supplemental policy	Doctor's appointments will vary with completion of chemotherapy; keep a list of questions for each visit to the doctor
Monthly appointments with heart doctor, J.B. White, M.D. (972-555-7212)	Dr. White will check heart's response to the chemotherapy and monitor blood pressure	Medications will be adjusted as needed; complications will be avoided	Paid by Medicare and supplemental policy	Dr. White shares medical reports with Dr. Smith; keep a list of questions for each visit to the doctor
Laboratory Studies/Blood Samples Hemoglobin Hematocrit Comprehensive Metabolic profile	Blood tests will be scheduled weekly during chemotherapy to check the body's response to the medication	The dosage of chemotherapy will be adjusted, as needed; other medications will be prescribed, as needed	Paid by Medicare and supplemental policy	The care manager will arrange for blood work to be completed at the same time as visits to the oncologist to limit travel
Nutritional status evaluation	Appetite will be affected by the chemotherapy and food will not taste as good	Food choices will be listed and appetite improvement should be reported	Care Options 1. Private clinic associated with Dr. Smith ($45/visit) 2. Classes at hospital every Thursday night at 7:30 for 4 weeks ($25 for classes)	Select the private clinic; Medicare does not cover this expense and it will be an out-of-pocket cost

MEDICATIONS

Pharmacist: Dot Harvey, Harvey Pharmacy, (972) 555-7312

Medication/Dose	Why Prescribed	Times	Cost	Comments
Oxycontin, one tablet every 12 hours	Pain relief	8 A.M. 9 P.M.	$71.91/month (60 tablets)	This is a strong medication that will relieve pain and cause drowsiness

(continued)

MEDICATIONS (Continued)

Medication/Dose	Why Prescribed	Times	Cost	Comments
Oxycodone, one or two tablets every 3–4 hours for increasing pain	Pain relief	11 A.M. 3 P.M. 7 P.M. Midnight 4 A.M.	$146.86/month (120 tablets)	This medication is for break-through pain and should be taken on an as needed basis; if patient becomes dizzy, confused, or constipated, talk with Dr. Smith

Note: This approach was repeated for all medications prescribed for Mr. R. The pharmacy he used was selected by Mr. R. and his brother because (1) pricing was competitive, (2) the pharmacy provided home delivery, and (3) a senior discount was provided to persons with greater than four long-term prescriptions. Cost was an issue, since total noncovered medications totaled approximately $700/month.

HOME CARE ASSISTANCE

Care/Need	Rationale	Outcome	Costs	Comments
Meal planning/preparation	Poor intake; poor appetite	Increased intake; improved energy levels; improved function	$0	Neighbors have organized to provide 15 meals/week; Mrs. K. will meet with patient on Thursdays at 10:00 A.M. to prepare a grocery list; Kurt R. will complete shopping
Homemaker services	Decreased strength has limited patient's ability to care for his home as he wishes it to be done	Laundry and cleaning completed	$45/week	Patient requested 3 hours, once weekly, at $15/hour; interviewed two persons from his church and selected one to hire; outcomes will be monitored by the care manager
Home care/skilled[a]	Provide comfort and personal care	Pain management and personal comfort	Medicare coverage	Patient requested hospice care at home at a time deemed appropriate by him and his family

[a] Mr. R. died peacefully at his home, surrounded by friends and family.

CONCLUSION

Life care planning benefits at risk geriatric populations (see Table 21.3). Those who are identified after assessment in medium- to high-risk categories are prime candidates for life care planning. As an outcome of care/case management, life care planning enhances individual/patient education, facilitates integration of services, decreases stress, and encourages use of and access to community resources. With an aging population, life care planning offers a valuable tool for those facing long-term health care needs resulting from catastrophic injury or chronic illness.

Table 21.3   At-Risk Geriatric Population

Category	High Risk	Medium Risk	Low Risk
Characteristics	75 years or older, assisted living, 2 or 3 comorbidities, major functional limitations, 2 or more acute inpatient stays in past 12 months, multiple physician contacts, dialysis, day treatment, home health services	Newly diagnosed chronic illness, 2 or 3 comorbidities, lifestyle change	Lifeline, support system in place, compromised financial status
Case management	Intensive	Active	Maintenance
Frequency	2 weeks or more	Monthly	6–8 weeks

RESOURCES

Accessible Home Page
www.homemods.org

Administration on Aging
330 Independence Ave. SW
Washington, DC 20201
(202) 619-0724
www.aoa.gov

Age of Reason
www.ageofreason.com

Agency for Health Care Policy and Research
http://ahcpr.gov

Aging Network Services
www.agingnets.com

Aging Research & Training News
www.bpinews.com/hr/pages/art.htm

AGS Foundation for Health in Aging
770 Lexington Ave., Suite 300
New York, NY 10021
(800) 247-4779
www.healthinaging.org

Alzheimer's Association
(800) 272-3900
www.alz.org

Alzheimer's Disease Education and Referral
Center at the National Institute of Aging
www.alzheimers.org

American Association of Homes and Services for the Aging
901 E St. NW, Suite 500
Washington, DC 20004-2001
(202) 783-2242
www.aahsa.org

American Association for Geriatric Psychiatry
www.aagpgpa.org

American Association of Retired Persons (AARP)
601 E St. NW
Washington, DC 20049
(202) 434-2277
(800) 424-3410
www.aarp.org

AARP: Coping with Grief and Loss
www.aarp.org/griefandloss

American Bar Association Commission on the Legal Programs of the Elderly
www.abanet.org

American Cancer Society
www.cancer.org

American Geriatrics Society
Empire State Building
350 Fifth Ave., Suite 801
New York, NY 10118
(212) 308-1414
www.americangeriatrics.org

American Society on Aging
833 Market St., Suite 511
San Francisco, CA 94103-1824
(415) 974-9600
www.asaging.org

Andrus Foundation
www.andrus.org

ARCH National Resource Center for Respite Care and Crisis Care Services
Chapel Hill Training–Outreach Center
800 Eastowne Dr., Suite 105
Chapel Hill, NC 27514
(888) 671-2594
www.chtop.com/archbroc.htm

Arthritis Foundation
www.arthritis.org

Assisted Living Federation of America
www.alfa.org

Association for Gerontology in Higher Education
www.aghe.org

Benefits Checkup
www.benfitscheckup.com

Brookdale Center on Aging
www.brookdale.org

California Department of Aging
www.aging.state.ca.us

Cancer Center
www.cancercenter.com

Care for You
www.carethere.com

Caregiver Survival Resources
www.caregiver911.com

CaregiverZone.com
www.caregiverzone.com

Caregiving Online
www.caregiving.com

Caregiving Supplies
www.blvd.com
www.coast-resources.com
www.dynamic-living.com

CarePlanner
www.careplanner.org

Case Management Resource Guide
www.cmrg.com/index.htm

Center for Eldercare
www.elderweb.com

Centerwatch
www.centerwatch.com

Children of Aging Parents
1609 Woodbourne Rd., #302A
Levittown, PA 19057
(215) 945-6900
(800) 227-7294

Citizens for a Sound Economy
www.cse.org

Clinical Trials
www.clinicaltrials.com

Consumer Consortium on Assisted Living
http://ccal.org

Elder Abuse Prevention
www.oaktrees.org/elder

Eldercare.com
www.eldercare.com

Eldercare Locator
927 15th St. NW, 6th Floor
Washington, DC 20005
(800) 677-1666
www.aoa.gov

ElderCare Online
www.ec-online.net

Elderhostel
www.elderhostel.org

ElderSearch.com
(856) 722-9910
Enjoying Retirement, MetLife
www.metlife.com

Elder Support Network
557 Cranbury Rd., Suite 2
East Brunswick, NJ 08816
(732) 432-7120
www.ajfca.org

ExtendedCare.com
www.extendedcare.com.com/asp/default.asp

Family Care America
www.familycareamerica.com

Family Caregiver Alliance
690 Market St., Suite 601
San Francisco, CA 94104
(415) 434-3388
www.fria.org

French Foundation for Alzheimer's Research
(800) 477-2243

Friends and Relatives of the Institutionalized Aged
11 John St.
New York, NY 10038
(212) 732-4455
www.fria.org

Geriatric Education Center
www.hcoa.org/nagec

The Gerontological Society of America
www.geron.org

GriefNet
www.rivendell.org

Guide to Retirement Living
www.retirement-living.com/main.html

Health A to Z
www.healthatoz.com

Health Answers
www.healthanswers.com

Health Care Financing Administration
www.hcfa.gov

Healthfinder
www.healthfinder.gov

Healthy Aging
www.healthandage.com

Home Care Page
www.ptct.com

Home Health
www.e-homehealth.com

Hospice Foundation of America
www.hospicefoundation.org

John Hopkins Intelihealth
www.Intelihealth.com

Long Term Care Insurance Buyer's Advocate
www.ltcibuyersadvocate.com

Long Term Care Insurance Decision Assistance Center
www.longtermcareinsurance.org

Mature Mart
www.maturemart.com

Mayo Clinic
www.mayo.edu/geriatrics-rst/Drug.html

MedBank of Maryland, Inc.
www.medbankmd.org

Medicine Program
http://themedicineprogram.com

MEDLINEplus
www.nlm.nih.gov/medlineplus

MedSite
www.medsite.com

National Academy of Elder Law Attorneys
www.naela.org

National Academy Press
www.nap.edu

National Academy of Social Insurance
www.nasi.org

National Asian Pacific Center on Aging
1511 Third Ave., #914
Melbourne Tower
Seattle, WA 98101
(206) 624-1221

National Association of Area Agencies on Aging
927 15th St. NW
Washington, DC 20056
(202) 296-8130
www.N4A.org

The National Association of Geriatric Care Managers
1604 N. Country Club Rd.
Tucson, AZ 85716
(520) 881-8008
www.caremanager.org

National Association for Hispanic Elderly
1452 W. Temple St., Suite 100
Los Angeles, CA 90026-1724
(213) 487-1922

National Association for HomeCare Online
www.nahc.org

National Association of State Units on Aging
1225 I St. NW, Suite 725
Washington, DC 20005
(202) 898-2578

National Cancer Institute
http://cancernet.nci.nih.gov

National Center on Elder Abuse
(800) 677-1116

National Clearinghouse for Alcohol and Drug Information Prevention Online
www.health.org/index.htm

National Committee to Preserve Social Security and Medicare
www.ncpssm.org

National Council on the Aging
409 Third St. SW
Washington, DC 20024
(202) 479-1200
www.ncoa.org

National Family Caregiver Alliance
www.caregiver.org

National Family Caregivers Association
10400 Connecticut Ave., Suite 500
Kensington, MD 20895
(301) 942-6430
(800) 896-3650 (for family caregivers)
www.nfcacares.org

National Health Information Center
(800) 336-4797

National Hospice Organization
1700 Diagonal Rd., Suite 300
Alexandria, VA 22314
(703) 243-5900
(800) 658-8898
www.nho.org

National Institute on Aging
(800) 222-2225
www.nih.gov/nia

National Library of Medicine (PubMed)
www.ncbi.nlm.nih.gov/PubMed

National Long-Term Care Resource Center
www.hsr.umn.edu

National Policy and Resource Center on Nutrition and Aging
www.fiu.edu/~nutreldr

National Rehabilitation Information Center
(800) 346-2742

National Respite Locator Service
800 Eastowne Dr., #105
Chapel Hill, NC 27514
(919) 490-5577
(800) 773-5433
www.chtop.com/locator.htm

National Senior Citizen's Law Center
1101 14th St. NW, Suite 400
Washington, DC 20005
(202) 289-6976
www.nsclc.org

National Senior Sports Association
www.amgolftour.com

Nursing Home Information
www.nursinghomeinfo.com

Nutrition Analysis Tool
www.ag.uiuc.edu/~food-lab/nat

Oncology
www.oncology.com

Searchpointe
Senior Housing Net
http://ccal.org

SeniorCom
www.senior.com

SeniorLaw Home Page
www.seniorlaw.com

SeniorLink
www.seniorlink.com

Senior Linkage Line
(800) 333-2433

SeniorNet
www.seniornet.com

Senior Options
www.senioroptions.com

Senior Sites
www.seniorsites.com

Social Security Administration
www.ssa.gov

TheHelpWeb
www.imaginarylandscape.com/helpweb/www/www.html

Thirdage.com
www.thirdage.com/care/index.html

United Seniors Health Cooperative
409 Third St. NW, 2nd Floor
Washington, DC 20024
(202) 479-6973
www.ushc-online.org

Web of Care
www.webofcare.com

Women's Health
www.womenshealth.org

World Wide Web, Beginner's Central
http://northernwebs.com/bc

REFERENCES

Administration of Aging. (1999). A Profile of Older Americans. Available at http://aoa.gov/stats/profile/orfil99.html.

Cohen, R. & Van Nostrand, J. (1995). Trends in the health of older Americans: United States, 1994. *Vital Health Statistics*, 3, 3–7.

Fowler, F. & Machisko, F. (1997). The geriatric continium. *Continuing Care*, 1, 20–23.

McCollom, P. (2000). Life care planning: a tool for elder care management. *The Case Manager*, January/February, 37–40.

U.S. Department of Health and Human Services. (2000). *Healthy People 2010*, DHHS Publication PHS 91-50212. Washington, DC: U.S. Government Printing Office.

III

FORENSIC
CONSIDERATIONS

22

FORENSIC ISSUES FOR LIFE CARE PLANNERS

Roger O. Weed

INTRODUCTION

This chapter will summarize some of the issues that the life care planner must consider in order to practice in the area of forensic rehabilitation and may offer a somewhat different perspective than that offered in the chapters authored by attorneys. Clearly, the life care plan (LCP) is used for more than litigation (Deutsch & Sawyer, 2003; Riddick & Weed, 1996; Weed, 1994, 2003; Weed & Field, 1994). Historically the care plan has been used in setting reserves for insurance companies, assisting workers' compensation companies with assessing future care costs associated with work-related disabilities, estimating the cost of future care for health care insurance companies, and providing the client and family with an outline of future care (Deutsch & Sawyer, 2003; Weed & Field, 1994). In the event that inadequate funding is available, the life care plan can become the road map for care. On many occasions the future care plan is not fully funded; therefore, the life care plan can be used to prioritize treatment so that available funding is used most appropriately. In a simplistic way, the life care plan is used to identify needs that can be translated into a budget so that the most important items are given the highest priority.

Since life care plans are used in a variety of jurisdictions, the appropriate "rules" must be considered. Probably the most comprehensive setting is in personal injury litigation (Weed & Berens, 2002). In the litigation arena, the life care plan must consider the entire person and his or her situation. Only items that have economic value are included. For example, hedonic damages, such as the loss of pleasure of life or choice, are not included in this format. This chapter is not intended to provide a comprehensive analysis for items and issues that do not lend themselves to economic projections; the reader is referred to Brookshire and Smith (1990) for a more detailed discussion of this specialized area. It must also be recognized that many states have different legal rules with regard to evidence and testimony. Indeed, federal rules are interpreted differently across the U.S. This chapter is intended to address common issues and topics associated with civil litigation.

0-8493-1511-5/04/$0.00+$1.50
© 2004 by CRC Press LLC

According to *Black's Law Dictionary* (Black, 1990), forensic rehabilitation refers to the practice of rehabilitation principles in legal settings. This short dissertation will discuss the relationship between rehabilitation and the courts, expert witness roles, and selected terms that may be important to the rehabilitation consultant within the legal system.

Rehabilitation experts are relatively new to the courtroom. Indeed, rehabilitation counselors historically were trained specifically to work in public agencies and were often shielded from acting as expert witnesses in personal injury litigation (Weed & Field, 2001). The first entry into the rehabilitation private sector, which involved nurses, was initiated on a larger scale in the late 1960s, when International Rehabilitation Associates, now Intracorp, was formed by an insurance company to help process and manage insurance claims. By the 1990s, private-sector rehabilitation has extended into almost all areas of disability care, including workers' compensation, long-term disability, Social Security disability insurance, health insurance, railroad (Federal Employees Liability Act), longshore workers, Jones Act, and personal injury litigation (Weed & Field, 2001). Although there is considerable similarity across jurisdictions, there are a number of differences the rehabilitation expert should know about before stepping into court.

For example, the word *disability* is defined differently in various systems. In public rehabilitation, *disability* usually refers to the medical condition, which establishes eligibility for services, indicating that the client is able to perform work and benefit from rehabilitation services (Weed & Field, 2001). When Social Security determines a person is disabled, the person is deemed unable to perform "substantial gainful activity" and may qualify for government support. In workers' compensation systems, some states have provision for disability that may be permanent or temporary, as well as partial or total. As with the word *disability*, terminology can make a significant difference and it is important for the rehabilitation expert to understand the meaning of words used in the courtroom.

Although this author recommends specific credentials in support of life care planning consulting and testimony, it is not necessary for the rehabilitation professional to be certified or possess a certain level of education to be considered an expert. According to legal precedence (*Kim Manufacturing v. Superior Metal Treating*, 1976), an "expert witness is one who by reason of education or specialized experience possesses superior knowledge respecting a subject about which persons having no particular training are incapable of forming an accurate opinion or deducing correct conclusion." Therefore, an attorney may retain someone for personal injury litigation who would not be considered an expert in some states for workers' compensation or as a vocational expert (VE) for the Social Security system.

EARNINGS CAPACITY ANALYSIS

Often one element of damages is the loss of earnings capacity (Field & Weed, 1988; Weed, 2002b; Weed & Field, 2001). If the life care planner is not independently qualified to opine about this aspect of the case, he may associate with a vocational expert. In order to provide an expert opinion regarding the loss of potential earnings, the expert must be prepared to provide an assessment of the person's earnings capacity. Although a separate chapter addresses the details for what must be evaluated to arrive at a vocational opinion, generally accepted methods for determining loss of earnings capacity include the following:

1. The most common method assumes the client has a work history. The rehabilitation professional scrutinizes vocational and medical records, perhaps supplemented by testing, and provides a professional opinion regarding preincident and postincident earnings capacity. Obviously, this is not useful for a client with limited or no work history.
2. The Labor Market Access method, developed by Field and Field (1992), uses federal data regarding worker traits and the *Dictionary of Occupational Titles (DOT)* (U.S. Department of Labor, 1991). A computer program can be used to help sort through more than 70 worker traits for the more than 12,000 job titles preincident vs. postincident. This process identifies the number of preincident vs. postincident jobs, preincident and postincident average earnings, and other information that can be used as a basis for the expert opinion. It may be useful to be aware of the new World Wide Web O*Net (http://online.onetcenter.org) developed by the federal government, which is expected to replace the *Dictionary of Occupational Titles*. However, at the time of this publication, there are numerous problems associated with using the O*Net in Social Security and personal injury pre- vs. postinjury opinions, and the aging *DOT* remains the resource of choice.
3. To determine earnings capacity for children and others who may not have ample work history, an extensive review of the client's background is useful. This may include school records, scrutiny of the parents and extended family with regard to work and education, and educational or neuropsychological testing. In acquired brain injury pediatric cases, preincident vs. postincident ability to be educated can be applied (Weed, 2000b).
4. Another common method, known as L-P-E, identifies the client's probability of life (L), probability of labor force participation (P), and probability of employment (E). For more information on this method, the professional is directed to *Economic/Hedonic Damages: The Practice Book for Plaintiff and Defense Attorneys*, by Brookshire and Smith (1990).

A more detailed explanation of these areas can be found in *The Rehabilitation Consultant's Handbook* (Weed & Field, 2001), the *Encyclopedia of Disability and Rehabilitation* (Weed, 1995), and Chapters 4 and 11.

HEDONIC DAMAGES

Another domain that some rehabilitation experts address is the loss of pleasures or choices in life, known as hedonic damages. Methods include describing to the jury the client's situation regarding pain, loss of access to the labor market, psychological effects, loss of consortium, and other factors, to provide the jury with guidelines. However, since hedonic damages cannot be specifically or directly translated into a dollar amount, this item is rarely a part of the life care plan report.

Table 22.1 Elements for Future Care Damages

- When does treatment start?
- What is the frequency of sessions?
- What is the cost per session (if relevant)?
- When does treatment stop?
- Additional costs such as evaluations, tests, laboratory, or medications?
- Any other needs/costs?

Table 22.2 Example Entry for Future Care Damages

- Psychological evaluation in June 2003 at $600
- Expect counseling to begin in July 2003 at 1 time/week, 1-hour session, for 26 weeks at $100/hour, then expect group counseling for 2 years (48 sessions/) at $40/session
- Expect medication, Prozac, 1 tablet of 20 mg/day for life expectancy, at $53.86 per month
- Expect psychiatrist follow-up for medication 4 times/year beginning January 2004 at $150 for the initial visit, then $75 for each visit thereafter to life

LIFE CARE PLAN

Regardless of the topic, the expert must be able to quantify damages in a way that provides the economist, if one is used, or the jury with the necessary information to project costs over time (Dillman, 1987). These data are used to help determine the amount of award to the client, if the party against whom the suit is lodged is found at fault. To ascertain the needs and costs of future care, particularly for serious medical conditions and catastrophic injuries, the life care plan was originally published by Deutsch and Raffa in *Damages in Tort Action* (1981). This method organizes topics according to various categories (see Chapter 1 for an overview and Table 22.1 and Table 22.2) that outline expected treatment, start and stop dates, costs, and other information that will provide the jury with an understanding of the treatment plan. The format is designed to develop a comprehensive rehabilitation plan that includes the necessary information to project the expense, usually with the help of an economist, in order to arrive at a bottom-line figure.

REPORT WRITING

Some general report writing issues were discussed in the chapters written by the attorneys. Of special interest in this author's view is the 1993 ruling known as the Daubert decision (*Daubert v. Merrell Dow*). This decision implied that any testimony in federal court offered by a scientific expert must be founded on a methodology or underlying reasoning that is scientifically valid and can be properly applied to the facts of the issue. Considerations included whether the theory or technique has been subjected to peer review and publication. This theory was extended to expert opinions by the Kumho Tire opinion (1999). (Some states have adopted this federal court ruling, so experts may face a Daubert challenge in state court cases.) Although this topic has been addressed in preceding chapters, it is important to emphasize that proper foundations must be provided to a plan. Since many life care planners either have failed to undergo specific training or do not follow published guidelines, the importance of continuing education, developing standards and methodologies, and publishing guidelines specific to our industry is underscored (Feldbaum, 1997).

One important aspect of the report is inclusion of appropriate details for the jury to determine the cost of future care and effects on vocational opportunities, including earnings capacity. Assuming that an expert has developed all of the necessary data and opinions relative to damages in a personal injury case, it is appropriate to offer a rationale to encompass the issues that should be addressed in a written report. The RAPEL methodology (Table 22.3) is designed to address the relevant topics for personal injury litigation in a rational and commonsense way as well as a format for displaying the information to the jury.

Table 22.3   The RAPEL Method: A Commonsense Approach to Life Care Planning and Earnings Capacity Analysis

Rehabilitation plan   Determine the rehabilitation plan based on the client's vocational and functional limitations, vocational strengths, emotional functioning, and cognitive capabilities. This may include testing, counseling, training fees, rehab technology, job analysis, job coaching, placement, and other needs for increasing employment potential. Also consider reasonable accommodation. A life care plan may be needed for catastrophic injuries.

Access to the labor market   Determine the client's access to the labor market. Methods include the transferability of skills (or worker trait) analysis, disability statistics, and experience. Some professionals use computer programs to help manage large amounts of data. Access loss may also represent the client's loss of choice and is particularly relevant if earnings potential is based on very few positions.

Placeability   This represents the likelihood that the client could be successfully placed in a job. This is where the "rubber meets the road." Consider employment statistics for people with disabilities, employment data for the specific medical condition (if available), economic situation of the community (may include a labor market survey), and availability (not just existence) of jobs in chosen occupations. Note that the client's attitude, personality, and other factors will influence the ultimate outcome.

Earnings capacity   Based on the above, what is the preincident capacity to earn compared to the postincident capacity to earn. Methods include analysis of the specific job titles or class of jobs that a person could have engaged in pre- vs. postincident, the ability to be educated (sometimes useful for people with acquired brain injury), family history for pediatric injuries, and computer analysis based on the individual's worker traits.

   Special consideration applies to children, women with limited or no work history, people who choose to work below their capacity (e.g., highly educated persons who are farmers), and military trained.

Labor force participation   This represents the client's work life expectancy. Determine the amount of time that is lost, if any, from the labor force as a result of the disability or retraining time. Issues include longer time to find employment, part-time vs. full-time employment, medical treatment or follow-up, earlier retirement, etc. Display data using specific dates or percentages. For example, an average of 4 hours a day may represent a 50% loss.

Reprinted with permission. Weed & Field, 1994/2001.

Rehabilitation Plan

This section includes the life care plan that comprehensively outlines the expected future medical and related care of the client (see previous chapters for topics). This section may also include, as applicable, additional future testing, counseling, training fees, rehabilitation technology, labor market survey costs, job analysis, job coaching, placement, and other needs for improving the client's potential for employment.

For expert testimony, the life care planner is expected to follow established procedures and ethics (see www.IALCP.com and www.cdec1.com for specifics, as well as Appendices I and II). Experts who elect not to be specifically certified in life care planning (CLCP) are not subject to complaints that can be reviewed or disciplined by the certification board (Weed, 2001a).

For example, one noncertified expert completed an updated life care plan for a client with a brain injury. Although the client had measurably improved from the first plan to the second, the updated plan was approximately double the cost of the first. Upon deposition, one explanation offered was that he was simply acting in an administrative role by writing down what the medical professionals told him. The second plan included a new expert, and he did not ask questions, collaborate, or otherwise participate in the development of the life care plan (in either the first or second plan). As a result, at least one plan was not an accurate representation of needs. Essentially, he reported that the attorney should depose the experts on whom he relied to try and ferret out the reasons for substantial changes. This stance seems to be an abdication of one of the major roles the qualified life care planner is expected to play. The qualified life care planner is expected to know what questions to ask, have enough knowledge about the disability to have a sense of what is reasonable, and be an active participant in the process. Further, according to one peer-reviewed article on the reliability of life care plans, professionals who conduct their life care planning practice according to published procedures should not observe significant differences between original and updated life care plans (Sutton et al., 2002; also see Chapter 28).

In a second example, the noncertified plaintiff's life care planner compiled a future care plan without consulting, collaborating with, or soliciting recommendations from treating professions to which he had access. As a result, when the physicians were deposed, their recommendations were very different from those in the written plan. When deposed, the expert proclaimed that he had been doing life care plans for many years and did not need to consult with others.

In summary, the *qualified* life care planner is neither a secretary nor a know-it-all. (See Weed, 2002a, "The Life Care Planner: Secretary, Know-It-All, or General Contractor? One Person's Perspective," for a more comprehensive discussion on this topic.) The expert needs to understand life care planning procedures, have knowledge about specific disabilities, and adhere to the profession's rules and ethics to develop a comprehensive and reliable life care plan. When conducted properly, the life care plan is a valuable road map of care that can also be utilized to resolve disputes.

Although ethics is covered in Chapter 26, there are LCP-specific issues and topics that may be relevant in this section. Certainly within a reasonable range, professionals in the life care planning profession can have differing opinions and philosophies. Some, particularly people who choose not to pursue the certified life care planner credential, seem to be most likely to push the boundaries (Berens & Weed, 2001). Indeed, in the Life Care Planning Summit of 2000, sponsored by several organizations and many different life care planning professionals, there were many topics that achieved consensus by all 100 plus participants present (Weed & Berens, 2001). One item that has wide acceptance is the need for medical foundation for relevant plan entries. First, it must be explicitly noted that every life care plan entry is not medical. Certainly nursing, allied health, vocational, psychological, case management, and other opinions can be offered by professionals who have the credentials to do so. However, many life care plan needs are within the realm of physicians to prescribe. The way to obtain medical foundation can be manyfold. The most obvious is to collaborate with a physician (or several if differing specialties are required). Other options include soliciting recommendations via letter or fax (keeping careful documentation), requesting the attorney to ask the physician questions in deposition if one does not have access to the physician (such as consulting for the defense), relying upon published medical research specific to the disability for opinions, and searching the client's medical records for recommendations.

When consulting with attorneys about another's life care plan, one recommended strategy to help organize data and reveal the foundation for recommendations is a matrix of data containing a minimum of three columns. The first column is for each life care plan recommendation by the other expert, the second is for supporting documentation (medical records, depositions, report contents, day-in-the-life videos, etc.), and the third is for comments (see Table 22.4 for a basic example). In some cases it may be appropriate to add a column for research-related information. It may also be useful to add a column when the expert plan being reviewed has been updated. This will allow the reader to see at a glance what the changes are for each category. Also to be included are general comments at the end.[1]

For occasions where comparison of two opposing life care plans is desirable, the two plans can be displayed side by side, with a column for foundation. See Table 22.5 for a limited example where the plaintiff's life care planner did not collaborate with, or utilize existing medical records and testimony from, the treating physician for the life care plan.

A third potential review technique is to compare the other expert's procedures (to the extent possible) with the published procedures. See Table 22.6 for the general outline.

Access to Labor Market (Employability)

In many of these cases, an individual may very well be able to return to a job that is custom-designed around his disability or with an employer who is interested in helping an employee with mild to moderate cognitive deficits (Weed, 1988; Weed & Field, 1994/2001). However, the client may not have access to the same level of vocational choices he or she did prior to the incident. In essence, the client might appear to have no particular loss of earnings capacity, but at the

---

[1] Thanks to Debbie Berens for the layout design for Tables 24.4 through 24.6.

Table 22.4 Example Basic Matrix for Determining Foundation for Life Care Plan Recommendations

Plan Entry	Recommendation Based on Records Review	Comment
Counseling 1 time/week for 2 years	No recommendation found in records	Unknown psychological foundation; the nurse consultant is *not* certified or licensed in a counseling field
Physiatrist 4 times/year to life	Dr. Doodue's deposition of May 10, 2003, p. 33, line 20, says 2 times/year to life	Dr. Doodue is the treating physiatrist and reported that she was not contacted with regard to her recommendations
Attendant care 4 hours/day to age 60, then 8 hours/day	Dr. Doodue's deposition of May 10, 2003, p. 49, lines 18–20, says the L2 spinal cord injury (SCI) client will require "some attendant care for household activities"	SCI research for anticipated attendant care for an L2 level is 0–1 hour/day; see Blackwell et al., 2001, p. 246 (copy included)

Comment: Records reveal a recommendation for ankle-foot orthoses (AFOs) for both legs, which was not included in plan.

same time be at high risk for losing a job and then having a significant problem locating suitable employment. The access to labor market can be determined through a variety of means. The Labor Market Access Plus 1992 computer program (Field & Field, 1992) is one tool used to assist in determining, based on worker traits, the client's ability to choose in the labor market. For example, one client may have a 50% personal loss of access to the labor market and another individual may have a 95% personal loss of access to the labor market. Obviously, an individual who has personal access to 5% of the labor market should be employable or placeable; however, the difficulty factor for suitable or sustained employment has increased significantly. By placing a loss of access percentage to the labor market, one can sensitize the reader or jury to the potential difficulty for placement. Generally, this is described in a particular percentage loss of access to the client's *personal* labor market rather than to the national labor market. Few unimpaired people have access to 100% of the labor market, and this is a common error assumed by the uneducated observer (Woodrich & Patterson, 2003).

Placeability

This represents the likelihood that the client will be successfully placed in a job with or without rehabilitation support or rehabilitation consultant assistance. One may need to conduct a labor market survey, job analysis, or, in pediatric cases, rely upon statistical data to opine about ultimate placeability. The economic condition of the community may also be a factor. It is important that the rehabilitation consultant recognize that the client's personality, cognitive limitations, and other factors certainly influence the ultimate outcome. For adults, the

Table 22.5 Example Comparison Matrix of Future Care Recommendations

Recommendation	Penny Money, Ph.D. (Plaintiff's LCP)	Roger Weed, Ph.D. (Defense LCP)	Medical Records/Deposition of Boat Dock, M.D. (Treating Physiatrist)
Physiatrist	2 times/year	1–2 times/year average to life expectancy	1–2 times/year for medication management
Primary care physician	Internist: 1 time initially, then 2 times/year to life expectancy	4–5 times/year to life expectancy (deduct average yearly medical care for general population)	4–5 times/year for general medical care (which includes a preexisting condition)
Orthopedic evaluation	1 time initially (by surgeon), then 1–2 times/year to life expectancy	Optional for complications, if any; year initiated and frequency unknown	*May need* if develops degenerative spine/joint disease and/or scoliosis; no need at present
Medical testing	No reference	Yearly lab tests to life expectancy Renal function studies every 3 months to life expectancy	Routine diagnostic testing Renal function studies every 3 months

rehabilitationist may find that it is useful to include an opinion about jobs that are available (actual openings) in addition to jobs that exist but are not currently available to the client — if it is likely that the client will have worker traits that match various job titles. Matching to a job title does not suggest that the person can indeed be placed in a particular occupation. Other factors, such as location, experience, education, and personality, can adversely impact placement. Also, many jobs that may be appropriate for the client are difficult to obtain. The vocational opportunity may be highly competitive or there may be very few positions available. On the other hand, jobs may exist that the client with a disability may be able to do even though on paper (through review of worker traits based on government statistics) it would appear to the contrary.

Earnings Capacity

Based on the rehabilitation plan, access to the labor market, and placeability factors, the client may or may not be employable in the labor market. If employment is likely, an estimate of the earnings potential is important. In general, the difference between wage loss and earnings capacity analysis for an individual is that which he or she can reasonably attain and hold. For example, consider a 17-year-old who delivers papers for an income when he is catastrophically

Table 22.6 Comparison Matrix of Published Step-by-Step Procedures for Life Care Planning and Expert's Procedures

Published Step-by-Step Procedures for Life Care Planning	*Comments Regarding Expert's Procedures*
(Source: Step-by-Step Procedure for Life Care Planning, Table 1.3 of this volume.)	(Based on records, report, deposition transcript, etc.)

Case Intake:
  1. When you talked with the referral source, did you record the basic referral information?
  2. Time frames discussed?
  3. Financial/billing agreement?
  4. Retainer received (if appropriate)?
  5. Arrange for information release?	

Medical Records: 1. Complete wpn requested including lab reports and x-rays	

Supporting Documentation:
  1. Are there depositions of client, family, or treatment team that may be useful?
  2. Day-in-the-life-of videotapes
  3. And if vocational issues to be included in report — school records (including test scores)?
  4. Vocational and employment records?
  5. Tax returns, if appropriate?	

Initial Interview Arrangements:
  1. Is the interview to be held at the client's residence?
  2. Have you arranged for all appropriate people to attend the initial interview (spouse, parents, siblings)?
  3. Did you allow 3–5 hours for the initial interview?	

Initial Interview Materials:
  1. Do you have the initial interview form for each topic to be covered?
  2. Supplemental form for pediatric cases, CP, traumatic brain injury (TBI), and spinal cord injury (SCI) as needed?
  3. Do you have a copy of the life care plan checklist?
  4. Example plan to show the client?
  5. Camera or video camcorder to record living situation, medications, supplies, equipment, and other documentation useful for developing a plan?	

Table 22.6 (Continued) Comparison Matrix of Published Step-by-Step Procedures for Life Care Planning and Expert's Procedures

Published Step-by-Step Procedures for Life Care Planning	Comments Regarding Expert's Procedures
Consulting with Therapeutic Team Members: 1. Have you consulted with and solicited treatment recommendations from appropriate therapeutic team members (if appropriate)?	
Preparing Preliminary Life Care Plan Opinions: 1. Do you have information that can be used to project future care costs? 2. Frequency of service or treatment? 3. Duration? 4. Base cost? 5. Source of information? 6. Vendors?	
Filling in the Holes: 1. Do you need additional medical or other evaluations to complete the plan? 2. Have you obtained the approval to retain services of additional sources from the referral source? 3. Have you composed a letter outlining the right questions to assure you are soliciting the needed information?	
Researching Costs and Sources: 1. Have you contacted local sources for costs of treatment, medications, supplies, and equipment? 2. Or do you have catalogs or flyers? 3. For children, are there services that might be covered, in part, through the school system?	
Finalizing the Life Care Plan: 1. Did you confirm your projections with the client and/or family? 2. Treatment team members (if appropriate)? 3. Can the economist project the costs based on the plan? 4. Do you need to coordinate with a vocational expert?	
Last but Not Least: 1. Have you distributed the plan to all appropriate parties (client [if clinically appropriate], referral source, attorney, and economist, if there is one)?	

impaired and is never able to work again. Certainly, the earnings history from the paper delivery does not represent the individual's capacity. On the other hand, a 55-year-old union truck driver may exhibit an earnings history that is consistent with his capacity. Considerations include whether the individual is a child or an adult and, if an adult, the industry for which he or she is best suited. For example, a drywall hanger of marginal intelligence may very well reach his earnings potential by the time he reaches his late 20s or early 30s. On the other hand, an attorney may not reach her potential until late in her career.

Labor Force Participation

This category represents an opinion about the client's anticipated work life expectancy. Usually an individual who has a reduced life expectancy will also be expected to have a reduced work life expectancy. At the other end of the spectrum, the client's participation in the labor force may be unchanged. An individual may also be expected to work 6 hours per day rather than 8 hours per day, which represents a 25% loss of normal work life expectancy. Some clients have demonstrated consistent extra income by working overtime, and this situation can be considered in this arena as well. Generally speaking, the counselor will express the opinion of loss by percentage or perhaps a number of years. It is usually the economist who makes the actual economic projections. This particular area is quite complicated, and most vocational counselors are not prepared to address the subtleties and complexities of economic projections (Dillman, 1987). However, for additional general information, though an aging resource, the counselor can obtain information about work life estimates in *Worklife Estimates: Effects of Race and Education* (Bulletin 2254, U.S. DOL, 1986).

In order to assure that experts cover the relevant areas and have the background to offer opinions, the following two checklists have been developed (see Table 22.7 and Table 22.8).

Table 22.7   Checklist for Review of Life Care Plans

√   **Was a complete set of medical and other relevant records provided with referral?** Did narrative report accompany LCP? Deposition transcripts of client, family, and/or treatment team provided? Day-in-the-life-of or other videotapes of client? Photographs of client? Deposition of life care planning expert?

√   **Does LCP follow published standards and procedures?** Refer to IALCP website (http://www.IALCP.com) for published standards for life care planners. Use of published or standard checklists, forms, charts, etc.? Collaborative effort? Potential complications referenced on appropriate page and not included in LCP?

√   **Are entries in LCP appropriate for disability/injury?** Input obtained from treatment team or consulting physician(s), if appropriate? Medical, psychological, and/or neuropsychological foundation established? Standards of care for the specific disability referenced, if applicable? Life care planner's recommendations within his or her area of expertise? Medical/therapeutic recommendations within respective providers' area of expertise? Preventive and rehabilitative goals? All areas related to disability included? Costs related to disability only and not related to general or routine care or preexisting conditions? Costs based on geographic area or other appropriate database?

(continued)

Table 22.7 (Continued)   Checklist for Review of Life Care Plans

√   **Overlaps?** Are same or similar services listed more than once under different categories? Can one provider accomplish two recommendations and be more cost effective (e.g., qualified speech therapist or occupational therapist to also do assistive technology evaluation, primary care physician to also do urinalyses, etc.)? Time frames for services chronological or mutually exclusive?

√   **In-home/facility care?** For in-home pediatric care, are adjustments made for time child is at school and for time parents normally are expected to be available to parent a child? Adjustments made as child gets older and normally would require less assistance? Level of care appropriate to client's needs? (In general, minimum LPN for G-tube management, bowel/bladder program, trach care, medication administration, and cut/clean toe nails; CNA/PCA/HHA for activities of daily living (ADL), meal preparation, laundry, housekeeping, driving, and safety/supervision at home. Also refer to each state's Nurse Practice Act for specific requirements.) Do agencies surveyed provide CNA II or have special rules that allow trained CNAs to provide some skilled care under supervision of RN/LPN? Consideration made to potential negotiated cost reduction with home health agency if long-term contract? Parents/family expected to provide some of the care? Lawn/yard care and exterior/interior home maintenance included as adult? For residential community living program/facility, is average yearly cost of individual room and board deducted from per diem rate?

√   **Appropriate cost deductions made or noted to economist with regard to general expenses incurred without disability?** For wheelchair-accessible van, cost of average vehicle or trade-in value of family vehicle deducted? Accessible home, cost of average home in local area deducted? Dental/medical care, cost of routine care recommended for general population deducted? Adaptive clothing allowance, average yearly cost of clothing for general population deducted? Adaptive leisure equipment allowance, average yearly cost of recreation/leisure activities of general population deducted? Total enteral nutrition, average yearly cost of food consumption for general same-age population deducted? Alternatively, is a distinction made that the recommended services in the plan are over and above those that are recommended for the general population?

√   **Are costs calculated correctly?** Is the math correct? Source of cost information known or documented? If economic calculations are included, is life care planner qualified to make such calculations? Are costs of as needed services/items included in plan? Are costs of potential complications included?

√   **Vocationally relevant items?** Are vocational issues addressed or deferred to qualified vocational specialist for vocational considerations?

√   **Plan confirmation?** Plan reviewed/confirmed/endorsed by physician(s) and/or treatment team, if access is available? Client/family, if access available? Future updates expected?

√   **Aesthetics?** Are plan entries easy to read, follow, and understand? Does plan overall look professional and make sense? Minimal to no typographical errors or date errors? Is the information presented clearly, logically, and with sufficient detail? Consistency between narrative report, records, and plan entries?

© 2002 by Debra E. Berens, M.S., C.R.C., C.C.M., C.L.C.P., and Roger O. Weed, Ph.D., C.R.C., L.P.C., C.C.M., C.D.M.S., C.L.C.P. Reprinted with permission.

Table 22.8   Checklist for Review of Life Care Planner Qualifications and Practices (a.k.a. Checklist for Selecting a Life Care Planner)

√   Professional's **qualifications**?

- ■ **Education**, including degrees and continuing education? If doctorate, was the university accredited? (Some have mail-order degrees or diplomas from "universities" that are not accredited.)
- ■ **Training** specific to life care planning?
- ■ **Work** experience?
- ■ **Life care planning** experience?
- ■ **Research** knowledge and experience?
- ■ **Certifications or licenses?** Generally accepted rehabilitation certifications include CLCP (certified life care planner), CRC (certified rehabilitation counselor), CDMS (certified disability management specialist), CVE (certified vocational evaluator), CRRN (certified rehabilitation registered nurse), CCM (certified case manager), diplomat or fellow ABVE (American Board of Vocational Experts), CLNC (certified legal nurse consultant).
- ■ **Forensic experience** (if appropriate)? Familiar with the rules pertaining to experts? Have they testified? Do they have a list of cases for which they testified at deposition or trial for the previous 4 years? Plaintiff/defense ratio?

√   Prospective consultant's **awareness** of life care planning?

- ■ Are they a **board-certified** life care planner? Refer to Commission on Health Care Certification website (www.CDEC1.com) for list of CLCPs.
- ■ Have they achieved the **certificate** in life care planning offered through the University of Florida?
- ■ Have they completed **courses** offered by a noted program on life care planning (e.g., Rehabilitation Training Institute, Intelicus, Medipro, University of Florida, IARP, et al.)?
- ■ Can they cite life care planning **references**?
- ■ Do they know some of the **professionals** associated with life care planning publications and training?

√   **Commitment** to the profession?

- ■ Do they belong to professional **organization(s)** with focus on life care planning such as International Academy of Life Care Planners (IALCP), www.IALCP.com? Do they belong to a disability-specific organization? (Are they legitimate or fringe organizations such as a for-profit owned by an individual or group with little recognition or substance?)
- ■ Do they **participate** in professional development?
- ■ Have they **contributed** their time and effort by volunteering services to clients in need, speaking, holding office with professional organizations, writing articles, chapters, or books?
- ■ Have they received **awards, honors, peer recognition**?

(continued)

Table 22.8 (Continued)   Checklist for Review of Life Care Planner Qualifications and Practices (a.k.a. Checklist for Selecting a Life Care Planner)

√   **Industry** experience?

- Workers' compensation or federal Office of Workers' Compensation Programs?
- Personal injury?
- Social Security?
- State rehabilitation?
- Longshore workers? Jones Act? Federal Employees Liability Act (FELA)?
- Long-term and short-term disability?
- Specialize in a particular disability?

√   **Medical foundation** for opinions established?

- Use established published **checklists and forms**?
- Routinely consult with a **physician** as part of the team and/or have medical literature relevant to client?
- Include other **health professionals** as appropriate (e.g., OT, PT, SLT, RT, audiology, neuropsychology, etc.)?

√   **Other?**

- What and how do they **bill** for their services? Do they charge different rates for interview, records review, deposition, or trial time?
- Current curriculum **vita**?
- History of **ethics complaints or arrests**?

Original checklist developed by Roger O. Weed, Ph.D., and revised by Debra E. Berens, M.S., C.R.C., C.C.M., C.L.C.P., and Roger O. Weed, Ph.D., 2002. Reprinted with permission.

CONCLUSION

This chapter has outlined many of the topics and issues that the life care planner must consider when developing opinions for civil litigation cases. The expert is in an excellent position to assist in resolving litigation by soliciting information that addresses almost all of the damage aspects of the case. Knowing the health care industry and effectively analyzing the needs and researching the future care and costs associated with a complex injury are specialized services that offer a true enhancement to the profession. When completed objectively and professionally, the care plan will assist the jury with a clear understanding of the needs of the client as well as provide the road map of care for the client and family.

REFERENCES

Berens, D. & Weed, R. (2001). Ethics update for rehabilitation counselors in the private sector. *Journal of Applied Rehabilitation Counseling*, 32, 27–32.

Black, H. (1990). *Black's Law Dictionary*, 6th ed. St. Paul, MN: West Publishing.

Blackwell, T., Krause, J., Winkler, T., & Stiens, S. (2001). *Spinal Cord Injury Desk Reference: Guidelines for Life Care Planning and Case Management*. New York: Demos.

Brookshire, M. & Smith, S. (1990). *Economic/Hedonic Damages: The Practice Book for Plaintiff and Defense Attorneys.* Cincinnati, OH: Anderson Publishing.

Daubert v. Merrell Dow. (1993). 125 L Ed 2d 469.

Deutsch, P. & Raffa, F. (1981). *Damages in Tort Action,* Vols. 8 & 9. New York: Matthew Bender.

Deutsch, P. & Sawyer, H. (2003). *Guide to Rehabilitation.* White Plains, NY: Ahab Press.

Dillman, E. (1987). The necessary economic and vocational interface in personal injury cases. *Journal of Private Sector Rehabilitation,* 2, 121–142.

Feldbaum, C. (1997). The Daubert decision and its interaction with the federal rules. *Journal of Forensic Vocational Assessment,* 1, 49–73.

Field, T. & Field, J. (1992). *Labor Market Access Plus 1992.* Athens, GA: Elliott & Fitzpatrick (computer program).

Field, T. & Weed, R. (1988). *Transferability of Work Skills.* Athens, GA: Georgia Southern.

Kim Manufacturing, Inc., v. Superior Metal Treating, Inc. (1976). 537 S W Reporter, 2d 424.

Kumho Tire Co. v. Carmichael. (1999). 526 U.S. 137.

Riddick, S. & Weed, R. (1996). The life care planning process for managing catastrophically impaired patients. In *Case Studies in Nursing Case Management,* 61–91. Blanchett, S., Ed., Sudbury, MA: Jones & Bartlett.

Sutton, A., Deutsch, P., Weed, R., & Berens, D. (2002). Reliability of life care plans: a comparison of original and updated plans. *Journal of Life Care Planning,* 1, 187–194.

U.S. Department of Labor (1991). *Dictionary of Occupational Titles,* 4th ed. Washington, D.C.: U.S. Government Printing.

Weed, R. (1988). Earnings vs. earnings capacity: the labor market access method. *Journal of Private Sector Rehabilitation,* 3, 57–64.

Weed, R. (1994). Life care plans: expanding the horizons. *Journal of Private Sector Rehabilitation,* 9, 47–50.

Weed, R. (1995). Forensic rehabilitation. In A.E. Dell Orto & R.P. Marinelle, Eds., *Encyclopedia of Disability and Rehabilitation,* 326–330. New York: Macmillan.

Weed, R. (2000a). Ethics in rehabilitation opinions and testimony. *Rehabilitation Counseling Bulletin,* 43, 215–218, 245.

Weed, R. (2000b). The worth of a child: earnings capacity and rehabilitation planning for pediatric personal injury litigation cases. *The Rehabilitation Professional,* 8, 29–43.

Weed, R. (2002a). The life care planner: secretary, know-it-all, or general contractor? One person's perspective. *Journal of Life Care Planning,* 1, 173-177.

Weed, R. (2002b). The assessment of transferable work skills in forensic settings. *Journal of Forensic Vocational Analysis,* 5, 1–4 (special issue editorial).

Weed, R. (January 2003). Life care planning for workers with injuries. *Rehab News,* 13–21 (Georgia State Board of Workers' Compensation newsletter).

Weed, R. & Berens, D., Eds. (2001). *Life Care Planning Summit 2000 Proceedings.* Athens, GA: Elliott & Fitzpatrick Vocational Services.

Weed, R. & Berens, D. (2002). Ethics in life care planning. In P. Deutsch, Ed., *The Expert's Role as an Educator Continues: Meeting the Demands under Daubert,* 59–67. White Plains, NY: Ahab Press.

Weed, R. & Field, T. (1994/2001). *The Rehabilitation Consultant's Handbook,* 3rd. ed. Athens, GA: Elliott & Fitzpatrick Vocational Services.

Woodrich, F. & Patterson, J.B. (2003). Ethical objectivity in forensic rehabilitation. *The Rehabilitation Professional,* 11, 41–47.

23

A PERSONAL PERSPECTIVE OF LIFE CARE PLANNING

Raymond L. Arrona and Mamie Walters, as told to Anna N. Herrington

INTRODUCTION

This chapter is a brief telling of Anita Arrona's story. On September 7, 1987, Anita was returning home from visiting her boyfriend when a drunk driver hit her. Her injuries were profound and included open brain trauma, severe brain contusion of the left and right frontal lobes, supraorbital fractures of her left and right eyes, multiple blunt trauma to the chest, hydrocephalus, pleural effusion of the left lung, fractured right clavicle, and severe spasticity with minimal control of bodily functions. By October 5, 1987, infected frontal lobe brain tissue was removed and a shunt was inserted to drain off excess fluid. Her left eye was unsalvageable. After 3 months and multiple surgeries, it became evident that Anita would never achieve independence, and the family's attorney retained the services of a life care planner to develop an outline of future expected care. Over the years, although severely brain injured, hemiparetic, and blind in the left eye, her medical situation has stabilized and she has learned to speak a few words. She resides in a wheelchair, which requires an attendant's service to move her. She is totally dependent on others for her well-being.

Anita's journey since her injury in 1987 has involved many factors: family and friends, high moral standards and strong values, and a solid plan. First, Anita's father, Ray Arrona, has been and continues to be her warrior in the many battles that must be fought to obtain what she needs. Mamie Walters, a family friend who has turned professional caregiver, has been devoted to seeking out creative therapeutic methods to enhance Anita's abilities and is committed to her growth. Second, Anita and Ray have had strong coping resources based on deep-rooted beliefs in optimism, honesty, perseverance, stubbornness, hard work, and faith in God. Last, on Anita's journey, has been the pragmatic vehicle — the life care plan. Anita's life care plan has been the essential road map, though detours are sometimes taken, of her often arduous journey.

0-8493-1511-5/04/$0.00+$1.50
© 2004 by CRC Press LLC

RAY ARRONA: MY DAUGHTER'S STORY

Let me begin with one of the codes by which I live my life: *be responsive.* A story I heard at a recent conference illustrates this well. There was a first mate that came to his captain advising him that the ship was going to be under attack and inquiring as to what to do. The captain told the first mate to run and get his (the captain's) red shirt. So he got the red shirt, they engaged in battle, and they won. About a week or two passed and the first mate returned to the captain and warned him of a pending battle with pirates. Once again the first mate asked, "What do you advise?" Again the captain replied, "I want you to bring my red shirt." So, they engaged in battle and wiped out all the pirates. When putting everything away the first mate was curious and asked the captain, "Can you please tell me about this red shirt? Every time you put this red shirt on we seem to do well. I wonder if there is some point in this." The captain told him that it "was the leadership thing." The captain explained that if he happens to get stabbed while under attack or is hit by a volley, "I don't want the men to see me get hurt and bleed so I can continue to lead them through the battle." That's pretty wise. Another month passes and the first mate rushed to the captain shouting, "Captain, Captain, I have news of yet another battle. There are pirates on starboard, on the bow, and on the port side! What shall I do?" So the captain says, "Will you please get me my brown pants?"

I tell this story to express the importance of a quick and smart response. I have found that being ready for the battle has been of immense importance in my life. I was born and raised in Miami, AZ, a copper-mining community about 80 miles east of Phoenix. Being Hispanic, I grew up in a strict and disciplined home. At home I learned the importance of a good attitude. I learned about making good choices and taking responsibility for those choices. I learned to believe strongly in myself. Now, I am 50 years old and I know these early lessons have assisted me through my life. I worked while attending college at Arizona State University and had plans to pursue a pre-med curriculum. That was in 1964. However, my plans changed when I met Anita's mother in 1965. Soon we were married and a year later, in November 1966, Anita was born.

I continued to work with my college employer, Wear-Ever, Inc., the first subsidiary of Alcoa, and later transferred to another subsidiary, Cutco. I have been associated with these two companies for nearly 30 years, though many changes have occurred. Our second child was another daughter, Andrea, who was born just about 11 months after Anita. Little did we know how short a time we would have with Andrea. Andrea, at 11 months, drowned in the bathtub. It was terrible. This tragedy was our first to experience as a family. I am not sure whether it prepared us for the future, but it certainly tightened the family.

Then there was the aftermath and our struggles. We had a son, my namesake, who was born on Christmas Day. You may remember the Apollo moonshot; it was somewhere around that time in 1968. Ray Jr. was 18 at the time of Anita's injury. (Ray is now married and has two children. He is in the Navy and lives in Seattle, WA.) For many different reasons, our marriage did not work and we were divorced in 1971.

I later met and married (October 1974) Sheri, the love of my life. We just recently celebrated 22 years of marriage. At the time of Anita's accident Sheri was

38 years of age. My employer offered me a promotion to a position that required transferring across the country to Atlanta, GA. We moved in 1976. Alyson was born to Sheri and me a year later in May 1977. Alyson, Anita's younger sister, was 10 years old and was in fifth grade at the time of the injury. Alyson probably has the most anger in the family about Anita's disaster, even to this day. Ryan, whom Anita used to take care of often, was born four years later in October 1981. At the time of the accident he was 5 and not really aware of what was happening.

It was during this period of time (1979) that Anita moved in with my parents in Miami, AZ, because of difficulties she was having with her mother. However, Anita did not realize how strict her grandparents would be, and we soon realized that it might be best for her to move to Atlanta to be with me. Anita moved in with us and enrolled as a junior at North Cobb High School in Kennesaw, GA. She graduated in May 1984. Anita is a very determined person — she has not lost this trait. She is a hard worker and has not lost that drive either. After school she worked several jobs with the goal of eventually attending court-reporting school. During this time she saved enough money to buy her dream car: a new, red, 1986 Toyota GT. Anita would not let anyone else drive or even touch that car. She loved that car.

It was Labor Day 1987, and since I am a football fanatic, I was glued to the television. At the end of the evening the news detailed Labor Day highway accidents. According to the report, the number of accidents was less than predicted. I thought, *This is really great*. Then the phone rang. The phone call was very similar to the one I received when I was working in Tucson and heard the news from an official at a local hospital about Andrea's accident. Although they would not say what was going on, I knew that something was terribly wrong. Anita had been visiting with her boyfriend, Dan, that evening of Labor Day and was on her way home. I called Dan and asked him what was going on. He did not know. Dan lived about half a mile from the hospital, and I asked him if he would please join me there. Upon arrival at the hospital, I was escorted into a private conference room, and as I walked in, I saw Dan talking with two professional men dressed in white. Later, I learned those were the neurosurgeons who were preparing for a lengthy, all-night operation on Anita. They informed me that Anita had been involved in a terrible auto accident that had crushed her skull. They said she was critical and was given only about a 20% chance to survive.

I felt all numb inside, as if I was living through a bad dream. That night was spent making emergency phone calls trying to find out what was happening because there was no information. I had a lot of support from Dan and his family; we prayed the rosary all night long together. We prayed that God would take care of Anita. The next morning the doctors came in and told us Anita had made it through the evening, but it was still touch-and-go. I was shocked when I went into the room. Tubes were inside of her, IVs, multiple machines that I had no idea what they were for, lights, monitors. I could barely find Anita because her body was very swollen. I felt a feeling of helplessness, not knowing what to do. I was overcome with feelings of despair, feelings of sorrow. As fate would have it, my mother had passed away the year before and Anita was planning to take a trip on that Labor Day to see my father. But the trip was postponed because of an American Legion conference that my dad, a veteran and an avid American

Legion member, wanted to attend. So, there was this anger about why things could not have been different. There was a lot of grief.

During the next few weeks, I was not really aware of what was taking place. There were many visitors and everyone was trying to understand what happened. I can recall staying up all night, sleeping on the floor, and waiting to be awakened for any news that we would have of Anita. There were many life-threatening decisions on Anita's behalf that needed to be made. She had edema, which at that time I had no idea what that was. There was pressure being caused by the cerebral spinal fluid because it was not draining properly; so we learned what edema was. It was to plague us throughout the next several months. There were several needed operations that required removing part of the brain to relieve building pressure. We learned what a shunt was — something that was where the fluid needs to drain back — and we learned what operation that was going to take. We learned what the left brain does and what the right brain does. Throughout several months we were just hoping that all parts of her body would work. We were hopeful that she would have movement on the right side of her body. We did see that, and it gave us a lot of hope that things were going to be all right and that Anita could return, by the grace of God, to the original Anita. However, many problems continued to appear. So, the hope for survival was in and out, in and out, and the prognosis changed day by day. She had good days and bad days.

Many people told us that quite often in a crisis, your emotions and intelligence do not work together. All I know is that we learned to measure gains in inches and seconds and minutes. Anita was in the hospital ICU for 9 months. Everyone was distraught; there was a lot of sadness, but the family pulled together. The many prayers and visits from my extended family were invaluable. I believe in prayer. It brought hope to our family. We had so much support: from our family, church, friends, and business associates sending cards, making visits and calls, and saying prayers. The hospital staff was supportive, especially the ICU nurses and the physicians. We had legal and financial support. We were truly blessed.

However, our family was under tremendous stress. Our family had changed. Most of the attention was on Anita. All talk was Anita. Being a husband had to go by the wayside. Though I did the best I could, being a father to all my children was sacrificed. I really did not have any idea how it would affect the other children. There was a different schedule that was imposed upon us. New schedules, new decisions, and emotions we had not experienced before. As parents, we were obligated to take care of Anita, even though she was an adult. We had a lot of bills to pay, unaware of where the money would come from. My business is commission based and, therefore, dependent on my being in the field to produce. Because I had become an independent contractor, I no longer had health insurance with the company. Our private-pay insurance did not cover Anita since she was not a full-time student. There were going to be a lot of things that were unclear to me. There were increased workloads for everyone in the family; we were stressed to the limit. We had no idea of what was ahead of us.

So what caused the accident? I can recall the second night that I was in ICU and a police officer came and talked to me. I thought he was very considerate to find out how Anita was doing. However, that was not his intention at all. The purpose of his visit was to serve me with a ticket, intended for Anita, for running a red light. Fortunately, there was an eyewitness who revealed the truth: Anita was broadsided by a college-age drunk driver who had run a red light. He was also on drugs at the time, and unfortunately, this was his third DUI offense.

I had no idea what was going to take place as far as Anita's litigation. The physician who had done the operation asked me if I had someone in mind, and I said no. He recommended an attorney who is very good with personal injury cases. However, I did not know he was good, I had never heard of him. My mind went through many things. I was unsure who to select and what to do, so I did what I was accustomed to doing and sought out other attorneys to see what their prices would be. I was told it would not cost me anything; however, it would be one third of whatever was awarded on a contingency basis. That blew my mind. I thought, *Anita needs all of this money.* I certainly can have an appreciation in retrospect. I did look for another attorney. I described the situation and he was willing to do it for a fixed cost and a certain percentage that was lower. However, as I talked with him, he thought we could make the records look like Anita was going to school at the time and work out something with the insurance. There was a part of me that was tempted to listen to that because I was desperate to find a way to preserve as many funds as I could. Thank God, I did not hire that individual. I found a good attorney, and it has worked out well in our case.

I learned how our courts work. There was to be a criminal trial and a civil trial. The criminal trial came first, and I do not know what effect the criminal trial had on our civil trial, but it was an ordeal. I came to the conclusion that our court system was not a justice system but an injustice system. Eyewitnesses had to be sought out to put together the actual scene of the accident, and we soon discovered the drunken driver who hit Anita was out of town on a vacation. He was out on bail. He never even spent one night in jail.

It was really hard for our family to sit in a courtroom with the man who hit Anita. He showed no remorse and neither did his family. That made it hard. Not once did they come and say they were sorry or anything at all. There were so many coincidental things that happened that would literally blow me away. One of the things is that the attorney that represented the defendant was a close friend of Anita's boyfriend. He did not know that Anita was the girl who had been hit, so he took the case. He happened to be an excellent attorney and I could not believe how things could be done in a way to make the innocent look guilty. There was a young lady in ICU who really gave a lot of care to our daughter. She worked in another hospital and was a close friend of Dan's family. She transferred to Kennestone. As fate would have it, her brother was working for the defendant. It was very emotional and distressing. After about a week of trial, the defendant decided to plead guilty. We never had a civil trial. That was settled out of court. The young man was sentenced to 5 years for a third offense, and we heard later that he was given 2 years to serve and after about 18 months was up for parole. We took an active role to ensure he served his full 2 years.

Based on the life care plan, a settlement was reached with the defendant and I was made Anita's legal guardian. I opted to select an irrevocable trust. The reason I did so is that if something happened to me, I could pretty much dictate who would be in charge of the financial affairs for Anita and also avoid temptations by either myself or anyone else to misuse those funds. I have used the trust, my attorney, and the professional rehabilitation consultant as my second conscience. The professional rehabilitation consultant/professional expert was very involved in the life care plan. It is amazing how many things he was right on target with and how important that was in supporting Anita's case.

Would Anita be better off now if she had not lived through the accident? What is her life going to be like? That almost seems unfair. There was a lot of anger in dealing with this situation and probably always will be. Will we ever totally recover from the catastrophic effects to our family, let alone Anita? Since the accident, my daughter Alyson has had to deal with much residual anger. A positive aspect is that time and being vocal has helped to dissolve much of that anger. My dad is from the old school and wanted to be a vigilante and come and shoot the drunk driver. Many times the emotions speak instead of the intelligence. Occasionally I pop in and out of that anger. Dealing with the resentment is hard, too. Why Anita? A beautiful person, a bright future, why us? My Alyson cries for the sister she lost and I grieve for my daughter.

It was becoming evident that Anita was coming to the end of her hospital stay. The people at the hospital were telling me to look for a long-term facility. That is when I started doing research and making trips. I have a whole bunch of files on everything. I went to Tennessee to Rebound and was impressed. I went to Florida to see a program they had there. I had heard about Peachtree Re-entry here in Atlanta, but I was told they would not take her. I visited Texas, but that was too far away. We settled on a facility near Birmingham, AL.

Because of Anita's condition at the time of transfer, she went into a Birmingham hospital and was later transferred to an Alabama facility. The quality of care went down. My gut feeling after awhile was that she was not getting the care we wanted. The people seemed to be superficial. That was the feeling I got. I was advised to get a case manager. I would offer the same advice. If you are ever in a similar situation, I urge you to hire an independent person or case manager that is your advocate and not use the facility's advocate.

Our case manager expressed dissatisfaction with the treatment that Anita was receiving and suggested we visit a brain injury program in Louisiana. We asked our initial life care planer to go with us and give us his professional opinion. We liked what we saw, so we moved Anita to Louisiana. Anita made many gains at the treatment facility. In fact, the first thing she ate since her accident was a communion, which was a great sign. A minister who worked at the facility administered this holy food. That is when Anita started eating.

A new facility had opened in Atlanta and I began to investigate the possibility of Anita returning "home." With the assistance of the initial life care planner, I obtained another case manager to study this possibility. When Anita was in Louisiana, it seemed as though the accident did not happen because she was a long distance away. Although I made trips, they could only be occasional, and we had to rely on and trust the quality of care of the facility. The family visitations were strained and the family seemed to be embarrassed of being with Anita in public. The involvement was guarded, and still is, though it is gradually getting better. A lot of it has to do with each family member maturing in his or her process of acceptance, as well as everyone remembering how much fun it is to be around Anita.

I have been very pleased with the things that I have obtained in the institutional setting, but I wanted something better for our daughter. We decided Anita's quality of life would improve if she lived in her own home. We tried to work with the doctors to set up a facility. There were many conflicts of interest that came about here in Georgia with doctors recommending clients to their own facilities, and we were hopeful that there would be a home environment. In trying to check out all our options, our life care planner and I made some more investigative trips. As it happened (God does work in mysterious ways) I was aware of a friend from work who had recently been outsourced (due to corporate downsizing). In fact, I was sending her resumes out throughout Atlanta trying to help her find a position because I was so convinced of her capabilities. Lightning struck my brain: What if I could convince our friend, Mamie Walters, to come to Atlanta and help us start a new program? Have Anita come out of Meadowbrook and go into her own home? Could we do this? Could we afford paying her? I confirmed the financial feasibility. We approached Mamie with the concept and she was interested. She came to Atlanta, and it has made a phenomenal difference.

There is hope for the future. One of the things we do in our business is to make measurable gains in a reasonable amount of time. That is by charting things, charting sales. We look for behavior that is going to enhance that increase. It requires positive thinking. Mamie and Anita have positive attitudes and it is evident by the progress Anita has made. She is tipping her chart.

So what about the future? Our long-term plans include the establishment of a licensed home with a home environment. However, as one might expect, there are obstacles (or a more positive interpretation is challenges). We want a home with a family atmosphere, a high quality of life, and a healthy, natural nutritional diet for the occupants. We are trying new ideas and approaches. I always laugh when I see Mamie coming up with something new and natural and noninvasive. I am so often humbled when her alternative therapies produce great results. Certainly there are going to be changes that are going to take place as time goes on. There are also many challenges that remain.

In conclusion, I would like to emphasize how much we all have learned from Anita during this whole ordeal. She has brought deeper meaning to perseverance, faith, determination, and love. One of the things that I always have done in my life is target areas in which there is control and in which there is potential for progress. I can look and find possibilities anywhere. I also like to identify areas in which there is no control and learn how to make adjustments or accept this lack of control. This concept is captured so well in the prayer of serenity.

> God grant me the serenity to accept the things that I cannot change,
> The courage to change the things that I can, and
> The wisdom to know the difference.
>
> **— Saint Francis of Assisi**

It is this prayer that has guided me throughout this ordeal and continues to be a source of comfort to me on my journey as Anita's dad.

MAMIE WALTERS: MY JOURNEY WITH ANITA

I remember one day a contractor was building a ramp at my home for Anita and he made the comment to me that if this accident had happened to him, he would just want to be dead. He could not see himself in this position, going through what Anita goes through and having people do for her what has to be done. My answer to him was "You don't get to be dead. You just deal with this every day. You just live with it. You have to adjust to it because you did survive." And that is what I have seen Anita do. What an inspiration she has been to me.

My children's father had passed away (1994), and it was our first holiday (Thanksgiving) without their Dad. Ray's family, being the dear family that they are, invited us to their home. We had a wonderful time. It was about 11:00 on Thanksgiving evening and just out of the blue Ray started discussing the possibility of me moving to Atlanta and working with Anita. Even though I had never worked with this type of client before, I had worked with Ray for many years and knew that we have had great success in the past in what we tried to achieve. I decided if he was willing, so was I. If it did not work out, we would both know we gave Anita our best effort and that was what really counted.

Once I made this decision, I returned to Orlando. One of the assignments Ray and I had given ourselves was to set our goals and objectives for the program and for Anita. At our next meeting, in January, we compared notes. As it turned out, our goals and objectives were almost identical, including the time frames. That was really exciting. Our original plan was to have Anita in her own home by the end of the year (1995). We actually had her home in 6 months.

I had experience in corporate forecasting for a number of years, and Ray is one of these math wizards. He also had been doing forecasting for about 30 years. We knew what we were doing. However, I believe the key to our progress was being of the same mind-set. Our singular vision allowed us to focus our energies and to be expedient in the pursuit of our goals.

One of the first things we did was to arrange for me to come to Meadowbrook and work with Anita. I did so for 6 weeks. I wanted to observe Anita's care and have some supervised hands-on experience. This observation and experience was vital in preparing for Anita's weekend visits with me. When I first began working with Anita, and the facility staff was in agreement, I noticed that Anita was very depressed. She had no initiative. Her arms were always folded and her head stayed down unless she was watching television. If she liked you, she smiled.

This was the Anita that I met. Her speech therapist said she just did not try to do any work. Her interpretation was that Anita felt like there was no reason to bother. There was not a lot of progress at Meadowbrook. We believed that there were many things that are possible in a home environment that are either not possible or practical or just not done in an institution. Ray and I were very excited about the possibilities.

In March 1995, I brought Anita home 2 days a week; in April, we increased to 3 days a week, and we continued this schedule through the end of June. I would bring her home from Friday night until Monday morning. In March, I was doing the care, the meals, everything. In April, I realized with the increase of 3 days that I might not be able to handle the care alone. My 17-year-old daughter, Ana, helped out and soon became very interested in assisting with Anita's care.

Anita's total transition time from institutional care, including her hospital stay, was 7H years. She has been home for almost 2 years now (Fall 1996).

My first objective for Anita, once she was home, was to increase her self-esteem. Without high self-esteem, she had little confidence. Without confidence, she had no initiative, and so it goes. I began by giving her control. Anytime I could give her control, I did. I bought different colored sheets so she could choose what color she wanted on her bed. I gave her a TV remote and CDs to choose for music. With more choice and independence, she began to have some self-respect and self-dignity. I let her know she was loved. As we worked together she gained trust and knew the things we were doing were for her own good (even the range of motion exercises, which she hated).

One of the challenges that Anita had was to drink enough fluids. She did not drink fluids. As a result, problems occurred. We wanted to increase her fluids. She drank V-8 juice but refused water and all other drinks, except sometimes a little pineapple juice. Currently Anita is drinking approximately 30 ounces of fluid a day, and she has been doing that for quite some time, and most of this is water. She has really come a long way with positive reinforcement and increased control. We took shopping trips so she could pick out some special drinking glasses for her water. Her favorite color is green, so we went on a shopping trip for green glasses. So simple, yet so effective.

Since Anita had a brain injury, I really did not know what she was capable of doing. I knew what I had been told. I knew that there was, supposedly, no place for her to go in her rehabilitation and progress. Her dad had taught her the word *hi*, and that was all she could say for about a year. Anita had not learned how to tap into her real voice, so her voice sounded really breathy. I would take her to the computer and she enjoyed it. I experimented and knew she could read. We made it fun. She has learned to type some words strictly from memory. This was a major accomplishment for Anita.

I believe this learning became possible with self-control, self-confidence, and the initiative to work. Once she started working and saw she could actually do things, she became more confident and more enthused about continuing to work. At this time she is reading a large number of words. We have organization skills activity where she will group flash cards using the words in categories. Her proficiency is about 85 to 90%, sometimes better. Anita presently has a vocabulary of about 20 different words and syllables that she speaks with her true voice. This is something I felt could happen. She has worked very hard.

Her grandfather was coming for a visit from Arizona and Anita dearly loves her grandfather. She is crazy about him. I asked her if she would like to greet her grandfather when he arrives. She nodded that she would work with me. In working with Anita I have learned how much she loves Elvis. We would practice to Elvis music. I did not know what I was going to get. We were having fun and were working at it. She started getting the "pa pa pa pa." From this we put a short sentence together. This was a giant step for Anita because of her severe apraxia. She eventually could say "Hi, Papa" and "Bye, Papa." I wondered if she would remember this when she saw her grandfather. A few weeks went by and we kept practicing. Her grandfather arrived and she said, "Hi, Papa," and when he got ready to leave she said, "Bye, Papa." There are some things money cannot buy because they are priceless, and that moment was one of them.

One of her words she learned was *hi*. We were working on the *pie* sound and I told her if she learned the word *pie* I would take her out to get some pie. I let her order it from the waitress. Her most current word is *sly*. That is because she is in love with Sylvester Stallone. Sometimes motivation gets easier and easier. Elvis is her romantic guy and Sylvester is her macho, hero guy. I told her if she could learn *sly*, I would take her to the movies. She worked and she said it, and so we went. I think it is important that if you do offer a reward, that it is given quickly. In her case, it has kept her going.

We have a Christian home where Anita lives. I believe that the mind, spirit, and body are intricately joined to make up the human being. In working with Anita I felt like the ball had been dropped in her spirituality. This is something Ray and I wanted to address. Today she enjoys Mass. She truly gets very excited about going to Mass. She loves gospel music. We try to address the spiritual side of Anita as a holistic approach to her care. Anita is very strong in her spirit and she is a survivor. I do not require my staff to go around saying Hail Mary's all day. They do not walk around with rosaries. We only provide for spiritual requests if the client wishes. I do ask the staff to play a rosary audiotape at nighttime for Anita because this is what she likes to hear. She likes gospel music, so they put in the tapes so she can hear that. These are the ways we are addressing her spiritual life. It is the belief in the importance of balancing the mental, the physical, and the spiritual.

When Anita came back to a home environment, her family visits increased. She dearly loves her family. Her strongest bonds are with her dad, her grandfather, her aunt, and her former boyfriend, Dan, who still comes to see her. Anita is quite social now and loves their visits. She also enjoys our emphasis on games, recreational outings, and community involvement.

Our home promotes prevention. One of the strongest results of our prevention approach has been the vast improvement in Anita's health through our nutritional program. Anita was plagued with upper respiratory infections, urinary tract infections, chronic conjunctivitis, and such. Now Anita experiences very few infections. Basically, we use only real food. There are no canned goods, no processed foods; our kitchen is stocked with fresh fruits and vegetables. We have eliminated meats, dairy products, and sugars from Anita's diet. Anita does not have a problem with swelling, her circulation is good, and she has had no skin breakdown since her return home. Her attention span has increased, her energy level has increased, and her stamina has improved. This has really helped with her therapy sessions.

If I had to select one aspect of the program that is essential, it would have to be teamwork. Teamwork started with the life care plan. That was our road map for Anita. When I came on board, it was essential that I have the life care plan available because my expertise is not in the medical field. I am not a certified case manager, rehabilitation specialist, or nurse. The life care plan was and is a main reference for Anita's life care. Also, the life care plan has been key in our financial success. We provide excellent care for minimal funds. The type of care we are providing costs approximately $250 to $300 per day. This does not include doctor visits, supplies, or medications. It does include 24-hour nursing care, bed pads and briefs, personal care for the individual, housekeeping duties, recreational and occupational reinforcement, and scheduled outings. We provide better care than the larger institutions with less money for this type and level of client.

Another vital aspect of our program is staff education and staff appreciation. If I explain to the staff the importance of why things need to be done, I find the job performance is good and their attitude is positive. I believe in staff recognition. The attitude at the home and the attitude of the staff is one of respect. We respect each other, we respect the clients, and we respect the guests coming into the home. We show a lot of dignity. The staff takes pride in what they are doing because they can see the results. We try to encourage each other, we try to encourage the client and not criticize.

We find that this attitude permeates the home and affects Anita's spirit. Although she continues to receive therapies and improvements are observed, the bottom line is that Anita is home — where she belongs.

EDITOR'S NOTE

Since this account was initially published, in the first edition of this book, the family has moved back to Arizona where they are closer to family. Anita continues to successfully live at "home" with 24-hour care. This story underscores the value of a dedicated and supportive family. The family, particularly the father, was thrown into a complex arena with little preparation. The event has irrevocably changed the family's and Anita's lives. Without the caring and unwavering problem-solving dedication, as well as diligent pursuit for improving Anita's life, it is unlikely that progress in her situation would have occurred.

24

A PLAINTIFF'S ATTORNEY'S PERSPECTIVE ON LIFE CARE PLANNING

Tyron C. Elliott

It is better to judge a man by his questions than by his answers.

— **Voltaire**

INTRODUCTION

Plaintiff's attorneys define themselves by their ability to ask the right questions, not only of their opposition, but also of themselves and their own clients. In the catastrophic case, the plaintiff's attorney understands that a myriad of questions may and should be asked about the future. Yet that same attorney is buffeted by thoughts that no real answers can be given. He or she fears that all attempts to probe the future or assist the trier of fact in probing the future will slide into that murky realm of the possible and away from the safe ground of the probable, where he or she must remain to prove a case. The attorney also knows that the more specific the questions become, the more difficult they are to answer. The safe thing to do then seems to be to generalize about future care and future needs and thus avoid these pitfalls.

Following this course leaves the attorney and his client ill-equipped to stand before the trier of fact and ask for specific compensation for the special damages for future medical and rehabilitation needs. He knows the judge or jury will be asking the next obvious question: What will those needs be, and how much can we expect that they will reasonably cost? The modern plaintiff's attorney must and should provide the judge or jury with all the evidence that exists on those issues.

As plaintiff's attorneys, we are accustomed to marshaling all our own evidence, tracking down its sources, and shaping our cases so that they can be fairly and clearly presented to the judge or jury. We are reluctant to say that in the catastrophic case, the medical and rehabilitation needs are too complex for us to

0-8493-1511-5/04/$0.00+$1.50
© 2004 by CRC Press LLC

attempt that marshaling of evidence. We do not know where to begin. We do not know what questions to ask.

Fortunately, we now have the life care plan and qualified persons able to prepare it. This specialization is being followed more and more by various rehabilitation professionals and nurses who, using their background training, become proficient at the business of working out a plan for the future medical and rehabilitation needs of the client. In working with the professional life care planner, the attorney does not abdicate the attorney's traditional role as the one who asks the critical questions and who marshals the evidence to prove a point. The attorney joins with the life care planner to make sure the right questions are asked. The skilled plaintiff's attorney recognizes that he needs the assistance of an equally skilled life care planner to identify those questions (Elliott, 1993).

ROLES OF THE FORENSIC EXPERT

There are generally two areas that the attorney must address in litigation: liability and damages. When a party is found liable, that party is determined to be at fault. The next task is to prove damages, or the costs associated with the incident. The rehabilitation professional may act as a *consultant*, which implies that he or she will work behind the scenes to assist the attorney with developing a case or reviewing the work of others (Riddick & Weed, 1996; Weed, 1995; Weed & Field, 2001). Although psychologists, rehabilitation counselors, neuropsychologists, physicians, therapists, and others offer these services, this seems to be a unique role for rehabilitation nurses and life care planners. Indeed, many larger law firms employ consultants on staff to conduct medical research, locate experts, develop deposition and trial questions, summarize medical records and depositions, and provide other litigation support services.

A more common role for the rehabilitation professional is to act as the *expert* and develop opinions, which will be offered as testimony. The rehabilitation expert will generally participate in the damages portion of litigation by assisting in establishing the cost of future care and the significance of the incident with regard to the person's ability to perform work (earnings capacity). Most life care planners are not qualified to offer opinions in the areas of future medical care costs and earnings capacity loss. Therefore, two experts will usually be retained to opine about these separate damages.

Life Care Plans in the Catastrophic Case

There are other very specific reasons why the plaintiff's attorney should use a life care plan in the catastrophic or neurolegal setting. It is an essential tool for settlement and trial preparation since it gives the insurance company and its counsel a clear look at what will be presented to the jury (Elliott, 1993; Taylor, 1996). It gives the plaintiff's attorney the comfort of knowing that those things that could be addressed have not been left to chance and uncovers items of damages that were not thought of by the attorney (Sbordone & Shepherd, 1991).

POTENTIAL PROBLEMS

Life care plans are becoming more and more acceptable to different courts, and they are increasingly required in specialized situations such as pediatric neurolitigation (Sellars, 1996). There are pitfalls, however, that must be watched for by the plaintiff's attorney. The attorney cannot assume that the life care planner in every instance understands the legal system to the extent that the planner can know what will or will not be properly received into evidence. It is tempting to assume that because you have found the life care planner, as a trial attorney, your job is over in that area. Nothing could be farther from the truth.

The attorney must make sure that the life care planner understands the need for a medical evidentiary foundation for each item in the plan. There have been cases where the entire plan was thrown out, and the award with it, because the attorney, and perhaps later the initial trier of fact, took the life care plan as the word of the life care planner and did not show or prove that the various items in the plan were there because they were authorized by medical personnel. In the case of *Diamond R. Fertilizer, et al. v. Jimmy L. Davis*, the court found that the lower court had approved a treatment plan that allowed the rehabilitation company that prepared the plan to determine the treatment needed. The court held that the authority for the plan must rest with the physicians, and it disallowed the plan. With no showing of medical necessity or physicians' orders, the plan provided for a TV, a VCR, a specially equipped van, a whirlpool, a hydraulic lift, and an environmental control unit for the client. The court found no justification and denied all of these items.

INSURANCE CONCERNS

Another area of care in crafting life care plans that the attorney must follow is in those cases where the funding is structured in dependence upon a specific health care policy and not upon general medical necessity. In the case of *Dempsey v. United States of America*, the plan provided for daily attendant home care. The lower court had mistakenly assumed that such care had been provided by the existing CHAMPUS policy that had to be offset. A close scrutiny by the appeals court showed that such care was not provided and the life care plan with that provision was approved. The attorney not only must see that the plan provides necessary care, but also must often prove that it is covered by insurance.

Logical Consistency of Life Care Plan

The attorney must also assume that the plan he or she uses may be scrutinized by the opposition or by the court for logical consistency. If there is illogic in its premises and if it is inconsistent, the plan may be considered flawed and not adopted at all. The plaintiff's attorney does not have to be a life care planner to read the plan in light of its logical underpinnings. For example, if a therapy, such as speech therapy, is proposed to terminate at a certain age and yet speech evaluations are proposed to continue beyond that age, there should be a very logical reason why the evaluations continue after the therapy is discontinued. This also applies to areas such as physical therapy and particularly applies to pediatric issues. If a child is to receive certain therapy only through childhood, evaluations that are pediatric in nature should not continue under the plan past childhood without specific explanation.

In the case of *Brewer v. Secretary of Health and Human Services,* the court applied just such a fine-tooth comb to the plan. Among other things, the court found that all parties and their life care planners had misread and miscalculated the dosage and amount of antiseizure medication. The court took it upon itself to research the issue and to determine the dosage of medication and the proper cost. The court also found that the replacement of assistive communicative devices was not coordinated to their useful life and that no proof was given for the number and type of devices. Finally, the court approved an award for counseling for siblings and parents, citing reasons of well-being for the patient, not the family itself, which the court based on an article from the *Journal of Head Trauma Rehabilitation.* None of these reasons had been advanced by the plaintiff.

THE ROLE OF THE PLAINTIFF ATTORNEY IN THE LIFE CARE PLAN

From the plaintiff's perspective, the life care plan is an integral tool in the proof of damages in neurolitigation or any other catastrophic injury. The attorney must continue to play an active role in making sure the plan fits the parameters for admission into evidence and that the plan meets the test of logic. The life care planner and the attorney must work as a team in reaching this goal. The plan cannot simply be drafted by the life care planner and then handed to the attorney, who, in turn, tenders it into evidence. It is not a chain letter to be passed on. It is a part of the mosaic of the case and must be viewed as such.

The life care planner also brings a new analysis and a fresh look to the legal case. If the plaintiff's attorney is open to examining new perspectives, new things are discovered about the damages aspect of the case. Some may be good for the case, such as an element of damages that should be sought but has been overlooked. Some may be bad for the case, such as the discovery of some exaggeration of an aspect of damages by the client, well intentioned or not. The life care planner is searching for different information than the attorney and, in reviewing the same material, will shed a new light on it for the attorney.

The level of objectivity of the life care planner is therefore very important. It is essential that the person doing the life care plan give the information to the attorney without sugar coating and without bias so that the attorney can adjust the theory of the case to the facts that are developed and not vice versa. This is particularly true in the area of employability. By using devices such as the functional capacities assessment and other tools, the vocational assessment as a component of the life care plan becomes the foundation for credibility. The jury can see what jobs the plaintiff may reasonably expect to perform in the future, how they are suited to the client, and why he or she cannot perform the tasks that would allow other employment. All this is integral to the solid life care plan. It shows thoroughness on the part of the plaintiff's team in bringing the facts to the decision maker on the other side, be that person an adjuster or a juror. The pitch that the plaintiff has compensation neuroses fades before the plain facts of what he or she can do, what he or she cannot do, and how this will affect life in the future (Elliott, 1999).

SPECIAL FORENSIC CONSIDERATIONS

It is useful for the rehabilitation expert to be sensitive to special rules and issues related to civil litigation. A few are listed below.

Hearsay

The ethical rehabilitation professional who practices in forensic settings provides a valuable contribution by establishing a reasonable treatment plan, helping to settle personal injury litigation, and providing the jury with information on which to base an award. Offering testimony is fraught with obstacles such as (1) introducing hearsay evidence and (2) developing appropriate exhibits for the courtroom. In general, hearsay refers to relying on information from another person that may be unreliable or inappropriate. Hearsay taken to the extreme can be applied to your personal identity. For example, you are likely to know your name because someone (your parent) told you your name many years ago. Rules of evidence (with special emphasis on 702 and 703) have been developed to address this problem (see Table 24.1 and http://www.law.harvard.edu/publications/evidenceiii/rules/702.htm).

As a result of *Daubert v. Merrell Dow*, Federal Rule of Evidence 702 has been amended to address the tests for admissibility of expert testimony. The new rule states:

> If scientific, technical, or other specialized knowledge will assist the trier of fact to understand the evidence or to determine a fact in issue, a witness qualified as an expert by knowledge, skill, experience, training, or education, may testify thereto in the form of an opinion or otherwise, if (1) the testimony is based upon sufficient facts or data, (2) the testimony is the product of reliable principles and methods, and (3) the witness has applied the principles and methods reliably to the facts of the case. Effective, December 1, 2000.

Table 24.1 Reducing Hearsay Challenges

- Are you qualified as an expert?
- Are you offering opinions that are in your area of expertise?
- Are you relying on facts and data that you and others in your professional field commonly rely upon?
- Are people employed or retained by you working under your direction and supervision?
- Have you provided a foundation for medical opinions by utilizing physicians for medical diagnosis?

In order to seek a uniform approach to the adoption of Rule 702 by the various states, the National Conference of Commissioners on Uniform Laws drafted what has been designated Uniform Rule 702 with the goal of creating a more uniform expert testimony admissibility standard across state jurisdictions (available at http://www.law.upenn.edu/bll/ulc/ure/evid1200.htm). The rule reads:

(a) <u>General Rule</u>. If a witness testimony is based on scientific, technical, or other specialized knowledge, the witness may testify in the form of an opinion or otherwise if the court deems the following are satisfied:

    (1) the testimony will assist the trier of fact in understanding evidence or determining a fact in issue;

    (2) the witness is qualified by knowledge, skill, experience, training, or education in the scientific, technical, or other specialized field;

    (3) the testimony is based upon principles or methods that are reasonably reliable, as established under subdivisions (b), (c), (d), or (e);

    (4) the testimony is based upon sufficient and reliable facts or data; and

    (5) the witness has applied the principles or methods reliably to the facts of the case.

(b) <u>Reliability deemed to exist</u>. A principle or method is reasonably reliable if its reliability has been established by controlling legislation or judicial decisions.

(c) <u>Presumption of reliability</u>. A principle or method is presumed to be reasonably reliable if its has substantial acceptance within the relevant scientific, technical, or specialized community. A party may rebut the presumption by proving that it is more probable than not that the principle or method is not reasonably reliable.

(d) <u>Presumption of unreliability.</u> A principle or method is presumed to be not reasonably reliable if it does not have substantial acceptance within the relevant scientific, technical, or specialized community. A party may rebut the presumption by proving that it is more probable than not that the principle or method is reasonably reliable.

(e) <u>Other reliability factors.</u> In determining the reliability of a principle or method, the court shall consider all relevant additional factors, which may include:

    (1) the extent to which the principle has been tested;

    (2) the adequacy of the research methods employed in testing the principle or method;

    (3) the extent to which the principle or method has been published and subjected to peer review;

    (4) the rate of error in the application of the principle or method;

    (5) the experience of the witness in the application of the principle or method;

(6) the extent to which the principle or method has gained acceptance within the relevant scientific, technical, or specialized
community; and

(7) the extent to which the witness's specialized field of knowledge has gained acceptance within the general scientific, technical, or specialized community.

At the time of this publication, the updated Uniform Rule 702 has been slow
to catch on; it would be wise for the practitioner to use this more detailed rule
in preparation for Daubert challenges or to make the same, since it is the most
comprehensive pronouncement on admissibility standards under Daubert that we
have seen. It appears that most states are waiting until further clarification appears
at the federal level before adopting these rules in their entirety. Even Uniform
Rule 702 does not provide a clear method for making the determinations required
under Daubert, and so far, life care plans have not reached the level of serious
challenge. If they become more critical to large verdicts with a cap on noneconomic damage, that may change.

Although the discussion below is based on federal rules, most states have
either adopted these rules in some form or established precedent through previous
legal cases. The old Rule 702 states that a witness qualified as an expert by
knowledge, skill, experience, training, or education may testify by offering an
expert opinion. Rule 703 allows the expert to rely on facts or data, which is not
entered as evidence, if the information is commonly relied upon by experts in
the field. Practically, this is demonstrated in two ways. First, the consultant may
hire a subcontractor or use an employee to develop research, assist in report
writing, and summarize medical records. As long as these professionals are
qualified and they work under direction and supervision by the lead consultant,
the information should be allowed in the courtroom. Second, it is common for
life care planners to rely upon physicians for treatment plans, vendors or catalogs
for costs, and other sources for the foundation of the plan. The key issue is related
to what the consultant and others in the field commonly do to conduct business
(see Weed & Field, 1994, for more Federal Rules of Evidence information).

Written Opinions

In most rehabilitation settings, it is expected that consultants will provide written
reports with conclusions and opinions. The same standard should apply to the
role of the expert witness. Attorneys may occasionally ask the expert to act as
an expert but not provide a written report. Although narratives may be optional,
conclusions, recommendations, and opinions should be provided in writing. In
this author's opinion, failure to follow the standards of the expert's industry reflects
badly and ultimately damages the profession as a whole. Experts who play the
game of challenging the attorney to guess what they will say at trial through
depositions are shortsighted. This has become enough of an issue that some
jurisdictions now require a written report.

Disclosing Prior Expert Testimony

A recent rule has been added to federal and other cases that may require revealing cases in which the consultant testified in deposition or trial during the previous 4 years (referred as Rule 26; see http://www.law.cornell.edu/rules/frcp/Rule26.htm). Data should include the case caption, the date of the deposition or trial, and the state in which the case was filed. This disclosure does not apply to cases where the life care planner was acting as a consultant or the expert did not testify.

Collateral Source

Collateral source rules vary from state to state and jurisdiction to jurisdiction (i.e., federal vs. state cases). In practical terms, collateral sources refer to rules that require that a personal injury award be offset by reasonable available services and products. Generally, this is represented in pediatric cases by including the free services that are available in the school system through the Individuals with Disabilities Education Act (IDEA). This may include special education, occupational therapy, physical therapy, speech and language therapy, aide services, and specialized equipment and supplies. Other options may include offsets for Medicaid or Medicare. The consultant is advised to discuss this issue with the attorney prior to rendering an opinion.

Interrogatory

An interrogatory is a list of questions that is submitted through an attorney usually to the client but sometimes to an expert. A series of questions is asked that is expected to elucidate the reason you were called as an expert. This is usually a prelude to a deposition. Generally the other side is attempting to discover what will be entered as evidence at a trial. This is a formal procedure that should not be taken lightly.

Deposition

The rehabilitation consultant's role at the deposition is similar to his role at a trial. The primary difference is the location and the lack of the presence of a judge. The deposition can be conducted at the office of the expert, at a court reporter's office, in the office of the attorney, and occasionally by telephone. A judge is not present to preside or to rule on objections by the counsels for plaintiff or defense. While clients may attend, their presence is uncommon.

There are two types of deposition that the expert is likely to face. One is an evidence deposition. The evidence deposition generally is called by the side that retained the expert. In this situation, either the attorney believes there is good reason to attempt to settle the case, or the expert will not appear live at trial. Both attorneys present their case similar to how it would be presented at trial. In some cases the expert may be videotaped, although more often than not, the deposition will be transcribed from an audiotape or other court recording method. Many physicians utilize this method. Another type of deposition is the discovery deposition. In this case the other side is attempting to uncover or discover what evidence is expected to be offered at trial. Usually the attorney that retains the expert being deposed does not ask questions of the specialist since the attorney does not want to give away any more information than necessary.

The attorney who requested the deposition initiates direct examination. Cross, redirect, and recross examination may follow. A certified court recorder records (and later transcribes) the entire testimony. Since a judge is not present to control the proceedings, objections by either side are stated. The rationale for such objections are given and discussed. The judge, prior to the submission of the testimony, will make a ruling on each objection into evidence at a trial. The rehabilitation expert should be aware that although the deposition appears to be a much more informal process, its content is equally important to that of the formal courtroom testimony. The entire deposition, or selected portions of its contents, may be read at the formal hearing or trial.

Note that some professionals find themselves in awkward positions. Many times opposing attorneys ask questions of experts that would not be allowed in trial when a judge is present. The experienced expert can usually set boundaries, but professionals new to the industry may not know what is proper. Seeking training in this specialized area is recommended in order to avoid compromising your reputation or offering opinions contrary to forensic rules. There may also be occasions where the expert is bordering on saying something that documents malpractice, such as incorrectly disclosing records that have been subpoenaed or providing confidential information about other clients. Remember, the attorney that retains the expert is not representing the expert. An expert should not expect personal legal advice from the attorney who hired him; if an expert makes this assumption, he is treading on dangerous legal territory. The expert is advised to consult *his* attorney if there are legal questions.

Subpoena

A subpoena is a formal legal request for records or appearance at a deposition or trial. It may or may not be a proper request. For example, the expert receives a subpoena for confidential records of a client. It happens to be a difficult client who is involved in litigation. Should the records be sent? The expert may decide that he must comply with the threatening warrant. However, the expert must first be clear on confidentiality. The expert should know that a judge does not usually review a subpoena for records. If the client has not signed a release, the expert should check with his own attorney before releasing the records. Recently, this author had a personal injury defense attorney subpoena him for a deposition. The expert was to appear at a specific date and time, but if he submitted records, the deposition would be canceled. The author contacted the attorney to tell him records would be released when a release of information was received. Ultimately, the deposition and the requested records were canceled when the request was disclosed to the client's attorney since the expert was not being called to testify. Another example involves a rehabilitation counselor who received a subpoena from a defense attorney for her records on a client. She felt compelled to send the records only to learn that the client's attorney was furious since she had also provided the other side with attorney work product, which was privileged communication. Generally, it is best for the rehabilitation professional to agree to provide information once the appropriateness is determined. This is accomplished by writing to the attorney who requested or subpoenaed the information and explaining that as soon as proper releases or a judge's order is received, the information will be provided promptly.

On the other hand, a subpoena for appearing in court as a witness carries a different expectation. If the individual is to appear as a witness to the event or accident, then it is expected that he or she appear or suffer possible warrant for arrest. On the other hand, if the individual is to appear as an expert witness, it is generally accepted that one cannot be forced to provide an expert opinion even though one may be required to appear.

Trial by Jury

The primary difference in a jury trial and other settings is the courtroom. At the jury trial, the expert is called to testify at the time the attorney deems to be the most critical for such testimony. The life care planner most frequently testifies without the benefit of hearing live testimony (referred to as sequestering), although in some courts the expert is allowed to sit in and listen to others testify.

The presence of a jury and the necessity to sit in the witness chair adds an air of sophistication and formality that matches no other legal setting. It becomes very easy to do those things that one should not and to forget to do those things that one should. The consultant should realize that the jury will not remember most of the testimony presented. What is remembered is the impression they held of the expert. Therefore, it is very important to avoid confrontation with the cross-examining attorney and become an advocate for one side over another. Remaining as objective as possible is vital but very difficult in the heat of the battle.

One more suggestion is to speak to the jury since the lawyer probably already knows the answer to the question. This is harder than it sounds. However, many juries have been sitting for days in a boring (usually) courtroom and may "doze off" at times. Speaking directly to the jury will help keep them on task and perhaps leave them with a better impression. There are several ways to display evidence to a jury to help convey your opinion in a more interesting way. For example, you may choose to write figures on a flip chart, blow up the life care plan or vocational opinions on a large chart that can be seen by the jury and others, use transparencies, make slides of the evidence, and, more recently, utilize computer-based displays. In general, it is recommended to use an educational approach by teaching the jury. This will be more interesting to the jury and will allow the expert to stand up and move around.

Recent Trends in Life Care Plan Value

There is a perception among plaintiff's attorneys that the relentless pursuit of a cap on noneconomic damages in civil cases will eventually bear some fruit and that, in most jurisdictions, they will be faced with a cap on the recovery of items such as pain and suffering. At both the federal and state level these issues are being renewed with new majorities in the House and Senate. As a consequence, many attorneys are already beginning to refocus their efforts on the maximization of economic losses to compensate for this change in the landscape. It is easy to see how the attorney must rethink the approach to catastrophic cases if a limit is to be applied for noneconomic losses. The juries will be asked, more than ever, to apportion their verdicts so that they must identify or allocate an amount to each category. Such a new approach means that life care plans become more important than ever as the keystone of an adequate recovery in the view of the plaintiff's attorney.

A variation on this theme is found in one of the recent federal cases to discuss a life care plan. In *Lebron v. United States*, No. 00-51101, 5th Circuit, decided January 5, 2002, the 5th Circuit Court of Appeals was reviewing a Federal Tort Claims Act case in which a life care plan had been used. In such cases the plaintiff must make a demand before filing suit. The demand is considered to set the limit of recovery and any recovery in excess of the demand in the principal case must be written down to the extent it exceeds the demand. In this case the demand was $20 million. The recovery was $20.6 million. The plaintiffs, in seeking to avoid the stricture of this rule, argued that they could not have known about certain damages at the time they filed the demand, citing the life care plan as it was later developed in proof of that fact. The court did not agree and reduced the award to the $20 million demand, pointing out that the case was known to be very complex from the beginning and nothing new developed after the demand was filed. The fact that the life care plan as produced was greater than anticipated was not adequate reason to change the rule as the court saw it. Had the focus been on the life care plan from the beginning, perhaps the result would have been different. Indicators are that life care plans will be involved in such catastrophic cases in the very early stages since so much more may be riding on them.

CONCLUSION

In the final analysis, the person receiving the life care plan for review or hearing it in testimony will filter that information through his or her own life experiences. If it contains items that just simply do not seem reasonable and necessary, those items will not be accepted. It will create an aura of skepticism about the entire plan. It is the job of the attorney working with the life care planner to analyze the plan and to search for items that may be perceived in this fashion. In many instances, the remedy is simply a matter of giving a proper explanation of why the item is needed, rather than an oblique reference to the source. Some items speak for themselves. Some require explanation if they are esoteric or very technical. It must be remembered by everyone involved in the process that communication is primary and essential.

The plaintiff's attorney in every case is sending a message in two parts: (1) the attorney must convince the opposing side of its obligation to pay money for damages, and (2) then must convince the opposing side how much it should pay. If the attorney is not certain about the future needs of the client, the attorney cannot maintain ardor in seeking that amount. To be effective, the attorney must first be convinced of the truth of the case and then must convince the opposing side. The life care plan is indispensable to that process. Properly done, the life care plan convinces the attorney. Properly presented, the life care plan convinces the jury. When the file is closed, the attorney will have to reflect on whether what was done was all that could be done to see that the client's life, all of the remainder of that life, was cared for in the best possible manner. It is often the life care plan that makes that reflection a source of satisfaction rather than regret.

REFERENCES

Brewer v. Secretary of Health and Human Services. (1996). Case 93-0092V, U.S. Court of Claims.

Daubert v. Merrell Dow. (1993). 125 L Ed 2nd 469.

Dempsey v. United States of America. (1994). 32 F.3d 1490.

Diamond R. Fertilizer, et al. v. Jimmy L. Davis. (1990). 567 So.2d 451.

Elliott, T. (1993). Life care plans: the legal perspective. *The Neurolaw Letter,* 2, 1, 3.

Elliott, T. (1999). Life care plans: a plaintiff's attorney's perspective. In R. Weed, Ed., *Life Care Planning and Case Management Handbook,* 371–379. Boca Raton, FL: CRC Press.

Lebron v. United States, No. 00-51101, 5th Circuit, decided January 5, 2002. Available at http://www.ca5.uscourts.gov/opinions/pub/00/00-51101-cv0.HTM.

Riddick, S. & Weed, R. (1996). The life care planning process for managing catastrophically impaired patients. In *Case Studies in Nursing Case Management,* 61–91. Blanchett, S., Ed., Sudbury, MA: Jones & Bartlett.

Sbordone, R. & Shepherd, J. (1991). The role of the neuropsychologist and life care planner in evaluating brain damage cases. *The Neurolaw Letter,* 1, 5.

Sellars, C. (1996). Life care planning for young children with brain injuries. *The Neurolaw Letter,* 6, 101, 106–107.

Taylor, S. (1996). Life care plans in court. *The Neurolaw Letter,* 5, 25, 28.

Uniform Rule 702. (2002). Available at http://www.law.upenn.edu/bll/ulc/ure/evid1200.htm.

Weed, R. (1995). Forensic rehabilitation. In A.E. Dell Orto & R.P. Marinelle, Eds., *Encyclopedia of Disability and Rehabilitation,* 326–330. New York: Macmillan.

Weed, R. & Field, T. (2001). *The Rehabilitation Consultant's Handbook,* 3rd ed. Athens, GA: E&F Vocational Services.

25

A DEFENSE ATTORNEY'S PERSPECTIVE ON LIFE CARE PLANNING

Lee D. Gunn IV and Tracy Raffles Gunn

INTRODUCTION

Counsel defending against serious injuries is likely to confront a life care plan presented by the plaintiff's attorney in an effort to quantify the various impacts upon the injured party's activities of daily living and quality of life.[1] A defendant must prepare early and thoroughly to rebut the plaintiff's various claims and identify areas of overreaching or weakness in the plan. This chapter will address the defense perspective on life care planning both in terms of attacking the plaintiff's life care plan and retaining a defense life care planning expert, either as a nontestifying consultant or to testify at trial.

Attacking the Plaintiff's Life Care Plan

Qualifications

The first step in attacking the plaintiff's life care plan is to determine whether the plaintiff's life care planner is, in fact, qualified to present the plan. This is a critical issue because an unqualified witness will not be accepted as an expert and will not be permitted to testify at trial. Thus, a successful attack on the plaintiff's life care planner's qualifications will result in the planner's entire testimony, and the plan itself, being kept from the jury's consideration.

There are two levels of qualification that will be required of a life care expert presenting a life care plan. First, the expert must be qualified generally in the area of life care planning. Second, the expert must be qualified to substantiate,

---

[1] The Federal Rules of Evidence apply only in federal courts, and different requirements may apply in certain state courts. However, the majority of states have patterned their rules of evidence after the federal rules and have adopted the case law interpreting the federal rules as persuasive in their respective jurisdictions.

0-8493-1511-5/04/$0.00+$1.50
© 2004 by CRC Press LLC

to the degree required under the particular jurisdiction's substantive law, the need for each element of care provided in the plan.

Qualifications as a Life Care Planning Expert Generally

Under the Federal Rules of Evidence,[2] a witness may establish his or her qualification as an expert by reason of "knowledge, skill, experience, training, or education[3]." The use of the disjunctive or in this list of the grounds for determining a proposed expert's qualification has been consistently held to permit qualification as an expert based on any one of these five factors. Thus, a properly qualified expert may have no practical experience in the particular area about which he or she testifies.[4] Similarly, a witness may qualify as an expert in a field in which he or she has no formal training, education, degree, or certification. In fact, at least one court has held that a skilled witness on a medical subject need not be duly licensed to practice medicine.[5] The determination of whether an individual qualifies as an expert is a decision for the trial court pursuant to Federal Rule of Evidence 104(a). This determination is left to the sound discretion of the trial court and will not be reversed on appeal absent an abuse of that discretion.[6]

Because life care planning is a relatively new profession, there are few written court decisions addressing the degree of experience, education, or other qualification required to properly establish a proposed witness as an expert life care planner. At least one court has held that attending two seminars on life care planning and compiling 25 life care plans is not sufficient to qualify an individual as an expert in life care planning.[7] Another court has determined that a rehabil-

---

[2] Federal Rule of Evidence 702, which governs the admissibility of expert testimony, provides as follows: "If scientific, technical, or other specialized knowledge will assist the trier of fact to understand the evidence or to determine a fact in issue, a witness qualified as an expert by knowledge, skill, experience, training, or education may testify thereto in the form of an opinion or otherwise."

Rule 702 serves several distinct functions. It establishes the authority to use expert testimony in general, sets forth the standard for admissibility of expert testimony in a given case, and addresses the qualifications necessary to accord a witness status as an expert. See generally *Coleman v. Parkline Corp.*, 844 F.2d 863, 865 (D.C. Circuit 1988); *Sterling v. Velsicol Chemical Corp.*, 855 F.2d 1188, 1208 (6th Circuit 1988).

[3] See *Gardner v. General Motors Corporation*, 507 F.2d 525, 528 (10th Circuit 1974); *United States v. Viglia*, 549 F.2d 335 (5th Circuit 1977), cert. denied, 434 U.S. 834, 98 S.Ct. 121, 54 L.Ed.2d 95 (1977); *Friendship Heights Association v. Vlastimil Koubek*, 785 F.2d 1154, 1160 (4th Circuit 1986); *Exum v. General Electric Company*, 819 F.2d 1158 (D.C. Circuit 1987).

[4] *Jenkins v. United States*, 307 F.2d 637, 644 (D.C. Circuit 1962).

[5] *Salem v. United States Lines Co.*, 370 U.S. 31, 35, 82 S.Ct. 1119, 1122, 8 L.Ed.2d 313 (1962); *Grindstaff v. Coleman*, 681 F.2d 740, 743 (11th Circuit 1982); *Dunn v. Sears, Roebuck and Company*, 639 F.2d 1171, 1174 (5th Circuit 1981), modified on other grounds, 645 F.2d 511 (5th Circuit 1981); *Mannino v. International Mfg. Co.*, 650 F.2d 846 (6th Circuit 1981).

[6] See *Fairchild v. United States*, 769 F.Supp. 964, 968 (W.D. La. 1991).

[7] See *Midway National Bank v. Estate of Bollmeyer*, 504 N.W.2d 59, 65 (Minn. App. 1993).

itation consultant who prepared 200 to 225 life care plans per year and held a bachelor's degree in psychology, a master's degree in rehabilitation counseling with a minor in behavioral psychology, and a Ph.D. in counseling psychology and a minor in rehabilitation counseling, with a subspecialty in severe orthopedic disabilities, was qualified by both his education and practical experience to testify as a life care planning expert.[8,9]

Between these two extremes, the lack of case law precedent on the issue leaves a gray area that will give rise to debate concerning the qualifications of a proposed life care planning expert. A life care planner seeking to testify for the plaintiff should be prepared to establish his or her qualifications by relevant training, education, or experience. A defense life care planning consultant can assist his or her client not only in analyzing the elements of the life care plan, but also in determining whether the plaintiff's proposed life care planning expert is in fact qualified as such.

Qualification to Present the Particular Life Care Plan

Rule 702 was written as a general grant of authority for the use of expert testimony and is therefore permissive in nature.[10] Therefore, in many applications of the expert witness rule, the threshold issue is whether the field of expertise is proper for expert testimony in court. Expert testimony is generally proper in any scientific field that has reached a level of general acceptance. Most courts have at least implicitly recognized that life care planning itself has reached such a degree of general acceptance as to be the proper subject of expert testimony. Thus, there should not usually be any question that expert testimony is generally permitted in conjunction with a life care plan.[11]

---

[8] Recently, the Commission on Disability Examiner Certification (CDEC) has created a program for life care planner certification (CLPC). Such a certification assures a threshold of knowledge and experience. Failure to be certified will not likely preclude the expert from testifying, but will serve as an important factor in arguing the respective weight to be given to competing life care plans. The CDEC may be contacted for more information at 13325 Queensgate Rd., Midlothian, VA 23113; (804) 359-3463. Also see Chapter 32 on credentialing.

[9] This perspective derives from the fact that expert testimony is treated as an exception to the general rule requiring witnesses to testify to facts instead of opinions. See generally McCormick, EVIDENCE 12, at 30 (3d ed. 1984).

[10] Note, however, that this general acceptance requirement can also impact the admissibility of a particular life care plan if the scientific bases for any elements of the plan are not generally accepted. This specific issue is discussed is more detail infra at notes 20 to 23 and accompanying text.

[11] See generally *International Brotherhood of Teamsters v. United States*, 431 U.S. 324, 97 S.Ct. 1843, 1851, 52 L.Ed.2d 396, 407 (1977) (recognizing that expert testimony is required in medical malpractice cases); *Randolph v. Collectramatic, Inc.*, 590 F.2d 844, 848 (10th Circuit 1979); *Huddell v. Levin*, 537 F.2d 726, 726 (3d Circuit 1976).

Conversely, however, the particular substantive law controlling a given case may *require* expert testimony regarding a certain issue. In these cases, expert testimony is not only permitted by rule 702 but is, in fact, required by the relevant substantive law.[12] For example, in cases involving claims of personal injury, courts around the country generally hold that expert testimony is required on the issue of whether treatment claimed as damages is medically necessary. Under this rule, many elements of a life care plan will often require qualified medical expert testimony in order to be properly presented to the jury as a claimed element of damages. In the vast majority of cases, this foundation requires testimony of a physician.

In many cases, plaintiffs seek to present a life care plan to the jury supported only by the testimony of a rehabilitation consultant or certified life care planner. The defense will likely take the position, and several courts have held, that each element of the life care plan must also be independently supported by a separately qualified expert's testimony as to that element's reasonableness and necessity in the given case. As one court stated, "[t]he responsibility for establishing a treatment plan rests with a claimant's authorized physicians."[13] Unless such requirements are enforced, the use of the life care planning expert will enable the plaintiff to circumvent the threshold for admissibility of each claimed element of damages

---

[12] *Diamond R. Fertilizer v. Davis*, 567 So.2d 451, 455 (Fla. 1st DCA 1990). In Diamond Fertilizer, the court held that it was reversible error to adopt a life care plan that was established by a rehabilitation counselor and that gave the counselor the discretion to oversee and supervise the claimant's medical and nursing home care, where the plan was supported solely by the counselor's own testimony without the testimony of any treating physician. The court emphasized that each element of a life care plan must be medically necessary and that, in most cases, medical expert testimony is required to establish medical necessity (567 So.2d at 455).

[13] See *Fairchild v. United States*, 769 F.Supp.964, 968 (W.D. La. 1991) (recognizing that each treatment element recommended by the life care planner must have independent record support); *First National Bank v. Kansas City Southern Railway Company*, 865 S.W.2d 719, 738 (Mo. App. 1993) (holding that a life care planner's testimony regarding the need for and costs of future attendant care should have been excluded due to the lack of a medical doctor's testimony establishing the need for such care on a medical basis) (analyzing the issue in terms of impermissible speculation on the question of damages); *Timmons v. Mass. Transp. Authority*, 591 N.E.2d 667, 670-71 (Mass. 1992) (holding that admission of vocational rehabilitation expert's opinion of future loss of earnings was prejudicial error because the expert assumed that the injury was permanent and this assumption was not supported by evidence). See also *Hobbs v. Harken*, 969 S.W.2d 318 (Mo. App. 1998); *Hines v. Sweet*, 567 S.W.2d 435, 438 (Mo. App. 1978). But see *National Bank v. Estate of Bollmeyer*, 504 N.W.2d 59, 65 (Minn. App. 1993) (holding that a qualified life care planner who has reviewed the plaintiff's medical records can testify to the plaintiff's need for future personal care services, and rejecting the argument that a medical doctor must testify regarding such need; the court did not state whether the medical evidence relied on by the life care planner established the plaintiff's need from a medical standpoint in the first instance).

It should be noted that an appellate court may permit a trial court less discretion in determining the scope of the life care planner's expertise than in permitting the expert to testify in the first instance. See, e.g., *First National Bank v. Kansas City Southern Railway Company*, 865 S.W.2d 719 (Mo. App. 1993) (allowing the trial court broad discretion in qualifying the expert but holding that the trial court committed reversible error in permitting the qualified life care planner to testify to matters requiring medical expertise).

in the plan. Thus, once the life care planner is properly qualified as an expert in the field of life care planning generally, the court will next consider whether the proposed expert is qualified as an expert in the relevant field for each element of the life care plan that is not supported by other evidence or another expert's testimony.

Failure by the plaintiff to properly limit the scope of the life care planner's proposed expertise may result in the entire plan and the planner's entire testimony being precluded or stricken.[14] A life care planner testifying for the plaintiff must therefore ensure not only that he or she is qualified to testify as a life care planner generally, but that he or she is qualified to testify concerning the necessity of any individual elements of the plan that are not independently supported by appropriate medical or other expert testimony. In many cases the plaintiff's life care planner can best serve his client by enlisting the services of the proper medical experts, rather than by attempting to support the plan based on his testimony alone.[15] A defendant's life care planning consultant can be of great assistance in helping defense counsel to identify any weaknesses in the plaintiff's proposed expert's qualifications to testify regarding the need for any given treatment element in the plan.

In general, a rehabilitation or habilitation expert will attempt to translate the physical or mental impairment into a disability in order to assess the effect upon the injured party's ability to participate in activities of daily living. It is the role of the physician to establish the existence of a physical or mental impairment, and it is inappropriate for a rehabilitation consultant to present opinion testimony as to the existence of a medical condition or its likely progression. Rather, the foundation for the impairment must be laid by a physician, including any expected complications or progression. This medical opinion can then be translated by the rehabilitation consultant into the disabling effects.

It should be noted that there may also be limitations on the authority of a life care planner to oversee and supervise the plaintiff's treatment. In one case, the court reversed an award that placed a rehabilitation counselor in charge of supervising the claimant's medical and nursing home care where there was insufficient independent medical evidence to support the award:

---

[14] See *Reddish v. Secretary of the Department of Health and Human Services*, 18 Cl. Ct. 366, 375 (U.S. Claims Court 1991) (noting that life care plan incorporated needs outlined by treating physicians); *Neher v. Secretary of the Department of Health and Human Services*, 23 Cl. Ct. 508 (U.S. Claims Court 1991) (damage award reversed because elements of life care plan were speculative and were duplicated by other award); *Ainos' Custom Slip Covers v. DeLucia*, 533 So.2d 862 (Fla. 1st DCA 1988) (reversing an order awarding the medical and nursing home services outlined in a life care plan where the testimony of the rehabilitation consultant was the sole support for the award and the medical witnesses testified that the claimant's current care was sufficient).

[15] *Ainos' Custom Slip Covers v. DeLucia*, 533 So.2d 862, 864 (Fla. 1st DCA 1988), review denied, 544 So.2d 199 (Fla. 1989). See also *Alpha Resins Corp. v. Townsend*, 606 So.2d 506 (Fla. 1st DCA 1992) (court retained jurisdiction to determine which elements of the life care were medically necessary).

The award is patently erroneous insofar as it purports to give a rehabilitation company authority to oversee and supervise claimant's medical
and nursing care. Such responsibility rests with a claimant's treating
physicians. Furthermore, although [the rehabilitation expert] was apparently competent to testify concerning his rehabilitation services, his
testimony was not sufficiently substantial to provide the sole support
for such a far-reaching award of rehabilitative oversight and authority.[16]

Foundational Objections, the Frye Standard, and Other Preclusions

In addition to challenging the plaintiff's expert's general and specific qualifications,
defense counsel should be aware of other potential grounds to exclude the
testimony. For example, an untimely disclosure of the intent to use a life care
plan can bar its introduction at trial.[17]

Likewise, even where there is no question regarding the expert's qualifications,
the expert's opinion must be supported by an adequate factual foundation.[18] The
expert's proper role is to provide opinion testimony based on facts that are of
record in the case. The lack of an adequate factual foundation requires that the
expert's testimony be stricken as based on speculation.[19] Such an issue may arise
if, for example, the life care planner intends to testify regarding the cost of certain
treatment but no medical evidence has been proffered to indicate that such
treatment is reasonable, necessary, or caused by the relevant accident. Such
foundational objections should be considered in cases where similar objections
to the life care planner's qualifications have been overruled.

The speculative nature of a life care plan can also preclude its admissibility if
the plan involves new or experimental treatments or novel theories of causation.
Frye v. United States[20] (the Frye rule) mandates that expert testimony deduced

---

[16] In *Department of Health and Rehabilitative Services v. J.B.*, 675 So.2d 241 (Fla. 4th DCA 1996),
the plaintiff's attorney represented to the defendant and to the court that he would not
introduce a life care plan at trial, and subsequently attempted to introduce such a plan at
trial. The court precluded the plaintiff from using the plan.

[17] *Randolph v. Laeisz*, 896 F.2d 964, 968 (5th Circuit 1990).

[18] *American Bearing Co., Inc., v. Litton Industries, Inc.*, 729 F.2d 943, 947 (3d Circuit 1984),
cert. denied, 469 U.S. 854, 105 S.Ct. 178, 83 L.Ed.2d 112 (1984); *Twin City Plaza, Inc., v.
Central Surety and Insurance Corporation*, 409 F.2d 1195, 1200 (8th Circuit 1969) ("When
basic foundational conditions are themselves conjecturally premised, it behooves a court to
remove the answer from one of admissible opinion to one of excludable speculation"); *Polk
v. Ford Motor Company*, 529 F.2d 259, 271 (8th Circuit 1976), cert. denied, 426 U.S. 907, 96
S.Ct. 2229, 48 L.Ed.2d 832 (1976) (an expert's opinion must be based on matters sufficient
"to take such testimony out of the realm of guesswork and speculation"). In *Randolph v.
Laeisz*, 896 F.2d 964, 968 (5th Circuit 1990), for example, the court held that a properly
qualified economist's testimony was inadmissible where the testimony was based on insufficient foundation. The economist had testified that lost wages should be reduced by a certain
percentage due to market conditions. The court held that because such market conditions
did not appear in the record, there was insufficient foundation for the expert's testimony.
The court found that the testimony was improperly admitted because the expert's testimony
served as substantive evidence rather than opinion interpreting facts in evidence.

[19] 293 F. 1013 (D.C. Circuit 1923).

[20] 293 F. at 1014.

from a scientific principle or discovery is only admissible if the principle or discovery is "sufficiently established to have gained general acceptance in the particular field in which it belongs."[21] While the U.S. Supreme Court has since adopted a slightly broader standard for admissibility of scientific evidence in federal courts,[22] all courts will apply some threshold requirements to the admissibility of novel scientific evidence. If the life care plan is based on a scientific theory that does not meet the threshold requirements, it can be excluded in whole or part. A Frye analysis can be applied not only to test the viability of the types of treatment and services claimed in the life care plan, but also to challenge the theory that the condition itself could have been caused by the particular event.[23]

Of course, defense counsel is advised to not only keep these potential exclusionary arguments in mind in analyzing the plaintiff's proffered life care plan, but also to ensure that any defense life care plan complies with each of these requirements and will be admissible.[24]

Cross-Examination of the Plaintiff's Expert

As courts increasingly relax the formal requirements for qualifications of expert testimony, and as scientific advances render more elements of a life care plan generally accepted, it may not be possible to completely exclude the expert from testifying.[25] Where the threshold requirements for qualification are met, any deficiency in the witness's knowledge, education, training, or experience is relevant only to the weight to be given his or her testimony, and not the admissibility of that testimony. Courts will often hold that a proposed expert of marginal qualification should be permitted to testify and the opposing party required to elicit the defects in his qualifications on cross-examination, rather than barring the testimony completely. Thus, when a life care expert is permitted to testify over defense objection, the expert should expect any weaknesses in his qualifications to be explored in detail on cross-examination.

---

[21] See *Daubert v. Merrill Dow Pharmaceuticals, Inc.*, 509 U.S. 579 (1993). Many states still apply the strict Frye test. See *Brim v. State*, 695 So.2d 268, 271-72 (Fla. 1997); *Hadden v. State*, 690 So.2d 573, 577 (Fla. 1997); *Flanagan v. State*, 625 So.2d 827, 829 n.2 (Fla. 1993); *Stokes v. State*, 548 So.2d 188, 193 (Fla. 1989).

[22] For example, in *Black v. Food Lion, Inc.*, 171 F.3d 308, 312-13 (5th Circuit 1999), the plaintiff's expert opined that her fibromyalgia resulted from a slip and fall accident. The defendant presented medical literature indicating that the scientific community had been unable to determine that trauma could be the cause of fibromyalgia. The court excluded the testimony even under the more liberal Daubert test, holding that "mere conjecture does not satisfy the standard for general acceptance" (171 F.3d at 313).

[23] See infra for a detailed discussion of the use of life care planning by the defense.

[24] See, e.g., *First National Bank v. Kansas City Southern Railway Company*, 865 S.W.2d 719 (Mo. App. 1993).

[25] In the instance of rehabilitation, an individual has a known ability that is lost due to the impairment, creating a disabling affect. In the art of habilitation, the counselor is seeking to develop skills unknown to the injured party prior to the impairment. Accordingly, the techniques required to rehabilitate persons differ from those to habilitate individuals. In this chapter the term *rehabilitation counselor* refers to both rehabilitative and habilitative counseling, unless noted to the contrary.

Defense counsel will determine whether the plaintiff's expert is state certified in rehabilitation, habilitation,[26] vocational rehabilitation, workers' compensation, or other form of counseling. A defendant will also find it helpful to determine whether the plaintiff's expert is a medical case manager. Oftentimes, plaintiffs will retain vocational rehabilitation consultants who have expanded their forensic practice into life care planning. Many plaintiffs' experts have never actively served as a patient advocate or coordinator of health services on behalf of an injured party. Establishing that the plaintiff's expert has done nothing more than read books and look at other life care plans in order to present a particular life care plan can be crippling to the plaintiff's case, even if the court finds the expert qualified to testify. A life care expert hired by the defendant to assist in preparing the defense case can assist his client by being familiar with all available training or education in the field, and making defense counsel aware of any such training or education that does not appear on the plaintiff's life care expert's resume.

Financial Bias

After the plaintiff's life care planner has overcome any qualification issues, the planner must avoid additional potential pitfalls. Financial bias is a common ground for defense efforts to discredit the plaintiff's experts, including the life care planner. The obvious financial bias of any expert is that he or she is being paid to present opinion testimony on behalf of the plaintiff.[27] Beyond the bias that all retained experts have, defense counsel will likely inquire about the amount of money received by the expert for litigation support services generally. Many jurisdictions require that the expert give a best estimate of the amount of money or percent of income received from litigation services as a whole. Under the Federal Rules (commonly referred to as Rule 26), the expert must disclose publications for the last 10 years, compensation paid for the study and testimony, and a listing of cases for which testimony was given in the last 4 years. Prior retention by the plaintiff's law firm is often a fruitful source of showing an ongoing business relationship that the life care planner presumably would not want to jeopardize by presenting conservative plans.

Another source of financial bias impeachment is the appearance of impropriety created by recommended self-referral. Some life care planners are involved in owned and operated rehabilitation centers. Where the life care plan is centered

---

[26] It should be noted that even where the relevant substantive law would permit compensation to the plaintiff for the fees of persons whose services were enlisted to obtain the award, a life care planner's fees may not be compensable. See *Southern Industries v. Chumey*, 613 So.2d 74 (Fla. 1st DCA 1993) (holding in a workers' compensation context that the life care planning services of a rehabilitation counselor and psychologist were not reasonably necessary to the procurement of benefits and therefore were not compensable expenses); *Frederick Electronics v. Pettijohn*, 619 So.2d 14 (Fla. 1st DCA 1993) (rehabilitation counselor and psychologist who developed life care plan did not qualify as a health care provider, and his services were therefore not reimbursable expenses in workers' compensation case).

[27] See *Compton v. West Volusia Hosp. Auth.*, 727 So.2d 379, 381 (Fla. 5th DCA 1999).

around such a program, this creates the appearance of a financial incentive on the part of the life care planner. In some egregious cases, defense counsel can successfully establish that the life care planner has engaged in self-referral of prior plaintiffs who have received settlements or judgment awards and entered into the life care planner's own facility programs. It can be devastating to the plaintiff's case for the jury to learn that the life care planner may receive a substantial amount of the life care plan funding by payment to a medical facility in which he or she owns a substantial interest.

Defense counsel should also be aware that the elements offered in the plaintiff's life care plan can impact other evidence and discovery in the case. For example, at least one court has held that where the plaintiff's life care plan included professional help to manage her assets, the plaintiff had put her economic condition at issue and was required to produce her personal financial records, which ordinarily would have been unavailable to the defense.[28]

Purpose of Retention

It is useful to establish why the rehabilitation consultant was retained by plaintiff's counsel. The obvious purpose is to support the plaintiff's litigation by providing a life care plan that can be used by an economist as a foundation to support a present value of economic loss.

Rather than sharing such candor, some rehabilitation consultants will attempt to present themselves as an advocate for the client, who is allegedly seeking advice regarding his future care needs and how they can be met. Defense counsel will establish carefully the extent to which the rehabilitation consultant has furthered advocacy of the client beyond obtaining the information necessary to prepare the plaintiff's life care plan. In the usual instance, nothing has been done to advocate on behalf of the client beyond the preparation of the life care plan report. For example, rarely will the plaintiff's expert have contacted an insurer or public assistance program in order to qualify the client for services. Such a line of inquiry can be most effective in instances where an insurer, the public school system, or other resource has provided a medical case manager who has not recommended the various therapies or other aspects of the plaintiff's life care plan.

Another area of recent aggressive attack is the failure of the life care planner to look at the injured party's circumstances in any real-world sense. Defense counsels are increasingly inquiring of the history of the life care planner's clients who actually follow through with the life care plan after a court recovery or large

---

[28] Such issues apparently do not create enough speculation to preclude admissibility of the plan itself. See *Ballance v. Wal-Mart Stores, Inc.*, 178 F.3d 1282 (unpublished disposition), 1999 WL 231653 (4th Circuit 1999) (trial court properly admitted life care plan testimony, despite defendant's claim that the life care plans are speculative because they are contingent upon future events and choices, such as whether the plaintiff has surgery and whether it is successful).

settlement.[29] Oftentimes, the catastrophic case takes several years to resolve. Life care planners need to be prepared to respond to defense counsel inquiry as to how the injured party is being presently cared for and the current economic cost for that level of care. Obviously, the life care planner must be prepared to explain why the proposed life care plan markedly differs from the current care plan and thereby justify the increased costs of the more intensive care.[30]

The Basis of the Opinions

The basis of an expert's opinions is another potential basis for criticism and cross-examination. In the discovery deposition, defense will establish the entirety of the work performed by the rehabilitation consultant in order to prepare the report and should determine that the work on the case is complete. Inquiry will be made regarding any interviews conducted and any authoritative text relied upon. A well-prepared life care expert will be able to demonstrate that he or she is familiar with all the relevant facts of the case.

Counsel should also determine at the time of the deposition that the rehabilitation consultant is not attempting to interpret any of the medical, psychological, or therapeutic assessments made, unless the rehabilitation consultant is qualified to do so. If the inclusion of some therapy, medical examination, diagnostic testing, or other aspect of the plan requires the opinion of a physician, psychologist, or other expert, it must be determined whether such a person has been contacted to validate those aspects of the life care plan. The more experienced rehabilitation consultant will have the life care plan reviewed by a physician in order to verify the inclusion of the various prescribed modalities. If this is not done, it can be a fertile source of cross-examination and perhaps, as discussed above, striking of some elements of the plan for lack of proper predicate.

Base Costing and Duplication

In most instances, the plaintiff's life care planner will attempt to identify a current cost for each aspect of the plan. Defense counsel will review the plan carefully

---

[29] Furthermore, the life care planner needs to be conversant regarding the stress being placed upon the current caregivers, especially when they are a spouse or parents, or some other family member. While the economist may talk about the economic cost to that caregiver, the role of the life care planner is to provide insight into the propriety of the care being given. In many instances, the life care planner will find that the parent or spouse is perfectly capable of giving adequate care with additional training and respite. In those situations, the life care planner should make that concession and remain objective. It is the role of the economist to extrapolate the cost to the family member of this type of care. In most jurisdictions, the court will allow evidence of the value of these services being provided by the family member and the jury will thus be able to consider the dollar value of this care in making an award.

[30] However, a defendant may be precluded from introducing evidence of the cost of an annuity to fund future medical expenses. See *North Broward Hospital District v. Bates*, 595 So.2d 578 (Fla. 4th DCA), rev. denied, 605 So.2d 1265 (Fla. 1992) (although evidence of the cost of an annuity to compute present value may be admitted in cases involving loss of future earning capacity and loss of support in wrongful death actions, the jury could not utilize an annuity approach in determining future medical damages).

to determine the reasonableness of each of these base cost assumptions. The defense rehabilitation consultant should also review the plan and point out any areas of weakness. Fertile ground for attack usually involves the failure of the plaintiff's plan to recognize the availability of bulk purchasing and long-term contractual rates. Many plaintiff's plans will set forth an hourly rate for home health aides, nursing services, and household services. Such hourly rates are then extrapolated by the plaintiff's economist, resulting in exorbitant annual costs. It is not unusual to be able to demonstrate that the annual cost of hourly services is more than double the cost of negotiated contract rates.[31]

Plaintiffs' life care plans also commonly provide for many duplications of services and supportive items. Duplication is not only a basis for attack of the life care plan in argument to the jury, but may also result in the court striking all or part of the plan.[32] All costs of the life care plan should therefore be carefully assessed and a determination made of whether the plaintiff is recognizing the fixed costs that would not be relatable to the injury event. For example, where a plaintiff's injury requires a special diet, the cost of the special diet should be offset by the normally expected food cost incurred by any individual. In instances of special transportation requirements, it is important to establish whether the plaintiff's plan has offset those transportation expenses that would have been normally incurred. Where group home residency is being recommended, the plaintiff's plan should set off for typical housing costs. The group home rate often includes laundry, food, and other expenses that may also be included in some other aspect of the plaintiff's economic analysis, such as lost earnings capacity.

Defense counsel should also explore with the plaintiff's expert any consideration given to the availability of public programs or collateral sources.[33] It should be noted that the collateral source rules of the particular jurisdiction may impact the permissible scope of such evidence.[34] In most states, the collateral source rule has been modified to allow defendants to set off insurance benefits provided without lien rights and benefits provided or available under public assistance programs from the damages awarded. The defendant's rehabilitation consultant should assist defense counsel in pointing out those matters called for by the plaintiff's plan for which there may be a government agency or other funding source not considered in the plaintiff's economic analysis.

For example, states receiving federal funds are required to provide comparable education opportunities to severely handicapped children until age 18. The public school system also makes available those therapies that are required to further the educational opportunities of the student. Therefore, the public school program

---

[31] *Neber v. Secretary of the Department of Health and Human Services*, 23 Cl. Ct. 508 (U.S. Claims Court 1991) (damage award reversed because elements of life care plan were speculative and were duplicated by other award).

[32] See generally *Cates v. Wilson*, 361 S.E.2d 734 (N.C. 1987) (noting that the plaintiff's life care planner testified both in the plaintiff's case in chief and on cross-examination by the defense regarding the availability of public facilities to meet the needs outlined in the life care plan).

[33] See generally *Cates v. Wilson*, 361 S.E.2d 734 (N.C. 1987).

[34] Life care plans are subject to the same requirements for pretrial disclosure as are applied to other evidence in the particular jurisdiction, and the life care plan may be stricken for failure to comply with such pretrial discovery requirements. See *Department of Health and Rehabilitative Services v. Spivak*, 675 So.2d 241 (Fla. 4th DCA 1996).

is an excellent resource for cases of catastrophic injury to infants and young children. Defense counsel should establish the plaintiff's rehabilitation consultant's position with respect to the consideration of these public programs and be prepared to rebut the plaintiff's expected contention that such programs are substandard and inappropriate for the particular client. The failure of a plaintiff's life care planner to recognize and take into account the availability and suitability of charitable and other publicly funded programs can cast doubt on an otherwise objectively prepared analysis.

Licensing Issues

To these authors' knowledge, no state has any specific licensing requirements for persons who author life care plans. As the majority of life care planning probably involves the medicolegal context, the lack of any standardized requirements and licensure makes the area fertile ground for those persons who wish to claim expertise for sale on the open market. Unlike recognized specialties that are subject to licensing requirements, the field is open to the unscrupulous expert who views the life care plan as a device to sell in the forensic marketplace. Without licensure, it is impossible to self-police those who are claiming to be life care planners. The long-term solution is the creation of a national standards organization that becomes recognized by the states and lobbies for enactment of statutory licensing. (Editor's note: There is a certification with ethics and standards. There is also the International Academy of Life Care Planners, which also publishes *Standards of Practice* guidelines. See separate chapters in this text.)

In the absence of separate licensure, life care planners must be mindful of the limitations that are imposed by related and existing state licensure laws. In most states, persons are required to hold one or more licenses before they may prescribe or perform various therapies. For example, a licensed vocational rehabilitation counselor is not qualified in the State of Florida to prescribe or perform physical therapy. Moreover, therapists licensed to perform physical therapy may only do so subject to intermittent physician reviews. Life care planners must therefore be mindful not to misrepresent to the client or the jury the ability to recommend the various treatment modalities that the life care planner is not independently qualified to opine as reasonable and necessary.

Due to the minimal organization within the life care planning profession, a myriad of qualifications are typically seen on the life care planner's resume. The life care planner's formal training may be as a vocational rehabilitation counselor, nurse, certified case manager, mental health counselor, or some combination of these and other professions. Thus, the ability of the life care planner to give specific opinions for care will vary with the type of case presented. For example, a vocational rehabilitation counselor who has no training in case management or nursing is not qualified to render a life care plan assessing the needs of a child with catastrophic birth-related injuries. The same life care planner may, however, be perfectly qualified to render a life care plan in the case of a less catastrophically injured plaintiff who simply requires modality seeking to reasonably accommodate the client in the workforce throughout his remaining work life. Conversely, a certified case manager with nursing experience in the long-term care of persons with impaired mobility would be well suited to the evaluation of the life care needs of the catastrophically injured child and ill-equipped to assess the needs of the less catastrophically injured worker. Thus, the life care planner seeking to provide services in a medicolegal context should assess his or her own limitations and accept cases accordingly.

Moreover, a certified case manager may be very well qualified to opine as to future durable goods requirements and perhaps the nursing care coverage required for the type of injury presented. This same case manager would, however, be required to defer to a qualified physician the issue of future surgeries and attendant complications, prescription medication, and prescribed therapies. Similarly, this life care planner should defer to an orthotist for the type of orthopedic bracing required and the various therapists involved in the care for the form and frequency of therapy provided. As the clinical care of the catastrophically injured person involves a multidisciplinary approach, the life care planner should not be hesitant to interact with and gain insight from these disciplines when creating a plan. In fact, the greatest service the life care planner can provide to a retaining attorney is to express the limitations of the planner to give opinions and encourage the retaining party's use of other experts to ensure a credible and legally sufficient foundation for the admission of the life care plan.

Many life care planners are unwilling to accept their own limitations for fear that it will erode their role. Such persons are encouraged to look at the other fields that are called upon to participate in the legal system. For example, economists were called upon to render opinions concerning future economic loss in catastrophically injured cases long before the assistance provided by life care planners today was available. In order to properly perform this assessment, the economist would frequently review the opinions of the health care providers, the costs provided therein, and the extrapolations required based upon this foundation of information.

The life care planner's role is to take this analysis to the next step and include a more holistic approach. The weakness of the economist's analysis historically was that it was incomplete in its scope. It is submitted that the life care planner is best able to assist the legal professional by using experience to dictate the probable needs that will be involved with a patient's future care. This ensures that the life care planner and attorney will research and consider all aspects of care in creating the life care plan. Just as most of the economist's report of future economic losses is predicated by facts gained from others, there is no weakness in a life care planner's relying upon information gained from other sources. Such reliance may make the difference between admissibility and inadmissibility of the life care planner's testimony.

THE DECISION TO RETAIN A DEFENSE REHABILITATION CONSULTANT

Because cases that are appropriate for plaintiff's use of a life care plan typically involve catastrophic physical injury or significant brain damage, the defense counsel is well advised to retain a defense rehabilitation consultant early in the case. Oftentimes courts do not require disclosure of experts' opinions until the months immediately preceding the trial.[35] As such, much of the discovery will be completed before the defendant has an opportunity to receive the plaintiff's life care plan.

In order to be properly prepared to rebut the plaintiff's plan and to determine whether to present a defense plan, it is vital that much of the groundwork be laid in the early portions of the case discovery. A defense rehabilitation consultant can provide early assistance by suggesting the various records that should be requested and identifying persons to be deposed in order to make the determinations necessary to evaluate the injured party's life care needs. In most cases, the defense rehabilitation consultant will not need to spend a significant amount of time or money to provide this initial assistance. Moreover, the dividends returned on this initial investment are paid in the form of easing the inevitably compressed final preparation toward trial.

The actual selection of a particular rehabilitation consultant requires a basic understanding of the types of injuries involved in the case and an investigation of those experts available and qualified to support the defense. The qualifications of any proposed rehabilitation consultant should be reviewed carefully by defense counsel. Most defense counsels will want to review the potential rehabilitation consultant's current curriculum vita and rate sheet. Defense counsel will likely request referrals from other attorneys who have hired the counselor, in order to confirm both the expert's qualifications and his abilities as a witness.

Ultimately, defense counsel must exercise judgment in determining the practical interplay of the retained rehabilitation expert with the overall theme of the defense and the other experts. For example, if the plaintiff has no in-state experts, then the defendant's theme may be to retain only local experts on all issues in order to point out the need for the plaintiff to go to other jurisdictions to get experts to support the case. As with the selection of any expert, the overall picture of the case must not be lost and the rehabilitation expert must make a good fit.

THE TESTIFYING DEFENDANT REHABILITATION CONSULTANT

The initial scope of retention is usually limited to service as a consulting expert to assist defense counsel in the rebuttal of the plaintiff's life care plan. In some cases, the defendant may want to take the next step and hire his or her own life care planning expert to testify at trial. The decision of whether to call a defense rehabilitation consultant at trial is troublesome and must be made on a case-by-case basis. Several factors affect this decision. First, a credible life care planner, even though testifying for the defense, will likely validate at least some of the plaintiff's plan. Defense counsel must weigh the price of validation of some or all of the plaintiff's plan with the benefit of attacking the credibility of those portions with which the defense rehabilitation consultant has substantial disagreement. Just as a defendant intends to elicit substantial concessions from the plaintiff's rehabilitation consultant on cross-examination, so too the plaintiff's counsel anticipates being able to reinforce much of the plaintiff's theory of the case through cross-examination of the defense expert.

---

[35] See Federal Rule of Civil Procedure 26(b)(4)(B).

A second and perhaps more important factor in deciding whether to call a defense rehabilitation consultant as a testifying expert is the impact of this decision on the discoverability of the expert's work and opinions. In most jurisdictions, the contributions of consulting experts who do not testify at trial are protected by the work-product privilege. For example, under the Federal Rules, a party can discover facts known or opinions held by another party's consulting experts only upon showing "exceptional circumstances under which it is impracticable for the party seeking discovery to obtain facts or opinions on the same subject by other means."[36] Absent such a showing of exceptional circumstances, which is extremely rare, the expert's work is protected from discovery.

However, such protection is usually not afforded to experts expected to testify at trial. Thus, in instances where the rehabilitation consultant may be called upon to testify, both defense counsel and the life care expert should be aware that matters that would have been protected as work product if prepared by a consulting expert may be stripped of that protection. Notes, memorandums, research, and other matters held by the consulting expert may, by the decision to have the expert testify at trial, be transformed into the discoverable file materials of a testifying expert.[37] These materials may outline a great deal of the defense theory of the case. The cost of disclosing these materials to the plaintiff prior to trial may outweigh the benefit of having a defense life care planner testify at trial.

Furthermore, under the Federal Rules, a party must automatically disclose the identity of all testifying experts, and each testifying expert must provide the opposing party with a report that contains:

> A complete statement of all opinions to be expressed and the basis and reasons therefore; the data or other information considered by the witness in forming the opinions; any exhibits to be used as a summary of or support for the opinions; the qualifications of the witness, including a list of all publications authored by the witness within the preceding ten years; the compensation to be paid for the study and the testimony; and a listing of any other cases in which the witness has testified as an expert at trial or by deposition within the preceding four years.[38]

This report must be provided 90 days prior to the trial date or at such other time as the court requires.[39] Additionally, the opposing party may depose any testifying expert, and the opposing party is entitled to take that deposition after the disclosure of the expert's report.[40] Such disclosure requirements and discovery opportunities are a substantial consideration in determining whether to retain a testifying life care expert for the defense.

In instances where the defense rehabilitation consultant will testify, it is imperative that a physical examination of the injured party occur, or that the court

---

[36] See Federal Rule of Civil Procedure 26(b)(4)(A).
[37] See Federal Rule of Civil Procedure 26(a)(2)(A),(B).
[38] See Federal Rule of Civil Procedure 26(a)(2)(C).
[39] See Federal Rule of Civil Procedure 26(b)(4)(A).
[40] See McCormick, EVIDENCE, 98 at 244 n. 5 (noting that more than 40 states recognize a physician–patient privilege).

be requested to allow such an examination. Otherwise, the plaintiff will make the often persuasive argument that the defense expert has not even seen his client. As the provision of care to severely injured persons continues to become more complex and specialized, it is essential to recognize a multidisciplinary approach and to allow the defense rehabilitation consultant access to the depositions and, if possible, the actual persons involved in the care and treatment of the injured party.

In catastrophic injury cases, it is advisable for defense counsel to work with the rehabilitation consultant to engage the services of the specialized physicians and therapists necessary for the overall assessment of the life care plan. However, many jurisdictions have patient–physician or other privileges that preclude defense-retained experts from meeting with the plaintiff's physicians and therapists.[41] Additionally, many treating physicians and therapists do not want to become involved in litigation and therefore refuse to be informally interviewed by a defense-retained rehabilitation consultant. In such situations, compiling a defense team is the only approach that will ensure a complete evidentiary foundation for a defense life care plan. Plaintiffs obviously have a distinct advantage in having access to treating physicians. The defense must minimize this advantage by putting together its own team of experts and, if permitted under the laws of the relevant jurisdiction, explaining to the jury why such assembly was necessary.

PRACTICAL CONSIDERATIONS: THE EFFECT ON THE JURY

It must be remembered by both plaintiff and defendant that the life care plan will not be presented in a vacuum. Issues of liability and causation can be affected by the credibility of the plaintiff's life care plan. Both plaintiff and defendant must be certain that they retain a well-qualified, knowledgeable rehabilitation or habilitation expert who will present an objective life care plan. Although the economic incentive to prepare an overreaching life care plan can be tempting to the plaintiff, the presentation of such a plan to the jury will often have a spillover effect on the overall view of the case. It may offend the jury and thereby swing a close liability case in favor of the defense. Defense counsel must therefore be prepared to take full advantage of the overreaching life care planner.

Conversely, the requirements of care for the injured party that are set forth in the life care plan directly affect the economic costs of the injury and indirectly affect the noneconomic losses by the life care plan's efforts at improving the quality of life. Defense counsel must therefore be cognizant that an attack on any aspect of the plan may be viewed as insensitive to the efforts at improving the plaintiff's quality of life. Just as the overreaching plaintiff can alienate a jury, the insensitive attack on elements of a plan for the benefit of the injured party can offend juries.

---

[41] Life care planning testimony may be relevant and helpful in cases other than personal injury cases. See, e.g., *Urbanek v. Urbanek*, 484 So.2d 597 (Fla. 4th DCA 1986) (using life care testimony in a marital dissolution case to analyze the wife's changed circumstances in setting alimony amounts). Life care plans are often used to establish reserves in workers' compensation claims.

CONCLUSION

Defense counsel involved in the catastrophic injury case in which the plaintiff relies upon a life care plan is advised to aggressively attack damages. This attack begins with early retention of defense experts, including a rehabilitation consultant. At a minimum, the defense rehabilitation consultant will be instrumental in preparation of early discovery and effective cross-examination of the plaintiff's expert. In instances where the plaintiff's life care plan warrants, the presentation of an alternative defense life care plan, and the early involvement and careful presentation of the defense rehabilitation consultant as a testifying expert can enhance the overall credibility of the defendant's case and provide the jury with a more reasonable economic alternative.

IV

GENERAL ISSUES

26

ETHICAL ISSUES FOR THE LIFE CARE PLANNER[1]

Roger O. Weed and Debra E. Berens

INTRODUCTION

According to *Black's Law Dictionary* (Black, 1990), *ethics* is defined as (1) a set of principles of right conduct, (2) a theory or a system of moral values, (3) the rules or standards governing the conduct of a person or members of a profession. A variation of this definition is found in *Merriam-Webster's Dictionary* (n.d.), which defines *ethics* as (1) the discipline dealing with what is good and bad and with moral duty and obligation, (2) a set of moral principles or values, (3) a theory or system of moral values, (4) the principles of conduct governing an individual or a group, or (5) a guiding philosophy.

According to at least one study (Swartz et al., 1996), ethical decision making undergirds all aspects of rehabilitation. This statement certainly holds true for the practice of life care planning as well and this chapter will focus on ethics issues specific to the life care planner with suggestions for minimizing potential problems. Also included are related standards and ethics for board-certified life care planners from the Commission on Health Care Certification (CHCC) and the International Academy of Life Care Planners (IALCP). According to *Merriam-Webster's Dictionary* (n.d.), a *standard* is defined as (1) something established by authority, custom, or general consent as a model or example, (2) something set up and established by authority as a rule for the measure of quantity, weight, extent, value, or quality, and (3) applies to any definite rule, principle, or measure established by authority.

As can be expected from a review of the technical definitions above, the interplay of ethics and standards is somewhat difficult to separate. However, based on the definitions, ethics-related observations directly related to life care planning are as follows:

---

[1] A majority of this chapter has also appeared in the monograph by Deutsch, McCollom, Weed & Berens (2002), *The expert's role as an educator continues: Meeting the demands under Daubert*, chapter 6, 59–67. Ahab Press, White Plains, NY. Reprinted with permission. Roger Weed and Debra Berens.

0-8493-1511-5/04/$0.00+$1.50
© 2004 by CRC Press LLC

1. **Right Conduct:** This premise is perhaps the most understandable. Most professionals know right behavior from wrong behavior, yet many influences are exerted on the life care planner when faced with insurance referrals, client advocacy, biased information provided by an attorney, etc. (Banja, 1994). The attorney, for instance, is hired as an advocate for one side of the case or the other (i.e., plaintiff vs. defense); however, the life care planner is ethically bound to be an objective professional who develops a future care plan based on the client's needs regardless of which side is paying the bill. It is especially relevant to clarify one's role at the outset, which can be done in the form of providing a Professional Disclosure Statement. Some professionals provide professional disclosure verbally and some by handing out printed information fact sheets or statements about the role and function of the life care planner and what the person with the disability can expect from an evaluation. For example, in personal injury litigation, the life care planner might be retained as a defense expert to conduct an independent evaluation, or as a plaintiff's expert to provide life care planning opinions without any expectation of implementation. In either instance, disclosure of the life care planner's role at the beginning of a case will help to minimize potential problems due to lack of the client's understanding or expectations of services provided.

2. *Moral Values:* The above dilemma can be further influenced by the life care planner's view of the world. For example, a life care planner retained by the plaintiff may privately hold the belief that insurance companies are thieves that deprive people of their rightful recovery and there is a need to "get as much as one can" for the client. Conversely, a life care planner retained by the defense may believe that plaintiff's attorneys get rich off the unfortunate circumstances of people with injuries and too many frivolous lawsuits are filed. These biases must be held in check with extra vigilance to ensure a proper and objective evaluation and conclusion.

3. *Rules or Standards of the Industry:* In an attempt to rectify some personal biases, industries and professions have developed agreed-upon rules or standards to govern professionals' behavior. Within the preview of the life care planner, there are many ethics codes and licensure laws that include rules regarding personal conduct. An example is the Standards and Code of Professional Ethics presented by the Commission on Health Care Certification, which include Rules of Professional Conduct that are "exacting standards which provide guidance in specific circumstances" (Standards and Code of Ethics, CHCC, 2002, provided in Appendix II).

GENERAL PROFESSIONAL DUTIES WITHIN HEALTH CARE

Many ethics guidelines overlap with each other and others have significant differences in the detail. However, there are several concepts that appear to apply across the board. According to Banja (1994, p. 86) and Blackwell (1999), the four commonalities are:

1. Autonomy, which refers to the client's right to information and voluntary decision making
2. Nonmaleficience, which is the client's right not to be harmed
3. Beneficence, which presumes that the client will receive appropriate care or services
4. Justice, which is the client's right to receive unbiased and nonprejudicial treatment

In accordance with these constructs, Shaw and Sawyer (2000) further divide the concepts into counseling and forensic environments. Although written for the certified rehabilitation counselor (CRC), several precepts apply to the life care planner. With regard to ethical priorities, the authors assert that professionals who practice in the counseling environment emphasize autonomy, nonmaleficience, and beneficence, whereas the forensic counselor emphasizes justice. The authors also observe that there are many other variations in roles that can constitute challenges. In general, confidentiality does not exist in the legal case, but failure to maintain confidentiality in a counseling relationship is a clear breach of ethics. Within the legal environment, the consultant must be accountable to the system (or attorney), whereas in the counseling environment, one is responsible to the client. The counseling relationship is expected to be supportive, whereas in the forensic setting the consulting relationship is evaluative in nature.

Further, based on the authors' experiences and review of the literature, several scenarios are regularly observed. The first is associated by going *outside of the area of expertise.* This can take the form of offering medical opinions, life expectancy projections, or economic valuations (distinguishing between economic summaries from present value calculations) without adequate knowledge, education, or foundation. Life care planners unfamiliar with the forensic setting may be seduced into offering opinions outside their area of expertise that can damage their credibility and, in a round-about way, damage the case. In the event of a plaintiff's expert, this action also can cause harm to the client.

A second scenario is associated with the life care planner who develops a relationship with the attorney such that he or she becomes the *hired gun.* This relationship can be cultivated with either plaintiff or defense attorneys where potential future referrals may be forthcoming. Also, some attorneys may be adept at providing biased information to the expert or inviting the expert to company parties or dinners just to "get to know them better" and to form a more friendly or social relationship rather than a professional, working relationship. This statement is not intended to suggest that a life care planner must not have a working lunch with a referral source, but that the ethical consultant will be ever aware of influences that may jade his or her professional opinion or give the perception of something other than a professional, nonbiased working relationship. In one case, a neuropsychologist admitted in deposition that she had invited the attorney who retained her services to her home for a lunch and swim party and that they had attended several personal social events together. In another, a rehabilitationist compiled a plan for an injured worker and he was married to the client's attorney. A third example is the case of a rehabilitation counselor who publicly claimed he was going to "kick the defense counsel's butt" in an upcoming trial. Although the reports and opinions by these professionals may very well have been appropriate and accurate, these statements and scenarios cast a shadow over the objectivity of the consultant's work.

A third scenario is the potential for errors and miscommunication because of *unclear expectations*. This is particularly a problem for the inexperienced life care planner who may take instruction from the referral source rather than have clear boundaries about his or her role. In general, it is more effective for the life care planner to assertively outline for the referral source what he or she is or is not qualified to do. In the writers' experience, it is better for the life care planner to clearly outline what the expectations are without relying on an attorney to "tell you what to do."

Life care planners need to exercise *due care* by diligently reviewing case materials, seeking appropriate research and information, and following a process consistent with standards of the industry that results in credible opinions and conclusions. Many consultants do not know what the established standards are (mostly because they are not members of the IALCP, are not board certified, and do not attend life care planning conferences) and therefore fail to follow them. It is reasonable to observe that a growing industry, such as life care planning, will attract entrepreneurs who will learn through trial and error; however, this method of learning can damage the industry unless effective intervention can occur, including education about accepted standards and procedures.

Life care planners who are new to the industry need to learn the specialty area (a.k.a. *literacy*). Unfortunately, many beginning care planners are seriously deficient in this area. There is a specialized vocabulary and knowledge base that must be learned and understood in order to be an effective life care planner. Also, different jurisdictions have different rules with regard to the life care plan. For example, in forensic and workers' compensation areas, differences exist between state laws and regulations as well as between state and federal rules of evidence, and it behooves the life care planner to be cognizant of the differences within the various jurisdictions in which he or she provides services. A case that the authors recently reviewed involved a life care plan developed as a result of a breach of contract lawsuit. Upon review of the plan and consultation with the attorney, it became apparent that the life care planner was not aware of, or perhaps familiar with, the rules specific to breach of contract law such that the plan included recommendations and costs that were not allowable under this particular jurisdiction, and this raised the question of accuracy of the life care plan and credibility of the life care planner who prepared it.

Another issue for the life care planner, even for the most experienced professional, is the potential problem with *dual relationships* (also related to dual roles or, more recently, multiple relationships or roles). The term *dual* implies that the professional not only serves in his or her primary role, but also establishes a second role with the client that may be viewed as harmful (Cottone, 2003). Although the issue of dual relationships historically has been a common topic in the ethics literature and is specifically addressed in the Standards of Practice for Life Care Planners (IALCP, 2001, reprinted in Appendix I), more recently the term *multiple relationships* has gained favor and implies two or more relationships with clients that could impair professional judgment or increase the risk of exploitation

(AAMFT Code of Ethics, 2001, subprinciple 1.3, as cited in Cottone, 2003). In the practice of life care planning, it may be common for the expert to develop a future care plan while also providing some case management and coordination services. Indeed, the Scope of Practice/Applications section of the Standards of Practice for Life Care Planners (IALCP, 2001) states, "the life care planner … may temporarily assume a peripheral role in the management of the case." Further, "the life care planner must take care to keep the life care planning function separate from caregiver and case manager functions" (III.A). In other situations, life care planners may use counseling skills to facilitate information gathering and reduce the client/family's psychological pain/anxiety when the real purpose is to obtain information to develop an expert opinion. In one example, a rehabilitation counselor proclaimed she was going to offer her services free to help an acquaintance in her divorce action because the acquaintance's "s.o.b. husband" was (in her opinion) mistreating her.

Shaw and Sawyer (2000) urge the life care planner to clarify the relationship, purpose, and roles at the outset. In the literature, such disclosure is referred to as professional disclosure (also noted above). Berens and Weed (2001) assert that a written Professional Disclosure Statement signed by the client is preferred and one of the best ways to uphold the life care planner's ethical obligation to inform clients of the process and ensure the client understands and gives consent to participate. The authors point out that professional disclosure such as this obviously applies to cases in which the life care planner has access to the client and his or her designee. In cases where the life care planner does not have client access or is serving as a consultant where no client interaction is allowed or expected, professional disclosure generally is not made or required.

EXAMPLE ETHICAL BRUSHES

Court rulings provide insight into ethical issues related to rehabilitation professionals providing expert testimony (Weed, 2000). For example, in *Fairchild v. United States*, 769 R. Supp. 964 (W.D. LA. 1991), the court awarded a sum of $150,000 instead of the $1.74 million requested because the rehabilitation plan was prepared by someone not considered an expert. The "expert" reportedly had attended two conferences on rehabilitation counseling and had prepared only 25 life care plans. No other training or education within the field of rehabilitation counseling or life care planning had been completed.

In *Elliott v. United States*, 877 F. Supp. 1569 (M.D. GA. 1992), the defense expert's opinion was disregarded because the expert had been a rehabilitation consultant for only a short time, had completed only five life care plans, and had never implemented a plan. Additionally, the care plan offered reportedly did not include a physician contact or a conservative view.

In *Norwest Bank, N.A. and Kenneth Frick v. K-mart Corporation*, United States District Court, Northern District of Indiana, South Bend Division (1997), the rehabilitation expert's opinion with regard to future care was excluded in part due to a lack of medical foundation, as well as an inability to produce evidence that the methodologies used to forecast the cost of future care were based on anything other than personal experience.

In a workers' compensation case, *Maria Teresa Palmer*, guardian ad litem *for J. Carmen Fuentes v. W. Brent Jackson d/b/a Jackson's Farming Company* (I.C. No. 859146, North Carolina),

> The life care planner did not travel to Mexico to evaluate plaintiff's home circumstances and was not familiar with the medical facilities which may be in the vicinity of plaintiff's home. Therefore, specific findings could not be made with respect to renovations which may be necessary to plaintiff's dwelling or specific medical and durable supplies and equipment. Further, while plaintiff would benefit from placement in a brain injury facility, there is insufficient evidence in the record on which any specific finding may be made of whether an appropriate facility is available for plaintiff.

However, in light of the unique contribution of the published procedures of a life care plan, the workers' compensation commission in this case concluded that a complete, current, and comprehensive life care plan would be beneficial.

In addition to published cases, there are other examples based on deposition testimony that are not readily available to the general reader. At least two recent cases reveal life care planners who admit no previous education specific to life care planning, few or no publications related to life care planning in their libraries, and no membership in professional organizations specific to life care planning. When asked about certification, at least one of the individuals claimed she does not need to be certified as a life care planner since she has years of experience and is certified in a related field. However, further examination of her credentials revealed she achieved certification as a case manager (CCM) and rehabilitation counselor (CRC) at the time the respective certifications were initially offered. Therefore, it may be presumed the individual was actually grandfathered in (i.e., took the certification exam but did not have to pass it in order to become certified). Grandfathering, as used in this context, does not apply to the board certification exam for life care planners (CLCP), and everyone who has the CLCP credential is required to take and pass the exam. Furthermore, CRC and CCM exams are not intended to evaluate qualifications to develop a life care plan, and indeed, there reportedly are few life care plan questions on those examinations.

Other examples of deponents' testimony include those that express claims that life care planners are only serving an administrative function where they, similar to a secretary, simply record what someone tells them (see also Weed, 2002). At the other extreme is the professional (who is not a physician) who asserts that he or she can develop a complex life care plan without consultation with medical or treating professionals (if he or she has access to them). Or a physician that develops a life care plan, including case management, nursing, vocational, and psychological opinions, without adequate corroborating foundation.

As noted in the Weed (2002) article, the competent life care planner is neither an administrative recorder nor a know-it-all. A better analogy may be general contractor or one who knows the big picture and which questions are relevant to ask of which professionals while building the care plan from a sound foundation to a completed comprehensive structure.

SUGGESTIONS FOR SUCCESS: GLOBAL

In order for the life care planning industry to thrive and expand, it is incumbent upon each individual life care planner to assume control over his or her practice and to practice within the ethical boundaries of the industry. Some suggestions to enhance the life care planner's ethical practice include:

- Join a professional organization specific to life care planning that includes ethics and standards of practice (e.g., International Academy of Life Care Planners). Belonging to organizations that primarily are nursing, rehabilitation counseling, or related professions are useful but may not be helpful for specific issues associated with providing an ethical foundation in life care planning. Professional organizations specific to life care planning also offer a process by which life care planners can be held accountable to ethics and standards within the industry.
- Pursue certification in life care planning. Although it is a voluntary process, certification affirms that the life care planner has completed the requisite education, experience, and training and has passed an exam that demonstrates he possesses a minimum competency to provide life care planning services. Also, certification offers a process for ethics complaints. Having this process will assist the life care planner in maintaining a continuing focus on life care planning professional ethics and standards of practice specific to the industry.
- Follow established standards of practice and ethics (see appendices at end of book) published by the CHCC, IALCP, or other organizations specific to life care planning.
- Expand one's knowledge base by attending conferences, summits, and specialty training specific to life care planning. Not only will the life care planner be kept current on the industry and acceptable practices (especially true if the consultant is not certified and has no continuing education requirements), but leaders in the field will become part of his or her professional network.
- Subscribe to the *Journal of Life Care Planning* to stay current with contemporary issues in life care planning. (Available from 706–548–8161)
- Be active in the industry. Join a committee for program planning, offer an article to the *Journal* or other relevant publications, or conduct or participate in research projects, e.g., do something that will enhance life care planning and give back to the profession.
- Develop a protocol for disclosing to clients various role(s) one might assume during the life care planning process.

SUGGESTIONS FOR SUCCESS: MALPRACTICE INSURANCE RELATED

The suggestions below were offered by National Professional Group, a malpractice insurance carrier, as cited in Weed et al. (2003, pp. 47–54). Although there are many overlapping topics, these are specific to avoiding ethical brushes with insurance claims.

- **Role with Account:** It is very important for hiring parties to clearly define the rehabilitation professional's role and the type of evaluation or services being requested. It is preferable that these assignments be in writing.

- **Role with Client:** In cases where the consultant is hired by the insured party's insurance carrier, professional disclosure must be made with the client and documented. The client must clearly understand the role of the consultant. For example, to evaluate and assist the client with return to work, to case manage, or to develop a life care plan.

- **Written Documentation:** Many times the individual retaining the consultant may send a cursory retention letter outlining services requested. If not, it is incumbent for the consultant to get the necessary information verbally and follow up with a written confirmation to the hiring party.

- **Scope of Service:** Misunderstandings can develop over the scope of service. Thus, the more accurate the consultant's documentation, the easier it is for a review committee or court to determine that the consultant acted appropriately.

- **Objectivity:** The consultant must remain objective and unbiased in the delivery of services and shall not accept assignments if the individual who retains the consultant's services attempts to influence the objectivity or outcome of the evaluation.

- **Contingency Fees:** Consultants shall not provide services on a contingency basis to prevent the appearance that the consultant's objectivity has been compromised at the prospect of financial gain.

- **Professional Fees:** If the consultant provides trial and deposition testimony, he or she will be cross-examined about professional fees. Fees should be standard for the services provided; exorbitant fees will compromise the consultant's credibility.

- **Communication:** Proper communication at all levels is critical, and it is important for the consultant to provide a clear explanation of what should be expected and the possible outcomes. Other areas of communication include ongoing progress, internal communication, external communication, fees, and fee structure. The consultant shall not tell a client that a co-worker made an error that caused the client's injury or that the client's problem could be worse.

- **Terminology:** Professionals have their own set of technical terminology, and it is easy to forget that laypeople may not completely understand those terms. It is important for professionals to use common terminology with clients and maintain a speaking manner that ensures the client is treated respectfully and that he or she understands what is being communicated. Provide booklets and pamphlets to encourage greater understanding among clients and to encourage clients to ask questions to avoid any confusion. Remember, the better the client is educated and understands the role of the consultant, the lower the chances for lawsuits.

- **Colleague Collaboration:** Quality collaboration helps detect areas of weaknesses in one's practice. An outside quality assessment from another professional perspective may help the consultant to recognize procedures that could be changed to benefit service delivery and potentially protect himself or herself from malpractice claims.

- **Continuing Education:** It is important to keep abreast of new advances in technology within a particular area of specialty. Therefore, continuing education, whether required by any board or certification, is crucial.
- **Common Sense:** Good common sense always is valuable in dealing with people referred for services and in maintaining good solid business practice.
- **Records:** Do not alter a client's record under any circumstances. Be careful about documentation and include the rationale for services or why in some cases a decision is made not to do something. Make sure to follow one's own policies and procedures in every case.
- **Client Respect:** Always treat clients properly and with respect. Never let the client feel he or she is unimportant or insignificant.
- **Consent:** Always obtain written informed consent from the client.
- **Confidentiality:** Be extraordinarily careful about confidential information. Oftentimes, rehabilitation professionals may be in an environment where unsuspecting family members or others may overhear the content of information that potentially could be damaging to the client.

CONCLUSION

In summary, the case examples described earlier in this chapter underscore the need to adhere to ethics and standards that are agreed upon and followed by competent life care planning professionals. Ethics statements represent judgments about morality, right or wrongness, good or bad, and dealing with everyday human situations. All possible situations or scenarios cannot be anticipated, and the life care planner with a solid ethics foundation will be able to approach those situations in a more ethical or correct manner, which likely will preserve his or her reputation and credibility while also minimizing the potential for ethics breaches or malpractice claims. As time passes, ethics statements seem to become more important. The Code of Professional Ethics for Rehabilitation Counselors (CRCC, 2001) essentially doubled in length from the previous code in an apparent continued attempt to address more issues based on a combination of ethics complaints, evolution and growth of the rehabilitation industry, and anticipated problems. Additionally, continuing education requirements to maintain CRC certification historically were based solely on rehabilitation-related topics requirements; however, effective July 1999, standards for recertification were made stronger in the area of ethics and now 10 clock hours of ethics continuing education is required for CRC recertification. On a related issue, professional nurses are bound to a Code of Professional Practice, promulgated by the American Nurses Association (ANA). Similarly, certified case managers (CCM) sign an agreement to practice under the Code of Professional Conduct published by the Commission for Case Manager Certification (Patricia McCollom, personal communication, September 6, 2002).

Life care planning professionals undergoing Daubert challenges or malpractice claims often will be held accountable to existing standards of practice regardless of whether they are certified or belong to an appropriate organization. On the other hand, if a life care planner commits an ethical violation but is not certified, the certification board has no jurisdiction even if a complaint is lodged. Certainly, life care planners will face ethical dilemmas and having knowledge and awareness of the accepted and published ethics as well as a network of knowledgeable colleagues to call upon to work through problems will reduce the risk of serious error. Indeed, knowledge reduces risk and fear.

A visual image one might keep in mind with regard to ethics is if the news crew from *60 Minutes* showed up at your office for an interview, would you feel comfortable with your opinions? Or, is your life care plan written so that experts from within the life care planning industry will conclude your work is reasonable and proper? Did you conduct yourself in a way that you would expect others to act toward you? If you can answer yes to these questions, perhaps many pages of ethic statements will be unnecessary.

REFERENCES

Banja, J. (1994). Professional or hired gun: the ethics of advocacy in life care planning. *NARPPS Journal*, 9, 86–90.

Berens, D.E. & Weed, R.O. (2001). Ethics update for rehabilitation counselors in the private sector. *Journal of Applied Rehabilitation Counseling*, 32(4), 27–32.

Black, H. (1990). *Black's Law Dictionary*, 6th ed. St. Paul, MN: West Publishing.

Blackwell, T. (1999). Ethical issues in life care planning. In R. Weed, Ed., *Life Care Planning and Case Management Handbook*, pp. 399–406. Boca Raton, FL: CRC Press.

Commission on Health Care Certification. (2002). Code of Professional Ethics. Available at http://www.cdec1.com.

Commission on Rehabilitation Counselor Certification. (2001). *Code of Professional Ethics for Rehabilitation Counselors*. Rolling Meadows, IL: CRCC.

Cottone, R.R. (2003). Detrimental therapist-client relationships — beyond thinking of "dual" or "multiple" roles: reflections on the 2001 AAMFT code of ethics. Manuscript submitted for publication to *Journal of Marital and Family Therapy*.

International Academy of Life Care Planners. (2000). Standards of Practice for Life Care Planners. Available at http://www.internationalacademyoflifecareplanners.com/life_care_planning_guidelines.html.

Merriam-Webster. (n.d.). Ethics. Retrieved September 4, 2002, from http://www.m-w.com/cgi-bin/dictionary.

Merriam-Webster. (n.d.). Standards. Retrieved July 31, 2003, from http://www.m-w.com/cgi-bin/dictionary?standards.

Shaw, L. & Sawyer, H. (2000). Ethics and forensic rehabilitation. In *Ethics for Rehabilitation Counselors*, 40–43. Available online at http://www.crccertification.org.

Swartz, J.L., Martin, W.E., & Blackwell, T.L. (1996). Maintaining an awareness of ethical standards in guiding professional behavior. *NARPPS Journal*, 11, 27–32.

Weed, R. (2000). Ethical issues in expert opinions and testimony. *Rehabilitation Counseling Bulletin*, 43, 215–218, 245.

Weed, R. (2002). The life care planner: secretary, know-it-all, or general contractor? One person's perspective. *Journal of Life Care Planning*, 1(2), 173–177.

Weed, R.O., Berens, D.E., & Pataky, S.K. (2003). Malpractice and ethics issues in private sector rehabilitation practice: an update for the 21st century. *RehabPro*, 11(1), 47–54.

27

RELIABILITY OF LIFE CARE PLANS: A COMPARISON OF ORIGINAL AND UPDATED PLANS[1]

Amy M. Sutton, Paul M. Deutsch, Roger O. Weed, and Debra E. Berens

ABSTRACT

This exploratory study examines the reliability of life care plans by comparing original and updated versions of 65 life care plans. The 65 anonymous participants, with varying diagnoses and backgrounds, each had an original and updated life care plan developed for them. The time between the original life care plan and the updated plan ranged from 1 to 5 years, with an average of 1.8 years. All life care plans were provided by two experienced and board-certified life care planners who follow the established standards and procedures within the industry, and the samples chosen included all applicable cases within the 5 years preceding the time the study began in Spring 2002. The Home/Facility Care and Routine Medical Care subsections of the life care plans were compared by assigning current year (2002) costs to the projected needs and then analyzing using a chi-square statistical analysis. These subsections were selected since virtually all cases had entries in these two areas. Results reveal that the chi-squares for both Home/Facility Care and Routine Medical Care between the original and updated life care plans were found to be not significant at the .05 level. These results provide further evidence of reliability over time of life care planning in the areas of home/facility care and routine medical care when using established procedures.

RELIABILITY OF LIFE CARE PLANS: A COMPARISON OF ORIGINAL AND UPDATED PLANS

To formulate an accurate depiction of an individual's current and future health care needs, a life care planner must integrate hundreds of pieces of information.

---

[1] This peer reviewed article originally appeared as Sutton, A., Deutsch, P., Weed, R., and Berens, D. (2002). Reliability of Life Care Plans: A Comparison of Original and Updated Plans in the *Journal of Life Care Planning*, 1(3), 187–194. Reprinted with permission.

0-8493-1511-5/04/$0.00+$1.50
© 2004 by CRC Press LLC

This requires commitment to a consistent and unbiased process and reliance on fact, research, and expertise to formulate a plan that can predict future needs with accuracy and reliability. A life care plan (LCP) has been defined as "a dynamic document based upon published standards of practice, comprehensive assessment, data analysis and research, which provides an organized, concise plan for current and future needs with associated costs, for individuals who have experienced catastrophic injury or have chronic health care needs" (combined definition, 1998, as cited in Weed, 1999, p. iii).

According to Deutsch (1994), the development of life care plans came as a response to multiple professional concerns. First, persons with disabilities and their families need a concise summary to plan for future needs. Second, a communication tool is needed with which all parties involved in a catastrophic injury case will be informed of these needs. Third, a planning approach in the field is needed rather than the traditional reactionary approach. Fourth, through the life care planning process, disabilities could be broken down into basic components to more carefully identify complex concerns. Finally, concerns specific to the person with a disability and his family, such as geographic location, preferences, and personal goals, need to be incorporated into a plan of care to ensure a realistic implementation. In response to these concerns, life care plans have become important tools in a number of different settings, including complex disease management, establishing insurance reserves, worker's compensation case management, health insurance managed care, resolution of personal injury claims, and facilitating client and family understanding of the long-term costs and effects of injuries and illnesses (Weed, 1994). To meet the demands of preparing such a plan, certain skills provided by life care planning training and certification programs, in combination with expertise in numerous areas, are recommended. Brodwin and Mas (1999) outline 12 areas of expertise: medical aspects of disability, foundations of rehabilitation counseling, case management, psychosocial aspects of disability, behavioral interventions, preventative care, equipment and supplies, educational and vocational implications of disability, assessment and evaluation, community resources and services, rehabilitation facilities, and expert witness testimony. Similarly, the published life care planning model includes several subsections that should be addressed in a LCP in order to provide the most comprehensive plan possible. Subsections include (Weed, 1998):

- Projected evaluations
- Therapeutic modalities
- Diagnostic testing
- Wheelchair needs, accessories, and maintenance
- Aids for independent functioning
- Orthotics
- Home furnishings and accessories
- Medications and supplies
- Home/facility care
- Routine medical care
- Transportation
- Health and strength maintenance
- Architectural renovations

- Potential complications
- Aggressive treatment or surgical intervention
- Orthopedic equipment needs
- Vocational planning

It is from this knowledge foundation that life care planning professionals are able to make future projections and confer with multiple care providers to develop the most accurate care plan possible.

As the field of life care planning has become more defined through training programs, publication, and widespread use, a need for research that examines the reliability and validity of life care plans has emerged (Countiss & Deutsch, 2002). Although much research involving case management exists and numerous articles have been written on life care planning, little research has been conducted specifically to evaluate the reliability and validity of life care plans. Reliability is expected from a life care plan due to its influential role in the clients' future care management. Demonstrating reliability of life care plans also provides a foundation for establishing predictive validity. Due to the comprehensive and predictive nature of a LCP and the extreme variability of the population served (e.g., varying diagnoses, age differences, available support systems, treating professionals, etc.), it is a challenge to measure the reliability of a LCP (Deutsch, 2002). However, one study, by McCollom and Crane (2001), surveyed 10 clients with spinal cord injuries who had a life care plan developed for them several years prior to the study. The authors concluded that a clear consistency was found between projected and actual needs. In comparison, the study presented in this article measures LCP reliability by evaluating existing LCPs of clients who, for a variety of reasons, have had a second LCP written 1 to 5 years after the first plan was completed. These second LCPs were updated and revised versions of the original LCPs based on the status of the client and the interventions, services, and complications that arose following the original LCP. By comparing the two plans and determining what has been revised, a measurement of change can be generated that provides professionals with information regarding those areas of a LCP that likely are not subject to change and those areas that are sensitive to the passage of time. The two major areas analyzed in this study include Home/Facility Care and Routine Medical Care. These areas were targeted for two reasons: (1) they are common among virtually all LCPs and (2) they comprise the bulk of the needs that can be tied to measurable data and costs in nearly every LCP. Based on a review of the literature, the following two hypotheses were formulated:

Hypothesis 1: There will be no significant difference between the Home/Facility Care costs of the original LCPs and the updated LCPs.

Hypothesis 2: There will be no significant difference between the Routine Medical Care costs of the original LCPs and the updated LCPs.

METHOD PARTICIPANTS

A total of 130 life care plans from 65 anonymous cases were obtained and analyzed. Each case had an original LCP (LCP 1) and an updated LCP (LCP 2). The diagnoses for the participants included a wide range of traumatic as well as chronic medical conditions such as acquired brain injury, spinal cord injury, birth defect, and pain syndromes. There were 44 males and 21 females of various ethnic backgrounds. Ages of participants ranged from 2 to 75, with an average age of 28 years. The years between LCP 1 and updated LCP 2 were 1 to 5, with an average of 1.8 years. The LCPs were obtained from two experienced and certified life care planners in private practice, both of whom maintain a policy of strict adherence to published life care planning processes, procedures, and standards. Due to the limited number of cases available, all LCPs that fit the criteria were included in the study. To maintain anonymity to the researcher, all LCPs were purged of names and replaced with case numbers. The study methodology was submitted to the Institutional Review Board (IRB) of Georgia State University for approval of human subject's research. Approval was obtained before the study was initiated.

PROCEDURE

Once all LCPs were reviewed, the projected needs outlined in the In-Home Care and Routine Medical Care subsections were extracted from each. A master list of all projected needs was generated and costs were assigned to the needs. The costs were obtained from a database of current health care costs from one specific region in the southeast U.S. during one specific time frame (2002). By using a consistent economic reference, all plans shared a common denominator with which they could be compared. As an example, the need for a home health aide was included in several LCPs, and an hourly rate for home health aide was determined from the database. Once all needs were assigned a cost, each LCP was again evaluated. If a LCP recommended a home health aide 5 days a week for 3 hours a day, 15 hours was multiplied by the cost from the database and then multiplied by the number of weeks per year the client was to receive the service. Finally, a total cost per year for the home health aide recommendation was determined. This methodology was followed for each recommendation in the Home/Facility Care and Routine Medical Care subsections until a complete list of annual costs for the two subsections was obtained. The costs were then totaled to create an overall annual cost for the subsection comprising the variables Home/Facility Care Costs 1, Home/Facility Care Costs 2, Routine Medical Care Costs 1, and Routine Medical Care Costs 2.

While executing the aforementioned method, a number of challenges became apparent. First, many recommendations were presented as a range rather than a specific number. For example, follow-up visits with a neurologist were recommended four to six times per year. For the purposes of data analysis, recommendations were averaged in each case. The entry for neurologist visits from the above example was then recorded as five times per year. Second, some of the recommendations were reported as less frequent than annually. For example, if magnetic resonance imaging (MRI) was recommended once every 1 to 2 years, it was averaged on a yearly basis that equates to 0.66 MRIs per year. As each LCP is a unique plan that is tailored to the individual, other challenges materialized. Often, life care plans make recommendations for time periods such as "from age 20–30, age 31–55, and age 56 to life expectancy." For this study, one specific time frame was chosen so that data analysis was consistent across all plans. The time frame in the study was determined to be the first year immediately following the updated LCP regardless of when the original LCP was created, because some recommendations would have been concluded before the second plan was completed. As such, recommendations that were one time only (i.e., urology consult — one time only) were included in the annual calculations only if the recommendation was to occur in the first year following the second LCP. This eliminated the concern that certain recommendations in the first plan may have been completed before the second plan was developed, thereby creating an inaccurate discrepancy in the cost between plans. Finally, many LCPs offer multiple options within a subsection. For example, within the Home/Facility Care subsection, Option 1 commonly relates to the client being cared for at home and Option 2 for the client to be cared for in a long-term-care facility. Statistical problems with averaging or totaling these different options, and the fact that some plans did not include both options, consequently led to the decision to consider only option 1 in this analysis. With these procedural problems addressed, the data corresponding to the previously identified variables were analyzed using the Statistical Package for the Social Sciences (SPSS) and Excel. Three researchers, to ensure accuracy, performed the data extraction and data entry.

RESULTS

Data points for the dependent variables did not fall into a normal distribution. Consequently, parametric tests such as analysis of variance, t-test, and repeated measures could not be used. Figure 27.1 and Figure 27.2 demonstrate this lack of normal distribution with the example of In-home Care and Routine Medical Care for the original life care plans (LCP 1). In particular, the distributions for each of the variables were skewed to the left, indicating that the majority of costs fell in lower-cost portions of the distribution, rather than the higher-cost ends. For this reason, the chi-square goodness-of-fit test is the most appropriate means of analyzing data that do not meet the normal distribution criteria. This test compares distributions and determines significant differences between the distributions. Costs were categorized into 10 bins according to frequency, and these were then analyzed. It was necessary to use these 10 categories due to the large range of the variables as well as the fact that absolute zeros were present in two of these ranges (see Table 27.1). The chi-square for Home/Facility Care variances between LCP 1 and LCP 2 was not significant at the .05 level (chi-square = .85, df = 9, p > .05). The chi-square for Routine Medical Care variances between LCP 1 and LCP 2 also was not significant at the .05 level (chi-square = 5.04, df = 9, p > .05). The critical value for both hypotheses was set at 16.919. These data indicate that differences between original and updated LCPs are not significant.

DISCUSSION

Any number of complications or technological advances, which are relatively impossible to predict and plan for, may affect a client's prescribed needs and components of the LCP. Some degree of change, therefore, is entirely probable. However, an overall reliability is expected from a life care plan due to the large psychosocial, medical, and financial investments entrusted in the plan. The results

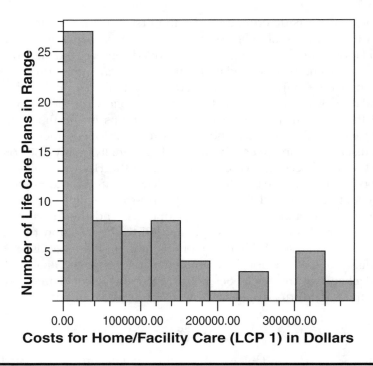

Figure 27.1   Distribution of actual costs for Home/Facility Care in ranges for original life care plans (LCP 1).

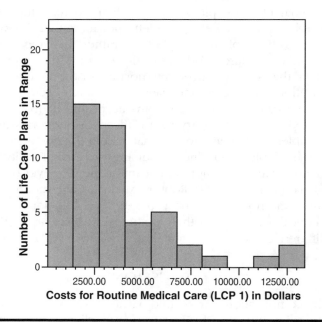

Figure 27.2   Distribution of actual costs for Routine Medical Care in ranges for original life care plans (LCP 1).

Table 27.1   Means, Standard Deviations, and Minimum and Maximum Values of Routine Medical Care and Home/Facility Care Costs for Original and Updated Life Care Plans (in dollars)

Variable	Minimum	Maximum	Mean	Standard Deviation
Home/Facility Care (LCP 1)	0.00	378,870.00	101,059.60	105,137.57
Home/Facility Care (LCP 2)	0.00	365,512.00	104,645.50	102,713.20
Routine Medical Care (LCP 1)	80.50	13,429.00	3,212.75	29,13.67
Routine Medical Care (LCP 2)	215.00	16,795.00	3,566.89	3,354.20

of this study indicate that for the two subsections analyzed, life care plan needs are resistant to the effects of time and therefore reliably predictive. Although projections made by the life care planner cannot be specifically validated by this study, projections remained consistent even after 1 or more years had passed. In order to specifically validate LCP plan entries, the various recommendations relied upon would be subject to further research design and analysis across multiple life care planners. However, it is clear from these data comparisons of LCP 1 and LCP 2 that agreement on entries implies that over time recommendations were appropriate. It is also clear that the results of this study alone do not imply the reliability of all life care plans, especially for uncertified professionals or those who fail to use established procedures; however, the study can be a springboard from which more research can be conducted. Another interesting finding is that total costs for the subsections Home/Facility Care and Routine Medical Care tend to fall in the less expensive direction of the distributions. This finding supports the proposition that life care plans are needs driven rather than cost driven, with a tendency toward conservative estimates of expenditures as opposed to liberal or inflated costs. One limitation of the study is that there were only two life care planners providing cases for review. Additionally, both of the life care planners are considered experts in the field and may not be representative of all life care planners. Both assert that they remain consistent in their approach and committed to following published standards and methodology. Similar studies in the future will be more valuable if a larger sample of certified life care planners with varying levels of experience who also adhere to the published standards of practice participate. Future research should also include a large enough sample to evaluate plan reliability based on diagnoses, gender, and age, among other factors. Other studies may take a similar approach as this investigation but look at other subsections of the life care plan, particularly if enough samples can be identified for similar disabilities or gender, and to distinguish differences between children and adults.

Although a few of the updated life care plans in the study had marked variations from their original life care plans, these variations did not affect the overall results of the study. For future research, these cases could be investigated from a qualitative perspective to determine why these updated plans reflected greater change. Change may occur for any number of reasons, such as the development of another medical condition, complications due to unforeseen events, failure to comply with the life care plan, changed physician recommendations, etc. Finally, a retrospective study to examine validity by determining what services were actually provided, what was needed, and what was projected would be valuable to determine recommendation validity.

This study underscores the effectiveness of future care forecasting where individual needs are identified and comprehensive treatment recommendations are documented when based on published models and procedures of life care planning. It appears that life care planners will benefit their clients by adopting a standardized approach to developing life care plans that is based on existing protocol designed for this specialized industry.

REFERENCES

Brodwin, M. & Mas, L. (1999). The rehabilitation counselor as life care planner. *The Journal of Forensic Vocational Assessment*, 2, 16–21.

Countiss, R.N. & Deutsch, P.M. (2002). The life care planner, the judge and Mr. Daubert. *Journal of Life Care Planning*, 1, 35–43.

Deutsch, P.M. (1994). Life care planning into the future. *NARPPS Journal*, 9, 79–84.

Deutsch, P.M. (May 2002). Life Care Planning Validation Research. Presentation at the Life Care Planning Summit 2002, Chicago.

McCollom, P. & Crane, R. (2001). Life care plans: accuracy over time. *The Case Manager*, 12, 85–87.

Weed, R.O. (1994). Life care plans: expanding the horizons. *NARPPS Journal*, 9, 47–50.

Weed, R.O. (1998). Life care planning: an overview. *Directions in Rehabilitation*, 9, 135–147.

Weed, R.O., Ed. (1999). *Life Care Planning and Case Management Handbook*. Boca Raton, FL: CRC Press.

28

AMERICANS WITH DISABILITIES ACT (ADA): FROM CASE LAW TO CASE MANAGEMENT AND LIFE CARE PLANNING PRACTICE

Lewis E. Vierling

BRINGING AN ADA PERSPECTIVE TO THE PRACTICE OF CASE MANAGEMENT AND LIFE CARE PLANNING

Catastrophic injury/illness does not necessarily equal disability under the Americans with Disabilities Act (ADA). After more than 10 years of enforcement and litigation, the courts are still struggling with the problem of proving whether an individual has a covered disability under ADA, and therefore is protected against discrimination. In fact, in the words of a judge at the First Circuit Court of Appeals in a recent decision, the word *disability* is considered to be a "term of art" (Heyburn, 2002). This clearly demonstrates the difficulty and subjectivity that has developed in defining disability under ADA.

Even though four prominent pieces of legislation were influential in forming the basis of ADA, there is no unified consensus concerning the meaning of a disability. For example, the Rehabilitation Act of 1973 (PL 93-112) provided for vocational rehabilitation services on a national scale to qualifying persons with disabilities. It also mandated employment of persons with disabilities in federal government jobs and most federally funded programs. Section 504 of the Rehabilitation Act, one of four sections, is considered to be "the underpinnings for the ADA" (Blanck, 1999). In summary, the section provides that people with disabilities have equal employment opportunities and prohibits the exclusion based on disability of otherwise qualified disabled persons from participation in any program or activity receiving federal financial assistance.

The Education for All Handicapped Children's Act, PL 94-142 (updated by PL 105-17 and termed the Individuals with Disabilities Education Act (IDEA)), had a strong influence in propelling the disabilities rights movement forward and was designed to educate and train children with severe disabilities who are likely to

0-8493-1511-5/04/$0.00+$1.50
© 2004 by CRC Press LLC

be placed into institutions (Blanck, 1999). Another important piece of legislation was the 1978 amendments to the Developmental Disabilities Assistance and Bill of Rights Act (PL 95-602). This legislation not only established a nationwide system of protection and advocacy, but also created a program of comprehensive services for persons with developmental disabilities. The Fair Housing Amendment Act of 1988, 42 USC 3601-3631, made it illegal to discriminate on the basis of disability in housing, real estate transactions, zoning, and the operation and services of apartments and condominiums. Despite the fact that the road to ADA has a long legal history that includes over 27 pieces of legislation (NCD, 1997), there is still no social consensus regarding what it means to be disabled (Diller, 1999).

The U.S. Supreme Court reviewed 16 specific ADA cases through its 2001–2002 term. Five of the 16 cases have dealt with clarifying the definition of disability. It is, however, absolutely clear that a medical diagnosis is not automatically considered to be a disability under the ADA. There is an inherent paradox in how the courts have opined regarding the definition of disability. For example, individuals who are severely ill or disabled and unable to perform the essential functions of a job under Title I of ADA are not protected. If an individual can do a particular job, he is not considered disabled and therefore not protected (Vierling, 2000a, 2000b, 2000c, 2000d, 2001a, 2001b, 2002a, 2002b, 2002c, 2002d).

There has been a transition in the intent of ADA. Congress, at the time of enactment, suggested that ADA should be a civil rights law that is inclusive and broadly interpreted. Through its review by the Supreme Court in the last 5 years, decisions have evolved to a currently very narrow interpretation. In fact, the court stated in the *Toyota v. Williams* decision that ADA should be "interpreted strictly to create a demanding standard for qualifying as disabled" (Vierling, 2002d).

National Council on Disability and ADA

In 1984, Congress established the National Council on Disability (NCD) to make recommendations to promote equal opportunity for persons with disabilities. In 1986, the NCD issued a report, "Toward Independence," recommending that a comprehensive law be passed. The NCD issued a follow-up report in 1988 entitled "On the Threshold of Independence," and the council published the draft bill of what was to become the Americans with Disabilities Act. A revised ADA Bill was sponsored by Senator Tom Harkin and Representative Tony Coelho in 1989. President George H. Bush signed into law on July 26, 1990, the Americans with Disabilities Act before an audience of more than 3000 American leaders from disability rights movements gathered on the White House lawn (Editor's note: The author of this chapter was an invitee.)

ADA DEFINITION OF DISABILITY AND THE FIVE TITLES

Disability, as defined in the ADA, is a physical or mental impairment that substantially limits one or more major life activities; a record of such an impairment; or regarded as having an impairment (as cited in Vierling, 2002d). The Equal Employment Opportunity Commission (EEOC) issued guidelines for complying with the ADA law. Within the EEOC's regulations was an expansion of the definition that was within the ADA legislation. The Supreme Court, however, has narrowed that definition considerably.

The ADA took affect July 26, 1992, 2 years after the signing by President George Bush. Title I of the ADA prohibits private employers, state and local governments, employment agencies, and labor unions from discriminating against qualified individuals with disabilities in job application procedures, hiring, firing, advancement, compensation, job training, and other terms, conditions, and privileges of employment. The following is a review of each major emphasis under all five titles and is not meant to be a full description of Titles I through V (Vierling, 2002d):

1. Title I: Employment — affecting employers having 15 or more employees
2. Title II: Public services — affecting all activities of state and local governments, with Subtitle B applicable to transportation provided by public entities
3. Title III: Public accommodations and services operated by private entities — affecting privately operated public accommodations, commercial facilities, and private entities offering certain examinations and courses
4. Title IV: Telecommunications — affecting telecommunications relaying services and closed captioning
5. Title V: Miscellaneous provisions — including the relationship of ADA to other laws, the requirements for technical assistance, the role of the Architectural and Transportation Barriers Compliance Board, the coverage of Congress, and some additional definitions regarding coverage

Major Life Activities and the Burden of Proof

The first requirement under an ADA claim is to prove that the individual has a disability. The difficulty is in proving that the impairment in question substantially limits a major life activity (MLA) such as caring for oneself, performing manual tasks, walking, seeing, hearing, speaking or breathing, learning, and working. Some of the Circuit Courts of Appeal and the Supreme Court have added reproduction, lifting, sitting, and standing to the list of major life activities. Very specific case law has developed around the issue of defining what is a disability. The five specific cases that have dealt with this definition are *Bragdon v. Abbott*; *Sutton v. United Airlines*; *Murphy v. UPS*; *Albertsons, Inc., v. Kirkingburg*; and *Toyota v. Williams* (Vierling, 2002d). The precedent that has been established by the Supreme Court is that there needs to be clear evidence to assist the court with a three-part analysis to determine whether a plaintiff has shown that he or she is substantially limited in a major life activity. After hearing the plaintiff's evidence in his or her burden-of-proof phase, the court applies the three-part analysis as follows (Vierling, 2002d):

1. The court must determine whether the plaintiff has an impairment under ADA.
2. It must identify the life activity on which the plaintiff relies in his or her case and determine if it constitutes a major life activity.
3. It must decide whether the impairment in question substantially limits the major life activity identified by the plaintiff.

It is important to note that the plaintiff must assert that he is substantially limited in a specific major life activity. Then it is apparent that the plaintiff must articulate with precision the impairment alleged and how that major life activity is affected by that impairment. In addition, the courts consider a number of other specific factors in their decision-making process. For example, when evaluating whether an impairment substantially limits a major life activity, the courts consider the nature and severity of the impairment; the duration or expected duration of the impairment; and the permanent or long-term impact or the expected permanent or long-term impact of, or resulting from, the impairment.

The courts require an individual assessment on a case-by-case basis. This means that both a case management plan and a life care plan must specifically address issues that are related to the definition of a disability. Those issues have been clearly delineated by the EEOC following clarification by the U.S. Supreme Court. For example, as a direct consequence of the Sutton, Murphy, and Kirkingburg decisions (Vierling, 2002d), the EEOC issued instructions for field offices regarding the analysis of ADA complaints and addressing the use of mitigating measures in considering whether a person is disabled (EEOC, 1999). These instructions changed the procedure for field office staff investigating individual complaints and appeared in the *Federal Register* in June 2000. The instructions to field offices summarize and explain how the Supreme Court cases impact the process of charges filed under ADA. The instructions emphasize "the individualized analysis that must be used in determining a charging party has a disability as defined by ADA and whether a person is qualified" (as cited in Vierling, 2002d).

Another important aspect of the developing ADA case law is that *individuals* are protected under ADA, not *specific disabilities*. Therefore, each individual has to be evaluated on a case-by-case basis to determine if the individual has a disability and is therefore protected.

UNDERSTANDING THE DEVELOPMENT OF CASE LAW

Precedent vs. Persuasive Authority

A distinction needs to be made between precedent vs. persuasive authority. In a legal sense, a precedent is "an earlier decision relevant to a case to be decided" (Elias & LevinKind, 1999). Once a court decides how a law should be applied to a particular set of facts, this decision controls later decisions by that and other courts. It is only a precedent as to a particular set of facts and the precise legal issues decided in light of those facts. The more the facts of legal issues vary between two cases, the less the effect of the precedent. If the circumstances of a current case match an earlier one, the previous case is considered a precedent and binding on the court.

Persuasive authority, on the other hand, is not binding on other courts, but if a case contains an analysis of legal issues and provides guidance for any court referring to it, it has persuasive authority. Generally speaking, the higher the court level, the more possibility for persuasive authority.

In rendering an opinion, a court may apply the prevailing interpretation of similar cases to the case being heard in its court. These cases said to be precedent, as discussed earlier, are established by certain types of courts. The principles that are derived from other court cases make up the body of case law applied in new cases. This is part of the legal tradition of common law.

Applying the principles from an earlier decision is the doctrine of *stare decisis* — "let the decision stand" (Vierling, 2002d). These principles are extracted from court decisions at a variety of levels. These decisions are pertinent to the field of rehabilitation. Case law further evolves as court cases are resolved. The following are examples of specific case law related to the definition of disability, employment, and reasonable accommodation (U.S. DOJ, 2003):

Definition of Disability
1. The effects of an impairment must substantially limit a major life activity presently, not potentially or hypothetically.
2. Courts must base their decision about whether an individual is considered disabled under ADA on detailed medical evidence, specific to the individual.
3. In satisfying the burden of proof, the individual must explain the degree of limitation the impairment imposes on the condition, manner, and duration under which he or she could perform the major life activity.
4. Temporary or nonchronic impairments of short duration, with little or no long-term or permanent impact, are generally not considered disabilities under ADA.
5. The central inquiry to determine disability under ADA is whether the individual is unable to perform the variety of tasks that are considered central to most people's daily lives.
6. The impairment must prevent or severely restrict activities of central importance to most people's daily lives.
7. Protection under ADA is restricted to people whose conditions are not readily corrected.

Employment
1. An employer is free to decide that physical characteristics or mental conditions that do not rise to the level of an impairment are preferable to others, just as it is free to decide that some limiting, but not substantially limiting, impairments make an individual less suited for a job.
2. If an employer's assumptions about an applicant's disability are unreasonable, or are not based upon a good-faith assessment of that individual's capabilities, and ultimately prove to be groundless, its refusal to hire will engender liability under ADA. An employer cannot exclusively defer to a physician's opinion without first pausing to assess the objective reasonableness of the physician's conclusions.
3. The date of an adverse employment action is the relevant date for determining whether a person is a qualified individual with a disability.
4. Disability determination must be based on a person's actual condition at the relevant date.
5. ADA does not entitle individuals to jobs that might jeopardize their health.
6. The individualized assessment of the ability of the individual to safely perform the essential functions of the job must be based on reasonable medical judgment that relies on the most current medical knowledge and on the best-available objective evidence.

7. An employer cannot evade its obligations under ADA by contracting personnel functions to a third party or parties.
8. The existence of a physician-imposed lifting restriction is insufficient to establish that an individual is precluded from working in the broad class of jobs necessary to establish the existence of a disability.

Reasonable Accommodation

1. Seniority systems prevail over reasonable accommodation. However, employees may identify special circumstances that lead to the employer providing reasonable accommodation.
2. The concept of providing reasonable accommodation is to accommodate a person's disability rather than accommodate the person with the disability.
3. The employer must make reasonable accommodations to the limitations of the disability rather than for those limitations.
4. Reasonable accommodation applies to obstacles exclusively related to the workplace.
5. Accommodations must be reasonable, feasible, and plausible.
6. Employers have a mandatory obligation to engage in an interactive process with employees regarding making reasonable accommodation.
7. The employer's obligation to be involved in the interactive process goes well beyond the first attempt and should continue when the employer is aware that the accommodation is not working.
8. The duty to accommodate is a continuing duty that is not exhausted by one effort and needs to consider each request by the employee.

The Effects of Supreme Court Decisions on Lower Courts

U.S. Supreme Court cases are precedent for all courts with respect to decisions involving the U.S. Constitution or any other aspect of federal law. Also, Appellate Court and Supreme Court cases are precedent with respect to future decisions by the same court. The U.S. Court of Appeals' cases are precedent for U.S. District Courts within their 12 circuits, plus a Federal Circuit Court. Opinions of the U.S. District Courts are never precedent for other courts. However, the decisions may have persuasive authority on other district courts' decisions. As noted above, generally speaking, the higher the court level, the more possibility for persuasive authority. State Supreme Court cases are precedent for courts within that state.

FROM CASE LAW TO PRACTICE: INTEGRATING COURT DECISIONS INTO THE PRACTICE OF CASE MANAGEMENT AND LIFE CARE PLANNING

The Role of Mitigating and Corrective Measures in Determining Disability

In June 1999, the Supreme Court rendered opinions on a trilogy of cases that have had a permanent impact on determining who is disabled (Vierling, 2002d). These decisions have created a new legal standard now used for defining disability under ADA. The most significant issue that the Supreme Court resolved was affirming the use of mitigating measures — such as medications, corrective lens, prosthetic devices, and the body's ability to compensate for an impairment — to determine disability.

In a vocational evaluation, case management report, or life care plan, the rehabilitation professional must consider whether the individual is using any mitigating or corrective measure. This is just as applicable to an individual who may have a prosthetic device because of an amputation as it is to an individual who may have a visual impairment. The Supreme Court has ruled and, therefore, it is case law that ADA requires courts to consider mitigating or corrective measures when determining whether an individual meets the statutory definition of disability. The plaintiff in ADA litigation must prove that his physical or mental impairment substantially limits any major life activity despite the use of corrective measures. Therefore, the individual's actual circumstances must be assessed. An individual who does not experience a substantial limitation in any major life activity when using mitigating measures does not meet the ADA's first definition of disability.

Mitigating measures may lessen or eliminate limitations caused by an impairment. Therefore, the court requires an assessment of both the positive and negative effects of mitigating or corrective measures. In that assessment process, it must be determined whether the mitigating or corrective measure fully controls a person's impairment.

Single Job vs. Class of Jobs

If a plaintiff/employee is relying on demonstrating a substantial limitation in the major life activity of work, he or she will need to satisfy this definition: he or she must be significantly restricted in the ability to perform either a class of jobs or a broad range of jobs in various classes, compared to the average person having comparable training, skills, and abilities. To satisfy this definition, the plaintiff/employee and his representative who is preparing either a vocational evaluation or a life care plan will need to present information on the number and types of available jobs from which he or she is disqualified that use similar training, knowledge, skills, or abilities and are within a reasonably accessible geographic area. This information will help the trier of fact to decide whether the individual's impairment rises to the level of a disability and therefore falls within the protected class under ADA. Clearly, it is crucial that the rehabilitation professionals provide very specific information well beyond a medical diagnosis or medical information from a physician.

Further Clarification from *Toyota v. Williams* Supreme Court Decision

In the *Toyota v. Williams* case (2002), the question before the Supreme Court was: What is the proper standard for determining whether an individual is substantially limited in performing manual tasks? Performing manual tasks is a specific major life activity. As a part of her case, Ms. Williams claimed that she was covered under ADA because her cumulative trauma injury prevented her from doing tasks associated with certain types of manual jobs. However, the Supreme Court said that the proper test for assessing whether an individual was substantially limited in performing manual tasks is whether the impairment prevents or restricts performing tasks that are of "central importance to most people's daily lives." In this decision, Justice Sandra Day O'Connor also made the distinction that routine or minor injuries not of a permanent or long-term nature are not protected under ADA.

In the Williams case, work as a major life activity was again questioned by the Supreme Court. The court's response to work as a major life activity has diminished the value of claiming it as an issue in an ADA claim. In addition, the Supreme Court said that the plaintiff must prove a disability by offering evidence that the limitation is substantial in terms of his own experience, reinforcing the standard that such assessments must be on a case-by-case basis. This, of course, reemphasizes that a full evaluation, whether it is a case management report, vocational evaluation, or life care plan, must be made by the rehabilitation professional. This decision supports the new legal standard relating to alleging a protected disability under ADA, if claiming a substantial limitation in the major life activity of performing manual tasks. Rehabilitation professionals will need to assess and review in their plan the individual's level of ability in performing manual tasks in his or her personal life. Manual tasks could include such things as ability to perform activities of daily living (ADL), housekeeping chores, and the ability to care for self and other family members. These are the types of real-world activities that the courts will be looking to assess.

In the Williams decision, published in January 2002, the Supreme Court stated that ADA should be "interpreted strictly to create a demanding standard for qualifying as disabled" (*Toyota v. Williams*, 2002).

Other Important Supreme Court Decisions

There are two other decisions that have created case law for which rehabilitation professionals should be familiar. In June 1999, the Supreme Court published its opinion in the *Olmstead Commissioner, Georgia Department of Human Resources v. L.C.* case, which has particular relevance to life care planners (*Olmstread v. L.C.*, 1999). In this case, the question presented to the Supreme Court was whether the public service portion of ADA compels the state to provide treatment and habilitation services for persons with mental disabilities in community placement when appropriate treatment and habilitation can also be provided to them in state and mental institutions? The second issue was that if ADA does include providing treatment and habilitation in community placement, does that exceed the enforcement power granted to Congress?

In a vote of 6 to 3, the Supreme Court determined that states are required to place people with mental disabilities in community settings rather than in institutions when the state's treatment professionals have determined that community placement is appropriate. This would also be under the condition that transfer from institutional care to a community-based program would not be opposed by the individual and that the placement can be reasonably accommodated. The state must also take into consideration the resources available and the needs of other individuals within the state facility.

On June 18, 2001, President George W. Bush signed Executive Order 1.3217, titled "Community-Based Alternatives for Individuals with Disabilities." This order provides assistance from the federal government to states to implement the Supreme Court decision in Olmstead. As a part of this program, the federal government awarded approximately $64 million in 2002 to support community living for people with disabilities. The goal of these grants was to assist people with disabilities to (Rubinger & Gardner, 2002):

1. Live in the most integrated community setting appropriate to their individual support requirements and preferences
2. Exercise meaningful choices about their living environments, the providers of services they receive, the types of support they use, and the manner by which services are provided
3. Obtain quality services in a manner as consistent as possible with their community preferences and priorities

As part of this initiative, President Bush is proposing increases in funding to help transition Americans with disabilities from institutions to community living. This is clearly another example of the integration of case law in providing valuable resources for rehabilitation professionals to assist their clientele.

The next decision to be discussed from the Supreme Court was *Cleveland v. Policy Management Systems Corporation* (1999). In this case, the question before the court was whether the application for, or receipt of, Social Security disability benefits precludes a person with a disability from bringing an ADA claim. The court recognized that there may be many situations in which the claim for Social Security disability benefits and an ADA claim may exist side by side. The court stated that because the qualification standards for Social Security benefits and ADA are not the same, an application for receiving Social Security benefits is not inconsistent with being a qualified individual with a disability under ADA. The court, however, did state that the plaintiff must provide an explanation that he or she can still perform the essential functions of the job with or without reasonable accommodation. The Cleveland case demonstrates to the rehabilitation professional the importance of providing reasonable accommodation under ADA. The rehabilitation professional should also be aware that there is the possibility that an individual receiving Social Security benefits would still be protected under ADA.

Court Decisions and Their Impact on Rehabilitation and Life Care Planning Practice

Whether rehabilitation professionals are serving in an advocacy role or as an objective evaluator, they have the responsibility to provide as accurate an assessment of the needs of the client as possible. Courts have provided specific guidelines in the form of case law to assist in making informed decisions in future cases. The life care planner needs to be knowledgeable about the case law to effectively provide appropriate data, particularly for vocational and expected future need opinions.

As already noted, court decisions affect EEOC's guidelines. The trilogy of decisions in 1999 was the impetus for the publication of new instructions to the field offices regarding analyzing charges addressing disability and who is qualified under ADA. Another example is the EEOC issuing new "Enforcement Guidelines on Reasonable Accommodation and Undue Hardship" under the Americans with Disabilities Act on October 17, 2002. These new guidelines were a direct result of the Supreme Court decision in the 2001–2002 term *U.S. Airways, Inc., v. Barnett* (2002). The updated enforcement guidelines revised the standard for reasonableness. The reasonableness of an accommodation is now evaluated not only by whether it is considered effective, but also feasible or plausible for the typical employer. In the Barnett decision, the Supreme Court suggested the possibility that special circumstances may exist for providing reasonable accommodations to an individual. Without the existence of any special circumstances, the court determined that it would be unreasonable for an employer to reassign an employee to another job, which would violate the seniority system.

Under the new standards from the Barnett decision, the plaintiff/employee has the burden to prove that an accommodation is reasonable. Then the burden shifts to the employer to provide case-specific evidence proving the accommodation would cause an undue hardship. The guidelines also provide examples of what would be reasonable and unreasonable accommodations. The rehabilitation professional can be a valuable asset by understanding the ADA case law and new legal standards.

Outcome of ADA Title I Cases

The rehabilitation professional should be aware that courts have decided in favor of employers in most ADA litigation cases. In surveys identifying court decisions from the year 2001, the *American Bar Association's Commission on Mental and Physical Disability Law Reporter* shows that employers prevailed in 95.7% of the cases (as cited in Vierling, 2002d). It was also noted that 80% of all employment cases are dismissed in motions for summary judgment. A motion for summary judgment is granted when the court believes no genuine issue of material fact exists. The party filing the motion is entitled to prevail as a matter of law. As a result, 80% of the ADA Title I cases never reach a jury. When they do, 95.7% of them are won by employers. Employers also prevail in 76% of the cases in administrative complaints with EEOC (EEOC, 2002). However, an estimated half of ADA disputes are settled before they are actually filed in court.

SUMMARY/CONCLUSIONS

As of the 2001–2002 term, the Supreme Court has provided decisions in 16 specific ADA cases. Five of the cases involved the definition of disability. These 16 cases have been reviewed before the court since the 1997–1998 Supreme Court term, and life care planners should be aware of these decisions. Of particular relevance is the Olmstead case, which may have implications for lifelong care of people with mental and developmental disabilities, since community-based programs may be legally required over institutional care. In addition, the vocational aspects of a life care plan may require a knowledgeable expert to ensure opinions are defensible.

These decisions have altered and, in many cases, narrowed the definition of disability and, consequently, who is protected under ADA. Matthew Diller, Fordham University law professor, has stated, "The courts have seized upon the definition of disability as a way to stop cases, and in effect, shield an employer's conduct from scrutiny" (1999). The courts have taken the position that ADA should be strictly interpreted, creating a demanding standard for qualifying as disabled. The records indicate that was not the intent of the Congress. As demonstrated, only a very small number of cases dealing with the actual discrimination issues are heard by a judge or jury.

The plaintiff/employee has the burden to prove that she has a disability as a gateway step to presenting her case before a judge or jury. This has proven to be a difficult step. The courts have provided very specific guidelines for presenting information within an evaluation to assist all parties concerned to understand the circumstances and needs of the plaintiff/employee. In practice, a detailed assessment based upon guidelines provided by ADA case law can be a valuable source of information for the judge or jury in adjudicating ADA cases. It has been demonstrated in this chapter that protection of people with disabilities under ADA is not automatic, even if one is in a catastrophic impairment situation.

REFERENCES

Allbright, A.L. (2001). *Employment Decisions under the ADA Title I: Survey Update, August 20, 2001.* Washington, DC: The Commission on Mental and Physical Disability Law Reporter.

Blanck, P.D. (1999). *Disability Law and Policy: A Collective Vision.* Washington, DC: ADA Commission on Mental and Physical Disability Law.

Bragdon v. Abbott. (June 15, 1998). No. 97-156.

Cleveland v. Policy Management Systems, Corp. (May 24, 1999). No. 97-1008.

Diller, M. (1999). Judges Don't Understand the ADA. Available at www.raggededgemagazine.com

EEOC. (July 26, 1999). Instructions for Field Offices: Analyzing ADA Charges after Supreme Court Decisions Addressing "Disability" and "Qualified." Available at www.eeoc.gov.

EEOC. (August 13, 2002). Report: Study of Litigation Program Fiscal Year 1997–2001. Available at www.eeoc.gov.

Elias, S. & LevinKind, S. (August 1999). *Legal Researcher: How to Find and Understand the Law,* 7th ed. Bertelsmann Industry Services, Inc. Berkeley, CA. Available at www.nolo.com.

Federal Register, Vol. 65, No. 11. (June 8, 2000). Rules and Regulations 36327: EEOC, 29 CFR Park 1630 Interpretive Guidance on Title I ADA.

Heyburn, Chief District Judge. *Cotter v. Ajilon Services, Inc.* (April 25, 2002). The Court of Appeals for the 6th Circuit, No. 00-2041.

Olmstead Commissioner, Georgia Department of Human Resources v. L.C. (June 1999). No. 98-0536.

Sutton, Karen & Hinton, Kimberly, v. United Airlines, Inc. (June 22, 1999). No. 97-1943.

Toyota Motors v. Williams. (January 8, 2002). No. 00-1089.

Rubinger, H. & Gardner, R. (May/June 2002). Tearing down the walls: new freedom initiative, *Continuing Care,* 21, 24–31.

U.S. Airways v. Barnett. (April 29, 2002). No. 00-1250.

U.S. DOJ (United States Department of Justice). (2003). ADA Definitions. Retrieved July 31, 2003, from www.usdoj.gov/crt/ada/.

Vierling, L. (2000a). The American with Disabilities Act: implications of Supreme Court decisions for case managers part 1. *The Case Manager,* 11, 47–49.

Vierling, L. (2000b). The American with Disabilities Act: implications of Supreme Court decisions for case managers part 2. *The Case Manager,* 11, 72–76.

Vierling, L. (2000c). The American with Disabilities Act: implications of Supreme Court decisions for case managers part 3. *The Case Manager,* 11, 65–68.

Vierling, L. (2000d). The American with Disabilities Act: implications of Supreme Court decisions for case managers part 4. *The Case Manager,* 11, 51–55.

Vierling, L. (2001a). The American with Disabilities Act: implications of Supreme Court decisions for case managers part 4, *The Case Manager,* 12, 77–82.

Vierling, L. (2001b). American with Disabilities update, *The Case Manager,*12, 20–21.

Vierling, L. (2002a). American with Disabilities update, *The Case Manager*, 13, 18–20.

Vierling, L. (2002b). American with Disabilities update, *The Case Manager*, 13, 21–23.

Vierling, L. (2002c). American with Disabilities update, *The Case Manager*, 13, 20–22.

Vierling, L. (2002d). *Court Decisions Involving the Americans with Disabilities Act: A Resource Guide for Rehabilitation Professionals*. Athens, GA: Elliott & Fitzpatrick, Inc.

Young, J., Ed. (July 26, 1997). *Equality of Opportunity: The Making of the American with Disabilities Act*, Appendix B, The Legal Road to the ADA. Washington, D.C.: National Council on Disability.

SUPREME COURT DECISIONS

Available from www.supct.law.cornell.edu:8080/supct.

Albertson's, Inc., v. Kirkingburg, No. 98-0591, June 22, 1999.

Barnes v. Gorman, No. 01-682, June 17, 2002.

Board of Trustees of the University of Alabama v. Garrett, No. 99-1240, February 21, 2001.

Bragdon v. Abbott, No. 97-156, June 15, 1998.

Buchannon Board & Care Home, Inc., v. West Virginia Department of Health and Human Resources, No. 99-1848, May 29, 2001.

Cleveland v. Policy Management Systems, Corp., No. 97-1008, May 24, 1999.

Chevron v. Echazabal, No. 00-1406, June 10, 2002.

EEOC v. Waffle House, Inc., No. 99-1823, January 15, 2002.

National Railroad Passenger Corp. v. Morgan, Abner, Jr., No. 00-1614, January 9, 2002.

Olmstead Commissioner, Georgia Department of Human Resources v. L.C., No. 98-0536, June 1999.

Pennsylvania Department of Corrections v. Yeskey, No. 97-634, June 15, 1998.

PGA Tour, Inc., v. Martin, No. 00-0024, May 29, 2001.

Sutton, Karen & Hinton, Kimberly, v. United Airlines, Inc., No. 97-1943, June 22, 1999.

Toyota Motors v. Williams, No. 00-1089, January 8, 2002.

U.S. Airways v. Barnett, No. 00-1250, April 29, 2002.

Vaughn L. Murphy v. United Parcel Service, Inc., No. 97-1992, June 22, 1999.

Wright v. Universal Maritime Service Corp., No. 97-0889, November 16, 1998.

IMPORTANT WEBSITES

Department of Justice — ADA Home
www.usdoj.gov/crt/ada/adahom1.htm

Equal Employment Opportunity Commission
www.eeoc.gov

The Federal Judiciary
www.uscourts.gov

Law News
www.law.com

The National Council on Disability
www.ncd.gov/index.html

U.S. Supreme Court of the United States
www.supremecourtus.gov

U.S. Supreme Court Collection
www.supct.law.cornell.edu:8080/supct

U.S. Supreme Court — Multimedia Media Database
http://oyez.nwu.edu

Washington Post Supreme Court News
www.washingtonpost.com

29

TECHNOLOGY AND LIFE CARE PLANNING

Randall L. Thomas

INTRODUCTION

Integrating emerging technology with professional skills provides a powerful tool for a successful life care planning practice (Thomas, 1992, 1994; Weed, 1995, 1996a, 1996b, 1996c). Today, the life care planner can access a wider scope of available resources and information to ascertain the most appropriate recommendations for the client. Previously, the professional did not have access to all possible resources, and the existing data usually required considerable time and effort to obtain. With today's technology, the professional can maximize efficiency and organization to produce a quality life care plan that best benefits the client's needs. This chapter presents guidelines for integrating today's emerging technology into a life care planning practice and provides practical information every life care planner should know.

As the Internet expands and more and more resources are made available to the general public via the Internet, the resources available to people with disabilities and those who work with them have also grown tremendously (Barros & Boyd, 1997). Because of rapid changes in technology, especially computer processors, hard drive capacity, and the Internet, integration of technology can be confusing and problematic to the life care planner. For example, determining which computer system to purchase, selecting the appropriate software and network capability, training staff, and knowing how to maintain the integrity of the data on the computer system are only a few of the critical decisions in this often difficult process. Therefore, integrating computer technology into a life care planning practice is not easy, and the temptation to avoid the transition may exist. Fortunately, emerging technology offers much more capability, convenience, and stronger computer hardware configurations that should remain functional and productive for the next 2 to 5 years. The professional can limit confusion regarding technology and take advantage of this increased ability by identifying needs within the practice and obtaining a better understanding of today's technology.

0-8493-1511-5/04/$0.00+$1.50
© 2004 by CRC Press LLC

INITIAL STEPS

The life care planner must first determine the professional and business goals in the practice before purchasing computer equipment. If the goal is to complete a maximum of two or three life care plans a year, including narrative and tabular printing of recommendations with associated costs, many of the commercially available word processing, spreadsheet, and database programs will suffice. The life care planner can construct simple databases to track information and resources. Commercial databases such as Microsoft Access and Filemaker Pro are readily adapted to provide simple, flat-file databases for resources and contacts. With professional programming, the databases can be customized to provide comprehensive relational databases for the life care planner.

On the other hand, if life care planning is to comprise a significant part of the practice, existing computer system and software may require upgrading. Computer hardware and software are now available that are reliable and cost-efficient. Access to this technology is essential because it allows production of a quality product that reflects current clinical knowledge and superior organization of information. This technology also enables the life care planner to create a summary table for costs during the client's lifetime, or on a year-by-year basis, while making the most productive use of staff time.

In short, technology impacts the life care planner in the following ways:

- Enhances the ability to organize professional contacts and resources in a logical, easy-to-find method
- Diminishes staff time for specialized reports or printouts
- Allows greater control over data integrity with less dependence on external computer experts and resources
- Increases ability to customize reporting formats and invoicing to referral sources
- Simplifies access to the Internet for research
- Enables access to state and national databases via the Internet
- Accesses and distributes information via personalized web pages on the Internet

The successful life care planner should be prepared to incorporate the above changes in a proactive manner to reach optimal efficiency (Thomas, 1994). Following are useful concepts that will enable the professional to begin these proactive responses and take charge of integrating technology into the life care planning process.

USE OF COMPUTERS IN A LIFE CARE PLANNING PRACTICE

Computers have become an essential tool for the life care planner. The recent generation of computers with very fast processors gives significant computing power to the small- or medium-size business. Current computers with their speed and improved operating systems allow the small company or solo practitioner to execute very sophisticated programs that were beyond consideration a few years ago.

Now it is possible to use software programs to accumulate all case management information resources and easily identify specific vendors, recommendations, and costs for items in a life care plan. Once resources and vendors are identified in an informational database, faxes can be quickly generated that allow the professional to quickly contact potential vendors for current costs. Upon obtaining the specific descriptions with costs and other pertinent information, these items can be easily translated into the traditional life care plan tables or into a customized life care plan report, depending upon the professional's preference. Retyping redundant information such as the recommendation and vendor is minimized (Thomas, 1994).

Because there are a variety of report requests, the life care planner is able to provide a report that meets the standards of life care planning as well as the requests of the referral source. For example, a referral source may wish to have a summary of the items and, in some cases, a summary of costs over the lifetime of the client. In the past, the life care plan narrative may have been completed in a word processing program. If a cost summary involving mathematical calculations were required, it would likely be completed in a spreadsheet such as Excel, or calculations would have been completed manually using a calculator. Now, all of this information can be completed at the same time in one software program.

Once appropriate software is installed, the professional will also become more familiar with multiple life care planning resources available on the Internet. E-mail communication has increased the sharing of information and the development of listservs has become an instantaneous help desk for the life care planner. By using the appropriate computer hardware and software, the life care planner will have a significant professional advantage. However, before the next hardware and software purchase, review the following guidelines in order to make wise decisions.

Computer Purchase Guidelines[1]

1. Purchase a computer with a processor speed of at least 1.5 gigahertz (GHz). If cost is not a significant factor, consider the fastest Pentium or Intel chip that is available.
2. Purchase a minimum hard drive capacity of 80 gigabytes (GB).
3. Purchase a minimum RAM (random access memory) of 512 megabytes (MB). If several software programs are used at one time, or digital photos are manipulated, or extensive Internet research is common, consider having more RAM installed at the time of purchase.
4. Purchase, at a minimum, a 17-inch monitor (preferably 19 inches). Some people prefer the flat monitors for space-saving purposes, and as the cost reduces, this may be a desirable option.
5. Purchase a laser printer with an installed Ethernet card. If color photos or text is included, inkjet printers have excellent quality and are relatively cheap. Because of the cost per page, it may be reasonable to have two

---

[1] See Appendix A for terminology definitions.

      printers: one laser for prints and speed and the other for color needs. Also, some all-in-one machines might be useful for color copies, color printing, and faxes.

6. Utilize a DSL line or cable modem for access to the Internet. The time savings is very significant when compared to a dial-up modem.

7. Network your computers at the office or home with an Ethernet network. Consider using the wireless networking referred to as Wi-Fi.

8. The most popular operating system is Windows XP, which is a more reliable and stable system than prior Windows systems. Have your staff trained on the Windows XP operating system.

9. Purchase an uninterruptible power source (UPS), which usually costs between $100 and $200. The UPS prevents sudden power outages on the computer and network equipment. Sudden power outages can result in loss or corruption of data. The UPS also serves as a surge protector.

10. Select a quality company from which to purchase computer and software products. Choose either (1) a reputable company, preferably one that will offer a 30-day, no-questions-asked, money-back guarantee, or (2) mail-order through a national company. Mail order companies such as Dell (800-424-1370) and Gateway (800-846-2059) offer a wide variety of products. Consider a 3-year support contract that includes toll-free 24-hour technical support. The cost of this additional service is approximately $200 and a very good investment.

11. Select a good data backup system and have a thorough understanding of its use. Some users install the data backup system with the hope it will never be used. Unfortunately, the user may not test the backup system until the dreaded hard drive crash occurs. One important quality of a backup system is that it is convenient and easy to use for both storing and restoring data. Utilizing a DVD burner is one method to archive data on your computer. Another is using larger Zip® disks. And don't forget to have an off-site copy of your data.

A DVD burner holds approximately 4.6 GB of information (approximately six regular CDs). One of its advantages is that the DVD can easily be read by other computers. This allows the user to save large files and then place the DVD in a safe location. Also, the professional can use a DVD or CD to mail data to other locations when it would not be practical to e-mail a 60- or 80-MB file. Another advantage of the DVD is that it allows instant access to archived files. A DVD reader/burner costs approximately $250. Successful life care planners recognize the ongoing need to protect their investments with appropriate staff training and data backup technologies.

Software

Software used to assist professionals is abundant in today's technology. Word processing programs such as Microsoft Word are a necessity for any office. Database programs that allow the user to design templates are also becoming popular. Such database programs include Microsoft Access and Filemaker Pro.

The professional may also explore spreadsheet capability and presentation software such as PowerPoint if the practice needs these. In addition, software programs incorporating the Merck Manual on CD-ROM, as well as other medically related software programs, can be beneficial to the life care planner (see Weed, 1995, 1996b, for examples).

While much of the software currently available is designed for home health agencies, specific software for case management and life care planning is now available. Software programs such as LCPStat were introduced in 1993 by TecSolutions, Inc. (www.LCP3.com). In approximately 2001, Life Care Writer by Computer Methods was made available as a Web-based service (www.lifecarewriter.com) and *Life Care Planning for the PC* by Ahab Press was released (www.ahab-press.com/lifecareplan.htm). In 2003, Total Life Care software by Compensation Economic Information Systems was made available for purchase (www.rehab-serv.com/tlc.htm). See Appendix B for websites and phone numbers for selected examples.

The above programs should be carefully reviewed by the life care planner considering a specialty software package for life care planning. The program should offer the user the ability to organize data and generate reports in an efficient and reliable manner. Such programs would also be a business advantage to those individuals using technology and life care planning. As with any software used in forensic settings, the user should be aware of any Daubert implications and be prepared to answer questions about the software from a Daubert standpoint (see Chapters 22, 24, and 25).

Another type of software that would be advantageous for the life care professional is a voice recognition technology (VRT) program. Voice recognition technology is not a new concept; however, it has only recently become popular because tremendous strides have been made in VRT, and computer hardware and software programs are now available at reasonable costs. VRT programs allow the professional to speak into a microphone and the computer will "type" at a rate of 50 to 125 words per minute with approximately 95% accuracy, increasing efficiency and reducing overhead in this high-technology approach to office tasks. Most VRT products are compatible with the major word processing, spreadsheet, and database programs. The minimum recommended configuration for most VRT programs is a Pentium II processor, 300-MHz speed, 256 MB of RAM, and 50 MB of available hard drive space. However, the program is much more effective with processor speeds of 1 GHz and RAM of 512.

There are a number of VRT products designed for Windows and Macintosh. Initially, the user should allow 2 hours for installation and "teaching" the VRT software the user's voice. Another 4 hours of practice and learning the software are necessary to maximize VRT productivity. There are a number of VRT products available, including programs by Via Voice® by IBM and Dragon Dictate®.

Also, Internet-related software include a variety of programs such as Real Audio, a software program that allows the user to listen to music or speech from an Internet site. The audio capacity will become more important as continuing educational programs and distance-learning strategies are introduced by professional associations and universities.

Computer Operating Systems

Most life care planners will be using the Windows XP operating system by Microsoft, Inc. Some users have hesitated to upgrade to Windows XP from prior Windows versions. However, Windows XP will most likely become the standard for most offices. With online system updates from Microsoft, the advantage for the life care planner using Windows XP will be significant.

Most of the software used by life care planners can be used on either the Macintosh or Windows operating system. However, most life care planners utilize the Microsoft operating system. With any of the new generation of operating systems from Microsoft and Apple, the user can access the Internet, receive e-mail, download files, and research the various databases. Although there has been concern over the future of the Macintosh computer and Apple Corporation, it is probable that the Macintosh operating system will remain a viable operating system for many years to come.

Other available operating systems include REDHAT and UNIX. It is important to note life care planners seldom use these systems because of limited software choices and the complexity of the systems. However, REDHAT and UNIX are powerful operating systems that are used by many large companies and experienced computer users.

Networking

Networking refers to the ability for several computers, in an office or at separate locations, to be electronically connected. The decision to network has become an easier one to make. Prior generations of computers were difficult to network. Windows XP and Macintosh have significant network capability built into their operating systems. For offices that have four or more people using the Internet or sharing the same life care planning databases, establishing a local area network is essential.

Once the decision to network is made, establishing the network should be relatively straightforward. A cable specialist will run cables, and a software specialist will set up the protocols for the computers to talk to each other. The user should be certain to ask that firewalls be installed to prevent unauthorized access to the computers via the Internet. Your computer consultant can advise on the most appropriate firewalls. And the user should be careful to save the various passwords associated with the modem and firewalls in a safe and secure location.

There will be a moderate cost for the initial network installation and associated hardware and software. There are also other costs involved such as ongoing maintenance and upgrades. In addition to the costs for the initial technology purchase (i.e., specific hardware or software products), there is also a commitment to staff training and development in the use of the network.

Using the Internet as a Resource

The Internet continues to grow in both volume and quality of information. It has become a useful medium for life care planners to locate medical specialists and resources (Thomas, 1996b). In addition, most medical centers have home pages that allow users to learn of services offered by specific facilities and to contact persons in these businesses. Data regarding specific medical fees by CPT code remain difficult to obtain over the Internet. Cost by DRG is easier to obtain but less useful in many cases than would be the cost by CPT codes.

For life care planners that have already attempted to find information on costs, there is a noticeable lack of printed materials providing cost by CPT codes, and materials that are available typically are expensive. Medical cost information is often proprietary and the publishers charge a premium price for the information in both printed form and access over the Internet. It is probable that databases with medical costs will eventually become available on the Internet. For example, one experienced professional has developed a Web-based site to assist with sharing of life care planning data in partial answer to this problem (www.careplanners.net). However, since the CPT codes and descriptors are copyrighted by the American Medical Association and are not in the public domain, there may be a long wait for a comprehensive data source.

The Internet will continue to expand access to medical and legal databases. Some of these databases have excellent information that is free of charge, whereas other databases such as the Lexus system of legal research will continue to be proprietary and have an associated fee. A general rule of thumb is that any printed information requiring payment will also require payment when obtained over the Internet.

To successfully use the Internet, a dial-up modem with telephone line, a cable modem, or a DSL line should be available that allows adequate speed of transmission of data. The DSL line and cable modem offer acceptable upload and download speed. In the author's opinion, the dial-up modem is typically too slow for surfing the Internet or sharing files.

DSL Telephone Lines

Users/computers can communicate over the Internet via telephone lines. Most telephone lines are composed of four copper wires (but only two wires are used for voice communication) that convey information. The size of the copper wire (and the fact that only two are used) limits the amount of information that can be sent or received by the computer/modem. DSL lines have become available in nearly all locations.

There are a number of considerations when choosing the DSL telephone line. The cost of DSL installation may vary from no charge to $300, depending on your local telephone provider. The DSL modem may cost from $100 to $300. The monthly DSL connection fee is approximately $60 without a static Internet protocol (IP) number, or $200 per month with five static IP numbers. DSL lines provide a cost-effective method for high-speed data transfer either for conventional Internet connections or for remote computing. The DSL telephone line allows approximately 5 to 10 times the amount of data to be transferred compared to the traditional modem telephone line.

Cable Modem

The television (TV) cable that is in your home or office has the capacity to transmit significantly more data than the DSL telephone line. A number of TV cable companies provide high-speed Internet access services via cable modem. Video conferencing and high-speed transmissions are also possible due to the bandwidth available with TV cable. Cost is typically lower than or competitive with DSL fees.

Internet Browsers

A browser is a software program that allows the user to view and access information on the Internet. At present, the most popular browser is Microsoft Internet Explorer®. Many individuals also use Netscape®. However, users still have to obtain Internet access via a local Internet access provider (Thomas, 1996a, 1996c) before using the above program to surf the Internet.

Internet Access Providers or Internet Service Providers

Internet service providers (ISPs) are prevalent in nearly all areas of the U.S. Use of ISP has become easier with the introduction of DSL and cable modem service. DSL and cable modem services provide unlimited access to the Internet, but with limits on how much data the user can upload. DSL providers typically limit the upload speed and allow higher download speeds. In contrast, cable modems typically do not cap the upload or download speeds; therefore, at times you may have fast download and fast upload speeds. But cable modems are similar to a telephone party line — if several people in your neighborhood log on to their cable modem, the download and upload speeds will diminish.

Internet Search Engines

Search engines are proprietary software programs that are accessed via the Internet and allow the user to list and enter key words for topics to be researched on the Internet. The search engine will review its database of Internet sites and provide the life care planner with domain names and uniform resource locators (URLs) of sites on the Internet that have information related to the key words. The life care planner can access a particular site by clicking on the site name. There is no charge to use the more popular search engines such as Google.com and alltheweb.com.

E-mail Communication

E-mail is another primary use of the Internet. E-mail means sending an electronic message to someone else that has an Internet or other e-mail address. This approach offers many advantages. For example, even though the U.S. Postal Service can deliver the same message, the exchange via e-mail occurs in a matter of seconds. Therefore, sending e-mail is essentially instantaneous, and typically there is no per message charge for e-mail. Also, once an account with the Internet provider is established, the user can send unlimited messages (Thomas, 1996a). Most Internet e-mail programs limit the size of attachments. This can affect sending large documents or photos.

There are software programs that will allow an Internet user to have a telephone conversation with another Internet user (Thomas, 1996b). These programs are in the early stages of development and quality of transmission varies but will continue to improve. The biggest advantage of this technology is that there will be no additional charge for an international phone call.

Videoconferencing

Videoconferencing will become a valuable tool during the next few years. As life care planners continue to purchase computers with faster processor and Internet access speeds, video compression programs are also becoming more effective. As a result, acceptable-quality videoconferences will be available over the Internet. Video quality will not be that of a television, but video on the computer screen will provide acceptable viewing for communication. In addition, as of the time of this chapter, some cell phones can communicate with other cell phones by sending video and voice.

Significant commercial value has been placed on videoconference software. Corporations (and life care planners) spend a significant amount of money for staff traveling to face-to-face meetings. The value placed on the face-to-face meeting is so significant that the life care planner and others will pay premium prices for reliable videoconference software and hardware.

For a summary of suggestions related to the above text, please refer to Table 29.1.

CONCLUSION

In summary, technology has a significant impact on the life care planning process. Technology continues to evolve that will allow more efficient and accurate completion of life care plans for individuals with catastrophic injuries. Computer hardware and software will allow quicker processing of reports and locating of appropriate resources. Use of software such as word processing, specialized programs for life care planning and case management, sources of information, and data on CD-ROM/DVD/Internet will continue to increase.

Implementing the use of computers and software into life care planning is more than simply buying a computer. There must also be an appropriate computer system, including hard drive capacity, processor speed, software, backup system, software/hardware maintenance, and staff training. Since data that are becoming available are more comprehensive, additional computing power will be required to process this data at a speed acceptable to the life care planner. This chapter contains guidelines and other information to encourage the successful integration of technology and life care planning and to provide the life care planner with necessary information.

Table 29.1   Practical Technology Hints for the Life Care Planner

■ Make sure you have firewall protection. If you have a full-time connection to the Internet with a DSL or cable modem, there will be several hundred attempts each day to access your computer.

■ Make sure you have virus protection — and keep it up to date.

■ Do not open e-mail attachments unless you are *sure* of their content. Even if the e-mail is from someone you know, attachments often are infected.

■ The monthly cost for a DSL or cable modem ($40 to $70) is worth the expense for the increased productivity.

■ New computers have adequate processing speed to run the numerous programs the life care planner will utilize.

■ A DVD burner for the additional cost of $175 to $225 is a good investment for the life care planner.

■ A DVD burner is a useful tool for backing up files for the life care planner.

■ Adobe Acrobat is a very useful tool for sending reports by e-mail that are printer ready. The full cost is approximately $200; $100 to upgrade from prior version.

■ When buying a new computer system, purchase *at least* 512 MB of RAM and 80 GB of hard drive.

■ Use www.whatismyip.com to identify the IP number for your computer when it is logged on to the Internet.

■ Use a router, not a hub, on your office Ethernet connection to the Internet. The hub allows greater security measures.

■ Wi-Fi is a wireless Ethernet connection that should be considered when networking your office.

■ A reasonable monthly fee to pay a company for Web hosting is $25 to $45 per month.

■ A reasonable cost to pay a Web developer to develop a website with approximately 10 web pages would be $500 to $1000.

■ A reasonable cost, on an annual basis, to pay a Web developer to update your website three to four times per year would be $75 per hour, with approximately 4 hours of update time per year.

■ Do not allow your Web developer to own your specific domain name. Perform a search on www.whois.com and discover who your domain name is owned by.

■ You can purchase domain names from www.register.com.

■ You register your domain name for 3 years and mark your calendar to renew the subscription. If your domain name registration expires, another company can purchase your domain name.

■ The approximate cost per year for registering and owning a domain name is $15 to $25.

REFERENCES

Barros-Bailey, M. & Boyd, D. (1997). *Internet Disability Resources: 1998*. White Plains, NY: Ahab Press (new edition should be available by time of this publication).

Thomas, R.L. (1992). The use of a computer in life care planning. *The Rehab Consultant*, 3, 4.

Thomas, R.L. (1994). Automation and life care planning. *The Case Manager*, 5, 77–82.

Thomas, R.L. (1996a). The Internet and You! Paper presented at the meeting of the National Association for Rehabilitation Professionals in the Private Sector, San Francisco, CA.

Thomas, R.L. (1996b). Research on the Internet. *The Case Manager*, 7, 42–43.

Thomas, R.L. (1996c). Surfing the Internet, part two: getting there on the World Wide Web. *Inside Case Management*, 3, 7–8.

Weed, R. (1995). Samples of practical technology for the case manager. *The Case Manager*, 6, 67–74.

Weed, R. (1996a). More practical technology for the case manager, part 4. *The Case Manager*, 7, 48–53.

Weed, R. (1996b). More practical technology for the case manager, part 3. *The Case Manager*, 7, 42, 44.

Weed, R. (1996c). More practical technology for the case manager, part 2. *The Case Manager*, 7, 41, 43.

APPENDIX A: SELECTED TECHNOLOGICAL DEFINITIONS

E-mail (electronic mail) Messages, usually text, sent from one person to another via computer. E-mail can also be sent automatically to a large number of addresses such as a mailing list.

FAQ (frequently asked question) Document that lists and answers the most common questions on a particular subject. There are hundreds of FAQs on subjects as diverse as pet grooming and cryptography. FAQs are usually written by people who are tired of answering the same questions over and over.

FTP (file transfer protocol) A very common method of moving files between two Internet sites. FTP is a special way to log in to another Internet site for the purposes of retrieving or sending files. There are many Internet sites that have established publicly accessible repositories of material that can be obtained using FTP, by logging in using the account name "anonymous." Thus, these sites are called anonymous FTP servers.

HTML (hypertext markup language) The coding language used to create hypertext documents for use on the World Wide Web. HTML looks like old-fashioned typesetting codes, where the user surrounds a block of text with codes that indicate how it should appear. Additionally in HTML, the user can specify that a block of text or a word is linked to another file on the Internet. HTML files are designed to be viewed using a World Wide Web client program, such as Netscape.

HTTP (hypertext transport protocol) Used to move hypertext files across the Internet. It requires a HTTP client program on one end and an HTTP server program on the other end. HTTP is the most important protocol used in the World Wide Web (WWW).

Hypertext Generally, any text that contains links to other documents, or words or phrases in the document, that can be chosen by a reader and that cause another document to be retrieved and displayed.

Internet telephony A category of hardware and software that enables people to use the Internet as the transmission medium for telephone calls. For users who have free or fixed-price Internet access, Internet telephony software essentially provides free telephone calls anywhere in the world. To date, however, Internet telephony does not offer the same quality of telephone service as direct telephone connections.

IP number An identifier for a computer or device on a TCP/IP network. Networks using the TCP/IP protocol route messages based on the IP address of the destination. The format of an IP address is a 32-bit numeric address written as four numbers separated by periods. Each number can be zero to 255. For example, 1.160.10.240 could be an IP address, An IP number is a unique number consisting of four parts separated by dots, e.g., 165.113.245.2. Every machine that is on the Internet has a unique IP number. Most machines also have one or more domain names that are easier for people to remember.

ISDN (Integrated Services Digital Network) Basically this is a way to move more data over existing regular phone lines. ISDN is rapidly becoming available to much of the U.S. and in most markets. It can provide speeds of roughly 128,000 bits per second (bps) over regular phone lines. In practice, most people will be limited to 56,000 or 64,000 bps.

ISP (Internet service provider) A company that provides access to the Internet. For a monthly fee, the service provider gives you a software package, username, password, and access phone number. Equipped with a modem, you can then log on to the Internet and browse the World Wide Web and USENET, and send and receive e-mail.

TCP/IP (transmission control protocol/Internet protocol) This is the suite of protocols that defines the Internet. Originally designed for the UNIX operating system, TCP/IP software is now available for every major type of computer operating system. To be truly on the Internet, the user's computer must have TCP/IP software.

URL (uniform resource locator) The standard way to give the address of any resource on the Internet that is part of the World Wide Web (WWW), e.g., http://www.matisse.net/seminars.html or telnet://well.sf.ca.us. The most common way to use a URL is to enter into a WWW browser program, such as Netscape or Lynx, and enter the URL address.

Wi-Fi (wireless fidelity) Wi-Fi is the popular term for a high-frequency wireless local area network (WLAN). The Wi-Fi technology is rapidly gaining acceptance in many companies as an alternative to a wired LAN. It can also be installed for a home network.

WWW (World Wide Web) The whole constellation of resources that can be accessed using FTP, HTTP, and some other tools.

APPENDIX B: SOFTWARE VENDORS

Elliott and Fitzpatrick
(800) 843-4977
(706) 548-8161
Fax: 706-546-8417
http://www.elliottfitzpatrick.com

IMA Technologies, Inc.
Case management software such as CaseTrakker
(800) 458-1114
Fax: 916-446-1157
http://www.casetrakker.com/

Life Care Planning for the PC
Ahab Press
http://www.ahabpress.com/lifecareplan.htm

Life Care Writer
Computer Methods
http://www.lifecarewriter.com/

O*Net (Occupational Information Network)
The automated online replacement for the *Dictionary of Occupational Titles*
http://online.onetcenter.org/

TecSolutions
LCPSTAT Case Management and Life Care Planning software for Windows and
    Macintosh
(601) 991-0551
Fax: 601-952-0072
www.LCP3.com

TIMESLIPS Corporation
Time and billing software
(800) 285-0999
Fax: 972-930-8938
http://www.timeslips.com/

Total Life Care Software
Compensation Economic Information Systems
http://www.rehabserv.com/tlc.htm

Voice Recognition Technology Companies

1. Dragon Dictate Systems offers Dragon Dictate Windows, http://www.scan-soft.com/
2. IBM offers IBM Via Voice, http://www-3.ibm.com/software/speech/

APPENDIX C: USE OF INTERNET SITES

One source of published information for the life care planner is *Disability Resources on the Internet: Collecting, Organizing, and Presenting in an Accessible Manner*, by Mary Barros-Bailey, Pauline G. Aguilar, and Michael R. Burks. See http://www.isoc.org/isoc/conferences/inet/99/proceedings/3l/3l_2.htm or www.ahabpress.com to purchase. This book provides a well-organized approach to Internet resources.

Since the number of useful sites on the Internet for life care planners has expanded exponentially, it is not reasonable to offer examples in this chapter. The life care planner is urged to learn the use of search engines (e.g., Google.com or alltheweb.com). The names and URL locations of web pages seem to change frequently. Therefore, the use of the search engines to identify valuable Web locations has become an effective tool if the URL is incorrect or out of date.

Simply enter the site name in the key word descriptor of the search engine. Then review the hits obtained by the search engine. By using this search method, the life care planner will be able to identify not only the requested site, but related sites as well. Once located, use of the bookmarks in the Web browser allows easy marking of the site location.

30

LIFE CARE PLANNING RESOURCES

Julie A. Kitchen and Elizabeth Brown

A plethora of information has been written over the years about resources that can and should be used in life care planning. As life care planners, we know that the person with the most accurate, accessible, and thorough resources is the winner in the life care planning arena. Without proper resources that are easily accessible, understandable, and updateable, the task of completing a competent, thorough, and accurate life care plan can be formidable. In the authors' experience, most life care planners spend the majority of their time researching information for the plan, rather than actually formulating the specific components for the plan. Therefore, the life care planner with the competitive edge is the one who has a multitude of data from a variety of sources, encompassing a large pool of information, rather than just the basics involved in setting up the outline for the recommendations for the life care plan.

There is an operative word that must be spoken and understood here, and that word is *accessible* resources. Just having the information available somewhere in the office is not enough. This will not help the expert during the stress of a deposition when asked to pull that source, or during a telephone conference with a referral source, asking for specifics on something referenced in the life care plan. Additionally, there are many topics not specifically covered in the life care plan itself that must also be readily available for conferencing, speaking, training, testifying, networking, and case managing. Remember that our role as life care planners is as educators — well-prepared, knowledgeable educators with an almost unlimited fund of knowledge and resources.

This chapter will outline some resources (which will in turn lead the reader to other resources) that will enable life care planners to expand their horizons and base of information. This chapter is not designed to outline specific individual sources for a specific problem. This chapter will globally outline information that will provide the life care planner/case manager with the fact source(s) needed to be well rounded and knowledgeable in all facets of the life care planning industry and that will provide a foundation upon which one can continually build a broad knowledge base.

0-8493-1511-5/04/$0.00+$1.50
© 2004 by CRC Press LLC

Just as the key to comprehensive life care planning is to develop and maintain a consistent methodology to analyze and process catastrophic cases, the key to resourcing and maintaining a database is just as important, and a consistent methodology must be used to obtain and maintain those sources. Otherwise, the professional will be mired in a deluge of information that is virtually useless if it is not accessible, updated, and maintained in such a fashion that the professional can have immediate access.

As professionals, we must keep abreast of technology available so as to benefit fully from what it can offer. This means being willing to investigate new technology, new data storage and retrieval systems. This is not to say that one cannot stay with a proven, successful method of data collection, retrieval, etc., but the professional must keep an open mind as to alternatives that are continually being developed. The professional is encouraged to seek out and evaluate a number of currently available software programs to determine which system (for case management, life care planning, resource data storage and retrieval, etc.) will best fit specific needs.

This chapter is also designed to make the task of researching easier and more user friendly. We will begin by starting at the beginning of the research process involved in the life care planning arena.

The process of researching requires the life care planner to do the following:

- Identify and define needed information
- Cultivate effective resources to locate information
- Organize, store, and retrieve valuable information

Therefore, let us break this down further by narrowing the scope a bit to make it more manageable. In order to identify and define needed information, the life care planner must look at the client specifics:

- Injury/disability
- Environment/location
- Client needs based on the disability:
    - Medical services
    - Nursing/assistance
    - Residential needs
    - Education/vocation
    - Miscellaneous services
    - Supplies/equipment
    - Allied health services

Defining client needs goes hand-in-hand with identifying those areas for inclusion in the life care plan. The authors' like to refer to the Area Cost Analysis Request form (see below) as a blueprint for the life care plan. It is in using this form that the planner begins mentally constructing the plan as the requested costing information is outlined. By checking off those items that require costing research, the planner is also constructing the various recommendations contained within the plan. See sample Area Cost Analysis Request below (also see Appendix A for a sample facility questionnaire).

Area Cost Analysis Request

Client: _____

Plaintiff: ___ Defense: ___ Age: ____ Sex: M F

Disability:___Area Code: _____

City: ___Nearest Metro Area: _____

Today's Date:___ Date Due: _____

Allied Health Professionals:

__ Dentist
__ Gastroenterologist
__ GP/internist
__ Neuro-ophthalmologist
__ Neurologist
__ Neuropsychologist
__ Neurosurgeon
__ Ophthalmologist
__ Orthopedist
__ Orthosurgeon
__ Otolaryngologist
__ Pain specialist
__ Pediatrician
__ Physiatrist
__ Plastic surgeon
__ Podiatrist
__ Psychiatrist
__ Psychologist
__ Pulmonologist
__ Rheumatologist
__ Urologist
__ Other: _____

Home Health: (See links to home health agencies)

Therapy: ____ PT, ____ OT, ____ ST, ____ Respiratory
Invasive procedures required? (Yes/No) Such as:
__ Catheter
__ Suction
__ IV therapy
__ Trach care
__ Tube feeding
__ Bowel program

Staffing:

HHA ____ Hourly, ____Visit
LPN ____ Hourly, ____Visit
RN ____ Hourly, ____Visit
__ Live-in (available/definition/last time staffed this level?)

(continued)

Area Cost Analysis Request (Continued)

Facility-Based Outpatient Therapy:

__ PT _____

__ OT _____

__ ST _____

__Respiratory therapy

__Aquatic therapy

__Therapeutic riding

__Recreational therapy

__Work hardening program

__Disabled driver

__Augmentative communication

__Assistive technology

__Other: _____

__Other: _____

__Other: _____

Miscellaneous Services:

__Handyman service

__Health club

__Home modification

__House cleaning

__Massage therapy

__Nutritionist

__Support group

__Other: _____

Educational Programs:

__Public school

__Summer program

__Private school

__College aid

__Tutor

__Camp__College: __AA __BA

__Vocational/technical: _____

Vocational Services:

__Vocational evaluation

__Vocational counseling

__Job coaching

__Sheltered work

__Supported work

__Day/activity program

Wage data research required (if providing a loss of earnings report):
 Occupation: _____

(continued)

Area Cost Analysis Request (Continued)

Programs/Facilities:

__Adult day care
__Day program __ABI __MR
__Assisted living facility
__Other:___
__ICF/MR or group home
__Long-term head injury
__Skilled nursing facility
__Supported living
__Transitional living __ SCI __ABI
__Neurobehavioral inpatient
__Chronic Pain :__Inpatient __Outpatient
__SCI rehab: __Inpatient __Outpatient
__SCI evaluation: __Inpatient __Outpatient

__Other

Facility Care Level:

Level of disability
Hours of supervision
ADLs:
Cues:
Aggressive
Ambulatory
Continent
Verbal
PVS
Trach
Vent dependent
Tube fed
Bowel program
Day program
Work program

Diagnostics:

__EEG
__EKG
__Evoked potential __Audio __Visual
__Pulmonary functions
__Renal scan
__Renal ultrasound
__Sleep study
__Swallow study
__Urodynamic studies
__CT: _____
__MRI: _____
__X-ray: _____
__Broncoscopy
__Colonoscopy
__Cystoscopy
__Endoscopy

Labs:

__Cardiac profile
__CBC (with diff.)
__Comp. metabolic panel
__Creatinine
__C&S
__LFT
__Lipid panel
__UA
__Chemical levels (what medication(s)): _____

(continued)

Area Cost Analysis Request (Continued)

Surgeries/Procedures:

__Botox
__Biofeedback
__FES
__Epidural block
__SCI fertility program: M F
__Gastrostomy
__PEG tube
__Trach revision
__Shunt revision
__Hip subluxation
__Hip replacement
__Knee replacement
__Baclofen pump
__Morphine pump
__Spinal stimulator
__Scoliosis surgery
__Diskectomy (cervical/thoracic/lumbar)
__Laminectomy (cervical/thoracic/lumbar)
__Spinal fusion (cervical/thoracic/lumbar)
__Scar revision (length of scar: ___)
__Stump revision
__Arthroscopy
__Contracture release
__Tendon release
__Hardware removal

Equipment:

__ECU
__Standers
__Cushions
__Ramp/lift
__Van conversion
__Assistive technology
__Augmentative communication device
__Pediatric equipment
__Orthotics
__Prosthetics
__Visual aids
__Wheelchair
__Specialized equipment: _____

Supplies:

Medications: _____
DME: _____

Copyright by authors. Reprinted with permission.

The above illustrates a sample form that can be used as a blueprint for the life care plan.

Once the needs are known, then researching the cost is in order. The Internet has certainly changed and shaped the way we research costs, but the telephone is still an important link when specific information needs to be acquired. E-mail is another valuable tool, and actually, some of the same tips on the art of obtaining telephone information is valuable in obtaining information via e-mail, since both, ideally, will be answered by a human on the other side. Do not underestimate the power of the spoken word. An outline of instrumental tips is located below.

THE ART OF OBTAINING INFORMATION BY TELEPHONE

- **First Impressions Count:** Do not be demanding, but humble, and with sincerity ask your questions.
- **Be Optimistic and Positive:** Do not let the person on the other end try to dismiss you by indicating he does not know the answer. Assume he does; he just might not know he knows. Be persuasive, but kind and optimistic.
- **Be Complimentary:** "I understand you are the area expert on such and such."
- **Be Persistent and Patient:** Do not give up. Continue to follow up on your contacts and respect their time requirements, if possible. (Beg when necessary.)
- **Be Personable:** No one enjoys talking to someone who is very stiff and all business. Throw in a bit of small talk to make both of you feel at ease. If the other person can feel your pain, so to speak, you have a much better chance of acquiring the needed information.
- **Be Flexible:** Go with the flow. If you are referred to yet another number to call, do so cheerfully. Eventually you will end up rewarded.

Now that we have reviewed the essential points involved with the art of obtaining information via telephone, let us look at some of the more practical matters in terms of locating information.

LOCATING HEALTH CARE PROFESSIONALS

When working outside of your geographical area, using the Web, go to the online Yellow Pages to begin your search for medical professionals or allied health professionals. Two examples are:

- InfoSpace: www.infospace.com
- The Real Yellow Pages: http://yp.bellsouth.net

To find certain *specific* specialists, such as a pain specialist, physiatrist, neuro-ophthalmologist, neuropsychologist, neurosurgeon, or nutritionist, special research tools are required. A useful tool to use to find specific specialists is the *National Trade and Professional Associations*. This text provides detailed contact and background information on over 7600 trade associations, professional societies, technical organizations, and labor unions in the U.S. It is available from:

Columbia Books, Inc.
P.O. Box 4668
Chestertown, MD 21690
(888) 265-0600
Fax: 410-810-0911
E-mail: info@columbiabooks.com

Another good general source includes the *Case Management Resource Guide* (www.cmrg.com). This guide can provide information for a number of programs and facilities, such as:

- Home care
- Rehabilitation
- Subacute care
- Nursing facilities
- Assisted living facilities
- Hospice
- Long-term acute care
- Hospitals
- Psychiatric and addiction

The following links will guide you to home health agencies. Always look to the national agencies first when researching costs. If there are no national agencies available, contact the closest agency for assistance. Many times, a national agency will service out-of-town areas for an additional transportation/travel charge.

Websites for specific agencies can direct you to specific offices in geographic locations served.

Home Health Links

- Gentiva (formerly Olsten): www.gentiva.com
- Interim Home Health: www.interimhealthcare.com
- Kelly Assisted Living: www.kellyassistedliving.com
- Maxim Home Health: www.maxhealth.com
- Nurse Finders: www.nursefinders.com

Other Useful Links

- Brain Injury Facility Locator: www.biausa.org
- United Cerebral Palsy Direct Services: www.ucp.org
- Spinal Cord Injury Rehabilitation Centers: www.spinalcord.uab.edu
- Commission on the Accreditation of Rehabilitation Facilities: www.carf.org/
- Shepherd Spinal Cord Injury Program: www.shepherd.org

- Miami Project: www.miami.edu/miami-project/5steps.htm
- National Spinal Cord Injury Association: www.spinalcord.org

LOCATING MISCELLANEOUS SERVICES

Search online Yellow Pages for:

- Handyman
- Health club
- House cleaning
- Massage therapy

LOCATING SCHOOLS/EDUCATIONAL SERVICES

- Preschools, public schools, private schools, school boards — online Yellow Pages: www.infospace.com
- Colleges and universities, by state: www.newsdirectory.com/college
- Tutor locator — Sylvan Learning Centers: (800)-Educate or www.educate.com
- Special needs camp: www.acacamps.org

VOCATIONAL REHABILITATION RESOURCES

- Department of Vocational Rehabilitation Offices by state: www.parac.org/svrp.html

GEOGRAPHICALLY SPECIFIC WAGE DATA

- Bureau of Labor Statistics: http://stats.bls.gov/oes/2001/oessrcma.htm (yearly metropolitan-area occupational employment and wage estimates)
- *Occupational Outlook Handbook*: http://www.bls.gov/oco/

FEDERAL INFORMATION

- Federal government: www.firstgov.gov
- Medicaid phone numbers: http://cms.hhs.gov/
- Social Security Administration: www.ssa.gov
- Federal government directory: www.lib.lsu.edu/gov/fedgov.html

WEB RESOURCES

- National Library of Medicine's MEDLINE database: www.nlm.nih.gov/databases
- National Clearinghouse of Rehabilitation Training Materials: www.nchrtm.okstate.edu/forms/mainquery.html

- National Center for Dissemination of Disability Research: www.ncddr.org
- U.S. Government consumer health information Healthfinder: www.health-finder.gov

STORING AND RETRIEVING INFORMATION — DATABASE

A life care plan database is an important aspect of what any successful life care planner/case manager will require. Below are several choices of products available:

LCP STAT
- A life care planning/case management software designed and initially authored by Randall Thomas, Ph.D., Madison, MS; (601) 956-3868 or (601)-946-0646; e-mail: Lcpstat@aol.com.

LCP STAT Lite
- Designed for life care planners. This product allows the user to print life care plans. It gives you the flexibility to create life care plan templates and begin a new plan with ease and fewer errors. This program is portable and allows the user to work on plans between offices and on laptops, and to e-mail them to other staff.
- Pop-up menus are editable by the user, and the life care plan title can be modified, i.e., Life Care Plan — Home Care Option. The LCP STAT Lite utilizes file tabs to move from one screen to another. This program does not include case management.

Resources Database
- This database is a separate file and allows the user to maintain resources (items and services) with unit costs or costs range. The user may identify a specific vendor, vendor address, and vendor city/state/zip code or geographical location. The user can also identify the specific medical impairment for which the item would be appropriate. The user can select specific items from resources and import those items into a life care plan.

Both the LCP STAT and Resources Database are designed for use on Windows 95/98/ME/2000/XP and Macintosh operating systems.

Life Care Planning for the PC
- A simple and effective life care planning program designed to work with Microsoft Word® or WordPerfect®, designed and authored by Ann Maniha, R.N., C.L.C.P. Contact: AHAB Press, www.ahabpress.com.

The Planner! Series of Life Care Planning Software from SaddlePoint Software include the following products:

- PlannerPro! — A complete package not only for the professional Life Care Planner, but for the Medicare Set-Aside Allocator as well. Features of the software include built-in calculation capabilities, reusable data, including reusable vendor databases, and 9216 LCP print format combinations. Numerous print options exist for the MSA output as well. Report print options include the ability to define 22 different fields within the printouts, including header, footer, title, and descriptive verbiage for the LCP fields. The software also has the capability to export a Life Care Plan or MSA created within the software into a Microsoft Word document. The print options for Word document exports include the ability to set the fonts and font characteristics of the output to Word, and the ability to define and set the types of tables into which the numeric output is inserted. Word options also include the ability to combine LCP numeric data within the LCP narrative, allowing the full editing capacity of Word to be employed within the Plan. The same ability to personally define the descriptive fields exists within the Word export option as well as the standard report option. PlannerPro! also has the capability to export Life Care Plans into PDF documents, allowing the quick and easy delivery of Life Care plans via the Internet or CDS. PlannerPro! requires Microsoft XP Professional or Windows 2000 Professional operating systems and Microsoft Office 2002 (Microsoft Word 2002) or above.

- PlannerExpress+ — Has all the features of PlannerPro! with the exception of the Word export capabilities noted above. PlannerExpress+ also has MSA creation and print capabilities as well. This software is optimally designed to install and run on most modern Windows operating systems. Features such as a Global Item Selection menu are included as well.
- PlannerExpress — Utilitarian software designed just for the thrifty Life Care Planner. This is a software package with basic needs of Life Care Planners in mind. PlannerExpress users have the calculation capabilities, reusable data capabilities and Global Item Selection features as PlannerPro! and PlannerExpress+, along with a variety of report print options.

It is extremely important to be well documented in your research and to be thorough and sure of the quality of information that was obtained. Make sure your definitions of job descriptions (live-in care, for example) are consistent with the agency's definition. Considerable anxiety and wasted time will be spared if you set up and follow a strict, structured methodology of information retrieval, collection, and storage.

SELECTED SPECIFIC RESOURCES

Examples that have proven valuable in the past are the following.

Paralyzed Veterans of America

PVA is another great source of information on a variety of topics related to long-term-care planning/case management of catastrophic disabilities. PVA publishes guides for the benefit of veterans with disabilities to help them understand the requirements for receiving benefits, services, equipment, and so forth, from the U.S. Department of Veterans Affairs (VA). The guides explain who is eligible to receive services and equipment and the process of application. It also describes the number and kinds of equipment that are available to veterans, depending upon their entitlement status. This includes wheelchairs, prosthetic and sensory aids, automotive grants/allowances, clothing allowances, and a multitude of other benefits. Of particular relevance to spinal cord injury are the monographs published under the title of *The Consortium for Spinal Cord Medicine, Clinical Practice Guidelines* (administrative and financial support provided by PVA). Topics include:

- Depression following SCI: A Clinical Practice Guideline for Primary Care Physicians
- Prevention of Thromboembolism in SCI
- Neurogenic Bowel Management in Adults with SCI
- Acute Management of Autonomic Dysreflexia: Adults with SCI Presenting to Health-Care Facilities
- Prevention of Thromboembolism in SCI
- Neurogenic Bowel: What You Should Know
- Outcomes following Traumatic SCI: Clinical Practice Guidelines for Health-Care Professionals

Contacting the Paralyzed Veterans of America at:

Paralyzed Veterans of America
801 18th St. NW
Washington, DC 20006-3517
PVA National Headquarters: (800) 424-8200
PVA Publications Distribution Center: (888) 860-7244
http://www.pva.org
E-mail: info@pva.org

Title 38: Veterans' Benefits

- http://www4.law.cornell.edu/uscode/
- http://www.access.gpo.gov/ecfr/
- http://www.nara.gov/fedreg/

To download these documents, scroll to "Federal Register Documents in the News" on the GPO Access Federal Register Page. You can also locate them by searching GPO's online *Federal Register* for the topic entry shown above.

To purchase a single copy or annual subscription of the *Federal Register*, contact:

Superintendent of Documents, U.S. Government Printing Office
(202) 512-1800
http://bookstore.gpo.gov/index.html (GPO's online bookstore)

You can also refer to copies of the *Federal Register* at any federal depository library and see page II for order information.

Special Needs Trust

Special needs settlements trusts have been in common usage since 1993 and have been used on behalf of individuals with disabilities in litigation since 1978. The trusts have received extensive attention lately and will continue to spark debate or changes over time.

Most trusts are established by court order for settlement or judgment proceeds received on behalf of a litigating party who is severely disabled. The trust's two basic purposes are:

■ To provide an ongoing management vehicle for the settlement proceeds to ensure that the funds allocated to the claimant with the disability are not subject to exploitation or waste
■ To preserve the claimant's eligibility (when properly drafted and in the appropriate situation) for local, state, or federal benefit programs, including Supplemental Security Income, under Title XVI, and Medicaid under Title XIX, of the Social Security Act (42 USC)

Congress amended the Medicaid statute in the 1993 Omnibus Budget Reconciliation Act (OBRA), now codified at 42 USC 396p(d)(4)(A), to expressly recognize the use of such trusts as a means of preserving Medicaid eligibility if certain conditions are met.

Part of the intrigue of a trust is the Medicaid lien. The medical needs of a person with a disability are often funded in part by Medicaid after, say, an accident and before the resolution of the case. Medicaid may be the only source of payment while liability is being contested. All attorneys should know that the Medicaid lien must be satisfied and discharged as part of the settlement process. Usually this process was left to the end of a suit, with the hopes that Medicaid will offer a substantial discount (often 30 to 50% or more of the actual lien). However, this discount may no longer be available. One can no longer leave the treatment of the Medicaid lien to the conclusion of a case. The Health Care Financing Authority (HCFA) appears to be taking a rather hard line of no compromise of the federal financial participation amount of Medicaid liens. Thus, to avoid the parties discovering at the end of a case that almost the entire recovery could go to the Medicaid lien, this lien must be examined at the front end of a case.

All of this is quite confusing. Each state is handled differently, so there is no blanket answer to questions often posed. The authors suggest that the case manager/life care planner obtain additional information from William L.E. Dussault, Esq., William L.E. Dussault, P.P., Inc., 219 East Gales St., Seattle, WA 98102; (206) 324-4300. Mr. Dussault was one of the first to publish data on the special needs trusts and has a network of professionals that specialize in this area.

Additionally, one can read more about special needs trust in *Topics in Spinal Cord Injury Rehabilitation*, 6, 27–51, 2001 (Thomas Land Publishers, Birmingham, AL), and *The Special Needs Settlement Trust: A Tool for the Catastrophically Injured*, by William L.E. Dussault. Contact the author at (206) 324-4300, Seattle, WA.

University of Washington Spinal Cord Injury Update

This newsletter is supported by a grant from the National Institute of Disability and Rehabilitation Research, U.S. Department of Education, to the Northwest Regional Spinal Cord Injury System, one of the model SCI care systems nationwide. The newsletter is issued several times per year and is packed full of information that is a must for all life care planners/case managers.

This newsletter covers topics related to spinal cord injury (SCI) for both health care providers and consumers. Contact: http://depts.washington.edu/rehab/sci/update.shtml. Subscribe scirehab@u.washington.edu.

National Council on Disability

The *NCD Bulletin*, a monthly publication of the National Council on Disability (NCD), is free of charge and is also available in alternative formats on the Internet (http://www.ncd.gov). It brings you the latest issues and news affecting individuals with disabilities. Contact:

National Council on Disability
1331 F St. NW, Suite 850
Washington, DC 20004-1107
(202) 272-2004 (Voice)
(202) 272-2074 (TT)
Fax: 202-272-2022
http://www.ncd.gov

Information from HEATH National Clearinghouse on Postsecondary Education for Individuals with Disabilities

This newsletter is published three times a year. Contact:

The George Washington University
HEATH Resource Center
2121 K St. NW, Suite 220
Washington, DC 20037
(202) 973-0904 (Voice/TTY)
(800) 544-3284
Fax: 202-973-0908
E-mail: askheath@heath.gwu.edu

Viatical Settlements

A viatical settlement is a unique financial resource that allows individuals facing a life-threatening illness to sell their life insurance policy for cash, which can then be utilized for treatment and resources required as a result of the disability. For more information:

American Council on Life Insurance
1001 Pennsylvania Ave. NW
Washington, DC 20004-2599

National Association of Insurance Commissioners
444 North Capitol St. NW
Washington, DC 20001

National Viatical Association
1200 G St. NW, Suite 760
Washington, DC 20005

North American Securities Administrators Association
10 G St. NE, Suite 710
Washington, DC 20002

Viatical Association of America
1200 19th St. NW, Suite 300
Washington, DC 20036

Viatical and Life Settlement Association of America
viatical@cfl.rr.com

Through the Looking Glass: Resources for Parents with Disabilities

Persons with disabilities still experience discrimination when it comes to everyday issues, even such basic issues as the human rights associated with reproduction. The ability of mothers with a disability to care for their babies is questioned by health care professionals and the general population. Through the Looking Glass is a nonprofit organization founded by Megan Kirschbaum in Berkeley, CA, in 1982. It focuses on preventative services, professional training, and research concerning families with a disability or medical issue for either parent or child. Contact:

Through the Looking Glass
2198 Sixth St., Suite 100
Berkeley, CA 94710-2204
(800) 644-2666
TLG@lookingglass.org.

Telecommunications Accessibility

With the advent of the ADA, each state was required to implement a telecommunications system that is accessible to people with disabilities. In Florida, for example, Florida Telecommunications Relay, Inc. (FTRI), is a not-for-profit organization that administers a statewide Specialized Telecommunications Equipment Distribution Program for hearing-impaired, dual sensory-impaired (hearing and vision), and speech-impaired Florida citizens. The equipment provided through this program is loaned to all qualified citizens for as long as they need it, at no charge. The FTRI program provides basic access to the telecommunications network as mandated by the Telecommunications Access System Act of 1991 (TASA), Chapter 417, Section III, Florida Statutes.

Every state must have some type of system in place to provide accessible telecommunications. Contact your local telephone service information system, usually located inside the front cover of your local telephone book.

To learn more about Telecommunications Relay Service (TRS), visit the FCC's website at www.fcc.gov/cgb/dro/ trs.html. You can also contact:

Federal Communications Commission
Consumer & Governmental Affairs Bureau
445 12th St SW
Washington, DC 20554
(888) CALL-FCC (888-225-5322)
(888) TELL-FCC (888-835-5322) (TTY)
www.fcc.gov/cgb/

Directory for Exceptional Children

The *Directory for Exceptional Children* is an excellent resource that reflects the growing recognition of the multidimensional needs of exceptional children. Since the organization's beginning in 1954, each subsequent edition has grown. This is a resource for both families and professionals, with listings encompassing the entire range of developmental, organic, and emotional handicaps. Each listing conforms to a standardized format, making it convenient for referencing and easy comparison of programs.

The 14th edition of the *Directory* (2002) is a comprehensive survey of 2500 schools, facilities, and organizations across the U.S. serving children and young adults with developmental, emotional, physical, and medical disabilities. With 15 distinct chapters covering a range of disabilities, this work is an invaluable aid to parents and professionals seeking the optimal environment for special needs children.

Directory for Exceptional Children, 14th edition
$75, 1056 pages, 2001–2002
Porter Sargent Publishers Inc.
11 Beacon St., Suite 1400
Boston, MA 02108
(617) 523-1670
Fax: 617-523-1021
info@portersargent.com

Guide to Summer Camps and Summer Schools

The 28th edition covers the broad spectrum of recreational and educational summer opportunities. Facts from 1100 camps and schools, as well as programs for those with special needs or learning disabilities, make the *Guide* a comprehensive and convenient resource.

$27 paper, $45 cloth, 640 pages

Porter Sargent Publishers, Inc.
c/o IDS
300 Bedford St., Building B, Ste. 213
Manchester, NH 03101
800-342-7470
www.portersargent.com

GENERAL INFORMATION SOURCES

Topics in Spinal Cord Injury Rehabilitation

This journal is published quarterly by Thomas Land, www.thomasland.com. This is a peer-reviewed topical journal devoted to multidisciplinary commentary on the management of persons with disability because of an insult to the spinal cord. The topics presented are current on the treatment of patients with spinal paralysis. A special issue on life care planning, co-edited by Terry Winkler, M.D., and James S. Krause, Ph.D., is Volume 7, Number 4, published in Spring 2002.

Exceptional Parent: The Magazine for Families and Professionals

This magazine is published 12 times per year by Psy-Ed Corp., dba *Exceptional Parent Magazine*, 209 Harvard St., Ste. 303, Brookline, MA 2146-5005; (800) 562-1973 or (800) 247-8080. www.Eparent.com.

Yearly technology/communication/education issues are included with a subscription to the *Exceptional Parent*. This magazine is a must for any professional working with pediatrics. Not only are the magazines stocked with informative articles, but the resource sections alone are worth a subscription.

The Neurolaw Letter

This monthly newsletter is a must-read for attorneys and health care professionals involved in brain injury litigation. Each month, *The Neurolaw Letter* provides practice points, trial techniques, marketing strategies, and hands-on tips that are of immediate benefit to practitioners in this emerging area of jurisprudence. Issue after issue, some of the most respected legal and medical professionals in the field of brain injury offer their insights to recognizing, evaluating, and litigating these challenging cases. Subscription includes a three-ring binder. The annual subscription rate is $96 (12 monthly issues). Contact: http://www.braininjury-books.com/legal.html.

OTHER SOURCES

The sources mentioned in this chapter are certainly not a complete list of all resources available. The authors' goal was to present some sources of information that may not be commonly known among life care planning/case management professionals. Not mentioned, of course, are the vast resources available through the Internet. There have been entire books written on the sources that can be obtained through the Internet. For example, Ahab Press publishes an Internet guide that can be obtained through www.ahabpress.com.

A chapter on sources would not be complete without mentioning some of the authoritative data available pertaining to life care planning/case management. Certainly, *A Guide to Rehabilitation*, by Paul M. Deutsch and Horace Sawyer cannot be overlooked. This book, updated yearly, was formerly published by Matthew Bender, Inc., and is now published by Ahab Press, Inc., 2 Gannett Dr., Suite 102, White Plains, NY 10604; (914) 644-7400 or www.ahabpress.com.

Journal of Life Care Planning

This journal is dedicated to the professionals involved in life care planning. It is published by Elliott & Fitzpatrick, Inc., Athens, GA (http://www.elliottfitz-patrick.com/ or 706-548-8161). Life care planning has evolved into a complex and advanced specialty practice. The goal of this journal is to serve as a vehicle for promoting education and advanced practice. (Editor: Patricia McCollom, M.S., R.N., C.R.R.N., C.D.M.S., C.C.M., C.L.C.P.; LifeCare Economics, Ltd., Ankeny IA.) (Editor's note: A subscription to the *Journal* is included with the annual subscription to the International Academy of Life Care Planning, www.ialcp.com.)

Training/Certification in Life Care Planning

There is now a certification for life care planners (certified life care planner, or CLCP), which issued its first certification in March 1996. The certification is through the Commission on Health Care Certification (CHCC). Specific information on the CLCP examination can be obtained through V. Robert May III, Rh.D., Commissioner of Research and Statistics, (804) 272-9192 or www.cdec1.com. Also see Chapter 32 in this text.

CONCLUSION

This chapter on resources is designed to provide the life care planner with basic information to be prepared for the circumstances that occur in our profession. The heart and soul of the life care planning process is the ability to quickly and efficiently locate resources. Preparedness is the key to a successful life care planning experience.

APPENDIX A

Appendix A is designed to be a questionnaire format used when querying home health agencies on the services available and the related costs.

Nursing Research Format

Provider:

Telephone: _____ Fax: _____

Contact: _____ Title: _____

Areas of Service (Counties):

_____

_____

Is there a mileage charge in addition to hourly? ___Yes ___No. If Yes: ____/Mile

Rates: (Private-pay rate for all costs: ___Yes ___No)

HHA/hour: $_____ $_____ $_____

HHA/visit: $_____ $_____ $_____

LPN/hour: $_____ $_____ $_____

LPN/visit: $_____ $_____ $_____

RN/hour: $_____ $_____ $_____

RN/visit: $_____ $_____ $_____

Minimum # of hours per visit: _____

Live-in: ___Yes ___No Daily rate: $_____

Number of hands-on care hours per day with a live-in: _____

Number of uninterrupted sleep hours for a live-in per night: _____

Definition of live-in services as defined by this specific agency:

_____

_____

When was the last time this agency actually supplied a live-in? _____

_____

_____

Case Manager: $_____/hour

Therapies:

PT ___ Yes ___No $_____/visit

OT ___ Yes ___No $_____/visit

ST ___ Yes ___No $_____/visit

Recreational therapy: ___Yes___No $_____/visit

Other:

_____

_____

Nursing Research Format (Continued)

Transportation:

Can staff member transport patient? ___Yes ___No

Personal car? ___Yes ___No   Patient's car: ___Yes ___No

Skill Responsibilities:

Can Aide level:

Administer medications: ___Yes ___ No

Perform bowel stimulation: ___Yes ___ No

Administer G-tube feeds: ___Yes ___ No

Insert catheter: ___Yes ___ No

Trim finger/toe nails: ___Yes ___ No

Can LPN level:

Perform trach care: ___ Yes ___ No

Perform vent care: ___ Yes ___ No

Trim finger/toe nails: ___ Yes ___ No

An agency may have a policy that aides, trained by RNs, can do certain invasive procedures such as bowel stimulation, catheter changes, etc. Under this arrangement, it is the specific RN training the aide who is ultimately liable and responsible for the activities of the aide. *Therefore, in this agency, in practice, are the aides performing such services in their day-to-day activities?*

Is RN Supervision (included with):

   Live-in or aide care: one visit/_____ (week/month/quarter)

   LPN care: one visit/_____ (week/month/quarter)

Is there an extra charge for the RN supervision visit? ___Yes ___ No
If Yes: $_____/visit

Comments:

_____

_____

_____

Research By: _____ Date: _____

31

MEDICAL EQUIPMENT CHOICES AND THE ROLE OF THE REHAB EQUIPMENT SPECIALIST IN LIFE CARE PLANNING

Paul Amsterdam

INTRODUCTION

The importance of medical equipment in the life care plan has always been a function of the physical impairment of the individual client. The greater one's physical impairments, the more dependent he or she will be on medical equipment and other assistive technology.

This chapter will address the need for accurate assessments of rehab medical equipment in a life care plan. It discusses the various factors that must be considered in choosing the correct models and types of equipment. Common errors of equipment planning are noted from the author's experience in reviewing life care plans, with some solutions toward achieving more accurate results. The role of the rehab equipment specialist (rehab technology supplier or assistive technology supplier, RTS or ATS) is also discussed as a beneficial tool to the life care planner.

Medical equipment has parameters different from other factors of a life care plan. In almost all cases of permanent disability, if there is a need for certain medical equipment at the start of the plan, that expense will continue throughout the client's life expectancy. Medical equipment choices are a very dynamic function of a life care plan as well. Allowances must be made for changes in the type of equipment that will be needed. Some of these changes in equipment will be due to the aging of a client, while others from expected physical deterioration of the client. A good example of the latter is the overuse syndrome that becomes common in spinal cord injury clients after years of propelling a manual wheelchair (O'Leary and Sarkarati, 2000).

0-8493-1511-5/04/$0.00+$1.50
© 2004 by CRC Press LLC

Allowances must also be made for the repair and eventual replacement of each piece of equipment. Maintenance and replacement schedules vary for different types of equipment, and factors such as manufacturer's warranty, daily expected usage, and a client's environment will all play a part in assessing these variables. Maintenance and replacement schedules will be addressed later in this chapter.

Medical equipment is only one area of assistive technology that should be considered for an individual client. According to the Technology-Related Assistance for Individuals with Disabilities Act of 1988 (Tech Act), an assistive technology device is "any item, piece of equipment, or product system, whether acquired commercially, off the shelf, modified, or customized, that is used to increase, maintain, or improve the functional capabilities of individuals with disabilities." Other areas of assistive technology, such as augmentative and assistive communication systems, environmental control units, computer interface technology, and visual impairment technology may also be needed and considered for the client, but are not primarily discussed in this chapter.

FACTORS IN CHOOSING MEDICAL EQUIPMENT

The predominant factor in choosing the correct medical equipment will be the client's *diagnosis* and overall medical assessment. A chronic lumbar sprain requires little in the area of assistive technology, whereas a spinal cord injury resulting in some level of paralysis may require considerable equipment depending on the extent of the injury. The need for equipment is somewhat commensurate with the level of the spinal cord injury. The higher the overall break in the neurological pathway, the more severe the client's physical involvement; consequently, there will be greater reliance on assistive technology to solve mobility, activities of daily living (ADL), and other day-to-day independent functions.

Another factor in equipment needs is the *age* of the client. As previously noted, equipment will change as an individual ages, not only due to physical deterioration, but also as an individual's lifestyle changes. The 4-year-old born with cerebral palsy may start childhood using a therapeutic stroller for mobility, grow into a pediatric tilt-in-space manual wheelchair, and then through increased function, graduate into a motorized wheelchair.

This also leads to another factor in determining correct equipment. What are the *mobility needs* for a particular client? Is the client able to manually propel a manual wheelchair, or is powered mobility going to be the primary option for independence? If an attendant must push the client, will a standard wheelchair frame meet her needs, or will she require something more specialized, such as a reclining or tilt-in-space wheelchair frame.

Often overlooked factors in determining the correct choice in equipment are the *environment and lifestyle* of an individual client. The equipment required for a T2 paraplegic who is living independently in a rural or urban environment, and has a full-time vocation, will be vastly different than that for a client with the same level of injury who resides in a skilled nursing facility with no occupation. Environment and lifestyle must also be considered when estimating correct replacement schedules for a client's wheelchair, which will be discussed later in this chapter.

COMMON ERRORS IN EQUIPMENT RECOMMENDATIONS

The author has reviewed many life care plans for several years. The two most common errors found in the equipment recommendations are *omissions and exaggeration of need.*

Omissions

Omissions of equipment in a life care plan, especially in the plan created for the plaintiff, will hurt the client twofold. Primarily, by not including a needed type of equipment, the cost allowance for that equipment is not included in the client's immediate assistive technology needs. The omission is then multiplied as many as five times the current amount, by not being part of the economist's computations for replacements of the omitted item.

Omissions hurt the client in another way. A good life care plan is not just a list of medical costs, but as stated in the Life Care Planning Survey of 2002 is "a comprehensive plan for meeting the individualized and complex service needs resulting from the onset of a disability" (Neulicht et al., 2002). An omission of a certain type of assistive technology may lead a client away from a certain therapeutic road. For instance, the omission of any standing therapeutic aid from the plan for a quadriplegic may never guide the client toward a type of therapy that can be an important part of his daily life. As the benefits of standing have been shown to lessen the possibilities of skin breakdown, osteoporosis, and urinary tract infection, among other things (Stewart, 1992), the omission of the equipment needed for this therapy may very well alter the client's future physical health and need for additional medical services.

It should be noted that an omission in the plaintiff's plan does not necessarily mean the equipment should then be omitted in the defense plan. On the contrary, an objective plan should include all needed equipment necessary for proper functioning for the client, regardless of which side created the plan. In Glynn and Davis's (2001) article on physician-directed plans, they state there should be "no more variation from case to case" (whether plaintiff or defense requested).

How Do You Avoid Omissions?

A good first source to help objectively set some equipment choices for a life care plan is the expected functional outcomes tables assembled by the Consortium for Spinal Cord Medicine (1999). These tables delineate between different spinal cord levels of injury and what probable equipment would be needed for a variety of functional activities. These tables, however, are specifically limited to spinal cord diagnoses, and equipment choices are made in general terms, not specific ones.

Another way life care planners can avoid costly omissions in the type of equipment needed is to trace a day-in-the-life-of for their client. The idea here is to try and picture how the client must go through every aspect of her day.

When she wakes up in the morning, can she lift herself out of bed? If so, how? Does he require any sort of assistance, either a trapeze bar or safety rail, off the side of the bed?

Can transfers be done independently with the use of a transfer board, or is a caregiver required to use a hydraulic patient lift and sling?

Can she dress herself? Can she button her own shirts and zip her own pants? How does she get to the closet or drawers to get the clothes in the first place?

Specific questions should be asked as the client goes into every room in his house. Functional mobility, independence in activities of daily living, transportation, and bathroom safety must all be reviewed as the client goes through his daily routine. Vocational and quality of life interests must also be addressed to avoid costly omissions. Pressure relief issues, both in sitting and in the bed, must be reviewed; in addition, possible adjunct home exercise and therapies should be addressed. As each area of functional dependence is noted, there are a variety of equipment choices that can then be made.

Problems in Wheelchair Choice

The most common instances for omissions occur in the area of wheelchair choice. Because of the amount of complex variables when evaluating a client for a wheelchair, the lifetime choices of models and needed accessories must be examined carefully. There are many different types of manual wheelchairs: standard frames, lightweight, ultralight frames, and rigid ultralights. This does not include the more specialized frames such as recliners, super-low hemi-frames, and adult and pediatric tilt-in-space wheelchairs.

Motorized wheelchairs also are incredibly varied in model and overall function. As an example, in the year 2002, the three largest manufacturers of motorized wheelchairs in this country had over 40 distinct models (source: order forms from Invacare Corporation, Sunrise Medical, Pride Mobility). The price of these chairs ranged from $3000 to $30,000. If you are creating a plaintiff's plan, do all your spinal cord injuries get a $30,000 chair? Likewise, can the defense hold that the least expensive $3000 chair will meet all clients' power mobility needs?

The answer, of course, is that neither side should delegate choice of model by overall cost. Every client has a range of correct possible wheelchair models that must suit his or her physical and mobility needs. It is a function of the life care planner to determine either through his own research or the use of outside experts the correct types of wheelchairs needed and to be able to defend those choices.

Wheelchair Choices

For the purpose of funding durable medical equipment, the federal government's Medicare program created different allowances with numerical procedure codes to describe (and pay) for the different types of wheelchairs. These descriptive codes have now been almost universally used by most of the managed care organizations as a basis for their method of payment for wheelchairs. The codes (although we are not interested in the allowable prices associated with them) are a good method of breaking down wheelchairs into different descriptive categories for the life care planner to utilize as well. The planner should make an examination of her particular client's physical limitations, in regards to the choice of the correct wheelchair category.

Table 31.1 Manual Wheelchair Bases

Code Type	Description	Utilization	Samples/Price Range
K0001 — Standard wheelchair	Weight > 36 pounds Width = 16 or 18 inches Depth = 16 inches Arms = fixed or detachable Footrests = fixed of or swing-away	Clients who ambulate or are capable of standing pivot transfer; inexpensive choice for those who are not dependent on a wheelchair as their primary means of mobility, or must be pushed by care giver	Standard frame from all manufacturers — Invacare Tracers, E&J Vista, and Traveler From $300–700
K0002 — Hemi (low-seat) wheelchair	Weight > 36 pounds Seat height = 17 or 18 inches Width = 16 or 18 inches Depth = 16 inches Arms = fixed or detachable Footrests = swing-away	Primary need for clients with hemiplegia; enables client to propel chair with one or both feet	Invacare Tracer EX From $500–750
K0004 — High-strength lightweight frame	Weight < 34 pounds Width = Variable Depth = 14 or 16 inches Lifetime warranty on side frame and cross-braces Back height = adjustable	For individuals who are unable to functionally propel a standard manual frame; excellent choice for older client or for nonpropellers with older caregivers who must lift chair	Invacare 9000 XT Quickie Breezy Series From $850+
K0005 — Ultralight frame	Weight < 30 pounds Width = Variable Depth = Variable Lifetime warranty on side frame and cross-braces Adjustable rear-axle system	For highly active wheelchair user; spinal cord injuries, spina bifida, or any other client using a manual wheelchair as his or her primary means of mobility	Quickie 2 Quickie GPV and R2 Invacare MVP Invacare A4 and A6 All Tisport/Tilite Wheelchairs From $1600+
K0009 — Other manual wheelchair bases	May include tilt-in-space wheelchair frames or other custom-designed frames to meet individual needs	Clients with significant positioning issues, presssure issues, limitations in range of motion	Invacare Solara Quickie TS Freedom Design Libre From $3000+ (does not include a seating system)

Table 31.2 Motorized/Power Wheelchair Bases

Code Type	Description	Utilization	Samples/Price Range
K0010 — Standard–weight motorized wheelchairs	Frame = nonfolding Electronics = little adjustablitiy or prgrammability	Client is not able to functionally ambulate or propel a manual wheelchair; client should have good upper-extremity control without cause for future progression	Invacare Pronto M50
K0011 — Standard-weight motorized wheelchair with programmable controls	Electronics must have significant programmability to adjust parameters for speed, tremor dampening, acceleration, and braking; allows for advanced switch options	Clients with upper-extremity tone or spasticity problems; clients with a progressive disorder that neccessitates changing the parameters of the controls periodically; clients who cannot use other options	Invacare Storm Series Wheelchairs (Torque, Ranger, E&J Solaire) Quickie Models S-525 or 626 and Freestyle Pride 1121 or 1122 From $6000+
K0012 — Lightweight Portable Motorized Wheelchairs	Weight < 80 pounds Must include folding back or a collapsable frame	Excellent choice for clients with minimal power mobility needs but for some ease in transportation	Invacare Nutron R32LX/R50LX Quickie V-121 E&J Metro Power From $3600+
K0014 — Other motorized/power wheelchair bases	Motorized wheelchairs with advanced electronics to accommodate alternative drive controls or power-actuated seating systems	Additional therapeutic or pressure issues that neccessitate alternative power-actuated systems and drive controls	Invacare Arrow and TDX5 Pride Quantom models Quicke P-222 and S-646 Permobil Chairman From $15,000+

Questions to Consider

- Can the client functionally propel a manual wheelchair?
- Will the use of a lighter-weight frame benefit her overall mobility?
- Before advancing to a motorized chair, will the use of the manual wheelchair provide the client with his most probable means toward daily exercise, continued range of motion, and easier accessibility throughout his home, workplace, and via transportation?
- Will the client require customized programming or the use of specialized switches (i.e., sip and puff, head arrays) that necessitate a motorized wheelchair with higher-end electronic capabilities?
- Would the need for power-actuated positioning systems such as power recline, power tilt in space, or a standing frame be substantiated, or would these functions be generally unused by the client and perhaps just make the chair overly heavy and cumbersome (not to mention far more expensive)?

Accessories Required

By far the greatest omission seen in life care plans for wheelchair considerations is in the area of accessories. All of us have had the experience of wanting to buy a large item, such as an automobile. We may first be attracted to an ad claiming a very low sticker price. After going to the retailer, reviewing options and accessories, you could not drive out of the showroom without the automobile, now costing you sometimes thousands of dollars more. There is little difference when having to purchase a new wheelchair, only in the case of the wheelchair, many of those options may truly be a medical necessity for the overall function of your client. These accessories fall into the following adjunct consideration categories.

Pressure Reduction. There are currently over 200 different wheelchair cushions on the market today. The prices of these may range from $20 to $2000. In my experience, few will benefit from the quality of a $20 cushion, but just as few would ever require cushions in the $2000 category. One excellent guide to proper cushion choice is the use of a skin assessment system, such as the Braden scale. When skin risk is determined, the range and type of possible cushion choices can be both narrowed down and substantiated.

When noting a cushion for the life care report, like the wheelchair itself, a replacement schedule must be set up. Inexpensive foam cushions will have a far shorter replacement life than some of the more expensive pressure equalization cushions, such as a Roho or Jay 2. It should be noted that many of the higher-priced cushions have far longer warranties as well. On many life care plans, I have often seen replacement of a Roho cushion after only 2 years, when the manufacturer fully warranties this product for the same 2 years. Additional cushion covers should also be taken into account. Providing an extra cover initially with a cushion will substantially extend the overall replacement needs for the cushion, as well as provide for needed cleanliness issues.

Custom Therapeutic Seating Systems. Many clients require the use of therapeutic seating in the wheelchair. Limits in range of motion, weaknesses or excessive muscle tone, trunk instability, or spinal deformities may all necessitate adding some range of customized seat and back systems. This may include other features, such as thoracic or pelvic supports, abductor wedges, chest harness, specialized head supports, or upper-extremity support trays.

How much therapeutic seating your individual client will need may be something the life care planner should research with that client's former therapists or other rehab technology seating specialists, before noting it in the life care plan. (Also see section on utilizing references and outside experts at end of chapter.)

Prices for seating systems may be as low as $400 or over $6000. In many cases it is equal to or more than the frame of the wheelchair. It should require references to modifications for growth, repairs, and replacements. Consequently, this is one aspect of the equipment report that cannot be omitted.

Mobility and Accessibility Features. Many of the features we commonly see on a wheelchair, such as the armrests and footrests are not necessarily included in the base price of the wheelchair. Some chair models may include some of these as standard features, but there is a good chance the accessories needed by your client will not be the standard styles provided. A particular model of ultralight wheelchairs may have as many as six to eight different armrests or footrest configurations to choose from. This may add an additional $175 to $400 to the price of the chair.

The choice of wheels will vary from molded composite to lightweight spoke wheels. The choice of tires and front casters can make significant changes in both a wheelchair's performance and cost. Standard hand rims are made of either chrome or aluminum, but vinyl- or plastic-coated are also available. Projection hand rims in both vertical and offset styles may be a medical necessity for clients with limited fine-motor coordination. As noted on an ultralight wheelchair order form from TiSport Corporation, there is currently a set of ultralight, highly durable wheel spokes under the brand name Spinergy that will add over $600 to the base price of a wheelchair, but may greatly enhance the suspension and mobility for some active clients.

Some mobility and accessibility features for motorized wheelchairs are not so obvious. One particular feature commonly recommended is a swing-away joystick mount. Without this device, most clients using a motorized wheelchair would be unable to bring the chair up to a dining table or desk. The device will in turn add an additional $300 to $400 to the base price of the power chair. Some clients may also benefit from a power seat actuator. At the push of a lever, this system will allow the seat of the power chair to raise about 8 to 11 inches from its standard height to enable the client to reach items that would normally be inaccessible.

Safety Features. Most accessories needed for wheelchair safety are usually not that expensive, but one would be negligent to omit them in the wheelchair order. Seat belts and chest harnesses may be the first items that come to mind, but certainly most common is a pair of rear antitipping levers. As wheelchairs have gotten lighter and more adjustable, the antitippers have become more of a safety necessity. Clients who are amputees may also benefit from a chair that has been modified with amputee adapters to change the center of gravity on the rear wheels.

Convenience and ADL Features. There are many accessories that may not be considered medical necessities, yet greatly enhance a person's ability to carry on with normal activities of daily living. One must remember that a life care plan should reflect all necessary items and that services reflect their needs with consideration for the jurisdiction.

Some items that come to mind are backpacks and seat pouches for the client to easily carry items. Also available are fold-up luggage carriers and cup holders. For those who use a pair of crutches or cane for short-distance ambulation, a crutch or cane holder becomes a needed feature. One item overlooked in many life care plans for clients who actively propel wheelchairs is a good pair of wheelchair gloves. As the active user will wear out gloves quickly, at least two pairs per year should be allowed for in a plan.

Exaggeration of Needs

The second common error regarding equipment choices in a life care plan is exaggeration of needs. Gass and Gonzalez (2001) in their article discuss the overall effects of gross exaggeration to a life care plan. Where omissions may affect a plan by not allowing for certain needed equipment or specific features, gross exaggerations of equipment needs may affect the overall credibility of the entire life care plan.

A life care planner is not necessarily basing his equipment choices strictly on medical necessity, but must be able to justify these choices in relationship to the functional needs and abilities of his client. For example, it would be difficult to justify a $12,000 alternating-pressure/low-air-loss mattress replacement system for a client with full skin sensation, ability to independently weight shift and transfer, and no previous history of skin breakdown. Likewise, an expensive high-performance ultralight titanium wheelchair is not the proper choice for a client who does not have the cognitive ability to self-propel a manual wheelchair.

As previously noted, the choices and price range of motorized wheelchairs are enormous. Unfortunately, this seems to encourage some in life care planning to pick only from the top end of this range, without regard to true individual need. This author has had to write an opinion on a plaintiff's life care plan that recommended a $30,000 motorized wheelchair with a power-actuated standing frame for a client who independently stands and ambulates with forearm crutches throughout his residence. It would only take a few examples of this type of gross exaggeration for a defense attorney to question the credibility of all the equipment choices and perhaps the credibility of the life care planner.

SETTING STANDARDS OF PROTOCOL FOR REPLACEMENT SCHEDULES OF MEDICAL EQUIPMENT IN A LIFE CARE PLAN

One controversial factor in life care plans has been the replacement schedule allowances for medical equipment (R. Weed, personal communication, April 20, 2002). As it is fundamental that all equipment has a useable life expectancy, when listing medical equipment for a life care plan, it is likewise fundamental that each piece of equipment has a noted replacement schedule. This is especially true of the more major purchases such as beds, pressure support systems, and wheelchairs.

How crucial is the accuracy of the figures? As an example, consider the case of a 25-year-old tetraplegic who has a life care plan that lists a motorized wheelchair with a power-actuated tilt-in-space system and standing features, programmable controls, and other needed accessories. The manufacturer's list price is noted at $31,000. One life care planner projects replacement of the chair every 4 years, while the other life care planner says every 5 years. Based on a life expectancy of 69 years, the former planner allows for 10 replacement chairs; the latter only 8. The overall difference between the life care plans would be $62,000. This of course is not discounted to present value and does not take the economist's adjustments for inflation into account.

Even with less expensive equipment, such as a Jay pressure relief cushion with a list price of $425, the differences in replacement allowances can show some significant variances. In reviewing plans, the author has observed that replacement for these cushions ranges from 2 to 5 years. Continuing to use the above-noted client as an example, the 5-year allowance equates to eight replacement cushions at a total plan cost of $3400. The 2-year allowance equates to 20 replacement cushions at a total price of $8500 (not discounted to present value), for a difference of $5100 between the two plans.

Even more problematic than the variance in costs between plans is the lack of any accurate standards to compute replacement allowances. This lack of any prescribed standards can easily allow an attorney to question not only the accuracy of the replacement costs of a particular plan, but also the accuracy of the methods of computation for all other medical equipment costs and allowances.

So what factors must be taken into account when figuring replacement schedules for equipment? The first factor to consider is the manufacturer's warranty of the particular piece of equipment being recommended. The implied expectation of any warranty is that the piece of equipment will last throughout the length of the warranty period. If the equipment is defective, the warranty allows for replacement or compensation with little to no cost to the user. In our homes most of us utilize equipment far beyond the expiration of the manufacturer's warranty. It is not uncommon to have the same refrigerator, stove, or washer for over 10 years, while the warranty on these items may expire after only 1 year.

In the author's experience, many life care plans include replacements of certain items that do not even meet or barely exceed the manufacturer's warranty of the product. The aforementioned Jay cushion has a complete replacement warranty (other than the cover) for up to 2 years, and if properly maintained (occasional cleaning and kneading of the gel pad and replacements of covers), the cushion's life expectancy should at least double the warranty.

Most items referred to as durable medical equipment are well described. That is to say, they are quite durable. Most standard commodes, tub rails, tub benches, and folding walkers have a lifetime warranty; however, it should be noted that a lifetime warranty does not preclude a replacement allowance for these items. Over a period of time, any of these items will show excessive wear and tear. This is particularly true of any items with many moving parts that will become shaky with time, or items that have padding that can eventually tear or wear out. Some pieces of equipment such as a trapeze bar attached to a floor stand are so durable and their everyday usage sufficiently limited that their replacement can safely be expected to last 10 years or more.

In addition to the warranty and its relationship to replacement allowances, the life care planner must also take into account the need for repairs and maintenance to a piece of equipment. A pair of forearm crutches should last a client 3 years, but the crutch tips will have to be replaced perhaps twice a year. The Jay pressure relief cushion previously referenced has a longer life than many allow for, but the removable covers should be replaced yearly. (A better strategy is to allow for the purchase of two covers when first buying a cushion, in order to alternate their use while cleaning, and then allow for twice the replacement time, i.e., 2 years for each cover.)

Repairs vs. replacement becomes a far more complicated equation when one is considering more complex pieces of equipment with more parts, such as manual wheelchairs or power-actuated products, like electric hospital beds, air-powered support surfaces, and motorized wheelchairs.

When including a hospital bed in a life care plan, it is important to note that hospital beds have a lifetime warranty on all the welds of their frame (Invacare Corporation and Graham-Field, Inc., product warranty information, 2002). It is extremely rare for these frames to require repairs. Conversely, the mechanisms for adjustment, such as the shafts, motors, and hand controls, will require repair or replacement, and an allowance for maintenance should be made. Likewise, the mattress should be replaced every 4 to 5 years. There are certain factors that must be taken into account, such as the weight of the client, the daily usage of the bed (for less active clients), and the use of higher-end support surfaces or flotation mattresses that either put less stress on the mattress itself or entirely replace the standard hospital bed mattress. (The author has seen a number of life care plans allowing for replacement of hospital bed mattresses when the client is using none.)

Wheelchairs categorized as high-strength lightweight or ultralight must have a lifetime warranty on the side frame and cross-braces (Centers for Medicare and Medicaid Services, 2002). The other working parts of the chair are usually covered by a limited warranty of 1 year, excluding wear and tear or abuse. (The manufacturer many times upon return of a broken or defective part will determine if there was abuse of the product.) Likewise, there is a minimum of a 5-year to lifetime warranty for the frame of a motorized wheelchair, and the electrical components all have a life expectancy minimum of 1 to 2 years (Invacare Corporation, Sunrise Medical, and Pride Mobility Products Corporation product warranty information, 2002). When recommending either a manual or motorized wheelchair, the life care planner should include maintenance and repair allowances, but after time must consider that the frequency of repairs and the overall wear on the frame will necessitate a replacement of the equipment.

Determining the replacement allowance for a wheelchair is a process that currently seems to lack any standardization or protocol. In Kendall and Deutsch's (2002) article on research methodology, the authors state that life care planning is a "standardized process" (p. 158). They further assert that, "If Life Care Planning is a reliable tool in Case Management and the provision of patient care, then the results of a given LCP can be consistently replicated" (p. 157).

However, in reviewing life care plans, the author has observed that similar models of wheelchairs may be assigned a replacement with as little as 2 years or as great as every 10 years. Although there may be a valid reason for the 10-year replacement, such as a rarely used backup chair, the plan rarely includes any notation as to the justification for a replacement number given. As shown in the examples given in the beginning of the article, these variances, when multiplied by a young client's life expectancy, can add up to significant cost differences in opposing plans.

There are a variety of factors that will have an effect on the replacement allowance for a wheelchair. Some of these factors will reduce the life of a chair, while others will add to its life. It is necessary for the life care planner to consider which factors are inherent in an individual client's lifestyle and account for those factors in the life care plan. By using a standardized format, taking the factors noted below into a weighted scale for replacement allowance, both greater reliability for the individual life care plan and greater consistency, reliability, and validity for the life care planning process as a whole should be achieved.

Contributing Factors to Replacement Time for Wheelchairs

Age

The age of the client is the first contributing factor. Everyone's general activity level differs throughout different age ranges. The greater the activity level of an individual, the more wear and tear on the frame of a wheelchair.

Most children (4 to 16 years) are very active, and those children who are wheelchair dependent are no exception. They usually are attending school 5 days a week, and when not in classrooms, most are playing with other children. Athletic programs now include children in wheelchairs in a large variety of games and events. The Special Olympics and other athletic associations for children with disabilities are a part of many school and recreation programs nationwide.

Moreover, children grow. Growth is a factor that must be addressed in each child on an annual basis. This is not to say a child will require a replacement of the wheelchair each year, because the majority of pediatric wheelchair frames are built with adjustability for growth. A qualified RTS or ATS will always try to allow for a maximum amount of growth in relationship to the current measurements of a child. Sometimes, a child's measurements fall between two sizes of wheelchair frames, and less growth must be allowed for proper propulsion of a manual wheelchair. This is less of a concern in motorized wheelchairs, where the ability to reach a joystick is far more adjustable than the ability to properly reach two hand rims. In the author's experience, pediatric wheelchair frames generally will last the child from 4 to 5 years, with growth being modified and accounted for.

Growth also must be accounted for not just in the frame of a wheelchair, but also in any custom seating system for children. This too is easily accomplished through quality evaluations performed by rehabilitation professionals when first designing the seating system. All seating systems should have about 4 to 5 years of growth built into them. One exception to this rule is custom-molded seating systems, such as Contour U™ or the Otto Bock OBSS™ systems. As these systems are created utilizing an actual body mold of the child, there is far less available growth that can be built into them.

Young adults (ages 16 to 30) are also highly active, and from the teens through the early 20s, the average individual is still attending school. Many are propelling for longer distances, especially throughout college campuses. In general, this age group is far less sedentary, and the population who are wheelchair dependent are now spending far more of their time with able-bodied friends and out in the community than ever in the past. Most are in the same wheelchair for as much as 18 hours per day, 7 days per week. Some also have become involved in wheelchair sports on a far more aggressive level (although the more serious of these athletes will probably purchase or utilize a separate sports wheelchair for their particular game). Again, the greater the activity level, the more wear on the wheelchair overall.

Adults (ages 30 to 65) in general will tend to have a bit lower activity level. Many wheelchair-dependent individuals will be married, have families, and spend more time at home. Many who are working in offices are indoors in more confined spaces throughout the day, putting far less stress on the wheelchair frame. This is not to say that many individuals of this age range are not active in the community or their careers, but the stress on the wheelchair in this type of lifestyle is far less.

Senior citizens (over 65) as a rule have a lower activity level. Many who are using manual wheelchairs (even lightweight frames) may not have the endurance or strength as they age to manually propel the chair long distances or in more difficult outdoor environments. Many may not be able to self-propel at all and are pushed by an attendant. With such a lower activity level, the replacement schedule for the wheelchair should obviously decrease.

Environment

Where the wheelchair is being used will also affect its replacement allowance. A suburban and urban environment where there are mostly paved sidewalks, graded curb cuts between streets, and, thanks to the Americans with Disabilities Act, far more wheelchair-accessible buildings, puts only limited fatigue on the wheelchair. Clients who live in a more rural environment, with far less of the above-noted accommodations, will fatigue the frames of their chairs quicker. Hills, rocks, and soft earth not only put more wear and tear on the frame, but also require more frequent repairs to the chair.

On the other hand, individuals who live in a skilled nursing facility will put far less stress on the wheelchair. The linoleum floors, fully accessible environment, and inferred lower activity level will increase the overall lifetime of the wheelchair.

Behavior

How an individual behaves in a wheelchair can greatly influence its replacement. This factor is more relevant for those in manual wheelchairs, as an individual with uncontrolled behavioral problems should probably not be driving a motorized wheelchair. The first instance to consider is whether your client can self-propel a manual wheelchair at all. If the client does not self-propel, due to either physical or cognitive deficits, his overall activity level in the wheelchair will usually be far less than those who functionally propel their chairs.

Some individuals may exhibit hyperactive, athetoid, or extreme self-stimulation behavior. All of these behaviors, which may result from developmental delays or clients with serious head injuries, will stress parts of a wheelchair frame. The author works with a large population of institutionalized clients who all incessantly perform some type of self-stimulation behavior in their wheelchairs. For example, they may slam their bodies back and forth in a rocking motion for hours while seated in a chair, and others, if not controlled, may beat the sides of the wheelchair with their fists, or, in transferring, will forcefully propel themselves into or out of the chairs. Any of these extreme behaviors will have an effect on the lifetime of the chair.

Body Type

Clients who are obese or are close to the weight limitations of a certain wheelchair frame will obviously put more overall wear on the chair. Most wheelchairs come with a 250-pound weight limitation; however, there are custom bariatric frames that are capable of supporting an individual weighing between 600 and 1000 pounds. Obviously, the higher the weight limitation, the more it will compensate for this weight factor.

Lifestyle

How the client spends the majority of each week is another factor that should be considered. Does the client spend most of each day at home or does she go into an office or a school 5 days a week? If so, how is she transported? It should be noted that the very act of securing a wheelchair onto a van or school bus twice a day for a long ride will lead to some wear, as the vibrations on the frame will eventually cause the bolts to oval out the holes in the frame. Wheelchair manufacturers and research facilities routinely test their frames in a double-drum vibration sled to count how many cycles will lead to frame damage (Vitek et al., 2001; Johnson, 1996).

Lifestyle must also be reflected when choosing the appropriate model of wheelchair for the client. If the client is an active self-propeller, the chair prescribed should be a high-strength ultralight frame. Various studies have tested the durability and cost comparisons of different wheelchair frames, and it has been shown that ultralight rehabilitation wheelchairs are the most cost effective over the life of the wheelchair, costing 3.4 times less (dollars per life cycle) than depot (standard frame) wheelchairs and 2.3 times less (dollars per life cycle) than the lightweight wheelchairs tested in the study (Cooper et al., 1997). Likewise, if the client is obese or exhibits self-stimulation behavior, a heavy-duty or even custom-reinforced frame is required. Similar appropriateness of correct model selection must be assured in calculating the replacement of a motorized wheelchair.

One note in considering a lifestyle should be when your client has both a motorized and manual wheelchair. In most cases, the manual wheelchair will be used as a backup, so consequently, its overall use may be far more limited than the use of the motorized wheelchair throughout the week. This too must be taken into account when projecting replacement schedules.

Replacement Allowance Worksheets

The author first introduced the following worksheets to participants of the Life Care Planning Summit in Chicago, IL, on May 18, 2002. At that time, first drafts of the worksheets, based on available data, were sent to over 20 life care planners throughout the country for their comments on both accuracy and ease of use. Initial changes were made, and the worksheets were then sent to another eight volunteers for additional comments. Responses from the life care planning community from both mailings were about 20% of all those sent.

It is hoped by the author that the enclosed worksheets will be considered a tool to improve the overall reliability of life care plans in the area of wheelchair replacement. By accounting for the factors described in this chapter, the assigning of a replacement value for a wheelchair can be better defended with a more objective basis. It is further hoped that this tool can be adjusted and improved with time by communication with the author as various life care planners utilize and perhaps supplement the worksheets based on the uniqueness of their individual cases.

Estimated Replacement Schedule Assessment Form

Manual Wheelchair

All medical equipment will eventually wear out and must be replaced. The frequency of replacement is dependent on the individual using the equipment and various factors in his or her life. Two assumptions must be made for this worksheet:

1. The wheelchair frame is appropriate for the lifestyle of the client (i.e., if he is an active self-propeller, this should be a high-strength ultralight frame). If the client is obese or exhibits self-stimulation behavior, a heavy-duty reinforced frame may be required.
2. Routine maintenance is done on an annual or as needed basis.

The following worksheet will assist the rehabilitation consultant with evaluating the factors and how they affect the overall replacement schedule of each item. Each of the factors will either add to or subtract from the life of the equipment being used.

Identify factors that affect your client, and then apply them to the chart based on the *value* instructions. The adjusted replacement time in the lower-right-hand corner will be the estimated weighted replacement schedule for the particular piece of equipment.

Client Name: _____ Date of Birth: _____

Average replacement time: 5 years

Additional Determining Factors	Value	Effect on Replacement Time
Age: If client is …	Then +/–	From 5 years
4–16 years	–1 year	
16–30 years	–0.5 year	
30–65 years	No change	
>65 years	+1 year	
Environment: If client lives in …		
Suburban or urban	No change	
Rural environment	–0.5 year	
Skilled nursing facility	+1 year	
Behavior: If client …		
Can self-propel	No change	
Cannot self-propel	+1 year	
Has self-stimulation, athetoid, or other hyperactive behavior	–2 years	
Body Type: If client is …		
Over 250 pounds	–0.5 year	
Lifestyle: If client …		
Is highly active adult	–0.5 year	
Locks wheelchair into a van or school bus several times per week	–0.5 year	
Is using manual chair as a backup for a power chair	+2 years	
Adjusted replacement time	=	

© Copyright Rehab Equipment Consulting, Paul Amsterdam, A.T.S., 2002. Reprinted with permission of the author.

Estimated Replacement Schedule Assessment Form

Motorized Wheelchair

All medical equipment will eventually wear out and must be replaced. The frequency of replacement is dependent on the individual using the equipment and various factors in his or her life. Two assumptions must be made for this worksheet:

1. The appropriate model of motorized wheelchair has been chosen to meet the lifestyle, environment, and weight capacity of the client.
2. Routine maintenance is done on an annual or as needed basis.

The following worksheet will assist the rehabilitation consultant with evaluating the factors and how they affect the overall replacement schedule of each item. Each of the factors will either add to or subtract from the life of the equipment being used.

Identify factors that affect your client, and then apply them to the chart based on the *value* instructions. The adjusted replacement time in the lower-right-hand corner will be the estimated weighted replacement schedule for the particular piece of equipment.

Client Name: _____ Date of Birth: _____

Average replacement time: 5 years

Additional Determining Factors	Value	Effect on Replacement Time
Age: If client is …	Then +/–	From 5 years
4–14 years	–1 year	
14–30 years	–0.5 years	
30–65 years	No change	
>65 years	+1 year	
Environment: If client lives in …		
Suburban or urban	No change	
Rural environment	–0.5 years	
Skilled nursing facility	+1 years	
Body Type: If client is …		
Over 300 pounds	–0.5 years	
Very ataxic or has high muscle tone of upper extremities	–0.5 years	
Lifestyle: If client …		
Is highly active adult	–0.5 year	
Locks wheelchair into a van or school bus several times per week	–0.5 years	
Adjusted replacement time	=	

© Copyright Rehab Equipment Consulting, Paul Amsterdam, A.T.S., 2002. Reprinted with permission of the author.

USE OF REFERENCES AND SPECIALISTS

There are a variety of sources life care planners can use to create their list of the most optimal equipment and most accurate prices for their clients. One of the most common methods is to obtain the original list of equipment a client was provided when he or she left the rehab facility after the injury. Although this is an excellent first step, it may be far from a complete list of all the client's equipment needs. Some of the flaws with this method that must be recognized are:

- **Time Factor:** If a great deal of time has passed since the original equipment was provided to your client, her physical condition may have changed (either better or worse).
- **Environment or Vocational Changes:** The client may have moved to a different home that requires other types of equipment, or the life care plan may be providing for a new, more accessible environment, which may change some of the equipment choices. Current or future vocational options must be considered as well.
- **Funding Issues:** When the original equipment was provided, the client's funding source may not have allowed for higher-quality models, or a large segment of equipment, such as independently controlled ceiling lifts, environmental controls, or computer interfaces built into the power wheelchair. The life care plan must address all equipment to provide the client with the highest possibility of independent function.

Prices for medical equipment are another area of possible contention in the report. As previously noted, by omission of various accessories, the price of a particular wheelchair may be vastly inaccurate. A more important point is what source a life care planner uses to acquire prices. The author has seen a variety of different sources used for price submission to the plan:

1. Catalogs
2. Internet sites
3. Calls to medical equipment providers in the client's local area

There is a possible problem utilizing any of the above sources to obtain prices. Many catalog and Internet sites are quoting extremely discounted prices for equipment. Some of these prices may be a result of overstocked merchandise or a particular price passed on by a manufacturer. When the client finally (possibly years later) receives a judgment on his case, and must now purchase his or her own equipment, he or she may not be able to receive an equivalent discount as to what was originally quoted. Likewise, when a life care planner calls a local vendor and requests a price, he may not be sure if the price has been discounted or possibly increased.

It has been the author's contention in past articles and lectures (Amsterdam, 2001, 2002) that the most objective price that should be used for a life care plan is the manufacturer's suggested list price (MSLP). As this price is provided by every manufacturer and consistent throughout all 50 states, it provides the only true objective basis for accurate pricing. The MSLP is also always a price that the client should be able to obtain from any reputable equipment provider.

THE USE OF REHABILITATION EQUIPMENT SPECIALISTS AS CONSULTANTS

If a client's physical disabilities are more involved, it may be beneficial to consult with a rehab equipment specialist. It is important to realize that the medical equipment industry, like all other branches of health care, has many areas of specialization. There are medical equipment companies that specialize in respiratory supplies, others strictly in the enteral or IV therapy business, and some whose primary income are as physician or hospital suppliers. Any of these companies can buy and distribute wheelchairs and other durable medical equipment, although they may have little, other than cursory, knowledge in proper evaluation of a rehab client.

Rehab equipment suppliers (RTS) are individuals who specialize in the needs of clients with permanent disabilities. They are usually employed in a firm that is in the primary business of rehab medical equipment evaluation and distribution. An RTS can go through a national certification or credentialing process; the most recognized curriculum was developed through RESNA (the Rehabilitation Engineering and Assistive Technology Society of North America). Those passing this certification process attain the credentials of ATS (assistive technology supplier). A therapist who passes the same curriculum attains the credentials of ATP (assistive technology practitioner). If the individual is also a member in good standing with NRRTS (the National Registry of Rehabilitation Technology Suppliers, 2003), he or she may also be recognized through the trademarked credential of CRTS™ (certified rehab technology supplier). RESNA and NRRTS both provide a directory of certified specialists on their websites.

Certified ATS/CRTS™ specialists are working in rehabilitation hospitals, state developmental centers, and schools for children with disabilities, evaluating clients for equipment needs on a daily basis. Utilizing the expertise of a certified ATS will help you get the best idea of your client's current and future equipment needs. He or she can provide you with accurate pricing based on MSLP if requested, as well as help add greater defensibility to the equipment section of the overall plan.

CONCLUSION

For many with permanent disabilities, the lifetime use of rehabilitation medical equipment, such as a custom wheelchair, may be the one aspect that separates their lives from the rest of the able-bodied world. As technology improves, providing lighter materials and more functionality, new models of equipment will be continually introduced, and the job of the life care planner to include the correct type of equipment in a plan will only get more difficult. When equipment costs are a large segment of a particular life care plan, costly errors of omission and tendencies to exaggerate medical needs can be used by opposing attorneys as focal points of contention. Better systems of protocols must be used for replacement schedules, as well as the ascertaining of accurate prices. The use of rehab equipment experts is increasing in the life care planning industry, and life care planners who are working without such expertise may have a harder time defending their choices in a court of law.

REFERENCES

Amsterdam, P. (2001). Rehabilitation equipment needs in life care plans, *Academy Letter, International Academy of Life Care Planners*, 4, 2–3.

Amsterdam, P. (2002). Setting standards of protocol for replacement schedules of medical equipment in a life care plan. *Journal of Life Care Planning*, 1, 275–283.

Centers for Medicare and Medicaid Services. (June 1997, reprinted July 2002). Manual wheelchair base definitions, chap. 9. DMERC supplier manual (available at cms.hhs.gov).

Cooper, R., Gonzalez, J., Lawrence B., Renschler, A., Boninger, M., & Van Sickle, D. (1997). Performance of selected lightweight wheelchairs on ANSI/RESNA tests. *Archives of Physical Medicine and Rehab*, 78, 1138–1144.

Consortium for Spinal Cord Medicine. (1999). *Tables of Expected Functional Outcomes Clinical Practice Guidelines*, 13–20. Washington, DC: Paralyzed Veterans of America.

Gass, J. & Gonzalez, T. (2001). Using the life care plan to defend damage claims. In *General Cologne Re's Guide to Injury Management*, Vol. 3, *Life Care Planning*, 27–29. Available at www.gcr.com.

Glynn, G. & Davis, L. (2001). Physician directed life care planning: the concept, creation and challenge. In *General Cologne Re's Guide to Injury Management*, Vol. 3, *Life Care Planning*, 12. Available at www.gcr.com.

Graham-Field, Inc. (2002). Product warranty information. Atlanta, GA. (800) 347-5678. Available at www.grahamfield.com.

Invacare Corporation. (2002). Product order form information. Elyria, OH. (800) 333-6900. Available at www.invacare.com.

Invacare Corporation. (2002). Product warranty information. Elyria, OH. (800) 333-6900. Available at www.invacare.com.

Johnson, D. (June 1996). Simplified Strength Tests for Manual Wheelchairs for Developing Countries. RESNA Proceedings, 159. Available at http://www.dinf.ne.jp/doc/english/Us_Eu/conf/resna96/page159.htm.

Kendall, S. & Deutsch, P. (2002). Research methodology for life care planners. *Journal of Life Care Planning*, 1, 157–168.

NRRTS. (2003). CRTS™ Directory. Available at www.nrrts.org.

Neulicht, A., Riddick-Grisham, S., Hinton, L., Costantini, P., Thomas, R., & Goodrich, B. (2002). Life care planning survey 2001: process, methods, protocols. *Journal of Life Care Planning*, 1, 97–148.

O'Leary, J. & Sarkarati, M. (July 2000). Aging with SCI. *The Interdisciplinary Journal of Rehabilitation*. Available at www.rehapub.com.

Pride Mobility Products Corporation. (2002). Order form information. Exeter, PA. (800) 800-8596. Available at www.pridemobility.com.

Stewart, T. (1992). Physiological Aspects of Immobilization and Beneficial Effects on Passive Standing. Available at www.lifestandusa.com.

Sunrise Medical. (2002). Product order form information. Carlsbad, CA. (760) 930-1500. Available at www.sunrisemedical.com.

Sunrise Medical. (2002). Product warranty information. Carlsbad, CA. (760) 930-1500. Available at www.sunrisemedical.com.

Tech Act. (1988). Technology-Related Assistance for Individuals with Disabilities Act of 1988, PL 100-407, Section 3, 1988

TiSport Inc. (2002). Product information. Kennewick, WA. (509) 586-6117. Available at www.tisport.net.

Vitek, M., Cooper, R., Renschler, A., Algood, D., Ammer, W., & Wolf, E. (2001). Static, Impact and Fatigue Testing of Five Different Types of Electric Powered Wheelchairs. Department of Rehabilitation and Technology, University of Pittsburgh (RESNA slide presentation). Available at www.wheelchairnet.org.

32

THE COMMISSION ON HEALTH
CARE CERTIFICATION (CHCC):
CREDENTIALING IN LIFE CARE
PLANNING SERVICE DELIVERY

V. Robert May III and Peter Lubinskas

INTRODUCTION

The certification movement in life care planning service delivery was officially
established in the spring of 1996, with the first group test administration of the
certified life care planner (CLCP) examination delivered in Atlanta, GA, and San
Francisco. However, the movement actually began several years earlier with the
incorporation of the Commission on Disability Examiner Certification (CDEC) and
the establishment of the Board of Commissioners. The Commission on Health
Care Certification (CHCC) evolved from the CDEC as the premier certifying agency
in life care planning service delivery, after much organizational changes and
restructuring. Input from professionals certified in any one of the agency's two
certifications and the Board of Commissioners has contributed to the growth and
success of the CHCC in its certification specialty areas, especially in life care
planning service delivery. This chapter traces the development of the Commission
on Health Care Certification, from its days as a monolithic certifying agency trading
as the Commission on Disability Examiner Certification, to its current status in
health care service delivery as a multicertification agency. Furthermore, it reviews
the credentialing process that includes licensure, registration, and accreditation,
in addition to certification. Each of these credentialing processes is reviewed with
definitions and applications to their respective fields. The development of the
certification examination and the qualifications required of a rehabilitation professional to be approved as a certification candidate are detailed and discussed.
The examination has undergone numerous reviews with ongoing item reliability
and validation research, thus resulting in an ever-changing examination in terms
of content. The reader will find that the qualifications to sit for the CLCP
examination are extremely restricted, with a more recent application of policy

0-8493-1511-5/04/$0.00+$1.50
© 2004 by CRC Press LLC

that now excludes 2-year diploma nurses and individuals with associate's degrees in related health care professions. Finally, an overview of the CHCC ethics review process is offered with an accompanying case study synopsis. The commission has reviewed specific complaints from certified and noncertified practitioners alike and five case reviews are detailed with the commission's ruling for each ethical complaint.

Credentialing

Matkin (1985) noted that accountability operates on at least two levels: (1) the programs of service to be delivered and (2) the qualifications of practitioners providing those services. Credentialing refers to "evidence that attests to and provides assurance of the [skills and knowledge] of a person or program to perform specific services" (Matkin, 1985, p. 221). When reference is made to a program rather than an individual, skills and knowledge become less of an issue, leading instead to the demonstration of program or service relevant to the specific occupation with which it is associated. There are fours areas of credentials that have strong applications in rehabilitation: (1) certification, (2) licensure, (3) accreditation, and (4) registration.

Certification

Certification is the nonstatutory process by which a governmental or nongovernmental association or agency grants recognition to an individual for having met certain predetermined professional qualifications (Fritz & Mills, 1980; Matkin, 1985). Its purpose is to establish professional standards of practice by which individuals with disabilities and the general public can evaluate the qualifications of individuals practicing or administering the services within the field in which they have been certified (Leahy & Holt, 1993). Theoretically, certification allows the general public, or the consumer of services, to request a review from the certifying agency under which the practitioner is certified for any transgressions the consumer alleges he or she may have experienced from the practitioner. By reviewing the standards of practice established by the particular certifying agency, the administrative board can determine if a violation has occurred, and thus proceed with appropriate action. Keep in mind, however, that no certification board has the administrative power to limit one's practice; the board can only limit one's use of the title that the certifying agency awards and for which a set of professional activities are defined. As applied to the CHCC, a practitioner with his or her CLCP title revoked may continue to practice. How this individual addresses the revocation of a credential in deposition or during cross-examination and maintains credibility may be ineffectual at best, and potentially coupled with an unrecoverable career.

Licensure

Licensure is the statutory process by which governmental agencies (i.e., state or federal) grant permission to a person meeting predetermined qualifications to engage in a given occupation and use a particular title to perform specific functions

(Fritz & Mills, 1980). Licensing represents the most restrictive form of occupational regulation, since the regulating licensing board has the power to grant or withhold a license, thus potentially denying an individual the opportunity to earn a livelihood in his chosen occupation.

Unlike certification, licensing may be a requirement to practice. Approximately 11 states require licensing for counselors, including Alabama, Arkansas, Florida, Georgia, Idaho, Louisiana, Ohio, South Carolina, Tennessee, Texas, and Virginia. However, certification may be a selective requirement among insurance carriers or third-party payers before reimbursement for services can be authorized to a practitioner. This concept is reviewed later in this chapter.

Registration

Registration is solely dependent on licensure and certification, for without either, registration does not exist (Gianforte, 1976). Matkin (1985) noted that once licensing or certification credentials have been issued, the professional's name and other pertinent information are listed with other similarly designated members of a particular discipline. What is formed is a registry, or a document, which assists the general public in identifying qualified practitioners providing specific services. Some examples of registered professionals include registered occupational therapists (OTR) and rehabilitation therapists.

Gianforte (1976) noted that registration could be administered on a state or national level. The difference is in territorial assignment; registering on a national level assures reciprocity and the legal ability to practice in any jurisdiction, whereas state registration is territorially restrictive (Matkin, 1985).

Accreditation

Accreditation defines the requisite knowledge and skills to be addressed by training and educational programs responsible for preparing individuals to enter a specific occupational discipline (Matkin, 1985). This definition also applies to service delivery programs responsible for providing a set of designated activities to consumers. To summarize, accreditation addresses programs or services within a specific entity that advertises and offers such services, and *not* the practitioners responsible for service delivery or for teaching a specific curriculum within an educational institution. However, Matkin (1985) noted that one of the criteria for accreditation might stipulate that a credentialed practitioner perform the specified service within a designated program.

CERTIFICATION DEVELOPMENT

Prior to reviewing the CHCC structure, mission, objectives, standards of practice, and ethics review process, it is necessary to provide an overview of the development of the certification process. This review will aid in understanding the relationships that exist and are necessary between the varying certifying agencies. Without the support of the Commission on Rehabilitation Counselor Certification, the CHCC may never have developed the CLCP credential.

Certification in the field of rehabilitation is the oldest certifying process among allied health care professions, beginning in 1963 with a proposal by the Professional Standards Committee of the National Rehabilitation Counseling Association that a certification system be designed to bring accountability to rehabilitation counseling. Culminating from this early proposal was the establishment of the Commission on Rehabilitation Counselor Certification (CRCC), which was formally incorporated in January 1974 (Leahy & Holt, 1993). The CRCC was designated as a nongovernmental body of the rehabilitation service delivery profession, authorized to conduct certification activities on a nationwide basis, and administered independent of any supporting organization. Between 1974 and 1976, the CRCC concentrated on administrative duties, which involved the appointment of a policy and governing body and the development of a certification examination. Representatives, or commissioners, were appointed from the original sponsoring organizations (American Rehabilitation Counseling Association and the National Rehabilitation Counseling Association), as well as other rehabilitation organizations, which included the Council of Rehabilitation Education (CORE, an accreditation body), Council of State Administrators of Vocational Rehabilitation (CSAVR), National Association of Rehabilitation Facilities (NARF), National Association of Non-White Rehabilitation Workers (NANWRW), National Council on Rehabilitation Education (NCRE), and a representative from a national consumer organization.

The grandfathering period began during this early development period in which individuals took the examination and rated each question for its relevance to the practice of rehabilitation counseling. During this period, all persons who took the examination were awarded the certification credential. Through this grandfathering process, the commission was able to ensure the rehabilitation counseling profession that the certification examination focused on field-oriented content resulting in a criterion-referenced examination.

The first postgrandfathering certification examination was administered in April 1976, which preceded the development of the commission's certification maintenance plan. The maintenance plan was adopted in September 1977 and went into effect in 1978. It required that each certified counselor attain 150 contact hours of continuing education during his or her 5-year certification period or retake the certification examination. This figure has since been adjusted downward to 100 hours so that "certified rehabilitation counselors (CRC) [could] focus their continuing educational activities on quality programs and increase their ability to achieve re-certification" (Leahy & Holt, 1993, p. 75).

The National Commission on Health Certifying Agencies accredited the CRCC as a certifying body in 1980, thus awarding the CRCC credibility to its mission and process. Rehabilitation in the private sector was gaining momentum and notoriety at this time as well, and yet there was not a methodology for determining or monitoring accountability within the private sector of rehabilitation practitioners. The National Association of Rehabilitation Professionals in the Private Sector (NARPPS), now trading as the International Association of Rehabilitation Professionals (IARP), had established itself as the representative membership organization of private practitioners by 1980, complete with a rules committee, code of ethics, and behavioral review board. However, this professional organization had no means of determining who was accountable in the provision of services in private-sector rehabilitation given the diversity of the practitioners' educational training and backgrounds. For the first time in its service delivery history, the rehabilitation field experienced the presence of a new group of practitioners whose roles and functions prior to this period were assigned to medical and hospital settings, the registered or rehabilitation nurse. It was the rehabilitation nursing population that was the first professional group to work in the private rehabilitation sector (Lewin et al., 1979). Suttenfield (1983) noted that traditionally individuals practicing in the private rehabilitation sector came from one or the other of two primary educational and experiential backgrounds, nursing and vocational rehabilitation. The problem that the Commission on Rehabilitation Counselor Certification faced was that under its qualifying provisions of 1983, rehabilitation nurses could not qualify to become certified as rehabilitation service providers. To exclude nurses from certification meant excluding a whole specialty area from meeting account-ability criteria. Thus, the certified insurance rehabilitation specialist (CIRS) was developed, which established criteria specific to nurses and formally trained vocational rehabilitation case managers and practitioners that would allow both groups to qualify for certification. In December 1983, the Board for Rehabilitation Certification (BRC) was created to administer both the existing CRC and the new CIRS credentials. The CIRS credential has been renamed and is now known as the certified disability manager and specialist (CDMS).

It was not until 1987 that the Code of Professional Ethics for Rehabilitation Counselors was adopted, which included nurse practitioners certified under the CIRS credential. A disciplinary code was established as well, whose purpose was to address ethical complaints received by the CRCC from consumers and fellow professionals (Leahy & Holt, 1993).

A comprehensive restructuring of the CRCC took place in 1990, which resulted in the abolition of the Board for Rehabilitation Certification in favor of a more flexible, autonomous administrative organization, which was titled the Foundation for Rehabilitation Certification, Education, and Research. Its primary mission is to support the commission by staffing the administrative offices, conduct public relations activities, and conduct research and administer educational projects (Leahy & Holt, 1993).

The CRCC certification examination was initially researched in the early 1980s to ensure that some relevance and validity had been identified and achieved in terms of how the test related to field practice (Rubin et al., 1984). To ensure constant monitoring of the relevance and validity of the CRCC examination, the CRCC entered into a joint agreement with the Council on Rehabilitation Education (CORE) to conduct validation research of the examination process on a continuing schedule. With this joint effort, the CRCC established a research process that would provide ongoing validation of CRCC examination content and the curricular standards used in the accreditation of educational programs. Beginning in 1991, the first validation research from the joint CRCC and CORE agreement was completed by Szymanski et al. (1993), which "supported the validity of the knowledge areas currently included in the standards for rehabilitation counselor certification or rehabilitation counselor accreditation" (p. 118).

The current structure of the Commission on Rehabilitation Counselor Certifi-cation consists of 17 individuals appointed for 5-year rotating terms. These individuals are representatives of the primary rehabilitation supporting organiza-tions, which include (Leahy & Holt, 1993):

American Deafness and Rehabilitation Association (ADARA)
American Rehabilitation Counseling Association (ARCA)
Canadian Association of Rehabilitation Personnel (CARP)
Council on Rehabilitation Education (CORE)
Council of State Administrators of Vocational Rehabilitation (CSAVR)
National Association of Non-White Rehabilitation Workers (NANWRW)
National Association of Rehabilitation Facilities (NARF)
National Association of Rehabilitation Professionals in the Private Sector (NAR-PPS)
National Council on Rehabilitation Education (NCRE)
National Rehabilitation Counseling Association (NRCA)

These 17 commissioners elect an executive committee that is organized around four standing committees: (1) standards and credentials, (2) examinations and research, (3) external relations, and (4) ethics. Outside consultants are also used to assist with activities such as item writing and participation in cut-score workshops (Leahy & Holt, 1993).

CHCC DEVELOPMENT

The Commission on Health Care Certification (CHCC) was established originally as the Commission on Disability Examiner Certification (CDEC) in 1994, in response to the health care industry's need for certified clinical examiners in impairment and disability rating practices. The CDEC expanded rapidly over its first 8 years such that its name was updated in the spring of 2002 to that of the CHCC. The name change was necessary since the CDEC was offering certifications into other specialty areas of rehabilitation by 2001. Furthermore, generic reference was required under which each of its three certification credentials, as well as future credentials, could be classified.

In the early 1990s, credentialing in the specialty area of impairment rating and disability examination evolved as a result of meetings with allied health care providers around the country. Issues were discussed that focused primarily on clinical examiner credentials, validity and reliability of rating protocol, and the establishment of a testing board to oversee the impairment rating and disability examining credentialing process. The resulting credential was the certified disability examiner (CDE), with three levels that allow for the inclusion of all professionals who are involved in measuring functional performance of persons reporting impairment or disability. The Commission on Health Care Certification awards the certified disability examiner I, II, or III (CDE I, II, or III) credential to persons who have satisfied the educational program requirements and training standards established by the National Association of Disability Evaluating Professionals (NADEP), with all classroom instruction currently offered at regional locations around the country.

In 1995 the commission broadened its influence in the medical and rehabilitation marketplace by researching and developing a certification program in life care planning and related catastrophic case management. Currently, comprehensive training programs in life care planning have evolved to respond to this need for life care planning services as applied to catastrophic cases. Vocational/medical rehabilitation case managers and rehabilitation nurses have established themselves as consultants and case managers in these catastrophic cases and often detail the medical and rehabilitation needs of catastrophically disabled persons. Thus, the commission developed the certified life care planner (CLCP) credential in response to the rapid growth and influence of case management in catastrophic disabilities and managed care in today's health care insurance industry. Validity and reliability research of the CLCP credential has been completed through Southern Illinois University and is based specifically on the roles and function of case managers and rehabilitation nurses who provide this service as part of their case management structure. There was little literature in the professional journals that addressed life care planning in 1996, and the commission's research goals of identifying and establishing the background, education, and experience criteria required to competently develop life care plans have since been achieved.

The issue of who to test for the CLCP credential, or which group of allied health care professionals to accept, based on background, education, and experience of the individual(s) as applied to rehabilitation case management services, was not as much of an issue as one may have thought it to be. Basically, two groups have played dominant roles in developing private-sector case management services: (1) nurses and (2) vocational rehabilitation counselors/case managers. The question, however, continues in debate as to which group is best suited for what specialty area; in fact, this issue remains to be empirically defined.

Deutsch et al. (1986) noted that rehabilitation counselors are best suited for life care plan development because many of the skills and services provided by rehabilitation counselors are directly applicable to catastrophic disabilities and pediatric rehabilitation. Furthermore, rehabilitation counselors are uniquely qualified by definition: rehabilitation counselors often function as coordinators of interdisciplinary services and the care of the permanently injured patient.

Conversely, Powers (1994) provided support for the rehabilitation nurse's role in life care planning by delineating the roles of the nurse both as a case manager and as a life care planner. Blackwell et al. (1994a, 1994b) followed Suttenfield's (1983) contention that this specialty service belongs to two groups, nurses and rehabilitation counselors. Actually, who is best suited for predicting one's future medical and rehabilitative needs through life care planning is not important, nor does it have merit in the case for measuring accountability. What is important is that accountability be established, measured, and monitored with regard to all of the professionals who provide life care planning services. Measuring accountability is best established by:

- Defining the service to be monitored
- Identifying the service providers' roles and functions required to deliver the service
- Developing a field-tested certification examination
- Conducting validation research of the examination
- Establishing a code of ethics

The CRCC had experience in this process through its work in establishing accountability for rehabilitation counseling, though its work in researching the roles and functions of certified case managers (e.g., nurses and rehabilitation counselors) is incomplete at this writing. In spite of its work in certification, however, the CRCC declined to get involved with life care planning certification in late 1995 because of the limited population of life care planners compared to rehabilitation counselors in the public and private sectors. Also, the expense involved in developing a certification process could not be justified given the potential for its return on investment (Taylor, personal communication, November 1995). The Commission on Health Care Certification contacted Eda Holt, executive director of the CRCC, to discuss the plans of the CRCC for certifying rehabilitation professionals in life care planning service delivery. She responded in writing that the CRCC had concluded that life care planning certification was not in the best financial interest of the CRCC, and that the CHCC should proceed as it wished. Based on this blessing from the CRCC and with the knowledge that the CRCC had withdrawn any consideration for developing a certification credential in life care planning, the CHCC proceeded with total commitment in establishing such a certification credential.

The Commission on Health Care Certification did its homework in terms of identifying the need for life care planning certification before it made inquiries to the CRCC regarding its plans for developing life care planning certification. By the early 1990s, life care planning had made significant inroads in the field of rehabilitation (Deutsch, 1994). Comprehensive training programs in life care planning were developed through the National Association of Disability Evaluating Professionals (NADEP) and IARP. More significantly, life care planning had obtained formal academic recognition and acceptance through a joint venture, known as Intelicus, between the University of Florida and the Rehabilitation Training Institute from Ocoee, FL. The CHCC recognized the need for accountability in this now-credible service delivery system, and in 1994 began its research and development for life care planning certification.

Goals and Objectives

The Commission on Health Care Certification was established for the development and administration of well-researched, standardized tests designed to measure the clinical examiner's working knowledge and demonstration of the NADEP work disability evaluation model (impairment rating and functional capacity evaluation) and in life care plan development. The CHCC established several initial goals it considered relevant in developing and maintaining its mission. These goals are listed below in the context of how the CHCC was structured and with its current progress toward achieving these goals documented.

Goal 1

Develop a national test that measures the clinical practitioner's working knowledge of functional capacity and impairment rating practices as applied to the NADEP evaluation model. Because of the diversity of backgrounds, education, and training of persons who perform functional capacity evaluations and conduct impairment ratings (e.g., medical doctors, chiropractors, physical therapists, occupational therapists, dental surgeons, etc.), the CHCC designed the test for all allied health care providers by grouping specialties by categories. This grouping is based on an educational/training focus and does not represent a ranking based on ability or status. The categories are:

Category I: All physicians designated as primary care providers, subspecialists, or specialists in the administering of medical, dental, or chiropractic-related services. Specific physician groups include medical doctors (MD), osteopathic physicians (DO), dental surgeons (DDS), and chiropractors (DC).

Category II: All persons who provide assistance to physicians in the treatment of injured persons or whose practice is involved with providing symptom relief and function restoration through modality and therapeutic applications. These specialties include physical therapists, occupational therapists, speech pathologists, kinesiologists, physiologists, psychologists, and doctoral-level vocational evaluators.

Category III: All persons who are influential in the outcome of the injured person's disability litigation, including vocational evaluators, vocational case managers, rehabilitation nurses, and rehabilitation counselors. These individuals may assume various roles in the disability litigation process, such as performing functional capacity evaluations and labor market analyses, assisting in the placement of the injured worker back into the labor market, conducting psychometric testing, and managing the medical care/costs associated with the respective disability case.

The examination is structured such that the examinee is required to demonstrate working knowledge of research and resource utilization as well as one's examination skills applied to the NADEP model. The written examination consists of two case studies, which are presented with varying orthopedic and psychological problems. The examinee is required to respond to a series of inquiries about different aspects of the cases, and a review of the literature is required for each inquiry response. Each of the categories identified above has its own set of inquiries, with some crossover between categories since the material is directly related to the classroom content of the core courses. Thus, examinees are required to review the literature to respond to the inquiries, and apply their responses to fit the NADEP clinical examination protocol. The commissioners develop all inquiries, and they have the final approval of the examination content and list of inquiries before dissemination to the qualified certification candidates. Topics in which one's knowledge and expertise are measured on the written examination include:

1. Medical diagnoses/correlates to disability
2. Psychological disorders and correlates to disability
3. Examination tools, instruments, and work sample selection and utilization
4. Legislation impacting evaluation protocol
5. Report writing and results/performance interpretation
6. Practice theory and concepts

Goal 2

Develop a national test that measures the life care planner's working knowledge of medical systems, associated disabilities, and treatment/maintenance protocols required to sustain life within an acceptable comfort level. Similar to the CRCC testing format, the CLCP test is comprised of multiple-choice case scenarios that contain four distractors, one of which is considered the correct choice. All test answers are referenced within current professional literature from the medical, insurance, and rehabilitation professions. The certification candidate has two options for test administration:

1. Tests are administered within the certification candidate's local community college by proctor. The candidate is required to contact his or her local community college and arrange with the business office a date and time in which the candidate can secure a proctor and sit for the examination. The candidate is responsible for any proctor costs associated with this arrangement. This option is offered to the candidate as an attempt to minimize the expenses typically associated with travel and lodging when sitting for a certification examination administered at a national testing site. Once the candidate notifies the CHCC of the community college site and proctor, the examination is mailed to the proctor at the college address. All testing materials will remain with the proctor, who is charged with the responsibility of returning all testing materials to the CHCC office. CHCC reserves the right to approve the recommended proctor or select an alternative proctor at the specified community college.
2. When possible, two national sites are designated by CHCC for weekend test administration on an annual basis. Dates and locations of the national sites are obtained from the CHCC office and are posted on the CHCC website (www.cdec1.com).

The certification test is under its fourth revision, which was released on July 1, 2002. This revised test is comprised of four categories and associated topical areas, as well as a general items section, which include the following (percentage of test content is designated beside each category):

1. Medical interventions and complications associated with medical conditions — 53%
   a. Traumatic brain injury (TBI)
   b. Amputations
   c. Lower-back chronic pain
   d. Burns
   e. Vocational worksheet information
   f. Vocational resources
   g. Vocational tests
2. Legislative issues — 11%
   a. Americans with Disabilities Act
   b. Home Health Practice Act

3. Measurement and statistics — 4%
4. Psychological issues — 4%
5. General items — 28%
   a. Terms and definitions
   b. Life care planning charts
   c. Miscellaneous items

The test results for the CLCP are scored at the corporate office of the Commission on Health Care Certification. Passing cutoff criteria are determined statistically based on *t*-scores and raw scores, as well as mean scores of each testing group and standard deviations applied to the bell curve. Anyone not meeting the passing criteria may take the examination a total of three times within a 12-month period. If the passing cutoff score is not achieved after the third trial, a board review by the commissioners is undertaken to review the candidate's test performance, and recommendations are made regarding future certification arrangements (i.e., additional course work, recommended readings, etc.).

Goal 3

Conduct ongoing research in terms of test item validity and reliability. Such research ensures that both tests measure what they purport to measure and that the items are a fair representation of the knowledge required to measure impairment and disability and to develop life care plans.

The CHCC recognized early in its development phase that reliability needs to be established and validity research needs to be conducted to ensure that the test items are a fair representation of common knowledge regarding disability evaluation and life care plan development. The goal was that both tests should measure what they purport to measure. Currently, the Commission on Health Care Certification funds doctoral-level research at Southern Illinois University, Department of Rehabilitation, doctoral program (Rh.D.), to conduct the reliability and validity research for both examinations. This endeavor includes a complete role and function study of persons engaged in the practice of determining disability or rating impairment and developing life care plans. The significance of these studies is that finally, specific roles and functions of persons in medical and rehabilitation settings engaged in impairment rating, disability evaluation, and life care plan development are defined.

Regarding the CDE examination, the role and function study were completed and published in 1996, which resulted in the identification of the various categories of expertise, or specialty knowledge areas involved in clinical practice, and more specifically, the NADEP examination model (Washington, 1996). Because of Washington's research, the CHCC's three testing categories were operationally defined and structured. The CLCP study was completed in 1999 and published in 2000. Similar to the CDE examination, this study identified the roles and function of qualified professionals involved in providing life care planning services and related catastrophic care management.

Goal 4

Administer the examination within 6 weeks of (1) a clinical examiner completing the NADEP educational/training requirements necessary to sit for the CDE examination, and (2) a life care planner completing the required and approved training necessary prior to sitting for the CLCP examination. This will ensure that minimal delays will incur for a qualified candidate to achieve certification status upon completion of required courses.

Goal 5

Procure qualified commissioners to sit on the Board of Examiners to represent all CDE and CLCP candidates and certified professionals. Similar to the CRCC, the CHCC originally began with 12 commissioners representing specialty fields of practice in medicine and rehabilitation. In contrast to the CRCC, the CHCC opted to establish itself as a field-oriented, practical testing agency without input or representation from supportive field groups. In other words, the administration of the CHCC felt that being represented by supportive organizations would have the best interests of those organizations at the forefront rather than the interests of the clinical practitioner. The administration also felt that a political element would eventually surface that would impact any clinical-based decisions in a direction that would not be in the best interest of the field practitioner. However, the commission has been approached by several supporting organizations in rehabilitation for representation on the board, and consideration is under way for its inclusion.

Today, there are 14 commissioners representing 12 different specialty groups within the fields of medicine and rehabilitation. These include life care planning (commissioner of life care planning), kinesiology (commissioner of kinesiology and physiology), case management (commissioner of case management), chiropractic (commissioner of chiropractic), occupational medicine (commissioner of occupational medicine), occupational therapy (commissioner of occupational therapy), physical medicine and rehabilitation (commissioner of physical medicine and rehabilitation), psychology (commissioner of psychology), research design and statistics (commissioner of research design and statistics), physical therapy (commissioner of physical therapy), vocational evaluation (commissioner of vocational evaluation), and academia (commissioner of university studies). The commissioner of rehabilitation nurses and the commissioner of life care planning were added when the CHCC decided to fully commit to establishing a life care plan credential.

The CHCC was careful in its selection of commissioners and established the following selection criteria to be applied to all commissioner candidates regardless of specialty:

1. Commissioners must hold a current license in their respective field. If licensure is not required within the specialty field, then the individual must hold certification common to the respective field of specialty.
2. Clinicians who have been asked to serve as commissioners for the CDE credential must complete the mandatory courses offered by NADEP and pass the CDE certification exam. Regarding the CLCP credential, these commissioners must have met the qualification standards for life care planning developed at the University of Florida and have taken and passed the CLCP examination.

Goal 6

Disseminate test scores within a 6-week period after receiving the test from the respective certified disability examiner (CDE) and certified life care planner (CLCP) candidates. To date, test scores have been disseminated on a timely basis for the CLCP credential. However, the dissemination record for the CDE credential is averaging between 8 and 12 weeks due primarily to the essay style of the tests and the requirement of three reviewers (one of whom holds similar background, education, and training credentials of the certification candidate) to review each examination. The CHCC is actively pursuing a resolution to this dissemination problem through a major adaptation of the testing process to include a multiple-choice, 4-distractor, 100-item examination.

Goal 7

Establish and monitor recertification policies to measure continued competence and to enhance the continued competence of the certified disability examiner and certified life care planner. The CHCC contended that certified professionals should maintain a high level of skills and knowledge through professional development and continuing education. The CHCC certification maintenance program extends the status of a CDE I, II, or III and a CLCP at 3-year intervals. The renewal requirement is a total of 48 clock hours for each 3-year period of approved education/training. During the renewal process, documentation is required to validate that the education or training has been successfully completed. A second option for recertification is to retake the examination.

Education and training for maintaining certification as a CDE I, II, or III and as a CLCP must occur in specific areas relating to impairment rating and life care planning for each respective credential. Regarding CDE certification, these areas may include impairment rating, functional capacity evaluation, and any topic that may be reviewed in industrial rehabilitation and personal injury seminars. Topics may be specific to the clinician's area of specialty as well.

The topic areas for the CLCP credential may include, but not be limited to, various areas of the life care planning process, such as catastrophic disabilities and other disabilities requiring life care plans, case management related to catastrophic injuries, or life care plans. Topics in resource development for life care plans, vocational issues related to life care plans, rehabilitation testimony, and other legal issues relating to life care plans are accepted. Professional/legal issues related to developing and maintaining life care plans may include ethical issues and legal matters that confront the certified life care planner in the development and delivery of a life care plan.

Education and training for certification may be obtained from a number of potential sources, including in-service training programs, seminars and workshops, college and university courses, national and regional conferences, professional publications, and presentations related to the above areas.

CERTIFIED LIFE CARE PLANNER EXPERTISE/SKILL STANDARDS

The CHCC acknowledged in its development of the CLCP credential that the life care planner is required to possess certain knowledge and skills that typify and are required of the life care planning process. Practice standards were adopted from those established by the University of Florida–Gainesville, authored by Dr. Horace Sawyer, Chairperson, Department of Rehabilitation Counseling. These standards have been updated since the Turner et al. (2000) role and function research was completed. Based on its interpretation of these standards with direct application to the field, the CHCC surmised that life care plan development involves data collection, resource development, and planning strategies in an interdisciplinary rehabilitation environment. It concluded that such an innovative, interdisciplinary approach allows for valid documentation of the needs of catastrophically injured individuals and projects the costs of needed services, treatment, and equipment over the individual's lifespan. To competently develop a life care plan, the CHCC mandated that those persons who provide this service should become certified in this specialty area and have expertise in research, development, coordination, integration, interpretation, and management of life care plans for catastrophic disabilities.

The CHCC adopted the training program standards established by the University of Florida when considering the approval of submitted maintenance hours by certified life care planners. At the time of the development of these standards in 1995, the University of Florida presented the most comprehensive and complete training program in the country in life care planning service delivery. The views of the CHCC were that while the University of Florida's Intelicus program was comprehensive and all-inclusive, other programs were not as complete. Therefore, not all training programs met the standards for training necessary to minimize incompetence in the practice of life care planning. The CHCC adopted the following standards for training in life care planning as a guideline for continuing education units (CEUs) and program approval:

I. **Administrative/Faculty Content:** The mission and objectives of the training program shall be made available to program applicants, consumers, public and private agencies, academic institutions, and the interested public. The title program shall maintain admission policies, procedures, and materials consistent with the mission of the program. The training ratio of students to faculty on-site shall be no greater than 40:1. Training faculty shall be sufficiently and appropriately qualified through preparation and experience in life care planning and related case management. Training facilities and environments are appropriate to maximize training value and accessible for individuals with disabilities.

II. **Program Curriculum:** The curriculum for the training program shall provide the essential skills and areas of expertise to effectively research, develop, coordinate, interpret, and manage life care plans for catastrophic disabilities. Training seminars would include, but are not limited to, the following minimal areas of knowledge, skills, and expertise:

1. Orientation of life care planning and case management
   a. Definition and history of life care planning
   b. Overview of life care planning topics
   c. Role of medical, psychological, and rehabilitation professionals
   d. Issues of family dynamics
   e. Review of legislation relating to life care plans
   f. Issues and opportunities of case management
2. Assessment of rehabilitation potential
   a. Pediatric and early assessment
   b. Rehabilitation evaluation and special needs
   c. Interpretation of medical evaluations
   d. Personality and neuropsychological evaluation
   e. Physical and functional assessment
   f. Vocational assessment and earnings capacity analysis
3. Medical and rehabilitation aspects of disability
   a. Medical records analysis
   b. Early medical intervention and acute rehabilitation
   c. Medical aspects: spinal cord injury, traumatic brain injury, amputations, burns, psychiatric disabilities, chronic pain and back injuries, other catastrophic disabilities
   d. Behavioral aspects of disability
   e. Issues of neuropharmacology
   f. Long-term care considerations
   g. Issues of life expectancy
4. Development of life care plans
   a. Systematic process of life care planning
   b. Planning strategies and resource development
   c. Interview procedures and data collection
   d. Computer applications of life care planning
   e. Rehabilitation technology and applications
   f. Utilization of collateral sources
   g. Areas of life care planning
      i. Planning for evaluation and treatment
      ii. Equipment and aids for independent function
      iii. Orthotics and prosthetics
      iv. Drug/supply needs
      v. Home/facility care
      vi. Medical care routine/complications
      vii. Transportation
      viii. Architectural renovations
      ix. Leisure/recreational
5. Consultation in life care planning
   a. Utilization of rehabilitation experts
   b. Analysis of established life care plans
   c. Medical/legal consultation
   d. Development of reports and reporting procedures
   e. Case preparation for consultation, mediation, settlement, conference, and testimony

6. Professional and operational issues
   a. Process and issues of rehabilitation testimony
   b. Professional ethics and malpractice issues
   c. Operational and business practices
   d. Standard of practice in life care planning
   e. Public relations, marketing, and professional development
   f. Life care planning and research issues

More important for consideration are the underlying values related to the standards of practice for qualified professionals in life care planning. The CHCC supports and confirms the following value statements for life care plan development:

1. All individuals with catastrophic disabilities have worth and dignity.
2. Life care plans are designed to facilitate and maximize functional capacity and independence for persons with catastrophic disabilities.
3. The systematic process of life care planning and related catastrophic case management is conducted in an objective and fair manner within the context of family, community, and employment systems.
4. Comprehensive and integrated services are the focus of life care planning and are based on individual involvement, personal assets, and a sense of equal justice from all involved parties.

Qualification Standards for CLCP Examination Candidates

The CLCP certification is generic in the sense that it was developed without reference to specialty areas of training or a candidate's achieved degree level. The CHCC requires the following criteria to be met by all CLCP candidates in order to qualify to sit for the examination:

1. Each candidate must have a minimum of 120 hours of postgraduate or postspecialty degree training in life care planning or in areas that can be applied to the development of a life care plan or pertain to the service delivery applied to life care planning. There must be 16 hours of training specific to a basic orientation, methodology, and standards of practice in life care planning within the required 120 hours. Training hours acquired over a time frame of 5 years from the date of application are counted as valid for consideration. Documentation of such course work and participation verification is required in the form of attendance verification forms or curriculum documentation from the training agency.
2. Each candidate must meet the minimum academic requirements for his or her designated health care-related profession, and be certified, licensed, or meet the legal mandates of the candidate's respective state that allow him or her to practice service delivery within the definition of his or her designated health care-related profession.
3. Each candidate must satisfy an experience component in *one* of the following options:

■ Submit one life care plan with candidate's name displayed as author or co-author.
■ Graduation from an accredited training program, which includes practicum or internship, or which requires the development of an independent life care plan for review and critique by a faculty member who is a certified life care planner (CLCP).

4. Each candidate must hold the entry-level academic degree or certificate/diploma for his or her profession. Beginning January 1, 2003, the minimum academic degree accepted is that of a B.A. or B.S. in a related field.

QUALIFIED HEALTH CARE PROFESSIONAL

The designation of a health care professional must be specific to the care, treatment, or rehabilitation of individuals with significant disabilities and does not include such professions as attorney, generic educators, administrators, etc., but does include such professions as counseling and special education with appropriate qualifications.

This designation of qualified health care professional is based on a background of education, training, and practice qualifications. A background of only experience or designated job title is not accepted as a qualified health care professional for this credential. Completion of training in life care planning, experience developing life care plans, or being qualified in the court system would not provide credential qualification without meeting the criteria for a qualified health care professional.

Due to allied health care providers' unregulated status or professional status that varies among states, the following are offered as clarification for qualified status regarding the following professionals:

Rehabilitation counselor — CRC
Case manager — CCM
Counselor — NCC, CRC, or state license or state mandate to practice
Psychologist — state license or state mandate to practice
Special education — undergraduate or graduate degree in special education
Social worker — MSW or state license in social work
Nursing — undergraduate or graduate degree in nursing

Regarding graduate students holding a graduate degree, they may be deemed qualified, provided they hold a graduate degree from an accredited program with a focus in rehabilitation in one or more of the following areas: (1) counseling, (2) case management, (3) psychology, and (4) life care planning. They must also complete subcriterion b of the third bullet criteria as stated above.

Board Structure

As noted previously, the board consists of 14 commissioners representing backgrounds in all professions affiliated with impairment ratings, functional capacity evaluations, and life care planning. These commissioners serve as advisors to the

CHCC administration and serve on the other boards, including the Board of Examiners, the Ethics Review Board, and the Board of Test Development.

The Board of Examiners advises on the scoring of the examinations from both credentialing areas. The Ethics Review Board is in charge of writing the Ethical Standards of Practice for both credential areas. These standards consist of 10 canons that include:

1. Moral and legal standards
2. Disability examiners and life care planners/patient relationship
3. Patient advocacy
4. Professional relationships
5. Public statements/fees
6. Confidentiality
7. Assessment
8. Research activities
9. Competence
10. CDE and the CLCP credentials

The Ethics Review Board also developed procedures for processing ethical complaints, but noted that the primary responsibility of investigating such complaints rests with the accused's own professional association under which he or she holds certification or licensure.

All commissioners have input into these standards, and the CHCC included surveys from certified life care planners and certified disability examiners I, II, and III for their input. The Ethics Review Board has the final vote on which standards to include and editorial freedom in writing the final document for publication to the certified body of practitioners.

This board serves as a review board for consumer/practitioner complaints and allegations that may have surfaced in the course of one's practice. The board reviews each complaint and determines any penalties or fines that may be imposed on the certified practitioner. It has the power to remove one's certification status if the offense in question is proven to have occurred and thus merits such action.

The Board of Test Development oversees item writing for both tests. This is not to say that the CHCC does not accept input from certified field practitioners; it does. However, the commissioners who staff this board have the final say regarding the inclusion or exclusion of any test item.

National Compliance

Similar to the CRCC, the CHCC recognized the need to adhere to a national policy and standards regarding certification testing. The CHCC is in the application process to the National Commission for Certifying Agencies (NCCA) at this writing. This application process leads to the consideration of review and compliance with this agency's certification standards. The CHCC concluded that such an affiliation would ensure that the highest quality of testing standards and development would be maintained for persons desiring CHCC certification. Areas under which the NCCA evaluates and monitors an agency include: (1) administrative independence,

(2) bias, (3) continuing competence, (4) discipline, (5) education and certification, (6) eligibility for certification, (7) public members, (8) reliability, and (9) validity.

In essence, the Commission on Health Care Certification has attempted to cover all areas of certification in both fields of impairment rating/functional capacity evaluation and life care planning. Validity and reliability of its tests, or any tests for that matter, are essential ingredients of a credential that must withstand scrutiny at all professional levels, particularly when being scrutinized by the judicial system in which many of the CHCC's certified practitioners testify. More important, standards of practice have to be established to serve as guidelines when one's behavior has to be judged against another's complaint. Only through a committed effort on the part of the CHCC to define the roles of evaluators and life care planners can these services delivery systems be improved. The CHCC is young compared to the CRCC, as is its generic rehabilitation certification movement. The certification movement in life care planning is still in its infancy with much work ahead. Only through the continued recertification efforts and support of those who have completed the certification process in both areas of the CHCC will the credentialing movement establish a foothold in the rehabilitation profession.

Continuing Education Requirements

The CHCC certification maintenance program extends the CLCP status at 3-year intervals if the life care planner completes a total of 48 clock hours of approved education/training. Failure to renew certification will result in revocation of certified status. Information submitted that is false or misleading may also result in certification revocation. As of 2003, the renewal fee was $90 for each 3-year period. A second recertification option is to retake the examination. The 2002 fee for this option was $200.

Ethical Process, Case Studies, and Current Concerns

There is nothing more serious within the Commission on Health Care Certification than the ethical issues that are brought before the Ethics Review Board. Our major concerns regarding the present and future status of life care planning certification rest not with business issues such as daily revenues and expenses, but with the nature of complaints that have been reviewed and ruled upon by the Ethics Review Board. Similarly, this commission receives inquiries from CLCP professionals regarding their concerns pertaining to a colleague's or peer's professional training and competency, given the life care planning product they have reviewed of that respective individual. Though this is not an ethical issue, it is alarming that the CHCC continues to receive these inquiries of qualitative applications.

The Commission on Health Care Certification adopted its code of professional ethics with direction and input from documents pertaining to the codes and standards of and statements from the following professional organizations:

Commission on Rehabilitation Counselor Certification
National Association of Rehabilitation Professionals in the Private Sector
National Rehabilitation Administration Association
Virginia Board of Professional Counselors
North Carolina Board of Professional Counselors

The resulting Code of Ethics is published in the *Commission on Health Care Certification Standards and Guidelines Manual*, and the reader is encouraged to download this text from the CHCC website at www.cdec1.com, as space limitations in this chapter preclude the listing of the principles and rules. (See Appendix II for the standards and code of professional ethics.)

Process

The process for submitting a complaint is fairly simple. The complaint must be received on the business letterhead of the person filing the complaint, and it must be signed by the author. The complaint is read by the executive director and a determination is made regarding the CHCC's jurisdiction over the issue, and if the issue merits further review by the Ethics Review Board. If there is merit to the complaint, the executive director assembles a five-person-panel Ethics Review Board that is comprised of commissioners actively serving on the Board of Commissioners. Due to the multidisciplinary backgrounds of certified life care planners, the CHCC reserves the right to refer any allegation of ethical conduct violations to the accused's own professional organization or credentialing board for a preliminary review and investigation. This is not to say that the complaint cannot or will not be heard by the CHCC; rather, it is the executive committee's opinion that any complaint should be heard by the accused's professional organization or licensing board in all fairness to the accused, if it is determined that the CHCC has no jurisdiction over the complaint. If the accused's board finds in fact that a violation occurred, then the CHCC will proceed, at its own discretion, with its own investigation.

A complaint may be filed by any individual or organization. The complainant need not be credentialed by the CHCC, but the accused must be credentialed under the CHCC. If the complaint does not involve a CHCC-credentialed professional, the CHCC executive director will inform the complainant and may refer the complainant to another agency or association with proper jurisdiction.

Applicants for certification under the CHCC are required to provide information relative to ethical actions past or pending involving other associations or credentialing/licensing organizations. Falsification of any information in this area will lead to the following disciplinary termination of application and notification of the falsification to relevant licensing boards, certification boards, and applicant references. Regarding all infractions that are found to have merit of which the accused has been found guilty, the Ethics Committee is entitled to take any one of the following actions upon a confirmation of the alleged infraction(s):

1. **Revocation:** The Ethics Committee may revoke the credentials that the clinician obtained through the CHCC, with notification of revocation disseminated to his or her professional organizations and certification and licensing boards.
2. **Probation:** The committee may place the credentialed professional on probation, suspend certification, or reprimand or censure the individual. The credentialed professional may be requested to cease the challenged conduct, accept supervision, or seek rehabilitative or educational training or counseling.

The Ethics Committee may implement these requests by issuing any one of the following:

1. **Cease and Desist Order:** Require the accused to cease and desist the challenged behavior.
2. **Reprimand:** Reprimand when the committee has determined that there has been an ethics violation, but there has been no damage to another person.
3. **Censure:** Censure when the committee has determined that there has been an ethics violation, but the damage done to another person is not sufficient to warrant more serious action.
4. **Supervision Requirement:** Require that the accused receive supervision.
5. **Rehabilitation, Education, Training, or Counseling:** The accused may be required to undergo rehabilitative counseling/therapy, additional education, training, or personal counseling.
6. **Probation:** Require that the accused be placed on probation. Probation is defined as the relation that the CHCC has with the accused when the CHCC undertakes actively and systematically to monitor, for a specific length of time, the degree to which the accused complies with the Ethics Committee's requirements.
7. **Referral:** Referral to a relevant association or state board of examiners for action.
8. **Reapplication:** The Ethics Committee may recommend that the CHCC Executive Board deny reapplication.
9. **Notification of Other Organizations:** In the event that a CHCC-credentialed individual who has violated the code of professional ethics is certified by or a member of other recognized professional boards or associations or is authorized by governmental authority to practice in cognate disciplines, CHCC shall, at its discretion, send notice of disciplinary action to each other organization. The notice shall state that the disciplinary action was pursuant to the CHCC Code of Professional Ethics.

Credentialed professionals are obligated, in accordance to the CHCC Code of Professional Ethics, to cooperate with proceedings of CHCC for any alleged violation of the code of professional ethics. If the accused voluntarily relinquishes certification or fails to cooperate with an ethical inquiry in any way, the CHCC shall continue its investigation, noting in the final report the circumstances of the accused's failure to cooperate. If a complainant refuses to provide testimony, the complaint may be dismissed at the discretion of the CHCC, upon the application and agreement of the accused. The CHCC will not accept countercomplaints from an accused CHCC-credentialed individual during the course of an investigation of the initial complaint. However, in unusual circumstances, the CHCC may accept a countercomplaint during the investigative period of the initial complaint.

CASE STUDIES

The Commission on Health Care Certification has received numerous ethical inquiries and practice-related complaints from CHCC-certified and noncertified health care practitioners. Below, five of these case studies are presented, with direct application to the CHCC ethical review process. There are four closed cases with rulings and one case pending.

Case 200210

The commission (CHCC) received a written complaint from a plaintiff's attorney representing a young boy who was struck by a motor vehicle while crossing a pedestrian crosswalk. Consequently, the youth suffered a severe open head brain injury involving significant damage to a large portion of his right frontal lobe, with additional injury to his temporal and parietal lobes. The attorney conducted a search for a certified life care planner (CLCP) with extensive brain injury expertise. Due to time constraints, the life care plan had to be finalized within 3 months. Their search led them to a CLCP who claimed to have the qualifications necessary to complete the life care plan, was qualified as an expert witness, and would have the life care plan completed within 4 to 6 weeks. Soon after, the CLCP was sent the medical records and met with the attorney's client for 4 hours. According to the attorney, after months of failed communications, contractual disagreements, and other conflicts, the attorney decided to discontinue his firm's relationship with the CLCP and seek services elsewhere. Of grave concern to the attorney, however, was that his firm discovered that the CLCP had forwarded to the defendant's attorney several pages of information related to the case without their knowledge, authority, or consent. Following is the listing of the plaintiff counsel's complaints:

1. Failing to respect the relationship with the clients and their firm, and breaching the confidentiality of their relationship
2. Placing the firm's client's case in jeopardy by conduct calculated to cause harm to the client
3. Failing to communicate with their office and failing to respond to communication.
4. Failing to provide a completed life care plan in a timely fashion and within the time agreed to
5. Misrepresentation of the CLCP's qualifications for severely brain injured children
6. Failing to act with integrity and protect the welfare of the client
7. Failing to demonstrate any care or concern to achieve optimism, welfare, and benefit to the client
8. Failing to observe the privileged status of the client's relationship with their office
9. Failing to adhere to professional standards in billing and promotion of services
10. Breach of agreement.
11. Placing financial gain before the client's well-being
12. Failing to provide the benefit expected of a credentialed life care planner

Consequently, as with all allegations of questionable conduct, the CHCC executive director must confer with the Ethics Review Board regarding the legitimacy of the complaint, review the complaint with legal counsel once the committee has reviewed and affirmed the legitimacy of the complaint, acknowledge the complaint within 30 days of receipt, and direct a letter to the complainant acknowledging acceptance or rejection of the complaint. If a decision to accept the complaint is made, the executive director must assist the Ethics Review Board chairperson in assembling the appropriate committee members.

Referring to our case, the CHCC legal counsel and the Ethics Committee certified the complaint; therefore, a notice of complaint was sent to the accused. The accused CLCP responded in writing within the 30-day time frame. The CLCP rebuked the attorney's complaints stating it was the attorney who repeatedly failed to return all forms of communications. In addition, the CLCP was recently in collection actions with the attorney for failure to close on past-due accounts for the services she rendered in relation to the case. In an effort to locate an attorney to settle her collection actions, she had an initial consultation and faxed various documents relating to her collections case to her newly retained attorney, who happened to be representing the defendant in the case of the young boy who was struck by a motor vehicle. Soon after their initial consultation, the attorney contacted the CLCP and stated he could not accept her case due to a conflict of interest. The CLCP insisted she had no prior knowledge that the firm was involved in any part of the litigation related to the case, and that no information regarding the life care plan was communicated. The CLCP soon retained a new attorney for her collections case and the actions were settled by both parties. As part of the settlement, the attorney agreed to release the CLCP of and from all manner of action related to their relationship. Consequently, the attorney requested a withdrawal of his complaint. In essence, this case was settled without any opinion rendered by the Ethics Review Board, and therefore, no determination of fault was made on behalf of the plaintiff counsel.

Case 20001

A complaint was filed by a certified life care planner regarding the qualifications of a case manager listed on the website as being certified as a life care planner. The complaint noted that in spite of the individual passing the examination, this person had not met the criteria for qualifying to sit for the CLCP examination because this person did not possess any certifications or licenses in his or her respective field of practice (*CHCC Standards and Guidelines Manual*, p. 9). This complaint was followed by several more from other certified life care planners regarding peers who they felt did not meet the criteria for qualifying for the CLCP examination due to their lack of possessing certifications/licenses in their respective field of training prior to sitting for the examination.

This issue was brought before the entire Board of Commissioners, with input gathered from all commissioners regarding a new comprehensive review of records and subsequent penalties should the complaints prove to be valid. The volume of files from all persons who were certified as either life care planners (CLCPs) or disability examiners (CDE) was reviewed. The result was that the complaint was found to be valid. An additional seven more persons were found to have been admitted without carrying the primary certification or license credential as a result of the comprehensive file review. All persons were contacted and informed of the complaint and of the findings of the board through the file review process. They were given an opportunity to respond in writing to the complaint, as well as to forward to the commission any updates in their respective credentials. Additionally, the individuals were informed that their credential was rescinded pending their submission of proof that they had met the primary credential qualification criteria. They were given 12 months to satisfy this criteria. All eight persons successfully obtained the necessary primary certification credential; several had obtained it since receiving the CLCP credential.

Case 20022

A complaint was filed against a CLCP practitioner by a peer CLCP practitioner questioning whether the individual should have been certified as a life care planner based on responses she gave in a deposition. Additionally, the complaint stated that her life care plan was flawed and was not of the quality representative of a certified life care planner. The complaint filed was meticulous in its detail with supportive suppositions for each alleged infraction offered by the complainant. The CLCP in question was asked several questions in deposition regarding her certification status, her preparation in sitting for the examination, and what her qualifications were that allowed her to qualify to test and receive the credential. From the author's perspective, her answers were not flattering to herself as a nurse case manager or as a certified life care planner.

A review of the complaint with subsequent investigation determined that the allegations were valid to pursue, and a five-member Ethics Review Board was established to review each of the allegations forwarded to the CHCC. The respondent was contacted and requested to respond to the allegations in writing. Her file was reviewed, which included her qualifications, the life care plan that she submitted for review by the commission, and her test scores. After a lengthy and careful review, the board offered its opinion, authored by the Ethics chairperson, Dr. Horace Sawyer. He noted that the respondent had successfully met the 120 hours of training in her bachelor's and master's degrees. Dr. Sawyer noted that "while her training did not take place in an established life care plan training program, she demonstrated sufficient hours related to life care planning."

It was further noted that her graduate thesis was related directly to the assessment and planning issues for spinal cord injury, and her submitted life care plan was found to be appropriate for a catastrophic case involving quadriplegia. Dr. Sawyer concluded that "while responses made in the 2001 deposition of the respondent were ill-advised and unfortunate, they do not constitute grounds to jeopardize certification status, in the opinion of the committee.... As a result of the comprehensive evaluation, the committee determined and recommended no required actions in the case."

Case 20031 — A and B

A certified life care planner filed a complaint with the CHCC regarding two case managers who claimed CLCP status without evidence of submitting an application or sitting for the CLCP examination. This CLCP knew one of the persons and was sure that she never applied for the CLCP credential, and felt sure that the other person did not carry the credential as well. Because this complaint was more didactic in proof (either they did or did not), this case was handled administratively by the executive director.

A review of the CHCC databases for current CLCPs, CLCP applicants, and CLCP inquiries revealed that both persons (respondents) were not listed. This fact suggested that not only were they not CLCPs, but they had not made an inquiry regarding the CLCP credential and the qualification criteria. A letter was sent to both respondents apprising them of the complaint and that the CHCC requested that they cease and desist immediately from using the CLCP credential in either written or verbal forms, and that all reference to this credential be removed from their paper products. After several months of no response from either respondent, the CHCC sent a follow-up letter to both respondents. Their nonresponse strategy remained for another month, after which the CHCC filed formal complaints with all of these persons' regulatory and certification boards. These boards included their respective state nursing regulatory board (Professional Conduct/Ethics Review Boards) and the Legal Nurse Consulting Certification Board. To date, only one response has been received from the credentialing agencies, and still no response from the respondents. As a final penalty, it was decided that full disclosure of their infractions be displayed on the CHCC website. It was this case that established the CHCC's policy for displaying on the CHCC's website those persons' names as well as their e-mail or any written correspondence in which the credential was improperly referenced. The names of the individuals remain on the website pending the receipt of their assurance that they will no longer make such an unauthorized and false reference. If they do not respond to our inquiry, a formal complaint is filed with their respective state health professional regulatory board, which has been done in these two cases.

These cases remain open since a response from both parties has not been received, and the investigation from the State Board of Nursing remains ongoing from one of the cases. The names will remain on the website indefinitely pending a resolution satisfactory with the CHCC policy on unauthorized use of its credentials.

CONCLUSION

The Commission on Health Care Certification is dedicated to researching and developing valid certification credentials that meet the standards of health care practice within the varying training and professional backgrounds of its applicants. The CHCC recognizes that its certification programs are not self-sustaining and requires solid, research-based credentialing, which in turn perpetuates a well-defined service delivery system.

The integrity and future of credentialing in rehabilitation and life care planning rests with how well the certifying agency addresses ethical complaints while basing its decisions on well-developed standards. The CHCC has undertaken such a task in its development of ethical standards as applied to its certification policies. Only through monitoring the behaviors and conduct of those certified will the CHCC be able to protect the consumer from any conduct unbecoming of a professional certified by the CHCC. Although protection does not limit one's practice directly, it can influence one's appeal to referral sources through credential revocation or through any of the other penalties applied by the Ethics Review Board.

It is important for the practitioner to understand that being certified under this or any other certifying agency is not a revelation toward one's competency to deliver a specified service or the quality of that delivery. Rather, certification attests to the fact that the certified individual has met the minimal acceptable standards of practice for that particular service delivery system under which the individual is certified. Furthermore, it states that the individual is willing to accept those standards and to practice by the guidelines.

One of the CHCC's main concerns reflects on the quality of training currently being offered in life care planning service delivery. Frequently, we are posed the question of how someone was able to achieve life care planning certification, and yet produce such an inept, incompetent life care plan product. The authors of these inquiries are reminded of what defines certification — that it is not by any means a qualitative measure, but more of a quantitative measure in determining that the individual has met the minimum criteria for acceptance to sit for the examination, and that his or her score was above the minimum acceptable score.

Given that certification does not have the authority to regulate one's practice, nor does it incur the quality of one's skills to practice, the question remains as to why one should become certified. Matkin (1985) claimed that with all of the varying certification agencies and assigned credentials that are available in health care professions, dilution of credential impact within one's profession results with little accountability applied to the respective credential. Thomas (1993) concluded that the primary purpose of professional credentialing in rehabilitation "is not to protect the weak but rather to increase the power, authority, and [revenues] of the strong; none of the professional/traditional credentialing bodies in [rehabilitation] provide any protection whatsoever to clients" (p. 187). Rather, he concluded, certification is about eliminating competition and increasing one's market share.

While it is true that there are ample rehabilitation certifications to confuse both consumers and rehabilitation professionals, resolution of this dilemma rests with the practitioner determining which certification will directly impact his or her practice. For example, in private-sector settings that focus on litigation cases and subsequent deposition and court testimony, a rehabilitation nurse or case manager may do well holding certifications as certified rehabilitation registered nurse (CRRN) or certified rehabilitation counselor (CRC). However, when the practice offers life care planning services that require additional training and postgraduate hours, the current certifications seem to hold little prominence when the opposing expert witness in the case has met the qualifying standards and criteria to hold the certified life care planner (CLCP) credential. It does not take the referring legal community much time before realizing the significance of one credential over another, especially when one is service-oriented and specific to the legal community.

Another practical aspect for support of certification and credentialing in rehabilitation is that of selective requirement. Currently, the CRC credential for rehabilitation counselors and the CCM credential for nurses and counselor-trained rehabilitation case managers are becoming mandatory credentials among third-party payers of private-sector rehabilitation services. Although the respective states may not require the certification credentials, several major insurance companies have selected these two credentials as mandatory before payment for services can be authorized. Thus, the CRC and CCM are selectively required of practitioners in some states that do not require certification credentials.

A similar scenario is found in the negotiations the CHCC has had with several national insurance companies regarding their disability policies. The CHCC has proposed that functional capacity evaluators and impairment raters who carry the CDE I, II, and III credential perform the disability evaluations exclusively for the respective insurance company. The attraction of such an offer for these insurance companies is that the medical review officers located in the branch offices around the country will be assured of receiving a disability report that is consistent in content among all certified disability examiners, consistent in its format, and that the protocol used to determine the disability outcome is research based with established validity. The advantage of such an arrangement to the certified disability examiner I, II, or III is simply an enhanced referral base for disability examinations, thus increasing the practitioner's overall revenue base. Similarly, Hartford Insurance mandated to all of its field offices in 1998 that only certified life care planners are accepted consultants to manage its catastrophic cases. To summarize, the clinical practitioner needs to become credentialed and needs to select the credential that will best serve his or her practice.

The answer to the question of whether to pursue certification or to leave the process to one's peers is clear given today's market trends and reimbursement policies. The profession is demanding closer scrutiny of service delivery and thus is requiring its practitioners to become credentialed. Life care planning has experienced significant growth over the past 17 years, and the legal community demands credentialed experts in this field. The question of which credential to pursue is market driven and is best answered by the practitioner when considering which credential will best benefit his or her practice. If one's practice is engaged heavily in life care planning, then the CLCP credential is the obvious choice. On the other hand, third-party payers are demanding that case managers and rehabilitation consultants be certified even if state statutes do not require certification or licensure for rehabilitation practitioners.

We must not forget, however, the original intent of certification credentialing: to define one's profession or, in the case of life care planning, the service delivery system, and to provide some protection to the consumer through title regulation (Fritz & Mills, 1980). The latter is achieved by virtue of the third-party payment systems supporting the credentialing movement in rehabilitation and life care planning through the authorization of reimbursement contingent on one's certification status. The former is achieved through the respective credentialing agency's desire to produce a valid and reliable credential that is backed and supported by research from a university-level institution.

As demonstrated previously, the rehabilitation profession has a plethora of credentials (certifications) from which the clinical provider can choose. When deciding on the certification credential that would best meet one's career goals, the reader is advised to review the integrity of the certifying agency through a thorough background review. Let us not be pretentious and think that because there is a complex application process, official-looking forms, and letterhead from the certifying agency, which contains numerous highly degreed and well-trained professionals on the agency's advisory board, that the respective agency delivers a valid credentialing process. This is simply not the case. The "proof in the pudding" rests with the effort the certifying agency has taken to ensure that the profession receives an unbiased credential without any conflicts of interest attached. The following checklist is designed to help the professional resolve this dilemma:

1. **Accreditation:** Choose the credential that has made an application to the National Commission on Certifying Agencies (NCCA). This is the prominent regulatory agency for health care certification agencies under which all of those in the field of rehabilitation would be categorized.
2. **Research Support:** Choose a credential that has been investigated for validity and reliability. This process involves extensive research from a university-backed institution that has a research-oriented human services department. What role research has in credentialing is to establish the examination's validity and reliability as the examination content is applied to the field.
3. **Training Conflict:** Avoid those certifications that are advertised through a training agency. In other words, some training agencies advertise that the participant will become certified or will receive notification of being certified upon completion of the training program. These types of certifications usually do not require the participant to pass a certification test, but to just attend the training.

Finally, in this same genre, avoid agencies that mail out postcard announcements suggesting that the grandfathering period is about to expire, and that the professional needs to act promptly in order to ensure a place on the certification registry of that particular specialty area. The process usually requires the professional candidate to send in three letters of reference, complete the abbreviated application form, submit a curriculum vita, and, of course, a check. When one looks at the material closely, the credentialing agency is one that provides training as a primary function with certification as an added bonus. In these authors' opinion, this practice is totally unacceptable. However, there is apparently nothing illegal about a credentialing agency using this approach.

The integrity and future of credentialing in rehabilitation and life care planning rests with all rehabilitation practitioners and consumers of services (i.e., insurance carriers, attorneys, disabled persons, and employers). Our profession will not sustain itself without solid, research-based credentialing, which in turn perpetuates a well-defined service delivery system. More practitioners need to support their respective specialty credentialing processes, and in turn, these credentialing agencies need to respond readily to the needs of the consumer of services as well as the needs of those whom they certify.

CERTIFICATION INFORMATION

For information about certification in life care planning, contact:

Linda McKinley, BSN, RN, CLCP, CDMS, CCM
Executive Director
Commission of Disability Examiner Certification
13801 Village Mill Dr., Suite 204
Midlothian, VA 23113
(804) 378-7273
Fax: 804-378-7267
mayrehab@aol.com

REFERENCES

Blackwell, T., Powers, A., & Weed, R. (1994a). *Life Care Planning for Traumatic Brain Injury: A Resource Manual for Case Managers.* Athens, GA: Elliott & Fitzpatrick.

Blackwell, T., Weed, R., & Powers, A. (1994b). *Life Care Planning for Spinal Cord Injury: A Resource Manual for Case Managers.* Athens, GA: Elliott & Fitzpatrick.

Deutsch, P. (1994). Life care planning: into the future. *NARPPS Journal,* 9, 79–84.

Deutsch, P., Sawyer, H., Jenkins, W., & Kitchens, J. (1986). Life care planning in catastrophic case management. *Journal of Private Sector Rehabilitation,* 1, 13–27.

Fritz, B. & Mills, D. (1980). *Licensing and Certification of Psychologists and Counselors.* San Francisco: Jossey-Bass.

Gianforte, G. (1976). Certification: a challenge and a choice. *Journal of Rehabilitation,* 42, 15–17.

Leahy, M. & Holt, E. (1993). Certification in rehabilitation counseling: history and process. *Rehabilitation Counseling Bulletin,* 37, 71–80.

Lewin, S., Ramseur, J., & Sink, J. (1979). The role of private rehabilitation: founder, catalyst, competitor. *Journal of Rehabilitation,* 45, 16–19.

Matkin, R.E. (1985). *Insurance Rehabilitation.* Austin, TX: Pro-Ed.

Powers, A.S. (1994). Life care planning: the role of the legal nurse. *NARPPS Journal,* 9, 51–56.

Rubin, S., Matkin, R., Ashley, J., Beardsley, M., May, V., Onstott, K., & Puckett, F. (1984). Roles and functions of certified rehabilitation counselors. *Rehabilitation Counseling Bulletin,* 27, 199–224.

Suttenfield, C. (1983). Credentialing for rehab practitioners. *The Claimsman,* 7, 38–39.

Szymanski, E., Linkowski, D., Leahy, M., Diamond, E., & Thoreson, R. (1993). Human resource development: an examination of perceived training needs of certified rehabilitation counselors. *Rehabilitation Counseling Bulletin,* 37, 163–181.

Thomas, K. (1993). Professional credentialing: a doomsday machine without failsafe. *Rehabilitation Counseling Bulletin,* 37, 187–193.

Turner, T., Taylor, D., Rubin, S., & May, V. (2000). Job functions associated with the development of life care plans. *The Journal of Legal Nurse Consulting,* 11, 3–7.

Washington, C. (1996). An Investigation of the Job Roles of Work Disability Evaluating Professionals. Unpublished Dissertation. Southern Illinois University, Carbondale.

Appendix I

STANDARDS OF PRACTICE AND ETHICS FOR LIFE CARE PLANNERS

International Academy of Life Care Planners (IALCP)

Available online at http://www.ialcp.com/life_care_planning_guidelines.html.

I. Introduction
   A. Definition
      A life care plan is a dynamic document based upon published standards
      of practice, comprehensive assessment, data analysis and research,
      which provides an organized, concise plan for current and future needs
      with associated cost for individuals who have experienced catastrophic
      injury or have chronic health care needs.
   B. Historical Perspective
      The development of a comprehensive plan of care has always been
      considered an integral part of the rehabilitation process. This type of
      plan has historically been utilized by multiple disciplines, including the
      rehabilitation plan utilized by rehabilitation counselors, the nursing care
      plan utilized by nurses, and the medical treatment plan used by thera-
      peutic disciplines. Pursuant to rapid growth in medical technology and
      an increased emphasis on the cost of care, including concepts of
      managed care, information regarding the specific cost of care has
      become an increasingly more important aspect of health care. This
      process of developing a comprehensive plan and delineating costs has
      evolved over an extensive period of time and is now utilized by case
      managers, counselors, and other professionals in many sectors. This
      concept represents an acceptable and pragmatic approach to the delivery
      of services within myriad sectors of the health care delivery system.
         The concept of rehabilitation/life care plans has been utilized in a
      variety of health care and legal settings to provide information and
      documentation regarding the cost of services related to long-term care.
      These plans are also provided as valuable tools for rehabilitation plan-
      ning, geriatric services implementation, management of health care
      funds, discharge planning, educational planning, and long-term managed
      care.

0-8493-1511-5/04/$0.00+$1.50
© 2004 by CRC Press LLC

C. Transdisciplinary Perspective

Life care planning is a transdisciplinary specialty of practice within professional disciplines. Each discipline brings to the process of life care planning Professional Standards of Practice, which must be adhered to by the individual professional. Each professional works within specific standards of practice for their discipline to insure accountability, provide direction, and mandate responsibility for the standards for which they are accountable. These include, but are not limited to, activities related to quality of care, qualifications, collaboration, law, ethics, advocacy, resource utilization, and research. Moreover, each individual practitioner is responsible for following the Standards of Practice for Life Care Planning.

In addition, the individual practitioner must examine their qualifications as applied to each individual case. Therefore, a thorough knowledge of the disability and long-term care considerations by virtue of education and experience is a necessary component of the practitioner's competency for each individual case.

D. Education/Preparation/Certification

The life care planner should maintain appropriate professional credentials, including:

1. Membership in good standing within a professional health care or rehabilitation discipline.
2. Current professional licensure or National Board of Certification within a professional health care or rehabilitation discipline.
3. Completion of an accredited program in nursing, or a baccalaureate or higher-level educational program in a professional health care or rehabilitation discipline.
4. The professional discipline should provide sufficient education and training to ensure that the life care planner has an understanding of human anatomy and physiology, pathologies, the health care system, the role and function of health care disciplines and clinical practice guidelines (or standards of care). Examples of professional disciplines meeting this requirement include, but are not limited to, registered nurses, medical social workers, rehabilitation counselors, psychologists, physicians, and therapists in health-related disciplines.
5. Maintenance of specific continued education required to ensure the individual practitioner's licensure and certification.
6. Knowledge of professional legal requirements, including the legal principles of consent and confidentiality.

II. Philosophical Overview

The life care plan should be a working document that provides accurate and timely information which can be easily utilized by the client and interested parties. It should be a living document that can serve as a lifelong guide to assist in the delivery of health care services in a managed format. The care plan should be a collaborative effort among the various parties and should reflect goals that are preventative and rehabilitative in nature. As a dynamic document, the life care plan may require periodic updating to accommodate changes and should have quality outcomes as its goal.

Goals/Life Care Plans

A. To assist the client in achieving optimal outcomes by developing an appropriate plan of prevention and restoration. This may include recommendations for evaluations or treatment that may contribute to the client's level of wellness or provide information regarding treatment requirements.

B. To provide health education to the client and interested parties, when appropriate.

C. To develop accurate and timely cost information and specificity of service allocations that can be applied by the client and interested parties.

D. To develop options for care that may be necessary for alternative situations.

E. To communicate the life care plan and objectives to the client and interested parties.

F. To develop measurement tools which can be used to analyze outcomes.

G. To routinely develop comprehensive assessments of the projected goals of the life care plan, whenever possible.

III. Role and Functions of Life Care Planners

A. Scope of Practice/Applications

As a member of a professional health care discipline, the life care planner must remain within the scope of practice for that discipline as determined by state or national organizations. The functions associated with performing life care planning are within the scope of practice for health care professionals.

Analysis of data and evaluation of care recommendations are key elements in the functions of life care planning. In performing these tasks, the life care planner will communicate with a variety of health care professionals regarding a case and may temporarily assume a peripheral role in the management of the case. The life care planner must take care to keep the life care planning function separate from caregiver and case manager functions. The life care planner does not assume decision-making responsibility beyond the scope of his/her own professional discipline.

B. Specialty Skills

The life care planner must have skill and expertise in understanding the health care and rehabilitation needs addressed in a life care plan. Personal clinical knowledge and practice experience provides an excellent foundation for development of a credible life care plan. To enhance the quality of the life care plan, the life care planner must be able to locate appropriate resources when necessary. The life care planner provides a consistent, objective, thorough methodology for constructing the life care plan, while relying on appropriate medical information, resources, and personal expertise for developing the content of the life care plan. The life care planner relies on state-of-the-art knowledge and resources to develop a life care plan.

Specialized skills are required to successfully develop a life care plan. These include, but are not limited to, the ability to critically analyze data, manage large volumes of information, attend to details, demonstrate clear and thorough written and verbal communication skills, develop positive relationships, create and use networks for gathering information, work autonomously, and demonstrate a professional demeanor and appearance.

C. Functions

1. Data Collection
   a. Collects data that is systematic, comprehensive, and accurate.
   b. Collects data about biopsychosocial, financial, educational, and vocational status and needs.
   c. Obtains information from medical records, client/family/significant others, and appropriate treating or consulting health care professionals.

2. Assessment
   a. Analyzes data to determine client needs and consistency of care recommendations with standards of care.
   b. Assesses need for further evaluations or expert opinions.

3. Planning
   a. Follows a consistent method for organizing data, creating a narrative life care plan report and cost projections.
   b. Develops and uses written documentation tools for reports and tables.
   c. Develops recommendations for content of the life care plan tables for each client and a method for validating inclusion or exclusion of content.

4. Collaboration
   a. Develops positive relationships with all parties.
   b. Seeks expert opinions.
   c. Shares relevant information to aid in formulating recommendations and opinions.

5. Plan Development Research
   The research component of life care planning requires a consistent, valid, and reliable approach to data collection. The life care planner:
   a. Reviews current literature or other published sources to determine current standards of care and available care resources.
   b. Collaborates with other treating professionals regarding standards of care and recommendations for each client.
   c. Determines replacement frequency for appropriate items of care.
   d. Delineates options and costs for each aspect of care, using sources that are available in the client's geographic area.
   e. Considers appropriate criteria for care options:
      1) Maintains specific criteria for each aspect of care.
         Example: Residential facility
         a) Category (e.g., intermediate care facility/mental retardation)
         b) Population served

        c) Staff/client ratio

        d) Staff credentials

        e) Level of care

        f) Cost information (per diem inclusions, etc.)

        g) Descriptive data

            1) Method of selecting care choices and cost data is valid and reliable (i.e., objective, uses comparisons, relies upon statistical evidence and literature searches).

            2) An appropriate number of sources are researched to determine available choices and costs.

            3) When available, classification systems (e.g., ICD-9, CPT) are used to correlate care recommendations and costs.

            4) Care choices are made matching client characteristics with the ability of the service or product to meet client needs.

            5) Care choices are based on current state-of-the-art products and services that are reasonably available.

            6) Knowledge is maintained of care standards, services, and products through continuing education, literature, exhibits, etc.

6. Facilitation

    a. Maintains objectivity and assists others in resolving disagreements about appropriate content for the life care plan.

    b. Provides information about the life care planning process to involved parties to elicit cooperative participation.

7. Evaluation

    a. Reviews and revises the life care plan for internal consistency and completeness.

    b. Reviews the life care plan for consistency with standards of care and seeks resolution of inconsistencies.

    c. Provides follow-up consultation to ensure that the life care plan is understood and properly interpreted.

8. Testimony

    a. Acts as a consultant to legal proceedings, related to determining care needs and costs.

    b. Provides expert sworn testimony regarding development and content of the life care plan.

    c. Maintains up-to-date records about participation in sworn testimony.

IV. Standards of Performance

  A. Ethical

Ethics refers to a set of principals of "right" conduct, a theory or a system of moral values, or the rules or standards governing the conduct of a person or members of a profession. The primary goal of practice ethics is to protect clients, provide guidelines for practicing professionals, and to enhance the profession as a whole. Within the life care planning industry, all practitioners are members of one or more professional disciplines and/or are licensed or certified. It is expected that life care planners follow appropriate relevant ethical guidelines within their areas of professional practice and expertise.

Life care planners are expected to maintain appropriate confidentiality, avoid dual relationships, adequately advise clients of the role of the life care planner, and maintain competency in the profession.

1. Confidentiality: Appropriate confidentiality is a sensitive and important concept. Some professionals will have communications protected by "privilege" which is statutorily based in each state. For example, although no "life care planners" are currently covered by privilege, many may be professional counselors, licensed psychologists, or others who have the additional statutory protection. In addition, litigation has the additional component of attorney work product that may have an effect on what information may be disclosed. The life care planner must be thoroughly informed on this topic.

2. Dual relationships: A personal relationship with a client is not appropriate during the course of service. Developing life care plans for friends, co-workers, professional colleagues, or anyone where the objectivity and professionalism of the care plan is questioned should be avoided.

3. Client advisement of role: Each client should be fully informed about the role of the life care planner. For example, the client should be fully informed about who is requesting the life care plan as well as the confidentiality of communications. Also, life care planners who have dual role responsibilities should clarify that they are not acting as a case manager, psychologist, etc. and what the limits of their participation might be.

4. Competency: The life care planner is expected to accurately represent any information received for a particular case. Medical recommendations are to have an appropriate medical foundation. Research information that the life care planner has obtained for all aspects of care should be readily available for examination by appropriate reviewers.

B. Research

The life care plan will have as its basis the scientific principles of medicine and health care. The involvement of the life care planner in the area of research should include, but not be limited to, the following objectives:

1. The life care planner will strive to identify and participate in research independently or in collaboration with others, utilizing research tools and activities that will promote quality outcomes.

2. The life care planner will critique literature for application to life care planning.

3. The life care planner will use appropriate research findings in the development of life care plans.

Appendix II

STANDARDS AND CODE OF PROFESSIONAL ETHICS

Commission on Health Care Certification (CHCC)

Available online at http://www.cdec1.com.

The Code of Professional Ethics for Certified Life Care Planners (CLCP) is presented in the *CHCC Standards and Examination Guidelines,* and are reproduced in their entirety for the benefit of the reader. We thought it would be beneficial to the interested practitioner to display our standards on this web site for easy reference. These standards are those by which the Commission bases its decisions of its reviews of all complaints filed under this certification agency. These standards are based on the input of the 14 Commissioners who comprise this agency in addition to the professional organizations listed below.

CODE OF PROFESSIONAL ETHICS

Preamble

The Commission on Health Care Certification has adopted the Code of Professional Ethics with direction and input from documents from the Codes and Standards of and statements from the following professional organizations:

Commission on Rehabilitation Counselor Certification
International Association of Rehabilitation Professionals
National Rehabilitation Administration Association
Virginia Board of Professional Counselors
North Carolina Board of Professional Counselors

For purposes of clarification and consistency, Certified Disability Examiners, Categories I, II, and III (CDE I, II, III), and Certified Post Offer Evaluators (CPOE) are referenced as disability examiners in this section. Similarly, Certified Life Care Planners (CLCP) are referenced as life care planners.

Disability examiners and life care planners are committed to making fair and impartial assessments regarding the functional capabilities and needs of the

0-8493-1511-5/04/$0.00+$1.50
© 2004 by CRC Press LLC

referred individual, whether that individual is considered to be catastrophically injured or adventitiously injured with a manageable orthopaedic or neurological diagnosis. Life care plans are required to be thorough with competent research conducted for each identified category of need, and opinions and conclusions structured without regard for personal reimbursement resources. Similarly, the disability examiner is required to provide a detailed and thorough examination with conclusions and recommendations supported by tests or evaluation components that have established reliability and validity. Concluding opinions are based on the performance results over an entire test battery, and are not based on the results of one test within the examination protocol. The disability examiner is committed to render concluding opinions without regard for third-party reimbursement resource attitudes or biases.

Disability examiners and life care planners are obligated to perform activities within their respective certification areas which have been researched to suggest that these activities are an integral part of their roles and functions. For example, disability examiners are responsible for collecting and processing intake information, assessing physical and cognitive tolerances for work activities, and evaluating primarily neurological and orthopaedic disorders. Life care planners are required at the minimum to assess the client's medical and independent living service needs, assess their vocational feasibility and options, and to provide consulting services to the legal system. But above all, disability examiners and life care planners must demonstrate adherence to ethical standards and must ensure that the standards are enforced. The Code of Professional Ethics is designed to serve as a reference for professionals who carry CHCC certification credentials, thus ensuring that acceptable behavior and conduct are clarified, defined and maintained. The basic objective of the Code of Professional Ethics is to promote the welfare of service recipients by specifying and enforcing ethical behavior expected of disability examiners and life care planners.

The primary obligation of the disability examiner and life care planner is to the disabled person in question. Only when the disability examiner is requested to perform an independent medical examination does the obligation of the disability examiner shift to that of the referring party since there is no physician/patient relationship. The same principal applies to the life care planner when approached by the third party funding source to critique a previously written life care plan developed per the request of the disabled individual's legal representative. However, the disability examiner and the life care planner are obligated to communicate to the third party referral source any discoveries which may benefit the disabled person in question regarding additional rehabilitation or vocational options.

The Code of Professional Ethics consists of two types of standards; Principles and Rules of Professional Conduct. The Principles are general standards which provide a definition of the category under which specific rules are assigned. While the Principles are general in concept, the rules are exacting standards which provide guidance in specific circumstances.

Disability examiners and life care planners who violate the Professional Code of Ethics are subject to disciplinary action. A Rule violation is interpreted as a violation of the applicable Principle and any one of its general applicable principles. The CHCC considers the use of Certified Disability Examiner, Certified Life

Care Planner, and Certified Post Offer Evaluator a privilege, and reserves unto itself the power to suspend or to revoke the privilege or to approve other penalties for a Rule violation. Disciplinary penalties are imposed as warranted by the severity of the offense and circumstances. All disciplinary actions are undertaken in accordance with published procedures and penalties designed to assure the proper enforcement of the Code of Professional Ethics within the framework of due process and equal protection of the laws.

When there is reason to question the ethical propriety of specific behaviors, persons are encouraged to refrain from engaging in such behaviors until the matter has been clarified by the CHCC Ethics Committee. Certified Disability Examiners and Certified Life Care Planners who need assistance in interpreting the Code should request in writing an advisory opinion from the Commission on Health Care Certification. This applies to those professionals who are not certified under the CHCC as well, and these practitioners are encouraged to consult with their own individual professional organization regarding an interpretation of the Code and/or individual Rule as disseminated from the CHCC.

Principles and Associated Rules

Principle 1 — Moral and Legal Standards
Disability examiners and life care planners shall behave in legal, ethical, and moral manner in the conduct of their profession, maintaining the integrity of the Code of Professional Ethics and avoiding any behavior which would cause harm to others.

Rules of Professional Conduct

R1.1 Disability examiners and life care planners will obey the laws and statutes in the legal jurisdiction in which they practice and are subject to disciplinary action for any violation, the extent that such violation suggests the likelihood of professional misconduct.

R1.2 Disability examiners and life care planners will be familiar with, will observe, and will discuss with their clients the legal limitations of their services.

R1.3 Disability examiners and life care planners will be alert to legal parameters relevant to their practices and to disparities between legally mandated ethical and professional standards and the Code of Professional Ethics. Where such disparities exist, disability examiners and life care planners will follow the legal mandates and will formally communicate any disparities to the appropriate committee on professional ethics. In the absence of legal guidelines, the Code of Professional Ethics is binding.

R1.4 Disability examiners and life care planners will not engage in any act or omission of a dishonest, deceitful, or fraudulent nature in the conduct of their professional activities. They will not allow the pursuit of financial gain or other personal benefit to interfere with the exercise of sound professional judgment and skills, nor will disability examiners and life care planners abuse their relationships with clients to promote personal or financial gain of their employing agencies.

R1.5 Disability examiners and life care planners will understand and abide by the Principles and Rules of Professional Conduct which are prescribed in the Code of Professional Ethics.

R1.6 Disability examiners and life care planners will not advocate, sanction, participate in, cause to be accomplished, otherwise carry out through another, or condone any act which disability examiners and life care planners are prohibited from performing by the Code of Professional Ethics.

R1.7 Disability examiners and life care planners will avoid public behavior that clearly is in violation of accepted moral and ethical standards

R1.8 Disability examiners and life care planners will refuse to participate in employment practices which are inconsistent with the moral or legal standards regarding the treatment of employees or the public. Disability examiners and life care planners will not condone practices which result in illegal or otherwise unjustifiable discrimination on any basis in hiring, promotion, or training.

Principle 2 — Disability Examiners and Life Care Planners/Patient Relationship

Disability examiners and life care planners shall respect the integrity and protect the welfare of people and groups with whom they work. The primary obligation of disability examiners and life care planners is to their patients outside of independent medical examinations and independent review of care plans in which no physician/patient relationship exists.

Rules of Professional Conduct

R2.1 Disability examiners and life care planners will not misrepresent their role or competence to patients. Disability examiners and life care planners will provide information about their credentials, if requested, and will refer patients to other specialists as the needs dictate.

R2.2 Disability examiners and life care planners will avoid establishing dual relationships with patients that could impair one's professional judgment or increase the risk of exploitation. Sexual intimacies with patients are unethical and will not be tolerated by the CHCC.

R2.3 Disability examiners and life care planners are obligated to clarify the nature of their relationship to all involved parties when providing services at the request of a third party. Similarly and as expected, disability examiners and life care planners have an obligation to provide unbiased, objective opinions whether the evaluation or care planning service be requested by the third party or directly from the plaintiff counsel. Disability examiners and life care planners retained by third party referral sources will clearly define through written or oral means, the limits of their relationship, particularly in the areas of informed consent and legally privileged communications, to all involved individuals.

R2.4   Disability examiners' and life care planners' primary obligation and responsibility is to the catastrophically or non-catastrophically disabled person for whom assessment, evaluation, medical, and vocational and rehabilitation needs are being determined.

Principle 3 — Patient Advocacy

Life care planners shall serve as advocates for people with disabilities.

Rule of Professional Conduct

R3.1   The life care planner will further use his or her specialized knowledge and abilities to promote understanding and the general welfare of disabled persons in the community and to assist in efforts to expand the knowledge needed to serve disabled persons with increased effectiveness. This Rule applies only to life care planners rather than to disability evaluators since life care planners assume a "case manager" role and function in the development of care plans.

Principle 4 — Professional Relationships

Disability examiners and life care planners shall act with integrity in their relationships with colleagues, other organizations, agencies, institutions, referral sources, and other professions so as to facilitate the contribution of all specialists toward achieving optimum benefit for patients.

Rules of Professional Conduct

R4.1   Disability examiners and life care planners will ensure that there is a mutual understanding of the evaluation report or life care plan by all parties involved in the rehabilitation process of the individual in question.

R4.2   Life care planners will abide by and assist in the implementation of "team" decisions in formulating care plans and procedures.

R4.3   When transferring patients to other colleagues or agencies, life care planners will not commit the recipient of the case to any prescribed courses of action which may be specified in the care plan. Similarly, when disability examiners provide rehabilitation recommendations in their reports, they will not commit the recipient of the transferred case to any specified course of action.

R4.4   Disability examiners and life care planners, as referring professionals, will supply all information necessary for a cooperating agency or professional to begin service delivery, and will provide these records in a prompt manner.

R4.5   Disability examiners and life care planners will secure from other professionals all medical records and evaluation reports when such reports and records are essential for life care plan development or for evaluating function and impairment.

R4.6   Disability examiners and life care planners will not discuss with patients the reputations and/or competency of colleagues in a disparaging manner, nor will they provide judgments to the patients regarding the quality of treatment they may have received from other professionals.

R4.7   Disability examiners and life care planners will not exploit their professional relationships with supervisors, colleagues, students, residents, or employees sexually or otherwise, and will not engage in any form of sexual harassment, defined as repeated or deliberate comments, gestures, or physical contacts of a sexual nature undesired and unsolicited by recipients.

R4.8   Disability examiners and life care planners who employ or supervise other professionals or residents/students will facilitate professional development of such individuals through the provision of appropriate working conditions, timely evaluations, constructive consultations, and experience opportunities.

R4.9   Disability examiners and life care planners possessing knowledge of any rule violation of this Code of Professional Ethics is obligated to reveal, upon request, such information to the Commission on Health Care Certification unless the information is protected by law. Disability examiners and life care planners who have knowledge of ethical infractions by their peers or colleagues will attempt to resolve the issue with the professional in question given that the infraction appears to arise from the professional's lack of sensitivity, knowledge, or experience. However, if the infraction does not seem amenable to an informal solution, then the matter must be brought before the Ethical Committee of the CHCC.

Principle 5 — Public Statements/Fees

Disability examiners and life care planners shall adhere to professional standards in establishing fees and promoting their services.

Rules of Professional Conduct

R5.1   Disability examiners and life care planners will neither give nor receive a commission or rebate or any other form of remuneration for referral of patients for professional services.

R5.2   Disability examiners and life care planners who advertise their services to the general public will fairly and accurately present the material, avoiding misrepresentation through sensationalism, exaggeration, or superficiality. Any reporting of "numbers," such as average fee charged per patient for services, average length of involvement in the program, shall be derived directly from actual patient records and appropriate descriptive statistics used to report the outcome data in the respective advertisement.

R5.3   Disability examiners and life care planners are obligated to see all referred patients for the initial assessment and intake interview regardless of their ability to pay. If insurance coverage is nonexistent, disability examiners and life care planners are obligated to establish a mutually acceptable payment plan, or refer the individual promptly to a facility which accepts indigent patients.

Principle 6 — Confidentiality

Disability examiners and life care planners shall respect the confidentiality of information from clients in the course of their work.

Rules of Professional Conduct

R6.1   Disability examiners and life care planners will inform patients at the onset of the service to be provided of the limits of confidentiality.

R6.2   Disability examiners and life care planners will inform responsible authorities when the conditions or actions of patients indicate that there is clear and imminent danger to patients or others after advising patients that this must be done.

R6.3   Disability examiners and life care planners will not forward to another person or agency any confidential information without the written consent of patients or their legal guardians. This does not apply in the situation in which the third party funding source has requested a record review of independent medical/life care plan evaluation.

R6.4   Disability examiners and life care planners will safeguard the maintenance, storage, and disposal of patient records so that unauthorized persons shall not have access to these records.

R6.5   Disability examiners will include in their insurance sign-in sheets a statement regarding the requirement for biomechanical imaging regarding functional capacity evaluations and impairment ratings, of which the patient will sign indicating their acceptance of such policy. Life care planners will obtain written permission from the patient or patient's guardian for video or audio taping of any interview session and interaction they may have with the patient.

R6.6   Disability examiners and life care planners will persist in claiming the privileged status of confidential information obtained from patients, where communications are privileged by statute for disability examiners and life care planners.

Principle 7 — Assessment

Disability examiners and life care planners shall promote the welfare of patients in the selection, utilization, and interpretation of assessment measures.

Rules of Professional Conduct

R7.1   Disability examiners and life care planners will recognize that different tests demand different levels of competence for administration, scoring, and interpretation, and will recognize the limits of their competence and perform only those functions for which they are trained and licensed to perform by their respective states.

R7.2 Disability examiners and life care planners will investigate and utilize those tests or protocols which have established validity and reliability, and which are safe to administer to the patient given the patient's diagnosis and functional capabilities at the time of testing.

R7.3 Disability examiners and life care planners will comply with the Americans with Disabilities Act of 1990 in terms of normative data applications and usage in interpretation of results, and will abide by testing protocol structures/administration as outlined in this Federal legislation.

R7.4 Disability examiners and life care planners will make known the purpose of testing and the explicit use of the results to clients prior to administration. Test results may be disseminated to the patient provided the referral source approves of the patient having access to such information, whether it be a plaintiff or third party referral.

R7.5 Disability examiners and life care planners will administer tests under the same conditions that were established in their standardization. When tests are modified to assess a domain set of trait factors or to accommodate the patient's biomechanical limitations, such modifications must be documented at the time of interpretation in the report.

R7.6 The interpretation of data will be directly related to the particular goals of the evaluation, or referral questions submitted by the referral source.

R7.7 Disability examiners and life care planners will attempt to ensure, when utilizing computerized assessment services or software, that such services and software are based on appropriate research to establish the validity of the computer programs, software and procedures used in arriving at interpretations.

Principle 8 — Research Activities

Disability examiners and life care planners shall assist in efforts to improve upon evaluation and life care plan protocols through participation in research programs or through literature reviews.

Rules of Professional Conduct

R8.1 Disability examiners and life care planners will ensure that data for research meet rigid standards of validity, honesty, and protection of confidentiality.

R8.2 Disability examiners and life care planners will be aware of and responsive to all pertinent guidelines on research with human subjects. When planning any research activity dealing with human subjects, disability examiners and life care planners will ensure that research problems, design, and execution are in full compliance with such guidelines.

R8.3 Disability examiners and life care planners presenting case studies in class, professional meetings, or publications will confine the content to that which can be disguised to ensure full protection of the identity of patients.

R8.4 Disability examiners and life care planners will assign credit to those who have contributed to publications in proportion to their contribution, or as agreed upon with the senior author if the senior author is other than the CHCC credential professional.

Principle 9 — Competence

Disability examiners and life care planners shall establish and maintain their professional competencies at such a level that their patients receive the benefit of the highest quality of services the credentialed professional is capable of offering.

Rules of Professional Conduct

R9.1 Disability examiners and life care planners will function within the limits of their defined role, training, and technical competency and will accept only those positions for which they are professionally qualified.

R9.2 Disability examiners and life care planners will continuously strive through reading, attending professional meetings, and taking course instruction to keep abreast of new developments, concepts, and practices that are essential to providing the highest quality of services to their patients.

R9.3 Disability examiners and life care planners who are educators will perform their duties based on careful preparation so that their instruction is accurate, up-to-date, and scholarly.

R9.4 Disability examiners and life care planners who are educators will ensure that statements in catalogs and course outlines are accurate, particularly in terms of subject matter covered, bases for grading, and nature of classroom experiences.

R9.5 Disability examiners and life care planners who are educators will maintain high standards of knowledge and skill by presenting disability examiners and life care planners information fully and accurately.

Principle 10 — CDE, CPOE, and CLCP Credentials

Disability examiners and life care planners holding the Certified Disability Examiner and/or Certified Life Care Planner designation(s) shall honor the integrity and respect the limitations placed upon its use.

Rules of Professional Conduct

R10.1 Disability examiners and life care planners will use their certification designations only in accordance with the relevant guidelines promulgated by the Commission on Health Care Certification.

R10.2 Disability examiners and life care planners will not attribute to the mere possession of the designation depth or scope of knowledge, skill, and professional capabilities greater than those demonstrated by achievement of the CLCP or CDE designations.

R10.3   Disability examiners and life care planners will not write, speak, nor act in ways that lead others to believe CLCPs or CDEs are officially representing the Commission on Health Care Certification, unless such written permission has been granted by the CHCC.

R10.4   Disability examiners and life care planners will make no claims to unique skills or devices not available to others in the profession unless the special efficacy of such unique skills or device has been demonstrated scientifically accepted evidence.

R10.5   Disability examiners and life care planners will not initiate or support the candidacy of an individual for certification by the CHCC if the individual is known to engage in professional practices which violate the Code of Professional Ethics.

CHCC GUIDELINES AND PROCEDURES FOR PROCESSING ETHICAL COMPLAINTS

The Commission on Health Care Certification provides the following guidelines and procedures for processing alleged violations of the Code of Professional Ethics by disability examiners and life care planners credentialed under the CHCC. All allegations are heard by the CHCC Ethics Committee comprised of persons appointed by the Executive Director. Please be aware that the hearing process should not be construed as a legal process designed to resolve legal issues, but rather an informal hearing process in which many legal structures and conventions are not observed.

Qualifying Statement

The Commission on Health Care Certification recognizes the many disciplines which comprise its certified professional groups. Therefore, the CHCC reserves the right to refer any allegation of ethical conduct violations to the accused's professional organization or credentialing board for a preliminary review and investigation. This is not to say that the complaint cannot or will not be heard by the CHCC; rather, it is the Executive Committee's opinion that any complaint should be heard initially by the accused's professional organization or licensing board in all fairness to the accused. If the accused's board finds in fact that a violation occurred, then the CHCC will proceed, at its own discretion, with its own investigation.

1.00 Jurisdiction

1.A   Types of Complaints: A complaint may be filed by any individual or organization (referred hereinafter as "complainant"). The complainant need not be credentialed by the CHCC, but the accused must be credentialed under the CHCC.

1.B   Anonymous Complaints: The CHCC will not honor or investigate any complaint which is not signed, or which the complainant is not identified.

1.C Non-Credentialed Complaints: If the complaint does not involve a CHCC credentialed professional, the CHCC Executive Director will inform the complainant and may refer the complainant to another agency or association with proper jurisdiction.

1.D CHCC Certification Applicants: Applicants for certification under the CHCC are required to provide information relative to ethical actions past or pending involving other associations or credentialing/licensing organizations. Falsification of any information in this area will lead to the following disciplinary actions: termination of application and notification of the falsification to relevant licensing boards, certification boards, and applicant references.

2.00 Disciplinary Actions/Options

The Ethics Committee is entitled to take any one of the following actions upon a confirmation of the alleged infraction(s):

2.A Revocation: The Ethics Committee may revoke the credentials which the clinician obtained through the CHCC, with notification of revocation disseminated to his or her professional organizations, certification and licensing boards.

2.B Probation: The committee may place the credentialed professional on probation, suspend certification, or may reprimand or censure the individual. The credentialed professional may be requested to cease the challenged conduct, accept supervision, or seek rehabilitative or educational training or counseling.

The Ethics Committee may implement these requests by issuing:

2.B.1 Cease and Desist Order: Require the accused to cease and desist the challenged behavior.

2.B.2 Reprimand: Reprimand when the Committee has determined that there has been an ethics violation but there has been no damage to another person.

2.B.3 Censure: Censure when the Committee has determined that there has been an ethics violation but the damage done to another person is not sufficient to warrant more serious action.

2.B.4 Supervision Requirement: Require that the accused receive supervision.

2.B.5 Rehabilitation, Education, Training, or Counseling: The accused may be required to undergo rehabilitative counseling/therapy, additional education, training, or personal counseling.

2.B.6 Probation: Require that the accused be placed on probation. Probation is defined as the relation that the CHCC has with the accused when the CHCC undertakes actively and systematically to monitor, for a specific length of time, the degree to which the accused complies with the Ethics Committee's requirements.

2.B.7 Referral: Referral to a relevant association or state board of examiners for action.

2.C   Reapplication: The Ethics Committee may recommend that the CHCC Executive Board deny reapplication.

2.D   Notification of Other Organizations: In the event that a CHCC credentialed individual who has violated the Code of Professional Ethics is certified by or a member of other recognized professional boards or associations or is authorized by governmental authority to practice in cognate disciplines, CHCC shall, at its discretion, send notice of disciplinary action to each other organization. The notice shall state that the disciplinary action was pursuant to the CHCC Code of Professional Ethics.

3.00 CHCC and CHCC Credentialed Professionals Responsibilities

3.A   Cooperation: CHCC credentialed professionals are obligated, in accordance to the CHCC Code of Professional Ethics, to cooperate with proceedings of CHCC for any alleged violation of the Code of Professional Ethics. If the accused voluntarily relinquishes certification or fails to cooperate with an ethical inquiry in any way, the CHCC shall continue its investigation, noting in the final report the circumstances of the accused's failure to cooperate.

3.B   Refusal of Testimony: If a complainant refuses to provide testimony, the complaint may be dismissed at the discretion of the CHCC, upon the application and agreement of the accused.

3.C   Countercomplaints: The CHCC will not accept countercomplaints from an accused CHCC credentialed individual during the course of an investigation of the initial complaint. However, in unusual circumstances, the CHCC may accept a countercomplaint during the investigative period of the initial complaint.

4.00 Processing of Complaints by CHCC

4.A   Initial Action by CHCC Executive Administrator
     4.A.1   Ascertain the certification status of the accused.
     4.A.2   Confer with Ethics Committee regarding the legitimacy of the complaint.
     4.A.3   Review complaint with legal counsel once Committee has reviewed and affirmed the legitimacy of the complaint.

4.B   Acknowledgment of Complaint: Within thirty (30) days of receipt of a formal complaint, the CHCC Executive Administrator shall:
     4.B.1   Direct a letter to the complainant acknowledging acceptance or rejection of the complaint.
     4.B.2   If a decision to accept the complaint is made, assist the Ethics Committee Chairperson to assemble the appropriate committee members.
     4.B.3   If the complaint is certified in the Ethics Committee and approved by the CHCC legal counsel, the Executive Administrator shall send a notice of complaint to the accused. The notice shall be:
         1) sent by certified mail;

2) marked "Confidential";

3) shall state the portion of the Code of Professional Ethics relevant to the allegations of the complaint;

4) shall enclose a copy of the complaint;

5) shall enclose a copy of the CHCC's Code of Professional Ethics;

6) shall direct the accused to respond to the allegations in writing, within thirty (30) days, and state whether the accused requests a hearing before the Ethics Committee;

7) shall inform the accused that failure to respond in writing within 30 days may result in termination of his or her certification.

Appendix III

BIBLIOGRAPHY OF LIFE CARE PLANNING AND RELATED PUBLICATIONS

Arrona, R. & Walters, M. (1999). A personal perspective of life care planning. In R. Weed, Ed., *Life Care Planning and Case Management Handbook*, 359–370. Boca Raton, FL: CRC Press.

Babitsky, S., Mangraviti, J., & Todd, C. (2000). *The Comprehensive Forensic Services Manual: The Essential Resources for All Experts*. Falmouth, MA: SEAK, Inc.

Banja, J. (1995). Professional or hired gun? The ethics of advocacy in life care planning. *Journal of Private Sector Rehabilitation*, 9, 85–90.

Barker, E. (1999). Life care planning. *RN*, 62, 58–61.

Bee, C.M. (1995). Case management and the life care plan. *Inside Life Care Planning*, 1(2), 4.

Berens, D. & Weed, R. (1999). The role of the vocational counselor in life care planning. In R. Weed, Ed., *Life Care Planning and Case Management Handbook*, 31–49. Boca Raton, FL: CRC Press.

Blackwell, T.L. (1995). An ethical decision making model for life care planners. *The Rehabilitation Professional*, 3, 18, 28.

Blackwell, T.L. (1995). Ethical principles for life care planners. *Inside Life Care Planning*, 1(2), 1, 9.

Blackwell, T. (1999). Ethical issues in life care planning. In R. Weed, Ed., *Life Care Planning and Case Management Handbook*, 399–406. Boca Raton, FL: CRC Press.

Blackwell, T., Jayne, K., Thomas, R., & Weiford, T. (1995). Life care planning. *The Rehabilitation Professional*, 3(6), 17–20.

Blackwell, T., Krause, J., Winkler, T., & Stiens, S. (2001). *Spinal Cord Injury Desk Reference: Guidelines for Life Care Planning and Case Management*. New York: Demos Medical Publishing.

Blackwell, T.L., Millington, M.J., & Guglielmo, D.E. (1999). Vocational aspects of life care planning for people with spinal cord injury. *Work: A Journal of Prevention, Assessment, and Rehabilitation*, 13, 13–19.

Blackwell, T., Sluis-Powers, A., & Weed, R. (1994). *Life Care Planning for the Brain Injured* (foreword by James S. Brady). Athens, GA: E&F Vocational Services.

Blackwell, T., Weed, R., & Sluis-Powers, A. (1994). *Life Care Planning for the Spinal Cord Injured*. Athens, GA: E&F Vocational Services.

Bogart, J., Ed. (1998). *Legal Nurse Consulting: Principles and Practice*. Boca Raton, FL: CRC Press.

Bonfiglio, R. (1999). The role of the physiatrist in life care planning. In R. Weed, Ed., *Life Care Planning and Case Management Handbook*, 15–22. Boca Raton, FL: CRC Press.

Brodwin, M. & Mas, L. (1999). The rehabilitation counselor as life care planner. *The Journal of Forensic Vocational Assessment*, 2, 16–21.

Brookshire, M. & Smith, S. (1990). *Economic/Hedonic Damages: The Practice Book for Plaintiff and Defense Attorneys*. Cincinnati, OH: Anderson Publishing Co.

Brown, M. & Helm, P. (1999). Life care planning for the burn patient. In R. Weed, Ed., *Life Care Planning and Case Management Handbook*, 247–262. Boca Raton, FL: CRC Press.

0-8493-1511-5/04/$0.00+$1.50
© 2004 by CRC Press LLC

Burke, W. (1995). The rehabilitation expert: analysis and management of brain injury and other neurological disorders. In W. Burke, Ed., *The Handbook of Forensic Rehabilitation*. Houston, TX: HDI Publishers.

Burke, W. (1995). Defense of rehabilitation and life care plans. In D. Price & P. Lees-Haley, Eds., *The Insurer's Handbook of Psychological Injury Claims*, 311–323. Seattle, WA: Claims Books.

Carter, M., Hooks, K., Jolley, L., Kessler, M., & Stelling, J. (1998). *Alabama's Life Care Planning for Catastrophic Injuries*. Eau Claire, WI: Lorman Education Services.

Consortium for Spinal Cord Medicine Clinical Practice Guidelines. (1999). *Outcomes Following Traumatic Spinal Cord Injury: Clinical Practice Guidelines for Health-Care Professionals*. Paralyzed Veterans of America. [Available www.pva.org]

Davis v. Ford Motor Co., 128 F.3d 631 (8th Circuit 1997).

Dempsy v. United States, 32 F.3d 1490 (11th Circuit 1994).

Deutsch, P.M. (1983). Burns. In P. Deutsch and F. Raffa, Eds., *Damages in Tort Actions*, Vol. 9. New York: Matthew Bender.

Deutsch, P.M. (1984). Central nervous system impairments: brain injury. In P. Deutsch and F. Raffa, Eds., *Damages in Tort Actions*, Vol. 9. New York: Matthew Bender.

Deutsch, P.M. (1984). Guide for occupational exploration and dictionary of occupational titles analysis: an appendix. In P. Deutsch and F. Raffa, Eds., *Damages in Tort Actions*, Vol. 9. New York: Matthew Bender.

Deutsch, P.M. (1984). Update and research on costs of case management. In P. Deutsch and F. Raffa, Eds., *Damages in Tort Actions*, Vols. 8, 9, & 10. New York: Matthew Bender.

Deutsch, P.M. (1985). Rehabilitation testimony. In P. Deutsch and F. Raffa, Eds., *Damages in Tort Actions*. New York: Matthew Bender.

Deutsch, P.M. (1985). *Rehabilitation Testimony: Maintaining a Professional Perspective*. New York: Matthew Bender (monograph) .

Deutsch, P.M. (1986). Burns. In P. Deutsch and H. Sawyer, Eds., *A Guide to Rehabilitation*. New York: Matthew Bender.

Deutsch, P.M. (1986). Cardiovascular impairments. In P. Deutsch and H. Sawyer, Eds., *A Guide to Rehabilitation*. New York: Matthew Bender.

Deutsch, P.M. (1986). Pulmonary impairments. In P. Deutsch and H. Sawyer, Eds., *A Guide to Rehabilitation*. New York: Matthew Bender.

Deutsch, P.M. (1986). Spinal cord injury update. In P. Deutsch and F. Raffa, Eds., *Damages in Tort Actions*. New York: Matthew Bender.

Deutsch, P.M. (1987). Ventilator dependency. In P. Deutsch and H. Sawyer, Eds., *A Guide to Rehabilitation*. New York: Matthew Bender.

Deutsch, P.M. (1990). *A Guide to Rehabilitation Testimony*. Orlando, FL: PMD Press.

Deutsch, P.M. (1990). Life care planning. In *The Coma: Emerging Patient*. Hanley & Belfus, Inc.

Deutsch, P.M., Ed. (1991). *The Rehab Consultant*. Orlando, FL: Paul M. Deutsch Press, Inc.

Deutsch, P.M. (1992). Life expectancy in catastrophic disability: issues and parameters for the rehabilitation professional. *NARPPS Journal*, 7(2).

Deutsch, P.M. (1992). Life expectancy in catastrophic disability: issues and parameters for the rehabilitation professional. In P. Deutsch and H. Sawyer, Eds., *A Guide to Rehabilitation*. New York: Matthew Bender.

Deutsch, P.M. (1992). Life care planning: its growth and development. In *Viewpoints: An Update on Issues in Head Injury Rehabilitation*. San Marcus, TX: Tangram.

Deutsch, P.M. (1992). Profile. *The Case Manager*, 3, 60–62, 64–66, 68–69.

Deutsch, P.M. (1994). Life care planning into the future. *NARPPS Journal*, 9(2), 79–84.

Deutsch, P.M. (1995). Life care planning. In A.E. Dell Orto & R.P. Marinelle, Eds., *Encyclopedia of Disability and Rehabilitation*, 436–443. New York: Macmillan.

Deutsch, P.M. (1996). Life care planning into the 21st century: can we meet the standards? *Journal of Forensic Rehabilitation*, I, I.

Deutsch, P.M. (1999). Learning to question research: a methodology for analysis. In P. Deutsch and H. Sawyer, Eds., *A Guide to Rehabilitation*. New York: Matthew Bender (includes an analysis of the statistical conclusions from the National Spinal Cord Data Research Center).

Deutsch, P. & Fralish, K. (1993). *Innovations in Head Injury Rehabilitation*, 2 vols. New York: Matthew Bender.

Deutsch, P.M. & Kitchen, J.A. (1994). Rehabilitation technology. In P. Deutsch and H. Sawyer, Eds., *A Guide to Rehabilitation*. New York: Matthew Bender.

Deutsch, P.M., Kitchen, J.A., & Cody, S.L. (1989). Life care planning and the discharge process. In *Viewpoints: An Updateon Issues in Head Injury Rehabilitation*, Vol. XIII. San Marcus, TX: Tangram.

Deutsch, P., Kitchen, J. & Morgan, N. (1988). Life care planning and catastrophic case management. *Head Injury Reporter*, 1.

Deutsch, P.M., Kitchen, J.A., & Sammarco, D. (1993). Life care planning and AIDS. In P. Deutsch and H. Sawyer, Eds., *A Guide to Rehabilitation*. New York: Matthew Bender.

Deutsch, P. & Raffa, F. (1981). *Damages in Tort Actions*, Vol. 8. New York: Matthew Bender.

Deutsch, P. & Raffa, F. (1982). *Damages in Tort Actions*, Vol. 9. New York: Matthew Bender.

Deutsch, P. & Reid, C. (2001). *The Catastrophic Injury Handbook*. American Board of Disability Analysts, Dubuque, IA: Kendall/Hunt Publisher.

Deutsch, P.M. & Sawyer, H.W. (1985). *A Guide to Rehabilitation*, 2 vols. New York: Matthew Bender.

Deutsch, P. & Sawyer, H. (1999). *A Guide to Rehabilitation*. Purchase, NY: Ahab Press.

Deutsch, P.M., Sawyer, H.W., Jenkins, W.M., & Kitchen, J.A. (1986). Life care planning in catastrophic case management. *Journal of Private Sector Rehabilitation*, 1(1), 13–27.

Deutsch, P., Weed, R., Kitchen, J. & Sluis, A. (1989). *Life Care Plans for the Spinal Cord Injured: A Step by Step Guide*. Athens, GA: E&F Vocational Services.

Dillman, E. (1987). The necessary economic and vocational interface in personal injury cases. *Journal of Private Sector Rehabilitation*, 2, 121–142.

Dillman, E. (1994). Economic perspective of life care planning. *Journal of Private Sector Rehabilitation*, 9, 63–68.

Dillman, E. (1999). The role of the economist in life care planning. In R. Weed, Ed., *Life Care Planning and Case Management Handbook*, 175–190. Boca Raton, FL: CRC Press.

Elliott, T. (1995). The plaintiff's view of the life care plan for the catastrophic case. *Journal of Private Sector Rehabilitation*, 9, 69–72.

Elliott, T. (1997). Life care plans: the legal perspective. *The Neurolaw Letter*, 1, 2.

Elliott, T. (1999). A plaintiff's attorney's perspective on life care planning. In R. Weed, Ed., *Life Care Planning and Case Management Handbook*, 371–380. Boca Raton, FL: CRC Press.

Evans, R. (1996). Commentary and an illustration on the use of outcome data in life care planning for persons with acquired neurological injuries. *Neurorehabilitation*, 7, 157–162.

Evans, R. (1997). The role of the neuropsychologist in life care planning for the brain injured population. *The Journal of Care Management*, 3(5), 46–47, 49.

Evans, R. (1999). The role of the neuropsychologist in life care planning. In R. Weed, Ed., *Life Care Planning and Case Management Handbook*, 65–76. Boca Raton, FL: CRC Press.

Field, T., Garner, J., & Jayne, K. (2000). *A Resource for Rehabilitation Consultants on the Daubert and Kumbo Rulings*. Athens, GA: Elliott & Fitzpatrick.

Gamboa, A. & Hanak, M. (1991). Catastrophic injuries, catastrophic costs: the life care plan. *Trial*, 27, 59–63.

Gladstone, V., Higdon, L., & Weed, R. (1999). The role of the audiologist in life care planning. In R. Weed, Ed., *Life Care Planning and Case Management Handbook*, 151–174. Boca Raton, FL: CRC Press.

Gunn, L. (1994). Life care planning: a defense perspective. *Journal of Private Sector Rehabilitation*, 9, 73–78.

Gunn, L. & Gunn, T. (1999). A defense attorney's perspective on life care planning. In R. Weed, Ed., *Life Care Planning and Case Management Handbook*, 381–398. Boca Raton, FL: CRC Press.

Hoffman, L. (1997). Checklist to help clients select a life care planner. *Case Manager Advisor*, 8, supplement.

Iyer, P., Bogart, J, & Beerman, J. (1996). The legal process: a view for the hot seat. *Neurorehabilitation*, 7, 137–149.

Iyer, P. & Yudkoff, M. (1996). Working with nursing expert witnesses. In P. Iyer, Ed., *Nursing Malpractice*, 797–865. Tucson, AZ: Lawyers and Judges Publishing Co.

Kitchen, J. (1999). Life care planning for the HIV/AIDS patient. In R. Weed, Ed., *Life Care Planning and Case Management Handbook*, 263–296. Boca Raton, FL: CRC Press.

Kitchen, J. (1999). Life care planning resources. In R. Weed, Ed., *Life Care Planning and Case Management Handbook*, 459–488. Boca Raton, FL: CRC Press.

Kitchen, J.A., Deutsch, P.M., & Cody, S.A. (1989). *Life Care Planning for the Brain Damaged Infant: A Step by Step Guide*. Orlando, FL: PMD Press.

Lane, G. & Weed, R. (1999). Life care planning for transplantation patients. In R. Weed, Ed., *Life Care Planning and Case Management Handbook*, 325–334. Boca Raton, FL: CRC Press.

May, R. (1999). The certification movement in rehabilitation and life care planning. In R. Weed, Ed., *Life Care Planning and Case Management Handbook*, 435–458. Boca Raton, FL: CRC Press.

May, V.R., Tuner, T.N., Taylor, D.W., & Rubin, S.E. (2000). The life care planning process and certification: current trends in health care management, part 1. *The Journal of Care Management*, 6, 38–49.

May, V.R., Tuner, T.N., Taylor, D.W., & Rubin, S.E. (2000). The life care planning process and certification: current trends in health care management, part 2. *The Journal of Care Management*, 6, 9–20.

Mayo, C. (1994). Life care planning: an overview for professionals. In C. Simkins, Ed., *Analysis, Understanding and Presentation of Cases Involving Traumatic Brain Injury*, 125–140. Washington, DC: National Head Injury Foundation.

McCaigue, I.S. (1999). The role of the occupational therapist in life care planning. In R. Weed, Ed., *Life Care Planning and Case Management Handbook*, 77–113. Boca Raton, FL: CRC Press.

McCollom, P. (1997). Life care planning; Case management. In *Advanced Rehabilitation Nursing Practice: A Core Curriculum*. AMC Publishing (contributor and reviewer). [Available www.rehabnurse.org]

McCollom, P. (1998). Ethical case management: humanizing reality. *Case Review*, July/August.

McCollom, P. (1998). Life care planning in workers' compensation cases. *Case Review*, 4, 70–72.

McCollom, P. (1999). Life care planning 101. *The Journal of Care Management*, 5, 24, 27.

McCollom, P. (2000). Life care planning practice: external influences. *The Case Manager*, 11, 62–63.

McCollom, P. (2000). Life care planning in elder care management. *The Case Manager*, 11, 37–40.

McCollom, P. (2000). Proposed practice guidelines for excellence in life care planning. *The Case Manager*, 11, 67–71.

McCollom, P. & Casuto, D. (1999). Life care planning. In M.E. O'Keefe, Ed., *Nursing Practice and Law*, chap. 23. Pensacola, FL: American Association of Nurse Attorneys.

McCollom, P. & Crane, R. (2001). Life care plans: accuracy over time. *The Case Manager*, 12, 85–87.

McCoy, D. (1995). The purpose of a life care plan. *Inside Life Care Planning*, 1(2), 1, 9.

Meier, R. (1999). Life care planning for the amputee. In R. Weed, Ed., *Life Care Planning and Case Management Handbook*, 191–204. Boca Raton, FL: CRC Press.

Miksis v. Howard et al. 106 F.3d 754 (7th Circuit 1997).

Peddle, A. (1999). The role of the physical therapist in life care planning. In R. Weed, Ed., *Life Care Planning and Case Management Handbook*, 115–128. Boca Raton, FL: CRC Press.

Penberthy, A. & Priest, J. (1989). Life care planning: an introduction. *Journal of Private Sector Rehabilitation*, 4(3).

Provder, E. (1993). Life care plans: documenting damages in catastrophic injury cases. *Trial Diplomacy Journal*, 16, 5–13.

Reid, C., Deutsch, P., & Kitchen, J. (1997). Life Care Planning and Case Management with AIDS Patients. In P. Deutsch & H. Sawyer, Eds., *Guide to Rehabilitation*. New York: Matthew Bender.

Reid, C., Deutsch, P., Kitchen, J., & Aznavoorian, K. (1997). Life Care Planning and Case Management. In P. Deutsch & H. Sawyer, Eds., *Guide to Rehabilitation*. New York: Matthew Bender.

Reid, C., Deutsch, P., Kitchen, J., & Aznavoorian, K. (1999). Life care planning. In F. Chan & M. Leahy, Eds., *Healthcare and Disability Case Management*, 415–453. Lake Zurich, IL: Vocational Consultants Press.

Rice, J., Hicks, P., & Wiehe, V. (2000). Life care planning: a role for social workers. *Social Work in Health Care*, 31, 85–94.

Riddick, S. (1993). Life care planning. In R. Howe, Ed., *Case Management for Health Care Professionals*, chap. 10. Chicago, IL: Precept Press.

Riddick, S. & Roughan, J. (October 1992). The ultimate discharge plan: the case management approach to life care planning. *Continuing Care Magazine* (feature article).

Riddick, S. & Weed, R. (1996). The life care planning process for managing catastrophically impaired patients. In S. Bancett & D. Flarey, Eds., *Case Studies in Nursing Case Management*, 61–91. Gaithersburg, MD: Aspen Publishers.

Riddick, S. & Weed, R. (1999). The role of the nurse case manager in life care planning. In R. Weed, Ed., *Life Care Planning and Case Management Handbook*, 23–30. Boca Raton, FL: CRC Press.

Riddick-Grisham, S. & Weed, R. (1996). Life care planning process for managing catastrophically impaired patient. In S. Bancett & D. Flarey, Eds., *Case Studies in Nursing Case Management*, 61–91. Gaithersburg, MD: Aspen Publishers.

Sbordone, R. & Shepherd, J. (1991). The role of the neuropsychologist and life care planner in evaluating brain damage cases. *The Neurolaw Letter*, 1, 5.

Sellars, C. & Burke, W. (1995). Pediatric brain injury: analysis, planning and management. In W. Burke, Ed., *The Handbook of Forensic Rehabilitation*, Houston, TX: HDI Publishers.

Shepherd, J. & Pittman, W. (1995). Mediation and the role of the life care planner. *Journal of Private Sector Rehabilitation*, 9, 91–92.

Sherer, M., Madison, C., & Hannay, H. (2000). A review of outcome after moderate and severe closed head injury with an introduction to life care planning. *The Journal of Head Trauma Rehabilitation*, 15, 767–779.

Sluis-Power, A. (1994). Life care planning: the role of the legal nurse. *Journal of Private Sector Rehabilitation*, 9(2), 51–56.

Sluis-Power, A. (1999). The role of the psychologist in life care planning. In R. Weed, Ed., *Life Care Planning and Case Management Handbook*, 51–64. Boca Raton, FL: CRC Press.

Sorenson v. Miller, 97 F.3d 1452 (6th Circuit 1996).

Taylor, S. (1997). *Neurolaw: Brain and Spinal Cord Injuries*. New York: ATLA Press.

Theriot v. Sprinkle, 30 F.3d 136 (7th Circuit, 1994).

Thomas, R. (1998). Expert testimony: are you an expert witness? *Inside Case Management*, 5(9).

Thomas, R.L. (1992). The use of computer in life care planning. *The Rehabilitation Consultant*, 3.

Thomas, R.L. (1994). Automation and life care planning. *The Case Manager*, 5.

Thomas, R.L. (1995). Computer software for life care planning. *The Rehabilitation Professional*. 3, 20.

Thomas, R.L. (1995). Making the most of computers for life care planning. *Inside Life Care Planning*, 1.

Thomas, R. (1999). Technology and life care planning. In R. Weed, Ed., *Life Care Planning and Case Management Handbook*, 407–434. Boca Raton, FL: CRC Press.

Thomas, R. (1999). Life care planning: defining procedures and process. *NARPPS Forensic News*, 2(1).

Thomas, R.L. & Busby, L.D. (1996). Legal nurse consulting from a life care planning perspective. *The Journal of Legal Nurse Consulting*, 7, 10–13.

Thomas, R.L. & Kitchen, J. (1996). Private hire: the real costs. *Inside Life Care Planning*, 1, 1, 3–4.

Thomas, R. & Kitchen, J. (1997). Life care planning: a comparison of private hire and agency costs. *The Rehabilitation Professional/NARPPS Journal*, 12, 47–52.

Turner, T.N., Taylor, D.W., Rubin, S.E., & May, V.R. (2000). Job functions associated with the development of life care plans. *Journal of Legal Nurse Consulting*, 11, 3–7.

Voogt, R.D. (1988). Life care planning. Viewpoints, 10, Tangram Rehabilitation Network, 1.

Voogt, R.D. (1994). Cost of long term health care. In C. Simkins, Ed., *Analysis, Understanding and Presentation of Cases Involving Traumatic Brain Injury*, 229–238. Washington, DC: National Head Injury Foundation.

Voogt, R.D. (1995). Controversial issues in life care planning. *Inside Life Care Planning*, 1, 9.

Voogt, R.D. (1996). Quality of life: an aspect of life care planning and long-term care. *Neurorehabilitation*, 7, 95–117.

Voogt, R.D. (1997). Economic and legal aspects of neuropsychological rehabilitation. In J. Leon Carrion, Ed., *Neuropsychological Rehabilitation: Fundamentals, Directions and Innovations*. Boca Raton, FL: St. Lucie Press.

Voogt, R.D. (1999). Brain injury litigation: what is the missing link in defining damages? *The Neurolaw Letter*, 9, 1, 4.

Voogt, R.D. (2000). Support care: the battleground in traumatic brain injury cases. *The Neurolaw Letter*, 9, 57, 59–60.

Voogt, R.D. & Groteguth, M.L. (1990). Damages: rehabilitation and life care needs after a traumatic brain injury. *American Jurisprudence Proof of Facts*, 3rd Ser., Vol. 9.

Waaland, P. & Riddick-Grisham, S. (1996). School services: a resource often utilized in pediatric life care planning. *Inside Life Care Planning*, 1.

Ward, J. & Krueger, K. (1994). *Establishing Damages in Catastrophic Injury Litigation*. Tucson, AZ: Lawyers & Judges Publishing Co.

Ward, T. & Weed, R. (1999). Life care planning issues for people with chronic pain. In R. Weed, Ed., *Life Care Planning and Case Management Handbook*, 205–227. Boca Raton, FL: CRC Press.

Watkins, C. (1999). The role of the speech-language pathologist and assistive technology in life care planning. In R. Weed, Ed., *Life Care Planning and Case Management Handbook*, 129–150. Boca Raton, FL: CRC Press.

Weed, R. (1989). Life care planning questions and answers. *Life Care Facts*, 1, 5–6.

Weed, R. (1990). Marketing of life care planning services. *Life Care Facts*, 2, 1–2.

Weed, R. (1991). Support for recreation and leisure activities in life care plans. *The Rehab Consultant*, 3, 1–3.

Weed, R. (1992). Working with the life care planner. *Orthotist & Prosthetist Business News*, 1, 5.

Weed, R. (1992). Orthotist and prosthetist roles in life care plans. *Orthotist & Prosthetist Business News*, 1, 4.

Weed, R. (1992). Economist's role and ethical issues in life care planning. *Orthotist & Prosthetist Business News*, 1, 4.

Weed, R. (1994). Life care plans: expanding the horizons. *Journal of Private Sector Rehabilitation*, 9, 47–50.

Weed, R. (1995). Objectivity in life care planning. *Inside Life Care Planning*, 1, 1–5.

Weed, R. (1995). Life care plans as a managed care tool. *Medical Interface*, 8, 111–118.

Weed, R. (1995). *Interview: Inside Life Care Planning*, 1, 6–7. Boca Raton, FL: CRC Press.

Weed, R. (1996). Life care planning and earnings capacity analysis for brain injured clients involved in personal injury litigation utilizing the RAPEL method. *Neurorehabilitation*, 7, 119–135.

Weed, R. (1997). Life care planning standards update. *Neurolaw Letter*, 7, 17, 21.

Weed, R. (1997). Comments regarding "life care planning for young children with brain injuries." *Neurolaw Letter*, 6, 112.

Weed, R. (1997). Life Care Planning. Ocoee FL: Intelicus (audiotape CEU).

Weed, R. (1998). Life care planning: an overview. *Directions in Rehabilitation*, 9, 135–147.

Weed, R. (1998). Aging with a brain injury: the effects on life care plans and vocational opinions. *The Rehabilitation Professional*, 6, 30–34.

Weed, R., Ed. (1999). *Life Care Planning and Case Management Handbook*. Boca Raton, FL: CRC Press.

Weed, R. (1999). Forensic issues for life care planners. In R. Weed, Ed., *Life Care Planning and Case Management Handbook*, 351–357. Boca Raton, FL: CRC Press.

Weed, R. (2001). Contemporary life care planning for persons with amputation. *Orthotics & Prosthetist Business News*, 10, 20–22, 24, 26, 28, 30 (cover story).

Weed, R. (2002). Life care planning procedures and the roles of various health care providers. *Topics in Spinal Cord Injury Rehabilitation*, 7, 5–20.

Weed, R. & Berens, D., Eds. (2001). *Life Care Planning Summit 2000 Proceedings*. Athens, GA: Elliott & Fitzpatrick.

Weed, R. & Field, T. (1994). *The Rehabilitation Consultant's Handbook*, 2nd ed. Athens, GA: E&F Vocational Services.

Weed, R. & Field, T. (2001). *The Rehabilitation Consultant's Handbook*, 3rd ed. Athens, GA: E&F Vocational Services.

Weed, R. & Riddick, S. (1992). Life care plans as a case management tool. *The Individual Case Manager Journal*, 3, 26–35 (cover photo and feature article).

Weed, R. & Riddick S. (1992). Life care plans as a case management tool. *Rehab Prose*, 8, 3–4.

Weed, R. & Sluis, A. (1990). *Life Care Plans for the Amputee: A Step by Step Guide*. Boca Raton, FL: CRC Press.

Whiteneck, G. et al. (1993). *Aging with Spinal Cord Injury*. New York: Demos Publications.

Whitmore, M. (1996). Utilization of the life care plan in personal injury litigation: case evaluation and funding design in the catastrophic needs case. *Neurorehabilitation*, 7, 151–156.

Williams, J.M. & Burlew, L.D. (1995). *Dealing with Catastrophic Injury: A Developmental Perspective on Life Care Planning*. Santa Cruz, CA: American Board of Vocational Experts.

Winkler, T. (1999). Life care planning for the visually impaired. In R. Weed, Ed., *Life Care Planning and Case Management Handbook*, 335–350. Boca Raton, FL: CRC Press.

Winkler, T. & Weed, R. (1999). Life care planning for spinal cord injury. In R. Weed, Ed., *Life Care Planning and Case Management Handbook*, 297–324. Boca Raton, FL: CRC Press.

Young, J. & Weed, R. (1999). Life care planning for acquired brain injury. In R. Weed, Ed., *Life Care Planning and Case Management Handbook*, 229–246. Boca Raton, FL: CRC Press.

Yudkoff, M. (1998). The life care planning expert. In J. Bogart, Ed., *Legal Nurse Consulting: Principles and Practice*, 657–686. Boca Raton, FL: CRC Press.

Zasler, C. (1996). Primer for the rehabilitation professional on the life care planning process. *Neurorehabilitation*, 7, 79–93.

Zasler, N. (1994). A physiatric perspective on life care planning. *Journal of Private Sector Rehabilitation*, 9, 57–62.

Zasler, N. (1995). Physiatry and the life care planner. *Inside Life Care Planning*, 1(1), 1, 8.

INDEX

P